FAULKNER
A BIOGRAPHY

1

> I was not only the oldest but a boy, the third generation of old-
> est son from Grandfather's father. . . .
>
> —"Sepulture South: Gaslight," *USWF* (451)

HE was a colicky baby. In the heat of the insect-loud September and
October darkness he would keep his mother awake almost every night. She
would rock him steadily, the tiny woman in her kitchen chair. According
to family lore, it was a straight chair, and with each forward motion the
front legs would strike the floor with a sharp report that echoed through
the open windows. She and her husband had lived in New Albany for almost a year now, but they did not know many people. They were stand-
offish, thought some of the neighbors, and after hearing the sound again
and again, one said, "Those Falkners sure are the queerest folks. They chop
kindlin' all night on the kitchen floor."[1] For the whole first year of his life
the baby would wake with the colic, and his small, strong mother would
hold him in her arms and rock him. It was as if auguries already hovered
around the cradle: sensitivity, pain, love, and clannishness.

Maud Falkner had gone into labor on Saturday, the twenty-fifth. Her
mother, Lelia Butler, had come from Oxford, thirty-five miles to the west,
to be with her. At eleven o'clock that night the doctor emerged from the
bedroom to tell Murry Falkner that he had a son. John Wesley Thompson
Falkner and his wife, Sallie Murry, lost no time journeying from Oxford
to see their first grandchild. With Maud's consent, Murry asked his father
to choose a name for the baby. Theirs was a family that favored traditional
names, and J. W. T. Falkner thought immediately of his own father, Colonel William Clark Falkner, dead now nearly eight years. "I'd like to name
him for Father," said "The Young Colonel" to his son, "but Father hated
'Clark.' " He thought a minute. "Here's what we'll do. We'll call him
William, but we'll use your middle name." So when the Methodist minister
christened the baby, he named him William Cuthbert Falkner.

In spite of the colic, he thrived enough in three months for his mother to take him to Oxford. Like most Southern roads, north Mississippi's were wretched in the year 1897, and the best way to make the short journey was not in an uncomfortable buggy but by train. One rode the St. Louis–San Francisco Railroad thirty-five miles northwest to Holly Springs and changed there to the Illinois Central for the remaining thirty miles south to Oxford. During that visit Maud dressed the infant in layers of elaborate white hand-stitched clothes and took him to the Sanders & Sweeny photographic studio. There Mr. Sweeny made a portrait of him in her arms. A small child with very little hair, he gazed into the camera lens wide-eyed and solemn. His eyes were so dark a brown they were almost black, like those of his mother and his great-grandfather, "The Old Colonel." Dressed all in white, eyes hidden as she gazed upon her baby, Maud wore, draped over her head, a mantle that fell in soft folds about her neck and down over her shoulders: a perfect madonna and child.

Maud Falkner would see to it that there was a photographic record of her family. Seven and a half months later, grasping a stick of peppermint candy, her baby smiled over the back of a wicker chair. Again the eyes were wide, and this time the camera caught another distinctive feature: the fold of skin that started over the inner portion of the upper eyelid and curved down to cover the outer edge. The next year's portrait, when he was two, posed him on the arm of a rattan chair, where he balanced himself casually and smiled an elfin smile. Although the hair was wispy blond and the little-boy features now gave promise of the generous Falkner nose, his looks favored Maud Falkner. The mouth was small and thin, and the eyes were bright and hooded like his mother's. By the time of this portrait his life had changed, for now his family had moved and grown.

JOHN WESLEY THOMPSON FALKNER had been the first of the family to go to college. Entering the University of Mississippi in Oxford after its reopening at the end of the war, he had gone on to gain admission to the Mississippi bar in 1869. In September of that same year the tall, dark-eyed twenty-one-year-old lawyer had married sprightly Sallie Murry. She was one month shy of eighteen. The following August their first child, Murry Cuthbert, was born. He was followed a little more than a year later by a sister, Mary Holland, and nearly five years after her by a brother, J. W. T. Falkner, Jr. Then, in 1885, the family moved to Oxford. Each of the Young Colonel's children was offered his educational opportunity. But with his first-born, it did not take. At the age of seventeen Murry had been sent to the university, but his passion was the Gulf & Ship Island Railroad.

As the Ripley Railroad Company, it had been incorporated in 1857, but little was done to begin construction, and then the war made that impossible. In its aftermath, when the beginnings of recovery lent impetus to new ventures, the state legislature chartered a new Ripley Railroad Company. One of the thirty-six incorporators that spring of 1871 was Colonel

William C. Falkner. Encouraged by the prospect of state payments of
$4,000 per mile of track, the investors envisioned a railroad that would
stretch twenty-one miles north from Ripley to the Tennessee line and then
four miles further to Middleton, where it would connect with the Memphis & Charleston. This time the project went forward. Four days before
the state deadline, one of the road's two funnel-stacked wood-burning
engines pulled into Ripley with its whistle shrieking triumphantly. The
road was affectionately called "The Doodlebug line" because its small
twenty-ton engines ran on narrow-gauge track. The size of the track and
the fact that not all of its twenty-five miles were within the state delayed
the payment of the state bounty. It was difficult to make ends meet, and
within two years the bonds went into default. It was not until a dozen
years later, in 1886, that the railroad began to show any signs of renewed
promise. This time Colonel Falkner gained control of the company and
used convict labor to push it south toward the neighboring county seats of
New Albany and Pontotoc. Characteristically, he antagonized many as he
moved ahead with vigor and vision toward his dream of a railroad that
would link the small town of Ripley with Chicago and the Gulf of Mexico.
The plans were already set to transform the Gulf & Ship Island into the
grander Gulf & Chicago Railroad.

By early May of 1888 a passenger could board the train in Middleton,
Tennessee, at 7:45 A.M. and arrive in New Albany, nearly forty-five miles
away, at 11:10 A.M. By Independence Day the line was complete to
Pontotoc. In celebration, the Colonel made a speech and his daughter,
Effie, drove in the silver spike. Two trains a day would run the length of
the line—each way—and the Colonel could stand on the platform at the
other end of the line and hear the conductor sing out, "All aboard for Wal-
nut, Tiplersville, Falkner, Ripley, Blue Mountain, Guyton, Cotton Plant,
New Albany, Ingomar, Cherry Creek, and Pontotoc!" And some of the
names: Falkner, Guyton, Ingomar—from his family, from that of a friend,
from his book *The White Rose of Memphis*—must have sounded particularly sweet to his ear. Fifty years later his great-grandson would say,
"The people could call the towns whatever they wanted, but, by God, he
would name the depots."[2] Now a passenger could make the sixty-three-
mile journey from Middleton to Pontotoc in five hours and five minutes.
Call it the Doodlebug line who would, the Colonel had built his railroad.

Murry Falkner would look at it with longing each time he returned
home from the university. Vacations would find him on the line in whatever capacity he could manage. As one of his sons would put it, "the railroad was his first and lasting love. . . . They would send him to Ole Miss
and the next thing they would know he would be back on the railroad.
After two years of trying to keep him in classes they gave up."[3] He not
only loved the work, he had a talent for it too.

Murry Falkner rose through the ranks. Beginning in 1888 he had shoveled coal. He worked his way up to the peaked cap and gauntlets of an

engineer, and by September 1890 he was a conductor on one of the trains, transferred to Pontotoc, where the railroad served that town of 535 souls. As a youth he had dreamed of the life of a cowboy, the kind lived briefly by the black sheep of the family, his great-uncle Henry, the Colonel's eldest child by his second wife. But now he had found his true vocation. That did not mean, though, that his life was serene.

He was a robust man, like his father, just a bit under six feet and close to 180 pounds. His eyes were blue rather than brown, but he too was large-nosed and strong-jawed. With his wavy hair and pleasant aspect, he was an attractive young man. The daughter of Dr. Fontaine found him so, and she would go out riding with him in the smart gig he kept. High-spirited Pat Fontaine disliked the clothes one of her father's patients had made for her to pay off her bill, and Murry Falkner was drawn into the back-biting that developed between the two women. The seamstress, Mollie Walker, had a brother named Elias who kept a grocery store but made most of his money gambling. When Pat asked Murry to tell 'Lias to make Mollie stop talking about her, the two men came to blows. Murry was the one who walked away, leaving his antagonist on the ground, but the next day, when Murry turned from his stool at Herron's drugstore counter, he was looking into the barrel of 'Lias Walker's twelve-gauge shotgun. The blast gouged a hole in his back the size of half a grapefruit. As Walker stood over him with a pistol, Falkner groaned, "Don't shoot me any more. You've already killed me." Walker said, "I want to be damned sure," and pulled the trigger. The slug knocked out teeth, damaging the jaw, and lodged against bone near the roof of Murry's mouth.

J. W. T. Falkner got there as fast as he could. As his anger mounted he began to drink. When he finally found Walker hiding in the back of a hardware store, he jammed a big Navy revolver into his belly. It clicked six straight times. By then Walker had managed to draw his own pistol and fire. Then he fled, leaving Falkner to nurse a bleeding hand. "If he had hit me in the stomach, it wouldn't have hurt so much," the victim said later.

Meanwhile Sallie Murry had arrived at Nelson's Boarding House to sit by the son that the doctors now despaired of. "Can I try something?" she asked them. She poured a vial of asafetida into his mouth. He gagged on the brown, oniony gum resin and began to vomit. Suddenly there was a clink in the basin. It was the bullet, and no hemorrhage followed. He had escaped a death similar to the Old Colonel's two years earlier. Sallie Murry took her angry convalescent husband home with her, and not long afterward her son followed.

THE work on the railroad left Murry Falkner time of his own, and he spent some of it, in the fall of 1895, on a hunting trip with his father and three congenial companions. There was more to enjoy than just the pursuit of the plentiful supply of birds, squirrels, and wild turkeys. Ripley was a strong temperance town which saw little social drinking and almost none in mixed company. In hunting camp father and son could indulge a mutual taste for bonded bourbon, one shared by the Old Colonel. It was a taste they could not always control, one which sometimes took the father to Memphis, where his wife would commit him to the therapy of the Keeley cure. The same treatment lay ahead for the son, though neither he nor his bride-to-be could have known it when Murry Falkner was courting Maud Butler in the spring of 1896.

They slipped off on Sunday evening, November 8, to be married on the quiet in the Methodist parsonage, and the next morning they left for New Albany to set up housekeeping in the frame house at the corner of Jefferson and Cleveland. The Oxford *Eagle* reported that "The young couple took their relatives and friends somewhat by surprise, but their congratulations and good wishes were nonetheless sincere. . . ."[4] There were no congratulations from one relative: the bride's mother. Lelia Butler expressed her disapproval by addressing her letters "Miss Maud Butler, in care of Mr. Murry Falkner."

Lelia Swift Butler was an Arkansas girl whose father-in-law, Captain Charles G. Butler, was the surveyor who had laid out the town of Oxford, an influential Baptist and prosperous property owner.[5] His son, Charles E. Butler, was at one time sheriff of Lafayette County. He was an unfortunate man, however, who was in deep financial trouble by 1888 and not long afterward disappeared, leaving his wife penniless. Her son, Sherwood, had a wife to take care of, so Lelia Butler had to depend on relatives, shuttling from one to another, until her daughter, Maud, graduated from the Women's College in Columbus, Mississippi, and undertook to support both of them, working for a time as a secretary. It was when she returned with her mother from that job in Texarkana that a visit to a friend, Holland Falkner, set in motion Murry's courtship. Lelia Butler resented "Buddy" Falkner's intrusion into the close relationship she and her daughter had shared. Though he was a straightforward young man, he was often gruff and inclined to silence. But more important, he had inherited the family vice of heavy drinking. (His sister-in-law would say, "Buddy did drink a lot, but he was a fine person.") Lelia Butler finally managed to deal with her feelings, perhaps pressed by necessity, to the extent that she was there under her daugher's roof when Willie was born and would be there often in later years.

Murry Falkner had every reason to be satisfied with the Gulf & Chicago. At New Albany, a town of 548 inhabitants, he had served as general passenger agent. In November 1898 he was appointed auditor and treasurer and placed in charge of the Traffic and Freight Claim Departments. That December, or shortly thereafter, Murry moved his family to Ripley, where he would be discharging his new responsibilities. There, in the seat of Tippah County, where the Old Colonel had left the strong impress of his powerful personality, they took up residence in a house on Quality Ridge, two doors from Murry's grandparents, Dr. John Young Murry and his wife. In early May, Lelia Butler arrived, and on June 26 her daughter presented Murry Falkner with another son.

They named him Murry C. Falkner, Jr., even though the middle initial did not stand for Cuthbert but for Charles, after his grandmother's half brother, Dr. Charlie Murry, the county health officer. The baby's father nicknamed him Jack. He had his brother's coloring, and though he did not suffer from colic, he was puny and had to be coaxed to eat. That job was taken on by Lelia Butler, whom Willie called Damuddy.

The elder Falkners made their ritual visit, returning to Ripley in October, the *Eagle* reported, because of "the illness of their little grandson, Willie Falkner."[6] The child recovered quickly, however, and they were soon able to return to Oxford, where the Young Colonel's legal practice was flourishing, especially in criminal law. Though his investments had grown more extensive and diversified, he continued to serve as president of his father's railroad based fifty miles and two counties away. An outsider, a blustery man, and an obvious drinker, he had met some resentment in Oxford, a town with strong temperance sentiment. More than that, he could not trace his line much beyond his father, who was "that man from Ripley" to some Oxonians. But he had distinguished himself at the university and at the bar. With a successful political career already under way, he was a powerful man in the community.

The strong ties of kinship were reinforced by frequent visits. Before Jack Falkner was a year old, his parents took him and his brother to Oxford to visit their grandparents in "The Big Place," the handsome home the Young Colonel had built for his beloved Sallie Murry. Back in Ripley, they saw the Murrys almost daily. The Old Colonel's oldest daughter by his second marriage, Willie Medora, still lived in Ripley with her husband, Dr. Nat Carter, and her daughters, Natalie and Vance. Young William Falkner even went by himself once to spend the night there, or part of it. "I was suddenly taken with one of those spells of loneliness and nameless sorrow that children suffer," he would recall, "for what or because of what they do not know. And Vannye and Natalie brought me home, with a kerosene lamp. I remember how Vannye's hair looked in the light—like honey. Vannye was impersonal; quite aloof: she was holding the lamp. Natalie was quick and dark. She was touching me. She must have carried me."[7]

IF J. W. T. Falkner was flourishing in the new century, so was his eldest son, though somewhat more modestly. Murry had bought into the Ripley Drug Company, and he owned a farm west of town. Two of his passions were horses and bird dogs. Now he was raising his own dogs and traveling to Tennessee to watch the field trials determine the national champion. His home was busier than ever, and early summer of 1901 saw the return of Lelia Butler. On September 24, one day before Willie Falkner's fourth birthday, his brother John Wesley Thompson Falkner III was born.

They would call him Johncy, and he would prove the most robust infant of all Maud Falkner's children. But these were years when infant mortality was high in a region where news of approaching yellow fever could nearly empty a town or invoke a shotgun quarantine to prevent anyone from entering it. Less than a week after Johncy's birth, Sallie Murry Falkner was back in Ripley, for Willie was seriously ill with scarlet fever. Before the crisis had passed they nearly lost him, and his brother Jack as well. It was two weeks before their grandmother returned to Oxford, after which Murry Falkner hired a trained nurse to care for them.

The Murrys had of course done their part in helping, and now shared the general relief. Dr. John Young Murry was not usually a demonstrative man. A Confederate veteran and one of the chief men of Ripley, he was a figure of real authority. His eldest grandson would later say that the old man spoke Gaelic and wore the kilt at times and even possessed a claymore. And if he felt like it, he knitted, as was perfectly proper for men of the highlands. He was kind and gentle to the children, and when the Young Colonel gave Willie a Shetland pony to celebrate his recovery, Dr. Murry had Mr. Cheek make a special saddle in his shop down by the depot. The Murrys were faithful churchgoers, and their observances at home always included grace before meals. It may have been in the aftermath of his recovery that Willie insisted on saying the blessing. It was one he knew by heart. He said:

> "Now I lay me down to sleep;
> I pray the Lord my soul to keep.
> If I should die before I wake,
> I pray the Lord my soul to take."

Before they could say their amens he spoke again. "W. C. Falkner," he concluded. Later Granny said to her husband, "He sent his petition up signed."[8]

Murry Falkner's relief that fall may well have been mixed with anxiety on another score. There had been reports just before the Old Colonel's death in 1889 that he had been planning to sell the railroad. But the Young Colonel had continued to run it for the benefit of all the Old Colonel's beneficiaries. It had been a profitable venture, but now, after a dozen years, his other interests were making increasing demands. His reputation continued to grow. "If you want to kill somebody," said courthouse regulars, "kill him Saturday night, call Johnnie on Sunday, and he'll get you off." A state senator and trustee of the University of Mississippi, he also owned a farm and extensive real estate and was now busy helping to organize a telephone company. But he had personal worries, serious ones. Sallie Murry Falkner was suffering from poor health. Her complaint would at first be diagnosed as stomach catarrh, but the treatments afforded her little relief.

J. W. T. Falkner might well have grown weary of the responsibility of running the railroad but felt unwilling to turn it over to Murry, who was still conscientiously working for it in Ripley. Or he may have wanted his eldest son in Oxford to help him. His other son, John junior (whom the family called "John, honey"), would follow in his father's footsteps to the University of Mississippi Law School, and the Young Colonel may have envisioned a family enterprise.

Whatever the reason, he told Murry that he was selling the railroad and that he wanted him to move to Oxford. Johncy Falkner would later say that his father's response was to ride thirty miles northeast of Ripley to Corinth, the seat of Alcorn County, to see a banker he knew. When the man heard there was a railroad for sale he laughed, thinking it was a joke—the idea that anyone would sell a profitable business like a railroad. Quick-tempered Murry Falkner was offended, Johncy said, and stalked out, leaving behind his best chance to save the only job he would ever love.

His father had promised to set him up in business in Oxford, but he was not cut out to be a merchant. He was an inarticulate man who was not very adept in personal relationships. None of his virtues—courage, hard work at his chosen profession, honesty, punctuality—could serve him in this crisis. This was probably one of the times when he longed for that life that had appealed to him since boyhood. He owned well-thumbed copies of Cooper's *The Pioneers* and *The Pathfinder*, of Peter B. Kyne's *The Pride of Palomar*. He could see himself as a cowboy riding the range, but he could not support a wife and three children that way. Somehow he would have to find the money to move west and raise cattle himself. At this point Maud Falkner put her small foot down firmly. She would not allow him to uproot his family for an uncertain life in the West. Murry Falkner acquiesced to what must have seemed pressure from every side. But he never forgave his strong-minded wife for denying him the chance, when the career he loved was taken away, to try one that had always fascinated him.

On September 22, 1902, the Falkners left Ripley. Symbolically, the three little boys left with their mother, riding the line their father had served to New Albany, where Willie had first seen the light of day. From there they rode the line founded by another Confederate soldier, General Nathan Bedford Forrest, to Holly Springs, and then completed their two-day journey on the cars of the Illinois Central into Oxford. Murry Falkner brought the household goods over the primitive roads by wagon. His family was in Oxford for Willie's fifth birthday. None of the turmoil or sense of dislocation came through in the sprightly item in the Oxford *Eagle*: "Mr. Murry Falkner and wife and their interesting family have removed from Ripley to Oxford and occupy the residence formerly occupied by Colonel J. W. T. Falkner."[9]

2

There is a ridge; you drive beyond Seminary Hill and in time
you come upon it: a mild unhurried farm road presently mounting to cross the ridge and on to join the main highway leading
from Jefferson to the world. And now, looking back and down,
you see all Yoknapatawpha. . . .

—The Town (315)

WHEN they arrived in Oxford, Jack Falkner was stunned. "We descended
from the coach, and Bill and I were speechless with wonder; never had
we seen so many people, so many horses and carriages, and so much
movement everywhere. And the lights—arc lights! The first we had ever
seen. As we drove to Grandfather's house by way of the town square we
noticed the fine board sidewalks which extended the whole way. More
than that, people were walking along them and it was already past nine
o'clock at night. We could hardly wait to see these wonderful sights
by daylight."[1]

Exploring the square by daylight, these new residents of Lafayette
County began quickly to acquire a sense of place. This was a county seat
of over 1,800 inhabitants. Oxford's courthouse and square were far more impressive than Ripley's. The four-faced clock under the large dome looked
out to North Street and South Street, to the large, comfortable white
clapboard houses, some of them twisted into the most fashionable Victorian
shapes, with cupolas and scrollwork and lightning rods. Others were
simple and straight, and for this part of the country, quite old. The Isom
place had been built in 1835, with slave and Indian labor, for Dr. T. D.
Isom, one of the earliest settlers, dead now only four months. The Wendel
house on Depot Street, just off the square, had been built in 1848 on land
bought from Ho-Kah, a Chickasaw who held her patent from the U.S.
government. Three-quarters of a mile south was the Bailey place, shady
and wooded, a haven for small animals and a favorite spot of picnickers

and game-playing children. The sturdy and symmetrical two-story plantation-style home was ennobled by a Greek portico and four wooden columns, with a second-story balcony set between them. Built in 1848 by an English architect for Robert B. Shegog, it was similar to three or four others in the city and county. Only a few houses rose to the three-story eminence of the home J. W. T. Falkner had built for Sallie Murry.

A little over a half-mile west of the square, the trains of the Illinois Central would signal their stops at the depot with distinctive whistles. Just across the railroad tracks, a mile west of the courthouse, lay the campus of the University of Mississippi (familiarly known as Ole Miss), with its scattering of Greek Revival and Georgian buildings, set among magnolias, dogwoods, redbud, and tall shade trees on a square mile of elevated rolling land. Beyond Oxford and the university lay the county.

Lafayette County was almost square, roughly twenty-five miles on each side. Slightly off center to the west was the city, the railroad tracks running between it and the university and angling off a bit to the southwest. Meandering across the northern border was the dark, slow-moving Tallahatchie River, with its thickets and swamps, black bottom land and stands of trees. Flowing into the river in the northwest corner of the county was Toby Tubby Creek, named for the old Chickasaw chief. The Tallahatchie formed the northernmost of three irregular, roughly parallel bands. The center one was the road linking Oxford with Pontotoc on the east and Batesville in Panola County on the west. The southernmost band, about eight miles south of Oxford, was the Yocona River (pronounced Yocknee), much smaller than the Tallahatchie, and bearing, on old maps, the Chickasaw name Yockeney-Patafa.

In Tippah, the Falkner boys had lived in a county that was less than one-third Negro. In Lafayette, nearly 10,000 of the county's 22,000 inhabitants were black. Directly or indirectly, the livelihood of all of them depended upon cotton. Here the fields did not stretch away, vast and flat to the horizon, as they did in the Delta. There were some good-sized plantations but there were also small patches, slanting down to a ravine or stuck precariously on the side of a hill. But cotton was an unrotated crop which badly taxed the land. And though the creek bottoms were largely heavy forest, erosion had left gulches and bare hills noted in reports by cavalry troopers as far back as the war.

Though for the fortunate, there would be shopping trips to Memphis, most Oxford residents patronized the merchants on the square, who would wait for the Saturday crowds. Drawn up around the courthouse, reins hitched to the iron chain looped to the wooden posts, wagons would be piled high with watermelons, tomatoes, corn, and other produce in season. While a woman shopped at the dry-goods store or a drugstore, her husband could poke around the hardware stores and then idle away some time with friends leaning against the courthouse. If he wanted a drink, he stepped into a secluded spot to share with a friend a bottle of powerful colorless whiskey made from local corn. A Negro farm hand or sawmill worker might head for Freedman Town—the seven blocks adjoining the railroad tracks in the town's northwest quadrant. There he could find convivial companionship and even the not uncommon violence that would attract the attention, finally, of the sheriff.

By the Saturday after their arrival, the Falkners had begun to settle into their new house, though people still called it "the old Johnny Brown place." It was on Second South Street, one block west and six blocks south of the courthouse on a lot that occupied the whole block, 400 feet wide and stretching 1,000 feet to where a wood began. The back half, divided from the front by the same kind of crisscross panel fence which enclosed the whole property, provided pasture and a barn. Set well back from the street was the house, a big one with a fireplace in every room but the kitchen. It was rather ornate, with latticework at the bottom of the porch that stretched across the front, and with elaborate trim where the porch supports met the roof. The extra-large windows were flanked by tall shutters.

The family needed the added space the house provided, for Lelia Butler had moved in to stay. Her piety continued unabated, and it may have contributed to her son-in-law's abjuring profanity on Sunday and refusing to touch a playing card on that day, even to build a card house for the children. Damuddy had brought her easel with her, a reminder, perhaps, of the scholarship she had won in 1890 to study sculpture in Rome, a chance declined because, she said, she had to take care of her daughter. She spent a good deal of time at the easel, and once she carved a nine-inch-high doll and dressed it in a blue policeman's outfit. Willie named it Patrick O'Leary and played with it in the roomy attic on rainy days.

Maud Falkner needed even more help than her mother could provide, however, in taking care of her three active sons. The help came in a form as diminutive as her own. Caroline Barr had been a house servant of the Young Colonel before going to work for Murry Falkner. She had traveled to Oxford with the family and moved into a cabin in the back-yard. She was a neat black woman weighing less than a hundred pounds. Born into slavery sometime around 1840, she had been freed at sixteen. Though she could not read or write, she had a fund of stories about old times before the war, and the days afterward too, when the riders of the Ku Klux Klan appeared claiming they were dead Confederates momentarily escaping the flames of hell to ride the night. Her own children raised and grown, she became a second mother to Willie, Jack, and Johncy. They loved her stories and they loved her. In her starched dress, ironed apron, and immaculate headcloth, she was second in authority over the children to Miss Maud. She addressed the head of the house as "Mist' Murry" and his parents as "Miss Sallie" and "Kunnel." She called young William Falkner "Mimmie," adopting Johncy's version of his brother's name. To the children she was Mammy Callie; to some of her friends,

Callie Watermelon. She had a wide circle of friends and acquaintances of both races in Oxford. In the Falkner home, she was soon a fixture in her rocking chair, a member of the intimate circle around the parlor fireplace.

The Falkner boys now saw much of their aunt Holland. A trim woman who stood five feet two, she was an accomplished rider, completely fearless, and still the best friend of Maud Butler Falkner. To Willie and her other nephews she was Auntee (Aun-tee, with the "a" as in "father" and the accent on the second syllable), and they returned the fierce loyalty she gave. Her life was more precarious than they could know, for though her husband, Dr. James Porter Wilkins, seemed secure as county health officer, the early signs of consumption had already appeared. Their daughter, Sallie Murry Wilkins, was not only cousin to the Falkner boys, she was one of their best friends. Murry Falkner would say to his sister, "Huldy, I'll give you any two of my boys for your girl." She was with them almost as often as if she had been a member of their household.

For the children, the firmament of adult authority included—now more than ever—J. W. T. and Sallie Murry Falkner. He was the classic figure of the Southern Gentleman, wearing a large panama hat and dressing all in white in the hot season. He would draw large cigars from the vest adorned with a heavy gold watch chain, and he swung a sturdy gold-headed stick as he walked. Sallie Murry was still ailing, but there was nothing of the pallid invalid about her. Like her independent brother, Dr. Will Murry, she was frank and outspoken, but she presided over The Big Place with grace and charm, entertaining often for her church groups, the book club, and the United Daughters of the Confederacy.

The Young Colonel was busier than ever. A city alderman, university trustee, and state senator, he would announce in the spring of 1903 for another term in the Senate. It was turning into a prosperous year for Mississippi, and perhaps in anticipation of an even heavier practice, the firm of Falkner and Shands had taken in a twenty-seven-year-old lawyer named Lee Maurice Russell. His home place was Dallas, a hamlet in the red clay hills of the county's southeastern corner. He had grown up as the son of a poor farmer, but his fierce ambition had pushed him along the rutted roads to the shabby schoolhouses and finally to the university. There he had been the butt of cruelty from the sons of the well-to-do, particularly fraternity boys. Now he was practicing law and cultivating a following among the inarticulate farmers, who saw him as one of their own. When the election was held in August, however, these voters threw their strength, not to Russell's employer, but to G. R. Hightower. In a portent of things to come, a movement some would call the revolt of the rednecks, Hightower won, and J. W. T. Falkner ran third and last.

It was a mortifying defeat, and he would never again run for any office beyond a local one, but he was at no loss for other activities. He was one of the incorporators of the Oxford Oil Mill Company. He bought a transfer line and renamed it the Falkner Transfer Company. That October he bought the Opera House. John Falkner, Jr., and Lee Russell would manage the Opera House, and Murry Falkner would run the transfer company and part of the oil mill business too. Like his father, John junior enjoyed politics, and he would become increasingly involved in state affairs. The Falkner family's activities were widening in scope: law, farming, real estate, and business.

It was a good time for the children. They were growing through a certain kind of nineteenth-century American childhood, one of large families and ample houses, of simplicity yet plenty in all the important things. It was a small-town childhood where, apart from church and school activities, children pretty much made their own diversions. But their lives were touched by the world outside through the offerings of the Opera House. Each year Ford's Minstrels played to a capacity audience. There was the edification and entertainment of *Ten Nights in a Barroom*, with such other popular standbys as *Peck's Bad Boy* and *East Lynne*. There were even occasional trips to go to Memphis shows. William Falkner loved seeing *Ben Hur* there "because it had live horses in it and a camel and I'd never seen a camel before."[2]

It was still the horse-drawn age in Oxford, and Billy—as he was now called—and Jack had their own ponies. Mammy Callie would take the children out into the woods, where she would teach them how to recognize the different birds. In the spring she would allow them to climb trees—"bird nesting" to find eggs to add to their growing collection. On rainy days the Falkner boys might go to The Big Place to play with Sallie Murry. She and Auntee had moved into the massive white clapboard house on South Street after the end of James Wilkins' struggle with tuberculosis, and by now Auntee had begun gradually to take over the running of the household from her ailing mother. She might send the four children up to play in the fully floored attic where they could even roller-skate if they wanted to. In the linen closet on the second floor they used a huge cedar chest to play ship, with Billy as the Captain, Sallie Murry as the Wife, Jack as the Sailor, and Johncy, the hapless youngest, as the Baby with a bottle full of water. Sometimes Sallie Murry's solitary companion would be Billy. He would play his games of the imagination with Patrick O'Leary while Sallie Murry would play hers with her dolls.

Sometimes a new friend would bring her dolls, and they would have to themselves all of the big screened-in porch that spanned the front and one side of the house. Her name was Lida Estelle Oldham, and her family had moved to Oxford that fall of 1903 from Kosciusko, ninety miles due south in the center of the state.

The Oldhams were different from most of their neighbors, not just because they were newcomers, but because they were Republicans. They had distinguished connections on both sides of the family: the legendary Sam Houston, a Confederate general, an Episcopal bishop, and a congressman. But even though the Radical Republican rule was almost thirty years past, memories were long, and there were few Republicans who would be spared the hostility of most of their fellow Mississippians. But the Oldhams were an addition to Oxford. Lem Oldham, a law graduate of the University of Mississippi, was a well-turned-out if somewhat pompous man, and his wife, Lida, was an accomplished woman. She had studied piano at the Cincinnati Conservatory and was teaching Estelle and her little sister, Melvina Victoria—"Tochie"—to play too. She entertained often and graciously, aided principally by her cook, Cynthia, who was freed of other tasks by Magnolia, who looked after the children. Magnolia would curl Estelle's long hair by twirling it around a broom handle, keeping her still by telling her to look out the parlor window to see what was going on in South Street. One day her seven-year-old charge saw a family procession go by—the Falkners on their way to The Big Place. The little girl pointed to the boy in the lead, the oldest one, on a Shetland pony. " 'Nolia," she said, "see that little boy? I'm going to marry him when I grow up." 'Nolia grunted and kept on twirling the soft hair. "Folks what say they goin' to get married while they little," she said, "is sho to grow up to be ol' maids." Estelle said nothing, carefully watching the procession move out of sight.

For the elder Falkners the visits to The Big Place were depressing, for Sallie Murry's pain and weakness were now obvious, as was her husband's growing deafness. But both Murry and Maud worked hard, and any pleasure they had must have seemed hard-won. It came in varied forms. Although she had been raised a Baptist, she had had her own children baptized in her husband's Methodist Church, where they faithfully attended Sunday School. Maud Falkner enjoyed the annual Camp Meeting, at which ministers from Holly Springs, Water Valley, and even as far away as Memphis labored over the souls of the faithful encamped in cottages and tents around the tabernacle in the woods. In August 1905 the Camp Meeting was crowned by thirty-five conversions. The zeal that produced them was reflected in a religious census two years later which revealed that "there were only 180 unconverted persons in the community, ⅔ of this number being under the age of 12 years."[3] Maud took strength and pleasure from her church, but even more pleasure from her books. She read Shakespeare and Balzac, Conrad, and other fiction writers of the day, and like her mother-in-law, she greatly admired Tennyson and Browning. As her children came of age she encouraged them to read, drawing upon the large library of the Young Colonel as well as the books she had accumulated over the years.

Murry Falkner's pleasures were much different. Leaving the railroad had been difficult enough, but his distress was compounded by the physical uprooting that followed. And then, in his new town, he had been plunged into a variety of unfamiliar enterprises. The first had been to superintend the grading of North Street. Not long afterward he bought O. I. Grady's

Livery Stable, and later took out an ad in the *Eagle* as manager of the Falkner Transfer Company. By 1905 the company was running a daily hack between Oxford and the university, and he had the added responsibility of managing the Oxford Oil Mill Company. But he had congenial company at the stable. Jack Falkner would recall, "a gang of Negroes to attend to the horses, two white men to drive the hacks, and always two to ten cronies to sit about the comfortable stove in his office and tell tall tales about animals, hunting and fishing, applying themselves to the ever-present crock of good drinking whiskey. . . ."[4]

From time to time the dark side of Murry Falkner's nature would erupt into violence. Not six months after his arrival in Oxford he and Dick Oliver, the dark-haired, mustachioed, hot-tempered constable of Lafayette County's Beat One, ran afoul of each other. Words came to blows, attracting a crowd which did nothing to stop them. The grueling struggle ended with a shattering crash as Falkner knocked Oliver through the window of John's Grocery. But there was a curious aftermath. Not only did the two men become friends, but Murry Falkner assumed a kind of responsibility for Dick Oliver, helping him from time to time for the rest of his life, a responsibility Murry's eldest son would assume in his turn.

A man's man in many ways, Murry Falkner preferred hunting camp to Camp Meeting, and he vastly preferred the "Club House" in the Tallahatchie bottom to the Falkner cottage near the tabernacle. He and Lex Ramey and sometimes John junior would slip off to hunt squirrels and rabbits, even an occasional deer or, more rarely, a bear. He enjoyed taking his sons with him to follow the hounds and listen to their voices as they chased possums by night. He took the boys to the Club House too, but on occasion his wife came along. It may have been anxiety about his drinking that took Maud into the Tallahatchie bottom on what should have been an outing for males only. What a shame, Faulkner would reflect later, that father and sons couldn't have gone there to hunt by themselves.

The union of the small, firm-minded woman and the big, gruff, inarticulate man was a difficult one. They were bound together by the memories of their courtship, by the ten years of their marriage, by their three sons, and by the whole web of personal and community sanctions that were particularly strong in a small Southern town. But it must have seemed now to both that there was as much to separate them. Maud read the classics and Murry read Westerns. Their working hours presented a strong contrast: the stable and the home. And there was the drinking: Murry had the family taste for it, and he must have turned to it not only for pleasure but for solace from past disappointments and present problems. Sometimes he would be unable to contain himself. He would think about the beckoning West, about prairies and cattle, and he would storm and shout. Maud Falkner would remain silent until her husband had stalked out or the storm had blown over. In her character she combined courage and stoicism, born in part of the years when she had to support both herself and her deserted mother. She detested whiskey—what it did to her husband and to the family. And when the drinking got seriously out of hand, it would be she who would have to deal with it. Like her mother-in-law, she would take her husband for treatment at the Keeley Institute, fifteen miles from Memphis.

Sixty years later Jack Falkner would remember those trips, which probably began when he was about seven. He remembered them with a good deal of pleasure, for he and his two brothers would ride the train to Memphis and then enjoy the sights on the streetcar line between the city and the institute. Then, while their father was being treated, they would stay in quarters the institute provided for patients' families. As long as they promised not to leave the streetcar, they could while away the time seeing the sights. From that vantage point they caught their first view of the Mississippi. Mammy Callie could have supervised the children at home, but Maud Falkner doubtless hoped that the boys would experience these trips as object lessons. The sight of a drunken father could hardly have failed to make some impression, but it did not serve to keep them from drinking heavily in later life. The example worked in just the opposite way from what Maud Falkner intended.

Mammy Callie gave love and devotion, and the children themselves were a close-knit group. What sort of parental love did they know in these crucial early years? Murry Falkner would tell his sons stories about hunting, about animals, and all three displayed the love of horses and dogs that he felt. He read the newspaper comic strips to them, and in a particularly good mood he might even stand by the piano and sing an old favorite of his, "The Glow-worm." But much of the time there would be a wall between them. At the table, vigorously eating the fried foods he loved, he would be silent until he put down his napkin. Perhaps the most loving of his boys was Jack, but looking back, even Jack realized "how little I actually came to know him, and perhaps, even less to understand him." It went deeper than that. "He was not an easy man to know," Jack recalled. "His capacity for affection was limited, but I'm sure that to such extent as it allowed he loved us all."[5] By the time Billy was entering adolescence the signs of conflict would be clear.

What of their mother? She had her silent side too, and at times a tartness that stung. She was shy and insecure. As one of her granddaughters would put it years later, she was "often afraid of strange people and situations. She masked her vulnerability with a cold hard manner."[6] Outwardly she sometimes appeared arrogant, brusque and self-assured, like the Old Colonel. She placed a sign in her kitchen printed in block crayon letters on a narrow stick of gray-green wood. It read, "DON'T COMPLAIN—DON'T EXPLAIN." It bespoke the kind of rigor that inculcated Christian virtues and prompted her to tell her first grandson, "You've got a back just like the Old Colonel, but you've got to be a better man than he was."

As her boys became men, Maud Falkner showed her love in ways that were perfectly clear, despite a habitual restraint, and in tragedy she would be utterly devastated. People said that her first-born was the apple of her eye, but when his achievements overshadowed those of another son, she declared herself equally proud of both. One friend said later that all the Falkner boys were too close to their mother, that they were emotionally tied to her. If this was to some extent true, it was certainly reciprocal, at least to the extent that when the boys married, their wives would have a difficult time with their mother-in-law. And many years later, when her eldest was ill, he was treated for a combination of complaints by a physician who looked for psychiatric as well as neurological symptoms. He conjectured that his patient might not have received enough love from his mother. When he tried to open up this area, Faulkner characteristically responded only with icy silence. There was no such suspicion in Jack's mind, recalling the way he had seen his brother look at their mother "with steady, open affection . . . a thousand times. . . ."[7]

It is difficult to penetrate the depths, seventy years later, of the psychic bonds between a reserved mother and an often quiet child who would become a frequently silent man. He was the oldest, and older children traditionally are made to bear more responsibility than younger ones, at least in their early years. And it is axiomatically difficult for them to compete with babies, particularly if some aspect of their earliest days and months is precarious, as was the case with Jack and would be the case with the fourth of the Falkner boys when he came along. If such a situation could produce anxiety or even perhaps some resentment, it could also produce a wish to earn love through different ways, both by conventional gifts and gifts of achievement. If some of these factors operated in the case of Billy Falkner, there was one pattern he would share with many men. It was true that he would be at maturity the shortest of the Falkner boys, and this would determine in part his choices among women. But it seems significant that most of the women he loved resembled his mother in some way: in stature, in features, or in temperament.

LIKE all the other mothers in Oxford, Maud Falkner was concerned in the summer of 1905 about the wave of yellow fever that began in New Orleans and had Oxford under a shotgun quarantine by August. But the crisis passed with the coming of cooler weather. Then she was caught up in special preparations: her first-born would begin school in September.

... standing at the corner when the dismissal bell rang, standing there while the kindergarten then the first-grade children
streamed past . . . then the second grade, standing there while
the Lilliputian flow divided. . . . the rules of the school and of
respectable decorum . . . the empty room itself smelling of chalk
and anguished cerebration and the dry inflexibility of facts. . . .

—*The Town* (144–145)

MAUD FALKNER had her sons' photograph taken that fall at the studio
over Leavell's Plain & Fancy Grocery. She and Mammy Callie had dressed
them in their black-velvet best—jackets buttoned tight at the neck, with
no shirt showing. William sat erect, looking almost plump, turned nearly
full-face toward the camera. (It could scarcely have been more different
from two other photos in the family album: in one he was climbing a
tree; in another, standing on his head.) The Butler cast to his features
was clearer now than ever, with the snapping black eyes, the thin mouth
concealing spiky baby teeth, and the fair hair parted precisely in the
middle. Bright and alert-looking, he skipped the beginners' grade, or chart
class, and went right into first grade on September 25, 1905, his eighth
birthday.

The Oxford Graded School stood two blocks west of the square on
Jackson Avenue, a two-story brick building that housed the chart class
and seven primary grades on the first floor and the three-grade high
school on the second. Each classroom was dominated by the teacher's
desk on a small platform looking out over the double desks, each one
seating two children. Heat flowed out from a wood-burning iron stove.
Billy's teacher was Miss Annie Chandler, whose students loved her.
Precocious in drawing and painting, Billy presented her with three watercolors. She gave him *The Clansman: An Historical Romance of the
Ku Klux Klan,* by Thomas Dixon, Jr. Hers was not an easy job, in school

or at home. She lived with her family on Pierce Avenue, a few blocks southeast of the Falkners. She and her sisters were charged with the care of their brother, Edwin, who could be seen playing in their front yard behind a high fence. The family had learned early in his childhood that Edwin was retarded. He would never be normal, though he lived past the age of thirty. Annie Chandler gave to her pupils the kind of love that her family gave its own perennial child.

Billy was an honor-roll student, and his report card throughout the year would show no grades below Perfect or Excellent. He worked conscientiously at reading, spelling, writing, and arithmetic, but he apparently liked drawing best. In the back of his first-grade reader he drew a locomotive and tender in great detail and sketched abbreviated engines at the front. One Sunday when Damuddy took him to the Baptist Church he drew a whole train in one of the hymnals before she noticed what he was doing.

His deportment in school was graded 80 at the end of the year, but it was not as high at home. He enjoyed playing tricks on his brothers. Once when he and Jack lost baby teeth—each worth a dime from the tooth fairy—Billy held his in his hand for a moment over the outdoor well and then told Jack, "I dropped mine in." Jack walked over and tossed his in. Then Billy opened his palm. There was the tooth. "I didn't," he said. He showed a fertile imagination for childhood games and enlisting others to test them.[1] Entertainment came in the form of family excursions. At about two o'clock, after an ample Sunday dinner, Murry Falkner would get out the trap and take his family for a ride in the country. On other days they might drive three miles northwest of the square and fish for catfish in muddy Davidson's Creek. When Grandfather would take Billy, Jack, Johncy, and Sallie Murry out in the surrey, they might just drive to another part of the creek, called Davidson's Bottom, where the worst mischance might be a false step or a push that could result in wet stockings or muddy drawers. Neighborhood children would often join in the play in the Falkners' big front yard. There Damuddy might help them to build miniature villages. One of the children remembered the way Billy could make do like Damuddy, his imagination seizing on whatever they could find as he led the group in improvisation.

Pretending was often fused with history for the Falkner boys. For years their grandfather had helped old soldiers and widows to fill out pension forms. He was the organizer and first commander of the Lamar Camp of the Sons of Confederate Veterans, and his wife was a past president of the Albert Sidney Johnston Chapter of the United Daughters of the Confederacy. Her loyalties embroiled her in controversy. It was the boast of the University of Mississippi that its students, "organized as the University Greys, reached the highest point of the Confederacy, forty-seven yards beyond the farthest point reached by Pickett's men at Gettysburg."[2] But that spring of 1906, when the town learned that the marble monument, nearly thirty feet high, would raise the figure of a Confederate scout on the campus instead of the square, Sallie Murry Falkner was indignant. Certainly the Greys deserved credit, but they weren't the only soldiers from Lafayette County, and it wasn't just university money that was putting up the monument. But the planners went ahead despite objections such as hers, and the dedication became a grand occasion, celebrated with a regimental band, the veterans, and the other ladies of the Albert Sidney Johnston Chapter. Adamantly unmollified, Sallie Murry took the most drastic step she could think of: she resigned from the U.D.C. It must have been indignation like hers that lay behind the resolution adopted in June by the United Confederate Veterans to erect another monument in the courthouse square, but she would not live to see it, for the ailment that had been called catarrh of the stomach was clearly cancer. A private nurse and special foods could do but little to ease her suffering.

Distraught as he was, J. W. T. Falkner did his best to keep up with his other obligations. One was to make plans for a September reunion of General Edward C. Walthall's brigade, whose members had fought under Forrest and particularly distinguished themselves at Lookout Mountain. Fully 3,000 gathered, hardly enough to consume 2,500 pounds of barbecued meat plus hundreds of pies and custards. The Young Colonel was used to this kind of hospitality, for periodically he would sponsor a reunion of W. C. Falkner's Partisan Rangers. He would put many of them up in his home, lining the upstairs halls with cots. Everyone would be pressed into service, including Leslie Oliver and the others who worked for Murry Falkner in another new business: an ice plant near the oil mill. The three small Falkner boys were fascinated to see the veterans and hear their martial reminiscences. The ample food and drink helped prompt one of the men of the Old Colonel's regiment to rise and recall campaigns fought forty years ago. He remembered the danger and the hardship, but with his own version of the rhetoric that had inspired the whole South in those long-gone days, he asserted that his service and sacrifice were a privilege of the highest order. "Now what air more noble," he asked with a flourish, "than to lie on the field of battle with your car-case filled with canyon balls?" From time to time thereafter Billy would fix Jack with an imperious glance and repeat the orator's question, at which they would both double up with laughter.

It was different, though, when they would sit on Grandfather's big front porch in the gathering twilight and listen to his tales of those far-off days when he was fourteen and a blue-uniformed patrol might ride up to the house and demand all they had. He would retell the stories of "Kunnel Falkner," as he always called his father, about the fighting in Virginia early in the war. Then, the next day, as Billy and Jack rode Fancy and Angel Face, they would be Jeb Stuart and Stonewall Jackson leading the gallant horsemen and gray-clad columns in the Shenandoah Valley. The tales seized upon their imaginations, especially that of the eldest, who was now beginning to rival Mammy Callie at telling stories, some true and some invented. Some of his drawings were now keyed to such tales. And when he would be promoted to third grade, skipping the second, and Miss Laura Eades would ask him what he wanted to be when he grew up, he would answer, "I want to be a writer like my great-granddaddy."

Whenever the question was posed, his answer would be the same. At the age of nine he had found his vocation. Jack would later say that the classroom avowal was "in accord with his character and his dreams."[3] In that Deep South milieu, in a small town where the mystique of The Lost Cause was nurtured by the United Confederate Veterans and the United Daughters of the Confederacy, where the nearby battlefield of Shiloh and the local cemeteries were mute memorials, Billy Falkner's response was remarkable for singling out that one thread of life that was so varied and spectacular. In 1851, at the age of twenty-six, William Clark Falkner had privately published *The Siege of Monterey*, a poem that drew upon his equivocal record as a first lieutenant in the Mexican War and upon his love for his wife-to-be. Before the year was out he paid for the publication of *The Spanish Heroine*, a novel as amateurish as *The Siege of Monterey*. It was a decade and a half before he wrote at length again, a play this time, in the wake of the war's destruction, to raise funds to help reopen the Ripley Female Academy. *The Lost Diamond* of 1867 had a good deal of the melodrama of the earlier works. His imagination as untrammeled as ever, he presented in the fifth of the play's eight scenes "The Battle of Manassas. Thrilling scenes on the bloody field." The ending followed the convention of the time in uniting the Blue and the Gray through the persons of the romantic leads. Almost fifteen years passed before he produced his greatest success, *The White Rose of Memphis*. Colonel Falkner paid for its serialization in the Ripley *Advertiser* in 1881. This time he hit the jackpot. With a Mississippi riverboat journey for a setting, Falkner's characters—costumed for a masquerade ball—took turns telling stories, but a central plot involved violence, betrayal, and true love rewarded. One critic would call it "a murder mystery plus two romances, with some absurdities and overblown rhetoric, but also some good characters and gripping scenes." The range of quotations, allusions, and references was surprising for a largely self-educated man. Drawing on nearly three dozen writers, he had quoted most from Shakespeare, the Bible, and Sir Walter Scott, in that order.[4] It would remain in print for nearly three decades, in thirty-five editions that sold approximately 160,000 copies.[5] A novel, *The Little Brick Church*, and *Rapid Ramblings in Europe*, a book of travel sketches, would appear before his violent death.

Later, as a grown man nearing forty, William Faulkner would not overvalue his great-grandfather's major work. *The White Rose of Memphis* was to him an ardently romantic novel with "the men all brave and the women all pure," the work of a man without humor or much sensibility.[6] But he certainly would not undervalue the force of his personality. "The feeling in Ripley did not die out with Colonel Falkner's death and Thurmond's leaving," he said. "I can remember myself, when I was a boy in Ripley, there were some people who would pass on the other side of the street to avoid speaking—that sort of thing."[7] Though the Old Colonel had died eight years before Billy Falkner was born, he felt he knew why this animus continued: that his ambitious and arrogant ancestor had provoked one-time partner Richard J. Thurmond and goaded him into murder, Still, the old man seized on his imagination through an almost mythic quality. "People at Ripley talk of him as if he were still alive, up in the hills some place, and might come in at any time," he said. "There's nothing left in the old place, the house is gone and the plantation boundaries, nothing left of his work but a statue. But he rode through that country like a living force. I like it better that way."[8] Ten years later he felt it more strongly. "My great-grandfather, whose name I bear, was a considerable figure in his time and provincial milieu," he told one correspondent; "we have a citation in James Longstreet's longhand as his corps commander after 2nd Manassas. He built the first railroad in our county, wrote a few books, made grand European tour of his time, died in a duel and the county raised a marble effigy which still stands in Tippah County."[9] Now Faulkner was enlarging the legend with the duel and the statue erected by a grateful citizenry.

It is hard to know with any certainty the total picture Faulkner had in his early years of this ancestor who loomed so over the whole family. Records indicate that one set of his forebears originally settled in Granville County, North Carolina, around 1750, and that they came from Maryland. One genealogical historian has written that "there is the strong possibility that the immigrant ancestors were John and Elizabeth Faulkner who arrived in Maryland in January of 1665 on the ship *Agreement* out of Bristol." The descendants would variously identify their lineage as Scottish, Ulster Irish, and French Huguenot. Although the 1790 census spelled the name Faulkner, in other records it appeared as Falkner, Folkner, Fortner, Forkner, and probably Falconer. On June 1, 1816, William Joseph Faulkner married Caroline Word in Surry County, North Carolina. She was the daughter of Thomas Adam Word, whose forebears were thought to have come from Wales around 1652. He was a prominent surveyor, the high sheriff of Surry County about 1800, and head of one of the county's most cultivated families. (His son, Thomas Jefferson Word, would become a Mississippi congressman.) In 1817 a son, Thomas Anderson, was born to Caroline and Joseph Faulkner, as he was called.[10] During the next several years the family moved to Virginia and then decided to try Tennessee. On the way they had to stop in Knox County, Tennessee, on July 6, 1825, for the arrival of their fourth child, William

Clark Faulkner. They stayed there for about ten years, which saw the birth of two more boys. Later in the decade, sometime before 1839, they picked up again and traveled through Tennessee, southern Kentucky, and Illinois to Ste. Genevieve, Missouri. The town was a stopping point for immigrants who would make their way across the river and head west. The Faulkners settled there, where Caroline Faulkner would give birth to two more children. It was in Ste. Genevieve that the saga of William Clark Faulkner began.

About 1841 he set out from home on foot to find his aunt, Justiania Word Thompson, and her husband in Ripley, Mississippi. There were three versions of his motives. One was that he sought better opportunities to support his widowed mother and her other children. (The records suggest that his father died about 1842.) Two other versions were that he had hit his brother with a hoe and feared he had killed him, or that his father had whipped him severely for bloodying young James Faulkner's head. When he reached Ripley, one story has it, he found that his uncle was in Pontotoc awaiting trial for murder. John Wesley Thompson was said to have argued his own defense and won acquittal. In any case, he adopted the boy, who was identified in local records as a resident of Ripley by June 1845. By the time he was twenty he was reading law himself and earning money however he could, including working at the jail. There he showed his resourcefulness by writing the life of a convicted ax murderer, supposedly splitting the proceeds with the family of the convict after hawking the pamphlet at the very moment and place where the trap was sprung. He went off to fight in Mexico and returned missing the first joints of three fingers and a good deal of blood from the foot struck by another musket ball. There was strong suspicion that the mission which took him into ambush had been amatory rather than military. On his discharge, dated October 6, 1847, his name was still spelled Faulkner. At some point thereafter, he dropped the "u." Eighty years later the Colonel's namesake would make the notation on a form: "(surname originally Faulkner)." One of his other descendants would say that there were "some no-account folks" in another part of the state who spelled their name Faulkner, and he didn't want to be confused with them.

Back home, he passed the bar, married Holland Pearce, and fathered John Wesley Thompson Falkner. Half a year later, in the spring of 1849, Robert Hindman, a member of Falkner's company in the war, accused Falkner of blackballing him for membership in the Knights of Temperance. He pulled a revolver, they grappled, and the gun misfired. Falkner killed him with his knife. To the Hindmans, this was murder; to Falkner, self-defense—and the jury agreed with Falkner. But misfortune dogged him. Three weeks after the killing, his wife died of consumption. When he took his ailing son to his Aunt Justiania, her husband said they would take the baby only on condition that he stay with them even if Falkner remarried. He had to agree. When he found a new love, Elizabeth Vance, who had helped him years before when he was seeking his uncle, her parents objected. Their disapproval was not lessened by events of February 1851. A partisan of the Hindmans named Erasmus Morris quarreled with Falkner over a house rental. The two argued violently, and suddenly Falkner drew his pistol and shot Morris dead. Thomas C. Hindman, Jr., the brother of his earlier victim, tried the case against Falkner, but again the jury was sympathetic. After the acquittal, Hindman's father tried to shoot Falkner, but missed. Understandably, Falkner found this a good time to make several business trips, and by October he was able to marry Lizzie Vance secretly. By the next August the two had started a family.

Dabbling in politics, Falkner by 1855 had switched from the Whigs to the Know-Nothing party and run unsuccessfully against John Wesley Thompson for the state legislature. The next year, when he wrenched a gun away from one of his friends who was trying to shoot Thomas C. Hindman, Sr., the near-victim challenged Falkner to a duel, which was averted only through the good offices of the editor of the Memphis *Appeal*. Now Falkner seemed to have breathing space. There was no imminent danger and his affairs prospered. A slaveowner since Holland Pearce had come to him with her dowry, he bought and sold slaves, practiced law, farmed, and invested in land. By 1859 he was worth $50,000, had fathered three children, and held a brigadier general's commission in the militia. He was about to enter upon a spectacular phase of his turbulent life.

When Mississippi seceded he lost out in the election of the four militia brigadier generals and had to settle for a captaincy in a company he had helped raise, the Magnolia Rifles. When they were merged with other units to form the 2nd Mississippi Infantry Regiment, he was elected colonel. Whipping his raw recruits into shape, he was promoted to brigadier general but declined the command two days later because it would separate him from his regiment. Ironically, he would spend the rest of his military career politicking to regain the stars he had renounced. But he made a gallant regimental commander. At the battle of the First Manassas, not far from Stonewall Jackson, he helped to repulse Union General Irwin McDowell's final assault and win the day. He lost two horses from under him, and when he seized a third mount, General Beauregard saw him flash by. One correspondent wrote that the Louisianan shouted, "Go ahead, you hero with the black plume; *history shall never forget you!*" It was the high point of his life. General Joseph E. Johnston commended his courage and leadership, but this did him little good in the regimental elections the next April. He was a martinet to the men, who saw his gallantry as recklessness that cost needless casualties. When they elected a new commander, he did the only thing his pride would permit: he left to raise a regiment to lead against the Yankees on his home ground.

By the summer of 1862 he had done it. The First Mississippi Partisan

Rangers numbered seven hundred men at peak strength and fought guerrilla-style in northeast Mississippi and southern Tennessee. In August, Falkner even led them in a daring pell-mell attack on the forces of General Philip Sheridan, but his struggle to keep his outnumbered command together was made harder by Confederate conscription officers raiding partisan units to bring regular regiments up to strength. Then, in April 1863, the outnumbered Rangers were decimated by a regiment of Wisconsin cavalry, and that was practically the end of Falkner's military career. A legend grew that he rode with General Nathan Bedford Forrest in the last years of the war, but it seems clear that he went underground, running the blockade around Memphis to bring back vital supplies such as salt and quinine, as well as other profitable commodities. In the dark year of 1864, when furious General A. J. Smith burned Oxford and Ripley, Falkner's home was one of those destroyed, but he recouped his fortunes quickly at the war's end.

Postwar peacetime was no less turbulent for him than the early years. He plunged into his law practice, involved himself deeply in the plans for the railroad, and found time for political activity too, including the harassment of Negro voters. Lizzie presented him with four more children between 1868 and 1874, but in 1878 his eldest went to join in the family plot the two little ones who had died in 1861. William Henry Falkner was a handsome ne'er-do-well who had been forced to leave one university and then gambled away the money to enroll him in another. According to family lore, he returned to Ripley and resumed an affair with the young wife of a crippled jeweler. When (in this contested account) the cuckold shot the betrayer, he followed protocol and called on the father. "Colonel," he said, "I hate to have to tell you this, but I had to kill Henry." After a moment's silence the Colonel was said to have replied, "That's all right. I'm afraid I would have had to do it myself anyway." But gunplay was not yet over in the Falkner family.

Triumph and tragedy came close upon one another as Colonel Falkner approached his middle sixties. He had published a book and raised money in New York, shaken Grover Cleveland's hand in Washington and done the grand tour in Europe. By the fall of 1889, when he was buying other lines to merge with his railroad, he was also running for the state legislature. Bitterly against him was Richard J. Thurmond, the former partner whom Falkner had forced out of the railroad. There had been words and even blows between them before November 5, 1889, when Falkner won the seat by an overwhelming majority. That afternoon in Ripley he strolled down toward the square. No longer would he carry a pistol, and he had made a new will. Talking with a friend, he stopped near Dick Thurmond's office. Later, some would declare Falkner looked in through the window and made a move toward his pocket. A bystander would say that Falkner turned and suddenly Thurmond was at his side. But there was no dispute about what happened next. Thurmond was holding a

.44 pistol at point-blank range. "Dick, what are you doing?" Falkner said. "Don't shoot!" Thurmond fired and Falkner dropped to the pavement, blood streaming from his mouth. He looked up and spoke before he lost consciousness. "Why did you do it, Dick?" he asked. Falkner lingered until the next night. He was buried with the most elaborate ceremony Tippah County had ever seen.

The following February, after many postponements and much maneuvering, Thurmond was tried and acquitted, and not long afterward he left the county for good. In due course a monument was raised over Falkner's grave: a pediment six feet square and fourteen feet high, with an eight-foot statue rising above it. It had been carved of Italian marble in Carrara from the Colonel's photographs and measurements. He had ordered it himself in the expectation, some said, that his grateful townsmen would erect it in the square. His great-grandson would visit the family plot from time to time. As a mature man, when Faulkner became the head of the clan, he would see to the repair of the weather-stained monument, and in his work he would commemorate its subject far more durably than Carrara marble ever could.

What image, then, did the growing boy carry in his mind of this ancestor whom he had never seen, yet who loomed so large? He saw in him a role-model of sorts: his own height at maturity, with features and carriage like his own. The Old Colonel did many things in his life, and if it was a career of tragedy mixed with triumph, it was a life which left its mark. Lawyer, planter, soldier, politician, railroad builder, and writer— he truly excelled at none of them, but there was a dynamism in him which made him a legend. What the boy would extract from it was not the dashing figure of the Knight with the Black Plume but that of the writer. He might speak of duels and civic monuments instead of murders and cemetery effigies, but he would see the total figure clearly, and he would perceive its arrogance and fatal haughty pride. The great-grandfather would give his descendant priceless material for his work, and he in turn would confer upon his ancestor a kind of immortality.

... So they in the hearse could not be dead: it must be something like sleep: a trick played on people ... tricked into that helpless coma for some dreadful and inscrutable joke until the dirt was packed down, to strain and thrash and cry in the airless dark, to not escape forever. So that night I had something very like hysterics. ...

But that was past now. ...

And three or four times a year I would come back, I would not know why, alone to look at them, not just at Grandfather and Grandmother but at all of them looming among the lush green of summer and the regal blaze of fall and the rain and ruin of winter before spring would bloom again, stained now, a little darkened by time and weather and endurance but still serene, impervious, remote, gazing at nothing. ...

—"Sepulture South: Gaslight," *USWF* (452, 455)

THE sense of mortality hung heavily over The Big Place in the fall of 1906. Sallie Murry Falkner had often entertained the Women's Book Club there, and once she had read them verses of her own. Answering the question "What is the best time in a woman's life?" the long poem was a kind of happy variant on the seven ages of man. Now she lay upstairs in the big bedroom, her writing confined to her diary. The last entry in her failing hand accepted death with resignation and looked forward to "unfading light in the Land of Life." Forty-eight hours later she was gone, four days before Christmas. Holland Wilkins and Maud Falkner herded the children to the back of the house on the day of the funeral, but John Wesley Thompson Falkner asked that they come into the parlor. So Billy and Sallie Murry Wilkins stood there with Jack and Johncy to hear the minister's funeral service for their grandmother. Then they rode with the others to St. Peter's Cemetery through the cold rain of the darkening December afternoon.

Later, Holland Wilkins tried to set the house back to rights. Maud

Falkner helped as best she could, for Holland herself was not a particularly robust woman, outspoken though she might be. There was in her, some thought, a strain of melancholia and hypochondria which could only have been aggravated during her mother's long illness.

In the silent house Auntee's father had already begun to retreat further into his deafness and his memories. During the days to come they would see him sitting in his chair, tracing with his finger upon the empty air the name "Sallie." Often he would walk alone to the cemetery to stand before her monument, gazing at the marble medallion that bore her likeness and at the epitaph he had chosen: *The heart of her husband doth safely trust in her. Her children arise and call her Blessed. Her husband also, and he praiseth her.*

Spring brought no lifting of the family's mood of grief and oppression, for now, as Damuddy sought comfort in her church and her Bible, she knew that she too was suffering from cancer. Maud Falkner was nursing her, looking after her as she had done so many times since girlhood. Sometimes her brother and his wife, Addie, would relieve her. They even took Damuddy to Memphis for treatment, but as the days passed, her grandsons could see how thin and shrunken she was becoming. She was anxious to see them, though she had little strength to talk, and she tried never to let them see her take the morphine that the doctor measured out. She died in the twilight of the first day of June, and they buried her the next day after a funeral service in Maud Falkner's parlor, which the children most probably did not attend. The grim and unsettling effects of Damuddy's lengthy ordeal must only have been increased when the three boys were sent to The Big Place while their own home was being fumigated to expunge the lingering traces of illness.

But in the perennial alternating rhythm, life was asserting itself over death as the fragrance of wisteria mingled with the heavy perfume of the gardenias and the blooming tuberoses. Maud Falkner was now awaiting her fourth child, and in the heat of midsummer he arrived on August 15, two days before his father's birthday. "He's my birthday present," Murry Falkner proudly told the men at his livery stable. Faithful to custom, he walked over to The Big Place and shouted through his father's deafness. What did he think they should name the baby? The Colonel thought back to the engaging and handsome half brother, dead now almost forty years. "Let's name him Henry," he said. When Murry Falkner relayed the suggestion to his wife, she thought of Henry and the gambling and the jeweler's wife. "Over my dead body," she replied. The boy was named for Damuddy: Dean Swift Falkner. In a few months his mother would be thirty-six, but now, whether by design or the workings of nature, her family was complete. She and Mammy Callie concentrated on the baby, and his elder brothers were now freer than they had ever been before to follow their own pursuits.

That was one side of the new situation: more freedom from adult supervision and discipline, which came not only from Murry and Maud but also from Mammy Callie, who would give orders as quickly as their mother would. But there must have been another side too, especially for Billy. One of his friends would say later that Murry was a silent man who ruled his boys pretty rigidly. "I know he did William," Bob Farley remembered. "Nobody gave him much trouble except William." Maud expected a good deal from her eldest, and if she thought he had led his brothers into devilment, his punishment would be appropriately harsher than theirs. But if he had felt displaced by Jack and then Johncy, if he had felt loss at the death of Sallie Murry, the matriarch, and the death of Damuddy, who had played with him and made blue-coated Patrick O'Leary for him, how did he feel now, when yet another baby lessened still further the attention he received not only from his mother but also from Mammy Callie, his second mother? He still had his brothers and his friends and his inner life, but it was no wonder that the silence which people saw as characteristic of his father would become a trait consonant with elements of his own psyche.

Billy was a quick and enthusiastic reader, but in the long days of summer he and his brothers would be outdoors most of the time. Some mornings they would slip out before daybreak, to see the fruit trains carrying strawberries north. Positioned on a high bank south of the station, they would know both the engine and the hand on the whistle when the first sounds came from the train laboring up the grade at Thacker's Mountain seven miles away. When it speeded up on the straightaway into town, Jack remembered, "the magnificent whistle spilled and spread out its song upon the quiet countryside, at once lonely, lovely, and unforgettable."[1] Reluctantly they would make their way home to breakfast.

Much of their entertainment came from stories. Sometimes the Colonel would take his four grandchildren out in the surrey to his farm in the country north of town. Billy would always seek out the Negro blacksmith on the place, listening to the man tell about old times in the county as he hammered the glowing plowshare or ax head. And of course, Mammy Callie had her seemingly inexhaustible fund of stories—memories of her girlhood on the Barr plantation under "Ole Mistis" before the war, and eerie experiences involving wolves and other varmints in the Tallahatchie Bottom. Billy would join in, and some of his tales seemed to enthrall even Mammy. Other stories came in written form that year in Miss May McGuire's fourth-grade class, but as 1907 became 1908 nothing they read had the vividness of a true happening they would hear about just before the next school year began. It was grislier than anything either Mammy Callie or Billy could have told, and as it swept through the county, it drew in its wake an aftermath terrible and violent.

Mrs. Mattie McMillan and her three children had moved into a rented cottage one mile north of town to be close to her husband, who was lodged in the county jail. On the morning of September 8 he asked Nelse Patton, a Negro trusty, to carry a message to her. It was said later that Patton was drunk and that he made advances, which Mattie Mc-Millan repulsed. When he angrily refused to leave, she reached for the pistol lying in the top bureau drawer. Before she could grasp it, Patton slashed her with a razor blow that nearly took her head off. As she rushed screaming from the house, her seventeen-year-old daughter came running from nearby. Patton seized her, but she wrenched free and fled to neighbors. They telephoned the sheriff, who immediately called Linburn Cullen and other deputies. Two of Cullen's sons, John and Jencks, disobeyed their father and raced out to try to intercept Patton. They met him near the wooded Toby Tubby Bottom, and when he tried to run past them, fifteen-year-old John Cullen raised his gun and shouted to him to halt. When he kept coming, Cullen fired and hit him with both loads of squirrel shot. Then the two boys stood guard until the posse came up. In Patton's pocket was a nicked and bloody razor, a piece broken from it that was later found in one of the dead woman's vertebrae.

By sundown a murmuring crowd of hundreds had gathered around the jail. From its porch, a judge and several ministers exhorted the men to go home and let the law take its course. But then a friend of J. W. T. Falkner sprang to the porch. He was W. V. Sullivan, a former United States senator. He harangued the crowd, which now numbered close to 2,000 people, and by eight o'clock, had turned it into a mob. Drawing his revolver, he handed it to a deputy sheriff. "Shoot Patton," he told him, "and shoot to kill!" The mob surged to the windows and boosted John Cullen and the sons of some of the other guards through them. They held their fathers while the doors were flung open. Because the sheriff had hidden his keys, the men labored with crowbars and pickaxes to break through a wall and reach Patton's darkened cell. When the first three rushed in, he battered them down with an iron bed railing. Then, as he crouched in a dark corner, refusing the order to come out, a volley of pistol shots echoed through the cell block. They dragged the body out through the powder smoke, castrated it, and mutilated the head. By a rope tied around Nelse Patton's neck, they dragged him behind a car to the square. Then they hung his naked body from a tree. The next morning Linburn Cullen bought a pair of overalls and clothed it. The coroner's jury found that "the said Nelse Patton came to his death from gunshot or pistol wounds inflicted by parties to us unknown."

When Miss Kate Kimmons' fifth-grade class was organized that September of 1908, if the boys standing around the playground wanted to know more about what had happened, Hal Cullen, the brother of the boy who had fired the first shot, could tell them. He was a good friend of Billy Falkner, who would visit him out in the country and go with him and his brothers to hunt bullfrogs and cottonmouth moccasins with a .22 rifle. Intelligent, imaginative, and sensitive behind that quiet manner,

Billy Falkner could not but have been impressed by that double tale of savagery and death. When a dramatization of Dixon's *The Clansman* came to town in October, he must have recognized in some of its incendiary scenes (which would provoke riots, on film in *The Birth of a Nation*) the same emotions which had seethed through Lafayette County and Oxford seven weeks before.

He must have been changing rapidly as he entered adolescence and the outside world impinged more and more upon his extraordinary consciousness. These changes were not translated into better grades, in part because Kate Kimmons, an excellent teacher, was stricter than her predecessors. In mid-October, Billy made the honor roll, but in contrast to previous years, this was the last time his name appeared there.[2]

His social consciousness was developing in a very personal way. "I more or less grew up in my father's livery stable," he would recall. "Being the eldest of four boys, I escaped my mother's influence pretty easy, since my father thought it was fine for me to apprentice to the business."[3] In a piece of fiction which no doubt enlarged on experience, he would write of a boy whose father "loved horses better than books or learning; he owned a livery stable, and here the boy grew up, impregnated with the violent ammoniac odor of horses."[4] He even bought one of his own, he later said, not like Fancy, the pony of his childhood, but a real and dangerous horse, the offspring of wild, range-bred Texas mustangs. As he would tell it, he went to the auction with one of his father's employees, a huge man with a boy's mind named Buster Callicoat. He paid $4.75 and bought one of the pintos, then realized that "it was a wild animal, it was a wild beast, it wasn't a domestic animal at all." When they harnessed the pinto to a cart, he exploded out of the barn. Buster threw Billy from the cart and then jumped out an instant before the horse destroyed it and ran wild for a mile. "But we kept that horse," Faulkner said, "and gentled him to where I finally rode him."[5]

The schoolroom must have seemed impossibly confining in September 1909. The response was predictable, and it would color the entire sense of school for this one-time honor-roll student. "I never did like school," he would say, "and I stopped going to school as soon as I got big enough to play hooky and not be caught at it."[6] His seatmate, Ralph Muckenfuss, noticed that though he was still outwardly quiet and well-behaved, he never seemed to do any work. He seemed to care for nothing but his writing and drawing. Ralph watched as Billy drew a cowboy being bucked over a corral fence by his horse. Such pictures now served to illustrate stories he was writing. This did not mean that his intellectual development was in suspension or that he was reading less. He may have been reading more. He went to his uncle John, now on the verge of his career as a lawyer. "I just browsed through those books of his," he would remember. "I don't know, maybe I learned a bit about the law. I remember I was very interested in Roman Law." Once his flight from the schoolroom—and perhaps from his family as well—took him back to Ripley. "I ran away to a doctor in the family and I browsed through his books. I learned plenty from them. I was interested in the brain. I learned that it had parts—a section for speech, for touch, and so on." When he could not play hooky, he would forget school in other ways. On the weekend he would go out to the country to hunt with Hal Cullen, or wander over to see the Colonel, who sometimes would get out mementos of the Old Colonel—his cane, the machete he brought back from the Mexican War, his silver watch, the pipe he was smoking the day he was shot—and Billy would examine them. He would listen to the stories and the bits of poems the old man sometimes recited. "I would sit there with him on the gallery," the grandson remembered. "He would have his feet up on the balustrade and a horse would come and put his head between his feet. And a Negro would come and bring Grandpappy drinks." If it happened to be a toddy he was drinking, Billy would be allowed to drink the "heeltaps"—the last little bit of diluted liquid in the glass.

So there was more fuel for his imagination from other sources as he began to draw away from formal schooling. Some of it was provided in yet other ways by the Colonel, who bought a 1909 Buick touring car. It was chauffeured by Chess Carothers, a freckled mocha-colored man. For family excursions all the way to Memphis, he would pack the tool kit with extra fuel, spare parts, chains, a lantern, rope, a hammer, and a hatchet. But sometimes they would bog down in a sand bed five miles north of town in Hurricane Creek Bottom and his furious employer would have to pay three dollars to two men—standing by, with mules, waiting for such a misfortune—to pull the Buick out. There were other excursions. In October 1910 the Colonel had become president of the newly organized First National Bank of Oxford, and he seemed to consider it *his* bank. Late one night, returning to Oxford with several of his cronies, all high-spirited and tipsy, he ordered Chess to drive around the square. On one of their circuits, he ordered Chess to stop and fetch a brick he saw lying near the board walk, then told him to drive by the bank slowly. Steadying himself, the Colonel took aim and flung the brick through the shiny front plate-glass window. Later that night one of his companions asked him why he had done it. Buoyed up by still more bourbon, he replied, "It was my Buick, my brick, and my bank."[7]

Other forms of motion were there to fascinate and even challenge Billy Falkner. One of his friends, John Ralph Markette, had a father who was an engineer on the Illinois Central. Mr. Markette let them ride in his cab and sometimes even hold the open throttle. But by now the airplane had begun to exercise the strongest grip on their imaginations. Under Billy's directions they built one, from plans in *The American Boy*, out of beanpoles, slats, bailing wire, wrapping paper, and paste. With the plane perched at the edge of the deepest ditch at the far end of the pasture, the crew grunted and sweated to get Billy airborne. With a last lunge they launched it. It pitched as the tail rose and then swung through an arc and thumped upside down into the bottom of the ditch in a flutter of paper and beanpoles. Billy silently picked his way out of the shattered fuselage as Jack, Johncy, and Sallie Murry looked on, dumb with disappointment. He did not go back to his aeronautical drawing board, but he continued to fill pages with pictures of goggled men in their frail, angular machines. By now there were air shows even in Memphis, and the *Commercial Appeal* was full of pictures: Louis Bleriot, the monoplane he had designed, and a Frenchman who was flying it in America. This was obviously material for stories as well as pictures.

Billy's proficiency with both was growing. One of his chores in the winter of 1910 and 1911 was to bring in buckets of coal for the fireplaces. Maud Falkner began to notice that every day her son was bringing home a husky boy named Fritz McElroy. She watched as Fritz loaded two buckets at the coal shed and carried them to the house. During the repeated trips she never saw Billy raise a hand to help, though he seemed to be talking constantly. She finally discovered what was happening. Billy was telling stories to Fritz and breaking them off at a suspenseful point to bring him back the next day. There were enough so that Fritz carried his coal most of the winter. Others were also noticing his powers of invention. Looking back, Sallie Murry said, "It got so that when Billy told you something, you never knew if it was the truth or just something he'd made up."[8] He managed, however, to harness his imagination to the needs of the schoolroom enough for Miss Minnie Porter to recommend his promotion at the end of his sixth-grade year in June 1911.

He was leaving the world of childhood, and he knew it. The family would still make the trip back to Ripley for periodic visits. His great-grandfather, Dr. John Young Murry, a gallant veteran who had survived murderous fighting as a company commander and then regimental surgeon of the 34th Mississippi in Walthall's brigade, was now a very old man, a Presbyterian patriarch with a long beard. Faulkner would recall that he was "a man of inflexible principles. One of them was, everybody, children on up through all adults present, had to have a verse from the Bible ready and glib at tongue-tip . . . if you didn't have your scripture verse ready, you didn't have any breakfast; you would be excused long enough to leave the room and swot one up. . . ." But the old man was not an easy taskmaster. "It had to be an authentic, correct verse. While we were little, it could be the same one, once you had it down good, morning after morning, until you got a little older and bigger, when one morning (by this time you would be pretty glib at it, galloping through without even listening to yourself since you were already . . . among the ham and steak and fried chicken and grits and sweet potatoes and two or three kinds of hot bread) you would suddenly find his eye on you—very blue, very kind and gentle, and even now not stern so much as inflexible; and next morning you had a new verse. In a way, that was when you discovered that your childhood was over; you had outgrown it and entered the world."⁹

Billy was changing. Maud Falkner had noticed a stoop developing in his shoulders. The solution was clear. There were pictures of it in the newspaper every week: shoulder braces, a canvas vest with laces in the back. It was a corsetlike contraption that made the rough-and-tumble games harder to play. But that concerned him less now than it would have earlier. When Billy Falkner had first become interested in the new girl on South Street, his brother remembered, he "tried to attract her attention by being the loudest one, the daringest. But the more he tried the more mussed he got, and sweaty, and dirtier, and Estelle simply wasn't interested." Two grades ahead of him, she disdained these childish antics. Later Billy discovered that he really liked wearing stylish clothes, and he was particularly proud of some the Colonel had bought him that resembled his own. Now he "found that Estelle liked him better neat and with her listening Bill found he could talk. From then on he spent more and more time down at her house, being with her and talking to her and listening to her play. She was an accomplished pianist even then. . . ."¹⁰

Estelle Oldham enjoyed his gifts too. On the north side of the square was Davidson and Wardlaw's, a combined bookstore and jewelry shop. People would stop in to buy or just to browse in the small but comfortably furnished back room. Billy and Estelle would see each other there after school. Often she would be reading fashion magazines and he would be reading poetry. They discovered, though, that poetry was a love they shared. His interest in it had been fostered by his mother, who encouraged him to read the English poets and who loved the work of Burns and nature poems such as Thomson's *The Seasons*.¹¹ From time to time he would bring her a book. "Look here," he would say, "I found something you might like." One day he handed her a few sheets of paper which bore verses, rather formal, with a good deal of pastoral imagery. Periodically he would bring her more of his poetry. One day he gave her two sheets carefully bound together and covered with lines written in his upright yet flowing hand.

"Which one do you like better?" he asked.

Estelle read them both carefully and then pointed to the right-hand page. "This one," she answered.

"You may not be a poetess," he said, "but you're a darn good literary critic." He smiled. "Those are from 'The Song of Solomon.' The others are mine."

Almost ten years later he would write, "I read and employed verse, firstly, for the purpose of furthering various philanderings in which I was engaged, secondly, to complete a youthful gesture I was then making, of being 'different' in a small town."¹² The cynicism of these words probably came from the pain he felt from what he thought was unrequited love. And the calculated use of his verses may have actually come a bit later. His verse was romantic and would remain so for years, and it is likely that for every erotic line, like those of Solomon, there were many that spoke in terms of the comparatively chaste longings of the shepherds and shepherdesses and fauns and nymphs who had caught his imagination. He could not then have known how much of his verse would serve as a vehicle not just for the traditional lover's laments, but for laments that were real to him and very deeply felt, conveying a melancholy much like that his family felt when Sallie Murry, and then Damuddy, just a few short years before, had made mortality such a reality for all of them.

But of course he could know none of this now, and as he grew more independent, saw less of school and less of the stable, he must have felt that his writing would help somehow to carry him into the new world into which he was moving.

5

... that April morning when you woke up and you would think how April was the best, the very best time of all not to have to go to school, until you would think *Except in the fall* with the weather brisk and not-cold at the same time and the trees all yellow and red and you could go hunting all day long; and then you would think *Except in the winter* with the Christmas holidays over and now nothing to look forward to until summer; and you would think how no time is the best time to not have to go to school and so school is a good thing after all because without it there wouldn't be any holidays or vacations.

—*The Town* (301–302)

HE felt increasingly bored with the world of the schoolroom that fall of 1911, even though he now moved from one room and teacher to another for seventh-grade English, history, and mathematics. The curriculum was below his level, for one thing. He would read *The Arkansas Traveller* with Myrtle Ramey for fun, but the book he was enthusiastic about was *Moby-Dick.* "It's one of the best books ever written," he told his brother, but Jack decided he didn't care for Melville and put it down unfinished. He and his brother shared a taste for comic novels, just as his mother liked the serious novelists he did and Estelle enjoyed some of the same poetry that moved him. But it would be two years before a new friendship would provide a mind as keen as his own to supply the excitement of a sympathetic response to new literary experience. And before that would happen, as he moved into the higher grades, his alienation would prompt some of the students at the Oxford High School to tease him and call him "quair."

Murry Falkner's indifference to formal education placed the burden of parental encouragement and discipline squarely upon his wife. Principal George G. Hurst had written a strong letter urging parents to see to it that homework got done, and Maud Falkner was quick to comply.

Every evening after supper she faithfully cleared the round table in Billy and Jack's bedroom and then placed at its center a freshly cleaned and filled oil lamp. Billy would provide his pocketknife and Jack would sharpen the pencils, prolonging the process as long as possible before starting the evening's work. Maud Falkner knew that Billy's reluctance at home was only a pale reflection of his performance at school. Ralph Muckenfuss thought his sometime deskmate was "the laziest boy I ever saw. He was generally almost inert." Ralph was making the mistake many others would make, unaware that the static exterior masked a dynamic interior, an interior world of far-reaching imagination mixed with daydreams. When he did manifest some activity, "he would do nothing but write and draw —drawings for his stories." Here Ralph Muckenfuss was perceptive. "He couldn't help it. I don't think he could have kept from writing. It was an obsession." Some mornings after he left home with his brothers he would simply skip school. When she learned of a transgression, Maud Falkner would take him to task, and he would listen submissively. "He never struck back at her," Johncy remembered. "If he couldn't turn her off with a laugh, he simply stood there and listened."[1]

But she continued to encourage him with his drawing and painting. The June issue of *St. Nicholas* magazine had announced a drawing contest, specifying "India ink, very black writing-ink or wash" as the medium. The names of the winners appeared in the November issue. His was not among them, but "William Faulkner" was listed among the many who "because of the merit of their entry, did deserve the encouragement of seeing their name in print."[2]

The only aspects of school that appealed to Billy were extracurricular. The high school had added an eleventh grade, and when a group began planning a yearbook for the class of 1913, he did several pen-and-ink sketches for it, some gently caricaturing students and teachers, most of them comic, with appropriate captions for the classroom scenes, but a few of them embodying the familiar high-school refrains of appreciation of learning and idealistic dedication to the future. The project was never completed and he was probably not disappointed. Throughout his life he would derive pleasure from planning, often when he must have known that the plans were like some of his daydreams. Besides, this was more fun than English class. "Bill showed absolutely no interest in the education being offered," his classmate Watson Campbell would recall. "He gazed out the window and answered the simplest question with 'I don't know.' This attitude on his part made me despise him, as it insulted beautiful Pearl Hickey, the teacher, with whom I was deeply in love."[3]

By this time he seems to have distanced himself from his parents more than any of his brothers would ever do. Again it may have been his keen intelligence that was responsible, his faculty for observing people closely and pondering the keystones of character and personality. He would always treat his mother with a combination of love and respect and care, even though he could see with perfect clarity the rigid standards coupled with the quirks and cranks that made her and Auntee, and other Southern women like them, at once the pride and the bane of their families. For the most part at loggerheads with his father, unable to see his good points and meet him with affection as Jack could, Billy seems to have taken no pains to avoid conflict and even to have gone out of his way to affront him. There is no evidence that he saw him as a rival for Maud Falkner's love, and his shrewd observation could not have missed the behavior which must have revealed Maud Falkner's reservations about her husband. Billy's love for her would shine through the letters he would write from distant places. For his father he would eventually develop a kind of tolerance and understanding, but these qualities, too, would await a distant future day.

Billy must have seen that things were not easy for his father. As the number of automobiles in Lafayette County grew, Murry Falkner's livery-stable business declined. Casting about for something to replace it, he obtained the Standard Oil agency, which supplied coal oil for the county's lamps. But this was not even a stopgap. In 1912, when he sold their home and moved to another house on South Street, some of the proceeds from the sale may well have gone into the purchase of a hardware store on the square. This was a less congenial vocation, if anything, than the livery stable. Jack Falkner realized "that Father was not a natural-born salesman—of hardware or anything else. In fact, he told us several times that he never heard of a Falkner who could sell a stove to an Eskimo or a camel to an Arab."[4] Murry was overlooking the fact that his father and grandfather had been highly successful selling varied ventures to many investors. Billy did not shun his father's store. Like his grandfather outside his bank, he would prop an old kitchen chair on its back legs against the storefront and sit there for hours looking out over the square. And he still shared his father's love of horses and dogs, using Murry Falkner's own Damascus steel gun to hunt rabbits and, later, bigger game in the approaches to the Delta in Panola County just to the west.

The differences between Murry Falkner's values and his own must have been clearest when he visited Estelle Oldham. Maud Falkner was usually too busy now to play the piano, whereas Lida Oldham was teaching her daughters, even six-year-old Dorothy. Sometimes Tochie might take her place at the keyboard, or Estelle might play, not just for her family but for the callers who had begun to appear in increasing numbers. Estelle was a year and a half older than he. She had worn long dresses before other girls had, and she was already popular enough to be invited to the house parties of prominent families in Jackson, the state capital. In Oxford she shone at the dances given by Myrtle Ramey's cousins, Marvel and Lucille. At such affairs a fond parent might spend $75 to bring from Memphis the band of an amiable forty-year-old Negro

named W. C. Handy, who would lead his group with his golden trumpet, or sometimes, in a kind of intermission, sit alone at the piano, fingering the rich chords and catchy rhythms of his own songs, such as
"Memphis Blues" and "St. Louis Blues." Estelle's card was always full
at such dance parties. Billy generally cut an uneasy figure on the dance
floor, but he was easily one of the most presentable.

He would dress carefully, knotting rich silk ties beneath high starched
white collars. There was a kind of dandyism that came out now, and
he had a graceful slim figure that the tight clothes flattered. His looks
were changing too. Sometimes he would comb his hair in a high pompa-
dourlike style without part above his generous forehead. His mouth still
looked narrow and set, and his eyes were somehow even keener. The
face seemed to have lengthened and narrowed. If it had lost the symmetry and charm of the little-boy face, it was still a striking one. But if
he showed promise, Estelle showed early bloom.

It did not go unobserved at the university. There she had caught the
eye of a tallish, handsome senior with dark hair and dark eyes. Cornell
Sidney Franklin had come to the university from Columbus, Mississippi.
He had distinguished himself from the start, and now he was president
of the class of 1913, captain of the track team, and member of a dozen
other college organizations. One of them was a social club called The
Outlaws, and when the annual, *Ole Miss*, came out for 1913, the caption
beneath Franklin's photograph named him as its "Chairman." The photographs showed these "Outlaws" as anything but desperadoes—young
men in full-dress suits and young women in evening gowns. One of the
prettiest, her photograph labeled "Sponsor," was his date, Estelle Oldham.
The motto under Franklin's vita in the annual was "The Glass of Fashion
and the Mold of Form." Estelle enjoyed his attentions as she did those
of her other beaux, and as a college senior, he provided an entree into a
world which must have seemed glamorous to her, a world that most of
the others, including Billy Falkner, could know only as observers. One
friend would say, "Estelle liked handsome men, and the handsomer they
were, the better she liked them." And no one could deny that Cornell
Sidney Franklin was indeed handsome.

It was therefore natural that prosperous Lem Oldham and his wife
should think about the benefits of a private-school education for their
two girls. In early 1913 they had decided that Tochie, a promising musi-
cian, should have the benefit of Immaculata in Washington, even if it
was a Catholic school. When they talked of Virginia schools for Estelle,
she favored Episcopalian Stuart Hall, in Staunton, but Presbyterian Lem
Oldham insisted on Staunton's Mary Baldwin College. So Estelle had gone
to Virginia's Blue Ridge Mountains to study English, French, geometry,
chemistry, and piano while Billy was gritting his teeth and enduring the
ninth-grade rigors of the Oxford High School. He wrote letters to
Staunton, sometimes with little drawings enclosed or sketches in ink on

the sheets themselves. He waited for the vacations and her return. She was so popular, though, that he could not count on having her to himself.

Estelle had continued to see Cornell Franklin. The university had a two-year Law School which permitted undergraduates in their senior year to take junior law, with credit toward both the A.B. and LL.B. degrees. Franklin had done this, and in the spring of 1914 he received his law degree. The legend under his picture in *Ole Miss* for 1914 read, "I want to grow as beautiful as God meant me to be." Estelle would say later that Cornell had proposed marriage to her and that she had light-heartedly accepted, with no more serious intentions than when she had accepted from other admirers the little gold fraternity pins with their Greek letters and tiny jewels. Besides, he was not only leaving the university, he was leaving the country. On the advice of his uncle Malcolm, who was Collector of the port of Honolulu, he was sailing for Hawaii.

In this year when Cornell Franklin was preparing to begin his career as a practicing attorney, Billy Falkner was running for election as president of his Boy Scout troop—and lost by one vote. If he had felt unease at the attentions paid the girl he loved by such a threatening rival, he did not confide them to anyone, and his feelings for her continued to grow stronger. He must have been relieved when she decided that one year at Mary Baldwin—shut in with all those girls—was all she could stand. At least, now he would not have to depend on so frail a thread as correspondence. When she came home he was at the Oldhams' house nearly every day. She had other gentleman callers, of course, and she would receive the attentions of still others when she entered the University of Mississippi in the fall.

As Estelle's world had begun to widen, so did his, also through the influence of an older man, another student and lawyer-to-be. His name was Philip Avery Stone. He had come into Falkner's life at a crucial time. He was able to supply what neither Maud Falkner nor Estelle Oldham could for this dreamy, talented young man—so obviously drifting, yet seeking. Stone would have a strong and positive impact upon his sensibility, and for the better part of twenty years their relationship would be intimate and important.

CHAPTER

6

From his sorry jacket he drew a battered "Shropshire Lad" and as he handed it to me he quoted the one beginning, "Into my heart an air that kills—" telling us he kind of thought it was the best he had seen.

"Why don't you go home?" I asked him.

"I will, some day. But that ain't why I liked that one. I like it because the man that wrote it felt that way, and didn't care who knew it."

—"Out of Nazareth," *NOS* (48–49)

At this time the young man's attitude of mind was that of most of the other young men in the world who had been around twenty-one years of age in April, 1917, even though at times he did admit to himself that he was possibly using the fact that he had been nineteen on that day as an excuse to follow the avocation he was coming more and more to know would be forever his true one: to be a tramp, a harmless possessionless vagabond.

—"Mississippi," *ESPL* (21)

PHIL STONE was four years older and more than four inches taller than William Falkner. Though each knew who the other was, there had never been any occasion for them to meet. Their families, though, had a fair amount in common. The Stones had come from Wilkes County, in north Georgia; Phil's mother, Rosa Alston, was descended from an old, established line at the top of the social hierarchy of Panola County. Miss Rosa was an introspective woman with a tendency to hypochondria, whereas James Stone, her husband, was a big man with a commanding manner whose honorary title of "General" may have come from these qualities as well as from his job as general counsel to the Illinois Central Railroad. His law practice and banking business had prospered, and his sons would follow him into the law. General Stone was a hunter and fisherman with tastes that men like J. W. T. Falkner and Murry Falkner shared. (His

periodic drinking bouts required nursing and subsequent recuperation at
Iuka Springs if not the Keeley Institute.)[1] The families had been friends
for years, and people said that "Miss Rosie" Stone and Sallie Murry
Falkner ran the Methodist Church.

James Stone had wanted his son to have the benefits of both Southern
and Northern education. Phil did not disappoint him. He earned his B.A.,
cum laude, from the University of Mississippi, and in June 1914 returned
home with another B.A., again cum laude, from Yale. Although a career
in the law lay ahead of him, his real delight was literature, and he had
come back from New Haven filled with enthusiasm for the new novelists
and poets. He was determined that his discoveries be shared by his friends,
and the one he cared most about was a lively and beautiful young woman
named Katrina Carter. She had told him that he ought to know "this
little Falkner boy who writes; he's always telling stories." One of the
others who would be part of the animated group on the Carters' side
porch was Estelle Oldham. Headed for the square, Falkner would hear
her voice and cross the street so that Katrina would notice him and invite
him to join them. Then he would tell stories to the girls in the porch
swing.

Finally Katrina brought him and Phil Stone together by telling Phil
that Billy Falkner wrote poetry but knew no one in Oxford who could
tell him what to do with his poems. So one Saturday afternoon, Stone
walked over to the Falkner house and was given the meticulously written
verses. Falkner sat there silently as Stone settled himself with them. He
found himself reading with growing excitement. "Anybody could have
seen that he had real talent," Stone would recall. "It was perfectly obvious."[2] Not only was he talented, he was also committed, like Stone, who
later recorded that they "talked day and night of writing and the summer
was very pleasant."[3] He immediately set out to give the aspiring poet
encouragement, advice, and models for study.

Phil Stone was uniquely fitted to serve as William Falkner's friend and
mentor. He was a compulsive talker, a man who loved to teach and tell
stories. Moved by impulses toward literary creation but lacking the drive
to carry them through to fruition, he could satisfy them only vicariously.
He would later say of himself, "I'm like an elaborate, intricate piece of
machinery which doesn't quite work."[4] He was a complex man and
unlike anyone the boy had ever known. There was pride and vanity in
his makeup, along with the humor and capacity for friendship. Combining dogmatism and intuition, he had a multifaceted, quicksilvery mind.
He was full of probing questions and specific criticisms. Billy Falkner
was a good listener, and it was a time in his life when he was particularly
open to learning. He was still an avid reader, but he was now ready for
a change of direction. Like Stone, Falkner could be analytical, but his
mode of thought and perception was already moving toward the deeply
meditative. But for all the striking differences between these two South-

Colonel William Clark Falkner

*Colonel William C. Falkner's monument,
Ripley, Mississippi*

John Wesley Thompson Falkner

Sallie Murry Falkner

Murry Cuthbert Falkner

Maud Butler and Holland Falkner Wilkins

*William Cuthbert Falkner,
aged eleven months*

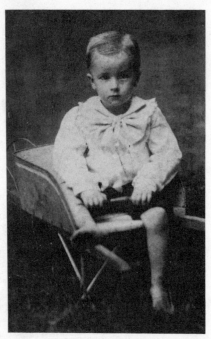

*William Cuthbert Falkner,
aged three years*

*William, Murry, and John Falkner, in front of their home
on Second South Street, c. 1905*

Murry, William, John, and Dean Falkner,
c. 1910–1911

William Falkner, 1914

Cornell Franklin in Ole Miss, *1913*

Estelle Oldham in Ole Miss, *1917*

Phil Stone in Ole Miss, *1914*

Ben Wasson in Ole Miss, *1921*

Caroline Barr ("Mammy Callie")

Ned Barnett ("Uncle Ned")

William Faulkner,
December 1918

Cadet Faulkner

Drawings by Faulkner for Ole Miss, 1919–1920

erners, they were complementary, and they functioned on a basis of a
common culture, attitudes, and feelings. Billy Falkner continued to visit
the Oldhams' home regularly, but now he was often with Phil at General
Stone's spacious old home. Stone would recall that he gave his friend
Keats and Swinburne to read, but also "a number of the then moderns,
such as Conrad Aiken and the Imagists. . . ."⁵ The young high-school
dropout was receiving something comparable to a college tutorial in
poetry, especially modern poetry.

From the summer of 1914, when Phil Stone returned home to work
for an LL.B. at the university, the relationship between the two men
broadened and deepened. They would read and talk in the big six-
columned house once occupied by Lucius Quintus Cincinnatus Lamar.
This revered hero had left the Union with his state to become a Confederate leader. After the war he had fought against Reconstruction and
become the architect of Democratic resurgence in Mississippi. Some of
his books were still in the library. It was pleasurable to take down from
the shelf a first edition of Algernon Charles Swinburne's *Laus Veneris*
and to see on the flyleaf the gift inscription from Jefferson Davis to
Lamar. Other books on the same shelves had belonged to Lamar's father-
in-law, Augustus Longstreet. Some days before Stone went off to class
he would put a stack of books in the family's Studebaker touring car;
besides a play of Sophocles and some of Plato's works, there might be
volumes by Roman philosophers, dramatists, or poets. On other days
there would be books on English literature or German works in translation. Then Stone would turn the car over to Bill, who would drive out
along a country road to some quiet, shady spot and spend the day reading.
When the two men were together, they might stride off on long cross-
country walks, covering as much as fifteen miles over the unpaved roads
and red clay hills of Lafayette County. Falkner liked the sounds and
rhythms of Greek poetry, and sometimes, as they walked along University
Avenue toward the campus or turned back through the woods toward
the Stone home on College Hill Road, Phil Stone would raise his voice
in the lines of Oedipus' lament.

Phil Stone derived intense pleasure from the teaching as well as the
friendship. As he recalled it years later, he said he drilled the younger
man in punctuation and lectured him on goals as well as grammar. "There
was no one but me with whom William Faulkner could discuss his
literary plans and hopes and his technical trials and aspirations." He
preached "that true greatness was in creating great things and not in
pretending them; that the only road to literary success was by sure,
patient, hard intelligent work," and he emphasized "the idea of avoiding
the contemporary literary cliques with their febrile, twittering barrenness, the idea of literature growing from its own natural soil, and the
dread of the easy but bottomless pit of surface technical cleverness."⁶
Not only would he lecture Bill about writing, but he would take him to

see a practicing writer, his admired friend Stark Young, who taught at the University of Texas but returned home to spend each summer with his father. "I owe my education," Stone would say, "to Greek and to playing poker. It was Mr. Stark Young who opened my mind when we would come home here in the summers. . . ."[7] Now Falkner would sit and listen to the developing writer-teacher and the talkative law student-litterateur.

It was not surprising that some who knew both of the younger men might say, "It was Phil who educated Bill."[8] Jack Falkner, who still shared a room with his brother, took a less sweeping view. "I'm certain he had such friends, and I'm certain he would not have disdained any suggestions they might have made, but he was perfectly capable of making his own selections, and I'm certain that, to a large extent, [that] is what he did."[9] Falkner had been reading widely for years before he met Stone, and he had also begun to imitate certain poets. And though the punctuation of his prose would strike a friend as shockingly eclectic as much as ten years later, he would scarcely have found a comma as unrecognizable as Stone thought he did. With Falkner's capacity for silence, someone as voluble as Stone could well go on at his rapid rate assuming that what he was saying was new to a hearer who might already be acquainted with it. But Falkner eagerly consumed books which offered him models at this uncertain point in his career. Some time later he would write, "I was subject to the usual proselyting of an older person, but the strings were pulled so casually as scarcely to influence my point of view."[10]

Where did the truth lie? Obviously, somewhere in between. Stone opened new vistas for Falkner—with his knowledge, his brilliant talk, and most of all, his books. Even though another friend would say of Falkner, half a dozen years afterward, that he seemed to be groping intellectually, he was a highly individualistic genius who could not have been pushed far in any direction in which he did not want to go. In the years to come, William Faulkner would testify to the special relationship with the dedications of three novels. Stone, less assertive, would say, "I just carried water to the elephant."[11] Faulkner would say, much later, "I don't hold with the mute inglorious Miltons. . . . I think if you're going to write, you're going to write and nothing will stop you."[12] Whatever the final balance, the relationship was pervasive—intellectual, aesthetic, social—and long-lasting, and it came at a crucial time in Billy Falkner's life.

The dedications of the novels that would come a quarter of a century later testified to the fascination both men felt with Mississippi history, particularly that of The Lost Cause. Stone could mark the accelerating process of change by what he heard in the family law office. Falkner must have heard much of the same in his grandfather's and his uncle John's conversations about county and state politics. But with Stone's combination of voracious reading and love of anecdote, he must have missed little of the revolt of the "rednecks" as it could be seen in Lafayette County. As he and Billy Falkner took their walks, Stone would talk. He knew the stories of country people who were laboriously pulling themselves up by their bootstraps, as J. W. T. Falkner's young colleague Lee Russell had done with his mother's help. For some of these strivers, the two privileged young men had a kind of admiration. Others among the rednecks seemed monsters of acquisitiveness and boorishness. For them they felt contempt and a kind of wonder.

The power of the Delta Bourbons, or aristocrats such as Leroy Percy, was steadily being eroded by Populist-style orators—demagogues, said many—such as James Kimble Vardaman and rascals such as Theodore "The Man" Bilbo. The Falkners supported Vardaman and helped with the rallies held for him in Oxford when he waged his vigorous campaigns with violent rhetoric reinforced by ample and spicy barbecues. But the lines between the political and the social were clearly drawn in Oxford, at least by John Wesley Thompson Falkner. Lee Russell's story was well known—how he had been a "goat" at Ole Miss, frozen out of the fraternities and insulted by their members, how he had conceived a hatred for them and the caste system which they represented, and how he nursed his revenge with a plan to destroy them. After he had joined the Young Colonel's law firm he had won a seat in the legislature. His bill to abolish fraternities at state schools had been passed, and now, in the fall of 1915, had been state law for three years. More important, Theodore Bilbo was readying himself to occupy the governor's chair and Lee Russell was his lieutenant governor-elect.

One Sunday afternoon Russell walked up the front porch steps of The Big Place and rapped on the screen door until the sound penetrated the Colonel's deafness. He opened the door and asked Lee Russell what he wanted.

"To pay a visit," his caller said.

The irascible old man drew himself up stiffly. "Sir," he said, "our relations are business and political, not social." And he slammed the door.

By now Billy Falkner's relations with school were mainly athletic. "I hung around school just to play baseball and football," he later said, "and then I quit." He was barely five feet five inches tall, and though he had not really begun to fill out, he was well coordinated. He played quarterback when he returned to school in September 1915 for what should have been his final, eleventh-grade, year.

His last season mixed pain and glory. Its high point came against Holly Springs. Oxford's left end was a lean, hard country boy named Benjamin McDaniel, whom his teammates called "Possum." He was tremendously strong, but incapable of catching a perfectly thrown pass. That Saturday, Billy directed his attack with confidence. Possum's ferocious defensive play helped keep Holly Springs' ground game stymied, so they began to pass. Suddenly, to the amazement of everyone, Possum intercepted the ball and sprinted hard—for his own goal line. As Johncy Falkner watched, horrified, he saw Billy recover quickly from his shock and launch himself in a desperation tackle. The two went down with a crash. Johncy said that Billy got up with a nose that was already bleeding but that he got credit for saving the game, at the cost of a broken nose. Years later McDaniel would say that he did not remember the incident, since there were so many fractured bones in those years. On one occasion Faulkner would say that he sustained the injury in what was to him a more glamorous, though probably fictitious, plane crash. There was no doubt of the injury, though, for a 1914 photo showed a generous but symmetrical nose, whereas one taken in 1918 showed the conspicuous hump. It probably does not matter exactly how his honorable wound was sustained, but the aftermath was an early example of the way in which legends would begin to accrue around this young man.

It was probably that same fall that Falkner's association with the Stone family led to a further widening of his experience. General Stone owned a hunting camp about thirty miles west of Oxford, just below Batesville, in 1,500 acres of the dense woods and rich bottom land of the Tallahatchie River. Though Phil had been a sickly child, by the time he was thirteen he had persuaded his father to let him go with the others in their yearly hunt for deer and bear. When he was fifteen, as he took his place on the stand, a bear materialized before him in the gloom of the autumn woods. He fired two blasts. Opening his eyes, he saw the bear's bulk on the ground. Then his father rode up, followed by some of the other hunters. "They smeared my face with blood," he remembered, "as they always do with your first bear. I never wanted to wash it off any more."[13] Not many years later he ceased to enjoy the taking of life and turned against the hunt, but Falkner relished hearing about the Stone camp, and when he was invited to go along, he joined the hunters for their yearly journey westward.

It was a region rich with stories as well as game. Major Philip S. Alston had served under Bedford Forrest, but he had survived the war to marry a girl who was a Potts. Her paternal grandfather was a Methodist circuit rider reputed to have owned ten miles along the Tallahatchie. His twin sons, Theophilus and Amodeus Potts, were Phil Stone's great-uncles. The Stones had settled some rich bottom land near Uncle Buck and Uncle Buddy's land, and the Illinois Central ran a line into the area and put in Stone stop as an accommodation. Each November, General Stone would lead the expedition to the camp, and there the tents would be pegged out and the barbecue pits dug before the hunters followed the wagonloads of equipment into the big woods. Wide intersecting paths would be hacked through the canebrakes so the hunters could take their assigned stands and wait for the dogs to drive the deer past them. But a bear could make his way through the thickest canebrake. After the disastrous fires in the Delta in 1914, the bears began to migrate, but the hunters would still see one from time to time, and they told stories about others. One of them was an immense and crafty old animal who was unmistakable by his track, which showed where two toes from his front left paw had been lost in the jaws of some trap. Old Reel Foot was both secure and deadly in his domain. The hunters told about the prodigious numbers of dogs who had tried unsuccessfully to bay him in his tangled vine-and-thicket lair, and how many of them had died from the slashes of his raking claws. The veterans of the camp knew these stories well: Uncle Ad Bush, the old Negro cook who would wake them at four for scalding coffee and hot flapjacks; Buster Callicoat, whose brute strength was as useful in General Stone's camp as it had been in Murry Falkner's livery stable. Once Bill Falkner was sent to Memphis with Buster to replenish the whiskey supply. When they returned, Buster had the whiskey and also "the partially wrapped corset he had bought as a present for his wife trailing under his arm."[14] In his quiet withdrawn way Falkner enjoyed the camaraderie of the camp as the men sat around the evening fire, smoking, passing the whiskey, and telling tales of other hunts and other times. He smoked his pipe and shared the whiskey.

He was showing a capacity for violent contrasts in dress. Young Ben Wasson had met him when he began his freshman year at Ole Miss. He saw him as "a small, slight fellow. He was wearing a pair of baggy, gray flannel trousers, a rather shabby tweed jacket and heavy brown brogans. . . ." As he talked, Ben noticed his thin, straight mouth, his aquiline nose, and the way his eyes were "very brown and somewhat almond shaped and very penetrating." Falkner dazzled handsome young Ben Wasson with his knowledge of A. E. Housman. "I had never known anyone who loved poetry enough to be so bold as to quote it." When they parted, Ben told him in his almost excessively courteous way how much he had enjoyed their meeting. Falkner looked at him with amusement. "Ah," he said, "we seem to have a young Sir Galahad on a rocking horse come to our college campus." But he looked Wasson up later and they discussed poetry, fiction, and philosophy, and their mutual love for Beethoven. Though Phil Stone had departed for New Haven, Bill Falkner was still a frequent and welcome visitor at the Stone home, and he would take Wasson with him sometimes. In a way he was playing out his own relationship with Stone. Sometimes he dazzled Ben with brilliant observations, very likely trying out phrases he had honed with the care he gave to his verses. But what Ben would remember most was his "innate kindness and gentleness. . . ."[15]

THE deepest parts of Falkner's life were involved with his writing, his reading, and Estelle Oldham. Quoting Housman in his conversation, he was imitating him in his writing. There were still strong traces of the poet he had discovered at sixteen, Algernon Charles Swinburne. "Or rather," he would write, "Swinburne discovered me, springing from some tortured undergrowth of my adolescence, like a highwayman, making me his slave." Neither Keats nor Shelley had moved him as Swinburne did, and when he was nearing the end of this phase of his development, he found new inspiration: It was a copy of *A Shropshire Lad*, "and when I opened it I discovered there the secret after which the moderns course howling like curs. . . . Here was reason for being born into a fantastic world: discovering the splendor of fortitude, the beauty of being of the soil like a tree about which fools might howl and which winds of disillusion and death and despair might strip, leaving it bleak, without bitterness; beautiful in sadness." From there, he said, he would go on to Shakespeare, Spenser, and the Elizabethans; and then to Keats, taking particular joy in "Ode to a Nightingale" and "Ode on a Grecian Urn." But it seems doubtful that any body of poetry ever again struck him with such force as Housman's did.[16]

At bottom, Falkner was writing as a Romantic, perhaps even a Late Romantic, but the unmistakable imprints of Swinburne and Housman were there in line after line of his often large and flowing hand in these months of the year 1916. There were clear borrowings from Swinburne poems such as "In the Orchard" and the famous chorus from "Atalanta in Calydon." Again and again he would use the images of faun and nymph in forest or field. The world-weariness of the poet complaining of un-requited love or the fatality of the languid woman who disdained his passion would dominate many of his poems. As he explored other veins, it was a small step from Swinburne's heavy Scots speech in poems such as "The Bloody Son" to the modified Shropshire dialect in some of Housman's ballads. Falkner wrote one narrative ballad about a highway-man and another controlled by the image of a hanged felon much like that in Housman's "On moonlit heath and lonesome bank." And one of the poet's best-known themes, the bittersweet passion of love and the fickleness of lovers, moved young William Falkner to whole-hearted imitation in another series of poems.

Phil Stone would call the work of these years the poetry of youth. Experimenting and imitating, Falkner was drawn to Swinburne's combi-nation of luxuriance and melancholy, to Housman's cynicism about love and pessimism over the human condition. But his own avoidances and preferences were there too. There was nothing of the Swinburnian gro-tesque and bizarre, and rather than Housman's plaintive and sometimes equivocal passion, there was a frank heterosexual eroticism. Falkner could enjoy dark gardens as much as Swinburne. He could glory, like Housman, in tree and bush and flower. But why, at seventeen and eighteen and nineteen, should he have felt so often such a pervasive melancholy? Was it a late-adolescent malaise, a pose, or just a fairly common literary posture?

He would write later of reading Edmund Spenser. If he read that poet's

"Mutablility" cantos in these years, he would have found much in them. Old Dr. John Young Murry, the great-grandfather who had been a fixture of his childhood years, was gone now, gathered to his fathers. In November little Ned Oldham, Estelle's nearly nine-year-old brother and Dean Falkner's fellow possum hunter, came home after a hunt complaining of pain. Dr. Culley thought the feverish boy was showing a touch of malaria. It was probably a streptococcal throat infection, and by the time a Memphis specialist diagnosed an acute attack of rheumatic fever, it was too late. Bill Falkner grieved with the Oldhams on Christmas Day of 1916, the child's birthday.

Other changes simply accelerated processes already begun. If Falkner had felt at a disadvantage with his brothers earlier, there was little reason to revise his estimate of his place in the family picture now. Jack was taller, Johncy was better-looking, and Dean was a sunny, happy-go-lucky child petted by everyone. Now he, the eldest, was indicating, sometimes subtly, sometimes overtly, that there were certain family standards to which he did not intend to conform. Murry Falkner must have found it increasingly hard to understand him. Bill once confided to Stone that he found his father a dull man. He also had reason to resent him. When word got back to Murry Falkner that Bill had driven the family car fast enough to leave grocer Will Mize behind in a cloud of choking dust, he upbraided his son for his discourtesy, and Bill never asked for the car again. The town photographer would later say that Maud Falkner told him that her husband, in rough teasing, would call Bill "Snake-Lips." The hostility that was there beneath the surface would sometimes erupt into the open. He enjoyed playing the university's nine-hole golf course, even though it was essentially a huge pasture with the greens, fashioned of oiled sand, fenced to keep the cows off. At one point in his seemingly aimless youth, Falkner sold cold drinks at a stand at the course, but he far preferred the pleasure of playing to the pocket money he could earn. Sometimes his high-school classmate Watson Campbell would join him. "To circumvent the blue laws concerning activity on the Sabbath," he recalled, "Bill, Bill's brother Jack, and I would play the back seven on the golf course. One Sunday as we approached the sixth green, having already played our drives, here came Bill's father in a rage. Shaking a big walking stick and uttering all sorts of threats, he came toward us. Jack and I picked up our balls and turned tail. Not Bill. He carefully selected an iron, cried 'fore' and addressed the ball directly toward his father." Hurrying down the road away from the course, Watson and Jack didn't wait to see what happened.[17]

On one occasion Murry Falkner made an overture when the two sat on the front gallery.

"I understand you smoke now," he said.

"Yes, sir," his son answered.

"Here," his father said, reaching into his pocket. "Try a good cigar."

"Thank you, sir," he said. Pulling out his pipe, he broke the cigar in half, stuffing one half into the pipe and the other into his pocket. The son would remember the incident to the end of his life. "He never gave me another," he said.

He loved his mother and his brothers, but he must have felt an increasing intellectual distance from them. And apart from Estelle and Stone and Wasson—perhaps a few others—there was no one with whom he could communicate on any deeper level. He could be a good companion and a witty friend, but the tendencies toward silence and withdrawal seemed to increase. In the autobiographical bit of fiction about the boy who had grown up in his father's livery stable, Faulkner would write that the boy had been unselfconscious as he "had gone through grammar school and one year in high school with girls and boys . . . whose fathers were lawyers and doctors and merchants—all genteel professions, with starched collars." But all that had changed, he wrote, with his growing sexuality, producing, as he looked at the blossoming girls who were his classmates, "a feeling of defiant inferiority."[18] If he felt intellectually superior to almost all those he knew, no doubt he still felt somewhat inferior socially to the friends with professional fathers. The vicissitudes of his father's business career never threatened the integrity of family life, and friends thought of him as a fine man in his own right, but Bill Falkner was still the son of a man rather often regarded as the unfortunate offspring of a brilliant father, a prodigious cyclical drinker shifting from one business to another without much success.

It seemed to most of his family that this son gave no sign of doing even as much with his life as his father had with his. John Wesley Thompson Falkner no longer had a railroad to provide jobs for his kinsmen, but he was one of the founders and the first president of the First National Bank of Oxford. So now, as Phil Stone was at Yale working on his second LL.B., William Falkner went to work as a bookkeeper. His duties "essentially were to post demand debits and demand credits—checks drawn or deposits made by bank customers. These were posted in the large cash books on a daily basis."[19]

Once more he was confined indoors, as he had been at school. Jack never saw him at his job, but once, thinking about it, he laughed and said, "I bet he didn't do much." Estelle Oldham imagined him sitting in a back room with his feet on a table, reading. No one would be likely to bother the founder's grandson, but it was still a profoundly unsatisfactory situation. He didn't want *any* sort of gainful job at that time, and he certainly lacked the skills to be a teller or bookkeeper, though there was a draftsmanlike neatness about any figures or columns that he drew. He told Estelle that he hated the bank. Money, he told her, was a contemptible thing to work for. It didn't take long for the rest of his family to learn the sort of job he was doing. His uncle John would say, "He just *wouldn't* work."[20] Cooped up, he thought of Estelle's freedom at the university. In the fall of 1914 she had entered the B.S. program and added German and psychology to the college French and English she had begun at Mary Baldwin. A year later she added history and domestic science, though she withdrew from the latter. She preferred the extracurricular side of school life just as much as Billy had. She was not only one of "Les Danseuses" of the Girls' Cotillion Club but secretary of the group as well. He would later write, "Quit school and went to work in Grandfather's bank. . . ." "Learned the medicinal value of his liquor. Grandfather thought it was the janitor. Hard on the janitor."[21]

The liquor had for him a more than medicinal value. It helped when, as in the bank, he had to endure a situation he detested until he could escape it. In hunting camp it helped him to overcome his habitual shyness. Like the other men in his family, he also drank whiskey because he liked the taste and the feeling it gave him. Like them, he often drank too much of it. Stone could understand. In the spring of his senior year at Ole Miss he had begun to drink hard—a quart of bourbon a day. He continued for almost a year before he was frightened into sobriety: on two occasions he passed out before he realized he was drunk. In the summer of 1914, when his friendship with Falkner began, Stone was staying away from friends who drank. He would abstain for a dozen years more, but he was not shocked at this developing behavior pattern in Bill Falkner.[22]

Now approaching twenty, Bill was only five feet five and a half inches tall and his genes would limit him to only one half-inch more. In a splurge of dandyism he used his bookkeeper's salary to buy elegant shoes and a good lounge suit. But not even a twenty-five-dollar "Styleplus" suit of tails could make him look taller. They could earn for him from some town wit the sobriquet of "The Count," but evening dress could not create the illusion of the good looks that had disappeared when, with the changes brought by adolescence, his face seemed to drop away, below the cheekbones, to a narrow and immature thinness, and below the large Falkner nose his mouth seemed even smaller and straighter. And there was Estelle. He loved her and felt there was still an understanding between them, even though she went on seeing other boys, some as attractive as Cornell Franklin. He was too acute not to feel anxiety and uncertainty about that part of his future as well as other areas. So if anyone had taxed him with the melancholy in his verse, he might have answered with Housman that the world had

> much less good than ill,
> And while the sun and moon endure
> Luck's a chance, but trouble's sure . . .

When it came, it came as a bitter blow. Through the remainder of 1917 they went on as they had done before. He would often go to dances with her, though he did not dance and she danced superbly. Her card would always be full, but sometimes she would save a dance and sit it out with him. She was wearing his gold ring with the gothic *F* carved on it—even when she went out with others, including his brother Jack, who was so silent that Estelle had to do most of the talking. She saw a good deal of a charming student from the Delta whom she thought part Creole. He proposed and she accepted him in the same way she had given what Cornell Franklin had thought was a favorable response three years before. Her father was furious. "You can't marry him," he said. "Don't you realize he has Negro blood?" She quickly put the boy out of her mind. Then, as the holiday season approached, Cornell Franklin was back in her mind and the midst of her life.

He had done as well in Honolulu as he had in Mississippi. With his uncle's help he had set up his practice, and it soon flourished. A gregarious partygoer with a passion for gambling, he lived a social life as full as his professional life, and the latter was very full. By December 1917 he was assistant district attorney in Honolulu, a major in the National Guard, and judge advocate general of the Hawaiian Territorial Forces. There was even the prospect of a federal judgeship. He had continued to write to Estelle, and now his letters came more frequently. By the end of his university career, one of Estelle's friends, Ella Somerville, had called Cornell the catch of the year. Before he had left, some had the impression that he and Estelle were courting. Now, at home, his mother, Mrs. William Hairston, talked with her good friend Lida Oldham, and found that they both thought it would be wonderful if Cornell and Estelle were to marry. Mrs. Hairston sent Estelle a double diamond ring, and Cornell wrote her that it was her engagement ring. He was coming home in April, he said, to marry her. She would later say that this news came as a complete surprise. Thinking back, a friend would say, "I don't think anybody else was surprised."[23]

Estelle Oldham was caught up in events she could not seem to control. Mrs. Oldham asked her daughter why she didn't wear Cornell's beautiful ring, and Estelle said she couldn't find it. Frantic searching produced it from the bottom of a dresser drawer. The unhappy girl sat huddled with her distraught sweetheart. "I suppose I *am* engaged to Cornell now," she told Falkner, "but I'm ready to elope with you." According to one friend, at some point they took out a marriage license, but he decided against elopement.[24] "No," he said, "we'll have to get your father's consent." He decided they would have to inform both fathers, and when he did, both of them exploded.

There were objections both spoken and unspoken. For one thing, how could Bill support the two of them? His prospects at the bank certainly didn't appear promising. Relations between the two families were amicable at best. The Falkners might well feel a deep political antipathy, and the Oldhams thought all the Falkners were too democratic. That was why

Lida Oldham wouldn't let Estelle and her younger sister, Tochie, go to Sallie Murry's dances: she invited ordinary Oxford boys rather than the ones Miss Lida regarded as coming from the best families. Murry and Maud Falkner could not forbid their son to marry the Oldhams' eldest daughter, but they would do all they could to discourage him. If they had to, Lem and Lida Oldham would forbid their daughter to marry the Falkners' eldest son, and they would do all they could to see that she married Cornell Franklin when he returned that April. Sitting in the grape arbor behind The Big Place, Bill and Estelle tried to find a way out of the impasse. If they were to marry, they would have to elope, but they had decided not to do that. Somewhere in the future they would find a proper way.

WHEN Phil Stone came home from New Haven for the Christmas holidays, he found Falkner despondent. Phil knew that Bill had long been sick of the job at the bank, but there was something more which, in his reticent fashion, he would not discuss. Stone resumed his courtship of Katrina Carter, from whom Phil probably learned what was troubling Bill.

As for Estelle, everything seemed to be conspiring against her, closing in around her. Tochie was to be married to Lieutenant Peter Allen when he returned from France. Wouldn't it be nice, Lida Oldham must have thought, if Tochie's older sister were married first, in the spring. Estelle Oldham found that Cornell's best advocate was his mother. Estelle had once visited her home, when she was fourteen. She had paid no heed to Cornell and went out with a boy her own age. But she had loved Mrs. Hairston, whom she had found to be a beautiful and charming woman. As she talked with her now, she thought her even more so. Cornell wrote again, looking ahead to the wedding, to the honeymoon, and to their life together in Hawaii. Family pressure increased, and by late March it had been arranged that Lida Estelle Oldham would become the bride of Cornell Sidney Franklin on the evening of April 18, 1918.

Bill still brought her verses. One set he had lettered beautifully on a single white sheet folded into four. On the back, in pen and ink, he had drawn a sketchily dressed nymph listening to the crouching satyr playing his pipe at her feet. In the upper left-hand corner a Mephistophelian face looked down upon the scene. Inside, two short poems, "Dawn" and "An Orchid," faced each other. The front section of the folded sheet bore the title "A Song." It introduced a poem he had written and rewritten. The poet was powerless before the beloved's beguiling image. He concluded

> It is vain to implore me
>   I have given my treasures of art
> Even though she choose to ignore me
>   And my heart.[25]

Gradually Bill began to realize that the wedding was actually going to take place. As his brother put it, "his world went to pieces.²⁶ Mixed with his pain and sense of loss was bitterness toward Estelle. Somehow, he felt, she could have resisted the pressures to marry a man she didn't love. Or had her fickle heart betrayed them? Torn and anguished, she told him that she did not prefer Cornell to him, but she did not know what she should do or, at this point, what she could do. But she was unable to reach him as he retreated from her into his silence and pain.

He retreated from Oxford as well, spending days in Memphis, in Charleston, and Clarksdale. He tried, without success, to enlist for pilot training. In late March, Phil Stone learned of the attempt. Fearing that his friend might turn back and try for elopement, convinced that marriage would spell the end of his chances as a writer, Stone called Maud Falkner from New Haven and told her he thought Bill should come up and stay with him until the crisis had passed. Furious, Maud Falkner called Estelle and berated her for what she thought was her part in Bill's foolhardy action. There was plenty of time yet for him to go to war. In September he would be twenty-one and then he would be drafted. She lectured her son. In the meantime he could get away; he could visit his friend and see another part of the country. He could see Yale University. He agreed to go. On Saturday, March 30, he posted his own deposit of $30 to his account and a $3 check against it. He cashed checks for $24.05 and $1 and left the bank for good without waiting for the end of Saturday's shortened business day.²⁷

With his mother and his brothers he drove to Memphis and boarded the train. Back home, across the widening miles, his sweetheart awaited the bridegroom coming to claim her. Bill traveled on, beyond Mississippi, beyond Tennessee, into a new phase of his life.

I quit moving around and went to the window and drew the curtains aside and watched them running for the chapel. . . .

. . . I began to listen for the chimes . . . the bitten shadows of the elms flowing upon my hand. And then as I turned into the quad the chimes did begin and I went on while the notes came up like ripples on a pool and passed me and went on. . . .

—*The Sound and the Fury* (96, 212)

He was a strange mixture of fear and pride as he opened the throttle wide and pushed the stick forward—fear that he would wreck the machine landing, and pride that he was on his own at last. He was no physical coward, his fear was that he would show himself up before his less fortunate friends to whom he had talked largely of spins and side slips and gliding angles.

—"Landing in Luck," *EPP* (43–44)

WILLIAM FALKNER had been reading prose as well as poetry. He and Stone admired Balzac, and Falkner had written his name in his copy of the volume containing *Les Chouans* and *A Passion in the Desert*. He had read light fiction as well as serious novels. He probably knew Owen Johnson's *Stover at Yale* and some of the novels in Burt L. Standish's series about Frank Merriwell, many set at the university in New Haven. And of course Phil Stone had told him about Yale. It was a different school now, however, from the one Stone had first seen nearly half a dozen years earlier. The leafy elms still rose above the old brick quadrangles, but there were far fewer students to jam the Yale Bowl on a late fall afternoon for "The "Game" with Harvard, fewer freshmen and sophomores to battle in the brutal "Fence Rush," and fewer junior fraternity men to robe themselves for processions that would call for the newly elected sophomores. The exodus had begun in the early years of the war—some volunteers in the

British and French armies, others into ambulance units—before the men in American khaki had begun flooding into training camps. By the fall of 1917 only 2,100 students were enrolled, and nearly half of these were in the ROTC or the Yale Naval Training Unit. By early April, when Falkner arrived in New Haven, ROTC men were being ordered to the training camps, and in less than half a year there would be only 200 students in civilian clothes.

But it was still a chance for Falkner to immerse himself in the atmosphere of a great university. He had spent a good deal of time on the campus of Ole Miss, and he had friends there who had often invited him to their rooms. He had some of the same advantages here—the chance to mingle with people interested in things that interested him, to read and dream in an environment of mental adventuring without having to attend classes. He moved into Stone's quarters in a rooming house owned by two old-maid sisters. It was close to places the two friends enjoyed. One was the three-year-old Brick Row Print and Book Shop, where Stone had bought first editions of Pound, Eliot, Robinson, and Masefield as investments.[1] The other was Mory's, the student gathering place celebrated in "The Whiffenpoof Song." Stone wrote home in a tone that was meant to be reassuring but succeeded in being patronizing. "He is a fine, intelligent little fellow," he said, "and I am sure he will amount to something."[2] Stone continued with his own one-man tutorials. He had fallen under the spell of William Butler Yeats, and he would read aloud, trying to imitate the way Yeats chanted his poetry. There were poets at Yale among Stone's friends and acquaintances. There was the precocious nineteen-year-old Stephen Vincent Benét, whose early work echoed Browning, Amy Lowell, and Alfred Noyes but who was finding his own unique voice. And there was Robert Hillyer, who not only was already accomplished as a poet, but also had undergone fascinating experiences in the war.

Falkner would not be entirely free to do as he wished in New Haven, however, for there was little or nothing left of his bookkeeper's salary. So, on April 10, he was back at work. One of Stone's friends, a blue-collar worker at the Winchester Repeating Arms Company, provided the contact, and now, once again, more of Falkner's day was spent at a high desk before ruled ledgers, his pen at the service of profit and loss rather than of the muse. In the company records his name was spelled Faulkner, either in error or as the first step in a stratagem soon to be attempted.[3]

But neither business nor poetry, nor anything of his new surroundings, could keep his mind from the past in the middle of that month of April 1918. Even if no one wrote to describe them, he could imagine the round of parties that celebrated Estelle's forthcoming marriage. What he could not know was something she would remember vividly years later. She wept the night before her wedding. A sympathetic great-aunt sat with her as they talked much of the night away. As the sky lightened on the morning of April 18, her aunt began to dress.

"I'm going to go to your father and make him call this wedding off," she told her niece.

"No, you mustn't do that," said the bride-to-be. "Daddy will be furious. It's too late." If she regretted the broken romance with Falkner, she regretted other things too—the freedom and the good times, the dance cards that were always filled, the house parties in Jackson and the Delta. According to Ben Wasson, "she was the butterfly of the Delta," and Sallie Murry Wilkins said she was "as pretty as a little partridge." The men had flocked about her, and she had loved it. Talking charmingly, dancing enchantingly, she had flitted on her brightly colored careless wings. She had laughed and said what she pleased, and suddenly the net had closed around her. But perhaps its gauze would not be so confining, after all. Besides, she had passed her twenty-second birthday, and though she would never be an old maid, it would not do for her to remain single for too long when younger girls such as Tochie bloomed and married. Life in Honolulu with a houseful of servants and the society of cosmoplitan friends had a certain allure, and if she was not ready for the sacramental bond that would tie her to a husband—to this husband—he was still what Ella Somerville had called him: the catch of the year. And there would be dances and house parties in Hawaii too, and much more that Oxford could not offer. Trapped as she now was, unhappy as she was over all that was ending, she could go only in the direction in which she was being drawn by forces she seemed unable to resist.

A little after seven o'clock that evening, walking carefully in her satin brocade, carrying her court train, Estelle entered the vestibule of the First Presbyterian Church with her attendants. She stood waiting for the organ peal, a coronet of orange blossoms in her hair and a shower of orchids and lilies of the valley in her shaking hand. As the chords filled the church the distraught girl turned to Katrina Carter. "I don't know if I love Cornell," the bridesmaid heard her say. Years later Estelle would say that Cornell married her knowing that she did *not* love him. Whatever the feelings in her divided mind and heart, time had run out for her. She put her hand on Lem Oldham's arm and advanced toward the rose-decorated altar where her groom, resplendent in white full dress with gold braid and saber, waited for her. The chauffeur who had brought her to the church drove them back to the Oldham home for the reception. It was Johncy Falkner. When he drove them to the station he said his goodbyes with the others and watched the receding lights of the 9:40 that carried the newlyweds to Memphis. By June 1, Major and Mrs. Cornell Franklin were at home, 5,000 miles away in Honolulu.

In the cool spring of Connecticut, Falkner went on with his divided life, with the ledgers by day and the reading and writing and talk by night. On the weekends he was free to roam, sometimes with Stone, sometimes without him. But he did have to think ahead. He planned to stay there until

Stone finished his work for the LL.B. in the summer, and to stay on, perhaps even until September, if the bill for lowering the draft age to eighteen
had not gone through. At twenty-one, when he was eligible for the draft
under existing law, he would enter service at home. An artillery unit at
Yale was staffed by French and American officers and two others who
were disabled veterans of the Canadian field artillery. Stone had friends
among this officer corps, and when they heard of Falkner's intention they
urged him to try for the RAF. For over a year now the Royal Air Force
had been working to equip twenty squadrons in Canada with the American
"Flying Jenny" to train pilots for the Western Front. Falkner found the
idea intriguing. Before leaving home he had told Jack that he hoped to find
a way to get into service "other than by enlisting as a private."[4] For one
with a taste for smart, trim clothes, what could be more attractive than the
slim boots, shining leather harness, and light blue of the RAF?

Though he had been in no rush to enlist during the last few months, his
imagination had earlier been seized by the idea of combat in the clouds.
"This was 1915 and '16," he would later recall. "I had seen an aeroplane
and my mind was filled with names: Ball, and Immelman and Boelcke, and
Guynemer and Bishop, and I was waiting, biding, until I would be old
enough or free enough or anyway could get to France and become glorious and beribboned too."[5] As recently as February the Oxford *Eagle* had
run a series called "The Training of an Air Man," describing "the thrill of
the first flight" and the pilot's progress toward the final goals: "a commission in the air service, and a place in the battle skies of France."[6] In March
he had told a Clarksdale friend, Eula Dorothy Wilcox, about his attempt to
enlist for pilot training in the Aviation Section of the United States Army's
Signal Corps. "Dot," he had said, "do you know anything that would
make me grow tall?" He had even stuffed himself with bananas, but they
had rejected him, he said, as too short and too light. But the official requirements at that time specified only that candidates had to be between
nineteen and thirty and stated that they could be "light in weight and
youthful in appearance."[7] Johncy Falkner would attribute his brother's
rejection to the lack of two years of college. However, no actual records
seem to have survived as evidence of an attempt to enlist, though both
Stone and Maud Falkner had reacted violently to the report that he had
made one. His imagination would come into play strongly in the military
career he was about to embark on, even at the outset.

Stone's situation was somewhat different from Falkner's. He wrote his
mother that he had been placed in the "Judge Advocate General's reserve"
with a draft classification of Class V, Division D. This would permit him
to finish out the year and receive his law degree and subsequently a commission.[8] He had already turned twenty-five, however, and if his mother
was understandably relieved at his deferment, there were those in Oxford
who thought it strange that he was not in uniform. With most able-bodied
students gone from the campus, both he and Falkner must have felt in-

creasingly uncomfortable about their civilian status. The quickest avenue to military service seemed to be through Canadian recruiters, a plan Stone would say they had already hatched in Oxford at Christmas time.

According to Stone's later accounts, they assumed that they would have to pass themselves off as Englishmen, or at least as "territorials," if Falkner were to join the Royal Air Force and Stone the Royal Artillery. One of the men at Stone's table at the Commons was an Englishman named Reed, who offered to drill them at mealtime on pronunciation and usage. Since they could not master all the nuances of the British "public school" accent, he suggested that they pose as Canadians. Stone concurred, but Falkner went on asking for the salt and discussing the weather in the best English accent he could muster. Stone said they devised other evidence: letters of reference which they wrote and mailed to their tutor's sister in London, who would post them to the New York recruiting office. They were purportedly the testimonials of a Reverend Mr. Edward Twimberly-Thorndyke, who called them "godfearing young Christian gentlemen."

The deception did not end there. When Falkner traveled to New York on June 14 he altered the facts he gave to the enlistment officer on Lord Wellesley's staff on Fifth Avenue in no less than half a dozen instances. He began with spelling, for he was now William Cuthbert Faulkner. His birthplace was Finchley, in the county of Middlesex, England. His Royal Air Force Certificate of Service recorded the information that he had been born on May 25, 1898, into the Church of England. His mother now resided in Oxford, Mississippi, and her name was also spelled Faulkner. He had certainly passed himself off as an Englishman, but why was he eight months younger than William Falkner of Oxford? Had he hoped it might mitigate the facts of his height and weight if they would count against him, that a lenient officer might think he had more time to grow? Whatever the case, he would enter upon active service with the rank of "Private II," with his "trade in Royal Air Force" put down as "Cadet for Pilot." The Royal Air Force might not be the romantic, glamorous Royal Flying Corps of the early years of the war, but it was still an elite combat force which he would join at the Recruits' Depot in Toronto on Tuesday, July 9. Returning to New Haven, he quit his job at Winchester. Stone's second LL.B. was voted him on June 19, and the two were free to leave New Haven. Stone would defer his attempt at enlistment for nearly six weeks, and ultimately fail to serve in either the British or the American army.

WHEN the two men had returned to Oxford that June it must have seemed a town of missing faces. Estelle and Tochie were gone. Jack was in Marine training at Quantico and Johncy was working in a power plant in Alabama. Faulkner visited Stone and his other friends, went on a few outings, and read: Harry Leon Wilson's *Ruggles of Red Gap*, James Branch Cabell's *The Rivet in Grandfather's Neck* (with whose artist-hero Faulkner doubtless empathized), and Kipling's "The Man Who Would Be King." And he read about the war—the ghastly slaughter in the war of attrition on the Western Front and the aerial warfare which was so different, a form of conflict in which one could still hear echoes of knightly combats of men descended from that ideal for him and Stone and so many other Southerners before them: the legendary Chevalier de Bayard, the sixteenth-century *"chevalier sans peur et sans reproche."* But by now the idea of military heroism had become inextricably linked with death, and with living intensely over a short timespan. As one veteran put it, "In those years death itself exerted a curious magnetism on young men . . . and death became a romantic dream for the new generation of American writers."[9] One such writer was John Dos Passos. When lawyers tried to discuss plans for his father's estate, he had asked, "but what use was an income to a man who expected to get killed within the year?"[10] Young men like Alan Seeger wrote poems such as "I Have a Rendezvous with Death," and many, like him, kept it.

At the Recruits' Depot in Toronto, Faulkner was issued the rough wool uniform, including the large greatcoat and white-banded overseas cap that identified him as a cadet. Canadians Albert Monson and J. M. Hinchley noticed him immediately. "Naturally we all knew Faulkner," the latter would remember. He was noticeable for his "diminutive physique, his feeble moustache, his rich Southern drawl, which Monson thought was English. . . ."[11] After two weeks of military drill and lectures on basics such as discipline and hygiene, they were ordered to Cadet Wing, a tent city of 1,600 men at Long Branch, just west of Toronto on Lake Ontario. Now the parade-ground drill and physical training were only adjuncts to the main curriculum: wireless telegraphy, topography, and air-force law. Writing home to his mother in late August, Faulkner told her, "I am trying to learn to walk and salute nasty, like a British officer."[12] By early September, when long route marches were hardening the cadets, he wrote her that the weather had turned and that he had to wear all his shirts and sweaters at once to keep warm. But the rugged training agreed with him, and he told her he had gained so much weight that his uniforms were tight even without the added layers of clothing. This did not show in a photograph, however, where he still looked like a boy in his mid-teens in spite of a shadowy mustache.

By September 20 he and the other members of Course 42 were at the No. 4 School of Military Aeronautics in Wycliffe College at the University of Toronto. To Monson and another Canadian, Justin Herbert Dyer, he seemed well-mannered, quiet, and intellectually inclined. Monson still thought he was British—alert, quick, and generally "just an outstanding little fellow."[13] Hinchley had received the impression that Faulkner had been a student at Yale. He also remembered his singing ballads and reciting unprintable limericks. On one occasion, when Faulkner received a check from home, he bought drinks for his four roommates and wound up conducting a one-man drill on the sidewalk, calling out commands loudly and then executing them smartly. Monson later said that he sometimes felt that Faulkner might be assuming an air of confidence he did not actually feel, and that he might be overcompensating for his shortness and his generally unimpressive appearance.

He seemed to read little beyond course texts, but his class notes were impeccable. Aircraft rigging, theory of flight, aerial navigation, motors, bomb raiding, signaling, artillery observation, reconnaisance, and photography—all these were recorded in his neat handwriting. The notes on motors and navigation, on tactics and weapons were detailed, and the accompanying sketches—like one of the Flying Jenny—were almost as precise as manufacturers' schematic drawings. There was a list of sixteen Allied military aircraft with their specifications. One was the Sopwith Camel, and though there were no Camels in Canada's RAF training command, this aircraft would loom large in Faulkner's imagination and memory.

His drawings were not limited to military equipment. Monson recalled that whenever Faulkner had the chance "he would take his notebook out and quickly sketch the officers or N.C.O.'s who were taking the parade or giving the lecture."[14] Other drawings must have had imaginary or photographic models. Several were of soldiers of varying nationalities. One sketch showed a pilot waiting in the cockpit of his single-seater biplane while one crewman held the lower wing and another grasped the propeller blade. The aircraft was shorter and stubbier than the Curtiss Jenny. It looked like the Sopwith Camel. It may have sprung from the same impulse that produced an incomplete ten-line poem in one of his notebooks. He called it "The Ace," and began with the darkness that would precede a dawn patrol. Then, with the mist rising in the dawning,

> The sun light
> Paints him as he stalks, huge through the morning
> In his fleece and leather, gilds his bright
> Hair and his cigarette.
>
> Makes gold his fleece and leather, and his bright
> Hair.
>   Then, like a shooting star,[15]

He stopped there, perhaps as the squadron fell out for close-order drill, or as the notes of "Last Post" sounded through the northern darkness.

Could he have sat in such a plane himself, or seen another there? How much of "the conquest of the air" that had been described so rhapsodically in the Oxford *Eagle* did he experience before the Armistice of November 11 put an end to that already archaic form of man-to-man jousting over "the battle skies of France"? The letters Maud Falkner received during that month suggested that he had experienced a good deal. He wrote that he had gone on a "joy ride" in August and later had rides from other friends. He had finished ground school on November 13, he wrote, and had begun to fly at more frequent intervals. On November 22 he went aloft, a day when he was "so cold he had to be helped out of the cockpit." Two days later he made another flight, and by November 30, he told Miss Maud, he had four hours of solo time in his log. He was glad, he said, that the war had lasted long enough for him to get flight training.[16] One year later his first published fiction would appear in *The Mississippian*: a 2,500-word short story entitled "Landing in Luck." The scene is an aerodrome near "Borden," the protagonist a young man named Thompson, who growls about his instructor, Mr. Bessing, a "blasted Englishman." Still inept after more than seven hours' instruction, Cadet Thompson is finally pushed into the air alone. He loses a wheel on a bad takeoff and then freezes in terror as he comes in for a landing. Miraculously escaping injury, he is credited by Bessing with skill he does not possess. The story ends with the new "barracks ace" lording it over his fellow cadets.[17] A little more than six years later Faulkner would be at work on his first novel, *Mayday*, which would be published as *Soldiers' Pay*. He had begun with a character much like Thompson. Nineteen-year-old Julian Lowe, "known as 'One Wing' by the other embryonic aces of his flight," had accumulated forty-seven hours' flying time with only two weeks to go to earn his wings when the war had ended.[18]

Faulkner's later accounts of his experiences made these fictional uses of autobiography pale. His brother Jack said Bill told him how he celebrated the armistice: "I took up a rotary-motored Spad with a crock of bourbon in the cockpit, gave diligent attention to both, and executed some reasonably adroit chandelles, an Immelman or two, and part of . . . a nearly perfect loop." Its chance of perfection was spoiled because "a hanger got in the way and I flew through the roof and ended up hanging on the rafters."[19] Johncy thought it was a Camel, which had gone only halfway through the roof. He also thought Bill had injured his leg in the crash. Later, Estelle's son, Malcolm, would say Faulkner told him he broke his nose in the accident. He told Phil Stone there were actually two of them in the plane and that they both hung from their seatbelts "trying to drink from a bottle upside down." Several years later he told Calvin Brown, Jr., that he had crashed in France, falling uninjured through a thatched roof and landing in the soup tureen of a peasant family's Sunday dinner. A dozen years later Faulkner would write that he wrecked not one but two aircraft.[20] No newspaper or surviving official record took note of such a crash.

How much danger had he faced? How much had he shared with the men who had risked their necks from the first moment they soared aloft in the fragile canvas, wood, and wire "kites" powered by rasping engines and fueled with highly flammable gas and oil? He knew the engines at firsthand from the Leaside airfield in north Toronto. There in tin sheds they had spun the propellers of bolted-down motors until they caught and roared into life. But they could not really count on flying until they finished the course at the School of Aeronautics and went on to Camp Borden, fifty miles northwest of Toronto, or to one of two others at Deseronto, 130 miles away. When the war ended, the members of Course 42 were still in Toronto. Hinchley remembered that one week later "orders came through to discontinue all flying in Canada and from that date we simply marked time while awaiting demobilization."[21] A week later over 2,000 cadets had been demobilized. Among the first of these were men from the school, and no one from Course 42 was posted to the camps where the flying training was now closed down. Monson and Dyer did not fly. Hinchley didn't either, and he would later say it seemed hardly credible to him that Faulkner could have been doing any solo flying. There was one possibility. In a letter in early September, Faulkner had mentioned to his mother a Lieutenant Todd, who had been allowed to skip ground school and been sent directly to the School of Aeronautics. If he had managed to go on from there to Camp Borden or one of the others for flight training, and if Faulkner had cultivated his acquaintance enough in the short time he had known him to visit Todd, he might possibly have flown with him. But this would have meant that Todd had acquired, rather quickly, enough hours to solo and that he would perform the doubtless unauthorized act of taking up a passenger. Or it would have meant that Todd had asked a qualified brother officer to give Faulkner a ride, or that this shy, reticent, and unprepossessing cadet had managed himself to ask some stranger—a pilot and an officer or some devil-may-care cadet—to give him a joy ride. In the RAF uniform he had heard no shots fired in anger, and the roar of the engines he had heard had been different from those he had dreamed of. And he would have to wait until he was a civilian again to know "the thrill of the first flight."

Jack Falkner had seen a very different war. By September 1918, Faulkner's nineteen-year-old brother was with the 5th Marine Regiment, a hardened survivor of the ferocious fighting at Belleau Wood and Soissons. In that same month he was in combat again at St.-Mihiel, and after a short time at the rear, was on his way to the Champagne sector. There he was badly gassed, but he doggedly managed to suffer through the immediate effects and to stay with his unit. They fought at Epinal, advancing over the blasted battlefields of 1914 and 1915. There was some time at the rear again in October, but the last night of that month found them on the edge of the Argonne Forest. In the early hours of November 1, bursting star shells signaled the beginning of a German barrage that came crashing down on the Marines' position. The "whiz-bang" from a German .77 exploded with a roar. His right knee laid open by a piece of shrapnel, a small fragment lodged against his skull, Private Jack Falkner was out of the war. His letters stopped coming, and soon Maud and Murry Falkner were frantic with worry. "Dad sort of went to pieces," Johncy remembered, "but Mother kept telling him, 'Hush, Buddy. He'll be back.'"[22] It was not until the week before Christmas, after Billy had returned home, that a letter at last arrived for Murry Falkner from Jack. It was a cheerful letter, with no mention of the gassing and little about the wounds. He had much to tell, he said, when he got home in the spring.

But the dark angel had not entirely overlooked Toronto. One of Faulkner's roommates had been fatally injured in a rugby match, and the great Spanish influenza epidemic of the autumn of 1918 had swept through the RAF command. More than a quarter of the officers and men at Long Branch came down with the flu. The School of Aeronautics was placed under quarantine, and a series of long marches was instituted to keep the men's resistance up. Cadet Faulkner proved impervious.

His Medical Boards examination on December 5 under the demobilization order showed that he had thrived in the RAF. He was fit, and pounds heavier. In the group photograph taken on November 18 he still had to wear the white cadet band on his overseas cap, but it was cocked rakishly on the side of his head, and though his expression was dour, the mustache was respectably dark. However, his groundwork was graded at a disappointing 70 percent. He was discharged "in consequence of being Surplus to R.A.F. requirements," and the column headed "Casualties, Wounds, Campaigns, Medals, Clasps, Decorations, Mentions, Etc." was simply stamped NIL. But he had an honorable discharge and $73.69 coming to him. He had a way to spend it, for he had already ordered a new uniform, not the coarse cloth the cadets wore, but an officer's uniform with the smart blue belted tunic, Sam Browne belt, two styles of trousers, two kinds of caps, a trench coat complete with flaps and equipment rings, and a cane and a swagger stick. On the left breast glittered a pair of wings, not of the Royal Air Force, but of its legendary predecessor, the Royal Flying Corps, and on the shoulders the pips of a lieutenant. It would be more than a year before he received a large parchment scroll which informed him that he had been gazetted Honorary Second Lieutenant and that he could wear the uniform only for military business "or on special occasion when attending ceremonials and entertainments of a military nature."[23] He was wearing the uniform when his family met him at the Oxford depot in early December and he wore it often after that, in whole or in part, at home and on the square, at dances and playing golf. He enjoyed taking the salute of other soldiers, and he posed for photographs in different combinations from his military wardrobe, a cigarette in his mouth, a handkerchief tucked in his sleeve, and the cane and gloves in his hand.

Why did he go through this elaborate charade? How could he wear the wings he had not earned, the pips that had not been awarded, the uniform of a rank he had not attained? And how could he let his family, still recovering from the anxiety and shock of Jack's being missing and wounded, think that he too had suffered grievous injury in the war? There were several possible answers. One was that he may have wanted to enjoy something of the aura that would greet Jack as a returning hero. Another was that the line between reality and imagination was not as compelling for him as it was for others—as Sallie Murry had said years before, when Billy said something, you couldn't tell whether it was true or he had just made it up. A more likely reason was that this uniform confirmed a dream that he would make real in appearance, though it was not so in actuality. It was not the first time that he had done this, and he would continue to enact roles for the rest of his life. He was a romantic and a dreamer. Moreover, he was still a physically unprepossessing young man, shorter than the rest, not handsome as he would become, and unsuccessful in love. He was not the first young man who would be transformed in the eyes of others when he wore a uniform and clothed himself in tales of heroic exploits. For all his shyness, he wanted attention. He wanted acclaim, and in a sense he wanted love. If his drawing and painting and writing were expressions of the deepest levels of his psyche, if they were activities that he pursued because he had to, they were also manifestations of the wish to be noticed and to be esteemed.

He got more than a uniform and a bit of money from his 179 days on active service with the RAF in Canada. He partook of the prestige of that elite group. Even if he had not fought or even flown, he *had* been an RAF man. He had enjoyed the chance to absorb some aspects of the British culture which he admired. Not only had he kept up with the exploits of the great British aces—Mannock, McCudden, and the Canadian Billy Bishop—he had heard the men who knew them speak about them. The training he had received conveyed the sense of combat and death, which his extraordinary imagination absorbed thoroughly. Some of it was virtually transmuted into his own experience, the comic as well as the grim. He would eventually pay a price for his masquerade; erroneous reports would get into biographical notes, for he gave the impression that he had been badly wounded in actual combat. In later years he would squirm and try in subtle ways to amend the record. He would talk about the dangers of just flying in those days, the strain it produced, and the way a man would wonder if he would be able to walk away from the next day's flight. The dangers, particularly in aircraft such as the Sopwith Camel, had been amply conveyed. This sense Faulkner also absorbed, so that whenever he spoke of it, the hearer could not doubt that it was something he had known firsthand, and in his vitals. The products of his 179 days—part of the triad he would cite so often: imagination, observation, and experience—would last him a lifetime.

Leaving Toronto for Oxford, he packed a shoulder patch lettered "Royal Flying Corps," a sixpence lucky piece, a bit of blue piping, and a tiny Union Jack. He also brought much more, stored in memory and imagination.

He suffered the same jaundice that many a more booted one than he did, from Flight Commanders through Generals to the ambrosial single-barred (not to mention that inexplicable beast of the field which the French so beautifully call an aspiring aviator); they had stopped the war on him.

—*Soldiers' Pay* (7)

So he was home again, in that time of freedom for the veteran who is not a professional soldier, when he can bask in whatever glory or prestige still attaches to him from his service and before he must engage in some kind of work or return to some sort of routine. His brothers enjoyed this part of his life almost as much as he did. Seventeen-year-old Johncy watched with pride as American soldiers, seeing his cap and belt, gave him the re-spect and salutes some of them reserved only for men who had been over-seas. Eleven-year-old Dean wore his Boy Scout uniform in a kind of imitation of his brother's RAF garb. James Nunnally, two years older than Dean Falkner, was fascinated. In contrast with the "frowsy, shapeless and shoddy garments" Oxonians had seen on American soldiers, Faulkner's uniform was "Bond Street-Piccadilly-tailored. . . ." He wore it with a kind of quiet superciliousness. The neatly trimmed new mustache "was startling enough in an era when a mustache, usually a handlebar, was a badge of the elderly, but the ultimate affront to convention was the swagger stick tucked nonchalantly under Faulkner's arm."[1] One friend recalled seeing him on the square "wearing his British uniform with all the regalia. He cut quite a swanky figure. . . . He gave the impression that he did not have a care or worry in this world, or give a damn about anything or anybody." Maud Falkner took snapshots of her son for her album in several different uniform combinations and poses—performing the manual of arms with a rifle, leaning lightly and casually, gloves in hand, on a rattan cane.

But by the end of the first week in January 1919 life in Oxford had more than palled. Writing Hubert Starr, a fellow law student and friend of Phil Stone in New Haven, Faulkner told him he had "had enough of his 'God forsaken' home town to last him the rest of his life" and feared that after his death he would be "returned to Oxford from Hell." He wanted to get away, but his mother was in "bad health" and wanted him to stay at least until Jack returned home. Although his parents didn't want him to leave, they "berated him for presumed weaknesses" but looked upon "any display of independence with a reaction approximating that of horror."[2]

By mid-March, Maud and Murry Falkner were full of anticipation of the return from the war of their hero son. In a surprisingly poetic strain, Murry Falkner wrote in a kind of journal, "The Fruit trees are in Bloom, & my Heart is blooming with thankfulness to the Ruler of all as he has brought my Boy back safely from overseas— He is today at Portsmouth Va & will be Home Soon—[.]" The next entry, about March 25, noted, "All the boys at home again & we are Happy & thankful."[3]

The eldest of the Falkner boys was spending as much time as he could away from home. Phil Stone was now living in Charleston with his brother, Jack, and Jack's wife, Myrtle, where the two men handled that branch of the family's legal firm. Faulkner liked Jack and Myrtle and he liked the Delta, densely forested and rich with dark soil and game and Indian lore. When he stayed with them he would slip easily into their family routine. He might play golf or be gone for days, walking over miles of Tallahatchie County, roaming, looking, and listening to the country people talk.

He saw old friends and made new ones. Dot Wilcox had her own home and her own beauty parlor in Clarksdale. Stone and Faulkner would often visit her, and she remembered them as inseparable. Faulkner liked Dot's friends, especially dark-haired, dark-eyed Reno DeVaux, who had run away from home in Mobile at seventeen. Both his mother and his parish priest had felt sure he was destined for the seminary, but the most compelling emotions moved him not at the altar but when he knelt to roll the dice in a crap game. He had made his living as a gambler, and now he owned Reno's Place in Clarksdale. He liked Phil Stone and even offered him a job playing for the house. Once Reno invited Faulkner to join a party going to New Orleans. When Faulkner told him he had only fifty cents in his pocket, Reno said, "That's all right. Come on along. I'll take care of it."

After they checked in at the Roosevelt Hotel, Reno realized that Faulkner could not dine in the Blue Room looking the way he did, so he bought him a new suit of clothes. Dot Wilcox threw the old clothes out the window, and two policemen came upstairs to investigate. Faulkner and Reno made the explanations and the policemen wound up having a drink with them.

It was a foot-loose life—Charleston, Clarksdale, New Orleans, Memphis —with the only limits imposed by his pocketbook, but he had friends to put him up, and he did not want or need much. His Canadian trench coat was more than enough for the Southern weather, and the pockets were capacious enough for a bottle of whiskey, a book or two, and his toothbrush. Years later he would say he was happier in these days than when he became a well-known writer.

His casual, free-and-easy life did not keep him from writing. He would later date a whole cycle of poems during April, May, and June of 1919 (though it may have been two or even three years later that he polished them to achieve their final form). They were pastoral eclogues linked together by observations on the seasons of the year and pervaded by melancholy meditations on youth, beauty, love, nature, and mutability. They were voiced by a marble faun, who mourned his lot in the prologue:

> Why am I not content? The sky
> Warms me and yet I cannot break
> My marble bonds. That quick keen snake
> Is free to come and go, while I
> Am prisoner to dream and sigh
> For things I know, yet cannot know. . . .[4]

As with most poems, the sources of these were complex. As one scholar observes, "Classical authors such as Pindar, Aristophanes, Plato, Herodotus, Virgil, Ovid, Lucan, Theocritus, and Apuleius often mentioned Pan and used him as a surrogate for the poet himself," as did Victorian aesthetes.[5] There were echoes of varied pastoral imagery and attitudes that had appealed to him in Swinburne and Housman. In some lines he struck the tones of a pensive Keats; in others, those of a melancholy Yeats. There were numerous unmistakable borrowings from Tennyson.[6] And while he echoed the Greek pastoral, he also borrowed imagery from a poem about another enervated figure: T. S. Eliot's "The Love Song of J. Alfred Prufrock." On the psychological level, the concept of the powerless lovelorn faun was one which might well have resonated with the emotional residue of the time when he too had lost his love. There was another process certainly at work. Though few perceived it, he was a genius whose mind was powerful enough to synthesize material from his wide if unsystematic reading. In their final form, one critic would say, these poems constituted "a carefully constructed exercise in pastoral, ironically implying the rejection of pastoral by modernity," with the faun "having the ironic capacity to discern his incapacity yet unable to do anything about it, a tortured creature of Pan, locked in himself like Prufrock. . . ."[7] (As Prufrock saw the mermaids "Combing the white hair of the waves blown back" so the faun saw the breeze "comb the wave-ponies' manes back. . . .")[8] The poems were peopled by other fauns and their nymphs, by shepherds and shepherdesses. They pined or dreamed in "quietude" by "ivied walls" in the "leafy shade" or the "westering sun." The diction and many of the images were actually closer to England than Mississippi. (One reason was probably a heavy indebtedness to "A Faun's Holiday," by an

Englishman named Robert Nichols, whose poems about warfare on the Western Front might first have attracted Faulkner.)[9] But there were some lines that showed close observation of nature. And if nothing else, these rather static poems showed an effort to master a number of verse forms and enough dedication for the writing and rewriting of hundreds of lines of poetry.

Stone resumed his role of five years earlier—continuing to encourage Faulkner, to read and discuss his work with him. Now he would also have it typed up by his secretary. They talked about other poets' work too. On one of their long walks in the country, Stone said he disliked the self-consciousness of Amy Lowell "and her gang of drum-beaters" because "they always had one eye on the ball and the other on the grandstand."[10] Faulkner smiled and said his "personal trouble as a poet seemed to be that he had one eye on the ball and the other eye on Babe Ruth."[11]

Faulkner was not an Imagist like Miss Lowell, but he was interested in images and particularly those combining various senses. One sheet of linen stationery contained only four lines:

> The darkness shakes its hair
> Stiffened with music, vagrant formless gleams
> Like dreams to haunt our dreams, a threading of violins
> and horns draw sensuously in darkness.[12]

An idea similar to that underlying the cycle of pastoral poems, one that may have dated from his time in Canada, gave him the basis for an ambitious poem that went through several versions. The final one began:

> I follow through the singing trees
> Her streaming clouded hair and face
> And lascivious dreaming knees. . . .[13]

In it he tried to link two situations: the lover pursuing his impassioned nymph and sharing her ecstatic flight, then, solitary and melancholy, watching moon-blanched dancers whirling past as he longed for escape and transcendance. He took his title from a work Stéphane Mallarmé, a French Symbolist, had published forty-three years before: "L'Apres-Midi d'un Faune." But the title was about all Faulkner had borrowed, for Mallarmé's symbolist eclogue can be interpreted, in one view, "as a complex ironic variation on a traditional pastoral theme: the pastoral protagonist as poet." In it the faun narrates two erotic adventures, both of them "extravagant attempts on the part of a sexually inexperienced faun to make his entry on the sexual stage of life with a uniquely memorable seduction; each attempt at seduction ends with the comic deflation of the faun's male ego."[14] As for the content, Faulkner's borrowings from Nichol's "A Faun's Holiday" were even clearer here than in his cycle of pastoral poems. Stone's secretary typed the poem, and they sent it to *The New Republic*.

The magazine paid $15 and published it in the issue of August 6. Stone quickly put other poems in the mail, but they all came back with rejections. Annoyed at these editors, they copied out John Clare's "Lines from a Northampton Asylum" and sent them in to *The New Republic*. The poem was returned without comment. The next time they copied out Coleridge's "Kubla Khan." Again the proffered work was rejected, but this time the editor added a note. "We like your poem, Mr. Coleridge," he wrote, "but we don't think it gets anywhere much."[15]

If Faulkner was disappointed at the failure of this hoax, he was amused by the success of another. In 1916, Arthur Davison Ficke and Witter Bynner had satirized contemporary "schools" of poetry in *Spectra: A Book of Poetic Experiments*. Writing as Emanuel Morgan and Anne Knish, of the Pittsburgh "Spectrists," they had deceived many, including William Carlos Williams and Amy Lowell (whom they had parodied), until they were exposed in *The New York Times Book Review* in June 1918. Faulkner thought it one of the best hoaxes he knew.[16]

ALTHOUGH Faulkner's passive grieving lovers had a precedent in poetic convention, some of the melancholy of his lines, that spring, may well have come from personal feeling. In "A Dead Dancer" he tried with long conversational lines to convey an emotion of exquisite sadness at the death of beauty, of youth, and of love. In the spring of 1918, Lieutenant Pete Allen had returned to Oxford as a hero and veteran of trench warfare after six months in France. He had claimed Tochie Oldham as his bride. Estelle Franklin, a newlywed of six weeks, was her matron of honor. The war danger past for Pete, the young couple had gone off to Georgia, where he was assigned as an instructor at Camp Gordon. By October she was happily pregnant. But the second wave of the great influenza epidemic had struck, and by mid-month Tochie, not long past the age of twenty, was dead. It must have seemed incredible to all of them that fall, and to Bill Faulkner when he returned, that someone as gay and brave and young as Tochie could so suddenly be gone.

When Estelle returned home to be with her grieving parents, she brought her baby with her, Tochie's namesake, Victoria. Estelle settled in for her visit, and once again Faulkner was often at the Oldham house. He liked to sit and watch little Victoria, who had been given the name "Cho-Cho" (butterfly) by her Chinese amah. In a way, it was worse that Estelle was home again, back in the house where she had played the piano for him so often, in the arbor where, little more than a year before, they had talked about marrying. Now she was the mother of someone else's child. He gave her the small black-covered Modern Library edition of Swinburne's poems which he had brought back from Toronto. He had drawn a pair of RAF wings in it and written his name there, together with "S of A," where he had trained, and "Borden," the post he had never reached. This last entry was a memento of the death of one set of hopes. The love poems of Swinburne recalled the death of another. Below the earlier lines on the flyleaf he inscribed the book to her, but the inscription was so passionate that she tore off the bottom half of the page so she could take the volume with her when she and Cho-Cho left for Hawaii near the end of September. All of his feelings of loss and longing, of love and rejection could indeed be objectified in figures such as that of the marble faun who could see others experiencing passions denied to him.

Something of his behavior with his male friends may have been a reaction. He and Stone and Jim Kyle Hudson often made a threesome, and though Stone had abjured hunting and was still off liquor, Hudson and Faulkner enjoyed both greatly. Several times, according to Hudson's son, they went "for three or four-week stretches out to the Tallahatchie and up into the wilds in boats; sleeping in tents, waited on by Negro servants, the men would hunt and fish all day and drink and play poker all night."[17] When young Jim Nunnally could provide a car, he and Faulkner and others would go to parties, sometimes to cabins out in the county where the principal refreshment would come from a zinc washtub of newly distilled "white lightning." After a few tin dipperfuls, Faulkner might stand on the hood of the car as they drove home. Arms outstretched, he would demonstrate how an aircraft turned and banked, and Nunnally would turn to follow his directions. "His ability to stand atop the jouncing car was uncanny," Nunnally remembered, but late one night the two got their signals mixed and Faulkner landed in a ditch on his head. That was the end of the "body-flying."[18]

For all of these diversions, Oxford must have seemed pale and empty to Faulkner after Estelle's departure. His situation at home was no better. His mother's love was constant, and his brothers still admired him, but he was spending less time in the home where his father had given up trying to understand this young man who now even spelled his name differently from his own on some of the pictures he drew and the things he wrote. There was real affection between his father and Jack, who would start his letters home with a warm "Dear Pardner." Johncy and Dean were excellent athletes for whom Murry Falkner could cheer on high-school and then college fields, and he could go into the woods with Dean to hunt in a close companionship. Between him and his eldest son, however, there now seemed only distance. But a change in his life was coming which would affect that of his son.

When Lieutenant Governor Lee Russell had announced for the governorship, John Falkner, Jr., had put aside his other interests to manage his campaign in Lafayette County. He ran strongly and then won the run-off in mid-July. Old J. W. T. Falkner had not changed his ideas about their social status, but he had been glad enough, late in the previous year, to profit, if only indirectly, from this connection with a powerful state official.

The Colonel must have decided that he had lost all the money a father could be expected to lose in setting up a middle-aged son in a series of businesses. The University of Mississippi was growing, but J. C. Eskridge was still both secretary and proctor. Undoubtedly with the approval of Lee M. Russell, the post of assistant secretary was filled on December 1, 1918, by the appointment of Murry C. Falkner. The salary was adequate, and a house on the campus would be provided as soon as it was available. So that fall of 1919 the students paid their tuition to him. His job-shifting was over, and as time went on he would assume additional duties.

His eldest son would move with the rest of the family. Jack was entering the university under a new provision that returning veterans might be admitted even without the specified high-school units. He would do his undergraduate work and then study law at Ole Miss, as his uncle and grandfather had done. It must have come as a surprise to everyone when the student who had left school as soon as it suited him agreed to go back too. But William Faulkner chose nothing as restrictive as a pre-law course. He would be a special student, taking only what he chose. Perhaps he did it to please his mother and placate his father, as a gesture toward conforming to some recognizable pattern for a young man his age. Whatever it was, William Faulkner was once more entering—very tentatively—into the life of a student.

All our eyes and hearts look up to thee,
For here all our voiceless dreams are spun
Between thy walls, quiet in dignity
Lent by the spirits of them whose lives begun
Within thy portals. . . .

—"Alma Mater," *EPP* (6)

IN the fall of 1919, 592 students were enrolled in the University of Mississippi. The mile-square campus was modest but attractive, with its cluster of Georgian Revival buildings and its parklike expanse of tall trees and flowering shrubs. In the small faculty, the strengths and foibles of individual teachers stood out, and the most prominent members formed a kind of inner circle. Dr. Muckenfuss, the father of Faulkner's former deskmate, Ralph, was head of the Chemistry Department and, with the help of one assistant, taught all the courses in the curriculum. General Hemingway, of the Law School, was a big, hearty, Taft-like man who was notorious for his easy grading of athletes. A. L. Bondurant was a professor of Latin who was noted for his elaborate courtesy. Professor D. H. Bishop was head of the English Department. In his academic robes he wore an expression faintly reminiscent of the older Woodrow Wilson. Probably the most learned man on the faculty was Calvin S. Brown, who had two doctorates, one in geology and the other in comparative literature. He taught German, French, and Italian. A nature lover, he would often show slides to his students, and sometimes he would talk about music, trying to convey to them his own love for it.

It was probably predictable when the two Falkner boys entered school on September 19 that Jack would be an agreeable student who would work conscientiously and that Bill would do as he liked and annoy some members of both the faculty and the student body. Miss Maud said he had the greatest powers of concentration she had ever seen. She remembered when he could stand at the mantel in the living room and study while John and Dean played noisily at his feet. He had a highly retentive memory and an enormous capacity for work, as his tireless verse writing showed, but from the outset he did not overtax himself. He registered only for French, Spanish, and Professor Bishop's Shakespeare course. Some members of the faculty had urged him to take other courses and study for a degree, but he told them that all he was interested in was languages and English. It was hard to tell how much he studied the courses he did take, for he never volunteered comments or answered questions in class. One student, much later, recalled an exception: "Mr. Faulkner," Professor Bishop had asked, "what did Shakespeare mean when he put those words in the mouth of Othello?"

There was a pause before Faulkner replied. "How should I know?" he said. "That was nearly four hundred years ago, and I was not there." If the classmate's memory was accurate, it was a rude and arrogant answer for one so shy and reserved, although it may have been jarred from him in a moment of surprise, and as he grew older he would increasingly show himself capable of abrupt and often cutting replies to overtures he had not invited.

Another classmate recalled that "The story was that he never bothered to take examinations, and would have been dropped except for the fact that his father (whom everyone liked) was an administrative officer and that the Falkners were an old-time Mississippi family and among the leading lights in that part of the state."[1] This could scarcely have endeared him to classmates. Earlier, he had been called "the Count" for his manner of dress; now some called him that for what seemed his put-on airs.

It may be that after his time at Yale, his own small state university seemed to him in some ways provincial. If it did, he appears also to have felt a genuine loyalty to it, unless his poem "Alma Mater" was exclusively a technical exercise; and for a fundamentally reticent man, he entered into a surprising number of university activities. All of the Falkners had belonged to the Sigma Alpha Epsilon fraternity. In spite of Lee Russell's law, it was one of the three still operating sub rosa, though without houses. In spite of Faulkner's idiosyncratic behavior, the brothers were willing to extend a bid to him, and his uncle John told him he should accept it. He agreed without hesitation and finally went through the candlelit Masonic-style ceremony which made him a member of the Mississippi Gamma Chapter of Sigma Alpha Epsilon. Fellow pledge Ben Wasson had been awestricken. "Don't you think the ritual's beautiful?" he asked him afterward. "All that mythological hash?" Faulkner answered derisively.[2]

His college experience, like his wartime experience, would not be broad, but it would be enough for the needs of his writing. In a photograph of the membership he stood in the back row. All but one of the others were formally attired in suits. Wearing a sweater, he seemed, as in the RAF group photo, a boy trying to look like a man. But this would be another transitional period for him. In a photo of the A.E.F. Club taken later that academic year for *Ole Miss*, he looked away from the camera while the others stared straight into the lens. By then he had abandoned the pompadour hair style. Instead, he parted it precisely in the middle. An umbrella handle was hooked nonchalantly over his shoulder, and from beneath the now fuller mustache, there protruded a cigarette in a long holder.

In these years the university administration was attempting to broaden its base of support and service. Paul Rogers, a Baptist minister's son from Choctaw County, was a sophomore at Ole Miss. Two years earlier, when he had entered on what he called "a poor man's scholarship," it had set him apart from most of his fellow students. Ole Miss "was just beginning to be other than a rich man's school," he remembered, "though it seemed to me that most of the students were quite well-to-do. Gambling—craps— was the institutional pastime and several students would win or lose as much as five or ten thousand dollars per academic year." By 1919, with the return of the veterans to the campus, the tempo of other pastimes had predictably increased. Living in a dormitory, Rogers saw "lots of drinking . . . . On Saturday nights, after the students returned to Gordon Hall from whatever outside activities, there was much retching and vomiting. After Prohibition, the alcoholic beverages were perfume, toilet water and melted Sterno." But for all of Bill Faulkner's fondness for his grandfather's liquor at the bank and friends' corn whiskey in rural cabins, Rogers never saw "in Gordon Hall or elsewhere anything to suggest that William Faulkner was a drinker."[3]

As it turned out, he became a highly visible member of the student body through his writing and artwork. More than two years earlier he had done his first drawing for *Ole Miss*. It was a highly stylized picture of a dancing couple which introduced the "Social Activities" section of the number for 1916–1917. The next year he did two more, again the same kind of elongated figures often seen in magazines such as *The Smart Set*. They were not particularly original, but they were by far the best in the book. Louis Cochran had been appointed editor of *Ole Miss* for 1920, and he asked Faulkner to do five drawings. They were all signed with the "u" in his name, and they were unlike those he had done for the earlier annuals. Again his pen-and-ink drawings were smoothly professional: a full-page spring scene for "Organizations," another featuring Harlequin, Pierrette, and Mezzetino in the traditional commedia dell'arte costumes against a background of checkered parquet and tall candelabra for "Social Activities." The other two signed drawings were smaller: a couple doing the Charleston for "Red and Blue," the senior dancing club, and a captioned picture of a flirtatious Frenchwoman and an American officer for the A.E.F. Club. Listed as one of the six art editors was "W. Faulkner."

On some days he would go out into the country with his box of water colors and brushes. Often Ben Wasson would accompany him and watch him paint "simple and direct" compositions "rapidly with sure strokes. He painted blue sky with clouds, and he fancied trees in any season, though best of all . . . in the springtime—pale, soft greens, light blues. He also cared for unplowed fields, sometimes with birds flying above them." After a time he would put his work aside and take a book from his pocket and read aloud—Keats, Shelley, Yeats, and other favorites such as *A Midsummer Night's Dream*. Then he would return to his painting.[4]

Faulkner also contributed a poem to *Ole Miss* which gave further evidence of his efforts to expand his skills. In late October of 1919 he had published a revised version of "L'Apres-Midi d'un Faune" in *The Mississippian*, the student newspaper. Two weeks later "Cathay" appeared. Its first stanza was a meditation on the transience of power in the manner of Shelley's "Ozymandias," the second employing imagery of a somewhat Yeatsian cast. As with several other works he would publish in *The Mississippian*, Faulkner printed "Cathay" in the Oxford *Eagle* too, so that his readership, by local standards, must have been considerable. "Landing in Luck," his story of RAF flight training, appeared in *The Mississippian* on November 26 with another of his poems. Few readers would have known that "Sapphics" was a condensation of Swinburne's poem of the same title or that Faulkner had not attempted Swinburne's use of the classical Sapphic stanza, but no Mississippi student could have failed to notice the erotic nature of the material, especially the lovelorn poet's last vision of a cruel Aphrodite:

> She sees not the Lesbians kissing mouth
> To mouth across lute strings, drunken with singing,
> Nor the white feet of the Oceanides
> Shining and unsandalled.[5]

Two weeks later still another poem appeared in *The Mississippian* over the name "W. Faulkner." Much like a Petrarchan sonnet, "Fifty Years" was dominated by a familiar tone, that of a lamenting lover enthralled by a *belle dame sans merci*. The poem that appeared in the yearbook which contained the drawings had a more contemporary title, "To a Co-ed," but the references were more traditional, recalling both the Symbolists and François Villon.[6]

There were other poems, and one of them, "The Lilacs," quite different in form and content, foreshadowed future work. It also had its roots in experiences that came well before his time as a student at Ole Miss. (He had written the first tentative lines of this much revised dramatic mono-logue on leftover sheets of his father's hardware-store stationery.) From the first the tone was one of death in life, for he had chosen as his central figure one he would use again: the maimed soldier. It was as though he had thought back to the image of the pilot in the dawn. But this time he was a casualty who looked back to his brief and fatal glory. (When it was published nearly six years later, it would be dedicated "TO A . . . . . AND H . . . . . , ROYAL AIR FORCE.") Now the poem began:

> We sit, drinking tea
> Beneath the lilacs of a summer afternoon
> Comfortably at our ease
> With fresh linen napkins on our knees
> We are in Blighty
> And we sit, we three
> In diffident contentedness.

Though in England, the invalid thinks back to a night raid over Mannheim and to the May morning when he had been shot down. Visual elements of the first mission were rendered with imagery that was poetic but realistic. The substance of the second encounter, however, was not that of an aerial dogfight but rather of the pursuit "through the shimmering reaches of the sky" of "a white wanton near a brake. . . ." The flight and pursuit of "L'Apres-Midi d'un Faune" had been transposed to "a cloud forest. . . ." One critic would identify the nymph as Death and the poem not only as a dramatization of "the obvious death wish of so many of the young men, especially aviators, who eagerly left for the front," but also as an embodiment of "other themes such as the pursuit of an immortal woman by mortal man, metamorphosis, and the fragmentation of personality. . . ."[7] Though the speaker's mind wanders and his vision is impaired, his hearing is keen and he makes out the murmured words of sympathy. Like Eliot's enervated Prufrock among the women at another party, he is aware of

> Smooth-shouldered creatures in sheer scarves, that pass
> And eye us strangely as they pass.[8]

He hand-lettered and bound the poem with a dozen others—some of them had already appeared in *The Mississippian*; some would appear there subsequently—in a red velvet cover. He dated it "Jan. 1 1920," printed "THE LILACS/W. Faulkner" on the title page, and dedicated it to Phil Stone with the inscription, ". . . quand il fait Sombre."[9]

It seems likely that it was during the completion of this poem that Faulkner achieved the experience that had eluded him. Phil Stone was an expert poker player, and Faulkner had learned a good deal from watching him play for substantial stakes. Faulkner had gained enough confidence now in his own ability to play with some of the wealthy student gamblers Paul Rogers had observed. Another player like himself was Robert R. Buntin. "Baby" Buntin was a trained pilot. Finally Faulkner confided in him. "Everybody thinks I can fly," he told him, "but I can't." Buntin led a busy life, but Faulkner was persistent. "Baby," he would say, "let's sneak off and do some flying." So Buntin gave him lessons. Faulkner soon discovered that he had one of the problems of Cadet Thompson of "Landing in Luck." For all his coordination and sense of balance, he had trouble landing the plane properly—a problem that would plague him for the rest of his flying career. He would be angry with himself after a bumpy landing, and Buntin would take him around again.[10] Faulkner seems to have told no one of these sessions, and he would construct an elaborate story to explain why, as an ex-RAF pilot, he no longer flew: he had lost his nerve in a military plane crash, and he had to regain it before he could fly again.

On January 28 he published the first of nine poems which would appear beneath his name in *The Mississippian* during the second semester. He pointed up the relationship of "Une Ballade des Femmes Perdues" to François Villon's famous refrain "Mais où sont les neiges d'antan." Faulkner's speaker pondered lost love and then, in a voice like that of the marble faun, "old and alone," he sang "in the green dusk / Of lost ladies— Si vraiment charmant, charmant."[11] A week later, in "Naiads' Song," the nymphs of lakes, fountains, and streams sang like the Lorelei or like Yeats's immortals to his mortals, enticing them to easeful death. If Faulkner wondered about the impression that such poems, or the persona he had adopted, had created among his fellow students, a sequence of events soon provided unpleasant answers.

When Louis Cochran put Faulkner up for membership in the Scribblers of Sigma Upsilon, one of three literary societies, he was blackballed. Cochran felt "he had rather needlessly offended many of the students by what they thought his 'arrogance': the way he was believed 'to put on airs.' " He was capable of ignoring people he didn't like and shy enough to avoid people he didn't know. Sometimes the working of his powerful imagination would remove him completely from his immediate surroundings. An acquaintance would speak to him on the square and Faulkner would pass him in silence, leaving the other offended by what seemed rudeness. Louis Cochran knew that some "thought him queer," but Faulkner was always pleasant enough to Cochran, who knew that "during that period of his life Faulkner was almost painfully shy; he felt that many of the other students did not like him, and he retaliated by affecting a total indifference he did not totally feel."[12]

The animus behind the blackball did not remain behind the doors of the Scribblers' meeting. On February 25, *The Mississippian* printed "Fantouches," which Faulkner had subtitled "à Paul Verlaine."[13] (He had correctly spelled the title "Fantoches," but *The Mississippian*'s typesetter had added a "u.") It was a loose adaptation of the poem in English, with only the last line in French: "La lune ne garde aucune rancune [The moon holds no grudge]." Verse in this newspaper tended often toward humor employing rural dialects. The column next to "Fantouches" contained "A Pastoral Poem." The first stanza was a bad imitation of Poe imploring the beloved's mercy on a threatening night. In the awkward second stanza she was revealed to be a cow. It was signed by Drane Lester and Louis Jiggitts, two members of the Scribblers of Sigma Upsilon who also contributed a humor column called "The Hayseed Letters." Some thought that one or perhaps both had blackballed Faulkner. But he refused to let them get under his skin. Laughing at a reference they had made to him, he told Ben Wasson, "I reckon I'll survive Jiggitts and Lester." His mother, however, was furious. "They only call him 'Count No Count' because they're jealous of him and know he's smarter than all of them are put together," she fumed, and declared she would burn her copy of the paper.[14]

The Mississippian for March 3 published another of Faulkner's translations. He retained the original title, "Clair de Lune," and added the subtitle, "From PAUL VERLAINE." It was an accomplished job. Two inches below, in the same column, was "WHOTOUCHES," described as "Just a Parody on Count's 'Fantouches' by Count, Jr.," who was identified as "J." The poem ended "how long the old aucune raccoon!" Two weeks later the paper published a disdainful letter from Faulkner which called the parody valueless, vulgar, and stupid. Two of his own poems appeared in the same issue: "A Poplar," and "Streets," modeled on Verlaine's poem.

A month later he would publish "A Clymène," the last of his four translations from Verlaine. They had come, apparently, from a source other than his university French course. Phil Stone would later say that Faulkner had read a good many of his copies of works by French Symbolist poets, most of them in translation, and that he thought this had influenced Faulkner's verse.[15]

The rejoinder to Faulkner's contemptuous letter dismissing the parody came on March 24 in the form of a personal attack. Its title was "The Mushroom Poet," who was identified as "a peculiar person who calls himself William Faulkner." The writer, again identified only as "J," shifted from the poems to the man, and the same issue carried a poem by "L.M.J." which was another attack on the young man who dared to carry a cane and imitate French Symbolists. It appeared that Louis M. Jiggitts —fullback, debater, crack pistol shot, columnist, track captain, and cornet soloist—had almost, if not quite, come out in the open in his struggle to demolish by ridicule what to him seemed the living embodiment of affectation and foreign decadence on the campus of the University of Mississippi.

Faulkner had certainly made himself a clear target for such distrust and dislike. A few, such as Ben Wasson, found Faulkner impressive. In Ben's eyes "he sported a small neatly trimmed moustache which struck me as quite worldly and daring." From time to time he would notice Bill extract a handkerchief from his sleeve. "The British wear their handkerchiefs in their jacket sleeves,"[16] Bill told him. He had rather pronounced and sometimes expensive views regarding sartorial usage. At one point his bill at

Halle's men's store in Memphis was so high, his mother gave Sallie Murry a diamond ring to sell so that she could pay it. When Murry Falkner learned of it, he was furious with all three of them, but it was too late for him to do anything.

As spring bloomed, the attacks in *The Mississippian* continued. On April 7, "Cane De Looney," with the attribution "From Peruney Prune," concluded " 'Who is the beau-u-tiful man with cane?' coyly!" It was unsigned, but a paragraph on the same page, which was probably written by Jiggitts, asked that readers bear with the efforts of amateur poets and ended with the admonition "Just remember all our poetry is 'homemade' and that always lends a charm that 'bought' or borrowed goods can never have." The same issue contained a short, supercilious, and almost bored rejoinder by Faulkner to L.M.J. and another letter which, surprisingly, was a good-humored defense of Faulkner.

On May 12 there appeared a parody which had been promised three months earlier in another anonymous letter. When "Sapphics" had appeared in November, one of Paul Rogers' friends stopped him. "Hey," he said, "look what the Count's got in this issue of the paper." When Rogers began to read, he remembered, "The very first lines hit me, and I drew aside to finish the poem, knowing at last that I was not a poet and that Faulkner had the stuff in him—or thinking so at any rate." Not long afterward, however, browsing in the library, Rogers discovered the unacknowledged source of the poem when he came across a set of Swinburne's works. He confided his discovery to Drane Lester, his co-worker on the staff of *The Mississippian*, and they agreed not to tell anyone about the plagiarized poem the paper had published.[17] When Rogers completed his parody of Faulkner's work, it came out under one of his many pseudonyms, Lord Greyson, and was entitled "Une Ballade d'une Vache Perdue." It described the heifer, Betsy, lost and wandering far from home. In spite of an awkward refrain, it was much better than Jiggitts and Lester's clumsy effort, and the poet had enjoyed himself describing the pastoral scene and Betsy's "rounded curves" and "waving tresses" as "she stood there nude. . . ." It must have amused others besides its author. Not the least of these, apparently, was the author of "Une Ballade des Femmes Perdues," who, more than fifteen years later, would take up the subject in a piece he would call "Afternoon of a Cow."

Faulkner's last poems in *The Mississippian* for this year were much less exotic than the one which had elicited Lord Greyson's parody. They approached the college experience from completely opposite directions. "Study," which appeared on April 21, presented the thoughts of the student who doubted the worth of it all, whereas "Alma Mater," on May 12, was a sonnet filled with such reverence for both the institution and the rewards of learning that it seemed a technical exercise. If it contained a note peculiarly his own, it was a quality of dreamy languor that made Alma Mater so sensuous that she resembled a Symbolist mistress.

If Faulkner took stock at the end of his first year as a special student at the University of Mississippi, the results must have seemed to him mixed. His grades were uneven. At the end of the first semester, in spite of his purported refusal to take examinations, he received an A in French, a B in Spanish, and a D in English. According to his uncle John, he had once received a grade of 99 in English which was erroneously credited to Jack. When his father suggested that the record be put right, he declined. "Dad," he said, "I don't care what the mark is. I've got everything from the class up here," he added, tapping his temple. "Let them leave it the way it is. Maybe it will please Jack." He dropped the course for the second semester and earned another A in French and B in Spanish. His poems during the academic year showed a greater French influence than English, and his interest in French language and literature would remain strong throughout his life.

The reaction to his writing was something else. After his single and deceptive acceptance by *The New Republic*, professional outlets had closed to him. The town and college newspapers and the university annual provided his only acceptances. If there was admiration among a few readers, there was mockery and personal attack from others. It was intensely painful for the young artist and it would mark him for life. As late as the publication of his third novel he would be anxious for copies of reviews from his publisher. But criticism would soon elicit the same pain and hauteur that his rejoinders in *The Mississippian* had shown. He would say that he knew the faults of his work better than anyone else, that he was busy with new work by the time responses to the old came out. This was in some measure true, but it was also true that his sensitivity to adverse criticism made him too vulnerable to bear it.

He did not even like to talk about his work, though he would talk about writing and about other writers' work when he chose. He had reason to feel insecure about his personal appearance at this time in his life, and his dandyism was a manifestation of this feeling. He was still smarting from the loss of his great love, and none had come along to replace her. Not only did his work serve as outlet for these emotions, it constituted an attempt to compensate, to construct a persona through the development of his gifts as an artist which would have the power and the attractiveness which he felt he lacked. And so, though these local outlets provided him the chance to begin the creation of this artifact—much as Yeats had done earlier on a larger scale and was continuing to do now in his later years—there were risks and some pain. The printing of his drawings may have pleased him more than the publication of his poems. Reactions to poetry were highly subjective, and beauty—especially when it came to pastoral poetry and experimental verse in Oxford, Mississippi—really did tend to reside in the eye of the beholder. But let a bungler try to draw a sketch and all the world could see him for a bungler. Faulkner and anyone else who cared to look could see that his drawings were good. They might be imitative, but they showed talent. It was not surprising that he should soon go further than ever before in attempts to fuse the visual and the verbal.

His verse brought one accolade at the school year's end. To encourage young writers, Professor Calvin Brown had set up an annual prize carrying the substantial sum of ten dollars. In his diary for June 1 he wrote: "The little prize which I offered for the best poem went to William Faulkner." He did not note which poem had won, but the poet was indubitably richer for his labors. For once, his Muse had brought him something other than labor and brickbats.

10

"I learned in spite of the instructors we had. They were a bunch
of brokendown preachers: head full of dogma and intolerance
and a belly full of big meaningless words. English literature
course whittled Shakespeare down because he wrote about
whores without pointing a moral, and one instructor always insisted that the head devil in *Paradise Lost* was an inspired prophetic portrait of Darwin, and they wouldn't touch Byron with
a ten foot pole, and Swinburne was reduced to his mother and
his old standby, the ocean. . . . But in spite of it, I kind of got
interested in learning things."

—*Mosquitoes* (116)

As the landscape of William Faulkner's mind had been changing rapidly
and radically over these last few years, so had the exterior aspects of his
life. For one thing, Murry Falkner had moved his family into the house
the university had provided and thus out of Oxford and onto the campus,
to University, Mississippi, a legal and geographical entity separate from
the town, with a post office of its own. The Falkners moved into the old
Delta Psi house, almost a mile west of the square on the edge of the
campus. It faced the Grove, the central part of the campus, where the
statue of the Confederate soldier stood sentinel at one end of the large,
roughly oval expanse of tree-shaded lawn, and the massive, symmetrical
white-columned old Lyceum Building marked the boundary at the other
end.

Standing on a slight hill just across from Calvin Brown's home, the
three-story house was so solid and imposing that it reminded some of
the old Geology Building, with its extremely ornate architectural style.
The most notable feature was the round tower attached to the front at the
right. Rising to the top of the second story, it ended in a pointed conical
roof that made it look like the donjon of a medieval castle. Murry and
Maud Falkner had a downstairs bedroom. An old-fashioned circular

stairway led to the second floor where the boys had their rooms. For a time Bill had a back bedroom upstairs; then he exchanged it for the small room in the tower. Besides his bed and dresser, there was a table where he worked at his manuscripts. The room also accommodated the supply of liquor he laid in whenever he could afford it. For all its outlandish design, it was a spacious and comfortable house.

In town, their old house had been bought by Joe W. Parks, a one-time supervisor from Beat Two, out in Lafayette County, who had bought stock in the Colonel's bank and was now one of the three-man board of directors. A familiar figure with his steel-rimmed eyeglasses and bow tie, he was a shrewd investor who had become one of the most prosperous men in the community. T. W. Avent was another successful businessman who had joined the board, and his kinsman, J. E. Avent, was cashier. Early in that year of 1920 the latter had duly announced the annual meeting of stockholders of the First National Bank of Oxford. The Colonel had been doing business there in the same way during the ten years since its founding. He would sit in his office at the rear before his big, cluttered roll-top cherry desk, but often he would conduct bank business at a desk out front. Sometimes the forms he filled out were illegible, and often his deafness made a loan applicant shout out information he would have preferred to keep confidential. The Colonel was there every day, napping on a huge leather couch after the heavy noon meal, while Chess Carothers would guard his rest, catnapping himself in a big matching chair. The Colonel may not have been aware of it, but a number of his fellow stockholders had had enough of his style of commerce.

By the time they all gathered for the annual meeting, Joe Parks and several others had carefully worked out a plan. After the reading of the annual report, they broke it to the Colonel. They wanted him to resign as president. The old man reacted with shock and outrage, but he soon saw that he had little support. He agreed finally, but on his terms. They would have to buy a large block of his stock. This was exactly what they were prepared to do, and Joe Parks was elected president of John Wesley Thompson Falkner's bank. When the Colonel cooled down he did what he could to put the best possible face on things—but he brooded over his eviction. One day not long afterward, as he sat with a crony in a cane-bottom chair tilted against the front of the bank, his resentment exploded into action. He went to Relbue Price's hardware store for two tin buckets and then strode into the bank. He withdrew all the cash plus the papers and notes he kept there. His resentment against Parks overcoming his rivalry with General Jim Stone, he marched across the square and opened an account at the Bank of Oxford. He retained some of his stock, but he would not deal with the bank which had repudiated him.

All that had been salvaged of the family interest was the continuance of John Falkner, Jr., in the bank's affairs as head of the legal department. His star was still in the ascendant, and a grateful Governor Russell had appointed him Judge of the 3rd Judicial District of Mississippi. So the Falkner influence continued in the First National, just as the name was still one to be reckoned with in state politics, but the old man no longer sat in front of the bank and he no longer spent much time at his law office, where the practice was now directed by his son and his colleagues. Now even Chess Carothers, his chauffeur and companion, was gone, fatally burned in an explosion of gasoline vapor as he lay beneath the Colonel's Buick trying to repair it. There was little to occupy him as he retreated further into his deafness and his memories. "He was," thought Johncy Falkner, "the loneliest man I've ever known."[1] The forces which had taken him out of the forefront of town life were signs of the times. Old families like the Stones might well have pondered what was happening.

But the Colonel could at least console himself with the stability of his family. His widowed daughter still kept house for him. Judge Falkner, large-nosed and broad-browed, was prominent and prosperous. And Murry was finally secure with his state job at the university, where he would soon be promoted from assistant secretary to secretary. He still drank, and he was subject to occasional sprees, which he would sometimes try to shake off by rising early and riding a horse to clear the fumes of the hangover from his head. His small, determined wife was as vigilant as ever. She might not go with him on these therapeutic rides—though her eldest son would say she once had the best seat of any horsewoman in the county—but she did what she could to forestall such outbreaks. She would walk him home from his office in the Lyceum Building every day.

He was still as gruff as ever, but his manner did not keep his home from being a center of activity. The Falkner boys were busy with their comings and goings—active men, all of them, with a love for the outdoors, enthusiastic sportsmen who enjoyed golf, tennis, and baseball. Now that thirteen-year-old Dean was big enough to play the university course, the Falkner brothers would often make a foursome. Mr. Friedman, one of the merchants on the square, always called it the "golfing pasture," and it was quite literally the university pasture. There was one fence around the whole course to keep the cows in and another around each green to keep them out. On a good day Bill would say to his brothers, "Let's go out to the golfing pasture." His costume might comprise an expensive sport jacket, his RAF breeches, and heavy green wool stockings Miss Maud had knitted for him. Because of his stature and frame, power was not his forte, but he was accurate and consistent, able to take a pail of practice balls and stroke each one of them through an open space between tree limbs. He was the same kind of accurate player at tennis. He did not have a powerful smash, but he had quick reflexes and he was a persevering retriever. "He was the kind of player who would bedevil you to death," Jack Falkner said. He also used disconcerting tactics, becoming the first in his group to risk hitting the second serve as hard as the first. "With him it was all or nothing," Bob Farley said. But he played with style, almost as though he were a weekend guest at an English manor house. "When he scored a point," Hubert Lipscomb remembered, "he would always apologize." Baseball no longer interested him except as a spectator sport. Always the careful observer, he looked on one day, bemused at the intensity of the Baptist team and its fans. "I don't know what church God belongs to," he murmured to a friend, "but I know he isn't a Baptist because he permits the other sects to exist."

He would sometimes watch with Dean, but the games he enjoyed more were played by Dean and his friends: thirteen-year-old Robert Brown; his brother, Calvin junior, who was two years younger; and their friend Rip Van Santen. Calvin's mother, Ida Maud Brown, had received her middle name as a result of her mother's friendship with Maud Falkner, and she was always glad to see Billy Falkner. "He was a gentle, nice boy," she remembered, "quite shy and sensitive, and always courteous." The boys were delighted with his company, though he was a good ten years older. "I have never known a man less capable of sham," Calvin Brown recalled. "Billy never pretended to be 'one of us'—the difference in ages was too great to be overlooked. He accepted the leadership and authority that naturally fell to him, but he exercised them with a wisdom which was deeper than mere tact." His natural temperament stabilized the relationship "because he was never effusive or demonstrative; he was always somewhat aloof, even with close friends of his own age. Billy's attitude toward us boys was simply that of a close friend who keeps his distance because of a basic respect for the individual." He was no guide to youth: "we were simply four quite different persons that met with him to do things that all five of us enjoyed."

Their passion was games of skill, endurance, and woodcraft. Hare and hounds—or paper-chase, as they usually called it—was their favorite. The two hares would set off with a sack full of small bits of newspaper. Five minutes later the hounds would pursue them, trying to outthink them, to cut through a loop and thrust on ahead to where they might even get a glimpse of the quarry. When the pieces of paper were exhausted, the hares would drop the sack and sprint for the goal. After the hounds had retrieved the bag, they would cap their three-mile jog trot with a breakneck half-mile steeplechase. Faulkner enticed Stone into one of the Sunday afternoon hunts for a first and last time. "It nearly killed him," said Calvin Brown. Their stalking games were craftier. Split into two camps a few hundred yards apart, each group would try to steal the opposing flag that had been tied to a stick or a tree. Or a single player might be placed on a small hill, and the others would then approach stealthily, Indian-fashion, to seize him before he could spot them. If he called out someone's name and position, they were out of it, but if he called a wrong name, they won. One moonlit night in the pasture of the university chancellor, Calvin Brown closed in, silently cut a bush for camouflage, then pushed it ahead of him little by little. "It was a glorious moment when I finally seized him by the ankle," he remembered. Billy would never have simply let him win; that would have been a violation of their code. Later Calvin realized that Billy had probably begun working something out in his head as he sat there, while external reality faded around him. "This ability to lose himself in his own private world was one of the unheeded signs of things to come."

Another such foreshadowing was Billy's improvisation of chilling tales by the campfire. "The tone was one of supernatural horror, but always relieved by enough humor, fantasy, or irony to give the tale some aesthetic distance. . . . Billy set out to amuse us by terrifying us, and . . . he never failed to pull it off."[2] Obviously, the tales and the games that he enjoyed as much as the boys did formed a part of their boyhood that would profit them as men, and were also a part of his apprenticeship that would profit him as an artist. The motif of the hunt, in which the quarry was not animal but human, would appear often in his work. Surely it would owe something to those Sunday afternoons that found him with the hounds pursuing the quarry through Davidson's Bottom or slipping quietly with another hare through Bailey's Woods, with the pack in full cry less than five minutes behind him.

WHEN the students returned to the campus in the fall of 1920, William Faulkner felt even less enthusiasm than in the previous year. "Billy seemed to be faltering and groping his way," Maud Brown recalled later. "He told my husband that he felt his thinking was fuzzy and wondered whether studying mathematics would help him. My husband said he certainly thought it would."[3] Billy enrolled in a lower-level course, and for a few weeks he seemed interested, but then he began to cut classes and finally stopped going. At times, his friend Lowry Simmons remembered, no one knew where he was. He was repeating his earlier pattern: dropping out of a structured learning experience and periodically dropping out of the local scene entirely.

He was not alone, however, in feeling there was not enough intellectual stimulation on campus. Ben Wasson and Lucy Somerville, a lively and attractive girl from Ben's hometown of Greenville, decided to form a dramatic club. Faulkner was at the top of their list of prospective members. "Bill was planning to write a play," Lucy knew; "he was reading plays and he was interested in the drama as an art form and in all phases of the theatre."[4] As a matter of fact, he had already tried his hand at a one-act play in which an emancipated young woman rejected a worldly suitor in favor of another whom she considered dominating, though he was actually subservient. Faulkner talked with Lucy about particular plays he liked, such as George Bernard Shaw's *Candida*, but he also talked about plot and characterization, about actors and the theatre in general. "He had a wit," she remembered. "Somebody would go by and he would make a joke. But he was a very private person; he was looking inward. He was restless; he sat on a bench for ten or fifteen minutes, then had to move on."[5] Though Ole Miss was a small university in a small town, there had been no lack of dramatic performances. As one critic would put it, "drama was very much a part of Faulkner's experience of growing up. Various strands were enmeshed in that experience—in the early years the revival of the English and ancient classics; somewhat later, the independent theatre movement, and the art theatre movement, with its evolution from symbolism to expression."[6] And now the same kind of student interest that had brought forth The Carolina Players and The Wisconsin Players had created The Marionettes.

Before long the nucleus of the group had been augmented enough so that they could decide on their first play, Norman Lee Swartout's farce The Arrival of Kitty. They had one member of the football team, Phil Davidson, but they were short on men, and though Ben Wasson was handsome enough to play any lead, he was even smaller than Faulkner. The women were much more imposing, and looking at them with quizzical amusement, Faulkner said they had a collection of he-women and she-men. But they had a group, a play, and a name: The Marionettes. Lucy circulated among the members a volume called A Book of Marionettes, by Helen Haiman Joseph. It contained a clear and comprehensive history of the development of the marionette art form from ancient cultures up to modern times. Harlequin and Scaramouche were there with Pantalone, Columbine, and Pierrot. Whether from that inspiration or some other, Faulkner decided he would do a new play which the club might stage. Before the year was out it would take form, though it would not be remotely suitable for the he-women and she-men of The Marionettes.

Lucy Somerville was starved for current books, and Faulkner was glad to pass on to her some of those he had received from Stone. Her interest took her to Drane Lester at the office of The Mississippian, and they agreed on a column they would call "Books and Things." When she asked Bill to review William Alexander Percy's In April Once, he readily agreed. When it appeared on November 10, a few readers may have noted how even a volume of poetry could call up violent political associations in Mississippi. The author had accompanied his father, Senator Leroy Percy, through a violent campaign in which the self-appointed champion of the rednecks had soundly defeated the Delta aristocrat. Will Percy would later write one of the most vitriolic descriptions of Theodore G. Bilbo ever put on paper, but the work Faulkner now reviewed consisted of lyric and dramatic poetry. Faulkner's 500-word review was a curious mixture of high praise and sweeping dismissal which said as much about himself as it did about Percy. The poet had unfortunately been born out of his time, "like alas! how many of us—." He should have lived in Victorian England or the Italy of Swinburne. The verse displayed lyrical beauty achieved at the expense of strength. Faulkner concluded that the gold outweighed the dross but that the artist was "a violinist with an inferior instrument" whose work was destined for oblivion.[7] Other essays would show Faulkner's delight in phrase-making and the same taste for sweeping statements. The most charitable judgment was that his strictures upon Percy's work came from the high standard he set for poets, a standard he applied to himself as well as others, and one which would eventually convince him that poetry could not be his life's work. "Poetry above all must be first rate," he would say. And this was the standard he had applied to *In April Once*.

There could hardly have been a better paradigm of the extremes of Mississippi politics than that provided by the contrasting figures of William Alexander Percy and Lee M. Russell—the aristocrat and the Populist. As the former had impinged on William Faulkner's intellectual life that fall, so the latter did on his social life. When Russell moved into the governorship early that year, he was determined that the state's institutions of higher learning should be democratized. As president of the board of trustees, he would see to it that the university would no longer be a place where cotton-rich planters' sons came to play, lording it over red-necked boys whose fathers scrabbled out a marginal living on hill country farms.

The students were reminded that membership in secret societies was punishable by dismissal. In an edict that affected most of the student body, major dances were limited to three a year, and these would be shortened and strictly regulated. In late October the students burned Lee Russell in effigy. Four days later the governor and four members of the board were on campus to conduct an inquiry. After two days of questioning resentful students, they dismissed four and suspended one for burning the effigy. They further directed that within a week all students were to file their names and addresses together with the names of organizations to which they belonged and any information they possessed about fraternity activities. Anyone supplying false information or failing to file a declaration would be "shipped." By the time the deadline arrived, all but a handful of S.A.E.'s had resigned. The Falkner boys had resigned two days after the edict appeared. William's transcript was marked "Withdrawn from the University Nov. 5, 1920." He was probably glad of the chance to withdraw under circumstances to which his family could not object. He had endured more than enough of the classroom, and now the university was beginning to institute new procedures such as compulsory medical examination, measures which might well have seemed to him intrusions on his privacy.

The things he wanted to do there—contribute a poem or review to *The Mississippian*, spend time occasionally with The Marionettes—he could do just as well as a non-student. Still a valued member of the drama group, he steadfastly refused to go onstage, but he had no inhibitions at their meetings. At one play-reading session he read a passage from a Greek tragedy containing a reference to incest. Ben Wasson remembered Faulkner's comment "that incest was not the horrible, hideous crime it was thought to be." In the ensuing uproar Faulkner said "you'll have to admit it's lots better to have sex with a sister or a brother, a mother or a father, than with a complete stranger." The meeting ended abruptly, with several members departing in what Faulkner later called "high dudgeon."[8] This was an example, thought Ben, of the way Faulkner liked to scandalize people.

By the time his review of *In April Once* appeared, his tenuous connection had been severed. The absences Lowry Simmons had noted would increase, and during the next year his pattern of alternation—home and away—would grow more marked. He would indulge his taste for roaming and then return to his base. For despite his seeming lassitude and preoccupied air, he was still struggling to master certain poetic forms and also to experiment with drama.

11

"It's the word that overturns thrones and political parties and instigates vice crusades, not things: the Thing is merely the symbol for the Word. And more than that, think what a devil of a fix you and I'd be in were it not for words, were we to lose our faith in words. I'd have nothing to do all day long, and you'd have to work or starve to death."

—*Mosquitoes* (130)

WHEN Faulkner gave Ben Wasson his one-act play, Ben read it with growing unease. It was too amateurish even for The Marionettes. So he simply kept it without saying anything, and it remained unproduced and unpublished. Faulkner may well have been unconcerned about its reception, for he was working on a very different sort of play in late fall of 1920. Near the end of the year he showed it to Ben.

The Marionettes was as much a work of visual art as dramatic art. The black lettering of the slim 55-page book was fine and sharp, and the ten drawings were exquisitely thin-line pen-and-ink work. The parchment pages were stapled between cardboard covers with paper pasted over them. On both the cover and the title page he labeled the work "A Play in One Act." Lettered on the verso of the title page was the legend "First edition 1920."

If the text suggested the commedia dell'arte and the pantomime as adapted by Verlaine, together with his own particular influence and that of half a dozen other French Symbolists, the illustrations showed a Decadent influence. Faulkner owned a copy of Oscar Wilde's *Salome: A Tragedy in One Act*, illustrated by Aubrey Beardsley, and Ben Wasson knew that Faulkner "greatly admired the contents of *The Yellow Book*, which he had come by in some way or another."[1] It was not a conventional taste to which Beardsley appealed. As one writer put it, "A Beardsley drawing seems to hide, just beyond the observer's awareness, a sinister and abominable fascinating story. His strange cast of characters . . . [betrays] a complacent and mildly pleased ennui, a smoldering eroticism, a thoroughly refined and passive licentiousness."[2] Another writer would say that Faulkner responded to Beardsley's work with unusual intensity because he was "attuned to fin-de-siècle styles, of which Beardsley was a major creator," as well as shared qualities such as youth and "rebellion against Victorian staidness and prudery."[3] There was nothing, however, of Beardsley's grotesquerie—his sinisterly androgynous or grossly phallic human figures—in Faulkner's illustrations; his line was finer than the Englishman's, but he too employed controlled distortion, and his drawings constantly suggested more than they explicitly revealed. The first drawing frames a list of six "Persons": Pierrot, Marietta, Shade of Pierrot, A Grey Figure, A Lilac Figure, and Spirit of Autumn. The scene of the play is a garden with a pool and fountain where the moon looks down on a highly stylized figure of Pierrot in drunken sleep. He does not stir during the entire play, a dream in which Pierrot's desires are satisfied through the Shade of Pierrot. It begins in the "moon madness" of May with the Shade of Pierrot courting Marietta. After the two leave the garden, the Spirit of Autumn enters, playing a violin and relating the departure of the Summer. A garden nymph, pining for her lover, the Summer, sings a short, sad lyric. It is autumn, and A Grey Figure and A Lilac Figure speak of the coming of winter and the mortality of all things. They praise Marietta's beauty in language suggesting "The Song of Solomon," but Marietta, seemingly deserted by the Shade of Pierrot, looks ahead to the future and to aging; the words seem to echo Amy Lowell's "Patterns" and some of the imagery in Ezra Pound's translations of Chinese poems. The book's tailpiece—very like Beardsley's for *Salomé*—shows Marietta dead upon a bier before the stricken Shade of Pierrot. But in spite of the fact that Pierrot was the betrayer and Marietta the betrayed, they can be seen as "two sides of the same narcissistic coin, sterile and moribund in their selfish insistence on living exclusively for their own satisfaction."[4]

Indebted as Faulkner was to Beardsley, the execution of the implications of the finished work were clearly his own. Faulkner's figures are chaste and often austere, very different from Beardsley's combination of the sinister and the beautiful. And if Faulkner had borrowed from the pantomime, the commedia dell'arte, and Verlaine, the mood and lyrics were distinctly his own. It was the same melancholy that ran through his cycle of poems about the marble faun. And though the languishing sufferer this time was the girl rather than her suitor, the emotions were the same. The play was his own attempt at a private vision of beauty undone by betrayal and by time.

The Marionettes was obviously not a play for the little group at Ole Miss. When Lucy Somerville read it she thought it was an interesting literary effort but "totally impractical from the standpoint of production."[5] Ben Wasson had a very practical suggestion. If Faulkner made additional copies, Ben would try to sell them. Faulkner agreed, Ben recalled, so that he could buy some whiskey with the proceeds. (He did not, however, seem to Ben either "an excessive drinker [or] a regular one.")[6] Ben sold five copies at $5 apiece. As his commission, Faulkner gave him a copy for himself.[7] Faulkner later gave another to Russell Pigford, a brother S.A.E. One of these products of this enterprise that William Morris might have admired would increase in value—fifty years later—by five thousand percent.

WHEN The Marionettes successfully presented *The Arrival of Kitty* on the night of January 7, 1921, Faulkner worked on the staging. Much encouraged, they decided to do *Green Stockings*, a romantic play, in two months, and Bill Faulkner would work hard on that one too, as property manager. *The Arrival of Kitty* and *Green Stockings* clearly satisfied no aesthetic need for him, but rather provided the enjoyment of working with agreeable people, kindred spirits, giving something of the same kind of pleasure he could derive from joint labor to make a garden or build a boat.

His aesthetic feelings were revealed in *The Mississippian* in the winter of 1921 in an essay he wrote on Conrad Aiken's *Turns and Movies* (1916). He contemptuously dismissed Vachel Lindsay, Alfred Kreymborg, Carl Sandburg, and "the British nightingales," and said of Aiken, "He, alone of the entire yelping pack, seems to have a definite goal in mind." Amy Lowell's attempts at polyphonic prose were "merely literary flatulency," but Aiken had completed a cycle back to the Greeks while assimilating elements of the French Symbolists. In fifteen years, he thought, Aiken might emerge as "our first great poet. . . ."[8] Later Phil Stone voiced the opinion that though T. S. Eliot had a big influence on Faulkner, "Conrad Aiken had almost as much or more, as you can easily see from some of Bill's verse."[9]

Faulkner made no bones about it to Ben Wasson. When Ben showed him one of his verses alongside one of Aiken's, Faulkner said, "You're right, and a good thing it was that Mr. Aiken never read my plagiarism. Anyhow, you'll have to admit that I showed good taste in selecting such a good man to imitate." Ben remembered that he smiled as he tore his lines up. "I still think my own poem had some good things in it that belonged to me," he said.[10] It could have been one entitled "Eunice," which took its opening and closing lines word for word from Part II, Section XI of *Punch: The Immortal Liar*, which Knopf published in 1921—identical except that Aiken's girl was named Judy instead of Eunice. (A sketch called "The Hill," which Faulkner would publish thirteen months later in *The Mississippian*, would owe its last lines to

Section XV.) One of the passages the author of *The Marionettes* might have liked best comprised the last five lines of Aiken's book, in the section called "Mountebank Feels the Strings at His Heart";

> . . . The puppets lay huddled together,
> Arms over heads, contorted, just where he had dropped them;
> Inscrutable, silent, terrific, like those made eternal
> Who start without thought, at a motionless world without
>   meaning.[11]

A reader who was used to seeing Faulkner's work in *The Mississippian* or the Oxford *Eagle* might well have thought he was in a fallow period. His only poem in the former that spring—and his last one—was a light and satiric effort he entitled "Co-Education at Ole Miss."[12] The eleven-line proposal of Ernest to Ernestine combined diction at once slangy and archaic. It is possible that he simply tossed it off for fun, for he was engaged with something else: the longest series of poems he had yet assembled. Some were new and others had been composed the summer before or earlier. Estelle Franklin was coming home again that May, and the poems were for her.

He must have known how each year widened the gap between them. Her world was not only the exotic world of the Far East, it was also a world of wealth and glamour, of servants and house parties, where a well-married and attractive woman like Estelle would find many charming and accomplished dancing partners. The year before, the American governor in Honolulu had given a formal reception for a distinguished visitor: His Royal Highness, The Prince of Wales. The governor's two plain and aging daughters had been excited at the prospect, but the prince had preferred to dance with Estelle Franklin and a few other young matrons. Before he left he presented her with a souvenir: an autographed photo of the H.M.S. *Renown*. Faulkner could acknowledge all of this with his mind but not his heart. He and his brother Jack never mentioned the thwarted love affair, but it was scarcely out of mind. "I don't think Bill ever stopped thinking of her," Jack later reflected.[13]

By the time he gave his volume to Estelle it was summer, and the book had grown to eighty-eight pages. The neatly typed poems were bound carefully in boards covered with a brownish-green mottled paper. On the front and on the simple title page he had called it *Vision in Spring* and described it as "Manuscript Edition, 1921." He could well have subtitled the collection of fourteen numbered sections *Homage to T. S. Eliot*. In Poem II, the four-page "Interlude," the imagery of music and dream suggested both Aiken and Verlaine, but one line, as the speaker heard "The horned gates swing to, and clang," echoed "Sweeney Among the Nightingales." There were more resemblances in the twenty pages of "The World and Pierrot: A Nocturne." Pierrot's world was that of *The Marionettes*, but some of his meditations were like those in Eliot's

"The Love Song of J. Alfred Prufrock," which he had read in Stone's copy of *Poetry* when the poem had appeared there in June 1915.[14] Poem VI was untitled, perhaps because it followed "Prufrock" so clearly:

> Let us go, then; you and I, while evening grows
> And a delicate violet thins the rose
> That stains the sky:
> We will go alone there, you and I. . . .

In Section IX, "Love Song," no one who knew Eliot would have missed more paraphrase. But to one writer it is "the pivotal poem" in which "the subjective passive dreamer . . . repudiates his *pierrotique* mask" as Faulkner parodies both Eliot and himself.[15]

If there was any kind of unity linking the other poems, it was provided by the familiar motifs of love, loss, mortality and death, and the use of imagery and diction drawn from music. The six-page title poem with which the book began was clearly linked to "L'Apres-Midi d'un Faune." In Section XII, Faulkner invoked musical associations with his title, "Orpheus." It is a poem he carefully revised, and it begins and ends with Orpheus standing in the dusk, longing for his beloved Eudydice. "Philosophy" might have been written by a member of the English "graveyard school" of eighteenth-century poetry, but the book ends with a softer poem called "April," in which, to a nightingale's song, a slim girl goes to meet her shepherd.

The most intriguing poem of the book is Section XI, an untitled nine-page work which is clearly the best of the longer ones. It is couched in a modern idiom and seems somehow the most clearly personal. Here is no faun mourning a vanished nymph, but a man sitting by firelight, watching a lovely woman at the piano. The poet immediately establishes a tension between the melancholy yet sensual external environment and the hysterical turmoil in the man's mind. Faulkner follows extended musical metaphors through the first section, until, in its last line, the man's brain cracks. In the next movement—perhaps as in a piano sonata or tone poem—he moves into the mind of the woman at the keyboard, who wants to dream

> . . . back to a certain spring
> That blossomed in shattering slow fixations, cruel in beauty
> Of nights and days. . . .

Finally the music ceases. The man watches her as she mounts the stair, hungering for her. Then, suddenly, in the poem's last line, comes a surprising, even discordant, reversal:

> At the turn she stops, and shivers there,
> And hates him as he steadily mounts the stair.[16]

In one typed version of this poem, Faulkner entitled it "Marriage."

Vision in Spring was a gift which Estelle would take back to the Far East with her. Early that fall Cornell Franklin would join his wife and daughter. He had become a federal judge, transferring his court periodically from one of the Islands to another. But Warren G. Harding had declined to appoint him for another term, and after brief family visits, he and Estelle and Cho-Cho would move to Shanghai. If there was discord in Estelle's three-year-old marriage, had she told Bill about it? Often she had played for him by firelight, as she had also played for Cornell. Had Faulkner felt the same kind of turmoil, that summer of 1921, hearing her play again, that the man in the poem felt? Had Estelle ever felt the hatred that the woman in the poem felt as she watched the man—with the implication of sexual claims—following her to mount the stairs? The poem could have been another of the exercises Faulkner set for himself in that spring and summer, with the familiar Symbolist striving for musical effects and synesthesia. But even so, this would not have precluded his attributing to a character emotions that he himself had felt. And if Jack Falkner was right about his brother's deepest feelings, about his unwillingness and inability to abandon a love that seemed futile, this poem could indeed have been deeply personal.

He had brought another gift volume to the Oldham home: a copy of *The Marionettes*, inscribed "TO "CHO-CHO," / A TINY FLOWER OF THE FLAME, THE / ETERNAL GESTURE CHRYSTALLIZED; / THIS, A SHADOWY FUMBLING IN / WINDY DARKNESS, IS MOST RE- / SPECTFULLY TENDERED."[17] One critic has recently argued that *Vision in Spring* is of special importance, that though Faulkner's poetry is derivative, especially of Aiken, it is more stylistically sophisticated and psychologically revealing than has been thought. "Pierrot's character," she writes, "even when disguised, informs and animates the voices of many of Faulkner's discrete lyrics and all of his known sequences and sequence fragments." Thus his exploration of large formal structures and his adoption of the Pierrot mask—"providing Faulkner with a basic character-type possessed of multiple and often contradictory voices"—were crucial for fiction to come.[18]

Part of *Vision in Spring* was read by others. Faulkner took Section II of "The World and Pierrot," which concentrated on Columbine, and used it alone under the title "Nocturne" in *Ole Miss* for 1920–1921. He provided a black background, broken only by stars and moon, and drew Pierrot and Columbine rising out of the tops of tall candle flames. He had four other drawings in the annual. It was a craftsman's work, and he was apparently still thinking of some sort of gainful work as an artist.

FOR all his labor at the two crafts, Faulkner had time for roaming. In Charleston, Jack Stone had been appointed receiver in the bankruptcy of the Lamb-Fish Lumber Company. Phil Stone assisted his brother and sometimes Faulkner went with them to Clarksdale, to Memphis, and elsewhere. He would go with Phil to see Reno DeVaux and Dot Wilcox. Campus wits might call him "the Count," but Dot was concerned at his appearance, at his mismatched shoes and ragged elbows, and at the way he sometimes drank too much.

"Bill," she would say, "why do you want to go around looking like that? Don't you want to make something out of yourself?"

"All I want to do is write," he would reply quietly. "Who knows, someday you may see a headline in the newspapers, 'Tramp becomes famous.'" He would later tell another friend that after he lost Estelle "he quit caring how he dressed."[19]

Men like Reno DeVaux and his friend Lee Brown were not concerned about Faulkner's appearance. With the other gamblers, they prospered when crackdowns in Memphis drove the big games across the state line to Clarksdale, seventy miles south of the city. They always welcomed Faulkner, and through them he came to know a world far different from that of Oxford or Charleston. They flourished in the "New World," the bawdy district of Clarksdale across the Greenwood, Clarksdale and Memphis railroad tracks, where customers could gamble and drink in places such as Reno's café and disport themselves in any of the seven or eight of the district's whorehouses, as Reno and Lee and the rest called them. Lee's mistress was a woman who called herself Dorothy Ware. She had left her home in the northern Alabama hills when her father and brothers had threatened to kill a city man she had become involved with, and had made her way to Memphis on foot, where Mary Sharon had added her to the staff of girls in the two-story brownstone bordello she ran. One of Dorothy's customers was Lee Brown, and when they fell in love she left the house to become his mistress and supervise a house herself in Clarksdale.[20] In that environment, there were few to object to Faulkner's baggy pants or ragged elbows.

He would usually made himself presentable, however, when he accompanied Stone to Memphis. It was the metropolis for the entire surrounding area extending over much of Tennessee, Arkansas, and Mississippi. Before the bluff on which the city stood, a panorama had passed: "the French, the Spaniards, the Chickasaws, the Indian factors, the land speculators, the flatboatmen, the slave-traders, the Whig merchants, the Federal soldiers, the carpetbaggers, the doctors and priests who had died fighting the yellowjack. . . ."[21] The years after the devastating epidemic of 1878 had seen an influx of white and black country people. Many brought with them a propensity for violence that had helped make Memphis "the murder capital of the United States." As a result of reform, Edward H. Crump (originally from Holly Springs) became mayor of the city in 1909. He was beaten six years later, but in spite of his regaining the office, by 1921 Memphis was unquestionably the toughest town on the river.

If Beale Street meant music, it was in a district that also meant gambling and worse: ". . . three or four Memphis city blocks," Faulkner would later write, "in comparison with which Harlem is a movie set."[22] Gayoso Street had been notorious for its brothels before the turn of the century, and even under a reform administration, it was still the heart of the Tenderloin District, which lay closer to the downtown shopping area than any counterpart in a major American city. There, for more than three solid blocks it was lined with two-story brownstone houses. To the west, off Gayoso and parallel to the river, was Mulberry Street. There stood the lesser houses staffed with white girls and then, contiguous with them, the Negro houses. By 1921, Memphis had a population of over 162,000, and a not inconsiderable fraction of this downtown area depended on or did business with those establishments on the far west side of the old river town.

Phil Stone would go to Memphis for pleasure as well as business. He knew friends of Reno DeVaux there and enjoyed pitting his skill against professionals at the green baize-covered tables. He would pay visits to Gayoso Street or Mulberry Street, and sometimes he would take Bill Faulkner along with him, just as he had to similar, if more modest, places in Clarksdale. Faulkner enjoyed these trips and the brief immersion in such an alien atmosphere. He had always been interested in unusual and out-of-the ordinary people, and there were plenty of them in Memphis, as well as a greater variety of whiskey. Stone must have been, for him, a fascinating study in human psychology. His mother's youngest, Phil Stone felt that she had neither wanted him as a baby nor loved him as a child. "By the time I was five years old," he recalled, "I knew Miss Rosie was a fool and didn't care anything about me." He saw her as a cruel and selfish hypochondriac. Through his sickliness, his critical illnesses, she had fretted enough over him, Stone's wife would later say, to undermine his confidence in himself. Voluble, assertive, unquestionably brilliant, he was also a mass of insecurities. A particularly troublesome one came from his increasing baldness, so much so that he seemed to wear a hat all the time except when he was in court. With the girls of the brothels, however, he was expansive and at ease. He thought the cliché of their exotic appearance was "absurd." To him "they looked like middle-aged Baptist Sunday school teachers." He liked them.[23] It would become a commonplace that the mores of the Victorian age had made it impossible for many men to see women as other than either virgins or whores—as the lily or the rose. Though Victoria was long dead, in many ways the Victorian age still lived in north Mississippi, and many "respectable" men regularly visited houses of prostitution. The attitudes Phil Stone shared with them could not have been lost on Bill Faulkner.

Apparently he never went upstairs himself, but he was a familiar visitor on good terms with the madams and their girls. One night he took his brother Dean along and introduced him to a madam. Dean got to stay long enough to see the girls parade in the parlor. Then he was sent out. He thought "the lady" was nice and "the other ladies" were pretty.[24] In parlors such as these in Clarksdale and in Memphis, Faulkner lost some of his shyness. According to Stone, he would sit drinking beer and "carrying on foolishness" with Mary and some of the girls. He and Stone would tease Dorothy Ware about going to bed with them (as though she hadn't given that up for Lee Brown), and Mary Sharon would playfully try to talk Bill into going upstairs with her. When one of the other girls joined in, propositioning Faulkner in earnest, he replied, "No, thank you, ma'am, I'm on my vacation." The implication was that he was such a sexual prodigy that abstinence would be restful. Increasingly, Faulkner would play at this kind of humorous sexual boasting and invention, but apparently few of his listeners in Mary Sharon's parlor were deceived. One day when he and Stone and Lem Oldham and another lawyer were waiting to catch a train, the lawyer took them to Mary's for a beer, and then decided to go upstairs with one of the girls. But before he did, he asked the others if any of them had ever "had a good time with little Billy." Stone waited for a reaction, because he knew that Faulkner was sensitive about his size, but he just sat there and glowered.[25]

Bill rarely gambled on the excursions, but he was not impervious to temptation. On one occasion he embraced it almost fatalistically. Jack went to Memphis with him this time, sharing a room at the stately Hotel Peabody. When Bill returned at noontime, Jack saw that he had been drinking, and learned that he had lost close to a hundred dollars he had earned at odd jobs in Oxford. When Bill borrowed twenty more, all that Jack had, Jack asked if he thought this twenty would go the way of the others. Bill said, "It probably will. But I've got to go back." When Jack tried to point out the folly of throwing good money after bad, Bill received the advice in silence. A few minutes later, accompanied by Jack, he climbed the steps of a shabby brownstone on North Main. In a heat-filled room, the gamblers stood around a large sheet-covered table. Bill put his money down. The man with the dice threw an eleven, and the brothers were out on the street again. As far as Jack knew, this was Bill's last experience with the dice, but it was by no means his last visit to the purlieus of the Memphis netherworld.[26]

If Jack found it hard to understand how his brother could do some of the things he did, it was no wonder that Murry Falkner understood him even less. Bill's occasional odd jobs were the only signs that he could do anything other than write poems, draw pictures, and waste time with assorted characters located throughout half of Mississippi and part of Tennessee. Murry would get his son these jobs, and people would see him in unlikely places. He had an extraordinary sense of balance—sure-footed as a mountain goat, one of his kinsmen would say. When he walked the narrow third-story ledges of a university building, balancing himself with a paintbrush and bucket, other members of the crew called it his "dance of death."[27] Johncy recalled the occasion: "They were painting the law building, which had a steeple. No one else would paint the steeple, so Bill did. He tied himself to it with ropes and painted it from top to bottom. After that Mother told Dad not to get Bill any more jobs without talking it over with her first."[28] Johncy and Dean admired Bill, as always, but the only people who had any confidence in his eventual success were his mother and Phil Stone. "Mr. Murry," Stone said, "I'm not a writer, I never will be a writer, but I know one when I see one." The truth was that Murry Falkner thought this unconventional young lawyer was a bad influence on his son, and so he was doubly skeptical of what he might say. "He may not make a lot of money for you in your time," Stone declared, "but he's got the stuff." Stone told the same thing to others, and he would shake his head at the disbelief he met. "I'm a male Cassandra," he would say.

There was one other person in Oxford in the autumn of 1921 who sensed both the waste and the promise. That was Stark Young, back from a year's travel in Italy to visit his father before returning to his teaching at Amherst College. Young was still full of Italy and particularly enthusiastic about the work of Gabriele D'Annunzio, a swashbuckling aviator, public man, lover, and poet whose verbal tastes were not unlike those in Swinburne which had appealed to Faulkner. Stone and Faulkner both admired Young. If they were rare birds in the eyes of the average Oxford resident, Young was a true exotic. Faulkner brought his notebook for Young to read, and Young would remember pages of poems that "strove for great intensity of feeling." Faulkner would sometimes tell Young something of his life in Oxford. "It seemed more and more futile," Young said later, "that anyone so remarkable as he was should be thus bruised and wasted. . . ." He wanted to help. "I suggested that he come to New York and sleep on my sofa till Miss Prall, a friend of mine, manager of the bookshop in Lord and Taylor's corner, could find him a place there and he could find a room."[29]

Now Faulkner had a better escape than Memphis and Clarksdale. Once again he could put real distance between himself and home. Estelle had left. Stone was busy as a partner in the family firm and as an assistant to Lem Oldham, now U. S. District Attorney for the Northern District of Mississippi. Ben Wasson, with whom he used to stand at the railroad station, watching people in the dining cars and longing to go with them, had graduated and was practicing law.[30] As a general sense of dissatisfaction gnawed at him, his moodiness deepened. Stone urged him to go. In New York he could at least try to meet some editors and critics. He had done well so far as a self-taught artist, but if he wanted to go any further, he might well profit from professional instruction. So he decided to accept Young's offer, and Stone wrote Young that Bill was coming.

"I had one hundred dollars," Faulkner later said. "I had been painting, you know. So with sixty dollars of my stake spent for railroad fare I went to New York."[31]

"Greenwich Village. . . . a place with a few unimportant boundaries but no limitations where young people of any age go to
seek dreams."

—*The Town* (350)

LIKE most writers, Faulkner did not stop creating fiction when he moved
from the realm of imagination to what was supposed to be the realm of
fact. At any rate, his memories of the first part of his New York experience differed from Young's. In spite of his respect for Young, Faulkner
probably felt somewhat ambivalent about the older man. There were
tastes they did not share, as with the work of D'Annunzio. Neither Faulkner nor Stone could read him in Italian, whereas Young could. But this
did not stop them from feeling there was something ridiculous about
him and from laughing when Young defended him. There was also the
sixteen-year difference in their ages, and though they shared elements of
a common background, Young's personality and style suggested a high
degree of culture and refinement, where Faulkner, though normally courteous and thoughtful, had a good deal about him at this time that was
rough-hewn—some of it affectation and some real.

"Young wasn't at home," he later said. "He wasn't at home for a week.
Lived on my forty dollars till he got to town. Then I moved in on Young.
He had just one bedroom so I slept on an antique Italian sofa in his
front room. It was too short. I didn't learn until three years later that
Young lived in mortal terror that I would push the arm off that antique
sofa while I slept."[1] Young's recollections were not the same. For one
thing, Young said he had only one room. For another, "How . . . different
that homely denim sofa, bought at a sale, was from that of the interviews:
an antique I so preciously feared would be ruined by the wild young
genius!"[2]

The two men agreed, however, on a meeting that was very useful for

Faulkner in the fall of 1921 in New York and that would prove to be very important to him three years later in New Orleans. Young introduced him to his friend Elizabeth Prall, who was manager of the Doubleday bookstore at the corner of 38th Street and Fifth Avenue. It was, in effect, a kind of subsidiary of Lord & Taylor's department store, and books could be charged to Lord & Taylor accounts. Thanksgiving was coming and they usually had to hire more help for the Christmas rush. "Don't you want a nice young man from the South?" Young asked her. Elizabeth Prall was glad to take Young's recommendation, and she quickly found that Faulkner made a good clerk—polite, interested, and one of the best salesmen in the store. She would have him wait on old ladies, who loved him. "All the customers fell for him like a ton of bricks," she remembered. Soon they were sending the difficult customers to him. "They looked at him and were charmed."

Off duty he was rather different. Stark Young was shocked at how much liquor this short, slim twenty-four-year-old could consume. It was probably one of the reasons that Young did not insist he remain with him. Faulkner then found himself a room that cost $2.50 of his $11 weekly salary. It was near where Elizabeth Prall lived, but she thought it was a dreadful little room. He obviously saw it with different eyes, for the young poet was now residing in that American substitute for the Left Bank, Greenwich Village. There were many Village residents who followed the most ordinary and mundane pursuits, but to others it was not so much a place as a state of mind. Young men and women from all over came to that part of lower Manhattan to be freer of restraints, to embrace the cult of the new—whether in surrealist art or radical manifestoes—to try free expression and perhaps free love, but also to try to paint, sculpt, compose, or write.

The pages of New York magazines would prove no more accessible to Faulkner's writing than before, however. He was also working with pencil and colored crayon, and Elizabeth Prall thought his drawings were so good that he would be able to sell them easily. He planned to study in a night class in the hope that he could improve his skill, particularly at the kind of line drawings he saw in advertisements, to the point where he could support himself while he worked for recognition as a writer.[3] But there seems to be no evidence that he either sold a drawing or attended a night class.

But he could study his other craft by himself, continuing the intensive process by which, in the words of one scholar, "he succeeded in educating himself more thoroughly, and in some ways more systematically, than most college graduates are educated."[4] In the words of another, he was serving "an apprenticeship to Melville, Conrad, Balzac, Flaubert, Dickens, Dostoevsky, Cervantes,"[5] masters he would often name later in his life. He read his old favorites among the poets and continued to learn from contemporary ones, as he had done from the books and magazines Stone bought. He had already read a fair amount of literary criticism and responded to some of it with vehemence. In January, Ben Wasson had given him William Stanley Braithwaite's *Anthology of Magazine Verse for 1920 and Year Book of American Poetry*. Braithwaite's introduction had praised British poetry and materials for poetry at the expense of American. "Indian and negro materials," he wrote, "are in our poetry still hardly better than aspects of the exotic. No one who matters actually thinks that a national literature can be founded on such alien bases." Faulkner's marginal comment was "Good God."[6] In a few months he would publish an essay praising Eugene O'Neill for his use of language, the greatest source "of natural dramatic material" in America, where English was spoken with an "earthy strength" matched nowhere save in parts of Ireland, as John Millington Synge had shown.[7]

Faulkner had heard a good deal from Phil Stone on this subject. One book that had captivated Stone was Willard Huntington Wright's *The Creative Will: Studies in the Philosophy and the Syntax of Aesthetics*. He had given a copy to Faulkner on his twentieth birthday. Stone would later say he didn't think Faulkner had read any of it, but he would also declare that "the aesthetic theories set forth in that book, strained through my own mind, constitutes [*sic*] one of the most important influences on Bill's whole literary career."[8] In Faulkner's review of Aiken's *Turns and Movies* he had taken the same position as had Wright, that there was a science of aesthetics which could be applied to art. There were a number of Wright's observations that Faulkner could well have found congenial. He preferred emotional intensity to realism, and this was one of the reasons why, for instance, Zola could not match Balzac, whom both Stone and Faulkner thought of as the greatest artist in the field. "Balzac," Wright wrote, "creates first a terrain with an environmental climate; and the creatures which spring from this soil, and which are a part of it, create certain inescapable conditions, social, economic, and intellectual. Furthermore, the generations of characters that follow are, in turn, the inevitable offsprings of this later soil, fashioned by all that preceded them." A great artist was both an imitator and an innovator, but he was also a solitary who avoided groups and schools. He should write poetry as a preparation for writing prose, but he should be prepared for hostile reactions to both and for lack of recognition of his true merit. But there were inevitable rewards. In words that might have come from the first novel of James Joyce, whom Faulkner would come to venerate, Wright wrote, "In all great and profound aesthetic creation the artist is an omnipotent god who moulds and fashions the destiny of a new world, and leads it to an inevitable completion where it can stand alone, self-moving, independent. . . . In the fabrication of this cosmos the creator finds his exaltation. . . ."[9]

Whether or not Stone's championing of Wright's theories influenced Faulkner's thought and practice, his time in New York, which Stone had helped urge upon him, gave him the opportunity to think more deeply about prose fiction; a shy young man with two friends and a few acquaintances in a city of hurrying millions, he was thrown upon his own inner resources. He was now subject, even more than in Canada three years before, to the kind of experience that had helped shape the artists of the Southern Literary Renaissance. He found himself removed from the familiar environment and set down amid an alien culture. In this new world he could also absorb unfamiliar attitudes and discern different currents, which could help him to reassess what was best about his own world—to see not only its weaknesses but its strengths as they really were when seen from the outside rather than as they had been described by custom and codified by tradition at home.

Fiction that may date from this time includes two stories which represented very different styles: one employed the indigenous and the other was a formula story, using materials completely foreign to the author's experience and depending for the most part upon his reading. The latter, called "Love," was clearly apprentice work and very complicated. Set in 1921, it involved two plots linked by a girl. One of her suitors is a failed combat pilot who has lost his nerve (as Faulkner would say he himself had done); the other, a successful squadron commander reverently addressed as "Tuan" by his faithful Indochinese valet Das. The incomplete 49-page typescript was melodramatic and clearly derivative. There were hints of Conrad, but the clearest influence was one Faulkner would acknowledge in another context. Fourteen years later he would brush off a compliment on adventure stories he published in national magazines. "Third-rate Kipling," he would say brusquely. He was serving part of his apprenticeship in the writing of stories such as "Love." The other story, "Moonlight," had the advantages of a Southern setting and a believable though slight plot resting on an unsuccessful teenage attempt at seduction. Faulkner had enough confidence in this story to rework it later, and though it was never sold, it did foreshadow elements of stories and novels which would sell.

He was doubtless writing verse too, though here again it is difficult to assign specific poems with assurance to this time in his life. There was one poem, however, which he might well have written now, when no one would buy his work, and here, where he was twelve hundred miles from home. In "Two Puppets in a Fifth Avenue Window" he played imagistically with the forms of the clothing dummies, whose postures defy gravity and mimic emotion. The poet tells passers-by that they too are puppets at the mercy of forces which control them.[10]

He knew a few people in New York besides Young and Elizabeth Prall. On Faulkner's first visit to Ben Wasson in Greenville, he had gone along when Ben and his family visited William Alexander Percy for an afternoon of tennis. Ben knew that Percy had resented Faulkner's review of *In April Once*, and he also sensed dislike as soon as he introduced the two poets. But Percy did courteously invite Faulkner to be his doubles partner, even though Faulkner was barefoot. The game ended quickly and ingloriously, however, when Faulkner proved unable to stay on his feet, let alone hit the ball.[11] But now, in New York, Percy sought Faulkner out. He took him to the New York City Library and introduced him to a staff member. Faulkner also made a friend of a man named John K. Joice, who had been in the lumber business in the South. According to Joice's wife, they saw a good deal of Faulkner, especially at dinner at their house. He carried a cane and gave the impression he had been in the war. He was a struggling young writer, her husband said, who lived on a plantation but was having trouble making ends meet in New York. By the time he got around to asking for a loan, said Mrs. Joice, he had become a nuisance and she abruptly terminated the relationship.

At home, Miss Maud and Phil Stone were worried about him. He clearly was not doing any better in New York than he had done at home. Stone feared that he might slide into some sort of bohemian existence, cut off as he was from one of his fundamental sources of strength: the land and people of Mississippi. Stone went to work on his friend's behalf once more. That summer Lem Oldham had been appointed U. S. District Attorney. Shortly afterward Phil Stone was made Assistant District Attorney, and Oldham joined the Stone law firm. Together, Oldham and Stone appealed to U.S. Senator Pat Harrison, who finally promised the appointment of William Faulkner as postmaster at the university sub-station.[12] Stone wired Faulkner to come back. Faulkner wired back NO THANKS.

He must have faced a set of unattractive alternatives. He would have liked to stay in New York but he was tiring of his job. If he didn't stay on, he would probably have to go home. He put off deciding. Stone wired him again, and once again he responded NO THANKS. He later said he stayed "until I got fired. Think I was a little careless about making change or something." Elizabeth Prall remembered only that he finally drifted away, a valued salesman who was English-looking, reserved, "with his chin tucked down toward his collar." He had, however, become a bit impatient. When customers picked up books he disapproved of he would be abrupt. "Don't read that trash," he would tell them. "Read this," he would say, pressing other books on them. There was no problem about change or accounts. He had simply had enough of the retail end of the book trade.

Although both Miss Prall and Young would write about Faulkner's activities as they observed them during this short period of his life, there were stretches of this sojourn in the North that only he could have recorded, and apparently did not. In spite of his youth, he felt the call of the past, and according to one scholar, he made a journey into that past for a "rather poignant sojourn" in New Haven, a lengthier one than the weeks he spent in New York.[13] Here he revisited the scenes of his college-environment comradeship with Stone where he dreamed his dreams of RFC glory before that brief career was aborted and he had to return home. Apparently he was no more anxious to go back now, with another set of dreams unrealized, than he had been three and a half years before.

The fact that Stone knew these scenes and doubtless some of the people Faulkner was seeing in New Haven did not lessen his concern or assauage Maud Falkner's worries. Faulkner would later say that he had been "a dishwasher in various New England cities."[14] Stone had told him it was time he got to hell back home; if he stayed in New York, he would be around people who would talk the Great American Novel, not write it. Stone composed a third wire: it was time for him to return, accept the responsibility of a job, and do his writing on his own time. Faulkner capitulated. Later Stone would say, "I forced Bill to take the job over his own inclination and refusal. He made the damndest postmaster the world has ever seen."[15]

13

look, cynthia,
how abelard evaporates
the brow of time, and paris
tastes his bitter thumbs—

the worm grows fat, eviscerate,
but not on love, o cynthia.

—XXXII, *A Green Bough* (55)

IN early December of 1921 it was reported in the local papers that William Faulkner had returned from New York City, where he had been studying art for some time, and that he had been named acting postmaster for the University of Mississippi post office.[1] He had gone through the motions of taking the examination, and even though he was predictably not the high scorer, he was now on the federal payroll at a salary of $1,500 a year.[2] He might still have occasion to borrow from Stone from time to time, but no longer would he need the makeshift of painting steeples, clerking, or selling books and soft drinks.

The fourth-class station he took over was located in the University Store Building, a one-story brick structure which also housed the bookstore, barbershop, and soda fountain and constituted the closest thing to a student union on the campus. If any of Faulkner's clientele ever entertained the idea that he would make a good postmaster, they were soon disabused of it. One remembered that "he would sit in a rocking chair with a writing arm attached, in the back of the post office, and was continuously writing. Patrons would come to the window. . . . Faulkner would pay no attention to them. . . . They would rap on the counter with a coin to attract his attention, and finally he would begrudgingly get up to serve them." Jack Falkner was not surprised. "It never ceased to amaze us all," he said, that "here was a man so little attracted to mail that he never read his own being solemnly appointed . . . the custodian of that belonging to others. It was also amazing that under his trusteeship any mail ever actually got delivered."[3]

Faulkner did all he could to make the post office agreeable, however, for those behind the window. He appointed Jack and Sonny Bell as part-time clerks, and he was the most lenient of bosses. There were bridge games in the afternoon and a mah-jongg table for other times. When the weather was fair and business was slack, they would close the office and go out for a few holes of golf. Tea was served in the rear, where a desk, a swivel chair, and two straight chairs furnished what they called "the Reading Room." On the desk, as on a coffee table, lay the latest magazines. After a few days or so, when the staff and their friends had had time to read them, they were put into the boxes of the subscribers to whom they had been addressed.

Although the postmaster would sometimes do what he could to further a campus romance by slipping notes into the proper boxes, some other patrons voiced legitimate complaints. He would serve students he did not know, but he would not speak with them. By the spring of 1922 the chancellor's office began to receive inquiries from people about college catalogues they had requested. When Chancellor Joseph N. Powers, Murry Falkner's boss and friend, stopped by the post office to inquire, Faulkner explained what had happened.

"Well," he said, "the way I do: I put [them] in the cart that we take down the hill to the railroad station and when it gets full we take it down, and then I start on a new batch."

"Bill," said the chancellor, "we want the catalogs to go out every day."[4] Those deliveries improved, but not the handling of first-class, registered, or special-delivery mail.

Though some of the writing Faulkner was doing was doubtless aimed at magazines that lay on the desk-coffee table, he was able to place his work only with the familiar, non-paying outlet: *The Mississippian*. Early that year he wrote on Edna St. Vincent Millay's experimental play *Aria da Capo*. She had combined new and old in a harlequinade featuring Pierrot and Columbine which served as a frame for a pastoral tragedy. Not surprisingly, Faulkner praised it. He also took the opportunity to lambaste Amy Lowell and Carl Sandburg again. In early February he applauded Eugene O'Neill's use of the provincial and his use of language, and shortly thereafter employed the provincial himself in a plotless 800-word piece called "The Hill." It begins with phrases suggesting *The Marionettes* but quickly focuses on the nameless itinerant laborer breasting the hill, before it ends in a burst of pastoral lyricism. The work formed an important transition between the poetry behind and the fiction ahead. Faulkner was sketching familiar country with a combination of realistic description and symbolist imagery. It demonstrated, in an elementary form, what would become the central feature of his mature fictional technique: he thought and wrote in poetic terms within a realistic framework.

A week later more of his literary criticism appeared, entitled "American Drama: Inhibitions." America was wealthy in language and dramatic materials—"old Mississippi River days, and the romantic growth of railroads" were two obvious subjects. But contemporary writers did little with them. Mark Twain had used the river, but he was "a hack writer who would not have been considered fourth rate in Europe." O'Neill was writing about the sea and Pound was wasting his talent in London. American writers were victims, and their neuroticism was "the deadly fruit of the grafting of Sigmund Freud upon the dynamic chaos of a hodge-podge of nationalities." The situation would not improve, he was convinced, "so long as socialism, psycho-analysis and the aesthetic attitude are profitable as well as popular. . . ."[5]

It may have been about this time that Faulkner wrote a story with erotic overtones that would have interested a Freudian. All his life he would emphasize the importance of telling a story, as he was trying to do in "Adolescence," but here he was also exploiting, as he had not done before, the linguistic resources and the provincial quality he had extolled, drawing them from his own region. Juliet Bunden's childhood and parentless adolescence were tragic, and her love for a boy like herself was doomed. There was more grief than the story could bear, but the use of dialect, of realistic—even naturalistic—description leavened with poetic prose, held promise for the future. This was apparently one of many Faulkner works typed in Stone's office, sent out to magazines, and then returned to rest in his files.

He was accumulating other materials for fiction, even when he may not have realized it. By the summer of 1922, John Falkner had been appointed Judge of the 3rd District Court to fill a vacancy created by the death of Judge W. A. Roane. He had to run for the office in the fall, and he waged a vigorous campaign. He bought a Model-T Ford to cover the whole circuit, and his nephew William usually served as his chauffeur. A trip into Calhoun County required an overnight stop at Pittsboro, where the candidate's standard speech was followed by a series of events Johncy Faulkner would recount forty years later. "Bill was sitting on the front porch of the boardinghouse late that evening when some men brought in a string of calico ponies wired together with barbed wire." After the auction the next morning, the ponies bolted when the owners went into the lot to claim their new purchases. "Bill sat there on the porch of the boardinghouse and saw it all. One of them ran the length of the porch and he had to dive back into the hallway to get out of its path. He and Uncle John told us about it the next day when they went home."[6] It would be nearly ten years before these events got into his fiction. The results of the campaign itself were, of course, much more immediate.

Outspoken John Falkner lost, as he did every time he ran for office, and returned to his natural place as a behind-the-scenes power in Mississippi politics.

Although John Falkner was still the younger brother in his generation, he was now the chief man in the clan. In the two years since the Colonel had been forced out of the bank, his deafness had increased and his idleness had further isolated him from the life around him. Then one morning, as spring approached, he took to his bed after breakfast and never rose from it. The Falkner boys sat up with his body in their turn, keeping the vigil until the cortege formed to take him to St. Peter's Cemetery. As the lodge brothers stood there, preparing to throw their ritual shovels of dirt upon the coffin of this Mason of high degree, Jack Falkner stood watching. Then, "Bill turned to me and in a low voice told me to note the third and fourth men in the line. I recognized them as two individuals for whom the Colonel had as little admiration while alive as he probably now had in his grave. I nodded and Bill said, 'When the Colonel was alive he wouldn't speak to them. Now that he's dead, they throw dirt in his face.' "[7]

There were other changes in the family too. On September 2, Johncy married his long-time sweetheart, Lucille "Dolly" Ramey, and before another half-year was out, Jack would announce that he and Cecile Hargis had been secretly married in that same month. Now Bill and his fifteen-year-old brother Dean were the only unmarried Falkners.

During the next year, 1923, after the birth of Johncy's son, Jimmy, and Estelle Franklin's son, Malcolm, William Faulkner might have felt like William Butler Yeats, who apologized in his poem "Pardon, old fathers" for having reached the age of forty-nine with "nothing but a book" to show. Faulkner had been writing for years, and apart from contributions to student publications, all he had to show was the one poem in *The New Republic* and poem V of *Vision in Spring*, published by *The Double Dealer*, a New Orleans magazine, in its issue of June 1922. He would later tell an aspiring writer, "It takes you 200 rejections before you get up to zero." Whatever the actual number, he may have felt by now that he had reached that demarcation line. On December 15, 1922, he had published his last piece in *The Mississippian*, an essay on three novels by Joseph Hergesheimer.

It was June 20 when he wrote a short letter to The Four Seas Company of Boston, which had published several volumes of Conrad Aiken's poetry.[8] Faulkner was offering them *Orpheus and Other Poems*. They replied six days later but the letter was lost, and it was November before he received a copy of it. It told Faulkner that the company's editor thought there was some fine work in his manuscript despite the echoes of Housman and one or two others. They could not, however, afford to publish any more books of poetry that year, but if he could supply the manufacturing cost of the first edition, they would pay him a royalty on each copy sold. Within a week he replied. "As I have no money, I cannot very well guarantee the initial cost of publishing this mss.; besides, on re-reading some of the things, I see that they aren't particularly significant. And one may obtain no end of poor verse at a dollar and twenty-five cents per volume."[9] Six months earlier he had read some of the poems to a sympathetic student named J. D. Thames. "What happened to your book?" asked Thames, seeing Faulkner in the post office. "The publisher sent it back to me," Faulkner answered. "It's beautiful but it's not what they're reading." His face flushed. "Dammit, I'll write a book they'll read. If they want a book to remember, by God I'll write it."

WHEN Stone came home from Charleston on weekends, he and Faulkner would be there at the law office on Sunday afternoons with a group of young people they called "The Bunch." Often they would go out riding in Stone's car, Drusilla. To The Bunch, these two older men were obviously eccentric, but no one questioned their idiosyncrasies, and Edith Brown remembered, "we reacted with fury to criticism from 'outsiders' of Phil and Bill's right to do as they pleased."[10] Aspects of life in Clarksdale and Charleston still had an appeal. There were still the parties with Dorothy Ware, Lee Brown, Reno DeVaux, and their crowd. They were free spenders, and Stone, who more than paid his share, was always welcome. They would often plan in advance, as when Lee sent an invitation and added, "be sure and don't disappoint us . . . be sure and come over and bring the Poet."[11]

A particular attraction for Faulkner was a stenographer in the law office, Gertrude Stegbauer, who Stone thought was " a very pretty little girl." Johncy Falkner saw the initialed handkerchiefs she gave Bill for Christmas and the little booklet of poems Bill had lettered and bound for her in purple leather, and he thought she was in love with his brother. Looking back, Stone would say, "Bill fancied he was in love with her," but when he took her to dances he would invite Stone to go along.[12] Whether he felt insecure about his dancing, or something deeper—his potential as a lover or an emotional residue from his defeated courtship of Estelle—or whether he was simply following the pattern of group parties, as with The Bunch in Oxford and the crowd in Clarksdale, his campaign failed. Gertrude's responses cooled, and according to one of Stone's friends, Faulkner felt "considerable emotional stress. But he cured himself, he told Stone, by deliberately developing mental pictures of that otherwise idealized person in the least romantic regularly repeated acts of our species."[13] Like his assertion in the Memphis whorehouse that he was vacationing, it manifested part of a persona he was developing, that of a man who was cynical and hard-boiled about women—a rather transparent disguise for a psychology that was fundamentally romantic and vulnerable.

By now he had a car of his own. He had borrowed money to buy a Model-T Ford chassis, built a racer body on it, and then painted it yellow. After his week's work in the post office, he would pack his suitcase and golf clubs and drive the forty-five miles to Charleston. There he could walk the fairways, enjoy the hospitality of Jack and Myrtle Stone, and listen to the rapid-fire conversation of his mentor, gadfly, and admirer, Phil Stone. When Murry Falkner started thinking about a new red Buick convertible, Bill got his father to swap him his old one. Murry traded Bill's Ford in on the Buick, and Bill got his dark-green four-cylinder roadster, which he immediately painted white. He had other uses for it besides trips to Charleston and an occasional ride with a coed.

The feeling for young people that had drawn him to Calvin Brown and the others was still there in the help he gave the Presbyterian minister, the Reverend J. Allan Christian, and his troop of Boy Scouts. "He was especially good with Nature Study," Christian remembered, "and the boys ate it up." Often he would transport the scouts in his car, jamming them in on repeated trips to get the troop and its equipment to the depot for the train trip to summer camp at Waterford, twenty miles to the north, or to Warren Lakes, near Holly Springs. After a time Mr. Christian asked him to take over as scoutmaster. Sometimes when he was going to leave for a hike immediately after work, he would go to the post office dressed in his scoutmaster's uniform, including the campaign hat, instead of his usual tweed suit, collar and tie. He would tell eerie stories around the campfire, which the boys listened to with horrified delight. At other times he might be as quiet, preoccupied, and aloof as he would be walking across the square. Once, at a lake on Dr. Hedleston's property at College Hill, some of the scouts decided to see how impervious his quiet calm really was. His camping tastes were not spartan, and he had brought along a bedroll the boys considered fancy. One night they caught a grass snake and slipped it into the bedroll. They lay there listening, expectant. Suddenly their scoutmaster squirmed, and then leaped up with a burst of profanity. He recovered as they struggled to contain their laughter. "I'm sorry, boys," he said. "That snake must have wanted to find a warm place out of the cold."

His recreation in town often involved golf and drinking. Friends would see him on the course playing his usual slow, deliberate, and accurate game. One day A. P. Hudson and Faulkner went out to the course together. After they had gone around the nine holes twice, Faulkner asked Hudson home for a drink. In his room at the top of the small tower, Hudson saw manuscript sheets scattered on the worktable.

"What are you working on now?" he asked.

"This," Faulkner replied, picking up two sheets of his small printed script.

"Would you mind reading it?" Hudson asked.

As Hudson listened, glass in hand, Faulkner read, "in his shy, almost singing voice," a poem about a boy lying on a hill, his imagination taking him into the clouds where an eagle soared. He sailed past them,

> "And saw the fleeing canyons of the sky
> Tilt to banshee wire and slanted aileron,
> And his own lonely shape on scudding walls
> Where harp the ceaseless thunders of the sun."[14]

At age twenty-six he was using the remembered dreams of Billy Falkner, at age fifteen, and recasting them in verse that still employed musical imagery.

He had other poems on his mind too. Phil Stone had written The Four Seas Company on May 13, 1924, informing them that he had a manuscript by a young man of great talent. Would they publish this work by an unknown poet if he personally advanced the cost of publication? In less then a week they indicated interest and Stone sent off a manuscript entitled *The Marble Faun*. It consisted of the pastoral poems Faulkner had written earlier, most of them five years before, now reworked into a tighter cycle. In three weeks they replied that they found the manuscript excellent and that they would publish an edition of a thousand copies for $400. Stone replied that neither of them could put up that sum right now, but he thought they could soon. By July 19, Faulkner had entered the correspondence to say he thought he would be able to supply the money. (Stone would later say that it was he who supplied both the $400 and the book's title.) In two weeks the contracts arrived. Faulkner signed and sent along $200, with the remainder to be paid with the proofs. By August 20, Stone was writing again. He told President Edmund R. Brown that he would supply a short preface and six glossy photographs of the author. "Mr. Falkner is not so very keen at attending to business," he wrote, "and I shall probably have to handle most of the business matters connected with his part of the publication. . . ."[15]

To Ben Wasson, Faulkner displayed contradictory attitudes toward *The Marble Faun*. "I have one of much better stuff which I have held back on account of the other," he wrote. "I sent the thing to Knopf, who turned me down cold. Then I sent it to the Four Seas who were naive enough to take it." But when he arrived in Lake Washington, near Greenville, for the sitting Ben Wasson had arranged for the publicity photo, he was in high spirits and gave Ben the impression that he was confident of both a critical and a financial success.[16] Phil Stone wanted him to look "like a romantic poet . . . like Byron with his thrown-back head and flowing tie."[17] But Miss Willa Johnson, the brusque and mannish photographer, posed him in many positions, and the proof they chose showed him in profile, his tieless shirt open at the neck and his hair tousled. His tanned face had filled out a bit and the mustache was fuller. The nose and eyes still dominated a face that looked appraising, both wary and intense.

He typed the biographical sketch himself: "Born in Mississippi in 1897. Great-grandson of Col. W. C. Faulkner, C.S.A., author of 'The White Rose of Memphis,' 'Rapid Ramblings in Europe,' etc. Boyhood and youth were spent in Mississippi, since then has been (1) undergraduate (2) house painter (3) tramp, day laborer, dishwasher in various New England cities (4) Clerk in Lord and Taylor's book shop in New York City (5) bank- and postal clerk. Served during the war in the British Royal Air Force. A member of Sigma Alpha Epsilon Fraternity. Present temporary address, Oxford, Miss. 'The Marble Faun' was written in the spring of 1919."[18] For a creative writer, he had elaborated on the truth hardly at all. The most interesting touches were two: he had changed the spelling of the Old Colonel's name to accord with his own, and he had called his residence a temporary address. Stark Young had been in Oxford recently after two months in Italy, and one of Faulkner's friends, Ole Miss French teacher Eric Dawson, had sailed for Paris. But he had been cooped up in the post office for the better part of three years now, and must have longed for a change. And if he had not thought about that possibility himself, he had received a letter in the first days of September that would immediately have suggested it.

His conduct of the post-office business had been remarked in print as early as the spring of 1922. A drawing in *Ole Miss* showed three men selling stamps and handling mail. Under the legend "Postgraduate Club" appeared the motto "Never put the mail up on time." The hours were listed as "11:20 to 12:20 every Wednesday." "Diversion" was reported as "Read all the mail." Lately problems had been multiplying. The Reverend W. I. Hargis had failed to receive a letter from his bank and then his *Baptist Record* stopped coming. Finally he found several copies in the garbage can behind the post office. Complaints had gone beyond the local level. When Stone called Senator Pat Harrison to ask for help, Harrison said he thought they ought to fire him. "He needs the money, Mr. Pat," Stone pleaded. "He's going to quit pretty soon anyway."[19]

Faulkner was in worse odor than ever before. A freshman, doctor-to-be Dick McCool, was standing in the post office one day when one of the students who worked in the building pointed to a figure walking across the campus toward them. "He was dressed in worn cotton denim trousers, wearing sandals without socks and with a shirt that had not been buttoned completely, revealing the hair on his chest. He was also unshaven. The man then asked me if I knew who it was and I replied that I did not. Then he said, 'That is Bill Faulkner and he will never amount to a damn.' " It was the same verdict John Falkner had rendered earlier. Standing on the square in front of the First National Bank, leaning on the mailbox, he had told a group of men, "that damn Billy is not worth a Mississippi goddam—and never will be. . . . He's a Falkner and I hate to say it about my own nephew, but, hell, there's a black sheep in everybody's family and Billy's ours. Not worth a cent." Passing by, Phil Stone stopped to defend the nephew to his uncle as he had defended him to his father.

"No, sir, Judge Falkner," Stone said. "You're wrong about Bill. I'll make you a prediction. There'll be people coming to Oxford on account of Bill who would never have heard of the place except for Bill and what he writes."

"Ah, hell!" Falkner replied. "That goddam tripe Billy writes!" And he stalked off.[20]

In Corinth, Mississippi, Postal Inspector Mark Webster was prepared to agree with John Falkner's assessment of his nephew's worth, at least as a postal worker, On September 2, 1924, he sent him a three-page letter setting forth seven different categories of charges. He was to show cause, within five days, why he should not be removed as postmaster. One charge was "that you have a book being printed at the present time, the greater part of which was written while on duty at the post-office. . . ." Another was that one patron had been obliged to get a note from Murry Falkner before the postmaster would deliver a letter to him; another needed Murry Falkner's help to obtain a package. It was charged that Faulkner not only permitted unauthorized persons access to the office but also permitted cardplaying there. Moreover, he could be found playing golf during office hours. Webster had even learned about the garbage can at the rear of the building. In sum, the charge was "That you mistreat mail of all classes," and there were nearly three dozen names to substantiate it.[21]

There is no indication that Faulkner responded to the letter. One day not long afterward, he was playing out a rubber of bridge with George Healy, Skeet Kincannon, and Sonny Bell when they were disturbed by an insistent knocking at the General Delivery window. When Faulkner went to the window he found a stranger there, wordlessly holding out his credentials: it was Inspector Webster.

As the bridge players left the building and crossed the street, Skeet broke the silence. "Bill," he said, "don't you feel strange leaving this place for the last time this way? Next time we come here it'll be like everybody else. We'll have to treat the post office like a post office and not like a club."

Faulkner walked on in silence for a moment. Then he said, "I reckon I'll be at the beck and call of folks with money all my life, but thank God I won't ever again have to be at the beck and call of every son of a bitch who's got two cents to buy a stamp."

But the break was not that quick or that easy. There were accounts to be rendered and mail to be found. The inspector found a number of undelivered items. Later, recalling the inquiry into his handling of the incoming mail, Faulkner said, "I'm glad they didn't check the outgoing mail." Webster had lectured them about how the mail was a public trust, but he was understanding too, and the normally taciturn postmaster told him he was glad that the authorities had sent someone who had a sense of humor and who also realized what "a hell of a job" he had.[22] At last the business was concluded and he was allowed to resign. So on October 31 he turned over his keys and the $1,300 in cash and stock to his replacement.

The post-office job was not the only one Faulkner lost. His drinking was repugnant to one of the local ministers, not just on general principles but also because he was entrusted with the leadership of a more or less church-affiliated Boy Scout troop. Pressure was applied and he was relieved of those duties.

He must have regretted losing that job, but certainly not the other. No longer would he pay any attention at all to the demands of the clock or the routine of an employee's day. He was free now, he said, to be outdoors, once again the observer he had been for so long. People had called him a dreamer. Well, now he could smoke and dream on his own time. And he could write. His first book was in press, and he was formulating other plans in his mind.

14

—to look at the outdoors—the funerals, the passing, the people,
the freedom, the sunlight, the free air—

—Requiem for a Nun (198)

FAULKNER had kept in touch with Ben Wasson, who was practicing law
in Greenville. His letters to Ben were frank and sometimes amusing. In
one he said he knew he was a genius—as he had matter-of-factly informed
Estelle's sister, Dorothy, on the golf course one day. On his occasional
visits to Ben, they would walk along the oak-shaded streets down to the
high massive levee that held back the Mississippi. Sometimes they sat there,
looking out at the small boats and long barges on their way down to
New Orleans. On one visit, Faulkner brought along a copy of Sherwood
Anderson's *Horses and Men.* He had already written Ben how much he
admired the story "I'm a Fool." As they sat on the levee, Faulkner read
aloud one of the stories from the collection. Anderson had been living
in New Orleans, and he had returned from a trip that summer with his
new wife—the former Elizabeth Prall. Faulkner had kept in touch with
his one-time employer by way of Stark Young. Ben said he thought it
would be a fine idea for Faulkner to go to New Orleans and renew his
acquaintance with Miss Elizabeth and get to know her husband.

Faulkner knew New Orleans. Early in his postal service he had gone
there, attracted by the knowledge that exciting things were happening
in the old city. Young artists in revolt and champions of the arts had
responded vigorously to H. L. Mencken's kind of icon-smashing. When
he represented the South as a cultural wasteland in his famous essay "The
Sahara of the Bozart," many bright young Southerners were forced to
agree with him. Two Orleanians, Julius Weis Friend and Albert Goldstein, wanted to show that conditions could be changed, that their part
of the country could actually support a magazine like Mencken's own
The Smart Set, which he edited with George Jean Nathan. They named

theirs *The Double Dealer*. As Friend put it in their first issue, in January 1921, they were "scornful of politics," but in art they "shared the enthusiasm of the revolt" set off by the work of Joyce, Lawrence, Pound, and others. This magazine that would publish the poetry of Crane, Davidson, Ransom, Tate, and Warren, the prose of Symons, Wilder, and Anderson, appealed to Faulkner. During that winter Faulkner even went once to the offices of *The Double Dealer* in a business district near the French Quarter, to sit there, drinking from his bottle of whiskey, while the editors and their stream of guests talked literature. Another aspirant, a young would-be-poet, listened that Saturday afternoon as the talk turned to Shakespeare and *Hamlet*. It was only then that Faulkner spoke. "I could write a play like *Hamlet* if I wanted to," he said, and then lapsed back into silence.[1] Friend and Goldstein had liked his work well enough to accept his poem "Portrait" for *The Double Dealer*. When they published it the following June, printed beneath it on the same page was an abrupt four-line poem of harsh images called "Ultimately" by another young writer, Ernest M. Hemingway.

Faulkner could not have missed an essay Anderson published there in March. It was called "New Orleans, *The Double Dealer*, and the Modern Movement in America." Anderson had come to the city in early 1922 and liked it immediately. With its variety and unique charm, it presented a challenge to artists. As for the magazine, it worked against the standardization and falsification of the large-circulation periodicals. New Orleans, and especially the Vieux Carré, where he lived, represented the same saving individualism. He hoped that more artists would move there.

Faulkner was too independent to join a literary group, but he did feel the pull, he later said, that any young writer feels "to be with people that have the same problems and the same interests as him, that won't laugh at what he's trying to do, won't laugh at what he says no matter how foolish it might sound to the Philistine. . . ."[2] This was exactly the kind of ambience Anderson created. He and Elizabeth Prall Anderson would invite some young people—most of them artists—almost every Saturday night to join them for dinner in their apartment in the Pontalba Buildings, on the south side of Jackson Square in the heart of the Vieux Carré. Erected in 1849, the impressive and graceful buildings now housed a number of artists, but few could afford to refurbish and redecorate as attractively as Elizabeth Anderson was doing. It was there, probably in October or early November 1924 at the latest, that she greeted her former clerk and introduced him to her husband.

"I had gone to call on her," Faulkner later said. "I didn't think that I would see him at all, that he would probably be in his study working, but it happened that he was in the room at the time, and we talked and we liked one another from the start. . . ."[3] The author of *Winesburg, Ohio* and *Horses and Men* embodied a set of physical contradictions: his face combined oversensitivity and strength, his dress blended bohemia and the race track, and his figure was bulky yet somehow undersized. Two years before, in the New York apartment of Scott and Zelda Fitzgerald, he had struck John Dos Passos as "an appealing sort of man with curly graying hair and strangely soft wrinkles in his face." He had "large shadowed eyes and prominent eyebrows and a self-indulgent mouth." Faulkner was surprised, though, that he was such a short man; "when he was sitting behind a table . . . he looked like a big man, but when he stood up he wasn't. And I think that he maybe would like to have been more imposing-looking. . . ."[4]

It was clear that they shared similarities: the dark eyes and the small stature and, more important, the acute sensitivity and receptivity toward others and a way of projecting a certain image which reflected needs within the self. Both could be compulsive storytellers, and Anderson would usually dominate the gatherings of his younger friends with his tales, real and fictional. There was no way for him to know that his new friend had an imagination more untrammeled than his own and a habit of protean role-playing. When Hamilton Basso met Faulkner at dinner at the Andersons' apartment, they talked about the South, and as Faulkner talked about his home, Basso was struck by "his beautiful manners, his soft speech, his controlled intensity, and his astonishing capacity for hard drink."[5] Anderson learned more about Faulkner's capacity one night when he took him to visit a friend, "Aunt Rose" Arnold, one of the most colorful of New Orleans madams in the days before the military authorities had closed down Storyville, the red-light district just northwest of the Vieux Carré, in 1917. After a number of drinks, Anderson and Faulkner strolled along Chartres Street toward Aunt Rose's house, with its little patio at the rear where a banana tree grew. Anderson walked slowly because Faulkner was limping. New Orleans friends believed it was another token, like the silver plate in his head, of the terrible war wounds from a plane crash. And that night, after more drinks and conversation with Aunt Rose, Faulkner was able to curl up and sleep.

He was not just an agreeable companion for Anderson, he was material too. *Dark Laughter* was a novel in which, behind the frustration and seeking of his main characters, Anderson meant to have "the mysterious, detached laughter of the blacks." Providing a counterpoint to the neurotic rush of modern life would be the "dark, earthy laughter—the Negro, the earth, and the river. . . ."[6] Anderson was a Midwesterner—a man of Ohio, of Chicago—and he listened intently as Faulkner spoke of home in that soft Mississippi drawl, telling about the plantation and about their Negroes, who said they had all the white folks they could take care of. He may even have told Anderson, as he would tell others, of returning to Oxford to visit his illegitimate children. The persona of the literary aesthete was in abeyance, and what Anderson was seeing was that of the "lost generation" survivor and possibly that of a man who was sexually very experienced with women. Anderson wrote it up in a story called

"A Meeting South" about "a little Southern man" named David who was befriended by a retired madam called Aunt Sally. (Faulkner would use the name David in his own writing, investing it with autobiographical significance.) Anderson sent it on to his agent in New York.[7]

Returning home, Faulkner had turned over the post-office keys, cash, and stock to the new postmaster on October 30. He was occupied with old work and new. In October he had sent The Four Seas Company the remaining $200 to pay the costs of *The Marble Faun*, and he and Stone had corrected the proofs. It was Stone who had plunged into a frenzy of letter-writing and other kinds of promotional activity. When he wrote the Yale *Alumni Weekly* that the book would be published about November 1, he added, "This poet is my personal property and I urge all my friends and class-mates to buy his book."[8] Doubtless he meant to strike a jocular note, but the words suggested a very real and deeply proprietary feeling. Both men recognized the unique nature of their relationship, a friendship of shared aims and satisfactions. Even so, by its very nature, it would rest on a precarious balance.

November 1 passed and Stone intensified his promotional campaign, sending Four Seas a seven-and-a-half-page mailing list. Enclosed with a covering letter were copies of two articles he and Faulkner had submitted to *The New Republic*. Faulkner was soon going to Europe, Stone wrote, and he proposed to support himself by supplying articles each week to local papers. This was how other young writers, such as Ernest Hemingway, had made their way. By mid-December a New Orleans *Times-Picayune* account datelined "University, Miss." had noted that "William Faulkner is preparing to leave the University of Mississippi campus for England and Italy, where he will spend the winter months in study." Faulkner meanwhile wired his publisher: IF YOU HAVE NOT SHIPPED MY TEN FREE COPIES MARBLE FAUN AND IF CAN BE SHIPPED FOR GODS SAKE SHIP THEM AT ONCE AS THIS IS HOLDING UP MY SAILING EVERY DAY. WILLIAM FAULKNER.[9]

While he tried to contain his impatience he had been working on new verse—an Armistice Day poem and one he called "Mississippi Hills: My Epitaph." The latter comprised four stanzas, but the heart of the poem was in the second and third, which he would retain when he discarded the other two and, later, carefully revise:

> Let this soft mouth, shaped to the rain
> Be but golden grief for grieving's sake,
> And these green woods be dreaming here to wake
> Within my heart when I return again.
>
> Return I will: Where is there the death
> While in these blue hills slumbrous overhead
> I'm rooted like a tree? Though I be dead
> This soil that holds me fast will find me breath.[10]

This could have been a conventional poetic exercise, but the references to his home country which personalized it may have reflected something deeper. Not long after his twenty-seventh birthday in the September just past he had written a friend that though he had lost his post-office job, he was not much concerned about making a living: for almost a year he had harbored a deep presentiment that he would die before he was thirty.[11]

He put together a sampling of his other work in a sheaf of onionskin bearing carbon copies of twelve poems, which he presented to his old grade-school friend Myrtle Ramey. He autographed them and Stone did too, under the rather forbidding legend "Publication rights reserved. Not to be published without the written consent of the author or that of Phil Stone," for Stone was to be his agent while Faulkner was in Europe. Unlike the earlier cycle of pastoral poems, some of these were clearly American in image and diction. It was a Mississippi scene he painted in "Wild Geese," as the poet asked himself if he had not once been free like the birds, whose cries stirred his blood as they fled south, silhouetted against a November moon. It had the Housman touch again, but the scene if not the tone was more that of the county of Lafayette than the county of Shropshire. In another, an untitled poem of eight quatrains, his materials were native—a farmer, who "furrows the brown earth," a blackbird, whistling "against the shimmering azure of the wood," and the action was dynamic:

> Rabbit bursts, its flashing scut
> Muscled in erratic lines
> Of fright from furrow to rut.[12]

There were rather lugubrious poems, among them, "The Poet Goes Blind" and "Moon of Death," but there were others—sonnets such as "Indian Summer," with the dominant image of a courtesan; "March," with Eve contorted under the Serpent's glittering coils—which showed how much experimentation the poet had been doing in the six-year interval since he had written the poems he awaited within the covers of *The Marble Faun.*

There were of course other things to occupy him in these days of waiting. His brother Jack remembered that he had been sending stories to *The Saturday Evening Post*, and receiving them back again. One day when his mother handed him the latest rejection, he told her, "the day will come when they'll be glad to buy anything I write, and these too, without changing a word." And Estelle Franklin had returned early that month, with one-year-old Malcolm Argyle and his sister Victoria, now almost five, and Nyt Sung, the children's amah, an exotic reminder in Oxford of the alien land where she and Cornell lived the active life of the international set's upper echelon. In Shanghai, there were the dances, the parties, the games of mah-jongg for high stakes, but it was a life that could pall. Cornell was charming and now distinguished, and his business and social calendars were always full. He liked to drink and he liked to gamble. So did Estelle. There was a full staff to take care of running the house and the obligatory entertaining. But in spite of the children, in spite of all the activities they shared, there was a process of distancing between the two that would soon manifest itself, if indeed it had not already done so. Now she was back in Oxford, with her family to welcome her and make much of her visit. One of those who came to visit her, as on her previous returns, was Billy. But this time it was he who would soon leave Oxford.

The Marble Faun finally arrived, and he was free to make his final plans. On December 19 he held a copy of the slim green volume in his hands. The first one went to Maud Falkner, as well it might have, dedicated as it was "To My Mother." Another went to Estelle, another token of love, as his work so often was, whether he described it in cynical terms of "philandering" or whether he simply let it speak for what he felt, articulating his needs and yearnings in print as he did not do in spoken words. One copy was inscribed "To Major and Mrs. L. E. Oldham, with gratitude for many kindnesses, and a long and charming friendship. William Faulkner." Years before, Lida Oldham had set one of his poems to music. This book was palpable evidence that though he had not finally been an eligible suitor for their daughter's hand, he was, in fact, a real poet, and a published one. The Oldhams had their customary Christmas morning eggnog party. Bill was one of the guests, and as he often did, he wrote out a little poem for everyone there.

He saw the new year in, there among the blue hills he had celebrated in his "Epitaph," but his obligations and preparations were almost completed. On Saturday, January 3, Stone wrote Four Seas that he had easily sold seventy-five copies of *The Marble Faun* in Oxford and was ordering fifty more. In a few days he was going to start selling hard, but first there was a trip he had to make. William Faulkner was departing for New Orleans the next day, Stone wrote, and he was going along to see him off for Europe.

Above banana and palm the cathedral spires soared without perspective on the hot sky. Looking through the tall pickets into
Jackson Square was like looking into an aquarium—a moist and
motionless absinthe-cloudy green of all shades from ink black
to a thin and rigid feathering of silver on pomegranate and
mimosa. . . .

—*Mosquitoes* (48–49)

ALMOST exactly three years before, in the Reading Room at the back of
the post office, Faulkner could have picked up *The Double Dealer* for
February 1922 and read about "The Renaissance of the Vieux Carré."
T. P. Thompson wrote about the rest of the city of New Orleans as
well as the oldest part he had named in his title. "There is probably no
other place in the Western World," he claimed, "unless it be Quebec
or the City of Mexico, that carries so much of the atmosphere of romance
and history in its object matter: The picturesque architecture, the narrow streets, the old square—all are reminiscent of two European domi-
nations, modified by the American engineers, Gallier and Latrobe, during
the early nineteenth century—all, collectively and individually, have become a museum of Franco-Spanish colonial houses." But there was more
than a museum atmosphere: "at last the new day seems dawning and
New Orleans has gone up into its garret and is pulling down the best
that it has in the way of sentimental worth. Today we can say that the
ante-bellum grandeur of the early fifties is likely to be reproduced by a
post-bellum culture probably aroused by the world's latest conflict, and
an eminent desire to enjoy that freedom of intercourse which the Bohemian atmosphere of the old Square seems to inspire."[1]

The old square—it had been French (*La Place d'Armes*) in the seventeenth century and beyond, Spanish (*La Plaza de Armas*) for three decades late in the eighteenth, then American early in the nineteenth, then

Confederate and finally Federal for good: Jackson Square. The Vieux Carré—"the French Quarter"—looked almost as much Spanish as French. The wide carriage doorways and discreet archways in the irregular plaster- and stucco-covered houses followed the Spanish style. Brick walls en- closing paved courtyards and gardens full of flowering shrubs and trees suggested Castile rather than Orléans. The airy balconies with their wrought-iron filigree shaded tall shuttered windows, combining beauty and practicality to cope with the sultry climate.

The city had survived the war and Reconstruction and yellow jack, and now it held nearly 425,000 inhabitants. Not only was it continuing its forward surge as one of the leading banking and shipping centers of the "new South," but it was becoming the nation's second busiest port. In the rush of progress, many old structures had been torn down to make way for new. Around the turn of the century, however, a philanthropist began to restore some of the French Quarter's most valuable buildings, and writers and artists found it a cheap and congenial place to live and work. Many of the comfortable old two-story houses had been replaced by tenements that housed the flood of immigrants, and now the accents heard in the Vieux Carré were more often those of Sicily or Naples than of France or Spain. But this did not bother the writers and artists. As Anderson had written, "On the streets here the crowds have a more leisurely stride, the negro life issues a perpetual challenge to the artists, sailors from many lands come up from the water's edge and idle on the street corners, in the evening soft voices, speaking strange tongues, come drifting up to you out of the street."[2]

Like Greenwich Village in New York, the Vieux Carré was "discov- ered" in New Orleans. Indignation about neglect would become indig- nation over exploitation for the tourist trade. As prices rose, a little more of the old easygoing ambience vanished. But there was a corresponding increase in cultural activity, as with the thriving Drawing Room Players, who had founded the Little Theatre and had to move it from its Pontalba apartment to Le Petit Théâtre du Vieux Carré on St. Peter Street, where 500 people could sit and watch a play by someone as noted as Eugene O'Neill or by one of their own lively and imaginative young playwrights. There were the great restaurants such as Antoine's and Galatoire's for those who could afford them. For the artist hoarding his money while learning his craft, the Quarter had good, cheap restaurants. And though Prohibition might be the law of the land, few laws could be more inimical to the spirit and traditions of the Vieux Carré. And so the artist needed to fear the absence of something to drink no more than the lack of at least one good meal a day. This was the New Orleans to which William Faulkner came, at twenty-seven, in the first days of the new year of 1925.

After he and Stone checked in at the Lafayette Hotel, they went to call at the Andersons' attractive apartment at 540 B St. Peter Street on the second floor of the upper Pontalba Building. Although Sherwood

Anderson had already left to begin a speaking tour, Elizabeth Prall Anderson was still in town. She welcomed them and they invited her to go out with them. She did, and for three days they saw much of each other. It was very gay, and to her it later seemed as though they had laughed constantly. (Stone's gaiety concealed the fact that he was experiencing the same kind of pain his friend had endured nearly seven years before: Katrina Carter would be married later that month, to Jim Kyle Hudson.) Finally Stone had to return to Oxford. Faulkner still needed a place to stay, though, because he wanted to wait for a ship that would exchange work for passage. The Lafayette would be expensive, so Elizabeth Anderson invited him to stay in the apartment. They had a spare room, and anyway, Sherwood would be away for two months. Faulkner gratefully accepted. His considerate hostess would offer him coffee in the morning and invite him to share a meal now and then. The rest of the time he could eat cheaply and well in the aromatic restaurants of the Quarter. He was free to wander by the wharves and to stand looking at the pictures in the art shops, the odds and ends in the second-hand stores, and the greenery of the park by St. Louis Cathedral facing the square.

Three years earlier, when he had lived briefly in Greenwich Village, he had hoped to sell his work to New York editors. There were fewer potential outlets for it in New Orleans, but at least he had some acquaintances, and he was not so alone and unknown. *The Double Dealer* had, after all, printed his poem "Portrait" two and a half years before. Phil Stone had been assiduous in requesting the dispatch of review copies of *The Marble Faun* and in checking to see that they had arrived. Before he had left for home he had gone to see John McClure, who helped edit the magazine and also ran in the New Orleans *Times-Picayune* what one friend called "the best literary review page in any southern newspaper."[3] Short and slight, with curly hair above regular features, McClure was a sympathetic man whom people liked immediately. Now thirty-two, he wrote a good deal of poetry, and he was the acknowledged leader of the group that had welcomed Sherwood Anderson. He had received his copy of *The Marble Faun*, and on January 29 his review appeared.

He quoted in part from Phil Stone's 500-word preface, which was a curious mixture of somewhat patronizing praise and deprecation. "These are primarily the poems of youth and a simple heart," he had written. They had the defects of youth but a feeling for words and color and rhythm, and they gave promise of accurate observation and firm statement to come. The verse, declared Stone, was like the poet himself: imbued with the sunlight and color and sounds of Mississippi.[4] McClure gave a balanced appraisal. With long poems such as this, he said, the most a poet could hope for was to fail with honor, and this Faulkner had done. "The excellences of *The Marble Faun*," he wrote, "are sporadic charming couplets or passages sandwiched between stretches of creditable but not remarkable verse." Its deficiencies were those of youth, such as "diffuseness and overexuberance, impatient simile and metaphor," whereas its virtues lay in its author's possession to "an exceptional degree [of] imagination, emotion, a creative impulse in diction and a keen sense of rhythm and form." It was "a prophetic book" that readers should buy, and "One day they may be glad to have recognized a fine poet at his first appearance."[5]

McClure added that his readers would also do well to buy a new book of verse Faulkner was writing. For all of Faulkner's enjoyment of New Orleans and the impression that his drinking and storytelling about himself created, this was a time when he was working intensively. He was writing poetry, reading it, and reading criticism of it. Two essays he composed in early 1925 revealed a good deal of what he was feeling and the path along which he had come. In "On Criticism" he charged that his countryman as critic generally was a showman displaying his own virtuosity; the "English review criticises the book, the American the author." Finally it came down to the fact that the critic was competing with the artist, which was ludicrous, for "Surely, if there are two professions in which there should be no professional jealousy, they are prostitution and literature."[6] In "Verse Old and Nascent: A Pilgrimage" he wrote that a "youthful morbidity" had prevented him from appreciating Shelley and Keats the first time. He had first written verse to advance "various philanderings" and "to complete a youthful gesture . . . of being 'different' in a small town." (By now he was cynical: "Ah, women, with their hungry snatching little souls!" Though they appeared interested in art, what they really wanted was the artist.) So he had entered upon the pilgrimage which, starting with Swinburne, had taken him to "the moderns," of whom he could now read only Robinson, Frost, Aldington, and Aiken in his "minor music." Curiously enough, he did not mention Eliot. Paradoxically, it may have been because his indebtedness was too great. In Housman, he had then found what he thought the moderns had been fruitlessly seeking. From there, he said, he went on to Shakespeare, Spenser, the Elizabethans, then Shelley and Keats. Keats touched him most deeply. "Is there nowhere among us a Keats in embryo?" he asked. In the last four years modern verse had interested him only in its tendency "to revert to formal rhymes and conventional forms again."[7] It would be Keats and Housman, along with Eliot, who would be echoed most strikingly in his later work. It must have pleased Faulkner to see both of his own essays published in *The Double Dealer*, the first in the number for January-February and the second in that for April.

His poetic practice, as he worked toward the volume he thought of calling *The Greening Bough*, was now eclectic and varied as compared with *The Marble Faun*, though his favorite models and modes were often still in evidence. He would not wholly abandon poetry, but he wrote one friend that he had "passed the emotionally youthful stage necessary for it."[8] As he was shifting from poetry to prose, from romanticism to realism, the impulses toward withdrawal in his work would give way to engagement. As one critic would later observe, "In New Orleans Faulkner first found a place where he could at once be at home (as he probably had not been earlier in New Haven and New York) and be accepted (as he was not in Oxford). . . . Accepted as he was, Faulkner had less longing to escape to somewhere else."[9]

He was still intent on his European trip, but he had learned it would take longer to obtain passage on a freighter than he had expected. For the time being his lodging was free, and he hoped that a dollar a day would cover his other needs. He would have to earn some money or dip into the modest amount meant to cover his European expenses. He certainly couldn't expect much of an income from his poetry, but he might do better with prose. He had planned to write for local newspapers and magazines while he was abroad. Four Seas had unsurprisingly declined to buy a book of such articles in advance (Faulkner needed the cash, Stone wrote them, because he would be in Europe "at least two or three years"), but he might manage something in New Orleans, where people he knew were able to help him. He was seeing a good deal of John McClure and some of his convivial friends such as Roark Bradford, who was a reporter and feature writer on the *Times-Picayune*. A Louisianan, Bradford drew heavily for his own writing on experience which included plantation life near Baton Rouge. He was a genial host who had entertained Anderson, Lord Dunsany, and many another writer, both well-known and obscure, at his balconied three-story house on Royal Street. He invited Faulkner there, as well as to the newspaper offices. Though Faulkner enjoyed talking with Bradford and McClure at home or in a favorite café, he would be close-mouthed in larger groups, particularly when they were enlivened by someone as well-known as that self-appointed chastiser of "the booboisie," H. L. Mencken. Faulkner had been introduced to Colonel James Edmonds, the managing editor of the paper, and had made a good impression on him. Then, with Bradford's help, he became a freelance contributor. When he brought in a sketch that could serve as the first in a series, it was accepted, and before the end of January he had sold four more for a total of twenty dollars. At this rate, he thought, he might earn as much as ten dollars a week while he was in Europe. He entitled them "Sinbad in New Orleans," but this was changed to "The Mirror of Chartres Street," a play on "Mirrors of Washington," the title of a column the paper ran on the doings of notables on the national scene.[10] The first of his sketches appeared in the *Times-Picayune*'s Sunday magazine on February 8, 1925. Another would follow on each of the next three successive Sundays.

The first sketch appeared under a modification of the projected title for the series: "Mirrors of Chartres Street." It was about a man with eyes "as wild and soft as a faun's," who was, however, a gray-haired cripple, an agile alcoholic on a crutch. The sketches that followed ranged from a race-track story to a description of an immigrant who almost became a bank robber to a melodramatic story, called "Jealousy," of a husband who shot an innocent man.

In another, more closely connected sequence of pieces which would appear relatively early in Faulkner's stay in New Orleans, his narrator would ask, "where is that flesh, what hand holds that blood to shape this dream within me in marble or sound, on canvas or paper, and live?" Briefest of all the elements of the sequence, it was called "The Artist," and it ended "But to create! Which among ye who have not this fire, can know this joy, let it be ever so fleet?"[11] More than three decades later he would say that he thought the true writer was "completely amoral. He takes whatever he needs, and he does that openly and honestly because he himself hopes that what he does will be good enough so that after him people will take from him. . . ."[12] These early pieces were apt examples of these convictions. They were the work of a young man loaded with talent (but not all that young—he had already lived a year more than Keats), moving from one genre to another, and working in many modes. The projected title for the *Times-Picayune* emphasized observation of the contemporary scene, and Faulkner's use of the local— as with the attempts at rendering immigrant speech—showed that he was trying. But he was also ranging across an extraordinarily wide variety of models and references to do it. He would take from whoever suited him, from the classics to the Bible to the Elizabethans to the moderns, in the restless experimentation and remarkable capacity for work which would finally lead him to his métier.

The Double Dealer was in a sense a more central part of the lives of people like McClure than even the *Times-Picayune*, despite the fact that for nearly three years contributors had not been paid regularly for their work. Lillian Friend Marcus had recruited a group of "guarantors" whose monthly contributions of ten dollars were helping to keep the magazine nearly solvent. Sam Weis, the uncle of editor Julius Weis Friend, let them use the loft of a building he owned as their editorial offices, but Julius Friend still had to dip into his own pocket to see that all the bills were paid. It was really an extraordinary magazine, run on a shoestring though it was, offering the hospitality of its columns to the established, from Anderson to Amy Lowell and Arthur Symons, and to the comers, from Hemingway and Faulkner to Robert Penn Warren and Thornton Wilder. McClure and Weis and Albert Goldstein and their friends would gather in the loft's main room, furnished with a table, a borrowed type-writer, a huge couch, and one good chair. It was probably McClure who had typed out for the January-February issue the "Notes on Contributors" which had listed all the knockabout occupations Faulkner had relayed to Four Seas for publicity for *The Marble Faun* and another notation that clearly derived from Faulkner's Vieux Carré histrionics: "During the war he was with the British Air Force and made a brilliant record. He was severely wounded. To date his literary interest has been chiefly in poetry." His most sizable contribution to the issue was neither his essay nor his poem, but more prose fiction.

"New Orleans" was a 3,000-word piece comprising eleven sketches which had connecting links to much of his other work. They were monologues, exercises in quick characterization, by turns poetic and realistic; and though they were brief, they were obviously meant, like James Joyce's epiphanies, to illuminate the essence of the character's life or personality. One of Faulkner's great strengths as an artist—the combination of energy, determination, and ingenuity with which he worked and reworked his material, trying different approaches, almost never giving up as he salvaged elements from one piece for another—was manifest in these sketches. "Frankie and Johnny" was the impassioned 450-word speech of a young thug to his girlfriend, a combination of gangster, ragtime, jazz-baby argot and poetic imagery of wind and water. Faulkner had apparently condensed it for "New Orleans" from the second part of an untitled five-part story nearly ten times as long in which he had presented Frankie's dead father carefully if broadly, her demimondaine mother, the conflict between the two women, and Frankie's proud independence and determination in the face of her pregnancy. Faulkner had doubtless tried to sell the story, and could not—perhaps because it was too long, or certainly unsavory to some readers. Among the other sketches was the monologue of a troubled priest which expressed the two kinds of love, sacred and profane, in a series of rhapsodic phrases, one borrowed directly from an early poem in which he had imitated that old pagan Algernon Charles Swinburne.

Next to last in the sequence came the two callings he had juxtaposed in his essay "On Criticism": prostitution and literature. Shortest of all eleven segments was "The Artist," followed by "Magdalen," the latter an American incarnation of the second oldest profession. In the final sketch, "The Tourist," New Orleans was impressionistically described as "A courtesan, not old and yet no longer young," a seductress to whom all return.[13] The last lines were almost identical with a surprisingly regular Petrarchan sonnet Faulkner had written, entitled "New Orleans."

By the time "Jealousy" appeared in the *Times-Picayune* on March 1, Faulkner had left the city. Early that month Murry Falkner had made an entry in the journal he kept sporadically. Under the date of February 7 he had written, with unusual approbation of his eldest, "William is in New Orleans & doing well   has had a book of Poems published—expects to go abroad this year—." He made the next entry two weeks later: "We are expecting William home this week—."[14] This was a farewell visit before Bill Faulkner returned to New Orleans to sail for England. He had time to do three drawings for George Healy for a new satiric humor magazine to be called *The Scream*, and a little time to spend visiting Estelle at the Oldhams' home before he left.

In the first days of March he drove with Stone to Memphis. Stone had done his best to cultivate Miss Monte Cooper, reviewer for the *Commercial Appeal*, whom Stone called the self-styled "literary arbiter of Memphis." He was pleased when she invited Faulkner to a literary lunch, but when the time came, Faulkner failed to appear. The reason, Stone wrote a mutual friend, was that Faulkner was then engaged in the business of "getting drunk with his friend [Reno DeVaux], well-known Memphis gambler and road-house proprietor. . . ."[15] Miss Cooper did not forgive him, as her review in early April of *The Marble Faun* and his *Double Dealer* essays would show. Not only were the latter dogmatic, to her they contained "a sneering quality, especially in regard to women, that is half-baked and raw, and in one or two places faintly evil smelling." One turned from them, she wrote, to the poems, where "an undeniably sensitive nature, so evidently now abraded," expressed itself in clichés and outdated images, displaying occasionally "a real delicacy and pensive charm. . . ."[16]

By the time Faulkner returned to New Orleans the first week in March, Sherwood Anderson was also back. When Faulkner appeared in the familiar Pontalba apartment, according to Anderson's later account, he had changed his mind again and decided to stay in the city a bit longer before sailing. Faulkner "had on a big overcoat," Anderson wrote, "and it bulged strangely, so much that, at first glance, I thought he must be in some queer way deformed." The coat so swallowed him that it reminded Anderson of Abraham Lincoln's reaction to Alexander Stephens: "Did you ever see so much shuck for so little nubbin?" As Elizabeth Anderson recalled, Faulkner asked if he could move in again, but she said she was sorry, there really wasn't room enough. Faulkner asked Anderson if he could leave some of his things there while he was looking for a place. "His 'things,'" wrote Anderson, "consisted of some six or eight half gallon jars of moon liquor he had brought with him from the country and that were stowed in the pockets of the big coat." Anderson had an idea. "Look," he said, "our friend Bill Spratling has an extra room there in Pirates' Alley. Why don't you just move over there with him?"[17] Faulkner walked the two blocks north to investigate.

When he went around to what old Orleanians called Orleans Alley, he found that Spratling's address, 624, overlooked the green and pleasant expanse of St. Anthony's Garden, which lay behind and to the northwest of the cathedral. Spratling himself proved to be a dark twenty-four-year-old inclined to thinness, with a dour look about him. In a place and time where flair sometimes passed for talent, Bill Spratling had both, and a touch of genius besides. Born in New York State and orphaned at ten, he had spent an unhappy adolescence with relatives in Atlanta. Educated as an architect, he was now teaching at Tulane. Besides painting and drawing, he had an abundance of energy, which permitted him to do detail drawings for local architects. He was a raconteur who loved parties, and his apartment, like Roark Bradford's, was one of the main gathering places for the bright young spirits of the Quarter. Yes, he told Faulkner, there was an extra room on the first floor, across a little areaway from the bathroom, and he could share the kitchen with the other roomer on that floor. With a cot and bedding borrowed from the Andersons, he moved in.

Faulkner continued to see the Andersons and their friends. According to one writer, "Apparently he imbibed a new understanding of modern art from both Elizabeth Anderson whose brother taught aesthetics at Harvard and from Sherwood Anderson whose apprenticeship to Gertrude Stein was past history in 1925. . . . The artist Carolyn Durieux who lived in the New Orleans French Quarter during 1925 remembers that Faulkner seemed to consume modernism. Mrs. Durieux recalls that Faulkner mostly just listened to the debates about art that were a regular feature of life in the quarter; he seemed to be . . . 'just soaking it all up.' "[18] Anderson was still the strongest influence. In the afternoons, Faulkner later said, "we'd walk and he'd talk and I'd listen, we'd meet in the evenings and we'd go to a drinking place and we'd sit around till one or two o'clock drinking, and still me listening to him talking."[19] Anderson had spent part of his childhood in his father's livery stable. Neither man was interested much in facts, and they did not let them get in the way of imagination. These intersections of taste and experience led them into a brief collaboration. Once Faulkner found Anderson sitting on a bench in Jackson Square, laughing about a dream in which he had been walking country roads trying to swap a horse for a night's sleep. Faulkner would say that with a little help from him, Anderson invented other characters like the one in the dream. "One of them was supposed to be a descendant of Andrew Jackson, left in that Louisiana swamp after the Battle of Chalmette, no longer half-horse half-alligator but by now half-man half-sheep and presently half-shark. . . ."[20] They enjoyed their creation so much and it became so "unwieldy" that they decided to write it in the form of letters to each other. Faulkner wrote Anderson a three-page typed letter about Al Jackson and the sheep he raised in the swamp to make their fleece more luxuriant, only to find that in time they began to change until they resembled beavers and then alligators. The same thing happened to Al's son Claude, from herding the creatures in the swamp. Anderson replied by telling Faulkner about a former "fishherd" named Flu Balsam, who had traded his horse for a night's sleep and then joined Al Jackson. In his next letter, Faulkner described other members of the Jackson family, among them Herman Jackson, who, with Al's help, invented a way to make pearl buttons from fish scales but died as a result of convulsions after reading Sir Walter Scott's complete works in twelve and a half days.[21]

Faulkner did not keep the fun to himself. He told Stone about it, but by the time Stone relayed the information to The Four Seas Company that Faulkner had "postponed for some months his departure for Europe because of the fact that Sherwood Anderson has been kind enough to write a novel in collaboration with him,"[22] that situation had changed. Actually, the Al Jackson letters had come to an end. Faulkner later wrote that Anderson once told him, "You've got too much talent. You can do it too easy, in too many different ways. If you're not careful, you'll never write anything."[23] There were very practical reasons why there was no more time for the Al Jackson letters, even if both men had remained interested in them. Anderson was becoming caught up in the planning and writing of *Tar: A Midwestern Childhood*. As for Faulkner, Anderson knew he was no sluggard. "I used to hear his typewriter as I went through the passageway," he later recalled. "I heard it in the morning, in the afternoon and often late at night. He was always at it, pounding away."[24] Bill Spratling could certainly confirm Anderson's recollection. "By the time I would be up, say at seven, Bill would already be out on the little balcony over the garden tapping away on his portable, an invariable glass of alcohol-and-water at hand."[25]

As a matter of fact, when Faulkner had returned to New Orleans in early March he began working so intensively that neither his mother nor Stone heard from him. Finally Stone sent him a wire. It read, WHATS THE MATTER DO YOU HAVE A MISTRESS. Faulkner's reply was, YES AND SHES 30000 WORDS LONG. Subsequently, in the letter to Four Seas about the collaboration with Anderson, Stone mentioned that Faulkner was also writing a novel.[26]

16

Outside the window New Orleans, the vieux carré, brooded in
a faintly tarnished languor like an aging yet still beautiful courtesan in a smokefilled room, avid yet weary too of ardent ways.

—*Mosquitoes* (10)

His novel had begun with two, perhaps three, of the kind of sketches and
stories he had been teaching himself to write. Now he had taken the
further step of expanding and joining parts of them into an extended narrative. According to the scholar who would many years later discover
them incorporated into the novel's typescript, one recounts the meeting of
a satyrlike young man called Januarius Jones and a nameless Episcopalian
rector in the latter's garden. The incomplete story "develops the conversation between them, the contrast of youth and age, the beauty of the
garden, the rector's Utopian dream of an untroubling world, the story of
the prized rosebush . . . and finally the rector's revealing to Jones his son's
picture and mementoes."[1] The son, David, provided a link with the other
principal germinal story. If the setting of the first one, with its beautiful
garden, suggested that of *The Marionettes*, the military personnel of the
second recalled "Landing in Luck." The story "relates the escapade of
drunken American soldiers disrupting an apparently south-bound train
from Canada. . . ."[2] Its principal focus is on an engaging American enlisted
man called Yaphank. The linking character between the two stories—the
train conductor's aviator son who was killed in action—was for some reason deleted by Faulkner. He used this story to begin the novel, introducing
a wounded aviator, Howard, and a war widow, Mrs. Donaldson. As
Faulkner moved into the story, she became Margaret Powers. Both she and
Yaphank, whose name was Joe Gilligan, grow increasingly attached to the
aviator, who becomes Lieutenant Donald Mahon, the son of the rector in
the other story. He had obviously not died in aerial combat, but in another

change, Faulkner revealed his wound to be so serious that he could not live long after his return to his home in Georgia.

It may have been then, as Faulkner moved into his second chapter, that he made two pages of notes. On the first he wrote down the names of his principal characters and something of their attributes. "Cecily," he began, "with her luck in dramatizing herself, engaged to an aviator reported as dead." The last paragraph foreshadowed the book's last lines: "Wind wafting Feed thy sheep, O Jesus into the moonless world of space, beyond despair." On the other sheet he wrote a twenty-line synopsis of the action from the end of Chapter Two to the novel's fourth and final section.[3] According to one scholar, his working title for the book was *Mayday*.[4]

If he was following what would be for years his standard practice, he was composing in pen, adding and cutting as he reread, and then typing out a copy for further revision. He wrote by hand, he later said, because the words didn't feel right coming out on a typewriter. But he had to transcribe quickly because, as he said someone had put it, a sheet of his manuscript looked as though a caterpillar had fallen into the inkpot and then walked across the page. He probably did at least one typescript on this novel before he began the final one, shifting whole sections and chapters from one spot to another, as he would habitually do.

From Faulkner's first chapter, Anderson must have seen that the facility of the sketches and the imagery of the poems had carried over into the fiction. Faulkner did not hesitate to reuse, adapt, or repeat other material. As the epigraph of the book, he would use the last quatrain of "An Armistice Day Poem," which Stone had sent to *The Atlantic Monthly* the previous November:

> The hushèd plaint of wind in stricken trees
>   Shivers the grass in path and lane
> And Grief and Time are tideless golden seas—
>   Hush, hush! He's home again.

If elements in the story of Lieutenant Donald Mahon represented a kind of wish fulfillment, other elements and characters drew even more clearly on Faulkner's life and the people in it. The epigraph to the first chapter adapted humorous formulaic material from cadet life, and the first words of the text identified nineteen-year-old Flying Cadet Julian Lowe, who was clearly based on Cadet William Faulkner, down to the white cap band Faulkner had worn with the rest of his class. His trip home from Canada at the war's end gave him the setting and most of the action of this first chapter, and he apparently based "Yaphank," Private Joe Gilligan, on a man he met on the train, also grafting onto him some of Spratling's authoritarian qualities. The conductor's reference to his Marine son, not heard from for six months, suggests Murry Falkner's anxiety over Jack, just as the head wound from which Jack recovered suggests the terrible head wound from which Mahon will not. As one critic would point out, "Faulkner revealingly gave Mahon many of his own real or imagined characteristics. Mahon carries Housman's *A Shropshire Lad*, . . . he reads but has little formal education; he wears the uniform of a British officer; he has small hands; and he even looks like Faulkner, with a 'thin face,' a 'delicate pointed chin and wild, soft eyes.' " (67)[5] As Mahon—with his scarred brow and withered hand, his intermittent amnesia and incipient blindness—represents the combat hero his brother actually was and Faulkner could never be, so also he derives in part from stories Faulkner had heard in Canada, some of them from the instructors invalided home from combat on the Western Front. (Later that year, in the June issue, *The Double Dealer* would print "The Lilacs," and for this publication Faulkner would add the two subscripts: "TO A . . . . . AND H . . . . . , ROYAL AIR FORCE/ *August 1925*.[6]) Even Margaret Powers, the war widow who joins with Gilligan to see the moribund Mahon back to his home in Georgia, has a familiar aspect. In her and in Cecily Saunders—Mahon's pretty, vain, and heartless fiancée—Estelle Franklin would recognize a partial portrait of herself.

He was, of course, drawing also from literary and artistic frames of reference. Of Margaret Powers he wrote, "Beardsley would have sickened for her; he had drawn her so often. . . ." (31) At one point, Januarius Jones, the despicable foil for Mahon, makes a reply "like Jurgen." Faulkner had obviously read Cabell's best-known novel, and one critic would perceive resemblances to *Jurgen* "of so detailed a nature as to suggest that Faulkner intended the presentation of Januarius Jones as a kind of parody of Cabell's presentation of Jurgen. . . ."[7] Echoes of other favorites were there, unsurprisingly enough: Swinburne, Housman, and Eliot. But there were even more: Conrad and, according to the same critic, Joseph Hergesheimer (three of whose novels Faulkner had reviewed for *The Mississippian* three years earlier), and half a dozen other contemporaries as well.[8]

Throughout his life he would read the work of Hemingway as it came out, and he was aware of much of Fitzgerald's. The title of his manuscript may have been a coincidental choice that had nothing to do with Fitzgerald's 1920 story of returning soldiers that bore the same title. Almost all of the action of the novel took place during the first two weeks of April, Eliot's "cruelest month." When Eliot added his notes to *The Waste Land*, he wrote that one of the two works to which he was most deeply indebted in the poem was Sir James G. Frazer's great anthropological-mythological study *The Golden Bough*. Elizabeth Anderson had her copy of this work in the apartment, and Faulkner read it, or read in it. So if Faulkner's own range of adaptation and borrowing, of reference and allusion, was wide—from chants used for the cadence count of marching RAF cadet formations to the great myths of antiquity—there was good reason.

Anderson must have seen much of it in the growing manuscript, and he had a strict directive for Faulkner during the rest of the writing: Don't read the work of anyone else.

One problem that he had was how to keep up the intensive work on the novel and still earn the money he needed to keep from depleting his meager supply before he left for Europe. When he had just started on the novel, he did a short piece that he doubtless hoped would sell: "Literature and War," which mentioned two poets, Siegfried Sassoon and Rupert Brooke, and two novelists, Henri Barbusse and R. H. Mottram. It was rather unfocused, written in a tone of irony and world-weariness which carried contempt for Brooke's romanticism about war, with all its horrors, and respect for Mottram's use of "the late war to a successful literary end. . . ."[9] It was a further indication of the scope of his reading, and elements of these works would get into his own. The piece, however, remained unsold. Not so another. He won $10 by answering in 250 words or less the question "What Is the Matter with Marriage?" The New Orleans *Item-Tribune* printed his answer on April 4, 1925. The caption below his photograph read, "Poet, philosopher, student of life, WILLIAM FAULKNER says that passion is a fire which quickly burns itself out. Love is enduring, he believes, a fuel that feeds a never-dying fire." There was nothing wrong with marriage, said the young philosopher, it was the people who entered into it without being prepared to give and to understand. Full-face to the camera, thick hair *en brosse*, deep-eyed and fine-featured, almost handsome and very youthful, the romantic idealist had, for the moment, displaced the world-weary bohemian aesthete and wounded aviator.

Fortunately, the *Times-Picayune* resumed the purchase of his sketches and stories for the Sunday magazine. A day after his letter about marriage, "Cheest" appeared. It read almost as though Faulkner were doing his own 1,500-word version of the Anderson story he so admired, "I'm a Fool." Another story which Faulkner may have begun at this time again featured a wanderer and also suggested Anderson in its use of horses and a small-town Ohio setting. What was more interesting was the clearly autobiographical writing about the boy's great-grandfather who "came into the county afoot from the Tennessee Mountains, where he had killed a man," and a description of the boy's own childhood experience in his father's livery stable. He went on to an account of the boy's adolescence, troubled by sexual longings and feelings of social inferiority, and to his fondness for liquor. Soon after that, for whatever reason, the story broke off.[10]

From time to time Faulkner would relax with Spratling. Observing him as he sketched people, Faulkner perceived the difference between the talents they each had. In a piece that appeared on April 12, he lamented that Spratling's "hand has been shaped to the brush as mine (alas!) has not. . . ." (Near the story's end he would say "words are my meat and bread and drink. . . .") Called "Out of Nazareth," this was one of three pieces that Faulkner would get from his ramblings with Spratling as his friend sought material; the subject is a seventeen-year-old vagabond with a face so beautiful that Spratling offers to pay him to pose. He is an aspiring writer who shyly shows Faulkner his copy of *A Shropshire Lad* and then gives them a sketch he has written about his travels. Faulkner incorporated it into his story, calling it "blundering and childish and 'arty.' " This was true, but Faulkner's story now embodied a new use of the material from "The Hill," of three years before, so that this vagabond had the strength and closeness to the soil of the vagabond in "The Hill," but these qualities were now combined with poetic sensibility and faith. It was as if Faulkner had employed some of his own deepest feelings, though he had fleshed them in an aspirant who might have been found in Winesburg, Ohio. Another walk with Spratling took Faulkner to the door of a Negro brothel. He called this piece "Peter," after the son of Mabel, one of the prostitutes.[11] "Peter" remained unpublished, but "Episode," in which Spratling sketched an old woman whose expression resembled the Mona Lisa's, was purchased for publication in mid-August.

Every Sunday, from April 26 to May 31, a story appeared in the magazine section of the New Orleans *Times-Picayune* under the name of William Faulkner, and though two (the most interesting) were set in a gangster milieu, each was substantially different from the others, the work of a writer learning his trade. The first of this sequence was called "The Kingdom of God." This reference to the little children Christ spoke of, as reported in Mark 10:14, was not embodied literally in this story. The central character was a child in mind only, an idiot with eyes as "clear and blue as cornflowers, and utterly vacant of thought,"[12] who was kept quiet by the narcissus he held while his brother delivered bootleg liquor. It would be three years before Falkner returned to that character, but when he did, the idiot would be transfigured—not in his appearance, but in his function.

The next three stories were apprentice work which did not come off. "The Rosary" was a tale of hatred that could have suggested "A Cask of Amontillado" except that the instrument of ultimate torment was a saxophone. "The Cobbler," of the following Sunday, was an expanded version of the material in the section of the same name in "New Orleans." A sentimental tale of lost love, it contained material Faulkner would rework for the characterization of the Reverend Mr. Mahon in his first novel. "Chance," of May 17, was the account of a bum's brief affluence. Nothing but the title suggested Conrad. Faulkner may have been thinking of Anderson's stories, but he was certainly trying to learn to write commercial fiction quickly enough so that it would not seriously interfere with his work on the novel.

Given all of his concerns, the last two for the month of May were surprisingly good. "Sunset" appeared on May 24, 1925. It was a new departure for him, prefiguring stories to come. He began it with an item from the *Clarion-Eagle* about a nameless Negro. "No reason has been ascertained

Publicity photographs, late summer 1924,
for promotion of The Marble Faun

Estelle Franklin and Cho-Cho, Shanghai, c. 1924

Self-portrait, with Lottie Vernon White,
spring 1923

William Spratling's drawing
of himself and Faulkner
in New Orleans' Vieux Carré

Faulkner in Paris, 1925

*Faulkner in
New Orleans*

Part of page 87 of manuscript of
Flags in the Dust

Helen Baird

*Faulkner with Rosebud Stone,
Pascagoula, Mississippi,
summer 1926*

"Pon devil," Hnax said, and again: "Pon old Bayard. He used to hate an automobile like a snake. Wonder what he thinks about it." They drove on across the square, among lettered wagons and cars parked casually and without order. Hnax spoke again, muttering "He ought to have more consideration for the old fellow than that. Heedless fool."

"Yes," his sister agreed. "They're worried about Colonel Sartoris' heart, now. Everybody but him. He has them, that is."

"Wild fool," Hnax said again. "Damn scoundrel," Hnax said again.

"He goes with him," Narcissa answered.

"Old Bayard in an automobile?"

"Yes. Miss Jenny says it to keep Bayard from having his fool neck. But she says Colonel Sartoris doesn't know it, but that Bayard would just as soon break his too. That he probably will before it's all over." She drove on across the square, among lettered wagons and cars parked casually and without order. "I hate Bayard Sartoris," she said with sudden vehemence. "I hate all men." Hnax looked at her quietly.

"What's the matter? What's Bayard done to you?" But she didn't answer. She turned into another street, bordered ~~Hotty~~ by ~~paro~~ stores and lined with ~~negros~~ in lounging clumps, eating bananas ~~on~~ or small cakes from cardboard cartons. "He ought to have more consideration for the old fellow than that," Hnax said with petulant ~~displeasure~~ disapproval. "Heedless fool."

"Yes," his sister agreed quietly again. "They're worried about Colonel Sartoris' heart. Everybody but him and Bayard are, that is. Thank heaven there men don't belong to my family."

"Damn scoundrel," Hnax muttered.

_____

"What's the matter? What's Bayard done to you?" But she didn't answer. She turned into ~~mothers~~ street, bordered by ~~pavo~~ stores and lined with ~~many stores~~ of no story and shaded by metal awnings beneath which negroes lounged in clumps, skinning bananas or small florid cartons ; cheap cakes ; and then a gristmill driven by a spasmodic gasoline engine, and between it and a shuttered and silent cotton gin, an anvil clanged from the end of a short lane filled with wagons and lettered houses with a hand-painted. It oozed ~~chaff~~ and a sifting dust mote-like in the sun, and upon ~~the door~~ alone the door a ~~lettered~~
tediously— hand-painted sign: W. C. BEARD'S MILL. Between it and a shuttered and silent cotton gin an anvil clanged at from the end of a short lane filled with wagons and lettered horses and mules, and shaded by mulberry trees beneath which countrymen in overalls squalled. "He ought to have more consideration for that old fellow than that," Horace said. ~~with petulant~~ "Still, they've ~~went through something pretty~~ if just to gone through an experience that really well floats the humanities and verities. Give him a little time. But I personally can't see why Colonel Sartoris doesn't let him go so on and kill himself off, if that's what he wants. Sorry for New Jersey, though."

"Yes," his sister agreed, quietly again. "They're worried about Colonel Sartoris' heart. Everybody but him and Bayard are, that is. Thank heaven I have you instead ; no ; have you in a health." And she laid her hand swiftly and lightly on his knee.

"Dean old Narcy," he said. Then his face clouded again. "Damn scoundrel," he muttered. "Well, it's their trouble. How's Aunt Sally now?"

She told him, with a wealth ; trivialities, tapping him in the quiet happiness ; her affection. The shabby

Faulkner, early 1930's

Faulkner, summer 1931

William and Estelle Faulkner in front parlor, Rowan Oak

Faulkner at his desk in library at Rowan Oak

for the black's running amuck," the account read, "though it is believed that he was insane." In the 2,500 words that followed, Faulkner used a Conradian strategy. He was interested not so much in what happened as in why, and he gave away suspense to achieve psychological penetration. The protagonist is a country Negro who wants to return to the African homeland. Cheated by a riverboat captain who puts him off in a Louisiana field and tells him Africa is a mile away, he kills a farm animal he mistakes for a lion. Before he can leave "Africa" and return home, the National Guard machine gunners find him. Not only did Faulkner manage to enliven the terrible with the humorous, he handled the dialect with assurance and presented the Negro and his troubles realistically and sympathetically. "Sunset" showed how far he had come since his first contribution to the *Times-Picayune* three and a half months before. The next Sunday's piece was a reversion to earlier work. "The Kid Learns" was a 1,700-word expansion of the "Frankie and Johnny" segment of "New Orleans."[13] For Johnny's inevitable death scene, Faulkner did not use conventional gunplay. Instead, he mixed fantasy, symbol, and allusion. When an alluring girl steps from a doorway, "her eyes the color of sleep," Johnny thinks it is the sweetheart he has just left, and calls to her tentatively. As she takes his hand she identifies herself as "Little sister Death."[14] Narrated rapidly, with stilted gangster dialogue, the story is almost redeemed by the sudden shift from the realistic to the symbolic in the poetic ending. The real gain for Faulkner was the development of images he would use again.

He was working long hours to learn his craft, but he was still finding time for friendship and diversion. One day the city editor of the *Times-Picayune* asked Hamilton Basso to do a feature story on a group of barnstorming aviators who flew decrepit two-seater Wright Whirlwind airplanes and called themselves "The Gates Flying Circus." Basso took Faulkner along, and the half-dozen rides each of them cadged created a bond far stronger than literary tastes. "Nobody else in our crowd," Ham said, "had gone looping-the-loop in a bucket seat and open cockpit over the Mississippi River."[15] Faulkner had women friends too. Back in Oxford he had been interested enough in Shirley Kirkwood to send her love letters and poems. Bob Farley said that was nothing, though, for even in high school every boy had been in love with Shirley. She married and moved away. In his post-office days he had become interested in an attractive coed from Natchez named Elise Huntington. He would take her for drives and sketch her, but she married a boy in the medical school. He wrote letters to Mary Victoria Mills, Lida Oldham's niece, sometimes enclosing a sketch, sometimes a page of something he had written. Mary Vic thought he wrote because he was lonely. And there had been the unsuccessful courtship of Gertrude Stegbauer in Charleston. In New Orleans he had become friendly with a young writer named Anita Loos. She liked him, but not in any romantic way, and besides, she was busy working on a book about a young gold digger who was convinced that diamonds were a girl's best friend. Another young woman whom he told about his wartime injury was twenty-four-year-old Margery Kalom Gumbel, whose broker husband was also a *Double Dealer* contributor. She was an attractive girl whose large eyes and pale-gold hair made her a good subject for a charcoal portrait by Spratling. But she was ill and unhappy in New Orleans, and Faulkner was drawn to her. Standing beside her on a catwalk-like wharf stretching out into Lake Pontchartrain, he watched their friends swimming, splashing, and calling to each other. Without preamble, he said to her in his soft voice, "Margery, we believe in God, don't we?" She felt that he, too, was unhappy.

At parties, he seemed to dislike the noisy talk and the blaring phonograph. He would walk out into the soft night air and stand gazing at the dark trees of Jackson Square below the iron tracery of the shadowed balconies. One of the partygoers was a quiet twenty-three-year-old reporter from Pascagoula named James R. "Pete" Baird. Spratling welcomed him to his sometimes boisterous parties where everyone seemed to be talking at once, smoking and dipping their drinks from a large bowl of absinthe or Pernod poured over a big piece of ice. Spratling liked "Pete" Baird's twenty-one-year-old sister Helen, who struck people as elfin. Barely five feet tall, she had dark hair and skin. She was quick, with a volatile straightforward manner, and she could be amusing. She liked people who did not care about convention, who had talent and something of her own devil-may-care manner. The afternoon Faulkner met her she was wearing what Spratling called her don't-give-a-damn look. Their meeting was still vivid when Faulkner recalled it to her years later: "I remember a sullen-jawed yellow-eyed belligerent humorless gal in a linen dress and sunburned bare legs sitting on Spratling's balcony and not thinking even a hell of a little bit of me that afternoon, maybe already decided not to."[16] Bill Spratling good-naturedly said that he had been interested in her first and Faulkner had taken her away from him. Spratling was probably exaggerating both his own interest in Helen Baird and Faulkner's appeal to her. But Faulkner did feel a strong attraction to her.

There was plenty to do in that lively crowd. Faulkner would later mention spending a weekend with Anderson on a riverboat. Spratling remembered a day-trip to Grand Isle, forty-one miles east of the City Yacht Club, when Anderson kept up such a stream of conversation and anecdote that he spent most of the day on the prow of the boat to get away from it. Sherwood and Elizabeth Anderson formed the nucleus of a group of friends who, another time, rented the yacht *Josephine* for a day's outing to Mandeville, twenty-three miles due north across Lake Pontchartrain. But after they were under way the day darkened, the engine lost power, and they were stranded, near shore but short of Mandeville. Coughing from the engine smoke, scratching bites from the swarming mosquitoes, they found the main cabin a poor haven at best. It was dark when they finally got back to New Orleans. Almost everyone had mosquito bites and some were sunburned. Others had the makings of hangovers. Faulkner had considerable material for future use.

According to stories he would tell, these were days when he sailed the waters beyond New Orleans for profit as well as pleasure. Evidence of the brisk liquor trade in the Quarter was everywhere. Scotch, bourbon, and gin were available at Joe Cassio's grocery, at St. Peter and Royal streets, just as they were at Manuel and Teresa's, directly opposite. The customer could not always be sure, though, that the bottles' contents corresponded exactly with their labels. It was commonly believed that the readily available Cuban alcohol served as a base. Spratling's friend Keith Temple remembered that you would "go fishing and come back with a five-gallon can." This traffic appealed to Faulkner's imagination. Some of his amusement may have come from the idea of his working as a rumrunner while his brother Jack was serving as one of J. Edgar Hoover's original G-men. "I ran a launch," he would say, "out into the Gulf where the schooner from Cuba would bring the raw alcohol and bury it on a sand-spit and we'd dig it up and bring it back to the bootlegger and his mother—she was an Italian, she was a nice little old lady, and she was the expert, she would turn it into Scotch with a little creosote, and bourbon."[17] Neither Jack Falkner nor Bill Spratling believed these tales. It is possible that Faulkner went out into the Gulf under cover of darkness with a well-known supplier in the Quarter called Slim, who ran his own boats. If he did, it is likely that he went as a guest, much as The Poet had accompanied Stone to watch the big games in Memphis and Clarksdale. Whatever his actual experience, it was the bohemian and the war hero all over again. He wanted to create the image of a man who was brave and adventurous, who lived an exciting and sometimes dangerous life. And here again he had material for fiction.

So if there was water imagery in what he was writing, it was no wonder. He did one piece whose protagonist stood midway between the idiot of "The Kingdom of God" and the vagabond in "Out of Nazareth" and also anticipated elements of another work he would also call *Mayday*. The nameless protagonist of an eight-page typescript entitled "Nympholepsy" was, in fact, the solitary "tieless casual" of "The Hill" given greater awareness and an adventure only hinted at in the earlier sketch. The farm laborer again climbs a hill at sunset, but this time he glimpses not only the Ionic columns of a distant courthouse but also "a girl like defunctive music."[18] Giving unsuccessful chase, he narrowly escapes drowning in a stream.

By mid-April, Anderson must have been recognizing some of these elements in the growing typescript. By now Faulkner had sent Cadet Lowe on to his home and settled his major characters in Charlestown, Georgia, as Margaret Powers and Private Joe Gilligan have brought the dying Donald Mahon home to his father, Episcopal Rector Dr. Joseph Mahon. There, too, are Donald's reluctant fiancée, flapper Cecily Saunders, and his one-time mistress, Emmy, the rectory housemaid and cook. Faulkner was now examining closely a complex of personal relationships as they develop and change during Mahon's decline and death: Mahon and Margaret; Cecily and Emmy; Cecily and her town boyfriend, George Farr, and the goatlike Latin teacher, Januarius Jones. Margaret is still involved in varying degrees with Lowe, Mahon, and Gilligan; Jones is alternately pursuing Cecily and Emmy. At the same time, Faulkner was keeping these relationships integral to the plot: Will Cecily go back on her engagement to Mahon, yield to Jones, or run off with Farr? What effect will this have on the clearly failing Mahon? How can Margaret influence the course of these events, aided by Gilligan, who now obviously loves her?

He was still drawing on life as he went. ("The reason why Bill's characters are so real," Bob Farley would say, "is because they were real.") Reverend Mahon, big-boned and bulky, resembled Murry Falkner. The anguish George Farr felt over Cecily Saunders in 1919 owed something to that which Bill Falkner had felt over Estelle Oldham in 1918. The night fighting and gas attack undergone by Margaret Powers' dead husband was similar to Jack Falkner's experience in the Argonne. Faulkner was using his own personal first- and second-hand knowledge of the war to particularize all he had absorbed from his reading. He "organized a series of juxtapositions of episodes from war and peace," as one commentator puts it, "often to savagely ironic effect. They demonstrate that those who have been to war find themselves obscurely disqualified from participating in the life of the community to which they return. . . ."[19] This was the situation Hemingway treated in "Soldier's Home," and it was one Faulkner would explore in his own short stories.

So he ranged from the particular to the general, from the realistic to the mythical. Thinking of the wasteland of the war and *The Waste Land* of Eliot, he borrowed from other contemporaries. He may not have consciously imitated Fitzgerald as he interpolated popular songs ("I Wish That I Could Shimmy like My Sister Kate") to suggest time and tone, but other devices were clearly suggestive of the "Circe" chapter of Joyce's *Ulysses*; he was also learning from the man he would call one of the two "great writers" of his time.[20] At the same time, he was integrating into this complex of references those obsessive archetypes that had marked his poetry and prose from the start. As Donald Mahon had played faun to Emmy's nymph in his youth before the war, now Januarius Jones plays satyr to Cecily's "Hamadryad." (77) There was more here than Faulkner's interest in the pastoral and the primitive, in the faun as emblematic both of natural man and the artist. To one critic, "A possible explanation for Faulkner's having placed in his first novel two versions of the faun and two of the nymph might run something like this: In the modern world the pagan virtues are no longer viable. Donald Mahon's honesty gives place to Jones's brutal cynicism, and Emmy's spontaneous life of the senses yields to Cecily's calculated poses and gestures."[21]

In "Verse Old and Nascent," Faulkner had called for "something beautiful and passionate and sad,"[22] and as he drew his novel to a close, this seemed more and more what he was trying to create. After Cecily has run off with George, Margaret offers herself to Donald. Her blind bridegroom dreams away his life, and then, after a terrifying memory of the fatal aerial duel, he is suddenly gone. In this novel, one writer observes, he used aphorisms as a characterizing device, "epigrams of the sort made fashionable by Oscar Wilde."[23] The last one is delivered by Reverend Mahon to Gilligan: "God is circumstance," he said. "God is in this life. . . . We make our own heaven or hell in this world. Who knows: perhaps when we die we may not be required to go anywhere nor do anything at all. That would be heaven." (317) The two men grip each other's hands, weeping, as they speak inwardly and poetically to the lost Donald Mahon and the departed Margaret. Faulkner cut this odd tableau and ended with the set piece he had foreshadowed with the last line of his notes. It provided a counterpoise to the minister's heterodox beliefs: the soft sounds in the night of a choir of Negro voices singing "Feed thy Sheep, O Jesus." By about May 21 he completed his first draft. On page 473 he typed two last lines: "New Orleans/May 1925."[24] He had used his own longings and frustrations, the things he had read and the things he had written, exploring the "realistic theme of the returned soldier and playing it off against the mythic implications of the Wounded Hero figure . . . setting images of stasis and death (however honourable) against images of motion and life (however corrupt)," and using his version of that archetypal figure as "a moral touchstone by which the community . . . may be judged. . . ."[25]

Faulkner would later mention spending a weekend with Sherwood Anderson on a riverboat. That trip could have come now, as Faulkner relaxed from finishing his draft. But it appears that Anderson did not see the latter part of the novel. One reason was the way he was caught up in the writing of *Tar*. But apparently there were others. John H. McGinnis, the book editor of the Dallas *Morning News*, liked what he had read of Faulkner's and asked him to do an essay on Sherwood Anderson. In 2,000 words, Faulkner assessed seven of Anderson's major works. Did Anderson read the piece, which came out on April 26? If he did, it must have given this insecure writer good cause for uneasy reflections. Faulkner gave with one hand and took away with the other. Critics often wrote of Anderson in an international context. "I prefer to think of Mr. Anderson," wrote Faulkner, "as a lusty corn field in his native Ohio." One friend had called him "the Phallic Chekhov." Actually, to this Mississippian, he was unquestionably Middle Western, "as typical of Ohio in his way as Harding was in his." As if it were not enough that Faulkner had compared him with a dishonest President, Anderson came out in the piece as half genius and half fortunate bumbler. He made judgments which were no more palatable for being right: Anderson's best medium was the short story. In his novels he showed a bad ear and that failing abhorrent to most writers: "a fundamental lack of humor."[26] A quarter of a century later, Faulkner would write, "His mother had been a bound girl, his father a day laborer. . . ."[27] He was wrong on both counts. But if he still thought these were Anderson's antecedents, when his own were those of the petty aristocracy, such as it was, of north Mississippi, that very conviction must have made itself manifest to Anderson on some level. And even if Faulkner had not yet concluded, as he would later do, that "the great tragedy" of Anderson's character was that he "expected people to make fun of, ridicule him," the essay showed that he had arrived at the aesthetic judgment he would subsequently render: Anderson was "only a one- or two-book man. He had to believe that, if only he kept that style pure, then what the style contained would be pure too, the best." In 1925, with *Dark Laughter*, "he had reached the point where he should have stopped writing. . . ."[28]

Faulkner was already using Anderson for fiction. It was in another story the *Times-Picayune* didn't buy. The protagonist of the eight-page "Don Giovanni" was a department-store buyer of women's clothes named Herbie, a Prufrockian character determined to keep trying despite repeated failure. Needing counsel, he sought out a French Quarter friend, a writer named Morrison, who tried unsuccessfully to avoid him. Morrison suggested Anderson, even if not as pointedly as in a later story called "Artist at Home." A man who relied on verbal strategies as much as actions in his unsuccessful amours, Herbie may have owed something to the author, who was capable of caricaturing himself in his writing as well as his drawing. The latest mischance, related to Morrison by Herbie at the story's end, was ludicrous enough to show life triumphing over art. "I am trying to write a novel," Morrison said, "and you have damaged my vanity beyond repair."[29]

Anderson had become so involved with *Tar* that he had stopped answering his mail. Faulkner's work on his own manuscript had kept him from seeing Sherwood and Elizabeth. Faulkner would later say that when he met Elizabeth on the street and they exchanged news, the final upshot was that she relayed to him a message from her husband: "He said that he will make a trade with you. If he don't have to read it, he will tell his publisher to take it." Faulkner would say he gladly assented, but when Estelle Franklin recalled a more intimate account, the tone was different. "I'll do anything for him," were the words Faulkner heard, "so long as I don't have to read his damn manuscript." That stung. "Bill remembered those words," Estelle said. But he wasn't going to be foolish. Horace Liveright was a flamboyant and unpredictable impresario, but his firm published Anderson, Pound, and O'Neill, not to mention Freud and other distinguished Europeans. Boni & Liveright were soon to bring out Hemingway's *In Our Time* and Dreiser's *An American Tragedy*. Faulkner would accept Anderson's recommendation gladly. His first draft finished, he went on a three-day boat trip. Then he returned for a week of rewriting. By now, thought his friend Harold Levy, Faulkner looked gaunt. Ready for another change of scenery, he gave two chapters to Lillian Friend Marcus, who had offered to do some typing for him. The man who rented the other ground-floor room, a newspaper advertising man called Louie, also offered his help and that of a friend. Faulkner gave Louie a batch and left for Oxford.[30]

In four months he would be twenty-eight. He would later insist that he had not read Freud, though his writings referred to him and showed that, at the very least, he had heard a lot of talk about Freudian psychology. How much he retained from *The Golden Bough*, he alone would know. But it would be hard for even the most casual reader to forget the early passages about the grisly process by which the priest of the grove at Nemi succeeded his predecessor through ritual death.

He was well out from under his father's domination now. And one writer would say that this was the year in which the balance of the "heretofore complementary relationship" between Faulkner and Stone "shifted a degree or two. . . ."[31] This process of growth and hard-won independence was continuing. In the past three months, before he and Anderson had become so involved in their books, they had been together a good deal. Later, in early summer, leaving the Crescent City, again Faulkner did not see him at all.

17

... the [young] man ... in a pair of disreputable khaki slacks
and a sleeveless jersey undershirt and no hat in a region where
even young people believed the summer sun to be fatal, seen
usually walking barefoot along the beach at tide edge. ...

—*The Wild Palms* (5)

AFTER the variety of New Orleans, Oxford must have seemed quieter than
usual. Jack was away. Dean had his high-school friends, and Johncy and
Dolly were still living with the Falkners. Their small son, Jimmy, now had
something like the place Dean had occupied as a child, and Bill enjoyed
playing with him. Estelle's visit had lengthened, and she and her children
were still with the Oldhams. Stone may or may not have known the extent
of his friend's interest in Helen Baird. And he may or may not have suspected that all was not well between Estelle and Cornell. But he did think
that it would be good for Bill to have a vacation on the coast, away from
home, before he went abroad. Stone asked his sister-in-law, Myrtle Lewis
Stone, to invite Bill Faulkner down to Pascagoula, and he accepted.

The Stones were sitting out on the front porch one evening in early
June when Bill Faulkner came walking around the corner, carrying his
typewriter and little else. Myrtle Stone gave him something to eat after
his 300-mile trip and then showed him the side porch, where he would
sleep. He settled in for four days of relaxation before making the eighty-
mile trip back to New Orleans to collect the typing his friends had done.
By June 11 they had it ready for him, and he was able to return to
Pascagoula to finish his revising and retyping.[1] The accommodations at
"The Camp" were simple: four rooms partitioned off by screening, with
awning shades in each room to be lowered for privacy. Little Myrtle
Stone, Allie Jean, Jack, Jr., and Rosebud saw nothing unusual in a magnolia
and a live oak sticking right up through the board flooring and out the

roof. The pale sand ran right up to the door from the lapping waters of the bay, a hundred feet away. It was so shallow that a swimmer had to go out a hundred yards or more before the water was over his head. Back from the beaches among the scrub pine and oak were palmetto trees and small wild palms that grew right up out of the ground, with no trunk. If a plant survived, some sort of trunk eventually would evolve. When the southerly wind blew, it would whisper dryly through the palms. In the wind before a storm they would clash and rattle as the dry fronds rasped against each other.

Faulkner settled easily into the camp routine. He came and went like a member of the family. No one asked him about his writing and he never talked about it. He found a favorite work place on a sort of bluff where a board seat encircled a big oak. He would pull up a wooden bench to support his small typewriter and become absorbed in his slow, steady, two-finger tapping. With the novel in Grace Hudson's capable hands, he was free to do other work now that he had caught his breath. It may have been in the early morning, or when Rosebud and her four-year-old brother Jack went in for their naps, that Faulkner worked on a story which, like "Sunset," used rural rather than urban characters and scenes. "The Liar" was a 4,000-word commercial story with a surprise ending which fitted a standard formula for short detective fiction. The taleteller was a country-man named Ek, renowned for whoppers, who gave an account of a love-murder in the hills, which he had seen from a distance. As narrator, Faulkner adopted something of a patronizing tone toward these rural characters with nothing of the faun or dryad about them. But he was developing what would be an increasingly useful technique: the representation of country speech that would be faithful to accent, diction, and syntax, yet easily intelligible to the reader.[2]

Sometimes when he put away his typewriter, Faulkner would go for a swim with the children. He was a good companion, and they adored him. This was a help to Myrtle Stone because the law office kept Jack in Charleston during the week. Little Jack Stone remembered that when he and Rosebud got up from their naps, Faulkner "would take them on long walks along the tidal flats looking for soft-shell crabs and telling stories of pirate treasure." Some evenings, when the children's parents were talking with Myrtle Stone's parents, Pascagoula natives Frank and Gertrude Lewis, there would be more walks. One night Faulkner told them "The Legend of Sleepy Hollow," and it seemed to the children that the Headless Horse-man materialized there before their eyes, pounding down the beach and away to the horizon in the dusk. It chilled them, but they never tired of it.

He also had time for relaxation with adults that June. He liked Tom Kell, an easygoing, companionable man. He would see Ebb Ford, an exemplar of a familiar Southern type: a Rhodes scholar and a lawyer of great intelligence, erudition, and skill, living out his life in a small Southern

town. Poet Sam Gilmore came over from where he was staying at Pass
Christian one day, and he and Faulkner took a small boat out, only to find
that between them the best they could do was go around in circles. On
more enjoyable expeditions, a cousin of the Stones would sail his fifty-foot
yacht from Mobile. They would take *The Flying Cloud* out and drop
anchor within the sound of the surf on the islands that shielded the placid
inshore waters. There they could fish or swim. There was always food and
drink and usually a ukulele or guitar. When they weighed anchor, Jack
Stone would watch admiringly as Faulkner nimbly made his way out onto
the ten-foot bowsprit and stretched out full length, gazing into the waters
of the Gulf ahead of the curling wake. At night there were fishing parties,
when they would go out with spears and lines, their torches flickering
over the quiet water.

Faulkner had always enjoyed going barefoot, and the beach was the
perfect place for it. He might walk into town the same way, and simply
sit there looking, as he did on the square at home. That was the way he
would drive the Stones' car, and he might salute a young lady he knew by
sticking his foot out the window and wiggling his toes at her. He would
spend time lounging on the piers and in the places where the Pascagoula
fishermen congregated for a drink. Usually he wore a white shirt and
white duck trousers with a rope tied at the waist. His shock of dark-brown
hair with its red glint was often uncombed. He had a good meerschaum
pipe that summer, which contrasted with the beachcomber effect of his
appearance. The mustache was neat, but often there would be a dark
stubble on the thin cheeks.

He was often at Helen Baird's house. Her mother, Mary Lou Freeman
Baird, was a well-to-do widow who had bought the place one summer for
$12,000 because she like the roofline. Helen, born in 1904, had a fine
talent for sculpture. She would shape a wire form and wrap it in crepe
paper and paste so that it took the form of a horse, a man, or a woman. Her
mother had formed strong feelings about Helen's new admirer from
Mississippi. "How can you stand going around with someone who looks
like a wild man?" she would ask. But Helen set no great store by clothes
herself. As often as not she would be wearing a paint-smeared smock. She
did not hesitate to wear a bathing suit that revealed the scars of a terrible
childhood accident. "I was burned," she would say offhandedly, in her
direct, abrupt way, her voice just short of harshness. She could be good
company, though she said she generally couldn't stand people for more
than an hour. But like Faulkner, she preferred out-of-the-ordinary people
even though she had enjoyed the swirl of a Nashville debutante's life when
her turn had come. She had more than her share of beaux, bright attractive
men such as Guy Campbell Lyman, a young lawyer who moved in influential New Orleans circles. He accused her of collecting screwballs, and
she readily agreed that she did. She would later say of Bill Faulkner, "He

was one of my screwballs." With his short stature and that shock of hair, she said, "he reminded me of a fuzzy little animal." Her friends thought she tolerated him. She would lecture him about his drinking, and he would simply say, "I know."

But from the time of his four-day vacation in early June he had seen as much of her as he could. Faulkner was learning to sail, and he would invite her to go out with him.[3] Pete Baird would visit whenever he could get away from his sportswriting job at the *Times-Picayune*. Their brother, Kenneth, called "Josh" or "Gus," would sometimes join them, whittling on a special pipe he had designed. They would lie on the jetties while Bill told Helen stories, or sit on the swings of the screened porches and gaze at the indigo heavens. One night she said, "Look, the moon looks like a fingernail in the sky." Faulkner looked at it, then said, "May I use that?" This short, stocky, vivacious girl, with her dark hair and gypsylike look, could treat him cavalierly. Once when she failed to keep an appointment with him, she returned home to find he had been sitting at her door for four hours. "That's all right," he said. "I've been working." She was not surprised, for it seemed to her that writing was what he lived for. But whether she knew it or not, he had fallen in love with her.

She appealed to him for several reasons. There was something childlike about Helen Baird in her brusque honesty, and as he always found himself attracted to children and sympathetic to the ill or unhappy, so he could not fail to respond to the way this young girl accepted her maiming with the courage of disregard. And she was creative. As an artist he respected that. In the kind of reverse psychology which often operates in human relationships, her lack of interest in his writing probably made him more open to her—and he was a man to respond to women, as the strong erotic element in his love poetry showed. Of course, it was summer, too, and she was there. Sometimes they would swim together. Often they would go out on one of the piers on the east beach. As they lay in the sun he would make up stories to tell her. In "Verse Old and Nascent," he had presented himself as a cynical poet who used his work to further "various philandering." He had a copy of "The Lilacs" with him. After making a few corrections, he presented it to her. He was also writing something new, for her. When he would complete it a year hence, it would be a sequence of fifteen sonnets, lettered in his thin, fine presentation script, bound and entitled *Helen: A Courtship*. This was more than mere philandering.

An introductory poem and each of the first seven of the sonnets would bear at the bottom the notation: "PASCAGOULA — JUNE — 1925." How well Helen fitted the type Faulkner liked was shown in two poems especially. A twelve-line poem which introduced the set, "To Helen, Swimming," praised her body, "Her boy's breast and the plain flanks of a boy."[4] And in sonnet VI he could remark "the scarce-dreamed curving of her thighs" before he asked,

> And breasts: can breasts be ever small as these
> Twin timorous rabbits' quisitive soft repose?[5]

He did a brief self-portrait in the first poem, which recalled the sketches comparing Spratling's gift and his own. He even called it "BILL":

> Son of earth was he, and first and last
> His heart's whole dream was his, had he been wise,
> With space and light to feed it through his eyes,
> But with the gift of tongues he was accursed.

But in the sonnet's last line he found peace: "he's quiet, being with her."[6] Sonnet II began with Eve and ended with an echo of Housman. The next was a revised version of the poem which had appeared in *The Double Dealer* for April as "The Faun," which he had dedicated there to H. L., his Vieux Carré friend Harold Levy. (Faulkner had finished the poem in Levy's home, and when he typed it out he inscribed it to Levy "to whom credit is due for the above sonnet after my own inspiration had failed.") Now it was smoothly integrated into Helen's book. The best of this lot were V and VI, to one critic "some of the most interesting poetry that Faulkner ever wrote."[7] V was entitled "PROPOSAL." Ten years later, writing Helen about that summer of 1925 or the next, Faulkner would recall when "I would go and visit Mrs. Martin [her aunt] and tell her that I wanted to marry you." In this poem he envisioned an interview with Helen's mother in which he was strictly quizzed as a prospective bridegroom, while in his own thoughts, as the same critic writes, "What the young man can scarcely suppress is his feverish desire for physical union with the girl." In VI, as he answers the mother's questions while thinking of her daughter's knees and thighs and breasts, the poem captures again "the plight of a young writer who has great imagination and is wracked by intense emotion, but who has no financial prospects and who is thoroughly aware of the exact degree of estimation he can claim in the eyes of the world."[8] His usual fauns and satyrs pursue a luscious nubile nymph in IV, but in VII he rang a change on this pattern and personalized it. The two quatrains of the octave filled in the figure of a passionate centaur with his lyre. But then, in the sestet,

> Hail, O Beauty! Helen cries, and she
> Would stay the Centaur's rush that there might be
> In islanded repose beneath his sweep
> A beauty fixed and true, but she forgets
> The dream once touched must fade, and that regrets
> Buy only one thing sure: undoubtful sleep.[9]

No matter what the form of the poem, no matter what the image, one thing seemed clear: this was one nymph who was not yielding to the blandishments of this faun, in bush or brake, on beach or pier. He had more in mind than a summer seduction. He was in love with her. He asked her to marry him, and she refused.

As June began to draw to an end, Myrtle Stone made preparations to welcome a new set of guests to The Camp. On June 23, Faulkner had finally worked his way through the typescript of his novel.[10] With further minor revising and retyping, he could send it off. He packed his few things, made his brief goodbyes, and rode the train into the early summer heat of north Mississippi. Grace Hudson had worked long and carefully on the novel, and some of The Bunch were allowed to read it. "My chief reaction at the time," Edith Brown remembered, "was to be shocked at how badly it was punctuated. I offered to repunctuate it, and Bill said he didn't care, so I did. As I remember it Bill didn't seem to care a bit about that novel. . . ." What Edith Brown was probably seeing was something else, something that would become habitual and even more pronounced: the process of putting completed work behind him and becoming absorbed in new work at hand. He revealed his feelings about the book by bringing the typescript in for the post-office gang to read. But Baxter Elliott typed up an anecdote, either about Faulkner or about the work, and circulated it, and Faulkner never gave them another typescript to read. He had this one packaged and wrapped and sent it off to Boni & Liveright in New York. Grace Hudson was still busy, though, typing letters of introduction for Faulkner from Stone to T. S. Eliot, Arnold Bennett, Ezra Pound, James Joyce, and others. The fact that Stone knew none of them did not deter the Oxford impresario in the slightest.

After another round of goodbyes Faulkner took the train to Memphis for a few more visits before taking another train south. He stopped in to see his friend Arthur Halle at his clothing store and told him he was going to Italy.

"What are you going on, Bill?" asked Halle.

"I have fifty dollars for expenses going over," Faulkner replied.

"How can you go on so little to a strange country?"

"I'm going to write for the *Commercial Appeal*."

"How? You don't have a signed contract, do you?"

"You'll see," was all Faulkner said.

As one writer has speculated, he may well have intended a series of sketches which could bear titles such as "Sinbad in Paris" and the like.[11] He went to visit his great-aunt 'Bama, Alabama Leroy Falkner, the Old Colonel's youngest child, now Mrs. Walter B. McLean. "Baby Roy" had been her father's favorite, accompanying him on the European trip during which he had written the letters to Ripley's *Southern Sentinel* which were collected as *Rapid Ramblings in Europe*. She had always been drawn to Billy, not only by her pride in his work but also by his admiration for her adored father. She did not believe in helping people too much, however, for she thought they ought to work out their problems themselves. It would bring out the best in their character. But now she relented, perhaps thinking about that trip to Europe forty years before and the contrast between the affluent Colonel and his down-at-the-heels great-grandson. When Faulkner saw Dot Wilcox he said he had received an unexpected windfall. It was twenty dollars, which he had sewn into his trench coat. Dot didn't think much of his appearance. He was wearing old work shoes, and his plaid jacket hung on him with one elbow out. But he was not going first class, and he didn't think he would need much. He would be going on to France after Italy, and since the time of François Villon, poets had been able to make do with a good deal less than the bourgeois' minimum. He had already constructed the phrase he would use: *Je suis un poete.*

In New Orleans, Bill Spratling was busier than ever. *Architectural Forum* had asked him to do some articles on northern Italy, and he had already arranged passage. Faulkner apparently had given up the idea of finding a ship on which he could work his passage across. The *Times-Picayune* would publish "The Liar" in three weeks and "Episode" three weeks after that. No matter when he actually received the money for these stories, it was further evidence that he could keep earning. And there was Aunt 'Bama's twenty in his trench coat. On Tuesday, July 7, he and Spratling stood on the deck of the 3,600-ton *West Ivis* as it cleared the harbor and headed out into the Gulf, bound for Savannah, Genoa, and Naples.

18

It had been a gray day, a gray summer, a gray year. On the street old men wore overcoats, and in the Luxembourg Gardens . . . the women sat knitting in shawls and even the men playing croquet played in coats and capes, and in the sad gloom of the chestnut trees the dry click of balls, the random shouts of children, had that quality of autumn, gallant and evanescent and forlorn. From beyond the circle with its spurious Greek balustrade, clotted with movement, filled with a gray light of the same color and texture as the water which the fountain played into the pool, came a steady crash of music.

—*Sanctuary* (308)

COMPARED with Faulkner's original plan, this trip was luxurious. He and Spratling had compact cabins meant for officers in charge of cargo or the occasional traveler. They took their meals with the captain and his officers. "When we were some two days out in the calm waters of the gulf stream," Spratling later wrote, "one morning Faulkner appeared on deck with a mass of MS about four inches thick. This he laid on the deck and proceeded to dispose of by tearing in batches and dropping overboard."[1] Faulkner confirmed this. He said that one of his duties (he had none; he was inventing again) was throwing the garbage overboard. He threw some sonnets with it. "It made me feel clean,"[2] he said. He was obviously clearing his own decks for new work. But sonnets would be part of it, again for Helen.

The *West Ivis* tied up in Savannah on July 11. Faulkner whiled away some of the time copying inscriptions from tombstones in the Colonial Cemetery in Savannah before they departed three days later.[3] In six weeks he would be using the leisurely crossing in his fiction. "There was really very little time to be lonely at sea," he would write, "twenty days on a freighter pushing one empty horizon before and drawing another one behind, empty too save for a green carpet of wake unrolling across that blue monotone."⁴ At last they passed through the Straits of Gibraltar and steamed slowly past the Balearic Islands of the western Mediterranean. His thoughts were elsewhere, though, when he composed another sonnet dated "MAJORCA — JULY — 1925." Called "Virginity," it would be eighth in the sequence he would present to Helen Baird.⁵ Finally the Ligurian coast rose out of the distance, and the *West Ivis* entered the ancient port of Genoa. It was Sunday, August 2, 1925.

Spratling and Faulkner left the ship there. With the first mate and the chief engineer, they went to a cabaret, where they could change some currency. Very shortly they were joined by several companionable girls. They ordered a round of beer and soon Spratling was dancing. When he reached "that stage where everything seemed irresistibly amusing," he decided to drop some coins under the table to see what his dancing partner and her pimp and their companions would do. In the ensuing scramble and uproar the carabinieri suddenly materialized. Before the others realized it, Spratling had been whisked away to spend the night in Genoa's vermin-infested Palazzo Ducale jail. The next morning at his hearing a municipal official informed him that his offense was so grave— stamping on coins that bore a likeness of the king's face—that the only thing to do was expunge it from the record.

As Spratling walked blinking into the bright sunlight, Faulkner looked at him. "You no longer look so vulgarly healthy," he said.

Surprised at the tone of the comment, Spratling told him he sounded sore.

"What the hell," Faulkner said. "Why shouldn't I be? Missing an experience like that."⁶ When Faulkner wrote Ben Wasson about the incident, he made himself the protagonist.

Spratling took the train for Rome, but Faulkner traveled twenty miles east along the coast to see what Yeats called "Rapallo's thin line of broken mother-of-pearl." Ezra Pound—a champion of the new, both the art and the artist—lived there, reading Jefferson and John Adams and working on his *Cantos*. When Phil Stone had written to him, as Sherwood Anderson had earlier on behalf of Hemingway, he had hoped Pound would interest himself in still another promising young American. Apparently Faulkner never tried to see Pound in Rapallo. Spratling said later that they both wanted to see him, but Faulkner's shyness kept him from approaching the leader of the avant-garde by himself.

On August 5 he sent a postcard to his two-year-old nephew, Jimmy. He was going to leave Rapallo the next day, he said, to walk to Paris: "I have a knapsack—le sport baggage, they call it."⁷ Actually, he took the train for Milan, but then, he wrote his mother, "I looked out and saw Pavia." He got off the train and found a fifteenth-century inn called the Pesce-d'Oro. All around it "are old, old walls and gates through which mailed knights once rode, and where men-at-arms scurried over cobble stones."[8] Beyond the narrow streets and city walls, he wrote Aunt 'Bama, you saw "an old grey red-tiled bridge crossing a stream in quiet meadows where cows ruminate in a mild wonder at the world, and sunset like organ music dying away."[9] A day later he sent his mother a postcard from Milan, marveling at the Cathedral.

The next day he met Spratling in Stresa. Spratling had been doing his sketching for the *Architectural Forum* series, and sometimes Faulkner went along with him, as he had done in New Orleans. He would talk from time to time as Spratling concentrated on his subject. There were "only two basic compulsions on earth," he told Spratling once, "love and death." Spratling found these meditations distracting, but one he remembered very clearly. The subject was borrowing from life for art. "I don't take whole people," Faulkner told him, "I do this." He placed both palms together, fingers outstretched, then rotated his hands, inter-twining his fingers.[10]

The weather had turned cold and depressing and the town was full of American tourists. "I took my pack and typewriter and lit out for the mountains above Lake Maggiore,"[11] he told his mother. On August 9 he arrived at Sommariva, "a grand village on an Alp above Stresa." He wrote Aunt 'Bama that he "lived with the peasants, going out with them in the morning to cut grass . . . and then coming down the mountain at sunset, hearing the bells on the mule jingle and seeing half the world turning lilac with evening." But he was getting some work done, including "a sort of amusing travelogue."[12]

He had been writing poetry, too—more sonnets in the sequence to Helen. In Genoa he had written another like the one dated off Majorca, full of images of unrequited love, and of Death, which in these poems was cuckolder and cuckolded. In another dated "PAVIA — AUGUST — 1925" he employed the convention of the cruel mistress who would not yield to her lover, and the lover who had to make up in imagination what he lacked in reality. In the last line he told her, "Why, I've lain lonely nights and nights with you."[13] In a second sonnet from Pavia, there were more images of sleeping and waking and "deathless golden Helens" juxtaposed by implication to herself. His pain was such that he would wish to wake only when he could forget her shoulders, her hair, and "These grave small breasts like sleeping birds uncaged."[14] Two more bore the dating "LAGO MAGGIORE — AUGUST — 1925." The first was dominated by the imagery of fire and the second by that of hawks, but the burden was the same as in the previous poems. Marvell had put it in two lines to his coy mistress:

> The grave's a fine and private place,
> But none, I think, do there embrace.

There was nothing of the marble faun's gentle melancholy pastoral lament in these poems. They were a different kind of exercise—poems with compressed lines and muscular images—with a clear sense, too, of resentment as well as frustrated passion.

He traveled to Mottarone, but left quickly. "Switzerland is a big country club with a membership principally American,"[15] he told Aunt 'Bama. He was disgusted by the way his countrymen behaved and he didn't blame the Europeans for overcharging them. He was glad that the Italians thought he was English. Returning to Stresa, he joined Spratling and they boarded the train for Montreux. It had been too dark to see the Jungfrau, but when they stepped off the train in the morning, they saw the great snowy mass of Mont Blanc. "We climbed an Alp and called on a Russian princess," he wrote his mother, "daughter-in-law to a member of the Czar's family, and herself a daughter of the last Doge of Venice."[16] Since the last Doge of Venice had abdicated in 1797, either Faulkner had been taken in or he had invented something he thought might please Maud Falkner. They went on to Geneva, but Switzerland was simply too expensive, and on August 13 they took the train for Paris.

Like Switzerland, it seemed full of American tourists, and it took them two hours to find a hotel. Later they moved to a nice one, he wrote his mother, "on the left bank of the Seine, where the painters live."[17] It was close to the Luxembourg Gardens and the Louvre, and from the bridge one could see both Notre Dame and the Eiffel Tower. Room and board would cost only a dollar and a half a day. He was soon taking the city in eagerly. On Sunday, August 16, he had taken a *pacquebot* down the river past Auteuil and Meudon to Suresnes. Crossing the river, he had walked through the Bois de Boulogne, then up the avenue to the Place de l'Étoile and the Arc de Triomphe. He sat there for a while and then walked down the Champs Élysées to the Place de la Concorde and had lunch in a workingman's restaurant. He took the *Métro* to the Père Lachaise Cemetery. "Alfred de Musset is buried there, and all the French notables and royalty," he told his mother. "I went particularly to see Oscar Wilde's tomb, with a bas-relief by Jacob Epstein."[18] On his way home he stopped in the Luxembourg Gardens to observe the children sailing boats on the pool. Even grown men sailed boats, in miniature regattas, while their wives and children cheered. And after his supper he had enough energy, or excitement, left over to write a long letter to his mother.

He meant to work there. He planned to have his typewriter repaired and settle in for some time. Across from the cemetery he had sat in a café and drunk a beer. Smoking his pipe, he planned another article. He had already finished two, he told his mother. He may have meant the "travel things" he had mentioned starting in his previous letter. It seems unlikely that he would have called a story an article, but it could have been about this time that he completed the last two stories he would publish in the *Times-Picayune*, one on September 20 and the other a week later. For the first of these, unlike the previous "Episode" and "The Liar," he reverted to a city setting. "Country Mice," like Scott Fitzgerald's *The Great Gatsby*, was narrated by a man of some cultivation who had become the confidant of a bootlegger who drove an ostentatious car. The story of running liquor into New Haven for a Yale football game had a surprise ending in which the city slickers were fooled by country constables. The 3,700-word tale showed a distinctly Faulknerian trait: pleasure in a complicated plot with elements of mystery-story technique.[19]

He was unmistakably imitating Conrad in the other story, "Yo Ho and Two Bottles of Rum." The *Diana*, with her Chinese crewmen, plied some of the same waters as did the *Nan-Shan* with her cargo of two hundred coolies in Conrad's *Typhoon*. There were the same themes: the East's enervating effect on some white men, their attitude of superiority, and the inscrutability of the Orientals. But whereas Conrad's novella dealt ultimately with the terrible power of storm and sea plus the human capacity for stolid heroism, this 3,300-word story treated homicide and its aftermath with a callous flippancy as the farcical burial, if not the decomposition of the victim, was played for comedy.[20]

H E had lost little time in acquiring a few characteristics of Latin Quarter artists: some knowledge of Paris and some conversational French. "And—" he wrote his mother, "dont faint—I am growing a beard."[21] On August 18 he moved from the pension on Rue Jacob, which was "full of dull middle class very polite conventional people," to a top-floor room at 26 Rue Servandoni, "just around the corner from the Luxembourg gardens, where I can sit and write and watch the children."[22] He had made new friends and acquaintances. One was a photographer from New Orleans named William C. Odiorne, a quiet man with a broad forehead and a small mustache, known to his friends as "Cicero." He had lived in Paris for a year, doing a little portrait work in his sitting room, where friends such as Spratling often dropped in to see him. Occasionally they would stroll along the Left Bank by the bookstalls above the river. Although Spratling was busy with his own pursuits, he and Faulkner would sometimes walk to the St. Germain-des-Prés district to sit at one of the sidewalk tables of the famous Deux Magots and observe the life of the Quarter. Faulkner was living the life American writers read about. Walking with Odiorne, he would make a point of pausing near the Place de l'Odéon. Thirty years later Faulkner would say, "I knew of Joyce, and I would go to some effort to go to the café that he inhabited to look at him. But that was the only literary man that I remember seeing in Europe in those days."[23]

Actually, he saw more painters than writers—among them one who was going to have an exhibition in New York in the fall, and four Chicagoans, "kind of loud and young and jolly," he told his mother. Another painter, Bill Hoffmann, remembered Faulkner's enjoying himself at a party given by fellow artist Paul Berdanier in his Montparnasse

studio. He even recited a risqué poem. (None of his listeners could know
that it was the fifth sonnet in the sequence to Helen.) He was well placed
to see much of the work his friends were talking about. Nearby were the
Luxembourg galleries, with their Post-Impressionist paintings. There were
also many small galleries in the Quarter, some of them showing the work
of artists rejected by the Salon. There was a wide range of exhibitions,
from the cubist paintings of someone like André Lhoté to the strong
nudes of Jules Pascin. He spent a whole day in the Louvre, he wrote his
mother, "to see the Winged Victory and the Venus de Milo, the real ones,
and the Mona Lisa etc. It was fine, especially the paintings of the more-or-
less moderns, like Degas and Manet and Chavannes. Also went to a very
very modernist exhibition the other day—futurist and vorticist. I was
talking to a painter, a real one. He wont go to the exhibitions at all. He
says its all right to paint the damn things, but as far as looking at them,
he'd rather go to the Luxembourg gardens and watch the children sail
their boats. And I agree with him."[24] In the last week of August he told
her, "When it rains—as it has for a week almost,—I go to picture
galleries."[25] A month later, however, he was still looking at pictures. "I
have spent afternoon after afternoon in the Louvre," he told her. He
visited the Luxembourg again, seeing Rodin's museum and two private
collections of Matisse and Picasso, "as well as numberless young and
struggling moderns." Another Frenchman's work excited him: "And
Cezanne! That man dipped his brush in light like Tobe Caruthers [an
Oxford Negro of many talents] would dip his in red lead to paint a
lamp-post."[26]

Like Hemingway, who would name painters from whom he had learned,
Faulkner was absorbing insights from this medium. More than half a year
before, in "Mirrors of Chartres Street," he had demonstrated his acquaintance with the Vorticist school. Like its practitioners, according to one
Faulkner critic, Cézanne also believed "that circularity was a basic
principle in art and nature." But even more appealing was Cézanne's
belief that "the basic form in nature was the cone, the basic line circular."
This critic would go on to cite Faulkner's admiration for his "method
of painting directly with colored pigments, without the use of guiding
structural lines," and to argue that Faulkner "derived much of his sense
of curved form from Cézanne"—displaying another of his characteristics:
"largeness of effect, the powerful possession of space."[27] Arguments
could be made, too, for specific influences from Gauguin, Van Gogh, and
others. Again and again, in many different ways, he would declare the
artist's willingness to take from any source for his own work. Here, in
Paris, day after day, he was storing up images that would serve him for
the rest of his life.

He was also absorbing images associated more with the tastes of tourists
than Latin Quarter artists. He went to the Moulin Rouge and described

it disarmingly to his mother as "a music hall, a vaudeville, where ladies come out clothed principally in lip stick. Lots of bare beef, but that is only secondary." He may have known that only thirteen years earlier Nijinsky had shocked Parisian audiences with his explicitly sexual interpretation of the principal role in the Diaghilev ballet based on a Debussy composition which had borrowed its title and inspiration from Mallarmé's "L'Aprés-midi d'un Faune." He went on to tell his mother, "Their songs and dances are set to real music—there was one with not a rag on except a coat of gold paint who danced a ballet of Rimsky-Korsakoff's, a Persian thing; and two others, a man stained brown like a faun and a lady who had on at least 20 beads, I'll bet money, performed a short tone poem of the Scandinavian composer Sibelius. It was beautiful." Americans were obsessed with sex, he said. "All our paintings, our novels, our music, is concerned with it, sort of leering and winking and rubbing hands on it. But Latin people keep it where it belongs, in a secondary place. Their painting and music and literature has nothing to do with sex."[28] The phrase "bare beef" bespoke a deep-seated attitude about female nudity he would articulate many times. In conversation he might refer to "nekkid meat" on bathing beaches. As he preferred slimness to voluptuousness, so he also preferred the suggestion of sexual charms rather than their outright display—except, of course, in the intimate eroticism described in some of his sonnets.

When he finished writing the last two of the fifteen sonnets for Helen, there in Paris, it was almost as if the nude chorines and golden dancers and faunlike men brought home to him his own sexual stasis, at least with respect to Helen. In these last two poems it was death which was victorious over that other principal compulsion, love. In the first of the two, in "cruel April," a lover's voice from the grave, like one of Housman's, recalled pangs at twenty-one and "a grave sweet mouth to kiss" that was not his. In the second of them (begun in New Orleans), the grieving lover recalled past love and knew he would feel it still "Though warm in dark between the breasts of Death. . . ."[29] He had composed a version of this poem six months earlier in New Orleans.[30] Powerful though his feelings were for Helen Baird, this sequence was not wholly a spontaneous outpouring of passion, but in part, at least, a carefully crafted work employing a familiar poetic convention and profiting from the same kind of tireless revision that was characteristic of his work in prose. It would be several months before he could give her *Helen: A Courtship*.

He worked on other poems from time to time. One beginning "What'll I do today?" seemed an imitation of E. E. Cummings,[31] and another was "so modern that I dont know myself what it means. . . ."[32] The first may have been part of a book of poems for children he was planning, but his major effort had been toward prose from the time he had arrived in Paris. He had begun work on a novel he called *Mosquito*, and then put it away because "I dont think I am quite old enough to write it as it should be written—dont know quite enough about people."[33] But by August 23 he could tell his mother he was in the middle of another novel, "a grand one. This is new altogether. I just thought of it day before yesterday."[34] At some point he had begun a story called "Growing Pains" about an unhappy fourth-grader named Elmer Hodge. After five unsuccessful starts, he recast it as *Elmer* and introduced his title character as an aspiring artist, twenty days at sea on a freighter and now almost within sight of Sicily. He used Elmer's paints for transition to a long flashback into an insecure childhood in a shiftless migrant family redeemed only by an adored older sister named Jo-Addie, whose bed Elmer shared. Chapter Two employed the same strategy, opening on the freighter and then slipping into a flashback to Elmer's "bastard son" in Houston and his love for Myrtle Monson, whom he had met there in 1921. Still limping from a war wound, he had asked her to marry him, but she had simply sailed for Europe with her snobbish mother. (Faulkner knew that Mary Lou Baird had talked about taking Helen to Europe. If he stayed long enough, he might even meet them during their travels there.) But Elmer received none of the sympathy lavished on Donald Mahon. Instead, the treatment resembled that of Julian Lowe, as though Faulkner were again thinking of Huxleyan satire. The two chapters seemed to be employing personal experience enlarged by imagination: Helen's rebuff and her departure with her mother for Europe, the stories he told in New Orleans about his illegitimate children back home, and his tales about his hazardous war service. Spratling was an artist who had been orphaned, though he had been spared Elmer's experience of shiftless migrant parents. There were resemblances between the Hodge family and the Bunden family in "Adolescence." And as a sexual element had been prominent there and in the flight-pursuit sequences of his novel, so it was there in *Elmer*.

The flashback sequence of Chapter Three employed Elmer's fourth-grade year, especially his blind adoration of another boy, slender and beautiful and cruel as a god, who humiliated him. The fourth chapter was heavy with phallic imagery, from Elmer's fascination with cigar butts to the feel of his tubes of paint to the way "he would stand in a dull trance staring at a factory smokestack." But his psychosexuality had also been formed by seeing something of his mother in his beloved sister, whose "Dianalike" beauty was transfigured into his ideal. The next chapter introduced his sweetheart, Ethel, who was pregnant by him but chose to marry someone else. With the war, the wound, and the recovery treated in further long expository flashbacks, Faulkner brought Elmer up to date: "here was Paris: the Louvre, Cluny, the Salon; all that he had wanted for so long . . . that merry childish sophisticated cold-blooded dying city to which Cezanne was dragged by his friends like a reluctant cow, where Degas and Monet fought obscure points of color and life and love, cursing Bougereau and his curved pink female flesh, where

Matisse and Picasso yet painted ——."[35] (Though called "the 'master of the artistic pinup,'" Bougereau painted at least one picture that would have appealed to Faulkner: *Nymphes et satyre*, which showed "a dreamy but virile satyr being dragged into the water of a marsh by no fewer than four naked beauties. . . ."[36])

For *Elmer*, Faulkner had drawn upon portions of various personas he had himself employed and attributed to him what must have been some of his own impressions of Paris. In making Elmer the blunderer and *artist-manqué* he was, his occupation—painter not writer—provided for some emotional distance. (In his next novel he would use a sculptor to convey some of his own deep feelings about the representation of life through art.) In later years, when he drew himself, he would consistently employ caricature. So there was an element of self-parody in the character of Elmer Hodge. Faulkner could look into the mirror and see an "ugly ratty-looking face," and this may have been one reason why he had grown a beard, and now that it was filling in, he could say, "Makes me look sort of distinguished, like someone you'd care to know."[37] In his tiny pen-and-ink sketch, it was pointed and quite full. The mustache drooped a bit, and above the sharp ears was a full and tangled head of hair. It was like a sketch of the young Bernard Shaw—not so elongated and not so Mephistophelian, but instead, rather faunlike.

My beard is coming along fine. Makes me look sort of distinguished, like someone you'd care to know.

Billy

Pen-and-ink self-portrait in a letter home from Paris (Courtesy Mrs. Paul D. Summers, Jr.)

He was also feeling satisfaction about the novel, "going elegantly well,"[38] he reported, as it approached 30,000 words. He started a new chapter with a description of Venice and then appropriated Bill Spratling's misadventure in Genoa. Elmer's drunken stream of consciousness suggested a blend of *The Marionettes* and the "Circe" episode of Joyce's *Ulysses*. After closely following Spratling's incarceration and release, Faulkner began to move his characters with more purpose in the two chapters that followed. Elmer and Angelo (a friend from the prison episode) entrained for Paris. Then Faulkner put the novel away for a time. He would soon make a trip of his own, across the English Channel, before he resumed work on it, and when he did, the new material would take on an English cast with Mrs. Monson's social climbing. (Faulkner's resentment at Mrs. Baird's disapproval of him as a suitor, and his disappointment at Helen's rejection of him as a husband, would help provide an edge to his portrayal of Myrtle Monson and her mother, traveling in Europe as Helen Baird and her mother were planning to do the following year.) His bizarre English nobles would be matched by the dessicated aristocrats he sketched when he shifted the scene to Rapallo. With more than 31,000 carefully counted words already written, he would again put the novel aside.

When he was asked years later why he left *Elmer* unfinished, he answered that it was "funny, but not funny enough."[39] The English characters might have offered possibilities for more sustained comedy, but there was little about Elmer that was very funny. Faulkner seemed ambivalent—sympathetic toward him as a psychologically stunted child yet satirical toward him as a bumbling adult. Another difficulty came from the numerous subplots and settings, which did not fuse into a coherent narrative. But it was not a profitless exercise, as future uses would show.

Near the end of the first week in September he had written another piece. It was unseasonably cool, he had told his mother, and so he would don his trench coat and sit "in the garden. I have come to think of the Luxembourg as my garden now. I sit and write there, and walk around to watch the children, and the croquet games. I always carry a piece of bread to feed the sparrows." Of the new work he said, "I have just written such a beautiful thing that I am about to bust—2000 words about the Luxembourg gardens and death. It has a thin thread of plot, about a young woman, and it is poetry though written in prose form. I have worked on it for two whole days and every word is perfect. I havent slept hardly for two nights, thinking about it, comparing words, accepting and rejecting them, then changing again. But now it is perfect—a jewel. I am going to put it away for a week, then show it to someone for an opinion. So tomorrow I will wake up feeling rotten, I expect. Reaction. But its worth it, to have done a thing like this."[40] Four days later, when he wrote Aunt 'Bama, he still felt the same exultation: "I have finished the most beautiful short story in the world. So beautiful that when I finished it I went to look at myself in a mirror. And I thought, Did that ugly ratty-looking face, that mixture of childishness and unreliability and sublime vanity, imagine that? But I did. And the hand doesn't hold blood to improve on it."[41]

Another piece he now began showed that the productive period which had begun in New Orleans had not ended. After putting *Elmer* aside for the first time, he had written his mother, "am about to start another one— a sort of fairy tale that has been buzzing in my head."[42] It seems likely that he would call this tale *Mayday* too, and that elements of it would anticipate one of his greatest novels.

Aunt 'Bama's letter had informed him that relatives from Ripley would be coming to Paris: his Aunt Vannye—Mrs. Vance Carter Witt— and her daughter, Willie. "They are very nice," he confided to his mother, "of the purest Babbitt ray serene." They carried their guidebooks everywhere, but "Europe has made no impression on them whatever other than to give them a smug feeling of satisfaction for having 'done' it."[43] Something of his reaction to them may have gotten into his portrayal of those other American tourists, Myrtle Monson and her mother. He must have shown none of his feelings, though, for his aunt entertained him generously, and after he told her he was soon off on a trip, she gave him a birthday present of a thousand francs.

WHEN they had left and Spratling had returned home for the fall term, Faulkner set off on September 21 with a two-dollar railroad ticket to Rennes, 180 miles west-southwest of Paris in Brittany. From there he took the train northeast to Rouen and began what he called "a walking tour" that would take him northeast again to Buchy, then to the war zone— Amiens, Cantigny, Montdidier, and Compiègne. From there, his route would take him to Pont Sainte Maxence, Senlis, and Chantilly before his return to Paris ten days after he had left it.

It was a well-earned vacation after six weeks of intensive work, and apart from the change of scenery and general sightseeing, it provided Faulkner with a chance to do two very different things: to read and reflect on some literary criticism and to experience, at firsthand, the physical signs of that phenomenon which had so affected his imagination, the Great War on the Western Front. When he had packed his "sport baggage" he had included Ham Basso's copy of Ludwig Lewisohn's anthology *A Modern Book of Criticism*. He had by now added his own name on a flyleaf in pencil. As he read, he did something which was rare for him: he underlined and annotated. Lewisohn made it clear that the book was meant as ammunition for America's young liberal critics opposing those whom Lewisohn considered repressive and arrogant—the so-called American Humanists, chiefly Paul Elmer More, Irving Babbit, and Stuart P. Sherman. These were critics who, in the words of one literary historian, "tended to stand out against the increasing realism of modern literature, its interest in what they . . . considered sordid facets of human life, and wanted to measure it against past 'models' of decorum."[44] The excerpts and essays constituted four groups: French, German, English and Irish, and American.

Although Faulkner might have been expected to sympathize with Lewisohn's point of view, most of the six comments he made were critical, and some were even tinged with indignation and disgust, perhaps because his reaction to the war got mixed with his reaction to the criticism. His comments on Hugo von Hofmannsthal's "The Poet and His Hearer" revealed not only a resistance to his breathless hyperbolic enthusiasm, but also a violent antipathy to things German. Alfred Kerr's furious "The Critic as Creator" not only argued that the critic was as much an artist as the poet, it set him above the ruck of wretches struggling with their muses. At the end of the essay, Faulkner appended four one-sentence paragraphs. The representative second one read "Mencken on a hobby-horse; Billy Sunday having a nightmare in the Browning society."[45] In "Experience and Creation," Wilhelm Dilthey elevated Goethe to the supreme position for all subsequent poets and philosophers and declared that the foundations of poetic activity rested mainly on experience, insight into it, and the "widening and deepening of experience through ideas."[46] On the book's endpapers, Faulkner wrote an extended rejoinder beginning with the word "Bunk." He declared that Goethe was unique in that he deliberately made himself a poet, whereas Shakespeare, Shelley, Keats ("trying to seduce Fanny Brawne with words"), Verlaine, and Swinburne "all became poets by accident. What did they care about establishing any correlation between the important facts of hunger and sex and death and any sort of spiritual world? Bunk. A real poet hasn't got time to do that." He concluded with another salvo at German critics, ending grandly and illogically with the pronouncement: "Let the French who are aware of the utter unimportance of ideas make criticism."[47]

In spite of his reaction, Faulkner kept the book, and he may have derived more from it than he realized. Later in life, when people would ask him about the sources of the artist's work, he would invariably answer, "imagination, observation, and experience." Something of the ars poetica he evolved may have come from his brief, angry involvement with this small book in the first days of the fall of 1925. It doubtless also deepened the distrust he had expressed in "On Criticism." By now the practitioners of that form may have seemed to him to be the artist's natural enemies.

Even before he left on his trip he had felt enormous sympathy for the French, with their long lists of war dead in the churches and the new fighting going on in Morocco. Now, in the Amiens sector, where the last desperate German offensive in the spring of 1918 had killed half a million men, Faulkner saw the ravages with his own eyes: "it looks as if a cyclone had passed over the whole world at about 6 feet from the ground. Stubs of trees, and along the main road are piles of shell cases and unexploded shells and wire and bones that the farmers dig up." He was indignant that American senators were demanding the payment of war debts. "Poor France!" he wrote. The French, he told his mother, were heroic.[48] He would retain a lifelong admiration for things French, and he would use the sights he had just seen in short stories and, twenty years later, in the book he would sometimes call his "magnum o."

There were souvenirs from the trip. One was a sonnet entitled "Cathedral in the Rain." It was a verbal landscape—dominated by a "sad and silver music," by "this soundless sorrowing of trees"—experienced, according to the last line, "above Rouen, in the rain."[49] There were other kinds of memories. From Europe he had sent postcards and short notes to Phil Stone, for whom he would later describe an encounter in a hotel in Brittany. He told Stone that a fat woman had succeeded in getting into bed with him. But then, as Stone recalled the tale, "Bill said that he had such a picture of himself, the little man on top of this big fat woman, that he couldn't perform, and she got peeved."[50] When he rolled over with laughter, the woman angrily retrieved her clothes and left. Faulkner would always say that he could not go to bed with a woman he did not love, not to mention the fact that the woman he described was the opposite of his idea of female desirability. Like the tale about climbing an alp to visit the daughter of the last Doge of Venice, this was clearly another invention meant to amuse. The fantasies in the sonnets to Helen were clearer revelations of his psychosexual wishes and needs.

Stone knew, of course, how concerned Faulkner was about *Mayday*, and he was still doing his best to promote it. At about the time Faulkner arrived in Paris, Horace Liveright was writing Sherwood Anderson, who relayed the word to Stone. Two of the readers had been enthusiastic about the novel but the third had not. So Liveright was going to read it himself and decide. Anderson thought he would take it. He was not sure about the introduction that Stone had apparently suggested he might supply, but if Liveright wanted a jacket blurb, he wrote, "I'll be glad to do it, as I certainly admire Bill's talent."[51] When Faulkner had answered Aunt 'Bama's letter in early September, he had told her that Boni & Liveright had a novel of his which should appear in the fall. It is not clear if he had heard something definite or if it was a hunch, like Anderson's. But on his return to Paris, there was a letter waiting for him from Spratling. Faulkner told his mother, "he has seen Liveright and my novel is to be published."[52]

He had been an extraordinarily faithful correspondent. Miss Maud required weekly letters from her sons when they were away from Oxford.[53] Her eldest son—addressing her as "Dear Moms" and signing himself "Billy"—had done better than that. Early in his stay in Paris he had written her, "just remember when Sunday and Wednesday come, that I am allright, feeling fine, and sitting down at the table writing you a letter."[54] As his verses were meant to earn the love of the girls he courted, so these letters must have been a similar tribute. To his father, he had sent one postcard. It was from Chantilly, showing a pack of hounds in a forest with their handlers and pink-coated huntsmen. He wrote that this was "A sporting place peopled principally by English."[55] The English lords, dukes, grooms, and jockeys he had seen in the streets and bars of Chantilly may have piqued his imagination or firmed up a plan previously made. He wrote his mother that he was going to England for about a month, "to walk a bit before the bad weather sets in, in November." He thought that his finances were fine and that he would even be able to buy some clothes in London. "I will tell George V howdy for you," he said, "and that you was just too busy to write."[56]

London, that gray and timeless one: Saint Paul's brooding alone
above the City and across houses to the river bridged and invisible; the strand blooming like an odorless and colorless flower
already tarnished and old ere birth; Nelson fatuous and dim and
somehow beautiful with sheer height above the tamed somno-
lence of his stone lions; beggars with waxed moustaches and
frayed trousers in Piccadilly, importunate and bitter with
matches or shoelaces, or resigned and skillful with colored chalk
on the dirty pavement before Buckingham palace and autobusses
in dreadful and endless laden ellipses and the endless and aimless
moiling of mankind. . . .

—Elmer[1]

Not long after he stepped off the train in London on the morning of
October 7, he decided he would leave the next day. It was dirtier than
Pittsburgh and "awful expensive." And the spectacle of the widespread
unemployment was worse than the prices. But he was as assiduous in
London as he had been in Paris. "I've seen a lot: Buckingham Palace (the
King never came out, though) with sentries in scarlet tunics and steel
breast-plates on white horses, Westminster, the Tower, all those old
coffee houses where Ben Jonson and Addison and Marlowe sat and
talked, and Dickens' Bloomsbury, and Hounslow Heath where they
robbed the mail coaches, and Piccadilly and St. Paul's, and Trafalgar and
Mayfair—everything, almost, despite the fog. The sun has looked like a
half-spent orange all-day sucker." He was going south to Kent and west
to Devon and Cornwall. "But if I dont find things cheaper there," he
wrote Maud Falkner, "I'm going back to Paris until time to start home."[2]

Two days later he was in Kent, thirty miles southeast of London in
Tunbridge Wells. He was stunned at the amount the English ate, but not
at the way the Scots drank: "Whenever you hear anyone ask for
whiskey in a bar you can count on looking up and seeing a face that
looks like it had been left out doors for about 5 years." He didn't think

much of the nobles and commoners who came to drink the waters, but he found the Kentish countryside beautiful, with its sheep-filled meadows of deep green grass and its quiet lanes bordered by trees turning red and yellow. "Quietest most restful country under the sun," he thought. "No wonder Joseph Conrad could write fine books here."[3] But the prices were no better, "too dear," he would say, no matter how much he had wanted to see Devon and Cornwall too.

By the time Maud Falkner heard from him again, nearly a week had passed. He was back in France but had not yet returned to Paris. He wrote from Dieppe, where for two days, he said, he had been working on a Breton fishing boat, with a high sea running, the weather cold, and his hands raw all the time. Whether this was literally true or an experience imaginatively augmented—like his work as a rumrunner and a merchant seaman—it was now stored away in memory, and by October 16 he was ready to return to Paris. He was anxious to continue work on his novel and to see if there was some mail there for him from Liveright.

He was not disappointed. The novel was accepted, rechristened *Soldiers' Pay*, which Faulkner liked. Years later he would say that a $200 advance was enclosed, but no one would cash it until he went to the British consul and showed him his British army dogtag, whereupon the consul gave him the money. If indeed the money was forthcoming, it was a welcome addition to his dwindling capital. He had sold nothing more to the *Times-Picayune* or anyone else, and the English trip had taxed his resources. He did have one product of that trip, however, that he hoped he could turn into money.

Writing from Dieppe, he had told his mother, "I've written a queer short story, about a case of reincarnation."[4] It was very likely "The Leg," and though it would not appear for nine years, it was imbued with impressions from that fall in England—"tramping about that peaceful land," the narrator, Davy, said, "where in green petrification the old splendid bloody deeds, the spirits of the blundering courageous men, slumbered in every stone." Davy's flying as an aerial observer hearkened back to Faulkner's own wartime ambitions, but the complicated tale suggests James and Kipling in some of their efforts in the ghost-story genre. When he briefly took up *Elmer* again before putting it aside, describing Myrtle Monson's "humanness," he wrote that "Henry James would have called it vulgarity. . . ."[5]

He seems to have discarded the sonnet form, but two other poems showed him just as diverse in his poetic style as in his prose. In one long poem he combined tourism, the poignant beauty of the spring, antimilitarism, and a lament for the war dead. With no capitalization and no punctuation save parentheses, he seemed strongly indebted in E. E. Cummings. There was a pompous oratorical general on tour, while the dead of the late war lay beneath earth in which the new season blossomed forth:

                                              o spring
                        above unsapped convolvulae of hills april
                        a bee sipping perplexed with pleasure o spring
                        o wanton o cruel. . . .[6]

   "Ode to the Louver" was not just a parody, it was a burlesque of every
semi-literate poet who had ever indited lines under the influence of his
muse. The first of the six stanzas, with its apparatus and refrain, gives an
accurate sense of the rest of the production:

                        Ode to the Louver[1]
                        The Louver is on Rivoli street
                        You can take the cars or go by feet[2]
                        The river is very deep and wide
                        It is more than a 100 metters from either side
                        The boats on it is called a barge
                        They are big but not as large
                              As the Louver

   _____
   Orthurs notes. 1. Big house in Paris, France. Near city hall.
                   2. Foot dont rhyme with street.

Faulkner sent these six stanzas to Phil Stone with a letter for Stone to
enclose when he sent them to "Mr. H. Mencken, magazine orthur." The
writer was one Ernest V. Simms, whose address was the "Baptist Young
Peoples Union" in Paris. He was submitting this poem on behalf of
"Wm Faulkner," who wanted "to get a start at poetry."[7] There is no
evidence that Simms or Stone or Faulkner ever received an acknowledgment of this unsolicited submission. It was a joke that the two Mississippians enjoyed, like their attempt to sell "Kubla Khan" to _The New
Republic_. But if it was a joke on Mencken, there may have been two
other targets as well. One might have been T. S. Eliot, who would
eventually refer to the notes he appended to _The Waste Land_ as "bogus
scholarship." Another, according to one Faulkner scholar, was probably
Stone himself—like Simms, a reviser of Faulkner's work, a zealot whose
"enthusiasm could be stifling," and the dispenser of "a patronage which
in time could rankle even the humblest of men."[8]
   As the November days brought the Paris twilight earlier each evening,
illuminating the city with "just enough light in the sky to turn these
lovely faded green and gray and red roofs into a beautiful faint lavender
at sunset,"[9] Faulkner kept to his routine, writing, spending time in the
Luxembourg, occasionally seeing Odiorne and Bill Hoffmann and other
artists. Odiorne was now doing some portrait work. He did a formal one
of Faulkner and several others made outdoors. The portrait was done in
deep shadow. Faulkner held a pipe, the strong, shapely hand highlighted
more than the thin, bearded face. It was a meditative picture, with an

aura of dreamy silence in the dusk. In one of the outdoor photographs he stood near a church. In another, in the same pepper-and-salt suit and vest, he sat on a bench. It was as if Elmer Hodge had been transfigured into his own idealized image of the man he might become. Light fell on the thin face and ample Vandyke beard, the eyes narrowed, the expression speculative.

He packed his few belongings—his typewriter and manuscripts, the "bluish-grayish-green" Harris Tweed jacket he had bought from a West End tailor in London from his shrinking store of money, and a few souvenirs: postcards and coins. It was probably the morning of December 9 when he boarded the boat train for Cherbourg to make his third-class voyage home on the S.S. *Republic*.

It was a stormy crossing, and he must have been glad to walk down the gangplank when they tied up in Hoboken on December 19. He was back on American soil again after nearly half a *Wanderjahr* in Europe. He would draw on it in his fiction for a long time to come.

CHAPTER

20

They drove on and mounted the shady gradual hill toward the square, and Horace looked about happily on familiar scenes. Sidings with freight cars; the platform which in the fall would be laden with cotton bales in serried rotund ranks; the town power plant, a brick building from which there came a steady, unbroken humming and about which in the spring gnarled heaven-trees swung ragged lilac bloom against the harsh ocher and Indian red of a clay cut-bank.

—*Sartoris* (165)

BEFORE he caught the train for home, he stopped in at the brownstone on 48th Street between Fifth and Sixth avenues that housed Boni & Liveright. It seems that neither of the partners was there, nor editor in chief T. R. Smith, who had probably changed *Mayday* to *Soldiers' Pay*. But editor Manual Komroff, who was in charge of the firm's Modern Library list, greeted Faulkner cordially and ushered him into his office. They talked briefly about his novel, which Komroff had voted for only on the strength of Sherwood Anderson's recommendation. Faulkner said something about another manuscript. "It's not my department," Komroff said, "but I'll see it gets a good reading." Of the conversation that followed, Komroff remembered only Faulkner's telling him about an accident in which he had fallen out of an airplane and cracked his skull. Faulkner left, having actually seen something of the firm which was going to publish his first novel.

There was one unexpected, and unsatisfactory, meeting. Helen Baird was there. She had been successful in selling some of the figurines she made in New Orleans, and now she was trying to do the same in New York. She would later recall that her bearded would-be lover looked shabby and unkempt. Not long after seeing her, he returned home.[1]

When he stepped off the train, Maud Falkner and Mammy Callie and his three brothers were waiting for him. After his mother kissed him, she stepped back and took a good look at his bearded face. "Billy," she said, "what do you do with that thing at night, wear it inside the sheets or out?" She knew that he had been six months without benefit of dry cleaning and with a minimum of laundering. Once back home, Miss Maud said to her twenty-eight-year-old author, "For heaven's sake, Billy, take a bath."[2]

He moved into a room in the old Delta Psi house, across the hall from Johncy and Dolly, but it was natural that he should spend much of his time out from under his parents' roof. When the weather was good he went to the golf course. Coming up on one tee, Ella Somerville was startled to see a bearded man emerge from a hollow nearby. "What's the matter, Ella?" the man asked. "Did you think I was Jesus Christ?" Then she recognized William Faulkner, strolling about the familiar "golfing pasture." Not long afterward he was serving as chairman of the tournament committee for the university golf club. Teeing off one day on a 132-yard hole, he hit a straight drive that dropped just short of the green and then rolled up and over the ridge. When he and the others walked onto the green they finally found his ball—in the cup. His achievement was memorialized with a dozen new golf balls and a pipe bearing the inlaid legend "Hole in One."

But he was writing too, spending time on work both old and new. Two items in particular presented an interesting and significant juxtaposition. Estelle Franklin's copy of *Vision in Spring* needed rebinding. This he did, and on a blank page at the end he neatly lettered a fine line in India ink: "Rebound 25 January 1926. Oxford. Mississippi."[3] Exactly two days later, in the same meticulous script, he inscribed another token of love for another young woman. It was the little book, *Mayday*, for Helen Baird. Put together some months earlier, it was probably intended as a gift to be presented before Helen left for Europe in February.[4] This was far from the last time he would be romantically involved with more than one woman at the same time.

He thought of Helen, he once said, as a "flame."[5] He was still drawn to her, still in love with her after the months he had had to brood over the failure of his suit the previous summer. He told Ben Wasson about her and said, "It's hell being in love, ain't it?"[6] Unlike *The Marionettes*, this gift was one of a kind. To create it, he had drawn more than India ink from the black metal box lettered with his name that held his artist's tools. Besides the meticulous lettering of the forty-three pages of text and two pen-and-ink sketches on the endpapers, there were three full-page watercolor illustrations, all bound in thin boards covered with mottled paper that bore the exquisitely executed stylized titling: "MAYDAY / by / William Faulkner." Borrowing from his inscription of *The Marionettes* to Cho-Cho five years before, he dedicated it "to thee / O wise and lovely / this: a fumbling in darkness."

The title worked on several levels. It signified the day on which crucial action in the tale took place. It suggested growth and rebirth, yet it was an anglicized version of the international distress signal, which Faulkner certainly knew in RAF training. It was appropriate to the shifting tonal qualities of the narrative, where the romantic and the cynical, the hopeful and despairing were mixed. There were so many elements that if it did not finally achieve artistic fusion, it was a fascinating creation which would intrigue future students far more, apparently, than it did the recipient. As one critic would put it, "*Mayday* is an allegory of the author's disappointed love in which a young knight named Sir Galwyn of Arthgyl is given a vision of a perfect woman, 'all young and red and white, and with long shining hair like a column of fair sunny water.' (50) In company with the specters Hunger and Pain, Galwyn rides in search of his vision and encounters on the way three princesses, each of whom falls short of his ideal by her eagerness to seduce him. At the end of the quest he is instructed by the good Saint Francis that his vision exists only as 'Little Sister Death.' (87) To find her, and by finding her, relieve his frustration with an imperfect world, Galwyn enters the stream of oblivion and drowns himself."[7] There were clear affinities with earlier work, as references to Saint Francis and the evocation of "Frankie and Johnny" by the character Little Sister Death testified. There was also clear evidence of literary influences, according to another critic, most clearly that of James Branch Cabell in *Line of Love*, *The Cream of the Jest*, and especially *Jurgen*, which Faulkner had inscribed to Stone as a Christmas gift two years earlier in 1923. There were numerous parallels, but one particularly meaningful difference: "disillusioned about idealized romantic love as well as about continually emphasized sensuality, [Jurgen] is at last willing to settle down with his wife of ten years in the realization that they have much in common. But Faulkner in *Mayday* let Sir Galwyn find no such optimistic compromise. . . ."[8] This tale would eventually be read as embodying other themes as well, such as that of the Quest and similar mythic motifs, while one of its most fascinating aspects was the concern, in both theme and imagery, with time, death, and sex, with twilight, water, and shadow. Moreover, it clearly foreshadowed important elements of a novel to come whose most striking figure would end his life as Galwyn did. Faulkner had written from Paris that he had put *Mosquito* away because he was not old enough to write it as it should be written, that he did not yet know enough about people. *Mayday* was the kind of work that helped to prepare him for that major effort two years hence.

So while *Mayday* was fascinating for all of these reasons, it was perhaps most so for the insights it gave into its creator. D. H. Lawrence would say, "One sheds one's sickness in books." A reader of the sonnets to Helen might have read there the answer to Suckling's question: "Why so pale and wan, fond lover?" This book was the other side of the coin. This suitor was a successful seducer of three princesses whom he loved and left. (One of the sketches in the endpapers showed a bearded satyr piping for a nude beauty. This was not the last time Faulkner would draw such a figure in a context which made it suggest a part of himself.) And if there was a seeking after transcendence through the pursuit of an ideal of female beauty that ended in self-immolation, there was also the frequent tone of cynicism about women's frailty and inconstancy. There was something else that was quite remarkable, even if familiar in other forms. Granting that Faulkner had little money to buy gifts, granting that in some sense his work had been and would continue to be a way of gaining love, granting that it was meant to aid in seduction with an efficacy and eloquence that perfume or ornaments presumably could not match, this work, done in one version only and for one pair of eyes, showed the prodigality of his genius. It is true that he had written from Paris about a book for children, and that parts of *Mayday* may have evolved from the stories he had told—as one might to a child—the previous summer to Helen Baird on the secluded jetty. It is not impossible that he might even have envisioned some other ultimate use of part or all of this little book. But there was no sign that he had such intentions now. So here was an artist who, after recently completing the better part of a novel and composing poems, sketches, and short stories, had the energy and inventiveness to do fifty pages of exquisite work in yet another genre before he went on to still other projects.

DESPITE the increasing reputation which he would acquire for unwillingness to talk about his work, he would in fact share it, reading it aloud, as he had done with A. P. Hudson and Phil Stone, and reciting it, as he had done at the Paul Berdainier's party. He allowed previews of work in progress, as he had done with Odiorne in Paris, and he did this now with his brother, across the hall from him in the Falkners' campus home. It seemed to Johncy that Bill was working mostly on short stories. It appears likely that two which might have occupied him at this time drew on his recent European experience. It would be years before they appeared, but as the manuscripts show, there were several versions, in part because of a labor-saving technique he had evolved, cutting out passages from manuscript sheets and then carefully pasting the salvaged material onto another sheet, where he would write up to and then beyond it.

"Divorce in Naples" was interesting not only in itself but also for what it conceivably said about *Elmer*. It, too, made use of the Spratling incident in Genoa, suggesting that Faulkner may have been borrowing from *Elmer*, as if he had decided to abandon it. The story deals with two crew members on a thirty-four-day ocean crossing.[9] George is a large dark Greek, whose beloved Carl—a small, blond eighteen-year-old Philadelphian of Scandinavian descent—betrays him with a female prostitute. Their reconciliation is shadowed, however, by an indication of future heterosexual betrayals by Carl. A slight link between the two works was provided by Elmer's early homosexual preference before his sexual feelings were transferred to females: Ethel and Myrtle. A link in the raw material which the works employed would remain hidden. Many years later, describing his experience in the jail of Genoa's Palazzo Ducale, Spratling would add one incident to his account. There in the dark cell, another young prisoner had begged for his sexual favors, and Spratling had brusquely granted them.[10] Clearly, this fitted with the character of George rather than Elmer.

The other story, "Mistral," began with two young Americans—Don, aged twenty-three, and the narrator, twenty-two—who, on a walking tour, encountered a case of murder in an Alpine village. Numerous details had personal antecedents, from glimpses of roadside shrines to "a shooting coat of Harris tweed."[11] Writing about the passion of an anguished priest for his seductive ward, the murder of her fiancé, and the relationship between the girl and her guilty lover, Faulkner showed growing assurance in a developing technique which would become a hallmark: withholding information and working by implication rather than statement. This was not the last time Faulkner would use this narrator and Don. In a story called "Snow" they would encounter another case of love and death, this time in a Swiss, rather than an Italian, Alpine village. In "Evangeline," set in Mississippi rather than the Alps, they would try to unravel a more complex murder mystery having to do with a plantation owner named Colonel Sutpen and the tangled lives of his children.

Very different was an unfinished story which Faulkner remembered having begun after his return from Europe. Called "The Devil Beats His Wife," it was actually a series of fragments and notes focusing on a maid named Della who produced a reconciliation between the young husband and wife she worked for. It seems to have been written with an eye to the magazine market, featuring the stock character of the loving illiterate servant who is really wiser than those she serves.

By now he had caught up on the news of his Memphis friends. Dot Wilcox had been glad to see him and hear about his European travels. They talked about Reno DeVaux, whose roadhouse had been closed down. He had paid his $500 fine, and busied himself getting back into business. It may have been about this time that Faulkner heard in another night club a story told by a young woman who talked freely about her life, about moving from her village, called Cobbtown, to Memphis, where she had taken up with a rising young gangster. (He was probably Neal Kerens "Popeye" Pumphrey, a veteran criminal at twenty-three.) Although the gangster was said to be impotent, he still persisted in having relations with women, and he had raped one with a particularly bizarre object and kept her in a brothel. When the girl left, Faulkner brooded over the horrifying story. Still the romantic who wrote about nymphs and fauns, he was no libertine despite his eroticism. "Do you know what the trouble is with me?" he had once said to Dot Oldham. "I'm a puritan." He would continue to dwell on the girl's story.

Faulkner made use of a character named Popeye in a story he called "The Big Shot," and he may well have written it not long after the encounter in the night club. The threefold narrative frame was elaborate but the plot was simple. A political boss protected a gangster against yet another traffic violation, not knowing that the hit-and-run victim was his own daughter. It was a surprise-ending, formula story, but its base was social criticism. Southern cities have been aping Chicago and New York, says the reporter-narrator, though "there is still a kind of hearty clumsiness to our corruption, a kind of chaotic and exasperating innocence. . . ." What was more intriguing than form or plot was characterization. Popeye is "a slight man with a dead face and dead black hair and eyes and a delicate hooked little nose and no chin, crouching snarling behind the neat blue automatic. . . ." His protector, "this Volstead Napoleon, this little corporal of polling-booths," is the son of a Mississippi tenant farmer. The crucial experience of his life had occurred when he carried a message to the landowner, only to be told, "Dont you ever come to my front door again." This was the trauma that finally produced his power and wealth, though he still dips the cheapest snuff, seen in "the slow thrust of his lower lip." His daughter is a "thin creature, a little overdressed," with a face like a "little painted mask." Her father does not know who is really taking her to "the Chinese Gardens, the Gold Slippers" (one of Reno's places was The Crystal Gardens), and he doesn't care, "just so they were not bums, the Popeyes and Monks and Reds that he used. . . ."[12] In this one journeyman story, clearly related to the gangster stories for the *Times-Picayune,* Faulkner had drawn first studies for major characters in five major novels to come.

After some time in the Memphis orbit, it was time for him to travel south again, to New Orleans. He was there by the time *Soldiers' Pay* was published in an edition of 2,500 copies. It was just as well. Murry Falkner had been told that the book wasn't fit to read. So he refused to open it and went on with his Zane Grey. Phil Stone tried to give a gift copy to the university library—and they declined to accept it. Sallie Murry said her aunt wrote Billy and told him that leaving the country was about the best thing he could do. Glad that he had gone to New Orleans, Miss Maud confided to Auntee, "there wasn't anything else for Billy to do after that came out—he couldn't stay here."

Back in the Vieux Carré, Faulkner may have wondered if the reviewers would agree.

21

. . . one of the narrow, dim, balcony-hung one-way streets between Jackson Square and Royal Street in the Vieux Carre—a
wall of soft muted brick above which the crest of a cabbage
palm exploded raggedly and from beyond which came a heavy
smell of jasmine which seemed to lie visible upon the rich stagnant air already impregnated with the smell of sugar and bananas
and hemp from the docks, like inert wisps of fog or even paint.

—*The Wild Palms* (36)

FAULKNER moved into the roomy attic Spratling had rented at 632 St.
Peter Street, almost at the corner of Cabildo Alley and just diagonally
across the street from Le Petit Salon. One visitor remembered "a large
room, littered with odds and ends of painting paraphernalia, a palette,
uncleaned from the day before, an empty easel, empty bottles on the
floor, a low bed cut off from the rest of the room by drapery of indistinct design, carelessly thrown over a wire that stretched from one wall
to the other."[1] It was large enough for their parties, which were sometimes
enlivened by more than just talking and drinking. Oliver La Farge would
put on a beaded Indian headband and do "the Eagle dance" atop a table.
Ham Basso remembered Faulkner and the others playing "a fine game of
tag one night across the steeply angled roofs of a narrow block of the
Quarter. . . ."[2] As for the drinking, Faulkner's prowess did not seem
unusual. "*Everybody* was a heavy drinker then," said painter Louis
Andrews Fischer.

George Healy, now a member of the *Times-Picayune* staff, would see
him in the newsroom with Roark Bradford, Lyle Saxon, and some of the
others who were working on books as well as newspaper copy. But there
was one person Faulkner saw very little of. When Sherwood Anderson
returned from California in late February he wrote a friend, "Both I and
Elizabeth, my wife, are pretty sick of people."[3] He did not elaborate.
When Faulkner had seen the Andersons in February, they had talked to

him admiringly about Anita Loos's new book, *Gentlemen Prefer Blondes.* And on March 17 he inscribed a copy of *Soldiers' Pay* "To Sherwood and Elizabeth Anderson." Some years later he had either forgotten or blocked out the memory of the meeting, for he wrote Manuel Komroff that between the time when he left for Europe and then returned to New Orleans, Anderson "had taken umbrage at me . . . I never did know why, and wouldn't even speak."[4] Faulkner was right about Anderson's feeling, though characteristically, Anderson could not expunge all of his earlier feeling for Faulkner any more than he could for Hemingway. In April he wrote Liveright that he had seen a good review of *Soldiers' Pay* and hoped Liveright would encourage Faulkner to keep at work. Liveright was free to repeat some of the good things Anderson was saying about Faulkner, though Anderson himself could not say them. "I do not like the man personally very much," he wrote. "He was so nasty to me personally that I don't want to write him myself."[5]

What had caused the breach? Apparently there were specific personal factors. Elizabeth Anderson thought Faulkner had been rude to their close friend Ferdinand Schevill. Faulkner denied it. She was not surprised. Faulkner thought what he thought, and it was hard, if not impossible, for anyone to change his mind. He had a superiority complex, she said, and he let it show. Moreover, he was a complicated man with expensive tastes that he could not satisfy. This left scars on him, and perhaps increased what was already a supersensitivity. (Years later Estelle would advance another theory: Elizabeth Anderson had become interested in Faulkner, and when he did not respond, she resented it.) Spratling said that he and Faulkner had found Anderson's teenage son Bob "uppity," and to teach him a lesson, had stripped him of his clothes, painted part of him green, and locked him out on the street. Such behavior would have run counter to everything in Faulkner's past dealings with young people, from little ones to Boy Scouts to late adolescents, but if Faulkner just felt as Spratling said they did, a father could well be offended.

There were reasons for deeper antipathies. Not only would Anderson criticize the South, from the wealthy class to the former slave class, he thought Faulkner himself was poisoned with pernicious attitudes. He wrote later about a kind of insanity in "those decayed families making claim to aristocracy, often living very isolated lives in lonely run-down Southern towns, surrounded by Negroes." There was cruelty toward the Negroes, Anderson said, which often took the form of sexual aggression by white men. "Faulkner has got hold of the queer sort of insanity that results. He understands and draws clearly the little white businessman, the small white farmers: still at the same time, there is in him also a lot of the same old bunk about the South."[6]

In his final judgment of Anderson, Faulkner would recall how vulnerable he was, how he "expected people to make fun of, ridicule him."[7] Faulkner may not have realized that this was exactly what Anderson felt

Faulkner had done to him. He remembered Faulkner's telling him about sterility, about "the cross between the jack and the mare that produced the mule and [saying] that, as between the white man and the Negro woman, it was just the same."[8] There was the Dallas *Morning News* essay. If Anderson read it, he could scarcely have missed Faulkner's implied reservations along with the qualified praise. Moreover, Anderson felt Faulkner had made him look ridiculous in his *own* writing. In "A Meeting South" he had put into the character of David many of the things Faulkner had told him about himself, and all their friends in the Quarter apparently knew it. Much later, when Ben Wasson mentioned the breach in their friendship, Anderson told him it had stemmed from that—Faulkner had lied to him about the war injuries. This may have cut both ways. Faulkner would later say, "I think that when a writer reaches the point when he's got to write about people he knows, his friends, then he has reached the tragic point."[9]

On the deepest level, there were other causes, causes that went beyond Faulkner's resentment at Anderson's saying he would recommend Faulkner's "damn manuscript" if he didn't have to read it. Anderson praised Theodore Dreiser highly as a man whose books gave him courage, but he thought that a more awkward writer never lived and that he would remain an example to other artists even after his books were no longer read. Faulkner would render a similar, if more generous, verdict on Anderson. He would call him the father of his own generation but stylistically a fumbling and simplistic writer who was finally "only a one- or two-book man."[10] Faulkner would later say that the writer "don't want to be as good as his coevals, or even as good as Shakespeare, he wants to be better than Shakespeare."[11] Elizabeth Anderson would say, "Sherwood and Bill were too much alike. This probably caused the eventual coolness between them." It was true, but in that late winter and early spring of the year 1926, the growing differences were more important than the similarities. One was declining from the summit of his career while the other was beginning the ascent to his zenith. And both probably knew it.

IF Faulkner saw little of the Andersons and the *Double Dealer* crowd, he still frequented some of his earlier New Orleans haunts, the Franklin Street cabaret and establishments such as Manuel and Teresa's, at St. Peter and Royal, where you could buy the Cuban alcohol doctored to taste like bourbon, Scotch, or gin. It may well have been now that he used these industrious entrepreneurs in a story that started to become a novel. The first-person narrator was the engineer aboard a rumrunner, a former pilot adrift after the war. He called the story "Once Aboard the Lugger," and at some point he subtitled it "The Prohibition Industry in Southern Waters." As usual, he typed from his own manuscript, and by the time the action came to a close, it constituted 268 typescript pages. Much later he would speak of destroying two novels which didn't suit him. This was apparently one of them. Characteristically, however, he salvaged two segments. One described an expedition to an island in the Gulf where the crew braved wild cattle and vicious mosquitoes to dig up the illicit alcohol. The other ended the tale with two crew members shot by hijackers who fled at the approach of a Coast Guard cutter while the narrator dragged the bodies to the galley. One of the killers was like Popeye in "The Big Shot," a small man called a hophead but expert with an automatic pistol. Two years later Faulkner would unsuccessfully offer the first segment for magazine sale; but after another similar interval, this kind of story would have a spectacular result for his career.

A different branch of the federal government from the one in the story had been showing a persistent interest in Faulkner. In November the Comptroller General of the United States had written Murry Falkner that his absent son owed the Post Office Department $38.25. In early March the Comptroller informed Faulkner that unless the matter was settled, they would have to collect from his bondsmen. Stone wrote to their congressman, who replied that the figure was correct: Faulkner had made errors in the money-order accounts. Once again Faulkner turned to Stone for a loan to settle the matter. Since he was almost completely out of funds, it was time for him to return to Oxford, from necessity if not preference.

Faulkner must have wondered if the reviews of *Soldier's Pay*, which had been appearing since early April, would have any effect on the appraisal of his novel in his hometown. The good review which Anderson had mentioned to Liveright had appeared in *The New York Times*. The book's form was experimental, said the anonymous reviewer, but it was written with "hard intelligence as well as consummate pity," and it showed "a sensuous regard for the feeling of life that is quite Hellenic." It was a book that ranked among great conceptions of war and man.[12] In *The Literary Review*, Thomas Boyd said it stood alone among novels of disillusioned veterans. In other newspapers and magazines, there were complaints about the soldierly language and the straining for effect, but *The Independent* called it "an extraordinary performance."[13] Nearer home the reviews were even better. In his *Times-Picayune* column, John McClure called it the "most noteworthy first novel of the year," and for the reviewer in the *Item*, it was "the best written novel about the war."[14] In May, when Stone asked Boni & Liveright about sales, he learned that 2,084 of the 2,500-copy edition had been sold by the middle of the month.[15] It would be late summer, probably, by the time Faulkner saw any royalties, but the figures were encouraging, and they must have provided an added incentive to write another novel.

He turned again to New Orleans materials when he began one he called *Mosquitoes*, salvaging a title once more. But rather than drawing on the gangster milieu, he turned to a very different one—the world of art, of fiction, poetry, and sculpture. A good deal of the emotional energy that went into the novel came from his feeling for Helen Baird. He also drew freely on his own work and on that of many of the writers he had been reading over the past several years. He would expand the sort of discussions of art he had written into *Elmer* and he would find a place for the Al Jackson stories. Once again he would pay tribute to T. S. Eliot, more explicitly than ever before. As he had been conspicuously indebted principally to one novelist in *Mayday*, so it appeared that he was here indebted to another. For Christmas of 1923 he had given Stone an inscribed copy of Aldous Huxley's *Antic Hay*. One of the novels Stone had bought from the Brick Row Book Store, which Faulkner apparently read, was Huxley's *Crome Yellow*. A number of critics would later identify resemblances between the latter and the book Faulkner now began. As one would put it, they both depict "a brief period in the lives of a disparate group of people—men and women, artists and non-artists, old and young—brought together by a wealthy lady who herself has only a surface interest in the arts." Within each group there are similar characters —such as skeptical men and bluestocking women—and topics of discussion to which the members of both parties continually return: according to the same critic, sex, words, freedom, war, and art and emotion.[16] Another student of Faulkner's fiction would see further resemblances to work by Huxley as well as the possibility that some of the aesthetic arguments in Lewisohn's *A Modern Book of Criticism* got into the novel.[17] Still another would see pervasive influence by James Joyce.[18]

Mosquitoes was the most self-consciously literary novel he would ever write. Like its predecessor, it was loaded with epigrams in the manner of Wilde, though here they were assigned to characters rather than the authorial voice.[19] The book's novelist character would remark, "you don't commit suicide when you are disappointed in love. You write a book."[20] Although this one was not two pages old before Faulkner was borrowing from *The Waste Land*, he borrowed first from himself. From "Don Giovanni" he had taken Herbie, who now became Ernest Talliaferro. Miss Steinbauer, the object of Herbie's designs, would reappear provided with the first name Genevieve, shortened to Jenny. As Morrison became the writer Dawson Fairchild, the character of the nameless irascible writer in the short story would provide a basis for the sculptor Gordon. Behind them stood elements of people Faulkner had known: Gertrude Stegbauer, Sherwood Anderson, and Bill Spratling. Talliaferro was cut from the same pattern as Prufrock: aging, worried about his attire and his thinning hair. He was excited by women but unsuccessful despite a self-regenerating faith in the ultimate success of stratagems of seduction that were mainly verbal. His character also suggested that of Januarius Jones and, in some details, seemed quite close to Elmer Hodge. At one point he mused, "it was unbearable to believe that he had never had the power to stir women. . . ." (346) If he resembled Faulkner in his bad luck at romance, he was even more of an anti-hero than Elmer, a hanger-on, a garrulous nuisance a little like the annoying mosquitoes which reappeared throughout the novel.

As Hemingway's Paris friends had played the game of identifying the models for characters in *The Sun Also Rises*, so Faulkner's New Orleans friends would be able to do the same with *Mosquitoes*. If Talliaferro's friend Mrs. Maurier, an affected and self-congratulatory devotee of the arts, suggested the wealthy Elizabeth Werlein to some, her eighteen-year-old niece, Patricia Robyn, owed a good deal to Helen Baird, as her brother, Theodore "Josh" Robyn, owed something to Josh Baird. As Faulkner had introduced his characters—in Gordon's studio, in a restaurant called Broussard's—before he assembled them on the yacht that would provide the equivalent of the Huxleyan house party, they all had something familiar about them. Poet Mark Frost, "a tall, ghostly young man" (34) who occasionally produced short, cerebral, and obscure poems, suggested Samuel Louis Gilmore, a veteran contributor to *The Double Dealer*. With him at Fairchild's restaurant table was a man named Julius, who in some ways resembled Julius Weis Friend. Intelligent and discriminating, the Julius in the book had a sharp and perceptive sister called Mrs. Eva Wiseman, who could have been modeled after Friend's sister, Lillian Friend Marcus. Later, aboard Mrs. Maurier's yacht the *Nausikaa*, Faulkner would introduce a painter named Dorothy Jameson. There would be two more recognizable characters, one more so than the other. Major Ayers, an eccentric Englishman, was modeled on Colonel Charles Glenn Collins, a Scot with an extraordinary career of adventure and misadventure who had been an amusing companion on many occasions for Faulkner's friends in the Vieux Carré. Jenny Steinbauer's boyfriend, Pete Ginotta, was a good deal like the young man Faulkner remembered from one of the families in the liquor business in New Orleans. Reading the novel later, Sam Gilmore would remember that Collins had been aboard the *Josephine* that day, a year earlier, when they had set out for Mandeville, only to encounter rain, engine trouble, and clouds of mosquitoes. So had Lillian Friend Marcus and those leading spirits in organizing the expedition that day, Sherwood and Elizabeth Anderson. If Dorothy Jameson owed something to pretty Virginia Parker Nagle, it was not surprising, for it had been she, Gilmore recalled, who had left the *Josephine* with Faulkner to go "skirmishing around at Mandeville" in spite of the mosquitoes. Faulkner was putting his own memories to productive use.

He was putting his feelings to use in his portrait of Pat Robyn. Talliaferro is conscious of "the clean young odor of her, like that of young trees." (21) If she was, thus, like one of Faulkner's nymphs become a dryad, she was linked with a figure at once more generic and more personal for him. Faulkner quickly juxtaposed her to Gordon—awkward, arrogant, withdrawn, and unhappy—more truly the archetypal artist than any of the group Mrs. Maurier was gathering together. In his studio, which suggested Spratling's, Pat saw herself in the figure he was carving. The omniscient narrator had prepared the reader: "you got again un-tarnished and high and clean that sense of swiftness, of space encompassed; but on looking again it was as before: motionless and passionately eternal —the virginal breastless torso of a girl, headless, armless, legless, in marble temporarily caught and hushed yet passionate still for escape. . . ." (11) It was Faulkner's own Winged Victory of Samothrace, the archetype which he would continue to regard as the highest kind of female beauty. Because of her, Gordon agrees to join the party. Her appeal is powerful despite her plainness, as manifested in the careless bangs of her short, dark, coarse hair. Many of her attributes in both appearance and manner would remind other Orleanians of Helen Baird.

Her lack of full sexual maturity had a corollary in her dismissal of the attentions of various men and her doglike devotion to her brother. At times it seems almost the mindless imitativeness and devotion of a younger brother for an older one, but the sexual component becomes clear when she warns the voluptuous Jenny away from him. It was a relationship that looked back to the seemingly sexless, passionate bond between Jo-Addie and Elmer and forward to much more complicated brother-sister rela-tionships to come. Once he had the party abroad the *Nausikaa*, Faulkner would explore her sexuality further in a curious two-page passage. In the darkness of the cabin, Pat lies in the same bunk with Jenny, who is sleep-ing nude. As Pat caresses Jenny's flank, Jenny sighs in her sleep, turns, kisses Pat on the mouth and seems softly to envelop her. But then Pat jerks her mouth away and spits. After an argument about who "started it," Pat tells Jenny that only "common people" kiss that way and agrees to show her how nice people kiss, only to be interrupted as Mrs. Wiseman enters the dark cabin and stands there "staring at them with a dark intent speculation."[21] The sequence suggests the experimentation of children rather than overt lesbian behavior. Pat's only overt heterosexual loveplay consists of a ritualistic nip on her brother's ear. In spite of all of this, she exerts a powerful attraction on Gordon, and before the trip is over she will come to obsess a young steward named David.

When he finished his "Prologue" section, Faulkner began "The First Day" as Pat boards the yacht with Jenny and Pete Ginotta. In the interminable conversations aboard the *Nausikaa* it was clear that Dawson Fairchild, from Indiana, was modeled on Sherwood Anderson, from Ohio. Genial and gentle, he has a "blobby benign face." (245) He was warmly drawn, the center of any group in which he appeared, ruminating, spec-ulating, retelling the Al Jackson stories. Mrs. Wiseman's brother, Julius, tells her, "His writing seems fumbling, not because life is unclear to him, but because of his innate humorless belief that, though it bewilder him at times, life at bottom is sound and admirable and fine. . . ." (242) While the passengers occupy themselves with food and drink, with diversions such as swimming and cardplaying, Josh Robyn works assiduously at making a pipe (just as Josh Baird once did), finally borrowing a rod from the ship's steering mechanism in order to heat it and bore apertures in the pipe. As a result, by the morning of the voyage's second day, the *Nausikaa* has run aground. By evening, Pat has spent the interlude in the bunk with Jenny and then, at midnight, slipped out for a swim with David West, a steward aboard the yacht. Although he was tall, with a striking body, he had characteristics that suggested his creator. One was his name, which Faulkner used at times for characters who had certain affinities with himself. Another was that "he had done a little of everything and had just completed a voyage as messman on a freighter"[22] before Dawson Fairchild had befriended him in Jackson Park and persuaded Mrs. Maurier to hire him. Like Faulkner, he had lain above Lake Maggiore gazing at the boats far below and at the Alps above. And his feeling for Pat would in the end be as unrequited as Faulkner's thus far had been for Helen Baird.

It may have been about this time that Faulkner, perhaps feeling as immobilized by his lack of money as the *Nausikaa* was by malfunctioning steering gear, discussed the problem with Stone. The upshot was a letter from Faulkner to Horace Liveright asking for a $50 advance on the new novel. Stone's biographer suggests that he dictated most of it, in part because it praised the new work at the expense of *Soldiers' Pay*. "Just now I am stuck in the middle of this new novel," the letter continued, "and can't seem to go any further. I think I need a change of surroundings but have no money hence the request above."[23]

WHETHER or not Liveright complied, Faulkner could still savor a change of scenery through the hospitality of Jack and Myrtle Stone. Five-year-old William Evans Stone V was always pleased to see his uncle Phil's Model-T Ford pull up in front of his home in Charleston. He knew that while his uncle and his father talked business, Mister Bill, when he was not playing golf on the local links, would tell stories to him and his sisters. And Faulkner was apparently still as welcome among the adults as among the children. So it was natural that when the Stones prepared for the summer stay in Pascagoula, they should invite him to spend some time with them again. He was glad to accept the invitation. If he was stuck in the middle of the new novel, the working conditions on the coast would be conducive to his finishing it. There was another project too. He had started meticulously lettering the sonnet sequence he would bind for Helen Baird. She must have been in his thoughts with every manuscript page that set forth David's abject love for Pat. He would take the manuscript and the sonnets with him.

CHAPTER

22

"He was a white man, except he was awful sunburned and kind of shabby dressed—no necktie and hat. . . . He said he was a liar by profession, and he made good money at it, enough to own a Ford as soon as he got it paid out. I think he was crazy. Not dangerous: just crazy."

. . . "What was his name? Did he tell you?"

"Yes. . . . Wait. . . . Oh, yes: I remember—Faulkner, that was it."

"A book is the writer's secret life, the dark twin of a man: you can't reconcile them."

—*Mosquitoes* (145, 251)

IN the summer of 1926 the accommodations were considerably better than they had been the previous year at The Camp. Frank Lewis, Myrtle Stone's father, had taken the Baird house with a view to buying it. It was set back a hundred feet on a 110-by-500-foot lot, the front yard shaded by live oaks and oleanders, and the back thick with tall grass. Faulkner's room in the big two-story house was furnished with the essentials: a day bed, a chair, and a table for his typewriter. There was plenty of time for swimming and for telling the Stone children stories. One photograph shows him with clear-eyed little Rosebud, leaning close to her, protectively. In his working hours he continued with his ongoing story.

IN *Mosquitoes*, David West is as vulnerable to Pat Robyn as Faulkner was to Helen. The third day of the *Nausikaa*'s voyage proves an unmitigated disaster for the pair as the expedition Pat has planned bogs them down in seemingly unending swamps where they are tortured by mosquitoes and thirst. David carries Pat and cares for her, looking at her with "dumb yearning eyes." (171) After they make their eventual excruciating return, she to her part of the yacht, he to his, Dawson Fairchild sees David sitting on a coiled rope in the moonlight, holding something in his hands. When Fairchild comes nearer, he sees that it is "a slipper, a single slipper. . . ." (235) It was not the last time that Faulkner would use a slipper as a symbol of loveliness and of love bereft of hope. Now, as the summer sun rode high in the skies above Pascagoula's flat coastal plain, Faulkner had but to describe the voyage's last day and take his characters home to New Orleans.

When the fourth and final day of the voyage begins, David leaves. Consistent as the motif of the mosquitoes is that of the endless talk, droning on like the insects themselves. In a review of John Cowper Powys' novel *Ducdame*, for the *Times-Picayune* fifteen months earlier, Faulkner had written, "To gather fools into a circle: God has already done that . . . you do it at your own risk."[1] He had done it here, and Gordon thinks "Talk, talk, talk: the utter and heartbreaking stupidity of words." (186) Faulkner might have talked about literature and aesthetics with Stone and Wasson and Anderson, but more and more, as he grew older, he would agree with Gordon.

Faulkner shaped the "Epilogue" to match the "Prologue" as the yachting party disperses. He saved one fillip for the end. With the artist's powers of divination, Gordon has done a clay head of Mrs. Maurier that reveals essentials of her character. Faulkner briefly interpolated the story of her life, including an unhappy marriage to a man who sought respectability rather than love. For the source of his wealth, Faulkner used the legend of Katrina Carter's grandfather, who was supposed to have acquired a hundred thousand dollars in uncut Federal notes near the war's end. As Faulkner had borrowed from Eliot, Conrad, Aldous Huxley, and others earlier, he used something of Joyce in the next-to-last section. In impressionistic prose he followed Gordon, Fairchild, and Julius into the redlight district with something of the *Walpurgisnacht* effect of Joyce's "Circe" chapter in *Ulysses*. He split the unused, slightly rewritten "Don Giovanni" neatly in two, half of it early in the "Epilogue," the other half to bring the story to a close, so that finally, with Talliaferro's misfortunes the despair of both Fairchild and the writer who lives below him, Faulkner borrowed word-for-word from the short-story's ending with the telephone operator's jibe to Talliaferro: "You tell 'em, big boy; treat 'em rough." (349)

There were private references that few would understand—to the A.E.F. and Canadians—and some that would have been most meaningful for Helen Baird. There was one phrase that occurred twice in Gordon's stream of consciousness: "your name is like a little golden bell hung in my heart." (267–268) Faulkner had taken this from one with whom he could empathize, an unsuccessful large-nosed lover like himself: Cyrano de Bergerac, in the play of that same name by Edmond Rostand. One evening in August, the month in which the book's action was set, Faulkner wrote to Helen Baird, imploring her to return to Pascagoula from North Carolina. The illegibility showed that he had been drinking, but the sentiments were clear. "Helen," he wrote, "your name is a little golden bell hung in my heart. . . ." He told her about visiting her aunt, Mrs. Martin (to whom he could confide that he wanted to marry Helen), and about his work on the novel, chapters of it written in her front yard. "Your book is pretty near done," he told her. "I have made you another book," he went on. "It's sonnets I made you, all bound. . . . you must come back. . . ."[2] It was *Helen: A Courtship*, imprinted "SINGLE MANU-SCRIPT IMPRESSION / OXFORD — MISSISSIPPI — June 26."[3] But he never mailed the outspokenly erotic letter. It was written on the back of page 269 of the typescript of *Mosquitoes*. Each of the small lines in black ink was crossed out. Perhaps it was the morning after when, for whatever reason, he decided that the page belonged in his typescript and not in the mail.

He completed his 464-page typescript of *Mosquitoes* and dated it "Pascagoula, Miss / 1 Sept 1926." Then he made changes, corrections, and additions in his minuscule pen strokes. During the same week his mother and Dean visited him there. Soon the Stones would be returning to Charleston, and it was time for him to go too. Back in Oxford, tanned and barefoot, still wearing the white trousers, he looked to some of his friends like a beachcomber. He gave the typescript to Phil Stone, who added punctuation and corrections and passed it on to Sallie Simpson in his office for final typing. Faulkner added the last touches and sent the parcel off to Boni & Liveright.

Before the last weekend in September he was back in New Orleans, where he told an interviewer for the *Item* that he had returned to the Vieux Carré to plan his work for the winter. "He told of a summer spent working in a lumber mill," ran the account, "until a finger was injured, and then on the fishing boats of the Mississippi coast. At nights, after working hours, he wrote his new book."[4] His love life may have flagged, but not his imagination. He was going back to Oxford for a brief visit, the interviewer concluded, and then he would return at the end of September to spend the winter in the city.

WHEN Estelle Franklin returned home with her children that spring, her family had teased her about shuttling back and forth, calling her a commuter. But Lida Oldham must have known that things were not going well in Estelle's Shanghai household. In early July, Estelle had gone with the children to Monteagle, Tennessee, for the summer. When they returned, Major Oldham took her to pay a visit to Bob Farley in his law office. This was a delicate matter, and one of the reasons for their going to Bob was that he was a friend. Cornell had even offered him a job one summer to go out to Shanghai and work in his office. But now Cornell was thinking about divorce, about Estelle's obtaining one there in Mississippi. The problem was that this would create a scandal, for the only grounds on which it could be granted were those of adultery. It would be far better for the proceedings to take place in the International Mixed Court of Shanghai, where, after provision for the children and division of property, it could probably be done quite simply in the judge's chambers. But it would still be wise to avoid precipitate action. After further consultation with Cornell, it was agreed that Estelle should go back to Shanghai. She would stay there briefly and then go to Honolulu for what she thought of as a "probationary" period. After that, if she and Cornell felt there was no way to save their marriage, the final papers could be filed and the long legal process set in motion.

How had they come to this pass? The two had been strongly attracted to each other: the striking girl and the handsome man. They had gratified both parents with their marriage, even though the uncertain bride had greeted her wedding day in tears. They had followed the pattern for their time and class: the full formal wedding, followed in due course by the arrival of the children and the ascending career. Cornell was the able, affable, driving man of affairs; Estelle, the winsome, talented, graceful young woman who charmed everyone. Each was attracted to members of the opposite sex. Sallie Murry Wilkins said that Cornell had an affair with the wife of a naval officer. (The wife of the Dean of the College of Liberal Arts at the University of Mississippi said that the trouble with Sallie Murry was that "she always tells the truth.") One of Estelle's special friends was a Navy captain in Shanghai. Many years later she would say, "While Cornell had his lovers in China, you don't think I was sitting at home, do you?"

Qualities enchanting in courtship could be difficult in marriage. Estelle had been trained to be, had been expected to be, charming and popular. She had said what came to mind, what was easiest, even if it might cause complications later. For Cornell, with his lawyer's mind, this was a foreign form of discourse and action. Bill and Estelle's friend Ella Somerville had heard one of the effects of this. "Mother," Cornell complained to Mrs. Hairston, "if you could only tell when she's telling the truth. She lies all the time." There were other potential sources of conflict. Cornell gambled at cards and Estelle played mah-jongg for high stakes. The Oldhams had given her every advantage they could, and now, with Cornell's practice prospering even though he no longer held a judgeship, she could enjoy an even more comfortable standard of living. And she did enjoy it. "I love fine things," she would say. It was a fast life in a fast set, with frequent large dinner parties and much drinking. She and Cornell drank along with the rest. When Estelle realized that their difficulties were growing more serious, the emotional impact was apparently severe. The daughter of one of her friends would recall seeing Estelle shortly after an arrival back in Mississippi, with bandages on both wrists. If they were the marks of a suicide attempt, it was not the last time that Estelle would make such a gesture. So now she had her probationary period to go through. Fortunately, she had the support of her family and her mother-in-law. She would always love Mrs. Hairston, who would prove herself a remarkable woman through the vicissitudes to come.

And of course there was Bill. Ben Wasson might feel that Helen Baird was the love of his friend's life, but Jack Falkner felt that it was always Estelle. She could not know about *Mayday* and *Helen: A Courtship*, but she had *Vision in Spring* and all the other poems he had given her over the years. It was probably in late October, one scholar speculates, that he bound "a small, handsome pamphlet" containing "heavily revised and polished texts of 11 of the 12 sketches he had published in the January-February issue of *The Double Dealer* under the collective title 'New Orleans.'" He called it *Royal Street: New Orleans* and inscribed it "To Estelle, a / Lady, with / Respectful Admiration: / This." It was dated October 29. He had omitted "The Tourist," the final sketch of the original *Double Dealer* sequence, and substituted for it a new one called "Hong Li," which conformed to the others as "The Tourist" had not done, for it was also a brief monologue. In three paragraphs Hong Li talked of misfortune and bereavement, speaking of the wise husbandman who "destroys the seed of tares," adding, "so do I root out and destroy the tares which her dead and delicate feet sowed across my heart. . . ." But in the final one-line paragraph, emotion destroyed all his philosophy: "But Ehee, Ehee, her little feet."[5] If this line hearkened back to "A Dead Dancer" and one version of a song for *The Marionettes*,[6] the Oriental ambience of the piece would have had a very contemporary ring for Estelle. And as he had told stories to Myrtle Stone's children, so he had to hers. A few months hence, when he made yet another gift book—this time for Estelle's daughter, Victoria—his text would describe the little protagonist's mother: "beautiful, so slim and tall, with her grave unhapy eyes changeable as seawater and her slender hands. . . ."[7] Even if Estelle felt or hoped that at the end of the probationary period she might return with Victoria and Malcolm to their father and the glittering life in Shanghai, it must have been comforting to know that Bill was still there, in Oxford or New Orleans (regardless of Helen Baird in Pascagoula or Tennessee), still giving part of his love to her.

23

First, let me tell you something about our Quarter, the Vieux Carre. Do you know our quarter, with its narrow streets, its old wrought-iron balconies and its southern European atmosphere? An atmosphere of richness and soft laughter, you know.

—*Sherwood Anderson & Other Famous Creoles* (25)

FAULKNER had moved back into the attic apartment with Bill Spratling. Little had changed apart from the fact that Sherwood Anderson—now at his farm in Virginia and soon to leave for Europe—no longer occupied the same place in their lives. The Quarter was as lively as ever, with parties four or five nights a week and everyone talking, smoking, and dipping drinks out of whatever bowl the host put out. Some would buy a six-dollar bottle of Pernod from the Swiss who made it in the Quarter. They would pour it into a pitcher of crushed ice and add a little water. Spratling and Faulkner would make their own gin, using gallon cans of alcohol. They would put it in a barrel and roll it across the floor to aerate it, until the tenants below complained.

At one of Lillian Friend Marcus' parties, Faulkner saw Margery Gumbel. "I want to talk to you," he said. After they walked out onto a screened porch he told her that he had fallen in love with a girl named Helen. He described the way they had sat on the beach together. He talked on and on about her before they finally drifted back inside to the party. He showed a different face to Marc and Lucille Antony, who owned the building he lived in. At dinner one evening he was very amusing, telling them about a woman in Oxford he was going to marry—with the agreement that she would adopt all his illegitimate children. Dinner on another evening was most unusual: Faulkner invited Margery and Irving Gumbel, Lillian Friend Marcus, and Julius and Elise Friend to elegant Galatoire's for a celebration. Liveright had accepted *Mosquitoes* and sent him a check for an advance against royalties. He had needed to borrow a coat to go to dinner with the Antonys, and he did it again now, but he was a gracious host to the group, which included two guests who had served as models for characters in the novel which was going to pay the check.

His imagination was now busy with characters of a much different kind, and they peopled not just one story but two. One began in town, but then, in an extended flashback, dealt with Mississippi hill folk from the early yeoman stock, and with the new breed of unscrupulous tenant farmers who had appeared in the decades after the war. The other story was set principally in town and focused on the established class, but as the novel developed, elements of the two classes of country people would also appear. The county seat was the same for both stories: Jefferson. As Faulkner moved further into them he found it a process of discovery as well as invention. Long afterward he would say, "I discovered that my own little postage stamp of native soil was worth writing about and that I would never live long enough to exhaust it, and that by sublimating the actual into the apocryphal I would have complete liberty to use whatever talent I might have to its absolute top. It opened up a gold mine of other people. . . ."[1] Sherwood Anderson had been right.

Shortly before meeting Faulkner, Anderson had begun and then abandoned a biography of Lincoln, called *Father Abraham*. If Faulkner appropriated the title, this was the only borrowing. Faulkner was thinking not of Lincoln but of his namesake, the patriarch who led his people into the Land of Canaan, where they prospered greatly. The clan which Flem Snopes led displayed his own traits: cunning, rapacity, and utter amorality. The story began with Flem gazing from behind the plate-glass window of the Jefferson bank, whose presidency marked the pinnacle of his forty-five-year career. Then a long flashback showed Flem at its beginnings. A squat, shapeless man with unblinking eyes the color of stagnant water, a tobacco-stained mouth and steadily ruminant jaw, he was a part of the phenomenon in which poor whites had flocked to Vardaman, Bilbo, and Russell and put them in power. Lawyers like the Stones and the Falkners knew them well. As early as "The Big Shot," Faulkner had seen their possibilities for fiction, and he had borrowed some of Flem Snopes's attributes from Dal Martin. Now he had in mind a novel about them. Phil Stone would later say he had given Faulkner the idea for it, that "the real revolution in the South was not the race situation but the rise of the redneck, who did not have any of the scruples of the old aristocracy, to places of power and wealth."[2]

He set the story southeast of Jefferson "in the hill cradled cane and cypress jungles of Yocona River. . . ." The settlement of Frenchman's Bend was located in about the same relation to Jefferson as were the hamlets of Yocona and Tula to Oxford, ten and twelve miles away, respectively, lying a few miles northeast of Dallas, the birthplace of Lee M. Russell. (Not far from Yocona was an even smaller settlement called Dutch Bend or Dutchman's Bend—also two businesses: Varner's Store and Ratliff's Grocery.) The ruined grandeur of the forgotten Frenchman's mansion stands in contrast to the undistinguished affluence of Uncle Billy Varner—rich from monopoly, moneylending, and politics—and the monomaniacal drive toward wealth of Flem Snopes. Flem has risen from Varner's store clerk to son-in-law by marrying the pregnant Eula, a figure toward which Emmy, Myrtle, and Jenny had been tending: "a softly ample girl with eyes like cloudy hothouse grapes and a mouth always slightly open. . . ." (16)

As he had brought in kinsmen to batten on the descendants of the old Scotch-Irish settlers, so Flem took advantage of his honeymoon trip to Texas to return with a gaudy herd of varicolored ponies, beasts so wild that Buck, the Texan who herds them, needs a barbed-wire hackamore to secure them to the wagon. Alternating richly comic hyperbole and droll understatement, Faulkner described the way the ensuing horse auction victimizes the bargain-prone and gullible men of Frenchman's Bend and further enriches Snopes. He was now embellishing whatever he and his uncle John had seen from that boardinghouse veranda in Calhoun County four years before. Under the minute strokes of his pen the Snopeses proliferated. With 14,000 words already written, he began Section II with a favorite image: twilight. Henry Armstid and Vernon Turpin are convalescing from injuries inflicted by the horses as Turpin prepares to sue Flem. One new character was V. K. Suratt, whom he first called a "patent medicine drummer" before changing him to a sewing-machine agent. Shrewd, affable, and voluble, he seems the only man other than Uncle Billy Varner who might fathom some of Flem's designs.

On page 25, Faulkner made several false starts and deletions before stopping in mid-sentence halfway down the legal-size sheet. It had, however, been an extremely fruitful project. The material demanded realistic treatment, but in the rich texture of his prose, as he wrote about dawn-wet grass and moon-blanched dust, he was also drawing on the pastoral lyricism he loved, using it for counterpoint to enhance the realism, dialect, and humor. In Faulkner's career thus far, one critic would declare, he had written "nothing more ambitious or more successful."[3] A sketch on the back of page 8 is highly emblematic. It shows two lambs gamboling with two rocking-horse lambs, dancing to music piped by a seated faun. His profile is quite distinctly like William Faulkner's. It is a drawing such as he might have made to amuse Cho-Cho or Malcolm. But at the same time it suggests a verbal music employing a new kind of pastoral which would henceforth distinguish much of his work.

It was probably late 1926 or early 1927 when he turned from *Father Abraham* to another manuscript on which he had also been making progress. He would call it *Flags in the Dust*, and in it he was giving rein to his romantic imagination. That summer the *Eagle* had reprinted an article from *The Southern Sentinel* captioned "Dreams of Col. Falkner are

Real."[4] His railroad was now a part of Gulf, Mobile & Northern. Thirty pages into his manuscript Faulkner wrote, "now the railway belonged to a syndicate and there were more than two trains on it that ran from Lake Michigan to the Gulf of Mexico, completing his dream, while John Sartoris slept among martial cherubim. . . ."[5] Two years later, in a highly rhetorical and sometimes illegible sheet and a half of manuscript, he wrote, "having known twice before the agony of ink, nothing served but that I try by main strength to recreate between the covers of a book the world as I was already preparing to lose and regret, feeling, with the morbidity of the young, that I was not only on the verge of decrepitude, but that growing old was to be an experience peculiar to myself alone out of all the teeming world. . . . So I began to write, without much purpose, until I realised that to make it truly evocative it must be personal. . . . So I got some people, some I invented, others I created out of tales I learned of nigger cooks and stable boys of all ages. . . . Created, I say, because they are composed partly from what they were in actual life and partly from what they should have been and were not: thus I improved on God, who, dramatic though He be, has no sense, no feeling for, theatre."[6]

Although this novel was also set in Jefferson, its action traveled far beyond the borders of what Faulkner called Yocona County. It would be a far longer and fuller manuscript than those of *Soldiers' Pay* and *Mosquitoes*. It would be more complicated too, at every stage of composition and production. Like other Faulkner works, it may have begun as a short story, for very early in its composition Faulkner would introduce passages which may well have had an earlier, unitary, life of their own. In the manuscript Faulkner would preserve, page 1 began with old Bayard Sartoris musing in the attic over relics untouched for twenty years: the family Bible, a Toledo blade, Mechlin lace, two pipes, and a cavalry saber. His train of recollection would provide background for the present action, set just after the First World War. Meditating on the family's hereditary affinity for lost causes and fatal violence, the old man contemplated a line whose exploits went back to Agincourt. As early as the second page of his manuscript Faulkner introduced another generation of Sartorises, who, like their forebears, were named Bayard and John. The former had fallen at Manassas, whereas his brother had survived both the Mexican War and the War Between the States. To their widowed sister, Virginia Du Pre, Bayard had become, over the years, not only a brave cavalryman killed in "a prank of . . . heedless and reckless boys wild with their own youth" but the apotheosis of wild gallantry, an angel "valiantly and glamorously fallen and strayed. . . ."[7] After the Civil War the widower John Sartoris had married a girl who had ridden with his partisan troop. He had restored the land, built his railroad, killed carpetbaggers, disfranchised Negroes, and won a seat in the legislature. Tired of killing, he had fatalistically accepted the idea of death at the hands of his erstwhile partner turned bitter rival. By the time this death was accomplished, Faulkner was nineteen pages into the manuscript. As omniscient narrator, he had related all of this through old Bayard's memories and come up to the present generation: John Sartoris' grandsons: Bayard and Evelyn John, pursuit pilots in the Great War.

It may have been at this point that Faulkner went back to the beginning and added seven pages to precede page 1. (Numbered 01 to 06, with page 02 followed by pages 002 and 003, they could have been part of an earlier short story.)[8] Describing their exploits in France, he filled in their background as he concentrated on John's fatal recklessness in combat. (Like American Ace Raoul Lufbery, he leaped to his death from his burning plane.) This brother had antecedents in Donald Mahon and Josh Robyn, a brash, self-centered, and ruthless young man who was fascinating to his creator. With these twenty-six pages Faulkner had worked out in some detail the background of another saga antithetical to that of the Snopeses. He had set up the two poles in the social structure of this fictional county. As one critic would later remark, he was also working "from the two poles of history, the Civil War and World War I, dramatized respectively in the old Colonel and the young Bayard. . . ." And he had probably come to see something else, "that the center of his story would be not the death of John (Evelyn) but Bayard's reaction to John's death and that the locale would be Mississippi."[9]

Before he went home for Christmas he became involved in another project. It was a collection of sketches Spratling had made of people in the Quarter. Faulkner's 500-word Foreword to *Sherwood Anderson & Other Famous Creoles* was signed "W. F.," but it was an unmistakable parody of the style and some of the views of Anderson. The writer began with praise of the Quarter and a declaration of the kinship he felt with its artists. He had felt a fellowship on first meeting Spratling, but at their next encounter, wrote W. F., in sentences that may have had a certain ring for Anderson, "I had a kind of vision. I saw myself being let in for something. I saw myself incurring an obligation which I should later regret. . . ." He agreed, however, to serve as "a wheelhorse." On the facing page was a sketch of a large-headed, small-bodied man in garish clothes. Beside his chair was a book entitled *Tar* and below the caricature was the legend "Mister Sherwood Anderson."[10] Subjects of the forty-one sketches included Roark Bradford, John McClure, Lillian Marcus, and, in the last one, the two collaborators. On the wall hung an air rifle (sometimes used in a game of pot shots at passers-by in the streets below) and the legend "Viva Art." Below Faulkner's chair were three jugs.

In December they paid the Pelican Press to print 400 copies and sold them all in a week at a dollar and a half each. Spratling liked the Foreword, which seemed to him "a more subtle and sweeter parody on Anderson's writing style than was *The Torrents of Spring* where Hemingway permitted himself to sneer at Sherwood, a friend who had helped him to find a publisher. Faulkner's analysis was warm and delicate, as was his nature." His pleasure was short-lived, though, for Anderson was much more vulnerable, seven months after Hemingway's destructively intended parody, than Spratling had realized. When he saw Anderson, "Sherwood said he didn't think it was very funny. . . ."[11] Spratling had not found him angry, but he was hurt, Faulkner thought, and he later referred to his collaboration with Spratling as "the unhappy caricature affair." Neither he nor Hemingway "could have touched, ridiculed, his work itself," Faulkner said. "But we had made his style look ridiculous; and . . . he too must have known by then in his heart that there was nothing else left."[12] For those in the Quarter who were "hipped" on Freud, there could scarcely have been a more graphic example of the son asserting his freedom by slaying the father. In any event, the regret the collaborators felt was not sufficient to prevent them from obtaining a second printing of 150 more copies in January.

IT was a family Christmas that year in Oxford, with Cecile and Jack Falkner home from Atlanta, Jack's current FBI assignment. They fell back easily into their old habits, identifying planets in the night sky and sharing a drink together, when Bill might begin to sing his favorite song, "Yes, Sir, That's My Baby." Johncy, now an Ole Miss graduate serving as city engineer, was doing well. His son, Jimmy, received the kind of attention and petting that had always been Dean's portion. Dean was still his father's favorite, sharing his love of sports, horses, and railroads and disdaining formal education even though he was now a freshman at Ole Miss. Bill's relationship to him remained paternal as well fraternal, just as when he had been his scoutmaster. He wrote him amusing letters from New Orleans and made up vocabulary lists for him. As far as academics went, Dean's bent was toward drawing and writing. Bill told him that he could do sketches for his books. He also made corrections on some of his short stories. But the out-of-doors was Dean's great love. He was an expert marksman and hunter who never carried a watch because he told time by the sun. An intense competitor who had to be tactfully dissuaded from football because the coach did not think his five-foot eight-inch 125-pound frame could survive the college game, he would go on to excel as an outfielder. Blessed with an open, sunny disposition, he went on his own way. "Dean never met a stranger," one friend would say. Apparently his oldest brother was looking ahead, however, concerned, if not worried, about what this boy would do later, when he was no longer in the protected situation of the teenager whose father once shouted to him that he could have his car if he scored the winning run and then, seconds later, waited to hand him the keys when he crossed the plate after hitting a homer.

It would not have been surprising if Dean's intensity reminded his brother of John and Bayard Sartoris. If he had followed his standard practice, he had brought his manuscript home with him, and even if he gave himself a holiday from his usual intensive labor on a novel, he surely talked about the Sartorises with Phil Stone just as the two shared their amusement at the Snopeses and their prototypes. The Sartorises were outrageous in another way, and it was no accident that Bayard Sartoris, a foolhardy apotheosis of Southern chivalry fed on the romanticism of Sir Walter Scott, should also bear the name of the legendary Bayard, "Chevalier sans peur et sans reproche." Stone would later say, "I invented more of *Sartoris* than I did any of the other books."[13] Models, however, abounded in Oxford. Young Dr. Alford, who advised excising a wen on old Bayard's cheek, would remind some readers of young Dr. Ashford Little. Dr. Lucius Quintus Peabody, one of the oldest settlers, who advised against it, would remind others of Dr. A. A. Young, Stark Young's father. In the family they would later say there was no mistaking Grandfather as the model for old Bayard and Auntee as the original of Aunt Jenny. It was natural for Faulkner to use them. Character came out of family, he told Stone. Environment was important too, he granted, but it was mostly a matter of genetics. "You do the best you can," he said. He also used what would later be called the South's concept of the "extended family," for Simon, old Bayard's coachman, owed something to Ned Barnett, and his last name, Strother, was the same as that of another family of Falkner servants.

There was another family in Oxford that concerned him that January of 1927. Estelle had returned with Cho-Cho and Malcolm. The probationary period had been completed. When Estelle had first gone to see Bob Farley she had given him for his file two letters Cornell had written her. Farley would remember them as being gentle and warm. In spite of this continuing amicability the possibility of a reconciliation had failed, and Estelle had embarked for home as soon as the depositions were taken and the divorce papers filed. If all went without delay or hindrance, the decree would be granted and final in two years. Faulkner did what he could to help her in this difficult time. When he wrote Horace Liveright in February he told him about "a mss. by one who has no literary yearnings whatever and who did this just to pass the time. Some one is to see it, and it might as well be you, so I have persuaded the author to give you first shot at it. I think it is pretty fair."[14] It was a novel Estelle had written, called *White Beeches*. After Faulkner typed it, the manuscript went to Scribner's rather than Boni & Liveright. When it was returned, Estelle angrily burned it. Faulkner in turn was furious—with her, for destroying it after one rejection.

Early that same month he had taken another book to the Oldham house. It was for Cho-Cho, and it was another of his handmade volumes, typed rather than printed, and bound in varicolored paper. He dated it February 5, and four days later he gave it to her, inscribed "For his

dear friend / Victoria / on her eighth birthday / Bill he made / this Book."
His storytelling was one of the chief attractions at the birthday party.
Cho-Cho's first memories of Billy were bound up with his storytelling.
He would buy a five-cent box of vanilla wafers, and as they scrupulously
shared them on a walk in the woods, he would tell her about fairies and
other creatures who lived there. Out of this had come the gift he had
carried to the party that day. *The Wishing Tree* was a 47-page account
of the birthday of a little girl named Dulcie, who waked to see a strange
red-headed boy named Maurice standing by her bed. He quickly organizes
an expedition for her: her brother, Dicky; their maid, Alice; and George,
the boy who lives across the street. Seeking The Wishing Tree, they
find a castle and observe Maurice's magic at work. Like Lewis Carroll's
Alice, they are in peril for a short time when they shrink in size. Finally
arriving at what they think to be The Wishing Tree, they find it is "a
tall old man with a long shining beard like silver," covered with "birds
of all colors and kinds." The omniscient narrator calls him "the good
Saint Francis." The mellomax tree they had discovered earlier was
really The Wishing Tree. If they will give him the leaves they
plucked, he will replace them and give them each a bird instead. They
step through a river, and Dulcie wakes to find a caged bluebird her first
present of the day. It ended with a suitable moral: "if you are kind to
helpless things, you don't need a Wishing Tree to make things come
true."[15] It was the kind of tale they loved to hear Billy tell. It was also
another manifestation of his prodigious genius that could contrive a
novella out of pleasure and generosity, a tale for a child which also showed
clear links with the work he had written for adults in *Mayday, Mosquitoes, Father Abraham,* and *Flags in the Dust.*

   The Wishing Tree is the story in which Faulkner describes, on the
next to last page, the beautiful mother with the "grave unhappy eyes
changeable as seawater."[16] His own dominant emotional state seems often
to have been one of melancholy in these days. He dated one sonnet "14
March 1927" (ten days after Helen Baird's marriage to Guy C. Lyman).
It was called "Admonishes His Heart." He began with the words "Be
Still, my heart, be still," and ended with the line "Why did I wake?
When shall I sleep again?"[17] He was borrowing again from *A Shropshire
Lad*, from poem XLVIII, one of Housman's darkest. Though this was
one of Faulkner's favorite poems, his own sonnet—typed out in these
last days of winter during a brief break from his novel—must have been
something more than just an admiring gesture or a literary exercise.

   Composing a section in longhand, typing it, then beginning a new section, Faulkner was elaborating the plot of *Flags in the Dust* and thicken-
ing its texture through contrast between generations and classes. As
Colonel Sartoris represented a vanished order, so his son, old Bayard,
symbolizes one that is vanishing. Contrasted with his wild grandson,

young Bayard, racing about the countryside in his dangerous and symbolic roadster, old Bayard is as archaic as the buggy driven by old Simon. That the line shall not die is one of the overriding concerns of Aunt Jenny. To this end she subtly encourages Narcissa Benbow to think of young Bayard. At this point Faulkner reached back into what he would later call his "lumber-room" for additional characters. One is Byron Snopes, the bookkeeper at old Bayard's bank and author of obscene, anonymous letters to Narcissa.

Faulkner had models all around him. V. K. Suratt, the sewing-machine agent whom he had left in his buckboard on the last page of *Father Abraham*, reappeared. Maud Falkner thought she recognized his original immediately. "We had a June Suratt here," she told one visitor, "who sold sewing machines in Lafayette County from about 1910 to 1925. He lived in a little house just off the Square. On the bed of his wagon he had a little doghouse painted to look like a sewing machine as advertising. We used to see his wagon whenever he was in town. Billy used him in quite a few of his early stories."[18] More than one Lafayette County resident shared some of the characteristics of old Will Falls, who had served in the war under John Sartoris, and the salve Will uses to cure old Bayard's wen has the same properties as that passed down to Oxford resident Buck Collins. As to young Bayard's reckless driving, Murry Falkner used to race the train in from Harrykin Creek in his red Buick until one day he hit the bridge on the home stretch and Miss Maud made him stop.

Faulkner did make a deliberate attempt, however, to avoid the direct equation of the two milieus. Jefferson, he wrote, was twenty-five miles from Oxford. When he wrote that Belle Mitchell's house was located on "the most beautiful lot in Oxford," he immediately crossed out "Oxford" and substituted "Jefferson." A scholar born and raised there would conclude, "Faulkner habitually thinks of his characters as moving about Oxford and Lafayette County, and . . . he often uses the local scene effectively and accurately, though he never bows to it pedantically or slavishly."[19]

Bayard Sartoris' wildness was like that in the Old Colonel, who had killed two men; in his son Henry, who allegedly had killed and been shot to death like his father; in the Young Colonel, who had wanted to shoot his father's assailant and tried to shoot his son's; and in Murry Falkner, survivor of both pistol and shotgun wounds. William Faulkner had not shown these tendencies, perhaps because of his Butler genes. After some uncertainty he introduced a foil for Bayard. The character of Horace Benbow embodies a different set of traits, some clearly closer to Faulkner's own. A devotee of Keats, a dreamer referred to as "a poet," Horace has come home from Y.M.C.A. work in the war with a glass-blowing set on which, after four failures, he has produced "one almost perfect vase of clear amber," to which he applies the same phrase he used for his sister: "Thou still unravished bride of quietness."[20] He is glad that Narcissa, like the figure on Keats's Grecian urn, has consummated no marriage, and their relationship suggests the vaguely incestuous intimations between Jo-Addie and Elmer and Pat and Josh.

These two would turn to others, however—Narcissa to Bayard and Horace to Belle Mitchell, whose heavy sexuality is like Eula's but without its adolescent freshness. A lawyer who is a talker rather than a doer, Horace displays a "taut and delicate futility." (171) Two close friends of Faulkner's were lawyers. If Phil Stone seemed a volatile talker rather than a doer, Ben Wasson also differed from the stereotype of the small-town lawyer. Ben would later be asked, "Are you the original of Horace Benbow?" and he would answer with a smile, "I'm afraid so." Ben would remember the Oldhams' hospitality on Estelle Franklin's visits from the Far East. It seemed to him "constant open house," with tea and tennis and drinks served by Nyt Sung, Estelle's children's amah. Estelle helped entertain, often at the piano. Late one afternoon Ben stood behind her, turning the sheet-music pages. When at last she rose, they spontaneously embraced and kissed. Then Ben saw that Cho-Cho had entered the room, and he left in confusion. Apprehensive about gossip, he told Faulkner what had happened. After a silence his friend said, "Watch out, and remember, Bud, that Eve wasn't the only woman who handed out an apple, just the first one." Later, when Ben would read the scene in which Horace and Belle, embracing in the music room, were interrupted by Little Belle, he would experience a distinct sense of *déjà vu*.[21]

FAULKNER wrote on into the spring, and it seemed a promising one for him professionally. (He would soon make his first appearance in *Who's Who in America*.) His new manuscript was growing steadily and *Mosquitoes* was due to be published in late April or early May. A critic would later write that "One theme of *Mosquitoes* is that sexuality has been corrupted," with the novel's characters forming "an anthology of sex defects. . . ."[22] When he had received the galleys, he had found that four good-sized passages had been deleted. Ben Wasson would later say that the book had been badly cut. Faulkner had written Liveright a letter that sounded querulous to the publisher, but later assured him that he understood why the deletions were made and that he was not trying to complain.[23] The first one consisted of two pages of Fairchild's conversation in which Julius, "the Semitic man," told him that writing was a kind of perversion. The second was the episode in the bunk between Pat and Jenny. In the third, Pete complained that the voyage and its people "Damn near refined me out of my girl." The last excision came after Fairchild's remark that the population would decline if a man had to watch himself making love. To Mrs. Maurier's horror, Fairchild, the

Semitic man, and his sister, Mrs. Wiseman, worked variations on the theme of "a mechanical contrivance to do the work." The editorial pencil had left untouched, however, an erotic fantasy of the sculptor, Gordon, that one critic would particularly remark years later. He thinks of Pat Robyn, and "imagines himself an Israfel 'whose wings are waxed by the thin odorless moisture of her thighs,' a biologically precise reference to the functioning of the glands of Bartholin."[24] One of the books Phil Stone ordered from New Haven was *The Glands Regulating Personality*, by Dr. Louis Berman. It seems very likely that Faulkner read, remembered, and used it. It also seems clear from this novel and other writings that this poet, this limner of ethereal nymphs and delicate maenads, was moving more and more toward the depiction of women in the flesh, no matter what non-corporeal attributes they might have. "*Faulkner is the only major American fiction writer of the twenties and thirties*," wrote the same critic (a woman), "*who incorporates into his depiction of women the functioning of the organs of reproduction*."[25] Unfortunately, Horace Liveright, a rake in private life, was as a publisher not ready for such avant-garde sexuality.

The book was dedicated to a woman. "To Helen, Beautiful and Wise," he had written. When he sent it to Liveright he wrote, "I made the promise some time ago, and you can lie to women, you know, but you cant break promises you make 'em. That infringes on their own province. And besides, you dont dare."[26] This was the tough-guy face he would turn to the world, to belie, if he could, the vulnerability inside. One thing it did not conceal was an attitude deep-seated (with good reason) by now. His step-granddaughter would call it "his rather strong distrust of women."[27]

Publication day was April 30, 1927, and by mid-June the reviews were coming in. A good one by Conrad Aiken in the New York *Evening Post* was offset in a negative one by Ruth Suckow in the *World*. Liveright probably knew they had one good one in their pocket. Lillian Hellman was a young woman working in Liveright's office who had written an enthusiastic reader's report on *Mosquitoes*. She also did reviews for the New York *Herald Tribune*, and there she wrote that the novel had humor and style and "a brilliance that you can rightfully expect only in the writings of a few men."[28] The returns in July were less encouraging, even at home, where Donald Davidson told his Nashville *Tennessean* readers that the novel was an example of the Grotesque, and where even John McClure, in the *Times-Picayune*, found the book a disappointment after Faulkner's "extraordinary first novel." *Mosquitoes*, he thought, was playful but cruel, brilliant but shallow.[29]

The book had gone out into the world bearing the dedication "To Helen." Someone, presumably the author, had deleted the "Beautiful and Wise." By the time the author had inscribed a copy to Helen Baird, she was already Mrs. Guy C. Lyman. She put the book with his letters and poems and stories—all of which she would later sell to a collector.

More than thirty years later, meeting a mutual friend of Margery Gumbel at dinner, Faulkner would send her a message: "Tell her I will always remember those days with tears in my eyes." If there was time for tears now, there was no need for them. Instead, Faulkner had a world to make, in which he could interpret and transform the deeper reality he had known in north Mississippi—the world of the Sartorises.

CHAPTER

24

> But the world was opening out before him fearsome and sad and
> richly moribund, as though he were again an adolescent, and
> filled with shadowy shapes of dread and of delight not to be
> denied: he must go on, though the other footsteps sounded
> fainter and fainter in the darkness behind him and then not at
> all. Perhaps they had ceased, or turned into a byway.
>
> —*Flags in the Dust* (190)

THE Mississippi summer transformed the fields as he went on with *Flags in the Dust*, taking time for an occasional round of golf or a trip to Memphis. He and Dean slept on the screened-in porch on the cool east side of the Falkner home. He still took time to make vocabulary lists for Dean and to go over the stories Dean was writing.[1] In his own work, he was bringing Horace and Narcissa, both reluctant lovers, closer to Belle and Bayard, at the same time that he followed the destructive growth of Byron Snopes's lust for Narcissa. In late July he wrote Liveright that the new novel was progressing. "It is much better than that other stuff," he told him. "I believe that at last I have learned to control the stuff and fix it on something like rational truth."[2] He asked Liveright how the reviews of *Mosquitoes* were. He also mentioned that he had enough verse in manuscript for a book and wondered if Liveright could be prevailed upon to look at it. This was answered with a cautious affirmative, but Faulkner did not drop the novel to polish the poetry. Instead, he brought the Snopes subplot to an end with Byron driven from town by a juvenile blackmailer, and he showed Narcissa drawn still closer to Bayard in spite of her incestuous feelings for her brother and Bayard's clear death wish.

Many Oxonians had by now left for summer trips and vacations. Estelle, Cho-Cho, and Malcolm had gone to Columbus to visit Mrs. Hairston, and Faulkner headed for Pascagoula once more. It appears that he stayed on this time after the Stone family left, intent on finishing the novel there if he could. Tom Kell remembered Faulkner's staying at the Turnbull place and coming to his house for meals. As they strolled together or sailed to Round Island in Kell's skiff, Faulkner would talk with admiration about his grandfather and his uncle John, each embodying certain Sartoris characteristics much in his mind now. As the summer wore on, it seemed to Kell that Faulkner was running low on both money and liquor. Faulkner finally confided to Kell the fact that he owed several hundred dollars—to Stone. (Kell thought the sum was $725.) "Phil Stone lent me that money," Faulkner said, "but I'm not gonna be obligated to him. I'm gonna pay that money back. Nobody dictates to me what I can write and what I can't write." Kell did not ask for particulars. Instead, he invited Faulkner to stay with him and advanced him five dollars, which Faulkner used immediately for two gallons of moonshine. Noticing his guest's capacity for liquor, Kell was not surprised to see that he drank sometimes even when he was working.

By late September, Faulkner was in the final stages of his manuscript, with Bayard and Narcissa married and with some pages of comic relief intervening before the doom that was about to descend. It came with Simon's murder, old Bayard's death, Horace's marriage to Belle, and young Bayard's self-willed death as a test pilot the day of his son's birth. Holding her child, Benbow Sartoris, Narcissa realizes "as she never had before the blind tragedy of human events." (356) The last passages of the novel held echoes of Faulkner's verse. His omniscient narrator mused on "the Player, and the game He plays . . . He must have a name for His pawns, though. But perhaps Sartoris is the game itself—a game outmoded and played with pawns shaped too late and to an old dead pattern. . . . For there is death in the sound of it, and a glamorous fatality, like silver pennons downrushing at sunset, or a dying fall of horns along the road to Ronceveaux." (380) This Hardyesque image of characters as pawns moved by a superior power would recur in later fiction, well after the romanticism that infused the portrait of the Sartorises had faded.

He did more revising on this novel than on its two predecessors. He relocated five lengthy sequences and deleted (then or later) the description of John and Bayard in wartime England and of Bayard's first wife, Caroline. Deleted also was old Bayard's recapitulation of the long Sartoris genealogy. The novel would now open in present time, with Will Falls telling old Bayard about the Colonel's escape from the Yankees. On page 583 of his typescript he put down the date in pen: "29 September 1927."[3] He had finished this book of his "growing years" four days after his thirtieth birthday. On a Sunday, probably October 16, he wrote Liveright from Oxford. "At last and certainly," he told him, "I have written THE book, of which those other things were but foals. I believe it is the damdest best book you'll look at this year, and any other publisher." Thinking ahead, he asked Liveright to "smooth the printer's fur, cajole him, some way. He's been punctuating my stuff to death; giving me gratis quotation marks and premiums of commas that I dont need."[4]

Now he was ready to relax. "As usual, I am broke," he told his publisher, "and as usual, I want some money. I have a good reason, this time: I am going on an expedition with a lady friend, for purposes of biological research, so if by any means you can let me have the rest of the advance on this mss., for the love of Priapus do so."[5] At some point, probably early in the next year, when he wrote Aunt 'Bama asking her to pay the family a visit, he told her, "I have something—someone, I mean,—to show you. . . . Of course it's a woman. I would like to see you taken with her utter charm, and intrigued by her utter shallowness. Like a lovely vase. It isn't even empty, but is filled with something—well, a yeast cake in water is the nearest simile that occurs to me. She gets the days past for me, though. Thank God I've no money, or I'd marry her."[6] Nowhere in either letter did he mention the name of the lady.

While he waited for word from Liveright about *Flags in the Dust*, he probably took part in what would become for him a regular custom: the annual deer hunt at General Stone's camp below Batesville on the edge of the Delta. It was thirty miles from Oxford on the map, but because of the unpaved highways it took more than a hundred miles and two changes of trains to get there. "Because he was a writer," Johncy Falkner remembered, "at first the other hunters didn't know whether they'd get along with him or not." On the first trip he had proved himself, however, for he "asked no favors, just to be allowed to hunt with them and be one of them. They assigned him the most remote and least likely stand of all because, as a novice, that was all he rated. He took it without a word and stood fast till they came for him each evening."[7] He gained quick acceptance as well as valuable material for his fiction.

If he went to camp that year and returned at the usual time, he found Liveright's letter waiting for him on about the last day of November. The first four words told everything. "It is with sorrow in my heart that I write to tell you that three of us have read Flags in the Dust and don't believe that Boni and Liveright should publish it." The second sentence was even worse: "Furthermore, as a firm deeply interested in your work, we don't believe that you should offer it for publication." The rest of the letter went even further in its strictures about the book both he and Stone had expected to bring popular success. "Soldier's [*sic*] Pay was a very fine book and should have done better. Then Mosquitoes wasn't quite as good, showed little development in your spiritual growth and I think none in your art of writing. Now comes Flags in the Dust and we're frankly very much disappointed by it. It is diffuse and non-integral with neither very much plot development nor character development. . . . The story really doesn't get anywhere and has a thousand loose ends. If the book had plot and structure, we might suggest shortening and revisions but it is so diffuse that I don't think this would be any use."[8]

Two years later Faulkner still remembered his reaction vividly: "I was shocked: my first emotion was blind protest, then I became objective for an instant, like a parent who is told that its child is a thief or an idiot or a leper; for a dreadful moment I contemplated it with consternation and despair, then like the parent I hid my own eyes in the fury of denial."[9] Almost immediately, he asked for the manuscript so he could send it elsewhere. "I still believe it is the book which will make my name for me as a writer," he declared. As for the $200 advance, he could send them another manuscript: "I am working spasmodically on a book which will take three or four years to do; also I have started another which I shall finish by spring, I believe." The first was probably *Father Abraham*, and the second may have been one he had mentioned to Liveright earlier, "a collection of short stories of my townspeople."[10] He had doubtless hoped for individual magazine sales of such stories, but he had found no more success with them than with his novel.

When Liveright returned *Flags in the Dust*, Faulkner did not send it out again immediately. Two and a half months later he still had it, because he felt compelled to make sure they were both clear about his submitting it elsewhere. He had put aside the new novel to write some stories, which he had sent, he said, to an agent, who was Ben Wasson. "I have a belly full of writing, now," he told Liveright, "since you folks in the publishing business claim that a book like that last one I sent you is blah. I think now that I'll sell my typewriter and go to work—though God knows, it's sacrilege to waste that talent for idleness which I possess." At any rate, he had enough incentive "to light in and bang you out a book to suit you.—though it'll never be one as youngly glamorous as 'Soldiers' Pay' nor as trashily smart as 'Mosquitoes.' "[11] He told Aunt 'Bama what he had not told Liveright—that he was spending at least part of his time revising *Flags in the Dust*. "Every day or so I burn some of it up and rewrite it, and at present it is almost incoherent. So much so that I've got a little weary of it and I think I shall put it away for a while and forget about it."[12]

THOSE early months of the year 1928 were a time of change for him. He was well into his thirty-first year now, and many differences in his surroundings were evident. Johncy Falkner and his crews had transformed the muddy streets with gravel and tar. Sidewalks went in as new streets were laid down. More than two dozen new houses had been built within the last half-year. Old houses had been altered, one of them the dwelling that had provided more physical stability in Billy Falkner's life than any other. As the executor of J. W. T. Falkner's estate, John Falkner had rented The Big Place to his father-in-law, who had made it a boardinghouse. Neither that arrangement nor others proved profitable, so he bought Murry's and Auntee's interest in the house (Murry's on a note, Auntee's with money borrowed from Murry) in a complicated transaction which also gave Murry a building lot carved from the southern portion of the property. Uncle John moved the old house and sold the corner lot to the Standard Oil Company, which soon put in a modern service station. Then he cut up the old house into apartments. To William Faulkner, this must have been a change more radical than the electric lights and paved streets.

It was February 27 when Horace Liveright formally gave Faulkner permission to sell *Flags in the Dust* to another publisher. The firm would agree then to apply the advance to Faulkner's next novel. His reply was livelier than his previous ones. "I have got going on a novel," he wrote, "which, if I continue as I am going now, I will finish within eight weeks. Maybe it'll please you."[13]

In this time of intense creative activity, he seemed the same old Bill Faulkner to most Oxonians—taking an occasional odd job, such as lacquering Hugh Clayton's brass horn for five dollars with such a finish that Mississippi State bandsmen would cross the field to examine his "gold" instrument. He needed only a little money, he later said, "thanks to my father's unfailing kindness which supplied me with bread at need despite the outrage to his principles at having been of a bum progenitive."[14] To the father, his son's writing counted for little. He did not think he wrote well. Assisting Murry Falkner in his Ole Miss office was a personable former coed named Martha Ida Wiseman. Also coach of the women's basketball team, "Jack" Wiseman was fond of her employer, a very private man but an easygoing boss. He taught her to play poker, and on summer afternoons when business was slow, they would play together. Or he might send her home to make a fourth at Maud Falkner's bridge table. It was at such times that he pursued a private avocation. Cigar smoke wreathing his face, he would write in purple ink in a large Ole Miss ledger which he would carefully lock in the safe each night. He finally revealed it to Jack Wiseman. It was a novel with a very melodramatic story line patterned, she thought, after *The White Rose of Memphis*. Jack thought it was funny, but of course kept her opinion to herself.[15]

An acute observer such as Stark Young saw more deeply into the situation of Murry Falkner's son, and in *The Torches Flare*, which he published in 1928 and set in a thinly disguised Oxford, one of his characters clearly resembled Faulkner both in his appearance and in his family. To friends such as Maud and Calvin Brown, he might seem abstracted and distant, but he was still capable of entering their lives unexpectedly. Their youngest, Margaret, who suffered from a birth defect, was now afflicted with terminal cancer. From time to time Faulkner stopped at the Browns' home to tell this little girl stories that she enjoyed. One morning Calvin Brown found a parcel addressed to her inside the front screen door. It was a typescript of *The Wishing Tree*, inscribed to her, and often during these last six months of her life members of the family read it to her.

The few people who knew the real Bill Faulkner, the complex man beneath the façades with which he concealed and protected himself, would not have been surprised at this gesture of tenderness toward childhood, innocence, and suffering. What they could not have known was that these same elements were combining in his mind, that late winter and early spring of 1928, to produce what would be his first—and to many his greatest—masterpiece.

Sometimes I could put myself to sleep saying that over and over
until after the honeysuckle got all mixed up in it the whole
thing came to symbolise night and unrest I seemed to be lying
neither asleep nor awake looking down a long corridor of grey
halflight where all stable things had become shadowy paradoxical all I had done shadows all I had felt suffered taking visible
form antic and perverse mocking without relevance inherent
themselves with the denial of the significance they should have
affirmed thinking I was I was not who was not was not who.

—*The Sound and the Fury* (211)

THE new novel had grown in a way Faulkner had not anticipated. It had
not begun as a novel at all, he would always say afterward, but as a short
story. There were certainly affinities between earlier work and this new
one as it developed. Sir Galwyn, in *Mayday*, accompanied in his travels
by the two figures Hunger and Pain, had foreshadowed elements of a
major character in this book. One of Faulkner's friends, probably William
Odiorne, said that Faulkner let him read works in progress in Paris in
the fall of 1925 and that one of them "was about a girl and her brothers,
and became *The Sound and the Fury*."[1] It is very possible that the friend
may have read the germ of a different story, one that remained a story
rather than becoming a novel, for Faulkner's imagination was so fertile
and his memory so retentive that all his life he carried around with him
an enormous store of characters whose stories he would write down, as
he would say, "when he got around to it." But in any event, it seems
likely that he had started this story as he had some of those he had
mentioned to Liveright.

"Twilight" was the title which he gave to a story begun in late winter
or early spring of 1928. "I thought it could be done in ten pages," he
remembered later. The materials were ready to his hand—riding out to
the Colonel's farm in his carriage with Johncy, Jack, and Sallie Murry,

fishing in Davidson's Bottom or splashing in Burney Branch. It came out of a memory that almost certainly had its origins twenty years before, at the funeral of Lelia Swift Butler, on June 2, 1907. It was at first "a story without a plot," he would remember, "of some children being sent away from the house" because they were "too young to be told what was going on and they saw things only incidentally to the childish games they were playing, which was the lugubrious matter of removing the corpse from the house, etc., . . ."[2] It came in a rush: "Caddy had three brothers almost before I wrote her name on paper." In the dominant image, they looked up at their sister, at her muddy drawers as she climbed the tree, bolder, more adventurous than they, to see what was going on in the house that they had been kept from seeing. Then another image supervened: the brother and sister splashing in the brook, the sister falling, and the smallest brother crying until she stopped to comfort him. "When she did so, when she quit the water fight and stooped in her wet garments above him, the entire story . . . seemed to explode on the paper before me."[3] One scholar would later write, "this core story has the ghostly implications of the old problem of fix't fate, free will, and foreknowledge absolute—or, in more modern terms, circumstances, intelligence, and genetic memories. All that the Compson children were ever to be is implicit in their childhood."[4]

In this story, as in the others, Quentin, Caddy, and Jason would be there, readily available for his use. But then, he recalled, "the idea struck me to see how much more I could have got out of the idea of the blind, self-centeredness of innocence, typified by children, if one of those children had been truly innocent, that is, an idiot."[5] Just a few blocks away Miss Annie Chandler, his first-grade teacher, still lived, and her brother, Edwin Chandler, who could speak and play simple games but whose mind would never grow to adulthood as his body had done years before. Faulkner had seen him behind his iron fence since childhood. (Maud Falkner would visit Mrs. Chandler, taking Jimmy along with her to play with Edwin.) Nearly four years before, in "The Kingdom of God," he had pictured an idiot, sitting in a car, tightly gripping a narcissus. His face "was vague and dull and loose-lipped and his eyes were clear and blue as cornflowers, and utterly vacant of thought. . . ."[6] Faulkner had, of course, made enormous strides in technique in the interval, so that he would withhold physical description at first, and rather than overtly characterizing, he would present; he would show rather than tell.

Now another dimension opened out before him: "I became interested in the relationship of the idiot to the world . . . and just where could he get the tenderness, the help, to shield him in his innocence. . . . And so the character of his sister began to emerge. . . ."[7] The "symbology of the soiled drawers" showed what lay ahead: "the shame which she was to engender, which Quentin and Jason could not face: the one taking refuge in suicide, the other in vindictive rage which drove him to rob his bastard niece of the meager sums which Caddy could send her. For I had already gone on to night and the bedroom and Dilsey with the mudstained drawers scrubbing the naked backside of that doomed little girl . . . as though she already saw the dark future and the part she was to play in it trying to hold that crumbling household together."[8] There had been no lack of little girls to admire in his life. Sallie Murry had been almost as close as a sister—a plucky good sport of a girl, brought up in the sad home where her widowed mother kept house for her widower father. And just one house away had been Estelle Oldham—the oldest child in a family every bit as conscious of its status and lineage as the Compsons. The images began to fuse in a powerful and unexpected way, and years later the dominant one he would still think of as "the only thing in literature which would ever move me very much: Caddy climbing the pear tree to look in the window at her grandmother's funeral while Quentin and Jason and Benjy and the negroes looked up at the muddy seat of her drawers."[9] Faulkner would later write still another, shorter, essay in recollection, one he would harshly repudiate, perhaps because he had tossed it off—to oblige his publisher and because he needed the money—but there would be a general consistency over the years in all the things he wrote and said about the novel.[10]

On page 1 of his manuscript Faulkner wrote "April 7, 1928." Benjy Compson, tended by T. P., a year younger than himself and a member of the Gibson family employed by the Compsons, watches the golfers playing on what had once been the pasture he loved. From the beginning, Faulkner limited Benjy's narration to a set of capabilities defining his idiocy. He cannot reason. One time level replaces another through stimuli producing a shifting stream of consciousness like the normal association of ideas in reverie or nearing sleep, as with Stephen Dedalus and Leopold and Molly Bloom in *Ulysses*. Benjy can record, like a camera eye, but he cannot interpret. For him there is no causal relationship between the movement of his body and the movement of his shadow. When his clothing catches on a nail in the fence and T. P. moves to free him, present time is replaced by past time as Caddy performs the same function more than twenty years before.

On the first page Faulkner had introduced two time levels, without any punctuation or typography to distinguish them. He continued to introduce other times brought to Benjy's consciousness by different stimuli. Some of these time levels incapsulate incidents that could have stood alone as separate short stories. In one, occurring in November 1890, Benjy's name is changed from Maury. His handicap now obvious, his mother feels he should no longer retain the name of her brother, his namesake. This time level, that of the present—April 7, 1928—and that of Damuddy's funeral in the early fall of 1898 are the three principal ones. Ten others would be set in 1904, 1905, 1906, 1908, 1909, 1910, and 1912. On these levels, past events would supplant the present in Benjy's mind: Caddy and her lovers, her wedding, the day of Quentin's death, Mr. Compson's death. Thus Faulkner moved forward in time, so that the episode of the children during Damuddy's funeral had evolved into a study of the whole family over a thirty-year time span.

The writing was apparently an experience of unparalleled intensity for him. "One day I seemed to shut a door," he remembered five years afterward, "between me and all publishers' addresses and book lists. I said to myself, Now I can write. Now I can make myself a vase like that which the old Roman kept at his bedside and wore the rim slowly away with kissing it. So I, who never had a sister and was fated to lose my daughter in infancy, set out to make myself a beautiful and tragic little girl." It was radically different from the novels on the other side of that door, as different as the impulse he felt now each morning as he sat down before the accumulating pages—"that emotion definite and physical and yet nebulous to describe: that ecstasy, that eager and joyous faith and anticipation of surprise which the yet unmarred sheet beneath my hand held inviolate and unfailing, waiting for release."[11]

Apparently some of the emotional intensity that produced this radically different work, this immense leap in technique that would contribute to one critic's calling him "the greatest innovator in the history of American fiction,"[12] came from the very opposite of ecstasy. He was still smarting from the rejection of *Flags in the Dust*. But there was more than that. Five years after the description of the ecstasy, ten years after the completion of the novel, his French translator would reveal that Faulkner had told him that he was struggling with difficulties of an intimate nature —"Ecrit alors que l'auteur se debattait dans des difficultes d'ordre intime."[13] He did not reveal what they were.

What could they have been, apart from the rejection of the novel he had hoped would make his name for him? That he was now approaching thirty-one and found himself writing only for himself? This hardly seems intimate. Like most small towns, Oxford was a fertile breeding ground for gossip and rumors. Now that Estelle and her children were back in Oxford on what seemed a permanent basis, he was often at the Oldhams' home. From time to time when Estelle would go to Columbus to visit Mrs. Hairston, he might go down and see her during her stay there, welcomed as he was by her open-hearted, hospitable mother-in-law and her brother, Malcolm Franklin, who had been collecting Faulkner's work since the *Times-Picayune* stories. It was as if they had resumed the old relationship when he seemed always to be there, the ardent swain. There would be rumors long afterward about their relationship at this time, that it had encountered some sort of crisis. If this was true, neither he nor Estelle would have been likely to reveal it, especially this most private of men. If this did in fact happen, the crisis was somehow surmounted, but it is not hard to imagine how difficulties and anxieties would have made his writing an escape, and how these difficulties would have provided something else as well: an intensity and a sense of immediacy which would go directly into the rendering of the poignant life of his beleaguered character, his "heart's darling," Caddy Compson.

On page 33 he came to the end of the first section, Benjy's section. "Then the story was complete, finished," he later wrote. "There was Dilsey to be the future, to stand above the fallen ruins of the family like a ruined chimney, gaunt, patient and indomitable; and Benjy to be the past. He had to be an idiot so that, like Dilsey, he could be impervious to the future, though unlike her by refusing to accept it at all."[14] He had treated many major events in the lives of this Jefferson family, but as he looked at his manuscript—almost all of the two-inch left-hand margin of page 20, for example, was filled with additions—he saw that it was "incomprehensible, even I could not have told what was going on then, so I had to write another chapter. Then I decided to let Quentin tell his version of that same day, or that same occasion, so he told it."[15]

Although there were links between Quentin and Benjy, Faulkner could scarcely have picked two seemingly more dissimilar narrators. In contrast to the mind of the idiot, that of his psychotic older brother was filled with allusions to the Bible, to Shakespeare, and to numerous other works of literature. It may have been now that Faulkner took a fresh sheet, wrote "Twilight—Notes" at the top, and set down more than a dozen dates of births, deaths, and other events that he had been able to leave implied, free-floating, or unknown in Benjy's stream of consciousness. These were a means of keeping straight certain objective elements in an increasingly complex story. Quentin's psyche was apparently clear in Faulkner's mind from the beginning. He was always frank to say he wrote from his own experience. He would tell Malcolm Cowley that in all his books, "I am telling the same story over and over, which is myself and the world."[16] Others perceived this. "I have never known anyone who identified himself with his writings more than Bill did," said his brother Johncy. "Sometimes it was hard to tell which was which, which one Bill was, himself or the one in the story. And yet you knew somehow that the two of them were the same, they were one and inseparable."[17] So he had looked within himself to create Benjy. The treatment of the next brother involved a process which was both more complex and more intense. Many years later, to a young woman in whom he was romantically interested, Faulkner would say something which seemed, for him, extraordinarily revealing. He was talking about a book he wished he had written. "Ishmael is the witness in *Moby-Dick*," he said, "as I am Quentin in *The Sound and the Fury*." Even allowing for exaggeration, something of this assertion must have come from elements within his psyche.

Similarities and dissimilarities between author and character would appear as, bit by bit, he filled in the portrait, building it up, stroke by stroke, as that painter he so much admired, Cézanne, might have done. He dated Quentin's section "June 2, 1910," beginning with Quentin's memory of Benjy crying and pawing at Caddy's dress, signifying Benjy's awareness of her sexuality which obsesses Quentin and helps drive him to suicide. Six pages into the section, however, he started over, with Quentin waking to the last day of his life in his Harvard dormitory room. Faulkner would later use the initial six pages, but only after he had tried them in two more places in the section. Quentin thinks of his father's reflecting, how "down the long and lonely light-rays you might see Jesus walking, like. And the good Saint Francis that said Little Sister Death, that never had a sister."[18] This image, even more than that of twilight, echoes earlier work such as *Mayday* and *The Wishing Tree*, as, through his stream of consciousness, Quentin begins to elaborate his dependency upon his sister. The Compson children have grown up lacking parental love in a home poisoned by their mother's egocentrism and hypochondria and their alcoholic father's nihilism. One consequence is a superfraternal love that extends to incest fantasies on Quentin's part and is intensified by two rivals with whom he cannot compete: Dalton Ames, a man-of-the-world ex-soldier, and Herbert Head, a boorish businessman whom Caddy marries after becoming pregnant by another lover. Thus Faulkner was reworking, with greater intensity, the subject he had treated with other characters, from Jo-Addie and Elmer to Horace and Narcissa Benbow. Throughout these pages the images of honeysuckle and twilight waft in and out, symbolizing to Quentin his sister's promiscuity and his own approaching death.

Moving toward the end of Quentin's section, Faulkner brought present events to the foreground. A little Italian girl attaches herself to Quentin as he wanders in a small town outside Cambridge. In a familiar regional usage of the time, he calls her "sister," but he cannot help thinking of two others: Caddy and Little Sister Death. Ironically, he is accused of molesting her, to be rescued only through the help of his roommate, Shreve MacKenzie, a sympathetic Canadian, and others picnicking nearby. But by now his obsession with the past is so strong, his association of ideas so fragmented, that he attacks the hostess' son, another lady-killer like Dalton Ames. As Quentin's disintegration accelerates, Faulkner emphasizes it with syntax and punctuation. As with Benjy, he would switch from roman type to italics, and back to indicate time shifts, and whereas dialogue in present time would be put in quotations, past conversations would not. Sometimes he would omit all punctuation to denote the flowing stream of consciousness. In exchanges which Quentin remembers with strong emotion, initial lines might be left uncapitalized. As Quentin's tenuous hold on reality weakens and as he prepares for escape from time into the oblivion which he craves, the personal pronoun drops from upper case to lower. As in the Benjy section, sensory cues are enormously important. In one of Faulkner's favorite devices, synesthesia, Quentin's nose can "see" gasoline, and his hands can "see" the door to his room as he prepares to pass through it on his journey to the river. Once again twilight dominates his mind as he moves steadily toward his death by water.

The primary fact about Quentin's plight is his inability to find the kind of love he needs. Insecure about his masculinity, he mourns a lost time and a lost girl: the idealized Caddy of his childhood and early adolescence. Supersensitive, inward-turning, he has a melancholy habit of mind which increases his emotional dependency. Of their lives he thinks, *"My little sister had no. If I could say Mother. Mother"* (117) He loves and apparently trusts his father in a relationship that is affectionate but in no way sustaining. If William Faulkner had now seemingly regained the girl he had loved and lost, she was no longer the same girl, subject, like everything else, to time and change, her status as matron and mother very different from that of the maiden he had loved twenty years before. He had loved his cousin Sallie Murry, as had everyone else in the Falkner family, and though the ages of the Falkner and Compson children put Billy and Sallie Murry where Quentin and Caddy were, there was never any evidence of an extraordinary attachment between them, though the fact that they were cousins, rather than siblings, cousins who had played the roles of husband and wife in childhood games, may have lent to their relationship a touch of childhood eroticism which could very well have gone into the intense relationship between Quentin and Caddy.

As for the parents, Billy Falkner seems never to have had the kind of rapport with his father that make possible for Quentin the long and numerous talks with his father, listening and remembering as he watches the fireflies and scents the cigar smoke and wisteria and honeysuckle. As for his mother, though her son had found her a strict disciplinarian, he had loved her steadfastly. Even as he grew older and sometimes felt at odds with her, exasperated if amused, he gave her the love that she in part exacted, as with the requirement that her sons write her once a week when they were away from home. Even his daughter could see it. Many years later she would say, "I think that probably Pappy's idea of women —ladies—always revolved a great deal around Granny. She was just a very determined, tiny old lady that Pappy adored. Pappy admired so much in Granny and he didn't find it in my mother and I don't think he found it in anybody. I think that maybe all of these including my mother were just second place."[19] Many were his gifts of love, from childhood drawings and a penknife on her birthday for sharpening pencils, to the copies of all his books. He gave her a three-inch statuette of Atlas with the world on his back—actually a small clock set in a round metal case, the face covered with a magnifying crystal, a constant reminder of the burdens of time. It was an intriguing object that might have compelled Quentin Compson's attention as much as the profusion of timepieces he saw in a Cambridge watchmaker's window.

Faulkner had told Bill Spratling that he took traits from people and combined them in various characters. If Caddy owed something to Sallie

Murry Wilkins, she perhaps owed most of that ideal, embodied in all the dreamlike nymphs he had created in poems and stories over the years. One critic would call her "a dream of beauty wasted and destroyed."[20] He had known the agony of love as well as "the agony of ink," and he would love more than one woman with intensity during his life. But always it was his work that he loved most. Years later, one of this novel's most perceptive readers would discern elements in the character of Quentin Compson both personal and symbolic: "Faulkner was also writing about the Southern writer of his generation. . . . The love/hate relationship—hating because one loves, loving despite the faults—between Quentin Compson and Yoknapatawpha County comes deeply out of William Faulkner's situation, and it mirrors that of the modern Southern writer and the South."[21] In still another broad context with possible personal overtones, Faulkner "created a character who felt keenly what he feared was a lack of masculinity," linking this character with "what Faulkner felt was the artistic temperament, in contrast to the masculine man of action."[22] If Faulkner had earlier feared a lack of masculinity in himself, by now that fear had diminished or vanished. He would say that as an artist, he felt he could create better characters than God could, and that in creating them, he drew upon the triad of imagination, observation, and experience. He had drawn upon all of these for Quentin Compson. Perhaps Dalton Ames, like Bayard Sartoris, represented a part of what he would have liked to be. Perhaps Quentin Compson, like David, the *Nausikaa*'s steward, represented a part of what he feared he might be. And the whole world of literature was open to him. One writer would see another troubled youth in Quentin: Rodion Raskolnikov, in Dostoevsky's *Crime and Punishment*.[23] There was something of William Faulkner, in any event, in Quentin Compson. By the same token, and by close attention to the work itself, the reader would be able to see that there was also something of William Faulkner in Jason Compson, who was, with competition for the place only from his mother, the worst member of the family.

He was there, said Faulkner, for "counterpoint." Contemptuous of every member of his family, filled with hatred for Caddy over the bank position her illicit pregnancy cost him when Head divorced her, hostile toward many and suspicious toward all, Jason Compson might be a monster of cruelty and hypocrisy, but his mind works with a self-consistent logic. Once Faulkner starts him talking, he moves rapidly, flashing back to the past like his brothers. With a mind shallower than Quentin's, he is far closer to objective reality than either of his brothers. Thus the stream of present-time events stands in the forefront, with relevant prior information provided where necessary from his sardonic and sometimes humorous ruminations. It is Jason who gives the reader details of Mr. Compson's burial, Caddy's exile and her surreptitious visits to glimpse her daughter, Miss Quentin, being raised in her grandmother's loveless home beyond even the mention of her mother's name. The reader easily infers from Jason's self-exculpating recital the details of his embezzlement, over the years, of money sent by Caddy for her daughter. Jason takes the reader along as he pursues Miss Quentin and her lover into the country, then returns home, to "the decaying house" (355) where he counts the total of his savings and embezzlement. As the section ends, he is about to retire on Good Friday evening, unaware that the Resurrection Day of the Christian calendar will be for him one of unmitigated disaster.

Maud Falkner was characteristically frank when she was asked about Jason: "he talks just like my husband did. My husband had a hardware store uptown at one time. His way of talking was just like Jason's, same words and same style." He also employed a Negro named Jobus, "just like the character in the story. He was always after Jobus for not working hard enough, just like in the story."[24] The only person in the novel for whom Jason shows any warmth is his sometime mistress, a Memphis prostitute named Lorraine. Besides Lorraine, the only person who shows any warmth for Jason is his mother, Caroline Bascomb Compson, who feels him to be the only one of her children who not only is a Bascomb but does not take up against her with the others.

Phil Stone was as sure of the models for Jason and Mrs. Compson as Maud Falkner was of the model for Jason. Of Rosamond Stone he would say, "By the time I was five years old, I knew Miss Rosie was a fool. . . ." He would look on appalled at her treatment of an orphan niece and watch as she became a self-declared invalid retreating from life. Jason, said Stone, was modeled on his brother, James Stone, Jr. "Between him and my mother," he said, "there was a typical harmless but complete Oedipus and Jocasta complex. Anybody who knew Jim Stone could recognize him from the way Jason talks . . . and many have actually done so." Moreover, Stone would tell his son, Jim Stone was "completely irresponsible, was dishonest in small ways and was a prime chiseler."[25] From the time he had first come to know Miss Rosie, Faulkner had been amused by her, especially by her interest in catastrophes. Stone would remember his friend's saying, "Miss Rosie, did you read about all those folks that were killed in the steamboat accident?" Then he would watch her animated response. When he left, Stone would remember her comment, "I declare, that Billy Falkner is the nicest little boy."

There were early memories that Faulkner could use in creating this mother and son. Prefiguring Jason's adult money mania was his childish avarice, hands in his pockets even when it cost him a fall. Petted by Damuddy, Jack Falkner was a good boy, but he, too, would fall down walking with his hands in his pockets. Billy Falkner never had very much in his, though there was enough to buy clothes when he was playing the dandy, and he saved much of his post-office salary for his time in New Orleans and Europe. But in these present years there had not been much, as his loans from Stone and advances from Liveright had testified. Jason constantly complains about his responsibilities and financial burdens in supporting himself, his widowed mother, and the rest of the household. More than once Faulkner's fiction would prefigure events in his life. In less than four years he would find himself in Jason's position, and his own bitter complaints would sound much like Jason's. He would encounter burdens so heavy and frustrations so grinding that it would have taken another temperament than his to react differently. But he had the capacity to react as Jason did, with the same kind of morbid humor directed at the causes of his frustrations and the objects of his resentments. He could look into himself and find there something to help create this third Compson brother, just as he had felt some of Quentin's emotions earlier.

"So I wrote Quentin's and Jason's sections," he later said, "trying to clarify Benjy's. But I saw that I was merely temporising; That I should have to get completely out of the book. I realised that there would be compensations, that in a sense I could then give a final turn to the screw and extract some ultimate distillation. Yet it took me better than a month to take pen and write *The day dawned bleak and chill* before I did so."[26] He put it another way too: "by that time it was completely confusing. I knew that it was not anywhere near finished and then I had to write another section from the outside with an outsider, which was the writer, to tell what happened on that particular day."[27] Now, however, the day was not that of Damuddy's funeral but the one on which a long chain of events came to an end in the Compson family.

At the top of page 125, Faulkner wrote "April Eighth, 1928." It was Easter Sunday. As Faulkner completed the novel and then revised it, the days of Easter weekend would suggest possible parallels, a number of them ironic, between Christ's passion and death and the agonies of the Compsons. He had apparently begun the novel close to the beginning of the Lenten season, and he must by now have been writing in Oxford's hot summer, but like his characters, he was operating on several time levels, and now he moved to that special Easter Sunday. Midway through the first section had come the image of Caddy climbing up one tree. Near the end had come that of her daughter, Quentin, climbing down another. In this fourth section Faulkner would explore the aftermath of Quentin's escape with all of Jason's hoard—his own savings and her own money—and Jason's return from a fruitless pursuit.

Standing as a foil to Jason was Dilsey Gibson, sustaining the household from her central place in its kitchen, comforting Benjy as she took him to her church for Easter services, much as she had earlier tried to interpose her own body to protect Miss Quentin from Jason's attack. One black critic would later write that to the black reader, Dilsey was flawed with "stereotypical abasement," seen as she was in a familiar literary situation in which "a white girl, always adorable, and sometimes ravishing, passes through her youth into early maturity attended hand and foot by a black female who would be, in any event, according to an Aryan cult of beauty, neither adorable nor ravishing, nor ever a likely candidate for romantic love. The white mistress marries. Her own wedding occupies the black female more than the black female's own. The white mistress has children. These children take precedence over the black female's offspring in the black female's hierarchy of responsibilities. And when the white mistress, or any of her family, dies, the grief which devastates the black female is greater than the grief she exhibits at the passing of any black, kin of hers or not."[28] It is likely that Faulkner would have rejected this view on the grounds that Dilsey was the creature of his own imagination; also, that many black women in the South, for whatever reasons, had for more than a century enacted such roles. A prototype for Dilsey existed in his notes for "The Devil Beats His Wife," in which the maid, Della, dominated the action and physically resembled Dilsey. But much of Dilsey's love and devotion must have derived from Mammy Callie. Maud Falkner was forthright as usual. "Dilsey in that story is Mammy Callie. We all loved her. But I'll tell you one thing, she always wanted you to know she was a 'nigrah.' "[29] But diminutive Caroline Barr was nothing like her physically, and whereas Dilsey was steadfastly religious and monogamous, Mammy Callie had a salty vocabulary and a taste for men. Once again Faulkner had drawn on many sources in the creation of a unique and convincing character.

While Jason Compson provided most of the action of this last section, Dilsey provided its moral center, embodying the Christian virtues—above all, the ability to give love as well as labor. Returning from the Easter service, she weeps for broken lives. She had been there in the family when the boy Quentin had been born: she had been there when his namesake had fled: "I've seed de first en de last." (371) Entering the gate, "all of them looked up the drive at the square, paintless house with its rotting portico." (372) It is as though she foresees what the future holds: Mrs. Compson's death, Benjy's commitment to the asylum, and Jason's cutting the old home into apartments before selling it. At the end, after an aborted trip to the cemetery, Benjy sits quiet and serene. Like the idiot in "The Kingdom of God," he holds a broken narcissus and watches as "cornice and façade flowed smoothly once more from left to right; post and tree, window and doorway, and signboard, each in its ordered place." (401) But it is a static and sterile order, foreshadowing the end to come.

One night Faulkner had invited Stone to visit him. When he began to read, Stone immediately thought of Edwin Chandler, but he understood little. "I could not make head nor tail of it," he remembered. When he asked Faulkner for explanation, he replied, "Wait, just wait." Then later, "as soon as we got into the part about Quentin the whole thing began to unfold like a flower." This went on, Stone said, "three or four nights a week over a period of three or four months." It was an experience he came to cherish, as he sat "night after night in Bill's little room in the little tower of the old Delta Psi chapter house and had him read The Sound and the Fury to me page by page." When it was finished, Stone said, Faulkner had no title, even though "Twilight" was still there on the first sheet. They thought about it, Stone said, and then, "since it was a tale told by an idiot," he suggested that they borrow from *Macbeth* and call it *The Sound and the Fury*.[30] Faulkner's memory was different. The familiar words of the title had come one day "out of my unconscious. I adopted them immediately, without considering then that the rest of the Shakespearean quotation was as well suited, and maybe better, to my dark story of madness and hatred."[31] It had been a grueling process of creation. He had, he later said, "written my guts into *The Sound and the Fury* though I was not aware until the book was published that I had done so, because I had done it for pleasure."[32]

He had written it with a sense of liberation from any practical constraints. "I believed then that I would never be published again," Faulkner recalled. "I had stopped thinking of myself in publishing terms."[33] So he had written on, while in the distance there resounded the noise of other events that summer: the presidential conventions and the ensuing contest between Herbert Hoover and Alfred E. Smith. Well before the election took place he would learn that his assumption had, happily, been wrong. Despite his discouragement at the rejection of *Flags in the Dust*, he had not given up. According to one scholar, after making a fourth composite typescript out of various versions of the novel, he had typed and polished a first draft, which he had sent to Ben Wasson, who was working as a literary agent in New York for The American Play Company.[34] After trying several publishers, he had last given it to his friend Harrison Smith, an editor at Harcourt, Brace and Company, a man of considerable if sometimes eccentric charm and literary taste combined with a sharp business sense. He told Ben he had written a favorable report and that the decision was up to Alfred Harcourt. Smith took Ben in to see Harcourt, who said he was uncertain, that he liked the 600-page manuscript but was troubled by what seemed to him prolixity in both style and content.

"I don't think he can cut his work," he told Ben. "Will you do it for fifty dollars?"

Ben immediately agreed and then diffidently asked about an advance.

"How about three hundred dollars?" Harcourt asked. Ben accepted.

Ben sent the money to Faulkner and explained the conditions for his approval. He suggested that if Faulkner agreed, he should come to New York, to be there while Ben did the cutting. He could bring along whatever he was writing and maybe they could place that too.

Faulkner agreed, and the contract arrived, dated September 20, 1928, calling for delivery by October 7 of a novel of approximately 110,000 words to be called *Sartoris*. (The manuscript had been handled so much that the title page had been lost, and at first Smith had thought it was

Ben's work. At some point the new title had been devised.) Faulkner put his few presentable clothes in his suitcase and carefully wrapped the manuscript of his new novel and the pages he had revised and typed. He still owed money and the refusal of his next book to Boni & Liveright. If they didn't like *Flags in the Dust*, there wasn't much chance that they would like the new book. But maybe Harcourt, Brace would.

He said his goodbyes and boarded the train for Memphis and New York.

Now and then, with a long and fading reverberation, a subway train passed under their feet. Perhaps they thought momentarily of two green eyes tunneling violently through the earth without apparent propulsion or guidance, as though of their own unparalleled violence creating, like spaced beads on a string, lighted niches in whose wan and fleeting glare human figures like corpses set momentarily on end in a violated grave yard leaned in one streaming and rigid direction and flicked away.

—"Pennsylvania Station," *CSWF* (613–614)

BEN WASSON met him at the station, but couldn't put him up in his tiny room in a Greenwich Village brownstone at 146 MacDougal Street, just across from the Provincetown Playhouse. But he did know the ropes of the publishing world and he could certainly show his friend around. As for lodging, that could be managed through what was jocularly known as "the Southern Protective Association." Stark Young and Bill Spratling were there in the city. So was thirty-seven-year-old Lyle Saxon—a charming raconteur from New Orleans, whom Spratling had pictured in *Sherwood Anderson & Other Famous Creoles*—who was living on a thousand-dollar advance Hal Smith had paid him against royalties from a novel. His apartment, over a bookstore on Christopher Street near Sixth Avenue, was a favorite meeting place for members of the Association, and Saxon told Faulkner he could stay with him for a while.

When Ben mentioned cutting *Sartoris*, Faulkner surprised him with his vehement refusal to have anything to do with it. Two years later he remembered arguing with Ben: "I said, 'A cabbage has grown, matured. You look at that cabbage; it is not symmetrical; you say, I will trim this cabbage off and make it art; I will make it resemble a peacock or a pagoda or 3 doughnuts. Very good, I say; you do that, then the cabbage will be dead.'

" 'Then we'll make some kraut out of it,' he said. 'The same amount of sour kraut will feed twice as many people as cabbage.' A day or so later he came to me and showed me the mss. 'The trouble is,' he said, 'that you had about 6 books in here. You were trying to write them all at once.' He showed me what he meant, what he had done, and I realized for the first time that I had done better than I knew. . . ."[1]

Ben went ahead and cut the typescript, he said, by a quarter. He deleted a long passage of Narcissa's reflections about Bayard as a boy and shortened Bayard's balloon ascent. He did the same thing with other passages in which Narcissa conveyed background material. Several scenes involving Byron Snopes, Virgil Beard, and Mrs. Beard were cut. Long passages were also deleted in which Faulkner had described Byron's twin torments: his anonymous lust for Narcissa and Virgil's blackmail. His final flight from Jefferson to Frenchman's Bend disappeared, as did the brief appearances of I. O. Snopes and his son, Clarence. Horace's role was reduced: his one-time desire to become an Episcopalian minister, his sense of doom, his affair with Belle, a brief affair with her sister Joan, his prior involvements, his incestuous feelings toward Narcissa—all these were removed or drastically cut.

When Ben finished he gave the typescript to Faulkner, who told him he had done a good job. In spite of his earlier protestations that he wanted no part of the cutting, Faulkner did take a hand in the reshaping. Because the setting copy for the novel apparently did not survive, it is impossible to tell if Faulkner took time off from his work on *The Sound and the Fury* to add his own changes or if he made them later when he received the galleys. But there were a number of passages that are not in the typescript of *Flags in the Dust*. And there were substitutions of dialect words whose meanings Ben didn't know. So, in spite of himself, Faulkner had, in the end, taken a hand in the final shaping of this novel which had such personal significance for him.[2] Ben remembered that he even painted a water color for the dust jacket, "a Negro and a mule plowing a field in the springtime with a very springlike blue sky above, and I regret to say that the publisher decided against using it. . . ."[3] Faulkner added another personal touch: a dedication which, like that to *Mosquitoes*, was a gesture toward the past. It was to Sherwood Anderson, "through whose kindness I was first published, with the belief that this book will give him no reason to regret that fact."

Dealing with his publishing past, in the firm of Boni & Liveright, would not be quite so easy. There was still the matter of their advance to him and their technical right to first refusal on his next book. Bill Spratling would recount an amusing if improbable story of Faulkner's telling Horace Liveright that he found writing when he was "all sewed up" in a signed contract "inhibiting," at which Liveright obligingly threw the contract into the wastebasket.[4] Many years later Louis Kronenberger would remember that Faulkner did visit the firm's offices, and that it had been decided "to ask him to put [*Flags in the Dust*] aside and accept an advance on a new book." Kronenberger was delegated to make the offer, and he remembered talking about it "with increasing embarrassment as Faulkner said nothing." He sat there silently for what seemed hours before he courteously took his leave.[5] There are enough discrepancies in this account to make it suspect too. But the essential facts of the situation were probably simple. Having rejected *Flags in the Dust* on the grounds that it did not tell a story and tell it well, Horace Liveright would probably not have accepted *The Sound and the Fury*. A second rejection would have freed Faulkner from any further obligation. As for the advance, he wrote Aunt 'Bama, "I'm going to be published by white folks now. Harcourt Brace & Co bought me from Liveright. Much, much nicer there. Book will be out in Feb. Also another one, the damndest book I ever read. I dont believe anyone will publish it for 10 years. Harcourt swear they will, but I dont believe it."[6]

The assurance had probably come from Hal Smith, who had already discussed with Faulkner some of the technical problems raised by his new novel. One day, when the two sat with Ben Wasson in a speakeasy, Faulkner had tried to convince the others that different-colored inks would help the reader distinguish among the time levels. This idea was a by-product of the hard work he was doing, day after day, in the small furnished flat he had rented at 35 Vandam Street in Greenwich Village. He was making extensive revisions, striving especially to link the first, third, and fourth sections closer together. Early in Benjy's section, Luster, Benjy's current nurse, now reveals that today, April 7, 1928, is Benjy's thirty-third birthday and that there will be a small cake (bought by Dilsey) to celebrate it. Thus Faulkner opened out further possibilities of both direct and ironic Christian symbolism. (Some readers would later link him with "the suffering servant in Isaiah and with Billy Budd as Adam before the fall," but as one critic would point out, he was essentially unlike Christ although he was like other figures partaking of this archetype who "suffer innocently from evils they have not caused but that come to everyman as part of the human condition.")[7] Faulkner made a number of other consistent linked revisions.

New passages revealed that Luster was trying to find a golf ball he could sell to buy a ticket for a newly arrived carnival. Jason's refusal to give Luster one of his free tickets would add to the impact of Jason's stunning loss when Miss Quentin ran off with his hoard. Faulkner further refined Benjy's characterization and made the Negro characters' speech less dialectal than it had been. To help the reader distinguish time levels, he practically doubled the number of italicized passages.

He also increased them in the second section, simplifying and compressing wherever he could. There were many corrections, even some on the eight new pages he inserted into this section. He clarified the fact that Quentin had purchased two six-pound flatirons—to weight his body for his descent into the river. The prose—well-punctuated now and comprising chiefly simple and compound sentences—faithfully mirrored Quentin's state. Calmly and serenely mad, he was emotionally at rest, as Benjy was after his outburst near the end of his section.

There were fewer corrections and revisions in the novel's last two sections. On the last page (392) he wrote in the lower right-hand corner in blue ink: "New York, N.Y./October 1928." In Ben Wasson's room he flung the typescript on the bed and said, "Read this, Bud. It's a real son-of-a-bitch."

Now he could relax with Saxon and the others, and new friends such as Eric James Devine, an Ohioan working for an M.A. in journalism at Columbia who shared an apartment on Amsterdam Avenue at 111th Street with two other Columbia students—Robert Walton and Leon Scales. They were fascinated with the soft-spoken Faulkner, whose beautiful Harris Tweed overcoat with raglan sleeves had pockets that easily concealed two square bottles of bootleg gin. It took liquor, Devine had concluded, to warm him up. Scales was fascinated by Faulkner's "strange, almost hypnotic eyes, and yet his speech was as picturesque as that of anyone with whom I had ever talked. He usually spoke with a slow Southern drawl, but when he got excited, he would speak with a rapid staccato-like speech interspersed with profanity." On one evening, fortified by a square bottle labeled Gordon's Dry Gin (actually bathtub gin bought at a nearby delicatessen for one dollar), Faulkner broke his habitual silence and began to talk. Shoeless, sitting on the floor with the others, he began to tell them about a man who brought a herd of wild ponies into a Mississippi town. He was trying out *Father Abraham* on a new audience.

One night Jim Devine and Leon Scales decided to make the subway trip to Greenwich Village to see Faulkner. They knocked and waited, but there was no response. The door was locked, but there were lights on inside. When Scales lifted Devine up to the transom, he saw Faulkner stretched out on the floor, and near him some of the familiar square bottles, empty. They forced the door and roused Faulkner, and when they found that he had not eaten for a couple of days, decided to take him to their apartment. Slipping an overcoat around his shoulders, they got him to the 14th Street subway entrance. As they paused to rest, Faulkner sat on the curb, head in hands, looking very sick. He roused himself for a moment. "Don't make me go up to your place," he said. "I have never been upstate on the subway."

THIS sequence of events foreshadowed many repetitions. Ernest Hemingway would speak of the irresponsibility that comes after the awful responsibility of writing. There were other aftereffects: a feeling of exhaustion, of being spent, and an accompanying depression and lassitude. Liquor was an anodyne that would drown it all out. Years later Faulkner's daughter would say, "He used drinking as a safety valve. It had to come out some way and almost invariably at the end of a book." At first he would be "extremely active. He'd want to do things. And then, one morning he would be a little quieter than he had been and all of a sudden he would start on his poem that heralded one of these bouts coming on: 'When daisies pied and violets blue, and lady-smocks all silver-white . . .' on and on and on, and you knew that the next day he'd be drinking. That was just the beginning of it."[8] Shakespeare's song from *Love's Labours Lost* (or a recitation of *The Phoenix and the Turtle*) would signal the oncoming of the sickness, and it would last for a week, or ten days, or longer, until he was ready to sober up.

Why else did he drink? There were at least a half-dozen situations that would produce drinking. There was abstinence too. Before he was much older he would swear off completely for a year. Most of the time, however, he did drink, and for long periods his drinking, whether moderate or considerable, would be controlled. It would have had to be, for him to accomplish all the work he did. At times he might spend an evening or more in heavy drinking, after which it would take him a day or so to recover completely. There were also extended bouts. The family could deal with some of these; for others he would require hospitalization.

There was certainly a predisposition to drinking in his family and his culture. As Jack Falkner would later recall, there was no such thing as social drinking in their part of Mississippi. Liquor was bought from bootleggers and consumed sub rosa. As a result, the drinking tended to be hard and often ended in drunkenness. His great-grandfather was said to have been a heavy drinker, and his grandfather and his father engaged in bouts that could end in hospitalization. The Young Colonel continued to drink heavily until his death, and Murry Falkner would begin to abstain only when he began to suffer stomach trouble near the end of his life. The example of abstemious Great-grandfather Murry had not been very persuasive. All of Murry Falkner's sons drank, and to excess. Of the four, only Jack would finally give it up.

It has been suggested that drinking can be passed on, as money is inherited. Although it was assumed for years that there could be no biological inheritance, modern research seems to suggest a strong possibility that there is an inherited link and that one component of it, paradoxically, might be a lack of intolerance for alcohol. Whereas "large numbers of people are more or less 'protected' from becoming alcoholic because of genetically determined adverse physical reactions to alcohol," such as nausea, headache, and generalized malaise, others can tolerate it so well that they can drink large quantities that lead, only after prolonged drinking, to acute symptoms and ultimately to the complex behavior patterns characterized as alcoholism.[9] There was no doubt about Faulkner's extraordinary capacity, from the time he began drinking his grandfather's liquor to his subsequent exploits with "white mule" in Clarksdale and Lafayette County, with better whiskey in Reno DeVaux's Memphis-area night clubs, with homemade Pernod in the Vieux Carré or doctored Cuban alcohol in the brownstone bordellos of Mulberry or Gayoso Street. Whatever the mode of transmission of William Faulkner's taste and tolerance, the inheritance had certainly been conveyed. And he was constantly with fellow inheritors. One friend in the Vieux Carré, looking back later on the old days, would not recall him as an outstandingly heavy drinker. "We *all* drank hard," she said.

Like most people who drink, he drank because of the way liquor tasted and the way it made him feel. He had liked the flavor of the "heeltaps" that remained in his grandfather's toddy glass. He greatly enjoyed the taste of good bourbon, and by the time he reached mature years he was a discriminating wine drinker. He enjoyed drinking because it made him feel good. It could provide a sense of relaxation, of well-being, and even more. "When I have one martini," he would later tell a young actress, "I feel bigger, wiser, taller. When I have a second, I feel superlative. When I have more, there's no holding me."

He drank out of avoidance as well as for pleasure. He was a shy man who would wryly say he got claustrophobia in crowds. He was a private man who generally disliked questions about himself or his work. For many, liquor eases the apprehension that may accompany a crowd situation, and it probably acted this way for him. Liquor was for him an analgesic, an anesthetic. Distrusting physicians generally, he would dose himself with whiskey for anything from a sore throat to a bad back. Faced with equally unattractive alternatives, he would avoid the decision by removing himself from the situation through excessive drinking. When faced with an obligation come due, he might make himself incapable of meeting it. Unhappily, this strategy in the long run is likely to intensify the condition it is meant to remedy.

The onset might come at any time. "He'd go along for weeks or months at a normal gait," R. N. Linscott would write, and "then the craving would come. Most often he'd fight it off. But once in a while something would happen that would 'get me all of a turmoil inside,' and liquor seemed the only escape. . . . You would be aware of the symptoms of increasing tension—drumming fingers, evasive looks, monosyllabic replies to questions—then he'd disappear. . . ."[10] To another, Faulkner once said, "I feel as though all my nerve ends were exposed. . . ." Some of the bouts were predictable, as with the tension following the completion of a book when, as Sherwood Anderson put it, "You have been in one world and you are trying to return to another." In the years when he went on the November trip to hunting camp, he would experience a complete change of atmosphere, of scene, of company. There was always whiskey around the campfire. He would take a supply with him, and sometimes the drinks before supper, meant to chase the chill from long hours at a stand in the woods, would multiply until they kept him from the stand the next day and finally terminated the hunt for him.

Sometimes he would plan when to start, and he would often plan when he would stop. And he would not stop until then. Johncy thought there

were periods of faked drunkenness—when Bill was bored, when he wanted
to avoid work or to be waited on. And sometimes, when he was well into
a real bout, he would continue to exhibit all the effects even if the family
member or friend who was caring for him surreptitiously substituted tea
for whiskey. In the main, however, there was little that was fake about
these occasions, for they could be serious, prolonged, and always debilitating illnesses.

Their progress and effects were the familiar ones of the periodic heavy
drinker. Shortly after the cycle began he would lose interest in food.
When his supply of liquor, sometimes ingeniously cached, ran out, he
would become dependent upon others. Then he might bargain, accepting
an eggnog in exchange for another drink. He would retire to his bed,
sometimes dispensing with his pajama top, or bottoms, or both. He might
leave his room without his robe, to the discomfiture—if he happened to
be in a hotel—of guests and staff. Was this a kind of exhibitionism, the
other side of the privacy, the shyness, the withdrawal, once his inhibitions
had been erased with alcohol? It seems so. An extraordinary quality his
friends and family noted was his ability to later recall conversations during
intensive drinking. Not only that, he would remember clearly incidents
from the past, particularly old grievances. He would show an acute awareness of what was happening to him, and the reactions of those seeing him
in this condition. But this mattered little. The bout would go on until he
was ready to taper off, or until he was hospitalized.

The reactions following prolonged intensive drinking are far more
severe than just headache, nausea, and sensitivity to sound. They constitute
withdrawal symptoms very like those caused by other addictive agents.
Some of the symptoms arise from the sudden lessening of alcohol concentration in the blood. Others result from retention of body fluids, with
accompanying cerebral edema. First to appear is usually acute tremulous-
ness and nervousness, which may persist for days or even weeks. There
will often be insomnia. There may follow hallucinations and a distortion
of the time sense. The worst, of course, is delirium tremens: disordered
mental activity, hypersensitivity to random stimuli, and a pervasive sense
of terror produced by the flickering yet absolutely convincing hallucinations. There may be episodes of alcoholic epilepsy, after the irritation of
neuronal tissue from overfluidation, in which the brain produces a discharge of electricity that disorganizes the body's circuitry and muscular
control. The victim may suffer convulsive spasms marked by labored
breathing, blueness of the skin from lack of oxygen, and involuntary void-
ing. At one time or another, William Faulkner would experience all of
these effects.

The treatment would vary from home remedies to the ministrations of
specialized hospitals. The physician might have to treat several complaints,
not just intoxication and dehydration but perhaps malnutrition as well,
plus a cold or other infection contracted during the bout. Today the

physician will prescribe glucose, vitamins, antibiotics, and sedation. In the 1920's, and for most of the next two decades, some physicians would use paraldehyde as a sedative. An alcohol substitute, it was a powerful and addictive drug which could be administered in several forms, some of them characterized by an odor many patients found nearly unbearable. But it acted as a deep sedative for the victim suffering from acute nervousness, to be supplanted only later by tranquilizers and other drugs. Gradually the body's chemical balance would be restored, the medication would be reduced, and appetite would return. Convalescence could be completed in the hospital or at home, to which the patient would return, still a bit shaky and debilitated, with the tag end of a cold, and with a bottle of large vitamin capsules in his overnight bag. Faulkner would know this cycle too.

Severe and protracted drinking could bring in its wake other ills; gastritis, memory blackouts, cirrhosis of the liver. Faulkner was fortunate. Appetite and digestion never failed him upon his return to health, though after years of indulgence he would give up beer because he said it made him "liverish." He would remain a gourmet. The few blackouts that he would suffer later in life came from other causes, and there is no evidence that he developed cirrhosis. He had a strong constitution and was spared some of the extremities to which other writers among his contemporaries were reduced. But his drinking would produce the equivalent of one, or sometimes two, or even more, serious illnesses a year. His own euphemism for such an illness was "a collapse." In a way, it was just that.

Faulkner had been drinking for more than a dozen years when Jim Devine and Leon Scales found him on the floor of his apartment, and the pace had apparently been increasing. This was not the first time that he had experienced such a collapse, but there is no evidence that he had at this point been hospitalized for his drinking. That was yet to come, with the days, weekends, and weeks that he would lose in New York, California, and Mississippi, in France and England, in Egypt and Japan. It was good that he could not know the degree to which these agonies lay ahead of him, but he was too intelligent not to know that given the pattern he had already begun, there was little chance that he would escape the ravages of this personal demon.

FAULKNER's period of recuperation in Jim Devine's apartment, "upstate" at 111th Street, was more pleasant than others he would know. He was soon able to go out for breakfast with Devine and Scales, and before long he was back at work, writing after the others left. When guests dropped in during the evening, he would take off his shoes and tell stories that made him the center of attention—about his Mississippi youth and his Canadian service, in which, he said, he had cracked up two airplanes before they discovered he didn't know how to fly and washed him out. He told about the woman in New Orleans and the two children she had had by him, how some day he was going to go back and marry her. Later, when Scales read some of Faulkner's fiction, he had the feeling that he had heard the story before.

When he was well enough to leave, he did not return to his own place. Instead, he moved in with a young man he met at Lyle Saxon's. Owen Crump was a painter from Shreveport, Louisiana, who rented a fourth-floor studio with a skylight, fireplace, and bed at the corner of Sixth Avenue and MacDougal Street for $7.50 a week. The trains of the "el" roared by outside, shaking the whole building. Except for that, it was like being back in the Vieux Carré. After their quick and simple breakfast, Crump would move his easel to catch the morning light, and Faulkner would seat himself in the middle of the bed and begin writing in a small notebook. When he finished one, Crump remembered, he would drop it into a small valise. There on the floor was a bottle of bootleg gin, and Faulkner was recovered enough so that he would take an occasional sip as he wrote.

Lunch might come from a pot of stew cooked by Crump on a hotplate, made with leftover vegetables bought cheaply from pushcart vendors. There was strong black chicory-flavored Luzianne coffee Crump received from Shreveport. After lunch they would work until four or four-thirty. If Faulkner finished first, he might sit and watch Crump, sometimes mixing paints for him. Dinner might come from the same pot of stew, or, to vary the routine, they might walk a block to the Italian section to a restaurant and speakeasy called the Black Rabbit, where both the food and the prices were particularly good.

On Sunday afternoons Lyle Saxon might invite them out to eat, or they might attend a literary tea at one of the village salons—for the mounds of sandwiches and the drinks made with good liquor. Faulkner would be something of a celebrity, with two novels and a book of poems in print, another soon to be published, and still another being read at a publisher's. Again Faulkner would sit on the floor, cross-legged, his shoes beside him, telling some of his stories.

There were not a great many of these literary occasions. They went not just for the food but because, Crump said, "we were lonely." Small-town boys in the big city, they would take long walks—to Battery Park, to places where the famous had lived, seeking a little space as relief from the concrete and the looming buildings. Crump knew a girl at the Civic Repertory Theatre on 14th Street, where Eva Le Gallienne produced and sometimes starred in a variety of dramas. The girl could sometimes slip them in, and so, Crump said, "we haunted that place." Together they saw Chekhov's *The Cherry Orchard* and Barrie's *Peter Pan*, both starring Miss Le Gallienne.

Crump did not know what Faulkner was writing in those small dime-store notebooks. He thought that when Faulkner had enough of them, he would take them to Wasson's office for typing. With Wasson's help, he had met magazine editors he hoped would buy the stories. Afterward he could collect them in a book, as he had mentioned to Liveright. Alfred Dashiell, at *Scribner's* magazine, had rejected "Moonlight," but in late October, Faulkner went to see him, taking along three stories. "The Leg" and "Mistral" dated from his time in Europe; the third, "Bench for Two," dealt with vagrants seeking shelter from a New York winter night in Pennsylvania Station. In a letter to Aunt 'Bama. Faulkner had told her "Having a rotten time, as usual. I hate this place."[11] Even if he was now having a better time than when he wrote, something of the predominantly negative part of Faulkner's ambivalence toward New York came through in this last, uncharacteristic story. Dashiell declined all three.

It was probably the first week in November when Faulkner retrieved them and left two others: "Once Aboard the Lugger" and "As I Lay Dying." The first recounted the expedition for bootleg alcohol from the longer, earlier work of the same title. In "As I Lay Dying," the principal events of *Father Abraham* were condensed into twenty-one typed pages. He was reworking the Snopes family material which so fascinated him and Phil Stone when they talked about the actual doings of people like the Snopeses. The historical perspective interested Stone. There was, he thought, a curse on the land which could be expiated only over a long period of time, and the Snopeses were a part of the process. Drawing on the turns and twists of human behavior which Stone's daily legal practice showed him, and which Faulkner's uncle John knew from experience, the two would make up wild, outrageous stories of things that no Snopes counterpart might have done, but of which they thought them perfectly capable. "As I Lay Dying" was told by a man driving a team for his uncle during "our quadriennial vote-garnering itinerary," just as Faulkner had driven for his uncle John.[12] All the material of *Father Abraham* about the rise and subsequent career of Flem Snopes had been excluded and principal events were related in flashbacks. But Faulkner still had not found the right way to tell this story. Dashiell turned it down, along with "Once Aboard the Lugger."

This rejection may well have exhausted the stories Faulkner had with him or wanted to write. About December 8, however, he came back to the studio with two hundred-odd dollars. It was an advance, he told Crump. He would go home and supplement it by taking a janitor's job while he finished the book he was working on. "I'm gonna live and sleep in the basement where it's warm and finish the book," he said.

He was on his way home again with no definite word about *The Sound and the Fury*. He had not sold any of his short stories, but *Sartoris* would be out in perhaps six weeks, and the next mail might bring a contract for the new book or a check for a story. He would wait for success on his home ground.

CHAPTER

27

He walked to town and crossed the deserted square. He thought
of the other morning when he had crossed it. It was as though
there had not been any elapsed time between: the same gesture
of the lighted clock-face, the same vulture-like shadows in the
doorways; it might be the same morning and he had merely
crossed the square, about-faced and was returning. . . .

—*Sanctuary* (214)

THERE had been considerable activity while he was away. In a statewide
clean-up campaign, Oxford had been named "Cleanest Town" in Mississippi. At the university, construction had been finished on six new dormi-
tories and more work was planned. But politics provided the most news.
John Falkner had announced his candidacy in a special election for district
attorney of the 3rd District. The Jackson *Clarion-Ledger* endorsed Fred
M. Belk and denounced Falkner as "a red-hot Bilbo man" and credited him
with Bilbo's overwhelming majority in Lafayette County the previous
summer. Such charges did not keep the Stones, Lem Oldham, Bob Farley,
Taylor McElroy, and others from supporting Falkner in a full-page ad in
the Oxford *Eagle*. John Falkner asked Mac Reed to take a day off from
the Gathright drugstore to help in Chickasaw County, his former home.
Bill Faulkner again went along as driver on the sort of "vote-garnering
itinerary" he had mentioned in the version of the story of the spotted
horses which he had revised as "As I Lay Dying" and tried unsuccessfully
to sell to *Scribner's*. But in spite of their efforts, Belk won four of the seven
counties in the district. It looked as though what they said was true: John
Falkner was the best campaign manager in north Mississippi, but he
couldn't get himself elected.

Most of Faulkner's energies had been going into his work rather than
campaigning. He had mailed two more stories to Alfred Dashiell in mid-
December. "Once Aboard the Lugger" was not the earlier story of the
same title but a reworking of source material from which the earlier story

had also derived. He included another story called "Miss Zilphia Gant" though he was afraid it might be "too diffuse. . . ." He sent it in spite of being "quite sure that I have no feeling for short stories; that I shall never be able to write them, yet for some strange reason I continue to do so, and to try them on Scribners' with unflagging optimism."[1] A suggestive exploration of sexual pathology involving dreams and hysteria, it also echoed the eroticism of earlier works such as "Adolescence." Young Zilphia Gant is dominated and caught, however, by her mother, whose namesake she is, a woman deserted by her husband. Frustrated like her mother, the girl unsurprisingly becomes a copy of her. To one writer, "the terrible frustrations imposed on poor Zilphia by her demonic mother make of her a 'grotesque' (in the sense in which Sherwood Anderson used the word)."[2] Three days before Christmas, Dashiell returned both of these stories, but true to Faulkner's claim of unflagging optimism, he had sent him another called "Selvage." The idea was originally Estelle Franklin's, but when she had written it she had found it unsatisfactory. Faulkner had suggested that they rewrite it together, but Estelle had had enough of it. He decided to try it himself. Like Zilphia Gant and Jo-Addie Bundren, Corinthia Bowman was juxtaposed to a tyrannical parent-figure. Engaged to a dull young banker, she seduces a handsome Louisianan. Her horrified grandmother tells her he has Negro blood. (Perhaps Faulkner had known the Creole at Ole Miss whose proposal Estelle had accepted, only to be told by Lem Oldham that her dashing Jack had Negro blood.) At the story's end, after Corinthia has crashed their car, she gazes, bleeding, at the wreckage where the bodies of her two lovers lie. Dashiell received the story in late January or early December, but by the time he rejected it, Faulkner was involved in another novel.

Its roots were as intertwined as his motivation was complex. For the crucial incident he had gone back to the ghastly story he had heard in the night club about the girl who had been raped by an impotent gangster using a bizarre object. This novel would, in the long run, exact as much labor from him as any but the longest of his books, and it would give rise to questions which would be put to him endlessly thereafter. Out of self-defense he would devise formulaic answers: "Well, that book was basely conceived." He could be a jack-of-all-trades when he was single, but "then I got married," and to meet the new expenses "I thought of the most horrific idea I could think of and wrote it."[3] Or he would say that exhausted after *The Sound and the Fury*, he had stopped thinking of publishing, but when *Sartoris* was taken, he started thinking again of making money by writing. "I took a little time out," he would write, "and speculated what a person in Mississippi would believe to be current trends, chose what I thought was the right answer and invented the most horrific tale I could imagine and wrote it in about three weeks. . . ."[4] In comments to friends, he adopted the old tough-guy stance. He told one he wrote *Sanctuary* because he "liked the sound of dough rising." He told another, "I made a thorough and methodical study of everything on the list of best-sellers. When I thought I knew what the public wanted, I decided to give them a little more than they had been getting; stronger and rawer—more brutal. Guts and genitals."[5] Such remarks—in part inaccurate and in substance misleading—were to do the novel a great disservice, emphasizing for the uncritical reader its shocking aspect while distracting attention from its moral force and artistry.

The book's roots were truly multiform. The members of the Falkner family had enjoyed and exchanged mystery stories. During those summers in Pascagoula it seemed that all his friends were passing them about. Faulkner had already used the gangster milieu in short stories. Perhaps he could cash in on it now. This would not necessarily exclude another possibility: that it should also be a satisfying work of art. In *Father Abraham* and other stories, he had shown an awareness of the depth to which human beings could sink. "Billy looks around him," his mother would later say, "and he is heartsick at what he sees." There was much to see—from a sensational trial of Governor Lee Russell on scandalous charges, to Theodore Bilbo's latest exploits, to the new record for corruption in high places set a few years earlier by the administration of Warren Gamaliel Harding. At this juncture he may have considered something like a three-horse parlay: a spectacular mystery-detective-gangster story, a commercially successful novel, and a work of art that would mirror the corruption of society at large in the lives of a small number of people from different levels of society. For even wider relevance, one critic would later argue, he would consciously draw upon the folklore, legend, and myth—especially that of sacrificial death—which he had probably read about in Sir James G. Frazer's *The Golden Bough*.[6]

He could range from the further reaches of Yoknapatawpha County to Jefferson to Memphis. That city provided a rich source, undisputed claimant as it now was to the title "Murder Capital of the U.S.A." Its denizens made Al Capone and Legs Diamond look prosaic. "One-thumb" John Revinsky, "the Russian Fox," was a daring second-story man with a penchant for diamonds and no compunctions about murder. A valued associate was Mae Goodwin, queen of the Memphis underworld, a brothel madam who posed dreamily in a riding habit, a crop in her gauntleted hands, who doubled as a fence for stolen goods. The night she died, a bloody handprint with the thumb missing identified her lover as her murderer. Faulkner had not known Mae Goodwin, but he had known Mary Sharon, the Memphis madam Phil Stone remembered as "fat and flamboyant" with her hat "full of plumes."[7]

Not quite as spectacular as the Russian Fox was "Popeye" Pumphrey, who had beaten dozens of felony charges ranging from gambling to safecracking, a paradoxical figure: a temperate bootlegger and a handsome man pathologically shy with girls. Faulkner and Stone had often talked about Popeye Pumphrey with Dorothy Ware, who knew some of the racy details of his life.[8] Behind him was the shadow of the mob, only one of several. Reno DeVaux, supported by local men, was caught in the middle. Reno was burned out of the New Crystal Gardens and then The Showboat. He said it was an accident, but the newspapers reported that "one local whiskey faction backed by Al Capone's gang at Chicago and another faction backed by a New Orleans–St. Louis outfit are struggling for control."[9] Faulkner knew some of the roadhouses, casinos, and bordellos at firsthand. Not two years earlier he had drawn a $200 draft on Horace Liveright. He explained that he had bought twenty-five gallons of whiskey and buried it in the garden. "Two days later I went to Memphis, lost over three hundred dollars on a wheel, and gave a check for it." He counted on the whiskey to supplement his checking-account balance, but "one of our niggers had smelled the whisky out, dug it up, sold a little and had been caught and told where the rest of it was. So I lost all of it."[10] Liveright met the draft but asked Faulkner to let him know in advance next time. This personal experience of another kind was but a pale echo of events in Lafayette and surrounding counties. Lynchings and burnings were reported in the *Eagle* every year. Federal officers periodically destroyed "white mule machines," some of them losing their lives in the process. Unspeakable homicidal violence, sometimes within families, occurred in Lafayette County just as it did in more densely populated areas. If William Faulkner possessed a strain of misanthropy, there was much on the local, regional, and national scenes to feed it.

And there was another grisly *donneé* for his novel. One recent spring, when the Ole Miss baseball team had traveled seventy-five miles to Starkville to play archrival Mississippi A&M, one of the Ole Miss coeds had left the train even before the riotous weekend was fully under way. She was an extremely popular girl who lived just two blocks north of the University Avenue home where the Falkners had lived as boys. She had suffered some form of sexual outrage, and people talked about the incident covertly. If William Faulkner needed a bridge between Popeye's alleged Memphis atrocity and the milieu of Yoknapatawpha and the university, this would have provided it.

Much of his material had been ready for some time. He had already explored the psychology of Horace Benbow at length in *Flags in the Dust*. The parts of Horace's story which were deemphasized in *Sartoris*—his insecurities and anxieties, his sexual attitudes, especially toward his sister Narcissa—had continued to interest Faulkner. And even when he was writing *The Sound and the Fury*, the effects of deep-seated sexual obsessions, overt and latent, conscious and unconscious, had fascinated him in the character of Quentin Compson, who in some ways might have been a younger version of Horace Benbow. Here Horace would share the forefront of the story with Temple Drake, and two false starts began with her. Then Faulkner wrote a scene in which Horace talks with Lee Goodwin, a moonshiner jailed on a charge of murder. He quickly brought in Goodwin's common-law wife, Ruby Lamar, and their child. Then, as Horace explains the case to Narcissa and Aunt Jenny DuPre, he fills in more of Goodwin's story, that Goodwin fears a gunman named Popeye. Horace also reveals that he has walked out on his wife, the former Belle Mitchell, the heavily sensuous seductress whom Faulkner had introduced in *Flags in the Dust*. The signs of exhaustive experimentation would appear throughout the growing manuscript. Before page 11 would be permanently fixed in that sequence, it would bear seventeen other page numbers. All but 34 of the 139 pages in the completed manuscript would be tried in more than one place. By the time Faulkner reached page 80 there were fewer pasteins and shifts of pages, but he would try sixteen of the novel's twentyseven chapters in other sequences before achieving their final placement. And even when he reached the typing stage, he would continue to rearrange his material drastically.

By mid-April, Faulkner had hopes of finishing the novel in the summer. *Sartoris* had been published on January 31, 1929, with an initial printing of 1,998 copies. On April 8, when Alfred Harcourt asked if Faulkner would like to see the reviews that were coming in, he replied quickly that he would like that very much, for he had seen only one. "I live in a complete dearth of print save in its most innocent form," he explained. "The magazine store here carries nothing that has not either a woman in her underclothes or someone shooting someone else with a pistol on the cover; that includes newspapers too." The only response he could make to their request for ideas for selling the novel involved Mac Reed: "If you could permit him a consignment basis, he will sell a copy now and then for three or four years, as people here learn that I am a 'book-author.' I'd not like to deprive them of their Tanlac and Pinkham's Compound by tying Mr. Reed's capital up in books, you know."[11]

The early reviews were mixed, including those of the influential *New York Times* and New York *Herald Tribune*, better on the whole in the latter than the former, where the anonymous reviewer found the work uneven and loose as well as inconsistent in theme and character. The reviews continued mixed through the spring. The best was Donald Davidson's column, which appeared in Nashville, Knoxville, and Memphis. But he had reservations too. Even though "as a stylist and as an acute observer of human behavior" Faulkner was "the equal of any except three or four American novelists who stand at the very top," Davidson felt he had not yet found a theme or character that would fully exploit his gifts.[12] It would be years later that one critic would identify a problem that must have been felt by many of the novel's readers. It lay with the protagonist: "Bayard all too often appears to be merely an immature, romantic, and neurotic young man, a special case, too limited to be representative either of the Sartoris family traits or the plight of modern man. . . ."[13]

Faulkner was disappointed and discouraged by the reception of *Sartoris*. Phil Stone shared his feelings, but he still had faith in Faulkner's talent.

"Bill," he said, "forget about trying to please them. Just go on and write what you damn please."

"I think I not only won't make any money out of what I write," Faulkner said; "I won't ever get any recognition either." In spite of his discouragement, he was going ahead with *Sanctuary*. One spring evening when Stone went to see Faulkner in his small tower room, he had listened to Faulkner read from it. Though he felt absolutely sure that Faulkner was intent on shaping it into a work of art rather than a sensational potboiler, he was not convinced that this novel would do any more for Faulkner than *Sartoris* had.

"Bill," he said, "this won't sell. The day of the shocker is past."[14]

Discouraged as he had every right to be, Faulkner characteristically trusted his own judgment and went on with the book, though he referred to it with a sardonic edge in a letter to Ben Wasson. "I am now writing a book," he said bluntly, "about a girl who gets raped with a corn cob." But what really interested him was "how all this evil flowed off of her like water off a duck's back." And he was ready to generalize from this. "Women are completely impervious to evil," he wrote. It was curious that he should have said that the book was about Temple Drake when its primary focus in this first version was Horace Benbow, and Horace's reaction to evil, in others and in himself. One critic would see it as "essentially, a heavily Freudian study of Horace's sexual and emotional problems. . . ."[15]

He bettered his own estimate of the time the book would take him. The manuscript finished, he began the slow process of typing it with his two index fingers. Among the girls of The Bunch it was known as the "bad" book that Phil and Bill wouldn't let Sallie Simpson type.[16] On the title page he wrote in blue ink "Oxford, Miss./January–May, 1929." On page 358, the last page, he wrote a more precise date: "25 May 1929." He had employed a double strategy, grafting the shocking Pumphrey material onto expanded elements which had first appeared in *Flags in the Dust*. Horace Benbow stood in the forefront, and many of the novel's events would be as important for the way they impinged upon his sensibilities as for their intrinsic function in the plot. The cuts from *Flags in the Dust* had reduced the incestuous component of Horace's relationship with Narcissa. Now in Chapter II it was clear that Horace had married Belle Mitchell only when Narcissa refused to cancel her wedding to Bayard Sartoris. " 'Narcy,' he said, 'dont do it, Narcy. We both wont. . . . when I think what we . . . with this house, and all it— Dont you see we cant?' " Belle had even taunted him: " 'You're in love with your sister. What do the books call it? What sort of complex?' " Married to corrupt Belle Mitchell for ten years, Benbow is now a distinctly Prufrockian figure, seeing himself in a mirror as "a thin man in shabby mismatched clothes, with high evaporating temples beneath an untidy mist of fine, thin, unruly hair." He would say, "I lack courage: that was left out of me. The machinery is all here, but it wont run."[17] (Some years later that other lawyer Faulkner knew so well, Phil Stone, would tell his wife, "I'm like an elaborate, intricate piece of machinery which doesn't quite work."[18])

Like Quentin Compson, Horace Benbow had been a boy whose love for his invalid mother had been displaced onto his sister. Unlike Quentin, however, he could feel a sexual passion for other women too, including his stepdaughter, Little Belle. As she sat with boys in the hammock (like Caddy and then Miss Quentin in the swing), Horace would hear her dress "whispering to the delicate and urgent mammalian rifeness of that curious small flesh which he did not beget." Faulkner called on his memories to describe the appeal Ruby Lamar held for Horace: "there was something about her, something of that abject arrogance and cringing beneath all the lace and scent which he had felt when the inmates of brothels entered the parlor in the formal parade of shrill identical smiles through which the old lusts and the old despairs peeped. . . ."[19] Horace would struggle with these feelings, aghast at some, less aware of others, repressing still others when he could. By the standards of 1929 this novel certainly would be a shocker, with a gamut of sexuality that extended from rape to sadism to voyeurism to fraternal and quasi-paternal forms of incest wishes.

The first chapter placed Horace in the jail talking with his client, whiskey-maker Lee Goodwin, in the presence of his common-law wife, Ruby Lamar, a former Memphis prostitute. It also revealed that he had finally left Belle, setting out on foot from their home in the Delta, accidentally encountering Popeye, the Memphis bootlegger, just as grotesque but even more sinister than he had been in "The Big Shot." As Horace related these events to his sister and Aunt Jenny, it became clear that the women in his life embodied a kind of scale of good and evil. As Belle and Little Belle suggested a heavy sexuality that was both attractive and repelling, so Aunt Jenny suggested a kind of nobility and honor tempered by a pragmatic view of life. As the novel developed, Narcissa would show herself quite as capable of evil as Belle. The same thing would be true of the wronged Temple Drake when she appeared, whereas, paradoxically, qualities of courage, sacrifice, and love would manifest themselves in Ruby in spite of the wretched and debased life she lived. Temple would not appear until Chapter VI, in a flashback preceding her ordeal and the murder of the half-wit Tommy, with which Goodwin had been charged.

Employing what one scholar would call an "intricate pattern of flashbacks and shifting perspectives,"[20] Faulkner showed how Gowan Stevens' drunkenness had stranded Temple and himself at the Old Frenchman place. Then, alternating omniscient narration with that of Ruby, he carried the story forward beyond Temple's undescribed rape to Popeye's installation of her in Miss Reba's Memphis brothel, presumably to keep her undercover against the need for a respectable alibi for Tommy's murder. At this point Faulkner turned again to material exploited in *Flags in the Dust*: Snopeslore. Virgil and his friend Fonzo Winbush, country boys come to Memphis to barber college, provided comic relief at the brothel, amazed that the "landlady" from whom they rented their room had so many "daughters." Reba Rivers was another strong Faulkner creation for whom he seems to have drawn not only on his Memphis memories but also on a character he much admired: Dickens' Mrs. Sarah Gamp.[21] The murder of Red—brought by impotent Popeye to Temple as a surrogate lover—was related by the omniscient narrator; so, too, was the trial, at which Temple's callous perjury permitted Goodwin's conviction.

Faulkner had ended the novel quickly. Chapter XXV was Horace's letter telling Narcissa how he had fled Jefferson and returned to Belle after the jury's verdict. The next chapter was Narcissa's seventeen-line reply. The final one briefly recounted Popeye's conviction for a crime he had not committed and described his strange passivity in the face of death. In a sudden shift to the Luxembourg Gardens at twilight, Judge Drake sat with Temple as she gazed idly at her reflection, then closed her compact as "she seemed to follow with her eyes the waves of music, to dissolve into the dying brasses, across the pool and the opposite semicircle of trees where at sombre intervals the dead tranquil queens in stained marble mused, and on into the sky lying prone and vanquished in the embrace of the season of rain and death."[22] It was almost certainly a shortened version of the piece he had described to his mother in his letter from Paris four years before, the one about "the Luxembourg gardens and death."[23] But then he undercut this evocative passage, ending his book with a brief sardonic vignette of Popeye as the sheriff sprung the trap.

The novel's first readers were women. Estelle was outraged.

"It's horrible," she told him.

"It's meant to be," he answered. Then he added, "It will sell." Three women in Hal Smith's office read it. Evelyn Harter thought it was so shocking that she told Louise Bonino she didn't think they could publish it. Louise reached the same conclusion and told Hal Smith. Lenore Marshall was stunned by the novel's power, and in her reader's report she wrote, "It's a great book."

Smith's verdict was unequivocal. Faulkner would recall it in an unvarying phrase: " 'Good God, I can't publish this. We'd both be in jail.' " Faulkner would say that he told himself, "You're damned. You'll have to work now and then for the rest of your life."[24]

ESTELLE's divorce was now final. It seemed to some Oxonians that Bill Faulkner was always at the Oldhams', seeing Estelle, eating with the family, sometimes baby-sitting. He was there so much that some—probably some of the same ones who had called him "Count No 'Count"—now called him "Major Oldham's yard boy." Faulkner cared very little what people thought, but the Oldhams were far less impervious to public opinion. Lem Oldham was no happier now at the prospect of having Bill Faulkner as a son-in-law than he had been eleven years before, but one late spring day a family argument boiled over, and Dorothy Oldham tele-

phoned Bill Faulkner to tell him it was time he married her sister. The
Oldhams could no more have compelled Faulkner to do something than
could his own family. By now, however, Estelle was distraught, and Dot's
call may have provided a crucial impetus. Faulkner's hopes for *Sanctuary*
had been dashed, but he felt compelled to act. Encountering his brother
Jack, he told him, "I'm going to marry Estelle." Thinking of finances, Jack
counseled postponement. "I got what I deserved," he later recalled, "no
reply at all."[25]

Faulkner must have been acting from mixed motives. Jack and Johncy
felt that he had never stopped loving Estelle, no matter how embittered he
had been by her marriage to Cornell Franklin. Feelings of pride and
defiance, another kinsman would later say, had also impelled him to
"show" these people who had once said, in effect, that he wasn't good
enough to marry their daughter. At this critical juncture, he bared some
of his feelings to his publisher. "Hal," he wrote, "I want $500.00. I am
going to be married. Both want to and have to. THIS PART IS CON-
FIDENTIAL, UTTERLY. For my honor and the sanity—I believe life—
of a woman. This is not bunk; neither am I being sucked in. We grew up
together and I dont think she could fool me in this way; that is, make me
believe that her mental condition, her nerves, are this far gone. And no
question of pregna[n]cy: that would hardly move me: no one can face his
own bastard with more equanimity than I, having had some practice.
Neither is it a matter of a promise on my part; we have known one another
long enough to pay no attention to our promises. It's a situation which I
engendered and permitted to ripen which has become unbearable, and I
am tired of running from devilment I bring about. This sounds a little
insane, but I'm not in any shape to write letters now. I'll explain it better
when I see you." Years before he had boasted blithely of bastard children
to Sherwood Anderson and other New Orleans friends, but now his tone
was not only serious but desperate. He would give Smith a note "with ten
percent. interest or whatever you wish, due the first of next March, with
the reversion of all accruing royalty on the two novels of mine you have
in case I die, and I will promise in writing to deliver you a third novel
before that date; if it fails to please you, the note and interest to be paid on
the above date." He concluded, "I need not say this is confidential—the
reasons, I mean—and urgent. I believe it will be the last time I'll bother you
for money before time, because from now on I'll have to work. And I
work well under pressure—and a wife will be pressure enough for me.
Will you wire me Yes or No collect? If No, of course I'll understand."[26]
Whatever Harrison Smith's response was, Faulkner did not preserve it,
but Faulkner's cousin Sallie Murry would later say that her husband, Bob
Williams, lent Bill Faulkner the money to go on his honeymoon.

On June 20, 1929—in Maud Falkner's little Chevrolet, with Dot squeezed
in beside them—he and Estelle went to the courthouse for their wedding
license. Then he turned back toward the square. Estelle asked where they

were going. "To your father's office," he said. It was a point of honor that he tell Lem Oldham. He had already told his own unhappy parents and Phil Stone, who seemed more unhappy than they. Stone felt as he had eleven years before, that this step would be ruinous for his career. Faulkner had in all likelihood responded to Stone's strictures as he had to Jack Falkner's, and the breach in their once intimate friendship grew wider.

It was a brief interview. "Mr. Lem," said Faulkner, his back poker-straight, " 'Stelle and I are going to be married."

"Billy," said Major Oldham, "I've always been fond of you as a friend, but I don't want you marrying my daughter. But if you're determined, I won't stand in your way." Bill and Estelle were adults, and Major Oldham regularly received the support checks that came from Cornell in accordance with the divorce settlement, so there was no likelihood of hardship for the children. This point of honor satisfied, Faulkner returned to the car and headed west on North Depot Street for the road to College Hill.

They could not be married in Estelle's church. Old Reverend Edward McCrady was sorry, but the Episcopal Church was very firm about the remarriage of divorced persons. So they had turned to one of the best-liked ministers in the county, Winn David Hedleston, professor of philosophy and ethics at the university and pastor of the College Hill Presbyterian Church. He welcomed them and said he would get his wife to act as a witness with Dot. She was in the kitchen, both ample arms black with berry juice. She was making blackberry preserves, she said, but Estelle felt sure it was blackberry wine. They drove to the stately tree-shaded church a mile away. Its white Corinthian columns lent it strength and dignity, and its bright white interior, with the old slave gallery in the back, showed the care its builders had lavished on it nearly a century before. Dr. Hedleston's words sounded clearly in the near-empty church as he read the simple ceremony. Afterward he signed the marriage certificate in his shaky old-man's hand, and the tiny wedding party departed with the Hedlestons' congratulations. Mr. and Mrs. William Faulkner drove back to town, in the borrowed car, with borrowed money for the honeymoon, facing an uncertain future.

If there was anything to mitigate the uncertainty, it was *Sanctuary*'s predecessor. When Faulkner had inquired in February, Alfred Harcourt had replied that they doubted the salability of *The Sound and the Fury*. But then, he said, Hal Smith had explained that Faulkner had submitted it to him, not Harcourt Brace. Smith was planning a partnership with the English publisher Jonathan Cape. Ben Wasson was to join the firm as an editor. When Smith asked Harcourt for the book, Harcourt replied, "You're the only damn fool in New York who would publish it." The firm of Jonathan Cape and Harrison Smith (Faulkner's fourth publisher in just over four years) had promptly dispatched a contract providing a $200 advance. He would be able to correct proof, on his honeymoon, of the novel about "his heart's darling."[27]

28

. . . the days themselves were unchanged—the same stationary
recapitulation of golden interval between dawn and sunset, the
long quiet identical days, the immaculate monotonous hierarchy
of noons filled with the sun's hot honey. . . .

—The Wild Palms (110–111)

BACK in Oxford, he exchanged Miss Maud's car for Mr. Murry's. Malcolm
Franklin had joyfully informed the neighbors that "Mama and Mr. Bill
got married." Now they put him in the car and set off for Columbus,
eighty-five miles to the southeast.

When they finally pulled up in the driveway of Mrs. Hairston's house,
Cho-Cho raced out to greet them. After supper the bridal couple drove
twenty-five miles back in the direction of Oxford to spend their wedding
night in Aberdeen. The next day they returned, then set out for
Pascagoula with Malcolm. Cho-Cho and Mrs. Hairston would join them
in three weeks. But Mrs. Hairston insisted that they could not go on their
honeymoon without help; they must at least take Emma, her white-haired
servant of many years. They must also take some of her silver. Mrs.
Hairston genuinely liked Bill Faulkner, and as Estelle would later write,
"it was she who approved and applauded my marriage to Bill. She also
unhesitatingly upbraided my father for coldly insisting that I'd married
a wastrel."[1] She was determined to do all she could to see that this new
marriage worked out.

It took most of June 21 to cover the 190 miles through the hills, the
brief strip of prairie, and the long stretch of piney woods before the
flat green coastal meadows came into view. At last they turned down onto
the beachfront road in Pascagoula, where the flat sheen of the Gulf
stretched out to the boat-dotted horizon. Frank Lewis had rented them
the two-story Turnbull place on the east beach just three homes from
the bayou. The house itself was considerably run down, but Estelle, still

dressed in the styles of Honolulu and Shanghai, became a figure of considerable interest to the neighbors. Pascagoula was a rather casual place, but Mrs. Hermes Gautier gave a party to welcome Mrs. William Faulkner. Despite the heavy rain that afternoon, Estelle wore a black velvet dress with a big black hat to match. Her clothes, the other ladies agreed, were gorgeous. One neighbor thought that she and her husband dressed every night for dinner. They drank quite openly. In fact, the Faulkners caused quite a stir in Pascagoula.

They had known each other for over a quarter of a century, but they were learning new things about each other. Estelle realized that geniuses weren't like other people, but some of her husband's habits were curious. Undressing at night, he would put his clothes neatly on a chair and his shoes on the dresser for polishing. Yet sometimes he would go out wearing moccasins; other times he would be barefoot. He was tanning quickly, and would go without shaving for days at a time. His movements were as slow as ever, but he was always punctual, starting out well in advance because he hated to rush. His view of time was different from that of most people. "I have all eternity ahead, why worry hurrying to get things done today?" he said. "Time is a man-made convention." One convention they established was to avoid discussing politics: she was a Republican born and bred, and he was a Southern Democrat. Neither was likely to sway the other. His manner might vary from abruptness and aloofness to gallantry. Their neighbor, Mrs. Martin Shepherd, was charmed. To her he was "a regular Chesterfield." Estelle was used to his silences; he, to her conversational talents, which protected him on social occasions. To friends of earlier Pascagoula summers, such as Bill Lolo and Tom Kell, he seemed much the same. Once, when Kell commented on his new status, Faulkner confided, "Tom, they don't think we're gonna stick, but it is gonna stick." Kell would come to see them often, occasionally bringing his wife, Lola, along. His friendship—his readiness to take one or both of them for a ride in his car or to get the torches and other gear for flounder-fishing at night in the shallow water—was particularly valuable when work intruded on the honeymoon.

The proofs of *The Sound and the Fury* arrived in early July. In copyediting the manuscript, Ben Wasson had deleted all of the italics in the Benjy section and had instead introduced additional space between passages to indicate time shifts. He felt that the italic-roman system could differentiate only between two time levels, whereas Faulkner had used at least four. Faulkner angrily restored the italics, closed up the spaces, and italicized additional passages. He wrote Wasson that sometimes there were more than four dates involved and listed eight different times as examples. The trouble with the spacing, he wrote, was that "a break indicates an objective change in tempo, while the objective picture here should be a continuous whole, since the thought transference is subjective; i.e., in Ben's mind and not in the reader's eye. I think italics are necessary to establish for the reader Benjy's confusion; that unbroken-surfaced confusion of an idiot which is outwardly a dynamic and logical coherence. To gain this, by using breaks it will be necessary to write an induction for each transference. I wish publishing was advanced enough to use colored ink for such, as I argued with you and Hal in the speak-easy that day." Now the passages would have to be repunctuated. "You'd better see to that," he wrote, "since you're all for coherence. And dont make any more additions to the script, bud. I know you mean well, but so do I. I effaced the 2 or 3 you made." Later Faulkner sent two more letters with brief instructions. There was a penitent note in one of them. "Excuse recent letter," he told Ben. "Didnt mean to be stubborn and inconsiderate. Believe I am right, tho. And I was not blaming you with it. . . . Excuse it anyway. Estelle sends regards. Love to all. Bill."[2]

Working to promote the book, Wasson had sent a set of galleys to Evelyn Scott, another Cape & Smith author, who had just published *The Wave*, a huge experimental novel of the Civil War which had been enthusiastically praised as well as criticized. When she wrote Ben, she told him that *The Sound and the Fury* was "a novel with the qualities of greatness." She thought Benjy a "better idiot than Dostoevsky's," and he made her think of Blake's Lamb and his Tiger, of Christ and Adam. She found the other sections extraordinary too. When Hal Smith saw the letter, he said, "Let's make a pamphlet out of this." Expanding the letter into a six-page essay, Evelyn Scott called Faulkner's novel a tragedy with "all the spacious proportions of Greek art," a work which was "an important contribution to the permanent literature of fiction."[3] Ben began making up mailing lists, and Faulkner responded to his request with ten names in Oxford and half a dozen others.

Perhaps Evelyn Scott's response took some of the sting out of another *Scribner's* rejection. Alfred Dashiell thought it was hard to find the actual story in "Through the Window." The mainspring of the plot went back to *Flags in the Dust*. The obscene letters Byron Snopes had written to Narcissa and then stolen back had been obtained by the FBI agent investigating Byron's robbery of the Sartoris bank. As ransom for the letters, Narcissa had slept with the agent, and this knowledge killed Aunt Jenny. He would revise the story as "An Empress Passed," but it would be more than three years before it appeared as "There Was a Queen."

THREE weeks after the honeymooners arrived at Pascagoula, Mrs. Hairston, accompanied by Cho-Cho, came for her visit. She was an easy guest and made herself at home, enlivening things for Estelle by organizing a bridge party. The routine was still the same. The days were spent swimming, sunning, fishing, or just strolling the beach. Some eve-nings they might all get into the touring car Faulkner had bought and drive forty miles along the silvery beach, past Biloxi, to Gulfport for dinner. After a week Mrs. Hairston took the children back to Columbus, and Bill and Estelle took a brief trip of their own. They went to New Orleans and put up at the elegant old Monteleone. Estelle met newspaper friends of her husband, and others he had shanghaied aboard the *Nausikaa* in *Mosquitoes*. By the time they returned to Pascagoula, it was getting on toward late summer.

In spite of all the diversions, it had hardly been a relaxing honeymoon. There had been strains and emotional crises. One of them had frightened Mrs. Shepherd. She had watched Estelle, in one of her gorgeous silk dresses, walk down to the beach after an evening of heavy drinking. Suddenly she heard Bill call out to her husband, Martin, sitting there on the porch beside her. "She's going to drown herself!" he shouted. Shepherd ran down and into the shallow water, wading and stumbling more than the length of a block before he caught Estelle almost where the shelf of the beach dropped away at the channel. He said she fought him, but he was finally able to bring her to shore. They summoned Dr. Kell, who administered a sedative and ordered her to bed. In a few days she was better.

Was it a serious attempt at suicide or a kind of gesture? It seems not to have been the first time, and it would not be the last. At the very least, it was a dramatic if not desperate response to her problems. She faced an uncertain future. She was living now in a rundown house with one servant—borrowed like the silver they ate with. And it was clear that the life she had known in the Far East could never be duplicated in Oxford. But Cornell's money would provide for the children, and Faulkner had always been so loving that she could feel well assured that they would suffer much less than most children of broken homes. Some of her distress could have come from a feeling that she and her bridegroom had been forced into the marriage, or that they had been motivated by a sense of duty or pride or both. They loved each other, and he, now a mature man, could be a passionate lover. But they were separated by a dozen years and widely different experiences from the people they had been in the early period of their relationship.

There may have been other feelings, even harder to cope with. Not long after their imminent return to Oxford, young Malcolm Franklin would visit one of his friends, agog with stories of Cornell Franklin and his new wife, Dallas, visiting Mama and Mr. Bill: Dallas and Mr. Bill together in the garden, Cornell and Estelle in the parlor. Many years later Cho-Cho would say she thought her mother had believed that somehow Cornell would come back to her, and that many times she probably regretted marrying William Faulkner. It is not unlikely that the first of those pangs may have come in the house by the beach at Pascagoula. Both knew each other well enough to know when something was deeply wrong, perhaps even to sense the causes. And the drinking made matters worse.

Though taciturn, Faulkner could be sharp. Cho-Cho would remember, "he could say things that would cut you to the heart." Apart from his remark that he was Quentin Compson, Faulkner would almost always steadfastly disclaim responsibility for, or even agreement with, his characters. But in the novel he would start, almost as soon as they returned to Oxford, the book's most reliable character, Cash Bundren, convinced that his youngest brother was having an affair with a married woman, would say, "A fellow kind of hates to see [a young boy] wallowing in somebody else's mire. . . ."[4] A few years later, describing a wedding day beset with obvious difficulties, Faulkner's narrator would say, "Yes, she was weeping again now; it did, indeed, rain on that marriage."[5]

When they returned to Oxford, they rented the downstairs floor of Miss Elma Meek's house at 803 University Avenue. A small gray-haired woman with glasses and a rather sharp nose, Miss Elma had a surprisingly sweet smile and a keen sense of humor. She scrupulously kept up her large, imposing white house. On the high-ceilinged first floor the Faulkners had a drawing room, two bedrooms, a dining room, bath, and kitchen—all off the enormous twelve-foot-wide front hall which ran almost the full length of the house. Estelle's furniture had been shipped from Honolulu, and it filled the ample apartment. The children started school and Estelle assumed her duties. She had a girl to do the housework, and Cornell's child-support payments provided a nurse for the children. Estelle did the cooking, often preparing exotic Eastern dishes her husband loved, especially the hot curries seasoned with imported spices.

They fell into new routines. Every day Faulkner would walk to the old Delta Psi house for coffee with Miss Maud. It was the kind of filial duty that would increasingly typify his relations with his family. To Phil Stone it was further evidence that all the Falkner boys were tied to their mother—and resented it. This was probably responsible in part, Stone thought, for an animosity toward women that he saw in Bill. Stone's possessive feelings had abated little, and as his proprietary status—such as it was—declined further, his feeling of injury increased. Occasionally Estelle would go along on one of the visits, bringing a small gift to her new mother-in-law. She noticed, however, that Miss Maud would shortly fall silent, and she was sure this did not happen when Billy went by himself. She was right. Once young Jimmy Falkner heard her muttering to herself, "I don't see how my sons get along with those women they married!" Jack's childless marriage had turned out to be a bitterly unhappy one which would not last. At least Johncy's had given her grandchildren, and Dolly was as much opposed to drink as Maud Falkner herself. But Dolly always called her "Mrs. Falkner." Miss Maud was far from reconciled to this recent marriage. When Billy drank too much, she was likely to feel that Estelle encouraged him by her example. Over the long run, Estelle would see more of Maud Falkner than would her other daughters-in-law, but it would be no easy relationship.

Miss MAUD had given her eldest son a frail spindle-legged writing table. He placed it sideways at one of his parlor windows where the light would come in from his left. One story he probably worked on at that table was entitled "A Rose for Emily." A boyhood friend, John Cullen, thought Faulkner took much of this one from life: from the courtship of Miss Mary Louise Neilson by Captain Jack Hume, a Yankee who had arrived two years before to supervise the paving of Oxford's streets. They had married in spite of the Neilsons' objections. What Faulkner wrote about, Cullen thought, was "events that were expected but never actually happened."[6] The inferences from Homer Barron's jilting of Emily Wyatt and her purchase of arsenic were clear, but there was still a quality of mystery. Five pages from the end, however, Miss Emily spoke openly to her servant about the body of her betrayer lying upstairs. The dusty room suggested the expectation of bridal rites, much like that of Miss Haversham in *Great Expectations*, the novel by one of Faulkner's favorites, Charles Dickens. In a surprise-ending technique such as he had employed for the *Times-Picayune*, a strand of gray hair next to the corpse's pillow showed that this was a drama not only of fornication and murder but necrophilia as well. In October, Alfred Dashiell informed Faulkner that in spite of good characterization and an "unusual situation," the story did not fall within *Scribner's* "fiction needs." The letter was dated October 7, 1929, the publication day of *The Sound and the Fury*.[7]

The reviews were not long in coming in. The New York *World* gave qualified endorsement. But on October 13, Lyle Saxon wrote in the *Herald Tribune*, "I believe simply and sincerely that this is a great book." Like Evelyn Scott, he invoked Dostoevsky and Joyce. Later in the month the Boston *Evening Transcript*'s reviewer mentioned Euripides and saw the novel as Greek tragedy in north Mississippi. Favorable opinions would come later from *The New York Times* and *The Saturday Review of Literature*, but there were no commensurate sales. The total printing was 1,789—enough to satisfy all demand for the book for nearly a year and a half.

In Oxford, the novelist in all likelihood was working on short stories, but rejections, such as the recent one of "A Rose for Emily," must have showed him that he now had to bow to necessity. He found a job, his first steady employment since his resignation from the Postal Service nearly five years before. Every workday night he would report to the university power plant at six P.M. to work a twelve-hour shift. In spite of his schedule, Estelle and he had company. He wrote Aunt 'Bama, inviting her to come for a visit with her husband, Walter B. McLean. Other visitors that fall included Cornell and Dallas Franklin. Faulkner welcomed them politely, but before long he had had enough of their visit. He went to Memphis and returned home only after they left.

WHEN Faulkner planned to work away from his home workroom, he would roll up the segment he had begun, together with an ample supply of blank sheets, secure the roll with a sturdy elastic band, and put it in his pocket. On October 25, 1929, the day after panic had broken out on Wall Street, he took one of these sheets and wrote at the top in blue ink "As I Lay Dying." Then he underlined it twice and wrote the date in the upper right-hand corner.

The two-story thirty-year-old powerhouse of brick squatted beside the tall smokestack that rose above it. Inside, wrote one historian, the "electric generator symbolized the University's entrance into the technological age of the twentieth century."[8] The building compactly housed the furnaces, boilers, the huge wheel and belt, the pulley and dynamo, and the banks of equipment with their gauges and switches. Faulkner would later describe his laborious job. "I shoveled coal from the bunker into a wheelbarrow and wheeled it and dumped it where the fireman could put it into the boiler. About 11 o'clock the people would be going to bed, and so it did not take so much steam. Then we could rest, the fireman and I. He would sit in a chair and doze. I had invented a table out of a wheelbarrow in the coal bunker, just beyond a wall from where a dynamo ran. It made a deep, constant humming noise. There was no more work to do until about 4 A.M., when we would have to clean the fires and get up steam again."[9] This gave him enough time each night, he later said, so that he "could write another chapter by about 4 A.M."[10] The creative imagination had been at work again—as when he recalled crashing airplanes and swabbing decks. The job was supervisory, with two Negroes to provide the labor. Estelle recalled that he would go to work after dinner, immaculate, and return before breakfast, still immaculate. After eating he would sleep for about two hours, piecing out his rest with brief naps later in the day. Sometimes he would show her what he had written on his shift.

In writing *As I Lay Dying*, he felt none of the rapture he had experienced with *The Sound and the Fury*. Like *Sanctuary*, this was a "deliberate" book. "I set out deliberately to write a tour-de-force. Before I ever put pen to paper and set down the first word I knew what the last word would be. . . . Before I began I said, I am going to write a book by which, at a pinch, I can stand or fall if I never touch ink again." A year and a half before, sitting down each morning to *The Sound and the Fury*, he had felt a combination of faith and expectation and even ecstasy. "It was not there in As I Lay Dying. I said, It is because I knew too much about this book before I began to write it."[11] He had already used the title twice before for versions of the spotted-horses episode from *Father Abraham*. When asked about it, he would sometimes recite a line—"As I lay dying the woman with the dog's eyes would not close my eyelids for me as I descended into Hades." It was the speech of ghostly Agamemnon to Odysseus in the Eleventh Book of the *Odyssey*.

What Faulkner was doing night after night as he wrote to the hum of the powerhouse dynamo was to structure his novel around a family which had not appeared in *Father Abraham*. Anse and Addie Bundren had five children, the youngest of them—a girl and a small boy—sleeping together as Jo-Addie and Elmer Hodge had done in *Elmer*. Besides Henry Armstid, there were others from *Father Abraham*: Vernon Turpin, Will Varner, one of the Littlejohn family, and even one spotted horse (a descendant of the original herd, since the time was twenty-five years later), ridden by Jewel Bundren. There were numerous other echoes—phrases and even whole scenes—from the two earlier works. The idea from which the whole book grew, Allen Tate would remember Faulkner saying, was Anse Bundren's reflection that his troubles had come with the building of the road, that once it was built, it was easy for bad luck to find him. Young Vardaman Bundren might not have been too different from young Admiral Dewey Snopes if it had not been for the imminent traumatic loss of his dying mother, Addie. Faulkner had depicted sultry nubile country girls before, but in Dewey Dell Bundren he would outdo himself. If Cash, the quiet eldest son, was a recognizable country type, Darl at first glance might seem unfamiliar and utterly different from the other Bundrens. Actually, he was another representative of a type which had always fascinated Faulkner: the madman with poetic gifts.

As he later said, "I took this family and subjected them to the two greatest catastrophes which man can suffer—flood and fire, that's all. . . . That was written in six weeks without changing a word because I knew from the first where that was going."[12] In the first story, the disaster had sprung from duplicity, greed, and naïveté. Now, though obligation to the dead would be the ostensible motive, it was shiftless Anse's desire for false teeth and a new wife that would subject Addie's children and her own putrefying body to the twin catastrophes. Faulkner was still dealing with some of the same constants: the evil and folly of men, a spectacle mitigated only by indignation, compassion, and humor.

His title was now more closely linked to the story than it had been when he used it in the version of elements from *Father Abraham*. It was a woman now, rather than a man, stretched out supine as in death, but as Clytemnestra had betrayed her husband Agamemnon with Aegisthus, so Addie had betrayed Anse with the Reverend Whitfield, the father of Jewel. But her major aspect was that of a victim—dying on a corn-shuck mattress while her husband looked toward her burial.

The manuscript pages accumulating under the minuscule strokes of his pen made it clear that Faulkner did know exactly where he was going. There were far fewer canceled passages, marginal inserts, and paste-ins than in the manuscripts of his other novels. He may well have been using material from the lost 203 pages—whatever they were—that had preceded the seventeen-page version of the story he had called "As I Lay Dying." Here the dialect was not oppressively heavy, as it had been in that story, though the novel also employed an experimental style. He was using the stream-of-consciousness technique, though sparingly, and even when he used it for Darl, it was never as hard to follow as it had been with Benjy and Quentin. There would be a total of fifteen characters, whose fifty-nine interior monologues, varying from one line to several pages, were most often more like soliloquies or the direct address of Jason Compson than the flowing and shifting memories and meditations of Quentin. But as the narrators of that novel had turned toward a central female figure, Caddie, who had no segment of her own, so more than one of these characters Faulkner was creating was preoccupied with another female figure, dying Addie, who was given only one narrative segment.

Here Faulkner may have been indebted to another American writer, one whom Sherwood Anderson admired greatly. In 1915, Edgar Lee Masters had published *Spoon River Anthology*, a book of more than two hundred short poems consisting of epitaphs and soliloquies by and about characters now dead and speaking from a graveyard on an Illinois hillside. Faulkner would later refer to this book, and if he also knew the *Domesday Book*, which Masters published five years later, it could have contributed something to both the form and content of the new novel. As one scholar points out, in the *Domesday Book*, Masters concentrated on a character named Elinor Murray, early in the poem declaring his intent to make a record

> Of lives which have touched hers, what lives she touched;
> And how her death by surest logic touched
> This life or that, was cause of causes. . . .[13]

Early in *As I Lay Dying* a familiar motif in Faulkner's work appeared, an abnormal bond between a sister and brother, though it would be far from incestuous. As early as page 11 of the manuscript, Dewey Dell thought of the knowledge of Addie's death which Darl had telepathically shared with her. Another paragraph, full of curiously fetal imagery, revealed his knowledge that she was pregnant by her lover, Lafe. (Other similar imagery resembled lines in his poem "Pregnancy" and the story "Frankie and Johnny.") Faulkner canceled these two passages, but Darl's clairvoyance was clear. She would feel his eyes on her during the funeral trip to come, knowing not only her predicament but also, presumably, that her own ulterior motive for the trip was an abortion. Instead of the mutual empathy conveyed in the canceled passages, however, her feeling for her brother would change to destructive hostility.

Though Faulkner's principal characters were new, he reached back into what he called his lumber-room for others who not only served present purposes but also provided links to other work. "I found out," he later said, "that not only each book had to have a design but the whole output or sum of an artist's work had to have a design."[14] One such linking character was Doc Peabody, from *Sartoris*. Seventy years old, weighing over two hundred pounds, he sees himself "hauled up and down a damn mountain on a rope" (42), summoned by so inept a husband that he knows the wife must already be beyond his help. Like Shrevlin McCannon in his involvement with Quentin Compson, Peabody, with his combination of practicality and wisdom, would provide a counterweight to the tragic and bizarre elements in the Bundrens' recitals.

He was striving for a wide range of effects in these interior monologues. In some, such as those of Cora and Vernon Tull (changed from Turpin), the voices were authentic over their whole wide range of moods and tones. In others he imposed a convention upon the reader: a kind of poetic license whereby a character's thoughts would be rendered in language far beyond his capabilities—as he had done years before in the sketch "The Longshoreman." This was especially true of Darl, but it was also true of the child Vardaman, who could say of Jewel's horse, "I see him dissolve—legs, a rolling eye, a gaudy splotching like cold flames—and float upon the dark in fading solution. . . ." (55) But when they speak aloud, all of their speech is faithful to their class. In Darl's first soliloquy, he had begun "Father and I," but Faulkner changed it to "Pa and Vernon Tull." The first would have been right for Quentin Compson, but it was not right for Darl Bundren.

Addie Bundren dies at that Faulknerian time of day: twilight. Cash, the good carpenter, makes her coffin himself, completing the work in the downpour which creates the flood. It makes their route so circuitous that they even leave the county. "They came from some place out in Yoknapatawpha county," one man says, "trying to get to Jefferson with it." (193) In this narrative Faulkner had named his county.

He later said, "It's a Chickasaw Indian word meaning water runs slow through flat land."[15] It appeared on old maps, transliterated as Yockeney-Patafa, to be shortened in modern times to Yocona, the name the river now bore. According to one scholar, a native of Oxford, Faulkner "normally accepts the physical facts of Oxford and of Lafayette County as coinciding with those of his Jefferson and Yoknapatawpha County."[16] He would use many clearly identifiable places and geographical features, changing their names and usually altering their features. Eventually he called it his "apocryphal county," and it took on symbolic qualities which permitted it to stand for much more than Lafayette County or any other "real" one could.[17] It was through this countryside that the forty-mile journey lay toward Addie's family burying ground, the pathetic cortege soon followed by buzzards drawn by the corpse putrefying in the July heat.

Like most of the women in the novel, Cora Tull is incensed at these outrages visited on Addie's body, feeling them symbolic of the hard lot of a hill farmer's wife. When Vernon tells her that it was a log which upset the wagon in the river, Cora replies, "Log, fiddlesticks. It was the hand of God." (145) It may have been with this line in mind that Faulkner added a marginal insert to the preceding passage in which Darl described the actual event: "*It surged up out of the water and stood for an instant upright upon that surging and heaving desolation like Christ.*" (141) In revising the Benjy section of *The Sound and the Fury*, Faulkner had added overt Christian references. Now, however, just before the catastrophe of fire was to be visited upon the Bundrens, Faulkner deleted a passage heavy with Christian references. It was a portion of Darl's interior monologue in which he decided to set fire to Gillespie's barn to dispose of the rotting body: "Once when I was dead I heard the sad horns. I heard the sad suspirant they call Christ when the earth turned in slumber and slept again. . . . Once I was a little Child and I set up in dying. My father set me up in dying. It was a good business but I just wasn't the man for it. I hadn't the aptitude for it. For not all men are born carpenters, good carpenters, like Christ."[18] The deletion preserved the suspense about the cause of the fire and also worked as the other deletions had done: to reduce the irrational element in the interior monologues of the Bundren family.

Between the catastrophes of flood and fire, Faulkner placed the monologue of Addie Bundren. Flanked by the monologues of the garrulous, obtuse, and self-righteous Cora Tull and the sanctimonious Reverend Whitfield, Addie's words convey her deep sense of alienation and bitterness. They also reveal a source of tragedy like that of the Compsons: a father whose counsel was one of utter despair, who had told her "the reason for living is getting ready to stay dead." (67)

The trip to bury her (with borrowed shovels) in the family plot has proved a costly one, with the mules drowned in the river and Jewel's horse traded away to replace them. Dewey Dell has failed to obtain an abortion and Vardaman's emotional trauma has deepened. Cash's broken leg, sustained in the river disaster, has made him a cripple for life, and Darl, revealed as the arsonist, has been taken off to the state asylum. But Jewel has saved Addie from flood and fire, as she had predicted. And not only has Anse kept his promise to her, he has gained his ulterior objects: false teeth and a wife to replace her.

Faulkner completed the final five pages of the manuscript with no marginal inserts and only two passages from earlier sheets pasted onto the last page. Then he wrote at the bottom of page 107 "Oxford, Miss./ 11 December, 1929." Forty-seven days had elapsed since he had started. Typing it out, he did far less revision than he had with the earlier books. Though there were dozens of corrections in all, they were essentially minor. On January 12, 1930, it was completed. He sent off the original to Hal Smith, to whom he would dedicate the book. Then he bound the carbon copy with cardboard and mottled paper of blue, green, and cream nebulae and put it on his shelf.

THOUGH he had been working in what he would later call "this little, lost town," he was steadily gaining notice. His mail was heavier now, and in the aftermath of *The Sound and The Fury*, there had been days when as many as two dozen letters would arrive. The autumn number of *The Southwest Review* carried an article in which Medford Evans had written that "Oxford's most immediate claim to the notice of the literati is that it is the home of William Faulkner. . . . one of the most talked-about and most seldom talked-to persons in the community. He walks a great deal by himself, carries a cane, and wears a moustache. . . ."[19] In England, Arnold Bennett wrote that he had been told about William Faulkner's promise and had sent to New York for his books, but had received only *The Sound and The Fury*. On December 19 he wrote in the *Evening Standard* that Faulkner evidently had "great and original talent," but, influenced by Joyce, he was "exasperatingly, unimaginably difficult to read." Bennett was infuriated by the book but would not have missed it. If Faulkner emerged from "this youthful stage of eccentricity," he would find "wide appreciation." Faulkner even received two letters from another English writer, Osbert Sitwell, after *The Sound and the Fury*. It was the Welsh novelist Richard Hughes who had told Bennett about Faulkner. During Hughes's visit to America, Wasson and Smith had supplied him with copies of all of Faulkner's novels except *Sartoris*, and he had read them with excitement. When he returned to England he persuaded his own publishers, Chatto & Windus, to bring out these titles and offered to write the introductions himself.

With the typescript of *As I Lay Dying* in New York, he could concentrate on short stories for immediate income. He began to keep a record of submissions to magazines, using homemade ledger sheets to provide a record of the stories he sent out over nearly two years, beginning on January 23, 1930. He wrote at the top border the names of a dozen magazines and the names of Hal Smith and Ben Wasson, and then drew lines to form columns. At the top of six of the fourteen columns were titles without dates, presumably stories sent out earlier. With his new system he would circle a title when the story was accepted.

It may have been at this time that he wrote, or revised, a curious and highly experimental story, obscure yet apparently with a very personal meaning for him, "Carcassonne." It did not appear on the ledger sheet, and it could have been begun several years before. In three surviving versions there are clear affinities with elements of *Mosquitoes*, *The Sound and the Fury*, and *As I Lay Dying*, and perhaps another book not yet contemplated. According to one scholar, the ancient French city was probably suggested to Faulkner by Gustave Nadaud's poem under that title in which he used Carcassonne "as a symbol of an unreachable goal, of frustrated desire," a theme that would have appealed to Faulkner, asserting, as he had done in other works, "the Dream, the Ideal, the will to live, against inevitable defeat by death and oblivion. . . ."[20] Faulkner's setting, however, was a port called Rincon where a poet sleeps in a garret under a strip of tarred-paper roofing at the suffrance of a Mrs. Widdrington, wife of a Standard Oil Company manager. (In manuscript he called her Mrs. Maurier and the poet David, both names he had used in *Mosquitoes*. The poet's garret looked like the one Faulkner had shared with Spratling in New Orleans. It was also like the studio of Gordon in *Mosquitoes*, and he used some of the same phrases Gordon did.) And as Quentin Compson recalled his father's paraphrase of Housman's "Be still, my soul," so writes the same scholar, this poet seems to recall Housman's "The Immortal Part," for he carries on a dialogue with his own groaning skeleton. Knowing that he is, in Housman's phrase, "dying flesh and dying soul,"[21] he still aspires *"to perform something bold and tragical and austere,"* and he envisions himself *"on a buckskin pony with eyes like blue electricity and a mane like tangled fire, galloping up the hill and right off into the high heaven of the world."*[22] Years later Faulkner called the story fantasy and remarked, "that's a piece that I've always liked because there was the poet again."[23]

A story on the sending schedule many months later, embodying related materials, may also have been written earlier and subsequently revised. "Black Music" is also set in a port called Rincon. It was told by a self-exiled protagonist to the actual narrator, his intellectual superior, in the manner of some of those in the stories Faulkner had written in New Orleans in 1925. The protagonist described a vision of Pan which transformed him for one day into a "farn." Now a contented old man, he sleeps every night in a roll of tar paper in the attic of a building owned by Mrs. Widrington [*sic*] and her husband, local manager of the Universal Oil Company. The vision had appeared in the Virginia mountains, and the plot involved a New York couple who had moved there and begun to disrupt the ancient order of things. When Faulkner had seen Sherwood Anderson in early 1926, Anderson had just bought a farm in the ruggedly beautiful, isolated region of southwest Virginia close to Marion. But if the story owed something to Anderson and the mountains of Virginia, it may well have also owed something to Nadaud and his imagery of the blue mountains beyond which one can glimpse Carcassonne. In this story the two symbols merged: the forest animal and the fabled city.

THE first two stories he recorded on his submissions schedule in January 1930 had been sent out before: "The Big Shot" and "Miss Zilphia Gant." The third, called "Idyll in the Desert," was new. Like "Selvage," it had begun with an idea Estelle had explored but then abandoned. Faulkner had treated the theme before. Here it was a thirty-five-year-old woman who abandoned husband and children to nurse her tuberculous young lover back to health, only to die of his disease after he has abandoned her. Again Faulkner used two narrators, Lucas Crump, a mail rider, and the nameless interrogator who relayed the story to the reader. Crump combined the one of the Western tall-tale teller with something of V. K. Suratt's easy garrulousness. *Liberty* and *The American Mercury* rejected the story, but Faulkner characteristically refused to give up on it.

Near the end of January he submitted a story to *The Saturday Evening Post* entitled "Smoke." Always using "we" rather than "I," the nameless narrator speaks for Jefferson—its knowledge, guesses, and reactions, as in "A Rose for Emily." It is an ingenious story which reveals the murderer of a misanthrope to be a cringing nephew who has tried to cast the blame on the victim's disowned son. It introduced an important character: County Attorney Gavin Stevens, who cleverly leads the murderer into revealing himself. Stevens is "a Harvard graduate: a loose-jointed man with a mop of untidy iron-gray hair, who can discuss Einstein with college professors but who spends whole afternoons among the men squatting against the walls of country stores, talking to them in their idiom."[24] He seems markedly to resemble Phil Stone, but later, when he reappeared in other stories, some readers would say that every county seat had at least one lawyer like him—brilliant, loquacious, foreign-educated yet wedded forever to his own small town. As Faulkner's poetic language had expressed for the Bundrens what they could not articulate, so Stevens, in the words of one critic, "could express the sometimes inarticulate feelings of the community and give them utterance."[25] Like other stories Faulkner was now writing, "Smoke" looks backward as well as forward, for the desperate murderer had hired a grotesque Memphis thug who resembled no one so much as Popeye. The *Post* refused the story. Again, Faulkner would use elements of it later.

During this same period he was sending out a much revised story which was equally as ambitious technically, though in a different way. "A Fox-Hunt" was set in the Carolina hunting preserve of Harrison Blair, based perhaps on the estate of the legendary Paul Rainey (whom Murry Falkner had advised about his stables) who had stocked his eleven thousand acres with game for his guests. The action is actually brief. Symbolically, the vixen Blair has mercilessly pursued suggests Blair's unhappy, unfaithful wife, and the fox's death seems to prefigure ultimate disaster for her. Though action and symbol suggest theme and technique in some of D. H. Lawrence's stories, the point of view is Faulknerian, with the omniscient narrator following the action through the radically different perspectives of three sets of characters. A few technical phrases indicate an interest in fox-hunting, which eventually would burgeon, though it would be many years before Faulkner had either the time or the money for it.

One of the last of his undated submissions was "A Rose for Emily." It seems likely that he had now deleted the deathbed scene of Miss Emily, making the story tighter and more effective, and changed her name from Wyatt to Grierson. The story was taken by *Forum* for the April 1930 issue, his first story to appear in a national magazine. Obviously encouraged, he sent out eight more during the month of February.

Two of them, "Per Ardua" and "A Dangerous Man," were never sold. The former would meet better fortune later in revised form as "All the Dead Pilots." The latter was based on a story—apparently begun by Estelle—of a woman with a difficult past. Another unfortunate woman was the focus of "Drouth." She was Miss Minnie Cooper, once popular, now a neurotic spinster. Faulkner quickly switched to a barbershop buzzing with the rumor that she has been raped by a Negro. The mindless homicidal response, led by a war veteran named Plunkett, precipitates a lynching. In the last of the story's five sections Plunkett brutalizes his wife, another woman trapped like the wife in "A Fox-Hunt." This new, powerful, and violent story was quickly rejected by *The American Mercury*.

Plunkett's wartime exploits may have provided a link to the story called "Per Ardua," which Faulkner sent off on February 14. This story probably employed RAF lore as did another entitled "Thrift." In this one the exploits of a Highland peasant named Wully MacWryglinchbeath were played more for comedy than drama. It derived not only from the handling of dialects—Scots, Cockney, and upper-class English—but also from MacWryglinchbeath's monstrous avarice and miserliness. Faulkner was writing of an imagined Scotland and a wartime France which he knew only from books and stories. But he was dealing with a son of the same people who populated Yoknapatawpha County's Beat Four, a remote region inhabited, he would later write, by "people named Gowrie and McCallum and Fraser and Ingrum that used to be Ingraham and Workitt that used to be Urquhart," living on hills that seemed to hang suspended above the plateau, as the Scottish Highlands did.[26] MacWryglinchbeath's quiet parsimony, his taciturnity in the face of good fortune and bad, his close computation in money matters—all were precisely the characteristics one would see in Frenchman's Bend. *The Saturday Evening Post*, Faulkner's first choice because of its premium prices, accepted "Thrift" for September publication.

He sent out eight more stories in the month of March. "Ad Astra" also used RAF materials and probably *War Birds*, purportedly an anonymous American flier's diary, which had been serialized in *Liberty* in August 1926. It had emphasized the high casualty rate among airmen, their frenetic life on the ground, and the way the survivors were maimed psychologically if not physically. Speaking in present time, Faulkner's nameless narrator set his story immediately after the Armistice. His comrades are Bayard Sartoris, Gerald Bland, a self-proclaimed shanty Irishman named Monaghan, and two others: a huge belligerent Irishman named Comyn and a philosophical Indian called the subadar, probably based on a model Faulkner had met in New Haven. The story's action develops out of Monaghan's insistence on bringing into a French café a German he had shot down. The ending, after the ensuing riot, strikes a note like that of the ending in *Sanctuary*. It is the prisoner who interprets the meaning: "All this generation which fought in the war are dead tonight. But we do not yet know it."[27] This ironically titled story was too grim for *The American Mercury*, but Faulkner sent it to *American Caravan IV*, whose editors took it.

Faulkner pursued this theme and one of the characters into peacetime. In early March he sent "Point of Honor" to the *Post*, which rejected it, and two and a half weeks later he sent "Honor" (in all likelihood a revision) to *Scribner's*. Set in 1922, the story follows Monaghan as he barnstorms with an aerial circus. In a passage doubtless embodying Faulkner's memories of New Haven in 1918, he recalls "campuses full of British and French uniforms, and us all scared to death it would be over before we could get in and swank a pair of pilot's wings ourselves." Monaghan quotes the subadar, whose words he now understands, but the bulk of the story treats an illicit affair which has confirmed him as a drifter. The neat happy ending was probably tailored to the requirements of popular fiction. *Scribner's* rejected it.

On March 20 he tried *The American Mercury* again with "Hair," in which a drummer tells the story of a man named Hawkshaw, a barber who had heroically tried to prevent the lynching in "Drouth." Speaking in a conversational tone such as one of Sherwood Anderson's narrators might have used, he describes the quixotic Hawkshaw's fidelity to a dead fiancée and her parents. The *Mercury* very promptly sent the story back. In one passage the narrator quotes from a record Hawkshaw kept of the payments which finally canceled the mortgage on his fiancée's mother's home. This passage may have reflected something more than just the needs of the story.

Faulkner's income had been uncertain, and so were his prospects. But he wanted to take himself and Estelle and Cho-Cho and Malcolm out from under Miss Elma Meek's roof to a home of their own. It would take mortgage payments to do it, but he was going to buy the old Shegog place out on the Taylor Road, where he and Estelle had played as children.

29

> So it was finished then, down to the last plank and brick and
> wooden pin which they could make themselves. . . . surrounded
> by its formal gardens and promenades, its slave quarters and
> stables and smokehouses; wild turkey ranged within a mile of
> the house and deer came light and colored like smoke and left
> delicate prints in the formal beds. . . .
>
> —*Absalom, Absalom!* (39)

IN 1844, "Colonel" Robert R. Shegog purchased a tract of land that had
been sold eight years earlier by a Chickasaw named E-Ah-Nah-Yea, who
had received the land as a grant from the U.S. government. Shegog hired
William Turner, an English architect, to build a two-story Colonial-style
home. They picked an elevated site, the land sloping off around it to
bluffs and ravines. The house would face south. There, seven-tenths of a
mile from the courthouse, the land was cleared and the kiln built in which
slaves would bake brick for the foundation.

The L-shaped house rose slowly. It was sturdy and roomy, symmetrical
in front, with parlors on both sides of the wide entrance hall and a dining
room and kitchen extending back from the one on the right. Upstairs
were three bedrooms. The Grecian roof of the portico was supported
by four tall wooden columns. Above the Georgian front doors was a
balcony, and on either side, above the wide, open gallery, were two large
shuttered windows upstairs and downstairs. A professional gardener
landscaped the grounds, curving a long cedar-lined drive to approach
the house.

In 1872, Mrs. Julia Bailey bought the house and much of the land.
Over the years, parties of picnickers would follow the paths to the
springs in Bailey's Woods. For the boys of Oxford it was a special hunting
and swimming preserve, and perfect for games such as hare-and-hounds.
When Miss Ellen Bailey died in the house in 1923, Mrs. Sally Bailey Bryant
inherited it, and rented it to a series of tenants. Gradually it fell into dis-

repair, and for a time it was vacant. Then, in late May of 1928, Mr. and Mrs. Claude Anderson moved in. He plowed up the weeds and bushes and even the lawn to plant corn to feed the chickens and cows. The Andersons sold their products all over Oxford, but they let the house continue to deteriorate. Mice and squirrels scurried in the attic under the leaky roof. Beams were rotting and sagging. Stained and faded paper peeled from the cracking plaster on the once-bright walls.

When Mrs. Bryant learned that William Faulkner was interested in buying and restoring the house, she urged her husband to work something out, even though the Depression made money tight. Will Bryant took to Bill Faulkner, telling him about old times in north Mississippi, about families dead and gone, and about others whose descendants seemed little like their hardy, upright forebears. Finally he told Faulkner he could have the house and four acres of land for $6,000 at six percent interest, with no down payment. He would pay $75 a month. On April 12, 1930, Faulkner signed the papers and the house was his on a deed of trust.

LOOKING ahead to this new, fixed obligation, Faulkner sent out six stories in the month of April. "Drouth" was one of them, revised now, with the ominous weather symbolic and even contributory to the emotional climate which bred the storm of violence, functioning almost as the weather had in *As I Lay Dying*. In another revision, Faulkner explicitly named the town Jefferson, now apparently linking the stories within the general design, as with the novels. This story and "A Rose for Emily" were his best work in the form so far. *Scribner's* bought it for $200, and it would appear early the next year as "Dry September."

On April 22 he had sent to the *Post* a story entitled "Beyond the Gate." It was set in present time at beginning and ending but in the Hereafter during the midpart, where a newly arrived judge seeks his son among the departed. The judge is in part a composite of Estelle's step-grandfather and her father. The deathbed physician is Doc Peabody. Lem Oldham had lost his son at age nine; the judge in the story, at age ten. In an authentic but chilling touch, Faulkner had given the child in the story precisely the same epitaph as that on little Ned Oldham's tombstone in St. Peter's Cemetery. The nameless fictional judge, speaking to the spirit of the famous agnostic Robert Ingersoll, sounds just like Quentin Compson: "what I have been, I am; what I am, I shall be until that instant comes when I am not. And then I shall have never been. . . . *Non fui. Sum. Fui. Non sum.*"[1] Even when the judge finally meets his son, his skepticism still shows in his voice. Divided into seven sections, the story produced a disjointed, episodic effect. When Faulkner dealt with the supernatural in "The Leg," he succeeded in the tradition of the English horror story. This religio-philosophical approach had neither horror nor force. When the *Post* returned it, Faulkner filed it away.

He had better luck with "Honor," which *The American Mercury* accepted for July publication. He was anxious for the money but reluctant to supply the information that the editors liked to print about their contributors. "Sorry, I haven't got a picture," he wrote Wasson. "I dont intend to have one that I know of, either. About the biography. Dont tell the bastards anything. It cant matter to them. Tell them I was born of an alligator and a nigger slave at the Geneva peace conference two years ago. Or whatever you want to tell them."[2] Pressed for money, he sent out "Selvage" and "Equinox" ("Divorce in Naples" under an earlier title) in May. Both were returned.

On May 27 he sent a story to the *Post* which may have had its inception much earlier. It was probably after he stopped work on *Father Abraham* that he began a manuscript he called "Omar's Eighteenth Quatrain." The lines he cited were these:

> They say the Lion and the Lizard keep
> The Courts where Jamshyd gloried and drank deep:
>   And Bahram, that great Hunter—the Wild Ass
> Stamps o'er his Head, and he lies fast asleep.[3]

In the nine manuscript pages which survive, Suratt drives out with Henry Armstid and Vernon Tull to the Old Frenchman place, where they crawl to a spot from which they can watch unobserved in the darkness. Faulkner describes the legendary Frenchman and his domain in two paragraphs almost identical with two others in *Father Abraham*. They were not paste-ins. Certain people, certain incidents in Yoknapatawpha history, apparently came to his mind with only the most minor variations. Representing fragments of perhaps two versions, this one tells how the three men watch Flem Snopes digging in the abandoned garden. The story breaks off after Suratt fetches an ancient dowser named Uncle Dick to help find what Flem is seeking. Two versions later, the story was called "Lizards in Jamshyd's Courtyard." Two typescripts later, by the time the three realize Flem has duped them with the old "salted-mine" trick, they have already signed thousand-dollar notes to buy the place. Earlier, Suratt had gotten the better of Flem in a minor deal, but the greed that overcame his natural decency and his skepticism left him vulnerable. But he and Tull return to sanity, unlike Armstid, who is driven mad. Flem is, if anything, more devious here than he was in *Father Abraham*, even though these events apparently took place before he and Buck had brought the spotted horses into the country. The *Post* rejected the story, but Faulkner was far from done with it.

WHEN the Faulkners moved into the old Shegog place in June 1930, Faulkner may have thought ruefully of Suratt surveying the domain of which he was one-third owner. There was no electricity and no plumbing. Malcolm stared at it. He would remember that "It looked as if it was going to collapse with the next rainstorm or high wind."[4] Not far away was the outhouse with its old Sears, Roebuck catalogue. They would have to use oil lamps and fetch their water from the vine-covered wellhouse. Cho-Cho watched her mother sit on the front steps and cry, not only undone by the condition of her new home, now that it was a reality, but also convinced that they would henceforth be beyond the pale of social life in Oxford. But Cho-Cho and Malcolm loved it, she as the older realizing that Faulkner wanted them to have a real home. Years later Faulkner's daughter, Jill, would discern still another motive: it was "the symbol in Pappy's life of being somebody. . . . everybody in Oxford had remembered that Pappy's father ran a livery stable, and he had lived in this house up not too far from the livery stable, and this was just a way of thumbing his nose at Oxford. . . . a nice old house [that] had a certain substance and standing to it."[5] This came through in a letter to Ben Wasson. "I am content and I am happy," he wrote.[6] His new edifice needed a good deal of shoring up, however. There was work for everyone to do, and they plunged into it. The house needed new foundation beams and a new roof, plumbing, wiring, paper, paint, and screens. After a day's work in the July heat, they would go to the wellhouse to take their baths in tandem: Cho-Cho and her mother soaping themselves and rinsing each other with buckets of water, then Malcolm and his stepfather doing the same.

Handy with tools, Faulkner was determined to do as much as he could himself. When he began jacking up the house to replace some of the beams, he got Rusty Patterson to help him. Rusty was a dumpy, good-natured man who came of a good family but chose the life of occasional handyman. He was a storyteller somewhat in the style of V. K. Suratt. Sometimes he and Faulkner would take a break from their work under a mulberry tree with a pitcher of home brew. Johncy Falkner remembered that one day Rusty brought a bottle of corn whiskey to work. He and his employer sat there under the house, amid the beams, and had a drink. When it was gone, Faulkner went in the house for more. But the work got done. Rusty helped with the painting, and so did Joe Peacock, whose sister, Dewey Dell, had been a grammar-school classmate of Estelle's. In July, Faulkner charged over $100 at Elliott's lumberyard and one of the hardware stores and got the screens up. In August he charged $200 more for the roof and paid Evans Smith and W. B. Mayfield $85 for their labor. He was already planning an order at Sears, Roebuck to do the bath and the kitchen plumbing.

Meanwhile, almost unbidden, the staff was beginning to gather. Uncle Ned Barnett, who claimed he could remember the day the Yankees burned Ripley, took over as general factotum. As butler, he served at the table. As yard man, he milked and also cared for Faulkner's and Malcolm's horses. A man with a feeling for proper dress, he wore a tie when he milked or chopped kindling, and on other occasions he would appear in frock coats inherited from the Young Colonel. Mammy Callie was his opposite number, helping to look after the children and, when she felt like it, creaming butter and sugar for the cakes Estelle would bake in the big wood-burning kitchen range, over which Josie May, the Oldhams' cook, usually presided. Although Estelle often felt that Mammy Callie was more of a nuisance than a help in the kitchen, it was in the natural order of things that she should join the family. She had served Miss Maud and now she was serving her daughter-in-law. As for Uncle Ned, he was simply taking care of another generation of Falkners. William Faulkner accepted his role. There was no money for salaries in these early months, but he was responsible for their food, shelter, clothing, health care, and pay when he could afford it. That he should do this was exactly what Mammy Callie and Uncle Ned expected.

Their first guest was Miss Ella Somerville. They had sat by candlelight on the east gallery, looking out across the lawn to the abandoned sunken garden sloping down to the woods. There was still a long way to go, but they had accomplished a good deal. Estelle's furniture was all in place, her piano in the parlor. She had begun playing it again even though the strings were out of tune from travel and exposure. On some of these candlelit nights, Estelle remembered, they would hear music, notes that sounded like a piece played by a child. Cho-Cho and Malcolm shivered in their beds, for they knew it was the music of Judith Shegog, a beautiful girl, the story went, who fell to her death trying to elope with a Yankee officer. She was a friendly ghost, they were sure, but it was eerie to hear the faint piano notes drifting up the broad staircase in the still night.

It was not fitting that their new home should still be known as the old Shegog house or the Bailey place. Faulkner had read in Frazer's *The Golden Bough* about the way Scottish farmers put pieces of rowan tree over the doors of the cowhouses to prevent witches from casting spells and stealing the milk. Indigenous to Scotland and signifying peace and security, the tree actually is not an oak but a mountain ash. Faulkner named this portion of E-Ah-Nah-Yea's land "Rowanoak," and later had it engraved on stationery in Gothic script.

There had been a different kind of activity that summer which caused William Faulkner's father to move to a new residence. Chancellor Alfred Hume had been fighting Governor Bilbo's determined efforts to incorporate the university into his patronage system. Hume had courage and integrity but little political power, and in June, Bilbo had gained a majority in the board of trustees of the state university and colleges. All but two of the heads of these institutions were soon replaced. A number of heads of the university's schools and departments were among those, in the Oxford *Eagle*'s words, to "Feel Fall of the Political Axe."[7] Others, like Bob Farley, did not wait for the ax, but resigned. It was said that many state employees, furthermore, had been directed to make contributions to the Bilbo organization. Murry Falkner was one of them, perhaps because he was regarded within the organization as both a supporter and a beneficiary. His family believed that the amount was $500. His salary was $3,000 and he wrote to say that he could not meet the assessment. On June 26 the *Eagle* reported his statement that he would not reapply at the university, that "there is too much work attached to the position, and also that he is growing too old to keep up with it." The next month he contracted for the construction of a modest brick home on the same lot with The Big Place on South Lamar. His desk cleaned out and his working life finished, he got out one of his old railroad ledgers. From time to time he would paste on its lined pages the pictures of horses and dogs he had cut from magazines. His tastes in reading had not changed. Nor had those of some former colleagues. When a friend of his met a foursome of deans on the golf course, and he observed that pictures of "our Bill" were appearing in "highbrow publications," one of them moved closer and cupped his hand around his mouth. "We don't talk about him around here," he said.[8]

In London, after the publication of *Soldiers' Pay* that summer, the reaction to Faulkner's name was very different. In the *Evening Standard*, Arnold Bennett declared that "Faulkner is the coming man. He has inexhaustible invention, powerful imagination, a wondrous gift of characterisation, a finished skill in dialogue; and he writes generally like an angel. None of the arrived American stars can surpass him when he is at his best." Two days later another reviewer for the *Evening Standard* wrote that no first novel in the previous thirty years "had attained such perfection" and ranked the author above D. H. Lawrence and Ernest Hemingway.[9]

IF the story-sending schedule is any indication, Faulkner must have spent most of July repairing rather than writing. It was the twenty-fourth of the month before he recorded a submission, when he sent "Red Leaves" to *The Saturday Evening Post*. He was exploring a new stratum of Yoknapatawpha County, the Chickasaws. He chose one of the oldest tribal customs: the burial of the dead chief with his horse, his dog, and his body servant. Beyond the motif of the pursuit—with the quarry here being the slave, who did not want to die—he tried to convey the Indians' attitudes toward change, the white man, and the slaves. His presentation of the servant was distanced yet compassionate, a Guinea man who "had lived ninety days in a three-foot-high 'tween-deck in tropic latitudes, hearing from topside the drunken New England captain intoning aloud from a book which he did not recognize for ten years afterward to be the Bible."[10] He supplied names that sounded like authentic Chickasaw—Moketubbe and Ikkemotubbe—and some of these characters would reappear. He would later tell one of his editors that he had wondered how to render Indian speech into English. Finally, he said, he had found the answer in the way Hemingway translated Spanish dialogue into English.[11]

The *Post* took this story and paid him $750 for it. Now they could afford to put in electricity, and Estelle ordered an electric stove.

Faulkner's workroom was off the front hall to the left, his desk against the side wall placed next to one of the two windows looking out to the west. One night after dinner, when he turned on the bare bulb that dangled from the cord, Miss Ellen Bailey's hand-painted murals gleamed garishly in the harsh light: blue and pink flowers among green leaves, and gold peacocks on the black plaster fireplace. He stood there for a moment. Then he went out to the barn and returned with a pail of whitewash to cover the artwork. Shortly thereafter, John Phillips bricked in the fireplace and then did the plastering and wallpapering. Faulkner built bookcases on two of the walls for the piles of books that lay about on the floor.

In the next month Faulkner had an additional incentive: Estelle was expecting a baby in March. Dr. Culley was worried about her, for she had experienced a difficult time with both her babies, and now, suffering from anemia, she weighed less than a hundred pounds. He prescribed iron and calcium. She would have to be very careful.

In that month of August, Faulkner sent out four stories, none new. "The Peasants" was a reworking of *Father Abraham* that was more effective than any of its previous versions. Now, however, it ran to almost 15,000 words, and *Scribner's* rejected it. But the *Post* bought "Lizards in Jamshyd's Courtyard" for another $750.

The appearance of "Thrift" in the *Post* on September 6 was applauded by the Oxford *Eagle*. Faulkner was "fast gaining national and international recognition." An item on another page concerned Faulkner on the local scene. He was going to appear in a major role in *Corporal Eagen*, to be staged by the Universal Producing Company under the auspices of the Junior Chamber of Commerce for the benefit of the planned city park and playground. The play's action revolved around "Red Eagen, an Irish doughboy, and his screamingly funny Jewish buddy, Izzy Goldstein."[12] Jim Stone was a logical choice for Red Eagen. To everyone's surprise, Bill Faulkner agreed to play Izzy Goldstein.

After ten days of rehearsals, the show was presented in the grammar-school auditorium on Thursday night, September 11. Most of the heavy backstage traffic flowed toward a window, outside which a ladder led to a platform near the boiler room. There Ernest, the barbershop shoeshine boy, had set up a bar serving corn whiskey. This may have lent some of the liveliness to the Minstrel Chorus's rendition of "Over There" and perhaps caused a missed cue, which Izzy Goldstein turned into a big laugh with a fast ad lib. The show ran for two more nights and everybody enjoyed it: the enormous cast, their many relatives, and the rest of the audience. "I remember," said bit player Bill Harmon, "that we all commented on how well Bill Faulkner played his part."[13]

The *Eagle* had affirmed the success of *Corporal Eagen*. When it mentioned Faulkner again, a week later, it was on the editorial page. The writer noted Sherwood Anderson's *American Mercury* article calling Faulkner and Hemingway the "two most notable young writers who have come on in America since the war." He had known both rather intimately and quarreled with both, he wrote, but that didn't alter his attitude toward the writing. *The Sound and the Fury*, he said, was "a beautiful and sympathetic piece of work. . . ." The *Eagle*'s editorialist briefly reviewed Faulkner's books and looked forward to a new one.[14]

As I Lay Dying appeared on October 6, 1930, with an initial printing of 2,522 copies. Although some of the Eastern reviewers conceded that this novel was not as difficult as its predecessors, the Bundrens seemed almost as strange as Martians to others. The October reviews in the South were more sympathetic. The reviews the next month in the New York papers and magazines were much like the earlier ones. In *The Nation*, Clifton Fadiman called the novel "a psychological jig-saw puzzle" by a writer whose "cosmos is awry; but it is his own, self-created."[15] In spite of qualifications, other major reviews added to his stature, but once again, the praise would not be translated into substantial sales.

THE process of moving into the old Bailey place that summer, living now near the woods where they had played as children, may have had an effect on his work much more integral than simply intensifying the need to sell it. That summer or early fall his mind turned back to that fictional family which had also lived in a large, once-imposing house that had fallen into disrepair and dilapidation. Years later Faulkner would recall a story which he said he wrote sometime after *The Sound and the Fury*.[16] The crucial element in it, and another probably conceived about that time or a little later, was point of view: the way events in the adult world impinged on the consciousness of three children: Quentin, Caddy, and Jason Compson. The eight manuscript pages of "Never Done No Weeping When You Wanted to Laugh" concern the plight of their laundress and occasional cook, Nancy, terrified that her lover is about to murder her for her infidelities. Faulkner would eventually write at least three versions of this story, sharpening it each time and playing off the adult consciousness—the children's self-centered hypochondriachal mother and their callous father—against that of the children: specifically the degree of awareness of Caddy and Quentin of the nature of the desperate and tragic situation they are witnessing. In another story, called "A Justice," Grandfather Compson drives the children out to his farm, where Quentin spends the whole visit listening to the Negro-Indian blacksmith Sam Fathers tell the story which Quentin relays to the reader. It is an account of how Sam got his name. Looking back from a later perspective, Quentin recalls his feelings with an image which was one of the most persistent in his creator's imagination. "We went on," Quentin says of the ride home, "in that strange, faintly sinister suspension of twilight. . . ." When Grandfather asks what Sam had said, Quentin realizes he had not understood it: "I was just twelve then, and I would have to wait until I had passed on and through and beyond the suspension of twilight."[17]

One newcomer to Oxford who was enormously impressed with William Faulkner's fiction was a blond, statuesque young Georgian teaching in the junior high school. Emily Whitehurst had discovered *The Sound and the Fury* back home and it had electrified her. When Johncy Falkner took a group that included another young admirer, George Marion O'Donnell, out to Rowan Oak (Faulkner's alternate spelling), she went along eagerly. She would remember Faulkner's presence, especially his eyes, which "burned through the flesh and bone of everybody in front of him. . . ." At one point Mrs. Faulkner entered, wearing an exotic Chinese robe. Faulkner talked about remodeling the house. When some of the group began asking personal questions, Faulkner slipped into his strategy of fiction and fantasy. He recalled that during his RAF days he had crashed into a hangar, where he hung upside down. He had not been scared, but for an instant when time had stopped, he had died. His listeners stared. Not long afterward they left.[18] Emily Whitehurst was also impressed with Phil Stone, because he was Faulkner's friend and because he enjoyed talking literature and directing her reading, as he had done with Faulkner. He showed her one of the Faulkner manuscripts in his law office. "This is grand," he said. "Listen to it." Later she told Faulkner how stirring she thought that passage was. "It *is* rather fustian, isn't it?" he replied. When she confided that she wanted to write, he offered little support.

Even now his own acceptance rate was not encouraging. Of the thirty-seven submissions he had recorded in the first nine months of 1930, only six had been taken. On the publication day of *As I Lay Dying* he had sent "Never Done No Weeping When You Wanted to Laugh," retitled "That Evening Sun Go Down," to *Scribner's*. They rejected it. Two days earlier he had sent the *Post* "A Mountain Victory." It was straightforward but long: forty-two pages. It was the story of a Confederate officer and his Negro servant, returning home after the war, fatally ambushed by a Tennessee mountaineer. The *Post* accepted the story, but it would be more than two years before it appeared.

By the time Halloween came, the Faulkners were ready to give a party, and Cho-Cho invited all her friends. In spite of the decorations, refreshments, and games, they were most impressed by Faulkner's storytelling after he gathered them all in the large foyer. John Reed Holley could almost see beautiful Judith Shegog and her Yankee officer. Judith had been buried there at Rowan Oak, he said, and eventually her lover too. In after years, on each anniversary of her death, Judith would make a pilgrimage—from the upstairs hall down the stairs, out the door, and across the lawn to the grave. Arthur Guyton was spellbound: "I can remember to this very day Mr. Bill walking slowly and majestically down the steps with his eyes lifted slightly, completely steady . . . and his two hands raised enacting the movements of the girl, and all of us seeing her absolutely instead of him." When Faulkner asked if anyone would like to see the lovers' graves, John Reed and Arthur followed him into the October darkness. Suddenly "chains rattled and we saw a white sheet out under the magnolia trees to represent a ghost, and it would move."[19] Arthur recalled that the story "came so near disrupting the party that at its very end Mr. Bill . . . changed the subject to something gayer and soon had the mood of the party back on course."

When *Scribner's* refused "That Evening Sun Go Down," he sent it to *The American Mercury*. Editor H. L. Mencken liked it, but he was uneasy about Nancy's husband being named Jesus and about her pregnancy being discussed in explicit terms. Faulkner tried to meet Mencken's objections. He did change the man's name. He told Mencken that he kept the dialogue about the pregnancy because "it establishes Judah as a potential factor of the tragedy as soon as possible." Mencken could delete it if he wished. Faulkner did, however, remove the passage about Nancy's swollen belly containing a watermelon that came from somebody else's vine. "I reckon that's what would outrage Boston," he wrote.[20] After further cuts, Mencken printed the story in March 1931.

In November, Faulkner aimed four stories at the *Post*'s bigger fees. "Rose of Lebanon" began in the manner of *As I Lay Dying*, with alternating segments by Dr. Gavin Blount and Randolph Gordon. Blount had appeared in "The Big Shot." Through Gordon, the story explained Blount's obsessive devotion to the Chickasaw Guards' Ball and all it represented. The war was made intensely personal for him through his namesake, a great-uncle killed at Chickamauga. A kind of counterpoint was provided by the death of Gordon's father, not in the main raid on Federal stores at Holly Springs but by a shotgun blast during a raid on a henhouse. After the *Post* rejected it, Faulkner revised and sent it out twice, without success. But characteristically, he would get something usable from it. Just as it looked backward to the Carolina Bayard's death in *Sartoris*, so it anticipated the obsession of a character named Hightower in a novel Faulkner would begin in nine months' time. As if Gavin Blount reminded him of "The Big Shot," Faulkner reworked that story under the title "Dull Tale" and sent it to the *Post*, where it met the same negative response as did "Rose of Lebanon."

"The Hound" had certain affinities with *As I Lay Dying*, though it was more violent. It told how a poor white farmer named Ernest Cotton shot an arrogant neighbor, Houston, who had wronged him. After an unsuccessful attempt to conceal the body, Cotton was caught. In Conradian fashion, Faulkner described the murder at the outset and then concentrated on the murderer's psychology. When the *Post* rejected it, he mailed it to *Scribner's* on November 29. That same day he sent the *Post* "Indians Built a Fence," probably the same story he would revise as "A Justice." The *Post* declined it, thus completing its perfect record on Faulkner submissions for the month of November 1930: it had rejected all four of them.

It must have been about mid-November that Faulkner opened his post-office box to find the galley proofs of *Sanctuary*. In May the linotype operators had gotten as far as galley 4 when the setting copy for *As I Lay Dying* was given precedence. On November 3 the setting copy for *Sanctuary* had gone back on the rack. Smith had either undergone a change of heart about the book he said could land them in jail, or the worsening Depression may have persuaded him to gamble on it anyway. When Faulkner read the galleys through, it was a traumatic experience. "I read it and it was so badly written," he said, "it was cheaply approached. The very impulse that caused me to write the book was so apparent, every word; and then I said I cannot let this go."[21] This judgment, printed and spoken many times by Faulkner, would render the book a great disservice, for though the economic motive was strong in *Sanctuary*'s composition, it was hardly the slapdash mercenary process these words seemed to make it out to be. His harsh judgment derived in large part from his craftsman's conscience, and he was quick to see that there were discrepancies and loose ends in the story. Moreover, he now was not the same writer he had been then. *As I Lay Dying* had interposed itself, and "Rose of Lebanon," containing probably the earliest matter from which his next novel would grow. So when Faulkner, who never made a practice of rereading his novels, read the galleys, he was going back in time to much earlier work. And because of the importance of the Horace Benbow material, it was not as though he were just going back two years with *Sanctuary*; it was more like four or five years to *Flags in the Dust*.

So he wrote to Hal Smith and told him, "You can't print it like this; it's just a bad book."[22] But he could understand Smith's situation. They compromised: Faulkner would agree to its publication after he made whatever revisions he felt necessary, but he and the firm would share any costs above the normal ones for correcting proof.

"I tore the galleys down and rewrote the book," he said.[23] He discarded whole galleys from the sheaf of 103, cutting and pasting others to form new ones. His revisions were dictated by his own aesthetic reasons, not because of any concern for readers' sensibilities. As a matter of fact, events in the interim could have served only to reassure him that the corruption with which he had imbued the novel faithfully mirrored corruption in society at large. His father had lost his job in a "shakedown" ordered by a governor whose tax commissioner had been tried on impeachment charges. The governor had been involved in suspicious land purchases. Reno DeVaux had emerged from jail, prudently silent about the loss of his roadhouse from arson and determined to build on the ashes. Popeye Pumphrey had been wounded in gang warfare in Kansas City.[24] When Faulkner and Estelle went to Memphis, they saw the same spectacle of unlawful divertissement—doubtless under police protection. Estelle noticed that sometimes when they returned to the Peabody, her husband would scribble on a pad—impressions, notes, things to remember, she thought.

Faulkner must have been cynically amused at the ironic contrast between the lawlessness and the posture of society's guardians. Lloyd T. Binford had come a long way from his origins in Duck Hill, Mississippi. A Baptist Sunday School superintendent and member of the Memphis Board of Censors, he had even objected to the nature of certain passages in *King of Kings*, a film on the life of Christ. The name Faulkner gave to Miss Reba's deceased lover, who had come to live in the whorehouse, was Lucius Binford. And Miss Reba's white, wormlike dogs were called Miss Reba and Mr. Binford. There were many other such touches in the novel, but they served as a kind of counterpoint for the main theme, the depiction of a wasteland. But it was more than that. One critic would see it as "a remarkable and highly sophisticated blend of Eliot, Freud, Frazer, mythology, local color, and even 'current trends' in hard-boiled detective fiction."[25]

Though Faulkner left unrevised the horrors at the Old Frenchman place, he did reduce the incestuous element in the Horace-Narcissa relationship. Moreover, he made Temple's story central. His guiding principle, as the same critic put it, "seems to have been the felt need to get us outside Horace Benbow's cloyingly introspective, narcissistic personality."[26] He still served as actor and chorus, but he no longer dominated the book. The action began swiftly, with Horace meeting Popeye at the spring near the Old Frenchman place. His troubles with Belle were explored but he no longer dreamed of his mother and wept, as he had on galley 22, or dreamed he saw black matter run from Belle's mouth as it had from the dead Emma Bovary. In Chapter IV, Faulkner introduced Temple and followed her through the next ten chapters. Only after Popeye murdered Tommy and raped Temple did the story return to Benbow at the start of Chapter XV. The next twelve chapters alternated between two story lines. One was Benbow's investigation as he prepared to defend Goodwin against the charge of murdering Tommy. The other followed Popeye and Temple to Miss Reba's house and through Temple's affair with Red and his death at Popeye's hands. Both lines merged in Chapter XXIII when Benbow interviewed Temple at Miss Reba's, then fused again in Chapters XXVII through XXIX, where the horror increased. In a new segment, the falsely convicted Goodwin was burned to death by a mob. The chapter before last showed Benbow unhappily reunited with Belle. To the final one, Faulkner added a naturalistic capsule biography of Popeye. Grandson of a pyromaniac, son of a shopgirl and a syphilitic strikebreaker, he was stunted in childhood, deformed and impotent in adulthood. Now the story closed not with Popeye's flippant last words on the gallows but focused on the ruined Temple as the resonant brasses crashed in the Luxembourg Gardens. It had been an expensive revision. Faulkner's share of the cost, he said, came to $270, "at a time when I didn't have $270.00"[27]

The book now was actually more violent than before—nine murders occurred or were mentioned—but it was aesthetically more satisfying. The focus was clearer and transitions more explicit. One result was greater symmetry, with Horace and Popeye implicitly compared, each impotent in a different way. As one scholar would put it, "The early version is, essentially, a heavily Freudian study of Horace's sexual and emotional problems; in the revised text Horace's problems are of course very real and very much a part of the novel's meaning, but Faulkner's primary concern is the considerably larger problem of the nature of evil itself: the power of darkness, the insufficiency of light."[28] Parts of the novel would trouble some readers: Temple's motive for her perjury and Popeye's passivity at his approaching death.[29] And there were still some discrepancies in dating Benbow's visits to Memphis, but Faulkner had done the best he could with the book. He had paid "for the privilege of rewriting it, trying to make out of it something which would not shame *The Sound and the Fury* and *As I Lay Dying* too much. . . ." With an assurance that many readers would not even notice, he added, "and I made a fair job."[30]

Faulkner returned the galleys to New York in early December. Then he was able to mail out four short stories before Christmas. "A Death Drag" was new. In the second paragraph a "we" narrator, like the one who told "A Rose for Emily," describes what might almost have been the Oxford-Lafayette County Airport. "Our town is built upon hills, and the field, once a cotton field, is composed of forty acres of ridge and gully, upon which, by means of grading and filling, we managed to build an X-shaped runway into the prevailing winds."[31] One of the major characters of the story was a familiar projection of Faulkner. Mr. Warren is an ex-RAF pilot trained in Toronto and wounded overseas. Like Gavin Stevens, a man who knew the world but chose to live out his life in Jefferson, he is the only one able to understand the sufferings of the pilot, Jock, another drifter and war casualty like Monaghan and Bayard Sartoris. One of his two partners, a grotesque man named Ginsfarb, provides a bizarre kind of Weber and Fields comedy. Conversations with tramp aviators at the Memphis airport had probably supplied material for the story. In the midst of *As I Lay Dying*, he had written Hal Smith,

"A pilot in Memphis is going to give me enough dual bar to get a Mexican pilot's license, and I am going back to flying. Think I can make a nickle or so that way. Haven't flown a crate since 1918, but he tells me that with 3–4 hours dual, I can regain my clog."[32] He may well have resumed flying by this time. His interest in it would continue to grow, and it would provide more material for his writing.

CHRISTMAS EVE found Faulkner and Estelle in the Episcopal church. At services, he would conscientiously join in the hymns, and he even had a Book of Common Prayer in which Estelle would see him make an occasional notation. The next day they made much of Christmas in the traditional way, with a big tree, pine boughs in the hall, and holly and ivy from their own woods on the banister. Members of both the Oldham and Faulkner families came, some for a visit and some for dinner. It was a full day and a taxing one for Estelle, now in her sixth month of pregnancy.

Little of the Christmas glow persisted into the last days of December. He had not sold a story in over a month, and when he took stock he saw that his total from magazine sales in the last half of the year amounted to only $1,700. One day he went to Mac Reed at the Gathright-Reed drugstore and handed him a small brown velvet bag. "Mac," he said, "can you let me have ten dollars for this?" Mac looked at the $10 gold piece and said, "Surely, Bill." He didn't have that amount himself, so he advanced it from the store cash register. Mac did not ask when the coin would be redeemed, and Faulkner did not know when he could redeem it. Things were even worse for the Stones. On Monday morning, December 29, 1930, the Bank of Oxford did not open its doors. General Stone seemed a broken man at the meeting called to describe efforts to save the bank. His own debts amounted to $50,000. Phil Stone stood behind his father, but there seemed little he or anyone else could do.

There were a few encouraging notes. In Sinclair Lewis' Nobel Prize acceptance speech earlier in the month, he had singled out Faulkner for special praise. And a young bookstore owner in Milwaukee named Paul Romaine had written to ask if he could print a collection of some of Faulkner's things from *The Double Dealer*. Faulkner agreed. In the first week of January, *Scribner's* returned "The Hound" and "Indians Built a Fence." Associate editor Kyle Crichton wrote that they were "two of the finest stories we have had in months," but that their readers had been complaining about horror stories. But they remembered the story about the spotted horses, and if Faulkner could successfully cut it to 8,000 words, they could take it. They considered him, said Crichton, "one of the greatest writers alive."[33]

Meanwhile, in the offices of the brownstone at 139 East 46th Street, advertising copy was being prepared for Cape & Smith's new titles. The ads would feature *Sanctuary*, which, like Faulkner's earlier novels, was "a mosaic of furious evil, of cold brutality, of human viciousness and human hopelessness." It was a novel which was "hideously and terrifically —and therefore beautifully—great."[34]

In Oxford, William and Estelle Faulkner waited for the book, and the baby.

30

... then suddenly the corridor became full of sound, the myriad
minor voices of human fear and travail . . . the light sleeping at
all hours, the boredom, the wakeful and fretful ringing of little
bells between the hours of midnight and the dead slowing of •
dawn . . . the tinkle of the bells, the immediate sibilance of
rubber heels and starched skirts, the querulous murmur of voices
about nothing.

—*The Wild Palms* (299–300)

WHEN Estelle woke Bill on the bitter-cold night of Saturday, January
10, 1931, he thought she was imagining things; the baby wasn't due for
two months. But he telephoned ahead and drove Estelle to Dr. Culley's
hospital. The next day she gave birth to a tiny little girl with beautiful
features. They named her Alabama, and on Tuesday, Faulkner sent the
news by telegram to her namesake in Memphis. Estelle was too ill even
to see the baby, but Faulkner wanted her and their daughter at home
as soon as possible. There was no incubator at the hospital, and with a
trained nurse for Alabama and a practical nurse for Estelle, he thought
they would do just as well at Rowan Oak. John Culley was a good-
looking, dogmatic man whom Faulkner did not particularly like, but he
was a fine doctor and his wife, Nina, was one of Estelle's best friends.
He came every day because there were problems with the baby's digestive
system. At the end of the week he could see that Alabama's condition
was worsening. Faulkner and Dean went to Memphis for an incubator,
but it was too late. On Tuesday afternoon, January 20, the baby died.
Estelle had never seen her.

The family drove in three cars to St. Peter's Cemetery, and in the cold
January morning Murry Falkner prayed over the small grave. He was
usually abrupt and inarticulate, but Sallie Murry remembered that now
he offered a beautiful prayer. That afternoon the nurse brought Estelle
a sedative. Then Bill came in and sat beside the bed. He told her about

Alabama and wept—the first time she had ever seen him cry. She told him they would have another child.

"Bill," she said, "get you a drink."

"No," he said. "This is one time I'm not going to do it." Later Mr. Murry came to see her. The baby had looked like Billy, he said. Billy had held the casket on his lap all the way to the cemetery.

As he had promised, Faulkner did not turn to liquor, not immediately. But there was one curious aftermath: it was a persistent rumor in Oxford that Faulkner had shot Dr. Culley in the shoulder. Estelle felt that Dr. Culley was in no way culpable in Alabama's death, but Faulkner apparently brooded over the lack of an incubator and felt that the child should have had better care. The rumor persisted in various forms. Faulkner had not shot Dr. Culley, but apparently he had wanted to. The rumor had originated with him. One symbolic response was more positive. Not long afterward he made the donation of an incubator—to Dr. Bramlett's hospital, to be used free of charge when parents could not pay for it.

His grief would remain acute for that whole year. It may have been an attempt to assuage it that caused the only car wreck in his life. That summer, when Ben Wasson wrote that he had rheumatism, Faulkner replied that he had suffered from it too. "But last winter I laid my skull bare in a wreck, and after I was patched up I never had rheumatism again." It must have been the night Mac Reed looked up from the counter to see Faulkner standing there.

"Bill, you're all cut up," he said.

"Well, at last I did it," said Faulkner. "I deliberately ran my car into a telephone pole. I lost control and it was running away with me, so I headed for the pole and hit it dead center." Mac sat him down, cleaned him up, and applied iodine. When it stung, Faulkner began to curse. Surprised and nonplused, Mac threatened to call the constable.

"Hell," said Faulkner, "I'd rather spend the night in jail than be burned alive." Mac telephoned Phil Stone, who came and got Faulkner and drove him home. The next day he apologized.[1]

HE was back at work on his writing that same month of January, sending out revised stories and one new one called "The Brooch." If it was linked to past fiction, it also suggested elements from personal life. The young wife loves dancing and longs for it; the husband doesn't particularly care for it and isn't much good at it. They have just lost a child, in infancy. It is another tale of a girl harassed into profligacy by circumstances and an inflexible, malevolent older woman. The son (another one-time University of Virginia undergraduate) is dominated by the same woman: his mother. Faulkner had worked through different names and situations before he sent the story out, and much more revision would be necessary before he could sell it.

He had better luck with "The Peasants," revised according to Alfred

Dashiell's suggestion, with V. K. Surratt as narrator. He tried it first on the *Post*, however, under the new title "Aria Con Amore." When they rejected it, it went to Dashiell, who bought it for $400. He relaxed his strictures about length, however, and by the time Faulkner had revised it yet again, it ran close to 8,000 words. Dashiell asked for another title, and Faulkner supplied it, so that when the story appeared in the June number, it was called "Spotted Horses."

Faulkner's first appearance in the new year had come with "Dry September" in *Scribner's* for January. Not many of Dashiell's readers objected to its violence. This was not the case when Cape & Smith issued *Sanctuary* on February 9, 1931. From the first there were two major responses: horror at its subject matter and grudging admiration of its power. In a review in the New York *Sun* on the thirteenth, entitled "A Chamber of Horrors," Edwin Seaver called it "one of the most terrifying books I have ever read. And it is one of the most extraordinary." Two days later, in *The New York Times Book Review*, John Chamberlain wrote that it left him limp. The review was titled "Dostoevsky's Shadow in the Deep South." (Nine weeks later, when Bennett Cerf wrote that he wanted to see Faulkner's work in The Modern Library and offered copies of volumes in the series, Faulkner replied, "if you will send me what Dostoyefsky you have in the list, I will appreciate it very much. I have seen several reviews of my books in which a Dostoyefsky influence was found. I have never read Dostoyefsky, and so I would like to see the animal.")

The reviews kept coming as the spring wore on. Clifton Fadiman told *The Nation*'s readers that by this book alone Faulkner took his place in the first rank of younger American novelists. But Henry Seidel Canby wrote in *The Saturday Review of Literature* that in *Sanctuary* "sadism, if not anti-romance, has reached its American peak."[2] With the summer and fall came high praise for both work and author. Robert E. Sherwood extolled Faulkner's "prodigious genius" in this "great novel," and Alexander Woollcott told his radio audience that it was an "extraordinary" work of "grandeur."[3] Nearer to home, Julia K. Wetherill Baker had written her usual perceptive assessment for the *Times-Picayune*. Having earlier likened Faulkner to Joyce, she now saw him at home in the Greece of Euripides or the London of John Webster. She thought he was probably America's best living novelist but hazarded the opinion that he was very likely becoming a scandal in his native state. The Memphis *Evening Appeal*'s reviewer proved her right. *Sanctuary*, he declared, was a "devastating, inhuman monstrosity of a book that leaves one with the impression of having been vomited bodily from the sensual cruelty of its pages."[4]

It was not only the unsophisticated who reacted with shock. Scribner's distinguished editor Maxwell Perkins thought it was a "horrible book by a writer of great talent." His own star author, Ernest Hemingway, conceded that Faulkner was "damned good when good" though he was "often unnecessary." Perkins toyed with the idea of trying to lure him away from Cape & Smith, but then decided against it. John Hall Wheelock, another Scribner editor, thought he knew why: "because he was afraid of arousing Hemingway's jealousy." Hemingway found it easy to express confidence in the work of two other Perkins authors, Thomas Wolfe and Scott Fitzgerald, but, thought Wheelock, "in Hemingway's mind, there was no more room in Max's life for another power so threatening as William Faulkner."[5] Somewhat later another distinguished writer would pay the novel a different sort of compliment. "*Sanctuary*," wrote André Malraux, "is the intrusion of Greek tragedy into the detective story."[6]

The response at home was far different. Very few people in Oxford had read any of his books, but even if they had, they preferred idealized or at least complimentary fiction. Here was an author presenting the worst possible aspects of the modern South and its people, not to mention gratuitous horrors a gentleman wouldn't discuss. And this "artist" was one of their own. There were names for people like that, no matter how much outlanders and foreigners seemed to think of them. As for Oxford's being the original of Jefferson, that was the last thing to evoke any sense of pride. Even friends such as Bob Farley found the book repugnant. Sallie Murry was very direct with her cousin. "Do you think up that material when you're drunk?" she asked him. He looked her in the eye and answered, "Sallie Murry, I get a lot of it when I'm drunk." In Murry Falkner, shock was mingled with outrage. His own standard fare was still Zane Grey and James Oliver Curwood, and he thought that if Bill was going to write, he ought to write Western stories. In his own notebook he had typed out a humorous piece about "the Maker" and his creation of college students, the fairest work of his hand being the coed.[7] He had not read this book about a fictional coed and he did not intend to. Crossing the campus one day he saw a real coed carrying a copy of *Sanctuary* and stopped her. "It isn't fit for a nice girl to read," he told her.

The author's support came from the same ones who had backed him from the start or from early in his career. Mac Reed loyally stocked his books, but a buyer usually wanted his wrapped before he left the drugstore. Others sent their servants to buy their copies for them, but enough Oxford residents read this Faulkner novel, according to one literary historian, to make it "the primary topic of conversation," which "rapidly displaced local talk about the ever-worsening depression and Governor Theodore Bilbo's unjust firings of many respected and admired professors at the University of Mississippi."[8]

One afternoon a member of Maud Falkner's bridge foursome asked, "Why did Bill write a book like that?" The hostess drew herself up even straighter than usual. "My Billy writes what he has to write," she said.

It was the last word spoken until the ladies left at the end of the rubber, and Maud Falkner never spoke to the offender again.[9]

Phil Stone was delighted with the response. He would later reminisce about retyping rejected stories and selling them at a higher price. Then, Stone used to say, he told Faulkner he was on his own. "I have a living to make," he told him. Faulkner's schedule for the balance of 1931 belies Stone's story. Of three early stories sent out, not one was accepted. There had been some wish fulfillment in Stone's other comment, too. For some time before the spring of 1931, Faulkner had been "on his own," as far as any literary reliance on Stone went. As far as sales went, he had now hit another drought.

As usual, he continued his efforts. One of the results was a new story called "Artist at Home." The setting suggested "Black Music," and but for a few details, the protagonist might have been Sherwood Anderson at Ripshin Farm in Troutdale. Six years after Anderson had used Faulkner in "A Meeting South," Faulkner was returning the compliment. Roger Howes is an amiable, generous man with an unflagging desire to help other artists and an unfailing capacity for being betrayed and hurt. But when his wife, Anne, betrays him (in the spirit if not in the flesh) with a young poet named John Blair, it is in large part through Howes's own failure, not only as a husband but as an artist so far past his prime as to depend on people rather than the creative imagination—the melancholy state into which Anderson had fallen, in Faulkner's opinion. The impecunious poet suggests Faulkner when the Andersons first knew him, but he fails too, in his arrant and fatal romanticism, just as Howes failed. If Faulkner had drawn something from his present situation as a married artist dealing with both domestic and artistic problems, he had also made another attempt to deal with other destructive aspects of the artist's life. He sent "Artist at Home" to the *Post*, which rejected it.

He sold nothing in March or April. He missed his March 1 mortgage payment, and Will Bryant graciously granted his request to defer further payments until September. He heated his home with firewood he sawed and chopped, often with Johncy's help. And there were unpaid medical bills.

In early March he had sent to the *Post* another story of a girl balked by an older woman, despite the efforts of the title character to save her. It was called "Doctor Martino," and was rejected promptly. It seems likely that the materials of this story did not touch Faulkner as deeply as those of a story he sent out in late April under the title "All the Dead Pilots." It was probably a reworking of "Per Ardua."[10] The narrator was a nameless British officer, thinking in 1931 of photographs at the war's end and reflecting that all the old pilots were dead. The elegiac beginning could have drawn on patrons of Reno DeVaux's New Crystal Gardens: "lean young men who once swaggered," now lost and baffled,

no longer lean, now out of place in "this saxophone age of flying. . . ."[11]
Their wartime apotheosis was one who had never lived to be an anachronism: John Sartoris. The principal matter here is his rivalry with
his stupid squadron commander for the favors of Antoinette, a readily
available barmaid. In the end, neither lays permanent claim to her, and
the closing account of Sartoris' death is another apostrophe to such
men and moments. But something failed to jell: Sartoris comes through
not as a doomed hero but as a violent, self-centered ruffian, and his rival,
Captain Spoomer, is too hateful to be a comic figure as well as a villain. Faulkner was reworking material which had dominated his imagination at the time of *Flags in the Dust*, and it was not the last time he would
employ all his hard-won craftsman's skill to make this material salable.

The major project which occupied him in May was the sort of thing
Faulkner had proposed to Horace Liveright more than four years before:
"A collection of short stories of my townspeople."[12] It was a Cape &
Smith contract for "A Rose For Emily And Other Stories." Six Yoknapatawpha stories would form the middle portion, but for the beginning
he had to draw on four war stories, the last three set outside the United
States. One of them, called "Victory," went back to impressions he had
gleaned in his 1925 trip to England, with vignettes of Englishmen devastated by the war they had survived physically but not psychically. Typi-
cally, he had worked his way through at least two manuscripts and two
typescripts, all focusing on a working-class Scot named Alexander Gray
who had distinguished himself for savagery and heroism and then tries
unsuccessfully to survive as a demobilized Guards captain. One seventeen-
page excision from the manuscript described Gray's infantry patrol falling into a chalk cavern that still entombed Senegalese troops gassed in
1915. Faulkner deleted Gray's name, changed the tense from past to
present, and entitled his new story "Crevasse." He would complete the
book with early and late stories which had not sold, enough to match
the final title, *These 13*.

Business showed some other signs of picking up. Ben Wasson had sold
"The Hound" and "Fox Hunt" to *Harper's* for $400 apiece. In England,
Chatto & Windus published *The Sound and the Fury*, and in France,
Gallimard acquired the French rights to Faulkner's work, with the first
volume to be *As I Lay Dying*, already in the process of translation by
Maurice Coindreau, a Princeton professor who had written an article about
Faulkner's work which would appear in the *Nouvelle revue française* for
June.

ONE result of Faulkner's increasing visibility was the visit that July of
Marshall J. Smith, who came down from Memphis to interview him for
the *Press-Scimitar*. Over pitchers of Faulkner's home brew they talked
under the shady cedars. Many of Faulkner's answers were a familiar sort
of exercise in fiction and fantasy, most of which Smith seems to have

taken literally. Faulkner talked about *Sanctuary* and about writing *As I Lay Dying* to the hum of the power-plant dynamo. But then he said, "I haven't written a real novel yet. I'm too young in experience. . . . Perhaps in five years I can put it over. Perhaps write a *Tom Jones* or a *Clarissa Harlowe*."[13] Smith brought his camera, and Faulkner posed not only for a profile shot and a truculent head-on picture, a corncob pipe in his teeth, but also for one hoeing in his kitchen garden and another in which, smiling, with newspaper in hand, he entered the ramshackle privy superannuated by the new plumbing. The interview was read in Memphis on July 10.

It is not impossible that the visit from Smith—a writer come from the city to an old house in the country—may have helped inspire a new story called "Evangeline." The narrator was not new. He was the companion of Don in "Mistral," but now the setting was a Mississippi village rather than an Alpine settlement. This time the generating action sprang not from a murder but from a ghost. Joining Don, the narrator-writer learns about Colonel Sutpen, a long-dead settler who had built a mansion out in the country, and about his daughter, Judith. He learns, too, of the mysterious objections which Judith's brother, Henry, had made to her courtship by his friend Charles Bon, which had led to an open break between Henry and his father and barely aborted a duel with Bon. The Civil War had intervened, and when Henry returned from it, he had brought Bon back with him, "killed by the last shot of the war." A gnomelike mulatto woman named Raby tells the tale, but the part that affects Don most is a young black girl's account of a terrifying ghostly face she had seen in the house years later, just before Judith's burial. Don is sure the Negroes think her ghost still walks in the old house. Not only that, there is also a police dog who has patrolled the grounds during all the forty years since her death.

In the third section of the suspenseful tale, the narrator takes up where the departed Don has left off. Entering the house by night against Raby's warning, he discovers the secret: no ghost, but the moribund Henry Sutpen. Before the story ends in its seventh section with the flames that consume the old house, the narrator learns more. Found in the ruins is a metal case that had contained the picture of Judith she had given to Bon, a case she had unaccountably beaten shut when Henry brought Bon's body home. Prying it open, the narrator finds the picture of Bon's mulatto wife, whose face is very like that of the languorous mulatto in "Peter," written six years earlier. The tale had begun as a ghost story and ended as a tragic history of miscegenation. The title alluded to Longfellow's tragic poem about two separated lovers. The story fluctuated between ambiguity and portentousness, and it needed more space for effective treatment than its forty pages provided. A passage of the narrator's musings indicates one of the problems: "There was something more than just the relationship between Charles and the woman; something she hadn't told me and she was not going to tell. . . . And without it, the whole tale will be pointless, and so I am wasting my time."[14] The editors of the *Post* and the *Woman's Home Companion* agreed when Faulkner sent the story to them. But he would continue brooding over this dark history of Colonel Sutpen's children.

Scribner's, however, was encouraging, along other lines. Kyle Crichton had been telling Faulkner that they hoped for more stories about Flem Snopes. On August 11 he sent them "Centaur in Brass." It follows Flem's activities in Jefferson as he expands from the base provided by his half-interest in the restaurant Suratt had traded for his interest in the Old Frenchman place. Now Flem has a job in the power plant, from which he has stolen brass parts, and he forces the two Negro firemen to help him even while he sets them at odds. There is an element of the fabliau in young Turl's seduction of old Tom-Tom's wife, but this triangle of normal sexuality is contrasted with Flem's suspected debasement of his wife, Eula, through his silent complicity in her affair with Mayor Hoxey, who has appointed Flem superintendent of the municipal power plant. Faulkner was justifiably resentful when *Scribner's* rejected the story because, Crichton said, they wanted Flem triumphant, as he had been at the end of "Spotted Horses," rather than temporarily foiled, as he was at the end of "Centaur in Brass." In late August, Faulkner sent the story to *Harper's*, and they rejected it too.

Early that month Crichton had also rejected "Rose of Lebanon." If Faulkner responded as usual, he probably thought about reworking it. He was apparently taken with the family history he had invented and the way in which Gavin Blount's romanticizing of the past had twisted his life. In north Mississippi there had been many Confederate attempts to capture Yankee supplies, such as the one in which Blount's father lost his life. In one of them, Major General Earl Van Dorn had successfully raided Grant's stores at Holly Springs. What Faulkner did when he resumed work on this story was to move the engagement to Jefferson. For Gavin Blount he substituted Gail Hightower, a Doctor of Divinity but an amateur physician. It was in the Jefferson raid that Hightower's grandfather had received his death wound, a raid full of martial romanticism, like that in *Sartoris*. The grandson's obsession with these events draws him in turn to Jefferson to play out the second-hand drama of his life and take part in another drama far more powerful.

Beginning again, Faulkner took a sheet of his manuscript paper (with its two thin black lines that marked off a margin on top and at the left) and wrote the date, August 17. He printed the title, "Dark House," and underscored it with three pen strokes.[15] He was following his usual regimen of rising early, writing most of the morning, then spending the rest of the day in leisurely work about the place, riding, or whatever suited his fancy. In the late afternoon he and Estelle would have a before-dinner drink on the east gallery. As they sat there one day Estelle looked out across the grass to the bushes, warm in the afternoon sunlight, and to the sunken garden in the deep shade beyond. "Bill," she said, "does it ever seem to you that the light in August is different from any other time of the year?" He rose from his chair. "That's it," he said, and walked into the house. Soon he returned without explanation. Knowing her taciturn husband, Estelle said nothing.

He had gone to his worktable, struck out "Dark House" and substituted "Light in August." He would later say, "I used it because in my country in August there's a peculiar quality to light and that's what that title means."[16] It was not the first time he had used an impressionistic title, and he would actually provide elucidation as Hightower waited for the recurrent vision of the cavalry charge: "In the lambent suspension of August into which night is about to fully come it seems to engender and surround itself with a faint glow like a halo." (465) He had merged the quality of light that month with the time of day which had ever exercised a spell upon his own imagination: twilight.

He had apparently made several false starts. In one, Hightower and his bride rode the train to his new church in Jefferson. In another, he told her the story of his grandfather's death in the henhouse raid. In still another, Hightower paused in his writing and looked out at the shabby sign in his front yard. At some point, however, a character emerged who not only changed Hightower's function to one of counterpoint and linkage, but caused Faulkner to forget or conceal the fact that he had ever begun with him. "I began Light in August," he wrote about a year and a half later, "knowing no more about it than a young woman, pregnant, walking along a strange country road."[17] (There was still another discarded opening, with the arrest of a man named Brown, the alias of Lena's faithless lover.)[18] He hoped to feel the rapture of *The Sound and the Fury*. "It did not return. . . . I was now aware before each word was written down just what the people would do, since now I was deliberately choosing among possibilities and probabilities of behavior and weighing and measuring each choice by the scale of the Jameses and Conrads and Balzacs."[19] He was probably suffering from the condition he had described to Wasson that spring: "I need a change. I'm stale. Written out."[20] But his financial obligations did not cease just because he was tired. He went on with his new work.

Again there were links both to other works and to life. It was as if he had asked himself what might have happened if Dewey Dell Bundren had gone off to find her seducer. Except for Lena Grove's more placid temperament, she was a country girl much like Dewey Dell. Some of the same people, notably the Armstids, befriended both in their travels across Yoknapatawpha. One character, whose story was introduced after Lena's, was returning there after a long absence. Faulkner called him Joe Christmas. Chess Carothers had been light enough to pass for white in some places; prosperous Oxford shoemaker Rob Boles, almost anywhere. So could Christmas, but there the resemblance ended. A closer counterpart would have been Nelse Patton, razor-wielding slayer of a white woman and victim of a lynch mob. Christmas was everything Lena Grove was not: male, hostile, and death-bearing. But like her and Hightower, he was a product of his past. Tortured by his purported mixed blood in his quest for identity, he would show the terrible effects of the vicious prejudice and vindictive religiosity visited upon him from earliest childhood. Spinster Joanna Burden was another product of her past. Descendant of an abolitionist murdered by Colonel Sartoris, she lived in her dark house outside Jefferson, her life shadowed by the curse of the slavery her people had abominated. A quiet philanthropist, she would find in Christmas a focus for her cold Negrophilism and frenetic eroticism. (For comparisons, Faulkner reached back to that early favorite, Beardsley, and to Petronius.) One more person, Byron Bunch, completed the cast of Faulkner's major characters. A good man like Cash Bundren, he was undersized, scrupulously honorable, compassionate, and limited. *Light in August* would be one of Faulkner's longest manuscripts. As he moved his scores of players about, it would also be one of his most heavily reworked, so much so that it would be difficult later to trace his shifting narrative strategies. One scholar would argue that he first told the story of Bryon and Lena and Hightower in the present tense, perceiving only then the importance of Joe Christmas, and writing a long flashback to fill in the story of his youth. The marginal inserts, the cancellations, the interpolations, the discarded sheets and the paste-ons salvaged from others, all showed the combination of meticulousness and energy, the craftsman's care and the determination to make the work match the dream.[21]

IT is difficult to tell where he was in the manuscript as August became September. He made several magazine submissions in that month, but only one was taken, "Doctor Martino," by *Harper's*, for $500. He listed no others on his sending schedule for the rest of that year. It would be a while before he received any royalties from *These 13*. The book had come out on September 21, and the regular edition of 1,928 copies sold out before the end of the month, as did a signed edition of 299. The book was dedicated "To Estelle and Alabama." Again the reviews were mixed. But in early October, Dashiell bought "A Death-Drag" and Mencken accepted "Centaur in Brass." Money was still so scarce that he couldn't make full mortgage payments. However, outside Oxford there were signs that his stature was increasing.

At the suggestion of Ellen Glasgow, the grande dame of Southern letters, the University of Virginia was organizing a gathering of Southern writers. Professor James Southall Wilson, heading an informal committee which included Miss Glasgow, James Branch Cabell, DuBose Heyward, Thomas Wolfe, and Paul Green, had issued thirty-four invitations. Faulkner's was one of them, and Wilson hoped he could be with them on October 24 and 25. Julia Peterkin, Donald Davidson, the Laurence Stallingses, Sherwood Anderson, and Allen Tate had promised to attend. Wolfe would be there too, if he could make it. Faulkner replied that he was glad of "your letter's pleasing assurance that loopholes will be supplied to them who have peculiarities about social gambits." He was like the hound dog that stays under a country wagon on the square, he said. "He might be cajoled or scared out for a short distance, but first thing you know he has scuttled back under the wagon; maybe he growls at you a little. Well, that's me."[22] But he would plan to arrive on October 22.

He did not tell Wilson what he would tell one new friend when he got there, that Harrison Smith had provided a round-trip train ticket to New York and $100 expense money. Faulkner may not have known it, but Cape & Smith was in serious straits, and Jonathan Cape was arriving in New York on October 27. If anything should happen to the firm, William Faulkner would be one of the first whom rival publishers would approach, especially after *Sanctuary*. It seems probable that Smith wanted this author close to him until the increasingly fluid situation was stabilized.

As for Faulkner, he might talk about hound dogs, but in New York, whether he wished it or not, he would be a lion. Perhaps he could turn his new status to financial advantage.

... you accursed who are not satisfied with the world as it is
and so must try to rebuild the very floor you are standing on,
you keep on talking and shouting and gesturing at us until you
get us all fidgety and alarmed. So I believe that if art served any
purpose at all, it would at least keep the artists themselves
occupied.

—*Mosquitoes* (319–320)

PREPARATIONS were going forward in Charlottesville. Faulkner's arrival
was awaited with particular interest. There was not only the stir caused
by *Sanctuary* but also such growing critical attention as Granville Hick's
recent essay in *The Bookman* declaring that "The world of William
Faulkner echoes with the hideous trampling march of lust and disease,
brutality and death." Advancing a thesis that would haunt Faulkner
criticism, he suggested that Faulkner might be playing a game with his
readers: one could imagine him writing his stories straightforwardly
"then recasting them in some distorted form."[1] Faulkner's visit to Charlottesville and New York was heralded in Cape & Smith's "Literary
Notes," along with the word that *These 13* had just gone into a third
printing and that *Sanctuary* and *As I Lay Dying* would be coming out
in French.

He had a reservation at the Monticello Hotel on Court Square. A
Charlottesville *Daily Progress* reporter, Lewis Mattison, was waiting when
he stepped out of the taxi. "Are you Mr. Faulkner?" he asked. Faulkner
glanced to the left and and the right. "Know where I can get a drink?"
he asked. Faulkner bought a bottle of corn whiskey from Mattison's
supplier and invited the reporter to repair to the S.A.E. house with him.
They spent a congenial evening together, without, however, any of the
literary talk that Mattison hoped to use in the *Progress*. Faulkner had
set the tone for his whole visit.

The next morning he wrote Estelle. When his train had stopped at Bristol, Virginia, he had sent a telegram to Elizabeth Prall Anderson, in Marion, Virginia, where she and Sherwood had moved four years before and where she still lived despite Anderson's leaving her in 1929. He told Estelle that he had received no reply. "Maybe she is still mad at me," he wrote. There would be no word from her.

Faulkner liked his surroundings. "I can see the Blue Ridge from both of my windows. I can see all Charlottesville, and the University too. The fall coloring is splendid here—yellow hickory and red gum and sumach and laurel, with the blue-green pines. It's just grand." In the afternoon Hal Smith would arrive, and then on Friday morning the conference would begin with "a formal to-do."[2]

Playwright Paul Green, from Chapel Hill, North Carolina, 1927 Pulitzer Prize winner for *In Abraham's Bosom*, was an outgoing man with a thick shock of hair and a Roman profile. Faulkner accepted his offer of a ride to the first meeting. When Faulkner came down from his room he was wearing what Green took to be an aviator's cap. He had been in the Canadian Air Force, Faulkner explained.

Thirty-four writers assembled that morning. Even without Thomas Wolfe and Stark Young, it was an impressive gathering. Ellen Glasgow began it. Her friends, admiring her brown eyes and dark-bronze hair, spoke of her "autumn leaf" coloring. Although she was rather deaf, her manner was still urbane and assured. She discarded the set topic in a witty but rambling talk on the relation between historical and fictional truth. Faulkner sat on the edge of his chair, his elbows on his knees and his head between his hands. He had apparently fortified himself. From time to time, after particularly authoritative pronouncements, he would raise his head slightly and softly murmur, "I agree, I agree."[3] A lively discussion followed, but then, suddenly, as Sherwood Anderson put it, "the meeting got bad—long tiresome speeches from professors. Everyone began to think it was going to be like a dentists' convention."[4]

Things picked up that afternoon with tea at Castle Hill, one of the great houses of Albemarle County, built on an original grant from George II. It was the mansion of Amelie Rives, who had met her husband, painter Prince Pierre Troubetzkoy, at a London party given by Oscar Wilde. The author of a once-shocking novel called *The Quick or the Dead?*, she had been in her prime a "tiny but striking figure with masses of golden hair, violet eyes, and long flowing gowns . . . one of the most photographed women of her day."[5] Two young admirers of Faulkner had stopped at the Monticello Hotel to take him to Castle Hill. He was sitting on the curb waiting for them, tie askew, a mason jar at his side. When Lambert Davis, managing editor of *The Virginia Quarterly Review*, opened the car door, Faulkner eyed him for a moment. "Can we get a drink at Castle Hill?" he asked. Not long after they arrived, Davis and his companion, a young teacher named Dayton Kohler, realized that Faulkner was not with them. He had decided to view the upstairs of the historic mansion. When they finally found him it was time for him to pay his respects to the hostess. Nearly sixty now and suffering from rheumatic gout, Amelie Rives was often confined to her room and never allowed anyone to see her except by candlelight or firelight. Sitting at a beautiful table in her elegant room, she looked up at her guest.

"Mr. Faulkner," she said, "I have seen how you have walked through my house and looked through my rooms, but I've forgiven you because you were accompanied by genius."

"Would that some ten thousand people would say them same words to me, ma'am," he answered.

Emily Clark, who would record many of these doings for the New York *Herald Tribune* and *The Saturday Review of Books*, noted the presence at the dinner given that night at the Farmington Country Club of Harrison Smith and his celebrated author, who "attended meetings and parties intermittently, and was, beyond doubt, the focal point of every gaze, since this new and dazzling light of American letters had never before been in Virginia. . . ." She recalled how this "exponent of horror beyond all imaginable horrors, a gentle, low-voiced, slight young man, on his first evening astonished his admirers and interested spectators by merely murmuring, while conversation and argument raged around him, the placating phase, 'I dare say,' at frequent intervals; and by gently crooning 'Carry Me Back to Old Virginia,' in an automobile between Charlottesville and Farmington."[6]

Faulkner skipped the trip to Monticello, Jefferson's home, on Saturday morning. He managed to hear a talk by James Boyd, the author of *Drums*, but by the time of the afternoon reception at the Colonnade Club on "the Lawn" of Mr. Jefferson's "academical village," he seemed to have lost interest in receptions. Sherwood Anderson was watching him. "Bill Faulkner had arrived and got drunk," he wrote in one letter. "From time to time he appeared, got drunk again immediately, & disappeared. He kept asking everyone for drinks. If they didn't give him any, he drank his own."[7] But by Saturday evening Faulkner had recovered sufficiently to spend more time, relaxed and pleasant, with Lewis Mattison, who felt that "the whole visit was meaningless for him." What's more, "He didn't give a damn about Ellen Glasgow or any of them."

Paul Green had driven to Charlottesville from Chapel Hill with Milton J. Abernethy, a short, round-faced senior at the University of North Carolina who was co-owner of the Intimate Bookshop there and co-editor of a little magazine called *Contempo*. Like Davis and Kohler, he had tried to do his part in looking after Faulkner during the conference. Now he was going to ride with Green to New York, where Green had a play running. Green invited Faulkner and Smith to make the trip in his old

Buick. Smith gratefully accepted for both of them. Once under way, Faulkner grew talkative. He told Green and Abernethy that he had been having a good time with people who accused him of being influenced by James Joyce. He said he would always tell them he hadn't read Joyce. Then he recited from memory for his companions one of his favorite poems, "Watching the Needleboats at San Sabba"—by James Joyce. Later he extracted the manuscript of *Light in August* from a canvas bag and read some of it aloud. He asked Green to stop so he could replenish his liquor supply, and Green did. They stopped again in Washington at a service station when the old Buick developed engine trouble. When Faulkner genially offered a drink to a passing policeman, his companions looked at one another. It may have been at this point that Smith left to complete the trip by train. He did not fancy being under arrest in Washington when he ought to be in New York dealing with a business crisis.

It must have been Monday, October 26, when the others arrived there. Already Harold Guinzburg of The Viking Press had been trying to reach Faulkner, as had Alfred Knopf for his own publishing house and Bennett Cerf and Donald Klopfer for their new firm, Random House. Cerf had a concrete plan in mind. He wanted to publish *Sanctuary* in The Modern Library series. Faulkner found these messages and telephone calls distracting. He responded by drinking more heavily. Milton Abernethy quickly got in touch with Hal Smith, who immediately supplied money for two tickets on the *Henry R. Mallory*, leaving New York for Jacksonville the next day at dinner time. Smith asked Abernethy to get Faulkner aboard as soon as he could and to keep him in Jacksonville, or somewhere outside New York, until the pursuit cooled.

After a stop in Jacksonville, Abernethy invited Faulkner to spend some time with him in Chapel Hill. He put him up in a small second-floor room in the office building that housed the Intimate Bookshop and *Contempo*. It had occurred to Abernethy and Anthony Buttitta, his partner in both ventures, that this might be an unparalleled opportunity for *Contempo*. The manuscript of *Light in August* was still in the canvas bag. "While he had been sleeping," Buttitta recalled, "we tried to decipher the script, but we made no headway. We told him so. He laughed." He said Buttitta could visit him at Rowan Oak and choose some of his rejected manuscripts. Faulkner also agreed to let them put his name on the masthead as a contributing editor.[8]

He had been drinking heavily, but he was well enough to join a Sunday gathering at the home of Phillips Russell, who taught a writing class at the University of North Carolina. To the host's great pleasure, Faulkner agreed to meet his class the next day. He gave a short talk, and his "courtesy and absence of pose," Russell recalled, "made a good impression." Not long afterward, Faulkner and Abernethy left for Norfolk, where

on November 3 they boarded the *Henry R. Mallory* for the return to
New York.

FAULKNER had hardly checked in at the Hotel Century when the battle
of the publishers was joined again. On November 4 he wrote Estelle,
"I have been meeting people and being called on all day. And I have
taken in about 300.00 since I got here. It's just like I was some strange
and valuable beast, and I believe that I can make 1000.00 more in a month."
He did not name the source of the money, but he had written a check
on it that same day for mortgage payments, for material still owing for
the remodeling at Rowan Oak, and for Malcolm's tonsillectomy.[9] The
day's action even made the New York *World-Telegram*, where Harry
Hansen wrote that "rival publishers fought a merry battle yesterday for
the favors of William Faulkner, America's most promising author. . . .
half a dozen publishers had stormed Mr. Faulkner's door, offering as
high as twenty-five percent and generous advance royalties."[10] Nearly two
years later Faulkner would recall "guys waiting with contracts in their
hands and the advance and percentage left blank, outside my hotel door
when the waiter fetched the morning coffee."[11]

Hal Smith's Jacksonville stratagem had failed, and his business position
had changed dramatically, but in the midst of the turmoil he showed how
resourceful he could be. Evelyn Harter was one of the talented young
women he had brought into Cape & Smith. She saw Hal as "a rather
slightly built fellow," who "had a little nervous way of twitching his
nose when he had to make a decision, and he looked on the world with
sort of a gentle, ironical look, as if he found it all very amusing. He was
a marvelous man to work for. . . ." He was very different from Jonathan
Cape, "a big, heavy-set fellow with a sort of long, horsey face; and he
had his own ideas of 'how we do things in England, you know.' " Their
temperamental, artistic, and business differences had grown sharper as
the firm's condition worsened. As head of production in the small firm,
Evelyn Harter was close to all of its workings. It seemed to her that
when Cape, once in New York, "decided things were going to the bad,
and he couldn't tolerate Smith any longer, he booted him." Owning
fifty-one percent of the stock, he could do it. Smith's loyal staff—Evelyn,
Louise Bonino, and a few others—hated to see the end of this organization in the old brownstone where "everyone knew each other," and
the place "vibrated with enthusiasm and energy."[12] Smith did a courageous thing in the heart of the Depression: he took his staff with him
and founded a new house, Harrison Smith, Inc.

He wanted to retain his authors. Loyal Evelyn Harter thought that
Smith's advances to Faulkner had kept him going. They had actually represented a small, if important, part of Faulkner's income, but it may have
been in recognition of them, and Smith's faith in his work, that Faulkner
acted as he did. And there was something else. When a reporter caught

him after he had debarked from the *Mallory*, he told her that he liked only a few things about New York and that he was there just to see Harrison Smith, "my one friend in the North, one man I like."[13] So he turned down Knopf, Viking, and Random House and went with Harrison Smith, Inc.

Faulkner was also influenced by another possibility. He had written Estelle, "I have the assurance of a movie agent that I can go to California, to Hollywood and make 500.00 or 750.00 a week in the movies. I think the trip would do *you* a lot of good. We could live like counts at least on that, and you could dance and go about." If she liked the idea, he would talk to the agent. "Hal Smith will not want me to do it, but if all that money is out there, I might as well hack a little on the side and put the novel off."[14] Ben Wasson took Faulkner to see representatives of two studios. According to Faulkner's uncle John, an approach had been made by Tallulah Bankhead at the behest of her studio. In England she had played Sadie Thompson in *Rain*, and she had starred in *My Sin* for Paramount Pictures. "I seemed sentenced for life to playing tarts," she recalled, "reformed tarts or novice tarts."[15] When she told Faulkner that she admired his work and hoped he would come to Hollywood to write a screenplay for her, he supposedly replied, "I'd like to help a Southern girl who's climbin' to the top. But you're too pretty an' nice a girl to play in anything I'd write."[16] It may have been Wednesday, November 11, that he talked to a representative of Paramount. Two days later he wrote Estelle, "I am writing a movie for Tallullah [*sic*] Bankhead. How's that for high? The contract is to be signed today, for about $10,000.00. Like this: yesterday I wrote the outline, the synopsis, for which I am to get $500.00. Next I will elaborate the outline and put the action in, and I get $2500.00. Then I write the dialogue and get the rest of it." After that, he thought they would go to Hollywood. And there was even a play he might write for Bankhead.[17]

As the business activities had accelerated, so had the social engagements. Hal Smith had him to lunch at his apartment with Evelyn and Louise and Maurice Coindreau. Smith and his wife, Claire Spencer, invited him to their place in Farmington, Connecticut, for a weekend. He carried no bag, just a few articles in the pockets of his capacious trench coat. Unable to restrain his curiosity, Smith crept upstairs and looked into Faulkner's room to see how his meticulous butler, William, had dealt with this unorthodox guest. There on the bed, William had meticulously laid out all of Faulkner's things: pajamas, razor, toothbrush.

The competition was by no means convinced that Smith had Faulkner sewed up. George Oppenheimer, co-founder of The Viking Press, entertained Faulkner. Oppenheimer's friend, Dorothy Parker, had said to him, "Look after this guy." A diminutive bright-eyed brunette with a reputation for witty satirical verse and craftsmanlike short stories, and famous for a sharp and sometimes malicious tongue, she was completely taken by Faulkner. "He seemed so vulnerable, so helpless," she said. "You just wanted to protect him." This reaction would not have been unknown to Estelle or other members of his family. They felt him to be an expert at playing this role, one he had performed convincingly for Elizabeth Anderson—for a time—and would perform for many others again.

IT may have been through Dorothy Parker that Faulkner found an entrée into still another set. It included some of the wits who often congregated at the "round table" of the Hotel Algonquin. One member was a distinguished thirty-six-year-old banker named Robert Abercrombie Lovett. He and his striking blond wife often entertained in their handsome duplex apartment on 83rd Street overlooking the East River. Their guests might include *New Yorker* editor Harold Ross and some of those who wrote for him, such as Dorothy Parker and Robert Benchley. Playwrights Robert Sherwood and Marc Connelly were often there, and a gathering might include novelists John O'Hara and Joel Sayre, columnists Franklin P. Adams and Alexander Woollcott. They were dynamic people, fond of the theatre, of literature and music. It took very little to get them started, and they had what they remembered as screamingly funny evenings together. They welcomed Faulkner for his talent, but they grew fond of him, as Dorothy Parker had, for a variety of reasons, and they would see him often thereafter when he came to New York.

On one such evening the talk turned to celebrated units in the war. Lovett had won the Navy Cross for flying bombers as an American with the Royal Naval Air Service. To him, the most gallant as well as the most decorated were the three-man crews of the Coastal Motor Boats that operated against the German U-boat bases. The skipper would take his CMB in over the minefields at top speed to launch his torpedoes. They couldn't have been past their early twenties, Lovett remembered, with their long British prep-school scarves hanging down to their knees. On one joint operation Lovett and his crew in their lumbering Handley-Page won a DSO for a diversionary raid, drawing fire away from the CMB's, racing across the deadly minefield below. The casualty rate in those little cockleshells, out night after night in all kinds of foul weather with no rescue gear, was as high as that in the squadrons of pursuit aircraft at the front. On occasion, men of Lovett's group would come across some of these CMB boys lying drunk in the gutters of Dunkirk, having unwound from one mission or momentarily staving off the thought of the next. The Navy pilots would take these sailors home and with them to the squadron to recover. Walking back to the hotel that night with Ben Wasson, Faulkner could not get the story out of his mind. "Great God Almighty, Bud," he said, "think of those boys lying in that gutter—doomed." Faulkner would often say, later in life, that a story would worry and worry him until he had to put it down on paper. That process apparently began now, and it may have been through it that he made two more good friends.

Frank Sullivan was a short, plump, worried-looking man whom the *Saturday Review* called the best slapstick satirist then writing. A Cornell graduate who had served as an infantry lieutenant in France, he was now, at thirty-nine, writing three wide-ranging columns a week for the New York *World*. He shared an apartment on East 51st Street with Corey Ford, ten years his junior, who wrote for a number of magazines and appeared regularly in *Vanity Fair* as a literary critic under the pseudonym of John Riddell. A late riser, Sullivan entered the dining area one morning to find it already occupied. "I was mystified to see a strange, gnome-like figure, his back to me, sitting at the refectory table tapping away at a typewriter." Annie Moffitt, the housekeeper, told him that the guest "was Mr. Faulkner and that Mr. Wasson had brought him to the apartment to use the spare typewriter." Mrs. Moffitt disapproved not only of this break in the normal routine, but of the visitor's working in his stocking feet and throwing discarded sheets on the floor. Sullivan fortified himself with breakfast and then asked if Faulkner needed anything. He did not, only the quiet seclusion of their apartment while he finished a story for the *Post*. After a brief but pleasant conversation, Sullivan left him to his work.

It seems likely that the story was based on the one Faulkner had heard from Lovett. He also used Lovett for the center of consciousness, for the omniscient narrator was Captain Bogard, an RFC pilot who has the look of a Yale man. The element that had struck Faulkner most forcefully is there in the short story. Doomed, and knowing it, these boys drink themselves unconscious yet behave with superb nonchalance and coltish grace. They are dead at the end, yet in a dextrous strategy Faulkner managed to introduce adventure and comedy, walking a tightrope in his avoidance of farce, melodrama, and bathos. Faulkner counterpointed the enthusiastic playfulness of the English boys and the hard-bitten cynicism of the older Americans. But the cynicism gave way to outrage—unlike "The Lilacs," *Sartoris*, and "All the Dead Pilots"—when at the end Bogard dives in vengeance to bomb an enemy headquarters, thinking, "God! God! If they were all there—all the generals, the admirals, the presidents and the kings—theirs, ours—all of them."[18] It would be nearly two months before Faulkner would send "Turn About" to Ben Wasson, but Robert Lovett would be able to read it in early March of 1932 in *The Saturday Evening Post*.

Faulkner's need for the quiet of Sullivan and Ford's apartment was obvious from the letter he sent Estelle on November 13. "I have created quite a sensation," he told her. "I have had luncheons in my honor by magazine editors every day for a week now, besides evening parties, or people who want to see what I look like. In fact, I have learned with astonishment that I am now the most important figure in American letters. That is, I have the best future. Even Sinclair Lewis and Dreiser make engagements to see me, and Mencken is coming all the way up from

Baltimore to see me on Wednesday. I'm glad I'm level-headed, not very vain. But I dont think it has gone to my head. Anyway, I am writing." He ticked them off: *Light in August*, a short story for *Cosmopolitan*, the Bankhead screenplay, and a stage version of *Sanctuary* that he said was to go into rehearsal next week. And would Estelle please send him a big envelope from his workroom? It contained some poems.[19]

Estelle found it a disquieting letter, not just because it didn't sound like him, but because of the frenetic tone. When fully engaged on a piece, he was an extraordinarily intense worker, but this was too much. It sounded as though he was headed for another collapse. When she telephoned the Algonquin, the operator said he was not registered there. He had asked her to send the poems to him at 320 East 42nd Street, and she had not recognized it as the address of the Woodstock Towers, one of the residential hotels that formed Tudor City. Later he would tell her that he had stayed with Stark Young for three or four days. Young lived in the neighborhood, and Faulkner may have moved from there to this new temporary residence—into the unfamiliar environment of a twenty-eighth-floor New York apartment. Estelle was really not well enough to travel, but she could see that she might have to.

Could she have seen the New York *Herald Tribune*, she would have learned that he had submitted to an interview that day in Ben Wasson's office. She might not have been surprised that he named *Moby-Dick* and *The Nigger of the Narcissus* as his favorite novels and Ernest Hemingway as his most admired colleague, but she might have wondered at his saying, for publication in a New York daily, that Southern Negroes were childlike and that they would be better off "under the conditions of slavery . . . because they'd have someone to look after them." In the accompanying photograph he gazed directly into the lens with an annoyed expression that was almost truculent.[20]

The pace did not slacken. On Sunday he and Jim Devine might take a ferry to Hoboken, where the saloons were wide open and their favorite served its own beer and offered a free-lunch counter that featured an appetizing clam broth. Paul Green took him to the Martin Beck Theatre to see his play *The House of Connelly*. Afterward, on the street, Faulkner sketched the structure of the play for Green in pencil on the front wall of the theatre. As they walked on, Faulkner said he was dramatizing *Sanctuary* and that he was going to act in it. "What part are you going to play?" Green asked. "The corncob," Faulkner answered, laughing. A little later Faulkner turned abruptly into a florist's shop and emerged with a bouquet of roses and handed them to the astonished Green. "I just thought you might like some roses," Faulkner said. Ben Wasson took him to see *The Front Page* and Norman Bel Geddes' production of *Hamlet*. Faulkner disliked Ben Hecht and Charles MacArthur's newspaper melodrama. For one thing, it was too noisy. But as they left the theatre after *Hamlet* he suddenly stopped. "Well, sir," he said, "I've just crossed over Jordan." Bel Geddes was one of Ben's clients, and he eagerly agreed to meet Faulkner. When he made an ill-considered remark about *Sanctuary*, however, Faulkner froze. Ben quickly retrieved the situation by asking Bel Geddes to show them some masks he had made for a proposed dramatization of Dante's *Inferno*. Faulkner examined and admired them. "O'Neill had the right idea in *The Great God Brown*," he told his host. "Those masks he used for his characters made a small play into a big one. But your masks are incredibly lovely; they express emotion in a way no human being could express it. Maybe that's the way all plays should be done."[21]

THE longer Faulkner stayed in New York the more writers he met. One was Nathanael West, a tall, dark, mustachioed man who had published a fantastic novel called *The Dream Life of Balso Snell*. Though a sad and gentle man, he was a fanatical hunter who loved to talk about hunting rather than books. That was not the case with two others, Dashiell Hammett and Lillian Hellman. Both were Southerners. Hammett had an even more knockabout employment history than Faulkner. For eight years he had been a Pinkerton detective, an occupation that had served him well when he came to write *The Maltese Falcon* and *The Glass Key*, books which made him a leader in the school of detective fiction which coupled violence with psychological character study. That must have appealed to the author of "Smoke," but Hammett, for his part, wanted most to write "straight" novels. He had encouraged Lily Hellman in her ambition to become a playwright, and she had quickly fallen in love with him. There were long evenings of drinking and talking, and in the morning Faulkner might still be there, asleep on the couch. When Faulkner said that *Sanctuary* was a potboiler written to make money, Dash Hammett, who admired Faulkner, replied, "That's not so, a good writer doesn't write for money." They differed on politics, Hammett a confirmed Marxist and Faulkner an anti-radical Democrat, but they continued to enjoy each other's company at the same time that they presented difficulties to others.

One afternoon as they were finishing lunch with Bennett Cerf at Jack Kriendler and Charlie Burns's club at 21 West 52nd Street, they badgered Cerf into getting them an invitation to a dinner party that night at the Knopfs', where the guests would include Serge Koussevitzky and Willa Cather. Cerf told them it would be black-tie and asked where he should pick them up. "Right here," one of them answered. When Cerf returned they were still there, not in the least concerned about attending the black-tie party in their tweeds. Cerf lectured them about behaving themselves, and at the party they were quiet and polite, from time to time taking glasses from the trays offered them by the butler. Then Hammett slid quietly off the couch and passed out. Faulkner rose to his feet, announced his departure, and also passed out. When Hammett was removed to recuperate, Faulkner rose once more to announce his departure, only to subside onto the carpet again. Eventually Ben Wasson and others helped him to make his exit.

Somehow these events did not deter Cerf from entertaining a similar gathering at his apartment. Alfred Knopf had been out of town at the time of his wife's party, and he was glad of the chance to meet Faulkner. He brought with him half a dozen Faulkner first editions and, later in the evening, asked Faulkner to sign them. He had searched Sixth Avenue for them, he said, because most were out of print. Faulkner was silent for a moment. Then he said, "People stop me on the street and in elevators and ask me to sign books, but I can't afford to do this because special signed editions are part of my stock-in-trade. Aside from that, I only sign books for my friends." Horrified, Cerf interceded for his publishing rival and friend. "Well," Faulkner said, after a pause, "Mrs. Knopf has been very kind to me, so if you want to pick out one of them, I'll inscribe it for you." Accounts of both parties spread quickly. This was the kind of temperament—some would call it rudeness—which would add to the quickly growing body of Faulknerian lore.

If his drinking was unusual, so were his recuperative powers. On November 25 he appeared at Ben Wasson's office to write the introduction for The Modern Library edition of *Sanctuary*. "You know what I was saying when I wrote *Sanctuary*, don't you?" he asked Ben. "I was saying that women are impervious to evil." Giving the handwritten copy to Morty Goldman for typing, Ben could not quite believe what Faulkner had said. "Yes," he had insisted. "You remember how Temple sat with her father, Judge Drake, in the Luxembourg Gardens? How she sat there on a bench, so quiet and serene? And just as if none of those horrific things that happened to her in the old house and the corn crib or in the whore house with Popeye and her lover, Red, even occurred. She wasn't demoralized or touched by any of it. All of it was like water falling on a duck's back and sliding right off."[22] If the introduction showed contempt for the reading public together with bravado and a craftsman's pride in the finished work, there was also genuine regret. Many years later he said, "I was still ashamed of it when I wrote that preface, I still didn't like the book, and I am still sorry that I wrote the first version of it. And that was the reason for the preface."[23] He would receive $100 for it. Random House was paying him $400 more for "Idyll in the Desert," which they would publish in a special edition on December 8. And he was about a quarter done with *Light in August*, according to an interview published in *The New Yorker* on November 28. When the reporter asked him when he wrote, he gave an answer that would sound to some younger writers like a rule of the craft: "I write when the spirit moves me, and the spirit moves me every day."

Now his friends began to miss him for two or three days at a time. Jim Devine knew that sometimes the city would close in on him. When it did, he might get on a commuters' train and get off at some station in Connecticut that had woods nearby, to walk there in the autumn weather. Then one of the absences lengthened into several days. Finally, Hal Smith and Louise Bonino found him at the Hotel Algonquin. He seemed agitated, emotionally upset, and he did not want to be left alone. It was midnight when he decided that he had to replenish his whiskey supply. Smith got hold of Ben Wasson, and Ben wired Estelle to come to New York if she could, and as soon as possible. From Ben's perspective, it was a very different story. He would recall that Faulkner told him he thought a trip would be good for Estelle to get her mind off Alabama's death and her own poor health.

On November 30 she took the train from Memphis. Faulkner, Harold Guinzburg, and Wasson met her at Pennsylvania Station. "She seemed exhausted," Wasson would remember, "and her eyes were enormous in her thin face, but she was making every effort to be animated and was even a bit kittenish." To him it seemed that husband and wife were assessing each other with covert glances in the taxi on the way to the hotel.[24] Estelle would later say that, weary with fatigue and the drain of her persistent anemia, she felt like going straight to bed. Instead, she had to deal with invitations and ward off some of them, for her husband seemed on the verge of a complete collapse. He told her that he had had just about as much of this pressure as he could take. It was fortunate that he was staying at the Algonquin. It seemed that there were always celebrities there, but at the same time the atmosphere was comfortable. Host Frank Case catered to genius, and he even had a piano moved into their suite so Estelle could play. Dorothy Parker was living there, and Estelle went shopping with her. Faulkner recovered enough for them to go to dinner with the Guinzburgs and the Smiths, and they saw a good deal of Frank Sullivan and Robert Benchley, whom she liked. That was not the case with Claire Spencer, Hal Smith's wife. At one of the parties at the Algonquin, with Faulkner sitting on the floor, a glass of bourbon beside him, Claire and Estelle got into an argument that Evelyn Harter remembered as being very unpleasant.

The truth was that now Estelle was succumbing to the strain—the fatigue, the excitement, the drinking. Bennett Cerf remembered one party at his apartment on Central Park South when Estelle stood at a window gazing out over the glittering Manhattan skyline. He saw her shiver. "When I see all this beauty," she said, "I feel just like throwing myself out the window." Cerf quickly steered her away from the window. "Oh, now, Estelle, you don't mean that," he said. She stared at him, her large blue eyes wide. "What do you mean? *Of course I do*," she told him passionately."[25] Dorothy Parker took her shopping, but then, back at the Algonquin, to Dorothy's astonishment, Estelle became hysterical, tore her dress, and tried to jump out the window. To Marc Connelly she seemed "a very nervous girl who occasionally had some kind of slips of mental processes, of thinking, and so on." He would remember one particular night. "I don't know what she did, but it was something with which Bill was obviously familiar. And quite objectively, without a bit of reproachment in it, he looked at his wife and reached out and slapped her face very hard. . . . She went right back to completely normal conduct, and Bill, without any apologies or anything else, continued whatever he had been talking about."[26] What was the cause of this hysteria, if that was what it was, of the threat to throw herself out the window? Less than two months before, she had lost Alabama, after a precarious pregnancy. Her physical and emotional reserves must by now have been virtually depleted, but as she would view this New York trip later, she had to fend for both her husband and herself.

They continued to be entertained—by the Lovetts and the Dashiells, the Guinzburgs and the Connellys. Ben Wasson gave a party for them, and the Faulkners gave a party for some of the people who had entertained them. On December 10, the publication date of Random House's limited signed edition of "Idyll in the Desert," Bennett Cerf gave a farewell party for them. When Estelle grew bored with all the book talk and went in the next room to read, Cerf put a record on the phonograph and asked her to dance. They danced for a long time. Cerf was amusing and charming, so much so that when Estelle returned home, she would place a picture of him on the mantelpiece in her room, along with one of her husband. (Malcolm thought she did it to irritate Faulkner.)[27]

Faulkner must have boarded the train for home with some relief; Estelle, perhaps with some regret. They did not go straight back, but stopped in Baltimore at the invitation of Mencken, who joined them for dinner at their hotel. Estelle retired early and the two men went out for an evening of hard drinking. By December 14 the Faulkners were probably back in Oxford. He had been away almost eight weeks.

Four days later Leland Hayward, superagent and Ben Wasson's boss at the American Play Company, received a telegram from Culver City, California: DID YOU MENTION WILLIAM FAULKNER TO ME ON YOUR LAST TRIP HERE. IF SO IS HE AVAILABLE AND HOW MUCH. It was signed by Sam Marx, of Metro-Goldwyn-Mayer Studios.

32

We crossed the street toward home. And do you know what I
thought? I thought *It hasn't even changed.* Because it should
have. It should have been altered, even if only a little. I dont
mean it should have changed of itself, but that I, bringing back
to it what . . . must have changed in me, should have altered it.

—*The Reivers* (299)

"HOME again now, where it is quiet," he wrote Alfred Dashiell. "The
novel is going fine." What he wanted to know was, did Dashiell have a
story of his called "Smoke"?[1] Yes, he did, but they were regretfully returning it. It would be a month before Ben sold it to *Harper's*.

Home was certainly immeasurably quieter than New York, but the
journalistic attention and intrusions followed him. Louis Cochran, who
had once asked him to draw for *Ole Miss*, now asked for an interview.
Cochran drove up from Jackson on December 20, 1931, and found him
doing some carpentry. Cochran gathered more about Faulkner's recent
past than about his work: he was tired of literary people and parties,
"where everybody talks about what they are going to write, and no one
writes anything."[2] He told Cochran he might talk to Phil Stone if he
liked. Cochran did, and later sent a draft of his article to Stone. The
reply told more about Stone than it did about Faulkner. He had trained
Faulkner for years, he said. Now he saw lapses of literary taste and feared
that Faulkner would not return to his true strength, his roots in the soil
that Stone had referred to in his preface to *The Marble Faun*. As he put
it, "my present discouragement is due to the fact that Bill has not yet
come out of his adolescent groove."[3] Cochran did not use that comment,
and the description he gave of Faulkner could not have been more flat-
tering. His eyes were "luminous" in a "countenance that is at once remotely aloof and sensitive to every living thing."[4] *The Virginia Quarterly
Review* rejected the piece as unscholarly, but nine months later it would

find acceptance and a larger readership in the Memphis *Commercial Appeal*. Meanwhile, a national audience was able to read about Faulkner in the December number of *The Bookman*, in an expanded version of Marshall Smith's earlier piece, with eight photographs.

At home he was enjoying the pleasures of solitude. Thanking Bennett Cerf on December 27 for gift books, he wrote, "Xmas was quiet here. Estelle and the children are with her mother in town, and so I am alone in the house. I passed Christmas with a 3 foot back log on the fire, and a bowl of eggnog and a pipe and Tom Jones. That was a special dispensation, as I have been on the wagon since reaching home, and I shall stay on the wagon until the novel is written. It is going great guns."[5]

Before January was out another interviewer arrived, Henry Nash Smith, of the Southern Methodist University English Department. Nearly two years before, *The Southwest Review* had taken "Miss Zilphia Gant" but apparently had asked Faulkner's permission to print an expurgated version. After he refused, Stanley Marcus took it for a limited edition of the Book Club of Texas with an introduction to be written by Smith. Now in Jackson on an assignment for the Dallas *Morning News*, Smith used the introduction as a pretext and sought out Faulkner in Oxford. Faulkner talked more freely about his writing than he had done with Cochran. He was working not at one novel but two. Though he did not specify, it could have been one that would draw on his "roots"—the Snopes saga, which had been developing in a series of short stories. He refused, however, to be drawn into a discussion of his wartime experiences. He left Smith with one impression very like those of Cochran and Stone: he was "a quiet, courteous man, unobtrusive and not very much impressed with himself, a little amused at the sudden enthusiasm of Eastern cities for books a good deal like his earlier ones, which they did not even bother to read or dismissed without comment."[6] There was one unlooked-for sequel to the interview and the introduction. Smith was forced to resign from the university for associating with "so obscene a writer."[7]

Another visitor had arrived in the rainy days of early January. Anthony Buttitta had come to collect on the promises made in Chapel Hill. Very scrupulously Faulkner played the host as well as the author. One afternoon during Buttitta's brief stay, Faulkner took him out for a walk and pointed out, Buttitta recalled, places along the varied itineraries of Popeye, Lena Grove, and Addie Bundren. Before he left, Faulkner told him to take what he wanted from among a number of rejected manuscripts. He chose one story and ten poems, enough to fill three of *Contempo*'s four tabloid-size pages.

Even before Buttitta left Oxford, however, there were repercussions when Hal Smith learned about both *Contempo* and another forthcoming Faulkner item to be called *Salmagundi*. Moreover, Milton Abernethy talked of a limited edition of Faulkner's verse. *Salmagundi* was the collection Faulkner had agreed to when he told Paul Romaine that he could go ahead with the special edition under the imprint of his Milwaukee bookstore. It was to contain six poems and two essays, all but one of the poems first published in *The Double Dealer*, plus one four-line poem by Ernest Hemingway. Smith came down on Faulkner rather sharply. "This limited edition business is a most interesting racket but it should be handled with great care," he wrote him.[8] Faulkner's reply was a mixture of penitence and annoyance. "I'm sorry. I didn't realize at the time what I had got into. Goddamn the paper [*Contempo*] and goddamn me for getting mixed up with it and goddamn you for sending me off with . . . [Abernathy] in the shape I was in."[9] He tried to explain to Wasson how he had gotten himself into this predicament. "You know that state I seem to get into when people come to see me and I begin to visualize a kind of jail corridor of literary talk. I dont know what in hell it is, except I seem to lose all perspective and do things, like a coon in a tree. As long as they dont bother the hand full of leaves in front of his face, they can cut the whole tree down and haul it off."[10] That was why he had given Buttitta whatever he wanted. He wondered what he could do about it now, if anything. He swore he would never promise anything again without first asking Ben's permission. Smith wrote the Casanova Book Shop about *Salmagundi* and Faulkner wrote Buttitta about *Contempo*. But none of the annoyance, anxiety, or correspondence had any effect on either publication. *Contempo* came out on February 1, 1932, and *Salmagundi* three months later. After all the furor, Smith tried to reassure his troubled and troublesome author. "Some people like the verse in Contempo enormously," he wrote, "so it did not turn out so badly."[11]

Faulkner had written Dashiell that the novel was "going fine." But that was before the difficulties had distracted him. He had told Wasson he had wasted "ten novel chapters of energy and worry over that goldamn paper."[12] Now Smith and Wasson were both asking for the novel. He had to tell Ben he couldn't send it because it wasn't finished and none of it was typed. "It is going too well to break the thread and cast back, unless absolutely necessary. But I may strike a stale spell. Then I will type some."[13] He was declining a generous offer that Ben seemed to have obtained from Hollywood in order to stay in Oxford and finish the book. A $250 advance from Smith would tide him over briefly. He disliked asking for it, he told his publisher, but "it's either this, or put the novel aside and go whoring again with short stories. When it's convenient, send me another slug. I have been caught by taxes and insurance and flood and impecunious relatives all at once."[14]

There were other concerns and complications to preoccupy him. When the contract for *Light in August* arrived he checked carefully to be sure that the clause calling for submission of his next two books was stricken out. He had not read the contracts for his two previous books and mistakenly thought that each was for a single book. Smith had already agreed

to a book of verse, tentatively entitled *The Greening Bough*. Smith told
him he needed a manuscript from him to submit to Cape, apparently to
satisfy whatever agreement had been made when Faulkner left that firm
to go with Smith alone. So now, Faulkner realized, though the contract
for *Light in August* did not call for submission of his next two books,
the contract for the book of verse *did* call for such submission. He wrote
Ben that if this clause would bind him, he was going to write Hal to
have it stricken. As for the novel, he hoped to serialize it before publication. Should he tell Hal now? There was something else he was not
going to tell him. Hard-pressed, he was remembering those offers in
New York, especially Harold Guinzburg's. "About Harold," he wrote
Ben. "I wont go behind Hal's back. When I get ready to swap horses, I
will tell him. So suppose you dont say anything about it to him until
I get this other straight and give you the word."[15]

As Faulkner worked his way further into the novel, Joe Christmas had
taken an increasingly powerful hold upon his imagination. Lena Grove
was still an important figure, but now, linked to the Christmas plot
through her relationship with Lucas Burch–Joe Brown, her betrayer and
Christmas' cohort, she served more and more as counterpoint for the
obsessed and doomed Christmas. As she had brought with her more than
a hint of *As I Lay Dying*, so Christmas had brought with him more than
a suggestion of *Sanctuary*. There was not only the brothel but also sexual
psychopathology. For Lena the process is simple: love, children, marriage.
Christmas' sexual attitudes are strongly conditioned by his fear and hatred
of dominant women and his revulsion at female physiology.

Faulkner was concerned with several subjects: the individual's integration into communal life, black-white relationships, the effects of uncertainty and deprivation, and the impact of harsh Calvinistic religiosity
upon the psyche. But he was also concerned with what lay at the heart
of *Sanctuary*: the problem of evil, and some women's affinity for it.
Hightower's wife, denied his love and shut out of his life by his obsession,
had turned away from him, only to die under scandalous circumstances
in Memphis. (Some Oxonians said that the first wife of one local minister
had been like her.) Faulkner interpreted the actions of the dietitian who
persecutes the child Christmas in the Memphis orphanage partly in terms
of "her natural female infallibility for the spontaneous comprehension
of evil." (117) And many years later Christmas' deranged grandmother
would say, "I would think how the devil had conquered God." (356)
There were many links of tone and phrase with *Sanctuary*. Near the end,
like Lee Goodwin, Christmas will die violently in Jefferson after acqui-
escing to a trial with a foregone verdict of Guilty.

As with *As I Lay Dying*, Faulkner made effective use of tense, the
present for Lena and the past for Christmas, perhaps, as one critic would
write, because he "is locked in his past," shifting to the present for him

"at the very end, when acceptance of his fate . . . seems to bring him closer to Lena's world."[16] At one point, Faulkner printed "FIRST PERSON" and drew a long arrow to a passage he would revise in typing.

It appears from the manuscript that he was moving rapidly, and that by early February or thereabouts he must have been writing Christmas' death scene. If he had drawn on Nelse Patton's crime for Joanna Burden's death, there was another, ten years after it, which could have suggested Christmas' end. In September 1919, Leonard Burt had slashed his wife to death. On his way from the jail to the courthouse he made a break for it, and the chase was ended by the police officer's gunfire. No matter how much some of Faulkner's townsmen might want romance rather than realism, they could not accuse him of sheer invention for sensationalism. Faulkner had developed his character carefully, but he had also employed ambiguity. As a man, Christmas most often acts on the premise that he has Negro blood. As a child at the orphanage, he has been told by a Negro workman, "You'll live and you'll die and you wont never know." (363) Faulkner would later say, "that to me was the tragic, central idea of the story—that he didn't know what he was, and there was no way possible in life for him to find out."[17]

Faulkner took particular care with some details. The child had been found on the orphanage doorstep on Christmas, and the thirty-third year of his life, in Jefferson, was emphasized. Like Benjy Compson, he was beaten and castrated. But whereas Faulkner strengthened Benjy Compson's Christian analogues in rewriting, he did the opposite with Joe Christmas. In the typing he changed the date so that his death occurred at age thirty-six. He was too violent a man to be a true Christ-figure, but Faulkner obviously did want to increase the perception of his role as a victim by the use of Christian elements. Faulkner's sympathy was clear, particularly in episodes where the helpless child is at the mercy of the sluttish dietitian, his mad grandfather, and his harsh adoptive father.

As a man, Christmas thinks he exercises free will. When Joanna Burden asks that he change his life, he thinks, "No. If I give in now, I will deny all the thirty years that I have lived to make me what I chose to be." (250–251) But his history makes it clear that he has been shaped largely by his environment—though the propensity for violence that contributed to his tragedy may well have been inherited. As the net closes, self-appointed vigilante Percy Grimm follows in implacable pursuit, "as if the Player who moved him for pawn likewise found him breath." (437) Three times more Faulkner mentioned "the Player" before the siren's crescendo signaled the end of the pursuit with his death and mutilation, as, in a kind of ascension, the blood "seemed to rush out of his pale body like the rush of sparks from a rising rocket; upon that black blast the man seemed to rise soaring into their memories forever and ever." (440)

Faulkner ended with Lena Grove in the fabliau-like episode in which Bryon Bunch tries unsuccessfully to climb into her bed in the back of the furniture dealer's Tennessee-bound truck. Byron Bunch has served to link Lena's story with that of Christmas, and he has been responsible for involving Hightower in both their lives: the old disgraced minister performing an emergency delivery of Lena's child and trying to offer protection to Christmas an instant before Grimm's fusillade. Though now Hightower has slipped into the old paralyzing reveries, he has for a time been drawn into life by Byron and Lena and her child, and he has blessed them. Isolation, the strength of the past, the effects of virulent Calvinism— these were the forces which provided parallels. Hostility and warmth, barrenness and fecundity—these provided linking contrasts. As one critic found, "it is difficult to say categorically which is the protagonist. Lena may have been the germ of the novel and remain its alpha and omega, and Christmas may be the most absorbing character . . . but Hightower, in spite of his flaws and shortcomings, is the moral center."[18] It is on the notes of warmth, comedy, and acceptance—provided by Lena Grove, doubtless soon to be Lena Bunch—that the novel ends. In the lower left-hand corner he wrote "Oxford, Miss./19 Feb. 1932."

Ben Wasson asked for some of the typescript to show to magazines, but Faulkner was making changes as he went and could not send anything. By mid-March he was nearing the end of the revision and typing, and on page 527 the typescript came to an end. After final checking he prepared to take it to Mac Reed at the drugstore for wrapping. Most of the strain of completing the work was now behind him, but it may have been this time that he would refer to, years later, when he described a scene with Estelle. She was so angry with him, he said, that she threw the manuscript of *Light in August* out of the car, and he had to go back to pick up the scattered pages from the roadside.

He sent it to Ben by express, with the instructions, "If you can get $5000.00 with no changes, take it. If not, and the movie offer is still open, that should tide me along. If you cant get $5000.00, I reckon I'll just turn it over to Hal. . . . I hope you will like it. I believe it will stand up. . . . As you say, I have enough momentum to coast a while now; particularly as the next novel will take about 2 years in the writing." He was enjoying the feeling of work done, and relaxing. "Spring here;" he wrote in closing, "beans and peas and dogwood and wistaria next week."[19]

But Ben could not find an editor who would pay $5,000 for serial rights, without touching a word. The news from Smith was just as bleak. The firm owed him $4,000 in royalties from *Sanctuary*, but by the end of March it was in receivership. Another letter from New York was more encouraging. Ben Wasson's boss, Leland Hayward, sent Faulkner an MGM screenwriting contract for six weeks at $500 a week, starting May 1. Faulkner was reluctant to leave because he was still hoping for the royalty check, but before long, Cape & Smith had gone from receivership to liquidation. Hayward sent a new contract which called for him to report for work in Culver City on May 7.

The bank informed him that he was overdrawn by $500, and his credit was evaporating. When he wrote a three-dollar check in McCall's sporting-goods store, Mrs. McCall said she'd rather have cash. Faulkner said, "That signature will be worth more than three dollars," but she was unmoved. Long after this aborted transaction, Mr. McCall would tell his help, "Don't let that Falkner boy charge anything in the store." Now he did not even have the money to wire acceptance of the studio's offer. When he asked his uncle John for a five-dollar loan, Judge Falkner offered to lend him the five hundred. Faulkner declined. Fortunately, the studio sent him an advance, along with a ticket for a lower berth on a train to Culver City. Murry Falkner's reaction was one of surprise. "He was confounded that mere scribbling could earn five hundred dollars a week," Faulkner would later recall. "When I showed him the check, he asked if it was legal."

He didn't really want to go. But the Cape & Smith royalties were blocked and there were no magazine sales in the offing. No one wanted the serial rights to *Light in August* and it would be eight months before there were any royalties from the novel to begin paying off the advances he had drawn on it. Where else could he earn $500 a week? It would be like selling a short story every week for six weeks. He kissed his family goodbye and started on his journey west.

The sun, strained by the vague high soft almost nebulous California haze, fell upon the terrace with a kind of treacherous
unbrightness. The terrace, the sundrenched terra cotta tiles,
butted into a rough and savage shear of canyonwall bare yet
without dust, on or against which a solid mat of flowers
bloomed in fierce lush myriad-colored paradox as though in
place of being rooted into and drawing from the soil they lived
upon the air alone and had been merely leaned intact against
the sustenanceless lavawall by someone who would later return
and take them away.

—"Golden Land," *CSWF* (706–707)

IN 1932, Metro-Goldwyn-Mayer was the undisputed leader among
motion-picture companies. On fifty-three acres in Culver City, "on the
dusty outskirts of Los Angeles, opposite three gasoline stations and a
drug store," the studio produced forty feature films a year that grossed
more than $100 million annually and played before an estimated total
world audience of a billion persons.[1]

The shortened workday of Saturday, May 7, had nearly passed before
William Faulkner arrived. When he did arrive, things seemed to go
wrong from the very start. The first thing Sam Marx noticed was that
his head was cut and bleeding. He had been hit by a cab while he was
changing trains, he said—in New Orleans. To Marx it was obvious that
he had been drinking. Marx wanted to call a doctor, but Faulkner said
he didn't need one and that he wanted to get right to work.

"We're going to put you on a Wallace Beery picture," Marx told him.

"Who's he?" asked Faulkner.[2] "I've got an idea for Mickey Mouse."
Marx explained that Mickey Mouse films were made at the Walt Disney
Studios, and arranged for a screening of *The Champ*. Beery had starred
in it as a lovable prizefighter, and now he was to play a wrestler in *Flesh*.
Faulkner allowed himself to be led to the projection room by Marx's

office boy, who reappeared very shortly. Faulkner did not want to watch the film, and he kept talking. "Do you own a dog?" he asked the boy, who said no. Faulkner said, "Every boy should have a dog." He should be ashamed not to own a dog, and so should everybody else who didn't own a dog. The film was hardly under way when Faulkner said to the projectionist, "How do you stop this thing?" There was no use looking at it, he said, because he knew how it would turn out. Then he asked for the exit and left. Marx started an immediate search for him, but it proved fruitless.

He did not reappear until Monday, May 16. He had been wandering in Death Valley, he told Marx. How he had gotten there (150 miles due east), he did not say. "The truth is," he later said, "that I was scared. I was scared by the hullabaloo over my arrival, and . . . I got flustered."[3] Marx had his contract reinstated and asked him to work on original stories for the studio. He was given Office 27 in a rickety white structure called the Old Publicity Building. There he worked on a story that was not original in the sense Marx probably had in mind. Called *Manservant*, it was a reworking of "Love," which he had been unable to sell to magazines a dozen years before.

Faulkner began with the line "India, 1921. A remote British Army post." All of the characters were renamed but one: Das, the major's faithful servant. The plot was unchanged. He used newspaper dates to show the passage of time, and just before the jealous maid thrust a deadly phial into her stocking, he specified a close-up to show it labeled "Poison." He was trying to teach himself to write for the camera, and he carefully broke the 21-page treatment into sixty-one shots, describing the action in each of them, ending with the happily married major returning Das's ashes to his distant home. The treatment was ready for distribution by May 25, but it aroused no interest. One of the draft sheets bore on its other side an abandoned letter: "I am not settled good yet. I have not got used to this work. But I am as well as anyone can be in this bedlam."[4]

He had indeed been working. He had typed out a three-page synopsis called "Night Bird." It may have been the story he had written in New York for Tallulah Bankhead. The synopsis traced the shocking career of a professor's daughter, from college beaux to a husband to a sinister lover, through murder and miscarriage to her final status as a kept woman, a "night bird." In a thirteen-page treatment, retitled *The College Widow*, the girl's ambivalence in seeking thrills and fleeing danger suggested Temple Drake. Like *Manservant*, this treatment was not approved for the addition of full-scale dialogue. On June 1, just six days after the script department's mimeograph had turned out *The College Widow*, it produced copies of another Faulkner original entitled *Absolution*. This nine-page treatment gave evidence not only of hasty composition but of indebtedness to "All the Dead Pilots." The romantic triangle begun in early adolescence ended in flames on the Western Front, the love of the two men for each other destroyed—along with the life of one of them—by an unworthy woman. But this one was also worthless to MGM.

Marx finally decided to pair Faulkner with an experienced screen-writer, Ralph Graves. Faulkner wrote home that the script was for Wallace Beery and Robert Montgomery, and that he was to be "a sort of doctor, to repair the flaws in it."[5] *Flying the Mail* was an original story written by Graves and Bernard Fineman with an eye to another Beery success, *Min and Bill*, which had co-starred Marie Dressler as the other lovable marital battler. Mimeograph had this sixteen-page continuity treatment ready by June 3. This was another characteristic which set Faulkner apart from most studio writers: sheer productivity. In spite of it, Marx sent out a memo saying his contract was not going to be extended.

Faulkner had derived more pleasure from a few personal relationships, it seems, than from all of his professional activities. He had encountered Laurence Stallings, whom he had met in New York. A crapshooting Marine like Jack Falkner, Stallings had made captain by the time shrapnel wounds in Belleau Wood cost him a leg. Co-author of the play *What Price Glory?* and screenwriter of *The Big Parade*, he had credentials Faulkner admired. He admired them enough to let Stallings interview him and to tell him what he thought of Southern California. The only thing archaeologists would find, he said, were the iron spikes people from Iowa drove into the ground for pitching horseshoes. Stallings described him (doubtless tongue-in-cheek) as a model of decorum: "Unlike prac-tically everyone else, he has remained cold sober. He bought one book to read over his lonely nights. It was a second-hand twelve-volume . . . Cambridge edition of the Holy Bible."[6] Faulkner admired Stallings enough to start telling his war stories again.

Sam Marx began to have second thoughts and offered Faulkner a year's contract at the reduced figure of $250 a week. Faulkner refused it. His hand may have been strengthened by a transaction in New York. On June 16, Paramount Publix Corporation paid the American Play Company $750 for a four-month option on *Sanctuary* against a purchase price of nearly $7,000 more. Then Faulkner heard from the director Howard Hawks.

A year older than Faulkner, Hawks had gone to Phillips Exeter and Cornell, driven racing cars and flown Army planes before entering the film industry to produce action movies such as *Dawn Patrol*. An avid reader who shared Faulkner's taste for Conrad, he had known Faulkner's work from the time of *Soldiers' Pay*. He had liked "Turn About," bought the rights through his brother, William Hawks, and now he wanted the author to do the screenplay. When they met in Hawks's office they were a study in contrasts; Hawks was a slim, blond six-footer with a ruddy complexion that emphasized his pale-blue eyes. Faulkner said, "I've seen your name on a check." Then he sat silently while Hawks explained at length what he wanted him to do. By the time he finished, Faulkner's silence had begun to annoy him. In spite of this, he offered a drink and Faulkner accepted. When they finished, Faulkner rose to go.

"See you in five days," he said.

"It shouldn't take you that long to think about it," Hawks said.

"I mean to write it," answered Faulkner.

With enthusiasm he plunged into the treatment, and five days later Hawks took it to Irving Thalberg, his brother-in-law and the company's brilliant young vice-president in charge of production. Thalberg read it quickly. "Shoot it as it is," he told Hawks. "I feel as if I'd make tracks all over it if I touched it."

Sam Marx repeated his offer of $250 a week. Confident in Hawks and in his own ability to do a script from his story, Faulkner accepted. Within a week, however, there were complications. According to a film historian, "MGM made three or four [Joan] Crawford pictures a year at that time, and when she or a comparable star was ready for an assignment and no tailor-made scripts were in the works, it was customary to make a place for her in an ongoing production."[7] Thalberg decided that Joan Crawford had to be in "Turn About." After Hawks told Faulkner, he remained silent for a moment. Then he said thoughtfully, "I don't seem to remember a girl in the story." Without going into contract technicalities, Hawks simply said, "That's the picture business, Bill. We get the biggest stars we can, and Joan's a nice girl, too."

When Joan Crawford read the first draft, she asked Faulkner to write the same kind of clipped British dialogue for her that he had devised for his two midshipmen, Ronnie Smith and Claude Hope. He did, creating the role of Ann, Ronnie's sister, and laying the groundwork for a triangular relationship that would later be enlarged to include an American, Captain Bogard. As with *Absolution*, he began with childhood background material. But this time he had Hawks's experienced guidance, and the results were markedly different. His deepest feelings as an artist were still not engaged, however, even though materials that clearly derived from his fiction were involved, as with a childhood squabble which suggested the Compson children playing in the branch.

AGAIN the unexpected intervened. Murry Falkner had been going downhill for some time. The doctor had told him that he would have to stop drinking or it would kill him. All his life Murry had eaten fried foods, and now the doctor forbade them too. One day Dorothy Oldham saw him sitting on his porch, holding a head of lettuce as though it were an apple. "He thinks if he eats a bushel of lettuce," Bill had said, "it will help make up for all that fried fatback he's eaten over the years. It won't."

But the son saw deeper into his father's illness. Murry had adjusted to the loss of the railroad. He had finally given up the dream of being a cowboy. He had worked over the years at one business after another for which he was temperamentally unfit. And now he could no longer live vicariously through his sons' athletic feats. His wife had her painting —in an "American primitive" style—her bridge games and her reading. He had no such sustenance. And he apparently received little or none from her. Increasingly, she had become the dominant partner in their relationship. Murry had contracted for their new home at 510 South Lamar, but it was Maud who had planned it. If her husband had grown more passive with age, she had done the reverse. She had designed the house so that the gallery would be cool by four o'clock on summer afternoons, when they would rock there together in seeming congeniality. However much there was on those afternoons, there was less when the weather turned. Members of her family would laughingly say that she was not frugal, she was *cheap*. They would see her angry with her husband because he was always building fires in the fireplace to take the chill off. She had various ways of letting him know her feelings. Sometimes she would hide his phonograph records. Other times she would put them under the cushion of his favorite chair, where he would sit on them. He was often in discomfort if not actual pain, and he was not even supposed to touch the whiskey that might relieve some of it. The family would see him walking up and down his front gallery constantly, "almost like a demented person." But then, "he just gave up," said his son. "He got tired of living."

The summer heat was hard on him, and the heart condition he now had made it even harder. In the early morning of August 7 he suffered a sudden attack, and he was gone, ten days short of his sixty-second birthday. He was buried in St. Peter's Cemetery, beside his father. In the obituary notice his name was spelled "Faulkner." William Faulkner came home from Hollywood, fortunately still able to work on "Turn About" in Oxford and draw his MGM salary. "Things are going pretty well here," he wrote Hal Smith. "My father died last month, and what with getting his affairs straightened out and getting Hollywood out of my system by means of a judicious course of alcohol in mild though sufficient quantities before and after eating and lying down and getting up, I am not working now. But I seem to have a novel working in me; when the cool weather comes, I will probably start it. . . ."[8] Jack Falkner remembered that when their father died, "Bill considered himself as head of our clan, and so did we. It was a natural role for him, and he assumed it at once, without fanfare, but with dignity and purpose."[9] Jack and the others didn't know how he felt inside. "I hope to hell Paramount takes *Sanctuary*," he wrote Ben Wasson. "Dad left mother solvent for only about 1 year. Then it is me."[10]

He intended to try some short stories for additional income, but first he had to read the galleys of *Light in August*. The job proved more time-consuming and exasperating than he could have expected. Queries on the galleys failed to show the slightest understanding of the complexities of his style. At the beginning of Chapter 6—"Memory believes before knowing remembers,"—Hal Smith or some anonymous proofreader had written "Construction?" Obliterating the query, Faulkner wrote "O.K. damn it." Galleys later, when the reader boggled at a question used declaratively, Faulkner again furiously crossed out the query and wrote "O.K. as set, goddam it." Four galleys later, the conscientious proofreader questioned the verb in Calvin Burden's threat to his children "I'll frail the tar out of you." Like a berserk penman, Faulkner drew a line through the proffered alternative "flail" and scribbled "O.K. as set and written. Jesus Christ." On the whole, however, it was a good job. "I was too busy and too mad all the time I was in California to write you," he told Ben Wasson. "But now I am home again, eating watermelon on the back porch and watching it rain. I have just finished reading the galley of LIGHT IN AUGUST. I dont see anything wrong with it. I want it to stand as it is."[11]

At home he completed the second draft of "Turn About": 108 pages with dialogue and a good part for Joan Crawford. Further additions by Faulkner and Hawks brought this version, probably typed in Hawks's office, to 122 pages filed at MGM on August 24.[12] Now he had to start thinking about his return to Culver City to make the final changes Hawks would want. They had planned that Estelle would return with him, but now she knew that she was pregnant, and they could not risk her traveling. So he decided to take his mother and Dean with him instead, and at the end of September they drove west. On Monday, October 3, he reported for work again at the studio. At home, forwarding material for him, Estelle wrote a cautiously flirtatious letter to Hal Smith and brought him up to date: "he motored out, taking his mother and youngest brother to show them the world—or perhaps put them in the movies—who knows. . . ."[13]

THOUGH gone, Faulkner had been far from forgotten, particularly by the studio manager, a gaunt, worried man named M. E. Greenwood, a one-time faro dealer who always suspected that writers were trying to put something over on him. He had called Faulkner's absence to Irving Thalberg's attention twice, and it took written assurance from Marx to convince Thalberg that Hawks had approved Faulkner's being paid for writing at home. Faulkner went ahead with several new scenes, and completed them on October 22, 1932. Two more writers would work on the script, and in the screen credits, under the film's final title, *Today We Live*, "Story and Dialogue" would be attributed to William Faulkner.

Maud Falkner was more than ready to return home, though Dean had found a good deal to interest him, and Faulkner had enjoyed seeing Stallings again and hunting with Hawks. One of the director's friends, Clark Gable, had a .410 over-and-under shotgun that Faulkner admired so much he wanted one like it. The first time they had driven into the Imperial Valley for some dove-hunting, Hawks began to talk about books. He would remember the conversation clearly. Faulkner entered into it, but Gable remained silent. Finally he ventured a question.

"Mr. Faulkner," he said, "what do you think somebody should read if he wants to read the best modern books? Who would you say are the best living writers?"

After a moment, Faulkner answered. "Ernest Hemingway, Willa Cather, Thomas Mann, John Dos Passos, and myself."

Gable took a moment to absorb that information. "Oh," he said. "Do you write?"

"Yes, Mr. Gable," Faulkner replied. "What do you do?"[14]

As Faulkner prepared to return to Mississippi, Hawks suggested that he stay a bit longer and pick up some more money at scriptwriting. By now Paramount had taken up the option on *Sanctuary*, which would bring Faulkner more than $6,000, and he was as anxious to return home as his mother was. Bill Hawks, acting as Faulkner's agent, as he had in the sale of the rights to "Turn About," also urged him to stay, and Faulkner said he would let them know if he changed his mind. With his mother and brother, he set out for home, where his copies of *Light in August* and the reviews were waiting for him.

This was upland country, lying in tilted slopes against the
unbroken blue of the hills, but soon the road descended sheerly
into a valley of good broad fields richly somnolent in the level-
ing afternoon. . . .

Bayard stood for a while before his house. The white simplicity
of it dreamed unbroken among the ancient sunshot trees.

—*Sartoris* (6)

"I RECEIVED a copy of the printed book," he said, "and I found that I
didn't even want to see what kind of jacket Smith had put on it. I seemed
to have a vision of it and the other ones subsequent to The Sound and
the Fury ranked in order upon a shelf while I looked at the titled backs
of them with a flagging attention which was almost distaste . . . until at
last Attention itself seemed to say, Thank God I shall never need to open
any one of them again."[1] At his publishers', however, the notices were
read with keen interest by both Hal Smith and his partner in the new firm
of Harrison Smith and Robert Haas.

Faulkner might not be to the taste of many newspaper reviewers, but
the new book was widely reviewed at considerable length as the work
of a major writer. On October 8, 1932, the day before publication, Henry
Seidel Canby wrote in the *Saturday Review* that despite obscurity,
turgidity, and sloppiness, "it is a novel of extraordinary force and insight,
incredibly right in character studies, intensely vivid, rising sometimes to
poetry. . . ." Reviewers for the *Times* and the *Tribune* were even more
laudatory. Dissents would be registered by others such as Dorothy Van
Doren, who complained that Faulkner was still writing about people
whose actions take place "almost entirely in the viscera."[2] But the preponderantly favorable response was reflected in a summary on October
20 in the Oxford *Eagle*, which called *Light in August* Faulkner's greatest

work and noted that he was now "enjoying international fame for his early publications."

It may have been at this time, unwinding from his stay in Hollywood, that he worked on two short pieces. On a sheet of notebook paper he neatly lettered a title page:

The Golden Book
of Jefferson & Yoknapatawpha County
in Mississippi
as compiled by
William Faulkner of Rowanoak[3]

Having thus suggested something of the medieval scholar, genealogist, and gentleman, Faulkner went on to write a 700-word biography of Colonel John Sartoris. Adding new lore, Faulkner may have been writing, for his own pleasure, material which could also serve as a source for further fictions. The protagonist of the other work, called "With Caution and Dispatch," was John Sartoris, the great-grandson and ill-fated aviator. There were resemblances to both "All the Dead Pilots" and "Turn About." Once again, harebrained John Sartoris was pitted against a commanding officer for the same girl. The story broke off after Sartoris crash-landed his Camel on the deck of a Brazilian merchantman in the English Channel.

In early November, Alfred Dashiell bought "There Was a Queen" for *Scribner's* for $300, but this was not enough to keep Faulkner from haunting the post office in expectation of the check for the film rights to *Sanctuary*. Much of the Hollywood money had gone into Rowan Oak —new floors were one item—and suddenly he was back in his old familiar financial predicament. Howard Hawks had told Faulkner to let him know when he needed money. "I got in a jam," Faulkner later said, "and did." As a result of Leland Hayward's dealings with Sam Marx, Faulkner had been represented in Hollywood by the Selznick-Joyce agency. Now, when MGM offered to put him back on the payroll, they would continue to take their agent's fee, but so would William Hawks, who had acted for Faulkner when Howard Hawks put things in motion. It was the first instance of such double financial jeopardy to which Faulkner would lay himself open in his motion-picture dealings, but for the present he could resign himself to it, for his new salary was $600 a week.

Beginning on November 28, his time was charged to a property called "War Story." This designation actually covered several sources for the potential film. John McGavock Grider was a young Arkansan, a frequent visitor to Memphis, who had not waited for the United States to enter the Great War. He had joined the Royal Flying Corps, trained in England, and died in combat over France in June 1918. He had kept a diary of his experiences and those of some of his comrades among the 150 young Americans in the RFC who came to be called the Oxford Group. After his death, it came into the possession of one of his friends, Major Elliot White Springs, who enlarged and enlivened Grider's account with descriptions of parties and love affairs. In 1926 it was serialized in *Liberty* magazine as *War Birds*, the diary of an anonymous American aviator. That same year it was published in book form, with Springs as author, by the George H. Doran Co. To complete the sweep, Springs sold the film rights to MGM and collaborated with another writer on a treatment. It was not successful, but then Faulkner did an outline which Hawks liked. Such a job would have taken him very little time, and this may actually have preceded his being put back on the MGM payroll.[4] To the relatively straightforward story of three cadets and, finally, the death of one of them, Springs had added a British flier and a German who would shoot him down. Onto this, Faulkner would graft parts of "Ad Astra" and "All the Dead Pilots." It was probably late December when he finished typing the 100-page script and mailed it in. Hawks had once taken Faulkner to see a film at MGM that he hadn't enjoyed. "I don't like ghost stories," he had said. When the new script arrived, Hawks found that Faulkner had entitled it *A Ghost Story*. Now he told Hawks, "This is my idea of a ghost story."

The ghost was John Sartoris, and the script told how it was placated, as his son, Johnny, comes to accept Lothar Dorn, the German pilot who had killed him, and the ménage in which Johnny lives, which includes not only Dorn but also Antoinette Gaussart, the young woman John Sartoris had pursued in France, Johnny's mother, Caroline, and his uncle, Bayard Sartoris. At the end, Bayard's horse soars over a jump as John Sartoris soars above in his wartime Camel, saluting them, "his face bright, peaceful."[5] If it took a more hopeful view of future Sartoris prospects than *Flags in the Dust*, it was a first draft in a medium Faulkner was far from mastering. There were serious problems with narration, dialogue, and characterization. The war exercised such a powerful effect on Faulkner's emotions and imagination that even in his best fiction he was often close to melodrama and cliché when he treated it. Here, where he did not have the full resources of his versatile literary technique to help him, he had produced a script much of which, to one critic, was "out of control."[6] It was probably Hawks who divided the script into separate shots and numbered all 323 of them, who copy-edited the script into standard MGM house style, retitled it *War Birds*, and sent it to Mimeograph, where it would be copied early in the new year.

When Faulkner returned to his desk in the early days of 1933, it was to continue with revisions of "War Story," as the studio was still calling it. By late February his time was being charged to "Honor," his own story, which had previously been assigned to writer Harry Behn. Apparently, however, Faulkner did little more than read and return it, continuing with *War Birds*. By March 6, however, he had to accept a fifty-percent pay cut. A week later Sam Marx wanted to know if Faulkner was to be kept on. Hawks immediately interceded with L. B. Mayer, and the checks kept coming. Hawks felt that they could make *War Birds* into a screenworthy script, and he expected that Faulkner would return to the Coast by April, when Hawks would be finished with another picture he was then directing. By the end of March, Faulkner was working on another property.

It grew out of an idea he had suggested to Sam Marx. It was still without a title, and for the record, it was called *Mythical Latin-American Kingdom Story*. One writer has suggested that the background probably owed something to "the political unrest in Cuba between 1929 and 1933, when the Machado regime was embattled with terrorist and student groups."[7] As usual, he was drawing strongly upon imagination, mentioning once again a place called Rincon, where he had set "Carcassonne" and "Black Music." There was a barnstorming American flier whose meanness suggested John Sartoris. Plot similarities suggested another source in the work of the novelist Faulkner and Hawks both admired: Joseph Conrad's *Nostromo: A Tale of the Seaboard*. Marx stopped charging his time to the story in late April, but four months later Faulkner would send him a complete 110-page draft. It had some of the same flaws as *A Ghost Story*, a very melodramatic script with dialogue that was alternately stilted and rhetorically heroic. When Marx decided that it had no possibilities for the studio, Faulkner asked for permission to turn it into a novel. He never did. Almost fifty years later, however, when Marx would return to MGM, he would decide that *Mythical Latin-American Kingdom* did have possibilities as a film script.[8]

IT was not surprising that there was so much flying in Faulkner's script-writing, for on February 2 he had begun taking formal instruction. When he approached Vernon Omlie, he told him what he had said to Baby Buntin several years earlier. "He told me not to say anything about it," Omlie recalled. "He said he wanted to get back his nerve and learn to fly all over again before anybody knew what he was doing."[9] It was impossible to keep the lessons secret, though, and so Faulkner told reporters that not only did he have to regain the nerve lost in two plane crashes, he also had to catch up with all the advances in flying technology. He could not have chosen a better instructor than Captain Vernon C. Omlie, a veteran of Army flying and extensive barnstorming. Quiet and kindly, a virile six-footer with keen eyes set in a weathered face that gave him a faint resemblance to Gary Cooper, he was married to a tiny woman whom he had met a dozen years earlier in Minnesota. Fascinated by an air show in her teens, Phoebe Fairgrave had bought an airplane with a small inheritance and then hired Vernon Omlie to teach her to fly it. Before long they were putting on air shows, with Phoebe as wing-walker swinging from one plane to another, then jumping, cutting away her parachute and falling free until she popped open a second one. They went on the road with the Phoebe Fairgrave–Glenn Messner Flying Circus. Business dwindled and Messner departed.[10] Then one day, broke and stranded in Memphis, they started a flying school and took on all sorts of charter jobs. Now they were celebrities, their Memphis apartment filled with mementos: the photos of fliers and their planes, the trophies they had won, the iron mouthpiece by which Phoebe—her hair cropped and her face scarred—had swung from their ship in their barnstorming days. The two were living embodiments of a whole way of life that fascinated Faulkner.

He was not the best pupil. Though they would fly every week but one over the next two months, some weeks as many as four times, Omlie saw that Faulkner had trouble getting back what he thought to be his old touch. "I had quite a time with Bill," he told another pilot. It took seventeen hours of dual instruction, substantially more than the average number, before Faulkner finally soloed in Omlie's Waco F biplane on April 20, nearly fourteen years after he had entered the RAF. He learned to recover from stalls and spins, but he did not enjoy aerobatics, and his preference would always be for straight and level flight. Over the years, his problems with landings would produce several mishaps involving damage to undercarriage and propeller, but he had finally fulfilled a boyhood dream, and he was gaining valuable material for fiction, even when he was just sitting and listening to the veterans engaged in "hangar flying."

His solo flight was one of three events which made that April an exceptional month. On April 20, Harrison Smith and Robert Haas published *A Green Bough*, which began with "The Lilacs" and included among its forty-eight poems the one about the lad who once lay "upon an adolescent hill" and dreamed of flying among "the fleeing canyons of the sky."[11] As early as January 1932, Faulkner had begun arranging the poems carefully, grouping them, he had written Smith, to "supply some demarcation between separate and distinct moods and methods. . . ."[12] He had drawn on the little books he had made for Estelle and Helen Baird and on the collection he had given Myrtle Ramey. He told Smith, "I chose the best ms and built a volume just like a novel."[13] The sequel to *The Marble Faun*, announced so confidently eight years before, had at last appeared, with six of the poems bought for separate publication by *The New Republic*, almost fourteen years after his debut there with "L'Apres-Midi d'un Faune." There was a wide variety in *A Green Bough*: ballad-style poems such as those he had written in his teens and experimental ones that suggested E. E. Cummings. There were more love poems than any other kind, from short lyrics and passionate sonnets to the long poem of love and hate in which the distraught lover, "laxly reclining" in the firelight, watched the beloved leave the room to mount the stair. In spite of his careful organization, it seemed an anthology rather than a coherent collection. The few reviews could not have changed his own assessment that the work was second-rate. "I've often thought that I wrote the novels because I found I couldn't write the poetry," he would say later, "that maybe I wanted to be a poet, maybe I think of myself as a poet, and I failed at that . . . so I did the next best thing."[14] He had asked Horace Liveright if he could print his poems, and now he was pleased when Hal Smith did. But with the exception of one brief effort, a dozen years later, he was through with verse. He would never publish another poem.

The other special event gave him the least pleasure of the three. On April 12, "Turn About," retitled *Today We Live*, had its national premiere in Oxford at the Lyric Theatre, owned by Sallie Murry's husband, Bob Williams. Faulkner even responded to Williams' address of welcome, briefly telling the capacity crowd about the differences between writing novels and screenplays. A Memphis reporter noted that "Faulkner brought his immediate family . . . together with his 'hired-help,' whom he wanted to show, he said, 'that he worked sometimes.'"[15] The Oxford *Eagle* reported that *Sanctuary*, retitled *The Story of Temple Drake*, might also have an Oxford premiere. George Raft, veteran portrayer of numerous hardened killers, had declined the part of Popeye on the grounds that it would mean "professional suicide." Phil "Moon" Mullen, son of the *Eagle*'s new owner, thought that Faulkner made sex disgusting, and wondered, "How can they make a moving picture out of . . . *Sanctuary*?" A few weeks later, however, he told his readers that the author was being praised in the London *Times* and that "Few Oxford people realize the distinction of having as a native son, William Faulkner."[16] Not many Oxonians read Faulkner's work. Mullen tried to keep up with it, and over the next two decades he would provide a barometer of Oxford's reactions to William Faulkner.

Meanwhile, things had been happening at the studio. In mid-April the salary cut had been restored, and in the last days of the month he had been assigned to do a script for *Louisiana Lou* from a play by Lea David Freeman called *Ruby*. It was the story of a rich would-be writer who alienated his father by marrying a dance-hall hostess and left with her for a shrimp camp in Louisiana's bayou country to research a book. The complicated tale became heavily freighted with intrigue before it ended with murder.[17] Apparently Marx felt that because Faulkner was a Southerner, his talents might be more profitably employed in Cajun country than in some mythical Latin-American kingdom. The director was Tod Browning, a thin man with a wax-tipped mustache and a brooding expression. His credits included the original *Dracula*, and he excelled at films such as *The Freaks*, starring Lon Chaney. Before Faulkner went off the picture he would actually do a 62-page script for Browning, only to be followed by nine other writers before it was completed and released as *Lazy River*.[18] By the time Faulkner was getting into his script, however, the studio had had enough of his working at home, and he was ordered to report to Browning in New Orleans.

The subsequent events passed into Hollywood lore, and though Faulkner denied some of the accounts, his recounting helped perpetuate them. With the baby's arrival close at hand, he wanted to leave home now less than ever, but he decided, he later said, to follow the studio's telegram to the letter and take the first plane to New Orleans. A train would have put him there in eight hours. "But I obeyed the studio and went to Memphis, where an airplane did occasionally go to New Orleans. Three days later one did." Once he got there, the continuity writer refused to let him see his story line until he showed the writer some dialogue. When he placed the problem before Browning, he was told not to worry and to get a good night's sleep. Every day thereafter, Faulkner said, they would make the long boat trip out to the false-front set above the waters of the bayou just in time to have lunch and then turn around for the trip that would return them to New Orleans before dark. The story's climax came in two telegrams. The first, Faulkner said, read, FAULKNER IS FIRED. MGM STUDIO. After Browning assured Faulkner that he would obtain his reinstatement and an apology, the second arrived: BROWNING IS FIRED. MGM STUDIO.[19] The truth was simpler and not nearly so entertaining. A little over a week after Faulkner had arrived in New Orleans, Marx had wired a query to Browning about the lack of progress with the script. Browning replied, PARTY REFERRED TO . . . BRILLIANT CAPABLE MAN BUT HAD UNFORTUNATE START.[20] Moreover, the dialogue was unsatisfactory and Faulkner did not want to go to Culver City. In a gentle telegram, Marx terminated Faulkner's contract as of mid-May, with a promise to put him back on salary any time he was ready to return to California. By May 9 he was back in Oxford.

COMPLETING additional material he had promised Browning, Faulkner began flying again with Omlie almost every week in a big, powerful Waco C cabin cruiser. By now he wanted a plane of his own, but there was another purchase that had to come first out of what remained from the $8,000 he had cleared this year at MGM. From Sallie Bailey Bryant he bought three lots adjoining Rowan Oak for $2,500 and an $800 note.

Gossip columnist Walter Winchell had reported in the New York *Daily Mirror* that the Faulkners were "anticipating a blessed expense," and that they planned to name him Bill. On Friday evening, June 23, the moon rose large and bright in the clear starry sky. It was so nice that they decided to go for a ride. He drove northeast, out to the College Hill Road and past the church where they were married. As he turned back toward home, Estelle said, "Billy, you'd better go right on to the hospital." About daybreak she gave birth to a girl weighing scarcely more than five pounds, but she did not need the incubator which her father had presented to Dr. Bramlett two years before.

When Faulkner came in to visit on Saturday morning he found Estelle disappointed over the baby's sex. He told her she mustn't feel that way. "There are too many Faulkner boys anyway," he said. They named their daughter Jill. When Dr. Bramlett gave permission for other visitors, Malcolm remembered that his stepfather appeared at school and asked that he be released early to go and see his new sister. Malcolm was surprised to see that he was wearing his RAF uniform, which he usually reserved for his walk around the square on Armistice Day.[21]

When Estelle and Jill came home, they were accompanied by a nurse, Miss Bee. She was joined by Narcissus McEwen, who was a few inches over five feet and a substantial number of pounds over two hundred. Jill was small, but she was a robust eater, and soon Miss Bee was able to leave, with good-natured Mammy McEwen serving as Jill's wet nurse. The child had been welcomed ceremoniously to Rowan Oak. John Phillips recalled that Faulkner took all the servants upstairs. He filled all the shot glasses on a tray and handed them around. "Now," he said, "we'll drink a toast to little Miss Jill."[22]

Anyone could see that he adored the child. In one of her earliest pictures he held her, coated and bonneted, as he sat on the brick steps of the front gallery. Fatherhood had come late to him. He was now nearly thirty-six, and to some who saw him with his daughter, then and later, familiar phrases about paternal love would come to mind. She was more than the apple of his eye; she was what he would call his fictional child Caddy Compson: "my heart's darling."

Three days after Jill's birth he had written to Ben Wasson. "Well, bud," he said, "we've got us a gal baby named Jill. Born Saturday and both well."[23] Then he turned to business. Seven months earlier, Bennett Cerf had asked him to write an introduction for a special limited edition of *The Sound and The Fury*. Now he was willing to do it for the $750 Cerf had offered. It was to be printed by the Grabhorn Press, which was famous for beautiful work, and Faulkner hoped they would use different-colored inks. Cerf agreed and wrote Edwin Grabhorn that they wanted three separate colors to distinguish between Benjy's childhood and adolescence and present time. "Faulkner himself is marking this section so that the printer will know exactly what color each paragraph must appear in. Personally, I think the three colors should be black, maroon, and either dark blue or dark green. . . ." Faulkner would supply the introduction in a couple of weeks and the color division even sooner.

It was mid-August, however, before Wasson received the introduction with a covering letter. "The enclosed explains itself. I have worked on it a good deal, like on a poem almost, and I think it is all right now. See what Bennett thinks and let me know."[24] It had gone through at least three stages. He abandoned one draft that began with a reference to Cerf's wish for the introduction. He wrote a thousand words, beginning "Art is no part of southern life." The Old South had been killed by the war and the "New South" was merely a land of immigrants trying to remake it along Northern lines. Southern writers, he said, needed "to talk, to tell, since oratory is our heritage. We seem to try in the simple furious breathing (or writing) span of the individual to draw a savage indictment of the contemporary scene or to escape from it into a make-believe region of swords and magnolias and mockingbirds which perhaps never existed anywhere. . . . That cold intellect which can write with calm and complete detachment and gusto of its contemporary scene is not among us; I do not believe there lives the Southern writer who can say without lying that writing is any fun to him. Perhaps we do not want it to be."[25]

Now he turned to his own career. "I seem to have tried both of the courses" he said of *The Sound and the Fury*. When he went on to finish that retrospective passage he dated it 19 August 1933. Then he reworked it, reducing it by half, excising the portion on art in the South and employing a broader, more flamboyant style. He had learned something about writing with *Soldiers' Pay*, but it was with this book that he had learned to use all that he had read: "in a series of delayed repercussions like summer thunder, I discovered the Flauberts and Dostoievskys and Conrads whose books I had read ten years ago."[26] He wrote that he had read nothing since and seemed to have learned nothing since. He no longer felt in writing the rapture which that book had brought him, but the memory of it still moved him. On August 24, Wasson sent the introduction to Cerf, and four days later Cerf received, marked for three-color printing, what Faulkner told him was his only copy of *The Sound and the Fury*.

He had found time for other projects besides the introduction. When he had told Ben Wasson about Jill's birth he had also written, "Working spasmodically at a novel." It was probably the one he had mentioned to Laurence Stallings in California about the Snopes family, and it may now have borne the Balzacian title *The Peasants*. In mid-July he received a check from Hal Smith along with a contract for the new book, but he wrote that he would not cash the check until he had Smith's response to his request that his royalty rate be increased. He also objected to giving the first option on his next novel. He did not mind giving Smith an option, but this one was to a company. "Vide the J. Cape affair, excusing which I would not be needing two thousand dollars now, not having got a cent of the four thousand odd which their royalty statement showed for April of last year. That's why I dont like option clauses; though if you insist, etc." This was the kind of negotiation which should have been handled by Ben Wasson, but Faulkner had the habit of interposing himself between his agent and editors and publishers and making deals which would later prove disadvantageous. He also told Smith, "I have turned out three short stories since I quit the movies, so I have not forgot how to write during my sojourn downriver."[27] He would often use metaphors of field-hands or slaves for his dealings with the film studios. Sometimes they would be more dramatic. He would later tell another writer, a young friend, "Always take the people seriously, but never take the work seriously. Hollywood is the only place on earth where you can get stabbed in the back while you're climbing a ladder."[28]

One of the three stories Faulkner mentioned to Smith was a reworking of *Manservant*. Another may have been "Lo!"—which picked up the father of Saucier Weddel, the protagonist of "A Mountain Victory." In "Lo!" Francis Weddel, a half-white Chickasaw chief, led a tribal journey to bring his nephew, who had murdered a cheating white man, before the Great White Father himself. It was a humorous story in which Faulkner was exploring another facet of the Indian dimension of his fictional world. None of the three stories sold. Not one had been published since January. He went back to his files, looking for others he could send out again.

He made a few changes in "Artist at Home," and *Story* took it for August publication. He reread "Beyond the Gate" and started it all over again. (One scholar would provide evidence that he incorporated elements from a very similar prize-winning story by Wilbur Daniel Steele.[29]) In the ending he made it clear that the Judge's whole experience—his visit to the Hereafter—was probably a moment's fantasy in his brain on the brink of death. *Harper's* bought it, but the editor wanted further clarification. Faulkner wrote Ben Wasson, stating what seemed to him the story's obvious implications: "the agnostic progresses far enough into heaven to find one whom his intelligence, if not his logic, could accept as Christ, and who even offers him an actual sight and meeting with his dead son in exchange for the surrender of his logic, agnosticism. But he naturally and humanly prefers the sorrow with which he has lived so long that it not only does not hurt anymore, but is perhaps even a pleasure, to the uncertainty of change, even when it means that he may gain his son again." Faulkner felt irritated and frustrated. "It is a tour de force in esoteria: it cant be anything else. I have mulled it over for two days now, without yet seeing just how I can operate on it and insert a gland." If the editor could "tell us just what he would like to have inserted, I'll invent some way to do it."[30] If Faulkner performed any surgery, it was minor, for the only discernible difference, when the story appeared as "Beyond" in September, was a lengthening of the last paragraph which made it clear that the Judge, back in his bed, was composing his limbs in his final repose.

WHEN the color-marked copy of *The Sound and the Fury* reached Bennett Cerf, he sent Wasson a $500 check against the agreed price for the signed edition. The project would eventually collapse, and the marked copy would disappear. In his letter to Cerf, Faulkner had written, "We are getting along fine. I hope to see you this fall."[31] He may have been counting on the money from the special edition to pay for the trip. He did not tell Cerf how he intended to accomplish the thousand-mile journey. He was planning to pilot his own plane. Flying now with regularity, he was making up for what he had missed, living in actuality some of the experiences he had known only in imagination.

35

The engines are long since throttled back; the overcast sinks slowly upward with no semblance whatever of speed until suddenly you see the aircraft's shadow scudding the cotton hillocks; and now speed has returned again, aircraft and shadow now rushing toward one another as toward one mutual headlong destruction.

—"Impressions of Japan," *ESPL* (76)

Two days after Jill's birth he was flying the big Waco again with Vernon. Eleven weeks later he was taking her and her mother and her nurse up for joyrides. When the Memphis *Press-Scimitar* reported it, Dr. Bramlett phoned Estelle and scolded her. But Jill showed no ill effects, and in early fall of 1933 they would drive up to Memphis once a week, take a suite at the Peabody and see their friends, and fly. Other days he would drive to Memphis and take Johncy's boys, ten-year-old Jimmy and five-year-old "Chooky," up with him in the big cabin craft with its clear numbers: NC13413. And later that fall he bought it, his own ship at last. He had entered into an arrangement with Omlie. Vernon could use the plane from time to time as he taught Dean to fly. Johncy and Jack were pilots now, and Faulkner had agreed to put up the money for Dean's flight instruction.

He was concerned about his brother. He was fond of Jack and Johncy, but he loved Dean. He had tried to be a father to him even before Murry Falkner had died. He had written him comic letters when he was away and made vocabulary lists and corrected his hunting stories for him when he was at home. A talented athlete—star outfielder, sub-par golfer, and crack shot—Dean was made for the out-of-doors and not the classroom. His teachers at the university knew he would never be there at the start of duck season or bird season or deer season. When he dropped out of school in the spring of 1928, Murry got him jobs and Dean lost them. "Dad got me a job with the contractor building our new house," he told Cousin Sue

Price, "but somehow I managed to drop a brick on one of the fellows' heads, so I got fired." Sue's father told her, "Buddy told Dean the other day he almost got him another job, but a fellow had just got it a few minutes before, and Dean said, 'Whew! What a narrow escape!' " And his father laughed. When Bill had vacated the tower room in the Delta Psi house, Dean had moved into it. Often he went about barefoot, in old clothes, and he imitated some of his brother's other eccentricities. He was fiercely loyal, defending Bill's work and asserting that he would write "the great American novel." Dean would take care of him when he was drunk, and when he went to the Writers' Conference in Charlottesville, Dean had stayed at Rowan Oak—keeping a poker game running in an upstairs bedroom. He tried school again, shifting from the demanding Engineering curriculum to Liberal Arts. The graduation exercises for 1931 listed him as a graduate, though not even his family was sure that he actually received a diploma. His father gave up on the idea of construction jobs and insisted that he take a commercial art course from *Modern Illustrating*. He was good at that, with a keen eye and a gifted hand.

When his father died, he became his mother's mainstay. He had a steady girlfriend, pretty Jeanette Hargis, his faithful rooter in the pickup baseball games he loved. But the deepest part of his life was bound up with his mother. "He was a grown man," his daughter would write, "twenty-five years old, without employment, as dependent on his mother for his livelihood as she was on him for emotional security. He loved her and he was caught." Bill saw all of this. So did Mrs. Hargis, and a year later she broke up the relationship between Dean and Jeanette, even though Dean by then was running the Gulf Service Station, which she owned. "He was bored, sad, lonely, and tired for the first time in his life." Faulkner, as head of the clan, was determined to do something. He saw that now his brother's life "was without direction or purpose," and that each day his mother "grew more dependent on her youngest son."[1]

Faulkner took Dean flying with him whenever he could. Sue Price said they went to Mexico once. Bill got drunk, and Dean couldn't sober Bill up and he couldn't fly the plane. It may have been then, Sue thought, that Dean decided to learn to fly. He was encouraged by his brother, who in the last week of September came in for a landing at Batesville that flipped the plane over on its back, bending the propeller and breaking ribs in the top wing. "I am not superstitious," Faulkner told a reporter. "The airplane's number has two 13's in it, and we got it ready to fly again on Friday the 13th."[2]

HAL SMITH might well have felt some trepidation for one of the firm's prize authors, and for the royalties advanced on an unnamed novel. "I have been at the Snopes book," Faulkner wrote him in October, "but I have another bee now, and a good title, I think: REQUIEM FOR A NUN. It will be about a nigger woman. It will be a little on the esoteric side, like

AS I LAY DYING." Smith had proposed a book of short stories, and Faulkner said he would let him know. "I shall have to peg away at the novel slowly, since I am broke again, with two families to support now, since my father died, and so I shall have to write a short story every so often or go back to Hollywood, which I dont want to do. They are flirting with me again, but if I can make a nickel from time to time with short stories, I will give them the go-by."[3] They were able to discuss their plans when Smith came down for Jill's christening later that October. A week later Smith went to New Orleans. He returned to Rowan Oak for some hunting, but Faulkner was drinking, and after a few days he went on to New York.

It may have been now, looking back through his files for stories, as he told Smith he would do, that Faulkner took up "Evangeline." This time he approached the material by way of Wash Jones, a malaria-ridden poor white who "looked after" Colonel Sutpen's plantation while Sutpen has been away at the war. At its end, with his wife dead, his son killed, Sutpen has returned, determined to rebuild and beget another son. Idolizing Sutpen, Jones has watched the sixty-year-old man's seduction of his fifteen-year-old granddaughter, confident that Sutpen will "make it right." When she bears a daughter, Jones realizes that Sutpen cares less for her than for the mare which has just foaled. The omniscient narrator conveys Jones's devastating realization: "*Better if his kind and mine too had never drawn the breath of life on this earth. Better that all who remain of us be blasted from the face of earth than that another Wash Jones should see his whole life shredded from him and shrivel away like a dried shuck thrown onto the fire.*"[4] He kills Sutpen with his scythe. After killing his granddaughter and the baby, he burns their shack and goes out to his death swinging his scythe at the posse. During the next three years Faulkner would be musing over the forces which brought Colonel Sutpen and Wash Jones to that apocalyptic moment by the warped shack in the river bottom. The story brought an immediate return when *Harper's* bought "Wash" on November 2 for $350.

The day before, he and Dean and Vernon Omlie had taken off for New York. Faulkner logged four hours on the two-day trip. After they checked in at the Algonquin, he attended to business. As usual, there were magazine editors to see. Ben Wasson was about to join a Hollywood agency, and his assistant, Morton Goldman, was planning to start his own agency. Faulkner agreed to let Goldman handle his stories. Hal Smith discussed his ideas for the book of short stories, and Bennett Cerf wanted to go over some of the details for the limited edition of *The Sound and the Fury*. The gregarious Cerf gave a cocktail party for Faulkner. When he arrived late, it was clear that he had already been celebrating. Nearly a month afterward Faulkner wrote his host, "I'm mighty sorry I made more or less of a fiasco of my part of the afternoon at your place. I was sick. It had started coming on soon after I got to New York, and I made the mistake of trying to carry on on liquor until I could get back home."[5]

He was hardly back at Rowan Oak before it was time for hunting camp. Near the end of the third week of November he set out for General Stone's lodge, in the Tallahatchie bottom thirty miles west of Oxford. At the Batesville train station, the wagons were waiting to carry the hunters and their gear to the lodge, where old Ad, the cook, and his helper, Curtis, were already established. But Faulkner did not find in hunting camp the recreation and relaxation he sought. He was now plagued with a familiar ailment, a prolonged bout of hiccups after his continued drinking. They could go on until he could neither eat, drink, nor sleep. He would try any remedy that was suggested, but the hiccups would usually run their course in three or four days. Now, however, they persisted, and his alarmed companions took him back to Batesville, where they finally stopped. From home he wrote Goldman, "I am expecting to be notified that I have permanently ruined my stomach and must live from now on upon bread and milk. I hope not, but I still feel pretty bad, though I am working all right."[6]

He was using his hunting-camp misery in a story called "A Bear Hunt," in which Suratt tells how Lucius Provine tried various methods to cure his hiccups in Major de Spain's hunting camp. It was a complicated story that ended when some Chickasaws scare them out of him. This tale drew upon several strata of Yoknapatawpha County: the Indians, the blacks, the aristocracy and their friends, and the poor whites in their good and bad aspects as exemplified in Suratt and Provine. The *Post* bought it for $900.

He went to his files for "Bench for Two," rewrote it and retitled it "Pennsylvania Station," and sent it off to Goldman, who finally placed it with *The American Mercury* for $200. Though Goldman felt it a privilege to represent Faulkner, he found him a difficult client. At New York parties like those in November, Faulkner would be approached by three different editors and agree to do something for each of them. It seemed to Goldman that Faulkner lived in self-created confusion. When he made his own deals, he might accept $200 for a story which would have brought more elsewhere. Goldman felt that both the advances and the royalty rates on the book contracts were too low. He would ask Faulkner to let him negotiate the agreements for books, but Faulkner would go ahead and sign the contract Smith offered anyway. It was a frustrating situation.

Faulkner had written Goldman that he had just sent Smith "a long unpublished story" for the planned collection. It may have been one which derived from Faulkner's struggles on the Rue Servandoni with *Elmer*. He had not given up on it. He had made three short, false starts, but at some point he had telescoped most of the action into fifty-seven pages entitled "A Portrait of Elmer." In a passage which suggests Leopold Bloom's outhouse scene in *Ulysses*, Elmer's painting career and the story come to an end. In desperate necessity, Elmer presses into final use the only picture he has managed to paint. (To one critic, the picture was very like one of Faulkner's illustrations in *Mayday*, and Elmer was a parodic self-portrait of Faulkner as a young artist.[7]) Though the scene does not come off, this version shows more finesse in the compression, flashbacks, and internal monologue, and Faulkner would later ask Goldman to try to sell it.

In mid-December he had begun work on the novel about the black woman, with the title he liked: *Requiem for a Nun*. One scene-setting suggested portions of *Sanctuary* and "That Evening Sun." Another beginning placed the woman and her husband in Gavin Stevens' law office. After a page and a half he put it aside, probably to write a comic story which he hoped would sell quickly to the *Post*, as "A Bear Hunt" had done. "Mule in the Yard" grew out of I. O. Snopes's practice of arranging for livestock to wander onto the railroad tracks so that he can sue for damages. This time Snopes is bested by a doughty railroad widow named Mrs. Mannie Hait, who is much like Maud Littlejohn of "Spotted Horses." Though the story is straightforward technically, it is far from conventional, with some of the grim humor arising out of the mangling of man and mule. It would be three months before it sold—to *Scribner's*, for $300.

It was a thin Christmas that year. Faulkner had told Goldman that he was living on credit. Hal Smith proposed a job for some quick earnings: an introduction to Smith & Haas's forthcoming publication of *Man's Fate*. "I dont read French easily enough to do justice to Malraux' book," Faulkner replied in late January of 1934. "About the novel. I still think that SNOPES will take about two years of steady work. I could finish the other one in good time, if only the Snopes stuff would lie quiet, which it wont do. However, I will have my taxes and insurance paid and off my mind by March first. Then I intend to settle down to the novel and finish it."[8]

When Faulkner sat down to his desk in early February, intent on earning money for his taxes and his mother's, and Estelle's parents' if they called on him for help, he went back to another story that had lain in his files. Calling the new work *A Dark House* (his leftover title from *Light in August*), he substituted two characters named Chisholm and Burke for the I-narrator and his friend Don of "Evangeline." Then he employed a new strategy as Burke tells Chisholm about Wash Jones. The manuscript ended after three pages. On February 11, Faulkner dated a fresh sheet and began again. He set the scene in the hot hotel room and wrote dialogue between the two; then he stopped after a page and a half. He started again, working along the same lines, and stopped after three-quarters of a page. He was groping for another approach, and before the day was over, he found it.

He had to move through at least two more steps. First he substituted Quentin Compson as narrator, telling the story to Shreve. Then he abandoned that beginning, dated another sheet, and composed a letter received by Quentin from his father dated January 12, 1910. "*My dear son*," it begins, "*Miss Rosa Coldfield was buried yesterday. She had been in a coma for about a week and two days ago she died without regaining conscious-*

ness. . . ." Mr. Compson goes on with a series of reflections on death which reverberate in the consciousness of "the two separate people in me, che Quentin Compson preparing for Harvard in the South, the deep South dead since 1886 and peopled with old garrulous baffled ghosts . . . and the Quentin Compson who was still too young to deserve yet to be a ghost. . . ." Then, at the start of the second paragraph, the hot hotel room is transformed in a flashback into the "office" in the home of Rosa Coldfield, Sutpen's sister-in-law. The problem of solving the mystery and understanding its larger implications would still devolve ultimately upon Quentin (and Shreve, when he made his appearance), but the mystery would be explored by other characters too.[9]

It must have been at this point that Faulkner wrote Smith again. "I believe that I have a head start on the novel," he began. "I have put both the Snopes and the Nun one aside. The one I am writing now will be called DARK HOUSE or something of that nature. It is the more or less violent breakup of a household or family from 1860 to about 1910. It is not as heavy as it sounds. The story is an anecdote which occurred during and right after the civil war; the climax is another anecdote which happened about 1910 and which explains the story. Roughly, the theme is a man who outraged the land, and the land then turned and destroyed the man's family. Quentin Compson, of the Sound & Fury, tells it, or ties it together; he is the protagonist so that it is not complete apocrypha. I use him because it is just before he is to commit suicide because of his sister, and I use his bitterness which he has projected on the South in the form of hatred of it and its people to get more out of the story itself than a historical novel would be. To keep the hoop skirts and plug hats out, you might say. I believe I can promise it for fall." He needed $1,500, and as if to reassure Smith, he added, "I'm still sober and still writing. On the wagon since November now."[10] This may, in fact, have been the beginning of a year's abstinence he imposed on himself when Jill was a very little girl. He wanted to show he could do it, he told Estelle.

IN mid-December he had finally earned his pilot's license. He continued to enjoy the hangar flying, sitting in the small lounges that faced the runways in Oxford and Memphis, smoking and talking with the other pilots. At the Memphis airport, on January 29, returning from Batesville, he must have heard a good deal about the coming dedication of New Orleans' Shushan Airport. Beginning February 14, it would be celebrated with speeches, races, and other aerial events. At Mardi Gras, floats illustrating "Conquest of the Air" would move down the crowded streets, bearing effigies ranging from Icarus' failure to Lindbergh's triumph. Faulkner and Omlie decided to go. They met in Batesville and flew the Waco to Jackson, and on the fifteenth, their red cabin cruiser touched down on the runway in New Orleans.

36

At the end of each lap would come the mounting and then fading snarl and snore of engines as the aeroplanes came up and
zoomed and banked away, leaving once more the scuffle and
murmur of feet on tile and the voice of the announcer reverber-
ant and sonorous within the domed shell of glass and steel in a
running commentary to which apparently none listened. . . .

—*Pylon* (26)

WHEN Faulkner and Omlie arrived, people were still talking about events
the day before at the new airport built on land laboriously reclaimed from
Lake Pontchartrain. Michel De Troyat, billed as the "European acrobatic
champion," had given a spectacular exhibition and Clem Sohn performed
an 8,000-foot free fall before opening his parachute for a safe descent. Jack
Monahan was caught in a cross wind, however, that blew him against the
seawall and knocked him out of the competition. That night Captain Merle
Nelson took off with pyrotechnic attachments firing from his wings to
give his "comet plane" effect. Dangerously close to the ground, he went
into a loop at what seemed full throttle. He went up and over, but something went wrong as he tried to pull out, and he plowed into the ground
and burst into flames. New Orleans *Item* reporter Hermann B. Deutsch
wrote up the crash in detail. Faulkner would accompany him often for the
rest of the meet, seeing a great deal through the entrée Deutsch provided.

The star of Thursday's events was Jimmy Wedell, a young airplane
designer and builder from nearby Patterson, Louisiana. When Deutsch
introduced them, Faulkner met a different sort of pilot from the barnstormers and tramp aviators at the meet. Wedell was a racer who felt that
developments in racing planes today could be applied to passenger aircraft
tomorrow.

The mishaps continued. On Thursday, Roger Donrae's engine cut out as
he rounded the home pylon and he barely made a dead-stick landing. On

Friday, Harold Neumann passed the home pylon just as his engine failed. He missed the runway but managed to crash-land in a pool of water. For a moment he was trapped in the cockpit. He was quickly released, however, and then embraced by his wife, their baby in her arms. Deutsch was on the spot again.

Because of delays caused by the bad weather, Omlie could not wait for the end of the meet. Faulkner now went to stay with Roark Bradford and his wife, Mary Rose. But though Faulkner moved his suitcase from the hotel, after a day or so the Bradfords did not see him. By this time men and machines were wearing out, but Jimmy Wedell seemed impervious as he set a world's record on Saturday over a 100-kilometer course. That same day Ben Grew went up for a jumping exhibition, piloted by a twenty-seven-year-old Ohio barnstormer named Charles N. Kenily in what Deutsch called a "stick-and-string airplane." As Kenily's wife sat watching, their child in her lap, Grew slowly stepped out onto the wing. Prematurely the white silk chute popped out and instantly became entangled with the tail surfaces. The announcer froze in mid-sentence as Grew either jumped or was pulled off the wing. As the plane's controls lost response, spectators saw Kenily stand up and look at Grew. The plane swiftly lost altitude as Grew dangled beneath it. Suddenly Kenily plummeted into the lake an instant before the plane submerged in a geyser of spray. Grew's smashed body was recovered. Kenily's was never found.

While Deutsch wrote the story, Faulkner was out with other friends who probably included Guy and Helen Baird Lyman, now living in New Orleans. When he appeared at the Bradfords' early Sunday morning, he looked ravenous and hung over. After he consumed a large breakfast, he launched into what seemed to Mary Rose a disjointed, nightmarish tale of accepting a ride from two motorcyclists, a man and a woman. They were aviators at the meet, and he had joined them in drinking, flying, and carousing. Later that day he took off for Batesville, not waiting to see Merle Nelson's ashes scattered from a plane over Lake Pontchartrain.

What Faulkner carried away with him was not the conception of commercial aviation projected in the gaudy decorations of the new air terminal, but the sense that the men he had seen were rather like the curiously superannuated fliers of "All the Dead Pilots." He would always remember "those frantic little aeroplanes which dashed around the country and people wanted just enough money to live, to get to the next place to race again. Something frenetic and in a way almost immoral about it. That they were outside the range of God, not only of respectability, of love, but of God too."[1]

The following Sunday and the Sunday after that he was back in Memphis flying again. One Saturday evening after dinner with Aunt 'Bama and Uncle Walter McLean, Faulkner asked Estelle what she wanted to do. She wasn't dressed properly for the dance at the country club, and she knew he wanted to retire early so he could fly in the morning. Then she thought of something. "I want to go and see Miss Reba and Mr. Binford on Mulberry Street," she said. Faulkner told her that was no place to take a lady. She pleaded to go and Aunt 'Bama even joined in on her side, but Faulkner lapsed into stony silence. "Couldn't you just call and see if it would be all right?" Estelle asked him. "No," he said shortly. But as they walked to the elevator after bidding the McLeans goodnight, he asked Estelle if she was sure she wanted to go. When she firmly answered yes, he made a telephone call to announce their visit. A Negro maid opened the door of the big frame house and showed them into an unoccupied parlor full of tawdry furniture. Then their hostess entered. The original of Miss Reba was about fifty. She wore a dress that might have been elegant had it not been stretched to tent-size. Though it was early, she held a tankard in her large hand and she was already tipsy. "I'm so glad you come along with Bill, dearie," she said to Estelle. "Won't you have some beer? I always drink beer this time of evening. Then I switch to gin later. It makes the gin go so much farther." As they settled into an exchange of small talk, Estelle's disappointment grew. There was clearly no prospect of any excitement or diversion. After twenty minutes she was ready to leave. The big woman saw them to the door, full of cordialities as they said goodnight.

They made the trip to Memphis often as winter became spring. Dean had moved in with Vernon and showed signs of becoming the best pilot of the four Faulkner brothers. On the last weekend in March he was in charge of an air circus sponsored by the merchants of Oxford, and four weeks later they staged another at Ripley, with Vernon performing stunts, George Goff jumping, and Faulkner flying Vernon's Waco F. Bright orange circulars billed the show as "William Faulkner's (Famous Author) Air Circus." One of Faulkner's group, according to the newspaper, was "a Negro pilot whom they call Black Eagle."[2] He was Narcissus McEwen's brother, George. Johncy remembered that George would come to work at Rowan Oak wearing the helmet and goggles Faulkner had bought him, "just to remind Bill that they could go flying instead of whatever Bill laid out for him to do that day."[3]

THIS kind of activity, understandably, was getting into Faulkner's writing. In late April he completed a story about barnstorming fliers called "This Kind of Courage," but Alfred Dashiell at *Scribner's* found it too mannered and complicated. Faulkner did not take the time to make the revisions Dashiell suggested. He considered a series of pieces to be called *A Child's Garden of Motion Picture Scripts*, burlesques of the way film writers would treat classic works. But fortunately, Dashiell bought "Mule in the Yard" for $300, and Faulkner did not have to carry out his idea.

During the winter and early spring of 1934 the book of short stories had been going through production. Smith and Faulkner had settled on fourteen, to be entitled *Doctor Martino and Other Stories*, the only unpublished ones being "The Leg" and "Black Music." The reviews, which began to appear in mid-April, tended to go to either extreme. The Boston *Transcript*'s anonymous reviewer found the volume bound together by "a single strand of horror" and complained that Faulkner did not show the virtuosity necessary to bring it off. The London *Times Literary Supplement*'s reviewer declared the stories uneven but their author "without doubt one of the most powerful, original and ingenious writers of fiction now at work."[4] In the Oxford *Eagle*, Moon Mullen reacted sympathetically after quoting *Time*'s verdict that the stories were "merely potboilers." But in a paragraph that suggested the ambivalence of a number of other Oxonians, Mullen had noted that one moviegoer, seeing *Lazy River* under the impression that it was a Faulkner screenplay, had commented with surprise, "Bedogged if it wasn't good!"[5]

Faulkner was the recipient that spring of additional publicity that revealed still other attitudes. Phil Mullen and his brother Dale launched a new publication on April 1 under the title *The Oxford Magazine*. It carried the first installment of a series called "William Faulkner, the Man and His Work"—by Phil Stone. He wrote that "perhaps twenty years of personal association with him, closer than is true of anyone else in the world, give me a better opportunity to record of him many things that no one else knows. . . ." To a subject jealous of his privacy and already resentful of any attempt to—as he would put it—"ride on his coat-tails," it was not a promising beginning. In his critical assessment, Stone gave with one hand and took away with the other. Faulkner was "one of the most outstanding of American prosewriters," but he was also "a simple-hearted country boy. . . ." Though he was "one of the most noted exponents . . . of modern technique" he had shown "no trace of genius," and Stone feared that "he has gone as far as he will ever go."[6] When the next issue appeared two months later, subscriptions were solicited on the basis that there would be at least six more issues, for it would take that many to carry Stone's "biography" of Faulkner. In this number, Stone described the careers of the Old Colonel and his son, noting, too, that the Young Colonel and Judge John Falkner were leaders in the Vardaman faction of Mississippi politics. Sketching "the 'Rise of the Redneck,'" Stone wrote, "It is this social and political upheaval that is the dominant theme of Faulkner's saga of the Snopes family . . . which work, if ever completed, may become his greatest book and possibly the grandest book of humor America has yet seen."[7] Five more months were to pass before the third number of the magazine appeared. There Stone discussed more of Faulkner's relatives and his relationship to Oxford. As for Stone himself, "You may be sure I kept his feet upon the ground. Nay, I stood upon his feet to keep them on the ground. Day after day for years . . . he had drilled into him the obvious truths that the world owed no man anything."[8] Stone's correspondence with Hal Smith indicated that he would not be averse to turning these pieces into a book. If Faulkner knew this, it must have been added cause for relief at the demise of the magazine after this third issue.

One of Maud Falkner's other sons was in the news during these months of 1934. FBI agent Jack Falkner had been assigned to a special squad. He went underground, living in disguise in a gangsters' hideout and engaging in battles fought with machine guns. He was there, months later, at the Biograph Theatre in Chicago when desperado John Dillinger died in a blaze of gunfire. Maud Falkner could be proud, but it was not easy to be the mother of these boys. Billy's life might not be as much at risk as those of the other three, but he was a source of pangs as well as pride. One friend would say, "I have seen Miss Maud with the tears running down the wrinkles on her face, crying because people in Oxford have been so ugly again to her Billy."

One writer to whom the people of Oxford were never ugly, though they might smile at some of his mannerisms, was Stark Young. In *The Oxford Magazine*, Ella Somerville had warmly praised his novel *So Red the Rose*, published in August. For Moon Mullen, in the *Eagle*, "The beauty, the luxury, the romance of the Old South, it's all there."[9] So why should Faulkner's fellow townsmen, few of them literary specialists, prefer Yoknapatawpha County to the Old Plantation? What they could not know, in the spring and summer of 1934, was that he was preparing something more to their liking.

ONE of the reasons Faulkner had not revised "This Kind of Courage" was that he had a new story on his mind, one centering on two boys and their families in the latter half of the Civil War. If it seemed promising, he could do three or four more. The two twelve-year-olds were Colonel Sartoris' son, Bayard, and Simon Strother's son, Ringo. One was white, the other black, but raised together from infancy, they were like brothers. The atmosphere and many of the events were ready to hand. Faulkner began the story in July 1863. In that year J. W. T. Falkner had been a boy of fourteen. His vivid memories of the war had been reinforced by his association with Confederate veterans, widows, and their families. Faulkner knew his grandfather's stories by heart. In his own new story Miss Rosa Millard, watching over the plantation for her absent son-in-law, John Sartoris, may have been modeled on Lizzie Vance Falkner. The climax owed something to the family tale about Lizzie Vance's supplying Yankee Colonel DeWitt Thomas with false information about Bedford Forrest's strength on that far-off day when he had whipped the Yankees so soundly at Brice's Crossroads. For the Strother family, Faulkner took the grandfather's name from his childhood playmate Joby Strother.

At the climax, Granny Millard's skirts conceal Bayard and Ringo from Colonel Dick, the Yankee officer whose horse they have just shot. A kind of comedy is provided by Granny's concern with family discipline in the face of the chaos around them. With Bayard as I-narrator, Faulkner was using a comfortable technique: youthful experience recounted in maturity. As in *The Sound and the Fury*, the elders were trying to keep something

With Jill on steps of front gallery, Rowan Oak

Faulkner with Waco

*With Meta Carpenter, Ben Wasson, and Dorothy Parker
on Marc Connelly's patio in Hollywood, 1935*

Two Warner Brothers employees:
Ruth Ford and William Faulkner

Meta Carpenter,
Hollywood, c. 1936

Howard Hawks, 1932

Phil and Emily Stone

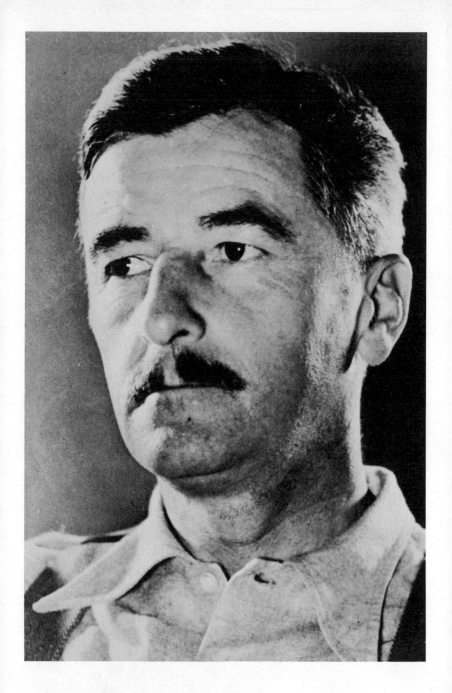

Faulkner, c. 1939

Receiving guests at hunt breakfast at Rowan Oak, May 8, 1938

Jill Faulkner on Lady Go-lightly, with her parents,
at House's Glendale stables

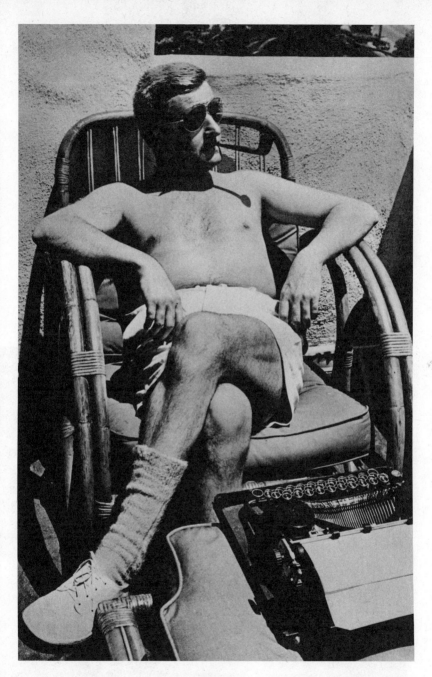

Hollywood

Christmas at Rowan Oak,
1948

Graduation garden party: Jill with her father and Hugh Goforth,
Mildred Murray Douglass, and Byron Gathright

from the children; this time it was not a burial but the knowledge of the imminent depredations of a hostile army. Faulkner called the 6,000-word story "Ambuscade" and sent it to Morty Goldman. The *Post* indicated enough interest for him to begin the second story.

In "Retreat" the boys were nearing fourteen, and their initiation proceeded apace. It was packed with action—a chest of silver and two mules lost to the Yankees, Colonel Sartoris' capture of one Yankee unit and his escape from another. By the end of the 8,000-word story, three generations—taught by the enemy—have become horse "borrowers": Bayard and Ringo, John Sartoris, and Granny Millard. Faulkner sent it to Goldman and told him that the *Post* could have the first two for $4,000 and the following three for $5,000 more.

He called the third story "Raid." Here Granny and the boys set out to find Colonel Dick and seek recompense for the silver and the mules. Faulkner introduced another major character: Drusilla Hawk, a young kinswoman, widowed by the war and wishing now only to leave her ravaged plantation to ride as a soldier with John Sartoris' troop and kill Yankees. In an ingenious twist of the plot, a clerical error has given Granny a requisition for ten chests of silver and one hundred and ten mules. By the end—under the necessity and stresses of survival in wartime —this model enforcer of proper behavior has herself become a transgressor, using forbidden language and appropriating property not hers. As the boys have passed through initiation into a species of corruption, so has she. One writer would see a whole historical process mirrored in their experience: "This war destroyed the basic integrity of the individuals in that society, the concepts of family unity essential to any stable social order, and finally undermined 'rules and orders, accepted habits and the convention of property' upon which the entire society was built."[10]

The editors of the *Post* agreed to the idea of a series, but suddenly there was a problem. Faulkner discovered that his plan would not work with just the three additional stories he had in mind. He needed to provide a bridge; he had to use some of his material to get him from what he called "the War-Silver-Mule business"[11] to the Reconstruction. Then another problem developed. Graeme Lorimer, of the *Post*'s editorial staff, would not offer as much for the series as Faulkner wanted. At this juncture the flirtation from Hollywood turned into a contract offer from Hawks: Universal Studios would hire him at $1,000 on a week-to-week basis. He may have been relieved to leave the stories for the time being, and he made plans to fly out.

One late June day, a shocking piece of news spread through the hangars and offices where fliers gathered. Jimmy Wedell was dead. On Sunday afternoon, the twenty-fourth, he had taken off to give a lesson at a field outside Patterson, Louisiana. He leveled off at three hundred feet when suddenly the plane dipped out of control and crashed. Survivor of the breakneck races around pylons, he had died teaching a beginner. Two days later Faulkner executed a three-page Last Will and Testament in Phil Stone's office. Everything would go to Estelle for her lifetime or until she remarried, except the income and manuscripts of *Soldiers' Pay* and *Sanctuary*, which would go to Maud Falkner. The principal of his estate was to be held intact for Jill. Her guardians, and the executors of the will, were to be "my Brother, M. C. Falkner, and my friend, Phil Stone."[12]

CHECKING into the Hollywood Roosevelt Hotel, he began work adapting Blaise Cendrars' novel *Sutter's Gold*. By July 7 he had finished a synopsis and hoped that after another week's work he could return home to do a final draft there. Writing Estelle, he enclosed a drawing for Jill in which a pair of wings was carrying him home to Rowan Oak with gifts for all the family and a small sack marked with a dollar sign. He signed the sketch "Your friend and admirer, Pappy."[13]

Five days later Estelle received another letter. "Finished another synopsis today," he wrote, "and am waiting now to hear about making a movie of the recent play, Mary of Scotland."[14] The prospect of an early return was fading, and he was already feeling the onset of loneliness and unease. But her letters had cheered him. "They were the nicest ones I ever had from you because they sounded happiest and like you had a good grip on yourself and are at peace."[15]

A week passed, with further delays. He wrote that he had made a draft of *Sutter's Gold* (which the legendary Sergei Eisenstein was supposed to direct), performed an emergency job for Hawks on a script for a Margaret Sullavan picture, and then waited for further developments on the Mary of Scotland story and corrections on the *Sutter's* script. Recognizing danger signals, he was more than anxious to leave. "I am getting nervous and a little jumpy to get home, at the fingernail chewing stage." There was one positive note: "Done a little on the novel from time to time."[16] Finally, he was free to leave, and on the scorchingly hot twenty-fourth of July he stepped off the aircraft in Memphis.

Once home, he had to deal not only with the script but also with his agent, his publisher, and one of his magazine customers. He brought Goldman up to date on his status and his dilemma: he had to finish the script, "keep the Post hot for a while longer,"[17] and get back to the novel, though that was also in an uncertain state. "I have a mass of stuff," he wrote Hal Smith in August, "but only one chapter that suits me; I am considering putting it aside and going back to REQUIEM FOR A NUN, which will be a short one, like AS I LAY DYING, while the present one will probably be longer than LIGHT IN AUGUST. I have a title for it which I like, by the way: ABSALOM, ABSALOM; the story is of a man who wanted a son through pride, and got too many of them and they destroyed him. . . ."[18] Inviting Smith down to deer camp, Faulkner felt a little pride himself, not just at the chance to show Mississippi to Smith, but also in the fact that he had not had a drink, he said, since Smith's visit the previous fall.

When he was able to return to the Bayard-Ringo series, he had no clear record of his part of the dealings with the *Post* to relay to Morty Goldman. But his feelings were clear. "As far as I am concerned," he told his agent, "while I have to write trash, I dont care who buys it, as long as they pay the best price I can get; doubtless the Post feels the same way about it; anytime that I sacrifice a high price to a lower one it will not be to refrain from antagonising the Post; it will be to write something better than a pulp series like this. . . . Hot as hell here; I have to work in front of a fan; I write with one hand and hold the paper down with the other."[19]

Drifting through the window would come the sounds of Malcolm Franklin, Art Guyton, and their friends from the swimming hole made by damming a gully at the spring in the lower end of the pasture. Some days he would knock off to play croquet or tennis with them on the court he had built. He had taught Art to play chess, and sometimes on the hot afternoons he would bring two glasses of lemonade for them as they sat in the shade over the board.

BY September he was able to resume flying. Often he would go with E. O. Champion, the twenty-seven-year-old service manager of the local Chevrolet agency. A self-taught aviation mechanic, Champ had a three-seat open-cockpit Command-Aire, a biplane especially popular with barnstormers for its reliability. They would go on cross-country flights together, and Champ would listen eagerly when Faulkner told about the dangers of flying Sopwith Camels in England. In mid-September, Faulkner and Vernon and Dean did a weekend aerial show at the Markette field, six miles south of town. At the end of October, Faulkner flew Champ to a job in Dyersburg, Tennessee. On the way back, one of the overhead valves lost a pin and he had to nurse the sputtering engine home on seven cylinders. He and the Black Eagle repaired the engine. A week later, after a short flight in the Waco, Faulkner made a notation in his logbook: "Accident Undercarriage Prop, Spar."[20] Although Johncy had the greatest respect for his brother's abilities as a navigator, he said that "every time he was out in his Waco by himself and went into some strange field he did something to it. Usually it never amounted to more than wiping off a wing tip or blowing a tire but he did it nearly every time."[21]

It was almost three weeks before Faulkner flew again. He had been making progress with the stories for the *Post*, galvanized by settlement of the money differences. The magazine had published the first three stories, and before the end of September he had mailed in "The Unvanquished" and "Vendée." The former was a 10,000-word story into which Faulkner had interpolated Snopes material that went back before the time of *Father Abraham*. Ab, Flem's father, sold back to Federal quartermasters the mules

Granny and Ringo commandeered with orders forged on stolen Federal stationery. Although Granny has used the profits to save the country's poor in the war's devastation, fraud and deceit have subtly corrupted her, and her natural self-assurance has become arrogance. This whole process, together with the wish to complete one last transaction to give John Sartoris a stake for postwar rebuilding, lead her into a fatal trap set up by Snopes's double dealing: an attempt to repossess four horses from marauders known as Grumby's Independents.

Taking his title from the coastal department in western France torn by a fratricidal royalist revolt in 1793, Faulkner devoted the 9,000-word "Vendée" to Bayard and Ringo's revenge. After Bayard shoots Grumby, the two boys fix his severed right hand to the board marking her grave so "she can lay good and quiet." Graeme Lorimer had not objected to Granny's walking into the trap, but now he objected to Grumby's motivation in the pursuit and showdown. With some resentment, Faulkner reworked the story and returned it.

On October 4 he sent in "Drusilla," again directly to the *Post*. Drawing on *Light in August*, he used Calvin Burden and his grandson, come to Jefferson to see that the newly franchised Negroes vote. The deaths of the Burdens at John Sartoris' hands are counterpointed with the comedy of Drusilla's struggle against respectability. Although her membership in John Sartoris' troop has been purely martial and platonic, she is finally forced into marriage. Faulkner may have gagged as he closed the happy-ending story with the regiment's rebel yell: " 'Yaaaaaay, Drusilla!' they hollered. 'Yaaaaaaay, John Sartoris! Yaaaaaay!' "[22] But within the 6,500 words he had developed a useful character in Uncle Buck McCaslin (who had helped track Grumby), and he had worked with another of a type always appealing to him: Drusilla, the masculinized woman—brave, hardy, and toughened by war and loss, but fundamentally still capable of love.

Faulkner sent Goldman one appeal he had received. "I like to help all these earnest magazines," he wrote, "but I have too goddamn many demands on me requiring and necessitating orthodox prostitution to have time to give it away save as it can be taken from me while I sleep, you might say. But fix him up if you can."[23]

He also asked Goldman to send him the story called "This Kind of Courage" because he was making a novel out of it. He would later say, "I'd got in trouble with *Absalom, Absalom!* and I had to get away from it for a while. . . ."[24] Only one chapter of the Sutpen story satisfied him, and so now he would switch to something easier, something at his fingertips, and for models he would use people he knew intimately.

The rest of this is composite. It is what we (groundlings, dwellers in and backbone of a small town interchangeable with and duplicate of ten thousand little dead clottings of human life about the land) saw, refined and clarified by the expert, the man who had himself seen his own lonely and scudding shadow upon the face of the puny and remote earth.

—"Death Drag," *CSWF* (197–198)

FOR nearly a decade barnstorming aviators had intrigued Faulkner. He had drawn fliers in uncertain pursuits in "Death Drag," in "Honor," and in *Flying the Mail* for MGM. Now he was involved himself, financially and emotionally. Two incidents in September 1934 had affected him particularly.

On the fifteenth, when he and Dean were getting the Waco gassed up in Memphis for the weekend air circus, Charlie Hayes introduced Faulkner to George Grider, an Annapolis midshipman. He had just soloed, after only a week, and he was John McGavock Grider's son. Even if he did not remind Faulkner of the father whose diary had provided the basis for *War Birds*, and even if he did not remind him of young John Sartoris, the tableau as he stood beside the plane for a snapshot might well have recalled the opening of "All the Dead Pilots," the pictures of the young men of 1918 beside their crates of wood, wire, and canvas. Charlie Hayes asked him to do a piece about the boy for the *Commercial Appeal*, and he did, not only describing their meeting but also telling the story of Mac Grider and *War Birds*, which moved him still.

An event two weeks later touched him much more deeply. Sunday evening, September 30, found Dean in Batesville after a weekend of barnstorming with Vernon and a jumper named Navy Sowell. Louise Hale had gone with them to Batesville. She was from the rugged northeast section of Lafayette County. In mid-June, just after soloing in Vernon's Waco F,

Dean was sitting over a Coke in Chilton's Drugstore on the square when his cousin, Sue Price, came in with Louise. Not long afterward, when Sue visited Memphis for a weekend, Dean told her to bring Louise along the next time she came. She did, and not only did Louise like Dean, she liked Vernon and the activities that revolved around him. She returned often that summer with Sue. "They would spend the afternoons at the airport, and late in the evening, when they would return to Dean and Omlie's apartment, they would find the apartment already filled with people and a party in progress. . . ."[1] Some afternoons Bill would drive up, and they would sit on chairs shaded by the hangar from the burning August sun: Bill and Estelle, and Narcissus, fanning herself and nursing Jill.

It was no wonder that Louise took to Dean. Happy-go-lucky, barefoot much of the time, he was a man, said his friend Charlie Hathorne, who never met a stranger. He would do anything to keep you laughing, Bill Harmon remembered, and when he was really tickled, he would roll on the ground with laughter. His good-natured charm made life easier for him than for his older brothers, but he made his way through this world of fliers on skill too. Not only was he checked out in all three planes Vernon used, he came to have, according to Jack Falkner, the "surest, most delicate touch of any pilot I ever knew."[2] He and Louise grew closer, and now she often went with him on out-of-town jobs.

Nine o'clock that Sunday evening found them in Batesville's Court-house Square. Dean got the jeweler to open his store, and bought a wedding ring. Then they crossed the street to the courthouse to be married, with Vernon and Navy for witnesses. It was ten o'clock by now, so they spent their wedding night at the hotel—in one big room with Vernon, Navy, and Jack's wife, Cecile. Two days later they broke the news, and everyone seemed pleased. Bill gave a dinner for them with both families present, and then they went on to Memphis.

Phoebe Omlie had taken a Washington job as the first woman appointed to the Bureau of Aeronautics, so Louise moved into the big apartment on Lamar Avenue. Dean and Vernon would go to the field every morning early, returning about five in time for drinks. Faulkner was with them often, still as paternal as when Dean was a bachelor. Louise could see that Dean worshipped his brother. He grew a mustache like Bill's and changed his name to Faulkner. When the family curse descended on Bill, Miss Maud would send for Dean to come and take care of him. Louise was prepared for this too. Shortly after their marriage Dean had said to her, "Mother and Bill will always come first."[3] Faulkner did his best for Dean. When federal WPA money was promised to equip the Oxford airfield for heavier traffic, Faulkner tried to enlist local support for the project and typed out a description of the responsibilities of an airport commissioner. He may have thought of himself for the job. Almost certainly he envisioned a time when Dean could run an air service company there.

*　　*　　*

IMMERSED as Faulkner was in aviation, it was not surprising that he should be writing about it. He was composing in longhand, as usual, then halting, in mid-stride almost, to go back and type up segments for mailing. Smith may have been anxious to set the book in type as quickly as possible to ensure an early publication date. By November 11, "Dedication of an Airport," the first chapter, was on his desk. Feinman Airport, built on land reclaimed from Lake Rambaud in New Valois, Franciana, was clearly modeled after its Louisiana counterpart. The same was true of several characters, including Lieutenant Frank Burnham, in his "Rocket Plane," and Matt Ord, world speed record holder. Faulkner opened with a tough, stocky, grease-stained mechanic named Jiggs, clearly appropriated from *Mythical Latin-American Kingdom Story*. His pilot, Roger Shumann, flew as well, if not as safely, as Vernon Omlie, living a hand-to-mouth existence racing in an obsolete airplane. Laverne Shumann's looks suggested something of Helen Baird, but she obviously owed more to Phoebe Omlie. Faulkner elaborated something more: a *ménage à trois* completed by Jack Holmes, a jumper. Faulkner added a touch of the grotesque with Laverne's taunting her six-year-old son, Jack, about his uncertain paternity. Throughout the novel, Faulkner's concern with the abnormal would be reiterated, from the fliers' life style to their fatalistic courage. A nameless reporter, modeled after Hermann Deutsch but grotesquely thin, completed the list of major characters. Like the fliers, he, too, was removed from the mass of mankind.

Just as Faulkner rejected the stereotyped romantic view of flying, so he portrayed the Mardi Gras festivities as noisy and tawdry. He was using consciously impressionistic description as in *Mosquitoes* and *Light in August*. Like Joyce, Dos Passos, and Wolfe, he used compound words— "lightpoised," "greasestained," "slantshimmered"—and like Eliot, he employed a gilded barge floating down the Nile. It was a Mardi Gras parade float rather than an imperial vessel, but it glided through a Waste Land just the same. By the end of the first chapter, the reporter, fascinated by Laverne, had offered the barnstormers the crowded hospitality of his small flat.

On November 23, Hal Smith received the second chapter. "An Evening in New Valois" opened with the death by fire of Burnham in his Rocket plane. Trying to explain people like Burnham and the Shumanns, the reporter tells his editor, "They aint human, you see. No ties; no place where you were born to have to go back to it now and then. . . ."[4] This would be a continuing process: the reporter's growing understanding and empathy for the fliers as he comes more desperately under Laverne's spell, trying to act as their interpreter and defender against the normal world. Two of the principal concerns in the novel were merged in one economical image: a stack of newspapers weighted down with a dollar watch. Both the fliers and the journalists are concerned with time, the latter with past causes and present effects, the former seemingly cut off from a coherent past and uncertain of a viable future. There is an added, almost hallucinatory, quality in their movement among the revelers, who suggest the grotesques of Beardsley: "grimacing and antic mimes dwarfed chalkwhite and forlorn. . . ." (53) The Hotel Terrebone (Faulkner's favorite was the Monteleone) suggests the Metropole of Eliot's *Waste Land*, with its aura of bought flesh, and Faulkner now used Anglo-Saxon four-letter words, along with the polysyllabic compounds, to describe it.

Faulkner's anti-modernist sentiments, so clear in his description of the Bauhaus-style airport with its inhuman noises, were now further generalized. They had been there in other work too, where electric lights were bloodless grapes and automobiles were stinking abominations. Here, where airplanes are "trim vicious fragile" (7) machines, there is a kind of unresolved ambivalence, for he had been a hero worshipper since childhood, when his imagination was stirred by the very names of airmen. In his artistic development he had placed a higher and higher valuation on the best of the past and on harmony with organic nature. He still admired people like Wedell and Omlie and wanted to be able to do the things they did. In some of his works he had used ambivalence and ambiguity profitably. Now it was probably making the work more difficult.

On November 25, Faulkner completed his 112-page manuscript of *Pylon*. It showed how fast he had been working—nearly every page bearing canceled lines or paragraphs, over half of them with marginal additions, and more than two dozen bearing paste-ons. Now, with a complete, coherent manuscript, he could concentrate his energies on the revisions and typing. On November 30 the third chapter arrived in New York.

"Night in the Vieux Carré" follows the reporter (fired after an unsuccessful appeal to his editor on behalf of the aviators) as he stops for a supply of absinthe, buying it from the same young hoodlum named Pete who had appeared in *Mosquitoes* and "Once Aboard the Lugger." Faulkner swiftly darkened his narrative, interpolating a seven-page flashback which describes the reporter's oft-married mother and suggests that he is just as cut off from a conventional family matrix as the fliers. Faulkner's account of the reporter's subsequent drunkenness is as harrowing as any such passage he would ever compose, and the jumper's abuse intensifies this vision of misery. "Tomorrow," which arrived in New York on December 5, carried the deteriorating situation further. The moment of weakness for Jiggs was described out of Faulkner's own bitterly acquired knowledge: "All he heard now was that thunderous silence and solitude in which man's spirit crosses the eternal repetitive rubicon of his vice in the instant after the terror and before the triumph becomes dismay—the moral and spiritual waif shrieking his feeble I-am-I into the desert of chance and disaster. He raised the jug. . . ." (118–119) Catastrophe caps disaster, with Shumann brought down after Jiggs's failure to perform engine repairs and the jumper injured just as Jack Monahan had been hurt against the seawall at Shushan Airport. In poignant counterpoint, Faulkner showed just how different Laverne was from glamorous fliers such as Jacqueline Cochran and Amelia Earhart: "all I want is just a house, a room, a cabin will do, a coalshed where I can know that next Monday and the Monday after that and the Monday after that. . . ." (165)

In the next chapter, which reached Smith on the twelfth, further counterpoint amplified Laverne's thoughts with a view of Matt Ord's "new neat little flowercluttered house," where "they could hear a dinnertable being set, and a woman's voice singing obviously to a small child." (168) The Ords have what the Omlies could easily have afforded, what Louise and Dean aspired to. With this fifth chapter's title, "And Tomorrow," Faulkner was just as clear in quoting Shakespeare as he had been with Eliot earlier. Shumann's efforts to buy a dangerous aircraft from Ord call up other lines in the passage from *Macbeth* which had given Faulkner his title for the Compsons' story: "all our yesterdays have lighted fools the way to dusty death." Faulkner's sympathies were so completely engaged with the fliers that even though Colonel Feinman's anti-government, anti-NRA views were congenial to his own, he made Feinman and his cohorts exploiters, with the fliers presented sympathetically in an adversary relationship just as hopeless as that of Dos Passos' Wobblies or Steinbeck's strikers. Before the final, manifoldly foreshadowed tragedy, Faulkner interpolated a flashback opposing love, if in a sensational form, to the death that would follow. It was a description of Laverne's first parachute jump when, in something like a farewell gesture, she had first climbed back into the cockpit and made love to Shumann as he flew the plane. Moments later, her blown skirts revealing her nakedness, she became a mythic image of desire: Venus descending from the clouds. Back in present time at the end of the chapter, the heroic Shumann flies the substitute craft until it disintegrates, plunging him to his death by water.

The last two chapters reached New York on December 15. In "Lovesong of J. A. Prufrock," Lent begins as the debris of Mardi Gras is removed from the city's streets and a crew dredges the lake for Shumann's body. Now the reporter's love for Laverne is merged with his grief for Shumann. The chapter ends with a passage evoking squalor and hopelessness, as Eliot had done not only in the poem which had given the chapter its title but also in "Preludes" and *The Waste Land*.

The novel ended with "The Scavengers," in which the reporter turns on his callous and cynical colleagues. In a passage that might have derived from "This Kind of Courage" he formulates the novel's final judgment: the fliers are not inhuman; they are, in fact, more truly human than those who scorn them. As the jumper and Laverne take her son to his paternal grandfather (a man who suggests Doc Hines), she knows that she is sacrificing for his present welfare any part she might have in his future. But as her own hard early life parallels that of Lena Grove, so this child's prospects recall those of Joe Christmas and Miss Quentin Compson. Some of the novel's ambiguity, and probably the author's ambivalence, was still unresolved. Faulkner was aghast at the bizarre and tragic shape of the lives of some people who flew. At the same time, he was a flier himself, and his brother made his living from the air. If he had known tramp pilots, he had known heroes such as Jimmy Wedell and Vernon Omlie. But in spite of images and sentiments which might exist in tension, his deepest feelings were clear—his admiration and compassion for these people, who were "outside the range of God, not only of respectability, of love, but of God too . . . as ephemeral as the butterfly. . . ."[5]

He could not yet relax for the Christmas holiday. He revised "Drusilla" and sent it to Morty Goldman. And he worried about *Pylon*. He wrote Smith, asking if there might be trouble over the resemblance of people and places in the book to actual counterparts. In a curious process of forgetting or denial, he admitted the use of New Orleans, Shushan Airport, and Jimmy Wedell, but declared, "the incidents in Pylon are all fiction. . . ." He told Smith, "You might decide whether there would be grounds for a suit, whether a suit would help sell the book, or whether to alter the location, etc., so there would be no grounds."[6] Smith was not worried. Besides, he would come down for a visit in January and they could change a few things here and there.

The galleys of *Pylon* were ready on January 9, and Smith brought them with him. The changes they made were negligible, substituting dots for Anglo-Saxon words for genitals, deleting modifying phrases and clauses, and adding material only when it clarified sequence or motive.

SMITH looked at some of Faulkner's other work during his stay. There was a story from Faulkner's last sojourn in California, called "Golden Land." Set in Beverly Hills, its every page seemed imbued with the distaste and unhappiness he had felt. The terrain, the climate, the architecture, the people, their behavior, their dress—all displeased him. Nebraska-born real estate man Ira Ewing is an alcoholic like Jiggs. In the morning he tremblingly shakes two aspirins "onto the glass shelf and set the tumbler into the rack and unstoppered the gin bottle and braced his knuckles against the wall in order to pour into the tumbler."[7] But this is the least unsavory thing about him. Both his children have been corrupted by too much money in childhood. His daughter is a Hollywood extra involved in a court trial over a sex orgy. On Ewing's orders, her true identity is given to a tabloid so that his photograph, also published there, will provide publicity for his business. Beside him, Miss Reba is a paragon of virtue. Here, as in *Pylon*, and in every reference he would ever make in his work, Hollywood is a symbol for corruption. Goldman had thought that "with its flavor of perversion" the story could probably be sold profitably only to *Cosmopolitan*, but Smith suggested that Faulkner try for another outlet between his customary extremes: The *Post* or *Harper's* and *Scribner's*. Smith tried to place "Golden Land," and in less than two months it was sold, but to the low-paying *American Mercury*.

Faulkner managed some quail-hunting in January before he had to turn once again to short stories. Johncy Falkner had written some of his own, stories he had first made up to tell seven-year-old Chooky. When they didn't sell, Maud Falkner made Bill promise to help. When Johncy brought the work to him, Bill said he thought they would be right for the *Post*. Johncy could tell that he had been annoyed to begin with, and when the *Post* refused the stories, Bill put Johncy in touch with Morty Goldman and returned to his own work. He hoped for a sale that would give him time to do some work on the novel, but he was not pressed enough to consent to a facsimile edition of *The Marionettes* or an article on lynching for *Vanity Fair*. "I am trying to bugger up an air story for Cosmopolitan," he wrote Goldman. "I must either hang something on them or on the Post; it all depends on which one I can invent first."[8]

As March came in, he was hard at work, and one of the new group of stories resembled those about the Compson children. The seven-year-old narrator, Georgie, as unscrupulous as young Jason Compson, serves his Uncle Rodney, who is quite as unscrupulous as Uncle Maury Bascomb. Domestic farce becomes domestic tragedy, however, in "That Will Be Fine," when Uncle Rodney, unluckier than Uncle Maury, is killed.

If the old-fashioned celebration of Christmas in the story drew on holidays at The Big Place and Ripley and Columbus, another story that March drew directly upon Oxford lore: the latter years of Uncle Bob Chilton, who had been killed that past September in an automobile accident. After the death of his brother, Uncle Top Chilton, he had run their drugstore with the aid of old Ad Bush, whose ice cream was as celebrated among children as his hunting-camp cookery was among their fathers. After a lifetime of hard work, Uncle Bob became "a good time papa to the pretty gold-diggers in Memphis," John Cullen said, crowding "all the living and fun he could into the short time he had to live."[9] The narrator of "Uncle Willy" is a fourteen-year-old boy full of loyalty and love for "the finest man I ever knew." Uncle Willy has been successively deprived of his drug habit and his substitute drinking habit by the forces of uprightness in the community. Left a near-bankrupt by the fat Memphis whore he had made his bride, Uncle Willy sells his last resources for a car, a tent, and an airplane; a chauffeur (like the Black Eagle) to fly the plane, and old Job (a tattletale like Uncle Ned Barnett) to do the chores. When his plan—to head west and live by barnstorming—is betrayed by Job, Uncle Willy takes the plane up and crashes it; death on his own terms is preferable to life on others'. Yoking comedy and violent death, the story looked backward to other condemnations of meddling born of smug religiosity and forward to two novels of runaways fleeing the law to seek adventure in the big world beyond north Mississippi.

He revised "The Brooch," making Howard Boyd's mother look a good deal like Mrs. Compson, and his wife, Amy, "a vivid daring girl whose later reputation was due more to folly . . . than to badness. . . ."[10] More important, he strengthened the ending, where Howard substituted suicide for despair. He added a passage unusual for him: 200 words on the effect on Howard of W. H. Hudson's romantic novel *Green Mansions*. To one critic, this treatment of "the sexually crippled male, tormented and bewildered . . . by his fantasy of an ideal female," ends appropriately as Howard makes a cave of Amy's blanket and places the pistol barrel in his mouth, the act "a successful fantasy, as he secures for himself in the anticipation and erotic excitement of death what he was never able to achieve in life."[11]

For another story that probably dates from this time, Faulkner turned to one of his favorite characters: Suratt, the itinerant sewing-machine salesman. In "Fool About a Horse," a nameless narrator relays Suratt's humorous story, told in the law office of "Grandfather," while a servant named Roskus operates the fan against the summer heat and serves the drinks. The losing encounter of Pap Suratt with Pat Stamper, the legendary horse trader, combined realistic elements with the tradition of the Southwestern tall tale.[12] It came from the same rich vein Faulkner had struck years before with the spotted-horses story, and it contained other echoes and perhaps foreshadowing. Roskus had worked for the Compson family, and it seems likely that "Grandfather" is Jason Lycurgus Compson, Jr., and that the retrospective narrator is his grandson, Quentin MacLachan Compson III. Quentin would also narrate *Absalom, Absalom!* and still another story that appears to date from this time which Faulkner called "Lion."

For "Lion," Faulkner drew again upon the tales of old hunters such as Ike Roberts and Bob Harkins. The events Quentin had experienced at sixteen were not related for comedy, as those in "A Bear Hunt" had been, but concentrated instead on Boon Hogganbeck and two animals who were almost mythic: Old Ben and Lion. The former was modeled on Old Reel Foot, hunted in Panola County for years, and the latter on a dog Faulkner would recall years later, "a tremendous big brute . . . must have weighed seventy-five or eighty pounds."[13] The narrative begins with comic notes, but soon the hunt is invested with meanings beyond the deaths of Lion and Old Ben.

ON January 30 the Mississippi Secretary of State had listed William Faulkner as one of the three incorporators of the Okatoba Hunting and Fishing Club, located on several thousand of General Stone's acres in the heart of the deer country near Batesville at the eastern edge of the Delta. Faulkner himself had typed up the articles of the charter, employing as much care as he had with the job description for an airport commissioner. The bylaws emphasized the protection of game, in part a reaction to the same historical process which saw asphalt roads and parking lots spreading over the land as forest and wildlife diminished.

It was good that the capital stock of the club had been no more than a hundred dollars, for his financial situation was worsening. Neither "Fool About a Horse" nor "The Brooch" had been taken. When he sent "Lion" to Goldman he added some information in confidence. He meant to travel east in the fall and try for a better arrangement with another publisher and give Smith the chance to match it. "I cannot and will not go on like this. I believe I have got enough fair literature in me yet to deserve reasonable freedom from bourgeoise material petty impediments and compulsion, without having to quit writing and go to the moving pictures every two years. The trouble about the movies is not so much the time I waste there but the time it takes me to recover and settle down again. . . ."[14] In April, when *The American Mercury* offered $250 for "That Will Be Fine," Faulkner answered, "Good God yes, let them have the story and do anything they want with it. . . . I couldn't wire you because I have no money to pay telegram with. Haven't had one cent since last story sold, wherever that was. . . . I am writing two stories a week now. I dont know how long I can keep it up."[15]

On top of the problems of tradesmen's bills and insurance premiums, the Bureau of Internal Revenue began to press him. There was only one escape. He began drinking. His mother reacted with more than her usual concern—he had been good for so long, even at Christmas, when Estelle had been under the weather herself. But Miss Maud's method of pouring the whiskey down the sink worked no better than it ever had. Dean couldn't come down, so she called Champ and asked him to see if he could do anything. Sitting at Faulkner's bedside, Champ said, "You know, Bill, you can't drink if you want to fly." Faulkner looked up at him, his face drawn, his eyes deeply circled. "If you say quit," he said, "I'll quit." He began to taper off and the bout was aborted.

His recovery coincided with one event and made possible another: the initial review of *Pylon* and the completion of *Absalom, Absalom!*.

38

"So maybe you will enter the literary profession as so many Southern gentlemen and gentlewomen too are doing now and maybe some day you will remember this and write about it. You will be married then I expect and perhaps your wife will want a new gown or a new chair for the house and you can write this and submit it to the magazines."

—*Absalom, Absalom!* (9–10)

THE reviews that began coming in on March 25, publication day, tended to praise Faulkner's power but deplore his assault on the reader's sensibilities. The objections ranged from Malcolm Cowley's deploring, in *The New Republic*, "unnecessary horror and violence" to Moon Mullen's frustration, in the Oxford *Eagle*, at "unintelligible" descriptive passages and an "inconceivable climax." Herschel Brickell, in the New York *Post*, called the novel "one of Mr. Faulkner's best executed pieces," but John Crowe Ransom concluded in the Nashville *Banner* that "William Faulkner is spent." In May, John Chamberlain objected in *Current History* to "deliberate obfuscations," but Hal Smith may have taken comfort in the June issue of *Esquire* at Ernest Hemingway's statement that he had been "reading and admiring *Pylon*. . . ."[1] On the whole, it was just as well that, by now, Faulkner generally did not read reviews of his work, and besides, he was at work on the next one.

On March 30 he had dated a sheet of his margin-lined paper and written at the top "*Absalom, Absalom!*." Though the dark house had vanished from the title, it would still be central to the novel. To one reader, it would become "what the scaffold is to Hawthorne's *The Scarlet Letter* and the *Pequod* is to Melville's *Moby-Dick*."[2] For another, the darkness itself would be central and pervasive, with "most of the major scenes in the novel . . . nocturnes, scenes occurring at night, or in the darkness of a shuttered house."[3] Faulkner would later say, "when I took it up again I almost rewrote the whole thing. I think that what I put down were inchoate fragments that wouldn't coalesce and then when I took it up again, as I remember, I rewrote it."[4] The earlier pages included two false starts, both set in Cambridge, Massachusetts, but he was able to salvage a number of paste-ons for the new manuscript.

He had his principal characters well in hand: the Sutpens, the Coldfields, the Joneses, and Quentin Compson. And there was much local history and lore for him to draw on. There had been a number of large landowners—Colonel Barr, the Potts twins, Alexander Hamilton Pegues. A brother, Colonel Thomas Pegues, had supposedly hired a French architect to build his house, and the big house built for Dr. Felix Grundy Shipp in the mid-1830's was still standing, a gaunt antique ruin eleven miles south of Oxford. There were two Wash Joneses in records from the nineteenth century, and more than one Oxford merchant had antecedents which went back to ante-bellum days. Faulkner's problem now was to interrelate these characters. His immediate concern was: Exactly what did Quentin (and some of the others) know, and how did they find it out? He sketched out a kind of flow chart of information: Charles Sutpen, at the top of his circle, was linked to Rosa Coldfield. He drew a line from her down to Quentin, who would learn things from his father (at the bottom of the diagram), who had in turn learned things from his father, General Compson, a confidant of Sutpen. The process would become more complex the further he worked his way into the novel.

From the beginning he signaled his method of supplying copious information about most of his principals, and though the retelling of events was set in 1910, just before Quentin went off to Harvard, Faulkner went back even before "Wash" to Sutpen's arrival in 1833. Now there was another son besides the one lost in the war. This was part of the story Quentin heard from Rosa Coldfield. It took Faulkner six attempts before he evolved her obsessed recital of the way this parvenu acquired his land and then built his house and grounds with a captive French architect and naked slaves. Rosa Coldfield's deepest bitterness was caused by Sutpen's marriage to her sister for respectability, his treatment of the sister and her two children, and finally, his consummate offense when, a widower, he made a scandalous proposal to Rosa.

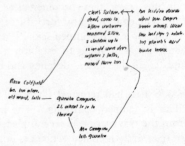

Notes for novel called *Dark House* and then *Absalom, Absalom!* (Courtesy Mrs. Paul D. Summers, Jr.)

She saw him as both a demonic figure and, like Wash Jones, a symbolic one. When Faulkner had told Hal Smith a year before about Quentin's function in the novel, he had explained that Quentin was projecting his bitterness about Caddy "on the South in the form of hatred of it and its people. . . ."⁵ His incestuous feelings would make him hypersensitive to certain characters and situations, but now he, too, saw Sutpen as a man who, properly understood, might yield symbolic truth. In *Sartoris*, Faulkner had shown one aspect of the Southern character—chivalric, foolish, and doomed. In *Father Abraham* and the Snopes stories he had treated the anti-Sartoris figure: the man bound by no scruples whatever. In the Bayard-Ringo series he had juxtaposed the two. Sutpen occupied a midpoint between them. To Quentin's father he was "underbred." He might accept what he took to be the code of the planter class, but no matter what their flaws, he would lack the gallantry of the Carolina Bayard Sartoris and the cultivation of Jason Lycurgus Compson II.

As Faulkner worked through the early spring, many of his artistic concerns were fusing to create a work of extraordinary power. He was writing at a high pitch of intensity, giving Rosa Coldfield a poetic and rhetorical style that often veered close to hysteria. And there was something of the frantic quality in *Pylon*. He did not neglect dramatic events and suspenseful chapter endings: Sutpen proving his mastery by fighting one of his slaves in a "raree show," and a further turn of the screw as his wife intrudes and the spectators are revealed to include not only Sutpen's small son but his two daughters—one white and one black. Using the procedure he employed with *Pylon*, Faulkner typed the chapter and sent it to Hal Smith in New York.

As the smell of honeysuckle had pervaded Quentin's section of *The Sound and the Fury*, the air is heavy in the twilight with the odor of wisteria as Quentin listens on the veranda to another narrator, one who is leisurely and masculine rather than shrill and feminine. Mr. Compson's subjective view of the Sutpen story was not necessarily closer to truth than Rosa Coldfield's, but it conveyed further information for Quentin to assess: Sutpen's early history in the county, but characterized through the town's speculation about the events and their meaning. And as Mr. Compson carries the story further, to Sutpen's consolidation of his position, his tragic flaw becomes clearer than it ever could through Rosa Coldfield, embittered by forty-three years of neurotic hatred. As Faulkner would put it later, Sutpen said, "I'm going to be the one that lives in the big house, I'm going to establish a dynasty, I don't care how, and he violated all the rules of decency and honor and pity and compassion. . . ."⁶

HAL SMITH had returned Chapter I with penciled comments. One read, "This is damned confusing." The new version Faulkner typed differed from the manuscript in several places. He moved the opening from 1910 to 1909 and tightened sentences for emphasis and logical sequence. In

Chapter II he sharpened his imagery and omitted details for powerful understatement. By June 29 this chapter was in New York and the manuscript pages of the third chapter were piling up.

This, too, was Mr. Compson's chapter, his narrative studded with allusions to mythological characters, even to "Greek tragedy." Introducing special information from his parents, he also speaks for the chorus: the townspeople of Jefferson. (In his Preface to the French edition of *Sanctuary*, André Malraux had perceived in it "the intrusion of Greek tragedy into the detective story." Speaking of *Pylon*, John Crowe Ransom had said, "William Faulkner is Greek." One critic would suggest that these tragic accents in this new novel could have owed something to a reworking of the *Oresteia* of Aeschylus by a dramatist Faulkner admired, Eugene O'Neill, in his *Mourning Becomes Electra*.[7]) All the others are seen in relation to Sutpen: his wife—as ephemeral as the fliers in *Pylon*—and his children, Judith and Henry, moving beyond adolescent closeness to an intimacy that would suggest Caddy and Quentin. His narrative swiftly advanced the exposition with the coming of Charles Bon to create a triangle, and the coming of the war, which Henry Sutpen hopes will resolve it. Faulkner was now almost at the point where "Wash" had begun, and in terms that suggested *Sartoris* as well as Greek tragedy, he wrote, "Fate, destiny, retribution, irony—the stage manager, call him what you will—was already striking the set. . . ."[8] This time his chapter ending held more surprise than suspense as Wash summons Rosa to Sutpen's Hundred with the news that "Henry has done shot that durn French feller. Kilt him dead as a beef." By July 22 the chapter was on Smith's desk.

At this point Faulkner had had to break off to concoct some stories to relieve the financial pressure, but by early August he was immersed in Chapter IV. He began it as omniscient narrator, returning to Mr. Compson and his son on their veranda and glancing briefly at Miss Rosa waiting in her dark house. Often Mr. Compson would describe events as he imagined them, combining fact and conjecture. More like Conrad than ever, Faulkner interpolated a three-page letter from Charles Bon to Judith, as Mr. Compson argues that Henry had repudiated the evidence of a bogus marriage of Bon to a New Orleans octoroon and then abandoned his birthright for love of Bon. His interpretation finds a supersensitive listener in Quentin, this version of a relationship in which a brother contemplated the courtship of a beloved sister. But this was even more complex than Quentin's own situation, for, according to Mr. Compson, the suitor and the brother loved each other. Later these psychological relationships would grow more complicated still. Preparing to end the chapter, with these two returned from the war, Faulkner realized that he had to change the end of Chapter III. He would delete the news of Bon's death, thus prolonging and heightening the suspense, and use it here at the end of Chapter IV for maximum effect. He finished typing the chapter and put it in the mail to Smith, who had it by August

19. It would be nearly two months before he would be able to work at the book consistently again.

LOOKING ahead in late July, he had told Goldman he would need at least $2,000 on September 1. He was even thinking of selling the manuscripts of his last five novels. "I hate like hell to sell it," he wrote, "but if I dont get some money somehow soon, I will be in danger of having some one put me in bankruptcy and I will then lose my house and insurance and all. So just ask around and see what the reaction is."[9] He rewrote "The Brooch," in accordance with Alfred Dashiell's suggestions, and *Scribner's* bought it along with "Fool About a Horse." But the pressure was not relieved. It may have been then that his desperation sent him back to a story whose beginnings could have gone back ten years to "The Devil Beats His Wife." A good deal later he had used the setting of his MGM treatment, *The College Widow*, for a synopsis he called "Christmas Tree." In a fifteen-page story he followed Howard Maxwell and Doris Houston to a happier ending than the one in *The College Widow*. It did not sell, and now under the title "Two Dollar Wife," he recounted their bizarre courtship and Maxwell's victory at dice aided by moonshine whiskey. It was purchased by *College Life*, where it would appear in January, described as "a pungent panorama of reckless youth. . . ." The tale of "madcap matrimony" was destined for thirty-five years of obscurity. By September 23, the situation was acute enough for him to go to New York to try a get a better deal from Smith or leave him.

The following Friday he sat down at the desk in his room in the Murray Hill Hotel and wrote Estelle. He had tried without success to sell the serial rights to *Absalom, Absalom!* to the *Mercury*. When Goldman could not arouse any interest at *Scribner's* or *Harper's*, Faulkner went to Hal Smith with the details of his situation. He owed nearly $1,700 in Oxford and Memphis, he was now providing $100 each month to his mother and to Lida Oldham, and tax payments and insurance premiums were coming due. He called Stark Young, and when they met for lunch, his discouragement was obvious. "I enjoyed seeing him very much," Young wrote Ella Somerville, but "He seemed bothered a good deal about his life down there. It all tallied with what you had told me."[10]

On Monday he wrote again to Estelle. He had talked at length with Smith and Haas and Harold Ober, Haas's Scarsdale neighbor and a successful literary agent who sometimes handled Smith & Haas business on West Coast trips. Smith had agreed to advance the bare minimum Faulkner needed, and if Smith could get Faulkner a film contract through Ober, Faulkner would go there for eight weeks to pay back the loan. "I have seen 2 shows," he reported, "dined out once, and I have a typewriter in my room and I am working on a story for Scribners. I drink in a very moderate way, two whiskeys before supper and no more, and

I am actually enjoying drinks now, and everyone is amazed at my temperateness."[11] On October 14 he was back home.

It would have been natural, on his return, for Faulkner to stop in at Phil Stone's office just off the square. If he did so, he did not find him there. Phil was in New Orleans preparing to take a bride. Emily Whitehurst had decided that teaching school in Oxford was not for her, but when Phil came down and asked her to return as his wife, she accepted. Sixteen years younger than her husband, she was full of admiration for his learning and assurance. Once back in Oxford, she moved into the old six-columned home of General Stone and Miss Rosie. She was bringing Phil, a talker and observer more than a doer, into the mainstream of life. And he was ready to give to her, a determinedly aspiring writer, the kind of encouragement and support he had given to Faulkner. But here the wished-for gifts of the magi were withheld: none of her novels would ever be published. He was forty-two, with parenthood and professional distinction still in store, but he would later tell her, "You've never known me when I was myself."[12] Years later she would discover what the psychic realities had been. "Phil Stone was burned out," she would say. "His life was over when I married him, but I didn't know it." Faulkner probably knew it, but he would remain faithful to the relationship, though it would become increasingly discordant.

THERE was some work on his desk to be attended to before he could return to his novel. He corrected the proofs of "The Brooch" for *Scribner's*. He read Bennett Cerf's reaction to the 57-page typescript of "A Portrait of Elmer." Cerf was sorry it had come too late for a limited Christmas edition. Faulkner was used to negative verdicts, but he must have reread another part of the letter: "I think we'd rather have you on our list than any other fiction writer living in America." More than that, Cerf said he had meant it when he told Faulkner on his New York trip that he could write his own ticket with Random House. And when he was ready, "we'll make everything so attractive for you that you simply won't be able to turn us down."

Returning to his manuscript, he started Chapter V of *Absalom, Absalom!*. Up to the last page, the narrator would again be Rosa Coldfield. Certain familiar refrains she uses over and over, but she also advances the narrative, watching Judith direct the building of her sweetheart's coffin, then plunging shockingly into present time, suddenly bringing to the surface the ulterior motive which Mr. Compson had suspected. Characteristically, she returns obsessively to the past almost in the same breath. With impassioned speech trembling on the brink of blank verse, she relives the effect of Sutpen, the Demon, upon her sister and herself. But there is one immediate thing Rosa Coldfield has to know, and she discloses it to Quentin in the chapter's last lines: there is something out at Sutpen's Hundred. "It has been out there for four years, living hidden in that house." (172) Faulkner had now brought this narrative of the past into the immediate present on this ominous, portentous note.

With Chapter VI, approaching the midpoint of his story, Faulkner placed increasing stress on interpretation, on the meaning of Sutpen's life as well as the psychological mechanisms behind his actions. To aid in this, he returned to an idea he had rejected when he had begun the novel: setting the scene in Quentin's Harvard dormitory room. And now he introduced the successor to those other, earlier interlocutors, Don and Burke, a familiar one, Quentin's roommate from *The Sound and the Fury*, Shreve MacKenzie. (In a typical oversight, he called him Shrevlin McCannon.) He became a co-analyst, conveying to the reader what Quentin had earlier told him. As Faulkner would later put it, "Shreve was the commentator that held the thing to something of reality. If Quentin had been let alone to tell it, it would have become completely unreal. It had to have a solvent to keep it real, keep it believable, creditable, otherwise it would have vanished into smoke and fury."[13] Like Conrad again, Faulkner shifted to omniscient narration for Quentin and Miss Rosa's night visit in late summer to Sutpen's Hundred, and he interpolated Mr. Compson's letter to Quentin that brought the news of Miss Rosa's recent death. Most striking, however, was the way, as Shreve threw himself into the problem, in which his diction became Hellenized like Mr. Compson's and his rhetoric high-flown like Miss Rosa's. Now this normally colloquial Canadian youth would see Sutpen as "a widowed Agamemnon to her Cassandra an ancient stiff-jointed Pyramus to her eager though untried Thisbe who could approach her in this unbidden April's compounded demonry and suggest that they breed together for test and sample and if it was a boy they would marry. . . ." (177) Recollection advanced the story further, with Bon's son (by the New Orleans "wife") raised by Judith and her black sister, Clytie, and with the deaths of Judith and the child in 1884 from smallpox. The story of the mulatto child's growth recapitulated much of Joe Christmas' tragic alienation. But as the chapter moved to an end, Faulkner was internalizing it more and more within Quentin's consciousness. Shreve has said to him, "*Tell about the South. What's it like there. What do they do there. Why do they live there. Why do they live at all. . . .*" (172) Now Quentin's thoughts, revolving obsessively around these events with a special meaning for him, become tinged with madness: "*Yes. I have heard too much, I have been told too much; I have had to listen too much, too long. . . .*" (207) But Faulkner was still withholding information to maintain suspense at the chapter's end: what *was* out there that night when Quentin and Miss Rosa visited Sutpen's Hundred?

AMONG the pieces Faulkner had written during these weeks of intense labor on his novel was a review of Jimmy Collins' book *Test Pilot*. He regretted the last chapter, an obituary written by Collins himself, who had been killed on a test flight. But that chapter contained the only line, Faulkner wrote, that arrested "the mind with the fine shock of poetry: 'The cold but vibrant fuselage was the last thing to feel my warm and living flesh.' "[14] Faulkner had hoped the book would provide a folklore of speed itself which, as he described it, sounded like what he had attempted in *Pylon.* Flying had come to occupy an ever larger place in his life and, in part from his example, in the lives of the other Faulkners too. In April, Dean had earned his transport license and was buying the Waco from Faulkner. In May, Johncy had earned his limited commercial license and was working toward his transport license. Vernon and Dean were doing air shows in Tennessee, Missouri, and Mississippi. They did one with Faulkner and three other pilots in Oxford in late April. Faulkner logged only two hours' time during that weekend, but it must have been further fulfillment of a dream. When he put on his leather jacket and white silk scarf and climbed into the cockpit, flying with men like Vernon, the townspeople who had called him Count No 'Count could see that he was a real pilot, even if they had to take his RAF credentials on faith. There were times, however, when he presented a problem for the others. One October weekend when he came to Memphis, Dean and Louise could see he had been drinking. On their flight to visit Johncy in Clarksdale, Bill took the stick. He said he wanted to land the plane, but when after twenty minutes he was still circling the field, Dean took over and made the landing.[15] But he remained the adoring brother, and on November 2 and 3, "The Flying Faulkners" staged an air show at Markette field. An added attraction was Willie Jones, billed as "the only Negro wing walker and parachute jumper in the world."

Dean and Louise were looking beyond this show. She was four months pregnant, and their life in Memphis was beginning to pall. A professional pilot often had to be away, and it was an uncertain life—giving instructions, flying charter jobs, putting on shows—not knowing what the next week would bring. They would sit at night and talk about it. "We must get out of this life," they told each other. They would start looking, but for the present they would have to continue as they were. After the Oxford show, Dean flew back to Memphis. The next weekend he would return to do another in Pontotoc.

Faulkner was too busy that weekend to get over to Pontotoc to help Dean and Navy Sowell, but Monday was Armistice Day and Dean would be coming to Oxford for a visit when the show was over. All day Saturday, Dean hauled passengers. Sunday morning was more of the same. Louise and Cecile decided to surprise Dean by driving down from Memphis. They arrived in time for the show, which was scheduled for two o'clock. Sometime after three o'clock rumors began to spread about an airplane crash somewhere over near Thaxton, about ten miles west of Pontotoc. The ringing of the telephone broke the Sunday silence at Rowan Oak. Faulkner answered. There had been a crash. Dean was dead.

39

... at last his body ceased trembling and he lay presently in
something like a tortured and fitful doze, surrounded by coiling
images and shapes of stubborn despair and the ceaseless striving
for ... not vindication so much as comprehension. ...

—*Sartoris* (321, 323)

HE had wanted to haul one more group of passengers before Navy's
jump started the show. Lamon Graham and the Warren brothers, excited at the prospect of seeing their farm from the air, climbed into the
bright-red cabin Waco. Dean taxied out, revved up the engine, and
took off. Louise and Cecile talked with Navy and a few others while
they waited. A half-hour passed, then a quarter of an hour more. Navy
decided to get in the car and drive out toward the Warrens' farm. Louise
and Cecile and the Caldwells got in with him.

Ten miles down the bumpy farm road they saw a pickup truck. When
Navy hailed the driver, he said he had seen a red airplane. It had crashed
in a pasture about a quarter of a mile away.[1] Clara Caldwell, Louise's
sister, held her back while Roger Caldwell and Navy leaped from the car
and raced toward the pasture. About thirty minutes later they returned,
walking slowly. They had found the Waco. All four men were dead.
Again Louise struggled to get out of the car, but Roger restrained her,
and they drove back to the airfield. From there friends took the women
to the home of C. D. Lemmons, who had flown in with Dean the day
before, and Louise was given a sedative. Then they made the telephone
calls to Oxford.

Maud Falkner was waiting when her eldest son drove up to the house.
They made the twenty-five-minute trip to Thaxton with no other passengers, both of them silent in their grief. The Lemmonses brought Louise
out to the car, and then Faulkner turned it around and headed back to
Oxford. Louise would remember her mother-in-law speaking only once.

She asked, "Did I ever do anything to make him unhappy?"[2] Instead of going straight to her home on South Lamar, Faulkner stopped first at Sallie Murry's and told her to take Auntee to stay with Miss Maud. Louise was put to bed, and as soon as Sallie Murry and Auntee arrived, Faulkner left for Pontotoc, a photograph of Dean in his pocket.

A crew had worked with shovels, blowtorches, and hacksaws on the wreckage of the Waco. The scene had been littered with debris—fragments of metal and canvas and wire, bits of equipment and garments and the men who had worn them. The plane had gone into the hard earth at a 45-degree angle to a depth of five or six feet. At last, just before darkness, they had cleared away the wreckage and taken the bodies to Carr's funeral home in Pontotoc. Faulkner did not know what grisly duty awaited him there, but if his mother was determined to look once more at her youngest, it was up to him to try to help spare her any agony he could. The Pontotoc undertaker could not perform the necessary reconstruction, and he had brought in George Garner, from Grenada, who had this kind of experience.

Each separate testimony that survived would be different: Dean's face was unbroken, or it was gouged by a piston; Dean's body was jammed up and foreshortened, or it was simply flattened. Faulkner's own account would be the grisliest of all: he had sat up all night with the undertaker, he would say, a bottle of whiskey at their side, reconstructing the shattered form where it had been placed in a bathtub. When they brought the body home to South Lamar the next morning, Faulkner called Sallie Murry into the living room. "Tell me if the job is all right so Mother can see him," he said. To Sallie Murry, the face looked a little too full and the mustache was not quite right. "Bill," she said quietly, "it's just a fine job, but it would be better if Aunt Maud didn't look anyway." She talked to her aunt herself and finally convinced her. Faulkner went in and sat on Louise's bed. "Knowing you like I do," he told her, "I know you'd want to remember Dean the way he was." And so the casket remained closed. The clan gathered, Jack from North Carolina, Johncy from Lambert, over in the Delta. That afternoon, after a short service there in the living room, Dean was buried in St. Peter's Cemetery. It was November 11, Armistice Day.

THERE were as many conflicting reports about the crash as there were about Dean's body. One reason was that the people who saw the plane go down were farmers, not fliers, and the experts had only their various reports and the mute evidence of the wreckage. There was agreement that the plane had spun in from about four thousand feet. After that there was only conjecture and contradiction. Some said a wing had come off the Waco; others, just a panel. Some thought this structural failure had caused the crash; others, that the defect itself had been caused by pilot error—not Dean's, but a passenger's. Twenty-four-year-old Lamon

Graham had taken instruction and presumably wanted to show the other two passengers that he could fly. When E. O. Champion peered into the wreckage, he saw the control wheel, which was movable, on the pilot's side, where Dean had locked it before takeoff. After Vernon Omlie examined what was left of the aircraft, he saw it was over to the right, in Lamon Graham's lap. He and Faulkner were convinced that when the plane began to spin—whatever caused the spin—Graham froze at the controls. Even if Dean had succeeded in pulling the locking pin at the top of the support column and switching the wheel back to his side, there would have been neither time nor altitude to pull out of the fatal spin. Weeks later, in Memphis, Omlie told a friend, "It will always be a mystery. No one will ever know for sure exactly what happened."[3]

William Faulkner knew all he needed to know about what had happened. It was his encouragement and example that had helped interest Dean in flying, and it was his plane that Dean had trained in with Vernon, his plane that Dean had finally bought. In the living room of their mother's little house, Bill had told Jack what had happened. Jack had never seen him so distraught. "Don't reproach yourself," he said. "What happened wasn't your fault. You weren't responsible for it." But his words did no good. Bill moved into the house with Louise and his mother, who had her sleeping pills at her bedside and said she just didn't know when she would take them all. Aunt Sue, Uncle John's wife, tried to comfort her. She remembered that Sis' Maud just said, "I've lived too long." Faulkner would do for her whatever she would let him. He would run Louise's bath for her and bring her a glass of warm milk at night. At breakfast one morning Louise said, "I can't eat. I dreamed the whole accident last night." A moment later he said, "You're lucky to have dreamed it only once. I dream it every night."[4]

He went on this way for three weeks, trying to comfort them at the same time that he tried to deal with his own grief and guilt. Then Louise saw that he had begun to drink. They sat there in the living room one quiet afternoon, talking about Dean. The tears welled up suddenly in his eyes and he began to shake with silent grief. "I've ruined your life," he said to her. "It's my fault." Louise began to sob. Maud Falkner walked into the room and realized what was happening. "Louise," she said, "you understand. He can't help it. He couldn't stand it anymore. He had to have some relief."[5]

He ordered the small marker for Dean's grave. There on the stone, beneath the name and the dates, was the epitaph he had chosen:

> I bare him on eagles'
> wings and brought him
> unto me.

For Oxonians steeped in the Bible, it was adapted from Exodus 19:4. For those who remembered *Sartoris*, it was the epitaph Faulkner had earlier given to that other ill-fated flier, John Sartoris. When Maud Falkner saw it, she did not like it. It was possible, thought one family member, that she felt it "a monument to William's grief and guilt. . . ."[6] A more acceptable tribute would come later, when the new airport, for which Faulkner had entertained such hopes, would be called the Dean Faulkner Memorial Airport.

Faulkner could not continue trying to drown his grief in whiskey, not with his mother and his pregnant sister-in-law to care for. And he had also brought with him to South Lamar the manuscript of *Absalom, Absalom!*. He had been able to find some relief from emotional stress in writing *The Sound and the Fury*, and now he tried it again at night in the quiet house. The bereaved mother and widow in their rooms, he spread out his pages on the dining-room table and wrote.

He started Chapter VII as omniscient narrator, but thereafter Quentin talks, with an occasional interruption as Shreve attempts to slow down the rush of the story. Flashbacks provide insight into the crucial events of Sutpen's life. Turned away from a Virginia planter's door by a Negro servant at age fourteen, he had run off to Haiti to earn the money to gain the land, the home, the trappings that he thought would make him equal to any. His trouble, according to General Compson, was "innocence." (240) Innocent of geography, human causality, and morality too, he could put aside his wife, his planter employer's daughter, because of her concealed taint of Negro blood which rendered her unfit to be the chatelaine of the domain he envisioned. He could say to General Compson, "I had a design in my mind. Whether it was a good or a bad design is beside the point; the question is, Where did I make the mistake in it. . . ." (263) Confronted with a new obstacle after the successful second marriage when Henry, as his catspaw, would not prevent Bon's courtship of Judith because of Bon's octoroon "wife," Sutpen apparently played another trump card. But this is only speculation on Shreve's part, and here once again Faulkner employed the device of withheld information. Faulkner interpolated passages from "Wash" before Quentin finally discloses the answer to Shreve's repeated question: Milly Jones's child, the innocent agent of retribution upon Sutpen, had been rejected because she was a girl, not a potential male heir. Brooding, withdrawing further into himself, Quentin thinks, "*I am listening to it all over again I shall have to never listen to anything else but this again forever. . . .*" (277)

On December 4, Faulkner wrote Goldman that he thought another month would see the novel done. The problem was that the advance was about gone and Smith, his new firm drifting into financial trouble, was anxious for repayment. Faulkner had agreed to switch over to film work in February if Smith obtained a contract for him. Ober had apparently had no luck in inquiring about screenwriting opportunities. With reluctance, yet with a sense, apparently, of bowing to the inevitable, Faulkner asked Goldman to pursue some inquiries he had in mind, and Faulkner would take the best contract, whether through Goldman, Smith, or Ober. It came sooner than he expected.

Once again the moving force was Howard Hawks, now working at Movietone City for Twentieth Century-Fox. It was the most attractive lot in the film industry. Most visible of the studio's five thousand employees were Shirley Temple, Fredric March, Ronald Colman, and Loretta Young. All this No. 2 studio needed to wrest the leadership from the giant of Culver City was better pictures, and five months earlier a nervous, dynamic writer-producer, Warner Brothers veteran Darryl Zanuck, had been brought in to provide those pictures. He had brought a French film called *Les Croix des Bois* principally for its actual battle footage. Hawks was developing a story, based on an account he had heard from a Verdun veteran, with the idea of taking the triumvirate he had used in *Dawn Patrol* and changing them from fliers into infantrymen. Zanuck's associate producer, Nunnally Johnson, had assigned Joel Sayre the job of developing the story line. When Zanuck decided they needed further help, Hawks asked Johnson if he could hire Faulkner. Whether or not he knew of Zanuck's concern about Faulkner's reputation for drinking, Johnson agreed, and Faulkner went on the payroll for four weeks at $1,000 a week beginning on Monday, December 16, 1935. This rugged individualist was now Twentieth Century-Fox Employee Number 27545.

Nunnally Johnson was a tall, thin, aristocratic-looking Georgian who had moved from journalism to screenwriting to producing. After he and Faulkner were introduced, Faulkner asked, "Do you mind if I have a drink? I have it with me." Johnson asked his secretary to bring glasses and water. As they sipped their drinks, Faulkner began to talk. "I've been through a rough experience," he said, and went on to relate the story of Dean's death, including the night at the funeral home in Pontotoc. They finished the pint together and then went out for more.

Faulkner found that he got along with others on the picture: Johnson's assistant, a bright twenty-six-year-old named David Hempstead, and Joel Sayre, a fine comic writer. And Howard Hawks's secretary, a twenty-eight-year-old Mississippi divorcée named Meta Dougherty Carpenter.[7] It was one of the important meetings of his life, that day when he walked into Howard Hawks's outer office, a meeting for which he had been made ready by events in the most private part of his life during the past half-dozen years.

IT had been a short honeymoon, that honeymoon on which his bride had attempted suicide, and the ensuing years had multiplied their problems—familial, financial, and emotional. Estelle had made the best of the move to Rowan Oak, working with the rest, gardening, putting up fruits and vegetables. Marvelously skillful with a needle, she had made baby clothes for Alabama, and then for Jill. But there were times when she would buy clothes, spending money they did not have, money her seething husband would have to try to earn with more potboiler stories. Cornell Franklin faithfully sent the child-support payments—to Major Oldham, and sometimes they did not reach William and Estelle Faulkner. Cho-Cho would recall that her stepfather was not welcome at her grandparents' home, in spite of—perhaps in part because of—the fact that he was now contributing to their support.

The trauma of Alabama's death had cut deep. Their nerves were raw in its aftermath, exacerbating points of conflict between Faulkner and Estelle, not just particular issues but antithetical elements in their personalities. When Buttitta had visited Rowan Oak he had heard them quarrel. She wanted him to dance, to go out with her. He wanted to stay home. Hollywood wanted him, and she wanted them both to go. He told her, "You're only looking for a good time. I don't want to go. I want to stay here. This is the only place I can write about."[8] She resented the constricted life she led. Once she sent her sister a parody of Scott's lines beginning "Breathes there a man with soul so dead. . . ." She described a scene of activity,

> While *he* in dignity sits alone,
> Aghast at the sound of e'en a trombone.
> And whiles his joyless hours away
> Reading a book—or maybe a play
> That very few people save he—understand—
> *This* breathing soul is my own hus-band![9]

There was not even a radio in the house, and Jill would reach her teens before her father succumbed to family pressure and allowed her to have a phonograph. Jill would remember "those early years [when] life was difficult for Mama. *She* had to cope with the gossip and the boredom. She was emotional and demonstrative. Pappy wasn't. Life for her was either way up or way down. . . . And she grew up in an era when being 'pretty' was extremely important. Her mother told her, 'Estelle, you're not beautiful, so you must be charming.' Sometimes, I guess, she came on too strong with the charm." And that charm, that attractiveness, was often lost on him. "Pappy would become so involved in his writing that his nearest, his dearest, weren't accepted. So Mama would paint and draw and sew, and play the piano and study French." Dinners could be lively, and afterward he might read to them—from Dickens, from Conrad, from the Bible. But sometimes dinners would be totally silent. Much later, looking back, Jill would think, "given his independent personality, he shouldn't have burdened himself with a family."[10]

Jill's birth had brought them together again, but only briefly. Half a dozen years later he would write of one of his characters, "he would marry someday and they too would own for their brief while that brief unsubstanced glory which inherently of itself cannot last and hence why glory. . . ."[11] If Faulkner shared this view with his narrator, it may have derived from an element in his makeup he might or might not have recognized. His daughter would say, "I think that probably Pappy's idea of women—ladies—always revolved a great deal around Granny. She was just a very determined, tiny old lady that Pappy adored. Pappy admired that so much in Granny and he didn't find it in my mother and I don't think he ever found it in anybody. I think that maybe all of these [women] including my mother were, just second place."[12] Still other factors had been at work in the years since Jill's birth. Estelle's health had been precarious. She was still anemic, and she had lost rather than regained any of the weight that had made Sallie Murry remember her in college days as "pretty as a little partridge." And there was the drinking. If his drinking made him a sometimes impossible husband, her drinking made her a sometimes unattractive wife. All of these factors, and others that could have been known to Faulkner alone, lay behind something he would very soon say to this new woman entering his life: under the same roof but in different beds, he and Estelle had not lived together as man and wife since Jill's birth.[13]

"Pappy liked ladies, liked women," his daughter would say, "plain and simple."[14] And this young woman was attractive: "That I was pretty enough, with blond hair that fell in a straight sweep to my shoulders, with a ninety-two-pound body as lean and as lithe as a ballerina's, and with a waist that was a handspan around, I knew without undue vanity."[15] There were other ways in which he was drawn to her. Not only did he hate leaving Oxford to go to California, he suffered from loneliness and homesickness once he was there. He would soon discover that Meta Carpenter had grown up on a plantation outside Tunica, in the Delta, just fifty-five miles northwest of Oxford. More than that, they were both "great-grandchildren of slave owners and descendants of Confederate soldiers." After they began to see each other often, Faulkner would turn to her after a trying day at the studio. "I could make him forget for hours on end that he was so far from home," Meta Carpenter would later write. "Together we recreated our own South. It helped make his life away from Oxford endurable."[16]

She had received the usual training of a young woman of her class, but she had a talent for music, and after sixteen years of study she hoped for a career as a pianist. Almost as soon as she had finished her schooling, however, she married Billy Carpenter, and the two of them had come to California in the early 1930's. They had separated not long afterward, and she had wound up living at the Studio Club, a haven for young women, and working for Howard Hawks. There in his outer office, her first meeting with William Faulkner was a polite one; the second, far from promising. It was two days later and he was drunk. He asked her out to dinner that night. Flustered, she retreated to Hawks's office and asked him to tell Faulkner she could not go out with him. She was not used to men who drank to excess. She was also unwilling to become involved with a married man, but Faulkner persisted.

One of her duties was typing scripts. When Faulkner's handwriting proved difficult, he was glad to come to the office to help her transcribe it. By the time she was able to do it on her own with the help of an occasional telephone call, they were on a first-name basis. Finally she accepted his invitation. He called for her at the Studio Club and took her to the Musso & Frank Grill, known as Musso Frank's to the many screenwriters who enjoyed its hearty dishes and generous drinks. He ordered one of his favorites, Cassoulet Toulousin, for them. That night he was open, conversational, charming. He wanted to know about her—her likes and dislikes, her hopes, what she thought of the life she was living, a well-brought-up girl from the Mississippi Delta in Hollywood. And he told her about Dean, about what he had been through. They strolled along Hollywood Bouvelard afterward, she the taller of the two by an inch, he taking her arm when they crossed a street. They went into a bookstore because he wanted to give her a copy of *A Green Bough*. He had to settle for *Sanctuary*, which he signed and dated for her. Before he took her home, she agreed to have dinner with him the next night.

He bought them an elegant, expensive dinner at LaRue's on Sunset Strip. This night he told her about the war, his combat missions in France, the crash, and the silver plate in his skull. He was enjoying himself enormously, he told her. He had known from the first that they were alike. They went to dinner again the next night, and on the weekend too. He had to see her every night, he said. She had saved his life in Hollywood; she had kept him sane. He told her stories and sang songs. He recited Swinburne and Housman. He showed her pictures of Jill, and he told her how he worried over her safety when Estelle was drinking. And he told her that there was no physical love in his life. Another week went by. He had not kissed her yet, but, she wrote, "womanwise, I sensed the tumult of his blood within him when we stood face to face, and the strain he felt at being close to a desirable young female."[17] They returned to Musso Frank's, to their favorite table, the middle booth on the left wall where no one entering could see them. One night after dinner they did not walk toward the bookstores and theatres. Instead, holding hands tightly, they walked toward Hollywood and Vine, toward his hotel. That night they became lovers. It was the beginning of an intermittent relationship—broken off and then resumed—over the next fifteen years.

AT the studio, he and Joel Sayre had gained Zanuck's approval on a story outline and had begun a first rough script called *Wooden Crosses*. A producer was delighted, Sayre knew, when a writer turned in five pages a day. Faulkner would sometimes bring his day's work with him in the morning—thirty-five pages' worth, Sayre estimated. Working at the studio he would write on a legal-size yellow pad. Sometimes he would call in the assigned secretary, a tall girl from Kansas named Julie Davies, and dictate from the yellow pad, tearing off the sheets and dropping them into the wastebasket. When he and Sayre had put in a good day's work they would relax and talk. Faulkner had taken to Sayre immediately. Two years younger than Faulkner, he had doctored his birth certificate at age sixteen to serve with the Canadian Expeditionary Force in Siberia. A superb factual reporter, he had covered New York gangsters for the *Herald Tribune* in the twenties. The wit and exuberant nature of this burly six-footer won him friends wherever he went. "Bill's head was full of stories about the Snopes family," Sayre would remember. He loved to hear them: "Once he said to me, 'Why, you know, they mail Snopeses to each other, take them down to the station and put tags on them.' " These stories provided welcome relief from the somber matter of the film, now called *The Road to Glory*. Their rough script, which they would complete by the year's end, would conclude with a procession of the dead. There were individuals, such as the sensitive pianist turned soldier, but the regiment went on, with a life of its own, in peace and in war, with its living and its dead. Even if Faulkner's custom had not been to celebrate heavily at holiday time, the screenwriting and this particular stript would have given all the impetus he needed.

There was one by-product of the storytelling and the celebrating which was probably unpremeditated. It was a present, a seventeen-page typescript Faulkner inscribed "To Joel Sayre / Xmas, 1935."[18] It was entitled "Afternoon of a Cow," and it was written, Faulkner would say, "one afternoon when I felt rotten with a terrible hangover, with no thought of publication, since the story is a ribald one."[19] One of the Snopes stories involved an idiot boy who fell in love with a cow. Some elements of this present to Sayre had their origins, however, as far back as 1919, when he had published "Une Ballade des Femmes Perdues" in *The Mississippian*, where it had been parodied three months later by "Lord Greyson" in "Une Ballade d'une Vache Perdue." In his childhood Faulkner had probably heard Professor Thomas C. Trueblood's Shakespearean recital, and in 1925 he had created Ernest V. Simms, who wrote H. L. Mencken from Paris in praise of William Faulkner. In "Afternoon of a Cow," Ernest V. Trueblood described his work as William Faulkner's amanuensis and recounted the trying incident which had elicited this piece. Both put-upon and prudish, he substituted dashes for his employer's profanities when a pasture fire drove Beulah, his cow, into a ravine. There, as they struggled to push and haul her free, her terror precipitated an outrage to her modesty: "Mr. Faulkner underneath received the full discharge of the poor creature's afternoon of anguish and despair." At the story's end, having bathed with saddle soap, seated wearing the summer blanket of his horse Stonewall, Faulkner sat, drinking his second julep of the afternoon. When he failed to tell Trueblood what he should write tomorrow, the amanuensis asked if he might employ the day's events, treating them in his own diction and style rather than Faulkner's. " 'By _____!' said Mr. Faulkner. 'You better had.' "[20] He had also used Malcolm, Jimmy, and his butler, Jack Oliver, in the story. He made fun of himself in this barnyard comedy, as he had done in other writing, though never this directly. He had enjoyed the parody of his style which Corey Ford had published in *Vanity Fair* in March 1932 under the title "Popeye the Pooh." In "Afternoon of a Cow" he showed that he could enjoy parodying himself.

This *jeu d'esprit* might have also provided some relaxation from the intense work on *Absalom, Absalom!*. Following his practice of rising early to work on the novel before reporting to the studio, he had moved into Chapter VIII, where the intensity increased once more as the two students immerse themselves more deeply in the reconstruction of the relationships among Sutpen's children: "So that now it was not two but four of them riding the two horses through the dark over the frozen December ruts of that Christmas Eve: four of them and then just two— Charles-Shreve and Quentin-Henry. . . ." (334) Quentin and Shreve still pursue their colloquy, with more weight added to their speculations —homing in on Henry's motive for killing Bon—by the supporting narration and exposition of the omniscient narrator. They infer Bon's motive: "*He need not even acknowledge me; I will let him understand just as quickly that he need not do that . . . just as he will let me know that quickly that I am his son. . . .*" (319) They imaginatively re-create Sutpen's playing his last trump card in a tent in Carolina: "*He must not marry her, Henry. . . . it was not until after he was born that I found out that his mother was part negro.*" (354–355) The chapter ended with Faulkner's slipping from the joint imaginative construct in italics back to roman type and the present tense as Shreve imagines Bon's death at the gates of Sutpen's Hundred.

One of the problems for Quentin and Shreve was to assess the reliability of the various narrators in order to arrive at the truth. However, one student of the novel would later observe that by now they themselves had become "too involved to render an authoritative verdict for the reader." And significantly, though Quentin talked about Sutpen, he was "far more interested in reconstructing the chain of cause and effect that leads to the murder of Charles Bon."[21] The spectacle of a man killing his sister's suitor would resonate strongly in Quentin's mind, particularly if he thought of his inability to use the pistol Dalton Ames had offered him that day at the bridge.

The final chapter was the shortest, as Faulkner moved quickly from the cold night of the Harvard dormitory room to the hot darkness of

Quentin and Miss Rosa's night visit to Sutpen's Hundred. Once there, a long italicized flashback followed Quentin up the stairs of the rotting mansion and into the room where lies the actual form of one of the ghosts that have so long haunted his psyche: seventy-year-old Henry Sutpen, wasting away, hidden there four years, fugitive still from the fratricide committed nearly forty-five years before. Now it is the omniscient narrator who reveals fragments of the brief conversation: explicitly, Henry's identity; by implication, his relationship to Bon. Lying in bed, Quentin trembles, thinking, "Nevermore of peace. Nevermore of peace. Nevermore Nevermore Nevermore." (373) The ending conveyed not only his precarious mental balance but also his ambivalence toward his land. (Nearly two decades later Faulkner would write of himself vis-à-vis the South, "Loving all of it even while he had to hate some of it. . . ."[22]) Now, as Shreve asks at the book's end, "Why do you hate the South?" Quentin answers, "*I dont! I dont hate it! I dont hate it!*" (378) And one of his remarks foreshadows the end he had met in *The Sound and the Fury*: "I am older at twenty than a lot of people who have died. . . ." (377)

In "Evangeline" the nameless narrator had fallen asleep against a column of the rotting mansion and then in his dream had questioned Henry Sutpen and Charles Bon to learn why Henry had killed Bon—only to be wakened as the flames consumed the old house. In *Absalom, Absalom!* Quentin, at Harvard, could only imagine that fatal fire, but by now the accounts of the whole long sequence of events seemed to him "to partake of that logic- and reason-flouting quality of a dream which the sleeper knows must have occurred, stillborn and complete, in a second, yet the very quality upon which it must depend to move the dreamer (verisimilitude) to credulity—horror or pleasure or amazement—depends as completely upon a formal recognition of and acceptance of elapsed and yet-elapsing time as music or a printed tale." (22)

Now that the manuscript was finished and the revisions on the draft of the screenplay were nearly complete, Faulkner's drinking began to increase. One day he handed Dave Hempstead a batch of pages covered with what Hempstead called Faulkner's "Carlovingian minuscule."

"I want you to read this," he said.

"What is it?" Hempstead asked.

"I think it's the best novel yet written by an American," Faulkner said. Hempstead did not want to be entrusted with Faulkner's only copy of his novel, but Faulkner insisted. The next morning Hempstead returned it to its author with relief. His condition, however, was worrisome, for he was reaching the stage where he would soon stop eating.

"Bill," said Hempstead, "how can you keep this up?"

"Dave," Faulkner answered quietly, "there's a lot of nourishment in an acre of corn."

He went to Hawks. "Am I through?" he asked.

"Yes, Bill, you are," his friend told him. Most of what he had done would not appear in the final script, but he had conscientiously tried to supply what Zanuck, Johnson, and Hawks had wanted.

His payroll card would show a brief notation for Tuesday, January 7, 1936: "Taken off temporarily due to illness." When he was able to travel, Meta Carpenter drove him to the train and he left for Mississippi.

Back at Rowan Oak, he continued to labor over the manuscript, reading it through and making further marginal additions and occasional deletions. He made three sets of notations at the bottom of the last page:

	Mississippi, 1935	Rowanoak.
Absalom, Absalom!	California, 1936	
	Mississippi, 1936	
		31 Jany 1936

William Faulkner[23]

Instead of being able to relax now for a bit, he must have felt a sense of urgency. The long process of revision and typing lay ahead, but he still owed money to Harrison Smith and he still had to meet his own expenses, with royalties from the novel still more than a year away, with a new advance unlikely, and no stories on hand likely to bring any substantial checks from the *Post* or *Harper's* or *Scribner's*. Hawks's covering up for him had left the door open for him to go back on salary. He was at home on borrowed time, and he must have felt that it would not be long before he had to head west again.

40

The sun was high. . . . the mountains stood serene and drab
against it; the city, the land, lay sprawled and myriad beneath
it—the land, the earth which spawned a thousand new faiths,
nostrums and cures each year but no disease to even disprove
them on—beneath the golden days unmarred by rain or weather,
the changeless monotonous beautiful days without end. . . .

"Golden Land," *CSWF* (725–726)

THE pressure, the frustration, the anxiety caught up with him again, and
he began to drink heavily once more. Visiting at Helen and Guy Lyman's
hunting place in Picayune, Mississippi, forty miles from New Orleans,
he departed from home in such a state that he left the manuscript of
Absalom, Absalom! behind him.[1] At Rowan Oak, Malcolm sat up with
him, but it became clear that they could not cope with the problem at
home. There was a small private sanitarium at Byhalia, fifty miles to the
north beyond Holly Springs, and they took him there. When he came
home several days later, he continued the regimen of rest and nourishment, and soon he was back at work on *Absalom, Absalom!*.

He was able to walk to the square again, to pick up his mail at the
post office, and to stop in to see his mother on the way home. Louise was
there, her baby due in less than two months. He was tender and solicitous
with her, his grief and guilt over the past mixed with his anticipation of
the future. The Falkner family seemed to run to boys. "What do you
think we'll do if the baby is a girl?" he said to Louise. He visited Phil
and Emily and read part of his new manuscript to them. Emily told him
that she had furnished the sitting room which she and Phil used on the
second floor of the Stone home.

"Yes," he said, "I can see another hand than Miss Rosie's here."

"You surprise me," Emily said. "Phil says you never see anything."

"I see everything," Faulkner replied. That was what his one-time classmate John Cullen would think, watching Faulkner in the square, stand-

ing "as if he were in a strange trance with his head tilted back and no expression in his eyes at all."[2]

If he gazed more intently than usual, it might have been because he knew that he would not be there to see the trees bud and bloom, to see the farmers plowing their fields and putting in the seed. On February 26, 1936, he was back at Twentieth Century-Fox. He was not needed on *The Road to Glory* (now retitled *Zero Hour*), and Nunnally Johnson wanted him for *Banjo on My Knee*, set on the Mississippi above Memphis. When Johnson had to turn to other duties, Dave Hempstead took over, and Faulkner turned in his pages to him, a tale of bargemen and shantymen which was romantic and violent by turns. "Bill wrote magnificent things," Hempstead remembered, "practically blank verse, sometimes two or three pages long. They were beautiful speeches, but they were written for actors like Tony Martin, and I couldn't show them to Zanuck." To Hempstead he seemed melancholy but without cynicism, sometimes observing the spectacle around him with dispassionate humor. At other times he gave the impression of being incredibly naïve. To those who were unsympathetic, he was simply an unpredictable drunk. The stories about him proliferated: bored at a party, he climbed down a trellis and made his escape; invited to another, he paired with comic actress Zasu Pitts to make the most vulnerable mixed doubles tennis team imaginable, she totally ineffectual, he barely able to navigate.

He had settled in at the Beverly Hills, a quiet Spanish-style hotel which catered to elderly permanent guests. By the time spring came, he needed a change from its particular ambience. He found it with Nathanael West, whose minor masterpiece *Miss Lonelyhearts* had made no money two years before, and who was writing scripts for Republic Studios (called Repulsive Studios by veterans). "I'm goin' pig-huntin'," Faulkner told Dave Hempstead. Later he would describe a rugged sport on Santa Cruz Island, where he and West would struggle through narrow tunnels of underbrush to hunt dangerous wild boars. When Hempstead met Faulkner and drove him back to the Beverly Hills, he was unshaven, clad in his hunting shirt, and carrying a borrowed weapon under his arm. As he crossed the lobby to pick up his room key, the clerk dropped to the floor with a cry, a salesman bolted from the lobby, and two spinsters fainted. The hotel had been robbed in his absence, and his entrance was taken to be the gunman's return. By the time Hempstead's story filtered back to Oxford and Moon Mullen printed it in the *Eagle*, it had become a part of the steadily accreting lore of Faulkner in Hollywood.

But his letters home were full of loneliness. The new script was coming along fine, he had written not long after his arrival but "I wish I was at home, still in the kitchen with my family around me and my hand full of Old Maid cards."[3] He was again earning $1,000 a week, but he hoped to be free to come home in a few weeks. Estelle could meet him in New Orleans for a two-week holiday, he wrote. At the same time, he was entertaining the possibility of another contract at a higher pay rate after *Banjo on My Knee*. But as it turned out, Zanuck threw out most of his script at the story conferences, and the most they would offer him was twenty weeks at $750 a week beginning August 1. The studio's wariness was clear in William Dover's instructions to the Contract Department: "Because of the past behavior of Faulkner we want to be sure that the behavior clause is potent."[4]

He decided to stay there, when he went off *Banjo on My Knee*, to wait for the new assignment he had been offered at his current salary beginning April 9: to be "loaned out" to work on *Gunga Din* at David Selznick's RKO Studios. Joel Sayre was the chief scriptwriter, and the director, George Stevens, was his friend. Corey Ford's description made the Writers' Building sound like a cell block, but Faulkner buckled down to work, and by late April he was able to write Estelle, "getting along allright and working hard. Have got my weight down to 140 and feel (and I hope, look) much better."[5]

He felt at home with the script for two reasons. When Hal Smith's friend Mrs. Sewell Haggard had complimented him on some of his short stories, he had said they were third-rate Kipling. He knew how to deal with this Kipling novel and with its main character. The trouble with some of the earlier writers on this picture, he said, was that they didn't understand that Gunga Din was "a colored man." But once again his contribution to the shooting script was not major. By mid-May, Faulkner was able to write home that he could leave about June 1. Jack Falkner was visiting him, and when Jack drove home to El Paso, he might be able to go with him. He sent love to all and concluded, "Damn this being an orphan."[6] There was no doubt that he missed his home and his family, that he missed Mississippi, but in Hollywood he was far from being an orphan.

FAULKNER's relationship with Meta Carpenter, begun during his work on *The Road to Glory*, had steadily grown more intense when he returned for *Banjo on My Knee* and *Gunga Din*. He was the ardent lover, reciting poems and writing out verses for her, sometimes his own, once a variation on part of Keats's "Ode on a Grecian Urn," another time, eight lines imperfectly remembered from *Ulysses*, "The Rogue's Delight in Praise of His Strolling Mort." (As Joyce did not acknowledge his seventeenth-century source, so Faulkner did not acknowledge Joyce as his.) Some of the verses were intensely sexual and completely explicit in their four-letter Anglo-Saxon words. As D. H. Lawrence's gamekeeper had done in *Lady Chatterley's Lover*, he devised proper names for the sexual organs of his beloved and himself. When Meta told him they needed other people in their life together, he reluctantly agreed to go to the beach with her friend Sally Richards, a pianist, and Sally's twenty-two-year-old lover, pianist John Crown. The two couples spent weekends in cottages of the

Miramar Hotel, in Santa Monica. There were mementos for Meta of those weekends: twenty-six fine-line pen-and-ink drawings of the two of them: before, during, and after love-making. To one who would see them many years later, "The basic concept of Faulkner's drawings was witty: Working at a film studio, Faulkner on a slack day, thinking of Meta while being paid to be there to make films, made drawings which suggest they are animation stills and would give the illusion of movement if seen in rapid sequence. As he was supposed to do in that office he made a movie."[7] If this aspect of their relationship provided humor and ribaldry, their affair was also, for him, a riot of the senses that curiously ranged from the explicit sexual word-play and graphically erotic drawings to gifts of hair ribbons and to pillows strewn in anticipation with petals of jasmine and gardenias.[8]

It was not easy for her. "With any other man," she wrote, "I would not have been afraid to ask questions . . . but not with Bill. From the beginning, I knew somehow that I had to be incurious. The insularity that he drew over himself like a second, tougher skin put him beyond common query." This gently nurtured daughter of the Delta could share the throes of physical passion with him, but she had to come to terms with the fact that the inner core of the man would remain beyond her ken. She felt it sometimes when he was with her and more keenly when he was away. During those lonely times she tried to "connect the warm, outgoing man of the letters with the man who was largely a cipher to me."[9] And she was caught in yet another dilemma. When he spoke of other writers, of his contemporaries, she was "painfully aware of my intellectual limitations," and so she held herself "to dazzling smiles when they were appropriate."[10] She wanted to be able to talk with him on this level, yet she also knew how he valued that quality of youth and inexperience that elicited the gifts of hair ribbons.

They had now passed the gardenia-and-jasmine phase of their relationship. She had seen him in the throes of delirium tremens, when he shuddered and screamed that the Jerries were going to shoot him down, and she had helped get him to the private hospital where he could ride out the ragged end of yet another debilitating drinking bout. Yet she told herself, "I could live with this man for the rest of my life . . . the dark moods, his lack of attention to me when his characters possessed his mind, his aversion to self-revelation that would be with him all his life, his coldness to others when they pressed in upon him—none of it would be more than I could rationalize."[11] There were things that could not but trouble her deeply. He complained bitterly about his wife, but he said he feared to sue for divorce because he would lose Jill in the process. Meta tried to anticipate his wishes and wants. When he gave her a dog, a cocker named Chloe, she was sure that meant she was to move from the Studio Club into an apartment where they could live together, but he told her it would be better if they had their own places. She wanted to be his wife, and she wanted to mother Jill, but there were so many areas that were off limits. He did not discuss his work with her. And though he told her what she had meant to him, "He had never been one for spoken sentiment out of bed, distrusting the flatness of the spoken word, resorting to French endearments when the playback of his own voice offended his ears. I knew he loved me by looks, by touch, by the poems and the letters, only seldom by what he said to me."[12]

Somehow, he could say clearly to Ben Wasson what he could not say to Meta herself. "That's the girl I'm in love with," he told Ben after he introduced him. "Can't get her out of my mind or system. And don't want to. . . . She's brought me peace of mind. I haven't said anything yet to Estelle, who's already suspicious, I think. I want to marry Meta." Faulkner could also talk about his work to Ben. After typing out pages of *Absalom, Absalom!* in an upstairs room of Ben's tiny rented Alpine château, Faulkner descended to the living room one day and told Ben, "It's a tortured story, and a torture to write it." But he had no trouble in expressing his feelings about Hollywood to both his lover and his friend. One afternoon when he descended after finishing his stint, he looked to see what Ben was reading. "Oh, Proust. *Swann's Way*," he said. "Swann! That pore misguided son of a bitch, and they call him a snob. I think he was just the opposite. Godamighty, what Odette did to him. To have crucified him would have brought him less hell, less anguish. In some ways Proust was lucky. He didn't ever have to contend with Hollywood for his bread and butter. I'd rather have spent my time in that corklined bedroom of his, asthma and all. Anytime."[13]

Some of the things Faulkner was able to say to Meta echoed the age-old cry of the man away from home, the man who was lonely and desperately in need of the solace of physical love. There was scant comfort in his promise to do what he could to seek his freedom. "I can't say what will happen or whether anything will happen," he told her. "If you had a grain of sense, you'd get shut of me right here and now, tell me to stay out of your life."[14] But she did not, as he surely hoped and perhaps expected. But she did wonder what was going to come of it, what would happen to her. There was one new possibility in her life. A tall, ungainly young Austrian pianist named Wolfgang Rebner had fallen in love with her, but she did not know how much of his love she could return. The answer depended on Bill Faulkner.

HE was home in plenty of time for Jill's birthday and his seventh wedding anniversary. He was not free to relax, however, for he had not finished typing and revising *Absalom, Absalom!*, though he must have been close to the end by now. His revised version of Chapter I had reached New York in early April. Hal Smith had apparently been sending sections of the novel to the printer as soon as they suited both editor and author. Criticism deriving from ignorance of Southern ways irritated

Faulkner, but he accepted a number of editorial cuts and simplified punctuation as well. Editor-author give-and-take went on frequently through most of the first half of the typescript. (When Smith commented, "I don't think one can wait for two and a half pages to find out what Henry (and not Bon) did," Faulkner granted the justice of his criticism, but when Smith wired him on June 3 to ask if they could put fifty pages of italics in Chapter V in roman type, Faulkner wired back NO.) Faulkner continued revising right to the end of the typescript. In the manuscript, Shreve's final speech had contained two references to Jim Bond, Charles Bon's feeble-minded grandson. Now Faulkner expanded these two references into six pages, visualizing Bond howling at the flames devouring the old Sutpen place.

Even after Faulkner had finished with the text, he continued to think about the book's complexity. He neatly lettered a chronology which began with Sutpen's birth in 1807 and concluded with the destruction of his house, dated as occurring in 1910. He wrote a genealogy that included seventeen characters with their vital statistics. Later he would type out the chronology and then add to it in pen the birth dates of four of the minor characters. He had this done by mid-May. A third reader's guide probably gave him more pleasure than either of the others. It was a map of Yoknapatawpha County. He drew the Tallahatchie at the north and the Yoknapatawpha at the south, bisecting the county vertically with John Sartoris' railroad. In the northwest corner, he wrote "Sutpen's Hundred, 12 mi." and balanced it to the southeast with Frenchman's Bend. He carefully identified twenty-seven places that figured in his fiction. He listed the county's area and population and then wrote "William Faulkner, Sole Owner & Proprietor." It cost his publisher an extra hundred dollars to print the map in two colors and tip it into the 6,000 copies of the first impression.[15] But it was worth it.

There was a special reason why this was going to be a beautifully made book. Late the previous year Bob Haas had broached the idea to Bennett Cerf that Random House buy Smith & Haas. On January 31, Random House announced that Smith and Haas would join the firm as partners. Bennett Cerf was delighted to have Faulkner at last: "we didn't think he'd *ever* be a commercial success," he remembered, "but he would be the greatest possible adornment to the Random House list." Cerf promised him a better deal. When the book came out, he would see what they could do.

Meanwhile, there were current money matters to deal with. *The American Mercury* had taken one version of the first chapter of the novel, but that wasn't enough. He told Goldman, "I seem to have got out of the habit of writing trash." Maybe he could copy something because "I can't seem to think of anything myself."[16] The financial pinch precipitated an action with effects he had not bargained for.

When the Memphis *Commercial Appeal* appeared on June 22, it carried an ad which also ran in the Oxford *Eagle* three days later. It read, "I will not be responsible for any debt incurred or bills made, or notes or checks signed by Mrs. William Faulkner or Mrs. Estelle Oldham Faulkner." It was signed by William Faulkner. He wrote Meta Carpenter that Estelle "had managed to find enough merchants whom I had not known to warn to run up or bring the total of bills up to about a thousand dollars, including some overstuffed furniture and a radio, the latter of which I had expressly forbidden to be brought into the house. So I have given myself (I have a small soul after all) a certain amount of sadistic pleasure in ejecting from the house pneumatic divans and Cab Calloways and so forth."[17] When Lem Oldham saw the ad he summoned his son-in-law to his second-floor office overlooking the square for a tongue-lashing. The next day reporters from Memphis appeared. *Time* magazine for July 6 reported, however, that Faulkner was found "helping his wife stage a birthday party for their three-year-old daughter, Jill. Denying any family ruckus, Author Faulkner explained: 'It's just a matter of protecting my credit until I can pay up my back debts.' " He canceled the scheduled reprintings of the ad.

No matter what had happened to his marriage, there was still his child. His love for her—intensified by the memory of the tiny lost baby—made him call her "the fat, pink pretty." He would draw pictures for her: a chicken, a goat, a mule—and a rear view of a large black pipe-smoking woman holding the hand of a small tousle-headed girl. Jill was growing up an outdoors child, like her father. She would often go on walks with Narcissus, whom she called Mammy Matewin. Her earliest memory was of looking up and seeing the underside of a horse and being pulled to safety by Mammy or her Pappy.

Faulkner could not bear the thought of another separation coming so soon. It was decided that they would be in California with him. He went out there first to look for housing. Then, on July 15, they set out, Jack Oliver driving a new Ford phaeton, with Narcissus sitting beside him. Jill's memory of that trip would be of sitting in the back seat with her mother, singing "Oh! Susanna" through the deserts and over the mountains all the way to California.

It was not easy to find a suitable place, but after a week of living in a hotel they found a house at 620 El Cerco, Huntington Palisades, just north of Santa Monica and six miles from the studio. They were a half-mile up from the ocean in a two-story rambling house of brown stone with a peaked shingled roof that gave it an oddly manorial appearance. Faulkner often took Jill down to the beach, where she would splash in her red bathing suit and he would try his own free-style crawl when he got beyond the breakers. But most of the time she played in their spacious backyard, her white bulldog lying on the sun-warmed flagstones. They had barely settled into the new quarters when the world intruded with two events, one unexpected and the other inevitable. On August 6 the papers reported the crash of a Chicago & Southern Airlines plane. The two pilots and six passengers of the *City of Memphis* had died in an emergency landing in the fog at St. Louis. One of the passengers had been on his way to Chicago to fly a new airplane back to Memphis. It was Vernon Omlie. Vernon's ghost summoned up another: Dean Faulkner in his flying helmet and goggles, squinting against the sun. Faulkner's memory was with his brother almost as much as that other lost pilot, John Sartoris, remained in the memory of Bayard.

If there were no ghosts when he went back to the Writers' Building, there was certainly some sense of *déjà vu*. It was another picture for Wallace Beery, called *The Last Slaver*, co-starring Warner Baxter and Mickey Rooney. His job was to supply "additional original dialogue" for the screenplay written by Lillian Hellman and Gladys Lehmann.[18] Through the hot summer he would come home from the studio fuming. By early September he was at work on *Splinter Fleet*. Zanuck had assigned Kathryn Scola to the picture to "keep an eye on the story line" while Faulkner worked on dialogue. She found him courteous, taciturn, and often morose. After he had read the treatment he told her that Gene Markey, the producer "told me to follow the story line, but I can't find the story line." Nonetheless, he did the best he could. "It was good Faulknerian dialogue," Markey remembered, "but it had nothing whatever to do with our story." He kept turning in his pages punctually, but sometimes the dialogue related more to aerial than naval warfare, as though Faulkner were caught in some dreamlike flashback, writing *War Birds* all over again for Howard Hawks. None of his work would survive when the picture was released two years later as *Submarine Patrol*.

Things were scarcely better at home than at the studio. Occasionally they might set off on an outing. One day he and Estelle and Jill got into the Ford with Narcissus, and Jack Oliver drove them south. At Tijuana they crossed into Mexico. Faulkner suggested to Jack that he park the car and then walk around to see the sights. Jack pulled over and parked but made no move to leave the car. "Mr. Bill," he said, "I've got the weak trembles. It's the first time I've ever set foot in a foreign country." Faulkner struggled to suppress his laughter. "The weak trembles" passed into the family vocabulary. But there was much more tension and anger in the family than laughter.

WHEN Faulkner first arrived in California in July, he had spent time with Meta. She was deeply disquieted at the prospect of Estelle's being there with him. "I kissed him and put up a brave Irene Dunne–Ann Harding face," Meta would write. "Hollywood movies of the 1930's were lessons in how to be noble and sacrificial." But once, at parting, when she lost patience and asked how long she had to wait for him to be free, he stared, then silently turned and left.[19] She had tantalizing glimpses of his other life. Once when Estelle was drinking, Meta spent a glorious day at the beach with him and Jill. When Estelle was ill again, Faulkner would call Meta, and she would take Jill to the park for a few hours. She loved the child and imagined herself as her mother. Once when there were visitors from Oxford, Faulkner asked her to join them for dinner, at the house, as Ben Wasson's date. Later she would regret what she came to think of as an invasion of Estelle Faulkner's home. She could eat almost nothing, but somehow she carried it off, while Faulkner showed not the slightest flicker of an expression that would have given them away. At the door, Estelle told Meta she hoped they would see much of each other and become friends. Meta thought her a "pale, sad, wasted creature" and found that she no longer hated her.[20]

Early the next morning Wasson's telephone rang. "You didn't fool me for a second, you and Billy," Estelle told him, furious. "I know that the person you brought to my house last night is Billy's girl out here and not your girl at all!" Later Faulkner telephoned to apologize for the call. "Ain't there something you can do to get her off my back?" he asked. "Get her a lover, anything, so she'll leave me alone."[21]

Meta Carpenter was now living her own version of *Back Street*, sleeping with her lover whenever they could manage it and at other times seeing him escorting his wife. At such times she did hate her, no matter how much she might tell herself she felt sorry for Estelle. Once he even asked her to invite Estelle and himself to a party she gave at the Studio Club. She did, and took Estelle on a tour of the place, through rooms where she and Faulkner had spent time together. New stresses began to appear in her own relationship with Faulkner, and some of them made her more aware of a kind of hollowness at the core. She realized more than ever that she knew more about him from his letters than from any words he spoke to her. Paradoxically, when he returned to her, "I was always disconcerted by the stoppage of communication. The great carapace was impenetrable, even in our most intimate moments, but at a distance there were soft areas."[22] He was concerned, though, over her relationship with Wolfgang Rebner, who would return soon from a long tour. One day when Faulkner appeared, she knew that there had been a violent argument at home. "He confided only what he wanted me to know of the clash between them," she recalled, but she was sure that he had finally opened the subject of divorce.[23] His answers to her questions convinced her that Estelle would fight for custody of Jill. Moreover, he felt that the financial penalties would be crushing. Later he told Meta that he had tried further persuasion, but that he had given up. Estelle had asked for his promise that he would stop seeing Meta, but he had refused. There was no hope of freedom for him for a long time.

Early in their stay Estelle and he had made an effort to be social. Clark Gable occasionally dropped in for a drink. He didn't have much to say, but he and Faulkner got along well and still hunted together. Joel Sayre remembered sitting in the large candlelit living room, having a drink with his host while Estelle sat at the piano in a long-sleeved gown. He remembered her playing "Just a Song at Twilight." Sometimes Sayre would bring his wife. The Ronald Colmans, Estelle's favorites, would come for dinner. But then things slid into blackouts, quarrels, and chaos. One morning when Faulkner arrived at the studio, David Hempstead noticed a mark in the middle of his forehead. Joel thought he saw lumps on his face.

"Bill," he said, "what happened?"

"I was just sitting there, reading *Time* magazine," Faulkner told him, "when Estelle came at me with a croquet mallet."

That September, Meta received her first marriage proposal from Rebner, and she began drawing closer to him though she was still sleeping with Faulkner. Finally she told Faulkner that it must stop. A week later he importuned her so violently that she appealed to her Aunt Ione to come and stay with her as her "protector" until her marriage to Rebner. Two days before the wedding, just minutes after her bridegroom-to-be had kissed her goodnight at midnight, Faulkner appeared, his haggard face disfigured by bloody scratches. It was the violent climax to a quarrel with Estelle over her, said Faulkner. They had been at a cocktail party at Joel Sayre's house. After a time Mrs. Sayre had helped Estelle to an upstairs room, where she lay down. Sayre later suggested that Faulkner take her home and then come back to relax and enjoy himself. When he did, Sayre saw the scratches on his face. Now, sitting on Meta's couch, he told her he wished her every happiness. But he would see her again. "You don't think I'm going to let you out of my life?" he said.[24]

ONCE again, there was work he could turn to. When he finished reading the galley proofs of *Absalom, Absalom!* he wrote Morty Goldman. "I am going to undertake to sell this book myself to the pictures," he told him. "I am going to ask one hundred thousand dollars for it or nothing, as I do not need to sell it now since I have a job."[25] By the time he placed a set of proofs on Nunnally Johnson's desk, he had cut his asking price in half. His terse note provided a little additional information. "It's about miscegenation," he wrote. It was to no avail. Nineteen hundred and thirty-six was not the year for miscegenation in motion pictures.

Random House sent the sheets for him to sign for a limited edition of 300 copies. He did not return them. When one of Meta's friends wrote her that Faulkner had been hospitalized for drinking, she knew it was from grief. Finally, on October 8, he informed New York that he had the flu but would sign the pages as quickly as possible. He kept back a few sheets spoiled by shaky writing. Another was quite legible, Number 1 of the 300, "inscribed for Meta Carpenter, wherever she may be." He also inscribed a set of galleys to her.[26]

Relieved to receive the pages, Bennett Cerf wrote him that the novel was "the greatest thing you have ever turned out." Nearly half a century later one student of American literature would call the novel "perhaps his supreme story of the human heart in conflict with itself."[27] To another, the treatment of Quentin Compson's anguish, first in *The Sound and the Fury* and now in *Absalom, Absalom!*, would represent "the high point in twentieth century American literature."[28] On October 26, with its unhappy and exhausted author still assigned to *Splinter Fleet*, *Absalom, Absalom!* was published, bearing on its jacket the assertion that it was Faulkner's most important and ambitious contribution to American literature.

41

. . . his very body was an empty hall echoing with sonorous defeated names; he was not a being, an entity, he was a commonwealth. He was a barracks filled with stubborn back-looking ghosts still recovering . . . from the fever which had cured the disease. . . .

—*Absalom, Absalom!* (12)

To Isabel Paterson, in the New York *Herald Tribune*, he was a Manichean and a Southern Orestes. To William Troy, in *The Nation*, he was a lyric poet. To Clifton Fadiman, in what was to became a notorious review in *The New Yorker*, William Faulkner was the author of "The most consistently boring novel by a reputable writer to come my way during the last decade." *Time*'s reviewer concurred on the novel's unreadability but at the same time called it "in some respects" his "most impressive novel."[1] In the South, *Absalom, Absalom!* received far less attention than *Pylon* had. If Faulkner had been disappointed at the failure of a magazine to serialize it or a studio to buy it, this reception in the press must have been close to devastating. In spite of the assertion in the book's flap copy that this was his greatest contribution to American literature, some of the people at Random House might have wondered just how much prestige William Faulkner was going to bring to their list, Bennett Cerf to the contrary notwithstanding. By mid-November a second and then a third printing had pushed the number of copies up over 10,000, but Faulkner must have been glad he was still on salary, even if for *Splinter Fleet*. But then, after ten days of no pages, he was taken off the payroll.

December must have drifted by in a kind of haze. Even if he had not felt like following his native custom of celebrating the holidays, the news from home could have tempted him back to the glass. General Stone had died of a heart attack at the hunting lodge near Batesville. Less than a month later his son, Jim, was dead of the same cause at the same place. Now approaching forty himself, Faulkner was becoming even more keenly aware of mortality. Near the end of the month, however, he wrote Goldman to say that he had "no stuff now, but am going to write some more short stories soon, also another novel in my bean."[2]

He broached another idea in a letter to Cerf on the same day. "I have a series of six stories about a white boy and a negro boy during the civil war," he wrote. "What do you think about getting them out as a book?"[3] The *Post* had published "The Unvanquished" in November and "Vendée" the next month. With the earlier four, they would form the greater part of the new book. He had consistently referred to these stories as pot-boilers, or trash. This way he could transform them from ephemeral magazine stories into a unified work that might last. The letter crossed two in the mail from Random House, both dated December 29.

One was from Hal Smith. He had resigned from Random House. He was absent-minded and unpredictable. His style was not their style, and he would be happier in another branch of publishing. But there were pangs. "I do not have to tell you," he wrote Faulkner, "what publishing your books has meant to me through all these years . . . or how important for the future and for literature your work has always seemed to me." Faulkner would continue to see him from time to time, but another link with the past was now dissolved. The other letter came from Robert Haas. Whereas Smith was outgoing and debonair, Haas was quiet and con-templative. A Yale man who had won the D.S.C. as an infantry captain, he had a thin aesthetic face and a manner that made one visitor think of a Florentine nobleman. To Evelyn Harter, Haas was a man of "absolute integrity and honesty."[4] He assured Faulkner that he and Bennett Cerf and Donald Klopfer were "among the most enthusiastic admirers of your work." Faulkner liked him, and he would come to rely increasingly upon his help and understanding.

WHATEVER work Faulkner got done on the Bayard and Ringo stories represented his only creative efforts in the early months of 1937. In late February he went back on the studio payroll, "Unassigned." On March 9 he began work on a film that would be called *Dance Hall*, but two days later he was once more listed as "Unassigned." Some of his energy went into moving from Huntington Palisades to a more modest but more con-venient house at 129 North Le Doux in Beverly Hills, a twelve-minute drive from the studio. He must have settled in there by the time he began a twelve-week assignment on Walter D. Edmonds' popular *Drums Along the Mohawk*.

Finding Edmonds' big novel of frontier life more congenial than *Splinter Fleet* or *Dance Hall*, he completed a 26-page treatment in three days. Once again Julie Davies was his typist. Bill Hawks told her that Faulkner's contract specified that he would be terminated if he did any drinking on the lot. If she ever noticed any warning signs, she was to call Hawks immediately. One day she found an unopened bottle of Courvoisier in his lower left-hand desk drawer. So it remained. Then, one mid-April day as she returned to her desk after lunch, she heard the unmistakable pop of a cork. When she heard the sound again five minutes later, she slipped out and called Hawks. When he arrived, he went into Faulkner's office and closed the door. Not long afterward, Hawks and Faulkner made a careful exit from the bungalow and the lot. On April 14 a pink slip went into the record with the notation "One week off for illness." One day Bill Spratling appeared unexpectedly and Estelle invited him to stay for dinner. After a few drinks Faulkner passed out. Spratling could see that they were miserable, and later Estelle showed him bruises on her arms. Spratling visited Faulkner the next day, in the Good Samaritan Hospital. By the time he was discharged and able to resume work, it was late April. The one week of illness had stretched into two— without pay.

But somehow, during the first half of the year 1937, he had managed to do most of the revisions of the stories for the new book. Beginning with "Ambuscade," he had thickened the texture of the prose at the same time that he tidied up, replacing pronouns with proper names and adding clarifying phrases. He filled in the portrait of Colonel John Sartoris. What Faulkner had sketched early in *Flags in the Dust* now received fuller treatment. And if he drew on imagination, he also drew on fact— some of the books in Colonel John Sartoris' office duplicated some of Colonel J. W. T. Falkner's: complete sets of Scott, Cooper, and Dumas. To "Retreat" he added comic material plus important passages about Uncle Buck and Uncle Buddy McCaslin. And another passage enlarged on one of the book's major concerns: the attributes of childhood and the process by which a child grows and matures. He expanded "Raid," as the boys saw more of the war's devastation and heard about the last Confederate locomotive of the ruined railroad, pursued by a Federal engine so that it was "like a meeting between two iron knights of the old time. . . ."[5] The seven-page recital of this heroism would contrast with the grim realities of combat and death that would mark their initiation from childhood into adulthood. He devised a new title for "The Unvanquished," calling it "Riposte in Tertio," a rather arcane reference to a fencing stroke so unsportsmanlike and deadly that it was outlawed before the sixteenth century.[6] The discarded title would become the name of the book. Only a few minor additions were made to "Vendée." A few passages in "Skirmish at Sartoris" served briefly to recapitulate Drusilla's traumatic loss of both fiancé and father early in the war. With these changes made, Faulkner was ready to send his typescript to New York.

Work dragged along at the studio, the scriptwriting solitude broken by an occasional story conference. Much later a younger writer asked Faulkner, "How did you ever stand those story conferences?" Faulkner answered, "I just kept telling myself, 'They're gonna pay me Saturday, they're gonna pay me Saturday.' " Soon there was little more for him at home than at the studio. Cho-Cho had married a handsome boy named Claude Selby, and they were expecting a baby in September. Cho-Cho wanted her mother back with her, and Estelle had had more than enough of California. So in late May she took Jill with her and returned to Mississippi. "I go home to that empty house in the afternoons," Faulkner wrote Cho-Cho, "and find her little toys scattered about . . . and I turn around and get out of there fast. . . ." The letter ended with a plea: "take care of my little baby for me, Sister. . . . I know I dont even have to ask this, I just need to repeat, because she is little and helpless and wants little save to be happy and loved and looked after, 'Take care of my little baby.' "⁷

THEN, for a brief time in late June, it was less lonely. Still teaching French at Princeton, Maurice Coindreau had resolved to undertake a French translation of *The Sound and the Fury*. Faulkner had been pleased enough with his translation of *As I Lay Dying* to wish him luck and offer "to draw up a chronology and genealogy and explanation, etc. if you need it, or anything else."⁸ Now, his first draft completed, Coindreau accepted Faulkner's invitation to stay with him so they could clear up some questions. "In the evening, after dinner, I would bombard Faulkner with questions," Coindreau remembered. Faulkner was drinking constantly, but to Coindreau he seemed unaffected by it. He "seemed to know *The Sound and the Fury* by heart, referring me to such-and-such a paragraph, to such-and-such a page, to find the key to some highly enigmatic obscurity." Only one passage baffled him. "I have absolutely no idea what I meant," he confessed.⁹

On Friday, June 25, the day before the week's visit ended, Narcissus served what Coindreau called "*un dîner planteureux*," Southern home cooking which did not strike Ben Wasson, one of the five guests, as particularly well prepared. Afterward, Faulkner offered to read. "This is a very original story," he told them. "It was written by a boy who has talent. I'm the hero, and I find it very comic." Coindreau listened intently. When Faulkner finished, twenty-five minutes later, there was silence.

"You haven't found it amusing?" he asked.

"Not particularly," one admitted.

"I find it too puzzling, too overwritten," said another.

Coindreau observed "*une neutralité respectueuse*." He had been working with Faulknerian prose long enough to recognize what he thought were certain "traps" Faulkner loved to set for his readers. What they had heard was "Afternoon of a Cow," and Coindreau was not surprised when Faulkner revealed himself as "*l'auteur de cette tragédie pastorale*." But Faulkner went on with the game, praising Ernest V. Trueblood but concluding, "since you didn't seem to find him funny, maybe I'll have to dispense with his services in the future." The next morning, as Coindreau was closing his suitcase, Faulkner handed him an inscribed first edition of *Absalom, Absalom!* and a carbon copy of the story, a *"souvenir de ce brave Trueblood."*[10]

Though he had gone off *Drums Along the Mohawk* and had been carried by the studio for the last ten days as "Unassigned," he still reported there each day. He wrote Estelle that he would hear in two weeks whether the studio would exercise its option and renew his contract. "I've had such nice letters from Rowan Oak," he told her, "that I have stopped worrying and now I can concentrate on just missing everybody."[11] He was also able to concentrate on finishing *The Unvanquished*. It had become apparent that the book needed one more story, one that would provide more density and resonance than "Skirmish at Sartoris," with its almost conventional happy ending, could supply. So Faulkner wrote "An Odor of Verbena" (at 12,500 words, the longest of the seven) to complete what "Ambuscade" had begun. He carried the action further into the period of the Reconstruction, as Bayard Sartoris is summoned home from his legal studies at the university to avenge the death of his father, dead at the hand of his business rival Ben Redmond. The parallels to events in Colonel William C. Falkner's life are clear: his war service, his death at the hands of Richard J. Thurmond. Bayard and Ringo now ride together as Henry Sutpen and Charles Bon had done, and like Bon, Bayard faces the prospect of violent death.

Questions of morality and ethics stated or implied in the previous stories are interwoven into the climactic action. Constituting herself a priestess of vengeance, Drusilla is ready to use even sexual power to move Bayard to fulfill her wishes. She praises Sartoris' dream: to benefit many, whereas Sutpen had been concerned only to benefit himself. Unlike her, the victim himself had realized how his means had contaminated the ends. "I have accomplished my aim," he had said, "and now I shall do a little moral housecleaning. I am tired of killing men, no matter what the necessity nor the end." (266) Torn like Henry Sutpen, ambivalent like Quentin Compson, Bayard Sartoris finds the courage to act and the strength to act rightly. Keenly conscious of the ritual vengeance expected of him, he tells his surrogate mother, Aunt Jenny Du Pre, "You see, I want to be thought well of." A generation closer than Quentin to the men of a heroic mold, sustained by love the younger man did not know, he is able to walk unarmed to face his father's murderer, and by sheer courage and moral force not only to stand while the other fires at him (to satisfy *his* code) and deliberately misses, but then to gain the triumph as Redmond flees his office and leaves Jefferson forever. At the end there is even a tribute from the departed Drusilla: a symbolic sprig of verbena, to her "the only scent you could smell above the smell of horses and courage. . . ." (253) It is not only an accolade to him but "an accolade of optimism too," Faulkner would later say, "a promise of renewal for next year."[12] This was one of the few works in which Faulkner would reverse his usual juxtaposition of past and present to the disadvantage of the present. Here, for the moment at least, the new code had prevailed, Christian non-violence over the revenge code of the Old Testament.

ON July 21, Faulkner wrote Estelle a short, terse letter. "Contract not taken up and renewed. Mammy and I will be home sometime between Aug 22–Sept 1, if we live and nothing happens."[13] A week later he wrote that he hoped to start home the week beginning August 15: "It's hot here and I dont feel very good, but I think it's mostly being tired of movies, worn out with them."[14] It was probably about this time that Jack Falkner received a call in El Paso. His brother had not been to the studio for several days. Some friends, Hempstead and Hawks, would try to check on him, but they were understandably not prepared to see him through a prolonged bout. One of them must have feared such a problem now.

When Jack arrived he could see that Faulkner was well into the cycle and that it would not end "until he himself decided that he had drunk enough for the time being." With Jack Oliver at the wheel, they drove out into the countryside. "Nobody would live in Hollywood," Faulkner told Jack irascibly, "except to get what money they could out of it." A few days later he decided to go back to work. He took Jack with him to the studio, where they had lunch in the commissary and then went to see some pictures being shot. Later Jack rented a four-place Fairchild and took his brother for a ride. When Jack asked him if he could pick out his house from the air, Faulkner replied that it was one among thousands and that "he found it practically impossible to distinguish even when driving along the street right in front of it."[15]

Ben Wasson was ready to go back to Mississippi, and if it had not been for his company, Faulkner would have made the trip alone. Narcissus McEwen and Jack Oliver had both decided they preferred living in California to the old life in Mississippi. Faulkner would be returning after many months of work that had been hard but profitable. Since January 1 he had earned $21,650. There was no immediate prospect of earnings like those from Twentieth Century-Fox, but he would be back home again, back at Rowan Oak. There he could see The Unvanquished through his end of the editorial process and get to work on the new novel he had mentioned to Morty Goldman. With a sense of relief he turned the Ford eastward toward home.

Faulkner spoke hardly at all as they left the city and drove past farms and ranches. When they reached the state line he stopped the car and gazed at the desert scene ahead of them. "Maybe on the Arizona part they might put up a sign saying 'Science Fiction Country,' " he said. "On the California side I'd suggest a sign to read: 'Abandon hope, all ye who enter here,' or however Dante said it. Well, it's behind me for a while, anyhow."[16] Before he put the car in motion again he took a bottle of bourbon from the glove compartment, the first of many he would consume on the trip. By the next day the monotony and heat and his persistent sorrow began to take their toll. Looking at his face, Ben thought it was wet with tears as well as sweat. Faulkner kept the bottle there on the seat beside him as they drove on past the mountains and sand hills, the cactus and tumbleweed. One day they passed a group of blank-faced Indians sitting by the highway. Faulkner mused on their griefs. "This was theirs," he said to Ben, "all of it. This whole country. We took it from them and shoved them off onto reservations. I reckon it's bad enough the way we treat the black folks. But they're like children and need looking after, expect to be looked after. Oh, hell, I don't know any answers for other people. I can't take care of my own problems."[17]

They drove on through the desert toward the Delta and the blue hills of Mississippi.

42

"He's free. He's done served his time out. . . ."

. . . he became quite still and looked about . . . temporarily lost in peace and hope. . . . and let his blank unseeing gaze go on and on unhampered. . . .

—*The Wild Palms* (80, 261, 263)

As if to greet him on his return home that August of 1937, there were two pieces within a week in the *Eagle* attesting to his growing fame and status as an unwilling tourist attraction. Settling back into the routine at Rowan Oak after thirteen months away, he found that he had no time to relax before coping with the continuous demands of domestic life. W. C. Bryant had been urging him for some time to buy four lots adjacent to his property which encompassed Bailey's Woods. He arranged for a survey. In recent years perfect strangers had begun the practice of driving up the bumpy rutted drive to observe the author of *Sanctuary* having a drink on the shaded east gallery in the cool of the day. Estelle had arranged for a wall to screen that area off, but a fierce summer storm had sent an oak crashing down, crumbling several courses of brick. Faulkner had it tidied up and began to train ivy to cover it.

Sometimes he would have to shift from the role of friend and companion to that of stepfather and disciplinarian. The proud possessor of a .22 rifle, Malcolm (now called Buddy or Mac) one day fired at a hawk in her nest high in a sycamore. When he proudly brought his trophy home, Faulkner made him go back and climb the tree to bring down the motherless baby hawks and wring their necks. Then he switched him with a riding crop and took the rifle away for six weeks. Ella Somerville was at some point distressed enough to tell a friend that Malcolm Franklin had come to her crying because his stepfather had beaten him cruelly. But Estelle raised no objection to his disciplining the children, and Mac would later say that any good attributes he possessed were due to his stepfather's crop and his gentleness. If there was no conflict in this area, there was stress in others, even if it was damped down most of the time in silence and avoidance.

On September 25 he would be forty. At some time prior to this birthday he wrote a six-page manuscript called "Wild Palms" which began with a forty-five-year-old doctor. The scene suggested Pascagoula, and there were a young man and woman living at the beach who were played off against the neighboring doctor and his gorgonlike wife. The couple were not honeymooners, however, but clearly tragic lovers. Suspense derived from the doctor's efforts to fathom the nature of her illness. A late night call for help by the man, a painter named Harry, reveals some of the answers but also leads the doctor to the brink of acknowledging a situation he cannot confront: the emptiness of his marriage and his life. The woman is hemorrhaging, and though the text did not make it explicit, the doctor apparently thinks it could be the result of an abortion. A parsimonious man, he even offers Harry money so the two can leave, not just so they can seek hospital treatment and flee if necessary, but also to get their passion and tragedy out of his life, to be no longer a reminder of its barrenness.

When Faulkner typed the story in twenty-two pages, he divided it into three numbered parts and expanded it throughout, chiefly in the third part. He named the woman Charlotte. He also enlarged upon the doctor's perceptions, especially the ambivalence and anxiety he feels: wanting to know why she behaves as she does yet dreading the revelation. "*Because I am at the wrong age for this* he thought." If he were twenty-five, he would not envy Harry because his own turn might still come. If he were sixty-five, it would do him no good to envy him "*because he has proof on the body of passion and of life that he is not dead. But I am now forty-five and I did not think that I had deserved this.*"[1]

If Faulkner sent the story out, no editor published it. But he did not give up on it. He took a new manuscript sheet with the printed margins, wrote "*The Wild Palms*" at the top and the numeral I below it. In the left-hand margin he wrote "Sept. 15, '37," as if beginning an extended work, the kind of notation he had made on other manuscripts. As he began, he followed the short story closely.[2] But he was ready for a break, for a return to New York, which he had not seen in nearly two years. As far as adult companionship went, Oxford must have seemed empty to him. When he had been in Hollywood, Phil Stone had sent him a manuscript of Emily's. Faulkner wrote back that she had a real story to tell but that she should burn the manuscript and start over, since she seemed obsessed with writing for its own sake rather than telling a story. In his reply, Stone said he would not go into detail because they were so much at odds about literary practice that he felt the truth was exactly the opposite of what Faulkner had said. And so Faulkner saw little or nothing of Stone. In New York he had friends to see, and if he needed an excuse, there was the matter of the contract for the new novel he had mentioned to Goldman.

Louise Bonino was still at Random House, and Jim Devine was still in New York. He was glad to see both of them again, as well as Haas and Cerf and Klopfer. He met a new member of the firm, a short, sad-looking, gentle-eyed man named Saxe Commins. Trained as a dentist, Commins had found that career unsatisfying. He had a strong literary bent, and after he performed a number of services over an extended period for one of his patients, Eugene O'Neill, the playwright had obtained an editorship for him with his publisher, Horace Liveright. Commins had moved on, after the failure of Boni & Liveright, to edit some of the works of Sherwood Anderson, Robinson Jeffers, and Theodore Dreiser. He had admired Faulkner's writing from the time he had read *Mosquitoes*, and he happily made room in his third-floor office for him to work on *The Unvanquished*. With Bob Haas, Faulkner went over financial arrangements, including a $1,000 advance on the next novel.

As with his other visits to the city, the pace of Faulkner's social activities quickly accelerated. He resumed his friendship with Hal Smith, who had joined *The Saturday Review of Literature*, and he saw a good deal of Jim Devine. The Haases entertained him and so did Cerf. He had received a letter from Meta, written a month after she and her husband had returned from an extended stay in Europe. Wolfgang Rebner's family had suffered at the hands of the Nazis in Germany, and he was now meeting discouragement in his continued efforts to make a career as a concert pianist in America. But he hoped his family's contacts would help him in New York. Meta's letter brought Faulkner up to date. She hoped he would save a day for them when he was next in New York. "Wolfi is anxious to meet you—he has read some of your books—and I long, dear friend, to see you again."[3]

When he telephoned her, his "voice, soft with wonder and love, still had the power to instantly pull me into it."[4] When they met for coffee, she was delighted to see that the two men apparently got along together. Puppeteer Bil Baird and his wife, Cora, entertained them at a party with Jim Devine, Corey Ford, and other friends. Baird made pen-and-ink drawings with wash coloring, each bearing a guest's name and a fanciful bawdy scene from a Faulkner novel. Faulkner went to hear Wolfgang Rebner practice. He went to lunch with him, and another time they were joined by architect Buckminster Fuller, who took them to his office and showed them his design for the all-metal prefabricated Dymaxion house. A genius whose range extended from architecture across a whole spectrum of disciplines, Fuller was especially receptive to the unusual when he saw it in others. "Geniuses remain children in that they retain all of their original SUPER-sensitivity," he later reflected. "They can also get hurt very easily. Often their hurt drives them instinctively to do beautiful work to preoccupy themselves—with the intense imaginative capabilities of children. But, there are times when the work is completed and they have nothing to block the hurt. I felt that Faulkner had been deeply hurt—probably in some love affair. I felt that he had something that kept hurting him—that drove him to write very, very beautifully to overcome the pain, not addressing his own hurt directly but simply to override it." His feelings were very clear about Faulkner: "I considered him to be a beautiful loner."[5]

Though he still disliked literary cocktail parties, he went to one of them, where people soon clustered around him. He was observed by another writer, who avoided him. It was Sherwood Anderson. Later Faulkner made his way over to him. "He took hold of my coat sleeve and pulled me aside," Anderson recalled. "He grinned. 'Sherwood, what the hell is the matter with you? Do you think I am also a Hemy,' he asked."[6] Faulkner remembered how he felt: "again there was that moment when he appeared taller, bigger than anything he ever wrote. . . . I knew that I had seen . . . a giant . . . even if he did make but the two or perhaps three gestures commensurate with gianthood."[7]

Buckminster Fuller had seen the melancholy beneath the exterior that so often seemed impassive. Wolfgang Rebner told Meta, after meeting Faulkner for the first time, that he thought he had been drinking steadily and for some time. As Faulkner's visit lengthened into November, Estelle began to worry. He did not answer the telephone or respond to messages. Morty Goldman could not reach him either, and he failed to appear for interviews. Jim Devine knew that Faulkner had been drinking heavily when he had last seen him a few days before. When Jim got the hotel manager to open his door, they found Faulkner face down on the floor, clad only in shorts, the cold November wind sweeping through the open window. In the small of his back, on the left side, was a third-degree burn the size of the palm of a hand. They lifted Faulkner onto the bed and Devine sent for a doctor. Faulkner had regained consciousness by the time the doctor arrived. Faulkner said that he had been sitting in the bathroom when he had fallen against a steam pipe. The doctor treated the burn and prescribed paraldehyde to carry him through the alcohol withdrawal. "Why do you do this?" he asked his famous patient. Debilitated from the drinking and wincing from the pain, Faulkner looked at him with that hooded glance, his jaw outthrust. "Because I like to," he said with a grimace. When the doctor left, Faulkner took the evil-smelling medicine in exchange for a drink. When he fell asleep, Devine left.

Meta and Wolfgang Rebner arrived and waited in the lobby nearly an hour for Faulkner to appear and take them to dinner. Finally they, too, gained admittance to his room and wakened him. He told her that he had started drinking that morning because he had been thinking of seeing her that night, belonging to someone else. After she sponged his face they left.

Devine returned the next day and got Faulkner to take a thick milk-shake enriched with two eggs in exchange for another drink. Besides his general debility and a cold, his nerves were on edge from the withdrawal process, and Devine wanted to distract him. When he asked whom he would like to see, Faulkner answered, "Joel Sayre or Sherwood Anderson." Before long Anderson arrived. Sitting at the bedside, he began talking in his quiet, easy way. What the doctor could not understand, this other storyteller could. He was warm and solicitous. He made no mention of his one-time protégé's illness; he was just visiting.

As soon as Faulkner recovered sufficiently, he invited Meta and Wolfgang to dinner in his room. Clad only in white shorts, he served the soup course. But Meta could see that he was in agony, and she and her husband decided to leave. She met him once more before he departed for home. Watching the swans from a Central Park bench, he offered her money to tide them over this difficult time. She declined with gratitude. She asked him if things were better at home, and he told her that a kind of truce existed. She told him that she loved her husband and his world, the life of music that she now had with him. But when he took her hand, she would remember, "a bolt of his great male energy coursed through me." Then he told her, "one of my characters has said, 'Between grief and nothing I will take grief.' "[8]

BOB HAAS had asked Jim Devine to make the return trip with Faulkner, and so they boarded the train for Memphis. Estelle met them there. On November 10, Devine wrote Haas from Oxford that Faulkner had not needed sedatives or liquor on the trip. But Faulkner's doctor "has been cutting off the dead tissue and later intends to graft on some skin. As a result, Bill has been in a very nervous state, but I don't think it will last long." It was a bleak November, sunless and cold, with gusty winds. When the furnace went out, they kept the fireplace blazing, and Devine read to his friend there in the library at Rowan Oak. When Devine finished "Carcassonne" he turned to Faulkner and asked, "What does it mean?" Curtly Faulkner answered, "It means anything you want it to mean." He added defensively that he had read a lot in the Bible and Shakespeare that he didn't understand. Later Devine managed to persuade him to sit for an interview on November 17 with a university student named Harold Burson. Faulkner told him that *The Unvanquished* would appear in February but that his best novel was "yet to be written." He was working on one now, he told Burson, and however long it took, he would stay at Rowan Oak until it was completed.[9]

He resumed work on *The Wild Palms* without missing a beat. Before going to New York he had left the manuscript on page 6 with a line ending with the syllable "ar-". Now he wrote in the left-hand margin "Nov 23, '37" and began the new line with "chaic." He was describing the doctor's nightshirt as he roused from his bed to answer Harry's call for help.[10] What had begun as a short story about the impact of passion on a provincial Baptist doctor was becoming a novel about tragic lovers.

On November 29, with Devine back in New York, Faulkner returned the contract for the novel to Haas. He thought he would be able to send it in by May 1, "though I cant give my word as to this, not having any great degree of peace in which to write."[11] Thematic elements in the novel would reflect this lack of peace, and it would be suggested on a symbolic level by a recurring image: "the palm fronds clashing with their wild dry bitter sound against the bright glitter of the water. . . ."[12] It was not hard for him to project the pain his principals felt. Not only did he still feel twinges in his back, but he would later declare that he wrote the book "to stave off what I thought was heart-break. . . ."[13]

As his novel grew, he fleshed out the characters. Now Charlotte demonstrated a kind of harsh masculinity that suggested Drusilla Sartoris, and her appearance recalled Helen Baird: a "dark-haired woman with queer hard yellow eyes in a face whose skin was drawn thin over prominent cheekbones and a heavy jaw. . . ." (5) The emotions she provokes in her lover, as their doomed affair moves toward its conclusion, must have been like some of those Faulkner felt when he could no longer have Meta Carpenter on his terms. But to one student of his life, "Faulkner had the novel in mind before he met Meta and was basing it on recollections of his frustrated love for Helen."[14] He was still in touch with her, if at lengthy intervals. He had first met Helen Baird in Pascagoula, and it was in such a coastal town that the novel began, with Charlotte Rittenmeyer hemorrhaging and intermittently delirious as Harry Wilbourne, her lover, seeks aid from the doctor who is their neighbor and landlord. Four days before Christmas, Faulkner wrote Haas, "The novel is coming pretty well; I found less trouble than I anticipated in getting back into the habit of writing, though I find that at forty I dont write quite as fast as I used to."[15] One of the alterations he made as he worked from the short-story material was to change the name of Martin, the doctor's real estate agent, to Cofer. The latter might be the name of a childhood friend, but the former was the name of Helen Baird's aunt, to whom he had confided his love in Pascagoula.

IT was a quiet Christmas that year. Claude Selby had left his wife and baby—born September 22 and named Victoria—and Faulkner did all he could to help Cho-Cho through the bitter winter. He gave her typing to do, read to her from Keats and *A Shropshire Lad*, and at night he did crossword puzzles with her. Later she would say, simply, "He kept me alive." And when her father had invited her to stay with him in Shanghai, Faulkner had encouraged her to go. He played with Jill and discussed Darwin with Mac, who had now begun reading in biology and anthropology under the spur of his stepfather's interest. By the big Christmas tree they read their cards and exchanged their presents. Then it was the new year.

He rejected the advice that he undergo skin grafting because he didn't want to be laid up during quail-shooting season and he didn't want to break his rhythm in the writing. So he sat at the small table in the library, his words punctuated by the twinges from the still-healing wound that would leave a large scar he would bear for the rest of his life. When he reached the end of the first section, he later said, "I realized suddenly that something was missing, it needed emphasis, something to lift it like counterpoint in music. So I wrote on the 'Old Man' story until 'The Wild Palms' story rose back to pitch." He would use this strategy for the rest of the book. When he felt that the main story would begin "to sag," he "raised it to pitch again with another section of its antithesis, which is the story of a man who got his love and spent the rest of the book fleeing from it, even to the extent of voluntarily going back to jail where he would be safe."[16] The counterpoint was quite clear, with the protagonist sent to rescue a pregnant woman not out of heroism but under orders, a chain-gang convict diverted from shoring up the levee in the disastrous flood of May 1927. The story began at the Parchman State Prison Farm, the setting he had used in "Monk," in which Gavin Stevens finally solved a murder committed but not instigated by the moron who gave the story its title when it appeared in *Scribner's* in May of 1937. In "Old Man" the protagonist—identified only as "the tall convict"—had landed in Parchman because he had been an inept romantic who had tried with outdated methods to rob a train in order to buy baubles for his faithless sweetheart. In many ways the antithesis of Harry Wilbourne, he is also a kind of double, a naïve country boy fated to disaster. Now Faulkner began to write scenes of great power as the rampaging river breaks its boundaries, set pieces of the kind he had not done since *As I Lay Dying*.

Returning to the story of Harry Wilbourne and Charlotte Rittenmeyer (set ten years later than that of the tall convict and the pregnant woman), Faulkner described the monastic intern's life which had made Harry so susceptible to love-at-first-sight for such an aggressive woman. He borrowed other characteristics from Helen Baird Lyman for Charlotte: burn scars, indifference to dress, and two small children. As Helen had been one girl with three brothers, so Charlotte was one among four. In an attic with a skylight like Bill Spratling's on St. Peter Street, Charlotte makes figurines of wire and papier-mâché to sell to stores, just as Helen had tried to market her nine-inch papier-mâché dolls. (But one of Charlotte's lines suggested other Faulkner women: she had married her husband because "you cant sleep with your brother." [40]) Nicknamed "Charley," she is in essence extremely feminine and intensely romantic. But she has a kind of strength that goes beyond her capacity for managing an illicit love affair. A female critic would later write, "One feels with

Charlotte the kind of sympathy and identification that one feels with real women grappling with the real world. But Charlotte Rittenmeyer, in the terms that Faulkner presents men, is a man in disguise. Or rather, perhaps more accurately, she is that always androgynous creature, the artist. In the love affair with Harry she is the aggressor, the experienced sexual creature, Harry the hesitant cloistered virgin."[17] In one of his poems to Helen, Faulkner had likened her to a flame, and he gave Charlotte the same intensity, though unlike Helen's feeling for himself, Charlotte sees Harry as a man with whom she could live literally for love rather than the domesticity she has known. Unwilling to settle for a tawdry assignation in a sleazy hotel, she nonetheless makes Harry ponder "that instinctive proficiency in and rapport for the mechanics of cohabitation even of innocent and unpracticed women. . . ." (54) As the novel's working title carried the idea of longing for a vanished homeland, so these scenes must have evoked for Faulkner the weekends at the bungalow on the Pacific shore where he had wanted Meta Carpenter to shut out the world.

In other essentially self-contained situations of high emotional intensity, Faulkner had introduced outsiders to lower the pitch and retain the reader's credence. Like Doc Peabody among the Bundrens and Shreve McCannon with Quentin Compson, a Chicago newspaperman named McCord performs that function here. Helping with the plot, he also supplies useful allusions. As McCord drinks with the lovers, Charlotte puns on the meat-packing name of Armour. McCord then adds, "Set, ye armourous sons, in a sea of hemingwaves." (97) In "The Snows of Kilimanjaro," Ernest Hemingway's dying protagonist—a failed writer named Harry being kept by his wealthy wife—had punned on the same name. A number of readers would discover analogies between this novel and *A Farewell to Arms.* Both Harry and Frederic Henry feel themselves victimized by society or fate after attempting to make a separate peace and live inner-directed lives. Both Charlotte and Catherine Barkley give all for love. But whereas Hemingway is totally in sympathy with his lovers, Faulkner could—while he felt compassion for Harry and some admiration for Charlotte—see quite clearly how destructive is the dream which Charlotte pursues, carrying Harry with her by force and example. But from the outset, their frail league against the world is as doomed as that of Roger and Laverne Shumann in *Pylon.*

Faulkner followed his lovers from New Orleans to Chicago to Wisconsin and back. He also continued to juxtapose the two male figures: Harry is static and the convict is dynamic; Harry is color-blind and the convict is a hemophiliac; Harry writes pulp stories and the convict reads pulp stories. Both have spent a quarter of their lives in abstinence under rigorous discipline. Now, surprised by passion, Harry looks about him at a world in which "we have got rid of love at last just as we have got rid of Christ." (136) Even more adrift from the familiar, the convict looks about him to see only the wild waste of waters.

BY the end of January, Faulkner was far enough into the novel so that he could go flying, but the pressure of a number of activities would keep him on the ground for three months after that. In early February he wrote the check that completed the deal for Bailey's Woods. He had also been waiting anxiously as Random House attorneys cleared the way for the sale of the film rights to *The Unvanquished* to Metro-Goldwyn-Mayer for $25,000. Not all of it would go to Faulkner, and the transaction would be marred by misunderstanding. Almost two years before, Faulkner had tried to explain to Morty Goldman that Hal Smith had handled sales of film and stage rights to the novels. Ben Wasson worked on magazine sales. Because Morty had handled sales of individual stories, he felt that he was entitled to a commission on the film sale. He offered a compromise, though, which Faulkner gratefully accepted "even though I do feel I have been screwed about 600.00 worth. But then, you probably feel you have been screwed 1,000.00, which is worse, I reckon."[18] Even after Goldman's $1,000 and Random House's $5,000, Faulkner had $19,000 of Hollywood money, earned in the way he preferred.

He did not want to put it in stocks or in an account where it might be dissipated little by little. He thought about buying an airplane. The answer was one he had mulled over for some time. Each of the Falkners in a direct line before him had owned farms. He would own one too. He could hunt the land as well as farm it. As for the actual work, that would provide a solution rather than a problem. Johncy and Dolly Falkner had been struggling to make a go of their one-plane airline. When Bill asked him if he would run the farm, Johncy began to scour Lafayette County for the right one.

Meanwhile, the reviewers were scrutinizing *The Unvanquished*. Clifton Fadiman predictably disliked the book, and in the New York *Herald Tribune* for February 20, Alfred Kazin likened him to "a willful, sullen child . . . losing himself in verbal murk." But favorable verdicts predominated, even in *Time* and *The New Republic* the next month. In the South, the novel was generally better received than any of its predecessors. Even so, some of the praise had an edge. Phil Mullen's brother, Dale, wrote in the *Eagle* that Oxonians would find this a book "that they can understand, can enjoy, can leave lying on their living room tables. . . ."[19]

Meanwhile, Johncy had finally found what they were looking for. It was a 320-acre farm seventeen miles northeast of the square near Woodson Ridge. Located in Beat Two, the toughest part of Lafayette County, it would provide a secure retreat from inquisitive tourists. The farm had been Joe Parks's home place. When he had moved into town he had bought Murry Falkner's North Street home, and now Murry Falkner's son, extending his roots into the Mississippi hills he had described in his verse, had reversed the process. "Bill found more than just a farm out there," Johncy wrote. "He found the kind of people he wrote about, hill people. They made their own whiskey from their own corn and . . . fought over elections and settled their own disputes."[20] William Faulkner was a pilot, as a number of his characters had been. Now, though he would not walk behind plow handles as the tall convict did, he, too, would be a farmer.

43

... the motionless uprush of the main ridge and the strong constant resinous downflow of the pines where the dogwood looked indeed like nuns now in the long green corridors, up and onto the last crest, the plateau and now he seemed to see his whole native land, his home—the dirt, the earth which had bred his bones and those of his fathers for six generations and was still shaping him into not just a man but a specific man, not just with a man's passions and aspirations and beliefs but the specific passions and hopes and convictions and ways of thinking and acting. . . .

—*Intruder in the Dust* (150–151)

He called it Greenfield Farm. On the hills were the blue-green pines, and on the bottom land, now rank with weeds and button willow, they would grow corn and hay for the stock. Johncy suggested that they raise cows and Uncle John agreed, but the owner was immovable. The apostrophe to the mule he had written into *Sartoris* still reflected an article of faith with him, and he put it strongly to his brother. "He said he had no feeling for cows. He wanted brood mares and a tack room with riding equipment in it. So we raised mules."[1] Johncy felt that there was not enough lime in the soil to produce strong-boned animals and he noted uneasily that many farmers were buying tractors. But Faulkner went ahead, and it would not be long before he could record in their studbook the servicing of the first mare. Greenfield Farm was in operation.

It was a welcome distraction from the lingering misery of the skin-grafting to which he had finally submitted at the end of February. In mid-March he wrote Haas, "I got it infected and had to have the wound scraped and constantly treated for the past two weeks, from which I am just recovering—bromides, etc. I have just got back at the book today, though I still feel pretty bad."[2] The book was perhaps a third done, and he could not now keep his promise of May delivery, and probably not June either.

Sitting at his table by the window, often wearing a buttoned sport shirt beneath a soft zippered pullover, he returned to the trials of the tall convict who found the woman he had been sent to rescue—perched in the branches of a tree above the waters of the flood. Like most Mississippians, Faulkner could remember vividly the flood eleven years before, the staggering disaster which had inundated over three million acres and caused nearly a quarter of a billion dollars' damage. As he had subjected the Bundrens to flood and fire, he now subjected the convict to flood, nosebleeds, and myriad hardships. One was that the woman "who could have been his sister" (148) is ready to go into labor at any moment. Stoically accepting this burden, he begins paddling, seeking "anything he might reach and surrender his charge to and turn his back on her forever, on all pregnant and female life forever. . . ." (153) Carried upstream on the Yazoo and then back downstream on the Mississippi past Vicksburg without knowing it, the convict meets his trials with quiet strength and courage: "if you just held on long enough a time would come in fear after which it would no longer be agony at all but merely a kind of horrible outrageous itching, as after you have been burned bad." (160) Flashing forward in time, Faulkner introduced another character to comment on the experience of the isolated couple, as he had done with McCord in the companion story. The questions of another convict (when the tall convict is safely back in Parchman) help carry the epic odyssey forward until the convict beaches his skiff on a snake-infested Indian mound barely in time for the woman to give birth to her child.

As Faulkner moved the convict's story in a great looping swing southward, he carried that of Harry and Charlotte westward to Utah, the region to which, in "Idyll in the Desert," another woman had followed her lover, also leaving her two children behind. Corresponding to the corrupt prison officials in Parchman is the corrupt mine owner who exploits the Polish miners whom Harry is ostensibly hired to treat. Another couple, even more passionately sexual than Harry and Charlotte, not only serve as foils but help prefigure the ending. With deep foreboding, Harry performs the abortion they request.

Faulkner took a break from time to time, going out to Greenfield Farm, where E. O. Champion checked over their Fordson tractor. Later he went up with Champ in his Command-Aire to fly over the farm. He told Johncy he wanted "to get a better picture of just what we had and how to develop it."[3] One evening in Ashford and Minnie Ruth Little's recreation room, after Ross Brown and Hugh Evans offered to supply the venison, Faulkner said Estelle could cook a hunt breakfast at Rowan Oak. The following Sunday morning a bizarrely dressed, giggling group of fourteen assembled for a half-mile ride down Second South Street to

Rowan Oak. Astride a Shetland pony, Sallie Murry Williams wore a flowered hat and veil, swallow-tailed coat, and tight white trousers tucked into embossed cowboy boots. Wearing a derby, shirtwaist, and long skirt, Maggie Brown rode a white mule side-saddle. At the gates of Rowan Oak, the procession was met by Uncle Ned Barnett, clad in a high-collared broadcloth coat and matching garments once owned by the Young Colonel. With a retinue of younger servants, he led the guests to the host, who was attired in a huntsman's cap, ruffled shirt, fawn-colored breeches, and a red velvet gold-braided cocktail jacket belonging to Sallie Murry. He lifted the hunting horn slung around his neck, blew a welcoming blast, and handed around shots of straight bourbon. The venison, Maggie Brown remembered, was delicious.

He resumed the story of the tall convict with keener contrapuntal strokes. Whereas Harry botches Charlotte's abortion, bringing on hemorrhage and infection, the tall convict cuts the infant's umbilical cord with a tin can and ties it off with a shoelace. Faulkner's description of this new nuclear family alluded to the "Ark out of Genesis" (232) and suggested a recapitulation of the history of the race. Faulkner's Christmas gift to Mac would be *The Origin of Species*; now he might have been drawing on *The Descent of Man* as the convict fashions an oar from a tree trunk by fire and later hunts alligators with a club like a "Thuringian mace," stalking "pleistocene nightmares up and down the secret inky channels. . . ." (255) In spite of the vindictiveness of "the cosmic joker" (264), the convict even manages to get into trouble over a woman at a sawmill before painfully making his way back to authority. The section ends with his succinct report of his stewardship: "Yonder's your boat, and here's the woman. But I never did find that bastard on the cottonhouse." (278)

The last section of "Wild Palms" ended the long flashback begun in the first section. If the operating-room scene suggests *A Farewell to Arms*, the scene of Harry in his cell parallels that of the convict in his, even to their nervous exhaustion. Building toward his ending, Faulkner had continued to work on the symbolic level. Charlotte's statuette of a little old man, called "the Bad Smell," has evoked for her the essence of a wasted life. And once again, as with a sound track under film action, Faulkner described "the black wind again, risible, jeering, constant," (291) in which Harry can hear "the threshing of the invisible palms, the wild dry sound of them." (295) If their passion has been strong like these hardy scrub growths, the black wind embodies all the societal pressure, the folly, and the bad luck which have conspired to destroy Charlotte's romantic dream which Harry has embraced. With a perception that suggests Darl Bundren's clairvoyance, Harry looks back to Charlotte's last interview with her husband, the man who actually offers him first a bail bond and then a cyanide capsule to avoid fifty years of imprisonment.

Refusing it, Harry thinks, *"Yes . . . between grief and nothing I will take grief."* (234)

But Faulkner chose not to end the book on that note. Paralleling what he had done at the end of Harry's story, employing contrast again, he returned to material treated earlier: the convict's relationship with the girl for whom he had robbed the train. She visits him once at Parchman and seven months later sends him a picture postcard—of her honeymoon hotel. The last line was heavy with anti-romanticism and misogyny: " 'Women, shit,' the tall convict said." At the bottom of page 213, Faulkner wrote

> Rowan Oak
> Oxford, Mississippi
> 15 June 1938

Many readers would close the book thinking beyond the convict's succinct comment. One critic would write, "In two complementary modes of expression, in two complexly related stories, Faulkner explores and dramatizes the ultimate questions of man's fate. What can man do in the face of the inevitable oblivion of death . . . ? What are the results and uses of suffering, freedom, human love? What does it mean to endure? to prevail?" And as for the two juxtaposed men, in this view, "The convict says No to life; Harry says No to death."[4] Still another would see this as a romance, composed of "two tales, each with its own innocent hero," both victims of a society which "seems to offer little scope for the heroism latent in the naive young hill man, or the almost ascetic dedication to passionate love latent in the young sobersides interne."[5]

Faulkner did some rewriting and sent his typescript off near the end of June. A fortnight later he would write Haas, "I have lived for the last six months in such a peculiar state of family complications and back complications that I still am not able to tell if the novel is all right or absolute drivel. To me, it was written just as if I had sat on the one side of a wall and the paper was on the other and my hand with the pen thrust through the wall and writing not only on invisible paper but in pitch darkness too, so that I could not even know if the pen still wrote on paper or not."[6]

THEY had celebrated Jill's birthday with the usual party and gifts, her father there to see her blow out the candles instead of being away in Hollywood. She loved being with him, listening to him read to her, loving the flow of the words even when she didn't understand them. Years later she would recognize the sound and rhythm of something she knew she had never read, and it would be the Dickens or Swinburne or Housman she had heard in her childhood. Sometimes when she went into the library she would find him lying down. When she would rouse him, he would tell her not to bother him; he was working, he would say, "thinking things up." Later, from the hall, she would see him sitting at his backless chair, feet twisted about the rounds, pecking slowly at his typewriter. In the evenings they might play dominoes or cards at the kitchen table. It could be wonderful being with him, just doing simple things. Then again he might be remote, aloof, as if she, or perhaps he, weren't there at all.

There was another celebration that summer, a Fourth of July barbecue at the farm. A three-foot pit was dug for a hickory fire and stoked for days. Faulkner chose for the feast a scrawny little bull called Black Buster. He was a favorite of Uncle Ned Barnett's but was non-productive, and Faulkner had bought a fine big pedigreed bull to service his cows. (He had agreed to raise cows though he still had no feeling for them.) On the morning of the third, Faulkner began basting the quarters with his own special barbecue sauce as they turned on the spits. By afternoon, some of the Negroes living nearby had come to help. When darkness fell Faulkner still sat there, half in shadow and half in the glow of the pit, basting the beef while the sauce dripped and sizzled, aromatic on the coals. They made an impromptu meal of crackers and sardines from the commissary, potatoes roasted in the ashes, and whiskey from the jugs that passed around. The next day at noon the savory ribs were ready. Baked potatoes and steaming sweet corn were heaped in platters on the board-and-trestle tables amid the profusion of pickle, relish, jams, and jellies. Uncle Ned appeared just as the guests began to arrive. Faulkner greeted him, and then, turning back to the pit, he happened to glance up the rise to the ridge not far away. He saw the little scrub bull trot across it. He looked at Uncle Ned.

"Who's that?" he asked.

"That's Black Buster," Uncle Ned said.

"Then who's this?" Faulkner asked, pointing to the quarter on the spit. "I thought I told you to kill Black Buster and I thought you told me you did." He realized now that he had not seen his pedigreed bull anywhere at any time since he had come out to the farm the day before.

"Master," the old man said, "I calls them all Black Buster." And he beat a quick retreat. Faulkner felt sick. His appetite was gone, and it was only later that he could again enter into the spirit of the holiday with his guests, who were eating and drinking, talking and laughing under the trees.

It was not the first time or the last that Uncle Ned confounded his employer. Jill considered him an informer, always ready to tell if she did something wrong, but she was fascinated by the costumes he would wear—high-crowned hats from the Old Colonel, broadcloth coats from his son. Sousing himself with toilet water, he would ask Estelle to drive him to town on Sundays to pursue an active social life, though he was nearly ninety. He had courted a woman named Ella and taken her to

Greenfield to live, and then, when divorce proceedings began, he had to turn to a friend to remember her name. Later that summer he came to Faulkner with an appeal: "Master, I ain't gonna live to see my crop. Give me the money to go home to Ripley and die." Faulkner complied, and subsequently bore the expense of having the crop gathered. Each year thereafter, Uncle Ned would complete the same transaction. He also enjoyed trading, and sometimes Faulkner would let him come along. The two "made a fatal combination at the mule sales," Jill would say, recalling a curious side of her father. "Anybody could sell him anything. He seemed to possess a kind of unflagging optimism and hope." Returning to display with satisfaction what was obviously unpromising stock, he would carefully point out qualities in the animal that all the others had overlooked. "He was a born sucker," Jill realized. "All his life he was always being taken."

To Johncy Falkner, his brother often seemed close-mouthed and dour that summer. One source of irritation was Bob Haas's objecting to the title and some of the words in the new novel. Faulkner wrote back that they could substitute dots for words such as the four-letter one in the book's last line. "This should whitewash it sufficiently, shouldn't it? It is only what people see that shocks them, not what they think or hear, and they will recognise these words or not and no harm done in either case. But these words are exactly the ones which my characters would have used and no other, and there are a few people whom I hope will read the book, among whom the preservation of my integrity as a faithful (even though not always successful) portrayer of living men and women is dear enough for me to wish not to betray it, even in trifles." He offered a solution: "why not let me swap you the objectionable words for the title? you to do as you see fit about the words, and let the title stand? . . ." The title page of the setting copy now bore, in typed block capitals, the title IF I FORGET THEE, JERUSALEM, a reference to the 137th Psalm's rendering of the pain of exile and longing. Faulkner explained, "It invented itself as a title for the chapter in which Charlotte died and where Wilbourne said 'Between grief and nothing I will take grief' and which is the theme of the whole book, the convict story being just counterpoint to sharpen it. . . ."[7] Haas agreed by return mail, but the matter was not settled.

In the latter part of August, Faulkner took his wife and daughter to the Gulf Coast for several days. By the time they returned, he had decided to read proof on the book in New York. It was the last week of September when he checked in at the Algonquin. On October 6, Faulkner wrote Estelle that the book's name would be *The Wild Palms*. He had found that Saxe Commins was also against his title, like Haas, who would later say he had been afraid it would hurt the book's sales by arousing anti-Semitic feeling.

It was not all business for Faulkner. Haas pitched horseshoes with him, and Commins took him to see Columbia play Army. At one crucial point in Columbia's last-minute game-winning drive, Faulkner leaned over and predicted the next play. When the Columbia quarterback called it, Commins congratulated him.

"From now on you'll always be known as the grandstand quarterback," he said.

"No," Faulkner replied, "I'll always be known as the corncob man."[8]

He went to Saks to shop for a kilt and bonnet for Jill. And he saw Meta Rebner again. Wolfgang was on tour as an accompanist and she was doubly glad to meet Faulkner for lunch. She poured out her troubles: the pressure of debts, her husband's fading hopes for a concert career, the way she sometimes felt excluded in the German culture of his family. And now Rebner was sometimes verbally abusive. She felt herself thin and unattractive, dressed in shabby clothes. Even so, she had felt when they met that he "wanted to take joy in me," but when their luncheon ended he said he was due back at Random House. She insisted on walking there with him, and on the street she broke down and cried. He stopped abruptly. " 'Buck up, Carpenter,' he said harshly. 'I've never seen you like this.' " When she met him the next day, she assumed a confident attitude. She asked him to help Rebner through the influential people he knew. "I see," Faulkner said. He arranged for her to meet Hal Smith and Bennett Cerf. Not long afterward he left for home.[9]

It was mid-October, in the interval between the last book and the next one, and he was free to enjoy the mild weather and to fly the Travel-Aire he had helped E. O. Champion buy. He was often out at the farm, where the harvest had been a fine one, though he did not give Johncy the credit his brother felt he deserved. One November day Faulkner noticed that the prices in the commissary had gone up. When Johncy told him that the wholesaler had raised his, Faulkner told him to mark theirs back down; "it was not the Negroes' fault that prices went up and he wasn't going to penalize them for it."[10] He would have to live on advances until royalties came in on *The Wild Palms*, but he was accepting financial responsibility for those dependent on him, just as he had been doing for the better part of ten years.

IT was time to turn to the next book. On November 7 he took a sheet of his manuscript paper with the two ruled margins and wrote at the top "BOOK ONE," then *Chapter One*, and below that, *Barn Burning*. This prologue centered on an embittered Ab Snopes and his ten-year-old son, Colonel Sartoris Snopes. As the father burns yet another barn to avenge what seems to him arrogance and injustice, Sarty Snopes repudiates his father's kerosene can as Bayard Sartoris had repudiated his father's derringer. Within ten days Faulkner had this segment written and typed.

He decided that it would make a good short story, and on November 19 it arrived at the office of Bob Haas's Scarsdale neighbor and long-time friend, literary agent Harold Ober. It would be March, however, before the story was taken by *Harper's*.

Ober and Faulkner could hardly have been more dissimilar. Ober was very tall, with blue eyes, a large lower lip, and beetling brows under carefully brushed gray hair. An oarsman at Harvard who had earned part of his tuition by tutoring, he had graduated with the class of 1905 and then gone to Paris because he wanted to write. When he realized after a prolonged stay that he did not have enough talent, he returned to America and became a literary agent. Most people thought he was far too gentlemanly to succeed in that profession, but the steely toughness of his New England forebears, combined with his integrity, decorum, and concern, helped to place him in charge of his own agency by 1929. Driving hard but honest bargains for his writers, he saw them through all manner of crises and did what he thought best for them—sometimes rather high-handedly. Among them were Corey Ford, Agatha Christie, Faith Baldwin, and Scott Fitzgerald, for whom he had provided extensive emotional and financial support, even taking his daughter into his own home for a crucial part of her growing years. Ober in some ways was like Faulkner. He was generous yet frugal. He was so shy that he might sit almost wordless at lunch with one of his authors. But many of his clients loved him, and they all trusted and leaned on him, as William Faulkner would do.

On December 15, Faulkner wrote Haas that he was about to run out of money. But rather than take the advance they had agreed on in a lump sum, he wanted $150 a month, so he would stay within it. Following his custom, he told Haas what Random House would eventually get for the money. It was a unique letter, reaching back eleven years or more to *Father Abraham* and forward to the completion of the Snopes saga. He said he was halfway through the first of three volumes, entitled *The Peasants*, which traced Flem Snopes's rise in Frenchman's Bend to a foothold in Jefferson. The next paragraph synopsized *Rus in Urbe*, in which Flem gradually ascended to the presidency of the bank, in part by blackmailing his wife's lover. Then in six paragraphs he traced out the plot of *Ilium Falling*, in which Flem brought in more relatives from the country to secure his flanks. Without naming her, he told how Eula Varner, pregnant by her first lover, would be married to Snopes for propriety's sake, and how her daughter would eventually meet the son of Colonel Sartoris Snopes and help to match him with the daughter of a collateral Snopes. The book would end in a double irony: their son would be the worst of all the Snopeses, and Flem—gorged on the town and incapable of enjoying anything—would play his final joke when, after his death, everything went to this degenerate Snopes. Neither Faulkner nor

Haas could know that it would be twenty years before the Snopes trilogy was completed and that the vein would ultimately be more heroic than ironic even if there was a good deal of dark comedy.

Haas readily agreed to the plan, and Faulkner began to concentrate on the complex composition of *The Peasants*. When he wrote Haas that he was "half through with it," he was referring in part to segments already written which he would link together, as in *The Unvanquished*. Borrowing phrases from the third paragraph of *Father Abraham*, he began with a panoramic, scene-setting description of Frenchman's Bend. He described its petty baronial lord, Uncle Billy Varner, his son Jody, and then plunged into his tale with Ab Snopes's rental of one of Varner's farms. Relevant material from "Barn Burning" would be recapitulated in dialogue as the chapter developed. Almost immediately Faulkner introduced one of the saga's themes: the contest between the Snopeses and non-Snopeses, though the line between the two was sometimes narrow, as with Jody, who plays with the idea of blackmailing Snopes out of his crop. Only too late does Jody realize that he is overmatched, and at the chapter's end Flem is installed as a clerk at Varner's store on the unspoken condition that Ab Snopes will abstain from burning any Varner barn.

The Varners have been warned of Ab's past by a familiar character. Faulkner would later say that the spotted-horses episode of *Father Abraham* "had created a character I fell in love with: the itinerant sewing-machine agent named Suratt. Later a man of that name turned up at home, so I changed my man to Ratliff for the reason that my whole town spent much of its time trying to decide just what living man I was writing about, the one literary criticism of the town being, 'How in the hell did he remember all that, and when did that happen anyway?' "[11] (Maud Falkner remembered that June Suratt had been selling sewing machines in Lafayette County as early as 1910. Faulkner would later say that after one of V. K. Suratt's appearances, he received a call from a lawyer telling him that another such appearance would be followed by a lawsuit.) So now it is V. K. Ratliff (another familiar Mississippi name) who tells Uncle Billy Varner how Ab Snopes got "soured." This was "Fool About a Horse" reworked, with the protagonist changed from Suratt's father to Ab Snopes. Originally this had been a comic tall tale, but now, in chapter form, its coda, in which Snopes brusquely rejects Ratliff's offer of renewed friendship, foreshadowed a different mode.

Chapter Three quickly established Flem's growing ascendancy over Jody Varner. It begins with a description of Flem which retains the unwinking eyes and purselike mouth of *Father Abraham*. Just as the machine-made black bow tie would remind some Oxonians of Joe Parks, Flem's face, especially his nose, would remind others of Earl Fudge. His business acumen would make others think of Thomas Edison Avent. He was grotesque in a physical sense and also in the deeper sense that Sherwood Anderson had described in "The Book of the Grotesque" in

Winesburg, Ohio, the result of cleaving to one "truth" to the exclusion of all others. Two more Snopeses from *Father Abraham* appear: a decent muscle-bound dullard named Eck and a weasel named I. O. Snopes who is constantly mouthing fractured proverbs. Faulkner would later say, laughing, "I used up all the proverbs I knew or could think up on I. O." He reintroduced a man named Houston, who had been the victim in "The Hound." His assailant-to-be was changed from Ernest Cotton to Mink Snopes, whom Ratliff called "a different kind of Snopes like a cotton-mouth is a different kind of snake." (91) It is Ratliff who brings him into the action by delivering a sewing machine which he implies has been ordered by his cousin Flem. (Johncy Falkner said that he had bought a sewing machine on time shortly after his marriage and that later the salesman had mistakenly dunned William Faulkner for the balance because of their resemblance.) Ratliff uses the note Mink gives him (payable by Flem) in an elaborate battle of wits with Flem over the purchase and sale of goats to a county newcomer starting a goat farm. The beneficiary of Ratliff's limited victory is a fair-haired slobbering idiot, Isaac Snopes, ward of his kinsman Flem. One of his aspects shows how far this pastoral is from those Faulkner wrote years before: the idiot has "pointed faun's ears. . . ." (86) Just as this second section of the chapter sets the situation for a later contest between Ratliff and Flem, so the brief final section foreshadows the bitter and violent one between Houston and Mink. In another augury of things to come, one of Ratliff's hearers has seen a figure seated, sovereignlike, before Varner's Old Frenchman place: "It was Flem Snopes. . . ." (91)

THE holidays were now upon them, and turning from conflict in fiction to conflicts in life, Faulkner tried to resolve some of them. In October he had tried to help Phil Stone work out a deal with Random House whereby Stone would use his political contacts to sell some of the sets left from an overprinting of the five-volume *Public Papers and Addresses of Franklin D. Roosevelt.* He had let Stone read *The Wild Palms* in typescript. Stone wrote a literary historian that he found it marred by "verboseness, obscureness, and unnecessary vulgarity." Perhaps in ignorance of Stone's verdict, Faulkner inscribed Malraux's *Man's Fate* to him and handed it to him with the comment "He's the best of us all." Stone and Emily had visited, bringing Faulkner's standard Christmas present of a striped tie. Phil and Emily had a child now, a son named Philip Alston, for whom Faulkner would stand as godfather. For the time, it was as though the couple's joy had helped restore elements of the old friendship between the two men.

Faulkner drove out to Greenfield with gifts for the four farm families and brought Johncy and Dolly back to town with him for Christmas. Jimmy and Chooky were living at Rowan Oak so they could go to school in Oxford, and the house was full of children. In the morning Faulkner presided over the distribution of the presents. Miss Maud came later, staying about fifteen minutes, as usual. Her son viewed her with a mixture of affection, exasperation, and amusement. Independent as always, she would not have a servant. Suspicious, she constantly felt that someone was trying to cheat her, and her day was made, one of her grandchildren would recall, when she could find an error in a shopping bill. But the holiday was for the most part harmonious, and so Christmas of 1938 passed.

The two brothers went out to the farm one sunny morning at the start of quail season. Johncy had located a few coveys of birds, but too many hunters had been there before them, and they did not down any. After that they posted the land and established conservation practices like those of the Okatoba Hunting and Fishing Club. The brief holiday respite was soon over. Faulkner would resume his intensive work on *The Peasants*, and as 1939 came in, so would the reviews of *The Wild Palms*. One of them would, of course, be in *Time: The Weekly Magazine*. But now his face would be on the cover.

CHAPTER

44

> And now, looking back and down, you see all Yoknapatawpha
> in the dying last of day beneath you. . . . on to where French-
> man's Bend lay beyond the southeastern horizon, cradle of
> Varners and ant-heap for the northwest crawl of Snopes. . . .
>
> —*The Town* (315, 317)

ON Thursday, January 19, 1939, Ralph Thompson delivered his verdict
in *The New York Times*: "William Faulkner has written another
tortured, bitter novel and again emerged the victor over his own sentence
structure." In ironic counterpoint, the same page carried the information
that the five new members of the National Institute of Arts and Letters
included William Faulkner, "the author of *Sanctuary*." Ben Ray Redman
and Clifton Fadiman found nothing to praise in the juxtaposition of the
novel's two stories. Malcolm Cowley concurred, and like the others, he
preferred the one about the tall convict, though he found him "the ideal
soldier for a fascist army." To Alfred Kazin, the novel's prose was a kind
of tortured poetry.[1] Shortly after the bound stacks of *Time* for January
23 were unloaded at the station, the drugstores around the square blossomed with William Faulkner's photograph. There on the cover in color,
he looked level-eyed and unsmiling at the camera, his mustache neatly
trimmed and his brown-gray hair waving slightly over his forehead.
Tieless, he wore the broad galluses of a country man. He had posed more
happily for a picture inside, his hand on Jill's bicycle and a broad grin
on his face. She had run to greet him that day seven weeks before when
he had returned from Memphis with Robert Cantwell, who had come to
research his cover story for *Time*. Driving his guest down in the Ford
Phaeton, Faulkner had responded freely when Cantwell mentioned the
Old Colonel. Faulkner said there was nothing left of his work now except
his statue, "But he rode through that country like a living force. I like
it better that way."[2] He had taken Cantwell to see Mammy Callie in her

cabin behind the big house at Rowan Oak. It was a pleasant visit, and it helped Cantwell to write a vivid piece. He began by placing Faulkner in the forefront of the Southern literary renaissance. He also gave an account of the Old Colonel, whose story had taken hold of his imagination. He included a short biography of the great-grandson, with a few contemporary notes about him as father, Southern landlord, and conservative Democrat. *The Wild Palms*, he wrote, was "conceived in the grand manner," and the portion about the tall convict was "a pulsing, racing story, a kind of hysterical *Huckleberry Finn*, its humor at once grotesque and shrewd, its moral at once grim and humane."[3] Once again the verdict had been rendered in favor of the story created simply as counterpoint for the one written to stave off what Faulkner had thought was heartbreak. But the article was still a landmark: extended and sympathetic treatment for him and his work from a middle-brow magazine of mass circulation.

Three days later Moon Mullen reported the reaction of most of his fellow townsmen in the *Eagle*. "Mr. Faulkner a great writer? Well, they sure wouldn't hire him to write a Chamber of Commerce booklet for the town." More than one Mississippian felt as he did. In Pascagoula, Ann Farnsworth told her friend Helen Baird Lyman that William Faulkner had a new book out. "Don't read it," Helen told her. "It's no good." When Ann read it she immediately recognized aspects of Helen in Charlotte Rittenmeyer.[4]

Cantwell had written that Faulkner regarded himself as "a social historian, who hopes that by recording the minute changes in Oxford's life he can suggest the changes that are transforming the whole South."[5] As Faulkner worked his way through *The Peasants*, he was writing about human experience as it manifested itself far beyond Yoknapatawpha and the American South and in times other than the early years of the twentieth century. In Chapter Four he was expanding rather than condensing, as he had done with the material of "Fool About a Horse." In *Father Abraham*, Eula Varner had been described as "rife and richly supine," but now she "suggested some symbology out of the old Dionysic times—honey in sunlight and bursting grapes, the writhen bleeding of the crushed fecundated vine beneath the hard rapacious trampling goat-hoof." (95) Now more than an instrument of the plot, she provides not only humor but a primal femaleness. She is Lena Grove and Dewey Dell Bundren raised several powers as, in an afterthought, Faulkner described her form as "a kaleidoscopic convolution of concentric mammalian ellipses." (100) There is humor, too, in the violent passion of a young hillman named Labove who plays football at Ole Miss to earn his education and equip his family with cleated shoes and varsity sweaters. (He looked much like Possum McDaniel, Faulkner's high-school teammate, who had gone on to play four years at Ole Miss.) Looking beyond his own bitter defeat, Labove can almost see Eula's future husband, "the crippled Vulcan to that Venus, who would not possess her but merely own her by the single strength which power gave, the dead power of money . . . as he might own . . . a field, say. . . ." (118–119) With this vision the atmosphere of the book started to darken.

Chapter Five began with what had been the substance of paragraph seven of *Father Abraham*: the country youths who flock around Eula. Now there was more violence and less humor as he introduced the lover who would plow the field Flem would own. Faulkner described young Hoake McCarron with an almost prodigal provision of background, but he dispensed with him quickly after he had fulfilled his function. The second of the chapter's two sections combined the elegiac and the fantastic. Ratliff meditates on the marriage of convenience ordered by Will Varner, linking "the splendid girl with her beautiful masklike face [to] the froglike creature which barely reached her shoulder. . . ." (147) Faulkner wrote and underlined eight lines in which Ratliff imagines Flem outsmarting the Prince of Darkness. Then a familiar thing happened: Faulkner's imagination took off and he wrote four more pages that end with the Prince hysterically fleeing his throne, leaving it to Flem. It was a virtuoso performance, a tall tale like that of Pat Stamper's defeat of Ab Snopes, but this one was enriched with a parody of elements of *Paradise Lost*, The Temptation on the Mount, and *The Temptation of St. Anthony* as well as echoes of *The Mysterious Stranger* and the Faust legend.

By early February he was able to write Haas that he had 215 typed pages and the manuscript was "in about the same condition as if I had all The Unvanquished except the last three stories, one of which needs to be written entire, the last two waiting for something to hang them onto it."[6] Before Faulkner got to "Spotted Horses" and "Lizards in Jamshyd's Courtyard," he would expand one of his stories and interweave it with yet another. Still regretting Eula's fate, Ratliff becomes aware of yet another outrage: the idiot Ike Snopes, copulating with a cow he loves, is being exhibited by his cousin Maud. (He had been christened Mordred. Faulkner was apparently enjoying the Snopeses' ingenuity in borrowing names from Arthurian legend as well as national history.) Here was a savage juxtaposition: this bestial love and Flem's relationship with the other quintessential female he had married only for gain.

On February 10, Faulkner began a new section, building a flashback to describe the affair between Ike and his beloved, for whom he undergoes trials not unworthy of a knight serving his lady. Here was the same situation which had provided the subject for Ernest V. Trueblood's "Afternoon of a Cow," but now Faulkner's troublesome Beulah was transformed into a bovine Astarte. He crossed out what he had written and began to expand Ike's quest in an extravagant style that shifted from the realistic description of "the slow planting and the plopping suck of each deliberate cloven mudspreading hoof" to the poetic vision of her as "integer of spring's concentrated climax, by it crowned, garlanded." (165, 168) The third section of the chapter ended with society's imposition of a folk solution to Ike's aberration: killing the cow and feeding him some of the meat. Somehow this spoliation, in spite of the grotesque element in this love, carries a sense of shameful loss, like the bartered and wasted richness of Eula.

By March 1, Faulkner was able to take some time for the first flying he had done since December, but very soon a crisis intruded. The debts that Phil Stone had assumed on his father's death were so heavy that he had not managed to reduce them very much. Now one of his creditors was about to foreclose on a note, and Stone had only a thousand dollars of the sum he needed. He turned to Faulkner, who turned to Random House. "I have a friend here," he wrote Haas. "I have known him all my life, never any question of mine and thine between us when either had it."[7] To raise the money, he would sign any contracts, sell or mortgage any of his manuscripts. By return mail, Haas sent him a check for $1,200 against royalties on Snopes. The $4,800 cash surrender value of a policy on the life of William Faulkner took care of the rest. The vectors in the Stone-Faulkner relationship, having begun to turn some time before, were now fully reversed.

In late March there was good news from Haas. *The Wild Palms* was selling more than a thousand copies a week and it had already topped the total sales of *Sanctuary*. There would be royalties enough by the November 1 due date to cover the $2,000 advance and the check that had gone to Stone. And *Harper's* was paying $400 for "Barn Burning." Faulkner was now able to make a trip in early April. For more than a month he had known that Meta Rebner's situation was worsening. She had undergone surgery, and when the incision reopened, Wolfgang had upbraided her for the expense of her return to the hospital. The clashes between them increased. When she threatened to leave, he told her he couldn't stop her. On March 6, Faulkner wrote Haas asking him to give Meta $150, to be charged against his royalties. It would cover her train fare to Kingman, Arizona, where her parents lived. Then he wired her to route herself through south Mississippi.

When the train stopped in New Orleans, he was there to meet her in a heavy rainstorm. He drove on through it, and shortly before midnight they checked into a hotel in the Vieux Carré. They were both soaked and she was running a fever. He gave her straight bourbon and made love to her. When they woke at noon, he declared her fever gone. The next day they strolled through the Quarter and he pointed out to her a tree he remembered, a bench in Jackson Square where he had composed a poem. He asked her to stay in New Orleans. He would come to her as often as he could. She said she was too ill, too run-down, and she needed time in Arizona to rest. Later, with the encouragement of her parents and the persuasion of Wolfgang's letters, she returned to New York, where she and her husband celebrated their reconciliation with lobster and champagne.

FAULKNER returned to Oxford and his manuscript. Before he had left he had begun on page 147 the chapter whose climax would be based on "The Hound." He described Houston at length. Much of his thirty-three-year lifespan was like that of Joe Christmas, with a harsh father and tender mother, initiation into sex by a Negro girl, and a twelve-year flight to escape both past and future before returning to meet his fate. It came first in the form of a girl who had steadfastly loved him, and then finally in an ambush by Mink Snopes—for impounding a skinny yearling Snopes had wintered at Houston's expense. (The murder bore resemblances to one that had occurred five miles south of Oxford thirty years before.) Faulkner was apparently working with a version of "The Hound" before him which provided identical wording in several phrases of the new version, but most of it he rewrote, interpolating new passages as he recapitulated the actions of Ernest Cotton, now Mink Snopes, in the aftermath of his murder of Houston.

Now Faulkner started Section 3 of the long chapter. He used phrases he had employed in his sketch "New Orleans," fourteen years before: "for the three weeks of Indian summer the ardor-wearied earth, ancient Lilith, reigned, throned and crowned amid the old invincible courtesan's formal defunction. . . ." (259) Mink Snopes awaits trial in the vain hope of rescue when Flem returns from his Texas honeymoon. As the chapter draws to a close, Ratliff notes the return of Eula and her child—her face not tragic, "just damned"—and the appearance of Ike Snopes dragging behind him a sentimental gift from Eck Snopes: "the battered wooden effigy of a cow such as children receive on Christmas." (265, 266) All Faulkner had to do now was fuse "Spotted Horses" and "Lizards in Jamshyd's Courtyard." At the beginning of the third week of April he sent Haas some new pages to be substituted for one he already had. "The book was getting too thin, diffuse," he wrote. "I have tightened it up, added some more here and there to give it density, make the people stand up." Before he put his typed letter in the envelope with the new pages, he took up his pen and added a single line below his signature. It read, "I am the best in America, by God."[8]

Ten days later that euphoria had vanished. In the aftermath of rescuing Phil Stone, he found his own finances in disarray. He was going to try for a $3,000 loan if he could get one from a Memphis bank by assigning future royalties from Random House. "God knows what I will do after it is gone," he wrote Haas wryly. "Maybe what I need is a bankruptcy, like a soldier needs delousing."[9] When the bank provided only $1,700, he knew what he would have to do: go back to what he called "boiling the pot." That was what he did for the next two months.

One paragraph in *The Peasants*, concerning the three founders of

Yoknapatawpha County, ended with the sole remaining descendant, Gavin Stevens, now county attorney. Faulkner cut the paragraph from the manuscript, rewrote it, and incorporated it into a story called "Hand Upon the Waters" in which Stevens solves the insurance murder of a feeble-minded fisherman who looks vaguely like Ike Snopes. The *Post* paid $1,000 for it. It was probably also at this time that he wrote "The Old People," a story of initiation which echoes elements of "A Justice." The young narrator has been taught by Sam Fathers, and when at twelve he kills his first deer, "Sam stooped and dipped his hands in the hot blood and wiped them back and forth across my face." But the climactic rite comes deeper into the big woods, where there suddenly appears a manifestation of all the game slain by hunters—an enormous buck that Sam hails like a totem animal: " 'Oleh, Chief,' he said. 'Grandfather.' " When the boy's father tries to explain to him how it could be that after he had killed his first deer, Sam had also shown him the same buck, it is in a passage that carries an echo of Harry Wilbourne's last speech to Charlotte's husband. "Think of all that has happened here, on this earth," the father tells the boy. "All the blood hot and fierce and strong for living, pleasuring. . . . But you can't be alive forever, and you always wear out life before you have completely exhausted the possibilities of living. And all that must be somewhere."[10] Though the story may have been tailored to sell as quickly as possible, Faulkner felt these sentiments deeply and would continue to hold them for the rest of his life. He sent this story to the *Post*, too, but this time he got a rejection.

The Fourth of July came, and with it another celebration at Greenfield Farm. Again there was the barbecue, and Negro singers in red bandannas. Faulkner continued to take a hand now and then in the affairs of the farm, recording in his studbook every month the mares serviced by their $600 jackass Big John. But he could not be away from his desk for long. He returned to *The Peasants* long enough to accumulate a new batch of pages, which he sent to New York in mid-August. But he had to write another story before he could get back at it uninterruptedly. It was probably "A Point of Law," a comic story involving a threefold conflict: the law vs. moonshiners, Roth Edmonds vs. his moonshining tenant farmers, and Lucas Beauchamp vs. his daughter Nat. The series of comic betrayals —a "Senegambian Montague and Capulet business"—may have amused Faulkner, but he doubtless considered it just as much a potboiler as any of the Bayard-Ringo series. He still hoped to complete the manuscript by early October, when he had to testify at a trial in Washington, and then go on to New York to polish the typescript. But there were the usual problems. "Do you suppose I can find a room," he asked his publishers, "about 50$ a month, where I can do as I like, go and come as I like. I could then buy liquor, and cadge grub from you all."[11]

It was about this time that *The Kenyon Review* appeared with an article in which George Marion O'Donnell asserted that Faulkner's works were held together by a great myth whose principle was "the Southern socio-economic ethical tradition." The influential essay compared the general meaning of his successful work with that in Dante's *Divina Commedia* and Sophocles' *Electra*. "The only close parallel in American literature is the better work of Nathaniel Hawthorne, whom Mr. Faulkner resembles in a great many ways."[12] As the summer wore on, the author himself continued to worry about boiling the pot.

As September came in, his main task was rewriting "Spotted Horses." Telling it now at greater length, he switched from Ratliff's voice back to the omniscient narration he had used in *Father Abraham*. This freed him to tap the resources of his own poetic prose and allowed him to pick up some of the motifs of earlier sections. He used all the events in *Father Abraham* and went on to the unsuccessful lawsuits brought by victims of the spotted ponies. He ended the chapter with another court case, one with a crucial sequel later in the trilogy. Finally on trial for Houston's murder, Mink waits in vain for his kinsman Flem to come to his aid.

The novel was not finished when Faulkner testified in Washington on October 10 in a suit whose plaintiff claimed that Twentieth Century-Fox had plagiarized a script of his in *The Road to Glory*. (The court would eventually find that the reverse was true.) In New York, over lunch at the Plaza, he told interviewer Michel Mok about coming events in the Snopes saga: Montgomery Ward Snopes's pornography studio and his role in the downfall of a kinsman, state Senator Clarence Snopes.[13] He had written Meta Rebner that he was coming, a letter that reiterated his unhappiness at home and his sexual longings, but apparently they did not meet. He did see other friends, though, the Lovetts, Hal Smith, and Smith's friend Mrs. Sewell Haggard—lively, interesting people who provided the kind of stimulus that made New York attractive to him, for brief periods.

Back in Oxford, he followed through on one conversation he had had in New York. In 1938 he had responded to an appeal from the League of American Writers by signing a short statement opposing General Franco and condemning fascist outrages. Vincent Sheean asked him for a contribution to a relief fund for the Spanish Loyalists. He responded on October 24 by sending him the manuscript of *Absalom, Absalom!* and offering him any of his first-draft typescripts. For a man who would later contemptuously recall being labeled "a Gothic fascist" by leftist literary warriors, it was quite a contribution.

The implications of foreign troubles had not been lost on him. One Sunday in the summer of the previous year, his mother had stopped by at Rowan Oak to find him pacing agitatedly.

"Billy, what's got into you?" she asked.

It was something he had read in the morning paper. "I'm afraid we're going to be in a war before we know it," he said.

"Oh, Billy, we're not," she said.

"Yes, Mother, we are. And the hell of it is, that boy is going to be in it," he said, pointing at Jimmy.

His reaction to facets of domestic politics was less liberal than his reaction to Spanish fascism. Responding to an earlier appeal by the National Retail Dry Goods Association, President Franklin D. Roosevelt had finally proclaimed that Thanksgiving would be celebrated on November 23 instead of November 30. Later Estelle would hear him say, "I never did care much for Thanksgiving after Mr. Roosevelt got through messing around with it." Out at Greenfield Farm two of his mules had names of a different kind from the rest. One was called Jim Farley; the other, Eleanor Roosevelt.

By December it was economics rather than politics that was distracting him. "I wasted a month writing two stories to sell to Sat. Eve. Post," he wrote Haas, "which they refused, obvious reason being that I need money, was trying hard to write mechanical stories in which I had no faith while my mind was on the novel. . . ." He had gotten back to the novel and thought he could make his planned delivery date of January 1. "This is provided I cant kick another plot story out of what I call my mind to write in meantime, though I believe I can do both by Jan. 1. By God, I have got to." The first O. Henry Memorial Award had gone to "Barn Burning" as the year's best short story. "If I have $500.00 from Random H. and the $300.00 prize and hang something on Post for $1000.00 by first of year, I will have a breather in which to invent salable stuff without having to haunt the post office for the check to pay coal and grocery bills with."[14] In a familiar irony, *The Atlantic Monthly* carried at this time an essay by Conrad Aiken in which he compared Faulkner with Balzac and declared, "what sets him above . . . all his American contemporaries, is his continuous preoccupation with the novel *as form* . . . and a degree of success with it which would clearly have commanded the interest and respect of Henry James himself."[15]

When he returned to the novel he must have had a typescript of "Lizards in Jamshyd's Courtyard" before him. He was able to dispense with introductory matter, and after inserting considerable new material leading up to Ratliff and Bookwright's realization that Flem had duped them into buying the Old Frenchman place with the salted-mine trick, he was able to conclude the section almost identically with the magazine version. Section 2 of this last chapter of the novel described the preparations for Flem's move to Jefferson and concluded as he drove three miles out of his way to observe the maddened Armstid still digging frantically for silver. As with *The Unvanquished*, the comic note of the linked stories was muted and supplanted by a darker one: in that novel, one of destruction and death; in this, greed and madness. He decided that the novel did not need a prologue and cut "Barn Burning" from its beginning.

Faulkner lent the typescript to Phil Stone, who was delighted to see transmuted there his original story of the idiot and the cow. Faulkner sent Saxe Commins new titles for the volumes of the trilogy: *The Hamlet, The Town,* and *The Mansion.* He divided *The Hamlet* into four books: "Flem," "Eula," "The Long Summer," and "The Peasants"—the last one not only the novel's erstwhile working title, but very possibly a tip of the hat to that master he had read as a youth: Honoré de Balzac.

As January 1940 came in, it turned bitter cold. By the twenty-fifth the temperature stood at zero and the snow lay half a foot deep. While logs crackled in the fireplace, Faulkner worked on galleys of *The Hamlet.* Then came a sudden interruption. On Saturday, January 27, as Mammy Callie sat in the kitchen while the cook bustled about getting supper, she suddenly collapsed. They carried her frail small form to her cabin nearby. It was a paralytic stroke, the doctor said. The vigil began, Estelle taking her turn with the others, as Mammy Callie's children and grandchildren made their way to Rowan Oak. Her illness was no surprise. She had been sick enough before for her kinfolks to gather. There had been times, late at night, when one of them would stick his head into the library and say, "She want de ice cream." And Faulkner would go out and drive to some "all night juke joint" where he could find the ice cream she craved. She lingered on until Wednesday, when, with Estelle at her bedside, she died without rousing from the coma.

Dressed in the fresh clean cap and apron she had requested, she lay in the parlor of Rowan Oak. A choral group sang "Swing Low, Sweet Chariot." Following another of Mammy Callie's requests, Faulkner delivered the eulogy to the weeping family. She had stood since his childhood "as a fount of authority over my conduct and of security for my physical welfare, and of active and constant affection and love," he said, concluding, "if there is a heaven, she has gone there."[16] (The next day, returning his galleys to Haas, he apologized for their lateness: with Mammy Callie's illness and death, "I have had little of heart or time either for work."[17] When Haas read the newspaper account with a transcription of the eulogy, he clipped it and sent it to Faulkner. In return, Faulkner sent him a 300-word typescript. With the divided consciousness of the artist, he told Haas that when he got it on paper "it turned out to be pretty good prose."[18]) Later, on her grave, Faulkner would have a marker erected on which, under her name and dates, the legend ran

MAMMY
Her white children
bless her.

* * *

HE was still busy with stories. Ober sold "A Point of Law" to *Collier's* for $1,000. In mid-February, Faulkner sent him one called "Gold Is Not Always" and followed that a week later with another called "The Fire on the Hearth." Again Lucas Beauchamp is the central character in what clearly could develop into another series of linked stories. He is still tight-fisted and cantankerous, stubborn and canny in an ultimately self-defeating way. Again his foil is the owner of the plantation: Carothers Edmonds—bluff, hot-tempered, easily upset, and twenty years his junior. A variation on a device in *The Hamlet* gives it a familiar ring. Lucas has become convinced that there is money hidden in the land and has enticed a St. Louis salesman out to the place with the prospect of selling one of his $300 divining machines. (In 1889 the Ripley *Advertiser* reported that a Negro had found $700 in gold near Hermanville. Uncle Jim Buddy Smith, who made moonshine whiskey on his place out near Greenfield Farm, claimed he knew where there was buried gold—hidden during the war, right there in Lafayette County.) After several complications, Lucas relies on the salted-mine trick—using fifty silver dollars, as Flem had done—to retrieve Edmonds' mule given as security and to gain title to the machine. It is a formula story done economically and adroitly. In "The Fire on the Hearth" (earlier written as "An Absolution" and "Apotheosis"), Lucas' obsession with his "finding box" drives his aged wife, Molly (alternately spelled "Mollie"), to the verge of divorce. Her portrayal was drawn directly from Mammy Callie, and her closeness to Edmonds was not unlike that of Mammy Callie to William Faulkner.

On March 14, Ober wrote him that *Collier's* had refused both stories. Almost by return mail, apparently, he sent Ober another, one of the most powerful he had ever written, entitled "Pantaloon in Black." All it had in common with the other two was the fact that its protagonist also lived on the Edmonds plantation. It was far from formula fiction, evoking, as its title suggested, the commedia dell'arte that had interested Faulkner as a young man. Here the Pantalone figure is not an old man cuckolded by a youthful rival but an enormously powerful young Negro, Rider, who loses his wife and cannot bear it, scorning religious consolation and exhausting the inadequate distractions of work and liquor and gambling before his suicidal murder of a cheating white man leads to the inevitable lynching—the climactic events not unlike those which had ended Nelse Patton's life long ago in Faulkner's childhood. In a fixative of irony, the last quarter of the story is a recital of the events by one of the deputies to his harsh, impatient wife. Unable to credit a Negro with such grief as Rider's, he misreads all of Rider's actions: "when it comes to the normal human feelings and sentiments of human beings, they might just as well be a damn herd of wild buffaloes."[19] Even toward the end of his life, Faulkner would talk of the difficulty of understanding Negroes' thoughts and feelings, compelled as they had been to develop patterns of concealment from white people. But his story showed a very different perception of the inner lives of black people from that in the portrayal of Caspey and Simon Strother a dozen years earlier in *Sartoris*. Eight days after Ober sent the story to *Collier's*, in mid-March, they replied that it was the strongest story of Faulkner's they had seen in many years, but there was no place in the magazine for such excellent work.

By now the author's copies of *The Hamlet*, bearing the dedication "To Phil Stone," had arrived at Rowan Oak. The author must have felt more concern than usual about the reviews to come, for upon them would largely depend the sales which could relieve the increasing pressures he was feeling. The first major ones began to appear at the end of March.

45

... what he remembered as dense river bottom jungle and rich farm land, is now an artificial lake twenty-five miles long: a flood control project for the cotton fields below the huge earth dam, with a few more outboard-powered fishing skiffs on it each year, and at last a sailboat. . . . the middleaging (now a professional fiction-writer: who had wanted to remain the tramp and the possessionless vagabond of his young manhood but time and success and the hardening of his arteries had beaten him). . . .

—"Mississippi," *ESPL* (35)

ON Sunday, March 31, 1940, Milton Rugoff wrote about the Snopeses in the book section of the New York *Herald Tribune*: "We watch them with the morbid absorption that marks men staring into a pit alive with lizards and nameless crawling things, except that here and there we have the painful consciousness of human kinship. . . ." The next day, however, in *The New York Times*, Ralph Thompson gave the novel its best review: "nothing short of superb—subtle and yet direct, humorous, homely, brilliantly evocative of a decaying South in the generation after the Civil War. . . . In this book," he concluded, "he is unsurpassable." On April 6, Clifton Fadiman informed his readers in *The New Yorker* that he had spent part of the week "weaving through *The Hamlet*" and that he had emerged, shaken, from "the intense murk of its sentences" with the conclusion that the author was suffering from the d.t.'s. A week later Malcolm Cowley told his readers in *The New Republic* that *The Hamlet* was Faulkner's best book since *Sanctuary*. His writing in the novel was praised by both Memphis dailies. In the *Eagle*, Moon Mullen relayed to his readers a few of the comments in *Time*, which compared the Oxford novelist to Shakespeare but remarked that only God and possibly William Faulkner knew what the essential subject of the novel was.

* * *

By late April, Faulkner's financial plight had worsened, so that he now faced the most acute crisis he had ever encountered. He wrote Haas that he needed $1,000 now and $9,000 more, perhaps in monthly payments of $400. Of the six stories he had written by March 16 only one had sold. To him, the effort and time were wasted, "as well as the time since March 15 which I have spent mortgaging my mares and colts one at a time to pay food and electricity and washing and such, and watching each mail train in hopes of a check." He would have to keep writing trash, he said. "I have a blood-and-thunder mystery novel which should sell (they usually do) but I dont dare devote six months to writing, haven't got six months to devote to it. I have another in mind in method similar to THE UNVAN-QUISHED, but since the chapters which I have written and tried to sell as short stories have not sold, I haven't the time to continue with it." He hoped that Random House could agree to his plan, even at $300 a month. "If not, can I have your blessing to try somewhere else for some similar arrangement?"[1]

Haas responded quickly. Through April 30 they had sold 6,780 copies of *The Hamlet*, but advances would eat most of that up. The best they could do was a three-book contract which would provide $1,000 now and $8,000 over the next three years. Faulkner was grateful for the response, he wrote Haas a few days later. Then he launched into a kind of capsule autobiography. "Every so often, in spite of judgment and all else, I take these fits of sort of raging and impotent exasperation at this really quite alarming paradox which my life reveals: Beginning at the age of thirty I, an artist, a sincere one and of the first class, who should be free even of his own economic responsibilities and with no moral conscience at all, began to become the sole, principal and partial support—food, shelter, heat, clothes, medicine, kotex, school fees, toilet paper and picture shows—of my mother, . . . brother and his wife and two sons, another brother's widow and child, a wife of my own and two step children, my own child; I inherited my father's debts and his dependents, white and black without inheriting yet from anyone one inch of land or one stick of furniture or one cent of money; the only thing I ever got for nothing, after the first pair of long pants I received (cost: $7.50) was the $300.00 O. Henry prize last year. I bought without help from anyone the house I live in and all the furniture; I bought my farm the same way. I am 42 years old and I have already paid for four funerals and will certainly pay for one more and in all likelihood two more beside that, provided none of the people in mine or my wife's family my superior in age outlive me, before I ever come to my own."[2] He was overstating the extent and constancy of the demands on him (and some of his relatives would deny and bitterly resent it), but not by much.

He knew, he said, that this kind of raging did no good. He asked for the thousand dollars now, and as soon as he began to draw the regular stipend he would begin a novel. True to his astonishing fertility of invention, the one he described was neither the mystery novel nor the one from the linked stories. "It is a sort of Huck Finn—a normal boy of about twelve or thirteen, a big, warmhearted, courageous, honest, utterly unreliable white man with the mentality of a child, an old negro family servant, opinionated, querulous, selfish, fairly unscrupulous, and in his second childhood, and a prostitute not very young anymore and with a great deal of character and generosity and common sense, and a stolen race horse which none of them actually intended to steal. The story is how they travel for a thousand miles from hand to mouth trying to get away from the police long enough to return the horse." In the elapsing weeks the boy "goes through in miniature all the experiences of youth which mold the man's character. They happen to be the very experiences which in his middle class parents' eyes stand for debauchery and degeneracy and actual criminality; through them he learned courage and honor and generosity and pride and pity."[3] By return mail a check for $1,000 arrived with the new contracts. Haas liked the story very much.

It was early June before Faulkner returned the contracts, and when he did, he was thinking about more than writing. "What a hell of a time we are facing. I got my uniform out the other day. I can button it, even after twenty-two years; the wings look as brave as they ever did. I swore then when I took it off in '19, that I would never wear another. . . . But now I dont know. Of course I could do no good, would last about two minutes in combat. But my feeling now is better so; that what will be left after this one will certainly not be worth living for." He linked this feeling to a complaint that was unusual for him. "Maybe the watching of all this coming to a head for the last year is why I cant write, dont seem to want to write, that is. But I can still write. That is, I haven't said at 42 all that is in the cards for me to say. And that wont do any good either, but surely it is still possible to scratch the face of the supreme Obliteration and leave a decipherable scar of some sort."[4]

He had said that he thought he was about to get at a book of some sort, but money problems absorbed the energy that could have gone into writing. In the continuing correspondence he told Haas that he had tried tentatively for a Hollywood job, but that appeared to be out. In late May he had proposed a collection of his magazine stories since 1933, and now he proposed it again, with an arrangement which would actually constitute a new advance of $2,400. Haas made the best calculations he could, but the advance he could offer fell substantially short of this new figure. On Friday, June 7, Faulkner replied in a three-page, single-spaced letter. Itemizing his debts and expenses against his assets, he concluded that though a $1,000 advance on the new novel would be welcome, what he still needed was $9,000 over two years or $5,000 over one—a gamble on his literary output. He did not want to part with his most substantial asset, "35 acres of wooded parkland inside Oxford corporate limits" until he was convinced there was no other way. He still thought the book of stories was a good idea. He didn't want to spoil their relationship with a proposition accepted out of friendship which would leave "a bitter taste in the mouth." So he wanted Haas's consent to his trying to sell the book elsewhere, even if he had to sign a contract for more than that. He told Haas that "years ago, before I knew you . . . a publisher intimated to me that I could almost write my own ticket with him."[5] He mailed the letter and began mulling over another he might write to see if Harold Guinzburg's verbal offer of 1931 still held.

On Saturday he drove out to Greenfield and worked for a while amid the commissary smells of cheese and tobacco and leather. Charlie McJunkin came in, and Faulkner neatly itemized his $4.80 worth of purchases in a small ledger. He must have reflected, as Charlie took the flour, sugar, lard, and other items, that he had been doing the same thing with Random House.

By Thursday he had Haas's reply. *Absalom, Absalom!* had earned Faulkner $3,037, *The Hamlet*, $2,700—figures that did not justify the advance Faulkner needed. Haas hoped he would let them know the details before he signed anything with someone else.

Because Harold Guinzburg was out of town, Faulkner had no word until Tuesday, June 18. It came that evening in the form of a telegram accepting Faulkner's offer. Haas was away, so Cerf responded to Faulkner's wire. "All of us are absolutely sick at heart at the thought of your leaving Random House," he told him. He had telephoned Guinzburg, a gentleman and a great gambler. They were boyhood friends, and Cerf spoke frankly. If Viking could make Faulkner a better offer, Random House would bow out, and it was only fair that the reverse should also hold. Guinzburg agreed. Cerf wrote Faulkner that he had racked his brains, and offered a $1,000 advance on the book of short stories to tide him over. He asked him to keep one thing in mind as he weighed the offer: Random House had a considerable investment in their 2,500 copies of *The Hamlet* as well as earlier books in stock. Faulkner did not even need to sleep on it. "I cant use one publisher to blackjack another into advancing me money which that second publisher had otherwise declined to advance," he wrote Cerf.[6] He would come to New York to settle the details.

It was not nearly as easy as Faulkner had expected. On Tuesday, June 25, he talked with Guinzburg, but Guinzburg felt that he could do nothing until he talked with Cerf about the matter of the plates for *The Hamlet* and the existing stock of copies, which Cerf valued at about $2,900 and which Viking Press would be expected to buy if Faulkner were to go with them. Cerf was out of town and Guinzburg had to leave immediately. He would see Cerf on the following Monday and write Faulkner about the results. Meanwhile, Faulkner would get the $1,000 advance from Haas and return home.

Before leaving, he conferred with Ober about his stories. He met Hal

Smith and Jim Devine, who offered to drive him to the airport. Instead, they wound up on Smith's thirty-eight-foot ketch and decided to make a night of it. They cast off for a cruise to Greenwich and on the way consumed all the liquor aboard. The next morning Devine photographed Faulkner—bare-chested, rope marks on his back from sleeping on deck, and the look of a man irate with the world in general.

On July 3, Faulkner received a letter from Guinzburg. Cerf had asked $1,500 for the plates and stock of *The Hamlet*. Guinzburg said this could not be considered an excessive amount, but it would mean "investing that additional sum to an amount [$6,000] which was already considerably larger than a conservative business approach would have warranted." He would regretfully have to withdraw his offer, but if Faulkner ever wanted to renew their talk, he would "always be ready to do so."

BACK where he had started from and out of pocket one trip to New York, Faulkner could do nothing but try once more for short-story sales. In New York he had told Ober to keep offering "the negro stories." The next day, after having been declined by seven magazines, "The Old People" was purchased by *Harper's* for $400. Just before he had left for New York, Faulkner had sent another story directly to the *Post*. Set a few years before the Civil War, "Almost" follows Uncle Buck McCaslin as he chases a slave named Tomey's Turl to the neighboring Prim plantation where his sweetheart lives. There it is the hunter who is trapped, extricated at last from an enforced marriage compact with Miss Sophonsiba Prim by Uncle Buddy McCaslin in a winning poker game with her brother, Jason Prim. The story is narrated by Uncle Buck's companion, a boy named Bayard, age nine at the time of the action. Most of the characters are white, but there are links with the Negro stories, and Faulkner had written this one with the emphasis entirely on the comic. When the *Post* returned it to Ober, he wrote Faulkner that some clarification should make it salable.

He was working on it when a visitor came to call. Dan Brennan was a young Minnesotan who had gone from pulp-magazine stories of aerial combat to the writings of Faulkner. The previous summer he had hitchhiked into Oxford and telephoned Rowan Oak. Something about his young voice had made Estelle ask him to come out. Faulkner had taken him on a picnic before he left the next day. Now Faulkner welcomed him back. When Brennan asked if he could sit in the library while Faulkner wrote, his host agreed. It was a comfortable room, aromatic with the new mixture Faulkner had begun using six months before. It was Dunhill's A10528, a blend of thirteen different tobaccos that sold for six dollars a pound. It was a smoke he deeply enjoyed. Taking a wooden match from a box held in a metal rectangle bearing RAF wings, he would push the diminishing tobacco down into the briar, relighting it until he would tap out the last fine gray ash. Entering a room he had left, one could tell he had been there by the strong, rich, heavy aroma. Brennan read from the books on the shelves along the wall and made himself at home. When Faulkner finished about three o'clock, Brennan had a souvenir. He retrieved fifteen pages of a revised version of "Almost" from the wastebasket, and Faulkner inscribed them with the date, July 19, 1940. The first page had been typed on the back of two paragraphs from another story called "Go Down, Moses," which was about a Negro funeral.

"Where'd you get the idea for it?" Brennan asked.

"I was down to the station last week," Faulkner told him, "and a coffin came in off the train."[7] Faulkner sent this story to the *Post*, even though it had none of the comedy of the ones they had most recently bought. The story began with a young Negro about to be electrocuted in Illinois for murder. To his grandmother, Aunt Mollie Beauchamp, he had been sold into Egypt, and Pharaoh has sent his body home, where it can be afforded the burial demanded by Mollie and paid for by Gavin Stevens and others. Unlike "Pantaloon in Black," where the connection with the other Negro stories is only through place, "Go Down, Moses" fills in more material in the gradually accreting history of the black Beauchamps and McCaslins, and shows some of the bonds which link them to white families. The title came from the spiritual which Faulkner had known all his life, a musical form fresh in his mind from those sung at Mammy Callie's funeral service. Faulkner may have thought of it for another reason. *Gone With the Wind* had played in Oxford in March, and if Faulkner went to see it, he could not have missed the Negro chorus in the sound track, in the chaos just before the fall of Atlanta, singing "Go Down, Moses." (One reaction to the film had amused him. Auntee had paid seventy-five cents for a reserved seat, only to stalk out of the theatre the first time Sherman's name was mentioned.)

The *Post* rejected "Go Down, Moses," but Faulkner persisted. On August 5 he sent them "Tomorrow," another of Gavin Stevens' cases, narrated by his nephew Chick, age twelve at the time of the action. It is ultimately another detective story of character and fate, rather than fact, in which Chick repeats a dictum of his uncle: "it don't take many words to tell the sum of any human experience; that somebody has already done it in eight: He was born, he suffered and he died."[8] The "somebody" was Joseph Conrad.

Because Faulkner had assumed that Guinzburg had also written Random House, Bennett Cerf remained in a state of suspense until late July. When he finally wrote asking what the decision was, Faulkner brought him up to date. If he could sell some stories and get through until mid-November, when he could begin to collect on his cotton and tenant crops, he could make it. One more long story would complete the book to be made out of the linked series, but that would be a novella, and there was no time to write that now, and it might be best anyway to publish it after the Huck

Finn novel. "It will be impossible to get at it though before next year at the earliest, unless lightning in some form strikes me a golden blow."[9] Fortune responded with a series of taps. On August 9, Ober sent Faulkner his own check for $400 for the sale of "Pantaloon in Black" so that he would not have to wait for payment from *Harper's*. Four days later Ober wrote that the *Post* was buying "Tomorrow" for $1,000. Less than a month later *The Atlantic Monthly* would pay $300 for "Gold Is Not Always," and a few days after that, *Collier's* would pay $1,000 for "Go Down, Moses." He had survived the acute phase of this crisis, but he could not yet cease writing magazine stories.

One of his stories produced an unlooked-for effect. When "A Point of Law" appeared, Miss Maud and Johncy found so many close resemblances between it and one of Johncy's stories that they were convinced Bill had appropriated the plot. "Look, Mother," Johncy said. "Bill didn't steal my story. A writer doesn't know where his stories come from except out of his mind. . . . He doesn't try to remember where each part came from." His mother stopped pacing, sat down, and looked at her son. "Johncy, Billy told me that a long time ago, except he called it stealing."[10] She still felt responsible for insisting that Bill read Johncy's stories.

Faulkner suggested that his brother use his experiences as the engineer on Oxford's WPA construction projects in a novel. When it was done, he wrote Bennett Cerf, who said they would be glad to read it. They did not take it, but Ober made some suggestions for revision and later sold it to Harcourt, Brace, which would bring it out as *Men Working*. When Johncy went to New York to meet his new publishers, *Saturday Evening Post* editor Stuart Rose mentioned his famous brother. "My brother is the most-even-tempered man in the world," Johncy told him, "mad as a hornet all the time." Johncy's editor asked if he would mind spelling his name the way his brother did, because it would help sell the book. Johncy cheerfully agreed. One unexpected result in Oxford was that thereafter he got his mail immediately rather than after it had first gone to his uncle, who bore the same name.

It was a busy summer for the whole family. In Shanghai late that July, Cho-Cho married William Francis Fielden, a tall, handsome young American who worked for the British-American Tobacco Company. Just about that time Jack had flown to Oxford to leave his two-place yellow-and-black cabin Aeronca there before he took up his new FBI assignment in Alaska. Jack had tried unsuccessfully to volunteer for RAF pilot training, and when he requested activation of his reserve commission and transfer to the Air Corps, J. Edgar Hoover blocked it because he needed experienced agents at home.

More and more the war was impinging on Faulkner's life. Every time he picked up the *Eagle*, there were photographs of local boys off to the service. His copies of *The Manchester Guardian* and the *Commercial Appeal* were full of dispatches from fighting abroad. Early that fall he wrote Haas, "I still have the novel in mind, may get at it when bad weather stops farming and flying and I become better adjusted mentally to the condition of this destruction-bent world. Saxon fighting Saxon, Latin against Latin, Mongol with a Slav ally fighting a Mongol who is the ally of a Saxon-Latin ally of the first Slav; nigger fighting nigger at the behest of white men; one democracy trying to blow the other democracy's fleet off the seas."[11] That October he made eleven flights, piloting four different aircraft as he worked on figure-eights, spot-landings, and instrument flying. He also gave himself a refresher course in Morse code. He told Haas he thought he would teach a course in radio and navigation at a CAA primary flying school attached to the university. And he was trying to get a National Guard commission.

But soon he had to break off to boil the pot again. Late in the month the annual county fair had brought the carnival to town, including an illusion called "Santaita, the Headless Wonder." In his story he used another illusionist, once billed as "Signor Canova, Master of Illusion. He Disappears While You Watch Him." Gavin Stevens discovered that Canova had not used that title for ten years, however, when he solved the two murders the man had concealed with his old skills. Again Chick narrated. These stories were forming themselves into a pattern. Faulkner was not using the detective mode for the kind of weightier purposes that had shaped *Absalom, Absalom!*, but the writing challenged his ingenuity, and he must have been thinking of their possibilities for collection in another book. Unfortunately for present purposes, "An Error in Chemistry" did not sell and it would be five years before it did.

There was a new diversion he enjoyed that mild early fall. He had seen Art Guyton building an eighteen-foot sailboat in his backyard, and the first-year medical student had invited him to sail when it was finished. At last he hauled the 800-pound craft twenty-five miles to the northwest, where she rode evenly on the twenty-mile-long Sardis Reservoir, her twenty-nine-foot mast sloop-rigged and carrying 230 square feet of sail. Art knew little about sailing, and when Faulkner went out with him, Art was particularly impressed by Mr. Bill's nautical terminology. There were other, familiar diversions too. Faulkner took the children on hayrides, and after they built a bonfire out in the country he would tell stories and lead them in songs such as "Old MacDonald Had a Farm." At other times he might lead a horseback-riding group of Jill and five or six others, setting out along a favorite trail.

Jill would start second grade that fall. She was growing into a shy child —pretty like her mother and quiet like her father. He remembered taking other children on walks and telling them stories: the Stone children, Cho-Cho and Malcolm. Now he had a child of his own, but when he spent time with her it was often after he had emerged from a spell of concentrated work or of depression, or sometimes after the drinking which the depression had brought on.

NOVEMBER brought hunting. The timber companies had denuded the land where General Stone's camp had stood, so now they had to travel 150 miles south to the Big Sunflower River in the Delta near Anguilla. Bob Harkins led them on his forty-ninth consecutive hunt. "Old Man Bob" Evans, Uncle Bud Miller, and Ike Roberts followed him in the hierarchy of the hunt. Then came the younger men, such as Felix Linder and William Faulkner. Negotiating the last eight miles by motorboat, they would pitch their tents and make camp. At first, they would eat pork, but before a full day passed, old Ad Bush would be cooking squirrel and coon. They would go out in the four-o'clock darkness, making their way through the thick brush into the deep woods, the leashed dogs sniffing and barking. Then the drive would begin, the hunters poised at their stands for the dash of the buck. At the end of the long day they would sit around the campfire drinking whiskey, waiting to eat the plain, hearty fare at the rough-hewn table. After clean-up chores, the storytelling and the nickel poker would while away the short evenings. Faulkner enjoyed it, hardly distinguishable from the others in his stained hunting clothes and worn slouch hat. He told some of the memorable tales, but most of the time he would listen, and often he would sit reading a book. He might scribble a note now and again, but whenever anyone began an off-color story, he would unobtrusively make his way off by himself.

He would drink moderately at first. Then his tempo would speed up. It may have been on this hunt that Ad Bush went to Uncle Bud one morning and told him he ought to go and take a look at Mr. Bill. Miller found him unconscious and ashen. Their alarm mounted because they were afraid he had suffered a kidney seizure of some sort. As they tried to figure out a way to get him out quickly, the sound of a motorboat reached them—"the best sound I ever heard in my life," Red Brite called it.[12] Back in Oxford, Dr. Culley told them a few more hours would have been too late. Alcohol, together with the weeks and months of worry and irritation, had done its work. Brite did not know if it was a perforated ulcer the doctor had feared, but whatever it was, it had been a close call.

If this was the year it happened, he recovered in surprisingly short order. By December 16, Ober had a hunting story from him entitled "Delta Autumn." It focused chiefly on Uncle Ike McCaslin and on one of his juniors on the annual hunt, Don Boyd. The climax comes when a light-colored Negro woman appears seeking Boyd, the father of her infant son. But he has repudiated them, leaving only money for her when he goes out to his stand. Struggling with moral outrage at Boyd's behavior, Uncle Ike is still unable to admit the idea of intermarriage until some distant future. Boyd's killing of a doe serves to point up for Ike the ravaging of the woods.

The cynical Boyd feels that the country is doomed too—to foreign or domestic fascism. Ike still has faith enough that its defenders would rise up, but the implication seems clear that he may not live to see them and that he certainly will not see many more hunts. Whether or not Faulkner was doing so consciously, he was creating a group of hunting stories from ante-bellum days over a century into present time, and the events taking place on the literal level—in each manifestation of the hunt or chase— carried implications which brought into focus moral and political problems in the historical process gripping the modern world.

By the early days of January he was beleaguered again. The worsening state of international affairs was manifested on his very doorstep when, late in the old year, Cho-Cho and little Vicki returned, having left China with other dependents of American businessmen. When Faulkner looked at his checkbook and his accumulated bills and obligations, he knew he was once more close to the desperate expedients he had contemplated in the summer. On January 16 he sent a telegram to Harold Ober: WIRE ME COLLECT WHAT POSSIBILITY OF ANY SUM WHATEVER AND WHEN FROM ANY MSS OF MINE YOU HAVE. URGENTLY NEED ONE HUNDRED BY SATURDAY.[13] Ober wired the money immediately. Faulkner returned to his short-story writing and thought again about the collection. He would plunge into Civil Defense work and try again for a commission. But as a further, desperate, hedge against disaster, he would try once more to go back to Hollywood.

46

> . . . his native land; he was born of it and his bones will sleep in
> it; loving it even while hating some of it: the river jungle and
> the bordering hills where still a child he had ridden behind his
> father on the horse . . . the wilderness, the two weeks in the
> woods, in camp, the rough food and the rough sleeping, the life
> of men and horses and hounds, not to slay the game but to pur-
> sue it, touch and let go, never satiety. . . .
>
> —"Mississippi," *ESPL* (36)

"Thank you for the money," he wrote Ober on January 18, 1941. "I did
not intend the wire to ask for a loan, but I have used the money and I
thank you for it. . . . When I wired you I did not have $15.00 to pay
electricity bill with, keep my lights burning."[1] That was how he now had
to think: which past-due bills came first? At the month's end he wrote
Will Lewis refusing to sign postdated checks Lewis had sent to be applied
against his bill at Neilson's department store. He reminded Lewis that he
had tried in the summer to explain about a government tax claim for an
additional $1,600 on his 1937 Hollywood income. Five days before Christ-
mas the second half of that amount had been demanded with threats of
penalties. If he were to sign any postdated checks or notes, they would
go to those who had supplied his family with food and heat. He enclosed
a $10 check and would send more when he could. If Lewis wouldn't
accept this, he could sue and be damned. If he did, Faulkner would try
to protect the creditors he mentioned. Then, after the government was
through with him, Neilson's could have what was left. They might even
get an autographed book. It would be worth a lot more, Faulkner said,
than his signature on a postdated check.[2]

It was the depth of winter now, with the fields showing only the bare
bushes and stalks of last year's cotton and corn. The country at large was
stirring with war preparations, but there was still no indication of a satis-

factory job for him to do. It was at bleak times like this that he was apt to retire with a supply of Old Crow to accomplish his flight from the outer world and to still his inner turmoil. He might escape for a week, or two weeks, or more.

The season dragged along. He went to New Orleans about his taxes. By now Helen Baird Lyman had some sense of the world's view of this one-time would-be lover, and she and Guy Lyman probably figured in this business trip. On February 19 he sent Estelle a birthday telegram.

As the year turned toward spring, life quickened. In the uncertain weather of late February or early March, as many as a hundred people would have a barbecue out at Sardis Reservoir. Faulkner would join in the songfests around a bonfire, and when the group was small he might sing a solo, usually his favorite, "Water Boy."

In early March he was still working at stories to keep the fires going on his hearth and in his kitchen. "The Tall Men" was set out in the county, but he could not exclude the way politics and war were affecting even its most remote residents. The action is straightforward: a federal investigator, arriving to serve a warrant on the two youngest McCallum boys for failing to register for the draft, is detained while their father's injured leg is amputated. Fuming about people who will do anything to get on the relief rolls, the investigator learns from the marshal that these are people who have refused a federal cotton subsidy with the proud reply "We can make out," who have no commerce with the big world's "loud grabble and snatch of AAA and WPA and a dozen other three-letter reasons for a man not to work." The story gave Faulkner a chance to update the views on modernization he had been expressing since his first comments on electric lighting and the motorcar. The virtues of the McCallums made clearer the weakening he saw in the moral fiber of other descendants of the once-independent Scotch-Irish who had emigrated to find freedom as well as better lives. "Life's a pretty durn valuable thing," the old marshal says near the end. "I don't mean just getting along from one WPA relief check to the next one, but honor and pride and discipline that make a man worth preserving, make him of any value. . . . Maybe it takes trouble, bad trouble, to teach it back to us. . . ."[3] The McCallums also demonstrate something else in this deeply felt story. The boys had simply neglected to register for the draft. But in the eyes of their father, if the situation is serious enough for an investigator to come after them, they can make only one response. They leave with the marshal and the investigator to go and enlist. Faulkner must have felt a ray of spring sunshine when Ober sold the story to the *Post* almost immediately for $1,000.

The earlier stories were still on his mind. "Last year I mentioned a volume, collected short stories," he wrote Haas in early May, "general theme being relationship between white and negro races here." He wondered if the time was right for such a book. He would begin with "The Fire and the Hearth" and follow it with "Pantaloon in Black," "The Old People,"

"Delta Autumn," and then "Go Down, Moses," which would give the book its title. Would such a book ease the financial situation between them enough for him to gamble the time and effort, "or shall I hold off until I can earn enough from short stories, or collect enough of the loan I made the friend two years ago to write a new novel?"[4] Haas was quick to encourage him. The book should earn him about $1,500, and they would be glad to send him advances against that amount. Faulkner immediately set to work.

There was a good deal of adaptation and revision to do. Ober had been unable to sell "Almost." Under the title "Was," Faulkner used it to begin the volume. The first-person narrator, eight-year-old Bayard, was replaced by nine-year-old McCaslin Edmonds, and Faulkner told the story in the third person as young "Cass" Edmonds experienced it. Theophilus McCaslin, still pursuing Tomey's Turl, was his great-uncle Buck. Miss Sophonsiba was a Beauchamp, not a Prim, and her brother Jason was now Hubert Beauchamp. An introductory segment identified Cass as the elder cousin of a boy who had heard of but not seen these events: Isaac "Ike" McCaslin, who would figure importantly in stories to come. Several of them would prove much more difficult to adapt than this one had been.

WISTERIA bloomed alongside Cape Jasmine as late spring turned into summer. Jill's school year ended and she was awarded a Music Prize Card for exemplary piano practice. On June 18, Ben Wasson came to visit, bringing with him a young sergeant on furlough. Shelby Foote was an aspiring Greenville writer, and he had brought his copy of *The Hamlet* with him. When Ben asked Faulkner to sign it, Faulkner complied cordially. They stayed for dinner, which Estelle served in the sunken garden she had designed off the west gallery. Faulkner told them a little about the new book, but the conversation was casual. Foote would soon report back to camp, and Ben had just about decided to enlist in the Navy. It must have seemed to Faulkner that everybody was going but him. He was flying, but he was restless. He had told Haas that the Civilian Pilot Training program was not enough, and he still thought about trying to get into the Air Corps. Mayor Bob Williams had appointed him aircraft warning chief for the area, and by late that month his organizational work put him behind with *Go Down, Moses*.

He had an office over a drugstore on the square, with a desk, a telephone, and a map of the county on the wall. He got social-studies teacher Charles Nelson to go out into the county with him to explain why aircraft spotters had to be recruited. On other occasions Judge Taylor McElroy went out with him, and McElroy noticed that Faulkner took notes at some of the meetings. At the end of the month, completing the organizing, he used one of his favorite quotations, from Irish patriot John Philpot Curran: "God hath vouchsafed man liberty only under condition of eternal vigilance, which condition if he break it, servitude is the consequence of his crime, the punishment of his guilt."

Another reason that *Go Down, Moses* was going more slowly than he had expected was the amount of rewriting involved. In revising "A Point of Law" to become the first chapter of "The Fire and the Hearth," he introduced new material about the buried treasure and laid groundwork for the major concern he had mentioned to Haas: the relationship between the white and black families. In a long flashback, he detailed the relationship between Lucas Beauchamp and Zack Edmonds, the son of McCaslin Edmonds. Molly had gone to Zack Edmonds' house to care for his infant son, Carothers, after the death of the mother. By the time Lucas demands her return, nearly six months later, he feels so dishonored that only blood can assuage his pride. Only a misfire saves Edmonds from death by gunshot and Lucas from a rope. The proud and haughty descendant of old L. Q. C. McCaslin, Lucas is imprisoned in his caste by his black skin. The third and fourth sections of the rewritten story completed the comic business of the counterstroke in which Lucas' daughter and her husband plant a still on Lucas' place, but there was much less of the comic about him now than there had been in the magazine version.

The revision of "Gold Is Not Always" was simpler, but the third and last chapter of "The Fire and the Hearth" was a different matter. Faulkner added to the Negro side of the genealogy as Ike McCaslin attempts to distribute L. Q. C. McCaslin's legacy to his black descendants. (At some point Faulkner sketched out a genealogical chart for himself as he got deeper into

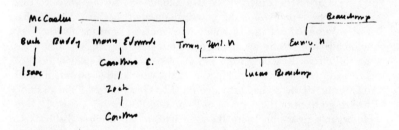

Author's tentative McCaslin-Beauchamp genealogy for *Go Down, Moses* (Courtesy William Faulkner Collections, University of Virginia Library)

the tangled relationships.) He pictured the two cousins, Ike and Lucas, together, and then employed another extended flashback to paint poignantly other injustices and sorrows endured by the black line. As Lucas and Zack had been raised almost as brothers, so are Lucas' son, Henry, and Roth's son, Carothers, the latter delivered by Molly and nursed at her breast with her own child. But one day in childhood, when "the old curse of his fathers, the old haughty ancestral pride" descended upon Carothers, he repudiated the black child and "entered his heritage. He ate its bitter fruit." (111, 114) Even in his adulthood, Molly would be the only mother Carothers would ever know. And if Lucas is a crotchety old man, often an antagonist, it seems, as well as a tenant, he is to Carothers *"more like old Carothers than all the rest of us put together, including old Carothers.* (118) His speech, close now to standard English, shows something of the pride and independence he has inherited from his arrogant white grandfather.

Faulkner was able, apparently, to type "Pantaloon in Black" from a copy of the story manuscript. This took him to page 159 of his typescript, but his pace slowed down immediately when he took up "The Old People." He had to make numerous changes so the new characterizations would function in terms of the progression of events in the book—which was not quite a plot—and again in terms of the black-white theme. The nameless young narrator of the *Harper's* version became Ike McCaslin, and Faulkner used third-person narration in juxtaposing him to Cass Edmonds, just as Cass had been juxtaposed to Ike's father, Uncle Buck McCaslin, in "Was." Ike's true father-surrogate, however, is Sam Fathers. As "The Fire and the Hearth" had treated bondage, "The Old People" treats liberation. Released from service in town to spend what remains of his life in the big woods, Sam trains Ike in the lore of the wilderness and the hunt, preparing him in turn for his liberation from the constraints of town life and town thinking. From a hunting story with quasi-mystical overtones, it became a story of an initiation which would have profound consequences.

According to plan, he took up "Delta Autumn" next, transforming Don Boyd into Carothers (called "Roth") Edmonds. He further revealed that the woman he repudiates is the granddaughter of Tennie's Jim, so that Roth has wronged not just an anonymous mulatto woman, but the very same blood wronged by his great-great-great-grandfather. The wheel has come full circle. Reaching page 200 of his typescript, Faulkner decided that he had to change his plan. He wanted the same kind of powerful effect "An Odor of Verbena" had provided for *The Unvanquished*. But to do it, he had to go back to the material of "The Old People."

He began a new story with Ike aged sixteen, but using a flashback to recapitulate earlier material, he again evoked the mystique of the hunt as he had done in "Lion." He used it as his working title. Abandoning gun and watch, finally even compass and stick, deep in the big woods the boy is vouchsafed a glimpse of Old Ben. This is his second acceptance, like that of a candidate past his novitiate and ready for new vows. This was Section 1. Faulkner sent it off to New York, where it arrived on July 25, 1941.

As he began the second section, he reworked more material from "Lion." In *Harper's*, narrator Quentin Compson was sixteen and Ike McCaslin an old man. Now the boy is Ike, in his thirteenth year when the great dog, Lion, makes his fated appearance. Ike and Sam have hunted Ben with a fyce dog that has the courage but not the size for the job. Ike's failure to fire at Old Ben from point-blank range marks his commitment, like Sam's, to this annual ritual drama in a way others cannot understand. Ben was more than quarry, linked as he was with the spirit of the vanishing wilderness.

If Faulkner had looked for further evidence of the day-by-day disappearance of the past, it was clearly to be seen that August. Earlier in the year the old Cumberland Presbyterian Church on South Street had been demolished to make way for a Kroger supermarket. Now they were tearing down the Lafayette Springs Hotel, a part of the county's social life for over a century, where Sallie Murry Falkner had taken him and the others as children. And now the Illinois Central discontinued all passenger service through Oxford. He could never again board a train at the depot for Memphis or New Orleans, as he had done to go off to Canada, to New York, or to set off for Europe. The disappearance of the wilderness was no isolated phenomenon.

By early September, Section 2 of the story was in New York. Faulkner went ahead as Ike McCaslin, in the coldest December of his sixteen years, waits for the climax. After providing comic relief and building suspense with a whiskey-buying mission that took Boon and Ike to Memphis, Faulkner showed the climactic combat joined in some of the most effective writing he ever produced. In at the kill, Ike sees Lion leap at Ben's throat an instant before Boon flings himself on his back as his knife seeks Ben's heart. When the three fall, it is not simply superb action, it evokes a sense of the classic and massive, a final struggle such as that of the Laocoön, set not on the Trojan shore but deep in the big woods of north Mississippi. Faulkner completed the section with a shift of tone and mood as from one symphonic movement to another, and drew it to a close as the great dog and the old priest of the woods follow Old Ben in death.

Not all of Faulkner's working time had been devoted to the steadily lengthening novella. He had written two outlines for motion pictures, but no summons had followed from the West Coast. Most of his advance on the book had been used up, and it was obvious what he had to do. Instead of trying a mystery story such as "An Error in Chemistry," which still had not sold, he turned to the material on his desk in search of a salable piece. As he rewrote, the young hunter was not called Ike; he is simply "the boy," and McCaslin Edmonds' dialogue is given to "his father." It ends not with death but with another rite of initiation successfully completed. Striving to learn the hunter's humility and pride, the boy has experienced them, and courage too, in the attack of the fyce on the bear. When he is unable to understand, however, why neither he nor Sam had shot Old Ben, his father quotes Keats to him: " 'She cannot fade, though thou hast not thy bliss. For ever wilt thou love, and she be fair.' " Through his forbearance, Ike has ensured that he can continue to attain his partial joy, like the lover on the poet's Grecian urn. The *Post* was interested in the story, but an editor told Ober that if "the boy could realize that what the bear, the dog, Sam, and he did, came from the heart, and therefore was truth, because his father had said truth was all things that touch the human heart, it would go a long way toward increasing the number of appreciative readers." With no carbon of the story, Faulkner made the change from memory and sent it in almost by return mail. On November 14, Ober informed him that the *Post* had bought the story for $1,000. It would be called "The Bear," as would the chapter in the book.

THE gold and bronze of the asters and chrysanthemums had faded as the fall colors brightened and changed outside his window. He emerged occasionally into the exterior world to take up his other roles. He took Jill to the carnival and occasionally to mystery films at the early evening show on Saturdays. He would sometimes amuse her by mimicking some of the mannerisms they had seen on the screen. (At *The Phantom of the Opera*, however, when she screamed in delighted horror, her father moved away from her. Finally he left the theatre.) He rode little now, but some days when she mounted her pony he would be there, leaning on the paddock rail.

Haas had hoped they could have all of the manuscript by December 1 so they could publish on March 1. But the magazine story had taken time and now he had to go back and revise "Was," adding, tightening, and preparing for heavily philosophical sequences to come. And there was something else. Stephen Longstreet, a writer he had met at Random House, had found an agent, William Herndon, who was sure he could help Faulkner in Hollywood. That spring Herndon had tried, without success, to sell some of his work for screen stories. In the fall Faulkner suddenly heard from him again after Herndon had talked with producer Robert Buckner at Warner Brothers. The result was a nineteen-page treatment in which Faulkner showed what he would do to doctor a sick script based on *The Damned Don't Cry*, Harry C. Hervey's novel about a poor-white girl from Savannah. It was as though her family were Compsons born on the wrong side of the tracks. He also wrote five story lines, each running between twenty and twenty-five pages, for Herndon to try to sell. With this done, he must have been more than ready to go to hunting camp. Arenza "Renzi" McJunkin, one of his tenants on the farm, would be his companion and body servant on such occasions, in part to see that he returned to Oxford in condition to resume his unfinished work.

Shortly after his return he wrote Haas to explain one reason for the delay. "There is more meat in it than I thought, a section now that I am going to be proud of and which requires careful writing and rewriting to get it exactly right."[5] He thought he could send in the rest by December 15, and as it turned out, he came close to his estimate. He supplied careful instructions at the beginning of Section 4 of "The Bear," which began on page 253 of his typescript. "Set as written, without caps or stops at beginning and end of paragraphs unless put there by me. . . ." It was a carefully planned strategy. At age twenty-one, Ike is to repudiate the land which is his heritage. But in turning it over to his second cousin and other father-surrogate, McCaslin Edmonds, he has to explain his renunciation. His long disquisition ranges back over the lives of his ancestors and the moral questions they embodied in the relations between slaves and masters. To encompass this long argument, compressing time as it does, Faulkner eliminated the need for italics after the beginning of the section by starting his paragraphs in the lower case and ending them without periods (except for dialogue and flashbacks) in order to give a sense of continuity. Remembering, perhaps, Ben Wasson's attempts to be helpful with the setting copy of *The Sound and the Fury*, he wrote, "Note to Printer: . . . DO NOT CHANGE PUNCTUATION NOR CONSTRUCTION."

Sitting in the plantation commissary, Ike elaborates his argument to his cousin. The land was never his nor his ancestors'; "because on the instant when Ikkemotubbe discovered, realised, that he could sell it for money, on that instant it ceased ever to have been his forever . . . and the man who bought it bought nothing." God had created man not to own the earth, but to be "His overseer . . . [and] to hold the earth mutual and intact in the communal anonymity of brotherhood. . . ." (257) He has discovered how far man has departed from brotherhood: in the commissary ledgers, in the painfully scrawled entries of the old man and of his sons, Buck and Buddy —entries about the black people whom the old man owned and upon whom he begat children, even upon his own mulatto daughter. The ledgers' account is a "chronicle which was a whole land in miniature, which multiplied and compounded was the entire South. . . ." (293)

Faulkner knew the plantation system, not just from stories he had heard but also from books he had read, such as *The Southern Plantation Overseer*, which he had borrowed from plantation owner Will Bryant nearly two years before.[6] Old ledgers were common in commissaries, and one in a general store in Taylor even bore an entry for a Carothers Edmonds. And Faulkner had an intimate knowledge of this symbolic artifact from his own ledger in the commissary where for the past two years he had made all the purchase entries for half a dozen black families. Some of his fellow townsmen might think Greenfield Farm was a plaything Faulkner used for posing as a farmer, but it was an avocation which not only satisfied a deep need but also provided experience which was translated directly into fiction. In the rest of the long section, Faulkner described how Ike's renunciation also costs him his marriage. He has already taken up the carpenter's tools in an imitation of Christ. He will remain a celibate, a kind of priest of the big woods, instructing many surrogate sons over the years, as Sam Fathers had instructed him.

Faulkner set the fifth and last section of "The Bear" a year and a half after the death of Old Ben, reworking the last part of "Lion" as he forged another link to the early sections. Now it is Ike who says "Chief . . . Grandfather" to a totem animal as Sam had done in "The Old People," but it is not to the great buck but to a sinister totem animal: a huge old snake.

Mixing the comic and the ironic at the end, Faulkner used a personal experience. One day a hunter had warned him away from a tree before which
he was repairing his rifle; the squirrels in the tree, the hunter said, were
his.[7] Here it is Boon Hogganbeck, maladroit with firearms as always, ham-
mering the disjointed barrel of his gun against the jammed breech and
shouting, not knowing it is Ike behind him, "Dont touch a one of them!
They're mine!" (331)

When he finished rewriting "Delta Autumn". it was three times as long
as the magazine version, which had finally sold—for $25 to *Story*. Roth's
killing of the doe, coming after the heroic pursuit of the legendary bear,
helps emphasize the change in the men who hunt the ravished woods.
Again Ike McCaslin serves as conscience: "No wonder the ruined woods
I used to know dont cry for retribution! he thought: The people who
have destroyed it will accomplish its revenge." (364) And Roth's rejection
of the woman who has borne his child shows that the malign spirit of
Lucius Quintus Carothers McCaslin still survives.

Saxe Commins was editing the typescript. Faulkner instructed him to
renumber the pages of the copy of "Go Down, Moses," which he already
had, to follow "Delta Autumn." That completed the book. "Wish I had
money to come up there and go through it with you," he wrote Commins.
"I think it's good stuff. But then I always do."[8]

On January 21, 1942, he sent Haas a dedication for the book, and it was
as though the tragic face of Mollie Beauchamp was still there in his mind.
He had written:

To Mammy
CAROLINE BARR
Mississippi
[1840–1940]
Who was born in slavery and who
gave to my family a fidelity without
stint or calculation of recompense
and to my childhood an immeasurable
devotion and love

He was thinking about more than the book now. "This world is bitched
proper this time, isn't it?" he went on. He had done his Civil Defense work,
which must have seemed more serious in the wake of Pearl Harbor. But
that was not enough. He had a chance to teach air navigation in the Navy
as a civilian. "If I can get my affairs here established, I think I'll take it."[9]

He had always liked acting the soldier, as when he wore the RAF blue
at parties and dances in Lafayette County. Aged forty-four, he knew more
about war now than he had then, but he still wanted to go, if for different
reasons. While Commins went ahead with *Go Down, Moses*, the author
would be trying somehow to get into the service.

47

> . . . the R.A.F. names and the machines they flew: Malan and
> Aitken and Finucane and Spitfire and Beaufighter and Hurricane
> and Buerling and Deere and the foreigners too like the Amer-
> icans who wouldn't wait and the Poles and Frenchmen who
> declined to be whipped: Daymond and Wzlewski and Closter-
> mann. . . .
>
> —*The Mansion* (244)

WHEN Bill Fielden was able to join his family at Rowan Oak, after sailing in convoy from Shanghai two months earlier, his meeting with his wife's mother and stepfather was not propitious. Both were drinking heavily, but it was not long before they recovered. When the weather warmed up they organized softball games, with Bill Fielden pitching for one of the children's teams and Faulkner for the other. Afterward they would sit in the shade with their Cokes and cold beer. When Faulkner decided they should have a Victory Garden, Bill and Malcolm cleared out the tough cocoa grass near the kitchen, and since it was too far to bring mules in from the farm, and there was no gas for the small tractor, they devised another method. Bill was big and strong and young, so Faulkner rigged up a harness. Bill would lean into the traces while Faulkner followed at the plow handles behind them. When they finished, they would move into the shade for the cold beer.

IN the months before the spring weather broke, Faulkner had performed his usual labors at the desk and produced another Gavin Stevens story entitled "Knight's Gambit." Narrated again by Stevens' nephew, Charles Weddel, it showed a growing fondness for these two familiar characters and reflected his own current preoccupations. "It is a love story," Faulkner would later write, "in which Stevens prevents a crime (murder) not for justice but to gain (he is now fifty plus) the childhood sweetheart which he lost 20 years ago."[1] Soon afterward Ober received another story. "Two Soldiers" employed one of Faulkner's favorite devices. He used a narrator, not quite nine, who idolizes the older brother determined to go off to defend his country. It was a touching story which followed the not entirely naïve narrator's unauthorized trip to Memphis so he could "chop the wood and tote the water" for his brother Pete and the other soldiers. Faulkner's aim was unerring. The *Post* bought it immediately for $1,000. "Knight's Gambit" was rejected by *Harper's* because of "obscurity and complexity."

He addressed the war more directly in "Snow," which Ober received on February 17. Like "Evangeline," it shows Don and the nameless young narrator trying to solve a mystery, and like "Mistral," their story is once again set in the Alps, but this time the villain is a brutal Nazi. It was refused on the same grounds as "Knight's Gambit."

Through the spring and early summer of 1942, Faulkner would have three principal concerns, alternatives with shifting priorities from week to week and sometimes from day to day: selling enough stories to meet the current crisis, trying for a screenwriting job, or seeking a commission.

The next story that he completed was "My Grandmother Millard and General Bedford Forrest and the Battle of Harrykin Creek." In it Granny Millard employs Cousin Melisandre to use Mrs. Compson's stratagem of saving the family silver by sitting on it in an outhouse guarded by her Negro cook. When the Yankees see through the trick, she is saved by a Confederate lieutenant who falls in love with her. Faulkner thought it had not only humor but a message: "a willingness to pull up the pants and carry on, no matter with whom, let alone what." He was concerned, however, that the "can motif"[2] might present problems for the *Post*. He was right.

He decided to write a sequel to a story the *Post* did like. He returned to the Grier family of "Two Soldiers," and in "Shall Not Perish" he again extolled the dignity, patriotism, self-sacrifice, love, and compassion of these hill people. There is no humor in this story, for it deals with the reactions of the boy and his mother to the death of Pete Grier, Yoknapatawpha County's first casualty. Faulkner was obviously composing what he hoped would be a commercial story, but into it he was putting some of his own deepest feelings embellished with borrowings from national events and local color. Almost by return mail he learned that he had missed again: the boy's language was "overwrought and artificial." He revised it and sent it to Ober three times, without success.

A story he sent along with the third revision may have been composed on the screened-in porch of "The Lodge," the cabin at Greenfield. There he could check on the farming that Renzi supervised and do his own work far from the sound of a telephone and a little farther, perhaps, from the thought of his bills. The setting could have been prompted by the Greenfield blacksmith shop, suggesting as it did the old man who had been the model for Sam Fathers. Whatever it was, Faulkner turned once more to the county's Chickasaw Indians of the old days. "A Courtship" is a sly story, told by a nameless Indian, of the epic feats performed by Ikkemotubbe and David Hogganbeck contesting for Herman Basket's sister, an Indian maiden as beautiful and sedentary as the young Eula Varner. Ober enjoyed it but warned Faulkner that it would be hard for most magazines to use it. Ober was right.

Meanwhile, the reviews of *Go Down, Moses* had been coming in. Faulkner had thanked Haas for his author's copies, but he would later recall his shock at seeing a subtitle: *And Other Stories*. "Moses is indeed a novel,"[3] he would write, but most of the reviewers took the subtitle at face value. As usual, the reviews were mixed. In early May, William Abraham wrote in the Boston *Globe* that the stories "represent William Faulkner at his best. Which is equivalent to saying the best we have." A week later in *The New York Times*, seeing the unitary nature of the book, Horace Gregory was almost as laudatory. The reviewers for the *Herald Tribune* and *The Saturday Review of Literature* made the usual objections to obscurity and difficulty, while *Time* gave with one hand and took away with the other: he was "the most gifted of living U.S. writers," to be mentioned in the same breath with Twain, Melville, and Joyce, though nothing yet had guaranteed him "the sure, sound permanence of any of these men."[4]

When Cerf asked him if he had seen any reviews, Faulkner said he had not. When he turned to a paper these days, it was the war news that occupied him. His grade-school seatmate, Ralph Muckenfuss, was now an Army doctor in England. Jack had finally managed to get free of the FBI to take a commission in counterintelligence, and he would soon embark for England. Now Johncy was talking about getting a Navy commission. Jill would remember her father putting on his uniform from time to time, fishing his lucky sixpence out of the box where he kept his studs and putting it in his pocket. "I am going before a Navy board and Medical for a commission, N.R.," he had written Haas in March. "I will go to the Bureau of Aeronautics, Washington, for a job."[5] Estelle tried to talk him out of it—they didn't need him, she said—but he asked Haas for a $100 loan and flew to Washington. He was met by Joel Sayre, who would become a war correspondent. They went out together, but Faulkner must have kept a tight rein on himself. If the medical board had any suspicion of a drinking problem, it would have been the end of his chances.

After Faulkner had returned home, Cerf wrote in early June that Bob Haas was on temporary duty as a major in the National Guard and that Don Klopfer had just been commissioned a captain in the Army Air Corps. Faulkner replied that the Air Corps had turned him down for some reason, but he hadn't given up hope. He had been offered a Navy lieutenant's desk job in Washington, he said, but "I want to stay out doors if possible, want to go to California."[6] If he could get out there, he thought, he might be able to do what Herndon had not: sell himself to the movies again.

The problem permeated his thoughts. At the end of the third week in June he sent Ober part of a revision of "Knight's Gambit" which indicated that the finished version might run as long as seventy-five pages. He was not yet on a first-name basis with Ober, but as writer to his agent, like penitent to his confessor, he poured out his troubles. "I have another shot at a comm. but haven't even the r.r. fare to New Orleans to take examination. I know where the trouble lies in what I write now. I have been buried here for three years now for lack of money and I am stale." He complained about the family obligations he bore to people "most of whom I dont like and with none of whom I have anything in common, even to make conversation about." He tried to end on a humorous note: "I believe I have discovered the reason inherent in human nature why warfare will never be abolished: it's the only condition under which a man who is not a scoundrel can escape for a while from his female kin."[7] By the time he sent in the rest of the story, three days later, he had concluded that even a commission would not save him. Writing Cerf the next day, he was beset with visions of bankruptcy and ruin. The notes he had given his creditors would soon come due and he would lose everything. "I have 60¢ in my pocket, and that is literally all. . . . I have reached the point where I had better go to Cal. with just r.r. fare if I can do no better."[8]

Now began a flurry of letters and telegrams in the most confused and heated negotiation of his career. Harold Ober was represented on the West Coast by H. N. Swanson, a tall and strikingly handsome man who wore a flower in his lapel and favored regimental ties. At Ober's request, Faulkner supplied details about his screenwriting career for Swanson's use. "Once I get away from here where creditors cannot hound me all the time," he wrote, "I think I can write and sell again."[9] (These letters marked one milestone: after nearly four years the shy and reserved client and agent were finally addressing each other by their first names.) At the month's end Cerf wrote that there was a possibility at Warner Brothers. Ober wrote that Faulkner might get to California if he could obtain a writing assignment in a government campaign to recruit glider pilots. Faulkner sent his thanks and told Ober he would be interested if that was the only way he could get there.

Even in the teeth of this crisis he had to keep writing; he could not indulge himself by giving way to despair or oblivion. In a manifestation of the extraordinary capabilities of the artist, he wrote one of his funniest stories. It was called "Shingles for the Lord" and it was narrated by the youngest Grier boy again. His father, Res, is a brother under the skin to Anse Bundren. He and Solon Quick are the antithesis of the proud, self-sufficient McCallums of "The Tall Men." Quick to embrace WPA terminology and benefits, the two engage in a battle of wits over work for the church and full ownership of a dog they share. Grier proves his ineptitude by inadvertently setting the church on fire. At the story's end the gutted church and its old pastor—Reverend Whitfield, a far more admirable man than he had been in *As I Lay Dying*—embody traits Faulkner had praised before: "jest indestructibility, endurability. . . ."[10] Faulkner showed something of this latter quality in a situation unusual for this dedicated artist. At one point he had drunk too much to sit at his desk, and so he dictated to Bill Fielden. But he was well enough to do the 21-page typescript, on the back of still another typed version, in time to get it to Harold Ober's office on Friday, July 17.

On July 11, Ober had wired Faulkner that there was something pretty definite in the works in Hollywood and that he should wire Swanson authority to go ahead. What none of them knew was that William Herndon had been at work too. Unlike Swanson, who had many prominent clients to serve, Herndon, only in his twenties, had scarcely any clients, but he admired William Faulkner and worked persistently on his behalf with people such as James J. Geller, the head of Warner Brothers' story department, who also admired Faulkner's work. He helped get Jack Warner's ear for a special project Herndon was promoting—a picture about the leader of the Free French: General Charles de Gaulle. When Herndon showed "Turn About" to Warner, he liked it. The assigned producer, Robert Buckner, was a writer himself and a Faulkner admirer. "I want him on this picture," he said. Herndon was ready to sign a contract for $200 a week, but Buckner helped to set it at $300. It was at this point that Swanson stepped in as Faulkner's agent.

Faulkner had wired Swanson the authority to act for him and sent Herndon a telegram telling him he did not have a valid contract. On Friday morning, July 17, Faulkner received Herndon's reply and transmitted it to Ober in a telegram of his own. Herndon said that he had made the deal, and if Faulkner did not wire Geller that Herndon represented him, he would make trouble. The next morning's mail brought Herndon's detailed statement of his case and corroborating letters from Geller and Buckner. Faulkner replied that he wished he had gotten the letter before the wire. "You accused me of deliberate underhand dealing, which is not true, and inferred that I could be forced by threats into doing what is right, which I will take from no man." He was asking Ober to make "some equitable adjustment" that would end their relationship. "If this is not satisfactory to you, then make good your threat and cause whatever trouble you wish."[11] Another letter from Herndon compounded the problem. "As he expresses it," Faulkner told Ober, "I have failed in integrity toward him. I was not aware of this at the time, yet and strangely enough perhaps even if it is not true, I do not like to be accused of it." Now he decided what he had to do: wire Herndon and the studio to close the deal, and he would settle with Herndon when he reached the Coast. He would pay Swanson's commission too. "It has come to point where for my own peace I must deal with Herndon myself. . . . Otherwise, I'll bust."[12] Characteristically, Ober said that neither he nor Swanson would take any commission. On July 22, Faulkner wired his acceptance to Warner Brothers. He would go on the payroll on Monday, July 27, at $300 a week.

He quickly made his preparations for departure. He sent off a revised version of "Snow," now in first-person form. The anti-Nazi sentiments were still clear, but more effective because they were less heavy-handed. If it sold, if anything sold, Ober was to wait for a new address. *"I do not want checks to come here in my absence,"* he wrote *"as they will be misapplied."*[13] He put in his suitcase a small book with alphabetized pages bearing the names of all his creditors and the amounts he owed them.

HE had told Ober and Cerf and Haas that he needed a change, and now he was going to get one. He may have looked around him for a moment with a different feeling—at the parlor where, a month before, thirty guests had celebrated his daughter's ninth birthday; at the shady place out under the pear tree where they would all gather around a watermelon bought on the square, he and Estelle and Jill, Malcom and Cho-Cho, Bill and Vicki, Boojack the maid and her daughter, Li'l Estelle, Jill's playmate. He straightened his desk and put things away: his pilot's log, with no entries since June and no more to come that year; the Greenfield studbook, with one entry in early May, the last in this record of a dream begun with such high hopes four years before. And he would keep no more accounts in the commissary ledger.

Jimmy and Malcolm would be going to boot camp and basic training before long. Jack Falkner was in London, assigned to the huge SHAEF Headquarters in Grosvenor Square; he had what he wanted—he was in for the duration. Now the oldest of the Falkner boys prepared to leave. He had asked for $200 and a ten-week guarantee; he had gotten $300. What he did not realize was that his contract, when all the options were added up, would run for years.

48

... from time to time, had he looked, he could have seen the
city in the bright soft vague hazy sunlight, random, scattered
about the arid earth like so many gay scraps of paper blown
without order, with its curious air of being rootless—of houses
bright beautiful and gay, without basements or foundations,
lightly attached to a few inches of light penetrable earth, lighter
even than dust and laid lightly in turn upon the profound and
primeval lava, which one good hard rain would wash forever
from the sight and memory of man as a firehose flushes down a
gutter. . . .

"Golden Land," *CSWF* (719)

SATURDAY evening at twilight when Meta Rebner drove home to her
apartment she found Faulkner sitting on the steps before her door, his
luggage beside him. He had written her that he would return, but she
had not believed it. Her friend Henriette Martin had told her he had
been blackballed at the studios because of his drinking. He had continued
to write her at intervals after his last departure, and she had depended on
his letters. "What I no longer received from my husband," she realized,
"I found in Faulkner's letters, all tenderness and affection."[1] When she
had finally decided to divorce Wolfgang Rebner, Faulkner had replied
only that he hoped she would not be lonely. But as soon as Cerf had
written Faulkner that something was in the works at Warner Brothers,
he had immediately informed Meta, in letters that were passionately and
specifically erotic. After the divorce, when Rebner fell ill with pneumonia,
she had asked her aunt Ione to come from Phoenix to nurse him. Rebner
wanted Meta back, and her aunt said she thought the marriage had not
worked because Meta had still been in love with Faulkner. "I just thought
I could go on to another life without closing him out," she told her aunt.[2]
  They went to Musso Frank's and the headwaiter seated them at their
favorite booth against the wall. She was free once again, as she had been

six years before when they had first met. He looked middle-aged to her now, and he was returning to earn a quarter of what he had earned when he was younger. After dinner, when they returned to her apartment, she told him he could live there with her. She waited for his answer. Finally he said, "I don't think you really want that." She thought the problem was Estelle, but he told her it was not that. If they lived together, they would lose "the mystery of each other." She agreed to his terms. When they had begun their affair, she had thought he would marry her when he was free. "Now," she realized, "I looked for nothing at all, asked for nothing at all, except his love and his emotional support. He was my lover, my rock; it was not enough, but I made it enough."[3]

On Monday morning he reported to the West Coast studios of Warner Brothers Pictures, Inc., in Burbank—135 acres, girded with walls like a medieval city. Later the head of the stenographic pool said, "When we saw this little man, quiet and grey, who was sweet and kind and soft-spoken, we said, '*This* is a *talent*?' " Studios employees were used to more flamboyance in this business run by autocratic Harry Warner and his brothers Abe and Jack. (Of Harry, Jack would write, "He had the toughness of a brothel madam. . . ."[4]) They had brought in sound with *The Jazz Singer* in 1927, and ten years later they owned more square feet of sound stages than any other studio. They led the industry in gross assets, but theirs was no lavish MGM-style operation. Abe Warner proudly thought of the studio as the Ford of the movies, leading the low-priced field with a standard, reliable product. Though there had been expensive films like *Zola* and even a few extravaganzas such as *Adventures of Robin Hood*, the money was made largely through frugal story-buying, avoidance of retakes, and iron repression of "temperament." They made money with *42nd Street* and other new-style musical films, with *Little Caesar* and other gangster pictures. Exposés of injustice and corruption won for Warner Brothers pictures the designation "most admired" in a poll of Hollywood writers.[5]

In spite of production-line philosophy, the studio employed forty of the best writers in motion pictures. There were Western specialists like Frank Gruber; novelists, including James Hilton—famous for *Lost Horizon, Random Harvest, Goodbye, Mr. Chips*; and political activists such as Alvah Bessie and Dalton Trumbo. Steve Longstreet was there, and so were a number of bright younger writers, among them, A. I. Bezzerides and Jo Pagano. These were some of the co-workers among whom Faulkner took his place two months before his forty-fifth birthday.

That first day of work he learned the full nature of the agreement Herndon had negotiated for him. "It is a long series of options, 13-13-26-26, then a series of 52 week options,"[6] he wrote Ober. He was installed on the first floor of the Writers' Building in a corner office in "the Ward," a group of six small offices opening off the big room in the center for the six secretaries. The workday ran from 9:30 to 5:40, with quitting time at one on Saturdays. In defiance of the front office, there were hot plates and refrigerators, gin rummy and crap games. When Owen Crump came to look Faulkner up in midafternoon, he found him asleep on the couch. Crump came back later to take him home for dinner. Faulkner insisted on a detour to see a horse in a Riverside stable. Finally, after drinks, Lucille Crump served dinner. Faulkner fell asleep, and Crump got him onto the sofa. It was one o'clock when he roused him to take him home. Crump never saw him again.

FAULKNER had rented a top-floor room with an adjoining terrace for $15 a week at the Highland Hotel at Highland Avenue and Franklin. It was just two blocks from Hollywood Boulevard and the business district, but he had a panoramic view of the Hollywood hills. On the corner he could get the bus that covered the three miles to the studio in less than a half-hour. A dozen miles to the southwest was Pacific Palisades, where he had lived five years before. Now, one of its temporary residents was among the most celebrated in Hollywood. He was Thomas Mann, whom Faulkner admired as "the foremost literary artist of his time,"[7] but he would not think of trying to meet him any more than he would have sought a meeting with Joyce in Paris seventeen years earlier. Frank Gruber would recall that among the discerning studio writers, Faulkner was regarded as "a writer who would live. He was spoken of as Hemingway was." To others he was a $300-a-week man where the top salaries were $2,500. He set conscientiously to work.

First there were conferences with Robert Buckner. A Richmond native who had graduated from the University of Virginia, Buckner had earned his M.D. before he realized that he was more interested in journalism and fiction. Later, moving from Boni & Liveright to Hollywood, he had shifted from writing to producing. He had already produced *Mission to Moscow*, and he was a logical choice for *The De Gaulle Story*. They had begun with a copy of De Gaulle's book on tank warfare. Faulkner took pages of notes in their story conference and set to work. He was to do the whole story line, treatment, and finally, the dialogued script. When Buckner went through the early material, he was uneasy for contradictory reasons. On the one hand, it seemed to him that Faulkner was treating the general as a symbol, as a modern Joan of Arc rather than the leading character in a high-budget action picture. On the other hand, Faulkner had put a whole tank battle into his outline.

"Bill," said Buckner, "where do you think we're going to get the money to do a scene like that?"

"I don't know," Faulkner answered quietly, "but it was important in De Gaulle's life and I know you fellows will find a way to do it."

Two weeks later Faulkner gave Buckner a 39-page treatment, tracing De Gaulle's career to the fall of France, then concentrating on his leadership, and ending with the Allied invasion of Europe. For help with action to balance the tendency toward large events and symbolic characters, Buckner brought in Frederick Faust, the enormously prolific "King of the Pulps" who wrote *Destry Rides Again* and more than a hundred other books under the name Max Brand. He had begun as a poet, and his admiration for Faulkner was close to hero worship. The two proved congenial. One lunchtime at Musso Frank's, Buckner listened as Faust ordered Myer's dark rum and Faulkner asked for Old Grand-Dad. When they began to discuss the best vehicle for a good, solid, two days' oblivion, Buckner thought it was like hearing two masters discussing stocks and bonds. The collaboration was short-lived, however, for soon Faust left for Italy, where he died as a war correspondent.

Other afternoons found Faulkner with more new friends among the screenwriters—English novelist and Imagist poet Richard Aldington and playwright Tom Job, who had an extraordinary memory. Sometimes they would play a game of quotations, and Faulkner would be the only one who could keep up with him. On the lot they would eat in the Green Room of the commissary with the stars and the major contract players. One day Alvah Bessie remarked that a Russian pilot could certainly use Faulkner's navigator's aeronautical wristwatch. Another day a young screenwriter described to the table a seduction he had recently accomplished. When he finished, Faulkner said, "I don't like it here," and walked out. From then on he ate among the minor actors, extras, and workmen—the lights and grips.

In mid-September, Howard Hawks wanted him. He was making *Air Force*, and he was dissatisfied with the ending, the death of the pilot of the Flying Fortress, his crew clustered about his cot. Hawks needed Faulkner for the kind of movie work he did best. "With a script that didn't work," one of the other writers said, "he would take a key scene and make it go. . . . What Bill did was to make the whole picture better." In Faulkner's rewrite, Quincannon's crew still gathered about him, but now in his last delirium they went through the cockpit checklist in a kind of litany of flight, and he died as the plane headed west. Faulkner finished his two days of work by patching up another scene. The problem solved, Hawks went ahead with his shooting.

The two men spent more time together that fall. As one writer put it, "Both enjoyed hunting, drinking, and telling stories; they even dressed in a similar manner (a fondness for comfortable tweeds) and often struck their co-workers as meticulous, stoic, and reserved."[8] They also had the bonds of flying and fascination with World War I, an overpowering personal and cultural experience for both as well as material for art. Faulkner went along when Hawks took his son and daughter fishing on Big Bear Lake in the mountains of southeast California. The fifth member of the party was Hawks's beautiful wife, "Slim." Next time, when they drove to Calexico, a hot dusty town on the Mexican border, for some bird-shooting, Clark Gable joined them. On the 200-mile trip back to Los Angeles, Faulkner and Gable shared a bottle of bourbon— very jolly and then very sleepy, Slim remembered. But this time Faulkner did not stop, and it was some days before he passed through his saturation point, with medical assistance. On occasions such as this, his admirer in the main building, James J. Geller, would report him sick.

One evening Hawks took Gable and Faulkner to a dinner party in Sullivan Canyon above Beverly Hills. Among the guests was Robert A. Lovett, whom Faulkner had not seen for years and who was now Assistant Secretary of War for Air. When Faulkner said he wanted to get into the war, Lovett did not take the bait. When he tried again a few days later, Lovett tried to discourage him on the grounds of age and physical requirements. When Faulkner tried a different approach, it wound up on Lovett's desk, where it stopped. "I will not approve making a Public Relations Officer out of William Faulkner," his friend said.

His weekends were usually uncertain. Then under contract to Warner Brothers was actress Ruth Ford, a former Ole Miss coed who had dated Dean Faulkner. He would visit her and play with her small daughter, Shelley. Sometimes the Buckners would entertain him at their home in Encino, where he would swim with their six-year-old daughter and four-year-old son. He would sit and talk with them as adults, and they loved it. He would compliment Bob Buckner on his juleps, and his wife— whom Faulkner called "Miss Mary"—on the Smithfield ham. Meta Rebner started to notice a change when he was with her. "The great difference," she recognized, "was that he pretended not to need me as impellingly as he once had for companionship." As they broke the pattern of seeing each other on a regular basis, she realized that her dependence on him was not as strong as it had been. "I wanted to see him when I could no longer stay away from him, when I was vital and undrooping, when I had ardor of my own."[9]

By mid-October, Faulkner had three principal characters in his script: De Gaulle, a fanatical follower, and the zealot's brother. The 96-page screenplay, now called *Free France*, ended with a huge bombing raid. He was done with the dialogue in November. When Buckner read the 153-page screenplay, his original misgivings returned because Faulkner's "natural circumlocutious style and endless sentences were diametrically opposed to the stringent, telegraphic needs of pictures." In retrospect, there was "an odd offbeat note, almost 'nouvelle vague' a la Fellini and Bergman." But that was not what was needed for a war picture in 1942. Faulkner and Buckner were saved by an unexpected turn of events. As De Gaulle proved himself increasingly troublesome to Churchill, the Prime Minister let Franklin Roosevelt know his feelings. They were communicated to Jack Warner, who considered himself court jester to the White House, and the picture was closed down. When the car pool brought Faulkner to work the next day, it would not be to write about the man who considered himself the embodiment of France.

The car was an old Willys belonging to Albert Isaac Bezzerides. He had published a novel about truckers called *The Long Haul*, and when Warner Brothers bought the screen rights, he helped write the script for the film, retitled *They Drive by Night*. He had been fascinated with Faulkner's work since he had read *As I Lay Dying* as a college student. He knew Meta Rebner, and five years earlier, seeing him one evening at a table with her, he had introduced himself and blurted out his admiration for Faulkner's books. Meeting him again, as a fellow inmate of the Ward, "Buzz" Bezzerides had offered better transportation than the bus, and Faulkner had accepted. He would come to figure in Faulkner's life as more than a faithful car-pool driver.

SHORTLY after Faulkner's arrival at Warner Brothers, Ober had informed him that the *Post* had bought "Shingles for the Lord" for $1,000. There had been nothing since then, but after the news came that Captain Eddie Rickenbacker had survived three weeks in a life raft after a plane crash in the Pacific, Faulkner was moved to write a long free-verse poem about the famous World War I fighter pilot. He was not flying in this war, but he had shown himself tougher than many younger men. Faulkner called it "Old Ace" and sent it off to Ober. He asked for a copy of "Tomorrow" to do a treatment in hopes of selling it, and told Ober he planned to go home on December 14 on four weeks' leave.

He wrote his mother explaining why he needed permission for this leave. The studio had picked up his option at the end of the first thirteen weeks. At the end of the second thirteen weeks he would get a raise if they picked it up again. Geller had assured him that they would tear up the contract Herndon had negotiated if he did well, and he thought he had done well for them this time. Each of Jill's letters asked when he was coming home. She missed the songs he sang to her—"Oh, Dear, What Can the Matter Be?" and one that began "Will ye go, lassie, go, to gather wild mountain heather?" And she missed his stories. He had told her a whole series involving a squirrel named Virgil Jones who played the guitar. She wondered what "Vurchill" was doing, so he made a phonograph record about the squirrel's further adventures and sent it to her. He told her he would come home as soon as he could.

Geller had assigned him to a picture alternately entitled *Liberator Story* and *Life and Death of a Bomber*. Faulkner dutifully toured a B-24 factory in San Diego and submitted four typed pages of notes. Ten days later he was shifted to a thriller called *Background to Danger*. Producer Jerry Wald remembered that they had not been able to determine what was wrong with the script. Faulkner said, "I know what's the matter— too much running around." Then, said Wald, Faulkner wrote some new scenes and made the picture work.[10] This was a two-week assignment. Then he went back to *Liberator Story*.

Time dragged as he waited for word about the Christmas leave. At the studio, he seemed to Buckner aloof without condescension. "He walked," the producer felt, "in a cloud of his own making." With a few he was able to unbend. The last time he had been in Hollywood he had met screenwriter Jo Pagano and his wife, Jean. At a party, Pagano had heard Jack Warner boast, "I've got America's best writer for $300 a week." Later Jo invited Faulkner to his Toluca Lake home. Faulkner had told Bezzerides, "Bud, you have talent, you ought to write more." To Jo Pagano he said, "Get out of this town." There was no question in his mind: if a man wanted to write fiction, he ought to get himself out of Hollywood and do it. If an artist did go there, he had to be careful. "Go take their money," he would tell Shelby Foote. "Always take the people seriously, but never take the work seriously. Hollywood is the only place on earth where you can get stabbed in the back while you're climbing a ladder."[11] To most of the people for whom and with whom he worked, he was an honest craftsman who did his best to give full value for value received. The crucial distinction for him was that in his own métier he was an artist, a solitary worker in a lonely craft whose novels and stories stood by themselves over his name alone. The function of the screenwriter in this cooperative and sometimes chaotic medium was entirely different, and not for him. If he had had money enough, like Hemingway, he would never have touched a Hollywood film script.

Early that December, when Malcolm wrote that he was going to enlist in the Army, Faulkner told him in a long letter "when I can, I am going too, maybe only to prove to myself that I can do . . . as much as anyone else can to make secure the manner of living I prefer. . . ." He drew a picture of Hollywood full of the kind of grotesques Nathanael West had depicted in *The Day of the Locust*. As for the place itself, "its economy and geography was fixed and invented by the automobile," and now, with gasoline rationing, the automobile for a time at least was "as dead as the mastodon," and so, too, would the town be. Looking ahead, he told Malcolm, "We must see that the old Laodicean smell doesn't rise again. . . ." After the young men had preserved liberty and freedom, there would come the time for older men, "the ones like me who are articulate in the national voice. . . ."[12] Other events would reinforce this feeling that he would have to speak out, as Mann had done, on political issues rather than confining his utterances only to his art.

FAULKNER had shown sufficient progress on *Liberator Story* for Jack Warner to grant him leave with pay for a month beginning December 14, and he promised that he would send a first draft of the story by Christmas. Meta Rebner had to come to terms with his going home to spend the holidays with his family, and she sent with him a gift for Jill.

His timing was good. After an absence of nearly five months, he was there to go with his wife to see *A Fairy Conspiracy*, with Golden Locks played by their daughter. He and Bill Fielden went out to the farm and cut three scrub cedars. Faulkner drew from all of them to make one "splinter tree." They decorated the banisters with holly, ivy, and pine boughs, and brought in a yule log. On Christmas Eve they went to the midnight service at St. Peter's Episcopal Church, and the next morning they celebrated the holiday. That was a wonderful Christmas, Bill Fielden remembered.

It was good to hear the slow deliberate tapping of his typewriter in the morning, and often, during his persistent bouts of insomnia, it could be heard at night when he might go downstairs and work. Then, as the sky outside began to grow lighter, the aroma of frying bacon and eggs would waft through the house. In the evenings after supper, he and Jill and Estelle might sit at the kitchen table and play hearts or a Greek game like rummy he had learned from Bezzerides. It was wonderful for Jill, but too soon he had to go back to Hollywood.

When Faulkner returned to the studio in January 1943 he found that they had picked up his option for the next twenty-six-week period, at the specified contractual increase of $50 a week. So much for Geller's promise of a better contract. As if to remind him how far he had slipped, a letter awaiting him from Ober informed him that the only buyer for "My Grandmother Millard" was *Story*, at $50. He had done a treatment of *Absalom, Absalom!* which was probably the basis for a 62-page screenplay entitled *Revolt in the Earth*, which bore his name and that of Dudley Murphy. It had been making the rounds at Warner Brothers. When it reached Bob Buckner he sent it back to Faulkner with a note. He thought it had no possibilities whatever, and it was so bad that he hoped Faulkner would not let it circulate with his name on it.

By January 23 he had finished his work on *Life and Death of a Bomber*. He had divided it into three acts whose moral was that personal and private sacrifices had to be made to win the war and its goals. It contained what one writer would call "a rather bloodless adultery story...."[13] If there had been some relevance for him in *Life and Death of a Bomber*, his next assignment, on a picture engaging the energies of a whole series of writers, must have seemed bizarre. *Northern Pursuit* was to star Errol Flynn as a Royal Canadian Mounted Policeman opposing a party of Germans who would reach Hudson's Bay by submarine and then make their way to a hidden airplane in order to bomb the canal at Sault Ste. Marie and disrupt Detroit's war work. In a letter to tell his mother that he was depositing $100 to her account, he wrote that he was working on a movie that was to star Errol Flynn, now that the jury had "fumigated" him at the end of his trial in a sensational statutory rape case. Three weeks into the story Faulkner wrote Haas, "I am well and quite busy, surrounded by snow, dogs, Indians, Red Coats, and Nazi spies." It may have been partly under the influence of his own script that he had decided, he told Haas, to try for the Ferry Command.[14]

If he did not learn much about global warfare from the script, he did learn something about screenwriting politics. To the surprise of most of the picture's writers, the final credits went not to Robert Rossen and Frank Gruber but to Gruber and Alvah Bessie. Tom Job and Faulkner showed this to Gruber. All they knew about Bessie was that he had fought in the Spanish Civil War and written for *The New Masses*. Regarded by many as primarily a Communist party functionary, he had no screen credits so far and his contract option time was fast approaching. "Look what these bastards are doing," Job told Gruber. Rossen had given his credit to Bessie. It didn't matter to Gruber, but at the insistence of Job and Faulkner, he went to Geller. It turned out that Rossen had every right to give his credit away. But Gruber and the others felt it was a Communist conspiracy. Faulkner, he recalled, was very outspoken. "I know what Faulkner's opinion was of Communists," he said.

His work and his life seemed to have little continuity other than the slow process of trying to earn enough money to free himself. He did thirty-eight pages on *Deep Valley*, with one scene set in a convict labor camp, and wrote a 50-page treatment of *Country Lawyer*, in which he changed the setting from New York State to Yoknapatawpha County. Unsurprisingly, it went unproduced.

He continued to solace himself from time to time in the usual way, as a familiar consequence testified in early April when he wrote to Cho-Cho and Bill Fielden, now settled in Tennessee. "I have had, still have, and apparently will have for the next few decades, the damned worst bloody rotten bad cold in human captivity. . . . I am a rachitic old man in the last stages of loco-motor ataxia. But . . . I can still invent a little something now and then that is photogenic, and I can still certainly sign my name to my salary check each Saturday."[15] Cho-Cho thought back to the time when her husband had joined them at Rowan Oak and had been jobless for five months. Pappy must have wondered where the next dollar was coming from, with a dozen white dependents to support and close to that number of black ones. She and Pappy had certainly had their conflicts, and there had been times when he had hurt her, but she knew that he was "the best friend I ever had."

If Cho-Cho and Bill were settled, the rest of the family was in flux. Jack was in Tunisia, Johncy had obtained a Navy commission, and Jimmy was finishing pre-flight. Faulkner sent him his goggles, his leather flying jacket, and one of his RAF pips as a good-luck piece. His letter carried something of the same kind of emotion that had gone into "Two Soldiers." It was another letter to a surrogate son, one with Falkner blood in his veins. He signed it with the name Jimmy had been taught to use in childhood, "Brother Will." In mid-May, Malcolm was ready to leave. "Buddy, my dear son," his stepfather wrote, "I should have helped give you a send-off." Again he wrote about the goals he had been trying to dramatize in his scripts, and about the parts they would play when the war was over. "Take my love with you," he told him, "which was constant even at the times when, as a man-child and a man, we wouldn't quite understand each other." Bill Fielden wrote to tell him what Rowan Oak had meant in his life, and Faulkner told Bill how much his letter had moved him. He did not know when he would be home again. Meanwhile, Bill should see *Air Force*. Faulkner mentioned the scenes in it he had written. In his cups, he uncharacteristically wrote an admiring letter to Eudora Welty, a Mississippian who published her third book that year. "I have just bought the collection named GREEN something," he informed her. "Do you mind telling me about your background? My address [Warner Bros.] is below, until July."[16] Jill wrote regularly. She cried a lot, she said, when she learned he would not be home soon. She wondered if she could have her knee-length hair cut. It cost him a pang, but he gave his consent, and "since Pappy knows and can remember and see in his mind whenever he wants to every single day you ever lived, whether he was there to look at you or not, why, any time he wants to he can imagine . . . how you looked then."[17]

In his letter he told Jill about the new picture he was immersed in. "It will last about 3 hours, and the studio has allowed Mr Hawks 3 and ½ million dollars to make it, with 3 or 4 directors and about all the big stars."[18] It was called *Battle Cry*, and it was to celebrate British, French, American, and Russian contributions to the coming victory. He and Hawks had done a rough outline, and by late April he had gone on to do 140 pages on his own. But they were scrapped and he was told to start over from the beginning. By early June he had completed a 231-page script, but it still wasn't right. Geller brought in another writer, a twenty-six-year-old named Steve Fisher, at a salary of $800 a week. He had written the successful screenplay for *Destination Tokyo* and he was to infuse some of the same qualities into *Battle Cry*. He knew nothing of Faulkner's work, and it took some straight talk from Hawks to ensure a workable collaboration. By June 21 they had finished "complete temporary script No. 3."

That same day Faulkner wrote Harold Ober, "I seem to have pulled something out of the hat at last here." A well-connected agent had offered to represent him. He thought this meant the option on his contract would be taken up, and he hoped he could renegotiate it at a better salary that would even permit him to "pension off" Herndon. If things looked promising he would let Ober know and get in touch with his West Coast representative, H. N. Swanson.[19] One afternoon soon afterward Meta Rebner looked up from her duties as script girl to see Buzz Bezzerides on the set. Faulkner had passed out in his office, he told her. When they went there, they found Faulkner with his head on the desk, a whiskey bottle by the typewriter and scenario pages scattered about the room. "There's a bathhouse on Cahuenga at Yucca where they'll dry him out,"[20] she told Buzz. Supporting him, one on each side, they managed to get

Faulkner safely out of the studio. Later he told Meta what had happened. Warner Brothers had taken up his option, but only at the usual $50-a-week increase and with no possibility of renegotiation. His salary was fixed at $400 a week for the next fifty-two weeks.

Then, in early July, word came that must have made the war stories in the film scripts seem like idle play. Bob Haas's son had been lost in his torpedo bomber on anti-submarine duty off Casablanca. Faulkner typed out a draft and then wrote to Haas on a single white sheet in pen. "Bob, dear boy," he began, and went on to tell him that "the sympathy is already yours without letters, from any friend, and some of the pride belongs to all the ex-airmen whom time has altered into grounded old men, and some of the grief is theirs too whose blood flies in this war." Perhaps the young ones would hold two places for them in Valhalla, "not because we were heroes or not heroes, but because we loved them."[21] Brooding over this death, he wrote Malcolm about the Haases, father and son, and the daughter who was flying planes in the Women's Ferry Squadron. "All Jews. I just hope I dont run into some hundred percent American Legionnaire until I feel better." Then he mentioned the Negro pilots who had flown a successful combat mission on the same day that twenty Negroes died in a race riot in Detroit. "A change will come out of this war. If it doesn't, if the politicians and the people who run this country are not forced to make good the shibboleth they glibly talk about freedom, liberty, human rights, then you young men who live through it will have wasted your precious time, and those who dont live through it will have died in vain."[22]

BY early August, Faulkner was looking past *Battle Cry* to what suddenly seemed a glittering prospect. Hawks was going to form his own production unit with Faulkner as his writer, he wrote Estelle, and they would make a team that would command "at least two million from any studio with which to make any picture we cook up . . . and divide the profits from it."[23] The studio had promised that when he wrote a successful picture they would destroy the seven-year contract. This was his chance. They were working as a unit already, trying to cut costs and prepare for a shooting date of September 15. The correspondence between Estelle and him had been sporadic and uneven, sometimes with discord when she wrote that she needed extra money and he supplied it with urgings that she be careful. Her reply to his optimistic letter must have seemed perverse to him. "Your letter sounded so cheerful that it made us all feel good. I've a notion that Mr. Hawks must have his old secretary back and that once again you're finding California worth while—Don't misunderstand this, and write back that I begrudge you pleasure—I truly do not. . . . Suppose I've lived so long now with the knowledge that it has become a familiar and doesn't frighten me as it did."[24] In an irony that could have come from a Warner Brothers script, Estelle could not know that in these years, when Meta Rebner thought of her situation, she felt "I had the short end of the stick, the sweepings, the leavings. His wife and daughter had everything."[25]

He wrote his mother about his enthusiasm for the work he was doing for Hawks. He told her that he admired Hawks's operation, that the producer protected him so that he did not have to work under a fore-man. Hawks, he said, was "a coldblooded" man, and as long as it was profitable for him, he would keep Faulkner on the payroll. Estelle's letter was still rankling him as he wrote. He was working there to support his dear ones, he told Miss Maud, and he didn't like it when he was suspected of just having fun.[26]

Howard Hawks was said to have a contract that gave him more inde-pendence than most producers. But now there was concern as costs continued to mount. Then there were rumors of a confrontation. One morning Steve Fisher picked up a trade journal and read that Hawks had walked off the lot. Soon the word came through that the script which Hawks and Faulkner were working on was off. That day, Fisher remem-bered, Faulkner walked across the street into a bar.

He asked for a six-month leave of absence, and Geller endorsed the request. After he went off *Battle Cry* on August 13 they could let him go home with an option to extend his contract by however long he stayed away. It was up to Jack Warner.

Faulkner was still talking motion pictures, though not, at the moment, with Warner Brothers or Hawks. Legends had grown up after World War I about the Unknown Soldier, and director Henry Hathaway had been trying to work the subject into a film script. He had tried the idea on several writers, with sometimes bizarre results, and one had stalked out with the comment "The only thing that would satisfy you would be if your unknown soldier was Jesus Christ!" It was not until later that Hathaway began to mull over that exit line. He had gone into partner-ship with producer William Bacher, and they decided to try the idea on Faulkner. Some of his friends attempted to dissuade him, but Bacher was a hypnotic talker, and with *Battle Cry* down the drain, the chances for Hawks's million-dollar deals seemed to have paled. And now Bacher was offering a three-way profit-sharing arrangement. As for his con-tract, he could write the story as a detailed synopsis and do the screen-play when his status with Warner Brothers was cleared up. And he could also do it as a play or novel, with the rights remaining entirely his.

He had not sold anything since *Story* had bought "Shall Not Perish" three months before for $25. Bacher offered him a $1,000 advance. Then, in mid-August, Geller told him Warner had approved a three months' leave without pay. Faulkner quickly wound up his affairs and bought his ticket to Memphis. He was beginning a project that would be far more complicated and protracted than he could possibly have imagined.

49

> . . . the places that men and women have lived in and loved . . .
> all the little places quiet enough to be lived in and loved and
> the names of them before they were quiet enough, and the
> names of the deeds that made them quiet enough and the names
> of the men and the women who did the deeds, who lasted and
> endured. . . .
>
> —"Shall Not Perish," *CSWF* (114)

IT was a while before he could concentrate on the writing. At Greenfield Farm there was cotton to be picked, hauled, and ginned, and at
Rowan Oak there were repairs to be made. But no matter what problems
he now had to deal with in Oxford, they were infinitely preferable to
those in California. "I'd rather stay home and be poor than go out there
and write for movies and be rich," he told E. O. Champion.

It was October 30 before he wrote Ober and told him about his new
project. "It is a fable, an indictment of war perhaps." It would be about
ten to fifteen thousand words long. When Geller wrote that his leave
would soon be up, Faulkner requested a three-month extension on the
grounds of illness, and it was granted. In mid-November he sent fifty-
one pages to Ober and the carbon to his backers. "This is about half of
it," he told his agent. "It continues on, through the Three Temptations,
the Crucifixion, the Resurrection. The Epilogue is an Armistice Day
ceremony at the tomb of the Unknown Soldier." He wanted to use it as
a magazine story, as part of a collection, and finally as a play. "I will
smooth it out, give the characters names, remove the primer-like biblical
references and explanations, and let the story reveal its Christ-analogy
through understatement."[1]

It was a subdued and prayerful celebration of Christ's birth in Oxford
that year. Nine Lafayette County boys had died, and when the *Eagle*
printed a "G.I. issue," there was page after page of young faces smiling

out under the visors, caps, and helmets. The Fieldens were at Rowan Oak for the holidays, and on Christmas, Louise and Dean joined them. Dean was ten now, and like Jill and Vicki, she called her uncle "Pappy." He tried to be that to her, never losing his sense of responsibility for his brother's death. He would tell Dean stories about his exploits. "Dean," he would say, "your father was a rainbow."

IN the springlike weather of early February he prepared for his return to California. Before the middle of the month he was back at Warner Brothers, where he found himself so busy that it was nearly ten weeks before he was in touch with his agent again. "As soon as I got here," he wrote Ober, "Howard Hawks asked for me. . . . As usual, he had a script, threw it away and asked for me."[2] When Ernest Hemingway had told Hawks he needed money but declined Hawks's invitation to Hollywood, Hawks told him, "I'll take your worst book and make a good movie out of it, and you'll make money on it." When Hemingway asked him which book it was, Hawks named *To Have and Have Not*. Hemingway sold him the screen rights, and Hawks assembled his own unit, using Warner Brothers financing and facilities.

Faulkner was glad to be working for Hawks again, even if on salary rather than profit-sharing, but after only three days he was needed for work on the adaptation of Colonel Robert Lee Scott's autobiographical novel *God Is My Co-Pilot*. Steve Fisher had done a first script treating General Claire Chennault's Flying Tigers in Burma, but a new approach was wanted. Faulkner devised one involving a protagonist with a past to expiate—injustice to his child and the child's dead mother. But he made clear to producer Hal Wallis his lack of interest in the project, and in the ensuing conflict he began to drink, just one week after he had reported for work. Fortunately for him, he had moved from the Highland Hotel, accepting Buzz and Yvonne Bezzerides' offer of the spare room in their house just north of Santa Monica. Buzz got him home and somehow managed to abort the drinking bout over the weekend. The situation was saved when Faulkner was reassigned to Hawks, very possibly through the good offices, once again, of James J. Geller.

The set of *To Have and Have Not* was a happy one, said the leading lady. "Bogie's got a new girl friend," Faulkner told Ruth Ford. "She's like a young colt." The actress was Lauren Bacall, a tall, straight-faced young woman with a surprisingly deep voice. Her forty-five-year-old leading man, Humphrey Bogart, was a veteran of the Broadway stage. A short, balding man with a slight speech impediment, he had played gangsters and then broadened his range as a romantic lead in *Casablanca*. He had a cool independence and a disdain for sham and hypocrisy. He also had a talent for friendship with a small group of people as iconoclastic as himself. Faulkner and Bogart got on immediately, as Faulkner did with another member of the cast, Southerner Hoagy Carmichael, and often the three would lunch together. Faulkner liked Carmichael's piano-playing and his wit. Observing shapely young starlets hurrying by one day, Carmichael turned to look and then said, in his gravelly voice, "Women ain't like men. They're one-dog people." It was a remark Faulkner would repeat with amusement. The relationships were companionable in part because of Hawks's method. "I set the picture up on the set," Hawks remembered.

He and Hemingway had worked on the story line on Hemingway's boat in Cuba. The previous fall, Hawks had put a veteran scriptwriter, Jules Furthman, on the project. A $2,500-a-week scenarist whose credits included *Treasure Island* and *Mutiny on the Bounty*, he could remember almost everything he had ever seen in a picture, and Hawks valued him for the way he could use that backlog. He had completed the final screenplay by late January or early February, so that when Faulkner went to work on February 22, Furthman's final 151-page screenplay was there as the basis for a shooting script.

The principal reason Hawks discarded that script apparently related more to politics than to art. Furthman's fidelity to Hemingway's novel had caused the problem. As a script girl on the picture, Meta Rebner learned what it was: "A film about an American who smuggled rum and revolutionaries between Havana and Key West, and in which the Cuban flag was raised, would deeply embarrass the government," and the studio's dependence on the government for help in war pictures under production made it imperative to avoid trouble.[3] So this time Hawks needed Faulkner not just for individual scenes, but to reshape the whole script. And so, according to one student of the picture, "it was Faulkner who thought of switching the location to Martinique, who condensed the figure of "Slim" out of two women in the previous screenplays . . . and who was most interested in the anti-Vichy elements of the new story."[4]

There were story conferences in Hawks's office, with Faulkner sitting on the couch puffing his pipe, but he would be "the sole author of the Second Revised Final."[5] Though Faulkner considered Furthman's script a kind of inspired hackwork, he admired his inventiveness and economy. Years later Faulkner would recall a device Furthman used to swiftly characterize Bogart's initial assessment of Bacall. "She looks at Bogart to light her cigarette," Faulkner would say. "Bogart looks at her for a minute, sizes her up, then tosses her the matches for her to light her own cigarette." Faulkner, on the other hand, still had not mastered the "telegraphic style." He was keeping ahead of Hawks with one day's shooting script, but once Lauren Bacall saw him walk onto the set with a new scene that contained an unbroken six-page speech. Bogart looked at it.

"I'm supposed to say all that?" he asked incredulously.

"Bill," interposed Hawks before Faulkner could replay, "that's fine." In such a situation Bogart and Hawks would do a revision. Other times

Hawks would say, "Bill, I know you can get the meat out of this for us." And Faulkner would go back to Hawks's office, where he preferred to remain anyway.

In his room in Bezzerides' house he worked on other matters. He completed his 1943 tax return on a gross income close to $12,000 and filed a declaration estimating income for 1944 at fifty percent more. He thought about new quarters for himself and for Jill and Estelle too, if he could manage to bring them out again. It may have been late March when he wrote Estelle that he had a single room in a private home closer to Hollywood and providing a better base for apartment hunting. He was still on Bezzerides' route for a ride to work in the morning, but after work he would head for Musso Frank's. There he would meet friends, sometimes the Paganos, and often a new couple, screenwriter Owen Francis and his Southern-born wife, Betty. "Many a night Bill did all the talking," she remembered, "about down home, the people and things," often drawing on his "grand repertoire of stories about little woods animals which gave us a breath of fresh air in Hollywood."

SPRING held no charm for Faulkner that year in the unchanging California sunlight. He expected to be through with the Hawks film by mid-May, but he felt no assurance that he would return to his fable. The war, with its "sublimation and glorification of all the cave instincts," he wrote Ober, was usurping the place of art. "It's too bad I lived now though," still too young to be unmoved by the trumpets, but too old to follow their call, and thus able only to wait for them to cease. "I have a considerable talent, perhaps as good as any coeval. But I am 46 now. So what I will mean soon by 'have' is 'had.' "[6] At times like this, his course was predictable, but now he tried to provide some hedge against disaster. One of his new friends that year, Edmund Kohn, an artist in a sergeant's uniform, waited for him at 5:30 one Sunday afternoon at the Roosevelt Hotel. He arrived, accompanied by a man in a dark suit carrying a small black bag who walked behind him. Faulkner introduced him as Mr. Nielsen. At dinner Faulkner spoke little, but he made one vehement comment. "They worship death here," he told Kohn. "They don't worship money, they worship death." His mood brightened when they left the restaurant. As they strolled down the street, Faulkner put his arm around Kohn and began reciting "The Phoenix and the Turtle." If Kohn had not already noticed that Faulkner had been drinking, the loving recitation of this favorite poem could have told him. At the Chapeau Rouge, at Faulkner's insistence, Mr. Nielsen produced a bottle of bourbon from the black bag. When Faulkner excused himself, Nielsen turned to Kohn. "You must be wondering who I am," he said. "I'm a nurse. Mr. Faulkner hired me to see that he got to work on Monday."

By May 1 he had completed a 118-page script, and by May 13, the revisions. The feat he had performed for Hawks was reflected in the new deference he received in the offices, on the back lot, and in the commissary. His reaction would not have surprised Johncy Faulkner. "All this head bowin' and foot scrapin'," he said to Meta Rebner. "Nobody looked at me before this, and if it's a flop, none of them will look my way again."[7] But *To Have and Have Not* was no flop, even if there was no praise for the script at the film's release five months later. What emerged, despite the work of so many people, was Hawks's plain style. As one writer would put it, "the casual viewer of the film would hardly recognize any trace of the two great novelists."[8]

Now he could look ahead. "I think I have found an apartment," he had written Cho-Cho, "a little cubbyhole but in a quiet, convenient *not Hollywood* neighborhood, with no yard, etc. But after several years of Rowan Oak and trees and grounds, maybe Big and Little Miss will enjoy living in a city apartment, with nothing to break the silence but the shriek of brakes and the crash of colliding automobiles, and police car and fire wagon sirens, and the sounds of other tenants. . . . They may like it. At least we will be together. . . ."[9] Their separation presented numerous problems, even including the mail. At one point he wrote Phil Stone that Major Oldham still had his post-office-box key. He asked Stone to please see that his mail went into a separate box, "since I trust him just about as much as God does." He told Stone to put Estelle's mail in his box so that Major Oldham could have something to go through. Stone replied that the postmaster was a friend of his and that there would be no problem.

If the arrival of Estelle and Jill on June 1 was something he could look forward to, Meta Rebner understandably felt differently. "Why did they have to intrude on my poor little piece of earth with Bill?" she asked.[10] When she told him her feelings, he said they could go on as if nothing had changed. She said this would change everything for her. As her voice began to rise, she saw people at other tables looking. She drove him to his hotel in silence. When she got to her apartment, the phone was ringing. He wanted to keep on seeing her, he said, on any terms, when his family arrived. She told him that it would be too painful, that it was time for them to part, and hung up. "I couldn't cry anymore. It was over."[11]

For him, something else, in a part of his life that had seemed dormant, was beginning. He had come across a letter which had lain in his desk for nearly three months. It was from Malcolm Cowley, who had been contemplating a long essay on Faulkner to "redress the balance between his worth and his reputation." He hoped to come to Oxford to talk with him.[12] Faulkner apologized for the delay and explained it. Unless he recognized a return address, "I open the envelopes to get the return postage stamps (if any) and dump the letters into a desk drawer, to be read when (usually twice a year) the drawer overflows." As for the proposed piece, he would like that very much. "I think (at 46) that I have worked too hard at my (elected or doomed, I dont know which) trade, with pride but I believe not vanity, with plenty of ego but with humility too (being a poet, of course I give no fart for glory) to leave no better mark on this our pointless chronicle than I seem to be about to leave." He had reservations about any biographical material, but Cowley would be welcome to come out and share his cubbyhole to discuss other things.[13]

On Monday, May 15, he was assigned to a new picture called *The Damned Don't Cry*. "It is one of the usual turkeys (a novel, good title but little else) which (God knows why) studios pay 40,000 dollars for," he wrote Ober. The producer was Jerry Wald, who remembered how Faulkner had helped him with *Background to Danger* and turned to him again, handing over the file already swollen with three rejected screenplays. Wald was a Hollywood phenomenon whom Jack Warner had brought to the Coast at eighteen. Constantly on the watch for new material, he had a combination of restless energy and feverish curiosity which to some made him the industry's most engaging producer. Supposedly the model for aggressive, amoral Sammy Glick in Budd Schulberg's novel *What Makes Sammy Run?*, he was harsh with a number of writers, but not with Faulkner. When Faulkner told him what he thought, Wald instructed him to throw the script away, because what he wanted was "some 'Faulkner' " in the picture.[14] Faulkner thought he had already created what Wald wanted in "The Brooch" and hoped he could sell it to the studio. Wald told him to write a treatment first, and they would see if the studio was interested. By early June, Faulkner had completed it in seventy-nine pages.

Wald was assigned to another picture, *The Adventures of Don Juan*, with a file containing two rejected scenarios. He took Faulkner with him. Full of clichés in both form and language, the script must have presented one of the most excruciating tasks Faulkner had faced. After three weeks, management decided that enough time had been spent on this project; also, that there was no use for Faulkner's amalgam of *The Damned Don't Cry* and "The Brooch."

ESTELLE and Jill arrived late, but they moved into the pink adobe apartment house in time to celebrate Jill's eleventh birthday on June 24, 1944. They were located in East Hollywood, off Sunset Boulevard near the Cedars of Lebanon Hospital. Sometimes they would go for a walk and play a round of miniature golf and then buy hot dogs with chili from a street vendor. Faulkner noticed that he and Estelle were the only adults he could see walking with a child; the others had dogs on leashes. Providentially, they were able to get out into the country at least two or three days a week. Faulkner had ridden from time to time at Jack House's Glendale Stables, just north of Griffith Park, and he had asked Jack to be on the lookout for a gentle little mare for Jill. She would ride to the studio with her father and from there to the stables on a bus. Each week she went to a riding school also attended by a young actress, Elizabeth Taylor. Sometimes Estelle would go along to sit and sew fancy under-things for her daughter. One morning when Jill arrived, the little mare was there, a good-tempered bay with a blazed face and a black mane and tail. Lady Go-lightly had been running the range in Colorado, where she had picked up distemper and other ills. Faulkner paid the veterinarian's bills, and after Lady recovered, Jill hardly ever rode another horse.

In early July he worked on a remake of *The Amazing Dr. Clitterhouse*, changing the title character from a surgeon to a psychiatrist whose schizophrenic career in crime had sprung from a desire to remedy injustice. After a week's work that produced two treatments, he was shifted to another remake, a version of *The Petrified Forest* in which escaped Nazis replaced the criminals of the original. He and Bezzerides were supposed to give the picture some class, but they felt contempt for what seemed to them a lame idea, and occasionally they would write a scene for their own amusement. In one, the fleeing Nazis commandeered a gas truck, and when, at the end of a running gunfight, the police roared up to the smoking ruins, there were the Nazis—in blackface. "Which way to Memphis?" one of them asked. "Too bad I can't shoot this," said the amused producer regretfully. By early August the two humorists were off the picture.

One weekend they took their families to Venice, where Zoe and Jill dived and splashed while their fathers took pictures. In one, Jill was just emerging from the water. Faulkner looked at it in silence. "It's over very soon. This is the end of it," he said. "She'll grow into a woman," he added, his tone melancholy. One day Estelle asked Buzz if Bill had ever told him anything about their relationship. "Something went wrong," she said. She began to cry. "I don't know what went wrong. We used to go fishing together. We loved each other."

Faulkner was reassigned to *God Is My Co-Pilot*, and he would come home from the studio in a black humor—furious or depressed, or both. Hal Wallis had not forgotten his earlier dealings with this recalcitrant writer, and he scheduled a story conference, which Faulkner awaited with dread. Sylvia Rosenthal had been his secretary for three months; she found him morose and uncommunicative, but sober. The day of the conference arrived, and a call summoned him to Wallis' office. When Faulkner failed to take the call, she went into his office. She was horrified to see that he was in no condition to go. As she tried to help him collect himself, Bezzerides appeared. After a half-hour Faulkner declared he was ready. "Bud," he said, "take me over there and push me in." Bezzerides got him started in the right direction and then peered through the blinds with Sylvia and waited. After another half-hour Faulkner reappeared and woodenly followed a painfully straight line back to his own office.

Once inside, he collapsed. Bezzerides got him home, but it was an exceedingly grim period in the small apartment, one that affected Estelle as deeply—and sometimes almost as disastrously—as it did her husband.

His time was charged to Wallis' picture for five days, and then he was shifted back to *Fog over London*, the remake of the Clitterhouse story. Then, after two weeks, his luck changed. One day when he and Hawks had been talking about murder mysteries, Raymond Chandler's *The Big Sleep* was mentioned. Hawks proposed to Jack Warner that they use it as another vehicle for the successful Bogart-Bacall team, and Warner approved the idea. Faulkner was paired with Leigh Brackett, a young writer on her first important assignment. "It's not supposed to be a great work of art," Hawks told them, "just keep it going."

As they began dramatizing this story about Philip Marlowe, Chandler's tough private eye, Leigh Brackett found herself completely in awe of her co-worker in the adjoining office. He laid out the work in alternate sections, and she would remember his turning out "masses of material, but his dialogue did not fit comfortably the actors' mouths and was often changed on the set. Amazingly (to me, after breaking my teeth on some of his novels) he was a master at story-construction." One morning when she entered his office he offered her a cup of the very black and strong coffee from the pot he kept hot. She noticed, to her surprise, that he was reading the Bible. Although he could well have picked it up to read the New Testament for the fable, what he mentioned was the Old Testament. He smiled. "I always enjoy reading about the rainbow-colored backside of God," he told her.[15]

It was good he had this work to do, for Jill and Estelle were preparing to leave as schooltime approached. Jill went out to the stables to ride Lady one last time, and then, on September 7, he put them on the train and waved goodbye. Less than two hours later he sent Estelle a telegram to be delivered en route: ARE YOU ALL RIGHT. WIRE ME COLLECT STUDIO. BILLY.

News from New York was hardly inspiriting. Cowley wrote that he had tried to sell the article in advance to the *Atlantic*, but they had declined. Among writers, he told Faulkner, there was nothing but admiration for his work, but among publishers the consensus was that it would never sell. Cowley had better luck with *The New York Times Book Review*, and on October 29 part of his essay appeared there, entitled "William Faulkner's Human Comedy." Cowley compared him to Balzac and declared that no living American author could match him for intensity and scope. It was a melancholy fact, however, that almost all of his work was out of print. Cowley then wrote him, asking if his approach to the symbolism in his works made sense. Faulkner replied that he had been primarily telling a story, but unconsciously the incidents came to form a structure symbolically applicable to the history of the South. But the South was not very important to him; he just happened to know it. To him, he told Cowley, "life is a phenomenon but not a novelty, the same frantic steeplechase toward nothing everywhere and man stinks the same stink no matter where in time."[16] He had seen the piece in the *Times*, he said, and he had liked it.

That was more than he could say of his next assignment. James M. Cain's story of a divorcée and her lovers, *Mildred Pierce*, had been undertaken by Jerry Wald and temporarily renamed *House on the Sand*. When he had a completed script in hand, he asked for Faulkner to make changes. By November 18, the end of his first week, Faulkner had reworked much of it. Then, at a story conference, he met the director, Mike Curtiz, known to some as a "butcher." After his lengthy comments elicited only silence from Faulkner, he turned on him. "Why don't you say something?" he said. Faulkner rose and left the room without answering. Back in his office, he began drinking. It took Jo Pagano and another writer, Tom Reed, to get him off the lot safely.

HE was back with Bezzerides, and by now Buzz was using the tactic of cutting off the supply once Faulkner was into the cycle. Faulkner would try to bargain with him. Once Buzz entered the room to find that Faulkner had piled all of his novels on the coffee table and autographed them. "Now will you give me a drink?" he asked. A doctor told Bezzerides that if Faulkner did not have heart trouble, this kind of habitual excess could bring it on. Bezzerides appealed to him. "Don't go that way, Bill. You're too precious." It seemed to make no impression, and Buzz walked away. When he returned, Faulkner was gone and two of the bookshelves were bare. From the porch he caught sight of Faulkner straining to carry two sacks up the nearby hill.

"Bill, what are you doing?" he called out.

Faulkner answered through gritted teeth. "I want to see if I've got a bad heart or not."

At this stage Buzz knew he could no longer deal with the situation. Muscled like a wrestler, he simply picked Faulkner up and headed for the car to take him to a private hospital in the Valley. Faulkner twisted in Bezzerides' enveloping grasp.

"Bill, what are you trying to do?"

"I'm trying to get down," Faulkner said.

Buzz stood there and began to laugh. Then Faulkner did too. Bezzerides took him on out to the car. It was in the aftermath of one of these bouts, out walking with Bezzerides, that he suddenly burst out, "God damn! Why do I do it?" And Buzz had said, "The only one who can tell is you."

He would plead against hospitalization and feel that the people who had helped put him in the sanitarium had somehow betrayed him. On one occasion Jo Pagano felt his reproaches. There may have been something of this when Faulkner moved that fall, although it was also true that he had appreciated the Bezzerideses' hospitality and did not want to impose himself on them. Henriette Martin, Meta Rebner's friend, told him that her family could let him have a room with its own bath and private entrance. Later she told Meta he was living there and that he always asked about her. Then, when actor Victor Jory told Meta that he had seen Faulkner at Musso's, in his cups but genuinely miserable and wanting her back, she decided she had made a mistake.

The next morning she drove out to Ridpath Drive, north of Sunset Boulevard and west of the Hollywood district. She was parked there when he emerged to wait for his car-pool ride to work. She took him to the studio, and thereafter they were lovers once again, with weekend trips to the beach and relaxation with the Paganos, the Crowns, and other friends.

Neither Wald nor Curtiz needed him after December 2, though there was some rewriting on *The Big Sleep*. With the holidays approaching, Faulkner was more restless than ever to be home. Besides that, Jill had broken her ankle and he wanted to see for himself that it was healing properly. And there was the constant deep concern about his own work. There was the fable, still incomplete. "I'll never get it written in this town," he told Meta. "Sometimes I think if I do one more treatment or screenplay, I'll lose whatever power I have as writer."[17] He asked Geller for a six-month suspension beginning December 13, and it was granted.

He left without even cleaning out his desk. When Jerry Wald looked through it he found a number of bottles and a lined legal-size yellow pad. In Faulkner's minute handwriting he read a series of phrases: "Boy meets girl. . . . Boy sues girl," which went on and on. On the train, traveling across Arizona and New Mexico and eastward toward home, Faulkner kept his end of the bargain. On December 15 he finished the last of twelve typed pages of changes for *The Big Sleep*. His covering note to Geller read,

The following rewritten and additional scenes for *The Big Sleep* were done by the author in respectful joy and happy admiration after he had gone off salary and while on his way back to Mississippi. With grateful thanks to the studio for the cheerful and crowded day coach which alone saved him from wasting his time in dull and profitless rest and sleep.

With love,

WILLIAM FAULKNER[18]

> . . . his attitude showed not so much indolence, but fatigue,
> physical exhaustion. Except that it was not spent exhaustion, but
> the contrary: with something tense behind it, so that the exhaus-
> tion did not seem to possess him, but rather he seemed to wear
> it. . . .
>
> —*A Fable* (60)

HE was under his own roof again, where, when people telephoned, the houseboy would say to them, "Mr. Faulkner tole me to tell you he ain't here." He was Norfleet Strother, the stepson of Wallace Lyles. A few years before, when Wallace's son Broadus was born, Wallace told Faulkner, "I finally got that boy to take care of you when you' an ole man." Faulkner must have wondered occasionally how he could provide for all his dependents until he reached that time.

There were some professionals who wanted to help. A group of his admirers at Doubleday, Doran had told Ivan von Auw, Jr., at Ober's office, that to help Faulkner avoid a return to California, the company would advance $5,000 for a nonfiction book on the Mississippi River. Faulkner was warmly grateful, but he told Ober he would have to think about it. "I am 47. I have 3 more books of my own I want to write. I am like an aging mare, who has say three more gestations in her before her time is over, and doesn't want to spend one of them breeding what she considers . . . a mule." If he took money for anything less than his best, "the whole purpose of the offer would be exploded, as I would still be morally and spiritually in Hollywood."[1] In a month he would try to decide.

On January 10, 1945, he proposed a solution to Cerf and Haas. "All my writing life I have been a poet without education," he wrote, "who possessed only instinct and a fierce conviction and belief in the worth and truth of what he was doing, and an illimitable courage for rhetoric (personal pleasure in it too: I admit it) and who knew and cared for little else." Now it was different. "I am writing and rewriting, weighing every word, which I never did before; I used to bang it on like an apprentice paper hanger and never look back."[2] As he wrote this he was forgetting the way he had measured each choice for *Light in August* "by the scale of the Jameses and Conrads and Balzacs."[3] What he was telling his publishers may actually have been a rationalization of—or a conscious or unconscious refusal to recognize—the fact that this new book lacked the force that had propelled those other works up from the depths of his psyche. Unlike them, this was a *willed* book, and the deliberation was actually a compensation for a lack of spontaneity. The principal worry he articulated was the habitual one. "As usual, I may run out of money before the six months are up. If I do, I'll either have to pot boil, or go back to the salt mine; in either case, I'll have to put this aside."[4] He must have looked with dread and horror not just at the prospect of writing whatever the studio told him to instead of writing his novel, but also at the destructive collapses he knew would come—at more lost days and nights in the hushed rooms and twilit corridors of hospitals in the Valley. Could he count on the firm, he asked, for an advance of two or three thousand dollars if he needed it in March? Haas replied promptly that he could. Faulkner then wrote Ober that he would put aside the possibility of "the River book" for Doubleday. "I will carry on with this fable," he told him."[5] It was clear in his mind. "The argument," he explained to Ober, was that "in the middle of that war, Christ (some movement in mankind which wished to stop war forever) reappeared and was crucified again. We are repeating, we are in the midst of war again. Suppose Christ gives us one more chance, will we crucify him again, perhaps for the last time."[6]

Through that cold, rainy January he drove ahead with the manuscript. By the time the forsythia and jonquils were yellowing the bushes and beds outside his window, he had written 100,000 words. In mid-March he told Ober that he had rewritten them down to about 15,000. "It will take some time yet to finish the mss. It may be my epic poem. Good story: the crucifixion and the resurrection." Warner Brothers had given him another extension, but he would have to go back about June 1. "I had my usual vague foundationless dream of getting enough money to live on out of it while I wrote and finished it," he concluded. "But I ought to know now I dont sell and never will earn enough outside of pictures to stay out of debt."[7]

That was what Cowley had told him the publishers said of his work. In print that April, Cowley made the same judgment Faulkner had made. "For all the weaknesses of his own poems," he wrote in a piece in the *Saturday Review* on April 14, "he is an epic or bardic poet in prose, a creator of myths that he weaves together into a legend of the South."[8] One of the letters Cowley received came from Oxford. It was from Phil

Stone. He told Cowley it was the best piece he had read yet, but he was "all wet about a number of things." *The Wild Palms* and *Absalom, Absalom!* "were absolutely ruined because of the fact that Faulkner apparently lacks any comprehensive sense of design." The incident with the cow ruined *The Hamlet*, and the trouble with his later books was "that he keeps on rewriting *Sanctuary*." All the characters talked like William Faulkner, and as for his famous prose style, it was "really not a style in the proper sense but merely a personal mannerism."

SOME of Faulkner's own reading that winter and spring may have been an indication of his mood as he prepared for a return to the Coast. He had put his name in Douglas Southall Freeman's four-volume biography of Robert E. Lee. In June he inscribed his name in a biography of a doughty, tenacious fighter, a Memphian skilled at living off the country and achieving his objectives despite consistently heavy odds; the book was Robert Selph Henry's *"First with the Most": Forrest*. Faulkner was going back to the studio to do Warner Brothers work and his own work too, and not necessarily in that order.

On Thursday, June 7, he went back on the payroll at a new salary of $500 a week for fifty-two weeks. He was now earning what he had earned thirteen years before when he had come to Hollywood for the first time. Without enthusiasm he attacked his first assignment, a treatment of Stephen Longstreet's new novel, *Stallion Road*, which focused on a ranch owner who was an expert veterinarian, gambler, and lover. By late July he had completed a 134-page screenplay, but there was the inevitable request for changes, and so he went back to the beginning again.

He had returned to his room in Bezzerides' home, and Buzz saw the kind of self-discipline Faulkner could apply when it came to his work. He would rise at four o'clock, and by eight he would have put in his day's work on the fable before they left for Burbank, where he would put in his day's work on *Stallion Road*. There was even a reserve he could tap for still more work. Jean Renoir was directing a picture called *The Southerner*. Nunnally Johnson had worked on the screenplay but was not available for the additions Renoir wanted. Zachary Scott, who would star in the film, recalled that Faulkner had told him he considered Renoir the best of contemporary directors. The director reciprocated Faulkner's admiration, and when the two met, Renoir told him about his problems with the script. Faulkner took it home with him, and two of the film's scenes would show Faulkner's touch: the first lighting of the fire on the hearth and the catching of a wily old catfish. It was not surprising that Faulkner was more interested in a young family of tenant farmers than in his normal screenwriting fare.

But this was a brief challenge. He and Meta Rebner had resumed their old relationship, but he had little joy to give her. "Hollywood irked him more than ever," she saw. "He rarely smiled or chuckled. He was downcast."⁹ Estelle complained about his letters. He replied that he had been busy working on a picture for Ginger Rogers. He had worked with Buzz to do a 50-page treatment of "Barn Burning" in the hope of selling it to a studio. He told Estelle that now, with Buzz not working, he spent a total of three hours a day riding back and forth from the house to the studio. "I'm doing all this to try to make enough money to get the hell out of this place and come back home and fix Missy's room and paint the house and do the other things we need," he told her. He had made a special effort early after his arrival to write her mother, who was grieving over the death of Major Oldham that May. He told Lida Oldham about the weather and variety of exotic flowers there. "It all looks pretty fine," he wrote, "a lot of magnolia blooms but the magnolia leaves are a lighter shade of green, almost sickly, not like our strong deep green." Being busy helped him to pass the days he was marking off on the calendar, "but I do miss my family in the evenings."¹⁰

In early August he received some good news from New York. The Viking Press had finally decided that it would be a good idea for Cowley to edit a collection of Faulkner's works for the Viking *Portable Library* series. He could not have enjoyed Cowley's telling him that this came at a time when all of his books except *Sanctuary* were out of print, but he could take some comfort from a conversation Cowley recounted with a new French dramatist named Jean Paul Sartre: "What he said about you was, '*Pour les jeunes en France, Faulkner c'est un dieu.*' Roll that over on your tongue." Faulkner responded promptly. "By all means let us make a Golden Book of my apocryphal county. I have thought of spending my old age doing something of that nature: an alphabetical, rambling genealogy of the people, father to son to son." Catching something of Cowley's excitement, he began to look back over the range of his pageant, describing the origins of some of the stories and novels. He drew a rough map to show the ancient boundary between Choctaw and Chickasaw lands. "Wish to hell we could spend three days together with these books." He concluded, "Write me any way I can help."¹¹

His situation in Hollywood was just the opposite. It grew more depressing and infuriating with every passing week. It particularly rankled him that Herndon's weekly commission now amounted to $50. Faulkner wrote him offering $500 in settlement. Herndon replied that his total commissions over the life of the contract amounted to $21,320, but that he would settle for $10,000 to be paid at the rate of $100 a week over a two-year period. The agent-client relationship would probably hold only so long as Faulkner stayed at Warner Brothers, but if he simply abrogated the contract, no other studio would touch him for fear of legal action from Warner Brothers. A letter to Ober on August 20 revealed the depths of his depression. "I think I have had about all of Hollywood I can stand," he told him. "I feel bad, depressed, dreadful sense of wasting time, I imagine most of the symptoms of some kind of blow-up or collapse. . . .

Feeling as I do, I am actually becoming afraid to stay here much longer. For some time I have expected, at a certain age, to reach that period (in the early fifties) which most artists seem to reach where they admit at last that there is no solution to life and that it is not, and perhaps never was, worth the living." Again he repeated, without mentioning his name, the things Cowley had told him: almost all his books were out of print and it appeared that they would never make a living for him. He wondered if he could do some sort of editorial work, or "some sort of hack-writing at home. . . ."[12] Faithful as always, Ober said he would have his lawyer check Faulkner's legal position in case he decided to come home. He could still draw a $5,000 advance for the Mississippi River book, and *Ellery Queen's Mystery Magazine* would pay $300 for "An Error in Chemistry" and enter it in a contest if he would clear up some ambiguity in it. In a week Ober received the story, rewritten.

THE California summer wore on. One day as Faulkner stood waiting for the Burbank bus, novelist and scriptwriter Paul Wellman saw him and asked how he was. "I'll be glad when I get back home," Faulkner answered. "Nobody here does anything. There's nobody here with any roots. Even the houses are built out of mud and chicken wire. Nothin' ever happens an' after a while a couple of leaves fall off a tree and then it'll be another year."[13]

By September 1 he had finished revisions on a 151-page script of *Stallion Road*. When the producer read it, he gave a copy to Longstreet and asked him to do the adaptation. "I thought it was a magnificent thing," Longstreet recalled, "wild, wonderful, mad. Utterly impossible to be made into the trite movie of the period. . . . Today it could be made as a *New Wave* film."[14] That was the end of Faulkner's part in *Stallion Road*. Longstreet said that they had been promised Bogart and Bacall for the film but that they got Ronald Reagan and Alexis Smith. An imaginative raconteur, Longstreet said that it turned out to be a bad film of which one New York critic said, "If you're a horse, you will like this picture." Then, said Longstreet, Faulkner sent a telegram to Reagan, saying, "My horse didn't like it."[15]

Mid-September came with a repetition of the previous month's pattern of events: good news from the East and increasing dissatisfaction with his immediate situation. Cowley wrote that Viking had completed the negotiations for rights with Random House and that he was hard at work on the book. Again Cowley quoted Sartre: in a drunken conversation Hemingway had insisted to the Frenchman that Faulkner was better than he was. And Hemingway had written Cowley that Faulkner had the most talent of them all, that "I would have been happy just to have managed him."[16]

Faulkner had gone to the story department to talk to Finlay McDermid, who had replaced Geller. "Finlay," he said, "I've got a mare that's going to foal, and I want it to foal in Mississippi. I've got a trailer for it, and when that mare goes to Mississippi, I'd like to go with it." McDermid had the legal department draw up an agreement, but it specified that Faulkner was going on six months' leave to complete a novel and that Warner Brothers would have first chance on the motion-picture rights. Obviously, he could not do that to Bacher and Hathaway. "Finlay," he said, "I've got ink poisoning." Herndon had said that if he stopped paying his commission, he would sue. The studio said he could go home on leave only if he signed the assignment of rights. On the afternoon of Tuesday, September 18, he cleaned out his desk and left the studio at the close of business.

Faulkner had known for a year now that he was going to take Lady home with him. He had known it ever since that summer day when Jill had looked up at him and said, "Pappy, I've got to have that horse. It hurts my heart." Lady Go-lightly had not been inexpensive, with the veterinarian's bills and stud fees. They couldn't tell if the breeding had taken, but now she had a heavy look about her. For $125 he bought a small two-wheeled horse trailer. For $350 more, Newt House, the son of stable-owner Jack House, agreed to haul it to Mississippi behind his Cadillac.

Other matters were more difficult. He had to tell Meta he was through with Hollywood. (When Cowley had relayed Hemingway's comments to him, he had told him that Hemingway was lonely and unhappy, perhaps because of his third divorce, and that Faulkner should write to him. Faulkner had replied that he would, that Hemingway had his sympathy. "Poor bloke, to have to marry three times to find out that marriage is a failure, and the only way to get any peace out of it is (if you are fool enough to marry at all) keep the first one and stay as far away from her as much as you can, with the hope of some day outliving her. At least you will be safe then from any other one marrying you—which is bound to happen if you ever divorce her. Apparently man can be cured of drugs, drink, gambling, biting his nails and picking his nose, but not of marrying."[17]) Meta was angry and resentful. "He had promised me that when Jill was old enough—she was twelve now—he would move for a divorce." She would not now subject Jill to the trauma of the courtroom, she told herself, "But Bill had forgotten his promise. I could not forgive him that. When he reached for me in the night, I pushed him away." He sent her a letter of apology and entreaty, and she forgave him. "My face on our last night together was worshipful."[18]

AFTER supper on Friday night, September 21, Bezzerides drove Faulkner out to the stable, where they hitched up the trailer and with difficulty got Lady into it. About midnight Faulkner climbed into the back seat of the Cadillac, with Newt at the wheel and his wife, Maxine, beside him. Buzz waved as they drove off. To him it seemed a symbolic flight—as if his friend were fleeing Babylon, the place that might destroy him, taking with him at least something precious to his daughter.

They headed for El Paso at the top of the speed limit. In the back seat Faulkner alternated between napping and talking—about Oxford, about Rowan Oak, about his smokehouse and the way he cured his hams. After the overnight stop at a motel, they set off the next morning, and when the highway leveled out on the plateaus, Newt put his foot down on the accelerator. Anything that slowed them down was intolerable to Faulkner, and they stopped only for food and fuel.

It was after midnight, Monday, when the big dusty Cadillac pulled the trailer slowly over the rutted, cedar-lined drive. Jill walked sleepily down the stairs in her nightgown and out onto the gallery. Suddenly she was awake, running out to the trailer. When they unloaded it, Faulkner stood silently and watched. "It's my horse," Jill said, her arms around Lady, "it's my horse."

If he had experienced in Hollywood his own Dark Night of the Soul, if he had felt ready to conclude "that there is no solution to life and that it is not, and perhaps never was, worth the living," at least he had escaped to return home once more. Now he was free to return to his fable, to complete it if he could, and to try to show that what he had once done, he could still do.

51

... there were new people in the town now, strangers, outlanders, living in new minute glass-walled houses set as neat and
orderly and antiseptic as cribs in a nursery ward, in new sub-
divisions named Fairfield or Longwood or Halcyon Acres which
had once been the lawn or back yard or kitchen garden of the
old residences. . . .

—*Requiem for a Nun* (249)

HE had returned home in time for his forty-eighth birthday. Things
seemed to be settling down. At least the family was all accounted for.
Major Jack Falkner had come back from Algeria, accompanied by his
new wife, Suzanne, a petite blond Frenchwoman who would bring him
something of the happiness that had eluded him in his disastrous first
marriage. Johncy was in a naval hospital, where he would remain for
another year, recovering from a jeep accident that would leave him
scarred and limping. Victoria (she no longer wanted to be called Cho-
Cho) and Bill Fielden were returning to China, but Malcolm and Jimmy
would soon be home. Maud Falkner and Auntee were seemingly the
same, still going faithfully to the picture show every time it changed,
alternating between the Ritz and the Lyric.

By the first week in October, Faulkner was preparing to plunge into
his work again. He had promised Malcolm Cowley that he would write a
few pages of synopsis of the first three sections of *The Sound and the
Fury* to provide background for the Dilsey section, which Cowley wanted
to excerpt for the Viking *Portable Library* volume of the work of William
Faulkner. In the crisp mid-October days that followed the first frost, he
completed it: a 30-page genealogy of the Compson family spanning two
centuries, from the Battle of Culloden in 1745 onward. "I should have
done this when I wrote the book," he told Cowley."[1] There was one
passage as symptomatic of his feelings as his retreat from Los Angeles

with Lady in tow. Of Caddy, whom he would many times call "my heart's darling," he wrote, "Married 1920 to a minor movingpicture magnate, Hollywood California. Divorced by mutual agreement, Mexico 1925."[2] The Hollywood experience had marked a further stage in her deterioration, and on some level his own psyche had been perilously close to the same thing. He wrote Cowley that "it took me about a week to get Hollywood out of my lungs," but he thought this piece was "really pretty good. . . . Maybe I am just happy that that damned west coast place has not cheapened my soul as much as I probably believed it was going to do."[3]

Hollywood was much in his mind, and it was epitomized in the form of a major rather than a "minor movingpicture magnate": Jack Warner, a smoker of big cigars, who sported a deep tan and a pencil-line mustache, whose shirts flashed with ruby cuff links and tiepins. Faulkner now made a direct appeal, using his military title of "Colonel Warner." He began with his overriding concern: "I feel that I have made a bust at moving picture writing and therefore have mis-spent and will continue to mis-spend time which at my age I cannot afford." He was unhappy not with the studio, he said, but with the type of work. "So I repeat my request that the studio release me. . . . I know my request will receive fair consideration, and I hope favorable."[4] One week later R. J. Obringer replied. The answer was no, and would he please sign the leave agreement. For Faulkner this was a kind of warfare of nervous attrition. The specter of insolvency was always before his eyes, and his problems with the novel were complicated by Warner's wanting the film rights when they were already assigned. He wrote Haas that he was to say nothing about this other than that "Warner seems to insist he owns everything I write, and so Faulkner wont do any writing until he finds out just how much of his soul he no longer owns."[5] But he did return to the fable before the Christmas preparations began, and he sent sixty-five pages for Haas to read and transmit to Ober. "I think it's all right," he wrote, "maybe good enough for me to quit writing books on, though I probably wont quit yet."[6]

It was a good Christmas, and one of the best parts of it was the return of Jimmy Faulkner, now a twenty-two-year-old lieutenant, smart in his Marine uniform. His uncle had looked forward to this homecoming. He had known that there had been a crash and later a medal. With engaging but frustrating reticence Jimmy had resisted attempts to get the story from him. Finally they learned: his F4U Corsair had been hit in the dense flak thrown up against a tactical support mission over Okinawa, and he had waited for rescue, bobbing about in his life raft, from morning until afternoon. The RAF pip his uncle had given him for luck had gone to the bottom with the Corsair.

Malcolm Franklin had served as a combat medic with the infantry in Europe, and all that he had experienced during the war made Christmas even more special and memorable than ever. "On Christmas Faulkner was always a fastidious dresser," he remembered. "To start the stocking-opening ritual in Mama's room, he wore an elegant and ornate silk Chinese robe. In this he would have his breakfast. Even for the early part of the ceremony of the tree he would be so dressed, for by nine-thirty the young people were there beside the tree in the parlour. It was at this time that Mama would make her appearance wearing a lovely Chinese wrapper in soft, muted pastel shades." Faulkner would offer a prayer and distribute the gifts. For himself, he would accept from his family only gifts of pipe-cleaners of various kinds and colors, except for an occasional handkerchief from Estelle. The rest of Christmas Day was punctuated by visits from friends, with drinks ladled out from the ruby-red punch bowl filled with Faulkner's special recipe of "apples, bourbon, dry burgundy and soda water, chilled by a generous portion of ice chunks."[7] Wallace Lyles was there on duty, ready to drive home guests no longer able to drive themselves.

FAULKNER had drawn a map of Yoknapatawpha County for Cowley to include in *The Portable Faulkner* and had with some reluctance supplied information about himself. When Cowley sent him the text of his introduction, Faulkner found it "all right, sound and correct and penetrating," but he hoped Cowley would cut what amounted to about four pages. "I'm old-fashioned and probably a little mad too; I dont like having my private life and affairs available to just any and everyone who has the price of the vehicle it's printed in, or a friend who bought it and will lend it to him."[8] When Cowley explained that he thought the biographical matter, including the information that Faulkner's plane had been damaged in combat, was so important that it should remain, Faulkner's reply was sharper: "You're going to bugger up a fine dignified distinguished book with that war business."[9] The persona of the maimed war hero had been one thing when he was an obscure aspirant in New Orleans; now it was different—nothing should detract from the body of work accomplished. He would make it clear that he had not crashed in combat, but his having flown military aircraft in wartime was still too much a part of his personal myth to be surrendered. Cowley finally made the changes he wanted, and in the springlike weather of the latter part of February, Faulkner told Cowley how relieved he was, because "I would have preferred nothing at all prior to the instant I began to write, as though Faulkner and Typewriter were concomitant, coadjutant and without past on the moment they first faced each other at the suitable (nameless) table."[10]

HE felt no such relief about his other problems. At the beginning of the month he looked at his dwindling bank balance and feared he would have to go west again. And Obringer had sent him a letter bristling with legal terminology because Faulkner was now in default of his contract for failing to execute the September suspension agreement. The money was gone from the sale of "An Error in Chemistry"—the $300 plus $250 more for winning the second prize in the *Ellery Queen Mystery Magazine* contest. "What a commentary," he had written Harold Ober. "In France, I am the father of a literary movement. In Europe I am considered the best modern American and among the first of all writers. In America, I eke out a hack's motion picture wages by winning second prize in a manufactured mystery story contest."[11] Cowley had told him what Hemingway and Sartre thought of his work; later in the year Sartre would tell readers of *The Atlantic Monthly* how Faulkner had influenced writers such as himself and Simone de Beauvoir and Albert Camus, and how, in the early days of the Occupation, "the reading of novels by Faulkner and Hemingway became for some a symbol of resistance."[12] Unfortunately, this cut no ice with Jack Warner or the majority of the American reading public. As if deliberately to exacerbate his feelings, the National City Bank of New York sent a check to the Bank of Oxford that should have gone to Harold Ober. He set them straight in an outraged letter that ended:

Thanking you, I remain, and that this sort of harebrained recklessness with information will not some day bring you to grief, is the sincere hope and prayer of

Yours truly,
William Faulkner.[13]

It was this kind of accumulation of problems, anxieties, and frustrations that would produce one of his "collapses," as he sometimes called them. And it appears he did not escape one that February. They all dreaded it. Jill would hear him recite "The Phoenix and the Turtle" or that other harbinger "When daisies pied and violets blue," and she would know what was likely to follow. Once she appealed to him. "Think of me," she pleaded. But it was already too late, and he answered her with a phrase she would never forget. "Nobody remembers Shakespeare's children," he told her. Sometimes she would have to help him back into bed. Once, perhaps this time, he toppled all the way down the staircase. He was lucky that the fall didn't kill him.

Sometimes all the Negro help would leave, and Estelle would take Jill and go to stay at her mother's house. And there were times when Jill would find that both her parents had taken to their beds. On some occasions Faulkner would be hospitalized at Byhalia. On others, they could manage at home. Malcolm would sit with him, and often he would be up all night, fixing drinks at whatever intervals Faulkner called for them. For relief, Malcolm would send for Wallace Lyles, who would go directly upstairs, where Faulkner lay in the big double bed that had been Uncle Malcolm's —"Mr. Bill's drunk bed," Wallace called it. Faulkner trusted him, knowing that he would not put raw eggs in the drinks, as Estelle might, or Tabasco, as Malcolm sometimes did. Wallace would give him an honest drink, but as Malcolm knew, Wallace also "had the gift of conversation to hold him off a little longer, slowly laying the ground work to bring Pappy around." Wallace combined experience and hope. After he had been on duty for a time he was likely to say to Malcolm, "Mr. Bill ain't never leave off soon from one of these go-rounds. He restin' a little better now."[14] Faulkner would calculate when he wanted—or needed—to emerge from one of these bouts. After he did, Jill would observe that he would be very quiet for a few days. Then he would say to her, "Missy, I want to talk to you." And he would apologize.[15]

There was no time for an extended bout now. He rewrote "Knight's Gambit" in hopes of a sale and wrote Ober about a story he had read in *The Saturday Evening Post*. He thought he might be able to turn it into a vehicle for child star Margaret O'Brien to be used as some sort of lever with Warner Brothers and Herndon. But he really had little confidence in the idea himself, and so, he told Ober, he was writing the studio that he would return about March 15. He had sent along a 40-page synopsis (probably *Continuous Performance*, done with another screenwriter named Tom Reed and intended for Cary Grant or Fred MacMurray) which his collaborator thought was rotten but which he still hoped might sell.

As the Ides of March approached, Ober and Haas persuaded Faulkner to wait while they assessed various strategies. He canceled his train reservation but then concluded that he had better make another. At this point Harold Ober followed a pattern well known to some of his authors: he would quietly go ahead and do what he thought was best for them no matter what they thought. He wrote to Jacob Wilk at the Warner Brothers New York office. "I am sending you 64 pages of William Faulkner's novel," he told him, "at present entitled *Who?*. I think this will give you a good idea of what the novel is to be. . . . I hope that you can tell Mr. Warner about it while he is here and get his permission to let Faulkner finish the novel." If this was accomplished, he promised that Faulkner would thereafter fulfill the contract. At the same time, Bennett Cerf, a personal friend of Jack Warner, added his persuasion to Ober's efforts. Two days later, on March 28, Wilk sent a memo to the West Coast offices: Warner agreed to let Faulkner finish the novel; moreover, the studio was not interested in it as a movie. Ober gave him this news and more. Random House would provide the money to see him through the novel. He was to draw $1,000 now, with $500 to follow on May 1 and a like sum a month later. "I feel fine," he wrote Haas, "am happy now, thanks to Harold and you."[16]

He was free now to return to the fable, though his work on it in April convinced him that it might take as much as two years to get it right and that it would not be called *Who?*. Malcolm Cowley, however, had completed his book, and it was about now that it arrived. "The job is splendid," Faulkner wrote Cowley. "Damn you to hell anyway. But even if I had beat you to the idea, mine wouldn't have been this good. By God, I didn't know myself what I had tried to do, and how much I had succeeded."[17] Now Cowley waited to see if the reviews indicated success in the goal he had mentioned at the outset: a revaluation of Faulkner's work. On May 5, *The New York Times* gave it the front page of its *Book Review*. There, novelist Caroline Gordon declared, "William Faulkner, alone among contemporary novelists . . . has the distinguishing mark of the major novelist: the ability to create a variety of characters," and in general she shared Cowley's assessment of his work. As the days passed, however, there were no other sizable newspaper reviews, and magazine notices were slow in coming.

One of Cowley's other objectives had already been partly achieved, though paradoxically with considerable annoyance to the author. Earlier in the year Cowley had interested Robert N. Linscott, Random House's new senior editor, in the idea of new editions of *The Sound and the Fury* and *As I Lay Dying*. When Linscott had offered Faulkner $250 for a new introduction to the former, Faulkner had told Cowley, "I'll do almost anything for $250.00 or even $25.00, but I dont know how to write introductions."[18] He didn't want to read the novel again and he wished Linscott would use Cowley's introduction to *The Portable Faulkner*. "As you will see," he told him, "this appendix is the key to the whole book; after reading this, any reader will understand all the other sections." He rejected the idea, though, of calling the section a Foreword, for this would be "a deliberate pandering to those who wont make the effort to understand the book. Also, it actually is an appendix, not a foreword." And he was even surer now that he didn't like the pairing of the two novels: "It's as though we were saying 'This is a versatile guy; he can write in the same stream of consciousness style about princes and then peasants,' . . ."[19] Linscott had searched the Random House files without success for the introduction Faulkner had written for the projected Grabhorn Press edition of *The Sound and the Fury*. Then Cowley had suggested asking Hemingway to write one, but Faulkner was unequivocally opposed; "It seems to me in bad taste to ask him to write a preface to my stuff," he told Linscott. "It's like asking one race horse in the middle of a race to broadcast a blurb on another horse in the same running field."[20]

As Random House went through the task of moving from 20 East 57th Street to 457 Madison Avenue, the old introduction came to light and Linscott jubilantly sent it to him. Faulkner's answer was hardly the kind Linscott expected: "I had forgotten what smug false sentimental windy shit it was. I will return the money for it, I would be willing to return double the amount for the chance of getting it out of danger and destroyed."[21] It was another manifestation of his wish to efface the self and leave only the work. As a compromise, however, he wrote a new page based on the old material and sent it to Linscott. When Linscott asked for a balancing explanatory introduction for *As I Lay Dying*, Faulkner's patience had worn thin. "I'm no good at this," he told him. "To me, the book is its own prologue epilogue introduction preface argument and all." But if Linscott wanted a paragraph, he would "fire it in."[22] Linscott knew when to quit. The book would appear with just the Compson Appendix, and no introduction to either of the novels.

IN the spring of 1946, Faulkner began to experience the kind of attention from foreign quarters that Cowley had told him about. In early March a man appeared at the desk of Moon Mullen and told him, "I have come 7,000 miles, all the way from Sweden, to see your William Faulkner." He was Thorsten Jonsson, who had worked in New York as the correspondent of Stockholm's *Dagens Nyheter*, and was now touring the United States with a group of Swedish journalists. He had been one of the first to translate Faulkner's stories, to the warm praise of his countrymen. Faulkner received him courteously, and before leaving, Jonsson told his host, "Some day you will receive the Nobel Prize for Literature." Six weeks later Cowley wrote that Ilya Ehrenburg and two other Russian writers hoped to visit him. "What the hell can I do?" Faulkner wrote back. "Goddamn it I've spent almost fifty years trying to cure myself of the curse of human speech, all for nothing. Last month two damned Swedes, two days ago a confounded Chicago reporter, and now this one that cant even speak english. . . . I swear to Christ being in Hollywood was better than this where nobody knew me or cared a damn. I hate like hell to be in this state, I can even put up with mankind when I have time to adjust. But I do like to have the chance to invite people to come to look at me and see where I keep my tail or my other head or whatever the hell it is strangers want to come here for."[23]

This capacity for irascibility extended to all kinds of sensory intrusion. Aubrey Seay, the warm and hospitable proprietor of the Mansion restaurant, had already begun the practice of unplugging the gaudy jukebox whenever Faulkner entered. One day as Faulkner sat in the Gathright-Reed drugstore waiting for a prescription, he called to Aston Holley, the pharmacist on duty.

"Aston," he said, "do you have to have that radio on?"

"Why, no, Mr. Bill. I wasn't conscious of it," Aston said, "but I guess it is pretty loud. I'll switch it off."

Faulkner nodded. "Aston," he said, "it just looks like all the people of this world must have a lot of noise around them to keep them from thinking about things they should remember."

IN spite of the annoyances and distractions he felt, Faulkner was moving along with the manuscript. In early May he sent Haas a batch of fifty pages and at the end of the month, another of about the same size. "I believe now it's not just my best but perhaps the best of my time," he told him. It might take one or two hundred thousand words, though, and he wanted to stay at Rowan Oak working on it until the end of the year, but the money it would take would add up to an investment of about $6,000 for Random House, and he did not know if they wanted to get in that deep. But as he closed, he demonstrated again that curiously assertive judgment so uncharacteristic of him: "I believe I see a rosy future for this book, I mean it may sell, it will be a War and Peace close enough to home, our times, language, for Americans to really buy it."[24] Haas told him that the total investment would be closer to $8,000, but "let's all take our courage in both hands and who knows but that from this nettle danger we will pluck this flower safety (Shakespeare). You not only have my blessing on the project, then, but that of the whole house here."

By midsummer, with nearly 200 pages in Ober's hands, Faulkner slackened his pace somewhat, working alternately at Rowan Oak and Greenfield Farm, where the harvesting had begun. At his desk he was pushing ahead slowly through the hot August days, reworking the story and expanding it. One of his pages still showed signs of the original synopsis form: "The Corporal turns from the window; the men watching him, including Judas, look quickly away or down again." He was now reclaiming this material, treating it not in his screenwriter's voice but in his novelist's voice. He had apparently developed his organizing principle: one week's time would encompass the Corporal's leadership of the non-violent mutiny and then his Passion and Death. The days of the week would be the largest units, and within them would be segments equivalent to chapters.

Through the late summer, the routines were broken only by occasional visits and outdoor diversions. Aunt 'Bama had come down in her chauffeur-driven limousine for a three-day visit, her rapport with her younger kinsman still strong, still recalling for him the life of her father, the Old Colonel, and old times, such as that of the Highland claymore, the family heirloom she would some day pass on to him. Back with the Bureau and reassigned to New Orleans, Jack Falkner came for a visit with his wife. Faulkner had corresponded with Aunt 'Bama in French earlier in his life, and now he enjoyed trying his French with Suzanne. She found it rather stiff and formal, yet well-accented and spoken with care.

By early October he was nearly 250 pages into the fable, but there was no prospect in sight of finishing, so he put it aside for two months to do some profitable sub rosa screenwriting. (Labor troubles in Hollywood provided the opportunity, and his Warner Brothers contract necessitated the secrecy.) So he was ready for diversion that fall. Bob Farley had returned to the university as dean of the Law School, and some mornings, when the two would ride together, at some point Faulkner would say,

"Let's let 'em go, Bob," and gallop ahead. This always annoyed Farley, not simply because Faulkner had a blooded horse and Farley didn't, but because this seemed a dangerous procedure on a rutted country road. This pattern would become stronger, part of a psychological mechanism Faulkner would later realize was dangerous but somehow necessary to him, in some measure an attempt to assert vitality and deny the encroachments of age. He would later write of a man "who had wanted to remain the tramp and the possessionless vagabond of his young manhood. . . ."[25] Tied to debts, to a short-term script and a long-term novel, he was neither free nor possessionless. So, momentarily at least, he denied all these things in jolting his forty-nine-year-old bones on reckless morning gallops along the Old Taylor Road.

Soon it was hunting season. The previous year he had fired at an old buck and missed. This year he shot a small buck but missed "a magnificent stag. . . . He was a beautiful sight. I'm glad now he got away from me though I would have liked his head."[26] He was one of three who bagged larger game that year in the dense Delta woodland along the Sunflower River, 125 miles southwest of Oxford. He was steadily moving up in the hierarchy, behind Uncle Bob Harkins, now on his fifty-second hunt, behind Uncle Bud Miller and Lucky Pettis and Ike Roberts.

But if in the big woods he still felt "the old lift of the heart" that Uncle Ike McCaslin had felt, there was something else that he missed. Back home, he wrote Cowley, "It's a dull life here. I need some new people, above all probably a new young woman."[27] Malcolm Cowley would say of artists and writers, "Their sexual drives are probably stronger than those of the population as a whole and their inhibitions are weaker; I am far from the first to suspect that there is a connection between literature and libido."[28] If that was the case with this writer, the psychic energy was there, but he wanted to spend it on love rather than on art. The struggle with the fable had become a protracted one, a battle of attrition like the war in which he had set his story, and this was not the first time that he would manifest a wish, on some level of his mind, to retreat from it.

When Howard Hawks had begun work on *Wooden Crosses*, one of his ideas had been to take the airmen of *Dawn Patrol* and change them into infantrymen. Faulkner would use airmen in the fable, but his story, too, was preponderantly one of ground warfare. If this in some sense resonated with change beyond the needs of the story—something like the reference in the condolence letter to Bob Haas about "all the ex-airmen whom time has altered into grounded old men"—an incident that fall made it clearer. Flying with Jimmy one day, Faulkner took over the controls of the Taylorcraft to shoot a landing. When he turned onto the final leg of the approach, Jimmy sat up straighter: Faulkner was coming in so low that they were going to hit a clump of willow trees. Jimmy slammed the throttle forward and pulled back on the stick. Then he went around, made the approach, and landed the airplane. Neither of them mentioned the aborted landing, but William Faulkner's career as a pilot was over.

THERE were some gains as he took stock near the end of the year. In July, Cagney Productions had paid $3,750 for the rights to "Two Soldiers," and after protracted negotiations, RKO's purchase of "Death Drag" and "Honor" had netted him $6,600 more. In mid-December he received $3,500 for the sub rosa scriptwriting. And "Afternoon of a Cow" was finally sold —to *Furioso*, a small quarterly, for $100. For one bit of writing he wanted no fee—two lines for the war memorial in the square:

> THEY HELD NOT THEIRS, BUT ALL MEN'S LIBERTY
> THIS FAR FROM HOME, TO THIS LAST SACRIFICE

There were other losses too. Auntee had died in November. Model in part for Aunt Jenny Du Pre and Granny Millard, she was the one, Jack Falkner would write, "whose steadfast devotion never wavered, whose everlasting love never lessened. . . ."[29]

There had been signs nearer home than Paris that more appreciation was coming his way; the sense of his worth, obvious from the start to a few, was now becoming clearer to many. Kentucky novelist and poet Robert Penn Warren had read the stories and the books as they appeared. "I felt I'd discovered him, but everybody I know practically had discovered him."[30] And like his friends, other teachers, critics, and historians, Warren was passionately devoted to the work. That summer he had reviewed *The Portable Faulkner* in *The New Republic*. On a few points he differed with Cowley, but he acclaimed the re-presenting of this author whose work constituted "the most challenging single task in contemporary American literature for criticism to undertake." Faulkner could be put beside "the masters of our own past literature," and perhaps this book would mark a turning point in his reputation. "That will be of slight service to Faulkner, who, as much as any writer of our place and time, can rest in confidence. He can afford to wait. But can we?"[31]

That spring in Oxford a graduate student had steeled herself to overcome her nervous shyness and make her way up the long driveway to Rowan Oak. Just as she neared the house it seemed to Margaret Parker that a thousand dogs—hounds and Dalmatians—came rushing at her. She stood terrified while Faulkner climbed down from his tractor to rescue her. As her words tumbled out he guided her quietly to a seat on the front gallery and calmed her with a cigarette.

"Now," he asked her, "what is it you want me to do?"

"I want so much for you to come to my class in freshman English," she answered; "I hope you won't think I'm being rude to ask you. We're all so much interested in your work, but we really don't understand it as well as we'd like to." Half of her students, she said, were Naval Reserve trainees just transferred from the fleet. He told her he did not see what they would gain, but he would come if there were no publicity and no professors present. "Tell them not to expect a two-headed calf," he said.

The next afternoon his battered gray Ford touring car pulled up outside her classroom precisely at four. She began by asking about his reading. Pipe in hand, turned halfway from the class, he began to speak—quietly, slowly, and briefly. The four greatest influences on his work, he said, were the Old Testament, Melville, Dostoevsky, and Conrad. The topics broadened. His coevals—Wolfe, Hemingway, Steinbeck, Dos Passos, and Caldwell—were all trying to do the same thing, but Wolfe had come closest to success. Faulkner had promised Peggy Parker fifteen minutes; by the time he left an hour had passed. In the ensuing months she went out to see him several times—once with a composition by a pharmacist's mate—and each time found him "gentle, compassionate, and very nearly clairvoyant."

This spring, a year later, found him restless. Near the end of March he told Haas he had "about 300 correct pages." He wanted to come to New York, he told him, not just because he wanted a vacation, but because he wanted to take a whole evening and tell them all the story. "(What I mean by locale and contents is: the villian is historically the French army or all the allied armies of 1918, and the principal ones are [still historically though to me fabulous and imaginary] Foch, Haig, Pershing, et al.)"[32] At this juncture Haas apparently talked with Ober, who then told Faulkner that Haas would take his word about the manuscript and that he could count on $500 a month for another year. And besides, Warner Brothers would not make any trouble. Just about this time Faulkner came down with a case of influenza, and when he recovered, there seemed little to do other than resign himself to more steady plugging away at the manuscript.

Easter was quiet. No one took Jill to church or Sunday School, so she alternated among the churches of her friends. Her demeanor was still the same—quiet, with a withdrawn quality that seemed like aloofness but was actually shyness. She acted in school plays, but she had only one close friend, and she still suffered from her parents' equivocal position in Oxford. She had felt unwelcome in some schoolmates' homes, and at times she felt like a social outcast. What she wanted more than anything else was to be just like the others. Her mother was silently aghast when she brought home cheap pink rayon underthings from the dime store in preference to the embroidered lingerie in her drawer. She "ached for mediocrity," but when she tried to tell her father how hard her situation was, he told her, "You're lucky to be my daughter." But he had carefully lettered the invitations to her St. Valentine's Day dance at Rowan Oak. She would soon be fourteen, yet clinging to the symbolic vestiges of her childhood, he still hid the jelly beans and the colored eggs, and dutifully she still went hunting for them.

Early April brought another sign that Faulkner's position in Oxford was changing. The university English Department asked him to talk to their advanced students. After two refusals, Professor A. Wigfall Green renewed the appeal, with a promise that there would be no faculty members and no note-taking. Considering this for a moment, Faulkner replied, with what seemed like bravado, "I wouldn't think of doing such a thing except for money."[33] When Green immediately agreed, Faulkner laughed and then consented with a firm handclasp. A few days later chairman Alton Bryant put it in writing: six sessions for $250. By now Faulkner may have had second thoughts—and well he might, for the meetings would produce unforeseen consequences.

C H A P T E R

52

> . . . young men who had never been farther from Yoknapa-
> tawpha County than Memphis or New Orleans (and that not
> often), now talked glibly of street intersections in Asiatic and
> European capitals . . . living now (with now a wife and next
> year a wife and child and the year after that a wife and chil-
> dren) in automobile trailers or G.I. barracks on the outskirts of
> liberal arts colleges. . . .
>
> —*Requiem for a Nun* (246)

ON Monday morning, April 14, 1947, Faulkner met one class in the novel
and another in American literature. His answers to the students' questions
tended to be brief and assertive. He thought that James Joyce was the
father of modern literature and Sherwood Anderson the father of modern
American literature. There was a warmth in his comments about his one-
time mentor, now dead six years, as though he were perhaps atoning, or,
with maturity, seeing more kindly the man whose talent he had gauged
so critically. He was still developing a poetics of his own, but few of
his basic judgments would change. On Tuesday he met the other American literature section, and on the next day the class in modern literature.
After that one, he joined members of the English staff for coffee. Fifteen
minutes later he rose formally from the table. "I wish you gentlemen
would excuse me," he said. "I must go home and let the cow out." Forty
minutes later he was back to meet the class in creative writing. Much
of contemporary writing was trash, he thought, and "what one writes
must uplift the heart. . . ." When a student asked if he didn't feel that
he gave a distorted view of his own area, he answered, "Yes, and I'm
sorry. I feel I'm written out. I don't think I'll write much more."[1] When
pressed to rate his contemporaries and to include himself, he said that
all of them had failed to achieve the dream, but that judged on the
splendor of the failure, he would rank them: Wolfe, Faulkner, Dos Passos,
Hemingway, and Steinbeck. At the first session he had said he liked the

kind of courage Wolfe had—he had dared so much that his attempt had been doomed from the start, but this was the grandest kind of failure. (This was a judgment that would surprise Ben Wasson. He had heard Faulkner say that he liked Wolfe, that he was very good. But on other occasions he would say Wolfe was absurd: "it's like an elephant trying to do the hoochie-coochie."[2]) As for Hemingway, he had always been careful, never attempting anything he couldn't do; he was like a poker player who kept his cards close to his vest; he never made mistakes in fact, style, or diction. Finally, on Thursday morning, Faulkner met the Shakespeare class and the series was completed. He looked tired but victorious to Green, and he even managed a graceful response to their thanks: had he known how pleasant it would be, he would have paid for a chance to talk with the students.

He was, it turned out, going to have to pay for it. Green's promises that no professors would be present and no notes would be taken had not been kept. The university's new public-relations director, Marvin Black, recently arrived from California, encouraged two of the students to revise their notes for magazine publication. On Monday morning Black wrote a short release giving highlights of the sessions. Included were Faulkner's ranking of the novelists and his reasons for Hemingway's rating: "he has no courage, has never climbed out on a limb. He has never used a word where the reader might check his usage by a dictionary." The release was prepared for general distribution to wire services and newspapers, and on April 24 the *Eagle* ran it on the front page. When Faulkner learned of the students' projected magazine piece, he immediately asked Alton Bryant to see that it was stopped. When Bryant wrote him a reassuring letter, Faulkner explained his objections. "I just hate like hell to be jumbled head over heels into the high-pressure ballyhoo which even universities now believe they must employ: the damned eternal American BUY! BUY!! BUY!!! 'Try us first, our campus covers ONE WHOLE SQUARE MILE, you can see our water tank from twelve miles away, our football team almost beat A.&M.' we have WM FAULKNER at 6 (count them: 6) English classes.' That sort of thing I will resist with my last breath."[3] But Dr. Bryant had reassured him, and now it seemed that he could relax. He and Estelle even went fishing on Hurricane Creek, as they once used to do. Some Sundays that spring, friends would see them at St. Peter's Episcopal Church. Wearing a Harris Tweed jacket, Faulkner would escort his wife to the same pew near the front each time. He would sit there impassive, looking straight ahead.

On May 11 excerpts from Marvin Black's press release appeared in the New York *Herald Tribune*, and in due course Ernest Hemingway received his copy at his home in Cuba. Always vulnerable and sensitive to a slur, particularly depressed at the time, Hemingway was cut deeply when he read the assertion that he had "no courage." He started an angry letter to Faulkner, listing the places where he had been in battle, but it began to get too long. He wrote to his friend Brigadier General C. T. Lanham in late May, asking him to write Faulkner and tell him only what he actually knew about Hemingway under fire. A month later "Buck" Lanham sent Faulkner a three-page registered letter recounting examples of Hemingway's extraordinary heroism as a war correspondent with Lanham's 22nd Infantry Regiment.

Faulkner replied almost immediately to make it clear that he was sorry for the misunderstanding and pain the release had caused. He told Lanham that it was a garbled, incomplete version of what he had said: he knew of Hemingway's record in both wars and in Spain. But he was retracting only up to a point—the original comment "had no reference whatever to Hemingway as a man: only to his craftsmanship as a writer." He explained his judging on degrees of failure, that Hemingway was next to last "since he did not have the courage to get out on a limb as the others did, to risk bad taste, over-writing, dullness, etc." And he would take any other opportunity that offered to correct the misunderstanding. He sent a copy with a covering note to Hemingway. "I'm sorry of this damn stupid thing," he told him. "I was just making $250.00, I thought informally, not for publication, or I would have insisted on looking at the stuff before it was released. I have believed for years that the human voice has caused all human ills and I thought I had broken myself of talking. Maybe this will be my valedictory lesson." But he closed the brief note without an explicit retraction. "I hope it wont matter a damn to you. But if or when or whe[ne]ver it does, please accept another squirm from yours truly."[4]

It was a painful sequence for Faulkner, and not just because he had gone against basic misgivings when he had agreed to the sessions. Long before he had made a name, he had thought of Hemingway as the best of the young American writers. Then later Hemingway had sent him warm and cordial greetings through Paul Romaine at the time of the *Salmagundi* publication, and then later he had sung the praises that Cowley had relayed. Faulkner must have felt even worse in late July when he received a long, rambling, and generous letter from Hemingway addressing him as "Dear Bill." Especially under the circumstances, he could not have begun more warmly. "Awfully glad to hear from you and glad to have made contact. Your letter came tonight and please throw all the other stuff away, the misunderstanding, or will have to come up and we both trompel on it." He knew what Faulkner meant about Wolfe and Dos Passos, but he still couldn't agree. He assumed that Faulkner had been referring to *For Whom the Bell Tolls*, "a very cold one of mine," but he still thought parts of it would stand. Though it would probably bore him, he wished Faulkner would reread it because "as brother would like to know what you think." He used his favorite boxing metaphors for writing. "You are a better writer than Fielding or any of those other guys and you should just know it and keep on writing . . . don't fight with the poor pathological characters of our time (we won't name). You and I can both beat Flaubert who is our most respected, honored master." Hemingway was a writer who liked to have a drink when the day's work was done and sometimes to turn then to his correspondence. The longer the letter went on, the more clearly the drinking showed and the warmth and sense of comradeship grew stronger. "Anyway I am your Bro. if you want one that writes and I'd like us to keep in touch." He told about his sons and the misfortunes they had suffered, and then closed: "Have much regard for you. Would like to keep on writing [letters]. He signed it "Ernest Hemingway."[5] Apparently, Faulkner never replied.

In the aftermath of his appearances at the university Faulkner had been going ahead with what Marvin Black's news release had called a novel about the birth and death of Christ. It had gotten no easier. "I have just found another serious bug in the ms.," he had written Ober. Reporting to Haas, he said, "I have realised lately how much trash and junk writing for movies corrupted into my writing." It would be all right after revision, but even after that the writing would be "a slow thing compared to the speed I had once."[6] Returning half of the rewrite two weeks later, he felt better. "It's getting right now," he told Ober. "It was a tragedy of ideas, morals, before; now it's getting to be a tragedy of people."[7]

Buzz Bezzerides and his family came for a brief visit that July and provided a welcome distraction. Faulkner told Buzz that the Bureau of Internal Revenue had disallowed the exemptions he had claimed for his 1944 California residence, and to earn the $1,000 additional tax, he feared he would have to return to Warner Brothers, where the new fifty-two-week option had been taken up at precisely the rate called for in the original contract. He took Buzz for a ride to show him the town and the countryside, but Buzz would also see him in his workroom when Renzi or someone else came in, writing checks and then shaking his head at how quickly the money flowed out. His account was not the only thing being depleted. Once when he wanted to show Buzz a spring, he was unable to find it. Finally he remembered. "The bastard bulldozed it for a lake," he said. "They're doin' it to the whole country." They got back into the car, and he drove to the bootlegger's and bought some corn whiskey.

He continued to work and worry through July and into August. The pages piled up as he wrote in the early mornings before the hundred-degree noontime heat. "I am now in the middle of a hundred page new chapter which itself is a good story," he told Haas, "a complete novelette, about a white man and an old Negro preacher and the preacher's 14 year old grandson who stole a crippled racehorse and healed its broken leg and spent a year dodging from one little back country track to the next racing the horse before the police ever caught them, then the white man shot the horse. They did it not to win money but because (the horse was a valuable champion) its owner would have retired it to stud because of its ruined leg while the thieves knew that what the horse wanted to do was to run races: a champion: a giant among horses."[8] The white man was a British soldier who functioned in the Western Front segment of the plot. But when Faulkner introduced the old Negro and his grandson seeking the white man, he decided he had to explain the development of their relationship, in spite of the fact that he had already estimated that he would have to write a thousand pages in all to complete the novel. He had envisioned a similar plot in "Uncle Willy," and had used the extended flashback before, with Joe Christmas and other characters. This interpolation, however, would not be as functional or as clearly integrated into the thematic pattern of the novel. A number of factors may have been involved. It had been a dozen years since he had set any fiction outside the South, and then it had been a short story. Now he had nearly 400 pages of a novel set in Europe, in a milieu he knew chiefly from reading and only limited personal experience. This new story would put him back on home ground, but as the hot dry month of August turned into September, the work moved slowly.

He tried to understand why as he wrote again to Haas. "The reason may be 1. This is perhaps the last book I'll write and I am putting all the rest of it into it, or 2. It may contain the germs of several more books."[9] More than twenty years before, when Faulkner had found Sherwood Anderson sitting on a bench in Jackson Square and laughing about a dream in which he had been walking country roads trying to swap a horse for a night's sleep, he had concluded that it was no dream but instead a story symbolic of the dream of America which Anderson offered in his work. Faulkner's horse thieves had embarked upon their adventure because they knew the owner's plan for the old champion. In a sense, the creator of this tale had himself been at stud, spending his seed in Hollywood to produce offspring for which he cared little. Seven years ago, before that long servitude, he had written Bennett Cerf, "Hemingway and Dos Passos and I are veterans now; we should be fighting tooth and toenail to hold our places against young writers. But there are no young writers worth a damn that I know of."[10] Now it was five years since he had published a novel, and for many reasons he must have wanted to show that he was still the champion he had been. The trouble was, that with his financial problems eased as they had not been in years, the track on which he had first chosen to run was proving a slow one. He had turned aside from the main action of the fable, turned to another track of the kind he knew best, but now this one was also proving slow. It may have been natural for his mind to turn away from this vexing problem to a familiar one, but without the desperate intensity of other times. Once more he took up the old refrain: he would have to go back to Warner Brothers not just because of the taxes but also because "I want to buy another horse since pretty soon now I shall be too stiff in the joints for anything except old man's riding."[11]

HE fretted as his fiftieth birthday came and passed. He was alarmed at his slowness and frustrated by distractions. Servants had left for more profitable jobs, and much of his time had to be taken up with errands if the household was to function, with the result, he told Bob Haas, that "the typewriter is the least important thing in my daily life." Going by the synopsis he had sent them three years before, he had not quite finished the introduction, even though Ober had 400 pages and he had written probably a million words in all. Sometimes, he said, he thought the stuff was no good. Then, rereading the letter, he had a surge of confidence: "I am just getting older and dont write fast anymore," but, he added, "be assured that any time Random H. feels this has gone far enough, so do I."[12] To continue, he would need $1,500 in addition to the monthly $500. Once again Ober set to work to shear away the difficulties troubling his client. Haas informed Faulkner that "The amounts you are going to need are not too staggering," and besides, when the horse-race piece was finished, Ober might be able to place it for him.

In mid-October, Robert Linscott told Ober that *The Partisan Review* would probably be willing to pay $1,000 or more. Ober naturally thought first of magazines such as the *Post*, but he waited to see the material. It was almost mid-November when it came. Ninety pages in all, it contained extended passages of italics and it was punctuated so that it was all one sentence. Ober saw that there was no chance at magazines such as the *Post*, and he thought a two-paragraph introduction would help no matter where he submitted it. Faulkner wasn't anxious to do that, but he told Ober he was willing to allow almost any change an editor wanted to make. Then he went off to hunting camp.

When he returned on Thursday night, November 26, there was word that *The Partisan Review* would not take it without substantial changes. Friday morning he sent Ober a wire: LET PR EDIT AND CUT BUT NOT RE-WRITE IT. He followed this with a letter describing an introduction which would cut it to sixty pages. If that was too long, the editors could take what they wanted and print it as a fragment from the work. "Let me hear as soon as possible," he told Ober, "and I will get at the induction."[13] A week later he found that he had misunderstood. It wasn't a question of revisions—they didn't want the piece at all.

Now he needed reassurance from both his agent and his publisher, who had loyally urged him to go on but had offered no specific comments. "What is your opinion of this section in question?" he asked the former. "Dull? Too prolix? Diffuse?" His own theory was that the world was too battered, that man had not enough spiritual strength left to be concerned with art. He was convinced that "that magazine does not exist now which would have printed sections from Ulysses as in the 1920's." In the letter itself, questions asking reassurance alternated with explanations and expressions of confidence. But finally he concluded, "Might be worth while trying some of it in some 'precious' publication like school quarterlies or some such amateur payless medium. . . ."[14] Ober spared him what would have been a painful blow: *Partisan Review* editor Philip Rahv had rejected the piece not only because it was too long, but because they thought it read like a first draft—it just wasn't ready for publication.

When it came time to stop for the holidays, he was ready. He went to Greenfield for the Christmas tree, and he made programs for a tea dance for Jill at Miss Lida's on December 23. There were fewer servants this year to share in the festivities, but they still followed the old ways. If one person surprised another and said "Christmas gift!" first, the other had to give him something. By unspoken custom, the servants always won. With the men—Renzi, Wallace, Harry Hilliard—Faulkner would hand over a bottle of whiskey. "Here's your Santy Claus," he would say. This year there was one conspicuous absence: Uncle Ned. Malcolm had watched as Estelle went through his cedar chest. She discovered a carefully wrapped birthday cake she had baked for him four years before, "odds and ends of the Old Colonel's Confederate uniform, as well as cast offs from the rest of the Falkner family. My mother cried at the sight. So did Pappy— one of the few times I ever saw him cry."[15] Faulkner went to Ripley to see to the old man's burial in the same cemetery with the earlier generations of Falkners he had served.

If Ripley brought back the distant past, Faulkner needed no reminder of the recent past. He had felt like a mare, he had said, with just a few gestations left. Alone in his workroom, or lying wakeful in the early hours of the morning, he must have wondered if this gestation had not been disastrous from the beginning. He had been trading too much of his remaining time as an artist for Hollywood's money. Now perhaps he had done the same thing to himself in his own medium, the thing he had tried to avoid by refusing to write the book about the Mississippi River. He had to be aware of that most pernicious of traps, self-deception. Perhaps he was wasting his time; perhaps he would do better to turn to something closer to his own special métier.

As he surveyed his situation that snowy, icy mid-January of 1948, it must have had a disagreeable sameness about it. Ober had nearly 500 pages of the fable now, a manuscript so complicated that one page in the horse-race sequence was numbered 120-Z-42. Throughout were interlineations, cancellations, and directions in red crayon. To reorder this material would take retyping and further editing. He was loath to spend the money for one and the time for the other.

At the time of the last financial crisis, he had said that if he needed money or felt stale, he could take a week or so and write a short story.

At the beginning of February he told Harold Ober, "On Jan. 15th I put the big mss aside and I now have 60 pages on an approximate 120 page short novel set in my apocryphal Jefferson." He was very optimistic about magazine and book possibilities. "I hope the idea will please Bob," he added. "I've been on Random H's cuff a long time now."[16]

53

"Soon now this sort of thing wont even threaten anymore. It shouldn't now. It should never have. Yet it did last Saturday and it probably will again, perhaps once more, perhaps twice more. But then no more, it will be finished; the shame will still be there of course but then the whole chronicle of man's immortality is in the suffering he has endured, his struggle toward the stars in the stepping-stones of his expiations. . . . But it wont be next Tuesday. Yet people in the North believe it can be compelled even into next Monday by the simple ratification by votes of a printed paragraph. . . ."

—*Intruder in the Dust* (154–155)

SEVEN and a half years earlier Faulkner had told Haas about an idea: "a mystery story, original in that the solver is a negro, himself in jail for the murder and is about to be lynched, solves murder in self defense."[1] The basic subject matter of violence was familiar enough. Little more than a dozen years before, it had happened in Oxford. Elwood Higginbotham had confessed to killing Glen Roberts, a white man. While the jury was still out, a mob of about seventy-five white men with dirt-smudged faces took the prisoner from the county jail. A half-hour later his body hung from a tree on a country road. Wherever imagination needed help from life, there were local models. Lafayette County knew affluent Negroes: light-colored Rob Boles, who owned a shoe-repair shop and considerable property; Rob Herod, a self-reliant landowner out in the county whose dignity seemed to some to verge often on insolence. And of course, Uncle Ned Barnett had made his appearance in Lafayette County many years before.

Although it may have been the mob scene at the climax of the horse-race story that had brought this material once more to mind, there were several elements developing. "The story is a mystery-murder though the theme is more relationship between Negro and white," he told Ober, "specifically or rather the premise being that the white people in the south, before the North or the govt. or anyone else, owe and must pay a responsibility to the Negro." He was taking up one of the themes that had undergirded *Go Down, Moses*. To the anguish and compassion he had felt over past sins and despairs was now added the soul-searching of the war years. "But it's a story; nobody preaches in it."[2] He expected to finish it before the end of February, and he did, with a week to spare, but he was far from through. "Am rewriting it now," he told Haas, "a little more of a book than I thought at first so the rewrite will actually be the writing of it. . . ."[3]

There were occasional breaks in the routine. In late February, Ben Wasson came up from Greenville, bringing with him Hodding Carter, editor of the liberal *Democrat-Times*. They wanted something from Faulkner for a new enterprise, the Levee Press, and he gave them the horse-race piece for a signed limited edition. He would receive twenty-five percent of the proceeds, but he had another motive. "I want to do it mainly," he told Haas, "to confound the people who say nothing good out of Miss." The same impulse was apparent in the book, which would demonstrate that though racial problems were clear and present, there were Southerners who would work toward solving them, and that ultimately this was the best and perhaps the only really effective way. As for his progress, the 139-page original draft might go over 200 pages, and it was going well. "Is a good story, not just a document."[4]

He was working intensively, moving pages and sequences about, sometimes typing as many as three or four versions of a single page. At the beginning, his original strategy had undergone a shift. The story still centered on an adult in jeopardy—Lucas Beauchamp—but Faulkner returned to a favorite device: presenting events largely as perceived by a child or young person. Charles (Chick) Mallison, Jr., had observed Gavin Stevens at work in "Monk," "Tomorrow," and "An Error in Chemistry." Now Chick would have an opportunity for more and scarier detective work, but the story's deeper level lay in the realm of morality rather than adventure. Aleck Sander (the son of Paralee, Mrs. Mallison's cook) was to Chick as Ringo Strother had been to Bayard Sartoris. With one other character—Miss Eunice Habersham, a thin spinster well on in years—Faulkner had his principals. On page 1 he had used what would be a 24-page flashback: having fallen into a stream and then having been dried out and fed at Lucas' home, Chick had been unable to accept this hospitality with courtesy and had tried to repay it basely: with coins. Over the next four years he had tried to expunge the shame he felt. Then, in present time, Lucas reenters his life, jailed for the murder of Vinson Gowrie, member of a family from Beat Four—the most remote, fierce, and intractable of the five beats of Yoknapatawpha County.

By the end of the first week of April, Faulkner had begun the last chapter of the book. As the forsythia faded and the dogwood bloomed, he pressed on. While keeping Lucas Beauchamp's plight in the forefront, he was concentrating in the novel's psychological level on Chick Mallison's changing perception of Lucas as a man. Even the relatively enlightened Gavin Stevens shares something of the community's feeling that Lucas has always acted like a McCaslin instead of a Negro. As Chick gradually understands his own share of that feeling, he comes to perceive more about the plight of the Negro in the world of Yoknapatawpha County. In creating his effects, Faulkner was using a number of techniques he had employed as a scenarist. In the scene in Lucas' kitchen in the earlier version, according to one scholar, Faulkner stopped "and like a screen writer typed out a thematic statement of the novel. . . ."[5] Fortunately he deleted it and made the same point as Chick recalls the smell of the quilt in which he sat wrapped as his clothes dried that day. He wonders "if perhaps that smell were really not the odor of a race nor even actually of poverty but perhaps of a condition: an idea: a belief: an acceptance, a passive acceptance by them themselves of the idea that being Negroes they were not supposed to have facilities to wash properly or often or even to wash bathe often even without the facilities to do it with; that in fact it was a little to be preferred that they did not."[6] In "Pantaloon in Black" the sheriff's deputy had been unable to conceive of the depth of Rider's grief for Mannie. Learning, a year later, of Mollie's death, Chick finally understands why Lucas failed even to see him on the square one day. A further step is the recognition of Lucas' danger: "death by shameful violence of a man who would die not because he was a murderer but because his skin was black." (72) There would be still more, coming to terms with the way people of his own land could so renounce their humanity, also, pondering with his uncle the stance they should take when the rest of the country attempted with legislation to prevent such outrages.

There were numerous links with other work. A long passage about hunters might have come from "The Bear." Chick and Aleck Sander and Miss Habersham vs. nearly the whole county suggests Bayard and Ringo and Granny Millard vs. the Yankee army. One passage about Chick and Aleck Sander's attempted exhumation of a body is full of military metaphors that might have carried over from the fable, and one character from Howard Hawks's ill-fated *Battle Cry* could have contributed to the Chick-Lucas relationship.[7] Though groping toward new attitudes, Chick is just as Southern as the Quentin who told Shreve he would have to be born there to understand the South, and a touchstone for Chick is almost the same moment of history. With Quentin it was Pickett's charge; with Chick it is "the instant when it's still not yet two oclock on that July afternoon in 1863, the brigades are in position behind the rail fence, the guns are laid and ready in the woods and the furled flags are already loosened to break out . . . and it's all in the balance, it hasn't happened yet, it hasn't even begun yet. . . ." (194) It is the moment before the fateful charge, before the wave that carried them up the slope to the high tide of the Confederacy, with the farthest crest of that wave—an article of local lore and faith—Oxford's own University Greys suffering that day on the field of Gettysburg a casualty rate of one hundred percent. Compared with this legendary heroism is the base and brutal threat of the mob and the cowardice of its hasty, shamefaced dispersal after Miss Habersham and the two boys demonstrate Lucas' innocence. Chick Mallison is not only like the men of the Greys, he is also like that most personal of Faulkner's other surrogates, the poet of "Carcassonne," for Chick wants "to perform something passionate and brave and austere. . . ." (193)

Stylistically, Faulkner attempted to maintain suspense through withholding and then gradually revealing information, as he had done in *Absalom, Absalom!*. He used words as he had not done since *Pylon*, with neologisms such as *dismatchment* and *succumbence*, and though there was no stream of consciousness as chaotic as Quentin's, he interpolated an unpunctuated six-page passage in which Chick hears the present against the past. And as in other novels, Faulkner presented the central complex of events from several points of view. Lucas Beauchamp is seen differently by the Gowries, Sheriff Hampton, Chick, and Gavin Stevens. "I'm defending Lucas Beauchamp," Stevens tell his indignant, angry nephew. "I'm defending Sambo from the North and East and West—the outlanders who will fling him decades back not merely into injustice but into grief and agony and violence too by forcing on us laws based on the idea that man's injustice to man can be abolished overnight by police. . . . I only say that the injustice is ours, the South's. We must expiate and abolish it ourselves, alone and without help nor even (with thanks) advice." (203–204) Faulkner would deny that Gavin Stevens was his spokesman, but he was, like Stevens, a gradualist—a position that would provoke abuse and even threats. Later his uncle John would vehemently disclaim any role as model for the character. "Me, that nigger lovin' Stevens? Naw, I don't read Billy's books much. But he can write them if he wants to. I guess he makes money at it—writing those dirty books for Yankees!"[8]

By mid-April, Faulkner was nearly done, and though he had complained about his slowness, he had accomplished a great deal of meticulous rewriting and expansion in a remarkably brief time. Chapter Five, for instance, had gone through no fewer than five versions.[9] It was April 20 when he wrote Haas that the 321-page typescript was finished. "It started out to be a simple quick 150 page whodunit but jumped the traces, strikes me as being a pretty good study of a 16 year old boy who overnight became a man." Now he had everything but a title. For more than a month he had been soliciting suggestions. "I still dont have a title, haven't found that word yet which means substitution by sharp practice IN THE

DUST. Please . . . ask Saxe, Don, Bennett, anyone, think of other titles besides IN THE DUST if necessary."[10] He didn't like "Jugglery" or "Imposture" but he was considering "Intruder."

He hoped for a magazine serial sale; he also reworked the first chapter of the novel and about a third of the second chapter into a 26-page story called "Lucas Beauchamp" which Ober received on May 12.[11] *The Sewanee Review* had bought "A Courtship" for $200, but Ober could not place "Lucas Beauchamp." As for the serial sale, Bennett Cerf was thinking along other lines, and by mid-May he had expressions of interest from Warner Brothers and Cagney Productions. Faulkner thought the former ought to have first look at it "since they did not become stuffy about relinquishing claim to movie rights on what I do while off their pay. . . ."[12]

MEANWHILE the book had been going through the editorial process. Saxe Commins was involved in other work, so the manuscript was turned over to Albert Erskine, who had come to Random House from Reynal & Hitchcock the year before. He was a good choice. A Memphian who had studied at Louisiana State University and edited *The Southern Review* with Robert Penn Warren and Cleanth Brooks, he was quite familiar with Faulkner's country as well as his work. His queries were straightforward and uncomplicated, and by June 1, *Intruder in the Dust* had arrived at the printer's.

In Oxford, Faulkner was preparing for a debut of another kind. Hugh Evans was a retired Army colonel three years older than Faulkner, a little taller and heavier but like him in other ways. When he had run the Ole Miss ROTC. program, Evans had gone flying with Faulkner and Ross Brown. Now he and Brown and Ashford Little had pooled resources to build a houseboat. For the last six months they had been at work, and from time to time Faulkner would stop by Evans' backyard to help, first with the deck, and by spring, the brasswork and mahogany paneling. His most significant contribution, however, was to provide elaborately drawn and colored letters of marque which comically described the vessel's birth and transportation to Sardis Lake. He also provided the commissioning papers of the ship, now named, out of a compound of first names of the three wives, the *Minmagery*. In a fine eighteenth-century hand he wrote, "by these presents [they] constitute and appoint her to be a Ship of the Line in the Provisional Navy of the Confederate States of America. . . . Given under my Great Grandfather's sword this Twenty Fourth July 1948 at Oxford Mississippi. William C. Falkner II."[13] When the guests came aboard for the christening party they were greeted ceremoniously by a figure with a blackened mustache, a Navy cap, and a jacket bearing sunbursts of decorations which on close inspection proved to be Coca-Cola and Orange Crush bottle caps. Faulkner enjoyed the party.

That had not been the only occasion for celebration that month. The sale of "A Courtship" had been made through Albert Erskine, who with Bob Haas's permission had shown a copy of the manuscript of *Intruder in the Dust* to Carol Brandt, Eastern story editor of MGM. When the galleys went out for motion-picture-company bids, she immediately phoned Bennett Cerf and said, "I'll offer you fifty thousand dollars sight unseen for the new Faulkner." Cerf accepted. Jacob Wilk and two other companies' representatives protested that there had been no time to make a decision, but Cerf had received a bona-fide offer and the contracts were drawn up. After the Random House commission, Faulkner's share would be $40,000. In Oxford, he and Estelle celebrated. Sallie Murry Williams found him barefoot. "Anybody who can sell a book to the movies for $50,000," he happily told her, "he has a right to get drunk and dance in his bare feet."

When the celebration was over, he decided for tax purposes to take only $10,000 right away, the rest in three equal payments over the next three years. It was the beginning of financial security, but past experience prevented him from enjoying it fully. "Will see you this fall I think," he wrote Ober. "I want to come up and consult you and Bob both about what to do with this money so my friends and kinfolks dont or cant borrow and spend it."[14] There was one indulgence he would grant himself. After the 1944 income-tax claim proved to be less than he had feared, he went to the local Ford dealer. He had nursed the old car along until it was beyond repair, so now he bought an almost-new maroon station wagon with a wooden body. Then, when permission fees for reprinting portions of his work brought in another $1,000, he decided to buy a small garden tractor and put a new roof on Rowan Oak.

There were other signs that year—besides the movie sale and the new book—of his standing in the world beyond Lafayette County. In February, H. L. Mencken had written asking him to send a few of his novels to a professor preparing to lecture on him in his seminar at the University of Berlin. Professor Carvel Collins, preparing to conduct a seminar at Harvard University in the fall on the work of William Faulkner, came to Oxford that summer to check the Ole Miss library and something of Faulkner's milieu at firsthand and had a pleasant meeting with the author himself. Later, Professor James W. Webb would recall that about this time, perhaps in the fall, "the matter of an honorary degree for Faulkner was presented to the faculty. It was pointed out that the University of Mississippi had not practiced the policy of awarding honorary degrees. A vote was taken anyway. . . . but we lost by a very narrow margin."[15]

Faulkner was about to come back into the public eye as he had not done since *Sanctuary*. Roark Bradford had asked if he could do a piece on him for a magazine called *48*, and he had not been able to refuse. Robert Coughlan had asked Malcolm Cowley to do a profile on him for *Life*.

Hamilton Basso wrote asking his consent for a profile in *The New Yorker*. He scratched a reply on Basso's letter: "Oh hell no. Come down and visit whenever you can, but no piece in any paper about me as I am working tooth and nail at my lifetime ambition to be the last private individual on earth & expect every success since apparently there is no competition for the place."[16] Friends out of the past were welcome so long as they came in a personal capacity. One late September afternoon Helen Baird Lyman, on her way to Washington with her two sons, Guy and Jim, came by for a brief visit. For the son of this woman who had inspired those passionate poems nearly a quarter-century ago, he inscribed one of his author's copies of his new book: "To Jimbo Lyman from his old and tried friend William Faulkner." Unshaven and wearing work clothes, he seemed very old to young Jim Lyman.

Faulkner was looking forward to his long-deferred trip to New York. The ulcer that had bothered him was getting better, and he asked Bennett Cerf to book a room for him at the Algonquin if it had not changed too much. He declined Bennett's invitation to stay at his house. "I look forward to meeting your family," he told him, "but one purpose of my expedition is vacation from the nest-and-hearth business."[17] As he made his preparations, the reviews of *Intruder in the Dust* were beginning to appear.

The book received more immediate attention than anything he had previously published. In a long review in *The New Yorker*, Edmund Wilson felt that it contained "a kind of counterblast to the anti-lynching bill and to the civil-rights plank in the Democratic platform," but at the same time, it was "a new note to come from the South; and it may really represent something more than Faulkner's own courageous and generous spirit, some new stirring of public conscience." And though Wilson lamented Faulkner's residing "so far from such cities as produced the Flauberts, Joyces, and Jameses" and his resultant provinciality, he praised "the genius that produced the book, which sustains, like its predecessors, the polymorphous polychromatic vitality, the poetic truth to experience, of Faulkner's Balzacian chronicle of Yoknapatawpha County." Horace Gregory wrote on September 26 in the New York *Herald Tribune* book section that he thought Faulkner had turned isolation to his advantage, that *Intruder in the Dust* was one of his best short novels and that Lucas Beauchamp was "one of the most convincing characters in American fiction." The reviewer for *Time* thought the book not only "a triumphant work of art" but one which offered hope for the South.[18] Maxwell Geismar, however, in *The Saturday Review of Literature*, called the book Southern Gothic tainted by both Hollywood and Southern chauvinism.

At home, the response would be mixed. It was another case of bad public relations, courtesy of William Faulkner, but the novel did take a stand on outside intervention which would be congenial to all but the most liberal Southerners. On September 30 the *Eagle* reprinted Harvey Breit's accolade in *The New York Times* and a week afterward took note of magazine praise of "Oxford's great novelist." In New York his publishers happily took note not only of the reviews but also of the indication that *Intruder in the Dust* would sell over 15,000 copies in the trade edition.

WHEN Cerf met him at La Guardia Airport in the late afternoon of Monday, October 18, Faulkner's social calendar was already filling up. He had asked Cerf to tell Hal Smith to let Jim Devine know he was coming. That night he had a dinner date with Ruth Ford, whom he had not seen since he and she were both working at Warner Brothers. Slim and striking, with black hair and snapping brown eyes, she had grown into an actress of skill and authority. After an enjoyable evening he said, "Ruth, I've been your gentleman friend for quite a while now. Ain't it time I was promoted?" Ruth laughed. "Oh, Bill!" she said.

The following day he visited Random House's new offices in one wing of the imposing brownstone building on Madison Avenue between 50th and 51st streets. Faulkner liked the ornate rooms with their high ceilings and paneled walls softened with heavy drapes. Saxe Commins installed him in his small office on the third floor. Soon the word spread, and at one point there were five people there, with Faulkner listening to the animated conversation and affably putting in a word or a wry comment now and again. That evening the Haases gave a dinner party at their Fifth Avenue apartment, where Faulkner met, for the first time, Malcolm Cowley and his wife, Muriel. Don and Pat Klopfer were there too, with Bennett and Phyllis Cerf, Hal Smith, and Jim Devine. It was a dinner in style, served by two butlers, with a good deal of cognac afterward and even a little literary talk in which Faulkner joined. Hemingway had no courage to experiment, he told Cowley. "You have to take chances and put it down good or bad," he said.[19] After Malcolm and Muriel left at two o'clock, Faulkner and Devine continued the party at Hal Smith's place.

There were engagements the next day. After Don Klopfer took him to lunch at "21" he submitted to an interview with Ralph Thompson for *The New York Times*. He was reluctant, as usual, and a little edgy. Critic Richard Chase had just published an essay treating Faulkner's imagery primarily in terms of curves and lines. When Thompson asked Faulkner about it, he said he just wrote about people around Oxford who didn't care about what he wrote, though some of them tried to borrow some of the money they thought he made. He was better off before he published a novel, he said, because "in those days I was a free man. Had one pair of pants, one pair of shoes, and an old trench coat with a pocket big enough for a whiskey bottle. Now I get stacks of letters asking what I eat for breakfast and what about curves and linear discreteness."[20]

On Wednesday, Ruth Ford phoned him at the Algonquin to invite him to go to a party with her. When he declined she thought his voice sounded strange. She called him the next day, and again he wouldn't go out, and his voice sounded even stranger. There was no answer at all when the operator rang his room on Friday. By now other friends were concerned. When Ruth and Harvey Breit got the manager to let them into Faulkner's room, they found him semiconscious. Bob Haas was there, and Cowley had been there and had now returned. After Cowley got Faulkner into his clothes, Breit helped him downstairs and into the waiting ambulance. Ruth and Jim Devine came down and got into the ambulance with them. Up at 250th Street they saw him through the admissions procedure at the Fieldstone Sanitarium.

When Ruth and Breit returned the next morning, Faulkner reminded Harvey of nothing so much as a fox padding from one side of his cage to another. "You gotta get me out of here," he said. "You gotta get me out of here." The doctor was adamant, however, that he needed four or five days of recuperation. Finally, after they called the Cowleys, a solution was reached. Malcolm and Muriel would put him up at their home in Connecticut. Cowley drove down, and late that night they got him discharged. As they drove north, at every crossroads where there was a tavern Faulkner would suggest they stop and have a drink. Finally they reached a point where Harvey and Ruth could take the train back to New York. Then, in Sherman, Malcolm and Muriel got their guest settled in his room.

The Cowleys had seen friends go through this before. Artists, Malcolm would later write, "need strong egos to do good work. It may be that their working habits, if nothing else, often lead them into a manic-depressive cycle. During the manic phase they write or paint furiously, but then the words and visions stop coming and they fall into a depressed phase of guilt and self-questioning." Moreover, "artists and writers, as a tribal group, have certain defects of character. To be quite simple, they drink too much; all the older ones drink except the reformed alcoholics."[21] If this had happened at home, Estelle and Jill and the rest of his family would have felt no surprise: he did it after almost every book. He had simply brought the pressures and the process to New York with him.

So now the Cowleys helped him through the pangs of withdrawal. By Monday he was up, and Cowley would remember him that day: "he showed extreme self-control, pacing up and down the living room with beads of cold sweat on his forehead and not asking for a drink except at long intervals of perhaps three hours, and then only politely: 'Do you think I could have a beer, ma'am?'" He gave Cowley an impression of delicacy and fastidiousness, and at fifty-one, weighing 148 pounds, he could still wear a pair of young Robbie Cowley's pants with a 30-inch waist. He felt well enough to converse, and in a gesture of gratitude and friendship he told Cowley about his life and his work. Of the book he had finished he said that the voice of Gavin Stevens was not his voice but rather that of "the best type of liberal Southerners." And when he spoke of the book in progress, he told him the fable's entire plot. On Monday, Cowley took him for a long drive, crossing the foothills of the Taconic range and driving on into the Harlem Valley where the maples stood bare and the purple of the oaks reflected the mellow autumnal sunlight. The next day he drove him to Brewster, where Faulkner took the late morning train to New York.[22]

Cowley saw him again on Friday, October 29, for lunch, at which time he said nothing to contradict Cowley's impression that he was resigned to the *Life* article Robert Coughlan had asked Cowley to do. The next day, having bought from Abercrombie & Fitch a corduroy coat for riding, he boarded a plane for home, arriving there not long after a dozen long-stemmed roses arrived at Muriel Cowley's door.

THE day after Faulkner's return found him back in his workroom. Settling into the Oxford routine, he set to work on the fable again "though not too hard," he told Haas, "as our deer hunting camp opens next week and due to the deaths this past year of the two senior members, most of the work—getting the dogs and horses sent up, cooks, tents, feed etc., has fallen to my lot."[23] The following week he went off to deer camp on schedule.

Not long afterward, the phone rang one evening with the kind of long-distance intrusion he detested. When Estelle told him that it was a young college student who said she might fail a course if she couldn't speak with Mr. Faulkner, he relented and told Doyle Halford, 150 miles away at Mississippi College, some of the things she needed for her term paper. When she ran down the hall for more change, Faulkner told the operator to put the call on his bill. Then, after it was completed, he called her back. "I thought you might like to tell something about the story I'm writing now," he said. As she took notes he told her about a lawyer who solved a case and thus prevented a murder. His work was taking a new direction.

It was not the direction Haas, Erskine, and Cowley had expected. Three years before, while Faulkner was still meditating what would become the Compson Appendix, Cowley had suggested a book of stories arranged by cycles—the Indians, the Compsons, and others, and Faulkner had liked the idea very much. Early in 1948, Albert Erskine had suggested to Haas that they bring out a book of new Faulkner short stories and then follow it with a collected edition combining the new book with *These 13* and *Doctor Martino*, both now out of print. He gave Haas an annotated list of twenty-five stories with twelve recommended for inclusion. When Haas sent it to Faulkner, he replied that he wanted to make a few changes in the starred list and that he would go over it later.[24] By the time he had finished revising *Intruder in the Dust*, he had lost the list. Asking Haas for a copy, he told him, "I would like to mull over it, try to give this volume an integrated form of its own, like the Moses book if possible, or at least These 13."[25] When he had written Cowley to report on his trip home, he told him, "It wasn't too dull because I spent the time thinking about the collection of stories, the which the more I think about, the better I like."[26] Haas and Saxe Commins had worked over Erskine's list with Faulkner and devised a table of contents divided into six segments. On October 31, Faulkner had returned corrections for "Shingles for the Lord" and "A Bear Hunt" to Commins together with a change in the table of contents. It was on the plane home, however, that the section titles had fallen into place. "I kept on thinking," he wrote Commins, "why *Indians* when we had never said The Country *people* and the Village *people*, but only the *Country* and the *Village*. Then I thought, not *Indians* but *Wilderness*, and then suddenly the whole page stood right, each noun in character and tone and tune with every other and I imagine that now you have divined the word for the war section too: The Wasteland. . . ." The last two sections of the book would be called "The Middle Ground" and "Beyond."[27]

This was before he had returned to the fable once more, before he had gone to deer camp and before he had told Doyle Halford about the new story he was writing. There was more involved than just one story. Now he wrote Commins and asked him to talk with Cerf and Haas. "Maybe we are too previous with a collected Faulkner," he told him. "I am thinking of a 'Gavin Stevens' volume, more or less detective stories." Besides the ones already in print, "There is one more which no one has bought. The reason is, it is a novel which I tried to compress into short story length. It is a love story, in which Stevens prevents a crime (murder) not for justice but to gain (he is now fifty plus) the childhood sweetheart which he lost 20 years ago. It will probably run about 150 pages, which should make a volume as big as INTRUDER."[28] If they all agreed, he would get at it after Christmas and the book could be ready for fall publication.

A week later he had an enthusiastic letter of agreement from New York. He had still been unable to mount another offensive in his continuing struggle with the fable, but he knew now that he was far from being burned out, and he was in the process of creation once more.

54

> But above all, the courthouse: the center, the focus, the hub;
> sitting looming in the center of the county's circumference like
> a single cloud in its ring of horizon, laying its vast shadow to
> the uttermost rim of horizon; musing, brooding, symbolic and
> ponderable, tall as cloud, solid as rock, dominating all: protector
> of the weak, judiciate and curb of the passions and lusts, reposi-
> tory and guardian of the aspirations and the hopes. . . .
>
> —*Requiem for a Nun* (40)

HE went on writing as 1948 drew to a close, but there were a number of
other things that distracted him or made demands upon his time. He had
seen the piece Cowley had done for *Life* on Hemingway, but it was
January of the new year before he got in touch with Cowley about the
article that Cowley wanted to write about him. "I will protest to the
last: no photographs, no recorded documents. It is my ambition to be, as
a private individual, abolished and voided from history, leaving it markless,
no refuse save the printed books. . . . It is my aim, and every effort bent,
that the sum and history of my life, which in the same sentence is my
obit and epitaph too, shall be them both: He made the books and he
died."[1] It had cost him a considerable pang to refuse Cowley because
of the double debt he owed him. Correspondence with Ober and Haas
produced no such concern. Ober wanted to be sure Faulkner was getting
his share of the profits from Valerie Bettis' ballet based on *As I Lay
Dying*, and Haas consulted him about their preparations for reissuing *Go
Down, Moses*, *The Wild Palms*, and *The Hamlet*.

JANUARY went out with a six-inch snowfall, which remained to greet
MGM director Clarence Brown and four assistants when they arrived to
survey film locations. Brown had apparently been briefed on the hostility
some townspeople still felt despite Moon Mullen's earlier defense of
Faulkner's politics in the columns of the *Eagle* and his argument that the

filming of *Intruder in the Dust* would not only honor the city but also bring it thousands of dollars. As Faulkner would explain to Jim Devine later that year, people were saying, "We don't want no one comin' into our town to make no movie about lynchin'." But Brown, a native of Knoxville and a graduate of the University of Tennessee, pleaded his case eloquently. "We can make this film the most eloquent statement of the true Southern viewpoint of racial relations and racial problems ever sent out over the nation," he told the *Eagle*.[2] Chamber of Commerce president Sykes Haney predicted one-hundred-percent cooperation. (Lodging of the Negro actors "in the homes of Oxford's colored leaders" solved a practical and social problem.) The next issue of the *Eagle* contained a full-page ad by forty merchants declaring their pride in the fact that Oxford was to be the stage for the filming of "Mr. William Faulkner's Great Story, Intruder in the Dust."[3] Faulkner did his part by helping to scout locations, driving about through the county with Clarence Brown. The author and director got on well, for Brown had been a fighter pilot in World War I, and now a farmer as well as a moviemaker, he was a director much more like Howard Hawks than Mike Curtiz.

By March 9, Brown and his assistants had returned to Oxford in the vanguard of the fifty-five-member troupe that would remain through the thirty-one-day shooting schedule. Most interesting to the Oxonians was the casting office MGM opened in Bob Williams' Lyric Theatre Building. "Much excitement here," Faulkner wrote Jim Devine. "It's too bad I'm no longer young enough to cope with all the local girls who are ready and eager to glide into camera focus on their backs."[4] Brown had cast surveyors Edmund and Ephraim Lowe on sight as the Gowrie twins. Local merchants were cast for bit parts in the barbershop scene, and Mayor Bob Williams also had a couple of lines to say. Faulkner helped with the casting, arguing for "a fat sweating ordinary person" as the killer rather than the obvious heavy that Brown had chosen who might give the mystery away in the first scene. Brown agreed and switched two of the roles. As it turned out, Faulkner did more than that. He also read a copy of Ben Maddow's 113-page scenario. "Brown one of the best to work with I ever knew;" he later wrote Bennett Cerf, "right off he asked me to read the script and tell him what I wanted changed; I think he meant it. There was nothing to change. I rewrote, re-arranged, the dialogue in the jail cell sequences, and rewrote the scene in the sheriff's kitchen over the stove and the meat-slicing, and straightened out the tag, but that was all. I really believe Brown would have let me make almost any change I wanted to, but there was no need. This, of course, is for yours and Random H. private ear; I myself am so pleased with the job that I would like all the credit to stay where it is: with Brown and the cast." There was another reason for silence: Warner Brothers' fifty-two-week option would not expire until mid-July, and though he might choose not to work for them, he certainly could not work for MGM.[5]

He would view the whole spectacle with a mixture of amusement, boredom, and exasperation. His family was interested in the filming, however, and so he took his mother to the set one day and sat with her in the canvas chairs to watch Clarence Brown quietly direct his actors and crew. Jill persuaded him to go down to the square one evening to watch a night scene. She was quickly absorbed in it. Then, glancing at her father, she saw "under those nasty blue arc lights, a look of disgust on his face." Some movie problems amused him, though. He thought the clear and precise enunciation of Puerto Rican Juano Hernandez made Lucas Beauchamp sound Shakespearean, and so he helped Hernandez imitate a Mississippi Negro accent. Faulkner served as one of the hosts when they entertained the MGM people on the *Minmagary*. But this was not enough, and he told Estelle she had to entertain them too. She said she would if Aunt 'Bama came. The old lady was delighted to leave Memphis for the occasion and help, but there was a problem about Juano Hernandez. He was a fine actor and a cultivated man, but if they invited him, they would have to invite his Negro hosts in Oxford, and they felt they could not do that. So the whole crew, with the exception of the portrayer of Lucas Beauchamp, came out to Rowan Oak one evening. By late April, after a civic fish fry in their honor, they had packed up and left, having employed more than 500 local people and left an estimated $200,000 behind them. That would be all of *Intruder in the Dust* for Oxford until the October world premiere at the Lyric Theatre.

NEAR the end of February, Saxe Commins had asked Faulkner if they could have the new manuscript in May. As spring approached, however, there was another distraction besides the film-making, but this was a more pleasant one. Arthur Guyton had returned to academic medicine after the war, but in 1947 he had contracted the dreaded poliomyelitis. After convalescence and therapy, he went back to Oxford to teach, but he concluded that he would never again be able to sail his boat by himself. "Mr. Bill mentioned to me in passing that if ever I wanted to sell my sailboat, to let him know," Arthur remembered, and so he called him. "It was only a few hours later that he was already there to collect the boat, and not long thereafter he had it under sail." Bill and Victoria Fielden were back at Rowan Oak for the summer, and Bill spent days with Faulkner, scraping, caulking, and recaulking. Before long they were able to transport the graceful little sloop to Sardis. Before he launched it, he named it *Ring Dove*. Estelle said she knew where the name came from. It was that of a vessel once commanded by Captain Eliott in a story called "The End of the Tether" by another novelist-sailor: Joseph Conrad.[6]

On May Day, Faulkner wrote Commins that he was near the end of his rewriting. Earlier he had thought of using some Latin phrase suggesting the law, but now he had decided he would call the book *Knight's Gambit*, after the novella. The basic plot remained the same, as a boy tries to drive away a suitor ostensibly seeking his mother's hand but actually in love with his sister. When threats fail, he hits upon a murder weapon—a killer stallion where the victim would expect to find a tractable mare. The title referred to Argentinian Captain Sebastian Gualdres, a centaur-like horseman who appears to young Max Harriss capable of moving in two directions—toward his mother or his sister—like a knight on a chess-board. But it does not take Harriss long to divine Gualdres' real intention, for like Henry Sutpen and Quentin Compson, Max Harriss is supersensi-tive to anything concerning his sister. It is the third chessplayer, however, who is the subtlest of the three.

Outwardly, in spite of the thin face and shock of graying hair, Gavin Stevens resembled Phil Stone, with his distinction, his garrulity, and his fondness for classic Greek. Inwardly, Stevens was closer to Faulkner, who, when he had first written to Random House about the novella, told Commins that Stevens was "now fifty plus" and trying to regain "the childhood sweetheart which he lost 20 years ago."[7] The affinity in age was clear enough, and the sense of loss suggested the mood of his com-ment to Cowley that what he needed was "a new young woman." As in Faulkner's life, Stevens' sweetheart had also married an older man, had given him a boy and a girl, and had lived abroad for ten years before returning home to stay. Like Stevens, Faulkner had often found himself playing chess with youngsters—Malcolm Franklin and Arthur Guyton—who later went off to war, as would Chick Mallison.

There were numerous links to other Yoknapatawpha works. Rafe McCallum is still interested in dangerous horses, as he had been in Sartoris, and Captain Warren is still commenting on warfare, as he had done seven-teen years before in "Death Drag." As for technique, this novella was linked to other works by Faulkner's favorite device of the extended flashback. Here it set up in present time the working out of the two major problems: foreseeing and then frustrating Max's move against Gualdres, and then regaining the lost Melisandre Backus Harriss, direct descendant of the young woman who had so gallantly borne danger and embarrass-ment in "My Grandmother Millard and General Bedford Forrest and the Battle of Harrykin Creek." As Gavin Stevens describes a brief meeting with his love after their separation, he tells his nephew he can see the site of the meeting "simply by opening the right page in Conrad. . . ." (244) For the woman's grief, Faulkner had turned, it appeared, to one of Conrad's most memorable scenes: Captain Marlow's visit to Kurtz's "Intended" in Heart of Darkness. "Knight's Gambit" is a minor exercise which ties up further ends of the Yoknapatawpha saga, but in the fabric of the prose—in a reference to the "four-year tunnel of blood and excre-ment and fear in which that whole generation of the world's young men lived" (213)—there is something of that other work that had been hang-ing over him now for six years.

He finished the manuscript in mid-May, though he had completed two typescripts of the novella before he was satisfied. By June 2, Commins was writing back to him. An editor who believed in constant encouragement, he wrote, "I have just this minute finished with great excitement my reading of *Knight's Gambit*. You must know without my telling you how deeply affected I am by its layer upon layer of implication and throbbing narrative power. My hat is off to you, Sir." By mid-July, Faulkner would have the galley proofs, and they would be so clean that he could correct them without even altering his sailing schedule, which now took him out to Sardis Lake three days a week.

"I'm having a fine time with my sloop," he wrote Haas in early July, "am become a fair fresh water lake sailor, where a dozen different weathers can happen in 30 minutes: rain and thunder squalls this time of year, and pretty exciting for five or ten minutes. Have blown off a few stays, but no mast or canvas yet. I seem to have done a really expert caulking job on her hull. . . ."[8] It was not so expert, however, that he did not need the services of Jill, or one of the other two teenagers who served as his crew, to pump out the *Ring Dove* for him. And he had certain convictions, as master of his vessel, that made one of these youths refer to him as Captain Ahab. For one thing, he scorned carrying an outboard motor. As a result, on July 4, when the temperature soared to 105, they sat motionless at two o'clock as the sun beat down on the glazed lake. They were expecting guests at the house, and by afternoon Estelle was ill, but he still would not hail another boat for help. Sunset and darkness brought no breeze. Then at last, by moonlight, fitful winds filled the sails just enough to urge them into sluggish motion. The sailing party returned home at three o'clock in the morning. The next day he bought an outboard motor and stowed it away out of sight for emergencies.

Jill actually dreaded the sailing expeditions, but a protest had produced such an injured silence that she never objected again. He was trying to draw her into things they could share beyond literary favorites such as Swinburne, whose work they knew so well that they would often make a game of reciting alternate lines of a Swinburne poem.[9] When she learned to type, he began to give her material. One batch was for Saxe Commins, and she was told to do a good job. She had already begun tidying up punctuation here and there, and this time she did some editing. She thought it was much better, much clearer, by the time she finished. He was in no condition to read it, so she sent it off. When Commins replied, he asked Faulkner to tell Jill to leave his writing alone. Later Faulkner was able to see the humor of the situation. She was at loose ends that summer, and now he began to give her notes on what he was writing to see what she could develop from them. He offered to go over her work and help her get it published. At the same time, she thought he was ambivalent, wanting her to write but feeling that domesticity was good too.

The lines of communication were not always open. One hot day she wore shorts down to the square. When it was too late to turn away, she saw her father approaching. He passed her without a flicker of recognition. Two weeks later she saw him in front of the post office attired in a pith helmet, a threadbare shirt, and old khakis hacked off at the knee and cinched with a length of rope. When she reproached him for his treatment of her for wearing clean, perfectly respectable shorts, he said simply, "Missy, you've got a point." At home there was still no radio, and Jill could hear programs only at Miss Maud's house or the homes of friends. One day Bill Fielden said, "Pappy, if you don't let Jill have her fun at home, she'll go outside her home for it." And so Faulkner consented to Bill's giving her a phonograph, though she could not play it when her father was at home.[10] But her problems extended to a deeper level. She invited new friends from Memphis down to visit her. When they arrived, her father and mother were drinking. It was horribly embarrassing, but there was nothing she could do except sit there, seething. She would dream the same dream, sometimes twice a month. In twenty-four hours her legs were going to give out, or be cut off. She would never walk again, and she had to decide how she would spend those hours, with her father or her mother. As they both stood looking down at her while she tried to decide, she suddenly realized that neither of them really cared. That spring she had gone to Mardi Gras, and now she would visit other friends in Memphis from time to time. Like most children, she looked forward to independence, but sometimes she felt a longing which few of her friends would understand.

ONE of Malcolm Franklin's friends who had visited Rowan Oak over the years was John Reed Holley. In that hot August of 1949 his wife, Regina, invited her cousin down from Memphis with her date. Joan Williams was a slim, quiet girl of twenty, with reddish hair, and freckles, and eyes of a greenish blue. From her time at Miss Hutchinson's School for Girls she had been determined to pursue a writing career, and she had worked at it during a year's study at Southwestern and another at Chevy Chase Junior College. During her junior year at Bard College she had been named one of the winners in *Mademoiselle*'s college fiction contest, and her story, "Rain Later," would appear in the August issue. One of her friends had introduced her to *The Sound and the Fury*. She would remember the book's impact, knowing that its author "had thought, felt, and suffered everything I ever had. And I wanted him to tell me the reason for suffering: why some people had to, and others never did." (Her own unhappiness had helped precipitate an elopement and a marriage that was annulled.[11]) So she and the young man who had given her the book decided to try to see its author, and Regina Holley extended the invitation. After they reached Oxford, John Reed telephoned and asked Faulkner if he could bring his cousin, who wanted to be a writer, to Rowan Oak to meet him. Faulkner said no; the morning rain had slackened and he was going sailing. John Reed told his guests that they could at least see Rowan Oak. So later they turned in past the NO TRESPASSING sign and drove slowly between the dripping cedars. John Reed saw Faulkner out beyond the house in work clothes, so he parked the car and made his way out to talk to him. When he asked Faulkner if he would come and speak to Joan, he agreed cordially enough, but as they approached, Faulkner asked, "Well, what does she want to see? Why does she want to meet me? Does she want to see if I have two heads?" When he came to the car, Joan remembered, she looked away instantly, "mortified by our intrusion." She was further embarrassed when her friend asked if he might shake Faulkner's hand. "Whatever he saw of me in that instant was his only glimpse."[12]

The minute Joan entered her house in Memphis she began a letter explaining what had brought her to Rowan Oak. She had come because of the work. Her parents had bourgeois aspirations for her and they did not think she would ever do anything with it. She had wanted to find out things from him. Could she see him again? She told him not to be embarrassed about his drinking; her father drank too. Later he said that she even told him about her dog, which had recently been run over.

Meta Rebner would write of him, "His sexual key was the image of a young woman, fresh and fragrant of skin beneath her summer cotton dress, tremblingly responsive to his desire."[13] He was touched by Joan's letter and even apologetic. "Something charming came out of it, like something remembered out of youth: smell, scent, a flower, not in a garden but in the woods maybe, stumbled on by chance, with no past and no particular odor and already doomed for the first frost: until 30 years later a soiled battered bloke aged 50 years smells or remembers it, and at once he is 21 again and brave and clean and durable. I think you know enough now, already have enough; nothing to lack which a middle-aged writer could supply." But if she would write her questions to him, sooner or later he would answer them.

She wrote him after she returned to Bard. "These are the wrong questions," he replied. "A woman must ask these of a man while they are lying in bed together . . . when they are lying at peace or at least quiet or maybe on the edge of sleep so you'll have to wait, even to ask them. You may not find the answers even then; most dont. . . . I'd like to know if you ever do. Maybe you will tell me; that can be a good subject for the last letter you will need to write me." But she should not grieve over the problems. "The kindest thing the gods can give people at twenty . . . is a capacity to ask why, a passion for something better than vegetation, even if what they get by it is grief and pain." He would try to answer the questions, though. "Meanwhile, get Housman and read him again, read him a lot."

She was shocked and apprehensive at the scene he had set in the letter's first lines, yet at the same time she welcomed the paternal reassurance that followed his reference to satiated sexual passion. "I was not to him the oddity my parents thought me. To pass through childhood I'd invented at an early age the belief I would go someday to a place where people would love me, and I would not be hurt anymore. I could not keep myself from believing I was not worthless, as I was told at home I was."[14] One of the polarities that would run through their relationship had already developed in this initial exchange: she envisioned a nurturing teacher, whereas he desired a youthful lover. He wrote her that when he thought of her, he thought of Bougereau. This may well have been the first time in nearly twenty-five years that he had mentioned that name, since the time he was writing *Elmer* in Paris, the name of the Bougereau whose *Nymphes et satyre* portrayed "a dreamy but virile satyr being dragged into the water of a marsh by no fewer than four naked beauties. . . ."[15] If this reference was not a portent, something he would tell her later was: he had had to tear up the first letter, because his mail was never safe.[16]

ON Sunday night, October 9, the white-blue beam of an eight-million-candlepower searchlight probed the sky above the square. Three smaller ones threaded bands of light over the courthouse and a dozen more bathed the front of the newly painted Lyric Theatre to illuminate the square for newsreel cameras. The *Eagle*'s banner headline proclaimed WORLD PREMIERE EXCITEMENT READY TO BREAK. This rising tide of Hollywood-style press agentry brought back the feelings of disgust Faulkner had experienced during the filming and increased his determination to have nothing to do with the spectacle. But fifteen-year-old Jill got caught up in the excitement of the promotional "mammoth parade" and went home and saddled up Clipper and joined it. The music and the crowds made it fun, and she waved to people she knew. It was only on her way home that the enormity of what she had done hit her. When she rode into the paddock, her father was there. He cast one look at her and walked away.

The MGM publicity men wanted a photograph of Faulkner for an eighteen-inch blowup to go on the Lyric marquee. He told them to use a picture of the book, but finally consented to holding it as J. R. Cofield tripped his shutter. Both came out clearly: the book and its author, wearing a tweed jacket, a T-shirt, and a three-day growth of beard. He sedulously avoided all of Monday's activities, and on Tuesday he was in Memphis. By now the women of the family began to confederate. When he got home his mother told him to shave and change his clothes for the press conference at the Lyric. He shaved and then appeared, looking aloof and annoyed. After the barrage of flash bulbs, the questions began. They asked him what he had thought of the film at the sneak preview in Memphis the previous month. "I don't know much about movies," he said, "but I believe it's one of the best I've ever seen." He thought it was as true to the book as it could be, treating the material in a different medium. Clarence Brown had made a fine picture. "I wish I had made it," he told them.[17] After each response he would fall silent and moodily swirl the ice in his glass of club soda. He was not drinking until deer camp, he explained. "I go on the wagon every now and then. It's not good for a man to let habits get too much hold on him. I've quit smoking too." Before the conference broke up, Sallie Murry heard him make a disquieting remark: he had given away his tickets to the premiere. His mind fled all this hoopla—the string band and turkey luncheon, the premiere ball and grand march. It fled to deer camp and beyond. At some point in this frantic week he wrote Meta Rebner in tortured phrases that might have come from *The Wild Palms*: he loved her and dreamed of her often, but he knew now that "grief is the inevictable part of it, the thing that makes it cohere; that grief is the only thing you are capable of sustaining, keeping; that what is valuable is what you have lost, since then you never had the chance to wear out and so lose it shabbily. . . ." And he quoted again a sentence she knew by heart: "Between grief and nothing I will take grief."[18]

His mind might be elsewhere, but Sallie Murry Williams' mind was right there in Oxford, where her husband, Bob, had jokingly told Faulkner that if he hadn't written the book, they wouldn't have had to paint the theatre. She was uneasy at the signs that he planned to duck out. "William," she said, "you've got your money out of this and it doesn't mean anything to you, but it means a whole hell of a lot to us." He made no reply, and before he reached home, she had been on the phone to Estelle, who was almost in tears. Jill and Dean and Vicki had their new dresses and nylon stockings and could hardly wait. "He'll have to go," Sallie Murry said. "Get Aunt 'Bama." Aunt 'Bama immediately joined the confederation. She phoned her great-nephew and told him that she was on her way, wearing one of her best dresses, and he had better be properly attired to escort her. He was beaten and he knew it.

More than one of the reporters used the same lead: not since the Yankees burned the town had there been such excitement. From all over the county the searchlight beams could be seen sweeping the night sky. The University of Mississippi band played to the jammed throng until the radio announcers began to name the dignitaries as they entered the spotlights and passed into the theatre. In the very first group was Aunt 'Bama, gray-haired and hawk-faced, large and commanding, resplendent in the large hat and the fine, beaded dress. Her clean-shaven great-nephew was at her side, wearing a white shirt, tie, and tweed jacket with a white handkerchief in the breast pocket. After the speeches he rose from his sixth-row seat to acknowledge the applause with a formal bow, sat down, and had to rise again to what one reporter called "thunderous applause." The audience enjoyed the film, especially the Oxonians who appeared in it, even though many of them had watched the rushes each night during the filming. Besides liking the film as a whole, Faulkner shared something of their personal pleasure. He wrote Bennett Cerf, "I trained the horse (he is mine) to flinch back from the quicksand. The owl was also mine; I had more actors in the picture than anyone." It would ring up almost 8,000 admissions during its first-week run, more even than *Gone With the Wind*. The next day Faulkner wrote Sam Marx. "Ever since our mild fiasco of twenty years ago I have felt that accounts between me and MGM were not at balance, and my conscience hurt me at times." Now, though, "I may still be on MGM's cuff, but at least I am not quite so far up the sleeve."[19]

IT was quiet until time for deer-camp preparations, though indications of his enlarging reputation continued to reach Oxford. In New York his autograph was selling for $45, more than a Woodrow Wilson or a Sinclair Lewis. "A Courtship" had won the $300 first prize in the 1949 O. Henry short-story awards. Earlier, the *Commercial Appeal* had reprinted an assertion in the *Encyclopaedia Britannica Book of the Year*: "A critical phenomenon of note was the general acceptance of William Faulkner as the most distinguished living novelist. . . ."[20] This was not lost on Harry M. Campbell and Ruel E. Foster, two Ole Miss professors who were collaborating on a full-length book on the work of William Faulkner. Nor was it lost on the members of the Swedish Academy when the balloting began in Stockholm in early November for the Nobel Prize for Literature, though it would be a year before something of the circumstances would be known. Initially there was a long list of candidates which included Hemingway and Steinbeck, Pasternak and Sholokhov, Mauriac and Camus. The field narrowed until the vote appeared split among Sir Winston Churchill, Pär Lagerkvist, and William Faulkner. Then it swung in Faulkner's favor, but not in time for the prize for literature to be awarded that year.[21]

Whether aided by the consciousness of having indisputably "arrived," or the measure of financial security, or the increasing free time, Faulkner was again attempting to help novice writers, as he had tried to help an aspiring young black poet, Joe Brown, in Oxford five years before. He did this in spite of receiving increasingly abusive letters from one young man he had encouraged and then referred to Random House. He had sent Commins a letter from a Mississippi Negro who, while earning her living as a servant, had completed a manuscript. He had told her to send it to Commins, and he even told Commins that if he insisted, he would read it himself. Joan Williams was another aspirant he was going to try to help, though he would later tell her, "Earlier I was too busy writing to have had time for you."[22]

As for his own work, there was not a great deal of kindly treatment for *Knight's Gambit* such as the film version of *Intruder in the Dust* had received. Nelson Algren described the book in *The New York Times* as containing "six masterly whodunits hot from the master's hand," and Warren Beck praised plotting, characterization, and style in the Chicago

Tribune, but Edmund Wilson called it "very inferior Faulkner" in *The New Yorker*, and for Irving Howe, in *The Nation*, the stories were second rate. In the New York *Herald Tribune* book section, Malcolm Cowley gave Faulkner "a base on balls" for this literary time at bat.[23] Faulkner did not fare much better afield. Reporting on the annual hunt to Haas, he wrote, "missed my stag, three times, easy shots, couldn't get the rifle on him somehow. But it wasn't much of a head, so it was not too bad."[24]

As the year drew to its close, there was a letter from Memphis among the belated season's greetings. Asking questions by mail and waiting for answers that sometimes didn't come wasn't very satisfactory, and so Joan Williams wrote that she wanted to see him. He was tentative and cautious, because he wanted nothing that would leave "a bad taste in the mouth." He suggested an outing on the *Minmagary*, and on January 3 she drove to Oxford. Estelle was kind and polite, providing a picnic lunch, which they ate in the galley. Joan had brought some of her things for him to read, and she told him about what she wanted to do and about her problems, how it seemed to take her so long to get anything done. As they looked away over the stretch of brown water toward the shore's leafless trees and the bare hills beyond, he talked about his own growing years. She should never stop reading the Bible and Shakespeare. He would give her Malraux's *Man's Fate*. She told him that she was interested in French writers and that she already had Bergson's *Creative Evolution*. "Read it," he told her. "It helped me." Then the day began to wane, and he rowed them back to shore.

Before the end of her school vacation he rode the seventy miles to Memphis, where she waited for him, full of awe, in the freezing bus station. He asked her to take him to the Peabody Hotel, where he wanted to deliver some material to a typist. He still addressed her as "Miss Williams," and she was struck by his courtly manner. That meeting set the tone for all of their meetings in Memphis, clandestine and filled with "so much aimless driving." She even crossed the river to Arkansas and back and then parked on a bluff overlooking the Mississippi. She was frozen and cramped from so much driving, and when he put his hand on her arm she tensed in surprise, and he immediately withdrew it. "By the day's end," she would remember, "driven almost beyond endurance by cold and aimlessness, I took him to see my mother: the house being both warm and stationary was the only reason."[25] But he felt her awe of him and he thought he understood another component of her feelings. "I know," he said, "you want me to be your father."[26]

At the end of the week he wrote her at Bard. He had read her prize story "Rain Later," and he was touched by it, by the sense of sad frustration and isolation. "It's all right," he told her, "moving and true; the force, the passion, the controlled heat, will come in time." He had tried a week before that to reassure her about the slowness. "All right. Here is the idea: let's try if I can get the Joan W. written quicker. I don't mean, collaborate or rewrite it. . . . but, the two of us together . . . to get the good stuff out of Joan Williams. . . ."[27] He had mentioned Pygmalion, "creating not a cold and beautiful statue, in order to fall in love with it, but Pygmalion taking his love and creating a poet out of her—something like that. Will you risk it?" He would come to New York in early February. They would not work with her material; instead, like a Renaissance master, he would sketch in some broad outlines and she, the apprentice, would work within them. He would give her notes to write from, to see if she could develop them. They were part of an idea he had for some new work. He thought it was going to be a play.

. . . as Gavin Stevens, the town lawyer and the county amateur
Cincinnatus, was wont to say, if you would peruse in unbroken
—ay, overlapping—continuity the history of a community, look
not in the church registers and the courthouse records, but
beneath the successive layers of calcimine and creosote and
whitewash on the walls of the jail. . . .

—*Requiem for a Nun* (214)

On February 2 he checked in at the Algonquin and then went up to
Random House. In late January, Saxe Commins had written that he and
Donald Klopfer had been thinking about publishing the deferred volume
of short stories in August. "It's all right," Faulkner replied; "the stuff
stands up amazingly well after a few years, 10 and 20. I had forgotten a lot
of it; I spent a whole evening laughing to myself about the mules and the
shingles."[1] Now he listened while Commins told him about the plans for
the book. He approved them, and the business part of the trip was over.

A few days later Joan Williams came down from Bard, bringing three
friends with her. Over a drink at the Biltmore, she and Faulkner talked
about the story line of the play, but she would remember nothing of what
was said. Later he rode the train back to Annandale-on-Hudson to see her
and to see if Bard was a school Jill might like. Joan came back on February
7 to go to a dinner party Bob and Merle Haas gave for him. It was a lively
one that included the Comminses, Ruth Ford, Bob Linscott, and Hal
Smith, and brought back memories of those years when he had been one of
the young Southerners away from home. Joan mentioned the writers of
the Algonquin Round Table and he nodded. "They all came to New York
and stayed here," he said. Later, when the talk turned to Shakespeare, one
of the guests tried to recall an obscure sonnet. Faulkner identified it and
went on to quote what seemed to Joan "reams of obscure Shakespearean
sonnets from memory."

Bob and Merle Haas took him to see the Rembrandt show at the Wilden-
stein Gallery, and for nearly two hours they looked at the pictures, Faulkner moving slowly from one to another, silent and absorbed, his hands
clasped behind him. A number of them, like the etchings and drawings,
dealt with Biblical subjects. By the time they returned to the apartment
for a drink, the February dusk was falling on Fifth Avenue. Merle asked
him to stay to supper, and afterward he told them the whole story of the
fable. On an expedition to the Palette Art Shop she helped him select expensive Windsor Newton watercolors and sable brushes. Then she picked
out a fourteen-dollar pad of Darsh watercolor paper. He considered it.
"You know," he said, "I've got a lot of brown paper at home. I don't believe I need that."

Ruth Ford tried to see that he got to parties he would enjoy. One of
them seemed to her to present a fairly typical New York gathering of
literary and artistic people, though one of the guests, Isadora Duncan's
brother, Raymond, was clad in sandals and a white toga. In the circle
around Faulkner, columnist Rhea Talley heard him say that New York
was all right for a visit but he found it "inhuman." Driving along the
Hudson River at night, he had looked up at the windows and thought how
there was no one behind them, how everyone had gone downtown. "Why,
in New York," he said, "even the dogs look inhuman."[2] After one such
party Ruth and Faulkner left with Harvey Breit and slim, blond Truman
Capote to have a drink at her apartment. *Cosmopolitan* had just begun to
serialize *Across the River and Into the Trees*, and Capote was one of a
number of readers who could find little that was redeeming in it. After
listening in silence, Faulkner broke in. "Young man," he said, "I haven't
read this new one. And though it may not be the best thing Hemingway
ever wrote, I know it will be carefully done, and it will have quality." For
a few moments there was silence in the taxi.

FAULKNER boarded the train on Sunday, February 12, and by the time he
got off in Memphis, he had begun the first act of his play. On Monday he
mailed Joan three pages of notes penned on Algonquin stationery. In
sketchy form they set forth the opening curtain for Act One as a defend-
ant named Nancy pleaded guilty to the murder charge read against her.
Faulkner told Joan she could begin there with the exposition. "She is a
'nigger' woman," he wrote, "a known drunkard and dope user, a whore
with a jail record in the little town, always in trouble. Some time back she
seemed to have reformed, got a job as nurse to a child in the home of a
prominent young couple. Then one day suddenly and for no reason, she
murdered the child. And now she doesn't even seem sorry. She seems to be
making it almost impossible for the lawyer to save her."[3]

Many strands which had begun in different places now gathered to form
this new work. Nancy Mannigoe had appeared nearly twenty years earlier

in "That Evening Sun," where the ending clearly implied that her jealous husband was about to murder her for her infidelities. Setting the present action many years later did not trouble Faulkner at all. "These people I figure belong to me," he would say "and I have the right to move them about in time when I need them."[4] It would develop that Nancy's employers were Temple Drake and her husband, Gowan Stevens. Faulkner had not dismissed Temple from his mind when he left her at the end of *Sanctuary* hearing the sad brasses in the Luxembourg Gardens. He would say that he had thought about her future and asked himself, "What could a marriage come to which was founded on the vanity of a weak man? . . . And suddenly that seemed to me dramatic and worthwhile. . . ."[5] As long ago as 1933 he had mentioned to Hal Smith his main character and his title, *Requiem for a Nun*. Ten years later Ruth Ford had gotten up the courage to say, "The one thing I want most in the world is for you to write me a play." He had made no promises, but he had remembered Ruth's wish. One reason, Estelle Faulkner thought, was that Ruth had dated Dean, and that she was still linked with the memory of the lost brother.

It seems likely that other factors were also involved. Clarence Brown had found the experience of shooting *Intruder in the Dust* so revivifying that he wanted to do more such filming. His cinematographer, Robert Surtees, had been particularly excited by the possibilities for composition, especially the dome of the courthouse looming above the square. Back home, Brown had even told one visitor that he was mulling over an idea for another picture set in Oxford. It would be a love story, Moon Mullen had heard, that would be woven around the courthouse and would tell its story.[6] Faulkner would certainly be an obvious choice as scenarist from Brown's point of view. From his own, he had thought about using the fable in more than one genre, and it would be logical at this point to think about *Requiem for a Nun* in the same way. He had managed each year to exceed the $10,000 set aside from the sale of *Intruder in the Dust* and wound up borrowing from Random House against the next year's sum. "I dont seem to know my own strength with a pen and a check book,"[7] he had told Bob Haas when he had written to draw the last of the second ten thousand. Before the end of 1951 it would all be gone. He was still uncertain when he could finish the fable. He must have wondered if he could again, somehow, stave off a return to the Coast with more sub rosa work at home. He had been intrigued when Steve Longstreet had told him how short a time it had taken him to write *High Button Shoes* and how large the royalties had been. Perhaps he could do himself a favor, as well as Ruth Ford. And besides, there were the plans he had for his protégée.

Joan Williams was busy, though, with her undergraduate thesis at Bard, and so he went ahead alone. By late February he had the first act laid out in a twelve-page rough draft. "I think I like the play," he wrote her. He could not say the same thing about their relationship. He was keenly aware of the fact that she was twenty-one and he was fifty-three. He would try to be, he told her, "whatever you want me to be to you," but he warned her that he was "capable not only of imagining anything and everything, but even of hoping and believing it." When she was able to send some notes, he told her that "they are all right, so all right there is no need to comment on them."[8] She should continue working on the play—which he insisted was her play, too—but she also had to do her schoolwork, no matter how much she hated it. When she came home for spring vacation they could lay out the work to be done—much as he had with Leigh Brackett for *The Big Sleep*. "My being his collaborator on the play," Joan knew, "would also be an excuse to offer his people and mine for our seeing one another."[9]

By the end of the third week of March he had gotten into the second act, but it was moving slowly and he felt something was wrong with the character of Temple. The present dramatic situation grew out of her past, but he had to provide the lengthy and complicated exposition to make the action plausible without undercutting the revelations to come. Temple's dialogue was sharp and biting, and her character was much more forceful than it had been in *Sanctuary*, but even so, he was dissatisfied. Some of the trouble might have derived from the fact that it had been Nancy's tragedy that had first moved him and that Temple's story had been grafted onto it. It was just at this time that some of the elements of his story were recapitulated—if with certain factors in the equation reversed—in a particularly horrifying crime eighty miles to the south in Estelle's home county.

A thirty-eight-year-old white man named Leon Turner had murdered three Negro children. The state had asked the death penalty but the Attala County jury's disagreement had made life imprisonment the mandatory sentence. On March 26 the Memphis *Commercial Appeal* published a letter from William Faulkner. He was writing as one of "those of us who were born in Mississippi and have lived all our lives in it, who have continued to live in it forty and fifty and sixty years at some cost and sacrifice simply because we love Mississippi and its ways and customs and soil and people," as one of those who had defended it against attacks from outlanders, but who now felt shame and grief and fear. He hoped the jurors would be able to sleep without nightmares. In ten or fifteen years Turner would murder another child, "who it is to be hoped—and with grief and despair one says it—will this time at least be of his own color."[10] The response was not long in coming, in part from critics of long standing such as Frederick Sullens, the editor of the Jackson *Daily News*, whose paper had run a story on the letter under the title "Faulkner Shames Mississippi for Verdict in Trial of Leon Turner."[11] In the act Faulkner had just drafted, Gavin Stevens would tax Temple with holding the belief that "all human beings . . . stink."[12] And on more than one occasion Estelle had heard her husband say, "The human race stinks." If he had needed any reinforcement of this view, the spectacle of crime and punishment in Attala County would have provided it. Nancy Mannigoe would receive no such indulgent sentence. He would speak out with increasing frequency on the subject of justice to Negroes, with the result that his native state would become a more and more uncomfortable place for him to live. This kind of emotional upheaval usually cost him dearly. In mid-April, when he apologized to Ben Wasson for his delay in sending the horse-race piece for the Levee Press, his handwriting was shaky.

Late that month he could take such comfort as he might from a familiarly ironic situation: under attack at home, he was honored elsewhere. The American Academy of Arts and Letters was bestowing on him its William Dean Howells Medal, awarded only at five-year intervals in recognition of the most distinguished works of American fiction published during that period. When he sent his thanks to Mark Van Doren he explained why he could not be present to receive the award: "I am a farmer this time of year; up until he sells his crops, no Mississippi farmer has the time or money either to travel anywhere on. Also, I doubt if I know anything worth talking two minutes about."[13] In late spring he would send a formal letter of thanks to the secretary of the Academy when the medal arrived in the mail. He was pleased at this judgment by his peers, he said, but it still seemed to him impossible to evaluate a man's work. None of his had ever suited him, and he was always busy with another one, and he had thought that perhaps when he reached fifty he would be able to decide how good the work was. At that point his tone modulated into the elegiac and valedictory. "Then one day I was fifty and I looked back at it, and I decided that it was all pretty good—and then in the same instant I realised that that was the worst of all since that meant only that a little nearer now was the moment, instant, night: dark: sleep: when I would put it all away forever that I anguished and sweated over, and it would never trouble me anymore."[14]

Writing Joan in early May, he enclosed eighteen pages, carbon copies of passages from what would become Scenes I and II of Act Two. They were set in the governor's office at two in the morning, where he sits impassively listening to Temple Stevens and her husband's uncle Gavin. She had fled with her small son to California, only to return the night before Nancy's execution to try to save her. As the questioning flashes back and forth, layers of the past are peeled away, together with Temple's defenses and deceptions. The affinity, the positive liking for evil she had demonstrated at Miss Reba's Memphis bordello, had led her to hire Nancy Mannigoe, a sister in sin and "the only animal in Jefferson that spoke Temple Drake's language. . . ."(158) When Pete, the brother of her dead gangster lover, Red, appeared, what had begun as blackmail turned into passion. But Temple had misjudged Nancy, who hid money and jewels to forestall the guilty lovers' flight. The next scene was a flashback to the day of the murder as Temple again prepared to desert her family, precipitating the only action Nancy thought she had left, "trying to hold us together in a household," Temple said, "a family, that anybody should have known all the time couldn't possibly hold together. . . ." (188) At the end of the scene Nancy exited holding a blanket, leaving the stage bare. A minute later her scream resounded in the darkness from the baby's bedroom off-stage. The pages ended with stage directions for the third and last scene of Act Two.

WRITING term papers and preparing for examinations, Joan had no time to work on the materials Faulkner sent her, and besides, "at twenty-one my heart was not in trying seriously to rewrite Faulkner."[15] She thought that if he came to New York in the summer, perhaps she could spend some time there trying honestly to collaborate on this work. He told her that she would have a little trouble explaining that to her family. "You can begin to see now how it is almost impossible for a middleclass southerner to be anything but a middleclass southerner; how you have to fight your family for every inch of art you ever gain—at the very time when the whole tribe of them are hanging like so many buzzards over every penny you earn by it." Later Joan would reflect that he had projected onto her situation memories of his own. He had written Bob Haas for help in Joan's quest. She needed a foothold somewhere, perhaps in New York, "which you can then use like a club when needed. Once we have that for you, you can hold your own with family; you will have something of the same freedom you would get by marriage, without the complication of a husband who might also be a champion of middle class."

His own work continued to go slowly. Jim Devine dropped in for a two-day visit, and when he entered Faulkner's workroom the next morning, he found him gazing out toward the white-fenced paddock, green with new May grass. "You know," Faulkner told Devine, "there were a lot of days when I sat and looked out this window and knew I was workin'. Now I sit and look out this window and know I ain't workin'." The problem was deeper than the characterization of Temple. "I realise more than ever that I cant write a play," he told Haas in mid-May, "this may have to be rewritten by someone who can. It may be a novel as it is. . . . Maybe we can print it as a book first, let me reserve right to try a play first, that sort of thing."[16] It was not just a matter of structure. It was the problem he'd had with To Have and Have Not, when he would bring new dialogue onto the set and Bogie would say, "Bill, how am I supposed to say all that?" Some of the speeches for Temple and Gavin Stevens ran to a thousand words. And the stage directions had been getting longer too, for action as well as setting.

In the third scene of Act Two he began to come to grips with the implications of the horrendous events as Temple tries to grapple with the relationship between good and evil and the need to save her soul, "if I have a soul." (212) The scene that followed comprised the final act. Nancy Mannigoe is now a figure of tragic dignity. Through her, Faulkner confronts not only the problem of God's existence in a fallen world but also the dilemma of how He could permit such suffering. When Temple, recognizing that she has to beg forgiveness as well as grant it, asks Nancy if there is a Heaven where she might meet the child she has slain, she can only reply, "I dont know. But I believes." (268)

Looking ahead to the rewriting, he told Haas what he planned: "my version or complete job will be a story told in seven play-scenes, inside a novel; it will run about 200 typed double-spaced pages." In the summer he would set Joan to work to extract a "workable play script. Then get advice from some playwright who knows how to do it." He was now pleased with it: "an interesting experiment in form. I think it's all right."[17] But the form was still changing, and near the end of June he told Haas that he was writing "the three introductory chapters which hold the 3 acts together."

A few days later Faulkner sent the first of these chapters to Ober in the form of a twenty-four-page typescript called "A Name for the City." He was now giving full rein to the novelistic impulse. His scheme was to concentrate on the courthouse in the first of these chapters, the capitol in Jackson in the second, and the jail in Jefferson in the third. Summarizing the past, he felt despair and loathing as he looked at the present and the future. It was a view not unlike that of Ike McCaslin. In man's rapacity, he was consuming the earth at a phenomenal rate. And what he did not consume he would change irrevocably. Faulkner could see it changing before his eyes. The old Cumberland Presbyterian Church had given way to a supermarket, and though the courthouse had apparently been granted a reprieve (it was structurally sound and could be repaired, said a consulting engineer), he felt its days were numbered. What had been open land north of Oxford was now bulldozed into a subdivision known as Avent Acres. For twenty years, he wrote, Jefferson had been suffering from "a fever, a delirium in which it would confound forever seething with motion, and motion with progress." (4) He had begun the chapter in the late 1700's with the physical antecedents of the courthouse. For one critic, "The story of the founding of Jefferson . . . is in its broadest implications nothing less than a fable of the founding of Western Civilization—the creation of order out of the old primal chaos—and of the attendant ethical and moral problems."[18] Faulkner introduced the founders and the successors—bearing Yoknapatawpha names—before recounting the building of the courthouse and its rebuilding in 1863. He concluded with lines that echoed a passage from *Absalom, Absalom!* as the sparrows and pigeons swirled from the belfry at the clock's stroke as though the hour "instead of merely adding one puny infinitesimal more to the long weary increment since Genesis, had shattered the virgin pristine air with the first loud dingdong of time and doom." (48) The image probably owed something to a passage from the fable, and he would rework it in yet another context before the year was out. A week later *Harper's* bought the piece for $500 for the October Centennial Issue.

IF Faulkner could now feel some ease about this taxing work, Joan Williams was feeling a great deal of unease about the collaboration that was supposed to have contributed to it. At Easter when they had gone to a Memphis drive-in restaurant for lunch, one of Estelle's acquaintances had seen them. One day Joan received an invitation from Estelle to meet her in the Black Cat restaurant of the Peabody. When Estelle took Joan's arm for support she seemed so frail that Joan felt protective of her. But then, after the amenities, Joan was astonished to hear Estelle ask her if she wanted to marry her husband. She could give only a simple No in answer. That she wanted to be a writer seemed to Estelle no reason to want to see William Faulkner.

The meeting at the Black Cat was followed by other measures. Estelle intercepted one of Joan's letters. She wrote and telephoned her and her parents in Memphis. She began drinking when these tactics produced even more bitter quarrels with her husband, sometimes in front of their daughter and the servants. He took what countermeasures he could: retrieving Joan's letter and preventing Estelle from traveling to Memphis to see the Williamses. He told Estelle that his main aim now was to undo any harm he might have done Joan and to prevent any further upheaval, and for a time Estelle appeared conciliatory. He told Joan to send her letters to Quentin Compson, General Delivery, in Oxford, but then he decided that name might be too well known and suggested A. E. Holston instead. He told her that she might not want to continue their correspondence, that perhaps the best thing would be for her to have nothing more to do with him, though this was not what he wanted. They had gone too far with the play to stop now. She felt she had not done enough for it to be "their" play, but her dilemma lay deeper. Though by now he had in fact drifted into the role of Pygmalion, she did not want to be Galatea, at least not on the terms he seemed ultimately to have in mind. But neither was she willing to sever the connection. The correspondence continued. Near the end of August he told her that he was working on "the scaffolding stuff that holds my three acts in a book." He would send her the first section when it was finished so she could understand better what he was doing. He was trying to keep alive some sense of participation and continuity, but she was feeling a depression he could not break through.

THAT same month had seen the publication of *Collected Stories of William Faulkner*. It had been adopted by the Book-of-the-Month Club as an alternate fiction selection, and its description included a word portrait of the author as John Malcolm Brinnin had seen him in that summer of 1950: "Physically, Faulkner is of modest stature, erect, with pepper-gray hair and slightly sallow complexion; yet he gives an immediate impression of compact strength. When he speaks, he turns his head with a slow, angular, bird-like curiosity, a quality enhanced by the slightly beaked curve of his nose. He moves with exceptional grace and, whether he is sitting or standing, makes the characteristic gestures of cupping his right hand around his left elbow and holding his head sidewise. . . . Of all his physical attributes, his eyes—steady, almost expressionless—are most memorable." From the first major reviews, the reception was generally one of enthusiasm and often acclaim. Harry Sylvester helped set the tone in *The New York Times Book Review*, praising his "enormous gifts" and overflowing energy. And even after demurrers on the score of obscurity, "one thing remains to distinguish him above all American writers since James and perhaps since Melville—he simply knows so much more than they." On the same day in the New York *Herald Tribune*, Horace Gregory made a similar judgment and concluded, "He is more distinctly the master of a style than any writer of fiction living in America today."[19]

At home he was planning to employ his plain style on concerns both local and particular. There was going to be an election to determine whether, for the next five years, beer could be purchased legally. A committee of most of the town's clergymen published an advertisement in the *Eagle* proclaiming the evils of drinking and the potency of four-percent beer. Soon afterward Faulkner walked into the office of the *Eagle* and left a letter to the editor which was a four-point refutation combining chemistry, satire, and polemic. Beer had been voted out, he wrote, not because of its "obnoxiousness" but because "too many voters who drank beer or didn't object to other people drinking it, were absent in Europe and Asia defending Oxford where voters who preferred home to war could vote on beer in 1944." He concluded with a pointed reference to the clergymen and "the Founder of their Ministry . . . when He ordered them to keep out of temporal politics in His own words: 'Render unto Caesar the things that are Caesar's and to God the things that are God's.' "[20] When the issue for August 31 appeared without his letter, Faulkner asked Mullen why. "We just didn't want the *Eagle* to help you in jumping all over the preachers," Mullen told him. Faulkner looked at him in silence. Then he said, "Strike me some circulars." To help distribute the broadside, entitled "To the Voters of Oxford," he mobilized Johncy, Malcolm and his bride, Gloria, Dean, Vicki, and Broadus Lyles.

When beer was banned for five more years by a vote of 480 to 313, Faulkner wrote another letter, full of irony and acerbity, which the *Eagle* printed. It was better to stick to the old way, "better than to break up the long and happy marriage between dry voters and illicit sellers, for which our fair state supplies one of the last sanctuaries and strongholds." Actually, he wrote, his major objections were to a clergyman's assuming that he could make any statement and that no one would dare check on it, and to violations of their calling "by using, either openly or underhand, the weight and power of their office to try to influence a civil election."[21] Two months later the beer broadside appeared again, sent by an Oxonian to *The New Yorker*, where it was described as "probably the clearest and most concise prose ever written by the moody master of Yoknapatawpha County."[22]

The cotton was picked, ginned, baled, and shipped by now, the dust and white wisps everywhere sinking gradually into the earth with the first fall rains. The haying was finished at Greenfield, and now he would drive out there occasionally to check on the animals and the fences and to watch Renzi begin the autumn care of the earth. Later that September, Joan wrote him from Memphis. When he replied, he had an idea for her. A college senior receives a visit from a famous man come to spend the day with her. Despite their talk, their rapport, she is troubled when he leaves by a sense of inconclusiveness. "Then she finds why he came, what he wanted, and that he got it. She knows it the next day; she receives a telegram that he is dead, heart; she realises that he knew it was going to happen, and that what he wanted was to walk in April again for a day, an hour. . . . Write that one, fairly short, objectively, from the outside, 3rd person, but of course from the girl's point of view. You can do it. Write it for me."[23] At that time, however, she was thinking more about a magazine job that might give her a toehold in New York. He was pleased for her even though she called it a stupid job. And he tried to reassure her about the unfinished play. She had not failed him; he liked her as she was; he had faith that she would find herself and succeed. "It may have been partly that belief which drew me to begin with or maybe it's vanity: Lucifer's own pride: I dont, refuse to, believe that I can take you—a young woman—into my life (spirit) and not have her make something new under the sun whether she wills it or not."

AT Rowan Oak it was an active time as the leaves turned red and bronze and the October nights grew crisper. Jill was moving toward adulthood and independence, but Dean and Vicki, aged fourteen and twelve, had not yet left childhood wholly behind. They were cheerleaders for the junior high school Pee Wee football team, and Pappy would drive them to the Thursday afternoon games and enjoy them as much as they did. Vicki's parents were still in China, so he was father to all three girls, setting standards for them. From the age of ten or eleven on, they were expected to be knowledgeable. He would turn learning into a game as they recited in order the names of the twelve Caesars, Kentucky Derby winners, or the six wives of Henry VIII. Their grades at school seemed not to be important to him, but they knew he was proud of them when they came home with honor-roll report cards. And he was helping to form their manners as well as their minds. On Thanksgiving Day, seated at a card table, they ate with the adults in the dining room. Norfleet in his white coat made rapid trips from the kitchen and stood there by the table humming to himself as he held each steaming platter. They even had wine, and Pappy came to their table when it was time for the toast and told them how to do it.

It was wonderful to be with him outdoors. They would stop at a clearing, where he would unpack materials and build a fire. Soon he would be demonstrating the process of making a corn pone. An astronomy lesson was something to look forward to. After supper he might say, "This is gonna be a good night for shootin' stars." They would stand on a ridge and soon it would begin. "There's one!" they would call. "There's another!" He would point out the big stars and name the constellations wheeling overhead. Living with him was no idyll, however. He would take them to help him work on the *Ring Dove*. One day when they came about fast, Dean dropped the sponge she was holding. He showed his annoyance. "That was a good sponge," he fumed. "It cost twenty-five cents." Dean was in tears. But he could still enchant them. They loved his ghost stories, and when Halloween came he responded with their favorites.[24]

Right after Halloween they might ordinarily have gone on one of their mule-drawn wagon rides for a weenie roast out in the country, but they didn't go in November 1950. As early as the third, an Associated Press story named William Faulkner and Bertrand Russell as the top candidates for the Nobel Prize for Literature, the unawarded prize for 1949 as well as the present one. A storm of criticism had followed when the prize had been withheld. During the following year Faulkner's reputation had continued to grow, as it had done since *Light in August* had appeared in Swedish in 1944. Now novelist Gustaf Hellström, president of the Swedish Academy, reported to his colleagues that Faulkner reminded him "of two great Swedish novelists, Selma Lagerlöf and Hjalmar Bergman, who each in his own way had also transformed their rural family setting into a vast universal theatre lighted by magic and offering the spectacle of a humanity teeming with larger than life characters."[25]

Early Friday morning, November 10, the telephone rang at Rowan Oak. It was long distance, from New York. When Faulkner came to the phone in the pantry off the kitchen, it was Sven Åhman calling, New York correspondent of *Dagens Nyheter*. In Stockholm the Swedish Academy had issued a statement. It had resolved to confer upon William Faulkner the 1949 Nobel Prize "for his powerful and independent artistic contribution in America's new literature of the novel." It would carry an award amounting to $30,171.

When Åhman asked how he felt about the award, Faulkner gave a suitable if cautious answer. When Åhman asked if he was looking forward to the trip to Stockholm, there was a pause. "I won't be able to come to receive the prize myself," he said. "It's too far away. I am a farmer down here and I can't get away." After a few more questions which elicited increasingly brief answers, Ahman thanked him and the interview came to an end. Faulkner hung up the phone, standing there bemused for a moment in the once-more unbroken quiet of the morning.

56

I feel that this award was not made to me as a man, but to my work—a life's work in the agony and sweat of the human spirit, not for glory and least of all for profit, but to create out of the materials of the human spirit something which did not exist before.

—"Address upon Receiving the
Nobel Prize for Literature," *ESPL* (119)

FRIDAY, November 10, 1950, was a school day. With Estelle beside him, he drove Jill and Vicki to school. Jill would not hear the news until the principal called her out of class to tell her. Her father had planned to go fishing after he returned home, but it was not going to be that kind of a day.

Almost as soon as he was back at Rowan Oak, Phil Mullen phoned him. He had been asked to do the story for the Associated Press and he wanted to come out. Faulkner reluctantly agreed. Near the end of his questioning, Mullen said, "Bill, you're just not very excited over the award, are you? Don't you think much of it?" Faulkner answered slowly, his eyes sharp. "Well," he said, "they gave it to Sinclair Lewis and Old China Hand Pearl Buck, and they passed over Theodore Dreiser and Sherwood Anderson." Two hours later he walked into Mullen's office and slowly read the sheets of gray copy paper. He asked for only one correction. "Change that to I was a member of the RAF," he said. "I did not see any service."[1]

After picking up the mail he strolled home, chatting briefly with a few friends without any reference to the day's news. When Mac Reed went out to Rowan Oak, he found him in the pasture in the old jeep that pulled a lime-spreader behind it. Finally reaching the gate, Faulkner turned off the engine and came over. Mac said not a word but simply held out his hand. Faulkner gripped it hard. "Mac," he said, "I still can't believe it."[2]

He began his preparations for fishing, only to meet intense opposition from his family. The Nobel Foundation would surely call, and he had to show them the courtesy of being there. He reluctantly agreed, and after lunch, went out to the backyard to chop wood. At 2:15 the call came through. Once more he gave polite thanks. Then he went back to the woodpile. He was still there when a group of reporters arrived from Memphis. Estelle met them. The prize, she said, would be very welcome. "Anybody who comes down here can see we're not rich." Her husband told the reporters that he didn't know what he would do with the money, and he doubted that he would be able to go to Stockholm to receive the award. But he refused to make a statement about that until he sent one to Sweden.[3] By the next morning his resolution had hardened. When Johncy dropped in he told him, "There just isn't enough gas left in the tank to go all that distance."[4]

He seemed unmoved by the congratulatory messages and the voluminous press—the pride of the *Eagle* and the *Press-Scimitar* or the denunciation of the Jackson *Daily News*, asserting that "he is a propagandist of degradation and properly belongs in the privy school of literature." The most moving tribute in the *Eagle* came from Phil Stone, who said that Faulkner was even greater as a man than as a writer. "A lot of us talk about decency, about honor, about loyalty, about gratitude. Bill doesn't talk about these things; he lives them. Other people may desert you but not Bill, if he is your friend. People may persecute you and revile you but this would only bring Bill quickly to your side if he is your friend. If you are his friend and the mob should choose to crucify you, Bill would be there without summons. He would carry your cross up the hill for you."[5] Year after year, Faulkner would renew the notes that had saved Stone from bankruptcy, and year after year he would burn them at their unpaid expiration. Stone's last image suggested his feeling about the way life seemed to be closing in on him, while the world continued to open out, if belatedly, for his former comrade.

On the same day that the *Eagle* appeared with its editorial thanking Faulkner for the honor he had brought to Oxford, there was evidence in *The New York Times* that the work was also bringing more substantial rewards. Charles Poore wrote that more than 100,000 copies of Faulkner's books had been sold in Modern Library editions and that nearly two and a half million had been printed in paperback, with a third of a million more soon to come off the presses.

On that same day Faulkner wrote Sven Åhman that he had informed the secretary of the Swedish Academy that he would be unable to be present in Stockholm. He asked Åhman to explain to the Academy. He held that the award was made not to him but to his work of thirty years "to lift up or maybe comfort or anyway at least entertain, in its turn, man's heart." What remained after those thirty years of work was "not worth carrying from Mississippi to Sweden," though he hoped to find "an aim for the money high enough to be commensurate with the purpose and significance of its origin." He mailed the letter, saw to his guns, gear, and supplies, and left the next day for a week in deer camp.[6]

Once more the hunters journeyed 130 miles to the southwest. From the town of Anguilla they made their way by boat and then mule-drawn wagon to their campsite on Cypress Lake. Faulkner had said nothing, but his companions knew from a newspaper someone had brought along that he had won the Nobel Prize. That night they celebrated with one of his favorite hunting-camp meals, collards and coon simmered in an iron pot by Uncle Ike Roberts. It was Faulkner's turn to help with the dishes, so he donned the apron of sacking. "Bill," said Uncle Ike, "what would you do if that Swede ambassador came down here and handed you that money right now?" Faulkner answered with scarcely a pause. "I'd tell him to just put it on that table over there," he said, "and grab a dryin' rag and help out." That delighted everyone. Afterward Faulkner gave Renzi the key to his whiskey box and the hunters enjoyed a nightcap or two of Old Crow. Faulkner never slept in the tent in fair weather, so when they retired at about three o'clock after further nightcaps, he took his sleeping bag and bedded down nearby. The next morning brought sleet and snow, but the hunters were unperturbed.

Faulkner's equanimity was not shared in Stockholm, Washington, and Oxford. His advocates, who had worked hard to persuade the conservatives in the Swedish Academy, were disappointed, and the American Embassy was deeply distressed. Ambassador W. Walton Butterworth cabled Secretary of State John Foster Dulles. It was decided to get in touch with Muna Lee, not only a Foreign Service officer but also a poet and 1913 classmate of Phil Stone and Cornell Franklin at Ole Miss. She turned to one of the most distinguished female members of the bar in the South, Mrs. Joseph M. Howorth, of Cleveland, Mississippi, who, thirty years before as Lucy Somerville, had helped Ben Wasson organize The Marionettes. She suggested that Muna Lee try her cousin, Miss Ella Somerville, in Oxford. Miss Ella suggested working through Colonel Hugh Evans. He was out duck-hunting, but finally he telephoned to say he would try to persuade Faulkner when he returned from deer camp.

Meanwhile, the situation on Cypress Lake was sliding into a familiar pattern of deterioration. Uncle Ike Roberts had been trying to get Faulkner to take some nourishment along with the bourbon he demanded from Renzi, bartering diluted whiskey punch for soft-boiled eggs and coffee. He now was suffering from a heavy cold, and by the time they got him home to Rowan Oak in the early hours of Monday, November 27, it threatened to turn into pneumonia.[7]

It was with the help of Victoria and Bill Fielden, recently home from Hong Kong, that Estelle developed a successful argument. She had no wish to go to Stockholm herself, she said, but Jill wanted to go, and when would she have another chance like this? Actually, Jill was not at all anxious to go, but her father did not know this and finally capitulated. Now further subterfuge was added to persuasion as their transatlantic departure date of Wednesday, December 6, seemed to rush upon them. "I'll take my last drink at six o'clock Monday night," he told Estelle and Victoria. "Then I'll be ready to go to Memphis on Tuesday and on Wednesday we'll fly to New York." They helped him into the parlor, where Phil Mullen took his passport photograph. His face bristly with several days' stubble, his intense dark eyes pouched with fatigue, Faulkner glared at the lens with an expression of absolute irascibility. Then he retired to his room, occasionally allowing someone to feed him small portions of chicken soup. Jimmy Faulkner stopped in after they had hit on the ruse of setting the calendar ahead and he had reluctantly begun spacing his drinks farther apart. Taking more interest in things about him, he asked where Malcolm was. "He's at the high school football game," someone said without thinking. Faulkner raised himself on an elbow and glowered. "Somebody's been deceivin' me!" he said. "They don't play football games on Monday." He lay back. "I've got three more days to drink."[8]

Meanwhile, the others went ahead with the preparations. Jill signed both their passport applications and Estelle and Victoria helped her supplement her wardrobe. It occurred to Estelle that they had to supplement his wardrobe too, and so she phoned Saxe Commins.

"We've got to get him a dress suit," she told Saxe.

"What can I do?"

"Bill doesn't want to buy a suit, so I reckon we'll rent him one."

The long-distance line hummed while Commins waited. With Bill Fielden assisting, Estelle took the measurements and then read them all off to Commins. At a rental store a helpful tailor took a blue-black dress suit off the rack with a flourish. When Commins questioned the color, the man reassured him. "Only last month Cardinal Spellman's nephew had an audience with the Pope," he said. "He wore this suit, and this is the one I'll let you have."

There was one thing no one could do for him: his acceptance speech. Dictating to Bill Fielden, he referred to some other writers—Bill remembered Ernest Hemingway and John Dos Passos—and some phrases about man's destiny, one with something about "the last ding-dong of doom." The next day when he gave an interview in the parlor he repeated some of the things he had dictated. He said that the prize honored his work, and it was that which mattered, not the man or the name "so long as the work uplifted, strengthened or did something to other hearts."[9] When Cowley had suggested that he write a foreword for the book of collected stories, Faulkner said the only foreword he remembered was one he had read when he was about sixteen, by Henryk Sienkiewicz in the Polish Nobel Laureate's novel *Pan Michael*, he thought, and he paraphrased a sentence from it. It was the same sentence he was paraphrasing now. (There was another debt to the Polish novelist he never acknowledged: the image of the old Roman who wore away the rim of a lovely vase with kissing it.) When one interviewer turned to cosmic questions, Faulkner was pessimistic. "Man is faced with one question: Whether he's going to get blown up. There used to be problems of courage, honor, chastity, virtue," he said. "They don't exist any more. There are only 'angles.' " But he thought that somehow man would survive, that his voice would continue to be heard "even in the ruins and ashes." As for his personal feelings at the moment, "My soul isn't my own until the whole mess is over." He had even had to acquire a new outfit. "The suit I use for funerals wouldn't do to meet a king," he told the reporters.

What Faulkner described as the "hurrah and uproar here" continued, with the telephone ringing, telegrams arriving, and friends and relatives felicitating him on the prize and the trip he didn't want to take. The usual sleeplessness, nerves, and irritability of withdrawal made the whole business even more excruciating. It continued even to the moment of departure in the December darkness. Early as it was, there were friends to see them off after a hurried breakfast. Phil Stone shook his hand. "Now, Bill, you do right," he said. Faulkner glared at him. "I'm so damn sick and tired of hearin' that," he shot back. "Everybody from the Swedish ambassador to my damn nigger houseboy has been tellin' me to do right!"[10]

It was a long journey to Memphis as day came without sunrise on the icy roads, and they arrived at the airport just a half-hour before flight time. The reporters were waiting. Unshaven, his back to the wall, Faulkner patiently answered the same questions again, though he felt miserable from his cold. Soon flash bulbs flickered against the wetly glistening aircraft as the photographers recorded Estelle's goodbye kiss to her husband. Dosed with Dramamine, Jill fell asleep almost as soon as they took off. Her father had time now to rethink parts of his speech or doze off if he could. The whole process had begun its inexorable progress, and he would be locked into it for nearly two uninterrupted weeks.

After a stop at Knoxville, they finally touched down at La Guardia Airport late in the afternoon. Bob and Merle Haas were there to help them through the terminal, but they could not fend off the reporters. Faulkner's patience was wearing thin. At one point the specter of the old notoriety from *Sanctuary* reappeared. An aggressive woman zeroed in on him. "What do you consider the decadent aspect of American life today?" she asked. "It's what you're doing now, Miss," he snapped back. "It's this running people down, getting interviews and photographs just because they have done something."[11]

He looked like a sick man to Merle Haas, and after he and Jill were settled at the Algonquin she called her doctor to ask the proper dosage for some Aureomycin she had. He told her and cautioned against any alcohol. That night Faulkner was able to help Bob and Merle greet their guests, a glass of Jack Daniel's and water in his hand. It was a good-sized party.

Faulkner looked sober enough to Maurice Coindreau, but Malcolm Cowley discerned a peculiar look on his face. "Faulkner was polite but abstracted that evening," he remembered, "as if reserving his strength for a supreme ordeal. I thought he had the look to be found on the faces of British Tommies at Ypres, in photographs taken a moment before they went over the top."[12] The next day Faulkner had a temperature of 102 and the doctor ordered him to bed.

When Merle Haas and Jill returned to the Algonquin from shopping, an hour afterward, they found seven reporters with him and the room full of tobacco smoke. Faulkner was chain-smoking and telling stories. There was no rest for him that evening, either. He had gone to the Haases' party and he felt he should go to the one at the Cerfs'. As on the previous night, some of the guests felt moved to offer testimonials before they left the dinner table. Harvey Breit watched as John O'Hara rose, a portly red-faced man eight years Faulkner's junior. He launched into a long speech praising Faulkner as "our only living genius." Naming some of Faulkner's works, he declared, "We were running neck and neck until you pulled away and left me behind." He paused as if, thought Harvey, he was waiting for Faulkner to say, "No, no." When Faulkner spoke, it was in the tone he would use when he was agreeing with someone, saying something because a remark was expected, though his mind was miles away. "Yes, that's right," he murmured. As a climactic gesture, O'Hara drew a gold cigarette lighter from his pocket and held it up. "This belonged to my father," he said, "and I'd like you to have it." O'Hara handed him the gift and sat down to hear the reply. Faulkner gave the lighter a polite glance, pocketed it, and said, "Thank you." Later he would recall his dilemma to a friend. "I didn't want it but what could I do? I was cooked either way. If I took it, he could say, 'The son of a bitch *took* my father's lighter.' If I didn't, he could say, 'The son of a bitch wouldn't take my *father's* lighter.'" When Bennett Cerf told him he ought to write a thank-you note to O'Hara, another Random House author, Faulkner refused. "I didn't want his lighter," he said. "I didn't ask him for his lighter. Why should I write him a letter?"[13] Later he would tell one friend, "Don't ever repeat this, but John O'Hara is a Rutgers Scott Fitzgerald."

The next day was Friday, and at 11:30 that morning the *Harald Viking* took off for Stockholm. Jill looked out the window of their SAS DC-6 while her father took out a sheaf of Hotel Algonquin stationery and worked on expanding his notes into a manuscript for his Nobel Prize acceptance speech. The general fear of atomic annihilation had displaced problems of the spirit, had given no time "to learn the problems of the human heart in conflict with itself which alone can make good writing." The young labored under a curse—"they write not of the heart but of the glands; they write as though they stood among and watched the end of man." Again he used the cluster of doomsday images, borrowed very probably from Joseph Conrad. He held, though, that man would prevail and that it was the writer's duty to write about the virtues that would enable him to prevail, borrowing again from that other Polish novelist he admired, Henryk Sienkiewicz.

After stops in Newfoundland, Prestwick, and Oslo, the *Harald Viking* finally landed at Stockholm's Bromma Airport. There to greet them were Ambassador and Mrs. W. Walton Butterworth, Sten Tersmeden of the Swedish Foreign Office, and Gustaf Hellström and Anders Österling of the Swedish Academy. Faulkner's bearing, thought Österling, was almost military, as though he were subjecting himself to some firm discipline. A short ride through the green fir forest brought them to the city—busy, with broad streets, much glass and light, humming with energy—and to the ambassadorial residence.

Walton Butterworth personally set about making his unshaven guest at home. They talked about New Orleans, Butterworth's birthplace, and found that they had mutual friends in Guy and Helen Baird Lyman. Faulkner seemed tired and nervous, and Butterworth quickly put him in the hands of Geoffrey Button, who had been trained as a butler in one of the great houses of England. Butterworth mistakenly told Faulkner that Button had also served in the RAF. Faulkner seemed to take to him immediately. It was as though Button were Faulkner's batman, Butterworth thought.

Faulkner conducted himself well at the afternoon press conference, where Jill was interviewed too. To Butterworth this seventeen-year-old had a kind of sophisticated innocence. "Not a foot placed wrong during the whole questioning," he would recall. By the time they finished, it was dark outside. The winter night seemed to descend about three o'clock, Jill thought.[14] The next ordeal was a dinner party at the home of Kaj Bonnier, Faulkner's Swedish publisher. Another member of the firm called for them. As their taxi sped along the snow-lined streets and across bridges over the lake and the canals, Faulkner seemed to him like "a gentleman of the old school, like a perfect cavalier to his daughter." Kaj Bonnier was abed with the flu, so his wife, Ulla, and his brother, Tor, welcomed them into the spacious and tastefully furnished rooms. After the introductions Jill talked with her hostess while her father stood looking at pictures. This had the makings of a stand-off: the withdrawn novelist and the formal Swedes.

Fortunately, a catalyst soon appeared in the person of Mrs. Thorsten Jonsson, the widow of the man who had made the prediction in Oxford nearly five years before. Tall and chic, Else Jonsson had glossy red hair, eyes of a violet blue-gray, and finely shaped features set off by clear skin. Seeing Faulkner standing alone, she went directly to him, and soon they were talking easily. At the immaculate, candle- and flower-decorated dinner table, Tor Bonnier proposed a toast. "*Skäl*," he said, "to the man not with us, but the man most responsible for our gathering tonight." At that moment Else Jonsson felt alone and desolate in the midst of the people and the glitter. Faulkner had gathered from their conversation that she was a widow with a small child, but he had missed her name. Now, when they *skåled* each other before they set the glasses down, she felt sympathy and understanding from the man Thorsten Jonsson had so admired. Talking on the sofa after dinner, she felt as though they had been friends all their lives.

Riding back to the embassy, Jill heard bells in the frosty night. She looked out her window, and there was a sleigh drawn by a prancing horse. The editor of her high-school paper, she had been hired by Phil Mullen to do some stories from Sweden for the *Eagle*. That sight, she wrote, "was the perfect ending to a day that had laid the spell for the storybook-like atmosphere of the coming days."[15]

When Faulkner told Walton Butterworth that he had never given a speech and he was scared, the ambassador had offered the help of press attaché Wilfrid Fleisher. Faulkner accepted his advice that he insert some punctuation to permit him to stop for breath and Butterworth's suggestion that he shorten the speech. At lunch he was anxious and almost abstemious. "I want to do the right thing," he said.

As the presentation ceremony approached, Faulkner's nervousness grew. He had remembered neither the day's engagements nor any of the papers involved. Checking the room, Button found all the mail in the wastebasket, including the invitation to the king's dinner. He also retrieved the pencil drafts of the acceptance speech. When Button found him in the library, distracted, Faulkner turned to him. "What's this all about, Button?" he asked. "I can't stand this." But soon it was time for Button to help him into his evening clothes. At the door he handed him his opera hat. Faulkner put it on and buttoned his torn and oil-stained trench coat. He had refused to shave, and so his cheeks were stubbled as gray-white as they had been in hunting camp. Walton Butterworth sighed to himself. Well, he thought, except for that and the trench coat, the rest of his appearance was *comme il faut*.

At four o'clock the spotlighted steps to the Concert House were lined with people as the limousines drew up. Moving inside the hall, impressive with statues and tapestries, Faulkner joined the other waiting laureates and their sponsors. At the trumpet fanfare, the laureates filed in to take their places on the platform. Then, with all standing, the clear brass tones rang again, and the king and queen entered. Seated beside Faulkner was philosopher-mathematician Bertrand Russell, laureate in literature for the year 1950. Russell saw his uneasiness. "I therefore tried to make friends with him, but found it uphill work as he was shy and reticent," he would remember.

When Faulkner's turn came, Hellström read the presentation speech, calling him the "unrivaled master of all living British and American novelists as a deep psychologist" and "the greatest experimentalist among twentieth-century novelists."[16] At the fanfare of the Royal Swedish Symphony Orchestra, the whole audience rose as Faulkner stood and walked to the edge of the platform. But then, instead of descending the four steps to receive the diploma and medal and congratulations from the king, Faulkner froze. King Gustav Adolf, large and commanding, quickly walked to him and presented the award. This was apparently noticed by few, for to some, Faulkner appeared the most graceful of all the laureates as he made his bows. The banquet and the speech still lay ahead.

A half-mile away was Stadshuset, the Town Hall with colonnades and tower rising above the blue waters of Lake Mälar like the Doge's Palace on Venice's Grand Canal. "The dinner was held in a room as big as the entire high school in Oxford," Jill wrote. "The only light was from the thousands of candles in silver candelabra on each flower-decked table." With a blare of trumpets, black-coated squads of waiters entered holding trays aloft. With Swedish military precision they served the spectacular gourmet meal, which ended with ice-based ice cream in intricate shapes borne in on trays lighted by sparklers. The dinner music ceased, and it was time for the speeches.[17]

When Faulkner rose in his turn, "a small elegant figure, very far away," Else Jonsson thought that "his appearance was unforgettable." But it was immediately apparent that he was too far from the microphone. And there were the added difficulties of his Southern accent and rapid delivery. "We did not know what he said until the next morning," Else Jonsson remembered. Then, the impact of the hurried words was tremendous. Later one scholar would say that each year at Nobel time it would be recalled as the best speech ever given at a Nobel dinner. It was a stirring statement, but how had William Faulkner arrived at this position of seeming faith and affirmation?

A few years earlier he had started a letter to Bill Fielden recalling his prophecy in 1945 "that inside ten years the Russians would have run all the white people off the continent of Asia and Europe too."[18] He expected a third world war by 1952 or 1953 which would exhaust the earth so thoroughly as to bring in a hundred years of comparative peace after the frightful ruin. In the last paragraph of the 550-word speech he delivered this night of December 10, 1950, in winter-bound Stockholm, he declared that it was easy to say that man was immortal simply because he would survive the cataclysm of devastation. "I refuse to accept this," he declared. "I believe that man will not merely endure: he will prevail. He is immortal, not because he alone among creatures has an inexhaustible voice, but because he has a soul, a spirit capable of compassion and sacrifice and endurance."[19] How, in just a few years, did he get from the letter to the speech? How could he say that man would prevail, he whose works seemed to some principally a chronicle of failure, anguish, and despair?

He had been writing for a long time about endurance, epitomizing it in Dilsey and her kin. If he had written about avarice and lust and murder, he had also written about pity and compassion and love. Some of his characters had been defeated or destroyed, but there were others—such as Aunt Jenny Du Pre, Cash Bundren, Gavin Stevens, Lena Grove, and V. K. Ratliff—who had prevailed. Human beings might stink, as he had said, but there were redemptive qualities which would shine forth occasionally in the humblest as well as the greatest. He had not said that man would be able to avert a general holocaust, but rather that, endowed with a soul, he would be able to survive one, as the earlier forms of life he would describe at the beginning of *Requiem for a Nun*'s second act had been unable to do. Those most likely to survive might well be the humblest, who had plenty of experience at enduring. He had long been feeling the encroachment of the years and the intimations of mortality. As his work would be a scratch on the wall of oblivion, so this pronouncement was an assertion of life over death. As for man's capacity for nobility to match the baseness, he would assert it through the corporal in his fable, and in another form he was asserting it here in Stockholm's Town Hall.

Afterward, accepting the congratulations of those who came up to him in the gallery, he saw Else Jonsson and made his way to where she stood.

"How did I look?" he asked anxiously. "Did I behave all right?"

"Oh," she said, "you behaved beautifully."

Though the festival had passed its peak, it was not over. On Monday morning there was another gathering. That noon he took Else Jonsson to lunch, where they ordered the heavy Swedish Christmas food. Evening brought the Nobel family dinner and the subsequent audience in the Throne Room at the Palace. Jill would report that the king talked for a long time to her father, about farming and sailing and archaeology. When it came her turn, "He talked to me for several minutes," she wrote later, "but I was too excited to pay any attention to what he said." Afterward they had to go to a concert, but they slipped away as soon as they could.[20]

When Walton Butterworth offered Faulkner a drink back at the embassy, Faulkner accepted immediately. "Say when," Butterworth told him. He tilted the decanter, and the rich brown liquid kept going, *glug, glug, glug* until it looked to Butterworth as though the glass held about four ordinary drinks. Then Faulkner added a little water. It was, thought the ambassador, his way of saying "School is out." The ambassador was content.

The next morning brought the confusion of packing and other predeparture chores. Fleisher took him to Nobel House to pick up his thirty-thousand-dollar check. The previous evening Faulkner had said, "I'll put the medal behind glass, with the books." This morning he could not find it. Button discovered it in one of the potted palms at the residence. Faulkner thanked his valet for everything. "I'm coming back," he told him, "maybe next year." He wanted to do some sailing, he said, in the Stockholm archipelago. He and Jill made their farewells to the Butterworths and the others, then got in the car for Bromma and their flight to Paris. It had been a busy seventy-two hours. A week later the American Embassy would conclude that the "stars" of the Stockholm festivities had been Bertrand Russell and William Faulkner.

Now came more of the ostensible justification for the trip as he showed Jill the things he loved: the Luxembourg Gardens where he had watched the children sail their boats twenty-five years before, the Left Bank cafés where he had sipped beer as the lilac dusk descended. But Jill came down with the flu, and on December 15 they left for London. While Jill tried to recover, he went to see his English publishers. The next day they left London for Shannon. The BOAC stewardesses made up a berth for Jill, and she slept the whole way to New York. There they stayed overnight. When Bennett and Phyllis Cerf called to see them at the hotel, Jill felt well enough to help tell about their adventures. In the midst of the conversation Faulkner changed the subject.

"By the way, Bennett," he said, "that full-dress suit you rented for me. I think I'd like to keep it."

"Bill," Phyllis said, "what are you going to do with it?"

"Well," he answered, "I might stuff it and put it in the living room and charge people to come in and see it, or I might rent it out, but I want that suit."[21] Random House bought it for him.

BACK at Rowan Oak they discharged their obligations. After Jill recovered she completed her long account of the trip for the *Eagle* and wrote her thank-you notes. Her father did his. To Merle Haas he wrote, "We are at home again, lots of family, plenty of Xmas. . . . I dont at all regret going to Stockholm now. . . . I went, and did the best I knew to behave like a Swedish gentleman, and leave the best taste possible on the Swedish palate for Americans and Random House."[22]

Walking into Judge John Falkner's office one day, Faulkner said to his uncle, "I want you to do something with that damned money. I haven't earned it and I don't feel like it's mine. I want to give some money to the poor folks of Lafayette County." He had kept track of the careers of more than one Oxford Negro. Nearly a dozen years before he had noticed the energy and ambition of young James McGlowan, and he had talked with him about teaching Mammy Callie to read and write. Now principal of the Negro high school at Hernando, McGlowan was one of those Faulkner saw as leaders of their race in the crucial times ahead. Nearly $3,000 of the Nobel money would go to advance James McGlowan's education at Hampton College and the University of Michigan. Some of the funds would not be limited to county residents. Five hundred dollars went to establish a scholarship in the University of Mississippi's music department in the name of Dorothy Commins, Saxe's wife and an accomplished pianist.

There were other aftereffects from the trip. Father and daughter had been welcomed home by the high-school band and seven drum majorettes. Thirty-three Oxford merchants had done the same thing with a full-page ad in the *Eagle*. Several groups invited him to address them. The one he accepted was from the Lafayette County Farm Bureau, where he made what observations he could about Swedish agriculture. Sykes Haney proposed that they add three words to the legend on the city water tower to make it read OXFORD, HOME OF OLE MISS AND WILLIAM FAULKNER. The secretary of the Ole Miss Alumni Association objected, however, that there was a difference between an individual and a great institution. The solution was vastly preferable to Faulkner. The Chamber of Commerce invited him to a fish fry in his honor and he accepted with pleasure.

He was glad when the "hooraw" died down. He did have work to do. He had another batch of manuscript pages on his desk, and there was no reason why they couldn't become a play as well as a novel. It would certainly have no trouble getting a hearing now.

57

. . . one universe, one cosmos: contained in one America: one
towering frantic edifice poised like a card-house over the abyss
of the mortgaged generations. . . .

—*Requiem for a Nun* (247)

THEY brought in the new year of 1951 at Rowan Oak the way they had
done since the children were old enough to have a taste of champagne.
Each New Year's Eve, Jill and Dean and Vicki would wait for his toast.
Then, at midnight, he would raise his glass and say, "Here's to the
younger generation—they are our hope."

The gesture of hopefulness was no reliable index of his inner life in
these January days. "I still have the damned cold," he wrote Bob Haas,
"which I carried from deer camp to N.Y. to Europe and back."[1] But his
malaise was more than physical. In the aftermath of the Nobel Prize his
critics remained as vocal as ever. He sent Phil Mullen a clipping Ben
Wasson had mailed to him and a letter he himself had received. "The
letter is interesting," he noted wryly. "I fear that some of my fellow
Mississippians will never forgive that 30,000$ that durn foreign country
gave me for just sitting on my ass and writing stuff that makes my own
state ashamed to own me."[2] One day Dot Wilcox Conkling's phone rang,
and to her surprise it was Bill Faulkner in Memphis, asking her to lunch.
As they sat over their drinks she could not see that fame had done him
much good. "I was unhappy when I first met you," he said, "and I'm
more so now than ever." It was in his letters too, especially when he heard
occasionally from Joan Williams, still struggling to learn her craft. It was
a relationship of emotional ups and downs. She might send him a story
she had been working on, or they might meet briefly. His hopes would
rise again and he would send her love letters. One result was a kind of
desultory domestic guerrilla warfare. He knew that at some point letters
from Joan had been intercepted and that Estelle had copies of them. In

some moods he might give clear evidence of the relationship instead of concealing it. When Estelle responded to this provocation, the resulting conflict could drive him to such measures as dismantling the telephone so that she could not call Memphis. He wanted to finish *Requiem for a Nun*, but for the first three weeks of January he spent more time at Greenfield Farm than he did at his desk.

Then Howard Hawks called. He wanted him to come out and fix up a script entitled *The Left Hand of God*. It was based on a novel about a former army pilot who stayed in China at the end of World War II in the service of a war lord. Then, disguising himself as a priest to escape his employer's service, he underwent a transformation. Hawks told Faulkner that Warner Brothers would raise no objection to his working for Twentieth Century-Fox and that it would be a two-month job at a salary of $2,000 a week. Faulkner agreed to do it and proposed to Joan that she come with him. He had told her that he thought her problems with the writing were caused by something that was frozen inside her and that he wanted to be the one to cure her, to free her. But she decided she could not make the trip with him. He reassured her again that she would write some day, though he concluded that he seemed to be the wrong one to help her.

AFTER his return from Sweden, Faulkner had written Meta Rebner that they must see each other again. Miserable after five years of remarriage to Wolfgang, she wanted him too, and on January 29 a note arrived to tell her he was coming. Bezzerides met him at the airport the evening of February 1 and drove him to the Beverly-Carlton. He had telephoned Meta from the airport, and she came to him at the hotel. After five years, they were lovers again. As she dressed to return home, he gave her a copy of the excerpt from the fable which the Levee Press had just published under the title *Notes on a Horsethief*. He inscribed it "This is for my beloved."[3]

It did not take long for his old feelings about Hollywood to return. "This is a place that lacks ideas," he told one friend. "In Europe they asked me, what did I think? Out here they ask, 'Where did you get that hat?'" By mid-February the strain was beginning to show in a familiar way. A letter to Estelle about household affairs was just barely legible. One morning at nine o'clock Random House novelist Irwin Shaw saw Faulkner sitting in the Beverly-Carlton lobby, "looking a little lost. He said to me that he had six bottles of beer in his room and asked me to join him to knock them off." But Shaw had to leave, and so "He sat down again, waiting patiently for somebody else to help him with the beer." But he did not let himself go over the brink. On Sunday, March 4, he earned a bonus by finishing the script in four weeks. There would be at least a week of rewrite money, but he was looking forward to getting home. "Beautiful damned monotonous weather," he wrote Joan in early

March, "and I am getting quite tired of it, will be glad to farm again. . . ."[4] During these weeks he had seen few friends, but he had been with Meta nearly every night and on weekends. At the airport he made her promise that they would see each other again before the year was out, perhaps in the summer. Then his flight was announced and, $14,000 to the good, he departed for Mississippi.

There had been another advantage to his stay in California: it had provided a plausible excuse for avoiding personal acceptance of the 1950 National Book Award for Fiction, in recognition of the collected stories, and Commins had accepted it for him. His name had continued to appear in the press. A week after Faulkner's arrival in Hollywood, Charles Poore had written in *The New York Times* that *Notes on a Horsethief* was "at once a brilliantly told story of a manhunt and a subtly woven allegory on man's fate."[5] The month after his return he let Commins stand in for him at the Page One Awards ceremony of the Newspaper Guild of New York. He would take pleasure in accepting another award himself, when he would become an officer of the French Legion of Honor in the fall.

AT Stockholm, Faulkner had spoken about honor and courage, and in the last years of the war he had written Malcolm and Jimmy about the obligation of men like himself to speak out in the days to come. Such an occasion presented itself in late March. In Laurel, Mississippi, execution was approaching for Willie McGee, a Negro convicted of raping a white woman. The editor of the *Commercial Appeal* called Moon Mullen and read him a statement which women from the Civil Rights Congress had obtained from Faulkner. It seemed so strong that the editor thought it would hurt Faulkner, and he asked Mullen to go out and see him. After Mullen talked with him, Faulkner pointed at his typewriter. "Sit down and write what you think I should say," he told him. In the release Faulkner said it had not been proved that force and violence had been used, and so the penalty should not be death. That would make McGee a martyr, and this would serve the cause of the Civil Rights Congress representatives, who themselves were being "used."[6] Once more he was arousing the resentment his portrayal of Lucas Beauchamp had provoked, the same resentment caused by his letter about the Attala County crimes a year before. He was immediately reproached in print by a prominent Baptist minister and attacked by the district attorney, who declared that Faulkner either was "seduced by his own fictitious imaginations [*sic*] or has aligned himself with the Communists."[7] It was another step in the continuing process alienating him from most of his fellow Mississippians. But his conviction that Willie McGee was innocent of rape remained unshaken. It was the same feeling that came through in "Dry September," published a little over twenty years before. The same compassion he had shown for Will Mayes he now seemed to feel for Willie McGee.

He had been at work on his own fictional court case, in which Nancy

Mannigoe had been sentenced to death. As he had treated the history of the courthouse as prologue to Act One of *Requiem for a Nun*, so now he supplied "The Golden Dome" for Act Two. Taking from his book-shelf a copy of *Mississippi: A Guide to the Magnolia State*, he transcribed almost directly many of the historical facts. The segment requiring noth-ing from the guidebook was the best: Faulkner's own tracing of the evolution from earliest creation of this spot where eventually "this rounded knob, this gilded pustule" (99) would stand. He borrowed again from the guidebook at the end when he listed among "chronic" diversions the annual festivals. In the last line he wrote, "Diversions: acute: Religion, Politics." (111) *Requiem* was going pretty well, he wrote Else Jonsson. "I have one more to do, the big one (Verdun) and then I have a feeling I shall be through, can break the pencil and cast it all away, that I have spent 30 years anguishing and sweating over, never to trouble me again."[8]

In early March he had told Haas about plans he was making. He thought it would be a good idea for him to visit some of the places he was writing about, such as Verdun. On April 12 he flew to New York for the first phase of his journey. It was a good three-day visit. Again Bob and Merle Haas gave a party for him. After dinner, when the conversa-tion turned to modern poetry, Dorothy Commins said she objected to the obscurity of much of it. Albert Erskine—recalling words such as *defunctive* and *interdict* common to both "The Phoenix and the Turtle" and *Absalom, Absalom!*—said, "Well, Dorothy, few modern poems are as difficult as 'The Phoenix and the Turtle.'" With that, Faulkner's face lit up, and he launched into a recitation of Shakespeare's poem. This time it was not a harbinger of trouble, and on April 15 he took off for London.

Three senior partners of Chatto & Windus took him to dinner. The next day a fourth, Harold Raymond, took him to lunch. Raymond was a type of Englishman that Faulkner admired. An Oxford honors graduate, he had risen to the rank of major in the First World War, won the Military Cross, and earned mention three times in dispatches. Also present at lunch were his son, Piers, and Mrs. Raymond, who was a daughter of the Vicar of Ruislip. This was a milieu Faulkner had imagined more than once in his early fiction. Before his departure, Raymond repeated an invitation to their country place in Kent, and Faulkner said he hoped to visit there some day soon.

The Gallimard family provided hospitality in Paris. They were some-what discomfited, however, at his taciturnity. They found the help they needed in one of their employees, a dark, intense, and voluble young novelist-editor named Monique Salomon. She was one of the young in France for whom, as Cowley had told him, Faulkner was a god. Faulkner liked her, and she saw in him the sympathetic intuitiveness Else Jonsson had perceived in Stockholm. He asked her to dinner with her student husband, Jean-Jacques. For Faulkner it was the beginning of a close, warm, avuncular relationship.

The trees were blossoming in the warm Paris spring, soft sunlight opening buds and bathing pastel buildings where sidewalk tables were replacing the winter barricades. Else Jonsson was also a friend of Monique, and she fled Stockholm's frigid spring to join them. They would make a foursome often when, it seemed to Monique, Faulkner always wanted to do the same thing: drink martinis, order coq au vin, and then visit Chartres. To Monique his French seemed rather stiff and heavy. He liked phrases such as the *"Ils ne passeront pas"* of the defenders of Verdun. Now he spent a few days viewing the vast sarcophagi where lay so many who had made good that vow. Photographers snapped him as he slowly paced along roads leading to the forts, puffing his pipe and scanning the terrain where half a million had died. His imagination could translate the huge stone crosses and vaulted buildings into the dugouts and strong-points, the neatly trimmed greensward into the muck at the end of *"La Voie Sacrée"* which had saved France. He had performed this kind of feat before in stories such as "Crevasse." When he returned home, carrying military maps and the Medal of the City of Verdun, he would set about doing it again.

It was a leisurely return after his two-week stay. He paid a brief visit to Joan Williams at Bard and then, in the first days of May, he joined Bill and Victoria Fielden in Lexington, Kentucky. He was at Churchill Downs at five o'clock in the morning to see them exercise the horses. Doing his own handicapping, he won $60 over Thursday and Friday. On Saturday, for the running of the Kentucky Derby, he put money down for Haas, Klopfer, Cerf, and Commins as well as for himself. He had the winner, Count Turf. When he returned to Oxford he sent Haas a check together with a page of arithmetic explaining the bets and the winnings. His letter ended, "Your business always appreciated by the old firm at the old stand. Am getting to work on Requiem today."

He could not, however, give it his undivided attention. Jill had telephoned him in New York to say that the principal of the high school had asked if he would talk to her high-school class. It sounded like some sort of informal talk, and he found it difficult to refuse Jill anything within reason. On arriving home, he found that it was the featured address at the commencement ceremonies for her graduating class. He would have to write another speech, for a formal event before more than a thousand people. It was natural that there should be echoes of the Stockholm speech. Understandably, it was in a way more optimistic. He told them that in spite of "the forces in the world today which are trying to use man's fear to rob him of his individuality, his soul, trying to reduce him to an unthinking mass by fear and bribery," the young people, if they

could speak out without fear, could change the earth, and in one generation, so that the tyrants would vanish from the face of it.[9] Not everyone
could catch his rapid voice, soft even over the public-address system, but
the largest Oxford graduation audience had enthusiastically applauded the
shortest graduation address on record: four and a half minutes.

He had gone ahead with the introduction for Act Three of *Requiem
for a Nun*. "The Jail (Nor Even Yet Quite Relinquish——)" was the
longest of the three. It followed the old structure, from the ceding of the
Indian lands and the planting of cotton to secession, from war and reconstruction to the automobile, from the New Deal and World War II
to "One Nation." As he once more wrote in his own medium, his confidence in the work continued to revive. The narrative portions beginning
Acts Two and Three would be all one sentence, each paragraph ending
with a semicolon. It was the technique he had used in "The Bear" and
Notes on a Horsethief. He was taking pains to integrate these introductions into the dramatic structure, using metaphors of act, scene, and
curtain to describe historical change, and so he instructed Commins to see
that the numbers designating the acts preceded the prologues. He was
experimenting with form again as he supported his uncertain dramaturgy
with prologues encapsulating material treated piecemeal elsewhere. On
one level *Requiem for a Nun* would follow Temple Drake's destiny; on
another it would be a study in crime and punishment; on still another
it would ring in the vast processes of geological and historical change.
Ober had no trouble selling "The Jail" to *The Partisan Review*, but for
only $270.

In early June he was able to relax for a while. "The mss. is about finished," he wrote Else Jonsson. "I'll be glad; I am tired of ink and paper.
. . ."[10] He looked forward to a quiet summer of crops, cattle, and horses.
Then, in a little over a week, his plans changed suddenly and radically.
In the midst of his leisurely rewriting, Ruth Ford called. She had shown
her set of galleys to Lemuel Ayers, to many the best working stage designer on Broadway, and he wanted to produce the play. Excited, Faulkner wrote her that he would come up to New York in early July. He
already had extensive revision in mind. "I may not be playwright enough
to do it," he told her. "But I would like to try. . . . It will be pretty fine
if we can make a good vehicle for you. I would like to see that title in
lights, myself."[11]

He arrived in New York in early July. Again writing on Hotel Algonquin stationery, he sketched a brief synopsis of each of the acts. Ruth and
Lem Ayers tried to help in evening conferences. Ayers had studied the
play carefully, and the general thrust of his suggestions was toward suspense and action. He wanted the audience to wonder if Nancy really was
the murderess and to feel that there was real hope of saving her. This
would be a radical departure from Faulkner's original strategy of beginning with Nancy's admission of guilt and leaving only the motive and its

ramifications to be revealed. Faulkner wrote and rewrote, but he began to grow restive. He told them he was anxious to get back to see about things on the farm, and on July 11 he flew home.

There was plenty he could do there. Ayers sent him five pages of criticism and suggestions, and from time to time there were queries from Commins as the book moved along toward publication. He described his activities on the farm to Else Jonsson. "Have not had much time for sailing this summer; I am really quite busy, I mean, my time is filled."

The tranquillity of the summer was broken in early August. Ten weeks earlier Cowley had written him that research had begun in the offices of *Life* magazine for an article on William Faulkner. Bob Haas had suggested that such a piece might be valuable for the fall publication of *Requiem for a Nun*, but Faulkner was adamant. "I have deliberately buried myself in this little lost almost illiterate town, to keep out of the way so that news people wont notice and remember me," he wrote Haas. "If, in spite of that, this sort of thing comes down here, I not only wont co-operate, I will probably do whatever I can to impede and frustrate it."[12] A week later it became clear that he would have to adopt that strategy when a letter from Hal Smith announced that his friend Robert Coughlan would arrive on August 16. Faulkner immediately sent a wire asking Smith to prevent the trip, but it was too late.

Robert Coughlan was already in Oxford. One of the best writers in the *Time-Life* organization, he had carefully prepared for writing a 6,000-word profile to accompany a picture layout. When he introduced himself to Estelle through the screen door he saw a startled and horrified look cross her face. She told him that her husband would be back soon and closed the door. Before long the jeep came up the rutted lane and vanished at the back of the house. Coughlan knocked again. This time Faulkner appeared and held the screen door slightly ajar. He asked Coughlan to state his business. When he did, he asked him to leave. Coughlan stumbled into an apology. Then as he turned to go, he said, "I want you to know how much I admire your work, and I'm glad I had a chance to say hello to you anyway."

At this, Faulkner said that maybe he had spoken too harshly. "Maybe a few questions won't hurt as long as they're not personal," he said. He led Coughlan to the cane chairs on the gallery, and before long he was talking cordially, but always within the boundaries he had set. He said he understood the circumstances that had brought Coughlan to Mississippi and even offered him a cold beer. So they sat and talked through the hot Mississippi afternoon, drinking ice-cold Löwenbräu. Faulkner offered to show Coughlan some places like Frenchman's Bend later, and suggested he see Moon Mullen. Coughlan left almost elated.

Mullen was helpful, but Coughlan had gotten as far with Faulkner as he would during his nine-day stay in Oxford. When he next saw him, on the street, Faulkner passed him without speaking. It was not hard to guess why. Coughlan had not wanted to antagonize him, but he knew very well that the editors of *Life* were not going to print an extended literary essay, and so he had interviewed as many of Faulkner's friends and relatives as he could, and he had asked personal questions. Returning to New York, he was shifted to another assignment. He transcribed his notes from Oxford and carefully filed them away.

"THIS is the beginning of harvest," Faulkner wrote Else Jonsson near the end of August. He described in detail the process of haying, "all in the hot sun, temperature about 95—all chaff and dust and sweat, until sundown, then I come back to the house, have a shower and a drink and sit in the twilight with another drink until supper, then bed in the heat full of the sounds of bugs, until daylight, when I get up again and go back to another section of grass, to guess again whether I can cut it before it rains or not." He looked ahead. "In November, the corn is ripe; the same process for it; the gathering, stowing away, and always the cattle, to be vaccinated, inoculated, nursed."[13] Like the three Falkners before him, he owned a productive farm, and he had now worked his longer than any but the Old Colonel, and much more closely than he had done. Apparently he gained from it not only diversion but a kind of strength, with its constant and tangible reminder of the rhythm of the seasons and the perennial process of rebirth.

But there were limits to what it could give him and how much it could distract him. When Joan wrote again, he replied, "Dont be unhappy, damn it. Let me be the unhappy one; sometimes I think I have enough for all, for all the world, I mean, the capacity for it." It was more than a general malaise. "I am too old to have to miss a girl of twenty-three years old," he told her. "I should have earned the right to be free of that."

In the second week of September, he and Estelle would drive Jill up to Pine Manor Junior College, in Wellesley, Massachusetts. Afterward he might stay on in New York for further revision so the play could go into rehearsal. He would be there when the first notices of the novel appeared. On September 6, Moon Mullen reported the publication, to mixed reviews, of Harry M. Campbell and Ruel E. Foster's *William Faulkner: A Critical Appraisal*. He also noted something else: no less than nine other books on Faulkner were now being written. Sympathetic critics such as Campbell and Foster must have wondered if the new book would add force to the view implicit in some assessments of the more recent works—that Faulkner had passed his peak, and that he was now mainly repeating himself.

58

. . . the important thing is to believe in it even if you dont understand it, and then to try to tell it, put it down. It wont ever be quite right, but there is always next time; there's always more ink and paper, and something else to try to understand and tell. And that one probably wont be exactly right either, but there is a next one to that one, too. Because tomorrow America is going to be something different, something more and new to watch and listen to and try to understand; and, even if you cant understand, believe.

—"A Note on Sherwood Anderson," *ESPL* (8–9)

THEY left Oxford on Wednesday, September 12, and made their way north in easy stages. Bob Linscott had volunteered to guide them on the last leg. He thought it would be interesting to stay at the Wayside Inn in South Sudbury, Massachusetts, the site of Henry Wadsworth Longfellow's *Tales of a Wayside Inn*. It was now chiefly a museum, but Linscott made a special effort, and when they arrived the manager said the Faulkners could have Longfellow's big second-floor bedchamber, preserved just as it had been when he had worked there on his book. Faulkner declined politely. It would make him nervous to sleep in Longfellow's bed, he said. With that, they left. A few miles down the road it became clear that it was too late to find other suitable accommodations, so they had to return. The manager obligingly put him in a room adjoining the Longfellow bedchamber. Now thoroughly unnerved, Faulkner declined to sit before the open fire in the old barroom and drink cider as Linscott had planned. Instead he went out and walked the dark road until bedtime. But then he could not sleep. So he stayed awake all night reading mystery stories. Longfellow's ghost was too much for him, he told Linscott the next day. "I can't seem to like antiquity when it's self-conscious," he said.[1]

On the way back to New York they had the ambivalent feelings of many parents who have delivered a child to college for the first time. There was satisfaction. Estelle hadn't wanted Jill to duplicate her own confining experience at Mary Baldwin, and she was determined that her daughter should go outside the South for further education, and now they had seen to it. But there was nostalgia for her childhood—Jill seemed so grown up now. Jill's own feelings were all positive. She liked the school, especially its wonderful riding instructors. On a deeper level, she was glad to leave Oxford, where, despite having a good friend like classmate Mildred Murray Douglas, she had so often felt alone. And she was glad to escape the tensions, the meals eaten mainly in silence at the polished dining-room table where she would be the only channel of communication between her parents, the periodic crises, and the sense of living in the shadow of that increasingly weighty reputation—borne by a man nonetheless still equivocal to the parents of most of her contemporaries. Now she could be on her own.

As the Faulkners were heading south again, breaking the trip with an overnight stay with Don and Pat Klopfer, the reviews of *Requiem for a Nun* were beginning to appear. Faulkner contented himself with sending signed copies of the book to old friends—among them Helen Baird Lyman and Phil Stone (the latter still inscribed, as in former years, "with love")— but Saxe pored over every review. After early affirmation, they turned increasingly negative. *Time*'s reviewer said that Faulkner was probably the best novelist writing in America and saw his themes of atonement and redemption as a presentiment of a "modest yes" after years of the "big no in American writing. . . ." But Hal Smith, writing as sympathetically as he could in the *Saturday Review*, put his finger on elements that would trouble other reviewers. The long prose passages of this book —Faulkner's twentieth, he noted—showed him at his best. If it had been all novel, with no play, "his talent would have illuminated this strange woman," his "nun," Nancy Mannigoe. Whether he had managed this in the play remained in doubt. There was no doubt in Irving Howe's mind: the work would suffer from the same weaknesses on the stage. The tenor of Robert Penn Warren and Malcolm Cowley's comments was much the same.[2]

According to one scholar, the standard reading of the novel which would develop was one in which it would be seen as "Faulkner's fable of sacrifice and salvation, in which the morally vacuous Temple Drake is saved from herself by Nancy Mannigoe's selfless sacrifice and Gavin Stevens's intervention. At the same time . . . it is seen as a statement by Faulkner of his own beliefs, of his own late grappling with some form of Christian orthodoxy, vague though it be, and as a rejection of and perhaps an apology for the despair and pessimism of his early work." His own radically different view was that "Nancy's murder of Temple's baby is the most savage and reprehensible act of violence in all of William Faulkner's fiction; . . . that Stevens is not at all out to 'save' Temple but rather to crucify her; and that Temple rather than Nancy is at the moral center of the novel."[3] A work with sufficient complexity, or ambiguity, to provide the basis for such dissimilar interpretations would hardly be easy to adapt for the stage.

HE was back home on September 25, but not for long. He wanted to check on the farm and lay out things for Renzi to do during the first half of October, when he would be away again, this time in Cambridge, Massachusetts. At the story conferences in New York he had met a young man named Albert Marre, who, after working in the Harvard Veterans' Theater, had helped to form a professional repertory theatre on Brattle Square. Ruth Ford had played Lady Macbeth there, and she wanted Marre to direct the new play. He said he would be glad to. On October 2, Faulkner left home for Boston and moved into a suite at the Hotel Continental, one block from Harvard Square.

If Marre's appraisal was right, Faulkner's feelings were now very different from his excited response when Ruth had called him about Lem Ayers' interest. Ruth was masterminding the planning with vigor and determination. Marre thought Faulkner was being very sweet to her about it, but he also thought Faulkner felt the play was no good and was doing it only for Ruth. He and Marre soon settled into a routine. Every day they worked on the play when Marre could get free of his theatre duties. Often Faulkner would ask Marre to sit at the typewriter. "Albie," he would say, "dummy up the scene for me." Then Marre would write what he thought the dramatic point of the scene was and how the dialogue should work, intensely conscious of Faulkner standing behind him. Some mornings when Marre would arrive, Faulkner would hand him five or six pages. Once it was a brilliant scene between Temple and Pete, but it was not integrally related to the play. He was very agreeable about Marre's criticisms, but he knew it wasn't coming off, and Marre felt he was beginning to despair of ever making it work. Faulkner wrote Meta Rebner that he would like to come to Hollywood and spend two or three nights in bed with her, but he could not, because of the play.[4]

The result was predictable. Starting with beer at 7:30 in the morning, he was drinking at what Marre considered a spectacular level. He went to New York briefly. When he returned, Marre told him that Thornton Wilder had said he admired his work very much and wanted to meet him. Faulkner agreed, but he employed his gambit of silence (which had unnerved novelist Henry Green and critic Lionel Trilling at a New York party in April), and the result was a brilliant discourse by Wilder. It seemed to Marre that each time Wilder mentioned a particular Faulkner technique, Faulkner played the country boy. When Wilder described the way he had explicated the title of *Light in August* for Jean Paul Sartre, Faulkner said he had never thought of that. "It just sounded pretty," he said. At that point Wilder flushed and departed. "Bill," Marre said, "why did you have to be such a bastard?" Faulkner looked at Marre with what seemed to him a dark, wicked smile. All he said for reply was "He's a nice man. He's a gentle man, isn't he?"

In spite of the difficulties, they went ahead with plans for a trial run at the Brattle Theater, beginning January 10, and a New York opening on February 4. Faulkner was due in New Orleans near the end of the month for the Legion of Honor ceremony, so in mid-October he broke off and took his problems south with him, to return for more work on the play in early November.

As it turned out, he made not one but two visits to New Orleans. After stopping briefly at home to check on the farm, he drove down alone. He began his holiday with Helen and Guy Lyman, but he soon outdistanced them. A visitor to the city saw him as he issued from the Monteleone. First this observer was struck by his appearance in his white linen planter's suit. Then he held his breath as he saw Faulkner's unsteady gait take him within inches of death under a streetcar bearing the designation "Desire." Finally Lyman had to call George Healy for help. They succeeded in lodging their friend in Baptist Hospital, despite his protests. A few days later he was able to go home.

He had scarcely reached Rowan Oak when it was time to go back. Estelle had taken Maud Falkner to Memphis and helped her pick out a sapphire-blue dress and shoes to match. Her son made the trip in un-shined shoes, unpressed trousers, and the leather-patched jacket he often wore hunting. When Jack and Suzanne Falkner joined them at the French consulate, she was distressed to see the ensemble in which her brother-in-law was receiving an award from the Republic of France, but at least he had taken the trouble to write out a short acceptance speech, which he read in his slow French. An artist ought to receive with humility an award conferred on him by the country which had always been "la mere universelle des artists." The other two sentences were couched in similar sweeping terms.[5] Saturday night Hermann Deutsch took them to dinner at Antoine's, and the next day they left for home, the back of their new gray Plymouth station wagon packed with French chairs and love seats Estelle had found in antique shops.

Apparently still vacillating between pessimism and hope, Faulkner re-turned to Cambridge on November 5. He brought new material with him, but Marre saw a lack of continuity again. "Bill, it doesn't fit," he said. "Can you try to do it visually, as you would do scenes for a novel?"

"I'll try," he replied.

They would consider different possibilities for interaction among the characters, but it was usually frustrating. "I don't get the idea of what you mean about the action," Faulkner would say. "Dummy up the scene." Marre would begin to tell him what he meant. "No! Don't tell me," Faulkner would say. "Write the goddam thing." Marre would then sit at the typewriter and peck out "dead-ass lines," but Faulkner would lean over, scratch out words, add a few, and suddenly, thought Marre, the line was his and it had life. But Faulkner was glad when it came time for him to fly home and join the others at deer camp on the seventeenth. When he and Marre parted, neither of them had much hope that they could get a Broadway production out of the play.

HE had no better luck in the Delta than in Cambridge. He attended to camp logistics and hunting gear as usual, but returned home after a week, without meat and without even having seen a deer. He went out to Green-field, and he puttered around at Rowan Oak—"waiting (I suppose) to go back to Boston or somewhere," he wrote Else Jonsson, "to rewrite the damned play again, of which I am quite sick now, except that as soon as it works, the producer has agreed to take it to Europe which is to be in the spring."[6] These plans were tied to a festival scheduled by the French government. The play would be staged at the Théâtre des Champs-Élysées if only they could get it to France. Lem Ayers had signed the contracts, and Ober had sent them on to Faulkner. He made one thing clear in a letter to Ayers: "this play is for Ruth, the part . . . is hers until she herself refuses it."[7] He sent the contracts back to have the "Ford clause" included. "I have known Miss Ford a long time," he wrote Ober a few days later, "admire her rather terrifying determination to be an actress, and wrote this play for her to abet it."[8] He knew that having a reigning Broadway star in the role would make it easier to obtain finan-cial backing, but he had given Ruth his promise, and he would keep it.

It had been a quiet Christmas. Jill had brought a Pine Manor classmate home with her. As usual, her father had seen to the tree and the yule log, the holly and the ivy and the pine branches. It had been a good Christmas, he wrote Commins, but "I am getting bored, and shall get to work at something soon now." Since he asked for $15,000 "immediately after January 1st," he would have mobility if that was required. Actually, much of the sum would be spent at Rowan Oak. He had always worked in the library or occasionally upstairs in his bedroom. His concentration was so intense that he might skip meals, but there were often interrup-tions. If Renzi or George or Alvis came in from the farm to see him, they would not disturb him if he was dozing in a chair. If he was typing, however, they would not hesitate. What he planned now was a hall at the rear of the library that would open onto a room with a fireplace. There would be a spacious adjoining closet and a full bath which would back onto the rear hall opposite the dining room. When the workroom was completed later that winter, he would furnish it with the table his mother had given him, an elaborate desk he and Malcolm had built, a bookcase, and a bed. Besides the materials and accessories of his craft, the room would soon accommodate saddles, leather polish, and all the equip-ment of a serious pipe smoker. It was not to be called his study, because he did not study in it. It was "the office," the traditional name for the room in plantation houses where business was transacted.

The play once more asserted its claims. Marre telephoned to ask if he could come down to put together a working script. When he arrived, Faulkner was standing on the gallery in a tweed jacket, breeches, and boots, with a crop in his hand—looking, thought Marre, like a self-conscious English gentleman. He was also the gracious host, presiding at the dinner table, where Victoria had joined Jill and her friend. Marre explained that Ayers had been unable to raise the money because the book publication of *Requiem for a Nun* "had taken the original 'shine' off the thing." But he still planned to open the play in September. Meanwhile, Marre had gone ahead with the plans for the Paris opening on June 1. The festival sponsors would put up the equivalent of $7,000, but for a one-week run it would take $15,000 more, and now it seemed that there was only one source it could come from—the author. If it was successful, Marre had a promise of "second money" to continue, perhaps in London. Then they would own the play, with sets, to sell to an American producer. On the other hand, they could not take any francs out of France, and if Faulkner drew $15,000 from his Random House account, his income tax would skyrocket. He told Commins that he was inclined to risk it, mainly for Ruth, who had missed out on other work because of the play, which was "her last—best—chance to make tops as an actress." But he wanted Commins to consult with the others at Random House, and he ended with one cautionary sentence: "Think it over well."[9] When Commins called Faulkner, he gave the advice almost anyone but a somewhat stage-struck author might have expected: Don't do it. Marre took the revised script back to New York with him. Not long afterward he telephoned that he had promises of $7,500. How much could Faulkner add? When he wired back that he was prepared to put up $2,000, Marre continued looking for further backing.

THE tempo of his activities continued to slow as the winter days lengthened. Mornings he usually worked on the fable. One critic would see a connection with *Requiem for a Nun* in that both "are built around characters who deliberately break the laws of their civilization out of their convictions that they are obeying a higher law, and who just as deliberately sacrifice their own lives . . . in that belief. Both novels describe the ways in which the world reacts to and deals with these rebellions."[10]

Now and then he would drive into Memphis on occasional errands. There was a stretch of movie work in February, with the prospect of a trip to the Coast for conferences if he thought he could do anything with the script. He wrote Meta Rebner, hoping for a holiday together. By now she had divorced Wolfgang for the second time, and she waited for Faulkner to return. In *Go Down, Moses* the omniscient narrator had said, "women hope for so much. They never live too long to still believe that anything within the scope of their passionate wanting is likewise within the range of their passionate hope. . . ." (352) Meta's Aunt Ione tried to make her look ahead. "You'd settle for a month this year, a few weeks next year?" she asked. Meta nodded. "Yes," she said, "I think so."[11] But the script conferences didn't materialize, and when Meta worked out a plan for a weekend in New Orleans, Faulkner wrote that he couldn't leave Oxford.

Though the pace was slow, there was a kind of balance to his days—except when he was on horseback. "I stay busy, working at my big book, also farming," he wrote Else Jonsson as March came in. He was also training a filly named Temptress. He was leading her and riding her dam, Jill's gaited saddle mare called Peavine's Jewel, when Tempy jerked him off Jewel's back. "So there I was, lying flat on my back in a mud puddle, with a frantic horse in each hand. No harm though; I learned years ago how to fall off horses.[12] On mornings when Bob Farley could not join him he would ride alone. Now in his fifty-fifth year, he had added some weight at the waistline, and his upper back curved at the shoulders, appearing thickened and almost humped. On one of these mornings his horse was startled by some random sound and flung him from the saddle. He landed hard, half on his seat and half on his lower back. He made it home without assistance, but the pain grew severe and persisted for several days before it eased. Horses continued to appear in his writing. Replying to one of Joan's letters, he said she sounded "so down and depressed" that he thought of borrowing a white horse to "snatch you up and gallop off forever—provided of course that you would go, and I could find the white horse."

Part of his time at his desk that spring he spent on work other than his fable. Bob Farley had acted as the intermediary in conveying an invitation to speak at the annual meeting of the eighteen-county Delta Council of 3,000 cotton planters and businessmen. Faulkner told Farley that he was no good at that kind of thing, but when Farley told him that he had obtained an offer of $400 plus expenses, Faulkner agreed to go. In early April, however, with the meeting less than six weeks away, Faulkner called to say he had been thinking about going to Europe and he was not sure now about the speech. When Farley impatiently told him, "Lay it on the line, either one thing or the other," Faulkner asked for another week. It passed with no further word, and Farley assumed that the Delta Council still had a speaker for its annual meeting at Cleveland, Mississippi.

On the morning of May 15, Bob and Alice Farley drove up to Rowan Oak. Faulkner was waiting for them. He was wearing striped seersucker trousers, a badly frayed shirt, and the belted jacket he had bought in New York, which was now too small for him. His felt hat looked to Farley to date from about 1915.

"You ready to go to Cleveland?" he asked.

"Oh, is this the day?" Faulkner replied, his eyes glinting.

"It sure is."

"Can I go like this?"

"You can if you want to."

At Cleveland, Farley left his own hat in the car and got Faulkner to leave his too, but his clothes still made him a conspicuous figure amid the planters in their expensive suits. On the platform with their plump host, Governor Hugh White, and Governor James F. Byrnes of South Carolina, Faulkner looked like a handsome riverboat gambler between a fat banker and a lean deacon. When he rose to speak to the audience of 5,000, he sounded at first a little like the Mississippi farmer Bob Farley had thought he would impersonate. But then he shifted to the guarantees in the Declaration of Independence and the individual responsibilities they entailed. Quickly reviewing the westward drive of the independent pioneers, he launched into a sweeping attack on federal welfare programs. Now the descendants of those tough old ancestors placed so much emphasis on a new kind of security that they were willing to accept charity through relief rolls or political gravy troughs. The true heirs of American heroes were not those implicated in the current scandals bedeviling the Truman administration; they were those who would stand on their own feet. It was the position he had taken since the earliest days of the New Deal, and he had been writing it into his fiction in stories such as "Two Soldiers" and "Shingles for the Lord." When he sat down, there was a roar of applause. Governor Byrnes gave a point-by-point indictment of the Truman administration and called for a new political party that would represent the South. Though most of his views were congenial to Faulkner, Byrnes was a politician Faulkner did not admire. When Ben Wasson leaned over and said, "He's a Snopes," Faulkner replied, "He sho' is."

Faulkner seemed almost to enjoy the rest of the affair. He even told council president Maury Knowlton not to worry about the $400 fee, just to give him a few bottles of whiskey. They already had a case for him, and Knowlton was unsure about what to do. "Will he be insulted if we offer him money?" he asked Farley. "No," his friend growled, thoroughly annoyed after the bargaining and arranging he had done. On the way home he gave the check to Faulkner and said that just for that he was going to take half the whiskey. "Take the whole case, Bob," Faulkner said. "You ought to be my agent." Looking out the car windows at the green fields of young cotton whizzing by, he could afford to relax now. He could even feel some pleasant anticipation.

In spite of the uncertainty about the play, he, at least, would be going to Paris. The French government's plans for the *Oeuvres du XXe Siècle* festival were quite firm. Not only would there be ballets, concerts, and cultural exhibits, there would also be a writers' conference. They had offered to pay all his expenses, and he had told Joan that with his "Legion d'honneur and the Nobel and all the other hurrah," he did not feel that he could decline the invitation. "I will pay my own way," he wrote Else

Jonsson, "give that time to the festival which will meet my conscience. That is, I will be a free agent in Paris, as far as I believe now."[13] He wrote Monique Salomon to tell her he was coming, and asked Saxe Commins to book a direct flight for him via BOAC to Paris. On May 16 he was on his way.

. . . taking the long way, through the Luxembourg Gardens
again among the nursemaids . . . and the stained effigies of gods
and queens, into the rue Vaugirard, already looking ahead to
discern the narrow crevice which would be the rue Servandoni
and the garret which he had called home . . . the archway where
the ducal and princely carriages had used to pass . . . the old
faubourg of aristocrats. . . .

—*A Fable* (148–149)

In New York, Marre brought him up to date on their struggles with the
play. They had finally raised the money to take it to Paris. Ruth Ford's
handsome husband, the actor Zachary Scott, had started working on
Gavin Stevens' lines. Pavel Tchelitchew had made drawings for the costumes and sets, and Ruth's brother, poet Charles Henri Ford, was helping.
Even the air tickets were provided by a government agency. But then
disputes arose over script, sets, and design, and suddenly the whole project
was off. When they tried to sort things out, nobody seemed to want
the tickets back. So with a few others, Marre prepared to fly to Paris,
arranging to meet Faulkner there.

When Faulkner arrived at Le Bourget on May 19, 1952, Jean-Jacques
and Monique Salomon were there to meet him, even though their baby
was due in two weeks. They drove him back toward his small hotel in a
Right Bank residential district. Obviously enjoying himself, he gazed at
the kiosks, the sidewalk tables, and the May branches arching over the
streets. He was prepared for a four-week holiday.

That was how it began. Once again Else Jonsson accompanied him,
and again they made a foursome with the Salomons. Marre joined them.
He enjoyed watching Faulkner and listening to his French, which seemed
fluent, though Marre thought the accent execrable. Whether in an ordinary bistro or at one of the city's best restaurants, Faulkner was secure,

knowledgeably ordering both food and wine. One day as they sat over coffee he said to Marre, "I'm relieved we don't have to do the play. I don't think it's any good." Marre said that Ruth didn't agree. "I don't think this play is going to do Ruth any good," Faulkner replied, "but she can go ahead with it if she wants to."

He was in good form, even at a formal dinner given by the Gallimards, but soon things changed. He would later tell a physician that he had been thrown from a horse in Paris. Perhaps he had gone riding one morning in the Bois de Boulogne, but even if it was, instead, an aftereffect of the fall two months earlier on the Old Taylor Road, the pain in his back was real enough. Just as his obligations came due, he began to drink to ease it. Novelist Glenway Wescott heard that the officious secretary of the Writers' Congress went to Faulkner's hotel when he failed to respond to her summons. When she unceremoniously opened the door and began a harangue, Wescott was told, Faulkner raised himself in bed and flung a bottle, driving her precipitately down the stairs. He managed to make a brief appearance, in part because one of the other speakers was André Malraux. As Wescott listened to the latter's eloquence, he glanced at Faulkner, sitting there motionless, looking like a gray fox out of a fairy tale inexplicably set down amidst humans. When it was his turn, he rose to say that for years he had been convinced that the world would have to depend on French brains and American muscle, pointing to his temple and then his biceps as he spoke. His short talk received an ovation. Afterward he seemed to get on well with Malraux, who reciprocated Faulkner's admiration.

By May 27 his back was so bad that Monique had to take him to the Clinique Remy de Gourmont. A total of nine x-rays revealed the problem: he had a broken back. There were compression fractures of the twelfth dorsal vertebra and the first lumbar vertebra, in the small of his back. Some natural splinting had taken place because they were old fractures, but arthritic involvement was adding to the pain. It could have happened in the violent impact when he left the saddle and struck the ground in a sitting position. It could also have happened six years before when he had tumbled all the way down the stairs at Rowan Oak. Whatever the cause, he did not like the prescription: surgical fusion. A man with a lifelong distrust of doctors, he treated his farm animals with turpentine, and for humans, favored Epsom salts or silver nitrate. The most he would agree to was a few days of bed rest in the hospital.

His usual reaction followed: a compulsion to escape a situation where he felt caged. Besides, the Raymonds expected him at Biddenden, down in Kent, on June 1, and he was determined to go. He had planned to fly from there to Oslo, and Else had already obtained his ticket for him. Because Monique Salomon was just about ready to go into labor, Jean-Jacques took him—grim-faced and moving slowly and gingerly—to the plane. He arrived on time in the same Kentish countryside he had admired a quarter-century before, now in the rich green of late spring. The quiet day went well, but by the time he returned to London, his back was worse. He went to see the Raymonds' doctor in Upper Wimpole Street, but there was little he could do in one visit.

The cycle of pain and flight was tightening. He telephoned Else Jonsson in Stockholm and told her that he had nearly drowned in the bathtub there in the Hotel Normandie, though from what mischance he did not say. When he arrived at a hotel outside Oslo on June 4, Else saw to it that he began a program of therapy. Every day for a week he went to a masseur, he wrote Raymond, "until he relaxed the muscles and with his hand, set the bad vertebra back into place; the discomfort vanished at once. . . ."[1] Later he would say that it was the first time in years that he had been without any back pain at all.

Now his interest revived in the life around him. He observed both people and scenery with that bright hooded glance as he ate on the sunlit hotel terrace amid the peaks, the Oslo harbor just barely visible in the far blue distance. He could clearly see the tower and ramp of the great ski jump and the fir trees circling the 100,000-spectator Holmenkollen stadium where each year the world's finest skiers competed. He met Sigurd Hoel, who had written some of the first good Faulkner criticism in Scandinavia, and he liked him and his friends. It was a feeling for the rugged nationalistic Norwegians, who struck him as poor but proud, seeing in them something of his own north Mississippi countrymen. Far from the center of attention, he was able to relax. By the time he took the thirty-five-mile ride to Gardermoen Airport on June 14, he was almost back to normal. There was one item he would attend to later. In London he had been unable to find his air ticket to Oslo and so had bought another one. When he found the first one, he sent it to Monique in Paris, the only place where it could be redeemed. She was to buy a gift with it to be engraved "to my god-daughter from son beau papa or what you like." He sent it with love and gratitude.

BACK in New York, Faulkner felt well enough to go out to dinner with Albert Erskine and his friend Robert Penn Warren. As they enjoyed the food and wine at Charles à la Pomme Soufflé, Faulkner moved from monosyllables to conversation. He began to talk about the distinction between the fact of a thing and the truth of a thing, citing a number of narratives without mentioning the authors. As Faulkner described several scenes in detail, Warren recognized two of them as coming from a story and a novel of his own. After dinner the night was so fair that Faulkner suggested they go for a ferry ride. When they returned from Weehawken, Faulkner invited them into the bar of the New Weston, where he was staying. There their evening ended with two bottles of champagne.

When his plane touched down in Memphis at 6:30 P.M. on June 17,

With friends aboard the **Minmagary**

Sailing on Sardis

At the tiller

Joan Williams

"...*above all the courthouse: the center, the focus, the hub....*"

At Nobel ceremonies with Dr. Gustaf Hellström and Envoy Ståhle

Else Jonsson

The hunters: Faulkner between Red Brite and Ike Roberts

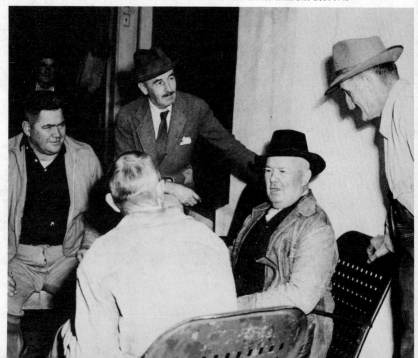

THURSDAY

VIII — Tae Runner goes to Paris to enlist the aid of the old Negro preachers. They return to the battalion, and persuade it to make the unarmed advance into No-man's Land, where an unarmed German force meets it, and both, except for the Runner, are destroyed by simultaneous British & German barrages. (~~Includes the story of the Sentry, the old Negro preacher and the stolen race horse.~~)

VIII — Levine hears about the unarmed British and German forces destroyed deliberately by their own barrages, and commits suicide.

VIII — The French Division Commander is executed by the three American privates.

VIII — The Last Supper of the Corporal and his squad.

VIII — The Old General offers the Corporal the Three Temptations. ~~The Corporal~~ to save himself. The Corporal refuses them

VIII — The French chaplain is sent to the Corporal to persuade the Corporal to accept Christianity & so repudiate his stand. The Priest fails, commits suicide.

Outline for A Fable *on the walls of Faulkner's office*

The master and mistress of Rowan Oak

Pre-wedding toast

Bride and groom

Random House partners: Donald Klopfer, Robert Haas, Bennett Cerf

Saxe Commins

Joan was there to meet him. They spent the evening together, and it was 2:30 in the morning when he finally reached Rowan Oak. When he wrote her two days later he was thinking of another unlikely pair, of "old eighty-year-old Goethe's pride and exultation at having conquered (I mean half-conquered anyway) a young and pretty woman. Only, in this case, there is a rather terrible amount of no-peace too. If we could meet whenever we liked, it might be different with me, though probably not. But as it is, I wont get any peace until we have finished the beginning of it. Maybe I can even do more for you then, after there is no more barrier, no more mystery, nothing to remain between."

At home for the first time in nearly five weeks, he found it too hot to work, but near the end of the week he was typing again—a letter that had its beginnings in Harvey Breit's request for a review of Ernest Hemingway's new novel, *The Old Man and the Sea*, for *The New York Times Book Review*. Faulkner had been keeping up with the work of his great contemporary. In Temple Drake's scene with the governor, she spoke of the girl in the Hemingway book who refused to accept the fact of rape—Maria, in *For Whom the Bell Tolls*, though she did not mention either name. And when Evelyn Waugh had written the editor of *Time* attacking the critics who had panned *Across the River and into the Trees*, Faulkner had sent a letter endorsing Waugh's statement. Now he resumed with the same tone. But first he recalled a remark which he attributed to Hemingway that "writers should stick together just as doctors and lawyers and wolves do." In a tangled sentence he went on to say that, in Hemingway's case, there was more wit than truth or necessity in the remark. Writers who when banded together were wolves, were singly only dogs. He felt it implied that Hemingway was a wolf who needed no pack. "So he does not need even this . . . from one who, regardless of how he rated what remained, has never doubted the integrity of it, and who has always affirmed that . . . the man who wrote MEN WITHOUT WOMEN and THE SUN ALSO RISES and A FARE-WELL TO ARMS and FOR WHOM THE BELL TOLLS and the rest of the African stuff and most of the rest of it; and that if even what remained had not been as honest and true as he could make it, then he himself would have burned the manuscript before the publisher ever saw it."[2] He mailed this strangely equivocal letter of praise to Saxe Commins to be forwarded to Harvey Breit.

The sequel provided further complications. Breit quoted the letter to Hemingway, telling him he planned to use it in a piece he was writting. Hemingway responded angrily. Reading and rereading the ambiguous phrasing and tangled syntax, he concluded that Faulkner had missed the point of what Hemingway had originally said and was calling him "just another dog." It was a betrayal, he told Breit, for writers knew each other's strengths and weaknesses, and these were *secrets profession-nels* which they should not reveal. Faulkner "is a good writer when he is good," he told Breit, "and could be better than anyone if he knew how to finish a book. . . ." When Faulkner won the Nobel Prize, Hemingway had sent him the best cable he could write, but it was never acknowledged. The prize, he thought, had ruined Faulkner as a writer. Hemingway always used to tell Europeans that Faulkner was the best American writer. "When they asked about my work, I would turn the conversation to his." And now he had written this patronizing letter. Hemingway asked Breit not to use it, spurning anything from the creator of "Anomatopeoio County."[3] Faulkner should have just refused to review the book, he said, and let it go at that.

A few months later an enterprising young man named Tom Carter asked Faulkner if he would review the novel for Washington and Lee University's journal, *Shenandoah*. Finally Faulkner sent him one paragraph. "His best," it began. "Time may show it to be the best single piece of any of us. . . ." But then a critical note crept in that recalled the value system in the Nobel Prize speech. Now Hemingway had "discovered God, a Creator. Until now, his men and women had made themselves, shaped themselves out of their own clay; their victories and defeats were at the hands of each other, just to prove to themselves or one another how tough they could be. But this time, he wrote about pity; about something somewhere that . . . made them all and loved them all and pitied them all."[4] Faulkner felt that most of Hemingway's work had been written from the wrong moral bases in a highly refined but essentially limited style. Hemingway felt that Faulkner had the most abundant natural gifts but that he had written too much, continuing when he was tired and then sometimes going on alcohol, adulterating the works with "tricks" and "rhetoric." Hemingway spoke of "getting in the ring" with Balzac and Tolstoy; Faulkner would say you wanted to be "better than Shakespeare." Perhaps the remarkable thing was that they expressed as much admiration for each other as they did.

Through the heat of late June and early July, Faulkner persisted in trying to help Joan with her writing. The previous winter, sending her a critique of a story he found static, he said, "I intend for you to win that prize, which is it? Harper's I think, $10,000 for a first novel? Then you wont have to ask anyone for permission to go where you like." He continued to offer criticism and encouragement when the work seemed to her to move too slowly. He had not been able to get her to try a novella he had in mind for her, and now he wanted her to collaborate on a television script. After several afternoons at her house, when they discussed story lines and names, the project evolved into seven pages called "The Graduation Dress," on which he did most of the work. He sent it to James Geller, and in late July, Geller sent a $500 check for it.

Joan's major interest was a story about a forty-year-old "loony" named Jake and his perception of the itinerant motion-picture show from which he was finally ejected. Faulkner thought this one was so good that he said he wouldn't even touch it, but he didn't like the title. He thought she should call it something like "Twilight." Then he suggested "The Morning and the Evening," out of Genesis, and that became the story's title. When they talked about Jake they compared him with Benjy Compson. Later Joan would think he was closer to Ike Snopes. Faulkner supplied a covering letter to go with the story to *Harper's.* It was written by a student of Faulkner, he said, and he hoped it would be looked at twice, if necessary. When they rejected it, he reread it and told her it was still all right. When Ober said he would try to place the story, Faulkner urged her to send it. But he did not give her a chance to rewrite it. "May send it to Ober," he wrote, "unless I can find some glaring fault which I can point out to you."[5] That was what he did a week and a half later.

But he was concerned with more than the story, concerned enough to write her four letters in one twenty-four-hour period and then two more a few days later. When he had returned from Europe his ardor had made them lovers, and though only briefly, it had been enough to add hope to his desire while it aroused all her impulses for flight. Now, meeting the same resistance he had met earlier, he felt that he had coerced her, and he was ready to resign that part of their relationship. He accepted the need she felt to meet new people, to escape, even to find someone else, someone free and young, whom she could trust and, in time, love. He would write Geller and Cerf to try to help her get away. And if their meetings since his return had meant goodbye, "that's all right too; haven't I been telling you something too: that between grief and nothing, I will take grief?"

Almost as soon as he had sent the letter he regretted it. He wrote another one but tore it up. In the next letter he asked her to forget the earlier one. "I still felt so rotten yesterday morning that I had to do something," he told her, "so suddenly I dug out the mss. of the big book and went to work at it; suddenly I remembered how I wrote THE WILD PALMS in order to try to stave off what I thought was heart-break too. And it didn't break then and so maybe it wont now, maybe it wont even have to break for a while yet, since the heart is a very tough and durable substance. . . ."[6] A letter from Joan showed that she had reacted as he had feared, but he wrote her that he refused to believe it was time for them to say goodbye. "Not goodbye, not yet. I will die some day before you do, but not yet." He wanted to look ahead, to their meeting again, to their being together. "The big book going well, but I need something, we agreed on that: something, someone, to write, not *to* but *for.*" He asked her to write him, to set a day for them to meet again.

AUGUST had been a bad month from the start. Estelle had been hospitalized in Memphis for an alcoholic episode, and he nearly wound up in the hospital too, though not from the same illness. The heat lay thick and shimmering on the roads, and in the fields the grain and hay began to turn dry and brown. For relief he and Malcolm drove out to Sardis. As he looked up to set a sail, the *Ring Dove* yawed and he went overboard. He described to Else Jonsson his efforts to swim and hold his hat with one hand "while yelling to the helmsman how to put about and run back and pick me up, which he finally did by running me down and of course the keel struck me across the back. So my back must be all right, to have stood that, so maybe I only imagine it hurts." When he wrote her again in two weeks he reported, "Back not much better; probably impossible with my nature and occupation—natural nervousness, inability to be still, inactive, and the farm-work, to take care of, though I am off horses, not been on one since I got home. Though probably the great trouble is unhappiness here, have lost heart for everything, farming and all, have not worked in a year now, stupid existence seeing what remains of life going to support parasites who do not even have the grace to be sycophants. Am tired, I suppose. Should either command myself to feel better, or change life itself, which I may do; if you should hear harsh things of me, dont believe all of them. . . ."[7] There was pain and discontent in nearly all his letters now.

He had written Meta Rebner twice about the masseur in Oslo, but now he told her about his inability to work. "I wish I could spend about two weeks with you," he wrote her, "lying on my face with the sun on my back. That would do more good than anything."[8] He began to brood about money as well as his sense of waste and loss. He didn't want to go back to Hollywood, he told Ober, but he would soon have to do some hack work of some kind or he would become a nuisance to his friends again. The big book was going well, but that was not enough to counteract the pain and depression.

By mid-September he was trying to forestall a collapse with beer and Seconal, but each day he felt worse. Then, on September 18, he suffered a convulsive seizure. They took him to Memphis, to the Gartly-Ramsay Hospital, a fifty-bed psychiatric hospital. There he told Dr. Dick C. McCool that his trouble had begun with injuries to his face, limbs, and back in a wartime plane crash, and the fall from the horse in Paris had aggravated the old condition. Now he was suffering from spasms of the deep spinal muscles all the way from his humped upper back on down. His range of spinal movement was only seventy percent of normal. Though a set of x-rays showed no new fractures, they revealed other old ones: mild compression fractures of dorsal vertebrae 8, 9, and 10. For some years now he had been walking around with five broken vertebrae in various stages of natural splinting, complicated by bone-lipping, spur formation, and moderately severe hypertrophic arthritis. They began withdrawing alcohol and administering Seconal in proper dosage for sleep and Pantopon for the pain. After a week of hot packs and massage he was feeling better. But then he had another convulsive seizure. When his physicians suggested a spinal tap for diagnostic purposes, he became frightened. Against their advice, he insisted on going home, and they released him on September 26.

A few days later he was able to deal with his correspondence. Ober had sent him a copy of a letter from the *Atlantic* accepting "The Morning and the Evening." Faulkner thanked him. "She has been my pupil 3 years now, when nobody else, her people, believed in her. I am happy to know my judgment was right."[9] Joan was working in New York for *Look* magazine, but on his advice she had gone to see Hal Smith. "He will do a great deal for me that doesn't cost actual cash money," he told her.[10] As for himself, he wanted to get on with the big book and a piece on Mississippi that *Holiday* magazine had asked for. "I still feel pretty bad," he told Ober, "but should improve from now on."[11] He was wrong.

Jimmy Faulkner would see him sitting on the fender before the hearth, his bare back to the open fire. With the pain the sleepless nights returned, and once more he began the beer and Seconal treatment. Then he fell, all the way down the stairs. Estelle appealed to Saxe Commins, who came down from Princeton. After nursing Faulkner for two days (and recording the details of his condition in his diary), Saxe took him back to Gartly-Ramsay.[12] Surprisingly, new x-rays showed no additional injury. Paraldehyde was administered as he was taken off alcohol. With the resumption of therapy, he began to improve. After several days he was sleeping and eating better. Occasionally he would go for a solitary stroll, a small, slow-moving figure in pajamas and bathrobe on the hospital grounds. He was fitted for a back brace, but his doctors felt that he would have to get used to living in pain as long as he refused surgery. On October 21 he was home again at Rowan Oak.

As he gradually came out of what he called a medication hangover, the nervousness and depression returned. "I have got to get to work," he wrote Joan, "and I am too unhappy here now; never in my life have I ever been so unhappy and depressed." He was pleased, though, that she was going to expand her story into a novel. But he warned her that leaving the middle class to be an artist would be hard. She would have to expect "scorn and horror and misunderstanding," but she would be all right, "because there is a God that looks after the true artist because there is nothing as important as the necessity to make things new and passionate and He knows it." He might have mentioned another god who treated the artist no differently from other mortals. He missed her. "I thought I was still the cat that walked by himself, needing nothing from anyone, or at least never letting them know it. But not anymore." Love had "destroyed forever that proud and self-sufficient beast."

THE movies came back into his life in early November. He had agreed to let the Ford Foundation make a documentary film on his apocryphal county for the television program *Omnibus*. Harry Behn had done a script which began with the Nobel Prize announcement and used a series of flashbacks. Phil Mullen had been engaged to portray himself and serve as both script collaborator and consultant. When he telephoned from his new job in Paris, Tennessee, Faulkner told him "Yes," he could come down with the script, "and bring some beer." Before Mullen departed a telegram arrived: DON'T FORGET THE SNAKE JUICE. Estelle wrote Dorothy Commins that the forthcoming filming was already a bother to him. "He is afraid his voice is bad, and that perhaps it is the wrong time of year— Ordinarily—all this would have been done with Billy's usual detachment and ease—but now, he seems actually to worry what people might think— Something so foreign to his nature—."[13] To the pleasure of director Howard T. Magwood and his ten-man crew, Faulkner showed himself to be a considerate host and an interested actor. He even offered Mullen some advice on reading his lines. He was at ease when he appeared with Mac Reed, but in a scene with Phil Stone he seemed stiff and distant. (Mullen thought he knew why. Stone now felt that Faulkner had developed "Nobelitis in the Head"[14] and he had been quoted by a reporter as saying that Faulkner was a great writer "but sometimes he is like a Negro preacher, using big words he doesn't know the meaning of. . . .") But Faulkner dutifully discharged his role, restaging Jill's high-school commencement speech and giving orders to Renzi out at Greenfield Farm. Magwood was amazed. "He's very good," he said. But Faulkner was relieved when the shooting for the seventeen-minute feature was completed and he could give directions for entertaining the crew. Mullen asked him what he was going to serve. "Some of my country ham I cured myself," he answered. "And it should be good—it costs me about fifty dollars per ham."

He had written Else Jonsson and Harold Ober that he might radically alter his life. In mid-November he left Oxford for Princeton. After a few days with Saxe and Dorothy Commins on Elm Road, he moved into a comfortable room at the Princeton Inn. He had agreed to do the piece on Mississippi for *Holiday*—7,500 words for $2,000—and he meant to get on with the fable. In spite of continued back pain, he was getting enough done to take time out for an interview, arranged through Commins' good offices, with an intense young Frenchman working for his Ph.D. at Princeton. Loïc Bouvard had prepared his questions carefully, and they came in a torrent, put with the obvious assumption that Bouvard was talking with a man of letters in the French sense who would try to answer with something of the same intensity and clarity. In a response that was unique for him, Faulkner tried to meet Bouvard on his own ground, perhaps thinking back to the literary discourse he had shared with Malraux and the others in Paris. When he had read Proust's *À la Recherche du Temps Perdu*, he said, "This is it!" and wished he had written it himself. He agreed with Valéry about the hardship involved in artistic creation and recalled Gide's comment that he admired "only those books whose authors had almost died in order to write them." As for himself, "Maybe I will end up in some kind of self-communion—a silence—faced with the certainty that I can no longer be understood. The artist must create his own language. . . . Sometimes I think of doing what Rimbaud did—yet, I will certainly keep on writing as long as I live." He had read Malraux's latest book on the psychology of art, but he did not know the work of Sartre and Camus. His feeling about some aspects of the human condition was nonetheless close to theirs. "Man is free and he is responsible, terribly responsible," he said. On the other hand, he disagreed with them at certain points. It was wrong, for instance, to do away with God. "I'm not talking about a personified or a mechanical God, but a God who is the most complete expression of mankind, a God who rests both in eternity and in the now . . . a deity very close to Bergson's." He agreed, he said, with "Bergson's theory of the fluidity of time. There is only the present moment, in which I include both the past and the future, and that is eternity." Bouvard left the interview in a state of exaltation and excitement.[15] In his room he wrote down everything he could recall, but it would be two years before it was distilled into a published article. In the process, some of the statements acquired a Gallic pithiness not characteristic of Faulkner's speech, but it was still a remarkable interview.

For a brief time it seemed that the relocation had produced some of the results Faulkner wanted. He was back at work on the fable. He saw Joan in New York and she visited him in Princeton, where they spent Thanksgiving with the Comminses. Closer to him and more dependent, she accepted him once more on his terms, but then he began to drink heavily again and suffered another collapse.

He was admitted to the Westhill Sanitarium, a private hospital located on a well-cared-for estate at Riverdale in the Bronx. At this point a doctor whom Joan had seen briefly offered to go to the hospital and visit him. Eric P. Mosse was a European-trained psychoanalyst who had written plays and novels. He specialized in the treatment of artists and he was particularly anxious to attend Faulkner because he admired his work. Diagnosing his illness as the result of drinking and depression, he advised electroshock therapy. Mosse told Mrs. Mosse that he administered a series of these treatments—perhaps six in all. In the aftermath of them, he said, Faulkner was gentle and affectionate. Mrs. Mosse remembered her husband's breaking into the middle of his day to drive at noon from his office in the city up to the sanitarium. After Faulkner was released in late November, Dr. Mosse's bill arrived. It amounted to several hundred dollars. Both Faulkner and Commins were furious. Mosse responded that each trip took him two hours, but he would accept whatever they thought was fair. Much later Jill would say that she had never had any indication that her father had undergone electroshock and that she doubted that he had. (Pappy never forgot anything. When he went on "a toot" he would remember all his grievances—who owed him money, who had failed to give him a drink, and so on. If somebody had clamped a pair of electrodes on his head and sent shocking currents of electricity through his brain, he would have mentioned it, and he never did.) Joan would say the same thing, adding that she was seeing Faulkner often at that time, and that she would have known if a series of such procedures had been performed. What was certain was Faulkner's outrage at the bill.

By early December he was staying at the New Weston, and sometimes when Saxe Commins appeared in the morning to open the doors at Random House, Faulkner would be there in the courtyard waiting for him. In Commins' small office he would begin typing, using his two index fingers steadily as the morning wore on. From time to time he would put his hands on his hips and, gritting his teeth, slowly straighten his back. In his narrative he was moving from the corporal and his squad of twelve to his followers waiting outside the prison. He was shifting from the doomed men to the power and authority that doomed them, represented in the Old Generalissimo, who would prove to be the corporal's father. The great stallion of *Notes on a Horsethief* and the men who served him had long since been further integrated into the sprawling narrative.

As the holidays approached, his mood was anything but joyous. His leave-taking in New York was grim, with Joan suffering from depression and with emotional distance between them once again. At home he did his shopping, checked things out at the farm, and spent time with Jill and Dean and Vicki. When he tried to work, he soon encountered the problems he had fled seven weeks before. "The initial momentum ran out," he wrote Commins, "and it is getting more and more difficult, a matter of deliberate will power, concentration, which can be deadly after a while."[16] He told Joan that it was not going as it should, "in a fine ecstatic rush" like an orgasm, but "by simple will power; I doubt if I can keep it up too long."[17] Nearly a week later, however, he was feeling much better. "Work is going damned well," he reported. "Am doing new stuff now: it is all right. I still have power and fire when I need it, thank God, who is good to me, lets me be able to write still and to be in love. . . ."[18]

He was not able to leave Rowan Oak for New York when he had hoped. Estelle had been suffering from cataracts for about a year, and she had finally decided to go ahead with the operations, the first on January 14 and the second a week later. He did his tax work and arranged matters at the farm, where the registered herd would go to Jimmy Faulkner's small farm. He was thinking in terms of his total financial situation, even considering the sale of his manuscripts once again and making provision for Jill even after she attained her majority. Hal Smith was to act for him if an attractive prospect appeared.

He left for New York on January 31, to occupy Smith's apartment until Smith returned from Bermuda and then to rent something in Manhattan or Princeton. He would be away for six months, perhaps longer. Apart from the enforced stays in Hollywood, this was the longest time he had planned away from home since Phil Stone had accompanied him to New Orleans in those distant days when he dreamed of making his reputation from Europe. Now he had the reputation without the resiliency and the capacity for hope. He felt a sense of release at his departure, but he was still in pain, and he knew that uncertain times, probably difficult times, lay ahead.

60

—the surrender, the relinquishment to and into the opium of
escaping, knowing in advance the inevitable tomorrow's inevitable physical agony; to have lost nothing of anguish but
instead only to have gained it; to have merely compounded
yesterday's spirit's and soul's laceration with tomorrow's hangover—

"Mr. Acarius," *USWF* (437)

WHEN Faulkner installed himself in Smith's third-floor apartment at 9
East 63rd Street, his visit seemed to begin well enough. He was grateful
to Smith but glad of his absence, for Smith was by now a crotchety old
man, by turns cordial and cold. Faulkner took Joan to the theatre and
seemed to enjoy it, though he dozed off before the final curtain. He had
been sleeping no better than usual, and not long afterward, as the back
pain grew worse, he turned to Smith's sideboard for an antidote. He
thought he found it in a bottle of forty-year-old applejack.

It was the start of another siege of intermittent but prolonged and
debilitating illness. When Joan and Bob Linscott discovered he was in
trouble, they sent for Ben Gilbert. "Dr. Broadway" had seen Faulkner
on his return from Norway, and their mutual liking had been immediate.
A man of enormous energy and zest, he was responsible with his staff
of doctors for a group of hotels and most of New York's major theatres.
He examined Faulkner, prescribed for him, and arranged for a nurse.
From time to time friends assisted. Albert Erskine went up to the apartment and couldn't help noticing that Faulkner was not too sick to take
an intense interest in the attractive nurse supervising his recovery.

It progressed well enough for him to accompany Saxe Commins to
the National Book Awards ceremony on February 7. With five hundred
other writers, critics, and publishers, he heard Ralph Ellison, Bernard

DeVoto, and Archibald MacLeish receive their awards. After a talk by Supreme Court Justice William O. Douglas, a noisy cocktail party began. *The New Yorker* reported that "the lion of the afternoon was . . . William Faulkner, who, very small and very handsome, with a voice that never rose above a whisper, stood with his back to the wall and gamely took on all comers." Another observer reported that "it was hard to get a word with him, so closely packed around him were his admirers. His famed reticence and dislike of publicity were much in evidence, as were his dignity, poise and shy friendliness."[1] Back at Smith's place, he continued drinking. The next day he was frightened. He had experienced another of what he would call "spells of complete forgetting." Joan and Linscott and Smith again called Ben Gilbert, who immediately made arrangements to hospitalize him.

They took him to the Charles B. Townes private hospital on Central Park West. Sick as he was, his remarkable memory was still operating, storing material away. He would recall the exterior and interior appearance, and the sensory details: "hearing the slow accumulation of the cloistral evening," seeing the pajama-clad men in the corridors. One would drift in and out of his room, sometimes during the night, singing to himself the same refrain: "Did you ever seen a dream walking?" Before long Faulkner was able to smile at the man's alcoholic nonchalance. In less than a week he got Commins to arrange for his discharge.

When he returned to the apartment, Smith slipped a note under the door of his room. It said he had behaved so badly that he would have to go elsewhere. The Haases took him in, and when Jill telephoned him there, he couldn't speak clearly or understand her. Bob Haas was concerned enough to make a doctor's appointment for him. His letters revealed his persistent worries and a theory he was developing. He told Else Jonsson "something is wrong with me; as you saw last spring, my nature has changed. I think now that when I fell off the horse last March, I may have struck my head too. I will know this week."[2] On the same day, February 22, 1953, he wrote the same thing to Monique and Jean-Jacques Salomon, in French, in a letter filled with nostalgia for happy times in Paris. Malcolm Franklin and his wife, Gloria, had called Commins about him. Faulkner explained his idea in a letter to them and told them he was glad they had called Saxe. "Remember," he wrote, "he will not lie to you about me. When anything serious happens, he will tell you." He told Meta Rebner that the injury would explain why he had repeated himself, as in letters to her. "I want to see you," he wrote, but he was working, earning money again for the first time in two years, and he felt he must stay in New York. But, he added, "I have not forgotten any of it, never will, never."[3]

On February 25 and March 2, Dr. Robert Hastings Melchionna performed a complete examination, which proved essentially normal. But because Faulkner described three episodes of blackout after heavy drinking that had been accompanied by retrograde amnesia, Melchionna ordered some special tests. Before they could be performed, however, Faulkner had to recuperate from another episode. Commins telephoned his wife and she met them at the door on a blustery March evening. Faulkner stood there, his hat in his hand, his handkerchief to his running nose. "Dorothy," he said, "I've misbehaved again." Saxe got him into bed and gave him an alcohol rubdown. Dorothy put him on aspirin dosage and left a jug of lemonade by his bed. Two days later he returned to New York.

As usual, it was too soon. Dr. Melchionna had him admitted to Doctors Hospital, where a colleague arranged for a series of tests. He was S. Bernard Wortis, professor and chairman of the department of psychiatry and neurology of the New York University medical school. When they read the x-rays, the skull was normal and there was nothing new in the spine. The liver function tests were normal. The spiky lines of the electroencephalogram showed some hypersensitivity in the brain waves but no indication of organic illness. After nearly a week they discharged him. Dr. Wortis felt that it was time to shift from the physical to the psychological.

On March 31, Faulkner went to the doctor's office for the initial visit. A tall, balding, imposing man, Wortis reviewed the medical findings and then began to try to draw his patient out. Faulkner seemed to talk easily, but when Wortis began to probe, on the theory that he might not have received enough love from his mother, Faulkner refused to talk. In spite of Faulkner's long-standing distrust of physicians in general and psychiatrists in particular, Wortis formed some strong impressions as the sessions went on. He felt that Faulkner had such an intense emotional responsiveness, such receptiveness for others and their problems, that life must be very painful for him. Obviously, his alcoholism was a narcotizing device to make it almost bearable for him. He was a man with a strong need for affection, one who hoped for some sort of emotional equilibrium but was uncertain of finding it. He was a man built to suffer, thought Wortis, to be unhappy and to make his contribution partly because of this. Faulkner gave his version of the first session to Else. "The tests show that a lobe or part of my brain is hypersensitive to intoxication." It was not just alcohol but also "worry, unhappiness, any form of mental unease, which produces less resistance to the alcohol."[4] Faulkner's brain was near the borderline of abnormality, the doctor had said, and if he himself had received such a report, he would stop drinking for three or four months and then have another test. Faulkner had a different reaction when the bill came: $450 for nine visits. "I remember only 3," Faulkner wrote Joan, "two of which I called at his office by his request, not mine. He is a psychiatrist; in my experience, psychiatrists will do anything. Stay with Melchionna, who is a simple doctor. He gave me a complete physical overhaul, charged $85 against Wortis's $450, out of which I got one bottle of Seconal capsules."

In spite of his troubles, Faulkner had done a considerable amount of work—at the Algonquin after leaving the Haases', then sometimes at Random House and sometimes at the Greenwich Village apartment he had sublet from writer Waldo Frank at 44 West 16th Street. His experience at the Townes hospital had produced a story called "Weekend Revisited"—a title that may have owed something to a novel he carried away with him from Malcolm Cowley's home after his recuperation four years earlier, Charles Jackson's *The Lost Weekend*. Faulkner's protagonist, Mr. Acarius, is a prosperous man beset with a sense of both an undistinguished life and impending nuclear doom. He makes his hospital arrangements and then deliberately drinks himself into it. It is a kind of Dostoevskian quest, in the hope of linking himself with other suffering men and coming to terms with the intolerable human condition. Instead, he meets in the hospital both farce and despair. *The New Yorker* refused the story and so did two other magazines.

He had better fortune with an essay on Sherwood Anderson, first intended as a foreword to a volume of his correspondence but sold instead by Ober to the *Atlantic* for $300 for June publication. Though clear about Anderson's limitations, it was a mellow, affectionate piece, with the acknowledgment that he had been "a giant in an earth populated to a great—too-great—extent by pygmies, even if he did make but the two or perhaps three gestures commensurate with gianthood."[5]

He wrote another, longer, retrospective piece that March. It was the one *Holiday* magazine had asked for through Ober. At the beginning he did in five-page capsule form what he had done in the prologues of *Requiem for a Nun*: he set forth the history of his land. Then he wrote in terms of his own childhood. He used the third person, however, rather than the first. Uncle Ned and Mammy were there, under their own names, but he was "the boy." He had described this kind of writing to Haas, actual happenings "improved" where fiction would help. (When Estelle would read a copy a year later, one month before *Holiday* published it in their April 1954 number, she would write Saxe that it "explains the two Bills—He is so definitely dual I think—Perhaps artists must needs be—."[6]) Mammy took on characteristics of Mollie Beauchamp, and the boy played games young Bayard Sartoris had played at the beginning of *The Unvanquished*. He borrowed from his own young manhood in Pascagoula and New Orleans. There was humor in the description of Art Guyton's launching of his sailboat, but the mood quickly turned elegiac with Mammy's decline and death. Mississippi was "his native land; he was born of it and his bones will sleep in it; loving it even while hating some of it. . . ."[7] On March 25 he took his typescript to Ober, 3,000 words longer than the editors of *Holiday* had expected.

"Am writing television scripts now," he told Else on March 31, "to have money to go somewhere and get at my own novel again."[8] He had done a script of "The Brooch" for the *Lux Video Theatre* and now he was doing one of "Shall Not Perish." For the William Morris agency he wrote a 26-page synopsis of "Old Man"—with a happy ending. The money was welcome, but his spirits began to dip still further, as they used to do in Hollywood.

On Saturday afternoon, April 18, Malcolm telephoned: Estelle had suffered a hemorrhage. They could not yet tell if it was the stomach or the esophagus. By midnight Jill had come down to the city from Welles-ley, and by six o'clock they were on the plane for Memphis. Estelle nearly succumbed to a second attack, and it took nine blood transfusions before she could return home from the Oxford Hospital. Faulkner thought it likely that the cause was impaired liver function because of drinking, but tests in early May were inconclusive. If it was an ulcer, it had by now healed, and with normal precautions, she should continue to recover.

During these weeks at home he wrote impassioned letters to Joan, looking forward to the time when he could fly north. But there at his desk he worked on the book too. It was going well, but at the same time he was able to step back from his immersion in it. He wrote, "I know now—believe now—that this may be the last major, ambitious work; there will be short things, of course. I know now that I am getting toward the end, the bottom of the barrel. The stuff is still good, but I know now there is not very much more of it, a little trash comes up constantly now, which must be sifted out. And now, at last, I have some perspective on all I have done. I mean, the work apart from me, the work which I did, apart from what I am. . . . And now I realise for the first time what an amazing gift I had: uneducated in every formal sense, without even very literate, let alone literary, companions, yet to have made the things I made. I dont know where it came from. I dont know why God or gods or whoever it was, selected me to be the vessel. Believe me, this is not humility, false modesty: it is simply amazement. I wonder if you have ever had that thought about the work and the country man whom you know as Bill Faulkner—what little connection there seems to be between them."[9]

But their relationship was still not what he hoped it would be. If it had grown more intense, it had also grown more complex and troubled. In earlier letters he had quoted to her the lines he had quoted years before to Helen Baird, the love words of Cyrano de Bergerac to Roxanne. He wrote his paraphrase in French to Joan: "*ton nom c'est comme une petit sonnette d'or / Pendant dans mon coeur. . . .*" And he had given her a little bell to wear on a chain over her heart. One of his favorite poems, one which echoed in his work as much as any other single one, was Keats's

"Ode on a Grecian Urn." He could not but have thought of it, especially during the first three years of frustrated ardor,

> Bold lover, never, never canst thou kiss,
> Though winning near the goal—yet, do not grieve;
> She cannot fade, though thou hast not thy bliss,
> Forever wilt thou love, and she be fair!

Finally there had been the bliss he had pursued, but now he sought again, unsuccessfully, the full, constant, passionate, physical relationship he craved. She was passionately pursuing the dream that had first brought her to his door, the dream of being a writer, which he had sought to help her fulfill. It had been a relationship in which literature and love had been inextricably mixed. He had urged her to write about themselves, to use their relationship as the basis for a story and for a novel. If either were to be based on the way they were now, in his eyes, it would be a sad tale. For now his portion was "crumbs and subterfuge." His reproach spoke to both tangled aspects of their relationship and their fictional projections: "without practising truth always you cannot write truth about Laurel and Almoner. . . ." He took her to see Victor Moore in a revival of *On Borrowed Time* and enjoyed it, though the growing distance between them probably gave the title a double meaning for him. Before the month was out he returned to Oxford. Writing Joan on June 1 at her Horatio Street address in New York, he began, "I dont know where you are." It was a short letter with no note of expectation or of hope.

A few days later he and Estelle left Oxford for Pine Manor, where he was to deliver the principal address at Jill's graduation. Picking up the theme of her high-school commencement speech, he said that the young people could work toward God's intention: to prove man's immortality and presumably complete the divine plan on earth "by means of free will and the capacity for decision. . . ." On this first level it was rather like an old-fashioned sermon, full of noble sentiments and general exhortations to virtue. On the private level it touched both personal and artistic concerns. Acting virtuously began at home, he said. "It means someone to offer the love and fidelity and respect to who is worthy of it, someone to be compatible with, whose dreams and hopes are your dreams and hopes. . . ." The artistic concern was reflected particularly in one thing he said about God's plan, the way he used even "the splendid dark incorrigible one, who possessed the arrogance and pride to demand with, and the temerity to object with, and the ambition to substitute with. . . ." It would remind men "that we are capable of revolt and change."[10] The "splendid dark incorrigible" angel he talked about was the same archetypal figure on which he was basing one of the main characters of the fable: the Generalissimo.

Back home in mid-June, he tried to make contact with Joan, and something like the tone of exhortation in the graduation speech came through in the letters. He told her not to be afraid and to learn to accept help. "I learned to write from other writers," he said. "Why should you refuse to?" He mentioned an idea they had discussed earlier, a writers' group, with himself as leader. "Will write more about the colony," he told her. "I could not do justice to a group which trusted me, and do my own work too. . . . If I stay with big book, the group will have to wait until next year, when I am free. But not you. We can, must meet again."[11] She sent him a story she was working on, and he sent it back with criticism, advice, and encouragement.

HE was set now for a solid ten-week pull with the fable. Through June and into the broiling weeks of July he would go into the office each morning while Estelle put up jellies, jams, and preserves, and Jill worked with the horses. At first it was discouraging. "The expected happened," he wrote Joan, "it ran dry after about two days, I was miserable, kept at it, the stuff was no good, I would destroy it every night and still try again tomorrow, very bad two weeks. . . ."[12] By the middle of July, however, it was "going beautifully." But he was ready to pack it up, to take it with him and work on it elsewhere if she would give the word—to Paris, where Hawks was talking of making a film, to Linscott's New England farm, to Mexico. He even had the car overhauled and two tires recapped, but the word did not come, and he remained in Oxford.

On August 4 he finished what he called the "Three Temptations Scene." He had already made clear the Christian analogues in the life of Stefan, the corporal: his ministering sisters, Mary and Martha; the men of his squad—Pierre, Paul, Jean, and the other nine; his illegitimate sonship to the supreme commander of all the Allied armies. He was now nearing the heart of this book which one writer would see as a study of "the nature and meaning of sacrifice."[13] Attempting to seduce the corporal from his sacrificial role, the Generalissimo offers him his life, his freedom, and finally the earth. Once the corporal withstands the temptation, the two are finally able to achieve partial agreement. In a passage full of echoes of the Nobel Prize speech, the Generalissimo affirms man's immortality even after "the last ding dong of doom. . . ." (354) When the corporal asserts that man will endure, his father declares that man will prevail. After the Transfiguration, Faulkner pressed on toward Crucifixion, Death, and Resurrection. With something like excitement, he told Commins he was nearing the end. "It is either nothing and I am blind in my dotage, or it is the best of my time. Damn it, I did have genius, Saxe. It just took me 55 years to find it out."[14]

He drove ahead through the shimmering heat of August. There was an outing on the *Minmagary*, visits from relatives and from friends of Jill, as in other summers. But then there came a change that would make this a different summer. Estelle thought he seemed frightfully unhappy at Rowan Oak, and she was increasingly embarrassed by his love affair. Jill had studied English and Spanish in summer school at Ole Miss, and now she wanted to attend the University of Mexico during the fall semester. Estelle would go along and play duenna and escape some of the unhappiness at Rowan Oak. Faulkner wrote Commins to send the money from his account, and on August 25, Jill and Estelle departed.

He worked on in the big house, alone but for the servants. He had looked forward to being free, but once again he was disappointed. He had seen Joan from time to time in Memphis or Holly Springs, but the trip he had hoped for had not materialized, and she had gone to Florida. She returned in early September, but when she failed to set a time to meet, he wrote her, "One of the nicest conveniences a woman can have is someone she can pick up when she needs or wants him; then when she doesn't, she can drop him and know that he will still be right there when she does need or want him again." Sometime, he warned her, he might break or not be there. Someone he had counted on was, in a sense, not there. A few days earlier Saxe Commins had suffered a heart attack. GLAD TO HEAR IT, Faulkner wired. BEGGED YOU LAST SPRING TO REST AND THE JOINT EXPLODE. MAYBE YOU WILL NOW. LOVE TO DOROTHY.[15]

THE book was almost finished, and now he had no one to show it to. He decided to visit Ben Wasson, so he put the manuscript in a big old cowhide briefcase, strapped it up, and got his outdoors man, Andrew Price, to drive him to Greenville. "When you finish a book you want to tell someone about it," he told Ben and his friends Bern Keating and his wife, Frankie. Ben was glad to see him, and he seemed so affable that the Keatings invited him to stay with them for a few days. They did not know him well enough to understand this near-euphoria. Faulkner was comfortable with Keating, an articulate writer-photographer, originally a Canadian and a Francophile like himself. Faulkner accepted his invitation to go with them to a party at the country club. It seemed to fit his mood, and on the way he chatted amiably. When they entered through a ballroom, it seemed to Keating that the teenage dance in progress suddenly stopped while everyone watched the small gray-haired man in the old-fashioned white pongee suit with the rosette in the buttonhole and the white handkerchief in the sleeve. Later, the party continued at Keating's house. Hand on his bulging briefcase, Faulkner declared, "This contains the manuscript of the book that is possibly the greatest of our time." When the guests showed eager interest, he took out the 700-odd pages, many of them typed on the backs of sheets from earlier versions. It was late when they retired. The next morning Faulkner appeared with a gash over his eye. Looking for the bathroom during the night, he had missed his footing in the unfamiliar hallway. Later in the day he began to talk about going to the Gulf Coast. Aware of the possible complications of such a trip, Ben and the Keatings decided to drive him to Oxford. He departed for home reluctantly, leaving his bloodstained tie behind and clutching the briefcase under his arm. He slept in the back seat of the car, rousing from time to time as he had done on the trip from New York to the Cowleys' home five years before.[16]

This time he demonstrated his remarkable recuperative powers in a shorter period, and by the time they reached Rowan Oak in the late afternoon, he was able to rouse himself and become the genial host, supervising the cooking of the steaks, mixing the salad himself, and—to Ben's amusement—taking pains about the temperature of the low-priced California wine. On the walls of Faulkner's office Keating saw the outline he had made of the Corporal's Passion week. Under Thursday he saw "The Last Supper," under Friday, his execution, under Saturday, his burial by Mary, Martha, and Magdalen. Faulkner agreed to some pictures, and the next day before they left Keating set up his Rolleiflex. Bouncing a strobe light off the white ceiling onto the white walls, he photographed Faulkner's carefully lettered legend. Some sheets of manuscripts keyed to it were still on the floor. Ben wisely took the precaution of calling Malcolm and Gloria before they left for Greenville.

Although the manuscript was not actually completed, he was now in the trough of the emotional wave that had crested the night before. To add to his misery the back pain was becoming acute again. He put himself back on the alcohol and Seconal regimen. Malcolm and Gloria soon were caring for him with the unreliable aid of the servants. By September 8 it was clear that he needed medical help. With the aid of Jimmy Faulkner, just back from flying combat in Korea, they took him to Gartly-Ramsay. On this admission they found that his appetite was good and that he asked for paraldehyde, not only for his nerves but for help with the alcohol withdrawal. He could no longer taper off on beer and will power, as he had done at the Cowleys'. Besides the back pain, he had abdominal distress and tenderness in the area of the liver. As usual, forty-eight hours into recuperation after the acute phase had passed, he grew impatient. The staff tried to reason with him and telephoned to enlist the family's help, but by that time he had already left. His file now bore the notation: "An acute and chronic alcoholic."

He had told Else Jonsson that Dr. Wortis had said his brain was hypersensitive to intoxication, and that his resistance to alcohol was lessened by "worry, unhappiness, and any form of mental unease." He was home in time to undergo in the most intense and massive form one of the things he dreaded most: invasion of privacy. On September 28, *Life* published the first part of Robert Coughlan's long essay, entitled "The Private World of William Faulkner." Coughlan had actually written out of admiration for the work, but several million people would read the abundant personal material too, material which the powerless subject would obviously detest. Coughlan had actually de-emphasized some of the comments he had received, including a harsh and extended critique of the man and the work from Phil Stone. Though there were numerous errors, Coughlan had tried to exercise care in his research, and as for the writing, his description of the man himself was the best ever written. That counted for little with Maud Falkner, whose photograph had been used without her permission. Irate, she canceled her subscription. As for her son, the knowledge that several million people were now privy to much of his life doubtless helped to lodge him once more in Wright's Sanitarium, the small private hospital at Byhalia, fifty miles north of Oxford. "The Man Behind the Faulkner Myth" concluded the essay in the issue for October 5, bringing his life and work up to the present.

He emerged from Wright's in time to reply to Phil Mullen's anxious disclaimer of responsibility. "I tried for years to prevent it," he wrote, "refused always, asked them to let me alone. It's too bad the individual in this country has no protection from journalism, I suppose they call it. But apparently he hasn't. There seems to be in this the same spirit which permits strangers to drive into my yard and pick up books or pipes I left in the chair where I had been sitting, as souvenirs." He had not actually read either article, but he did not need to. "What a commentary. Sweden gave me the Nobel Prize. France gave me the Legion d'Honneur. All my native land did for me was to invade my privacy over my protest and my plea. No wonder people in the rest of the world dont like us, since we seem to have neither taste nor courtesy, and know and believe in nothing but money and it doesn't much matter how you get it."[17]

HE must have felt that the only good thing that had happened to him, apart from his progress with the fable, was that Joan had drawn closer to him again. In mid-October they set out for New York together, but he was still so weak that she had to do all the driving the first day. The next day he was able to help, and when they reached the city, he was considerably better. After staying briefly with Bob Linscott in his 63rd Street apartment, he took a suite at Number One Fifth Avenue, off Washington Square, where Joan would sometimes work in the mornings. In spite of what he had told Wasson and the Keatings in Greenville, he had not finished his work, and he continued doggedly through October. When gossip columnist Earl Wilson interviewed him, he said he was now finishing a novel portraying Christ as a corporal in a famous French mutiny. It would be called *A Fable*, he said.

He did not lack for company. Jim Devine was married now, and his wife, Rita, had him to dinner. He would dine with Ruth Ford. He lunched with Budd Schulberg and argued amiably over books. He criticized *The Grapes of Wrath*, implicitly associating Schulberg with what he took to be Steinbeck's attitudes. At another lunch they disagreed amicably over Scott Fitzgerald. Schulberg greatly admired *Tender Is the Night,* but Faulkner thought Budd's own *roman à clef* about Fitz-gerald, *The Disenchanted,* was better. One night after dinner at the Klopfers', Irwin Shaw sat on the floor near Faulkner's chair listening carefully to Faulkner's soft speech, sensing a combination of "pride, watchfulness and silent privacy." Shaw recalled times when he had been so outraged with the final mishmash of films he'd worked on that he hated seeing his name on the screen credits. He wondered if Faulkner hadn't felt the same. "Son," Faulkner said, "in those days they didn't want my name on pictures."

One weekend he spent on Linscott's spartan farm near Williamsburg in the Berkshires of western Massachusetts. He was now close to this tall, humorous, craggy-faced New Englander, a widower nearly a dozen years older than himself. Linscott enjoyed his guest's pleasure at watch-ing beavers at work. Faulkner revealed himself in a different way when he ran his finger slowly along a row of his books on Linscott's shelf. "Not a bad monument for a man to leave behind him," he said. He even agreed to Linscott's setting up a luncheon with Robert Coughlan, who was a good guy, Linscott said, and who wanted to correct any errors he had made in the *Life* pieces, particularly since he was adding to the articles to publish them in book form. The meeting was friendly but ultimately inconclusive. When Coughlan asked if Faulkner would read the manu-script, he rather noncommittally agreed. Coughlan sent him a copy, but heard no more from him.

THE psychic energy he commanded was still going in the same directions as he worked at Random House into early November. He had received a letter from Meta, out of work and with no new film job in sight, ask-ing for a loan to tide her over. He had wired her the $150 she asked for. When she sent him half of it in repayment, he tore up the check and told her, "You can't possibly owe me anything like money. I remember too much." He also told her what he was doing: "Am just finishing what I think is the best work of my life and maybe of my time, a book, novel, fable."[18] If the achievement should fall short of this estimate, it would not be for lack of grandeur of conception. To one scholar, he had cre-ated, "a myth, an allegory, a sacred drama where the natural and super-natural fuse into an incarnational humanity replete with tensions, conflicts, and pressures."[19] One of his main modes of revision had always been to shift passages about, rewriting up to them or from them where necessary for continuity. This manuscript was so big, however, that he needed Commins' help, and by early November he was in Princeton. Commins was daunted, even though they had the outline from the walls of Faulk-ner's office at Rowan Oak, as well as a little calendar he had made of the month of May 1918. Once when Joan came down, there were pages spread out over desk, chair, and bed, and she tried to help sort them out by page and number. By November 4 he was able to cancel headings such as "May 4, 1918" and to leave instead only the legend "Tuesday Night." Finally he took his pen and at the bottom of page 654 he wrote "December 1944 Oxford, New York Princeton November 1953."

Working steadily all day and into the evening, they began to shift from text to makeup. The segments were to be divided by simple, nondenominational wooden crosses. There would be a single one on the dust jacket, which was to bear no note on the author. The color was to range from dark blue at the bottom to almost the color of a clear sky at the top. Now, as the sky outside paled and then brightened with the dawn, Commins typed up the notes about composition in a letter to Don Klopfer. The dedication would read simply "To my daughter, Jill." In it was the tone of parting which had sounded so often in the past two years. She would be twenty-one by the time the book appeared. "It was," he would later say, "just a way of saying, 'Good-bye to your childhood, you are grown now and you are on your own.' "[20] He looked at her now not just with love and pride but also with confidence. He told Jimmy Faulkner, "The Oldhams are very unstable people. I've been watching Jill carefully for a long time now, and she hasn't got any of the Oldham characteristics." Faulkner took Commins' letter and the manuscript with him to New York and, a decade after he had begun it, delivered it to Donald Klopfer at Random House.

As he finished this book, his psyche skipped the euphoria and went straight into the letdown. In the short Foreword to a collection Random House was bringing out as *The Faulkner Reader*, he wrote about reading in childhood Henryk Sienkiewicz's pronouncement that one wrote "to uplift man's heart" and "say No to death." He went on, "Some day he will be no more, which will not matter then, because isolated and itself invulnerable in the cold print remains that which is capable of engendering still the old deathless excitement in hearts and glands whose owners and custodians are generations from even the air he breathed and anguished in; if it was capable once, he knows that it will be capable and potent still long after there remains of him only a dead and fading name."[21] One evening at Joan's Horatio Street apartment he began to write from memory Housman's poem XLVIII from *A Shropshire Lad*. He did not write down the third quatrain, which Mr. Compson had paraphrased twenty-five years before to his son, but he reproduced the fourth in nearly perfect form:

> Look, earth and high heaven ail from the prime foundation
> All thoughts to rive the heart are here, and all are vain:
> Horror and scorn and hate and fear and indignation
> Why did I awake? When shall I sleep again?

One night when they were having dinner at The Colony, Dylan Thomas came to their table. They had spent part of an evening together in the spring, when Faulkner had been moved by Thomas' reading of his verse, and the two had gotten on well together afterward. They talked briefly and then Thomas left. On November 10 he was dead, of pneumonia brought on, said the doctor, by acute alcoholic "insult to the brain." They ought to go to Thomas' funeral, he told Joan, as a gesture of respect from one writer to another; Thomas would want them to do this. But they did not attend any memorial service.

Now he was seeing less and less of Joan. He did take her to see Arlene Dahl and José Ferrer in *Cyrano de Bergerac*. More than ever he must have empathized with the unsuccessful lover who was a master at words. And when Cyrano told Roxanne that her name was like a golden bell hung in his heart, it must have sounded like a knell in Faulkner's own. Now, as more and more she turned from him, he wrote that it was too painful; it would be better if they did not see each other. He still worried though, he said, about where she would turn when she needed him and he was gone. He had spoken to Linscott, and if she needed anything, she was to turn to him and he would help her.

He was thinking now of a literal as well as a metaphorical departure. Hawks's plans for a film in Paris had fallen through, but just before Faulkner had made his trip to Greenville, Hawks had called to say he had sold Jack Warner on the idea of a film to be called *Land of the Pharaohs*. From New York, Faulkner had agreed to work on the script with Hawks in Europe for two months beginning in December. He had told Klopfer and Linscott that he did not want to go, but he had to. "Hawks asked me," he said. "He's done me favors in the past, and I can't let him down now." He did not want to go to Europe and Africa. He did not want to return to Mississippi. He did not particularly want to stay in New York.

In the unsettling time of waiting for departure, he went to Princeton. At a party at the Comminses' the guests included Albert Einstein. The benign physicist found the novelist no more loquacious than had Bertrand Russell. He tried to find something they had in common to talk about. "You know," he finally said, "when I went to get the Nobel Prize, I arrived a day late." Faulkner would tell Commins he liked Einstein, finding him a truly gentle man, but he sat there, pipe in hand, saying little.

Though he had found it too painful to see Joan again, they were still in touch. She had finally told him that the physical differences due to their ages were too great. And he inferred that she had found a young man who might be the one she had been waiting for. But even in this kind of pain, he could not bear to think of her regretting what had been. "You did something fine and brave and generous, and the gods will love you for it. You'll see in time. Dont regret and grieve." But he was far from that kind of acceptance himself. A few days later, when he wrote that he was canceling two tentative engagements they had, there was a burst of recrimination. "You take too much, and are willing to give too little. . . . People have attributes like animals; you are a mixture of cat and mule and possum—the cat's secretiveness and self-centeredness, the mule's stubbornness to get what it wants no matter who or what suffers, the possum's nature of playing dead—running into sleep or its pretence—whenever it is faced with a situation which it thinks it is not going to like." But he still worried about what would happen to her, living among young people who only "go through the motions of art—talking about what they are going to do over drinks, even defacing paper and canvas when necessary, in order to escape the responsibility of living." In the letters he poured out to her he went through swings of mood and vacillating intention. He went from depression to denial and anger and then to the stirrings of hope. By turns he said he could see her again only on his terms, or that he would see her again on other terms when he felt he could bear it. He wrote that he had heard that Don Klopfer planned a farewell champagne lunch. Would she like to come to it? But there was some misunderstanding, for no such gathering had been planned, and this seeming opportunity he had clutched at now vanished.

Hawks had been sending him advance information about the Nile delta and the pyramids. All he had at this stage, Hawks would later remember, was the idea of the tombs and his Nobel Prize winner. Faulkner faithfully prepared to join him. Bob Linscott and his friend Elisabeth Shoemaker waited with him for boarding time on Monday night, November 30. He had expected others, but no one joined them. They watched as he walked to the plane—deliberate, small, and very much alone.

The aircraft cleared Idlewild, climbed to altitude, and turned on course high above the dark Atlantic. He had told Loïc Bouvard that he loved France and the French very much. But before he could try to recapture something of the past there, he had to spend time working with Hawks in Switzerland. He had talked about "breaking the pencil" when he felt he had said it all, perhaps after he had finished the big book which carried so many of his hopes. He must have wondered that night, looking at the blinking wing-lights beyond the droning engines, if that time had come. He had traveled at other times after finishing a book, but his travels now would be exhausting as he crisscrossed from one place to another, seeking escape more than discovery.

It is just dawn, daylight: that gray and lonely suspension filled with the peaceful and tentative waking of birds. The air, in-breathed, is like spring water. He breathes deep and slow, feeling with each breath himself diffuse in the neutral grayness, becoming one with loneliness and quiet that has never known fury or despair. 'That was all I wanted,' he thinks, in a quiet and slow amazement. 'That was all, for thirty years. That didn't seem to be a whole lot to ask in thirty years.'

—*Light in August* (313)

WHEN the New York plane arrived at Orly on December 1, Faulkner was not on it. Hawks and Harry Kurnitz, whom he had hired as a kind of backup scriptwriter, returned to the hotel. Their wait stretched into the next day. Finally, there was a knock at the door. Hawks opened it to find two gendarmes supporting his missing scenarist. They had found him in Montmartre with a nasty gash in his scalp. About to send him where any bibulous Parisian would await the judge, they noticed the Legion of Honor rosette in his buttonhole. After checking his passport they took him to a café for hot coffee. He had then been able to say, "Hawks—Plaza." The director thanked the policemen and helped Faulkner into bed.

The next day they started their journey south, and on December 4, crossed into Switzerland. They continued on through the Alps and into Italy until the blue outline of Lake Maggiore came into view. At Stresa they settled in for a two-week stay in a villa overlooking the lake. As Faulkner gradually pulled himself together, they began to fill in the story outline, sketching the characters of King Cheops, his queen, and the high priest. Kurnitz was a twenty-five-year veteran of the screenwriting craft. Tall, bespectacled, and curly-haired, he was a sensitive and amiable man. He would go on long walks with Faulkner past the summer villas of

Italian nobles, the tall pines dark green among the bare trees in the pale winter sunlight. A week after their arrival Faulkner was feeling optimistic. "Hawks has given me a share in this picture," he wrote Joan, "it will mean about $60,000. Also a share in two more to be made in Egypt— Solomon, and the Biblical story of Ruth. It looks like I will be rich at last."

If he was enthusiastic about the money, he was half-hearted about the project. Kurnitz found that gradually more and more of the work was falling to him, but he had long been a Faulkner admirer and collector, and he was glad to serve as workhorse in this collaboration. The story conferences with Hawks tended to be uncertain and tentative. For one thing, none of them had any idea how Pharaohs talked. Hawks could foresee Faulkner using Southern dialect, Kurnitz trying Shakespearean English, and himself having to try to make it colloquial.

By the time they left the stately lakeside quiet of Stresa for the expensive glitter of mountainous St. Moritz, Faulkner's depression had deepened. It was December 19 when they registered at the elegant Suvretta House in the clear cold air of the capital of Swiss winter sports. As Faulkner wrote to Joan that night the letters were sometimes shaky and indistinct, but the emotions were clear. "I am very happy to know that you are working," he told her, "and that you know that nothing basic has changed with us. It never will. . . . I believe you know that until I die, I will be the best friend you ever had."

As they entered Christmas week he tried to make the best of things. One of his first acts, Kurnitz remembered, was to commandeer a whole bin of thirty-six bottles of Montrachet. Each day at lunch with Kurnitz he would drink half a bottle, having begun the meal with an appetizer of two martinis. Though he left the winter sports to Hawks and his glamorous wife, Slim, one day he unaccountably bought a pair of ski boots, which he charged to Warner Brothers. (Retrospectively embarrassed, he would later refuse to discuss them with his family.)

Agent Charlie Feldman and his wife, Jean, were a part of the lively set that gathered around Hawks and Slim. At their Christmas Eve party, Feldman introduced Faulkner to Jean Stein, a striking, fine-featured nineteen-year-old with dark hair and eyes. Admiring his work enormously, she had asked Jean Feldman particularly to invite Faulkner to the party. Now, shy and almost breathless, she sat there looking at William Faulkner. Gentle with the young as usual, he began to draw her out, and soon she was talking rapidly. He became bored with the party and invited her to go to Midnight Mass. Afterward he saw her back to the Palace Hotel, and in the quiet of the early Christmas morning he walked back to the Suvretta House alone.

He hated the idea of spending the Christmas holiday among wealthy American tourists, so on the twenty-sixth he flew to Stockholm to spend some of it with Else Jonsson. He began to drink less, and he went to a masseur, who relieved him of the nagging pain in his back. "Stockholm Xmas was pleasant," he later reported to Joan. "I tried to stay obscure, in a small hotel, but in two days reporters with cameras followed me, and every morning there would be gangs of schoolchildren, and older people in the snow at the hotel door, asking for autographs." He also reported on Christmas Eve: "A curious thing happened, almost repetition, her name is even Jean. She is 19." He saw the new year in there in Stockholm. Then he flew to England for a visit with the Raymonds at Biddenden, in Kent. On January 6 he was back at the Suvretta House.

With the first draft of the script on its way to completion, it was time for Hawks to do his casting in Rome. Faulkner wired Monique and Jean-Jacques Salomon that he was coming and flew to Paris. Jean Stein was there, living with her uncle David in his house off the Étoile while she studied at the Sorbonne. When she joined Faulkner's group she could see that his young French friends idolized him. But it had to be a short stay, and on January 19 he boarded still another airplane and flew to Rome.

He registered at the Palazzo & Ambasciatori on the noisy and fashionable Via Veneto. He and Kurnitz went out together, stopping at the Excelsior to pick up Humphrey Bogart. Later they joined Lauren Bacall for drinks, and Faulkner seemed glad to see her. She asked him what he wanted to do when the picture was finished. "I think I would like to drive through the Loire Valley," he answered slowly, "tasting the wine of the country." Sometimes she would see him sitting alone at a table in the bar at George's, and she would leave him to his privacy. One night at Ristorante Passetto, she said, "Bill, why do you drink?" Perhaps because he liked her he answered. "When I have one martini," he said, "I feel bigger, wiser, taller. When I have a second, I feel superlative. When I have more, there's no holding me." To Kurnitz it seemed that Faulkner was enjoying himself in Rome. His spirits rose further when Jean Stein joined the group there. "She is charming, delightful, completely transparent, completely trustful," he would later write Commins. "I will not hurt her for any price. She doesn't want anything of me—only to love me, be in love."[1]

In early February they were able to begin the second draft of the scenario. At a party, surrounded by people from the American Embassy and some of Rome's cultural leaders, he said that this was not his medium. He was just Hawks's "patcher-upper," but "a competent man can switch with outside help, as I do. It is like translating from another language—films are visual while the novel is for the ear." People who took picture money but constantly carped about Hollywood outraged him. "If they have that attitude they should stay away." He was glad when someone changed the subject. "I've fallen in love with Rome," he said. "I want to see much more of it."[2]

He was reluctant to leave for Cairo as Hawks prepared his company for departure on February 10. He had written Monique that he was working, but that his heart dreamed constantly of his children and he hoped always to return to France in April. He asked Hawks if he could go to Cairo by way of Paris, and Hawks reluctantly agreed. In the early hours of February 15, Hawks and Kurnitz waited apprehensively in the Egyptian darkness. Just as they began to hear the distant drone of the engines, an ambulance pulled up to the arrival gate. Kurnitz thought he saw Hawks suddenly blanch. After the other passengers deplaned, the two found that the ambulance stretcher was indeed for their compatriot. In the depths of his moroseness at leaving Paris, he had managed to dispose of a bottle and a half of brandy on his way to Cairo. They lodged him in the Anglo-American Hospital, and as soon as they could, they transferred him to the Mena House, a tourist hotel near the pyramids where the company was staying.

From New York, Saxe Commins tried to keep Faulkner's family apprised of his concern with the final completion of *A Fable*, Faulkner's health, and his movements. Estelle replied that his letter gave her pause: "I was just on the verge of writing Bill that I was suing for divorce— . . . Bill has been at home very little the past four years, and a good bit of that time spent here, has been a nightmare of drunkenness—He must be very unhappy—so the only cure I know of is to help him get free—legally—Heaven only knows he has been free in every other sense—." (A month later she would thank Commins for his advice, apparently having decided against divorce.)[3]

Meanwhile, at the Mena House, Faulkner was making a very slow recovery. One morning Hawks sat down by his bed and asked him how he was. "Howard," he answered huskily, "I just can't seem to shake this cold." When Kurnitz checked on him another morning at six, Faulkner invited him to share a liter of beer that stood on his table. "It's good for my cold," he explained.

Kurnitz had finished the second draft, but Faulkner intended to do his part of the rewriting. "Feeling pretty well—working," he told Commins in a shaky note in late February, adding, "Dont think much of Egypt." Working in his room each day, he would give his lined yellow legal-size pages to Kurnitz, but it was clear that he was far from top form. In one scene, tension began to build between Pharaoh and Hamar until the angry high priest dared to touch Pharaoh's sacred person. Drawing himself up to his full height, Pharaoh commanded imperially, "Leave go of my arm." The sympathetic and protective Kurnitz did not pass these pages on to Hawks. By mid-March, Faulkner was doing better. "Worked very hard all this past week," he wrote Jean Stein, "finished script again, for the second time, yesterday." Hawks might tear the script up again, "But just maybe, maybe, he wont, by March 23rd I may, just may, be done with it. . . ."[4]

* * *

MARCH was a month of endings and beginnings. Since September, Joan Williams had been seeing Ezra Bowen, a vigorous young war veteran and sometime professional athlete. The son of historian Katherine Drinker Bowen, he was also a writer. They were married on March 6. When Commins wrote to inform Faulkner, he replied that Joan had written him there that she intended to marry. "I was not free to marry her, even if I had not been too old," he told his editor. "So I knew. I want her happy. If she is, I am the best friend Bowen ever had."[5]

On March 22, Jill wrote that she planned to marry. In February she had met a young West Point graduate named Paul Dilwyn Summers, Jr. A survivor of the bitter fighting at Pork Chop Ridge in Korea, he was now a first lieutenant stationed at Fort Bragg. When he had first been told that Jill was the daughter of William Faulkner, he had asked, "Who's he?" Hearing this, Jill had responded, "He's for me." Paul paid a visit to Oxford, and before long a courtship had begun. Now Paul wanted her parents' consent, and Jill asked her father to come home as soon as he could. With Paul she felt she had both love and security. Life with him would be totally different from the one she had known.

Faulkner talked with Hawks. He could finish the sequences he was now working on and then head home by way of Paris, returning for further rewriting if necessary. By now he was more trouble to Hawks than he was worth, and so he was able to take the night flight from Cairo on March 29. He had his wish, to be back in Paris in the spring, but he was able to derive little pleasure from it. On April 5, Monique Salomon and Else Jonsson took him to the American Hospital of Paris. When they visited him the next day he said he would jump out the window if they didn't get him out of there. They capitulated. As they were preparing to leave, the doctor said, "Do you know what kind of responsibility you're taking on yourselves?" Faulkner told Monique and Else that if he were in Oxford, he would have someone drive him out into the country, and he would be sober by the time he walked home. Returning to the Hotel Beaujolais, he began to display again the unusual recuperative powers that had amazed Harry Kurnitz, and a week later he was able to turn to some work of his own.

A Fable had not been out of his mind. Bennett Cerf had raised a question about Faulkner's acknowledgment at the beginning that the basic idea belonged to William Bacher and Henry Hathaway. Cerf wanted a release from Bacher from his first claim on motion-picture rights, but Faulkner replied that rather than asking him for this, he would relinquish his own picture rights to Bacher. "I love the book," he had written Commins in early February, "gave ten good years of my life to it: if any part of it should taste like dust on the tongue, I had better never have done it."[6] In the end there was no problem. Cerf concluded that it was an unlikely movie prospect, and the acknowledgment stayed. On

April 12, three months after he had given the galleys a cursory reading, he cabled Commins: FORGOT JUDAS MISERY DESIRE REWRITE ONE SECTION PLAN ARRIVE 20 APRIL OR WILL CABLE TO SEND SECTION HERE.[7] The last scene was in his mind too. Twice he wandered near the Arc de Triomphe searching for the exact location he had had in mind when he had written it. The second time Jean Stein watched him as he made several photographs. A few days later, as though paying final homage, he went once more to Verdun with Monique and Jean-Jacques.

He was back in New York on the twentieth. It may have been now that he composed a preface, as though he feared the novel might be misunderstood. "This is not a pacifist book," the first of the two long paragraphs began. "In fact, if this book had any aim or moral . . . it was to show by poetic analogy, allegory, that pacifism does not work; that to put an end to war, man must either find or invent something more powerful than war and man's aptitude for belligerence and his thirst for power at any cost, or use the fire itself to fight and destroy the fire with. . . ." In the second paragraph he did something unusual for him: he provided a gloss on three of his characters who represented the "trinity of man's conscience—Levine, the young English pilot, who symbolizes the nihilistic third; the old French Quartermaster General, who symbolizes the passive third; the British battalion runner, who symbolizes the active third. . . ." This concern had been there all along, when he had explained the plot in Musso Frank's to other screenwriters ten years before, when he had told the story to Dot Oldham, when he had read parts of it and explained it to Estelle and Jill. At some point Commins had the preface mimeographed for distribution and even considered using it on the dust jacket. Finally, however, the craftsman won out over the moralist, and the preface went into Commins' files. Even after his return to Mississippi he would continue mulling over ways to clarify the novel, as he had tried to do with *Absalom, Absalom!* by appending the Chronology, Genealogy, and map of Yoknapatawpha County. He would take photographs of what he called the "cross file" of events on the walls of the office for possible use in the book, but that idea was also discarded.[8]

By the last days of April, Faulkner was back at Rowan Oak after an absence of six months. In almost exactly four months his daughter would be married, and two weeks before that, *A Fable* would appear.

May walks in this garden, fair
As a girl veiled in her hair
And decked in tender green and gold;
And yet my marble heart is cold
Within these walls where people pass
Across the close-clipped emerald grass
To stare at me with stupid eyes
Or stand in noisy ecstasies. . . .

—*The Marble Faun* (50)

"I AM busy out of doors all day now," he wrote Jean Stein in early May, "trying to get back into proper physical condition again, already sunburned a little. . . . But mainly to get time passed. . . ."[1] By the end of the month he had seen to the farm and rented it for the next year so that he would be free again.

Early June brought the heat of full summer and the beginning of the nuptial events. The engagement was announced on June 10, 1954, with the wedding to take place on August 21 in St. Peter's Episcopal Church, where Jill had been confirmed and had later sung as a member of the choir. "I will need money, probably a ghastly amount," he wrote Commins. "Jill and her mother seem bent on making a production out of this, and her trousseau wedding stuff, bridesmaids' dresses, champagne etc will run to quite a piece of jack I fear."[2]

Publication of *A Fable* was now imminent, and the arrival of his author's copies brought him but short-lived pleasure. Donald Klopfer asked his cooperation for a *Time* cover story, and he immediately refused. He wanted no prying into his private life, he said. He knew he could not stop it because the individual could not protect himself from "one of the most fearful things in modern American life: the Freedom of the Press." But if the editor at *Time* persisted, "please warn him that I will be dug in to defend what remains of my privacy to the last bullet."[3] When

Cerf told him that the reporter was a trustworthy friend of his and that the story would have enormous value in promoting *A Fable*, Faulkner sent him an adamant telegram which ended ESTIMATE WHAT REFUSAL WILL COST RANDOM HOUSE AND I WILL PAY IT.[4] Cerf capitulated and wired back that the whole project was off. The telegraph wires had hardly stopped humming when *Newsweek* sent a man to Oxford to do a cover story. Phil Mullen telephoned to ask if Faulkner would see him and received an immediate no. In spite of this, Bill Emerson went out to Rowan Oak, where Estelle greeted him graciously. When Faulkner entered, Emerson thought "he looked like an unexpected apparition, his face covered with stubble, bare-chested and wearing slightly ragged shorts." Emerson told him he felt obliged to hear the refusal face-to-face. Because Faulkner tended to feel that the individual reporter, under orders from his editor, was in a sense powerless too, he remained courteous and took refuge in silence, though Emerson could see he was angry. Emerson put together his story as best he could. One photograph had already been provided, a stark portrait in which Faulkner's cropped hair gleamed silver against a deep-black background, his downward gaze musing, his jaw outthrust under the dark mustache. It might have been a picture of one of the damned, brooding silently in a far quiet reach of hell. It appeared on the cover of *Newsweek* on August 2, 1954, the publication day of *A Fable*.

"Faulkner's undertaking," one scholar would write much later, "was bolder than, if not as successful as, Milton's attempt to write the epic of the fall of man. . . . Utilizing a radical adaptation of the central part of the Christian myth," and presenting two exemplary fables—the one of the horsethieves and the other of the corporal and his father—he intended "to accomplish the transfer of the Christian myth into secular terms—into a fable illustrating man's imaginative power to transform his history into transcendent myth. . . ."[5] Where had all the materials come from?

He had of course drawn from his life. His time in Toronto had supplied RAF lore, and Jack's experiences had provided realistic detail for trench warfare. His memories of their absorption with reports of the battle of Verdun had been fused with his French walking tour of 1925 and his later visits to the actual battle site. He sent the runner through the Rue Servandoni, where he had lived that first time, and through the Rue de Vaugirard, where he had mailed postcards home. He was indebted to others' books (besides the Bible) and to his own. Only a few would have recognized the parallels with Humphrey Cobb's *Paths of Glory*, which Harold Guinzburg had given him in 1935. In that book a French regiment broke in a foredoomed assault, and in the end three of them were shot: two shady characters, and one good man who remarked, "Those posts make it look like the Crucifixion, don't they?"[6] Among his own books, *The Sound and the Fury* had drawn on Passion Week, and *Go Down, Moses* had presented Cass Edmonds and Ike McCaslin in a conflict of principle and authority which resembled that between the old general and the corporal. In *The Wild Palms*, Harry Wilbourne had lamented, "we have got rid of love at last just as we have got rid of Christ. . . . If Jesus returned today we would have to crucify him quick in our own defense. . . ." (136) (One of Faulkner's favorite novels was *The Brothers Karamazov*, and many readers of *A Fable* would detect resemblances to Dostoevsky's Grand Inquisitor sequence.) In the new novel, the military was the embodiment of anti-Christ, but as early as "Turnabout," Captain Bogard had wished he could kill "all the generals, the admirals, the presidents and the kings—theirs, ours—all of them."[7] For correspondences in central images and ideas, of course, the reader had only to look back from *Notes on a Horsethief* and the "Three Temptations" scenes to "The Bear" and the Nobel Prize speech.

His concerns were once more ultimately with freedom, peace, and the dignity and brotherhood of man. As in the New Testament, temporal power had triumphed over a manifestation of the spiritual, if not the divine. But the final meaning was clear. Though unresurrected, the corporal's body by a series of coincidences came to repose within the cenotaph of the Unknown Soldier. Under the eternal flame it symbolized not so much martial valor as the human capacity for sacrifice and love, qualities which would gain for man as much salvation as he could achieve. Nearby, even more faithful than Christ's disciples near the empty tomb, was the terribly maimed runner, another victim yet another manifestation of man's indomitable spirit.

One of the earliest reviews rendered what would be the most common verdict. A major novel by a major novelist, it showed many of his marvelous gifts but was difficult and murky; *A Fable* was a noble failure. It was Malcolm Cowley who said it kindly in the New York *Herald Tribune* on Sunday, August 1. Writing the same day in *The New York Times*, Carvel Collins analyzed it as "one of the important works of our major novelist." Late in the month, however, Charles Rolo wrote in the *Atlantic* that it was among the most "inaccessible" books Faulkner had written, "a heroically ambitious failure." For Leslie Fiedler in *The New Republic*, it failed at every point. Handing down his opinion in the pages of *The New Yorker*, Brendan Gill called it "a calamity," among other things. Reviews in major American newspapers tended to be warmer, and when Harvey Breit added up the score in late August, he could report that "the bouquets outweighted the brickbats by a comfortable margin."[8] In time the novel would receive close attention in extended literary analyses, some of them highly favorable. But no one echoed the author's nervously assertive vaunt that it might be his best work and the best of his time. Ironically, no one wanted it for a motion picture, not even Bacher. When Henry Hathaway finally read it he said, "I couldn't find my story. I didn't recognize anything."

Jill Faulkner would later say that she thought her father "was dissatisfied with it when it was finished. . . . The theme is religious, so this was to be a great work. But it wasn't. I think he knew it all along. He knew that he was out of his element. . . . he had made a big play about dedicating it. . . . But he never once mentioned it again."⁹

FAULKNER had often said he never read the reviews of a book because he was too busy with the next one. This time he was involved with something else: preparations for a trip at the behest of the United States government. An international writers' conference had been planned for August 9–21 as part of the celebration of the quadricentennial of the city of São Paulo. Robert Frost had agreed to go, and the staff of the American consulate hoped that Faulkner would join him. When Muna Lee put it to him as a public service, he consented. Writing Saxe Commins for the dinner jacket and trousers he had left in Princeton, he said he was going "to attend a centennial beanfeast, me to strike a blow of some sort for hemispheric solidarity."¹⁰ The trip would provide a good excuse to skip the pre-wedding hubbub, but Muna Lee saw that they had tapped his deep patriotic feelings.

The trip began so successfully as to allay any anxiety about the performance of this withdrawn and unpredictable artist. He left Memphis on August 6, and in Lima he spent a crowded twenty-four hours that included cultural visits and a press conference at which he revealed that the European writer he most admired was André Malraux and that the presidential candidate he had voted for was Adlai Stevenson. There was a cocktail party for forty that afternoon, with an interpreter to help them put questions to the honored guest. Early the next morning, after very little sleep, Faulkner boarded the plane for São Paulo. The gifts included two bottles of Peruvian brandy. Much of it was gone when he got off the plane that evening at seven. The officials greeting him presented him with two beautiful decanters of Brazilian brandy. When they went to a Russian restaurant for dinner, he skipped the food and contented himself with vodka. Forty-eight hours and one physician later, he was ready to resume the grind.

On the morning of Wednesday, the eleventh, he began a press conference with a reading of his Nobel Prize speech. He then spoke on behalf of solidarity and the need for attacking the world's most acute problem, the racial problem. The next day he was strong enough to visit a cathedral and a center for research on snake venoms, to put in a working luncheon and a working dinner, and to appear afterward before a capacity audience at the União Cultural Brazil-Estados Unidos, where he answered more questions about his writing habits, his ideas, and his tastes. After a few more visits and a few perfunctory remarks at the Writers' Congress plenary session, he departed on the morning of the fourteenth. One of the other delegates was sorry to see him go. "I looked forward so much to meeting Faulkner," Robert Frost told his daughter, "and I was so disappointed because I never saw him." Smiling, the eighty-year-old poet made a gesture of drinking. "I think he'd been doing something naughty," he said.

Actually, Faulkner was well enough to meet the Venezuelan press at a stopover in Caracas. He said that "he had been deeply impressed by the intellectual energy of the youth of South America." He wanted to know the region better and planned to begin studying Hispanic literature. After his return to Rowan Oak on Monday night, August 16, he wrote Harold E. Howland at the State Department to thank him, and said he had become interested in what he had been trying to do. He would be in New York in the fall and would be glad to make a report or discuss "further possibilities, situations, capacities, etc. in which I might do what I can to help give people of other countries a truer idea than they sometimes have of what the U. S. actually is." Reveling in the "most glowing accounts" of his success, State Department officers authorized "emergency payment of $98 medical expenses connection Faulkner visit" and looked ahead to future Latin-American triumphs by the creator of Yoknapatawpha County.

AT Rowan Oak again, he watched Jill make her preparations and plans. Most of her friends seemed to talk only about getting married; they would settle down in Oxford as a matter of course. Not so with Jill, even though her parents put Rowan Oak in her name that June. She had told herself that she wanted to go places and do things, and now she would. Paul had been separated from the Army and was preparing to enter the University of Virginia Law School, and so Charlottesville would be their new home. Her father was not anxious for her to marry, but he did not attempt to dissuade her. She knew that he was there, ready to support her in whatever she did. He worked outside in the August heat, up in a tree stringing Japanese lanterns. He went out to the paddock, with less useful results. "The colt I am training kicked with me yesterday when I wasn't watching for it and hurt my back again," he wrote Jean Stein, "not too bad though." The night before the wedding the groomsmen gathered in the darkness to serenade Jill with traditional West Point songs. At the end of the first refrain they heard coughing from behind the window. Then one of them realized they were serenading the father of the bride.

Guests streamed into town on the sunny morning of August 21, while presents kept arriving and flowers were delivered to both church and home. Ben Wasson helped his friend of thirty-five years dress for the wedding. Faulkner put on the dark striped trousers and the white shirt with its wing collar, and Ben lent a hand with the studs and links, the shining cravat and stickpin. Then Faulkner slipped into the gray double-breasted waistcoat and went down to the front hall to watch as Jill descended the stairs in her figured white satin gown and train, lace at her wrists, pearls at her throat, and the sheer white veil floating behind her from the satin cap that half covered her blond hair. "He had a bottle of champagne already there," she would remember, "and we drank champagne—the two of us, nobody else, drank champagne together."[11] Then they entered the limousine waiting to take them to St. Peter's. They walked to the church door, Jill smiling and self-possessed, her father silver-haired and bemused-looking in the uncomfortable finery. Vicki moved to her side as maid of honor, and Dean moved in behind with the other bridesmaids. Jill's young groom met her at the altar, and very soon her father had given her away.

Returning to Rowan Oak, they stood in the fragrance of gardenias and roses to greet the guests. To Shelby Foote, the bride's father seemed euphoric. "Isn't Jill the perfect virgin?" he asked. Estelle seemed dissolved at the wedding of her last, her youngest. In the well-trimmed garden Bern Keating snapped pictures—for the family only, Faulkner had said. Estelle, however, had extended an invitation to Jane Sanderson, of the *Commercial Appeal*. Estelle said she could bring a photographer but Bill mustn't know it, because he had barred the press. Before she left, Miss Sanderson gave in to an impulse. "I am a reporter for the *Commercial Appeal* in Memphis," she told Faulkner. "I have just covered your daughter's wedding." He stepped back and looked at her with what she thought was "a faint trace of amusement." He said, "Now they're coming in disguise."[12]

Reaction and letdown came quickly after the newlyweds departed for Mexico. A few friends stayed for supper. Faulkner had switched from champagne to whiskey, and he and Estelle were both drinking heavily. The next day when Saxe and Dorothy Commins said their goodbyes, he was in bed. "Don't worry," he said. "I'll see you in two weeks." But he would have to spend two days at Wright's Sanitarium in Byhalia before he could think about going to New York.

By September 10, Faulkner was back at the Algonquin for at least a month, during which he would see Jean Stein again and do some writing. Later in the month, congratulating Malcolm and Gloria on the birth of their son, Mark, he reported, "Earned $1000.00 TV last week, just finished a hunting story Post should buy, maybe $2000.00, am happy to be earning again and reassure myself that I can."[13] The first sum came from a CBS telecast of "An Error in Chemistry." The second one would come, he hoped, from a story with sources as diverse as any he had ever written about hunting camp.

Fellow hunters would recognize the locale of "Race at Morning." It was the kind of country they hunted each fall from their camp near Anguilla on the Sunflower River in Sharkey County, just twenty miles east of the Mississippi. The two protagonists—the deaf old man and the twelve-year-old boy who clutches him from behind, sharing his saddle so he can shout which way the dogs go—were recognizable. (They were Clarence Bernard and his helper, thought Red Brite; Jack Stone and his grandfather, thought Phil Stone.) So was the quarry: "The old deer would disappear about the beginning of the hunting season and return to his hide-out just after the season was over," wrote John Cullen, "just as William says, and that old buck's tracks were as large as William says they were."[14] The fictional buck is like the great stag of "The Old People" and Old Ben of "The Bear," though he does not have their transcendent qualities and clearly symbolic importance. Mister Ernest deliberately refrains from killing him when he might have. "Which would you rather have?" he asks the protesting boy. "His bloody head and hide on the kitchen floor yonder and half his meat in a pickup truck on the way to Yoknapatawpha County, or him with his head and hide and meat still together over yonder in that brake, waiting for next November for us to run him again?" Whereas "The Bear" demonstrates the inevitability of change and death, this story asserts the will toward life. Sam Fathers passes on skill and knowledge to Ike McCaslin; here, under happier circumstances, Mister Ernest does the same thing for the boy. In Peru and Brazil, Faulkner had spoken about the need to solve mankind's pressing problems. Mister Ernest explains to the boy that farming and hunting are not enough. He has to go to school "so you can belong to the business of mankind," so he can know about right and wrong "and be able to tell the folks that never had no chance to learn it."[15] The *Post* bettered Faulkner's prediction when Harold Ober sold it to editor Stuart Rose for $2,500.

He busied himself with several projects. When two young women asked him to make a recording for their new company, Caedmon Publishers, he replied, "My daughter got married and I need the money." So on the last day of September he reread the Nobel Prize speech and parts of *A Fable*, *As I Lay Dying*, and "Old Man" for a twelve-inch, long-playing record. In the office at Random House he was busy with another story which he called "By the People." The protagonists are a team: Gavin Stevens and V. K. Ratliff. The antagonist is a local politician named Homer X. Yarbry. The nameless narrator is a twenty-eight-year-old World War II veteran who calls Gavin his uncle and sounds like Chick Mallison. The problem is to defeat Yarbry in his congressional race against a gallant former officer who had won the Congressional Medal of Honor and lost a leg in Korea but suffered from the political liability of having commanded Negro troops. Borrowing from the text of Faulkner's speech at Jill's high-school commencement, Ratliff demonstrates both age's experience and youth's capacity for action. The battle against evil in Yoknapatawpha County was still going on a half-century after the events in *The Hamlet*. Faulkner made it more explicit when he changed Homer X. Yarbry to Clarence Eggleston Snopes, who had appeared in *Sanctuary*. A total of eight magazines would refuse the story on the grounds of its earthiness before it was finally purchased eight months later—by *Mademoiselle*, for $750.

It may have been at about this time that he composed another Yoknapatawpha story he called "Hog Pawn," which involves another returned veteran. The story focuses, however, on his sweetheart's father, a man so mean that a new Snopes feels no compunction about trying to murder him. This story would not be offered for sale until early 1955, and then unsuccessfully, but Faulkner would find a use for it eventually.

The idea of death was more profoundly present in another piece he did that fall. Anthony West had sent him a photograph Walker Evans had made in a shaded cemetery, a view from the rear of more than a half-dozen life-size marble effigies. "I think it's fine," Faulkner had told West. "Do you want to write anything about it?" West asked. Faulkner was noncommittal, but not long afterward West received a piece Faulkner had entitled "Sepulture South: Gaslight." It began with a kind of humor, but by the time he finished, it had gone from gentle recollection to deepest melancholy. The narrator recalls his grandfather's death and concomitantly one of the vagaries of Southern cooks: using a death in the family as the time to move from one employer to another. Faulkner went from there to the protocol and rituals of mourning. Laid out in his regimentals, Grandfather looks like Colonel Sartoris in "An Odor of Verbena." Among the mourners, Uncle Rodney is much like Maury Bascomb in *The Sound and the Fury* and probably identical with the character of the same name in "That Will Be Fine." But the narrator moves deeper as he personalizes the whole experience. Some day he, as the oldest male, will, like his father at Grandfather's death, ride to the cemetery on horseback. But even now those earlier generations are with him, for "three or four times a year I would come back, I would not know why, alone to look at them, not just at Grandfather and Grandmother but at all of them looming among the lush green of summer and the regal blaze of fall and the rain and ruin of winter before spring would bloom again, stained now, a little darkened by time and weather and endurance but still serene, impervious, remote, gazing at nothing, not like sentinels, not defending the living from the dead by means of their vast ton-measured weight and mass, but rather the dead from the living; shielding instead the vacant and dissolving bones, the harmless and defenseless dust, from the anguish and grief and inhumanity of mankind."[16] West had wanted the piece for *Harper's Bazaar*, and it would appear there in the December number.

At home again in mid-October, he continued to work, but the generating emotion was not grief but rage. By now he had read Robert Coughlan's study of his work and himself, and after his reading, Malcolm Franklin recalled, "he blew up." Under the title "The American Dream: What Has Happened to It?" he used his own experience as symptomatic and then generalized. "It goes back to that moment in our history," he wrote, "when we decided that the old simple moral verities over which taste and responsibility were the arbiters and controls, were obsolete and to be discarded."[17] He sent it to Commins in early November, but soon asked for it back. He had decided it was not an article but a lecture, perhaps one out of a total of five or six. "I have more and more offers to lecture," he told Commins, "my price is up to $1000.00 from colleges now, and I may take it up, use this one for the first of a series, to be a book later. . . ."[18] It was a different response from that of the diffident classroom visitor in Chapel Hill in 1931 and the rueful commentator on Hemingway's courage at Ole Miss in 1947.

Now he could relax for a while, but nothing seemed to catch his imagination, neither pleasure nor work. He wrote Jean Stein that he didn't particularly want to go to hunting camp, but since he was head of the club by inheritance, he would go. His feelings were like Mister Ernest's in "Race at Morning." He would not try for a kill. "I began to discover several years ago that I dont want to shoot deer," he wrote, "just to pursue them on a horse like in the story, and now I have discovered that I dont like to kill anything anymore, and probably wont, give the guns and gear away."[19] When he returned, Malcolm and Gloria were looking ahead to their son's first Christmas. In Manila, Bill and Victoria were preparing to celebrate the holiday with Estelle as their guest. In Charlottesville, Jill and Paul were making ready for their first Christmas in their own home. Faulkner saw to a few things, among them a set of his books bound in blue leather for Jill. Then he left for New York.

He went to parties there with Jean and took her with him to Princeton to spend Christmas with the Comminses. In the familiar holiday syndrome, he felt even worse. "Between grief and nothing," he told Jean, "I'll always take grief." Back in the city as the new year of 1955 began, he told Jean he had a feeling of "impending doom." There were traces of the oppression a week later in surroundings that would have dissipated it, at least temporarily, for many men. Having agreed to do a piece for *Sports Illustrated* on a hockey game between the New York Rangers and the Montreal Canadiens, he saw the artificial ice of Madison Square Garden as another manifestation of the kind of modernity he deplored. Out of the same feeling he had steadfastly refused to air-condition Rowan Oak against the brutal summer heat. "They're trying to do away with weather," he had said. Here the whole spectacle was to him symptomatic of what was happening to sport in America. It should be individual and out of doors; he could foresee the day when even hunting and fishing would be "indoors too beneath lights and the trapped pall of spectator tobacco. . . ."[20] The only mitigating emotion came from a sight that never failed to move him: hero-worshipping little boys impatiently awaiting their own hours of glory. Appearing in *Sports Illustrated* on January 24, "An Innocent at Rinkside" earned him a thousand dollars.

The vision of a day when even hunting would be carried on indoors may have called up the hunts of his young manhood. Whatever the impetus, it seemed a good time for a collection of his hunting stories. Faulkner would link them together with what he would call "interrupted catalysts," and it would be a deluxe volume illustrated by Edward Shenton, who had done the fine drawings for *The Unvanquished*. Faulkner used man's relationship to the wilderness, from the introduction to Act Two of *Requiem for a Nun*, to introduce "The Bear," omitting the complex fourth part of that novella. He prepared for "The Old People," with its great stag, by using material with still another totem animal: the snake that slashed the fleeing slave in "Red Leaves." To introduce "A Bear Hunt," Herman Basket told once more how Doom made the People move the abandoned steamboat, as he had done in "A Justice." Faulkner followed that story with material from "Mississippi," excerpting where he could and rewriting where he had to, again mirroring changes in the land and modulating into a description of the mighty river. A new passage which foresaw the last stand of the Big Woods was full of memories of the men and the animals who had run in them and who would not die. Then he wrote, "*Oh yes, he would think; me too. I've been too busy all my life trying not to waste any living, to have time left to die.*" (171) When he used the first person again in the last of the catalysts, after the final story, "Race at Morning," it was the voice of Ike McCaslin, with his lament for the Big Woods from "Delta Autumn," slightly rewritten. Fusing with the stories, the interrupted catalysts fulfill the dual function of providing historical perspective and emphasizing the elegaic note.

It was almost time now for Faulkner to start back to Oxford again, but first there was a public occasion he decided not to avoid. The later reviews and early critical essays on *A Fable* had continued to vary. Philip Blair Rice wrote in *The Kenyon Review* that though it was "an eccentric and dreamlike commentary on modern society, and artistically unachieved, it at times commands partial respect by the heat of the vision and the depth of the concern." But to Swiss scholar Heinrich Straumann, in *Anglia*, *A Fable* was for the European reader "the most important novel" Faulkner had written. He compared it with *War and Peace* and *Moby-Dick* and called it "a literary masterpiece" in its "absolute fusion of the philosophical with the epic development." What raised him above all his American coevals in the work was "the all-embracing nature of his subject-matter, the supension of his intellectual magnetic field between Manichaeism, Stoicism, and Christianity, and the meaningful references which are thoroughly worked out down to the smallest detail. It is a milestone in the history of American literature."[21] Though no American critic would call it his best book or the best of his time, the judges reviewing fiction for 1954 gave it the National Book Award.

On Tuesday, January 25, 1955, he and Commins made their way to the Hotel Commodore. Wearing a blue double-breasted suit and gray tie with maroon stripes, his rosette in his lapel, he entered the crush of more than seven hundred writers, critics, and publishers. "In all my experience," wrote Memphis columnist Paul Flowers, "I have never witnessed such a spectacle of personal discomfort." At award time, Faulkner looked to Flowers like a condemned man. When the citation was read—by his habitual critic Clifton Fadiman—he took two typewritten sheets from his pocket, donned his glasses, and gripped the sides of the rostrum. As usual, he raced through his speech. The main theme was the status of the artist in America. "In our culture, the pursuit of art is a peaceful hobby like breeding Dalmatians. . . . we stay out of trouble, keep out of the way of the practical and busy people who carry the burden of America."[22] Thus both were happy—the harmless artists and the powerful manipulators—until an occasion like the present one, when the artist might speak out before others of like mind against such things as the cult of success.

After a quick drink Faulkner left. Walking downtown with Harvey Breit, he kept thinking about his subject. "The artist is still a little like the old court jester," he told Harvey. "He's supposed to speak his vicious paradoxes with some sense in them, but he isn't part of whatever the fabric is that makes a nation. It is assumed that anyone who makes a million dollars has a unique gift, though he might have made it off some useless gadget." As he spoke about the impotence of the artist, he might have thought about his letters to Malcolm and Jimmy ten years before in which he told them that after the war people like himself would have to speak out. The trip to Peru and Brazil had apparently galvanized that impulse. "I might be going to Europe this spring," he told Harvey, "for the State Department." Breit thought that the Cold War and the Soviet emphasis on culture might have made people think about the contribution American artists could make. Faulkner was not sure Breit was right. "Unless," he said, "someone somewhere had enough sense to go to someone in a high position and said, 'Let's see Robert Frost instead of Henry Ford for a change.' "[23] On January 27 he left for home.

In frigid February, Edward Shenton's dummy for *Big Woods* arrived in Oxford. Faulkner typed out a page and a half of careful, detailed suggestions. Suggesting a headpiece for "A Bear Hunt," he wrote that it could be "something symbolical and allegorical . . . the wilderness, the Indian of the now, dispossessed of heritage, and in the background the shadowy figure of what he once was, the wild man, the king?" The next day he canceled two of the suggestions because he saw that the artist had been right in the first place.[24] However, Shenton liked the one for "A Bear Hunt" enough to follow it closely. Pleased with the book, Faulkner wrote Else Jonsson, "I had thought that perhaps with A FABLE, I would find myself empty of anything more to say, do. But I was wrong . . . and I have another one in mind I shall get at in time."[25]

One project that appeared as though it might take precedence was a half-hour television script for ABC about a man falsely accused of being a security risk during the McCarthy era. It would pay $2,500. He made a quick trip to New York in late February and produced a six-page synopsis. When the contracts arrived, however, they infuriated Faulkner and Ober. The author was forbidden to discuss the project with outsiders, he was subject to a "morals clause," and he would have to join a union. The network was informed that Faulkner did not wish to proceed with the project and that he refused to accept any of their money for what he had done.

Before returning home from New York he stopped in Philadelphia, where Jean Stein was working on the production of Tennessee Williams' *Cat on a Hot Tin Roof*. After opening night Faulkner sat at a table with Jean, the playwright, Christopher Isherwood, Gore Vidal, and Carson McCullers. The desultory conversation convinced Jean that the day of the literary salon was over. One reason for Faulkner's silence was his feeling that the play "was about the wrong people—the problems of children are not worth three acts," as he would say some time later. "The story was the old man, I thought, the father."[26] Another reason might have been stomach pain. He thought he had picked up a bug of some kind in Egypt. The contretemps with ABC may have aggravated it, and in mid-March he went into the hospital for tests, but they apparently proved negative.

THERE were other matters that caused distress that late winter and early spring of 1955. The *Minmagary* had disappeared from Sardis Reservoir without a trace, and some suspected that commercial fishermen had scuttled her because she had broken their trotlines. Man drowned the big woods to make a reservoir; then he littered the reservoir with trash; then he sank boats that floated on its waters. There was nothing in what Faulkner saw around him to convince him that what he had written in his fiction was anything but the absolute truth. His distress was acute, too, at a letter to the editor of the *Commercial Appeal* alleging that Negroes in Memphis slums were too shiftless to nail up the ratholes in their homes. He replied sharply in what was the first skirmish of a heated engagement.

In another letter exactly a month later, Faulkner came closer to the issue that exacerbated many Southerners, both black and white. In the previous year, when the U. S. Supreme Court had struck down the "separate but equal" doctrine in public education, Mississippians continued planning and financing the dual system. Faulkner began, "We Mississippians already know that our present schools are not good enough." He opposed stringent taxes to support an inadequate dual system and concluded, "how foolish in simple dollars and cents, let alone in wasted men and women, can we afford to be?"[27] The attacks came almost immediately. One man sent him a carbon copy of a letter he was sending to the *Commercial Appeal* in which he accused "Weeping Willie Faulkner" of cowardice, ignorance, and treachery. Before, Faulkner had simply been the writer who had betrayed his own land by peopling it with murderers, perverts, and idiots. By his attack on this shibboleth, he had made himself as vulnerable as Colonel Devries in "By the People." Anonymous callers phoned to curse him at odd hours. Johncy would write that because "none of us agreed with Bill's views we said, 'It serves him right. He ought to have known this would happen.' "28 Without naming names, Johncy wrote the *Commercial Appeal* in opposition, but people knew whom he was talking about. Jack felt that because of his FBI job he should not write public letters, but he did write to the editor asking special consideration for Johncy. It had been a cliché of fiction that the Civil War had set brother against brother. The civil rights conflict of the 1950's was doing it again.

In the month of April, Faulkner wrote three more letters in one two-week period. The first two amplified what he had already said. All students should receive with equality and freedom as much education as they could use. If there had to be two school systems, the first should be an academic system and the second a system of trade and craft schools. Faulkner said he had no degrees or diplomas. "Maybe that's why I have so much respect for education that I seem unable to sit quiet and watch it held subordinate in importance to an emotional state concerning the color of human skin."29 In the third letter he applauded one from a student willing to accept change. But what a commentary it was, he thought, that young Mississippians dared not sign their names to a statement running counter to parental opinion. By the time his third letter appeared in mid-April, he was at the other end of the continent, giving an address at the University of Oregon and repeating it at the University of Montana. It was the essay *Harper's* would publish in their July number as "On Privacy. The American Dream: What Happened to It."

Back from the Northwest, he was busy with a different kind of magazine piece. *Sports Illustrated* had offered him $2,000 and a week's expenses to report on the Kentucky Derby, and if the story was as good as they hoped it would be, he would receive a $500 bonus. He went to Louisville by way of New York, staying long enough to tell Commins about the new book he was planning and to see Ober. (As he left the city, the newspapers announced that *A Fable* had won the Pulitzer Prize for Literature.) He arrived in Louisville, where *Sports Illustrated* provided him with a $100-a-day chauffeured limousine, in time to begin what would be the most unusual piece the magazine had ever printed about a horse race.

"Kentucky: May: Saturday" was not so much a report on the eighty-first running of the Derby as a reaction to what it all meant. The first of the five parts set the historical perspective: "This saw Boone: the blue-grass, the virgin land rolling westward wave by dense wave from the Allegheny gaps. . . ." He envisioned the Indians and the pioneers, as he had just done in *Big Woods*. He used the log-cabin shrine where Lincoln was born to invoke both past martyrdom and present concerns—if one chose to think "that the man's voice is somewhere there too, speaking into the scene of his own nativity the simple and matchless prose with which he reminded us of our duties and responsibilities if we wished to continue as a nation." In the next section he described the favorite, the great horse assessing the track as Old Ben had the hunters in his land. (He was Nashua; and though Faulkner did not once name him, he bet on him.) The third act looked back to legendary champions and the fourth to the Running of the Derby on May 7. He began "The Day" with a disquisition on the horse, which, now obsolete for commerce, still supplied to man "something deep and profound in his emotional nature and need." In the last section he did not make explicit Nashua's loss to Swaps. Instead he tried to convey the emotional intensity of the race. "We who watched have seen too much," he wrote; "we must turn away now for a little time, even if only to assimilate, get used to living with, what we have seen and experienced."[30] The others could report the finish order and the times and the odds. He was trying to give not just the essence of the Derby as it had been for nearly a century, but also the essence of the horse race, using for his vehicle the archetypal experience in America's oldest classic. When the check came from *Sports Illustrated* it included the $500 bonus.

In New York, Faulkner had begun discharging an obligation to Howard Hawks. He submitted to two interviews. "Bill felt guilty about Egypt," Hawks said, "and as a result he practically did personal appearances for the movie." On Monday, June 13, he completed payment of his debt at a Memphis cocktail party for a preview of the film. All of his family was there while he posed sourly for photographs and submitted to questioning by the press. In the earlier sessions he had praised Hawks's vision and courage. Now he said other complimentary things, but finally he told one questioner that there was nothing new in *Land of the Pharaohs*. "It's *Red River* all over again," he said. "The Pharaoh is the cattle baron, his jewels are the cattle, and the Nile is the Red River. But the thing about Howard is, he knows it's the same movie, and he knows how to make it."[31]

One topic came up which bore no relation to the movie: the response to his letter about integration. There had been gratifying letters and calls, he said, but there had also been the bitter denunciations from people who preferred the impractical solution of ignoring the problem. "It's like living in Alaska and saying you don't like snow,"[32] Faulkner said. When he explained these anti-integration attitudes to Else Jonsson, he wrote, "I am doing what I can. I can see the possible time when I shall have to leave my native state, something as the Jew had to flee from Germany during Hitler."[33]

The brief times he spent in the office at Rowan Oak, both before and after the Memphis chore, were given to correspondence rather than the new book he had been meditating. One letter, unanswered for eleven weeks, was from Harold E. Howland, asking him to attend a seminar for thirty Japanese professors of English and American literature to be held in Nagano in August. In mid-May, in answer to a follow-up telegram, Faulkner had asked if he could go to Japan and then do something else for the State Department in Europe. "Will I need formal clothes," he asked, "or could I rent them there if needed? I could take a black tie with me." Delighted, the State Department representatives replied that it would supply anything he needed. He had written Meta Rebner about the trip, but her hopes were soon dashed when he wrote that he did not think he would be allowed to break his journey in Los Angeles. Later that year she would suddenly know that she would never see him again.

By mid-June anticipation was building in Japanese intellectual circles. In Tokyo, Acting Chief Public Affairs Officer G. Lewis Schmidt planned a schedule of ten days at Nagano, four at Kyoto, and five in Tokyo. He hoped that Faulkner would give three talks at Nagano and sit in on discussion groups. The largest textbook publisher in Japan had already requested permission for a book to be called *Faulkner at Nagano*. Faulkner agreed to the program, with reservations. If he went as a literary man, he would be a failure. "I will do better as a simple private individual, occupation unimportant, who is interested in and believes in people, humanity, and has some concern about man's condition and his future, if he is not careful."[34] To some, these sentiments would sound disingenuous. But the truth was that he was not a literary man in the sense that Gide, Malraux, Camus, and Sartre were with their command of literary criticism.

He had a little time to himself before he went to Washington for briefing and then departed for Japan near the end of the month. He transacted some business with Ober and executed two separate power-of-attorney documents to Saxe Commins. At some point, probably on his return from Washington, what he had done came home to him: his patriotic impulses, his wish to speak out on public issues, and his desire to get back to Europe had led him into the kind of situation that unnerved him. It would be worse than the trip to Stockholm. He began to drink. What had happened was clear to Dr. Chester McLarty: Faulkner didn't like these things but he felt an obligation to accept them. Once again he was the subject of intensive care.

He was able to board the American Airlines flight at 3:25 on Friday afternoon, July 29—just barely. In Los Angeles he would change to a Pan American flight which would deposit him in Tokyo twenty-four hours later on the first leg of a trip that would take him around the world before he saw Rowan Oak again.

63

. . . there is nothing to measure it against, nothing for memory and habit to say, 'Why, this looks like the word for house or home or happiness;' not even just cryptic but acrostic too, as though the splashed symbols of the characters held not mere communication but something urgent and important beyond just information, promising toward some ultimate wisdom or knowledge containing the secret of man's salvation.

—"Impressions of Japan," *ESPL* (76–77)

IT was a precarious arrival. When the plane touched down at Tokyo's Haneda Airport at 8:45 on Monday morning, August 1, 1955, he had consumed no solid food since leaving the United States. As they taxied up to the ramp the heat rose in waves and the temperature was in the nineties. When he emerged from the aircraft his face was grim. He would later describe his emotions very simply: "when I reached your country, I was frightened. I believed that you would be expecting something of me which I knew I did not possess. You would expect that literary man which I knew I was not. . . ."[1] He descended slowly, and was immediately surrounded by animated photographers and reporters. Donald Ranard and Clement Hurd got him through the crowd as quickly as they could. Then they sped away in the embassy car to the International House at Azabu, Tokyo.

With no allowance for jet lag, Faulkner's schedule began almost immediately. He arrived late for a courtesy call on the ambassador and then was forced to interrupt it for a sudden dash to the men's room. After lunch he was taken to see a Japanese-American cast rehearse *The Teahouse of the August Moon*, and at 4:30 there was a press conference-cocktail party where he appeared coatless to answer the questions of thirty newsmen about his opinions of Japan, Ernest Hemingway, the racial situation at home, and East-West cultural differences. He said he had a vast respect for Japanese culture and added, "I'm afraid a Westerner is going to be pretty gauche and look pretty stupid to the Japanese." Afterward there was a long radio and television interview conducted by a professor and a social critic. He did not want to go to the party on the town that evening but finally gave in. He sat there eating nothing, but he drank with the rest.

The next morning Dr. Leon Picon, in charge of the embassy's book program, appeared at Faulkner's room to take over. Faulkner showered and breakfasted, but he said he would not face the 170 guests who had been invited to a luncheon in his honor. He said his back was hurting, and he asked Picon to jump on it while he stretched out on the floor. Picon left for the luncheon. There he announced that the guest of honor was unable to attend due to an indisposition caused by the heat. "What kind?" asked one of the newsmen. "Canned or bottled?"

A reception at the residence that afternoon at 5:30 did nothing to salvage things. Ambassador and Mrs. John M. Allison had formally invited many prominent Japanese and members of the foreign community. Faulkner arrived too late for the reception line and then stationed himself, glass in hand, against a wall. He stood his ground silently until he had to flee behind the potted palms in an alcove, where nausea overtook him. Not long afterward Lew Schmidt received a memo from Allison which said, in effect, "Get him on the next plane out of here or show me reasons why you shouldn't." Schmidt and his colleagues were young, members of one of the finest units in the United States Information Service, and their morale was high. He typed out a statement to the ambassador and told Picon to sign it. It read, "Our resignations will be on your desk tomorrow morning. If we don't pull this off, you can make them effective." Picon added his signature and so did Ranard. Meanwhile, Faulkner had collapsed, and he had been bundled out of his room for emergency medical treatment.

When Leon Picon came to his room the next morning, Faulkner looked at him carefully. "Yesterday you were smiling," he said. "Today you're not. Why?" Picon told him. Faulkner looked at him again. "Leon, I'll keep faith with you," he said. "I won't let you down. The U. S. government commissioned me to do a job and I'll do it."

When he met six Japanese authors from the P.E.N. club that afternoon, glass in hand, he opened the conversation. He told them how much the climate and the scenery resembled those of Mississippi. He also told them that his land had been handed down from his forefathers, and that as head of his family, he had to look after it. "It was a singular experience," wrote Shohei Oh'oka, "to find a newly arrived foremost American author to belong to the type of an old-fashioned, virtuous, bashful and earnest literary man, which is about to disappear in Japan." Suekichi Aono paid him yet another compliment: he even *looked* Japanese.[2] On the next morning, August 4, Faulkner submitted to four consecutive forty-five-minute interviews. Earlier he had said that he knew a little of the haiku and waka forms in Japanese poetry. Now he said that the night before he had read part of Jun'ichiro Tanizaki's novel *Some Prefer Nettles*. "All the Japanese writers," he declared, "are more intellectual and better educated than I am. They are also very polite and gentle."[3] In the afternoon he met a group of reporters and literary critics. In the evening he gratefully boarded the night train for Nagano.

He arrived early the next morning in the popular summer resort near the "Japanese Alps," something over a hundred miles northwest of Tokyo. He and Picon had adjoining rooms at the Gomeikan Hotel, a typical *ryokan*, an inn which combined grace with functionalism. Outside was a small porch which led to an enclosed garden from which came the peaceful sound of water dropping from an artificial rain spout.

The fifty Japanese professors and their American faculty of four had reached a pitch of excitement even before Faulkner arrived at the Japan-America Cultural Center. His rapid reading of a two-page statement quickly lowered it. What he had said in Tokyo had been misconstrued. "American culture is not just success," he explained. "We desire and work to be successful in order to be generous with the fruits of that success."[4] A hush fell. Sitting in front were the *genro*, the older men whom the Americans called the "prestige professors." It would have been unthinkable for the younger teachers to ask questions before their elders spoke. When the first two questions came, on the safe ground of the Nobel Prize speech, Faulkner was able to answer in general affirmative terms. Another palpable silence lay on the air. After a few more questions, Professor Robert Jelliffe, Fulbright lecturer at Kobe College, called the session to a close. Faulkner began the next session with another two-page statement, this one about the artist's concerns. A series of questions followed about style and his reading preferences. Between long pauses many of the listeners sat in profound silence while the novelist concentrated on the lighting of his pipe. A week and a half more of this would be unbearable.

Faulkner finally hit on a solution. He went to two of the *genro* and asked their help in encouraging the younger people to ask their questions freely. It worked, producing wide-ranging questions. In a companion strategy, he turned his meals at the Gomeikan into working sessions, asking Leon Picon or the younger scholar assigned as translator, Ichiro Nishizaki, to invite one or two of the participants to join them. Faulkner had developed a taste for the Japanese rice wine, and an attractive young member of Picon's staff, Kyoko Sakairi, would attend to this, asking if a guest wanted more sake. With a rising inflection she would say "Please." To the Western ear, this sounded like "Dozo?" As the attentive host, Faulkner quickly took up the word. On one occasion, glancing at Nishizaki's empty cup, he said, "there sits the Professor, unnoticed, unsung, undoozoed." He liked the clear soup, the baked fish or shrimp fried tempura style, the chicken or pork, and the rice and fruit. He even enjoyed using the chopsticks, though when he was complimented he said, "I ate this way the first time I used them. What I can't understand is why I don't improve." After dinner he and Picon might stroll around the town in the cool of the evening. Other times Faulkner would have a Japanese bath, with one of the hotel's large hot pools all to himself. Then Picon would hear a tap at his door. When he opened it, Faulkner would ask, "How about a recap and a nightcap?" Their conversation on the small balcony would range beyond the day's work. It might be three or four hours after midnight when Faulkner would return to his room.

The formal sessions continued with a consideration of *Sanctuary*, a reading from a book in progress to be called *The American Dream*, and a discussion of the South. Yes, Faulkner said, there had been an aristocratic tradition like that of the samurai and there was, similarly, a peasantry. But as for the plight of the Negro, he thought it was based on economic rather than political or racial grounds: the fear that given equality before the law, the hard-working Negro would "take the white man's economy away from him." This discrimination was shameful, and if Americans were going to go about the world talking about freedom, they had to practice it at home.[5]

He was quite open to this strange culture. After strolling on the shady, beautifully tended grounds of the 1,400-year-old Buddhist Zenkoji Temple, Faulkner started a colloquy with schoolchildren. Then he put a series of interested questions to the Temple abbess and ate some Japanese cake. With Jun'ichi Nakamura, who had translated for him with the children, Faulkner strolled past a graceful fountain and a manicured garden. Then they paused to watch as sixty Japanese of all ages danced on a raised platform, swaying in the motion of the *bon-odori* meant to entertain the spirits of ancestors visiting during the festive season. At the archery court they watched the formal practice of this ancient samurai skill, applauding when one of the archers scored a bull's-eye. Faulkner was urged to try, and he accepted the short bow with interest. His first arrow hit the ground and the next two were wide of the target. "One more arrow!" he called. He missed again, but the newsreel coverage would show the arrow quivering in the target.

He was working much harder now than he had in Brazil, appearing frequently before diverse groups. On August 13 there was a meeting with a cross section of thirty people from Nagano at the inn. "All of you here have known American soldiers," he told them. "I am not a soldier, and I would like to talk to you not as a soldier and only incidentally as an American."[6] One of his hearers brought up a postwar outrage, and he responded sympathetically. When they asked about his books, he continued to make an obvious effort to answer clearly and at length.

He was going at a pace which would have worn down a younger man in better health, and Leon Picon tried to help him cope with it. When Faulkner's spirits flagged and he wanted a drink instead of another interview, Picon would say, "You're under contract to the U. S. government."

At other times he would mix a weak gin-and-tonic, and Faulkner would muster his forces and go to the scheduled meeting. Picon had noticed that Faulkner always seemed to do better when there was a pretty girl in the audience. Now he always saw to it that Kyoko Sakairi was there, or a slim, boyish-looking little student named Midori Sasaki, a twenty-four-year-old teaching assistant at the Hiroshima Women's College. Faulkner always seemed to be more on his mettle when they were there.

Welcome relief came on Sunday, August 14, when they traveled up into the snow-topped mountains to Lake Nojiri, which was swept by strong winds. The scene seemed totally alien to Faulkner. "It is only a skiff," he would write, "yet to the western eye it is as invincibly and irrevocably alien as a Chinese Junk . . . containing a woman in a kimono beneath an open paper parasol such as would have excited no comment in a sunny reach of the English Thames. . . ."[7] Suddenly he saw sailboats across the lake. "Leon, get me out of this," he said. "I see what I want." Soon he was out of his shoes and socks. With trousers rolled up he got them moving, and soon he and Leon were skimming along under the puffed white sails, racing Clem Hurd and George Alcott. He was in a good humor the whole day.

He continued to watch Midori Sasaki—striking, with her black hair, black eyes, and beautifully clear complexion that she protected from the sun with a dainty parasol. She also carried a folding fan, which she would use to conceal the quick and genuine blushes that signaled her frequent shy embarrassment at the attentions Faulkner sometimes showed her in the presence of older and prominent Japanese. Her high-pitched voice was little more than a whisper, and her hesitancy stemmed partly from modesty and partly from custom. She had been raised not only within the traditional Japanese concept of the place of woman, but in Hiroshima, where the art of feminine facial maneuver had not been lost. He had written out for her a page to be translated into Japanese. When her friends were impressed at this prized possession, she tore it into pieces so she could share it with them. Faulkner was moved. It was a kind of loyalty that had impressed him here. "I'm going to send this girl to the United States on a scholarship," he told Picon. He may have been influenced by her coming from the tragic city of Hiroshima, but he told Picon something more. All his life, he said, he had felt a special compassion for those who fell short of being tops. He had never said that his Nobel Prize fund was for the best; it was for those who would otherwise be overlooked. Midori was not the brightest, but she was the youngest. And she had loyalty.

As Faulkner's impressions of Japan began more and more to cohere, USIS film man Harry Keith was making his own record: Faulkner in *yukata*, the light summer-weight kimono; Faulkner pausing to gaze from a hilltop or standing meditatively by the goldfish pond. One day a camera followed him to a gruff old woman who sold pigeon feed near the Zenkoji Temple. Picon said he was going to tell her who the purchaser was. "No," said Faulkner, "this is refreshing." Now, seeing the camera, she put her hands up before her wrinkled face. Faulkner walked on with Picon, delighted. "Here's somebody who doesn't know what I am, care what I am, and doesn't give a god damn what I think of Ernest Hemingway." Just then a member of the crew called them back to retrace their steps. This time the old woman sold them the feed and stood unprotesting. After the filming Faulkner asked what had happened. "You'd be surprised what 2,000 yen will do," answered an enterprising member of the crew. "I don't care what they'll do," Faulkner said grimly, "I want to go home and take a bath."

Picon had been urging Faulkner to write down his impressions of Japan, and had entered in a notebook many of the things Faulkner said. Faulkner had finally used these notes, typing and dictating to Picon's secretary what he would call "Impressions of Japan," to be used as a narrative to bind the film footage together. He framed a series of eight vignettes between impressions of his aircraft arriving and departing. Of the faces, he said, "Van Gogh and Manet would have loved them. . . ."[8] There was a brief vignette of the geisha behind whose painted mask he saw "a gift for comedy, and more: for burlesque and caricature: for a sly and vicious revenge on the race of men." And the kimono, with its graceful and feminine concealment, he loved: "one unbroken chalice-shape of modesty proclaiming her femininity where nudity would merely parade her mammalian femaleness."[9] In the next-to-last place, before a final glance at the land, he put an apostrophe to loyalty, specifically inspired by his assiduous and faithful chambermaid and also, apparently, by Midori Sasaki.

On the last night of the seminar Faulkner and a few of the others sat in comradely relaxation at the Gomeikan as Kyoko Sakairi doozoed them once more. If Faulkner was expansive from a sense of relief, the embassy people were feeling a glow of satisfaction tinctured with something like amazement. The staff worked hard, Lew Schmidt wrote later, but "it might be said that Mr. Faulkner worked even harder and although he is unsociable by nature, he became the most sociable American at the seminar, all the while retaining most of the unpredictable qualities of his perverse personality."[10] This night they relaxed, looking ahead to Kyoto and then Tokyo again. Faulkner was looking beyond to the rest of his trip from Asia to Europe. Midori Sasaki reminded him of another girl, he said. Her name was Jean Stein, and one of the reasons he had agreed to the trip to Japan was so that he could return home by way of Europe and see Jean in Rome. They made ready to board the train for Kyoto.

A local carried them to Nagoya, where they transferred to the Tsubame express that rushed them westward. They had descended from the rugged alpine foothills into the valley where the long expanse of Lake Biwa signaled the end of the 300-mile journey to "the City of Purple Hills." They would spend four days here in this most classic of Japanese cities, the site of the emperor's court less than a century before and still the great repository of Japan's art. After a reception given by the president of Kyoto University, they enjoyed a leisurely dinner. Later, the two men were taken by members of the American consulate to a villa where they watched from a distance as the night sky glowed with the ritual *Daimonji Bon* fire.

The next three days were filled with public appearances and semi-private entertainment. Faulkner spoke to a total of nearly five hundred Japanese intellectuals, including writers, scholars, teachers, and newsmen. Again he emphasized Japanese-Southern similarities where he saw them: the idea of the family and the process of recovery after a devastating military defeat and occupation. He received individual plaudits and one standing ovation. "Eccentric and paradoxical, Faulkner left his audiences bewildered but filled with admiration," Lew Schmidt wrote later. "The trigger-like responses to all questions posed to him, seemingly deeply thought out yet rapid-fire, were so powerful in conviction that his listeners gasped with amazement."[11]

Several factors had combined to produce this effect. When he answered questions, he looked at the speaker, head up, and spoke into the microphone. By now he had heard some questions so many times that his answers took on the quality of aphorisms. He spoke with conviction, and sometimes he would end a sentence with a lift of his head and set of his jaw, as though anticipating opposition. And often his glacial silences between questions made the eloquence that much more effective when it came.

On Saturday morning the Tsubame express pulled out of the Kyoto station for the 400-mile trip due east along the coast to Tokyo. They looked fruitlessly for a glimpse of Mt. Fuji near Mishima, and now Faulkner was sitting, staring, his drink untasted. "Is anything wrong?" Picon asked him. He answered, without turning his head, "Here youth kept asking and I still don't know their problem."

In Tokyo the problem began to resolve itself. On Sunday evening Faulkner met with a group of 150 Japanese teachers and students. He appeared weary, but as the young people began to ask about the idea of a "lost generation" and about contemporary problems, he grew more animated. Afterward, walking out to the car with Picon, he said, "I know the problem now. It's all very familiar to me." The next day he typed out a 900-word message which he entitled "To the Youth of Japan." He had said some of it before. A hundred years ago, he began, the South had undergone a worse war and occupation than the Japanese had known. But now the whole country was stronger for this anguish. Young people in the South might then have asked the questions young Japanese were now asking about a hopeless future. The answer was that man was tough enough to prevail, and out of their experience the Japanese writers would speak "not a Japanese truth but a universal truth." He concluded with the subject that had ended "On Privacy"—the belief that man's hope had to be couched in freedom. Democracy was a clumsy method of social improvement, but it would do until a better one was found, "since man is stronger and tougher and more enduring than even his mistakes and blundering."[12]

Faulkner's last full day in Japan was a working day, with a reception, a bookstore autographing party, and the last press conference. The Picons and the Hurds gave a garden cocktail party for over a hundred Japanese literary people and members of the diplomatic corps. Before dinner, Kyoko Sakairi and Midori Sasaki excused themselves so that Midori could change into a kimono and obi with Kyoko's help. The only available place was Faulkner's room. Not long afterward the hotel manager, a former newspaperman and diplomat, told Picon he had been informed that the two young women were in Mr. Faulkner's room, and they must leave. Before Picon could explain, Faulkner tapped the man on the shoulder. "Listen, Mr. Innkeeper," he said, "there *are* two young women in my room, but I'm down here, and if I weren't already leaving here tomorrow, I wouldn't set foot in your inn again."

As for his impact on the other Japanese, one of them paid him the ultimate compliment: "Every Japanese—without any exception—was so attracted to him because of his Oriental, likeable, and sincere personality." Nearly ten years later an American professor would observe that whereas some Americans still talked about his drinking, "Japanese who were there spend all their time talking about what a great person he was. The Japanese who met him still light up when one mentions his name and they talk in awed tones about it—meeting him was obviously one of the great events of their lives."[13] The U.S. Department of State concluded that the mission had done more to better Japanese-American cultural relations than any other single act of the department.

ON Tuesday evening, August 23, Faulkner left for Manila. His plane gained altitude and turned south, climbing past the picture-postcard view of white-domed Mt. Fuji, over the Pacific, and on toward the blue reaches of the East China Sea. At the end of "Impressions of Japan" he had written, "now the aircraft lightens . . . into the overcast and then through it, the land, island gone now which memory will always know though eye no longer remembers. Sayonara."[14]

He had written Victoria and Bill Fielden that he would stay in their Manila home during his forty-eight-hour stopover. He was able to go sailing with Vicki, and he also had time to write Leon Picon about items he was missing: one coat, two waistcoats, three shirts, cuff links and studs. "I hope things will go well here," he concluded. "Will write from Rome, send a report, etc. and of course will do my best to uphold the old Japanese tradition."

Things went well enough, though not as smoothly as they had in Japan. He read parts of *The American Dream* to an audience of 4,000, but the public-address system failed in picking up his soft drawl. At a conference the following day he fielded a variety of questions. One girl wanted to know if the Biblical account of Adam and Eve in the Garden of Eden was true. Another asked, "As a representative of the American people, does your America believe that man has a soul confined in flesh?" He replied that he couldn't speak for America, but that he certainly did. He paid a courtesy call on President Ramón Magsaysay. Later he ventured into foreign policy: not only was the Filipino the best friend America had, "we will defend that friend and even go to the length of what might be mistakes." The conviction was growing upon him that America needed all the friends it could get. When his plane departed he left behind a reaction that USIS had hoped for: "a climate of respect in the small but articulate circle of journalists, writers, and intellectuals among whom unfortunately are some of the severest critics of American mores and policies." The audience which had expected to find him difficult "was extremely gratified to find him utterly sincere, kind, humble and unfailingly patient."

Manila had sent word ahead, and Jean Stein was there to meet him at Rome's Ciampino Airport. It was August 28, and for the first time in a month he had ten days to himself. He revisited Roman landmarks, strolling down the Spanish Steps, then posing in profile with the Castel Sant'Angelo as a backdrop. There was one function with a semi-official air about it. Ambassador Clare Boothe Luce gave a luncheon for him and invited Alberto Moravia, Ignazio Silone, and several other literary figures. They were anxious to talk to him, but he was so taciturn that the ambassador felt he was being extremely rude. The trouble he found with many writers, particularly European men of letters, was that they wanted to talk about writing. He had just had a whole month of that.

A series of events dispelled this taciturnity. On September 3 the United Press called him for a comment on the Emmett Till case. A fourteen-year-old Negro, Till had come from Chicago to vacation with relatives near Greenwood, Mississippi. Later, white men accused him of whistling at a white woman and making an obscene remark to her. When the boy disappeared, two relatives of the woman's husband were charged with his death. Faulkner made notes over the weekend and went on Monday morning to USIS, where he typed them up and asked for suggestions. On Tuesday, September 6, the 400-word statement was released to the press. It was couched not just in terms of the moral geopolitics he had been talking about for some time and which had struck him even more forcibly on this trip. "Perhaps the purpose of this sorry and tragic error," he said, "committed in my native Mississippi by two white adults on an afflicted Negro child is to prove to us whether or not we deserve to survive. Because if we in America have reached that point in our desperate culture when we must murder children, no matter for what reason or what color, we don't deserve to survive, and probably won't."[15] This was what he had been saying at the end of "On Privacy," stated now with greater urgency.

A few days later his official duties began: question-and-answer sessions with a hundred Romans on the ninth, with eighty-five Neapolitans on the twelfth, with fifty Milanese on the fourteenth. His visits to the three cities were covered by eighty daily newspapers and nearly a dozen weeklies. To USIS, this coverage was evidence that "Faulkner's presence in Italy was the cultural event of the summer." While USIS was evaluating his effectiveness, he was making some assessments of his own. He would later say, "the people in our State Department in Europe are intelligent people. They have learned by hard experience that the enemy, the opponent, is not the foreigner, it's in the State Department in Washington, the bureaucrats in Washington." One day an Italian had said to Faulkner, "You Americans know the Italian attitude toward women yet you send us a woman for an Ambassador. We know your attitude toward Negroes yet you send us a Negro for your Public Affairs Officer." This to Faulkner was symptomatic of "the sensitivity to conditions which the European has which the American doesn't have because the American is too fired always by the emotional situation."[16]

There was time for a few non-official functions as mid-September came on. His Italian publisher, Alberto Mondadori, entertained him and proposed a uniform edition of his complete works in Italian. Faulkner liked it enough to write Livio Garzante, who had published *Sartoris*, asking him to allow Mondadori to include that volume. For him this would be not just an acknowledgment of the warm response Italians had always given his work but also of "the affection and 'kinship' which I felt from my first sight of Italy, for Italy and Italians, as though we were kin, not just in spirit but in blood too."[17]

He left Italy on September 16 for Paris, by way of Munich, and two days later reached his destination. He had planned on two weeks there, and he had told USIS that they could have half of his time. The day after he arrived he found himself facing thirty French journalists in the office of William Weld, who noticed that Faulkner was avoiding complicated political questions. Faulkner had found that if he waited when a Communist journalist asked an argumentative question, a non-Communist colleague might answer him. When he wanted to turn aside a literary question, he would say he was a farmer and not a literary man.

On his own time he was enjoying himself. He was comfortable in the Hotel Beaujolais, and in the warm September mornings he would breakfast early and then read his newspaper under the chestnut trees in a garden of the Palais de l'Élysée. In this mood of golden Indian summer relaxation, he was ready to talk easily to a pretty girl if not to a room full of journalists. USIS had assigned Richard Grenier to look after him, and Grenier's wife, Cynthia, asked if she could interview him. She found him handsome, with a bearing that belied his fifty-eight years. She asked how he felt about his books' being read and discussed all over the world. "I like it." he answered. "If they believed in my world in America the way they do abroad, I could probably run one of my characters for President . . . maybe Flem Snopes."[18]

He was entertained in groups large and small. Jean Stein gave parties for him in the beautiful apartment of her uncle on the Avenue Newton. Anita Loos came one evening and reacquainted herself with Faulkner after the thirty-year lapse since they had met in the Vieux Carré. Then she had thought him too thin and unkempt, but now, with that gray-white hair, she thought he looked handsome and distinguished. Others were even more impressed. Monique Salomon—now Monique Lange after her divorce—recalled a dinner party Jean organized at which Tennessee Williams seemed worshipful. (One journalist would later say that Williams told Hemingway, "Those terrible, distraught eyes. They moved me to tears."[19]) If Faulkner was distraught, Monique thought it was because of a question Williams asked him about Negroes in the South. He refused to answer and remained silent for what seemed two hours. Later, she asked if he minded if she went with the others to another party. He laughed. "Go with your queers," he said.

The hospitality involving large groups tended to be overwhelming. The house of Gallimard invited four hundred to a cocktail party. Bill Weld ushered him to the garden behind their building on the Rue de l'Université. In a tree-shaded corner he handed Faulkner a glass of bourbon and water and told him he would bring on, one at a time, people he would presumably want to see. One of those anxious to meet him was Albert Camus, who had said, "Faulkner is the greatest writer in the world." Almost two years before, he had requested permission to adapt *Requiem for a Nun* for the French stage. By the time he was introduced, the line had already taken its toll, and he ran into what another called "that famous wall about which Paris has been talking for days . . . built of the most exquisite but the most obdurate politeness. . . . When you come up against it you find yourself gently pushed back to an immense distance from William Faulkner." He admired Camus, but now, claustrophobic and withdrawn, he merely shook his hand. Camus sadly withdrew. The process continued as the afternoon shadows lengthened. "It's appalling!" said one guest coming in from the dark garden. "I can't watch it; it's like seeing someone being tortured." At last the victim made his way inside. He hesitated. "I would like to say good-by to a Gallimard," he said.

They brought him two, but neither was the right one. Which one did he want?

"The one who looks a little sad," he told them, "the bald one."

"Ah," said another, "that one has gone to bed."

"It doesn't matter," said Faulkner, and made his way out to the freedom of the Rue de l'Université.[20]

His planned two weeks lengthened into three, and there were more parties before he left for London on October 7. In his four-day stay as a private citizen he visited Chatto & Windus and looked to his wardrobe, which by now included more than one English derby and prized suits such as the pepper-and-salt model made for him there. He checked in with USIS and did what he could for them before leaving for yet another assignment.

On October 12 his aircraft made its slow descent over the cold green northern seas and settled down onto the Reykjavik airport's main runway on the treeless island of Iceland. He plunged into a five-day program. This time he met some political questions head-on. When one reporter asked about the foreign army in their small country, he reminded him that the troops were there under the auspices of NATO rather than the United States. If they didn't like it, neither did the American soldiers. "Is it not better to have American forces here in the name of freedom," he asked, "than a Russian one in the name of aggression and violence, as in the Baltic states?" Before he left he called on the president and later received a copy of the Icelandic masterwork *Brennu-Njals Saga*, translated by Halldór Laxness and inscribed by twenty-four Icelandic and Scandinavian writers. In the margin of the official report on Faulkner's visit, one legation member wrote, "Just what the doctor ordered."

FAULKNER was back in the United States nearly three months after he had departed on his round-the-world mission. His duties would not be ended until after a debriefing in Washington, but that would not be onerous. There were odds and ends of business to attend to in New York, but he was thinking about home. Writing Else Jonsson on October 20, he told her, "I will go back to Mississippi soon and get to work again; I know I won't live long enough to write all I need to write about my imaginary country and county, so I must not waste what I have left."[21] There were other reasons, too, why he was thinking of Mississippi now. It had been a bad summer for Estelle, who had been hospitalized again after an alcoholic episode. In her health and her life she had reached a crossroads. She decided to join Alcoholics Anonymous. Jill had written her father from Rowan Oak that she had gone there for a rest but that she had also been glad to be there to give her mother what she needed from both of them: love and understanding and encouragement. Jill had been ill herself and only a few months into a precarious pregnancy that might not go to term. Malcolm had been seriously ill during the summer. Then, on October 23, there was a telephone call from Oxford. Maud Falkner had been rushed to the hospital suffering from a cerebral hemorrhage. She was almost eighty-five and her chances were not good. Her son boarded a plane for Memphis.

64

Home again, his native land; he was born of it and his bones
will sleep in it; loving it even while hating some of it. . . . the
intolerance and injustice: the lynching of Negroes not for the
crimes they committed but because their skins were black . . .
the inequality: the poor schools they had then when they had
any, the hovels they had to live in unless they wanted to live
outdoors: who could worship the white man's God but not in
the white man's church; pay taxes in the white man's courthouse but couldn't vote in it or for it; working by the white
man's clock but having to take his pay by the white man's
counting. . . .

—*"Mississippi,"* ESPL (36–37)

"It was a hemorrhage inside the skull," he wrote Jean Stein on the last day
of October, "relieved by opening veins, etc. in the neck. It was not completed, because she is too old—80 something. . . . she may live years yet or
go out in a [second]. I will get her settled here, then I will be free." Four
days later she was home with a nurse. "I am to read a paper at a historical
association meeting in Memphis the 10th, next Thursday. If Mother is still
all right I can come up then for a week or some such. . . ." She was a
spunky old lady, cantankerous and suspicious, but when it came to Billy,
her eldest, "the light of my life," she was tender as always. And he was
still the dutiful son whose letters, still addressed "Dear Moms," would
come to her faithfully. As she moved into convalescence, he was able to go
on with his plans for leaving.

He would read his paper at the Twenty-first Annual Meeting of the
Southern Historical Association. The men tried for the murder of Emmett
Till had been exonerated by local juries, and the outrage of some Northern
groups was matched only by the satisfaction of white supremacists in the
South. An integrated audience of more than five hundred, mostly teachers,
crowded the Hotel Peabody for the papers. Phil Davidson, a fellow mem-

ber of The Marionettes thirty-five years before, received no flicker of recognition when he spoke to Faulkner, who had much to be abstracted about as he prepared to deliver "On Fear" again. Even in his own family, everyone disagreed with his whole position. Most of it was as it had been at Nagano, but there was one conspicuously new sentence. "I am not convinced," he said, "that the Negro wants integration in the sense that some of us claim to fear he does."[1] He was a long way from Nagano now, and he was choosing his words carefully. He went on to emphasize his theory of the economic bases of segregation and then closed with the firm assertion that all Americans would soon have to make a choice between being slaves and being free, and that choosing to be free would involve abolishing the shame of segregation. According to one reporter, "spirited discussion" followed.

For some time to come, much of Faulkner's thought and energy would be absorbed in the mounting civil rights crisis. His Memphis address rankled many. To John Cullen and most of his neighbors, it was "a poor speech, poorly timed," but Cullen magnanimously conceded, "all men make mistakes, and Faulkner, I sincerely believe, made an honest mistake."[2] In this view, Cullen was in the minority. By the time Faulkner returned from his State Department debriefing, Jean Stein was in the Delta with her friend Marguerite Lamkin, who had been hired by Elia Kazan to help his actors develop authentic Southern accents for the film he was making called *Baby Doll.* "I get so much threatening fan mail," Faulkner wrote Jean, "so many nut angry telephone calls at 2 and 3 am from that country, that maybe I'll come over to the Delta to test them."[3] A few days later he wrote a statement for the pamphlet in which the Memphis speeches would be printed. "The question," he wrote, "is no longer white against black. It is no longer whether or not white blood shall remain pure, it is whether or not white people shall remain free." The three speakers and those who published the pamphlet would "accept contumely and the risk of violence"[4] because they refused to sit quietly by and see the South ruin itself once more over the Negro question.

Before the month was out he did go to the Delta. In Greenville, Jean had met Hodding Carter and Ben Wasson, who telephoned Faulkner and asked if a group of them could come for a visit. Ten members of the film company made the trip, including the director, Elia Kazan, and his beautiful wife, Mollie. Faulkner served them martinis. He was cordial and amusing and even answered equably Mollie Kazan's questions about Mississippi's racial climate.[5] By the time their visit ended, Faulkner had decided that he would show Jean other places that he liked. He took her to Vicksburg, and then, in New Orleans, to places in the French Quarter he had known thirty years before. On the Gulf Coast he met a ghost from the past. He had taken Jean to the Longfellow House at Pascagoula and pointed out the spot where the Stone Camp had stood. Now the cold autumn beach was deserted, except for one other figure. As they approached, he saw that it was Helen Baird Lyman. Widowed and ill, she had nonetheless retained her old tartness. Later, when she told Ann Farnsworth that she had met Bill Faulkner on the beach, she said, "He had some young girl with him. But you have to expect that." She painted a picture of him—looking much older than he actually did.

He was writing Jean again in early December. "I have just started on another novel," he told her, "the second Snopes volume." Seventeen years before, to the month, he had sketched for Bob Haas the whole Snopes saga, as he had conceived it at least ten years before that. Now he was recounting events since the end of *The Hamlet*. Once again he would rework episodes used in short stories to fit them into the narrative. He began *The Town* with a chapter in which Charles Mallison recounts events seen by his cousin, Gowan Stevens, as Flem studiously ignores the adultery of his wife, Eula Varner Snopes, with Jefferson's mayor, Manfred de Spain. This set up the rest of the chapter for a rewrite of "Centaur in Brass." With Ratliff supplying antecedent information, the manuscript grew, without difficulty yet without compulsion. Early in the new year of 1956 he sent some of it to Jean. She replied enthusiastically, and in mid-January he wrote her that it made him feel good. "Does it make you nervous to find out somebody needs you? . . . I still feel, as I did last year, that perhaps I have written myself out and all that remains now is the empty craftsmanship—no fire, force, passion anymore in the words and sentences. But as long as it pleases you, I will have to go on. . . ."[6] Her reaction did not buck him up for long, though, and near the end of the month he told her, "The book is going too good. I am afraid; my judgement may be dead and it is no good."[7]

THE events of that January of 1956 must have had an ironic tinge for him. In the years when he had felt a rocklike certainty about his talent, he had hoped vainly to nourish it with sales to the movies. Now, when he had persistent misgivings about his new work, motion-picture people were bidding for the old. In New York, Ober was holding a check for $3,500 for an option on *The Sound and the Fury*, and in California, Geller was working to get Jerry Wald to increase his offer of $3,500 for an option on *Pylon*. As it turned out, Universal International offered the $50,000 purchase price Ober had been trying to get out of Wald and Columbia. If they exercised their option on *The Sound and the Fury*, Faulkner would have to pay on almost $70,000 in movie sales in addition to taxes on royalties. He decided to go to New York in February to get some advice on investing his money.

He was thinking about another of his things for which he would receive a vastly smaller return but whose importance to him continued to grow. He sent Ober a copy of "On Fear: The South in Labor," with specific instructions not to try the slick magazines, "since on this subject, segregation, in the South here, the slick ones are automatically attaint." He had no ax to grind and he was anxious for credibility. "I am not trying to sell a point of view . . . NAACP or liberals or anybody else. I am simply trying to state, with compassion and grief, a condition, tragic, in the country where I was born and which I love, despite its faults."⁸ Ober sold it to John Fischer for *Harper's* for $350.

Harry Sions went to see him at Random House in hopes of getting another piece for *Holiday*, but the Snopes book was going too well for Faulkner to stop. Yet after rioting broke out at the University of Alabama over the admission of a young black woman named Autherine Lucy, he did stop to write a piece he called "A Letter to the North." Asserting a centrist position for himself, he addressed the activists. To those "who would compel immediate and unconditional integration" he said, "Go slow now. Stop now for a time, a moment."⁹ The Southerner needed time to assimilate the knowledge of what could happen if he did not institute integration himself. Without this pause, the South—with dissidents like himself drawn to the majority in its imposed role of underdog—would resist, even knowing that the cause was both doomed and wrong. When he gave the piece to Ober he wanted the fastest publication and the widest audience possible. For this reason, despite his feelings about *Life* magazine, he approved Ober's sale to them for $1,500, with publication at the end of February.

But this was not soon enough. A federal court had ordered the university to admit Miss Lucy by March 5, and the campus was in a ferment that was spreading over the whole state. Like many Alabamians, Faulkner was sure that if she set foot on the campus, she would not leave it alive. He was almost frantic at the approach of this crisis. He began to drink, but he continued to cast about for some means of trying to head off the disaster he foresaw. He had told Harold Ober he needed a forum. The office of Edward R. Murrow, the widely respected news commentator, had not responded, and the best anyone could manage was the prospect of an appearance on the *Tex and Jinx* conversation-and-interview program, carried only in the East, but a possible conduit to the NBC newsroom and the wire services. He was to meet one of Tex McCrary's staff on February 24.

Meanwhile, something else was developing. When the word went out that Faulkner was anxious to speak on this explosive subject, Philip Horton, of *The Reporter*, asked for an interview on February 21 to be conducted by Russell Warren Howe, who would also publish it in his paper, the London *Sunday Times*. Faulkner consented to meet Howe in Saxe Commins' office. (Trying to slow him down, Jean had thrown out some liquor. "Pouring out liquor," Faulkner told her, "is like burning books.") His answers closely followed what he had said in the essays for *Harper's* and *Life*. Gradually, however, as he described the warlike mood he had seen in the South, his comments grew more desperate. If Autherine Lucy went back to Tuscaloosa, she would die. "The government will send its troops and we'll be back at 1860." Another exchange showed his desperation. "As long as there's a middle road, all right," Howe quoted him as saying, "I'll be on it. But if it came to fighting I'd fight for Mississippi against the United States even if it meant going out into the street and shooting Negroes." He kept repeating to make himself clear. "I will go on saying that the Southerners are wrong and that their position is untenable, but if I have to make the same choice Robert E. Lee made then I'll make it."[10]

The repercussions were both immediate and prolonged. He would later tell Albert Erskine that Johncy had said that if the day came when they tried to get a colored child into a white school in Oxford, he would bar the way with a gun. Faulkner said he started thinking, if it came to shooting and my family were involved, where would I stand then? And he became so upset he started drinking. A month after the Howe interview he wrote out a statement for the press in which he said the comment about shooting Negroes was "more a misconstruction than a misquotation." He said the quoted statement was both "foolish and dangerous," and he repudiated the idea that the South was armed to resist. A month later, after further coverage of the controversy by *Time*, *Newsweek*, and *The Reporter*, he amplified the statement in a letter to the latter. "They are statements which no sober man would make," he wrote, "nor, it seems to me, any sane man believe."[11] In the same number for April 29, *The Reporter* carried Russell Howe's convincing rejoinder and assertion of accuracy. Saxe Commins did not dispute it.

The day after the Howe interview, Faulkner had a luncheon appointment with Joan Williams Bowen, but he canceled it abruptly. Almost a year later she would receive a letter of explanation. "I dont know now why I thought then that drinking could help, but that's what I was doing, a lot of it. I woke up that morning in an apartment not mine with just sense enough to tell you I couldn't make the luncheon, collapsed. Came to Friday and friends resuscitated me just in time to make a presentable appearance on the Tex Something, Tex and somebody like a Frankie and Johnny team on the air from the Waldorf and make my plea."[12] This time he sounded as if the mounting pressure was pushing him further to the right. He made a number of the points he had made earlier, but he said now that if Negroes could receive a good education in their own schools, the immediate problem would be solved in five years. Then, in a hundred years, complete integration could be achieved, and in three hundred years the black race would be assimilated into the white—two hundred years less than Gavin Stevens' estimate in a passage Faulkner had written in February 1949 for inclusion in later editions of *Intruder in the Dust*. His appearance on the *Tex and Jinx* show fell short of his hopes, however, for there was no mention of his plea by the wire services.

By now Faulkner had apparently concluded that he had done all he could do for society and it was time to get back to his novel. Working in Saxe Commins' office, he moved into the second and third chapters. He used Gavin Stevens to look back to the spotted horses and to show how Flem was now bringing more Snopeses into Jefferson. Switching to Charles Mallison, he worked to build the other plot that would counterpoint the rise of Snopesism: Gavin Stevens' devotion to the beautiful and doomed Eula Varner Snopes. Ratliff was there to see the portents of Snopesism, and Faulkner would increasingly use the give-and-take between Ratliff and Stevens to relate the advances of Snopesism and analyze its effects.

Now that he had passed through his most recent acute phase, he was able to relax and drink normally with his friends. Anthony West had him up to his farm in Stonington, Connecticut. One of West's most vivid memories would be of Faulkner's moving up so slowly on a fox and her cubs that she not only continued eating mulberries but glanced at him twice, and then, as she rounded up her brood to depart, "gave him another long steady stare, nodded, and was gone." What struck West was that "the fox so clearly recognized him as a fellow creature." Robert Linscott and his bride, Elisabeth Shoemaker, entertained Faulkner at the farm in the Berkshires. Occasionally he would speak of his work. He told them, "there are a couple of Snopeses I've got to deal with." He even looked ahead when he said, "I want to tell what happened to Quentin after she climbed out the window."[13] Back in the city, he mixed work and social engagements as usual. Sometimes he and Jean Stein would take Linscott to lunch or dinner at one of the quiet places Faulkner preferred. At George Plimpton's suggestion, Faulkner's conversations with Jean began to form the basis for a piece for *The Paris Review*, which Plimpton helped to edit.

The result was the most compendious and the best single Faulkner interview ever published. There were polished anecdotes and comments that rang like epigrams: "If a writer has to rob his mother, he will not hesitate; the *Ode on a Grecian Urn* is worth any number of old ladies." There was a kind of humor not too far from that of *As I Lay Dying* and *Sanctuary*: "I'd want to come back a buzzard. Nothing hates him or envies him or wants him or needs him. He is never bothered or in danger, and he can eat anything." Jean ended the interview, however, with a fundamental question: what made him begin the Yoknapatawpha saga? Well, he said, he wrote the first two novels because they were fun. But then, "Beginning with *Sartoris* I discovered that my own little postage stamp of native soil was worth writing about and that I would never live long enough to exhaust it, and by sublimating the actual into the aprocryphal I would have complete liberty to use whatever talent I might have to its absolute top. . . . I like to think of the world I created as being a kind of keystone in the Universe; that, as small as that keystone is, if it were ever taken away, the universe itself would collapse. My last book will be the Doomsday Book, the Golden Book, of Yoknapatawpha County. Then I shall break the pencil and I'll have to stop."[14] Faulkner worked on the final form of the interview with her in her apartment at 2 Sutton Place, high above the East River. He enjoyed some of the parties there, with guests

ranging from lively young people just beginning their careers to luminaries
such as Adlai Stevenson. George Plimpton would watch Faulkner, standing in a corner, observing. Faulkner was grateful for the devotion Jean
gave him, showing her his work, drawing sketches for her, inscribing her
copy of *A Fable*.

IT was a vastly different milieu he found when he returned to Mississippi
in early March. "A Letter to the North" appeared in *Life* on the fifth. One
night as he sat in an Oxford restaurant with Dean's widow, Louise Meadow,
and her friend Jane Coers, Jane started to talk about the wide influence
Faulkner had. But then she added that his mother was upset about the way
he was using it to stir people up. His face flushed in anger and he hit the
table with his hand, but instead of making any rejoinder, he just seethed
silently. One morning he met two small boys in Bailey's Woods. After a
brief but amiable chat, one of them—Clarence Moorer, who had a vague
idea about Faulkner's identity—said, "Mr. Faulkner, what is it that's so
different about you?" Faulkner told him to ask around. "Then come back
and tell me," he said, "and I'll tell you if it's right." The next time they
met, Faulkner asked Clarence if he had found anything out. "I asked two
people," the boy answered, "and all I could find out was that you're a
nigger-lover."

Fortunately, there was the new novel to divert him in the office when
he cared to turn to it. Outside, there was Tempy to train, though this
activity was a mixed blessing at best. He would go out to the paddock
wearing a polo player's belt to protect his tender back as he slammed down
onto the saddle after jumps that seemed to open a foot of daylight between the seat of his breeches and the saddle. Once she threw him, and he
landed so heavily that he was in pain for days. The old vertebral ache
returned, and he thought he had a cracked rib too. It turned out to be just
a bad bruise, but he was too sore to ride for days. In his habitual response
to pain, he turned to liquor. To add to the family's sense of oppression,
Lida Oldham died in late winter of 1956.

In mid-March he wrote Jean that his back was better, though he still
could not ride Tempy. The winter was over, he told her, with "flowers
everywhere and trees beginning to bud. Already redbud, 'Judas tree' and
dogwood soon."[15] But when the dogwood began to bloom in masses of
white in the groves around Rowan Oak, he would not be there to see it.
On Sunday, March 18, the effects of the accumulated anger, fear, frustration, injury, sickness, and drinking caught up with him. He began to
vomit blood and collapsed into unconsciousness. He was taken immediately
to the Baptist Hospital in Memphis, where they placed him in an oxygen
tent and started transfusions and intravenous feeding. When his brother
Jack came to see him, the doctor told Jack that if Faulkner didn't stop
drinking, it would eventually kill him. Jack had quit, and the doctor said
he should try to persuade his brother to do the same. But William Faulkner

was like their grandfather. He had suffered a hemorrhage before this, Sallie Murry thought, and when she had tried to tell him to stop he had said, "If I can't lead a normal life I'd just as soon be dead." Sitting on the uncomfortable hospital chair by the shining canopy that enclosed his brother, Jack told him what the doctor had said. Bill just smiled. Jack knew he would never quit.

Again Faulkner's strong constitution helped him to rally, and four days after he was admitted, he felt well enough to send a telegram of reassurance to Jean. Tests disclosed no ulcer. By Tuesday, March 27, he was able to dress and sit for a series of photographs by Richard C. Crowder, one of his doctors. Years before, Faulkner had written of Ratliff, after his gall bladder operation, "he had been sick and he showed it. . . ." Now, like Ratliff, he was mending, "the smooth brown of his face not pallid but merely a few shades lighter, cleaner looking. . . ."[16]

FAULKNER was well enough to leave for Charlottesville with Estelle in early April as the time approached for the birth of Jill's first child. Estelle settled herself to help, there at Fox Haven Farm, and he went on to New York, telephoning Estelle every night to ask for the news. His stomach was still troubling him and he was prey to depression and morbidity. One night he told Jean about Dean's death, sparing her none of the details of its ghastly aftermath. He went to see Dr. Ben Gilbert about his stomach, and sometimes he would have dinner with him and his wife, Anne. Gilbert could see that Faulkner was now straying from the strict diet that Dr. Crowder had prescribed for three months. Gilbert had enjoyed no more success with this patient than the other doctors had. And Faulkner resented questions about his drinking. "Never ask me why," he had once told Gilbert. "I don't know the answer. If I did I wouldn't do it."

On April 15, Jill gave birth to Paul D. Summers III, and Faulkner returned to Charlottesville. He would be almost as fond a grandparent as he had been a father, though Jill knew that his attitude toward children was a realistic one. Not long before, he had paraphrased Francis Bacon to her: "He who hath children hath given hostages to fortune."

He received two visitors at Fox Haven Farm that April from the University of Virginia. Emily Clark Balch had left a substantial sum for "the encouragement and production of American Literature," and it had been decided to use half of the income each year for a writer-in-residence program. Frederick L. Gwynn had made inquiries on behalf of the English Department. He considered William Faulkner the greatest American novelist, but he had little hope that he could be induced to accept a university appointment. Then one day Jill had said quite casually to a friend, "I think Pappy might be interested in that." When Gwynn wrote to Faulkner, he received a reply which not only indicated interest but gave a short listing of his needs. And when Gwynn went out to Fox Haven Farm, accompanied by Floyd Stovall, the chairman of the English Department, Faulkner repeated them. Stovall had said with some embarrassment that he doubted if they could raise $2,000. "Don't worry about money," Faulkner replied. "Don't pay me anything. It would only confuse my tax situation, and besides, I don't know whether I'll be any good at this or not. All I need is enough to buy a little whiskey and tobacco. Let me work at it awhile and we'll see how it goes." By the time they left he had agreed to come in the late winter and early spring of 1957 for eight to ten weeks.

With Jill and the baby continuing to thrive, he returned to New York for late April. On May 8 he went home to Oxford. When Jill had asked him how the book was going, he told her it wasn't. He had even given her material to develop into part of the novel for him. She had done some retyping of his pages from time to time, but she knew there were long stretches when he didn't work on it at all. The trouble, she thought, was that he didn't want to write that book. Now, alone at Rowan Oak while Estelle was in Charlottesville, he could try to come to grips with it again, but he felt no urgency about it. "Will be busy farming for a while now," he wrote Jean, "am drinking milk, eating properly, going to bed every night and sleeping until the damned noisy birds wake me about 4." One mockingbird was a particular pest. "We hear him all the time," he would tell one friend, "during the day and at night. He can imitate anything: other birds, horses, even trucks changing gear when they come up the Old Taylor Road. He's a real nuisance. But he probably figures, if we don't like it, we can always move." Later that month, the improvement he had expected had not materialized. "Now I dont even want to work on my book," he wrote Jean, "back is too painful to ride Tempy enough, so nothing to do but be a farmer while sitting in a car watching other people."[17]

As June came in, though, he was able to go sailing again, and he was back at work. Early that month he was able to send Commins what he reckoned to be a third of the manuscript. He might regard this as just the second volume in the Snopes trilogy, but he was still referring to so many other events in Yoknapatawpha history that it was as though he were trying to sum up in case there should be no other book after this one. His main concern was still the rise of Snopesism coupled with Stevens' resistance and his quixotic love for Eula. He continued alternating narrators as he carried the story to the point at which Flem Snopes prepares to move up to the vice-presidency of what had been Colonel Sartoris' bank. Gavin, seemingly vanquished by Eula's lover, Manfred de Spain, leaves for Heidelberg, then returns, only to find another female he can break his heart over —one almost, but not quite, like her mother: Linda Snopes. In Faulkner's covering letter he told Commins, "I still cant tell, it may be trash except for certain parts, though I think not. I still think it is funny, and at the end very moving; two women characters I am proud of."[18] He hoped to have it all in by December 1.

Immersed though he might be now in the re-creation of Jefferson as it was in about the year 1920, Faulkner could not shut out what was happening in Oxford and the country at large in 1956. Periodically he would discuss the situation with liberals such as James W. Silver, a history professor at Ole Miss, who had been principally responsible for Faulkner's speaking at the Southern Historical Association meeting in Memphis. One of Silver's friends was P. D. East, a newspaperman from near Hattiesburg who had a reputation like that of Hodding Carter for liberalism, intelligence, and fearlessness. One June day East and Silver went out to Rowan Oak. It was scorchingly hot, and so they took the *Ring Dove* out into Sardis Lake. Faulkner was interested in the possibility of forming a group of some sort in Mississippi, a bastion on the middle ground Faulkner saw as his own. They talked of forming a "Mississippi Moderates" group, but they concluded that they would probably spend all their time fending off attacks. Faulkner felt that one of their best chances lay with outstanding members of the current college generation. A group at Ole Miss had already done a series called "The Nigble Papers," in which they lampooned the Scotch-Irish claimed as forebears by many Mississippians.

When the three men returned to Rowan Oak, they gathered together a number of these papers and decided to use them as the basis for the first number of a semi-annual paper to be called *The Southern Reposure*. East volunteered to edit and pay for the first number, and it occupied him for much of the next month. From time to time he checked with Faulkner, whose taste for the lampoon had remained constant over the years. This time, however, the subjects included powerful men such as Mississippi Senator James O. Eastland. The three men did not use their own names. Instead, the publisher was listed as "Nathan Bedford Cooclose," and the masthead bore the bogus motto: " 'Know Ye The Truth And Be Ye Then Free' JOHN 3:16." Soon after the 10,000 copies were distributed, East visited Faulkner again. "East," said his co-founder, "you did a damned good job with that paper. I've sent copies to New York." But it was the first and last issue of *The Southern Reposure*.

During this time Faulkner had been doing more serious writing on this general subject than his collaboration on the remarks of Nathan Bedford Cooclose. Allan Morrison, an editor of *Ebony*, had written him in mid-June about the interview in *The Reporter*. In reply, Faulkner wrote a short essay answering the questions Morrison posed. He called it "A Letter to the Leaders of the Negro Race." It was an appeal for moderation that few of them would have wanted to hear. He urged them to follow Gandhi's way. "If I were a Negro, I would advise our elders and leaders to [follow] . . . a course of inflexible and unviolent flexibility directed against not just the schools but against all the public institutions from which we are interdict, as is being done against the Montgomery, Alabama, bus lines." The Negro's watchwords, he said, should be decency, quietness, courtesy, and dignity. "We must learn to deserve equality so that we can hold and keep it after we get it. We must learn responsibility, the responsibility of equality."[19] He had already been called a gradualist. This essay would serve only to affirm this label in the minds of white liberals and to discredit him with Negro activists.

A NUMBER of things had combined to keep Faulkner from doing much with the book from mid-June into early July. Besides his involvement in the civil rights crisis, he had taken his mother to Memphis twice for minor operations. In late May, President Eisenhower had asked citizen leaders of different professions to explore a "people-to-people" program which would help bridge international gaps widened by the Cold War. In mid-June, as an afterthought, he had asked Faulkner to head a section which would strive for better contacts between American and foreign writers. Faulkner had agreed to do it, and the preliminaries had taken time. In the heat of mid-July, it seemed to him that he had not gotten much work done constructively on anything except the *Ring Dove*. But then the old impulses began to reassert themselves. It was time now to turn from social controversy and concentrate his full attention on his true vocation, time to drive through to completion the work nearly thirty years old in conception and nearly fifteen years delayed in the writing.

By the end of the last week in July he was able to write Commins that though things were dull in Oxford, they were "good enough now since my novel is going pretty well." He was still proud of Eula and Linda Snopes. Eula is far from the bucolic Lilith she had been in *The Hamlet*. More sophisticated, more articulate, she is still the same figure of unparalleled sexuality—so much so that Gavin Stevens and his sister can think of her as both Helen and Semiramis. Gavin has projected his feelings for the mother onto the daughter, so that his old romantic impulse is now tinged with the parental. He sets to work "forming her mind" (179), lending her volumes of Donne and buying her ice-cream sodas after school. But as the relationship progresses, he stops himself abruptly with the reminder, "the County Attorney must not be actually *seen* running down his office stairs and across the street into a drugstore where a sixteen-year-old high-school junior waited." (207) He sends away for catalogues from women's colleges. He fears for her reputation and even proposes to her, only to learn that she loves him but doesn't want to marry anyone. He finds himself engaged in a covert struggle to help a vulnerable girl escape from what he takes to be the stultifying constrictions of family, town, and class. Faulkner had urged Joan Williams to use aspects of their relationship in her writing. Now, after an interval of a few years, he was doing it. But he was also employing literary materials from the past. Uncle Willy Christian appeared for the first time since the short story bearing his name twenty years before. Jason Compson appeared to collect for his mother the rent for the store which Montgomery Ward Snopes called "Atelier Monty" and used to show French postcards.

As mid-August approached, Faulkner continued with vigor. "Book is going splendidly," he wrote Jean. "Each time I begin to hope I am written out and can quit, I discover I am not at all cured and the sickness will probably kill me. . . ."[20] One reason why it might have been going easily was that by now he must have reached the place where he could interpolate "Mule in the Yard," of 1934. He grafted on a new ending, though, in which Mrs. Mannie Hait, the protagonist, was aided not only by Stevens but also by Flem Snopes, against his own kinsman I. O. Snopes. This emphasized a new factor in the Snopes saga, Flem's increasing desire not just for money and power, but also for respectability. With his flanks now secured, he could open his final covert assault upon his long-cherished objective: the presidency of Colonel Sartoris' bank. It would be Eula herself who would finally reveal how Flem manipulated Linda to produce the result he wanted.

By now Faulkner's emotions were deeply engaged in his narrative. "Just finishing the book," he wrote Jean on August 22. "It breaks my heart, I wrote one scene and almost cried. I thought it was just a funny book but I was wrong."[21] The initial impact comes from the suicide of Eula Varner Snopes—with the tragic waste of this life cut short at thirty-eight, and the effect of her death on those left behind. Charles Mallison sees the tears course down his uncle's cheeks as Stevens muses, "She was bored. She loved, had a capacity to love, for love, to give and accept love. Only she tried twice and failed twice to find somebody not just strong enough to deserve, earn it, match it, but even brave enough to accept it." (359)

In this last section of the novel Faulkner again drew heavily on family lore. Manfred de Spain is forced out of his bank, like John Wesley Thompson Falkner. Flem Snopes draws his money out of his own bank, as did John Wesley Thompson Falkner. The second line of Eula's epitaph is identical with that of Sallie Murry Falkner. After taking over the Sartoris bank, Flem Snopes buys Manfred de Spain's house, just as Joe Parks took over the Colonel's bank and moved into Murry Falkner's house.

He also drew on personal material. The will Linda makes in Flem's favor has been drawn by a young Oxford lawyer named Stone who had gone to school in New Haven. County attorney Gavin Stevens, "already white-headed" (317) stands on Seminary Hill and looks down on Jefferson and Yoknapatawpha County radiating out from it. This suggests very clearly the creator looking upon his creation. And it is as though Faulkner was summing up the saga once again.

The last chapter is narrated by Charles Mallison, one of the generation that would carry on the battle against Snopesism, though this quality has begun to change its appearance as Flem's quest for respectability leads him to effect the banishment of Montgomery Ward Snopes from Jefferson, as he had managed that of I. O. Snopes earlier. Ostensibly a grieving widower and now a deacon in the Baptist church, Flem has reached the estate Faulkner had used thirty years before as his starting point for *Father Abraham*. The last chapter, however, unfolds another threat to his hard-won eminence, and for this Faulkner had gone back at least twenty years. In Hollywood he had told Joel Sayre, "the Snopeses, you know, they mail them to each other, take them to the station and put tags on them." Now Faulkner told how Byron Snopes, the absconded bank cashier, mails to Flem his four dangerous offspring by a Mexican Apache squaw. Faulkner was ending on a savagely comic rather than a tragicomic note, but clearly uppermost for him as he completed his draft was the quixotic Gavin's feeling for the tragic Eula and her daughter.

Now, in the last days of August, Faulkner could afford to take a little time off before revising and retyping. There was always the *Ring Dove* and the farm, and always more work around Rowan Oak. He had planned a new barn, and when he found that all the local carpenters were working for housing contractors, he did his own manual labor in the blazing summer weather. With Norfleet's stepbrother, Broadus, to hand him the tools, he sawed and hammered. When Johncy no longer heard him, he strolled over to look at the structure. "He showed it to me with a great deal of satisfaction," John remembered, "for it stood, to him, as another evidence of his independence. . . . He pointed out the cupola he had added as an afterthought. He was so pleased with it that he said he thought he'd add a weathervane on top and a barn clock in the front."[22]

As September came in, it was time for him to resume his public role. He packed up his half-completed typescript, and by the second week of the month he was in Charlottesville with Jill, Paul, and his grandson, "Tad." On September 11 he was in Washington for three days' work on the People-to-People Program. The first day was taken up with speeches by the President, the Vice-President, and the Secretary of State. The assembled participants were informed again that this was to be a private effort rather than a federal program, that there was a need to penetrate the Iron Curtain with information about American efforts for a better life for all, and about the importance of showing that a system based on liberty was best. The second day's sessions showed that Faulkner's group was something of a catch-all, with representation not only for writers, the fine arts, and music, but also for religious groups and medical and health groups as well as hobbyists and the handicapped. Faulkner's only recorded contribution was that he thought writers were not going to unite and that he would get in touch with individual writers.

Fortunately, Donald Klopfer had already set things in motion. Saxe Commins agreed to help with the letter-writing, and Jean Ennis, the Random House publicity director, undertook the record-keeping. Harvey Breit consented to be co-chairman. Faulkner sent Breit a letter to go out to the writers they settled on. It solicited ideas and included a few of Faulkner's own in aid of the somewhat hazy goals. One was to anesthetize American vocal cords for a year. Another was to establish a fund to bring in 10,000 young Communists to the United States each year, at the end of which "Any installment plan automobiles or gadgets which they have undertaken would be impounded." After this, they would be supplanted by 10,000 more to be seduced by the American way of life. He concluded with a P.S.: "In a more serious vein, please read the enclosed one-page description of Mr. Eisenhower's purpose."[23]

Then he went back to Oxford and the task of finishing his novel. Returning to New York, he took it all with him and set up once more in Saxe Commins' office. There, in the last days of September, he completed his 478-page typescript.

Now he had to turn back to the People-to-People Program. He did so out of duty rather than conviction. Later, when Harvey Breit would ask him how he got into it, he would say, simply, "When your President asks you to do something, you do it." Nearly a third of the recipients of the letter Faulkner had sent to Breit wanted no part of the idea. Several of the twenty who accepted the invitation to participate—Robert Lowell and Waldo Frank among them—were frank to say that they had responded because of Faulkner. Conrad Aiken said the program should be dropped as unworkable, and Edmund Wilson wrote back that he was surprised that Faulkner was involved in such a scheme. A second form letter failed to elicit enough ideas to serve as a basis for a preliminary report and a meeting. So Faulkner and Breit sent out another on October 11 with a questionnaire. It comprised thirty suggestions, ranging from the one about anesthetizing American vocal cords to dropping the whole program or to electing presidential candidate Adlai Stevenson. They sent out fifty of them and waited. Faulkner took the train south to spend six weeks at home.

In Oxford things went quietly. Estelle had come to accept her situation, with its aloneness, just as she had finally accepted her alcoholism and striven to overcome it through the help of Alcoholics Anonymous. In early November she had written Saxe Commins, "I know, as you must, that Bill feels some sort of compulsion to be attached to some young woman at all times—it's Bill—At long last I am sensible enough to concede him the right to do as he pleases, and without recrimination—It is not that I don't care—(I wish it were not so)—but all of a sudden [I] feel sorry for him—wish he could know without words between us, that it's not very important after all—"[24]

On an occasional Sunday, worshippers at St. Peter's would see Estelle and Bill Faulkner at the 11 A.M. service, or sometimes Faulkner alone. He might take in a matinee at the Lyric if a Western or a mystery was playing. On many mornings he would go out to the paddock. "Am working with Tempy again," he wrote Jean Stein in late October, "have a series of jumps cut through the fences around the place so I have about a half mile steeple chase course." Two weeks later he was working Tempy every day, so much that he stayed "stiff and sore and stove up all the time now; she is very rough . . . has the same system for jumping everything: to jump as high and hard as she can. . . ." All these activities had not driven the uncertainties about the book from his thoughts. "I want to know how you liked Linda and Eula," he wrote. "You can tell me."

By the time he returned to New York in late November, Harvey Breit and Jean Ennis had collated the results of the questionnaire. Some recipients had clipped out Faulkner's signature, not knowing that it was machine-made. But forty-one responses had produced suggestions for various international exchanges and ideas, "ranging from the freeing of Ezra Pound to a sounder foreign policy," as Breit wrote the respondents over Faulkner's signature. On November 29 a group numbering just under two dozen met at Breit's house on East 64th Street.

To poet Donald Hall it seemed a curious gathering. Faulkner was seated near the door, with "no expressions of feeling in his facial expression at all and very little in the inflections of his voice. He was holding a gigantic Old Fashioned glass . . . which I later found out to be Jack Daniel's and a little bit of ice and nothing else. He drank at this regularly and it was refilled. He was extremely calm and quiet and his voice was not slurred. . . ." He said he thought they would all agree "that most committees, maybe all, are the last despair and cry of impotence." Besides, "we have spent all our lives already doing this very job which President Eisenhower discovered last year is a critical necessity. So there is not much more we can do." But he went on to restate one of his ideas. "Let's bring our enemies here to see this country as it is, instead of a false picture. Let them see what it is here that makes us write."

As the discussion began, Saul Bellow seemed incensed. "What's going to happen to these families when they go back?" he demanded. John Steinbeck asked about an airlift to the United States of refugees after the Hungarian uprising. Faulkner responded with a criticism of the Voice of America for encouraging people behind the Iron Curtain to think they could be free when, at the time of the uprising, this country failed to help them. Writers could propose all they liked, he said, but they had no pressure groups of million-member labor unions behind them. Edna Ferber and then Elmer Rice joined in the heated discussion. By now, thought Donald Hall, "the meeting was chaotic and pretty ridiculous." John Steinbeck thought they could do nothing, and he was convinced that the People-to-People Program was actually illegal. William Carlos Williams said he thought some beginnings could be made, and he made an eloquent plea for a recommendation that the government free Ezra Pound, who was still confined in Washington's St. Elizabeth's Hospital on the grounds of his being unable, by reason of insanity, to stand trial for wartime treason. Robert Hillyer sat glowering, ready to renew his battle with Williams on this point. As they began a heated argument, Saul Bellow joined in, angry and horrified at the implications of Pound's anti-Semitism, particularly after the Holocaust.

Then it was cocktail time. By now Harvey Breit was trying to derive what consensus he could from the discussion. It seemed to Hall that Faulkner had assented "mildly to most of the propositions about the Hungarians, about the dissemination of cheap books, about the freeing of Ezra Pound, and to offer his own contribution of fellowships to the automobile plants." A committee was formed, comprising Faulkner, Steinbeck, and Hall, to distribute a record of the discussion together with a draft of the proposals. As Hall left Breit's house one image remained clearly in his mind from the hours of talk: "William Faulkner himself, a small, tidy, delicate, aloof, stern, rigid, stony figure—delicate and stony at the same time . . . that small aloof figure sitting in his chair rather away from the rest of the people, holding that enormous glass from which he frequently took a long sip, and that quiet, mellow, bourbony voice coming out with its absurd proposals."

By December 3, Saxe Commins was able to send a draft of the paper to the three committee members. Faulkner replied from Oxford that as soon as everyone had a chance to respond to it, he would send a final version to the President. But he had little faith in Eisenhower's understanding of world conditions or in the administration's foreign policy. He wrote the editor of *The New York Times* that repudiation of the French-British-Israeli attack on Egypt after the Egyptian seizure of the Suez Canal was folly. "What this country needs right now," he wrote, "is not a golf player but a poker player."[25]

He was at home for the Christmas holidays even though he felt little holiday spirit that season. His stomach was bothering him again, so much that he thought he might have to go back on the bland diet, but it did not keep him from reading the galleys of the novel, now called *The Town*, and rewriting a page which went to the printer on January 2. Most of the communications bearing his name in the early days of 1957 were emanating from New York, however, for he was not yet through with his assignment. On January 2 copies of the "distillate of the discussion" went out to sixty-four people with a covering note over his signature. The responses came in with surprising promptness. They were in the main approving, though a number took strong exception to the proposal to free Ezra Pound. But the chairman of the writers' group was not finished. He and the others were summoned to New York by general chairman Charles E. Wilson, former president of the General Electric Company, for a meeting on February 4.

When Faulkner telephoned Harvey Breit, he sounded so depressed that Breit invited him to dinner. As soon as he arrived, Breit mixed him a drink, and as he sipped it, the trouble came out. Jean Stein had telephoned to say that she couldn't keep a date they had made. (Donald Klopfer had seen him recently in low spirits and remembered a thank-you note Faulkner had sent Pat Klopfer after they had entertained him and Jean. "To Pat," he had written, "who is always good to me whether I've been thrown over by a horse or a dame.") But though he was depressed, Faulkner felt well enough to eat two of Pat Breit's Cornish game hens. After the liqueurs, they switched back to whiskey as the desultory conversation veered to the next morning's meeting. Breit's uneasiness turned to alarm as Faulkner seemed to be saying that he planned to repudiate their recommendations. They didn't need any exchange of writers, he said, because writers all over the world understood each other. As for disseminating literature, "here's what we should do," he said. "We should get two stamps, and we take every book that goes out of this country and we stamp it 'True' or 'Not True.'"

"Bill," Breit said, "who's to say what's true and not true?"

"We'll get a committee of writers, and they'll know what's true and what's not."

When Harvey Breit called at the Algonquin the next morning, Faulkner looked terrible. And it seemed that he was prepared to stick to his "True-Not True" scheme. Breit was appalled at the prospect. Faulkner's perverseness was obviously due in part to the mood of black depression which had settled over him, but it may have been an example of a particularly Faulknerian sort of black humor. Sometimes there would flicker out from him a kind of mordant and sardonic wit or invention, and it did not matter to him who would suffer from its consequences. Inwardly writhing, looking for some way out of the dilemma, Breit made a desperate stab.

"Bill," he said, "I don't feel very well. I don't think I can take this meeting. Let's not go."

Faulkner considered this in silence. "Well," he said slowly, "let's just look in."

A sizable group of chairmen and staff members had already assembled when they reached the Metropolitan Club. Seating themselves near the back, Breit and Faulkner listened as Charles Wilson opened the meeting. Breit was searching his mind anew for ways to keep the chairman of the writers' group from making his disastrous pronouncement when Faulkner leaned toward him. "Let's get out of here," he said.

IN the following days there was good news and bad news. Ober had sold the last chapter of *The Town* to *The Saturday Evening Post* for $3,000. Wald and Columbia were exercising their option and purchasing the screen rights to *The Sound and the Fury* for $35,000. But Ober had to pass on the word to James J. Geller that he thought it would be at least a month before the author could sign the contracts. The cycle Harvey Breit had seen in its inception had gone into its next phase, and Ober thought it would require extended hospitalization before it ran its course.

He was reckoning without the combined forces of Benjamin A. Gilbert, M.D., Stanley W. Mackenzie, R.N., and the recuperative powers of William Faulkner. In mid-October the Charlottesville *Daily Progress* had published the news that William Faulkner would be writer-in-residence at the University of Virginia for the second semester of the 1956–57 academic year. Floyd Stovall had written Faulkner that the university would provide $2,000, most of which would go for rent, utilities, and a butler and maid. While still in New York, Faulkner had planned to reach

Charlottesville on February 1 for a few days of house-hunting with Estelle. He apparently was ready now for more stability in his domestic life. Estelle confided to the Comminses that she had offered him a divorce, but he did not take her up on it.[26]

Despite fears of precipitating a second coronary, Commins devotedly nursed him for three days, carefully recording the ordeal, until Mackenzie was found to relieve him.[27] On Saturday morning, February 9, Nurse Mackenzie took his patient to Ben Gilbert's office and from there to Penn Station. At 12:10 P.M. Faulkner was sitting in a roomette, pale and weary-looking but self-possessed, as the train pulled out on the first leg of the trip to Charlottesville. There, one week later, in the heart of rolling Albemarle County in the shadow of the Blue Ridge Mountains, he would embark on a new phase of his life.

Then, as though at signal, the fireflies. . . . And you stand
suzerain and solitary above the whole sum of your life beneath
that incessant ephemeral spangling. First is Jefferson, the center,
radiating weakly its puny glow into space; beyond it, enclosing
it, spreads the County, tied by the diverging roads to that center
as is the rim to the hub by its spokes, yourself detached as God
Himself for this moment above the cradle of your nativity and
of the men and women who made you, the record and chronicle of your native land proffered for your perusal in ring by
concentric ring like the ripples on living water above the dream-
less slumber of your past; you to preside unanguished and
immune above this miniature of man's passions and hopes and
disasters. . . .

—*The Town* (315-316)

THE University of Virginia had changed little in appearance since William Faulkner's brief sojourn there a quarter of a century before. Once
again he strolled the Lawn of Thomas Jefferson's "academical village."
Photographers were there on February 15, 1957, to frame him in their
lenses, looking off, keen-eyed, toward the Ragged Mountains in the distance, behind him the pillars of the Rotunda and bare oak branches against
the pale winter sky.

He began his work that morning. Walking slowly and directly—he
was like Judge Dunkinfield in *Knight's Gambit*: walking with "an erect
and dignified carriage which the Negroes called 'rearbackted'" (11)—
he entered Frederick Gwynn's class. He seated himself stiffly at the desk
before the sixteen graduate students of American fiction and the thirty
visitors. The session began with questions about the current assignment,
The Sound and the Fury. He answered carefully in his light, soft voice.
Then he would look down at the desk top, idly turning over a matchbox
housed in a small metal holder decorated with RAF wings. His calm
belied his feelings. "I'm terrified at first," he would say later, "because

I'm afraid it won't move." But the pace began to pick up and the questions ranged over other works. Soon the hour passed. He stood dour-faced by the door with a smiling Floyd Stovall as the pleased students and visitors filed out.

In the press conference that followed, Faulkner was more relaxed. He had lost none of his penchant for sharp remarks that made good copy. Just why, asked one reporter, did he accept the invitation to come to the university? "It was because I like your country," he answered, "I like Virginia, and I like Virginians. Because Virginians are all snobs, and I like snobs. A snob has to spend so much time being a snob that he has little left to meddle with you, and so it's very pleasant here." He agreed that being near his grandson was one of the advantages. Another reporter wondered what parts of the Southern tradition Faulkner hoped his grandson would carry on and what parts he would discard. He slowly relit his pipe. "I hope of course that he will cope with his environment as it changes," he said. "And, I hope that his mother and father will try to raise him without bigotry as much as can be done. He can have a Confederate battleflag if he wants it but he shouldn't take it too seriously."[1] After an hour of questioning, the lively conference ended, and Faulkner left with Gwynn.

A forty-one-year-old associate professor, Fred Gwynn was a good choice as chairman of the three-man committee administering the writer-in-residence program. A former torpedo-bomber pilot who had also served on the staff of Admiral William F. "Bull" Halsey, he was not only a scholar but a witty and congenial companion. Working with him was Joseph Blotner, an assistant professor six years his junior, who had done his war service as a B-17 bombardier in the 8th Air Force. Over coffee in Gwynn's office, Faulkner expressed polite interest in the wartime flying of these two English teachers. It was a good point of departure for their service together during Faulkner's tenure as writer-in-residence, far better than their mutual interest in literature. When the other member of the committee, Floyd Stovall, had written Faulkner in November, he had said the department would be glad to stand as a barrier between him and engagements outside his duties. Faulkner had gratefully accepted this offer, and it would usually fall to the two other committee members to carry it out. Gwynn was quick to perceive another obligation, one to all the students—living and yet unborn—who could not sit in those classrooms and hear William Faulkner talk about his work. Moreover, he wanted to ensure that Faulkner would not be misquoted or quoted out of context. When Gwynn suggested to Faulkner that for both of these reasons his sessions should be recorded, he readily agreed. So it was that when he and Blotner accompanied him to classes outside the English Department's home base of New Cabell Hall, one of them would be carrying a tape recorder. That year both of them wore raincoats that reminded some observers of sinister characters in adventure movies. The sight of two men of average height on either side of a smaller man, one of the two carrying a case, would provide material for the student humor magazine.

Faulkner was assigned a small faculty office where he would meet students who signed up for appointments. He would sit there with the door open, legs crossed, reading *The New York Times* through dark horn-rimmed glasses until a student or an occasional faculty member would knock diffidently. Whether the student wished to talk about his writing or literature in general, Faulkner usually went to some pains to answer the questions as fully as he could and often to ask about the visitor's own concerns. When the office hours were over, he would stroll down the corridor to Gwynn's office—which soon became "the Squadron Room"—where Blotner would join them for coffee. One day not long after Faulkner had assumed his duties, he put a question to Floyd Stovall: "Can I come in more often than two mornings a week?"

Some mornings he would read the letters that accumulated in his departmental mailbox. One day in late February he told Professor Atcheson Hench that his mail currently came mostly from old ladies criticizing his remark that Virginians were snobs. "I didn't mean any harm by that," he said. He had been right in anticipating respect for his privacy, and he received it out of polite consideration and often awe. And there had been none of the threats or insults that his stand on integration had evoked at home. When he answered his mail, he usually did so in the handsome two-story Georgian-style brick house on Rugby Road, just a twenty-minute walk from his office, which Jill had found for her parents. When *The Saturday Evening Post* wanted to send a photographer so they could run a picture with the last chapter of *The Town* (under the title "The Waifs"), he typed out a telegram that ended WILL SUBMIT FOR ONE THOUSAND DOLLARS CASH IN ADVANCE.[2] He wrote Joan Bowen that Saxe Commins had sent him the first copy of *The Town*. "It looks pretty good," he said. He would send her copy to her.

As February drew to a close his schedule remained easy. It was at a departmental reception for the Faulkners at the Colonnade Club that a touch of the old irascibility showed. Estelle stood in the receiving line wearing a flowered hat and frilly gown, the gracious Southern lady well-schooled in the art of conversation. He stood his ground as usual, suffering politely. He even brightened when one of the guests began talking hunting, fishing, and riding to him, but when another posed a literary question, he turned it aside brusquely. "I'm off duty now," he said.

He was in a good place to talk hunting. Parts of Albemarle County had been hunt country since the time of Lord Fairfax, and descendants of George Washington had ridden there. Dotted with modest mansions, Albemarle could stand comparison with any area of the Old Dominion. The Farmington and Keswick Hunt Clubs, like those of Middleburg and

Warrenton, preserved the customs of the European hunt. Faulkner had hunted Mississippi fashion, listening to hounds baying at night as they ran their quarry. Now, in this region boasting two hunts, he could try the real thing. He was barely six months away from his sixtieth birthday and he still needed the polo belt for the cracked vertebrae, but no such considerations would keep him away from the horses and hounds.

He went about it in a very practical way. Jill had been hunting for some time. Often she rode at Grover Vandevender's 500-acre horse farm and riding school in nearby Ivy. Grover raised beef cattle on the good grazing land and ran his horse business at the same time that he served as huntsman to the Farmington Hunt. Big and friendly, he had the weathered face of a man outdoors in all seasons. He and Faulkner took to each other immediately. Very soon Faulkner was a familiar figure there, in a tweed jacket with patched elbows, smoking his pipe, often sitting and observing on a plank atop the fence opposite the barn. Grover agreed to instruct him. Two years older and lame in bad weather from numerous fractures, Grover knew that almost-sixty was a somewhat advanced age for jumping large animals over stone and wood obstacles, but he put Faulkner on a safe, good-tempered mount called Sweet William. Faulkner was assiduous, and he made progress. In due course he joined Grover and some of the others for the "cubbing," in which puppies and grown hounds were taken out together to give the young dogs experience. Faulkner enjoyed this form of riding, but it was more than that. When the hunters took the field in the fall that year, he meant to be among them.

He made four university appearances during early March. In the first he read from "Spotted Horses" and then answered a question by looking back to the time when, with Buster Callicoat, he had bought just such an animal himself with $4.75 of his savings. Smiling, he described their attempts to "gentle" it and the ensuing disaster when they hitched it to a homemade cart. Everyone in the audience enjoyed the reminiscence, but none so much as those who had known the story first as Ike McCaslin's recollection of his debt to Boon Hogganbeck in Part 3 of "The Bear." The other sessions produced familiar responses, but each time there was usually something new as well. He politely turned stupid or inept questions into good ones, answering in words that were reflective, measured, and often a little sad. "I'm inclined to think," he told one of the classes, "that the only peace man knows is—he says, Why good gracious yesterday I was happy. . . . That maybe peace is only a condition in retrospect, when the subconscious had got rid of the gnats and the tacks and the broken glass in experience and has left only the peaceful pleasant things—that was peace. Maybe peace is not is, but was." At other times, as he sat there fingering a pipe under bright fluorescent lights that glanced off the white hair and aquiline nose, something of a gay indomitable spirit seemed to come through. After he had declined to say anything about Hemingway because he was still alive, one student asked if he would say something about his own writing. "No," he said, "I still haven't [completed] it, but I intend to live to be about a hundred years old, so I've got forty more years yet. By that time I'll answer your question if you're still around."[3]

Meanwhile, he was ready to go voyaging again. He had been unable to accept an invitation to visit Greece in September 1955, but now, in mid-February 1957, he had consulted the university and agreed to spend two weeks there in late March, when Dimitri Myrat would produce *Requiem for a Nun* in Athens' Kotopouli Theatre. He would make official appearances during one week and then enjoy a second week on his own. The mariner of Sardis Lake had not fulfilled his plan of returning to sail the Stockholm archipelago, but now he hoped to sail Homer's wine-dark sea.

WHEN Faulkner flew into Athens on the evening of March 17, he was greeted by Second Secretary Stephen Gebelt and Cultural Affairs Officer Duncan Emrich and his wife, Sally, of the American Embassy. To them it seemed ridiculous that Washington should have forwarded a copy of the department's advice on handling William Faulkner. Their first thought was to take him to one of the city's cultural centers, the bar of the Grande Bretagne, and they did so.

Faulkner began with assurance at the noon press conference the next day. After he had fielded the standard questions about segregation and fellow writers, he showed how adept he had become at combining avoidance and public relations.

"Do you have a message for the Greek people?" asked one of the journalists.

"What message can anyone give," Faulkner returned, "to a people who is already the bravest and toughest and most independent people? Your country is the cradle of civilized man. Your ancestors are the mothers and fathers of civilization, and of human liberty. What more do you want from me, an American farmer?"[4]

Two formal dinners and a call on Dimitri Myrat at the Kotopouli Theatre were followed by a formal call on the officers of the Athens Academy. This year its annual Gold Medal would go to the embattled people of Cyprus, the Silver Medal, to William Faulkner. After arrangements were made for the presentation on March 28, Faulkner, Emrich, and Gebelt departed for a luncheon given by the general secretary of the Merchant Marine. Then came an appearance at a reception given by the Association of Traffic Police of Athens. That evening Faulkner attended a performance of *Requiem for a Nun* at the Kotopouli and then gave a curtain speech to 1,200 members of the Workers Clubs of Athens. Such a schedule would inevitably lower his resistance. As he posed for photographs with Myrat and his wife—who played Gavin Stevens and

Temple Drake—American Ambassador George V. Allen wore a keenly speculative look as he gazed at the guest of honor.

The next day Faulkner was able to leave on a two-day trip to Delhi with Stephen Gebelt. He napped in the car, and whenever they stopped, there was always plenty of ouzo, the potent licorice-flavored liqueur of Greece. By the time they returned from their visit to the shrine of the great oracle, the industrialist Bodosakis Athanasiades had put his yacht, the *Jeannetta*, and its five-man crew at Duncan Emrich's disposal. It was stocked with Scotch and smoked salmon, champagne and caviar. This was the part of the trip Faulkner had been waiting for. They headed southwest from Piraeus, the port of Athens, and that night the *Jeannetta* tied up at Naupflion. The next day they motored to the site of ancient Mycenae. To First Secretary Lee Metcalf, Faulkner wore a poker face. Behind it, he was closely observing modern Greeks against the ancient background. As he would later put it, "The people seem to function against that past that for all its remoteness in time it was still inherent in the light, the resurgence of spring, you didn't expect to see the ghosts of the old Greeks, or expect to see the actual figures of the gods, but you had a sense that they were near and they were still powerful, not inimical, just powerful. That they themselves had reached and were enjoying a kind of a nirvana, they existed, but they were free of man's folly and trouble, of having to involve themselves in man's problem."[5]

After another night at Naupflion they set out for the Cyclades and the Aegean beyond. Emrich got Faulkner to begin work on his acceptance speech for the Silver Medal, but he stopped after writing three sentences. Emrich ruefully concluded that they were reaping the rewards of scoffing at Leon Picon's advice. Faulkner understandably preferred lolling on deck and sipping ouzo. He would take off his shirt and turn his aching back to the sun. Sally Emrich had given him a vigorous massage that seemed to ease the sore spots. "Miss Sally," he would say, "pound me some more." They coasted along through the lazy day, the sea calm and the sky a cloudless blue. "Did you ever think what life would be like if men could do this every day without worrying about the bomb?" he asked. "Hit me again, Miss Sally."

But on the morning of the twenty-sixth the weather started to change, and they began the voyage back to Piraeus. Sitting with Faulkner in the *Jeannetta*'s top forward lounge, Duncan Emrich got him to work on the acceptance speech again. Faulkner would start a phrase and Emrich would rough it into a sentence for his approval and write it down. By midmorning they had completed the speech in a page and a half, and Faulkner was happy to go back to the stern and join the others for ouzo and snacks on the semi-enclosed deck. By now they were heading into a very rough sea, and the captain told Emrich they had to turn back and make for Siros. Emrich had joined the others in the stern at the moment when the captain, turning, put the boat broadside to the sea. She heeled dangerously, and Emrich wondered if the top-heavy *Jeannetta* would recover, but she completed the turn before the next wave hit her.

They put into Siros in storm and rain and concluded that to be sure of reaching Athens in time, they would have to take the only vessel bound for Piraeus: a miserable island-hopping steamer, a dirty red-gray hulk that heaved even though she was berthed at the dock. They got under way in the teeming darkness, slogging out of the harbor and into the open sea while the wind screamed. In the middle of the night Emrich heard a knock on the door of their cramped cabin. It was Faulkner, dressed only in his shorts. He shouted over the roar of the wind, "They've got a little ouzo in the bar."

On deck the next morning in Piraeus, Faulkner seemed to Emrich "fresh as a daisy." That night he got through a formal dinner followed by a dance and reception with 150 guests. The morning of the twenty-eighth began with a session with a hundred Greek students. A photographer snapped him as he made his way through them. They were applauding, and there was a faint smile on his face. He had the air of a man slowly negotiating a tightrope, a ceremonial glass of ouzo in his hand. That night he received the scroll and Silver Medal of the academy. He accepted the medal, he said, as one chosen by the academy to represent the principle that man shall be free. "When the sun of Pericles cast the shadow of civilized man around the earth," he said, "that shadow curved until it touched America." Now he had come home to the source, back to the cradle of civilized man. He said he would tell his countrymen "that the qualities in the Greek race—toughness, bravery, independence and pride—are too valuable to lose. It is the duty of all men to see that they do not vanish from the earth."[6] For the next two weeks those words would be heard in newsreels throughout Greece.

The official functions continued for two more days. At the gala performance of *Requiem for a Nun*, he seemed to be dozing most of the time up to the intermission. He was taken backstage, to emerge for a curtain speech. When he stepped out between the curtains into the footlights' glare, he said a few words to the audience not about the play but about his reaction to their country. According to custom, he received a bouquet of flowers. He made his formal courtly bow to the ringing applause, and, composed, stood there for a moment, stiffly erect, holding the bouquet upside down.

Afterward he and Duncan and Sally Emrich went out on the town. The next morning, when the Emrichs got to the Grande Bretagne, it seemed to them that the suite was crowded and the bathroom a profusion of flowers. "Miss Sally," Faulkner said, "I didn't get much sleep last night. There was an awful noise and water all over. And I have to apologize about the carnations. When the bidet blew up there wasn't much I could do about the carnations." Soon it was time to go to the airport. Like the visit to Japan, this trip had been the best stroke that Americans could remember in their service there.

GETTING the medalist home was a more difficult problem. Faulkner checked in at the Algonquin and collapsed there. Saxe Commins went to his aid and found him, he noted on April 2, in a "near-state of catalepsy."[7] After Faulkner had revived somewhat, Commins put him on a train for Washington and wired Hal Howland that he was coming. Howland knew nothing of this, however, until Commins phoned him at the very moment that Faulkner, again virtually *hors de combat*, arrived at the Washington station. Providentially, Howland's friend, former basketball star Nat Holman, phoned him from the station a moment later. Holman then found Faulkner and took care of him until Howland arrived. Obviously, a State Department debriefing the next morning was out of the question, and Howland decided to take Faulkner to Charlottesville that night. He drove along Virginia's dark back roads, past Fairfax, past Culpeper, past Madison as Faulkner slept, rousing only for a stop at a service station men's room. He took a Miltown tablet, and soon they were speeding along the winding roads again in the moonless night. Suddenly, "Faulkner bounded from his seat, lifted the door handle, swung open the door and took one step into the night. A lunge and a wild grab and I had his coat tail. Yanking him back into his seat I shouted, 'Bill, are you trying to kill yourself? We're doing at least sixty!'

"Mr. Faulkner drawled: 'I was just going to ask the stewardess for a glass of water!' "

At last Howland turned in the drive at Rugby Road and delivered his charge to Estelle Faulkner and Malcolm Franklin. Almost immediately Faulkner revived and commanded Malcolm to fetch his Valpack. Then, Howland remembered, "Faulkner took out from amidst all his garments a brilliant, shiny silver helmet, a helmet such as those worn by proud Athenian warriors of Panhellenic days. He explained that the chief of police in Athens had given the helmet to him as a gift."[8] Faulkner put it on and modeled it for his family. It was three o'clock in the morning. After two or three cups of coffee, Howland headed back to Washington.

The next day Faulkner was out of circulation. The cycle begun in Greece ran its course in Virginia, and he landed in the hospital on April 7. To add to Estelle's troubles, Malcolm succumbed to the same complaint. But Faulkner demonstrated his recuperative powers once more, and inside a few days he was home again, helping to care for his stepson.

As spring flowered in Charlottesville, Faulkner became more and more a familiar figure, strolling up Rugby Road to the Grounds, gazing ahead abstractedly, politely answering the greetings of students who had sat in class with him. Their responses and those of the faculty and townspeople to his readings and classroom appearances had been so enthusiastic that the Writer-in-Residence Committee was thinking ahead to next year. There was another consideration, which Fred Gwynn had stated wryly in a memorandum. He enumerated the large fees which artists such as John Dos Passos and Thornton Wilder had received from other universities. For the coming year the funds from the Balch bequest to the university would probably provide no more than $2,000. Gwynn concluded that "we are in the paradoxical position of being able to afford only a Nobel and Pulitzer Prize winner." Faulkner seemed still to be enjoying himself, and the committee proposed to explore the idea of a second year.

His enormous appeal to Virginians was demonstrated again that April. On the fifteenth, visitors came by invitation from colleges all over the state to hear him. Prompted by a note from Gwynn, many of them had prepared questions. Near the end of the session one woman raised her hand. She began in a plaintive tone. "Mr. Faulkner," she said, "we read about all these symbols in your novels and short stories. Could you tell me just one symbol that I could take back to my class?" He smiled as he waited for the laughter to subside. "Well," he said, "since being at the University I have learned of several I was not aware of before." He stopped to think for a moment. "There's probably not one that I would use deliberately. I have used it only by reaching into the grab-bag to pick out something that I needed to finish a corner with, to nail a stake on a fence with. . . . And if it's a symbol, well and good. If not a symbol, well and good." Now another hand shot up. What about Old Ben, the bear? "Well, he was such an obvious symbol," Faulkner answered quickly. "He represented the vanishing wilderness. He was an obvious symbol."[9]

By April 25 it was time, in his words, to "put the show on the road," to the university's sister institution in Fredericksburg, Mary Washington College. The young women and their visitors listened in a hush to his reading from "Spotted Horses" and then acquitted themselves very well in the question period. Before the return journey to Charlottesville, he and Gwynn and Blotner stopped by a brick-walled cemetery where Confederate soldiers lay. Making their way through the grass under the newly fledged trees, they looked at the dark weathered stones, reading in the fading letters the names and regiments of the young whose bones had lain under the mounds for almost a century. Faulkner was silent, hands clasped behind him as he slowly walked between the graves. More than once he had told Virginians that he liked their country, that he was enjoying his sojourn in it. This was a part of that feeling, the sense of history in such places, arousing in many from the Deep South a veneration for the Old Dominion, for the places from which the forebears of so many Tennesseeans and Kentuckians and Mississippians had come.

After a considerable amount of Jack Daniel's and a good dinner, the three returned home well after dark.

ONE of the many ways the students of the university recognized Faulkner's presence was with a special issue of their humor magazine, *The Virginia Spectator*. The cover of the Writer-in-Residence Issue bore his likeness as rendered by art editor Al Carlson, a talented caricaturist. It pictured him long-nosed and spindly-legged, his cuffs over his knuckles, a book under his arm, and a rose in his lapel. He rested one hand on a broken Greek column and, smiling, looked ahead. When the editor handed him his copy of the magazine, Faulkner's face flushed as he began to shake with soundless laughter. He laughed until he was overcome with the paroxysm of coughing of the inveterate pipe smoker. Then he wiped his eyes, thanked the editor again, put the *Spectator* under his arm with his copy of the *Times*, and went home for lunch.

He could not have derived much pleasure, however, from the reviews of *The Town* that began appearing in May. Commins told him that they were very pleased with the early nationwide reviews, but the verdicts in the prime opinion-makers gave little cause for satisfaction. On May 5 the San Francisco *Chronicle*'s Lewis Vogler called the book merely "dull." On the same day Alfred Kazin had other adjectives in *The New York Times Book Review*: "Tired, drummed-up, boring, often merely frivolous," he wrote. There was a recognition of Faulkner's "astounding imagination" and "unflaggingly passionate mind," but the final verdict was emphatically negative: "The truth is not merely that *The Town* is a bad novel by a great writer, but also that Faulkner has less and less interest in writing what are called 'novels' at all." The following day, *Time*'s anonymous reviewer called him "a Manichaean and a Mississippian, a confused and magnificent novelist whose magnificence comes from his confusion and that of the people he has made his own." Late in the month Malcolm Cowley rendered a regretful verdict in *The New Republic*: "With the best will in the world, one finds it impossible to take a serious interest in the characters of *The Town*. For when characters go solemnly about their symbolic and rhetorical duties, ordinary relations among them are put out of the question. They communicate chiefly by striking attitudes at one another."[10]

Inevitably, Faulkner was asked for his reaction. One student queried a reviewer's comment that he seemed tired of the Yoknapatawpha County chronicle. Faulkner was silent for a moment. "I don't think that I am," he said finally, "though of course the last thing any writer will admit to himself is that he has scraped the bottom of the barrel and that he should quit. I don't quite believe that's true yet. But it's probably not tiredness, it's the fact that you shouldn't put off too long writing something which you think is worth writing, and this I have had in mind for thirty years now. So maybe it could be a little stale to me, though I don't think that's true, either."[11]

No matter what the reaction to this particular novel, Malcolm Cowley probably represented fairly the opinion of his peers when he asked Faulkner to present the Gold Medal for fiction to John Dos Passos. Faulkner had replied, "I hate like bejesus to face this sort of thing," but the vocation had been so kind to him that such a ceremony was part of his obligation in return. "So, if you are sure I am the man, I will take on the job and do the best I know."[12] He typed out a three-paragraph speech to deliver at the American Academy auditorium on May 22. It picked up ideas he had used in the now apparently abandoned project *The American Dream*. The artist had no place in the American culture or economy, he wrote, no place in "the mosaic of the American dream as it exists today. . . ." Perhaps this was a good thing, since it taught humility, and if so, none had been better trained in it than the recipient. It proved that in time, working through the humility and the oblivion, the writer and "the value of his life's work will be recognized and honored at least by his fellow craftsmen, as John Dos Passos and his life's work are at this moment."[13] With the speech in his pocket, he was ready for the ceremony.

It turned out to be even more of an ordeal than he had expected. There were tributes to departed members and other formalities before the cocktail hour that preceded the luncheon. "At lunch Faulkner sat next to my wife," Dos Passos recalled, "and she earned what seemed to be his undying gratitude by giving him her wine. The waiter must have thought she had great capacity because her glass was always empty." Halfway through the luncheon, Cowley, Faulkner, and Dos Passos were called into an adjoining room to rehearse the presentation of the medal. The ceremony began before they could return to finish lunch. The citations, inductions, and announcements seemed endless. When a long address followed, Faulkner left the platform in the middle of it to smoke in the Green Room. He returned to the platform, only to flee again. In the intervals he had expanded the last paragraph of his speech. When the time came and Cowley beamingly announced the award, Faulkner walked quickly to the podium. "Oratory," he said, "can't add anything to John Dos Passos' stature, and if I know anything about writers, he may be grateful for a little less of it. So I'll say, mine is the honor to partake of his in handing this medal to him. No man deserves it more."[14] He thrust the medal into Dos Passos' hand and returned to his seat.

Back in Charlottesville, two more public appearances concluded his official duties. In all, he had met with twenty-four diverse groups. By now his audiences were often responding as the Japanese had done at Nagano, with murmurs of admiration. At the end of the last session he stood there at the podium for a quarter-hour more, shaking hands with people who had come up to thank him. He seemed warmed by the obvious admiration and even affection he elicited. Not long afterward, however, at a party given by Paul Summers' parents, he would say that he liked the university but that he would not return because he thought someone new should be writer-in-residence; he doubted if he had anything more to give after four months. "I sat in an office and answered questions from students," he said, "questions that either a priest or a veterinarian could have answered."[15]

HE had leisure time in the late spring days, and in the sunny afternoons he and Blotner would often go to Little League baseball games. His pleasure in sports seemed to increase in direct proportion to their amateur nature. He recalled how he had pitched and played shortstop as a boy, and he followed these players' warm-ups closely, enjoying their postures and grimaces almost as much as the actual play itself. And there were other diversions. In mid-June the two men set out, accompanied by Paul Summers and Malcolm, for a tour of the Seven Days' battlefields. They took turns driving and made their way from Malvern Hill to Petersburg and Amelia Courthouse. Paul had brought along one of his West Point textbooks, and they would frequently consult it to orient themselves. Faulkner knew the battles in considerable detail, far better than the others. "This is where Pegram's battery came up," he said at one position, and on other slopes he pointed out where the various corps had been disposed. They looked at the plaques and stone shafts to regiments of long-dead soldiers and gazed at the rows of enormously heavy and inert cannon, pitted and faded with rust and weather. Inside the Petersburg Memorial they looked at Minié balls and bayonets, now so utterly static within the glass cases, and read the testimonials to the awful carnage of siege warfare in those dying days of the war. As the others looked— the lawyer, the herpetologist, and the English teacher—they could not help thinking how their companion had worked to make such material, by the power of his imagination and his words, come alive in works of art such as *The Unvanquished* and *Absalom, Absalom!*.

That evening the Faulkners gave a Squadron dinner on their terrace at Rugby Road, for the three-man squadron that had assembled so many times for coffee in Fred Gwynn's office, and for their wives. Estelle had prepared one of her celebrated curry dishes, using giant shrimp. She served quail eggs with it, and champagne. Dessert came and then brandy and coffee. By then it was full dark under the huge elm tree just come into leaf, and the Faulkners and their guests sat talking in contentment amid the candle flames in the spring night.

On the morning of June 26 he and Estelle pulled slowly out of the narrow driveway in the carefully loaded station wagon for the two-day drive back to Oxford. There would be a good deal to occupy him there. In his next-to-last session, one member of his audience had noted that Random House had announced a sequel to *The Town*.

"Do you like being under that kind of pressure?" he asked.

"The pressure is not actually from the publisher," Faulkner replied. When he had thought of the Snopeses he had known there was too much for one volume. Another auditor asked if he intended now to write the story of Eula's daughter. "Yes, sir," he said. "She's one of the most interesting people I've written about yet, I think. Her story will be in the next book."[16]

66

And you stand there—you, the old man, already white-headed
. . . while there rises up to you, proffered up to you, the spring
darkness . . . which, although it is of the dark itself, declines the
dark since dark is of the little death called sleeping. Because
look how, even though the last of west is no longer green and
all of firmament is now one unlidded studded slow-wheeling arc
and the last of earth-pooled visibility has drained away, there
still remains one faint diffusion, since everywhere you look
about the dark panorama you still see them, faint as whispers:
the faint and shapeless lambence of blooming dogwood returning loaned light to light as the phantoms of candles would.

—*The Town* (317)

Dot Oldham had seen to it that the grass was cut at Rowan Oak, the
shrubs trimmed, and the flowers tended. Roses clustered thick on the
brick wall by the east gallery, and the air was heavy with the fragrance
of the Cape jasmine bushes. But the farm was run-down, as he had feared,
and he would either have to let it go in 1958 or give it a little more attention at planting time. For now, though, it was a summer of leisure, and
any hard work he undertook was his own choice, like riding Tempy
and the other horses and fashioning a new wooden mast for the *Ring
Dove* that he and Malcolm stepped themselves.

Such business as arose was easily attended to. When Floyd Stovall extended an invitation for a second term as writer-in-residence, Faulkner
replied promptly. "It is far from my intent to relinquish whatever slight
hold I may have on U.va. Eng. Dept.," he wrote, "let alone ever to
accept without fighting displacement as THE writer-in-residence of the
University."[1] He proposed to arrive about February 1, to return home
from mid-March to mid-April, and then to come back for the rest of
the semester. Three weeks later it was all official. The University of Virginia would enjoy the services of William Faulkner at a cost of $1,600.

When he had accepted the first appointment he had told Floyd Stovall that money was not a consideration. This was equally true now, especially with Jerry Wald using part of *The Hamlet* as a vehicle for Paul Newman, Joanne Woodward, and Orson Welles under the title *The Long Hot Summer*.

There was one disquieting note, however, that sounded again for him that summer. He was now anticipating the development of militant Negro separatist movements. His first draft of a letter to the editor of the Memphis *Commercial Appeal* revealed a conviction he had not often expressed before. "I dont believe the Negro wants to mix with white people," he wrote. In his next draft he deleted that paragraph and took a different tack. "A few years ago, the Supreme Court rendered an opinion which we white Southerners didn't like, and we resisted it. As a result, last month Congress was offered a bill containing a good deal more danger to us all than the presence of Negro children in white schools or Negro votes in white ballot boxes. . . ." The bill did not pass. "As long as we continue to hold the Negro second class in citizenship—that is, subject to taxation and military service, yet denied the political right to vote for, and the economic and educational competence to be represented among those who tax and draft him—Congress will continue to be offered bills containing these same or similar dangers," and another time one would pass.[2]

The letter appeared on September 15. Three weeks later he sent one to Ober for transmittal to *The New York Times*. In it he was speaking to a national audience about the crisis which had culminated in President Eisenhower's sending federal troops to ensure school integration in Little Rock, Arkansas. The tragedy, he wrote, was that this action had brought out into the open "the fact that white people and Negroes do not like and trust each other, and perhaps never can." But perhaps this was not a tragedy, after all, if the races recognized that they had to "federate together, show a common unified front not for dull peace and amity, but for survival as a people and a nation."[3]

On Wednesday, November 13, he was back in Charlottesville, free of any duties at the university and at liberty to do whatever he liked. That Saturday he went to the Virginia–South Carolina football game. He rooted loyally for Virginia, which was suffering a protracted series of losing seasons and which promptly fell behind. Blotner said he was probably used to seeing better football, for the University of Mississippi perennially fielded a winning team. "I like this," he replied. "This is real amateur sport. At home they got a tame millionaire and he buys a team for them. That's professional sports. This is amateur." He even seemed to like the rather helter-skelter half-time entertainment. "It's better than seeing a fifth-rate floor show," he said. He even agreed to go on the air at half-time. His interviewer would be Virginia's celebrated football hero "Bullet Bill" Dudley. The two men provided a sharp contrast: Faulkner, looking like a trench-coated old nobleman, and Dudley, now an insurance man, bluff and amiable, his battered features showing the marks of his former calling. As Faulkner took his seat in the booth, Dudley made a brief introduction. "And so," he continued, "it's a real pleasure to have with us today Mr. William Faulkner, the winner of the Mobile Prize for Literature." Then, for the space of four or five minutes, the listeners of the regional radio football network were treated to the experience of hearing Bullet Bill Dudley talk literature and William Faulkner talk football.

The following Saturday was considerably different. He had developed a sore throat and, as usual, refused to see a doctor, insisting instead that Estelle paint it with Argyrol. The treatment failed, and as the pain increased, Faulkner resorted to his favorite remedy. Before long he was in a Richmond hospital undergoing treatment for a strep throat and the results of his bourbon therapy. As soon as he was able to travel, he and Estelle left for Oxford.

By early December he was feeling well enough to do some riding. He bought some bird dogs and waited for quail season, busying himself in the office occasionally. Early January of 1958 found him typing out his first draft of *The Mansion*, on the back of his typed first draft of *The Town*. He had begun by going back to *The Hamlet* for the Snopes he would play off against Flem: his cousin, Mink. He introduced him with lines like some he had used for Nancy Mannigoe in *Requiem for a Nun*. Chapter One began, "The jury said 'Guilty' and the Judge said 'Life' but he didn't hear them." (3) Then Faulkner doubled back for an extended flashback which culminated in the crime that earned Mink the life sentence: the murder of Jack Houston. But he was doing it at greater length than in *The Hamlet*, treating Mink more sympathetically and establishing character and motivation which would have to sustain much of the action as well as the final working out of the events of the whole trilogy.

If his efforts as an artist were absorbed that winter with the Snopes family, other energies were directed to the Falkner family. His mother still refused to have a nurse or even a servant when she convalesced from one of the frequent illnesses of old age. Johncy and Bill would take turns preparing her breakfast and bringing lunch and dinner trays from Dolly and Estelle. "Bill and I decided she even got enough of her own children at times and at such times we let her alone," Johncy said. "She was as hardheaded as Bill and I suppose that's where he got it from."[4] Faulkner's other familial duties took him outside of Oxford. He got A. B. Cullen to go to Ripley with him to clean the Old Colonel's monument. He even wanted Cullen to restore the effigy's damaged hand, though that proved impossible. In the previous spring he had begun talking about moving to Charlottesville permanently, and it was as if he were trying to settle all his accounts.

By late January he and Estelle were back in Charlottesville, renting a comfortable house on Minor Road, a pleasant tree-shaded street close to the university. His schedule for the new term was much like that of the previous year. He had been thinking ahead, however. One day during that term he had told Blotner, "I was thinking that it might be good to have some connection with the university after I'm through being writer-in-residence—if they can still use me, that is." That possibility was much in the minds of the committee members. Keeping his office hours in New Cabell Hall, he still read the *Times* when he had no callers. But this year he might also take from his trench-coat pocket a thick roll of plain white letter-size paper secured by an elastic band. It would consist of both typed and blank sheets. Soon anyone passing by would hear his slow tapping at Floyd Stovall's typewriter.

One day Gwynn asked, "Get any work done this morning?"

"Yes," he said, stirring his black coffee. "I haven't worked for so long that it's fun again. I got back to that Memphis whorehouse in *Sanctuary*, Miss Reba's. That's where I am right now. Senator Snopes is in Memphis and the nephew is going to barber college and they're trying to preserve his innocence."

"Eula's daughter went to New York," Fred said. "Is she back in Memphis?"

"No," Faulkner said. "That's the third-act curtain to the whole thing. She went to Spain with her husband in an ambulance unit and was deafened by a shell blast. In the last scene the Snopes who thought Flem didn't help him got out of jail and played on the fact that she couldn't hear anything and shot Flem in his chair when she was upstairs. Then when he was looking for a door to get away by, a door opened behind him and there she was. She said, 'Don't take that one. It's a closet. Take this one.' And he got away."

From the extraordinary recital of events from work in progress, delivered almost rapid-fire, he was now in Chapter Four of *The Mansion*. He had begun his second chapter with the same lines as the first, but with his necessary flashback concluded, he was free to set in motion the principal plot: Mink's entry into the Parchman State Prison Farm awaiting the day, twenty years hence, when he would be eligible for parole—so he could kill Flem. On January 29, Faulkner had begun Chapter Three in V. K. Ratliff's voice, recapitulating Montgomery Ward Snopes's pornographic-picture business and his incarceration in Parchman. In Chapter Four, Montgomery Ward takes up the story with his narration of the scheme by which Flem blackmails him into provoking Mink's unsuccessful escape attempt so that twenty more years will be added to his sentence. It was in this chapter that Faulkner had reintroduced Miss Reba, summarizing material from *Sanctuary*. She is still the hardened brothel madam, tough and maudlin by turns, but even through Montgomery Ward's cynical words, Faulkner managed to convey a new compassion for her. It was the kind of softening he had performed with Mink, who, dogged by unbelievably hard luck from birth, still tries to preserve what he can of dignity, "not being a rich man like Houston but only an independent one, asking no favors of any man, paying his own way." (8)

On February 13, the day on which Faulkner had talked about his novel in Fred Gwynn's office, Floyd Stovall had talked about Faulkner in Colgate W. Darden's office. The president of the University of Virginia dealt very briefly with Stovall's recommendation. While he appreciated Faulkner's contribution to the university, he felt that other writers might feel they, too, might obtain permanent connections with the university if William Faulkner did. Faulkner's friends felt there was more to it than this. The governor of Virginia had promulgated a doctrine of "massive resistance" to integration. It was not impossible that Faulkner's outspokenness on the subject might prove an embarrassment with the state legislature when it came time for appropriations.

If Darden did have any such reservations, he must have felt doubly sure of his own rectitude when he learned of a talk Faulkner gave to three university societies the next week. "A Word to Virginians" was an appeal that Virginia lead the whole South in what Faulkner thought the only practical response to the crisis. Even though it revealed a further hardening of earlier attitudes, it would still be anathema to Southern conservatives. The nation could not endure at peace in a largely hostile world, he said "with ten percent of its population arbitrarily unassimilated. . . ." He went on to explore the difficulties he foresaw. "Perhaps the Negro is not yet capable of more than second-class citizenship. His tragedy may be that so far he is competent for equality only in the ratio of his white blood." Much of the Negro's plight was the fault of the white man, who alone could "teach the Negro the responsibility of personal morality and rectitude—either by taking him into our white schools, or giving him white teachers in his own schools until we have taught the teachers of his own race to teach and train him in these hard and unpleasant habits." If not, there would be a crisis such as that at Little Rock each year. The place to begin, he said, was Virginia. The other states had failed to heed her counsel once before to their grief. He believed that this time they would follow "Mother Virginia."

In the animated discussion that followed, he granted that a lot of the trouble was being caused by irresponsible white people and that they needed education as well as the Negro. "But then, the Negro is not going to wait right now while the white man educates himself in order to educate the Negro. . . . The Negro is not going to wait any longer." His answers made it clear that he had moved to a more conservative position than the one he had advocated three years before. He thought it would be fifty years before the kind of integration advocated by the NAACP became real. Why not, asked one man, raise the Negro's economic and education standards while he was still segregated? That, replied Faulkner, was what he would like to do. "I would like to give him such good schools that he wouldn't want to go to the white schools. I would like to give him so much equality in his own race . . . and make him have to spend so much time being responsible for his own equality that he wouldn't have time to bother with the white man's." One problem was that the schools had been made into "a sort of national system of baby-sitters," and moreover, "to improve standards of education we've got to get some folks out of the schools, not get more in it that don't belong there."[5] The questioning went on for an hour.

What could have been another kind of conservatism in his thought surfaced when the State Department asked him to join a group of American writers in a visit to Russia. After pondering the idea long and seriously, he concluded that it would be of greater value "in the 'cold war' of human relationships" for him to decline. "The Russia with which I have, I hope, earned any right to spiritual kinship was the Russia which produced Dostoievsky, Tolstoy, Chekhov, Gogol, etc. That Russia is no longer there." To give "even the outward appearance of condoning the condition which the present Russian government has established, would be a betrayal . . . of their spiritual heirs who risk their lives with every page they write; and a lie in that it would condone the shame of them . . . who have had their souls destroyed for the privilege of writing in public." It was again the perennial theme of freedom. He regretted his decision, he said, because the Russians he had seen had been impressive. "If the Russians were free, they would probably conquer the earth."[6]

He had always been outspoken, and with age, though he mellowed in some ways, he was often more outspoken rather than less. Asked to help inaugurate National Book Week with a filmed meeting with a group of students, he consented, apparently under the mistaken impression that it was expected of him. When it was over, he turned to Blotner with his fierce, hawklike look, head back, and said in a high-pitched voice, "Pardon the language, but I just can't stand that Hollywood shit."

His humor was not improved by having to leave for Princeton on Saturday, March 1. The previous May the Princeton University Library had opened the largest and most impressive exhibit of his work ever presented, with hundreds of items including manuscripts, typescripts, proofs, published volumes, medals, and prizes. Not only was he conscious of the honor they had done him, he was aware of Commins' unofficial tie with Princeton, and when he had been working on *A Fable* in his home, he had promised classics professor Whitney J. Oates that he would meet with Princeton undergraduates for a $500 fee. In the group sessions he was able to use many of his now formulaic answers, but as usual, his talent for coining aphorisms manifested itself. Professor Lawrance Thompson remembered one especially serious student's question. "Mr. Faulkner," he said, "I have read all your books and short stories, and I want to know, is there one character that is saved by grace?" Faulkner considered for a moment. "Well," he said finally, "I have always thought of God as being in the wholesale rather than the retail business."

Harold Ober and Donald Klopfer came down for one of his seminars. After dinner at the Comminses' he asked their advice. What would they think of his buying a farm in Virginia? In a few days Klopfer wrote him that he hoped he would sell Rowan Oak and Greenfield Farm first. Ober took a more sanguine view. In 1957, Ruth Ford had opened *Requiem for a Nun* in London, where it had run well into the new year to rave notices. Besides, he wrote, "you have $50,000 coming to you definitely over the next four years from the picture sale of *The Sound and the Fury* and *The Hamlet* so it seems to me your real estate venture is perfectly safe." This prospect would continue to occupy him, with additional impetus of different kinds, and in a few months his resolve would be even stronger. "I have got a belly full of Oxford," he would tell Ober. "I cant keep tourists out of my front yard, rubber-necking at my house, and there is not one place in fifty miles that I have found where I can eat any food at all without having to listen to a juke box. I think I shall undertake to buy a Va place on credit, mortgage, and hope for the best. If the play makes some big gob of money, I can do it. Maybe I could mortgage a year in Hollywood for net $75,000.00."[7]

Faulkner was back at Rowan Oak before the end of March, overseeing the work at the farm and putting in time on his manuscript in the office. He returned to his other life in Charlottesville as the second half of April began. Strolling to the university, he would pass Jefferson's serpentine brick walls, the gardens behind them enclosing rosebushes offering tentative buds and an occasional apple tree fragrant with a snowstorm of blossoms. Shortly after he resumed his duties, he prepared another talk, which he delivered to the English Club on the twenty-fourth under the title "A Word to Young Writers." He began with a backward glance at the People-to-People Program. With all its various groups it was symptomatic, to him, of "the universal dilemma of mankind at this moment . . . the mystical belief, almost a religion, that individual man cannot speak to individual man because individual man can no longer exist." The artist's problem was that he ran "full-tilt into what might be called almost a universal will to regimentation," and so his tragedy was "that today he must even combat this pressure, waste some part of his puny but (if he is an artist) precious individual strength against this universal will to efface his individual humanity, in order to be an artist." The result was that "the young writer of today is compelled by the present state of our culture . . . to function in a kind of vacuum of the human race. His characters do not function, live, breathe, struggle, in that moil and seethe of simple humanity as did those of our predecessors who were the masters from whom we learned our craft. . . ." He found a perfect example in the best of the contemporary books, which he said he had begun reading only a short time ago. It was J. D. Salinger's *The Catcher in the Rye*, and Holden Caulfield was symptomatic: "His tragedy was that when he attempted to enter the human race, there was no human race there." He ended with a kind of echo and variant of the Nobel Prize speech. The writer's task was "to save man's humanity . . . to save the individual from anonymity before it is too late and humanity has vanished from the animal called man."[8] It was as though his obsession with freedom had grown stronger while his faith in man's power to endure had grown weaker.

As May came in and the end of the term approached, his remarks would sometimes take on a valedictory tone. Inevitably some questions and answers were repetitive, but there was usually something unexpected and provocative. In spite of a residual antipathy, he had agreed to meet with the University Hospital's residents in psychiatry and a few members of the department. One of them asked whether or not he had any idea where he learned psychology. "No sir, I don't," he answered, fingering his pipe. "Only what I have learned about it from listening to people that do know. What little of psychology I know the characters I have invented and playing poker have taught me. Freud I'm not familiar with."[9] And there were still answers like epigrams and aphorisms. "James Joyce," he told one group, "was one of the great men of my time. He was electrocuted by the divine fire. He, Thomas Mann, were the great writers of my time. He was probably—might have been the greatest, but he was electrocuted. He had more talent than he could control."[10] At his next-to-last session he was asked if he had enjoyed his stay in Virginia. "Well," he answered, "I have been in Albemarle County off and on for two or three years now, and I have seen a few Snopeses there. But I like Virginia and Virginians. The longer I stay in Albemarle County the more like Mississippians they behave, but they don't have some of the Mississippi vices. I said last year that I liked Virginians because they were snobs, and since they seem to think I'm all right then maybe I am all right."[11]

The end of William Faulkner's service as writer-in-residence at the University of Virginia brought mixed responses. Floyd Stovall walked up the Lawn once again to the president's pavilion to present the English Department's recommendation that Faulkner be made an honorary lecturer in American literature at the university. Colgate W. Darden told him, "There are no honorary positions at the University of Virginia." The Seven Society, an anonymous group whose main function lay in beneficences, chiefly to the university, left on Faulkner's doorstep a silver tray engraved in tribute to his contribution to the life of the university. There was a round of Squadron dinners with scrolls for the three members to commemorate the 1st Balch Experimental Hangar Flying Squadron. Faulkner designed the device, an adaptation of the RAF insignia, the citation, and the motto "Ad Astra Per Jack Daniel's." All were signed by "Ernest V. Trueblood, Adjutant," in a bold signature that completely disguised the penman's usual meticulous style.

Two weeks before he left he had handed Blotner a manila portfolio. "Here," he said brusquely, "read it." A quick glance showed that it was a typescript. It was the first third of his new novel, he said. It was also his only copy. It was returned the next day, having been read with enjoyment but with dispatch. He had completed Chapter Five, and with it the first of the book's three sections, which he would entitle "Mink." In this chapter the omniscient narrator followed Mink as he serves out the rest of his time. Released in 1948 at the age of sixty-three, he has acquired after his forty years' imprisonment a kind of tragic dignity. Now an anachronism knowing no close kin, he has been released on an appeal to the governor signed by Linda Snopes Kohl, a deafened widow who also has a score to settle with the man under whose roof she is living—Flem Snopes.

BACK at Rowan Oak, Faulkner worked on the novel's second section, entitled "Linda." He used the voice of V. K. Ratliff to recapitulate Eula Varner's brief affair with Hoake McCarron and then the principal events of *The Town*. He was not copying from an earlier version, as he had done with parts of *The Unvanquished* and *Go Down, Moses*, but rather describing again fictional events etched clearly and deeply in his memory, the principal one the tragic death of one of his most powerful creations, Eula Varner Snopes.

Another death occupied his thoughts in that summer of 1958. On July 17, Saxe Commins succumbed at sixty-six to a heart attack at the Elm Road home where Faulkner had stayed so often. There was not time for him and Estelle to arrive in Princeton for the services, and so Faulkner sent Dorothy a telegram: THE FINEST EPITAPH EVERYONE WHO EVER KNEW SAXE WILL HAVE TO SUBSCRIBE TO WHETHER HE WILL OR NOT QUOTE HE LOVED ME UNQUOTE.[12] Writing to Harold Ober nearly a month later, he told him, "We all miss Saxe. I will have to hunt up somebody else now who will stop anybody making the Wm Faulkner story the moment I have breathed my last."[13]

There was more than Saxe's death to make him think of breathing his last. He had been riding Tempy in the cool mornings and also in the evenings of that sultry August. "I have been trying to get my green hunter ready for a night horse show," he wrote Ober, "but she would not face the lights and crowd, tore a ligament loose in my groin so that my leg is rainbow-colored, red, purple, green, yellow, down to the knee. . . ."[14] But as soon as he could manage, he was back in the saddle, jumping fences set at three and a half to four feet. He was determined to do what he had planned despite the clear and obvious risks.

Faulkner took a week in mid-September to travel to Charlottesville with Estelle, who was anxious to help Jill with her house-hunting in anticipation of the birth of her second child three months hence. Back home, he wired Donald Klopfer about his brokerage account but included some information too: IN BACK STRETCH BUT WONT ETA UNTIL I CAN SEE THE WIRE. . . .[15] In Chapters Eight and Nine, Charles Mallison took over the narrative. Again the dense texture of Yoknapatawpha life is evident as characters appear from earlier novels and stories, but the thrust is forward with the activities of Linda Snopes Kohl, returned home after losing her husband in the Spanish Civil War and herself deafened by a shell burst. A card-carrying Communist, like Barton Kohl, she plunges into work to change the school system for the betterment of Negro students. It is finally the Negro principal himself who comes to Gavin Stevens to put a stop to it. Faulkner made him the advocate of a position the principal said was first taken by Booker T. Washington and George Washington Carver: that the Negro has to earn a place by his efforts to make the white man need him. Linda now receives an epithet more than once applied to her creator: she is a "Nigger Lover."

As Faulkner worked on into the fall, Gavin Stevens took over the narration in Chapter Ten. Faulkner had always admired Jack Falkner's bravery as an FBI agent, but now, as he described an FBI investigation of Linda, possibly instigated by Flem Snopes, he revealed again his devotion to individual liberty. (According to Johncy, Faulkner had once given a political contribution of $50 to a Danish house painter in Oxford named Gustaf Uth, whom he thought to be the state's only registered Communist, as "a tribute to a man standing against the other two million of us."[16]) As Faulkner advanced his story to 1941, Linda repeats two gambits of her mother's: she asks Stevens to marry her to protect her, and when he declines she asks him to marry someone else, wanting him to know what she had known. Like her mother, she has offered him her body, but again, he does not want the act unless she wants it in the same way he does. Drawing on the love and pain he had known not many years before, Faulkner wrote that Stevens tells her it is not necessary for them to sleep together, "because we are the 2 in all the world who can love each other without having to." (239) He completed the "Linda" section of the novel with the short eleventh chapter in which Charles Mallison summarizes the part of "Knight's Gambit" reuniting Stevens with Melisandre Backus, his early love. The pace picked up in Chapter Twelve as "Flem" begins with the omniscient narrator's description of Mink's journey from Parchman to Memphis, where he makes a purchase: a pistol and three cartridges.

THOUGH Estelle and Jill were in Charlottesville, he was still acting as father in Oxford as Dean Faulkner's wedding approached. He had seen her through her education and a trip to Europe, and now he would give her away at the altar and be host for the reception at Rowan Oak. There were still flowers in the gardens of Rowan Oak a few days before the wedding on November 9. Louise was cutting a bouquet when he came around the corner holding his side. "We mustn't tell anybody because we don't want anything to disturb this wedding," he said, "but I've just had a bad fall and I think I've broken a few ribs." He played host to the more than forty guests at the Saturday wedding-eve party, staying up until three. There were even more guests for breakfast the next morning. By noontime he was out in the paddock taking Tempy over the jumps, and by midafternoon he was in the striped trousers, cutaway, and ascot in which he had given Jill away. Riding to the church in the limousine, he kept Dean calm with conversation and stories. One of them was a shock. "I made up the story of Judith for Aunt Estelle and Buddy when we moved into Rowan Oak," he told her. "The house needed a ghost."

Later, after Dean and Jon Mallard had escaped by the route he had devised, and after the last of the 150 guests had departed, it was time to relax. "No more cheap champagne," he said. He got out a good bottle of red wine to go with a few of the hors d'ouevres that were left. After that he poured some whiskey on the rocks and then took them to Aubrey Seay's Mansion restaurant for steak.

Afterward there was one thing more to do. They took the altar flowers out to St. Peter's and laid them on Dean's grave. The flowers told his brother that he had seen his daughter through childhood and adolescence, from maidenhood to marriage. He had fulfilled the vow made twenty-three years before by the wreckage of the Waco. When they returned to the car, Faulkner bade the others goodnight and walked back alone, under the bare trees and the autumn starlight, to Rowan Oak.

As mid-November approached, Faulkner began to pack for his return to Charlottesville. His only obligation would be the additional week of student sessions he owed Princeton. He had the last section of his novel to complete, but he would have plenty of time for something else. The previous spring he had been invited to ride with Keswick, and he had enjoyed the few times he had been out. Now the hunt was preparing to take to the field again. He had not been working Tempy and bruising his bones for nothing. This time he was determined to follow with the rest when the huntsman sounded his horn.

. . . the men (one in a red coat, with a brass horn) and the women in the pants and boots on the thousand-dollar horses. . . .

And the next year there was an actual pack of hounds, fine ones, a little too fine to be simple dogs just as the horses were a little too fine to be simple horses, a little too clean, a little too (somehow) unaccustomed, living in weather-proof hutches with running water and special human beings to wait on them too like the horses did and had.

—*Knight's Gambit* (157-158)

By November 16, 1958, he was back at Princeton University for a total of six more days of preceptorials and student conferences. It was a hard-earned $500, but this was a promise he had made to Oates and to Saxe Commins. Still grieving, Dorothy Commins nonetheless gave a party for him, inviting mostly members of the Institute for Advanced Study. When she told him who was coming, he said, "Dorothy, I don't understand their world." During the evening he sat in a corner, responding to conversational attempts with yeses and noes. One of the physicists was J. Robert Oppenheimer, with whom Faulkner had sympathized when the loyalty controversy had swirled up around him. Now Oppenheimer joined him. "Mr. Faulkner," he said, "I saw your story 'The Brooch' on television, and I enjoyed it. I wonder what you think of television as a medium for the artist." When Faulkner watched television it was to see horse races, an occasional professional football game, and a favorite comedy series. But now he gave Oppenheimer a short answer. "Television is for niggers," he said.

He checked in at the Algonquin for the last three days of the month and worked on Chapter Thirteen of *The Mansion* at Random House before he took the train for Charlottesville. He was back in time for the Blessing of the Hounds, when guests from many parts of Virginia joined the huntsmen and hounds of the Keswick Hunt Club on the lawn before the Grace Episcopal Church in nearby Cismont, the front door of the church adorned on either side with shocks of corn. After the minister in full vestments performed the office, the hunt assembled on the rolling grounds of Kinloch, the handsome and imposing residence of Linton and Mary Massey, by now good friends of the Summerses and the Faulkners. Soon Faulkner was riding with them, as welcome at the Keswick Hunt Club at he was at Grover Vandevender's. And there were constant invitations to the homes of other riders. He and Estelle were renting a house on Ivy Lane in Farmington, among a number of other imposing homes near the Farmington Country Club, a few miles west of Charlottesville on the slopes of the Blue Ridge. At one cocktail party he met Mrs. Julio Galban, the mistress of Gallison Hall, which might have been pictured in some American equivalent of *The Stately Homes of England*. Short, forthright, and friendly, Evalyn Galban was a former nurse who had been born in a small Alabama town, and she and Faulkner immediately began talking easily. When she learned he was riding with Keswick, she asked why he was not riding with the Farmington Hunt Club. "I haven't been invited," he replied. "I'll arrange that," said Mrs. Galban, and she did.

Now he began to put down more roots in Albemarle County, according to local folklore, one of the four richest in America. The Keswick Hunt was the oldest in this part of Virginia, including members in the tradition of the legendary John Peel—in the saddle at daybreak and out after the fox in all weathers as long as the light lasted. The newer Farmington Hunt was originally more cosmopolitan, with elaborate breakfasts and generous stirrup cups. By now, however, the old differences were fading, and both had a varied membership. They included gentleman farmers from New York, hard-working horsemen, sporting academics, and a fair number of transplanted Europeans. In this diversity Faulkner would find himself talking one day with a retired diplomat, and on another, with a likable young ne'er-do-well who trafficked in moonshine whiskey. A few of the women bore titled names and a few others bore scandalous associations which would have been a distinct handicap in any Albemarle set other than this hard-riding, hard-drinking group. They were congenial hunters, most of whom rode as much for the chase as the kill, and at Farmington they didn't kill more than four or five times a year, sometimes perhaps twice in the season. This was just what Faulkner wanted: the sport more than the kill. He had left that with the slain deer years before.

He would appear at Grover Vandevender's door at six or seven in the morning, and the two would warm themselves before Grover's great stone fireplace and drink steaming black coffee. Then they would go out and mount. By now Grover knew well his friend's style in the hunting field, riding with his stirrups too long and his toes pointed out, taking the jumps with his knees out instead of tight to his mount. "He was all nerve," he said later. "He would follow anywhere through any kind of country and jumps." Another rider thought he had too much nerve, if that was what it was. He would see a small man coming on a big horse, flat out, and sometimes, at a log fence or a stone wall, there would be daylight between the rider and his saddle. "Man," said this hunter, "when I saw him I would get out of the way." The Master of the Hunt, English-born Dr. E. D. Vere Nicoll, knew that he was not a particularly good horseman but said he "had the courage of a lion and adored the hunt." And he was punctilious. With an Old World air he would come up, doff his hat, and say, "Good morning, Master." As the day's hunt wore on, others would peel off, but he would ride on with the Master, the Hunts-man, the whips, and the hounds. "It could rain or snow," Grover said, "but he stayed out to the last hound bark." Faulkner was now sixty-one years old. It gave Jill pleasure just to watch him when the others wore their pink coats and he dressed up too: his boots shined, his white stock neatly pinned, his black derby firmly settled on his head. In the coat would be two other indispensables, his tobacco pouch and his brandy flask. It was only now in these last few years, Jill sometimes thought, that she really got to know him and he got to know her.

Though he sent money to help with the expenses of his old comrades, he would never return to hunt in the Delta river bottoms in rainy November. Jumping his hunter over log fences and stone walls as the voices of the hounds rang clear in the crisp morning, he felt an excite-ment on those frosty hills and fields he had not known since his flying days. Stopping at one party on his way back from a hunt, he was still feeling it. When novelist Nancy Hale joined him, she said, "I don't see why you fool with those real horses when you've got your own horses inside. Do you *like* horses?" He looked at her with that intense black-eyed glance. "I'm scared to death of horses," he said, speaking rapidly, "that's why I can't leave them alone." It was like the reply he had made to his mother, when, after one of his falls, she had told him he should stop riding. "No, Mother," he said, "I love the thrill of the danger." He would tell another that the horses were necessary to him—their power and speed in the swift rush of the hunt lifting him in an exhilaration stronger than any drug.

But the hunting had not come at the expense of the novel, for by mid-December, Chapter Thirteen must have been almost completed. He began it with Charles Mallison's return from the war, but then he stopped to trace the tortuous process leading to his homecoming. An Air Force bombardier, he had endured more risks as a German prisoner of war than he had flying combat missions out of England. In the hangar-flying sessions in Cabell Hall, Blotner had told some of his war stories. Later, when the book was published, he said to Faulkner, "I enjoyed the part about Chick's experience in Germany." Faulkner smiled. "I used your story about being bombed in POW camp," he said. "I lifted that right from what you told me." In the rest of the chapter, Faulkner retold the story of Colonel Devries' defeat of Clarence Snopes through Ratliff's scatological stratagem. Some passages were almost identical with their counterparts in "By the People," but most of it was subtly changed, the language polished in still another retelling.

By now it was time to put the novel aside for the holiday season. It was a special one, for on December 2, Jill had given birth to her second boy. She and Paul had already determined that he was to be named for Pappy. Estelle knew that he considered Cuthbert a sissy name and disliked it wholeheartedly, but to her surprise, he said the baby should be named William Cuthbert Faulkner Summers. In Chapter Seven of *The Mansion* he had revealed Ratliff's given names: Vladimir Kyrilytch. In his family the first male of every generation had to receive the name of the first American progenitor—to ensure the family's luck. With perhaps something of the same sense of tradition, William Faulkner insisted that his grandson have the same first name borne by his own great-grandfather, the Old Colonel.

On New Year's Day of 1959 he was in the saddle as a guest of the Farmington Hunt. Even though he got separated from the rest, he had a fine time. A few days later he wrote Evalyn Galban to say how much he had enjoyed the day—"a pleasure and an honor too. I wish I could be a member of it." The next day he returned to Mississippi for a five-week stay. He settled into a routine: up early to work at his desk, then in the afternoon some riding or roaming over the countryside with Jimmy, combing the winter-brown fields and listening for the whir of quail wings. He would usually go to The Mansion for dinner, where Aubrey Seay would put an "Out of Order" sign on the jukebox as soon as he came in. Back home again, he would read for a while and then retire early in anticipation of possible insomnia and certain early rising.

Less than two weeks after his return he wrote Don Klopfer, "Am finishing first draft of mss. this week, will do about a month's cleaning up. . . . You should have it all by March."[1] He was writing all of the remaining chapters of "Flem" from the point of view of the omniscient narrator, weaving together many strands as he introduced new characters and unpublished material while he referred to old material. This process contributed to a virtual recapitulation of much of the Yoknapatawpha saga. In Chapter Fourteen he interpolated "Hog Pawn," the story Ober had been unable to sell four years earlier. The courtship of Essie Meadowfill by ex-Marine McKinley Smith provided a chance to expand the motif of the returned war veteran. The story's villainous Snopes is now identified as Orestes Snopes. The real estate deal which sets him and Old Man Meadowfill at odds gave Faulkner the opportunity to introduce another such deal: Jason Compson's sale of the old Compson place to Flem Snopes. And here Faulkner supplied completely new material revealing that Benjy had died when he set fire to the house. With his extensive expansion and revision of the story, he had set the stage for the climactic events of his final four chapters.

Chapter Fifteen focused on Linda Snopes and Gavin Stevens. Now apparently safe in his middle-age marriage to Melisandre Backus Harriss, he is still a self-made quixotic victim. (Not only was Don Quixote one of Faulkner's favorite characters, there was a good deal of him in Faulkner, said Estelle, as his anti-segregation battles had indicated.) Gavin is ready to tilt for Linda again. Showing by now the effects of the traumas of her life, drinking too much, she is another, like Drusilla Hawk and Joanna Burden, turned from the conventional pursuits of women, expending the energy of these blocked drives in surrogate ways. Chapter Sixteen revealed what they were: using Stevens—and through him others, including Ratliff —to obtain from the Governor the release of Mink Snopes from the Parchman Prison Farm. Faulkner heightened the suspense with Stevens' efforts to prevent a revenge murder, but then, characteristically, he sacrificed it a few pages later at the chapter's end by simply picturing Flem Snopes's bank with drawn shades and "the somber black-and-white-and-violet convolutions of tulle and ribbon and waxen asphodels fastened to the locked front door." (395) Now he would explore the How of the thing, as he had done so often in *Absalom, Absalom!* and other books.

On January 23 he sent a telegram to Estelle, hospitalized with bronchitis. FINISHED FIRST DRAFT AND AM HOMESICK FOR EVERYBODY, it read. VALENTINE'S LOVE. PAPPY.[2] His next to last chapter followed Mink on his last thirty miles to Jefferson, comforted by something like the bleak Calvinism of Joanna Burden and Simon McEachern, confident of revenge in his conviction that "*Old Moster jest punishes; He dont play jokes.*" (398) The chapter had the kind of big ending Faulkner often used: Mink's escape after the murder, as he had described it to Gwynn and Blotner that day in Cabell Hall. In the last chapter, with her mother's death avenged, Linda leaves Yoknapatawpha as had that other tragic figure, Caddy Compson, thirty-five years before. In the last dozen pages Stevens and Ratliff—"two old men themselves, approaching their sixties" (434)—drive out into the country to give Mink the money Linda has left for him. Stevens feels himself linked with Mink by complicity in his crime, but a greater kinship is that with all of suffering mankind. Driving toward the ruins of Mink's one-time home, Stevens and Ratliff talk about the human predicament.

" 'There aren't any morals,' Stevens said. 'People just do the best they can.'

'The pore sons of bitches,' Ratliff said.

'The poor sons of bitches,' Stevens said." (429)

After they hand the money to Mink, the focus shifts to him, no longer afraid of his old enemy, the land, the earth. He feels himself and all the travail of his blighted life flowing into it, where there is peace, joining those already there, "equal to any, good as any, brave as any, being inextricable from, anonymous with all of them: the beautiful, the splendid, the proud and the brave, right up on to the very top itself among the shining phantoms and dreams which are the milestones of the long human recording—Helen and the bishops, the kings and the unhomed angels, the scornful and graceless seraphim." (435–436) With this set piece, one of the best he ever wrote, he had come to the end of his long trilogy. It was typical that it incorporated imagery that had seized his imagination more than a third of a century earlier, that he had reworked three times before, and which he had first used in print in his essay on Eugene O'Neill in *The Mississippian* in 1922.

As he approached the completion of this long labor at Rowan Oak, so did Ruth Ford in New York, where on January 30, after seven years' effort, the curtain rose on *Requiem for a Nun*. He had written Ruth that though he could not be there, a contingent including Jill and Paul, Ella Somerville and Vicki would be there to "see you and do our Oxford cheering." In the last part of his letter he wrote, "God bless you. I only wish this play could be what you deserve." The London production had been a spectacular hit, with Ruth receiving extraordinary plaudits. Her opening-night performance had the same power, and she was supported brilliantly by Zachary Scott as Gavin Stevens and Bertice Reading as Nancy Mannigoe. The critic for the *World-Telegram & Sun*, Frank Aston, gave the kind of review they had received in London, and there was praise from Brooks Atkinson, Walter Kerr, and John McLain, but most of the critics dissented: the story was told rather than demonstrated, they said. In a word, it was undramatic. *Requiem for a Nun* closed at the end of February after forty-three performances.

FAULKNER shared something of Ruth's disappointment and possibly something of her outrage at the power of bad notices. It could scarcely have made him angrier, however, than two letters he had received early in the month. During the summer Mrs. Calvin S. Brown had written to him, apparently asking for permission to publish the copy of *The Wishing Tree* which Faulkner had made for Margaret thirty years before. When he did not reply, Jim Silver decided to help her, feeling that she needed the money. He sent out copies of the story, and not long afterward Ober sent Faulkner a copy of an inquiry he had received from Ralph Graves, articles editor of *Life*. Faulkner's reply went to Ober. When he had received Mrs. Brown's letter, he said, he didn't believe it. "When I told her the story (after [Margaret's] death) belonged to her, to do as she wanted with it, it never occurred to me that she would want to commercialise it. . . ." He assumed then that she wanted to sell the copy to a collector. "There were times when I needed money and could have sold it to an editor for publication, and didn't. Because of that doomed little child, I wont yet. But if Mrs. Brown wants to, and can be happy afterward, I wont stand in the way."[3] If he were to give permission for publication, he told Ober, it would be with what he had just written as a foreword. Silver went on to pursue the possibility in correspondence with Bennett Cerf and Albert Erskine, even though the story had been given to Victoria Franklin and the copy that Faulkner gave to the Browns carried no publication rights. Her children felt she did not understand this and opposed the whole idea, deploring what they regarded as a friend's meddling. Finally, nothing came of it.

In the same letter Faulkner told Ober, "By now I should certainly have got used to the fact that most of my erstwhile friends and acquaintances here believe I am rich from sheer blind chance, and are determined to have a little of it. I learned last week (he didn't tell me himself) that another one gathered up all the odds and ends of mine he had in his possession, and sold it to a Texas university; he needed money too evidently. So do I—the $6000.00 of my cancelled life insurance which paid a mortgage on his property 20 years ago which I'll never see again."[4] He had learned about the sale from James B. Meriwether, who as a graduate student had been one of those principally responsible for Princeton's Faulkner exhibit and who now, as a teacher at the University of Texas, was working to build up the library's holdings in his area. Meriwether had come to Faulkner and explained the purchase he was negotiating with Phil Stone because he wanted it to be aboveboard. He had offered to halt the transaction, or to see that Texas paid Faulkner the same amount they paid Stone, but Faulkner had declined. He wanted no part of such a sale for himself, and he failed to understand why some people were so interested "in the things a man does when he's learning to write."

The news Meriwether had brought must have been revealing as well as bitter and ironic. Though in recent years Stone had done occasional legal work for Faulkner, they had seen very little of each other. (Writing Anne Louise Davis, of the Ober office, about a codicil he had prepared, Stone said, "I am glad to do this and I do things like this for Bill free, but I have too much to do to run Bill down. Bill is just too much trouble sometimes anyway." He had just told one correspondent, "When he got the Nobel Prize he seemed to look down his nose at me," and in the last few years, he told another, Faulkner had become "insufferable."[5]) From time to time, perhaps in a kind of nostalgia, Faulkner would drop in at the small house off the square where Stone and his junior partners worked. As likely as not, Stone would send out word that he was busy. Faulkner would sit for a half-hour or so before he would rise slowly and leave. The partners could only speculate about why Stone acted as he did. One of his problems was that he had never done well enough to retire the debts he had assumed at the time of his father's collapse, and over the years he had been selling off parcel after parcel of Stone land, until, like Mr.

Compson, he had very little left. Faulkner went on tearing up the old promissory notes and accepting new ones he knew would never be redeemed.

Though he must have fumed, he apparently spent little time in useless anger. On the day he sent off the letter about *The Wishing Tree* to Ober, "Mink" arrived on Albert Erskine's desk at Random House. When Erskine read the first two chapters he was enthusiastic, but he was concerned about the discrepancies that appeared immediately between *The Mansion* and *The Town* and *The Hamlet*. This was a problem that had bothered Saxe Commins when he began reading the typescript of *The Town*, and he had gratefully accepted James Meriwether's help in identifying them. Now there were more. Erskine typed out a whole page of notes on discrepancies in the Mink Snopes–Houston story. Besides the intensive work ahead in studying and reconciling the three volumes, Erskine did not know how much editing Faulkner wanted or whether in fact they were meant to be a true trilogy, three novels that together constituted one work. Meriwether offered his help again, and Erskine wrote Faulkner that he favored accepting it. Faulkner replied that any help Erskine approved was all right with him. It was important that they know where problems existed, but his approach was different from his editor's. "What I am trying to say is, the essential truth of these people and their doings, is the thing; the facts are not too important."[6]

At the end of the first week of February, Erskine sent Faulkner a list of discrepancies between the first two volumes and the new manuscript. In his reply Faulkner established a general principle: if changing the new work to match the old caused the new work to suffer, they should change the old where they could, or ignore it. His idea was to make the changes in the next printing of *The Hamlet*, and then, "someday we may print the three volumes as a simultaneous trilogy, same binding, imprint, etc. and sell the old prints as antiques."[7] Along with the letter, he sent in the six chapters comprising "Linda," and he hoped to finish "Flem" in time to take it to New York about March 23. On March 9, three weeks after he was back in Charlottesville, he finished the typescript. Meanwhile Erskine had continued to wrestle with the discrepancies. He wrote Faulkner that Meriwether could come up from Texas for a week. Again Faulkner told Erskine that any procedure he decided on would be agreeable to him. But he was firm on one point: *The Mansion* was to be "the definitive" volume, with the other two of the trilogy to be adjusted to it in subsequent editions unless the discrepancy was "paradoxical and outrageous."[8] He still planned to check in at the Algonquin on March 23.

THERE had been other things on his mind while he was revising and retyping. With the help of friends such as Alexander Rives, who was a realtor as well as a fox hunter, Estelle had seen several places in the country. She had particularly liked Jumping Branch Farm, which was just across from Grover Vandevender on the Garth Road. Faulkner wrote Donald Klopfer that he was thinking of offering as much as $80,000 for it, but he would have to draw an additional $20,000 a year from Random House and Ober. What did Klopfer think? Klopfer told him that he had about $45,000 on deposit, that there was a constant flow of royalties, and $40,000 more to come over the next four years from the film rights to *The Sound and the Fury*. But he would advise waiting until the film rights to *Requiem for a Nun* were sold to Twentieth Century-Fox. By the time Faulkner reached Charlottesville, there was an offer from Ruth Ford, Zachary Scott, and Harvey Breit of $5,000 down and $45,000 more over four years for the motion-picture rights to *Light in August*. He accepted, and there was no reason to think that the deal for the rights to *Requiem for a Nun* would not go through. But now, for some reason—whether uncertainty or native caution or the memory of being land-poor with Rowan Oak—he began thinking of buying a place in town instead of a farm.

But his connections both in town and country were growing firmer. At Linton Massey's suggestion, librarian John C. Wyllie had released the news that William Faulkner had been appointed consultant on contemporary literature to the Alderman Library of the University of Virginia. In practical terms, this meant only that Faulkner would have the use of one of the fifth-floor faculty studies, but it would provide some sort of link with the university. In a newspaper release Faulkner was quoted as saying he was " 'delighted and honored' to be given a permanent connection with the University of Virginia." He used the study to complete his work on *The Mansion*.

In Farmington, Evalyn Galban had taken the hint in his note of thanks and proposed him for membership in the Farmington Hunt. He could have an out-of-town membership now and a local membership later. Writing his thanks from Mississippi, he had told her, "I will try to live up to the honor and the courtesy."[9] In the blank for "junior riders" he had listed his two grandsons. He was "looking forward to seeing all the Virginians who have made us so welcome."[10]

If he was distancing himself from Mississippi, his removal from Hollywood and its works was complete. When producer Jerry Wald implored him to appear on Edward R. Murrow's television program to publicize *The Sound and the Fury*, Faulkner told him to tell Murrow he had retired. Wald said that when a major New York newspaper asked Faulkner, through him, to write "some stories" about the picture, Faulkner replied, "Have Tennessee Williams write them." Not only would he not be at the film's world premiere in Jackson, he told one reporter that his contract specifically stated that he did not have to read the screenplay or see the picture.

* * *

Now that all of the typescript was in New York, he was free to please himself, even when it involved rough going. On March 4 he rode hard after the fox through a thicket, and that night one eye was still watering and blurry from a twig that had struck it. He had been riding a horse of Dr. Harry Hyer's named Tiffany, not as big or as strong as his own Powerhouse but a more graceful and promising jumper. He was looking forward to riding him in the Virginia hunter trials. At the Farmington hunter trials on Saturday the fourteenth, he rode Powerhouse. The footing was wet and uncertain, and his big hoofs threw up clods of earth as they moved swiftly around the curve to the first barrier. As Faulkner turned him hard for a straight run at it, Powerhouse lost his footing on the treacherous ground. Faulkner twisted free but landed hard on his right shoulder. Shaken, he rose slowly. Grover did not think he had broken anything, but Doug Nicoll phoned the resident on duty at the university hospital and sent him in.

Faulkner grumbled at leaving the trials to make the trip in to town, but the x-rays showed a shattered clavicle. As soon as the resident applied a figure-of-eight bandage and plaster and put his right arm in a sling, Faulkner slung his coat over his shoulder and returned to Farmington. Before the afternoon was over he was actually back in the saddle again. A fractured collarbone, he said, was "no worse than a hangnail." That was why, he said, "I don't intend to miss the last hunt of the season on Tuesday." In spite of his bravado, he was more grateful than usual for the Jack Daniel's at cocktail time.

He missed the last hunt of the season. But when the cast came off on March 17, he was mending nicely. He was still wearing a sling, though, three days later, when he watched the Virginia Field Hunter Championship Trials instead of riding in them. The previous season, Keswick Master Alexander Rives had let him ride his champion hunter, Wedgwood, twice. This day, as Faulkner watched him, he was determined to ride one of his own the next year.

Less than a week later, however, the picture had changed. He was in pain and he had developed a respiratory infection. Meriwether had flown in from Texas, and he and Erskine had gone through *The Mansion* together. It was clear that there was much adjusting of discrepancies to be done, but Faulkner was in no shape to participate in them. Doug Nicoll had given him a prescription for APC pills, but he had not had it filled. By the time he needed further medical attention, he was also suffering from the liberal use of bourbon to kill the pain. Leo Falk, his Charlottesville doctor, was away, and James B. Twyman saw him instead, both at home and at the office. Besides considerable swelling in the area of the collarbone, he also had a urinary tract infection. Twyman detected a prostate enlargement too, though to a degree not unusual for a man of his age. When he thumped him on the chest, the sound was one sometimes heard from an enlarged heart. The liver felt enlarged too, but the x-ray showed no enlargement, and apart from sulfa for the infection, the directions were the same ones he had received so many times before: abstinence, nourishment, and rest. As usual, he would follow them at his own pace.

It was clear now that a trip to New York was out of the question, and on April 6 he and Estelle left for Mississippi with a driver. Faulkner had checked a list of Memphis orthopedists with Doug Nicoll before he left, but when he arrived home he decided instead to put himself in the hands of one just a short distance down the Old Taylor road: Felix Linder, his childhood friend, who had retired and moved back to Oxford. When he asked Nicoll to write to Linder, Faulkner reported that he was still stiff and sore from bruises but that his strength was coming back. "I am anxious to work my two [horses] here," he wrote. "How much longer before I can risk riding again? I dont want to break myself up for good at a mere 61."[11] Nicoll's response was not encouraging. He had suffered a shattering of the collarbone rather than one clean break, and it would probably take about two months before he should ride again. By late April he must have realized how right Nicoll was. When he went to see Felix Linder he had literally wept with the pain. Felix relieved it somewhat by strapping him up. He offered to write a prescription for pain pills, but Faulkner refused it. He wrote Joan Bowen that he thought something was pressing against a nerve somewhere. He told her that he had not gotten much done. "I still have one more book I want to write. Now that I cant waste time with horses, I should get at it. Though I hope every day I can ride again."

Joan wrote him about the novel she was trying to complete and about her worry that people might say it was too much Faulkner. "Never give one goddam about what anybody says about the work," he replied, "if you KNOW you have done it as honestly and bravely and truly as you could. . . . Every writer is influenced by everything. Whatever touches him, from the telephone directory to God. I was in your life at an age which I think you will find was a very important experience, and of course it will show on you. But dont be afraid. There are worse people and experiences than me and ours to have influenced you. Dont be afraid. Do the work." He closed optimistically. "My arm is better. I think I can ride again soon."

Nicoll had told him that he should not count on riding until June. He was back at it by mid-May. Rising early, crossing the lawn from the office to the barn, he would saddle and mount with only the sound of birds or an occasional car to break the spring silence. "He was riding past the Linders' house," Johncy Faulkner wrote later, "and luckily Felix and Dewey were out in the yard. A piece of paper blew across the road right at the horse's feet. The horse spooked, shied out from under Bill, and he fell flat on his back on the pavement. It was a terrible fall." The

Linders took him home and put him to bed. Johncy was convinced he was bleeding internally, and he remembered that Felix said "the fall was enough to have killed him."[12] After a spell of bed rest he was up again, but one leg hurt so much that it pained him to walk. Six months later two x-rays made in the course of a checkup would show something new: an anterior compression fracture of the sixth dorsal vertebra. It was squashed, and it looked as though D4 might possibly be involved too. "I think he broke his back again," Nicoll said as he made notes in his record. It was impossible to tell whether Faulkner had smashed the vertebra on this May morning, but whatever the extent of the injury, it put him on crutches for more than two weeks.

Once again there was little for him to do but turn to his work. Early in the month Erskine had written him about new problems that had surfaced in reconciling the three volumes of the trilogy: "Sometimes they are of such a nature that I don't see how they can be changed in H to conform to M, since the contradictory details are functional in both places. . . ." In *The Hamlet*, Mink's first shotgun shell misfired, and it was the second one which killed Houston. Now the first one fired. Faulkner had a reason for the change. When Mink pulled the trigger at Flem, the first cartridge failed to fire. He thought two such mischances would be too many, and the second instance would provide more drama than the first. There was more than a touch of asperity in Faulkner's reaction to the problem Erskine had raised. He was "a veteran member of a living literature," he said, and for him "living" was equated with constant alternation, evolution, improvement. "So if what I write in 1958 aint better than what I wrote in 1938, I should have stopped writing twenty years ago; or, since 'being alive' equals 'motion,' I should be 20 years in the grave." He still insisted that if anything were to change, it would have to be *The Hamlet*. "Though, since I believe that fact had nothing to do with truth, I wouldn't even bother to change HAMLET." But he did offer one remedy. "If you like, we can make a foreword of the first paragraph [of this letter] and steal all the thunder beforehand."[13] They could thrash it all out when he and Estelle came up in June for the christening of William Cuthbert Faulkner Summers. One element of the front matter of the book would present no problem. The dedication would be simply "To Phil Stone." This was "for consistency"[14] with the other volumes of the trilogy.

Near the end of May he wrote Erskine that they would leave for Charlottesville on June 2 and that he would come up to New York five days later. "Have a rewrite idea for *Mink* in *Mansion* which will match the dud shells when he shot Houston in *Hamlet*," he told him, "and will lose nothing of *Mansion* story."[15] He was still stiff and sore when they started out, but he had postponed the trip as long as he could. The lease on the house on Ivy Lane had expired, and though they could stay with

Jill and Paul in their new home, it would not be a good arrangement for long, especially with a small boy and an infant in the house. If he was going to buy a place, he ought to do it now. Moreover, he certainly did not want to ask Jill to postpone the christening, and he most certainly wanted to be there when the name he bore, now spanning six generations, was passed on.

CHAPTER

68

And you, the old man, standing there while there rises to you, about you, suffocating you, the spring dark peopled and myriad . . . the cup, the bowl proffered once to the lips in youth and then no more; proffered to quench or sip or drain that lone one time and even that sometimes premature, too soon. Because the tragedy of life is, it must be premature, inconclusive and incon-cludable, in order to be life; it must be before itself, in advance of itself, to have been at all.

—*The Town* (317–318)

THREE days after their arrival, the Associated Press reported that William Faulkner had bought a home on Rugby Road in Charlottesville and would move into it in September. The closing would not actually take place until late August, but they had indeed settled on the handsome Georgian brick house they had first occupied in Charlottesville. Comfortable and convenient, it was fifteen minutes on foot from the university and twenty minutes by car from Grover's. It was a good investment which would also provide a base while they looked out in the county for a country place.

By the time the AP story appeared, he had checked in at the Algonquin for a week's work with Albert Erskine on *The Mansion*. When he walked into Random House he was moving more slowly than usual and carrying a cane. It would be weeks before he could abandon it, but when Cerf and Klopfer commiserated with him over the injury he pooh-poohed it. He settled down in Erskine's dark but comfortable office to get the work done. Although Erskine had worked on *Intruder in the Dust* and the early stages of *Collected Stories*, he was now entering into a new kind of relationship with the firm's most prestigious author. This was work he particularly enjoyed. Four months earlier, just coming to grips with the discrepancies, he had written Faulkner, "I've never been given an assign-ment that gave me more pleasure." In spite of Faulkner's near-irascibility in his letter about being "a veteran member of a living literature," he proved to be flexible as they worked over the manuscript. Whatever his idea was for matching up the Houston murder in *The Hamlet* and *The Mansion*, he abandoned his earlier determination and changed *The Mansion*, so that the first shell was a dud, as it had been in *The Hamlet*. They went on with the list of problem passages. Down the hall, Hiram Haydn was talking with Donald Klopfer in his office, and he was surprised when Faulkner came in. "I don't mean to interrupt you," Faulkner said to Klopfer, "but I feel I must tell you what has just happened." He went on to describe the progress they had made. "I got more help from Mr. Erskine in an hour than I've ever before experienced," he concluded.[1] Erskine was offering stylistic suggestions too. He had noticed that Faulkner had fallen into a mannerism that was not functional: putting a character's name after a pronoun when the antecedent was perfectly clear, as when he would write, "he, Chick Mallison, now seventeen." Now several younger writers seemed to be imitating him. Erskine pointed this out to Faulkner, and as they continued to move through the typescript Faulkner began to eliminate this construction, drawing lines through either pronoun or noun.

Faulkner spent the weekend in Charlottesville and then returned to put in another week's work. He and Erskine were now satisfied that they were doing as much as they could to remedy the most obvious disparities. Some would remain, and the small inconsistencies would not matter in the long run. As an additional hedge, however, Faulkner followed through on the suggestion he had made earlier and expanded the paragraph to "steal all the thunder beforehand" from anyone who wanted to carp. This was the summation, he wrote, of a work that had originated in 1925; "the purpose of this note is simply to notify the reader that the author has already found more discrepancies and contradictions than he hopes the reader will . . . due to the fact that the author has learned, he believes, more about the human heart and its dilemma than he knew thirty-four years ago; and is sure that, having lived with them that long time, he knows the characters in this chronicle better than he did then."

The book moved into production, and by mid-July, Faulkner would finish correcting the galleys. "We left most of the discrepancies cryptic enough in the other session to be corrected without much wrenching," he wrote in his covering note. "I think I have done this. . . . I can go through HAMLET and TOWN before next printing and make them match right up to the hilt of poetic license."[2] As with most of his other business relationships, this one became a personal association too. He would remain for the most part undemonstrative, and partly because of this, when he did show his feelings, it meant more. In the fall of the year, when Albert Erskine and his beautiful bride, Marisa, would send the Faulkners a wedding announcement, Faulkner would write back, "After having seen her once, anyone congratulates you; after knowing you as many years as I have, I can even risk congratulating her."[3]

A kind of corollary of the author's note in *The Mansion* was taking shape in Charlottesville that summer. Linton Massey and members of the University of Virginia Library were arranging an exhibit of Faulkner's works. Massey's own collection would serve as one of the bases, and Faulkner and Random House had agreed to supply other items. Massey provided six tentative titles for the show. Faulkner finally wrote down the one they would use:

William Faulkner
Man Working
1919 - 1959

He had told one of his Virginia classes that the writer "knows he has a short span of life, that the day will come when he must pass through the wall of oblivion, and he wants to leave a scratch on that wall— Kilroy was here—that somebody a hundred, a thousand years later will see."[4] This exhibit would help to make clear the proportion of William Faulkner's mark on that wall.

In Charlottesville he was especially aware of another kind of immortality. In the year they had lived on Ivy Lane, Jill would sometimes look up from her work to see her father walking more slowly than usual, pacing his steps to match the uncertain ones of his grandson. Now Tad was an active three-year-old. Jill knew that both times Pappy had been hoping for a girl. But during this visit she would look out the kitchen window and see her father lying in a lawn chair. He would be watching his two grandsons, a smile on his face and contentment in his dark eyes. "Pappy really changed," Jill thought. "He became so much easier for everyone to live with—not just family, but everybody. . . . he was a different man. . . . He was enjoying life."[5] He and Estelle stayed in Virginia until Little Will's christening on June 27. Godmother Mary Massey held the child in her arms. Standing at her elbow, Faulkner whispered the baptismal names to be sure they were pronounced in the proper order.

WHEN they returned to Oxford, Faulkner was still planning for his Virginia residence. He talked with Thomas Tullos, a friend of Dorothy Oldham and acquisitions librarian at Ole Miss, about the library he wanted to build. He wanted a set of Dickens and the Malay Edition of the works of Conrad, and Tommy offered to obtain them. On some evenings after dinner Faulkner would take down a volume from the shelf—perhaps Dickens or Cervantes—and read aloud to Tommy and Estelle and Dot, like a Victorian paterfamilias. The books were always old favorites. "I suppose I have about fifty that I read," he said. "I go in and out like you go into a room to meet old friends, to open the book in the middle and read for a little while. . . ."[6] He would enlist Erskine's help as well as Tullos' in building up a second library. He asked him for a baker's dozen of Modern Library "Giants," including a complete *Homer* and *Don Quixote*, a three-volume Gibbon, Boswell's *Johnson*, and the poems of Keats, Shelley, and Donne. He also asked for *Anna Karenina* and *War and Peace*, *Les Misérables* and *Moby-Dick*, *Tom Sawyer* and *Huckleberry Finn*. When the books came, he was disappointed with the *Homer* because he had wanted Pope's translation. Blotner ordered it for him from Blackwell's in England, along with another staple he wanted: Bishop Jeremy Taylor's *Holy Living* and *Holy Dying*—preferably in seventeenth-century editions. His love for reading would manifest itself in still another way that spring. In Charlottesville he would go to the local studio of Recording for the Blind to read "That Evening Sun," the first of several such volunteer stints.

There would be more than one new Faulkner first edition for Estelle to lock in the glass bookcase in the library at Rowan Oak that year. Gwynn and Blotner had transcribed and edited his recorded sessions at the university. Faulkner wrote Erskine when Ober asked if he could offer some of the material to magazines. He told him that Saxe Commins had not wanted any of it printed because "it would inevitably be taken as Faulkner's definitive opinion on Faulkner. I . . . was ready to agree to the publishing of it, but submitted to Saxe since he was my literary wet-nurse, etc. He finally agreed that the Univ of Va could print it in their own organ, but that if it were ever printed commercially, Random House should do it." Faulkner thought Erskine should check the material. "I didn't think it was all that important, myself. It was done impromptu, off the cuff, ad lib, no rehearsal; I just answered what sounded right and interesting, to the best of my recollection after elapsed years, at the moment."[7] Erskine liked the material, and so publication plans went forward for *Faulkner in the University*.

Faulkner reacted very differently to another title bearing his name. Professor Floyd Watkins, of Emory University, wrote Erskine that he had completed the editing of a manuscript by one of Faulkner's hunting friends called *Old Times in the Faulkner Country*. In it the unnamed author related a good deal of Lafayette County lore and many anecdotes about Faulkner. Though it was in the main favorable, there was material about Faulkner's drinking and the reasons why some of his neighbors disliked him, and Watkins wanted to know if Random House would be interested in the manuscript. Erskine sent the letter to Faulkner, who promptly suggested the reply that "Faulkner himself has already milked his private life of any or all interesting literary matter . . . and therefore the mss. will belong to the scavenger school of literature, and Random House doesn't want it."[8] Before he mailed the letter he learned that the author was John Cullen. In a postscript he told Erskine he thought there was no malice in it, probably just a desire to be literary and even the wish to gain Faulkner's approval of his work. "The sad thing is," he would tell one friend, "that that boy probably had a book of his own to write, but that fellow came down with his tape recorder and turned it into something else. Now he's just another one of these people riding on my coattails." Two years later the book would be published by the University of North Carolina Press, and it would be useful to many critics and scholars.

He had told Erskine, "Am riding again in late pm when it is bearable, am looking forward to fall and fox hunting in autumn countryside."[9] When he agreed to postpone the publication of his new novel so he could earn $2,500 from *Esquire* for the publication of the first two chapters, he told Ober, "Having, with *The Mansion*, finished the last of my planned labors; and, at 62, having to anticipate that moment when I shall have scraped the last minuscule from the bottom of the F. Barrel; and having undertaken a home in Virginia where I can break my neck least expensively fox hunting, I am interested in $2500.00 or for that matter, in $25." In spite of the jocular tone, he was thinking about making provisions for the future. He wanted to deed the Rugby Road house to Jill and leave the money in his broker's account to her children. He also wanted his manuscripts to go to Jill, and asked Ober to find out how to go about placing a valuation on them. He offered Jack Falkner a $10,000 loan toward a retirement home in Oxford, but as he expected, his independent brother declined it. When Bill Fielden sent him the interest on a loan, Faulkner wrote back, "I am trying to arrange my affairs, in case I break my neck fox hunting (also, I'm 62 years old now), so there wont be a lot of inheritance tax, and gift taxes, to pay." For this reason he might "endorse all the notes I hold of my children, family etc. as bad debts. . . . This is simply to advise you not to curse my memory if you find your note endorsed in this fashion."[10] He had told Joan Bowen that there was one more book he wanted to write, but with the completion of the Snopes trilogy, and with the vast labor of creation behind him, he meant to take what pleasure he could from life. It would be no old age spent by the fire, and if Tempy should refuse a jump or Powerhouse come a cropper some brisk morning, his affairs would be in order.

He would still heed the call of duty. When Muna Lee asked him to serve as "consultant" at the 7th National Conference of the U.S. National Commission for UNESCO in Denver he had reluctantly agreed. "I will go of course, be present. But I . . . would prefer not to have to listen to any one else's speech, last on earth to make another of them myself."[11] She saw to it that veteran Foreign Service Officer Abram Minell went along on the three-day trip. On their first evening together, Minell uncorked a bottle of Cutty Sark and they began to talk. Minell found himself reminiscing about his time on an LST on the China coast and about traveling after the war from Shanghai to the Great Wall. Soon Faulkner was talking about working as a sailor in his youth. When Minell repeated an earlier suggestion that Faulkner address a meeting, Faulkner said they should write it together. By the time Minell left at 2:30, Faulkner had written out a page on hotel stationery. At the plenary session on Friday, October 2, he delivered it—another celebration of individuality and freedom. Russia's Chairman, Nikita Khrushchev, had been wrong, he said, when he had told the West, "We will bury you." He went back to his Nobel Prize speech imagery: "The last sound on the worthless earth will be two human beings trying to launch a homemade space ship and already quarreling about where they are going next."[12] It seemed to Minell that most of the audience had found the two-minute talk profoundly moving and that when the session ended, everyone was talking about it. Having performed his duty, Faulkner left Colorado for Mississippi as soon as he could.

Three weeks later he and Estelle were back on Rugby Road in Charlottesville, where they would stay until New Year's. They had hardly settled in when, on the last day of October, word came that must have made Faulkner think again of the request he had so recently made that Harold Ober help him value his manuscripts for testamentary purposes. He had not seen as clearly as some of Ober's other clients the toll which a series of heart attacks had taken. Anne Louise Davis had written that Ober would be out of the office for a couple of weeks. Now a telegram brought word that he had died that morning. Saxe Commins, whom Faulkner had expected to outlive him, was gone. Now, in tall, taciturn Harold Ober, Faulkner had lost a friend as well as an agent, one who had patiently seen him through difficulties for more than twenty years. "Harold will be missed," he wrote Bob Haas a few days later, "maybe by not too many people, but by the sort of people I hope will miss me; there are not too many like that."[13]

So Harold Ober would not be there to see the chapters he had placed when they appeared in *Esquire*, nor the reviews of *The Mansion* when they began to appear in November. Many of them tended to say the same thing: Faulkner was the greatest living American novelist and parts of this novel were superb, but it did not rank with his best. Granville Hicks wrote that it was like the others Faulkner had written since 1948 in that "one feels in them strength of will and mastery of technique rather than the irresistible creative power that surged forth so miraculously in the earlier work."[14] It would be two years before the most subtle and judicious appraisal would come in a study of the whole trilogy, entitled *Man in Motion*, by that consistently perceptive Faulkner critic Warren Beck. Meanwhile, there were other testimonials to Faulkner's whole body of work. Four years earlier the London *Times* had called his hometown of Oxford "the literary capital of the English-speaking world."[15] Now the issue of *The New York Times Book Review* which carried Malcolm

Cowley's favorable review of this novel (by "an epic poet in prose") also printed a series of reports from major capitals on the worldwide influence of William Faulkner.[16]

MEANWHILE, the poet was spending the golden fall weather as a novice fox hunter, riding with Farmington and Keswick, hunting as often as four or five days a week. "It is very fine, very exciting," he wrote Joan. "Even at 62, I can still go harder and further and longer than some of the others. That is, I seem to have reached the point where all I have to risk is just my bones."[17] He was not risking his heart. In the spring he had written her, "I'm not going to see you again, at least now. It's too painful. . . . I love you but I can do it with less pain from a distance."

To his friends in the field he was a source of pleasure and worry. One morning Scottish-born David Yalden-Thomson dismounted at a jump to push Faulkner's mount from where he had pinned him at the bottom of a ditch. "That was a nasty spot you were in," said Yalden-Thomson. "Well," replied Faulkner, "as the others jumped over me it was very interestin' countin' the nails in the horses' shoes." From then on, Faulkner and the forty-year-old philosophy teacher began to see a good deal of each other. "One's heart was in one's mouth every time he went over a fence," Yalden-Thomson said. He had good coordination and great determination, "but he was so slight, so *light*, that no decent-sized hunter was really in his control once it was out of the canter. He would come swishing by one, face set, lips grim, completely out of control—trying, however, as hard as he could to look in perfect control of his animal. Then a little later he would come up beside one, and if he'd brushed you or bumped you, he would just grunt, 'Sorry.' " Yalden-Thomson also felt that Faulkner was like his own father, whom he resembled: "the same disregard for physical fear carried to a point where . . . one suspected a very self-destructive streak." But Faulkner was "a very old-fashioned type gentleman," and in the hunting field he was "a great opener of gates for others—he was in fact a most unselfish rider."

He insisted now on being on a first-name basis with David and Evalyn Galban and Harry Hyer. When Doug Nicoll's pretty young blond wife, Molly, consistently addressed him as "Mr. Faulkner," he asked her to call him "Uncle Will." Like David, Harry saw the steel under the companionable exterior. Faulkner was riding Quilter, a roan jumper of Grover's, when they came to a split-rail fence and Quilter refused. Faulkner catapulted off and onto the rails. Hyer saw him take the impact on his ribs and lower back, around toward the area of the kidney. His face went white. As he collected himself, Hyer offered to help. "I'll jump your horse over," he said. Immediately he saw that he had said the wrong thing. "I'll jump my own horse over," Faulkner said with hauteur.

If Quilter was a problem, so was Powerhouse. Hyer offered to help solve the problem of the second mount by selling him one of his own horses, Tiffany. Faulkner paid $1,500 for him, and in a few years he would be worth three times that much. Faulkner renamed him Fenceman and began riding him often. Now he was completely self-sufficient at his avocation, riding with two hunts on alternate jumpers four or five times a week. He continued to hunt in all weathers, and on one of the shortening fall afternoons it was cold enough for him to break his rule of not drinking before five under normal circumstances. When Ev Galban offered him her flask, he gratefully accepted a draught. By the end of the first week in December he was coughing and running a temperature. Leo Falk diagnosed it as pneumonia, started him on a course of antibiotics, and advised him to come in for an overdue checkup. A week later the x-ray showed that the medicine had knocked out the pneumonia. He did not bother with the examination.

At Christmas he gave inscribed copies of *The Mansion* to his friends. He had attended to gifts for the family members in Mississippi, and he had obtained enough of the McAlpine plaid to make kilts for Tad and Will and a smoking jacket for himself. He felt well enough for the Christmas ritual of having friends in for sangaree. When they arrived at 10:30 that morning, he met them at the door. Before one couple could hand him the plum pudding they had brought, he held out a package and said, "Here's your Santy Claus." It contained a bottle of Jack Daniel's. On the dining-room table stood the silver bowl, apple slices floating on the shimmering surface of the sangaree. He kept filling the silver cups of the dozen or so guests from the hunt, the county, the city, and the university.

As the new year of 1960 came in, Faulkner was thinking about his return to Mississippi. He would get in some bird-shooting, but more compelling reasons would keep him there until mid-February. One was that if he lived in the Rugby Road house for more than half the year, he would have to pay taxes in Virginia as well as Mississippi. And there was his mother's care. He worried about her. When one friend asked how she was, he said, "She keeps getting smaller and smaller and smaller." She was still as feisty and independent as she had been a few years before, when she had tripped over an orange crate at Kroger's while marketing and gotten Uncle John to sue the store and settle out of court for her. Every day she took a cold bath, and she kept the house at sixty-eight degrees. It was increasingly difficult for her to do for herself now, but whenever the family would engage a housekeeper-companion for her, she would immediately let her go. Faulkner knew he would have to try to make some permanent arrangement, and so on January 3 he boarded the train for Mississippi.

She was in the hospital when he got there, not only ill but also upset. Two years before, she had bought an inexpensive insurance policy. "She told me," he wrote Estelle, "with a kind [of] angry disbelief that John had told her he had paid Dr Holley some money on her bill. She didn't believe she could possibly have a bill, with her policy, somebody was cheating her, as usual. I smoothed her down, got hold of John and told him for God's sake why did he tell her, let her have her illusions . . . that I had never told her about the bills I paid, let her believe she could live in 1960 for 11 dollars a week if it made her happy."[18]

He relaxed, driving out into the country for bird-shooting. Jimmy Faulkner noticed how well-dressed he was, wearing the best hunting clothes, some of them from the L. L. Bean catalogue. He carried his Browning twelve-gauge over-and-under shotgun with its engraved breech, specially cut stock, and butt bearing a silver disc with his initials. But Jimmy noticed that his shooting was off. "I better get some hunting glasses," his uncle said.

He was not home for two weeks before he was sick again. When his temperature shot up to 103, Dorothy Oldham called Felix Linder, who gave him penicillin and told Dot and Jimmy to get someone to stay with him, partly because he had already started increasing his bourbon intake. Two days later the situation began to go out of control. When something like this had happened eight years before, he had ultimately used it in "Weekend Revisited." The events that now took place would amuse him even more, so much so that one of his first acts upon his recovery was to describe them in a two-and-a-half-page, single-spaced letter he typed out to Estelle. At her discretion she could read it to Linton Massey and to Blotner, who, he was sure, would enjoy the tale as much as he had. It covered the six days from the time he left Rowan Oak on Monday morning until he returned on Sunday. He didn't remember any of the first part of it, he wrote, because of the combination of fever, delirium, penicillin, and whiskey, but he had reconstructed the events. "John drove into the yard in an ambulance, came up to my bedside and said, 'I'm going to save you. The ambulance is waiting.' I probably said, 'Fine, I'd like a nice ride this morning.'" Installing his brother and himself in the back, John instructed the driver to take them to Byhalia, fifty miles away. Faulkner would not realize he was in Wright's Sanitarium until Friday night, but from what he had learned, John had insisted on checking in with his brother on their arrival and occupying the other bed in the room at a special rate. On Thursday night, when Faulkner had surfaced sufficiently to ask for a drink, his brother asked for one also. When they told him he could not have one because he had paid only for William Faulkner, he indignantly departed for Oxford, by taxi, stopping in Holly Springs to purchase two cases of beer. When Louise Meadow decided that Maud Falkner had to know about this adventure, Louise found that the news had already reached her there in the hospital. "If John has dropped Billy off at a hospital," she said to Louise, "he's probably some-where still riding around in the ambulance." Next, Louise went to John's house to inform his wife, Dolly. At that moment "John himself walked in the door behind her carrying his beer. Louise said she could have gone through the floor, but chose the door instead; nobody asked her to stop around." On Sunday morning Faulkner was discharged very readily by the doctor, from whom he had won thirty-five dollars in the Saturday-night poker game. When he felt well enough to visit his mother in the hospital, he met Dolly: "she never said beans: just beamed at me, a really good beam for four or five seconds—you know, like a tiger." Now he was staying in for a few days, but he was feeling pretty fair. "Keep this letter," he told his wife; "it's one of the funniest tales of good intent and human foolishness I know."[19]

There was little more of comic relief for him on this visit, however, and he was glad when the six weeks began to draw to a close. And if the knowledge that he had required intravenous feeding and medication at Byhalia had not given him pause, there was another memento mori in early February. Albert Camus died in an automobile accident, and Faulkner contributed a short tribute to *La Nouvelle Revue Française*'s "Hommage à Albert Camus." He wrote that Camus, in spite of denying God and being convinced of the absurd in human life, had spent his life "demanding of himself answers which only God could know. . . ." People would say he had died too young, but "When the door shut for him, he had already written on this side of it that which every artist who also carries through life with him that one same foreknowledge and hatred of death, is hoping to do: *I was here*."[20] A decade before, in *Requiem for a Nun*, he had described Cecilia Farmer, a frail young girl, scratching her name on a pane of glass one April day in 1861 as her way of saying *'Listen, stranger; this was myself: this was I.'* (262) Faulkner had spoken many times of man's desire to make his mark, his "Kilroy was here," on the wall of oblivion before passing through it. This death of another Nobel Laureate, an admired one, and one younger than himself, could only have intensified his own feelings of mortality in the depth of that winter of his sixty-third year. On February 12, in the teeth of a snow-storm, he left for Virginia.

In March he began to take part again in the life of the university. He spoke to a dozen Uruguayans on a State Department-sponsored trip. To everyone's surprise, he rattled off a short welcome in Spanish. He had obviously composed it beforehand and then memorized it. He was doing again what he had tried to do in so many places around the world, to make American culture understandable to foreigners insofar as he could from his own special vantage point, trying, too, to make friends for America. His growing conservatism did not show as clearly on this public occasion as it had in a private exchange shortly after his return. Paul and Elizabeth Pollard had worked for the Faulkners in Charlottesville. Now Pollard wrote asking his former employer to buy him a lifetime membership in the NAACP. Faulkner told Pollard that he was no longer contributing to that organization, that he felt it was following the wrong course. Once again he ranged himself with Booker T. Washington and George Washington

Carver. "As I see it," he wrote, "if the people of your race are to have equality and justice as human beings in our culture, the majority of them have got to be changed completely from the way they now act. . . . If the individual Negro does not do this by getting himself educated and trained in responsibility and morality, there will be more and more trouble between the two races."[21] He was using his money (his Nobel fund had a long list of beneficiaries) for individual cases, not for organizations. It was the last extended discussion of the subject he would put on paper. In May, however, after a reading before more than two hundred people at the university, he showed the other side of his ambivalent feelings when he spoke out against the closing of some Southern libraries to avoid integration. "I, too, feel the old inherited prejudices," he said, "but when the white man is driven by the old inherited prejudices to do the things he does, I think the whole black race is laughing at him."[22]

When he returned with Estelle to Mississippi in early June, it was to a quiet routine: riding in the morning, seeing to work at Rowan Oak and Greenfield Farm from time to time, occasionally sailing the *Ring Dove*. Early on Thursday he would drive Estelle to the store for her weekly grocery shopping. He was still paying his morning calls on his mother, but often he had to go to the hospital to do it, for it was clear that now, at eighty-eight, she was failing rapidly. She knew she was going to die, he told one friend later. "So I created a fairy tale for her. I would tell her about Heaven, and what it was going to be like, how nice it was going to be and how she would like it." It may have surprised him to learn that her conception of behavior in heaven was in some ways as unorthodox as the one he had created thirty years before in "Beyond the Gate." After one of his descriptions of the joys of the Blessed, she said she just didn't know how she would stand those robes all the time.[23] Then she asked him a direct question: "Will I have to see your father there?"

"No," he said, "not if you don't want to."

"That's good," she said. "I never did like him."

He would laugh as he told this later, but the sight of this small, once indomitable figure growing daily weaker, a prey to uncertainty and doubt, must have taken a greater emotional toll than he would admit.

There were occasional items of business to transact as the fall came in with the heat of late September. When Ruth Ford and Zachary Scott and Harvey Breit had been unable to arrange for the production of *Light in August*, he agreed to the deferment of this second payment or their sale of the rights to someone else. "Evidently the property is not too hot," he wrote to Ivan von Auw at the Ober office, "or they would have sold it."[24] One thing that had sold produced confusion. It was the television script called "The Graduation Dress," which James Geller had sold, bearing the names of William Faulkner and Joan Williams. Now the producer wanted Faulkner's help with promotional publicity using the National

Book Week film he had made at the University of Virginia. Faulkner told Anne Louise Davis that he really did not remember the script, but that it must have been a collaborative work with Joan Williams and that she should have all the credit, if possible. He was sending a copy of the letter to the University of Virginia, and he wanted Miss Davis to use her copy "to give Miss Williams her share of credit, and to stop anyone trying to exploit my name further than a collaborator on this single script, which ended the collaboration."[25]

In early October he and Estelle were preparing for their return to Charlottesville. But then, on the morning of the eleventh, when Louise brought Miss Maud her breakfast, she found her on the floor unconscious. The night before, she had been reading, and D. H. Lawrence's *Lady Chatterley's Lover* was still on her night table. But she had been stricken by a cerebral hemorrhage, and now she was in a coma. The family gathered quickly. She had made Sallie Murry promise that they would not keep her alive on glucose. So they instructed her doctors to stop the supportive measures, and waited. One day as Jack Falkner sat on the front steps of the hospital, Bill drove up. "Let's go in and see Mother," he said. They sat there for a few moments, watching the slight form under the sheet, motionless but for the faint breathing. Outside on the steps once more, Bill filled his pipe. "Then," recalled Jack, "with unlit pipe in one hand and unstruck match in the other, he gazed out at the unhurried traffic and asked me what my thoughts were on the hereafter." Jack explained them as best he could. Bill slowly drew the flame into the bowl. Not long before, he had written about what Albert Camus had said on *this* side of the closed door. Now, sitting in the mild October sunshine, he thought about death again. "Maybe each of us will become some sort of radio wave," he said.[26]

On the sixth day she slipped away. "Bill and John and I returned to her room," wrote Jack, "and one after the other, in the order in which she had given us life, we leaned over the bed and for the last time kissed the dear forehead in death as each had done so often in life."[27] Again they knew her wishes. "I want the simplest casket I can get," she had said. She had exacted another promise from Sallie Murry: no embalming, just a wooden box. "I want to get back to earth as fast as I can," she had told Jimmy. Billy picked out the casket. At the funeral only the family handled it; no outsider touched it until the undertaker's men took charge as it left the porch of the house on its way to its place beside Dean in St. Peter's Cemetery. For her eldest son, this was a kind of final severance. He knew that Jill would never return to Rowan Oak to live, but if things worked out, it would be taken care of within the family.

IT was time to go north again. In August, Floyd Stovall had proposed to President Edgar F. Shannon, Jr., that William Faulkner be appointed Balch Lecturer in American Literature. The duties he envisioned would include one public reading a year plus a few classroom question-and-answer sessions. Stovall proposed a one-year agreement to be renewed every year so long as Faulkner wished it. The annual stipend would be $250. In reply Faulkner asked Stovall, "Why does the University want to waste its money by paying me $250.00 for something I am going to do anyhow for free?" He would be back in Virginia for fox-hunting, he said, and concluded with "our best respectful compliments to Mrs Stovall and to all our other friends amid the groves of Acadame on the 5th floor."[28]

So they turned their red Rambler station wagon north again to Virginia, where William Faulkner owned a house, belonged to a hunt, and would soon assume his duties as a faculty member of Mr. Jefferson's university.

69

That was how, his uncle said, the man seemed a part of the horse he rode; that was the quality of the man who was a living part of the living horse; the composite creature might die, and would, and must, but only the horse would leave bones; in time the bones would crumble to dust and vanish into the earth, but the man would remain intact and impervious where they had lain.

—*Knight's Gambit* (165–166)

THEY were back in Charlottesville the last week of October 1960. He began to discharge the modest obligations of the new job, and he was often with his grandchildren. He did pictures for them, pen-and-ink drawings with wash coloring. One showed Pappy jumping a horse. Another showed a cow and a horse, with a four-line verse between the two. At drink time Jill and Paul might drop in at Rugby Road. Often Tad would be using his junior in a brotherly fashion, practicing flying tackles on him, rolling over him, in the immemorial fashion of older brothers. When Will would finally give way to tears, his grandfather would look down, smile, and shake his head. "If he sees two he'll see sixty," he would say. One thing that Will would do pleased him especially. "Listen to this," he said to one friend. Looking down at the small figure that looked like a miniature of himself, he said, "What's your name, boy?" Legs firmly planted, hands in his pockets, Will looked up. "Will Faulkner," he said.

Out at Grover's on days when they did not hunt, he would sometimes take his favorite place, sitting on the top plank of the fence, his feet on the mounting block, watching the children. That fall he and George Barkley organized the Buck Mountain Riding Club, and Grover joined them on the governing board. One of its main purposes was training the children. They would go on trail rides and stay out all afternoon, enjoying themselves so much that it was soon called the Fun Club. With dues and horse shows and some borrowed money, they began building a big room with a huge fireplace which would be the heart of the club. Faulkner took the minutes for the meetings, recording an afternoon's business on one page written in his small hand.

Some of the adults would ride together every morning. Faulkner was usually among them, these riders who were, in the words of surgeon Euclid M. Hanbury, Jr., a "band of brothers." Riding with them in the mornings and with others in the afternoons, he put in full days. One afternoon when Blotner stopped in at Rugby Road, Faulkner poured the first drink of the day with special pleasure. He had spent five hours on Powerhouse, he said, and he really needed it. He took the first swallow with obvious satisfaction. "It's a good thing that in a changing world there are some unchanging things you can count on," he said, "like the quality of Jack Daniel's."

From time to time he would give some indication of his thoughts about the changing world. One evening he walked the four blocks to Old Farm Road, where the Blotners lived. As the two men sat sipping port, Faulkner took a copy of the Manchester *Guardian* from his pocket and read aloud an account of the tributes paid in Parliament to Ernest Bevin, one of them from Winston Churchill. He began to muse on Churchill's greatness. "I wrote him once during the war," he recalled. "I said that his speeches would be studied by schoolboys when Hitler was forgotten." Then he turned to another page and pointed to a photograph of a party scene. There was Eleanor Roosevelt, smiling and talking to Marilyn Monroe. "She's something of the new age," he said, pointing to the latter, "wiggling even while she's standing still."

One day at Farmington, Doug Nicoll and Paul Bloch, the joint Masters of the Hunt, asked for a word with him. "Mr. Faulkner," said Nicoll, "we would consider it an honor if you would wear the buttons and colors of the Farmington Hunt." In hunting circles this would be regarded as a considerable distinction, especially for a relative newcomer. He seemed delighted, but he wanted some information. Exactly what did it mean? "Oh, it means that you wear the pink coat and top hat every Saturday when we hunt," Nicoll told him. Faulkner ordered the full-dress scarlet tail coat with its Belgian blue collar and wrote Jimmy to send him his top boots, the black ones with the tan tops. "Fox hunting is fine here," he wrote Albert Erskine, "country is beautiful. I have been awarded a pink coat, a splendor worthy of being photographed in."[1] Jill observed his reactions and preparations with pleasure. She did not have to hear him singing "D'ye ken John Peel?" in his fine light tenor to know he loved everything about the hunt. He was, she thought, like a convert: more ardent than many born to it.

He was riding a good deal with Harry Hyer, who was serving as a whip this year. On occasion he would join Harry in peeling off from the rest for a moment to rein in on a hill and look out over the country, his keen eyes scanning the distance and his ear tuned to the sounding off of the hounds as their music drifted up through the clear cold autumn air. They rode in easy comradeship, but Harry still had the faculty of unintentionally ruffling his friend. Once when they came to a locked gate where the dogs and horsemen moiled, Harry looked over his shoulder questioningly. "Ready to jump the fence, Will?" he asked. Faulkner bristled. "Indeed I am," he answered, and with that he clapped his spurs to Powerhouse and sailed over it. Not many days later Harry suddenly realized he was due at the hospital and there was no time to tell the Master or one of the other whips. So he wheeled his horse and went tearing down the mountain, jumping fences and gates at a dead gallop. As he reined in at Grover's stables, Faulkner came clattering up after him.

"Will," said Harry in surprise, "what are you doing here?"

"You mean you're not following the fox?"

"No, I've left the hunt."

"You know, you're supposed to tell the Master."

"I suddenly remembered I had to be at the hospital and there wasn't time."

Red-faced and furious, Faulkner switched his horse around. "God dammit, Harry," he said, "I've left one of the best hunts of the season to follow you halfway to work." He spurred Fenceman into a gallop and set off to rejoin the others.

When the Keswick Hunt assembled before the doors of Grace Church, decorated as usual with the sheaves, Faulkner was among them. In a photograph taken that day, he sat Powerhouse beside Grover, their pink coats a bright splash against the dun November countryside. His top boots shining, his white stock pinned beneath his chin, he grasped the reins firmly with pigskin gloves. Below the brim of the top hat his features were calmly composed, the mustache full and flowing as a guardsman's. He looked as elegant as the Old Colonel ever could have, even when he took the regiment north in '61.

A few days earlier the New York *Herald Tribune* had noted the forthcoming motion-picture remake of *Sanctuary*. Faulkner's position now was a far cry from that of the writer whose name, thirty years before, had been anathema to so many of his countrymen. What would they think now, could they see him, those who had called him Count No 'Count? Some in Charlottesville, aesthetes and intellectuals, sneered at what were to them affectations unworthy of a great writer. What they did not realize was that in a way he had adopted still another persona, like that of the wounded war veteran, the bohemian artist, and the working farmer. But this one gave him at least as much satisfaction as any of the others had, and it was at least as true, perhaps even more so, to fundamental elements in his makeup. Long ago he had written his mother, "country folks are my sort," and David Yalden-Thomson now saw clearly how much more at ease Faulkner was with unsophisticated huntsmen and grooms than with those who wanted to talk about Sartre or the stream of consciousness.

Before Hadrian's Tomb in Rome, 1954

With Japanese teachers at Nagano

At Manila Yacht Club with Bill and Vicki Fielden

Jean Stein

Rowan Oak at daybreak

Convalescing

March 20, 1962

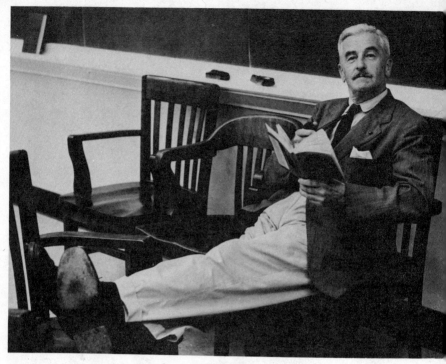

After a successful class meeting

With Joseph Blotner and Frederick L. Gwynn

In the paddock with Tempy

Schooling his horse

With Grover Vandevender, at his stable, before a hunt

"To Random House. Love and Kisses. Tally-ho. William Faulkner"

One of his favorite poets, William Butler Yeats, in "Under Ben Bulben" had exhorted the coming poets to sing, among others, "hard-riding country gentlemen." Faulkner took much of his material where he found it, and he told Harry Hyer that he was going to write an "allegorical" book about fox-hunting. But now, with a lifetime of the most intense artistic labor behind him, it pleased him to follow a pattern not unlike Henry Fielding's Squire Western or Squire Allworthy, whether it ever gave him material for his art or not. The new pink coat pleased Jill and Estelle as much as it did him. It was another closer tie to Charlottesville, and with Maud Falkner's death it make sense to cut out—or at least cut down—the long trips between Virginia and Mississippi.

THREE days after Christmas, Faulkner signed a codicil to the new will he had executed in Charlottesville six months before. It secured more firmly the Virginia connection, reading as it did, "I give and bequeath to the William Faulkner Foundation, Charlottesville, all of my manuscripts and other tangible personal property deposited at the Alderman Library." The foundation's aims were broadly philanthropic but they were centered on scholarships and grants, especially for worthy Mississippi Negroes, and for the encouragement of American literature, especially the novel. His gift of cash would provide for the scholarships and grants. His gift of the manuscripts—now that he could provide for Jill in a more conventional way—would give him a tax advantage, but it would also confer a great advantage on Faulkner scholars who would come in ever-increasing numbers to Charlottesville to study his work.

One of the first things he did after their return home in late December was to go—resplendent in his Farmington dress hunting costume—to J. R. Cofield, for the best portraits Cofield ever made of him. Nearly full length and in color, they showed the subject holding the coiled whip, his head back, a look of aristocratic hauteur on the strong features. He ordered two large portraits and seventeen smaller ones, leaving a mailing list of ten friends with Cofield.

Before leaving Virginia he had told David Yalden-Thomson, "Lock up your classroom and come on down." David accepted, and for ten days he and Faulkner went out after bobwhite quail. They would start six or seven coveys in the course of a day, and they brought back enough birds so that they got more than just exercise. In the course of the visit David learned about both the town and the county. Faulkner had told him about his nephew, Jimmy. "He got two DFC's, five Air Medals, and three court martials," he said. "He's a *good* boy." One evening Jimmy and his wife, Nan, took them to the country club for dinner. After they had ordered, a man rose from a nearby table and lurched over to them. If Faulkner would autograph a book for a friend, he said, he would let him shoot a deer on his place with a bow and arrow. "Maybe I couldn't hit the deer," said Faulkner.

"I'll put some corn on the ground and make it stand still," replied the drunk.

"Perhaps it wouldn't like corn."

"I'll tie it up for you."

"Shooting it would be great fun," said Faulkner with a freezing look as he turned away.

Baffled and disgruntled, the man returned to his table, where he fell over his chair. "All of his family have been game hogs," Faulkner told David. "He's a lying oaf who likes to pick fights, but he can't deal with a little mental quickness." It was revolting, he said, that you lost your privacy from drunks like that because you wrote books.

In the evenings after dinner they would sit and read in the library. For several evenings Faulkner read one book very slowly. It was *Dombey and Son*. He said you had to make a distinction between books which you could read fast and those you must read slowly. "*Great Expectations*," he said, "is one you must read very slowly." Sometimes he would fall into a storytelling mood and recount to David incidents both real and imaginary from his time in the RAF, in which David had also served. Other times he would exercise his gift for mimicry, which might be turned on an acquaintance or someone such as General Sir Douglas Haig in his famous Order of the Day issued April 11, 1918, in the teeth of the massive Ludendorff offensive: " 'With our backs to the wall,' " he said, in the English accent he had learned in New Haven in 1918, " 'and believing in the justice of our cause, each one of us must fight to the end. . . .' "[2]

One morning David watched his host as he went through a wicker hamper of mail. If he did not recognize a letter's return address, he would hold it to the light. If there did not appear to be a check or an envelope within, he would drop it in the wastebasket. David asked if he could be sure he was not throwing out any checks. "Oh, I'm really an expert at that," he answered. "I never miss a check and I never miss a stamped envelope." The pigeonholes in his desk were filled with envelopes divided according to the amount of postage. "I'm not sure that this small harvest of stamps makes it worth opening these letters," he said, "but I haven't bought a stamp for years." Other measures of his host's frugality —the way he could wear a pink coat one day and a tattered jacket the next—were familiar to David. It was part of a Highland pattern, and Faulkner displayed an extraordinary knowledge of Highland history and customs, as he had done thirty years before in "Thrift." It seemed to Highlander Yalden-Thomson that "Faulkner saw himself as a Highlander living in exile in Mississippi."

By mid-March, preparing for their return to Charlottesville, Faulkner was contemplating two changes of place with distinctly different feelings. On Rugby Road he and Estelle enjoyed the visits of their grandchildren, but though they had fenced in the terrace, they were uneasy about the traffic along the road. Paul and Jill were about to move eleven miles west

of Charlottesville to a thirty-acre property located between the Farmington and Keswick hunt country. They had made plans to enlarge the
house, and a cottage on the place could be enlarged for Jill's parents.
Naturally, the Faulkners would contribute to the cost of the purchase
and the improvements. The other prospective move involved a shorter
duration but a greater distance. In the summer of 1960, Muna Lee and
some of her colleagues had worked on a plan to cement United States–
Venezuelan relations. At her suggestion, Foreign Service Officer John M.
Vebber had broached the idea to the other directors of the North
American Association of Venezuela. When Vebber polled leading
Venezuelans, Faulkner was their overwhelming choice for a visit. In
September he had reluctantly agreed to the first two weeks of April.
Now, as the time approached, he was feeling increasing reluctance. For
one thing, "As I get older," he wrote Muna Lee, "I get more and more
frightened of aeroplanes." But he would go and do the best he could,
even though "I am still afraid I am the wrong bloke for this. . . . I am
not even interested in writing anymore: only in reading for pleasure the
old books I discovered when I was 18 years old."[3] Just then their travel
plans changed. Estelle developed a kidney infection and Chester McLarty
had to put her in the hospital. A week later she was still there, with her
recovery period unpredictable.

Bill Fielden's career in the tobacco business had taken him and Victoria
to Caracas. Faulkner wrote to say he was looking forward to seeing them
but also to explain why he would not be staying with them. "I have never
had any confidence in this visit," he wrote. "As I read it, it is a group of
North Americans who found they could make more net money living in
Venezuela than anywhere else, who wish to keep on making more net
money there even to the desperate length of paying the expenses for a
2 weeks' visit of a man like me who is neither interested in visiting
Venezuela nor in money either. . . . I have no hopes of the visit still. But
if, when, it fails, we dont want to have it said that the visit was a shabby
excuse for two deadhead weeks with my North American kinfolks and
their circle."[4]

Because of Estelle's illness they did not reach Charlottesville at all that
March, and Faulkner left for Caracas via New Orleans and Miami at the
beginning of April. The formal occasion for the visit was the Sesquicen-
tennial of Venezuelan Independence. The North American Association
had been assisted in its preparations by three of the country's leading
writers: Rómulo Gallegos, Arturo Uslar Pietri, and Arturo Croce. The
Venezuelan intellectual community might be anti-American on international issues, but for this visit they showed an almost unanimous accord
of anticipation. This was evident from the moment the reception committee of writers and reporters greeted Faulkner at Maiquetía Airport
in the early afternoon of Easter Sunday, April 2. Riding in to the city,
with the Cordillera de la Costa dominating the horizon, he might well

have thought of one of the writers he had told Muna Lee he had loved at eighteen: Joseph Conrad, who had set his *Nostromo* here at the edge of the continent.

Bill and Victoria took him home for some rest and relaxation, but the next morning it all began in the usual way, with a press conference. Public Affairs Officer Charles E. Harner would later say, "He handled the subject of racial problems in the United States with insight and sympathy." A warm welcome at President Rómulo Betancourt's official luncheon was followed that evening by a large cocktail party given by the N.A.A. at the luxurious country club. For the first time on this trip Faulkner began to resemble the harried lion in the Gallimards' Parisian garden. There was other cause for uneasiness, for when he had telephoned Jimmy to find out how Estelle was, he had learned that she had been moved to the University of Mississippi Medical Center in Jackson, where they would have to remove her infected kidney.

He carried on with his heavy schedule, which included a wreath for Bolivar, an exhibit for Faulkner, and a round-table discussion with more writers. His efforts did not go unappreciated by a group of journalists who had called him "*el hombre simpático.*" Working at his Spanish, he said he wanted "*saborear el vino de país.*" Some of the reporters began calling him simply "*El Premio.*" Formal recognition came with the award of the Order of Andrés Bello, the country's highest civilian decoration. After Faulkner read his short, graceful acceptance speech—in Spanish— he took from his buttonhole the prized rosette of the Legion of Honor and replaced it with that of the Order of Andrés Bello. The ceremonial meals and visits went on until the weekend, which he spent with Victoria and Bill, free of official functions until the Sunday-night concert in his honor by the Venezuelan Symphony.

On Monday morning, April 10, he and Victoria and Bill and Hugh Jencks, his interpreter, left by car on a four-day trip that took them west to Maracay. The next morning he rose early. Someone had found a horse for him, and he set out for an hour of the kind of sightseeing he liked best. But there were luncheons, receptions, and visits to Valencia and the University of Carabobo before a 250-mile flight the next morning over the mountain ranges that soared upward between Valencia and the sweep of Lake Maracaibo. He spent forty-eight hours in Maracaibo. On three of his visits students cheered him, but he had to handle hostile questions in a round-table discussion at the Universidad de Zulia, and later that after- noon other student questions had a distinct edge to them. But he was quiet and deliberate, and the sessions ended with cheers from his auditors. He obviously enjoyed himself at the open-air reception that night, eating and drinking Venezuelan style. Another mark of appreciation was portable: a two-foot-high bust of Don Quixote carved by Marcelino Pena in rich native wood.

The next day, Friday, April 14, the formal program came to an end back in Caracas with a cocktail party at the American Embassy. After another restful weekend with the Fieldens, he autographed books for several Venezuelans and stood at the Fieldens' door as host at a cocktail party on Sunday for all those who had worked on the arrangements. On Monday morning he flew home. Reassessing the visit, Charles Harner thought it "an enormous personal success." Faulkner did not "spare himself in the grinding schedule of the job he came to do," and as a result he had "rendered a high service to the United States." Both the embassy and his countrymen would be able to draw for a long time on the fund of good will the visit had engendered.

FAULKNER's cynical misgivings before the visit had given way to hopeful planning. He wrote some of the follow-up letters himself. In one he said he was glad that "el mission Venezuelano no fue fiasco, per un poco de succes. . . ." Later in the spring, with the help of Linton Massey and Professor Arnold Del Greco, he would make plans for a program whereby three judges in each participating Latin-American country would select an outstanding novel which had been published since World War II for an award from the William Faulkner Foundation, which would then use its influence to try to help effect translation and publication in the United States. There were other results: invitations to visit Mexico and Puerto Rico.

As usual, there was a pile of accumulated letters and parcels. From the Venezuelan trip came many volumes, several inscribed by their authors, but the one that pleased him most came from New York. It was Joan's novel, *The Morning and the Evening*—"at long last," as she said. The previous summer she had told him of its acceptance. "Splendid news," he had written her. "That not only justifies us but maybe absolves me of what harm and hurt I might have done you; maybe annoyance and exasperation are better words."

On May 9 the Faulkners returned to Charlottesville in time to await the birth of another grandchild. At the end of the month he arrived, A. Burks Summers III. It was then that Faulkner made his first appearance as Balch Lecturer in American Literature. He read from "The Courthouse" section of *Requiem for a Nun* and then answered questions. One revealed how, as he approached his sixty-fourth birthday, his literary tastes were changing with his age. Of all of Shakespeare's plays, the one he liked best now was *The Tempest*. Will Faulkner, trying to put himself into the mind of Will Shakespeare, said, "He said at last, 'I don't know the answer, so I will break my pencil and stop.'" He ran his hand back over his white hair. "At my age I know how he felt. You never will have the answers to the human condition, so you might as well give up."[6]

The next week brought word of another artist who had sought in vain the ultimate answers. On July 2, 1961, at his home near Ketchum, Idaho, Ernest Hemingway had placed the barrels of his favorite 12-gauge shotgun against his forehead and pulled both triggers. That Sunday the Faulkners were at Jill and Paul's. When Jill heard the first, incomplete report of Hemingway's death, she went out to the screened-in side porch and told her father. "It wasn't an accident," he told her immediately. "He killed himself." When Harry Hyer saw him at the stable on Monday morning he was still talking agitatedly about it. He had told Jean Stein that he thought Hemingway protested too much, that his show of fearlessness and virility was to some extent a cover-up. He continued to brood over it. To one friend he said that Hemingway was obviously sick, but there was something unmanly about what he had done. Then he made a curious remark: "It's bad when a man does something like that. It's like saying death is better than living with my wife." He was silent for a moment. "Hemingway's mistake," he went on, "was that he thought he had to marry all of them." The next time Red Hanbury saw Faulkner the reaction had crystallized further. "I don't like a man that takes the short way home," he said.

But if that death troubled him as midsummer of 1961 approached, he was deeply involved in life as it was embodied in the riders of the future. The Buck Mountain Riding Club was flourishing. They had added a bathroom onto the big clubroom with the huge stone fireplace, and they were working on a kitchen. On a small lake on his land Grover had built a four-deck wooden pier. At times there would be as many as a hundred people swarming over it. Some would be sunbathing on the top, others diving from the bottom, and still others swimming their ponies out into the lake. At night many of them would bring sleeping bags and spread them on the pier or the beds of the big hay wagons. Faulkner and Grover and other adults would roll themselves into horse blankets in one of the wagons still bedded with hay. When morning came Grover would wake them all with a blast on the hunting horn he was teaching Faulkner to blow. At other times Faulkner would arrive in the morning for the trail ride and stay all day.

He was still enjoying social life in town, continually revealing facets of his personality. At dinner at the Blotners' one night, he and his host were talking about aerial combat in World War I while Estelle carried on an animated conversation with Ted and Sally Turner, both artists. As Yvonne Blotner summoned her guests for dinner, her husband had just begun to recite the most stirring poem about aerial combat he knew, Yeats's "An Irish Airman Foresees His Death":

> "I know that I shall meet my fate
> Somewhere among the clouds above . . ."

Then suddenly he was stuck for the next line. Faulkner took it up almost without a pause:

"Those that I fight I do not hate,
Those that I guard I do not love,"

and then he completed the poem as they followed the others in to dinner. Over port and cigars the conversation turned to the insouciance of those pilots in the Camels and Bristols, and the contrasting precision of units such as the Guards regiments which relieved each other before Buckingham Palace with such snap and smartness in the execution of every command. "Yes," said Faulkner, and rising from the table, he briskly executed the hesitating half-step, stamp, halt, and turn of the officers exchanging the colors. He did it with the same élan he must have put into close-order drill forty-three years before in Toronto.

It was still early July, a few days later, when, as Blotner left Faulkner's home after drink time, Faulkner said, "Here's something for you to read," and handed him a tied manila folder. It proved to be the ribbon copy of three chapters entitled *The Horse Stealers: A Reminiscence*. It was set in 1905, and it began, "Grandfather said: . . ." Thereafter the text was all Grandfather, telling, as to his grandchildren, a story from his childhood more than a half-century before. At ages five and three, Tad and Will Summers were too young to follow this tale, but it was as if Faulkner had looked ahead to the time when they might. Grandfather was the protagonist of the story: ten-year-old Lucius Priest, who worked for his father, Maury, in his Jefferson livery stable while his three younger brothers were cared for at home by his mother and her helper, Aunt Callie.

The Priests represent the "cadet branch" of the McCaslin-Edmonds family, and familiar characters appear from the first. Boon Hogganbeck is there in the livery stable (like Buster Callicoat in Murry Falkner's stable), as rough a diamond and as poor a marksman as ever. Aunt Callie was of course based on Mammy Callie, and the coachman of "Boss" Priest, Lucius' grandfather, is Ned McCaslin, identified as Lucas Beauchamp's cousin and seeming to Jack Falkner to combine a good deal of Uncle Ned Barnett with something of Chess Carothers. Faulkner got things under way quickly with Boon's audacious scheme, which would give the novel its substance and struggle: the unauthorized borrowing of Boss Priest's new Winton Flyer with the ulterior motive of an expedition all the way to Memphis to visit the house of Miss Reba. Boon needs the connivance of Lucius, and the boy's gradual seduction by the promise and thrill of an automobile trip (and actually *driving* the machine) introduces the main theme of the novel: the loss of innocence through initiation. A corollary is the idea of gentlemanliness, not just manners, but also the deeper attributes, the virtues Faulkner had extolled in his Nobel Prize speech. With the end of the third chapter, the introductory phase was complete as Boon and Lucius set out in the Winton to face the trial and testing of

Hurricane Creek and Hell Creek Bottom on the road to the earthly paradise eighty-five miles away. Any reader who wanted to see mythic elements would find reason to do so, but the comic would be there quite clearly too. Some of that element is signaled by the discovery of a stowaway. " 'I wants a trip too,' Ned said. 'Hee hee hee.' "[7]

The developing novel had generic antecedents on more than one time level: in childhood Faulkner had ridden to Memphis with the rest of his family in the Young Colonel's Buick; there existed a whole sequence of photographs of one such trip, including a shot of the Colonel surveying his machine bogged down in a ditch deeper than the quagmire that temporarily frustrates Boon's expedition. That trip was fifty years ago. Faulkner had proposed to Haas, twenty-one years earlier, a novel about "a sort of Huck Finn," with other characters including an unreliable but courageous white man, a cantankerous old Negro servant, a compassionate whore, and a stolen race horse. Faulkner had told Haas that the boy "goes through in miniature all the experiences of youth which mold the man's character. . . . the very experiences which in his middle class parents' eyes stand for debauchery and degeneracy and actual criminality; through them he learned courage and honor and generosity and pride and pity."[8] Faulkner had used elements of his outline in other works, but now he was treating it fully. In his question-and-answer session at the university he had said that now his favorite play by Shakespeare was *The Tempest*. As that play had a happier ending than the great dramas of mid-career such as *Hamlet*, so would *The Horse Stealers* have a happier ending than such a novel as *Absalom, Absalom!*—at least if he followed his stated intention of two decades before.

When Blotner received the next installment a week and a half later, Faulkner said he was going to supply the jacket blurb himself. It would be a bogus excerpt for a review: " 'A very important statement—this book will become the Western world's Bible of free will and private enterprise.' E. V. Trueblood, *Oxford Eagle*, Mississippi." As he said it, he became convulsed and red-faced with his silent laughter. "This book gets funnier and funnier all the time," he said. He handed over the manila folder, containing the fourth and fifth chapters, and a paper bag containing a bottle of Pouilly-Fuissé, his favorite white wine.

The third chapter had taken the three heroes through the mudholes of Hurricane Creek. In the fourth chapter they find their strength and endurance insufficient to overcome the man-made quagmire at Hell Creek Bottom, and Lucius sees that in some exigencies there is no solution but money. When the travelers pass the night at Ballenbaugh's, Faulkner characteristically recounted its history, including the crucial role in it of the Reverend Hiram Hightower, the grandfather of Gail Hightower. In the fifth chapter, with their arrival in Memphis, he was able to introduce the other major character he had described to Haas: a big, pretty, gentle country girl named Corrie—one of Miss Reba's girls and the beloved of

Boon Hogganbeck. By now Lucius' initiation is moving on apace as he encounters not only smells he has not known before but also an unfamiliar helplessness in the face of cruelty, which he sees in Mr. Binford's treatment of one of the prostitutes. It suggested Ratliff's meditation in *The Mansion*: "the pore sons of bitches"—men and women caught, victims in extreme cases of the human predicament.

THE Faulkners returned to Rowan Oak in the last week in July. "Hot as hell here, as usual," he wrote Albert Erskine at the end of the month. "Now it's 64 years I have said I'll never spend another summer in Miss."[9] He went on a five-day horse-buying trip to Oklahoma, and he and Estelle entertained friends from the Memphis Hunt Club, but he returned to the novel with a burst of energy more sustained than any he had experienced in years. He had ended Chapter IV with Ned's appearance in Miss Reba's backyard holding a horse. In Chapter VI he revealed that Ned has swapped Boss Priest's car for the horse, and, moreover, that it is a stolen horse to begin with. Ned's strategy prepares for the trials to come: they will race the horse to win back the car.

Additional information and characters are introduced as Lucius' education makes a giant and sickening leap ahead in Chapter VII. Corrie's real name is revealed to be Everbe Corinthia—the name of one of Phil Stone's favorites in a Memphis brothel and the name of one of Faulkner's characters forty years before in "The Leg." This information comes from Corrie's fifteen-year-old nephew, Otis, stunted and steeped enough in evil to recall Popeye rather than Uncle Bud. When Otis also reveals what Corrie does and tells how he used a knothole for profit back in Arkansas to exhibit her doing it, Lucius attacks him. As Corrie treats Lucius' wounded fingers, Boon makes a comment Faulkner undoubtedly enjoyed writing: " 'Eleven years old,' he said, 'and already knife-cut in a whorehouse brawl. . . . I wish I had knowed you thirty years ago. With you to learn me when I was eleven years old, maybe by this time I'd had some sense too.' " (159)

In his eighth chapter Faulkner continued to explore the interaction of Lucius' initiation and his code of conduct. An unexpected result of the latter is Corrie's reaction to Lucius' championing of her: the resolve to abandon her profession and live virtuously. But now the story begins to darken as it deepens. Faulkner touched on the "pore sons of bitches" theme again with the introduction of harassment by a sadistic deputy sheriff after the group has succeeded in transporting the horse, called Acheron but renamed Lightning, to Parsham, Tennessee, where they will race him against his former possessors. With the increase in Lucius' knowledge and compassion, there has been a corollary loss: "I knew too much, had seen too much. I was a child no longer now; innocence and childhood were forever lost, forever gone from me." (175)

One of the obvious ways in which this novel was unlike its two predecessors was in the handling of point of view. Rather than several narrators, Faulkner had only one: Grandfather recounting events on one time level from the perspective of another a half-century later. This made asides and digressions easier and more natural, whether they were definitions of political parties, ratings of the intelligence of animals, an apostrophe to the mule recalling that in *Sartoris*, or railings against modernization.

Writing in the morning before the heat of the August day would reach its peak, Faulkner started Chapter X as Grandfather recounted the events of the day of the race. In the two chapters that followed, Faulkner wrote his way through the climax with Lucius' victorious ride on Lightning and on toward the story's resolution. The thirteenth chapter revealed changes wrought: Boon from lusty bachelor to husband-to-be, and Everbe Corinthia from virtuous whore to wife-to-be. But the primary focus remained on the boy. Holding Lucius while he weeps, Boss tells his grandson that he can atone for his lies by living with what he has done. In effect, Lucius has learned in Memphis and in Parsham something of the same code that his kinsman, Ike McCaslin, had learned in the big woods. "A gentleman can live through anything," his grandfather tells him. "A gentleman accepts the responsibilities of his actions and bears the burden of their consequences, even when he did not himself instigate them but only acquiesced to them, didn't say No though he knew he should." (302) The last lines form a short coda. As Lucius stands later looking into the crib, Everbe tells him the baby's name: Lucius Priest Hogganbeck. Faulkner had set this part of this grandfatherly tale in the same whorehouse as that of his most notorious novel, *Sanctuary*, but this time the consequences of initiation were quite different. After the fall there is a knowledge of evil but also of good, with the added components of compassion and the promise of maturity. At the bottom of page 300A he typed the date, "21 Aug 61."

After a few days' respite he was back at work. The revisions were minimal, and the biggest change was in the title. He had changed it to *The Reavers*, but he wrote Albert Erskine that there was an archaic Scottish spelling with a more "swashing" sound that he liked better. He thought he would call it *The Reivers*.

He walked down to Gathright-Reed, as he had done when he had finished other books, and asked Mac if he had something to wrap the manuscript in. Mac reached under the counter and produced the corrugated paper, the tape and wrapper and string. Faulkner leaned on the counter watching as Mac finished the job neatly and affixed the label Faulkner had brought with him. "I been aimin' to quit this foolishness," he told his old friend. He sent the parcel off just before his birthday.

IT was a little past mid-October when he and Estelle headed north again in the red Rambler. It looked like a busy autumn, what with moving to the cottage at Jill and Paul's Knole Farm, traveling to New York for a final check on the novel, and doing a few things for the university. And there would of course be the donning of the pink coat and top boots on those keen mornings when the dogs gave tongue as the poised fox on the hill listened for the first sounds of the chase. "He was enjoying life," his daughter would say. "I don't think he was being driven as much as he had been. . . . he had in a sense finished the creative side of his life and wanted to have something else."[10] A sixty-four-year-old man who had just completed his nineteenth novel had a right to spend however much time in the saddle he wanted, whether he had actually broken the pencil or not.

. . . that was something to see: the man and the horse fusing, joining, becoming one beast, then passing on beyond even that point, that juncture: not daring, but testing, almost physically palping at that point where even at mutually-compounding ultimate, concorded at absolute's uttermost, they must become violently two again. . . . It was as if the man knew that he himself was invulnerable and unbreakable, and of their two, only the horse could fail. . . .

—*Knight's Gambit* (167–168)

AFTER their return to Charlottesville on October 21, Faulkner sent Albert Erskine a list of changes in response to questions. A number of them were names. The depraved deputy sheriff became Butch Lovemaiden instead of Butch Lovelass. (There were two subscribers in the Oxford phone book named Lovelace and half a dozen named Lovelady.) In *The Town*, Faulkner had told how a mechanical genius named Mr. Buffaloe had handmade the first motorcar in Jefferson. In his typescript he had reintroduced this inventor but called him Mr. Bullock. Now Faulkner changed the name back to Buffaloe: perhaps a private gesture to honor John Buffaloe, who had handmade Oxford's first motorcar. He thought there would probably be a few more changes when he came up to go over the typescript on November 6. He told Erskine that he would not accept Bennett Cerf's invitation to stay with them. "I live up to my arse in delightful family," he wrote, "and I may want a holiday, at the Algonquin."[1]

By late October they were comfortably settled in the cottage at Knole Farm, just a few hundred feet from Jill and Paul's handsomely enlarged house. He and Paul went bird-shooting, and the hunt crowd welcomed them back. Besides the ordinary riding, there were the horse shows, such as the one at Upperville, where they would put up a tent with a bar and make a day of it. Faulkner would contribute his share in the form of a ham or a thirty-pound turkey. As usual, he spent time with the children as well as the adults, reading a section of the horse race in *The Reivers* to Molly Nicoll's Pony Club.

Near the end of the month Bennett Cerf wired that the Book-of-the-Month Club had chosen *The Reivers* as a future selection. Later that week Faulkner thanked him for the good news. "I am not working on anything at all now," he added, "busy with horses, fox hunting. I wont work until I get hot on something; too many writing blokes think they have got to show something on book stalls. I will wait until the stuff is ready, until I can follow instead of trying to drive it."[2] He had finished what he called the last of his planned labors, but he did not sound like a man who had decided to break the pencil.

He put off his trip to New York. Estelle had recovered from the kidney surgery, but she was still frail. She had abjured alcohol and she ate little, but she savored her strong black chicory-flavored coffee and her cigarettes as much as ever. She had enjoyed her roles as grandmother and as hostess to their Virginia friends, and she had continued to develop in other ways as well. She had been an avid reader for many years, and now her interest in religious and mystical writings extended from the books of C. S. Lewis to expositions of Zen Buddhism. And she was painting, using oils in a delicate, non-representational way. On one canvas she had attempted to capture the essence of Judith, and Victoria Fielden declared that that was exactly the way she herself had seen that gentle spirit in the upper hall at Rowan Oak.

Early on November 27, Faulkner checked in at the Algonquin for more work on *The Reivers*. Again the names of several subordinate characters were changed. Also, feeling that Lucius was perhaps a bit too young to absorb as much as he had, Faulkner changed his age from ten to eleven. Later he would supply the dedication—to the five children of Victoria, Malcolm, and Jill, thus further reinforcing the grandfatherly element of the book. The Ober office was working on the material too, so that the *Post* would carry an excerpt called "Hell Creek Crossing" in March and *Esquire* would print "Education of Lucius Priest" in May. When Faulkner and Erskine finished with *The Reivers*, they went to work on material Erskine had sent him a full year before: a five-page list of various matters treated in all three books of the Snopes trilogy, a three-page list of inconsistencies with a marked copy of *The Hamlet*, and a genealogy and character list from *The Mansion* to help in straightening out the differences. They got a good deal done before he returned home as December came in.

It would not prove a good month for the Faulkners. Estelle spent a week in the hospital to calm her ulcer. On December 14 he taped Irwin Russell's Negro dialect poem "Christmas Night in the Quarters" for a special holiday program on local radio station WELK. Faulkner read the long poem with skill and satisfaction, but it did his tender throat no good.

By Monday, December 18, he had developed an acute respiratory infection. He was having back trouble again, and so he began his usual course of bourbon therapy. Leo Falk gave him an injection of gamma globulin to protect him from the hepatitis Jill had contracted, and put him in the hospital. He showed improvement the next day, and x-rays showed no new injuries in his sore chest and pelvis. By Thursday he was extremely restive, and Falk reluctantly agreed to discharge him. When Estelle and Blotner arrived to help him with the process of leaving the hospital, he sat in the bedside armchair in what seemed a state of quiet exhaustion. On the night table lay his standard hospital reading: the Bible, Taylor's *Holy Living* and *Holy Dying*, and Boccaccio's *Decameron*. He was suffering from what he called a medication hangover, but there was more to take home with him along with the vials of vitamin pills. He might be able to enjoy a quiet Christmas with his family if he obeyed orders.

He did not. By the morning of Christmas Eve, both Leo Falk and Doug Nicoll thought he belonged in the Tucker Neurological and Psychiatric Hospital in Richmond. Paul Summers and Blotner took him there and turned him over to the admissions office and James Asa Shield. One of the hospital's four doctors, he was a tall, portly man with neatly combed white-gray hair and a close-clipped mustache. Master of Fox Hounds with the Deep Run Hunt, he radiated authority and competence. His examination revealed that all the vital signs were good for a man of sixty-four, the only serious negative indications being the pain he felt when Dr. Shield pressed the area of lumbar vertebrae 1, 2, and 3. They would follow the obvious indications: ordinary remedies for gastrointestinal discomfort, standard treatment for his cold, mild sedation, some heat, rest, and nourishment to build up his resistance.

He was back at the cottage at Knole Farm for the tag end of the year. Released on December 29, he had insisted that he did not want anyone to come for him, and so he had left the hospital later in the afternoon in time to catch the bus to Charlottesville. By New Year's Day, 1962, he thought he was practically well again. Two days later he bundled up and rode out on Fenceman. There was only a thin layer of snow on the wintry ground, but it was just enough to conceal the groundhog hole that Fenceman stepped into. Later he could not remember what had happened, but by the time he got home his left eye had begun to swell and he had a darkening purple lump on his forehead. He had also suffered dental injuries. Two nights later his rest was broken by coughing spells and chest pain. Leo Falk's Demerol had not relieved the back pain, and he was drinking again. On January 8 he was readmitted to the Tucker Hospital.

When Dr. Shield examined him, his eye was black and draining, and his forehead was plum-colored. He could not remember the moment when Fenceman tumbled down and flung him to the frozen ground, and this amnesia suggested some cerebral concussion. Two days later he was still complaining of chest pain and was also running a fever. Dr. Shield called in cardiologist Paul Camp. Putting his stethoscope to the patient's chest, he heard rales in the left lung. When he shifted to the heart, he detected a slight sinus tachycardia. That meant it was a little fast, and one area was louder than another, but it was still within the normal range, with no enlargement. The electrocardiogram showed a normal rhythm. As a matter of fact, it was a very good tracing for somebody his age. The x-rays showed the broken ribs on the left side, but the breaks were about five years old. The cold had produced pleurisy, or pneumonitis. Dr. Camp put him on the drug of choice, Combiotic—penicillin and streptomycin—administered every eight hours. In a few days he was free of fever. Before he left the hospital on January 15, Dr. Shield came in to see him. Faulkner told the doctor he had made a new resolve. "I'm going to stop being a damn fool and acting like a forty-five-year-old and start living as a sixty-five-year-old and perhaps live to be an eighty-five-year old." Three days later he and Estelle set out in the wintry weather for milder Mississippi, where they planned to stay until late March.

Mending there at Rowan Oak, he turned his attention to his dental problems. One night in Charlottesville he had amused his companions when he had asked John Coleman to stop at Rugby Road before they went on to their dinner engagement. "I've got to get my false teeth," he said.

"Why, Mr. Faulkner," said Julia Wilson, "I didn't know you had false teeth."

"Yes, ma'am," he said, "these are my talking teeth. My eating teeth are made by Sears, Roebuck."

Coleman parked in the driveway, and a few moments later Faulkner returned wearing the small partial plate he called his "Sears-Roebuckers." It had been made at the direction of Dr. Wilbur Abernethy, in Oxford, after he had extracted abscessed teeth. Now Faulkner went back to Abernethy. The examination revealed three broken teeth: the upper left central incisor, lateral incisor, and canine. He asked Faulkner to come back a week later, when he would extract the three damaged teeth and insert a removable partial plate to replace them and the two teeth on the old plate that had been anchored to the canine. A regular service Abernethy performed for him was to clean his teeth, turned brown by the heavy pipe-smoking. Now, as Abernethy handed him the wheel of tooth shades, Faulkner said, "Doctor, I want real white teeth. Every time I lose a tooth I want the whitest I can get, and finally I'll have a set of white teeth." He picked out the most brightly gleaming of the lot. When the plate was prepared, Abernethy toned down the brightness a bit, and Faulkner apparently did not notice it. His new teeth might not be as spectacular as the gleaming gold tooth of Minnie, Miss Reba's maid in

The Reivers, but these contrasting dental colors were almost as great. When he wrote Blotner, he said, "I feel now like I've got a mouse trap in my mouth. It dont hurt Jack Daniel though, thank God."[3]

On some of the winter days when he talked with Jimmy, he struck a different note from that when he told Abernethy about his long-range dental plans. He would drive out to Jimmy's farm in his old jeep and they would take to the fields. Faulkner had two beautiful new bird dogs, and Jimmy whistled when he learned they had cost five hundred dollars. "Whenever you can swap money for pleasure," his uncle told him, "do it." Jimmy thought he was shooting phenomenally. One day they went to Holly Springs and hunted on horseback. They started two birds out of a thicket and Faulkner swung his gun up. Leading the first one just enough, he brought it down with a quick shot. Then, swinging in an arc past the second bird, he pulled the other trigger and it came fluttering down for a double. When they returned, Jim invited him in for a drink, as usual. Faulkner looked at the sun. It was low on the horizon, so he followed his nephew into the house. They sat there before the fireplace savoring their drinks in silence. Then Faulkner began to talk. He said he had a premonition of death. Jimmy scoffed. "You'll outlive me," he said. But his uncle repeated it. Then he told Jimmy the things he wanted done after he was gone. Jimmy tried to tell him he'd be around a long time to do them himself, but Faulkner listed them one by one. He would do it again that winter.

There was not much current literary business to attend to. Erskine and Bertha Krantz had worked on the galleys of *The Reivers* at Random House, sending to Faulkner only four of the galleys with queries. Erskine had received approval of his plan to reissue *Sanctuary*, and he had sent Faulkner a list of errors and discrepancies they could correct in the resetting. Returning the material in early February, Faulkner was amenable to most of the suggestions and particularly endorsed one change: dropping the preface. He would still contend that he had started with the idea of writing the novel for money, but many readers had been misled by his deprecation. Many had missed his assertion at the end that with his revisions he had made it "a fair job." He was against prefaces on principle, and this novel could certainly stand on its own.

Among the Ole Miss faculty people he and Estelle saw were Bill Strickland, the chairman of the department of modern languages, and his French-born wife, Ginette. (Once when they had extended a dinner invitation, Faulkner asked if it would be all right if they came at eight. They arrived punctually, having spent the previous half-hour at Jim and Dutch Silver's house watching Faulkner's favorite television program *Car 54, Where Are You?*, which dramatized the adventures of two amiable, bumbling policemen.) Ginette's stepfather was a portrait painter named Murray Goldsborough, and they invited the Faulkners over to meet the Goldsboroughs on an afternoon in mid-March. The occasion was owing to an idea of James W. Webb, the chairman of the English Department. Webb thought a portrait would be a fine acquisition for the library's growing Faulkner Collection, carefully tended by Dot Oldham, now curator of the Mississippi Collection. At first Faulkner was so non-committal that Webb was increasingly uneasy. When Goldsborough said he would like to do the portrait in an academic cap and gown, Webb quickly said he thought an informal tweed jacket would be better—the way people saw Mr. Faulkner around town. Faulkner lit his pipe and drew on it. "This whole thing ain't my idea," he said. "It's the university's idea." But finally he agreed to it—in the jacket and not an academic gown.

Goldsborough's method was to work from photographs, and so the next afternoon, J. R. Cofield's son, Jack, made two dozen good ones. When the same group gathered as the Faulkners' guests two days later, there was an easy consensus. Pipe in one graceful hand, matchbox in the other, Quiet Birdman button in his lapel, Faulkner looked straight into the lens, at ease and pleasant, though unsmiling, the spectator of life speculating again—gazing, thinking, wondering. Estelle also liked another shot with a downward gaze. "I'd like to have a print of that one," she said. "He seems to be looking at his grandchildren playing on the floor." Goldsborough shortly returned to his Florida home and set to work from his photographs, notes, and sketches. In less than three months the portrait would be ready for hanging.

By early April he and Estelle were ready to make the trip back to Virginia. There was a special sense of leave-taking now, for they were determined to move there permanently. Looking back, Jill would say, "I think that he was torn at the idea of leaving Rowan Oak, but I really feel that Oxford had become almost unbearable to him. I don't think he had any regrets at all at leaving Oxford. . . . I think he had transferred his roots to Virginia. Because Virginia is old unlike [the way] Mississippi is old. Mississippi is old and in some ways ashamed of it. . . . Virginians are not like that. They enjoy some shabby old things. And Pappy was very happy with that. . . . That was the way he felt about so many things."[4] And Faulkner now knew what he wanted in Virginia, something like the country places they had looked at, one such as Red Acres, for instance, a 250-acre estate-farm. It might cost over $200,000, but they were 250 of the most beautiful acres in the Piedmont, not far from Farmington and the Blue Ridge. He had meant what he said to Jimmy about swapping money for pleasure.

Only two weeks after their arrival in Charlottesville, an Army DC-3 put down there on the nineteenth to fly the Faulkners and the Summerses to West Point for a two-day visit. It had been the idea of Major Joseph Fant, like Paul Summers a member of the class of 1951 and a veteran of Korea, now assigned to the United States Military Academy as an instructor in English. Faulkner had surprised everyone by agreeing.

Strolling beside the rock walls on the battlements overlooking the Hudson, he cut a trim figure, natty in pepper-and-salt suit, wearing glossy shoes and a black bowler, carrying a black umbrella. They toured the post before the black-tie dinner in the quarters of the superintendent, General William C. Westmoreland.

Afterward they went to Thayer Hall, where he read to an audience of 1,400. He began by saying he was going to "skip about a little to read about a horse race which to me is one of the funniest horse races I ever heard of."[5] He had always had this curious attitude toward his finished work, as though it were something completely outside himself, and he showed it particularly with this book. While Henri Cartier-Bresson took photographs, Faulkner read to the gray-clad cadets and their guests about Lucius and McWillie, and the two horses they rode, Acheron and Coppermine. At the end he bowed to the resounding applause, a small, elegant, silver-haired figure in his tuxedo, bending stiffly from the waist in the fashion of a small boy of fifty years ago or an aristocrat of the old school.

The warmth generated by the reading carried over into the rest of the evening's program. He was genial at the press conference, but he refused to be drawn into weighty discussion of the great imponderables. His reading of the books he liked best as a young man was, he said, no criticism of contemporary writing. "No, it's the glands—the mind has slowed down a little and it don't like new things. It likes the old things just like the old man wants his old shoes, his old pipe. He don't want a new one—the new one's better, he realizes that, but he don't want it. He wants the old one."[6]

The next day began before sunrise, with Faulkner and Paul Summers there in the Central Area at 5:45 before the reveille gun boomed to bring the cadets streaming out into ranks for the day's first formation. In the two classes he met that morning the questions were wide-ranging. His responses to a question about "Turnabout" showed the same vision he had manifested from Soldiers' Pay to A Fable. "War is a shabby, really impractical thing," he told the class, "and it takes a genius to conduct it with any sort of economy and efficiency." He tried to make clear the import of Captain Bogard's dive-bombing at the end: "it was a gesture of revolt against all the brassbound stupidity of the generals and admirals that sit safe in the dugouts and tell the young men to go there and do that. . . . something that probably every soldier in war has felt. They have cursed the whole lot of them—that my brother is the man I am trying to kill."[7]

When his presence was announced to the Corps at lunch in the cadet mess hall, "thunderous applause broke out," Fant recalled. As he sat there, the light streaming in on his white head from the mullioned windows behind him, he looked desperately weary, with deep lines ridging his brow. The night before he had been the genial, gentle old man; today he looked older than his years. He bade a warm goodbye to Westmoreland

and his staff. In early summer he would send his thank-you note, for all the courtesies and the pleasure of "watching our youngest daughter being fetched back to visit his alma mater by her husband . . . not as a guest of the class of '51 but among the very top brass hats themselves."[8]

He was free now for a month for his duties as Balch Lecturer at the University of Virginia. His schedule was light, but not for lack of demand. One day as he sat in Blotner's office, the head of the university information service called. *Newsweek* wanted to know why he had turned down President Kennedy's invitation to dinner at the White House, extended to fifty-one American Nobel Laureates and other American prize winners. (Estelle had wanted to go, and only one other, Reinhold Neibuhr, had declined, because of illness.[9]) Blotner assumed that Faulkner would not want to respond. Faulkner agreed, but then he changed his mind. "Tell them," he said, "I'm too old at my age to travel that far to eat with strangers." They both burst out laughing, and then Blotner relayed the quote. *Newsweek* used it, and so did the wire services.

THERE was one ceremony he could not get out of so easily, one that involved work too. Four months before, the National Institute of Arts and Letters had informed Faulkner that on May 24 it would award him its Gold Medal for Fiction, and Eudora Welty had agreed to make the presentation. He would naturally have to respond with some formal words of acceptance. A week after his return from West Point he could see this obligation beginning to come due. "I hate to swot up a speech for that Gold Medal," he said one day in Blotner's office. "I wish somebody would write one for me," he added, looking out the window. The hint was broad enough, and Blotner volunteered to supply a draft. The next week he provided a typed page employing images he thought Faulkner might like: the blue ribbons and gold medals of the old-fashioned county fairs. "Here's some bogus Faulkner," he said. "Maybe you can make something out of it." Faulkner pocketed it with thanks. Four days later he handed it back with a carbon of his own version. "Here's your copy," he said. "Maybe you can make some money out of it sometime." As soon as he left, Blotner read it anxiously. With relief he saw that Faulkner hadn't thrown out his material. He had merely done what Blotner had expected: transmuted the counterfeit Faulkner into the true sovereign metal.

When he arrived at the institute on May 24, Muriel Cowley greeted him. Soon Conrad Aiken, who had nominated Faulkner for the award, introduced himself and joined their little group. Faulkner admired the work of his fellow Southerner as much as he had when he had reviewed it for *The Mississippian* forty-one years before. He spoke the lines from "Discordants" which he had quoted in the review: " 'And bread I broke with you was more than bread.' " But Aiken responded, "No, Mr. Faulkner, I've changed the second line—it's *bed* I broke with you was more than bed." If Aiken was joking, Faulkner did not perceive it. He repeated his version of the line, and then Aiken repeated his. It was a standoff, Aiken later said, and they dropped it. At lunch, Muriel sat at his right, with critic Kenneth Burke on his left. Faulkner declined the small talk until someone led him onto the Virginia countryside, his riding, and his grandchildren. "That day he had a country look," Malcolm Cowley recalled later, "his face bronzed under the white hair and apparently glowing with health."[10]

Remembering how wearing Faulkner had found the Gold Medal presentation to Dos Passos, Cowley and the committee had scheduled the bestowal ceremony much earlier in the program. Faulkner moved with Eudora Welty and the others to the stage, sitting there before the thousand guests and the 240-odd members of the institute who had voted him the medal. It was a distinguished company, including Mark Van Doren and Kay Boyle, Glenway Wescott and Carl Van Vechten, Aldous Huxley and Robert Frost. Joan Williams Bowen was there too. For Faulkner, however, there was little in the program that was diverting. Leaning over to Eudora Welty from time to time, he kept saying, "When is it gonna be over?" Joan was among those receiving awards that day, for *The Morning and the Evening*, but when she walked up to the stage to receive her envelope from Malcolm Cowley, she thought Faulkner was asleep.

At last his part of the program came. Miss Welty made a short, graceful presentation to her fellow Mississippian. Then he rose, put on his glasses, and began to read from his single typed page. As Cowley listened, it seemed to him that this acceptance "had a tone of retrospection, of lament for the dignity and freedom of the past, that was not exactly new for him, but that seemed to have a new resonance."[11] Afterward Donald Klopfer took Faulkner home to dinner. There was little more to keep him in New York. The next day he had lunch with Jean Stein, now Mrs. William vanden Heuvel. Then he took the train home to Charlottesville.

THERE were many friends in town and in the country to see during the few days that remained before the trip back to Mississippi. He was not anxious to go. In spite of the illnesses, there had been good times. He had made a total of three public appearances, reading and answering questions. Before the last of them, he said to Blotner, "If I ever get to the point where I ought to quit, you be sure to tell me." The responses had been as admiring and enthusiastic as ever, and his friend told him he could not foresee that day's coming. And there were events in the sporting world, such as the Virginia Gold Cup, which he had enjoyed more than receiving a gold medal. That Saturday on May 5 when they had gone with Jill and Paul and a number of friends to the thirty-seventh running at the Broadview Course at Warrenton, the names of Mr. and Mrs. William Faulkner were listed among those of the other patrons at the back of the program. They watched the thoroughbreds—three- and four- and five-year-olds—through the long golden afternoon. For one whose imagination could produce the race between Acheron and Coppermine, this was a feast of the senses: the bays and blacks and chestnuts flashing past, soaring as their riders in the bright racing silks lifted them over the hedges and fences—speed and power and beauty fused together for brief moments of high tension. Later in the spring they went to the Campdown Races in Dodswell. Faulkner and David Yalden-Thomson and several of the others put numbered twists of paper into a cap, paid a dollar, and then drew a number for each race. "Bill won four times in a row," David remembered. "His eyes lit up like a little boy's with a rather wicked glitter in them as he pocketed our money and made some remark about the profits of horse racing."

Late one afternoon Evalyn Galban stopped by for him to autograph a copy of *The Reivers*. At the exhibit of his work in the library she had copied out "My Epitaph." She showed it to him and asked, "Did I punctuate it right?"

"Yes," he said, "but this line should be here. Do you want me to correct it?" He took her pen, crossed out the phrase "Though I be dead" where she had put it by itself, and wrote it in at its proper place at the end of the line above. Before she left he talked about the fall season. "I want to get back early," he said, "so I can go cubbin'."

He stopped in for a drink at the Blotners', where he seemed to enjoy sitting on the terrace that looked out toward the misty Blue Ridge. (When he had appeared unexpectedly one day and Blotner had ushered him out there, Yvonne Blotner had hurriedly apologized for a fresh stain on the flagstones left by their small daughter, who stood there listening. "Nancy had a little accident here," she said. "I mean," she added hastily, "she spilled her juice." Faulkner smiled. "Oh," he said. "That's good. For a minute I was afraid it was bourbon.") This day he had brought the Blotners' inscribed copy of *The Reivers* with him. They sat out on the terrace enjoying the fragrance of the new buds and blossoms. Yvonne Blotner excused herself to go in and start dinner, and the two men sat silently in the twilight. At last Faulkner rose, straightened his back, and said he had better be getting along. Inside, he stopped for a moment to say goodbye to Yvonne. Then she and her husband walked down the front path with him. There he halted and bent down to talk to six-year-old Nancy Blotner. "I had a little girl like you once," he said in his soft voice, "but she grew up on me."

After they saw him on his way, Yvonne said, "Did you hear what Mr. Faulkner said to me in the kitchen? He said, 'Come and see me in Mississippi, Miss Yvonne.'"

"That was nice," her husband said.

"There were tears in his eyes," his wife said.

Faulkner rode out to the Hunt Club, exchanging greetings en route, for in the short time that the Summerses had been at Knole, it seemed to Paul that his father-in-law had come to know every man, woman, child, and animal along that road. The last night he and Estelle went with a dozen friends on a picnic to a place Grover owned up in the mountains about fifteen miles from town. They had taken the hounds, too, and later they let them go and sat around the campfire listening to their music, just as in Mississippi. Others were welcome to White House dinners.

The next morning was May 30. He kissed his daughter and his grandchildren, and then he and Estelle got in the car, said their final goodbye, and drove down the long road and out of sight.

71

"Ever' now and then a feller has to walk up and spit in deestruction's face, sort of, fer his own good. He has to kind of put a
aidge on hisself, like he'd hold his ax to the grindstone. . . . Ef
a feller'll show his face to deestruction ever' now and then,
deestruction'll leave 'im be twell his time comes. Deestruction
likes to take a feller in the back."

—*Sartoris* (234–235)

A FEW days before they arrived home at the beginning of June, the first
major review of *The Reivers* had appeared. Writing in the New York
Herald Tribune book section on May 27, George Plimpton provided a
somewhat ambiguous assessment and took the first turn at what would
almost become a game with successive reviewers: naming boys' adventure
stories the book would call to mind. Though the reception would be
generally favorable, it would show that in some ways journalistic reviews
had changed relatively little in a third of a century. Whereas the mass
of early reviewers tended to say that Faulkner could be great if he
learned to control his talent, many would say in the latter part of his
career that it was too bad that a great writer could not control his talent.

Throughout the month of June the reviews kept coming in. On
Sunday, the third, Irving Howe wrote in *The New York Times Book
Review* that the novel was "a deliberately minor work" that was "almost
successful," that *The Reivers* was to "The Bear" as *Tom Sawyer* was to
Huckleberry Finn. On Monday the daily reviewers of the *Times* and the
Tribune had their say. Orville Prescott thought it was one of the best
Faulkner had written. Like Howe and a number of others, he called Ned
(a "guileful folk hero") the most appealing character. John K. Hutchens
also thought it a moral tale, one which reminded him of *The Motor Boys
Overland*. The review in *Time* on June 8 called Faulkner "a mellowed
Prospero" who proved "an engaging fellow." If some saw in "this
autumnal story" a retreat into anecdotal escapism, it was still "a work of

love." As the month wore on, opinions grew more divergent. When reviews would appear in England in the early fall, these divergencies would appear even more starkly, with Leslie Fiedler calling parts of the book "as bad as anything he has ever done," and V. S. Pritchett declaring it a "superlative book" which matched Mark Twain—the author most often invoked in comparisons.[1] If Faulkner had read any commentaries, one which might have diverted him was the "Report" by a Book-of-the-Month Club judge on the July selection. *The Reivers* was "a delightful" book, a "highly sophisticated folk comedy," a novel "about the meaning of virtue," wrote Clifton Fadiman.

MID-JUNE was a leisurely time for Faulkner. He worked with his horses in the paddock, spending a good deal of time with Stonewall, one of the horses he had bought in Oklahoma, who was proving unruly and hard to train. He called twice at Phil Stone's office, both times fruitlessly. He went again, and this time Stone came out to chat briefly. Early on Sunday morning, June 17, he saddled Stonewall and headed out to the bridle path that led through Bailey's Woods toward the site of Murry Falkner's ice plant and the by-pass that crossed the Old Taylor Road. The horse was skittish as usual, and he had to use the crop as well as the reins. He emerged from the woods and rode on down toward the weedy rubble of rusted machinery that remained of this enterprise he remembered from childhood. Then he turned Stonewall and started back for home. Suddenly, spooked by a sound or shadow, or just fractious, the animal arched his back and threw his rider. Faulkner landed on an earthen bank at the side of the road, taking the full force of the impact on his back. Stonewall stopped after a few steps and walked back to where he lay. Faulkner stretched his arm as far as he could to catch the reins, but he could not reach them. Stonewall nuzzled him, backed off, and stood there. Then he turned and headed for the trail through the woods.

Standing in the kitchen, Chrissie Price saw a riderless horse heading for the stable. She called Estelle, who sent her out in one direction and Andrew in the other. Estelle hurried out to the Rambler and turned right onto the Old Taylor Road. Before she had gone far she came upon her husband, limping angrily home. When they reached Rowan Oak, he strode painfully into the paddock, remounted Stonewall with Andrew's help, and rode him over the jumps.

Then he went down the road to Felix Linder's house. What Felix found was a very painful groin injury which would shortly begin turning colors. Faulkner described the whole sequence of events. When he told about getting back on the horse, Felix was horrified. "You were a fool to do that," he said. "You could have killed yourself."

"You don't think I'd let that damned horse conquer me, do you?" replied Faulkner. "I had to conquer him."

Some time before, the Faulkners had accepted an invitation to Bill

Green's house. They went in spite of the fact that Faulkner was now walking gingerly with the aid of a cane. When Estelle explained, Faulkner good-naturedly replied to questions about how he had handled Stonewall. "I know now why I was able to get him so cheap," he said. They stayed until seven o'clock. Hanging his cane on his left arm and laying his gloves across his wrist, he moved from one guest to another, shaking hands and saying goodbye. The Stricklands would soon be leaving to take a student group to France. Bill reminded Faulkner that he had promised to go along the next year when they went to Aubigny, Ginette's native place. Their friend, Comte Antoine De Voguë, wanted Faulkner to ride with him in his part of his province's hunt country. Faulkner said he would remember.

By Tuesday he was in bed. When Chester McLarty came out to examine him, Faulkner said it was his back again, though he said little about the recent fall. Chester told him that he could give him something for the pain, but that his back needed treatment and he should go to the Campbell Clinic in Memphis. Faulkner did not want to go to the Campbell Clinic any more now than he had in previous years. As for the pain, he had already had one injection for it, and that hadn't done much good. Estelle knew that he had a cache of things—Demerol, tranquilizers, gin—and that he would dose himself if it got too bad.

On Sunday morning, a week after the accident, Chester saw Faulkner in the post office. He looked pale, and Chester realized this was one of the few times he had seen him with a pallor. When he asked how he felt, Faulkner told him his back still bothered him and he needed a pain tablet at night to rest. Chester again urged him to go to Memphis, but Faulkner gave no indication that he would.

One day during the week he slowly walked the half-mile down to the Linders' house, where Felix was sitting on the porch. Apparently Bill just wanted to talk. He spoke directly.

"Felix," he said, "I don't want to die."

Felix looked at him, troubled. The times he had seen him, he had done it as a favor. He was retired and he could not take on an orthopedic case like this. "I could give you something to keep you from suffering," he said. "I could do that. I'll be glad to."

"That ain't what I want,"[2] Faulkner replied, and left Felix wondering just exactly what he did want. In *A Fable*, the old general had said, "nothing—not power nor glory nor wealth nor pleasure nor even freedom from pain, is as valuable as simple breathing, simply being alive even with all the regret of having to remember and the anguish of an irreparable worn-out body. . . ." (350) Felix could not know that Bill Faulkner had apparently seen, suddenly and close up, that wall of oblivion he had so often mentioned, and he did not want to pass through it.

Joan Bowen came to Oxford to visit her cousin Regina, who urged her to call Faulkner. Estelle answered and told her to come out right away. Estelle called her husband when Joan arrived and then ushered Dot Oldham off the porch where they had been sitting and left them alone. "I wish we had said something momentous," Joan would recall, "but we did not."[3] When he walked her to her car she noticed the same pallor Chester McLarty had observed.

On the last Wednesday in June, Jane Coers met him on the square. "How do you feel, Bill?" she asked. He grimaced. "If I sit down I'm not comfortable," he said. "If I lie down, I can't stand it." A few days later he was able to walk to the square. There he met Arthur Guyton and walked back with him to the Guyton house. As they covered the half-mile, Faulkner mentioned his fall. This was the first time, he said, that he had felt like walking all the way to the square and back. At that moment he looked to Arthur to be in perfect health, as spry as a man of fifty.

He was not as well as he looked. His back still hurt, and when he saw Jimmy he told him so. He had somewhat shakily inscribed Jimmy's copy of *The Reivers*. He had loved his nephew as a child, and their relationship had deepened as Jimmy had become a man. He had continued to fly as a member of the Marine Corps reserve, achieving the rank of lieutenant colonel. Whenever Faulkner had the occasion, he introduced Jimmy as Colonel Faulkner. If his own military service had been minimal, here was another Faulkner whose exploits could be mentioned with those of the Old Colonel. On this day Jimmy was recovering from the extraction of an impacted wisdom tooth. The dentist had given him some Darvon capsules and he offered to share them, but Faulkner declined them. Jimmy then asked why he didn't try some aspirin. "No," said Brother Will, with an absolutely straight face, "I don't want to get addicted to aspirin."

He dealt with some of his correspondence. Ginette Strickland had written him in French, and he replied in his own ungrammatical French, promising absolutely to visit Aubigny, perhaps in 1963. On June 29 he began a momentous correspondence. He wanted Red Acres. The handsome brick house, with its central portion nearly a century old, had a wide front veranda from which one could see for miles, the panorama of rolling hills and meadows like an eighteenth-century landscape. There were smaller houses and barns and outbuildings on the estate, as well as the nine box-stall stable with a groom's room. The taxes were low, but the asking price was $200,000. When Faulkner had given the carbon of the setting copy of *The Mansion* to the Masseys three years before, he had inscribed it "In recognition of the many favors they have done my family, favors which we will probably repay in the simple human fashion of increasing them." Now he made good his prediction.

He wrote via air-mail special delivery to catch Linton before he and Mary left for Europe. He wanted to know if he could count on Linton for $50,000 "on demand." He explained, "I wont blame you at all if you say No. Klopfer wants to say No too. But I want Red Acres. I will gamble on it, I mean, on my ability to swing it. I may fail. I may lose $15,000.00 on it. But I think I will try it."[4] Linton was wryly amused at his friend's assumption that he could immediately put his hands on $50,000 without liquidating any assets, but he assented by wire. He asked if they could not try working through Klopfer, but concluded, IN ANY CASE DEPEND ON ME. On July 2, Faulkner wired back that a conference was not necessary yet. COULD SOLO, he told Linton, BUT THIS ABOLISHES RISK OF POSSIBLE SACRIFICE IN PRESENT HOLDINGS TO MEET DEADLINE. BLESS YOU. BILL.[5]

Now he felt he could relax. Aubrey Seay had been trying to get him interested in the possibilities of Enid Lake, twenty miles southeast of Oxford, as a commercial investment. Aubrey came by and took him out to the lake for a cruise on Rex McRaney's houseboat. Politics was one of the subjects that came up on that quiet afternoon. Aubrey wondered if there would be trouble when a man named James Meredith enrolled in the fall to become the University of Mississippi's first Negro student of record. If there was trouble, Faulkner said, it would be "because of the people out in Beat Two who never went to the University or never intended to send their children to the University." The influence of this back-country, White Supremacy element had always been clear to Faulkner. Aubrey thought about the power of their prime representative, reactionary Governor Ross Barnett. "Rex," said Seay, "how was Barnett elected Governor?" Faulkner, who had been scanning the shore through binoculars, did not wait for McRaney to answer. "Eighty-two Beat Twos,"[6] he said. They had a few bourbons together and then headed home.

TUESDAY, July 3, began as a normal day. In the morning Faulkner walked down to the square. He checked the mail and then went over to the drugstore to see Mac Reed. He had Else Jonsson's copy of *The Reivers* with him. "I come off and forgot my glasses this morning," he told Mac. "Would you address this for me?" He already had the required foreign postal forms, but he was apologetic about asking Mac to do the extra work. "My back was hurting me so I just couldn't think of anything much this morning."[7] He thanked Mac, picked up his reserved copy of the *Commercial Appeal* and a package of tobacco and left.

That night he and Estelle appeared at The Mansion at their regular time. He ordered filet mignon as usual, but he told Aubrey things hadn't been tasting right. "The meat and the bread taste alike," he said. Even so, he looked fine to Aubrey, in spite of his complaints. Later that evening Jimmy stopped by to see how he was. He found that Leslie Oliver was there to help. Faulkner had begun drinking.

Independence Day dawned inauspiciously at Rowan Oak. When Jimmy telephoned at breakfast time, Oliver told him that Faulkner was still in bed. He was still drinking and he had been taking some of the prescription painkillers. Jimmy drove in and went up to his uncle's room. He sat and talked with him for a while. Before Jimmy left for home, he talked with Estelle. "What shall we do?" she asked. At this stage he was no more sure than she, so they decided to wait and see how Faulkner was the next day. That night when Chester McLarty made a routine call, he found that Faulkner's blood pressure was all right and that there were no alarming symptoms. But they did talk about sending him to the hospital.

The next day he was worse. His pain apparently was now close to unbearable, and his drinking was getting out of hand. And there was the problem of controlling the medication—the painkillers and tranquilizers that he had on his night table. When Jimmy telephoned, Estelle said, "Maybe it's time to go to Byhalia." After lunch Jimmy arrived and sat down on the bed to broach the idea to his uncle. To his surprise, he was ready to go. From what Jimmy could tell, he had not consumed more than a fifth and a half, and that would be relatively early in the cycle. But Jimmy concluded that his uncle did not want to mess with this one. He began to talk to Jimmy in earnest, but Jimmy could not make it out— whether he was giving him instructions or what. They packed his bag and helped him to dress.

It was different this time. He could walk and he was going to Byhalia earlier in the cycle. And there was his behavior. Dot Oldham thought he had appeared worried. J. R. Cofield said he had been so much nicer to people than ever before. Chrissie Price just thought he had been acting differently of late. She spoke to him when they stopped in the kitchen for a moment on the way out to the car. "Mr. Bill," she said in her plaintive voice, "do you want to go to the hospital?"

"I want to go home, Chrissie," he said. Chrissie thought she knew what he meant, and what he knew.

It had been a sweltering day, with the temperature driving on up to ninety-five as the afternoon sun beat down. It seemed no cooler now though it was nearing five o'clock as they drove out the gate, through town, and onto the Holly Springs road to the north. From Holly Springs they headed northwest on Route 78, and inside an hour they had covered the forty-nine miles to Byhalia. About a mile west of town on a gentle hill to the right was Wright's Sanitarium. They drove up the long drive to the main house, all white clapboard with green-trimmed shutters. Estelle and Jimmy helped him through the main entry, and they slowly made their way down the dark corridor to the foyer. Nearby were a few patients in robes, talking quietly and smoking, who fell silent as they watched. Estelle and Jimmy left him in a comfortable chair while they gave the information at the desk. He was admitted at 6 P.M., July 5, 1962.

A nurse in starched white prepared him for examination. The doctor appeared and greeted Estelle and Jimmy. Leonard D. Wright was just under medium height, a pleasant-looking man with a snub nose, bright blue eyes, and a ruddy complexion, his short brown hair flecked with gray. A no-nonsense physician, he was the son of a Tennessee country doctor and himself the father of two physicians. While Estelle and Jimmy watched, he checked Faulkner's blood pressure and heart. Both were normal. So was his chest, but he complained of pain there as well as in his back. It could have been associated with his heart, but there was no clinical indication that it was. He was able to tell Dr. Wright about the cause of his problem. He was jumping, he said, and his horse threw him on his back. Dr. Wright finished with the examination and put him in a room across from the first-floor station. The soft-spoken doctor noted that he was a quiet and tractable patient, humble even, who joked as they took care of him. He knew the attendant who was helping him. "Shorty," he said to him, "I need a pair of carpet slippers."

He was settled in his room and the nurse was to be with him. There was nothing more Estelle or Jimmy could do, so she kissed him, and then Jimmy went to his bedside, "Brother Will," he said. Faulkner's eyes lit up. "When you're ready to come home, let me know and I'll come for you." Earlier, his uncle's speech had been confused, and he had talked to Jimmy of sergeants and captains. Now he spoke quite clearly. "Yes, Jim," he said, "I will." With that, they left.

The ordinary routine of the first floor resumed. Dr. Wright started treatment with vitamins, Benadryl, and the other standard medications indicated. He felt there was no need for pain medicine. From across the hall drifted the sounds of a television set in a small lounge where a few patients watched. To the right was a simply furnished dining room where a sideboard held hot coffee. A few more patients sat there, drinking it, smoking, talking about the illnesses that had brought them there and about when they could go home again. Dr. Wright returned to his quarters behind the main building, and the sounds diminished as the quiet evening shift began.

The big clock ticked past midnight and July 6 came in—the Old Colonel's birthday—with no promise of a letup in the heat. Insects thumped against the screens while electric fans hummed here and there. Faulkner had been resting quietly. A few minutes after half past one, he stirred and then sat up on the side of his bed. Before the nurse could reach him he groaned and fell over. Within five minutes Dr. Wright was there, but he could not detect any pulse or heartbeat. He began external heart massage. He continued it for forty-five minutes, without results. He tried mouth-to-mouth resuscitation, again with no results. There was nothing more he could do. William Faulkner was gone.

THE ringing of the bedside telephone woke Estelle. She was stunned, devastated by the brief call. He had gone to the hospital so many times before, often sicker than he seemed yesterday, and when they had left he had seemed in no danger. Still half unbelieving, she telephoned Jimmy and asked him to call Jill and Blotner in Virginia. Now Jimmy took charge, grieving and furious with himself for not leaving his phone number at the sanitarium rather than Estelle's. Dressing rapidly, he began to make his calls. Then he drove quickly through the hot summer night over the dark roads toward town.

Chester McLarty had driven to Rowan Oak as soon as he received Jimmy's call. Not long after Jimmy got there, his father arrived and went upstairs. Chester was there, watching Estelle with concern as she walked the floor, her thin hands tightly clenched. John silently put his arms around her for a moment. "I can't believe it," she said. "I can't believe it. He's not gone. He's not gone."[8]

Jimmy and his father went downstairs to the foyer. John stood there without speaking, trying to absorb the reality of his brother's death, the finality of absence and loss in the paradoxical surroundings of the homely and familiar. Jimmy waited until his father spoke. "I'll go to the funeral home to be there when they bring him in," he said.

John sat on the steps of the Douglass Funeral Home and waited in the darkness. He thought of the time they had gone out to Byhalia in their own ambulance, men in their sixties helling around like boys. Boyhood came back as he looked out to the square—seeing the shortcut to school, the balloonist's ascension. Dean had made his last journey here. Now John was able to accept the fact that Bill, too, was gone. He sat there dreaming over the square as his brother had done, seeing not just Billy but the world he had created—Joe Christmas and Percy Grimm and Gail Hightower. At last he heard the sound of the returning ambulance.

Inside Douglass', John met Dick Elliott and Murry Sutherland and watched them place Bill's stretcher on a dolly. Dick Elliott, a thin, red-faced man, was both mayor of Oxford and mortician. The electric light glinting on his wire-framed spectacles, he asked John if they could go ahead with the embalming. He said they could, and the dolly noiselessly rolled away and the doors closed behind it. In the office he supplied the information for the death certificate. Dr. Wright called it a coronary occlusion. Later, again waiting outside on the steps, John thought about a thrombosis as it had been explained to him—"a stoppage," so that "the heart action can produce no blood flow through it. Without blood, the well goes dry, the pump stops. So it happened to Bill."[9] He used to joke about living to be a hundred, and he had survived his mother by only a few years. But he had outlived all the Falkner men who had gone before him, except Grandfather. Now he was with them.

Next there transpired a series of events which might have amused the author of *As I Lay Dying*. When the hearse brought Faulkner's body back to Rowan Oak, it lay in a closed, plain wooden coffin covered with silver-gray cotton felt. Jimmy had driven in to Douglass' and picked it out. It was exactly the kind of coffin they had chosen for Nanny and the kind her son had said he wanted too. The men wheeled the bier and coffin into the parlor, where Mammy Callie had lain. Maud Falkner had said she wanted the quickest and cheapest funeral possible: no one but the family, no flowers, and no fuss. John remembered that Bill said he wanted his to be "just like Mother's."[10] Jimmy and his father had gone home for a while, and in the parlor Sallie Murry Williams and Dot Oldham and Ella Somerville stood above the now-open coffin. To Ella, Bill looked "all squinched up" in it. When Sallie Murry went upstairs and asked Estelle if she didn't want a better coffin, Estelle said she thought she did and she would leave it to Jimmy. By the time Jimmy returned to Rowan Oak, Dot had sent the coffin back. Jimmy's face set, and he started into town. His brother, Chooky, forestalled him. "Don't," he said. Then they waited for William Faulkner to make his fourth trip through the square that morning. When he returned, he lay in a closed coffin of cypress covered in dark-gray wool felt, its large heavy silver-plated handles glinting in the parlor's subdued light. The vigil began. Jack Falkner had arrived from Mobile, tall, dignified, and sad-eyed. He was suffering from a bad cold, but he would take his turn with the others. Bill's kinsmen would sit there with him until he left his home for the last time, though no one would circulate a quid of tobacco as they had done when they sat up with Grandfather.

The telephone had been ringing in Virginia. Like her mother, Jill had been alone to receive the call. Paul was on temporary reserve duty in Louisville. A plane was chartered for Jill, and they would pick Paul up on the way. Edgar Shannon was out of town, and Blotner was asked to go with Jill to represent the University of Virginia. The morning was incongruously bright with the golden daylight, and Jill's dress incongruously black against her fair skin and bright hair. The two stepped into the sleek white Piper Aztec, and almost immediately the ground fled away. There was nothing to say to grief like hers. After all those years, her father had seemed to change and mellow, and a new life beckoned to him. But he had persisted in risking the vulnerable bones, and when the disaster he seemed almost to court had responded, he had treated it in the habitual destructive way. Hers were more than ordinary tears of grief, keen and bitter with a double sense of loss.

As the pilot taxied to the parking strip at the Oxford airport and shut off the engine, the heat waves were shimmering up from the dark asphalt in the afternoon sun. The sweating taxi driver said it had been ninety-five yesterday and it was even hotter today. It seemed incongruous, passing through the square, that it could seem so ordinary on this day. In a few moments the taxi turned down Garfield Avenue, and ahead were a few parked cars. The policeman waved the taxi past and into the rutted drive up to Rowan Oak.

At just about that time in Charlottesville, the university carillon broke the summer stillness. One of the customary hymns floated out over the Lawn, across the Ranges where a few students sat before their open doors.

The final measure died away, and then, after a pause, the slow, deliberate notes began to sound again. Onto the golden afternoon, close to what he always called the best time of day, there chimed a refrain the carillon had never sounded before. The clear bell tones floated slowly out toward the green fields and hedgerows, toward Grover's jumps and pastures, and on toward the far faint haze of the Blue Ridge beyond . . .

> *D'ye ken John Peel with his coat so gay?*
> *D'ye ken John Peel at the break of day?*
> *D'ye ken John Peel when he's far, far away,*
> *With his hounds and his horn in the morning?*

BY suppertime the clan was gathering, the kin by blood and kin by marriage. Aunt 'Bama was too infirm to come, but Bill and Victoria were on their way up from Caracas, and Malcolm from Charleston. All day the press had been coming into town, gathering what facts they could, making assumptions in their absence. Both Jimmy and Jack had refused to answer any questions, but that night, with Paul Flowers acting as intermediary, they met the press at The Mansion. Jack said what he knew his brother would have wanted him to say: "that we understood their mission and wished to cooperate with them, but that we could not permit them to make interviews or take photographs at his residence. We asked only that they handle their assignments with the understanding befitting the event."[11] Later, Dick Elliott told them the route that the funeral would take and where to stand to photograph the procession. The Falkner plot in the old part of St. Peter's was filled up, so the grave would be dug in the new part adjoining, down a slight slope. Elliott would put the press up above, in the old part of the cemetery. He repeated a message from the family: "Until he's buried he belongs to the family. After that he belongs to the world."

On Saturday morning the telephone calls and telegrams kept coming in, from the President, from fellow craftsmen such as Robert Frost and John Dos Passos. They would be followed by more letters and wires from many parts of the world. There were new arrivals at Rowan Oak all the morning, Linton and Mary Massey from Lake Placid, Bennett Cerf and Donald Klopfer from New York. "For twenty-five years," said Cerf, "Bill Faulkner has been trying to get me to come to Oxford, and I waited too late." On the square, in a booth in the Rexall drugstore, Shelby Foote and Joan Bowen sat silently stirring their coffee. Finally Joan said, "I'll miss just knowing that he's there."[12] At Rowan Oak, Dick Elliott had opened the coffin so that Andrew and Chrissie Price could say goodbye to Mister Bill, the last ones to look upon his face.

By noon the house was full of family and friends, many of whom had helped provide a bounteous buffet. People helped themselves to the turkey and ham, the subdued murmur of conversation rising above the whir of the electric fans. Among the mourners was novelist William Styron, sitting with others at the dining-room table. He looked around him: "The hour of the service is approaching and outside through the window the afternoon light casts black shadows of trembling oak leaves and cedar branches against the rich hot grass. From far off comes a mockingbird's rippling chant."[13]

Duncan Gray, Estelle's minister, had been with her earlier. At two o'clock, clad in white surplice, Book of Common Prayer in hand, he entered the parlor. With him in the room were the immediate family. The others watched from the adjoining dining room. A young man, though already balding and bespectacled, he began solemnly to intone the Order for the Burial of the Dead:

> "I know that my Redeemer liveth, and that he shall stand at the latter day upon the earth: and though this body be destroyed, yet shall I see God: whom I shall see for myself, and mine eyes shall behold, and not as a stranger."

The phrases rolled on over the small sounds of weeping. From the green leafiness outside drifted the careless bird notes again. Gray read from the 27th and 46th Psalms and then from St. Paul's Epistle to the Romans. At last all joined in The Lord's Prayer, and the service was ended.

Jack and John and his two sons went to the hearth and moved the coffin slowly from the parlor to the front gallery, where the hearse waited. The funeral cortege of sixteen cars moved very slowly between the cedars shading the long driveway. It passed through the gate with the sign he had lettered—PRIVATE—KEEP OUT—and into the road beyond. Then the cameras and the flash bulbs flared.

The slow patrol car led the hearse toward the square. Behind it followed Dick Elliott's car. Duncan Gray and Blotner rode with him, and Phil Stone. Tall and thin, with a fringe of silver hair combed over his high-domed skull, Stone seemed in constant movement, chattering incessantly as they moved up South Lamar and on into the square. On the border of the courthouse and under the drugstore awnings across the street stood people white and black, gazing at the shining limousine as it passed under the blazing sun. Stone chattered on, but the others in the car were silent as their thoughts turned inward. Stryon would record one such moment: "I am deep in memory, as if summoned there by a trumpet blast. Dilsey and Benjy and Luster and all the Compsons, Hightower and Byron Bunch and Flem Snopes and the gentle Lena Grove —all of these people and a score of others come swarming back comically and villainously and tragically in my mind with a . . . a sense of utter reality. . . . Suddenly, as the watchful and brooding faces of the townspeople sweep across my gaze, I am filled with a bitter grief."[14]

Soon they stopped on the sandy roadside gravel at the edge of the new part of the cemetery. On the hill above arched the shady cedars, beneath them the carpet-smooth turf and weathered markers of the Falkners. Up there stood the boxwood and magnolias. The newer slope was raw and red. But the Douglass canopy gave shade at the graveside, and soon Estelle sat there, her hand held tightly in her son's. Behind were the brothers. A further apron of shade covered the slope from two strong deep-rooted white oaks against the hot blue sky.

Near the open hearse door stood Mac Reed, Ben Wasson, blacksmith Earl Wortham, and other old friends. The gloved pallbearers took hold of the silver handles, Blotner last of the six, as befitted one who was not, like the others, connected to him by marriage or some distant tie of blood. They lifted and walked slowly, straining not to stumble over the ruts as the cameras whirred again, raucous as cicadas, from the hill above. Their brief task and last gesture ended beneath the canopy, the pallbearers stood there for Duncan Gray's final prayers. Then it was over.

The cars moved away from the raw clay slope, where in time the rains would anneal it and the sward would cover it. The monument would be set there, and in time the bushes and trees would grow to complement the giant oaks. Now the cortege swung through the square, past the granite gaze of the Confederate soldier looking ever to the south. The mourners returned to Rowan Oak where he no longer was. It had finally come, at last, that which he had anticipated so long: "the moment, instant, night: dark: sleep: when I would put it all away forever that I anguished and sweated over, and it would never trouble me anymore."[15] Where, then, was he now? He had written it forty-three years ago—

> If there be grief, then let it be but rain,
> And this but silver grief for grieving's sake,
> If these green woods be dreaming here to wake
> Within my heart, if I should rouse again.
>
> But I shall sleep, for where is any death
> While in these blue hills slumbrous overhead
> I'm rooted like a tree? Though I be dead,
> This earth that holds me fast will find me breath.[16]

NOTES

Books and Miscellaneous Collections of Work by Faulkner, editions cited here:

AA   *Absalom, Absalom!*. N.Y., Random House, 1936; N.Y., Modern Library, 1951; N.Y. Vintage, 1972.´

AGB   *A Green Bough*. N.Y., Harrison Smith and Robert Haas, 1933. *The Marble Faun and A Green Bough*. N.Y., Random House, 1965.

AILD   *As I Lay Dying*. N.Y., Random House, 1964; N.Y., Vintage, 1964.

BW   *Big Woods*. N.Y., Random House, 1955.

CSWF   *Collected Stories of William Faulkner*. N.Y., Random House, 1950; N.Y., Vintage, 1977.

DRM   *Doctor Martino and Other Stories*. N.Y., Harrison Smith and Robert Haas, 1934.

EPP   *Early Prose and Poetry*, ed. Carvel Collins. Boston, Little, Brown, 1962.

ESPL   *Essays, Speeches & Public Letters*, ed. James B. Meriwether. N.Y., Random House, 1966.

FAB   *A Fable*. N.Y., Random House, 1954 (fourth printing); N.Y., Modern Library, 1966.

FIU   *Faulkner in the University*, eds. Frederick L. Gwynn and Joseph L. Blotner. Charlottesville, University of Virginia Press, 1959; N.Y. Vintage, 1965.

FR   *The Faulkner Reader*. N.Y., Random House, 1954, N.Y., Modern Library, 1959.

FWP   *Faulkner at West Point*, eds. Joseph L. Fant III, and Robert Ashley. N.Y., Random House, 1964.

GDM   *Go Down, Moses and Other Stories*. N.Y., Random House, 1942. *Go Down, Moses*. N.Y., Modern Library, 1955.

HAM   *The Hamlet*. N.Y., Random House, 1954 (third edition).

HEL   *Helen: A Courtship and Mississippi Poems*. [New Orleans] Tulane University and [Oxford, Miss.] Yoknapatawpha Press, 1981, intros., Carvel Collins and Joseph Blotner.

IID   *Intruder in the Dust*, N.Y., Random House, 1948; N.Y., Modern Library, 1964; N.Y., Vintage, 1972.

KG   *Knight's Gambit*. N.Y., Random House, 1949.

LIA   *Light in August*. N.Y., Harrison Smith & Robert Haas, 1932; N.Y., Random House, 1967; N.Y., Vintage, 1972.

LIG   *Lion in the Garden: Interviews with William Faulkner, 1926–1962*, eds. James B. Meriwether and Michael Millgate. N.Y., Random House, 1968.

MAN   *The Mansion.* N.Y., Random House, 1959; N.Y., Vintage, 1965.
MAR   *The Marionettes: A Play in One Act.* Charlottesville, Va., The University
       Press of Virginia for the Bibliographical Society of the University of
       Virginia, ed. with intro. by Noel Polk, 1978.
MAY   *Mayday.* Notre Dame, Ind., University of Notre Dame Press, intro. Carvel
       Collins, 1980.
MOS   *Mosquitoes.* N.Y., Boni & Liveright, 1927; N.Y., Liveright, 1951.
NOS   *New Orleans Sketches*, ed. Carvel Collins. N.Y., Random House, 1968.
PYL   *Pylon.* N.Y., Harrison Smith and Robert Haas, 1935; N.Y., Random House,
       1965; N.Y., Modern Library, 1967.
REQ   *Requiem for a Nun.* N.Y., Random House, 1951 (third printing); N.Y.,
       Vintage, 1975.
REV   *The Reivers.* N.Y., Random House, 1962; N.Y., Vintage, 1966.
SAN   *Sanctuary.* N.Y., Random House, 1962; N.Y., Modern Library, 1964; N.Y.,
       Vintage, 1967.
SAR   *Sartoris.* N.Y., Harcourt, Brace, 1929; N.Y., Random House, 1956.
S&F   *The Sound and the Fury.* N.Y., Jonathan Cape and Harrison Smith, 1929;
       N.Y., Random House, 1966; N.Y., Modern Library, 1966.
SLWF   *Selected Letters of William Faulkner*, ed. Joseph Blotner. N.Y., Random
       House, 1977; N.Y., Vintage, 1978.
SP   *Soldiers' Pay.* N.Y., Boni & Liveright, 1926; N.Y., Liveright, 1951.
TMF   *The Marble Faun.* Boston, Four Seas, 1924.
       The Marble Faun and A Green Bough. N.Y., Random House, 1965.
T13   *These 13.* N.Y., Jonathan Cape & Harrison Smith, 1931.
TWN   *The Town.* N.Y., Vintage, 1961.
UNV   *The Unvanquished.* N.Y., Random House, 1938, 1966; N.Y., Vintage, 1966.
USWF   *Uncollected Stories of William Faulkner*, ed. Joseph Blotner. N.Y., Ran-
       dom House, 1979; N.Y., Vintage, 1980.
WP   *The Wild Palms.* N.Y., Random House, 1939; N.Y., Vintage, 1964.
WT   *The Wishing Tree.* N.Y., Random House, 1964.

Other Frequently Cited Sources:

ALG   *A Loving Gentleman: The Love Story of William Faulkner and Meta
       Carpenter*, Meta Carpenter Wilde and Orin Borsten. N.Y., Simon and
       Schuster, 1976.
BLRO   *Bitterweeds: Life at Rowan Oak with William Faulkner*, Malcolm Franklin.
       Irving, Tex., Society for the Study of Traditional Culture, 1977.
CF   "Chronicle of a Friendship: William Faulkner in New Orleans," William
       Spratling. *The Texas Quarterly*, IX (Spring 1966), 34–40; rept. *Sherwood
       Anderson & Other Famous Creoles.* Austin, Tex., University of Texas
       Press, 1966.
CNC   *Count No 'Count: Flashbacks to Faulkner*, Ben Wasson. Jackson, Miss.,
       University Press of Mississippi, 1983.
DSF   *Dean Swift Faulkner: A Biographical Study*, Dean Faulkner Wells. Ox-
       ford, Miss., University of Mississippi M.A. Thesis, 1975.
ENF   "Early Notices of Faulkner by Phil Stone and Louis Cochran," ed. James
       B. Meriwether. *MQ*, XVII (Summer 1964), 148–64.
F   *Faulkner: A Biography*, Joseph Blotner. N.Y., Random House, 1974.
FCF   *The Faulkner-Cowley File: Letters and Memories, 1944–1962*, Malcolm
       Cowley. N.Y., Viking Press, 1966.
FGBC   *Faulkner: A Comprehensive Guide to the Brodsky Collection*, eds. Louis
       Daniel Brodsky and Robert W. Hamblin. Jackson, Miss., University Press
       of Mississippi, 1983.

FMF   *Faulkner, Modernism and Film: Faulkner and Yoknapatawpha, 1978*, eds. Evans Harrington and Ann J. Abadie. Jackson, Miss., University Press of Mississippi, 1979.

FMS   *Faulkner's MGM Screenplays*, ed. Bruce F. Kawin. Knoxville, Tenn., University of Tennessee Press, 1982.

FOM   *The Falkners of Mississippi: A Memoir*, Murry C. Falkner. Baton Rouge, La., Louisiana State University Press, 1967.

FRGF   "The Faulkners: Recollections of a Gifted Family," Robert Cantwell. *New World Writing*. N.Y., New American Library, 1952; rept. *William Faulkner: Three Decades of Criticism*, eds. Frederick J. Hoffman and Olga Vickery. N.Y., Harcourt, Brace, 1963.

FYY   *Fifty Years of Yoknapatawpha: Faulkner and Yoknapatawpha, 1979*, eds. Doreen Fowler and Ann J. Abadie. Jackson, Miss., University Press of Mississippi, 1980.

IMCW   "An Interview with Meta Carpenter Wilde," Panthea Reid Broughton. *The Southern Review*, XVIII (Oct. 1982), 776–801.

M&M   *The Maker and the Myth: Faulkner and Yoknapatawpha, 1977*, eds. Evans Harrington and Ann J. Abadie. Jackson, Miss., University Press of Mississippi, 1978.

MBB   *My Brother Bill: An Affectionate Reminiscence*, John Faulkner. N.Y., Trident Press, 1963.

MCA   Memphis *Commercial Appeal*.

MPS   Memphis *Press-Scimitar*.

MQ   *Mississippi Quarterly*.

NYHT   New York *Herald Tribune*.

NYT   New York *Times*.

OFA   *The Origins of Faulkner's Art*, Judith L. Sensibar. Austin, Tex., University of Texas Press, 1984.

OTF   *Old Times in the Faulkner Country*, John B. Cullen, with Floyd Watkins. Chapel Hill, N.C., University of North Carolina Press, 1961.

OXE   Oxford *Eagle*.

PSY   *Phil Stone of Yoknapatawpha*, Susan Snell. Ann Arbor, Mich., University Microfilms, 1978.

PWWF   *The Private World of William Faulkner*, Robert Coughlan. N.Y., Harper & Brothers, 1954.

WFLP   *William Faulkner: A Life on Paper*, ed. Ann J. Abadie. Jackson, Miss., University Press of Mississippi, 1980.

WFO   *William Faulkner of Oxford*, eds. James W. Webb and A. Wigfall Green. Baton Rouge, La., Louisiana State University Press, 1965.

Repositories:

FCUM   William Faulkner Collection, John Davis Williams Library, The University of Mississippi.

FCVA   William Faulkner Foundation Collection, The University of Virginia Library. Unless otherwise noted, letters from Faulkner to Bennett Cerf, Saxe Commins, Anne Louise Davis, Albert Erskine, Morton Goldman, Robert K. Haas, Donald S. Klopfer, Robert Linscott, Horace Liveright, Mrs. Walter B. McLean, Harold Ober, Dorothy Olding, Harrison Smith, Ivan von Auw, Jr., Ben Wasson, and Joan Williams are in this collection, as well as letters from any of the above to Faulkner and to others. The collection also includes all unpublished class conferences at the University of Virginia.

HRCT   Humanities Research Center, The University of Texas at Austin.

JFSA   Jill Faulkner Summers Private Archive. This includes Faulkner's report cards, pilot's log, passports, various letters, drawings, and the like, and the Greenfield Farm commissary ledger and studbook.

MAETV   Mississippi Authority for Educational Television.

NYPL   New York Public Library, Henry W. and Albert A. Berg Collection, The Arents Collection, Astor, Lenox, and Tilden Foundations.

Each citation of institutions and individuals is made with the grateful thanks of the author. Where no repository is given for Faulkner letters to persons not listed above, the recipients themselves are the sources, and their help is again acknowledged with grateful thanks.

As stated in the Foreword, notes to this book refer for the most part to published sources. New interviews only are cited in the notes, identified by the symbol I and followed by the name of the interviewee and the date. Interviews first used in the two-volume *Faulkner: A Biography* are identified there.

All quotations from Faulkner's published and unpublished writings are made through the kind and gracious permission of Jill Faulkner Summers.

Foreword

[1] The apparatus of *Faulkner* of 1974 will provide information not included here, such as the names of people interviewed and quoted there. New interviews quoted in this book are listed in the notes, which, for the most part, I have confined to printed sources.

[2] Where this book quotes from a Faulkner letter appearing in both *Selected Letters of William Faulkner* and *Faulkner* (1974), the latter will also be cited if it supplies portions of the letter which are not included in *Selected Letters*. Bibliographical information for most of the works cited in this Foreword will be found in the Notes after the alphabetically listed acroynms for the titles. These acronym-abbreviations

will be used in all notes hereafter. The works in this Foreword not listed among those designated by acronym-abbreviations are cited in full immediately below.

[3] William Faulkner, *Sanctuary: The Original Text*, ed. Noel Polk (New York, Random House, 1981).

[4] *The Ghosts of Rowan Oak: William Faulkner's Ghost Stories for Children*, Recounted by Dean Faulkner Wells (Oxford, Miss., Yoknapatawpha Press, 1980).

[5] Dumas Malone, *Jefferson the Virginian* (Boston, 1948), p. vii; Merrill Peterson, *Thomas Jefferson and the New Nation* (New York, 1970), p. viii.

Chapter 1

[1] *MBB*, p. 11.

[2] *FRGF*, p. 55. I wish to acknowledge with gratitude the fact that much of the information in this volume on Col. William C. Falkner is drawn from Donald Philip Duclos' invaluable Ph.D. dissertation, *Son of Sorrow: The Life, Works and Influence of Colonel William C. Falkner, 1825–1889* (Ann Arbor, Mich., University Microfilms, 1962).

[3] *MBB*, p. 11.

[4] *OXE*, 12 Nov. 1896.

[5] Dean Franklin E. Moak to JB, 20 May 1980.

[6] *OXE*, 26 Oct. 1899.

[7] *SLWF*, p. 20.

[8] *MBB*, p. 12.

[9] *OXE*, 2 Oct. 1902.

Chapter 2

1 *FOM*, p. 4.
2 *FIU*, p. 285.
3 *OXE*, 24 Oct. 1907.
4 *FOM*, p. 10

5 *FOM*, p. 12.
6 *DSF*, p. 4.
7 *FOM*, p. 58.

Chapter 3

1 *MBB*, p. 57.
2 FRGF, p. 58.
3 *FOM*, p. 6.
4 Calvin S. Brown, "Colonel Falkner as General Reader: *The White Rose of Memphis*," *MQ*, XXX (Fall 1977), 585–95.
5 Robert Cantwell, Introduction, *The White Rose of Memphis* (New York, 1953), p. xxvi.

6 FRGF, p. 55.
7 FRGF, p. 56.
8 *Ibid.*
9 *SLWF*, pp. 211–12.
10 Franklin E. Moak, "William *Joseph* Faulkner," in *The Forkner Clan—Forkner/Fortner/Faulkner*, comp. Mona Forkner Paulas (Baltimore, Md., 1981), I, pp. 26–36.

Chapter 4

1 *FOM*, p. 80.
2 It is difficult to reconstruct all of Faulkner's school record with certainty.
3 *SLWF*, p. 212.
4 "And Now What's To Do," *A Faulkner Miscellany*, ed. James B. Meriwether (Jackson, Miss., 1974), p. 145.
5 *FIU*, p. 30.
6 Unpublished class conference at University of Virginia, June 5, 1957.

7 *FOM*, pp. 67–68.
8 *PWWF*, p. 34.
9 Jean Stein, "William Faulkner: An Interview," *The Paris Review*, (Spring 1956), 28–52, rept. *LIG*. See p. 250.
10 *MBB*, pp. 85, 122.
11 See Ilse Dusoir Lind, "Faulkner and Nature," *Faulkner Studies*, 1 (1980), pp. 113–14.
12 *EPP*, p. 115.

Chapter 5

1 *MBB*, p. 220.
2 Jack Ewing, "Collector Finds Consolation Stone," *The Faulkner Newsletter*, 1 (July–Sept. 1981), 2. The "u" did appear here, though it would be

years before Faulkner would follow this practice consistently.
3 Courtesy Franklin E. Moak.
4 *FOM*, p. 11.

Chapter 6

1 *PSY*, p. 44.
2 *PWWF*, pp. 38–39.
3 Phil Stone's "Autobiography," as quoted in *PSY*, p. 185.
4 *PSY*, p. 195.
5 Phil Stone, "I Know William Faulkner," *OXE*, 16 Nov. 1950, rept. 23 Feb. 1967.
6 Phil Stone, "William Faulkner: The Man and His Work," *The Oxford*

Magazine, I (1934), in three consecutive issues: 1 (April 1), 13–14; 2 (June 1), 11–15; 3 (Nov. 1), 3–10; rept. ENF, see pp. 162–63.
7 *Ibid.*
8 Emily Whitehurst Stone, "Faulkner Gets Started," *The Texas Quarterly*, VIII (Winter 1965), 143.
9 *FOM*, p. 18.
10 *EPP*, p. 116.

[11] Ford Foundation documentary film for *Omnibus* program, 1953.

[12] *FIU*, p. 24.

[13] Emily Whitehurst Stone, "How a Writer Finds His Material," *Harper's*, CCXXXI (Nov. 1965), 160–61.

[14] *MBB*, p. 92.

[15] Ben Wasson, "The Time Has Come," Greenville *Delta Democrat-Times*, 15 July 1962.

[16] *EPP*, pp. 114, 117.

[17] Courtesy Franklin E. Moak.

[18] *A Faulkner Miscellany*, p. 146.

[19] Thomas E. Lamar, "Debits and Credits in Faulkner's Hand Found in Old Bank Ledgers," *The Faulkner Newsletter*, 1 (July–Sept. 1981), 3.

[20] *PWWF*, p. 58.

[21] Marshall J. Smith, "Faulkner of Mississippi," *The Bookman*, 74 (Dec. 1931), 416; rept. *LIG*, pp. 8–15.

[22] *PSY*, p. 185.

[23] I: Robert J. Farley, 22 Dec. 1979.

[24] *MAY*, p. 11.

[25] JFSA.

[26] *MBB*, p. 133.

[27] Lamar, p. 3.

Chapter 7

[1] *PSY*, pp. 256, 261.

[2] Carvel Collins, "Faulkner's War Service and His Fiction," Modern Language Association lecture, New York, 28 Dec. 1966.

[3] *EPP*, p. 11.

[4] *FOM*, p. 89.

[5] *FR*, p. viii.

[6] *OXE*, 7 Feb. 1918.

[7] Elmer Parker to JB, 20 Nov. 1967.

[8] *PSY*, pp. 240, 244.

[9] Malcolm Cowley, "American Writers and the First World War," lecture at the University of Virginia, 1 Nov. 1967.

[10] John Dos Passos, *The Best of Times: An Informal Memoir* (New York, 1966), p. 46.

[11] Michael Millgate, "Faulkner in Toronto: A Further Note," *University of Toronto Quarterly*, XXXVII (Jan. 1968), 198.

[12] Collins, "Faulkner's War Service."

[13] Millgate, pp. 198–99.

[14] Michael Millgate, "William Faulkner, Cadet," *University of Toronto Quarterly*, XXXV (Jan. 1966), 123.

[15] JFSA.

[16] Collins, "Faulkner's War Service."

[17] *The Mississippian*, 26 Nov. 1919, rept. *EPP*, p. 41.

[18] *SP*, p. 5.

[19] *FOM*, pp. 90–91.

[20] *LIG*, pp. 7, 31.

[21] Millgate, "William Faulkner, Cadet," pp. 129–30.

[22] *MBB*, p. 197.

[23] JFSA.

Chapter 8

[1] James D. Nunnally, "Faulkner, With A 'U,'" *Mid-South Magazine* (*MCA*), 28 Sept. 1975, p. 6.

[2] As paraphrased in Carl Petersen, *On the Track of the Dixie Limited: Further Notes of a Faulkner Collector* (La Grange, Ill., 1979), pp. 16–17.

[3] Courtesy James M. Faulkner.

[4] *TMF*, p. 12.

[5] Patrick Samway, S.J., "Faulkner's Poetic Vision," *Faulkner and the Southern Renaissance: Faulkner and Yoknapatawpha, 1981*, eds. Doreen Fowler and Ann J. Abadie (Jackson, Miss., 1982), p. 218.

[6] *OFA*, Ch. 1, *passim*.

[7] Lewis P. Simpson, "Faulkner and the Southern Symbolism of Pastoral," *MQ*, XXVIII (Fall 1975), 411.

[8] *TMF*, p. 37.

[9] Robert Nichols, in *Ardours and Entrances* (London, 1917), pp. 69–136. See Michael Millgate, "Starting Out in the Twenties: Reflections on *Soldiers' Pay*," *Mosaic*, VII (Fall 1973), 5, and Martin Kreiswirth, "Faulkner's *The Marble Faun*: Dependence and Independence," *English Studies in Canada*, 6 (Fall 1980), 333–44.

[10] Faulkner had apparently rebound his

annotated copy of *Some Imagist Poets: An Anthology*, and he had certainly read it. *FGBC*, p. 13.

11 *TMF*, p. 8.

12 JFSA.

13 *EPP*, p. 39.

14 Steven F. Walker, "Mallarmé's Symbolist Eclogue: The 'Faune' as Pastoral," *PMLA*, 93 (Jan. 1978), 106.

15 Phil Stone to the editor, *Saturday Review*, XLII (27 June 1950), 23.

16 See William Jay Smith, *The Spectra Hoax* (Middletown, Conn., 1961), also *SLWF*, p. 32.

17 *PSY*, p. 215.

18 Nunnally, pp. 6–7.

Chapter 9

1 Louis Cochran, in *WFO*, p. 102.

2 *CNC*, p. 32.

3 Paul Rogers to JB, 7 April 1980.

4 *CNC*, p. 40.

5 *EPP*, p. 51.

6 *EPP*, p. 70.

7 Margaret Yonce, "Shot Down Last Spring: The Wounded Aviators of Faulkner's Wasteland," *MQ*, XXXI (Summer 1978), 362, 354–60.

8 *TMF*, pp. 7–11.

9 *FGBC*, pp. 23–24.

10 I: Mrs. Robert R. Buntin, 5 May 1975.

11 *EPP*, p. 54.

12 ENF, pp. 102–03.

13 One of Verlaine's best-known poems was "Le Faune," and in other works he employed Harlequin, Pierrot, and other traditional figures from the commedia dell' arte.

14 *CNC*, p. 42.

15 Phil Stone to James B. Meriwether, as quoted in Martin Kreiswirth, "Faulkner as Translator: His Versions of Verlaine," *MQ*, XXX (Summer 1977), 430. Kreiswirth writes that all four poems "appear in an index to the revised and enlarged edition of the most popular contemporary work on French symbolism, Arthur Symons' The Symbolist Movement in Literature." This book was likely to have been in Stone's library and "there are enough correspondences between Symons' and Faulkner's translations to suggest that the young poet was very familiar with Symons' versions." P. 430.

16 Wasson, "The Time Has Come."

17 Paul Rogers to JB, 6 March 1980.

Chapter 10

1 *MBB*, p. 73.

2 *WFO*, pp. 40–48.

3 *PWWF*, p. 3.

4 Lucy Somerville Howorth, "The Bill Faulkner I Knew," *The Delta Review*, 2 (July–Aug. 1965), 38.

5 "Judge Howorth Remembers Early Faulkner Days," *OXE*, 7 Aug. 1975, p. 3A.

6 Ilse Dusoir Lind, "Faulkner's Uses of Poetic Drama," *FMF*, p. 69.

7 *EPP*, pp. 71, 73.

8 *CNC*, pp. 52–53.

Chapter 11

1 *CNC*, p. 39.

2 Addison C. Bross, "*Soldiers' Pay* and the Work of Aubrey Beardsley," *The American Quarterly*, XIX (Spring 1967), 5.

3 Ilse Dusoir Lind, "The Effect of Painting on Faulkner's Poetic Form," in *FMF*, pp. 131–32.

4 *MAR*, p. xxx.

5 *OXE*, 7 Aug. 1975.

6 *CNC*, p. 49.

7 Ben Wasson, *A Memory of Marionettes*, p. vi, a pamphlet boxed with the facsimile edition *The Marionettes* (Oxford, Miss., 1975).

8 *EPP*, pp. 74–76.

9 Quoted in *PSY*, p. 182.

10 *CNC*, p. 41.

11 Conrad Aiken, *Punch: The Immortal Liar, Documents in His History* (New York, 1921), pp. 62–65, 67, 80.

12 *EPP*, p. 77.

13 *FOM*, p. 125.

14 *PSY*, p. 181.

15 See *OFA*, Chs. 10 and 11, *passim.*

16 JFSA.

17 *MAR*, p. 89.

18 Judith L. Sensibar to JB, 16 Aug. 1983.

19 *HEL*, p. 24.

20 *PSY*, pp. 314, 318.

21 Gerald M. Capers, Jr., *The Biography of a River Town: Memphis: Its Heroic Age* (Chapel Hill, N.C., 1939), p. 234.

22 *LIA*, p. 200.

23 *PSY*, pp. 1, 276, 314.

24 I: Louise Meadow, 19 Dec. 1979.

25 *PSY*, p. 315.

26 *FOM*, pp. 107–11.

27 Nunnally, p. 7.

28 *MBB*, p. 142.

29 Stark Young, "The New Year's Craw," *The New Republic*, LXXXXIII (12 Jan. 1938), 283; *The Pavilion: Of People and Times Remembered, of Stories and Places* (New York, 1951), p. 59; OXE, 30 Nov. 1950.

30 I: Dean Faulkner Wells, 19 Dec. 1979.

31 Marshall J. Smith, in *LIG*, p. 14.

Chapter 12

1 Marshall J. Smith, in *LIG*, p. 14.

2 Young, "The New Year's Craw," p. 283.

3 *MAY*, pp. 9–10.

4 Richard P. Adams, "The Apprenticeship of William Faulkner," *Tulane Studies in English*, XII (1962), 114.

5 Michael Millgate, "Faulkner's Masters," *Tulane Studies in English*, XXIII (1978), 155.

6 William Stanley Braithwaite, *Anthology of Magazine Verse for 1920 and Year Book of American Poetry* (Boston, 1920), pp. ix-xii. JFSA.

7 "American Drama: Eugene O'Neill," *The Mississippian*, 3 Feb. 1922, rept. *EPP*, pp. 86–89; *FR*, p. viii.

8 *ENF*, p. 141.

9 Willard Huntington Wright, *The Creative Will* (New York, 1915), p. 33 and *passim.* See Mick Gidley, "William Faulkner and Willard Huntington Wright's *The Creative Will*," *The Canadian Review of American Studies*, IX (Fall 1978), 169–77, also Hugh Kenner, "Faulkner and Joyce," in *FMF*, pp. 20–33.

10 HRCT. Cf. the lines quoted from Aiken's *Punch* on p. 154A above.

11 *CNC*, p. 63.

12 *PSY*, p. 332.

13 *MAY*, p. 9.

14 John McClure, "Literature—and Less," *NOTP*, 29 Jan. 1925.

15 *ENF*, p. 139.

Chapter 13

1 *The Mississippian*, 9 Dec. 1921, and clipping datelined "University, Miss., Dec. 2." JFSA.

2 *PSY*, p. 332.

3 *FOM*, pp. 111–12.

4 George Healy, Jr., in *WFO*, p. 58.

5 *EPP*, pp. 93–97.

6 *MBB*, pp. 158–59.

7 *FOM*, p. 111.

8 See *OFA*, Part Three.

9 *SLWF*, p. 6.

10 Edith B. Douds, in *WFO*, p. 53.

11 *PSY*, p. 322.

12 *PSY*, pp. 308–09.

13 *MAY*, p. 15.

14 XVIII, *AGB*, p. 40.

15 FCVA.

16 *CNC*, p. 66.

17 Emily Stone, "Faulkner Gets Started," p. 145.

18 FCVA.

19 Emily Stone, p. 147.

20 *PSY*, p. 329.

21 *The New Yorker*, 46 (21 Nov. 1970), 50.

22 *MCA*, 14 Dec. 1950.

Chapter 14

1 James K. Feibleman, "Literary New Orleans Between Wars," *The Southern Review*, I, N.S. (July 1965), 705–06.

2 *FIU*, p. 231.

3 *FIU*, p. 230.

4 Dos Passos, p. 141. Waldo Frank and Roger Sergel, as quoted in Irving Howe, *Sherwood Anderson* (New York, 1951), pp. 123, 241; *FIU*, p. 260.

5 Hamilton Basso, "William Faulkner: Man and Writer," *Saturday Review*, 45 (28 July 1962), 11.

6 *The Letters of Sherwood Anderson*, ed.

Howard Mumford Jones, with Walter B. Rideout (Boston, 1935), pp. 141–42.

7 Sherwood Anderson, "A Meeting South," *The Dial*, 78 (April 1925), 269–79; rept. *The Sherwood Anderson Reader*, ed. Paul Rosenfeld (Boston, 1947), pp. 274–84.

8 HRCT.

9 *SLWF*, p. 7.

10 See *AGB*, p. 67.

11 *HEL*, p. 75.

12 *AGB*, p. 27.

Chapter 15

1 T. P. Thompson, "The Renaissance of the Vieux Carré," *The Double Dealer*, III (Feb. 1922), 84–89.

2 Sherwood Anderson, "New Orleans, *The Double Dealer* and the Modern Movement in America," *The Double Dealer*, III (March 1922), 126.

3 Feibleman, pp. 706–07.

4 *TMF*, pp. 6–7.

5 McClure.

6 *EPP*, p. 112.

7 *EPP*, pp. 114–18.

8 *HEL*, p. 82.

9 Panthea Reid Broughton, "Faulkner's Cubist Novels," in *A Cosmos of My Own: Faulkner and Yoknapatawpha, 1980*, eds. Doreen Fowler and Ann J. Abadie (Jackson, Miss., 1981), p. 74.

10 See *NOS*, xix, xxvi, and James B. Meriwether's introductory note to "The Priest," *MQ*, XXIX (Summer 1976), 445–46.

11 *NOS*, p. 12.

12 *FIU*, pp. 20–21.

13 *NOS*, pp. 3–14.

14 Courtesy James M. Faulkner.

15 *PSY*, p. 420.

16 *MCA*, 5 April 1925.

17 Sherwood Anderson, *Memoirs* (New York, 1942), p. 473.

18 Broughton, p. 75.

19 *FIU*, p. 21.

20 *ESPL*, p. 7.

21 *USWF*, pp. 474–79.

22 HRCT.

23 *ESPL*, p. 7.

24 Sherwood Anderson, *We Moderns: Gotham Book Mart, 1920–1940* (New York, 1940), p. 29.

25 CF, p. 35.

26 HRCT.

Chapter 16

1 Margaret J. Yonce, "The Composition of *Soldiers' Pay*," *MQ*, XXXIII (Summer 1980), 295.

2 *Ibid.*, p. 300.

3 NYPL.

4 *NOS*, p. xxxi.

5 Judith Bryant Wittenberg, *Faulkner: The Transfiguration of Biography* (Lincoln, Neb., 1979), p. 46.

6 Rept. *AGB*, pp. 7–11.

7 Michael Millgate, *The Achievement of William Faulkner* (New York, 1965), pp. 63–64.

8 Millgate, "Starting Out in the Twenties," p. 5.

9 Michael Millgate, "Faulkner on the Literature of the First World War," *MQ*, XXVI (Summer 1973), 388.

10 "And Now What's To Do," *A Faulkner Miscellany*, p. 145.

11 *USWF*, pp. 489–94.
12 *NOS*, p. 55.
13 *NOS*, pp. 76–85.
14 *NOS*, pp. 86–91.
15 Basso, p. 11.
16 Courtesy William B. Wisdom Collection of William Faulkner, Tulane University Library.
17 *FIU*, p. 21.
18 NYPL.
19 Millgate, "Starting Out in the Twenties," p. 2.
20 *FIU*, p. 280.
21 Cleanth Brooks, *William Faulkner: Toward Yoknapatawpha and Beyond* (New Haven, 1978), p. 75.

22 *EPP*, p. 118.
23 Calvin S. Brown, "Faulkner as Aphorist," *Revue de Littérature, Comparée,* LIII (July-Sept. 1979), 287.
24 *HEL*, p. 16; FCVA.
25 Millgate, "Starting Out in the Twenties," p. 9.
26 *NOS*, pp. 132–39, 22, 132–33, 139, 134.
27 *ESPL*, p. 5.
28 *ESPL*, pp. 4–6.
29 NYPL.
30 *HEL*, pp. 16–17.
31 *PSY*, p. 447.

Chapter 17

1 *HEL*, p. 18.
2 *NOS*, pp. 92–103.
3 *HEL*, p. 17.
4 *HEL*, p. 111.
5 *HEL*, p. 117.
6 *HEL*, p. 112.

7 Brooks, p. 53.
8 *Ibid.*, p. 54.
9 *HEL*, p. 118.
10 *HEL*, p. 18.
11 *HEL*, p. 83.

Chapter 18

1 CF, p. 37.
2 *NOTP*, 13 Dec. 1953; *LIG*, p. 12.
3 *PSY*, p. 448.
4 *Elmer*, FCVA.
5 *HEL*, p. 119.
6 CF, pp. 37, 38.
7 *SLWF*, p. 8.
8 *SLWF*, p. 9.
9 *SWLF*, p. 19.
10 CF, p. 38.
11 *SWLF*, p. 10.
12 FCVA; *SLWF*, pp. 19–20.
13 *HEL*, p. 121.
14 *HEL*, p. 122.
15 *SLWF*, p. 19.
16 *SLWF*, p. 11.
17 *Ibid.*
18 *SLWF*, p. 12.
19 *NOS*, pp. 108–20.
20 *NOS*, pp. 121–31.
21 *SLWF*, p. 12.
22 *SLWF*, p. 13.
23 *FIU*, p. 58.
24 *SLWF*, p. 13.
25 *SLWF*, p. 14.

26 *SLWF*, p. 24.
27 *FMF*, pp. 141–43.
28 *SLWF*, p. 24.
29 *HEL*, p. 126.
30 NYPL.
31 JFSA.
32 *SLWF*, p. 17.
33 *SLWF*, p. 14.
34 *SLWF*, pp. 13–14.
35 FCVA.
36 Walker, p. 107.
37 *SLWF*, pp. 20, 18.
38 *SLWF*, p. 20.
39 James B. Meriwether, *The Literary Career of William Faulkner: A Bibliographical Study* (Princeton, N.J., 1961; Columbia, S.C., 1971), p. 81.
40 *SLWF*, p. 17.
41 *SLWF*, p. 20.
42 *SLWF*, p. 22.
43 *Ibid.*
44 Mick Gidley, "Some Notes on Faulkner's Reading," *Journal of American Studies,* IV (July 1970), 97.
45 JFSA.

46 *A Modern Book of Criticism*, ed. Ludwig Lewisohn (New York, 1919), p. 53.
47 JFSA.
48 *SLWF*, p. 28.
49 JFSA.
50 *PSY*, p. 448.

51 *The Letters of Sherwood Anderson*, pp. 145–46.
52 *SLWF*, p. 27.
53 *DSF*, p. 56.
54 *SLWF*, p. 15.
55 *SLWF*, p. 26.
56 *SLWF*, p. 27.

Chapter 19

1 FCVA.
2 *SLWF*, p. 29.
3 *SLWF*, p. 30.
4 *SLWF*, p. 31.
5 FCVA.
6 *AGB*, p. 21. Cf. Cummings' "Memorabilia," rept. *E. E. Cummings, Poems: 1923–1954* (New York, 1954), p. 183.

7 James B. Meriwether, "Faulkner's 'Ode to the Louver,'" *MQ*, XXVII (Summer 1974), 333–35.
8 *PSY*, pp. 443–47.
9 *SLWF*, p. 20.

Chapter 20

1 See *HEL*, p. 19.
2 *MBB*, p. 155.
3 JFSA.
4 *HEL*, p. 12.
5 *MAY*, p. 12.
6 *CNC*, p. 75.
7 James G. Watson, "Literary Self-Criticism: Faulkner in Fiction on Fiction," *The Southern Quarterly*, XX (Fall 1981), 51.

8 *MAY*, p. 19. See *HEL*, pp. 28–31.
9 The ship's cargo was the same as the *West Ivis*': "Texas cotton and Georgia resin." *CSWF*, pp. 879–80.
10 I: Spratling, 28 Jan. 1965.
11 *CSWF*, pp. 843–76.
12 *USWF*, pp. 504–25.

Chapter 21

1 James A. Wobbe, "How Faulkner Wrote Sonnet," New Orleans *Item*, (29 Aug. 1954), p. 18.
2 Basso, p. 12.
3 *The Letters of Sherwood Anderson*, p. 152.
4 *SLWF*, p. 293.
5 *The Letters of Sherwood Anderson*, p. 155.
6 Anderson, *Memoirs*, p. 474.
7 *ESPL*, p. 5.
8 Anderson, *Memoirs*, p. 474.
9 *LIG*, p. 120.
10 *ESPL*, p. 6.
11 Unpublished portion of class conference, University of Virginia, 15 May 1957.
12 *NYT Book Review*, 11 April 1926.
13 17 April 1926.
14 11 April 1926.
15 *PSY*, p. 453.

16 Edwin T. Arnold III, "Faulkner and Huxley: A Note on *Mosquitoes* and *Crome Yellow*," *MQ*, XXX (Summer 1977), 433–36.
17 Gidley, "Some Notes on Faulkner's Reading," pp. 97–100; Joyce W. Warren, "Faulkner's 'Portrait of the Artist,'" *MQ*, XIX (Summer 1966), 121–31.
18 Joyce W. Warren, "Faulkner's Portrait of the Artist,'" *MQ*, XIX (Summer 1966), 121–31.
19 See Brown, "Faulkner as Aphorist," p. 289.
20 *MOS*, p. 228.
21 FCVA.
22 See Carl Petersen, *Each in Its Ordered Place: A Faulkner Collector's Notebook* (Ann Arbor, Mich., 1975), p. 29.
23 *PSY*, p. 454.

Chapter 22

[1] Carvel Collins, "Faulkner's Review of *Ducdame*," *MQ*, XXVIII (Summer 1975), 345–46.

[2] FCVA.

[3] *HEL*, p. 12.

[4] *LIG*, pp. 3–4.

[5] Noel Polk, " 'Hong Li' and *Royal Street*: The New Orleans Sketches in Manuscript," *MQ*, XXVI (Summer 1973), 394–95. See also Noel Polk, "William Faulkner's 'Hong Li' and *Royal Street*," *The Library Chronicle of the University of Texas at Austin* (N.S. 13, 1980), 27–30.

[6] Judith L. Sensibar, "Pierrot and the Marble Faun: Another Fragment," *MQ*, XXXII (Summer 1979), 475–76.

[7] *WT*, p. 81.

Chapter 23

[1] *LIG*, p. 255.

[2] *Father Abraham*, ed. James B. Meriwether. New York: Red Ozier Press, 1983, p. 4; *PSY*, p. 475.

[3] *Father Abraham*, p. 7.

[4] *OXE*, 18 Aug. 1926; *SAR*, p. 43.

[5] FCVA.

[6] Joseph Blotner, "William Faulkner's Essay on the Composition of *Sartoris*," *The Yale University Library Gazette*, 47 (Jan. 1973), 122–23.

[7] FCVA.

[8] A sizable body of commentary has grown up about the vexed problem of this text. Among those exploring it are Stephen Dennis, "The Making of *Sartoris*: A Description and Discussion of the Manuscript and Composite Typescript of William Faulkner's Third Novel" (Ph.D. thesis, Cornell, 1969); Douglas Day, Introduction, *Flags in the Dust* (New York, 1973); Melvin R. Roberts, "Faulkner's *Flags in the Dust* and *Sartoris*: A Comparative Study of the Typescript and the Originally Published Novel" (Ph.D. thesis, Univ. of Texas, 1974); and George F. Hayhoe, "William Faulkner's *Flags in the Dust*," *MQ*, XXVIII (Summer 1975), 370–86. See also Max Putzel, "Evolution of Two Characters in Faulkner's Early and Unpublished Fiction," *The Southern Literary Journal*, 5 (Spring 1973), 47–63, and George F. Hayhoe, "The Rejected Manuscript Opening of *Flags in the Dust*," *MQ*, XXXIII (Summer 1980), 371–84.

[9] John Pilkington, *The Heart of Yoknapatawpha* (Jackson, Miss., 1981), pp. 9, 6.

[10] *Sherwood Anderson and Other Famous Creoles*, p. 43.

[11] CF, p. 36.

[12] *ESPL*, pp. 10, 6.

[13] Emily Stone, "Faulkner Gets Started," p. 143.

[14] *SLWF*, pp. 34–35.

[15] *WT*, pp. 74, 76, 82. Prof. James B. Meriwether is convinced that WF actually wrote *The Wishing Tree* for Margaret Brown. "Then later, for Cho-Cho's birthday, he made a revised and very elaborately produced copy for her." JBM to JB, 13 Nov. 1983. (See pp. 197–98 and pp. 207–08.)

[16] *WT*, p. 81.

[17] JFSA.

[18] James Dahl, "A Faulkner Reminiscence: Conversations with Mrs. Maud Falkner," *Journal of Modern Literature*, III (April 1974), 1028.

[19] Calvin S. Brown, *A Glossary of Faulkner's South* (New Haven, 1976), p. 241. See also Charles S. Aiken, "Faulkner's Yoknapatawpha County: Geographical Fact into Fiction," *The Geographical Review*, 67 (Jan. 1977), 1–21, and "Faulkner's Yoknapatawpha County: A Place in the American South," *The Geographical Review*, 69 (July 1979), 331–48.

[20] *SAR*, p. 182.

[21] *CNC*, p. 81.

[22] *MAY*, p. 34.

[23] *SLWF*, pp. 34–35.

[24] *MOS*, p. 48; Ilse Dusoir Lind, "Faulkner's Women," in *M&M*, p. 94.

[25] Lind, p. 92. See also Mick Gidley, "William Faulkner and Some Designs

of Naturalism," *Studies in American Fiction* (Spring 1979), 75–82.

26 *SLWF*, p. 34.

27 Victoria Black, "Faulkner and Women," in *The South & Faulkner's Yoknapatawpha: The Actual and the Apocryphal*, eds. Evans Harrington and Ann J. Abadie (Jackson, Miss., 1977), p. 150.

28 19 June 1927.

29 3 July 1927.

Chapter 24

1 Dean Faulkner Wells, "Faulkner Helped Young Brother Dean with Vocabulary Lessons," *The Faulkner Newsletter & Yoknapatawpha Review*, II (Jan.–March, 1982), 3.

2 *SLWF*, p. 37.

3 FCVA.

4 *SLWF*, p. 38.

5 FCVA.

6 FCVA.

7 *MBB*, pp. 157–58.

8 25 Nov. 1927. FCVA.

9 Blotner, "William Faulkner's Essay on the Composition of *Sartoris*," p. 123.

10 *SLWF*, pp. 39, 34.

11 *SLWF*, pp. 39–40.

12 *SLWF*, pp. 40–41.

13 *SLWF*, p. 40.

14 *SAN* (ML ed.), p. 5.

15 I: Martha Ida Wiseman, 9 Aug. 1982.

Chapter 25

1 *MAY*, p. 20. Collins does not name his source, but it seems likely that it was Odiorne.

2 *LIG*, p. 146.

3 "An Introduction to *The Sound And The Fury*," *MQ*, XXVI (Summer 1973), 413.

4 Leon Howard, "The Composition of *The Sound and the Fury*," *The Missouri Review*, V (Winter 1981–82), 115.

5 *LIG*, p. 146.

6 *NOS*, p. 55.

7 *LIG*, p. 146.

8 "An Introduction," *MQ*, pp. 413–14.

9 "An Introduction for *The Sound and the Fury*," ed. James B. Meriwether, *The Southern Review*, 8 (N.S., Autumn 1972), 710.

10 Faulkner wrote it in 1933 for a special edition Random House planned. He was paid for it, but the edition was not published and the introduction was lost until it was discovered by Robert Linscott in Random House's files in 1946. When it was sent to Faulkner, he replied, "I had forgotten what smug false sentimental windy shit it was," and offered to return the money to keep it out of print. (*SLWF*, p. 235) It was not published.

11 "An Introduction," *The Southern Review*, p. 709. For the source of Faulkner's allusion to the old Roman and his vase in Henryk Sienkiewicz's *Quo Vadis* and Pliny's *Natural History*, see James B. Meriwether, "The Old Roman and His Vase," *The Faulkner Newsletter*, II (Oct.–Dec. 1982), 2, 4.

12 Albert J. Guerard, "Faulkner the Innovator," in *M&M*, p. 71.

13 Maurice Coindreau, Introduction, *La bruit et la fureur* (Paris, 1938), p. 14.

14 "An Introduction," *MQ*, p. 414.

15 *LIG*, p. 147.

16 *SLWF*, p. 185.

17 *MBB*, p. 275.

18 *S&F*, p. 94.

19 *WFLP*, p. 105.

20 André Bleikasten, *The Most Splendid Failure: Faulkner's The Sound and the Fury* (Bloomington, Ind., 1976), p. 66.

21 Louis D. Rubin, Jr., "The Dixie Special: Faulkner and the Southern Literary Renascence," in *Faulkner and the Southern Renaissance: Faulkner and Yoknapatawpha, 1981*, eds. Ann J. Abadie and Doreen Fowler (Jackson, Miss., 1982), pp. 80, 87.

22 Louis D. Rubin, Jr., "William Faulkner: The Discovery of a Man's Vocation," in *Faulkner: Fifty Years After The Marble Faun*, ed. George H. Wolfe (University, Ala., 1976), p. 53.

23 Frederick L. Gwynn, "Faulkner's Raskolnikov," *Modern Fiction Studies,* IV (Summer 1958), 169–72.

24 Dahl, p. 1028.

25 *PSY*, pp. 1, 64, 189, 498, 78.

26 "An Introduction," *MQ*, p. 415.

27 *LIG*, p. 147.

28 Blyden Jackson, "Faulkner's Depiction of the Negro," *The University of Mississippi Studies in English,* 15 (1978), 38.

29 Dahl, p. 1028.

30 *PSY*, pp. 494–95, 497.

31 Maurice Coindreau, "Preface to 'The Sound and the Fury,'" *MQ*, XIX (Summer 1966), 109.

32 *SAN* (ML ed.), Introduction, p. vi.

33 *Ibid.*

34 See Merle Wallace Keiser, "*Flags in the Dust* and *Sartoris*," in *FYY*, pp. 44–70.

Chapter 26

1 Blotner, "William Faulkner's Essay on the Composition of *Sartoris*," p. 124.

2 See Day, Dennis, and Hayhoe, also William Boozer, "Footnotes on *Flags, Sartoris*," *MCA*, 18 Nov. 1973.

3 Courtesy MAETV.

4 CF, p. 16.

5 Louis Kronenberger, "Gambler in Publishing: Horace Liveright," *The Atlantic Monthly*, 215 (Jan. 1965), 94–104.

6 *SLWF*, p. 41.

7 John Pilkington, *The Heart of Yoknapatawpha* (Jackson, Miss., 1981), pp. 57–58.

8 *WFLP*, pp. 31–32.

9 "Alcoholism: Can it be Inherited?" United Press International, Detroit *Free Press*, 25 April 1979.

10 Robert N. Linscott, "Faulkner Without Fanfare," *Esquire*, LX (July, 1963), 36, 38.

11 *SLWF*, p. 41.

12 FCUM.

Chapter 27

1 *SLWF*, p. 42.

2 Giliane Morell, "Prisoners of the Inner World: Mother and Daughter in *Miss Zilphia Gant*," *MQ*, XXVIII (Summer 1975), 299.

3 *FIU*, pp. 90–91; *SAN* (ML ed.), Introduction, p. vi.

4 *SAN* (ML ed.), *ibid.*

5 Dr. J. Watson Campbell to Franklin E. Moak, 11 Dec. 1975, courtesy Dean Moak; Nunnally, p. 8.

6 See Thomas L. McHaney, "*Sanctuary* and Frazer's Slain Kings," *MQ*, XXIV (Summer 1971), 223–45.

7 *PSY*, p. 314.

8 *PSY*, p. 448.

9 *MCA*, 3 Dec. 1919.

10 *SLWF*, p. 37.

11 *SLWF*, p. 43.

12 Donald Davidson, Nashville *Tennessean*, 14 April 1929.

13 Pilkington, p. 32.

14 Emily Stone, "Faulkner Gets Started," p. 144.

15 Noel Polk, "Afterword," *Sanctuary: The Original Text* (New York, 1981), p. 304.

16 *PSY*, p. 353.

17 *Sanctuary: The Original Text*, pp. 55–56.

18 *PSY*, p. 195.

19 FCVA.

20 Gerald Langford, *Faulkner's Revision of "Sanctuary": A Collation of the Unrevised Galleys and the Published Book* (Austin, Tex., 1972), p. 7.

21 See Linda Kauffman, "The Madam and the Midwife: Reba Rivers and Sairey Gamp," *MQ*, XXX (Summer 1977), 395–401.

22 *Sanctuary: The Original Text*, p. 291.

23 *SLWF*, p. 17.

24 *SAN* (ML ed.), Introduction, p. vi.

25 *FOM*, p. 125.

26 NYPL.

27 Courtesy Harcourt Brace Jovanovich and The American Play Co.

Chapter 28

1 Estelle Faulkner, in *BLRO*, p. 8.
2 *SLWF*, pp. 44–46.
3 Evelyn Scott, *On William Faulkner's "The Sound and the Fury"* (New York, 1929), pp. 6, 5.
4 *AILD*, p. 125.
5 *AA*, p. 58.
6 *OTF*, p. 71.
7 Scribner Archive, Princeton University Library.
8 James B. Lloyd, *The University of Mississippi: The Formative Years, 1848–1906* (University, Miss., 1979), p. 71.
9 *SAN* (ML ed.), Introduction, p. vii.
10 Lawrence Stallings, "Faulkner in Hollywood," New York *Sun*, 3 Sept. 1932.
11 James B. Meriwether, "Faulkner, Lost and Found," *NYT Book Review*, (5 Nov. 1972), pp. 6–7.
12 *FIU*, p. 87.
13 Edgar Lee Masters, *Domesday Book* (New York, 1929), pp. 20–21, cited in Pilkington, p. 89.
14 *LIG*, p. 255.

15 *FIU*, p. 74.
16 Calvin S. Brown, "Faulkner's Localism," in *M&M*, p. 6.
17 See Charles S. Aiken, *passim*.
18 FCVA.
19 Medford Evans, "Oxford, Mississippi," *The Southwest Review*, XV (Autumn 1929), 46–63.
20 Noel Polk, "William Faulkner's 'Carcassonne,' " to appear in *Studies in American Fiction* (Spring 1984), ts., p. 40.
21 Polk, pp. 2–3; A. E. Housman, *The Collected Poems* (London, 1960), pp. 47–48.
22 *CSWF*, pp. 899, 895.
23 *FIU*, p. 22.
24 *KG*, p. 16.
25 Cleanth Brooks, "Gavin Stevens and the Chivalric Tradition," *The University of Mississippi Studies in English*, 15 (1978), 19.
26 *IID*, p. 148.
27 *CSWF*, p. 421.

Chapter 29

1 *CSWF*, p. 792.
2 *SLWF*, p. 48.
3 FCVA. Faulkner was drawing on the 3rd, 4th, or 5th edition of Edward FitzGerald's translation of *The Rubáiyát of Omar Khayyám*.
4 *BLRO*, p. 21.
5 Courtesy MAETV.
6 *CNC*, p. 98.
7 *OXE*, 19 June 1930.
8 *WFO*, p. 75.
9 Gordon Price-Stephens, "The British Reception of William Faulkner, 1929–1962," *MQ*, XVIII (Summer 1965), 122–23.
10 *CSWF*, p. 330.
11 William Styron, *NYT Book Review*, 6 May 1973, p. 10; 22 July 1973, p. 26.
12 *OXE*, 4 Sept. 1930.
13 *WFO*, p. 91.
14 *OXE*, 25 Sept. 1930; Sherwood Anderson, "They Come Bearing Gifts," *The American Mercury*, XXI (Oct. 1930), 129.
15 *The Nation*, 131 (5 Nov. 1930), 500.

16 Unpublished portion of class conference, University of Virginia, 15 Feb. 1957.
17 *CSWF*, p. 360.
18 Emily Stone, WFO, pp. 96–98.
19 John Reed Holley, *WFO*, p. 87.
20 *SLWF*, p. 49.
21 *LIG*, p. 123.
22 *Ibid*.
23 *SAN* (ML ed.), Introduction, p. vii.
24 *MCA*, 24 and 25 June 1929, 15 Aug. 1930.
25 Noel Polk, "Afterword," *Sanctuary: The Original Text*, p. 293.
26 Polk, "Afterword," p. 300.
27 Unpublished portion of class conference, University of Virginia, 15 April 1957.
28 Polk, "Afterword," p. 304.
29 To Calvin S. Brown, both would be clear: Temple's reprisal against Ruby for the way she had humiliated her at the Old Frenchman place and Popeye's "bored indifference to both life and death," that of a man incapable

of pleasure and filled with "a vague sense of the general meaninglessness of everything. . . ." "*Sanctuary*: From Confrontation to Peaceful Void," *Mosaic*, VII (Fall 1973), 88–90. To Cleanth Brooks, Temple acts out of "lassitude and docility" in the wake of her fear, her corruption, and her debilitating loss of Red. *William Faulk-ner: The Yoknapatawpha Country* (New Haven, 1963), p. 126.
30 *SAN* (ML ed.), Introduction, p. viii.
31 *CSWF*, p. 186.
32 NYPL.
33 Scribner Archive, Princeton University Library.
34 FCVA.

Chapter 30

1 I: W. M. Reed, 30 July 1979.
2 *The Nation*, CXXXII (15 April 1931), 422; *The Saturday Review of Literature*, VII (21 May 1931), 673.
3 Copy of Sherwood review, courtesy Dean Faulkner Wells.
4 26 March 1931.
5 A. Scott Berg, *Max Perkins: Editor of Genius* (New York, 1977), pp. 226–27.
6 André Malraux, "Préface à *Sanctuaire* de W. Faulkner," *Nouvelle revue française* (1 Nov. 1933), 744–47.
7 Courtesy James M. Faulkner.
8 Pilkington, p. 114.
9 *DSF*, p. 122.
10 See James B. Meriwether, "Faulkner's Correspondence with *Scribner's Magazine*," *Proof*, 3 (1973), 253–83.
11 *CSWF*, p. 511.

12 FCVA, 18 Feb. 1927.
13 *LIG*, p. 11.
14 *USWF*, p. 600.
15 FCVA.
16 *FIU*, p. 74.
17 Meriwether, "Faulkner Lost and Found," p. 7.
18 See François Pitavy, *Faulkner's "Light in August"* (Bloomington, Ind., 1973), p. 9.
19 Meriwether, "Faulkner Lost and Found," p. 7.
20 *SLWF*, p. 51.
21 Regina K. Fadiman, *Faulkner's "Light in August": A Description and Interpretation of the Revisions* (Charlottesville, Va., 1975), pp. 9–19 and *passim*.
22 *SLWF*, p. 51.

Chapter 31

1 "The Past and Future of William Faulkner," *The Bookman*, LXXIV (Sept. 1931), 17–24.
2 *SLWF*, p. 52.
3 Emily Clark, "A Week-end at Mr. Jefferson's University," *NYHT Books* (8 Nov. 1931), p. 1.
4 *Letters of Sherwood Anderson*, pp. 250–51, 254.
5 Helen Lojek, "The Southern Lady Gets a Divorce: 'Saner Feminism' in the Novels of Amelie Rives," *The Southern Literary Journal*, XII (Fall 1979), 54.
6 Clark, p. 1.
7 *Letters of Sherwood Anderson*, pp. 252–53.
8 Anthony J. Buttitta, "A Memoir of Faulkner in the Early Days of His Fame," San Francisco *Sunday Chronicle*, 15 July 1962, p. 20.
9 *SLWF*, p. 53.
10 5 Nov. 1931.
11 *SLWF*, p. 72.
12 *The Making of William Faulkner's Books, 1929–1937: An Interview with Evelyn Harter Glick*, Southern Studies Program (Columbia, S.C., 1979), pp. 2–3, 20–21.
13 Undated clipping, New York *World-Telegram*, probably 5 Nov. 1931.
14 *SLWF*, pp. 52–53.
15 Tallulah Bankhead, *Tallulah: My Autobiography* (New York, 1952), pp. 189–92.
16 *PWWF*, p. 106.
17 *SLWF*, p. 53.
18 *CSWF*, p. 509.

19 *SLWF*, pp. 53–54.
20 *LIG*, pp. 19–20.
21 *CNC*, pp. 112–13.
22 *CNC*, pp. 115–16.
23 Unpublished portion of class conference, University of Virginia, 27 April 1957.
24 *CNC*, p. 126.

25 Paul Gardner, "Faulkner Remembered," in *A Faulkner Perspective* (Franklin Center, Pa., 1976), p. 17.
26 *WFLP*, p. 68.
27 James B. Meriwether, in *The Making of William Faulkner's Books, 1929–1937*, p. 5.

Chapter 32

1 *SLWF*, p. 54.
2 *WFO*, p. 223.
3 *WFO*, p. 227.
4 *WFO*, p. 222.
5 FCVA.
6 *LIG*, pp. 28–32.
7 Quoted in Morell, p. 299.
8 FCVA.
9 *SLWF*, p. 55; F, p. 755.
10 *SLWF*, p. 56.

11 FCVA.
12 *SLWF*, p. 57.
13 *SLWF*, p. 59.
14 *Ibid*; F, p. 758.
15 *SLWF*, p. 60.
16 Pitavy, p. 48.
17 *FIU*, p. 72.
18 Pitavy, p. 54.
19 *SLWF*, p. 62.

Chapter 33

1 "Metro-Goldwyn-Mayer," *Fortune*, VI (Dec. 1932), 63, 51.
2 *FMS*, p. xxiv.
3 *NYT*, 23 Dec. 1932.
4 JFSA.
5 *SLWF*, p. 64. See also George Hayhoe, "Faulkner in Hollywood: A Checklist of His Film Scripts at the University of Virginia," *MQ*, XXXI (Summer 1978), 407–19, and "Faulkner in Hollywood: A Checklist of His Filmscripts at the University of Virginia: A Correction and Additions," *MQ*, XXXII (Summer 1979), 467–72.
6 Lawrence Stallings, "Faulkner in Hollywood," New York *Sun*, 3 Sept. 1932.

7 *FMS*, pp. xxx–xxxii.
8 NYPL.
9 *FOM*, pp. 200–01.
10 *SLWF*, p. 65.
11 *SLWF*, p. 66.
12 *FMS*, p. xxxii; Hayhoe, "Faulkner in Hollywood" (1978), p. 410.
13 JFSA.
14 Bruce F. Kawin suggests that Gable's and Faulkner's ignorance of each other's career may have been feigned, that "the 'dove hunts' were wild weekends in rented bungalows and that no one participated in them who was not well known to the others." *FMS*, p. xxviii.

Chapter 34

1 Meriwether, "Faulkner, Lost and Found," p. 7.
2 Dorothy Van Doren, *The Nation*, CXXXV (26 Oct. 1932), 402.
3 For a suggestion that Faulkner may have been indebted here to Edgar Lee Masters' *Domesday Book*, see Michael Millgate, "A Cosmos of My Own," in *FYY*, pp. 39–41; see also James B. Meriwether, "The Novel Faulkner Never Wrote: His *Golden Book* or *Doomsday Book*," *American Literature*, XLII (1970), 93–96.
4 *FMS*, p. 258.
5 *FMS*, p. 420.
6 *FMS*, p. 263.
7 *FMS*, p. 430.
8 Wayne Warga, "Sam Marx: Mole in King Louis' Mines," Los Angeles *Times*, 13 Feb. 1981, pp. 22–23.

9 Memphis *Evening Appeal*, 27 March 1933.
10 Paul R. Coppock, "Mid-South Memoirs—Those Daring Young Aviators," *MCA*, 19 Sept. 1982, p. G7.
11 *AGB*, p. 40.
12 *SLWF*, p. 54.
13 *SLWF*, p. 67.
14 *FIU*, p. 4.
15 *MCA*, 13 April 1933.
16 *OXE*, 9 and 23 March, 6 and 23 April 1933.
17 *FMS*, pp. 545–46.
18 *FMS*, pp. 546–47.
19 *LIG*, pp. 241–43.
20 Courtesy MGM.
21 *BLRO*, p. 46.
22 Courtesy Dean Faulkner Wells.
23 *SLWF*, p. 71.

24 *SLWF*, p. 74.
25 "An Introduction to *The Sound and the Fury*," *MQ*, XXVI (Summer 1973), 410, 412.
26 Meriwether, "Faulkner Lost and Found," p. 7.
27 *SLWF*, p. 72.
28 Shelby Foote, "Faulkner's Depiction of the Planter Aristocracy," in *The South and Faulkner's Yoknapatawpha*, p. 56.
29 Steele's story is called "Can't Cross Jordan By Myself." See Hassell A. Simpson, "Wilbur Daniel Steele's Influence on William Faulkner's Revision of 'Beyond,'" *MQ*, XXXIV (Summer 1981), 335–39.
30 *SLWF*, pp. 71–72.
31 *SLWF*, p. 74.

Chapter 35

1 *DSF*, pp. 135, 139, 140, and *passim*.
2 *MPS*, 11 and 26 Oct. 1933.
3 *SLWF*, p. 75.
4 *CSWF*, pp. 548–49.
5 FCVA.

6 FCVA.
7 Watson, p. 59.
8 *SLWF*, p. 78.
9 FCVA.
10 *SLWF*, pp. 78–79.

Chapter 36

1 *FIU*, p. 36.
2 Undated clipping, JFSA.
3 *MBB*, pp. 169–70.
4 Boston *Transcript*, 30 June 1934; London *Times Literary Supplement*, 13 Sept. 1934.
5 *OXE*, 3 May 1934.
6 ENF, pp. 149–50.
7 ENF, pp. 152–53.
8 ENF, pp. 162–63.
9 *OXE*, 6 Sept. 1934.
10 Thomas Daniel Young, "Pioneering on Principle," in *FMF*, pp. 47–48.
11 *SLWF*, p. 81.
12 JFSA.

13 *SLWF*, p, 81; *F*, p. 852.
14 *SLWF*, p. 82.
15 12 July 1934, JFSA.
16 *SLWF*, pp. 82–83.
17 *SLWF*, p. 83.
18 *SLWF*, p. 84.
19 *Ibid*.
20 JFSA.
21 *MBB*, p. 168.
22 Published as "Skirmish at Sartoris," in *Scribner's*, XCVII (April 1935), 193–200; *UNV*, p. 242.
23 *SLWF*, p. 85.
24 *FIU*, p. 36.

Chapter 37

1 *DSF*, p. 156.
2 *DSF*, p. 151. I am indebted to Dean Faulkner Wells for her kindness in making her notes available to me.
3 *DSF*, p. 165.

4 *PYL*, p. 46.
5 *FIU*, p. 36.
6 *SLWF*, pp. 86–87.
7 *CSWF*, p. 705.
8 *SLWF*, p. 89.

9 *OTF*, pp. 111–13.
10 *CSWF*, p. 648.
11 Sharon Smith Hult, "William Faulkner's 'The Brooch': The Journey to the Riolama," *MQ*, XXVII (Summer 1974), 291, 305.
12 Here Faulkner could have drawn on the kind of lore revealed in Dr. A. S. Alexander's *Horse Secrets*, advertised in the OXE for 20 Jan. 1910: "Learn how 'bishoping' is done, how a 'heaver' is 'shut,' and a 'roarer' is 'plugged,' how lameness, spavins, and sweeny are temporarily hidden. . . . In short, how to beat all the games of crooked auctioneers and dealers."
13 *FIU*, p. 59.
14 *SLWF*, p. 90.
15 *SLWF*, p. 91.

Chapter 38

1 *The New Republic*, 82 (10 April 1935), 254; *OXE*, 4 April 1935; *The Nashville Banner*, 24 March 1935); *Current History*, 42 (May 1935), xvi; *By-Line: Ernest Hemingway*, ed. William Whyte (New York, 1967), p. 200.
2 François L. Pitavy, "The Gothicism of *Absalom, Absalom!*," in *FYY*, p. 207.
3 Pilkington, p. 162.
4 *FIU*, p. 76.
5 *SLWF*, p. 79.
6 *FIU*, p. 35.
7 Judith Bryant Wittenberg, "Faulkner and Eugene O'Neill," *MQ*, XXXIII (Summer 1980), 336–40.
8 *AA*, pp. 72–73.
9 *SLWF*, p. 92.
10 John Pilkington, *Stark Young: A Life in the Arts, Letters* (Baton Rouge, La., 1975), p. 650.
11 *SLWF*, p. 93; *F*, p. 902.
12 *PSY*, p. 321.
13 *FIU*, p. 75.
14 *The American Mercury*, XXXVI (Nov. 1935), 370–72; rept. *ESPL*, p. 190. For a fuller, corrected text see James B. Meriwether, "The Uncut Text of Faulkner's Review of *Test Pilot*," *MQ*, XXXIII (Summer 1980), 385–89.
15 *DSF*, p. 171.

Chapter 39

1 See *DSF*, pp. 174–82.
2 *DSF*, p. 178.
3 *DSF*, p. 181.
4 *DSF*, p. 184.
5 *Ibid.*
6 *DSF*, p. 185.
7 *ALG*, pp. 15–16.
8 Buttitta, p. 20.
9 HRCT.
10 Gardner, pp. 14–15.
11 *GDM*, p. 326.
12 *WFLP*, p. 105.
13 *ALG*, p. 52.
14 *WFLP*, p. 104.
15 *ALG*, p. 27.
16 Meta Doherty Wilde, "An Unpublished Chapter from *A Loving Gentleman*," *MQ*, XXX (Summer 1977), 453.
17 *ALG*, p. 56.
18 Courtesy Richard J. Stonesifer.
19 *SLWF*, p. 245.
20 *USWF*, pp. 430, 434.
21 Pilkington, *The Heart of Yoknapatawpha*, pp. 180–81.
22 *ESPL*, p. 42.
23 FCVA.

Chapter 40

1 IMCW, p. 777.
2 *OTF*, p. 53.
3 *SLWF*, pp. 94–95.
4 Tom Dardis, *Some Time in the Sun* (New York, 1981), p. 273.
5 WF to EF, 28 April 1936, JFSA.
6 WF to EF, 16 May 1936, JFSA.
7 *HEL*, pp. 60–61.
8 *ALG*, pp. 59–79.
9 *ALG*, pp. 50, 101.

10 *ALG*, p. 131.
11 *ALG*, p. 137.
12 *ALG*, p. 248.
13 *CNC*, pp. 144, 131, 132.
14 *ALG*, p. 145.
15 Glick, p. 47.
16 *SLWF*, 95–96.
17 *ALG*, p. 103.
18 Dardis, p. 273.
19 *ALG*, pp. 166–67.
20 *ALG*, p. 173.
21 *CNC*, p. 149.

22 *ALG*, p. 181.
23 *ALG*, p. 183.
24 *ALG*, p. 195.
25 *SLWF*, p. 196.
26 IMCW, p. 782.
27 Brooks, *William Faulkner: Toward Yoknapatawpha and Beyond*, p. 328.
28 John T. Irwin, *Doubling and Incest / Repetition and Revenge: A Speculative Reading of Faulkner* (Baltimore, Md., 1975), p. 20.

Chapter 41

1 New York *Herald Tribune*, 25 Oct. 1936, p. 3; *The Nation*, CXLIII (31 Oct. 1936), 524; *The New Yorker*, 12 (31 Oct. 1936), 62–64.
2 *SLWF*, p. 97.
3 *SLWF*, pp. 97–98.
4 Glick, p. 20.
5 *UNV*, p. 111.
6 See Thomas Daniel Young, "Pioneering on Principle: or How a Traditional Society May Be Dissolved," in *FMF*, p. 41.
7 FCVA.

8 *SLWF*, p. 99.
9 Maurice Edgar Coindreau, "The Faulkner I knew," *Shenandoah*, XVI (Winter 1965), 29–30.
10 *Ibid.*, p. 29.
11 *F*, pp. 963–64; *SLWF*, p. 100.
12 *FIU*, pp. 255–56.
13 *SLWF*, p. 100.
14 *SLWF*, p. 101.
15 *FOM*, pp. 195–97.
16 *CNC*, p. 154.
17 *CNC*, p. 156.

Chapter 42

1 FCVA.
2 FCVA.
3 *ALG*, p. 218. However, Carvel Collins writes that Faulkner met Meta and Wolfgang Rebner at the dock on their arrival in New York. *HEL*, p. 89. Mrs. Wilde briefly concurs (IMCW, p. 794), but the present narrative follows the detailed circumstantial account she provides, with part of a letter as supporting evidence, in *ALG*, pp. 218–20. Evidence of WF's whereabouts in the late summer and fall of 1937 is supplied by his pilot's logbook, where he recorded the following flights: "9–1," from Memphis to "local"; "10–15," from Memphis to "local" (indicated by ditto marks); and "11–16," with columns for origination and destination filled with a notary public's certification of license renewal. JFSA.

4 *ALG*, p. 220.
5 Buckminster Fuller to JB, 23 Aug. 1979.
6 *Sherwood Anderson's Memoirs: A Critical Edition*, ed. Ray Lewis White (Chapel Hill, N.C., 1969), p. 466.
7 *ESPL*, p. 10.
8 *ALG*, p. 230.
9 *LIG*, pp. 33–34.
10 FCVA.
11 *SLWF*, p. 102.
12 *WP*, p. 8.
13 *SLWF*, p. 338.
14 *MAY*, p. 12.
15 *SLWF*, p. 102.
16 *LIG*, pp. 247–48.
17 Ellen Douglas, "Faulkner's Women," in *FYY*, p. 159.
18 *SLWF*, p. 105.
19 *OXE*, 24 Feb. 1938.
20 *MBB*, p. 177.

Chapter 43

[1] *MBB*, p. 177.
[2] *SLWF*, p. 105.
[3] *MBB*, p. 178.
[4] Thomas L. McHaney, *William Faulkner's "The Wild Palms": A Study* (Jackson, Miss., 1975), pp. xv, 194. For an argument that these two views embody Schopenhauer's pessimism vs. Nietzsche's affirmation, see pp. xviii-xix, 190, and *passim*.
[5] Brooks, *William Faulkner: Toward Yoknapatawpha and Beyond*, pp. 207, 229.
[6] *SLWF*, p. 106.
[7] *Ibid*. See also James B. Meriwether,

The Literary Career of William Faulkner: A Bibliographical Study (Princeton, N.J., 1961), pp. 28, 69.
[8] Harvey Breit, "A Sense of Faulkner," *The Partisan Review*, XVIII (Jan.-Feb. 1951), 91.
[9] *ALG*, pp, 236-38. On p. 794 of IMCW, Mrs. Wilde is quoted as saying that Wolfgang Rebner and her dog, Chloe, were also present. This account follows her detailed description of the incident in *ALG*.
[10] *MBB*, pp. 195-96.
[11] *SLWF*, p. 197.

Chapter 44

[1] Fadiman, *The New Yorker*, 21 Jan. 1939; Redman, *The Saturday Review of Literature*, 21 Jan. 1939; Cowley, *The New Republic*, 25 Jan. 1939; Kazin, *NYHT*, 22 Jan. 1939.
[2] *FRGF*, p. 56.
[3] *Time*, XXXIII (23 Jan. 1939), 45-48.
[4] *HEL*, p. 87.
[5] *FRGF*, p. 56.
[6] *SLWF*, pp. 109-10.
[7] *SLWF*, p. 111.
[8] *SLWF*, p. 113.
[9] *SLWF*, p. 114.
[10] *USWF*, pp. 211-12.
[11] *SLWF*, p. 114.

[12] George Marion O'Donnell, "Faulkner's Mythology," *The Kenyon Review*, I (Summer 1939), 285-99.
[13] Michel Mok, "The Squire of Oxford," New York *Post*, 17 Oct. 1939, rept. *LIG*, pp. 38-41.
[14] *SLWF*, p. 116.
[15] Conrad Aiken, "William Faulkner: The Novel as Form," *The Atlantic Monthly*, 164 (Nov. 1939), 650-54.
[16] *ESPL*, pp. 117-18.
[17] *SLWF*, p. 117.
[18] *ESPL*, p. 118.
[19] *USWF*, p. 252.

Chapter 45

[1] *SLWF*, p. 122.
[2] *SLWF*, pp. 122-23; *F*, p. 1044.
[3] *SLWF*, pp. 123-24.
[4] *SLWF*, p. 125.
[5] *SLWF*, pp. 127, 129.
[6] *SLWF*, p. 132.
[7] *LIG*, pp. 42-51.

[8] *KG*, p. 98.
[9] *SLWF*, p. 135.
[10] *MBB*, p. 207.
[11] *SLWF*, pp. 136-37.
[12] *WFO*, p. 157.
[13] *SLWF*, p. 138.

Chapter 46

[1] *SLWF*, pp. 138-39.
[2] Remarks by Judge E. Grady Jolly, "The Law and Southern Literature," Second Annual Law and Humanities

Conference, Jackson, Miss., 22 Oct. 1983.
[3] *CSWF*, pp. 57, 58, 60.
[4] *SLWF*, pp. 139-40.

5 *SLWF*, p. 146.
6 *The Southern Plantation Overseer, As Revealed in His Letters*, ed. John Spencer Bassett (Northampton, Mass., 1925).

7 See Carvel Collins, "A Fourth Book Review by Faulkner," *MQ*, XXVIII (Summer 1975), 339–42.
8 *SLWF*, p. 147.
9 *SLWF*, p. 148.

Chapter 47

1 *SLWF*, p. 280.
2 *SLWF*, p. 150.
3 *SLWF*, p. 284.
4 Boston *Globe*, 2 May 1942; *NYT Book Review*, 19 May 1942; *NYHT Books*, 17 May 1942; *The Saturday Review of Literature*, XXV (2 May 1942), 16; *Time*, XXXIX (11 May 1942), 95.
5 *SLWF*, p. 149.

6 *SLWF*, p. 152.
7 *SLWF*, p. 153.
8 *SLWF*, pp. 154–55.
9 *SLWF*, p. 155.
10 *CSWF*, p. 42.
11 *SLWF*, pp. 157–58.
12 *SLWF*, p. 160; *F*, p. 1112.
13 *SLWF*, p. 159.

Chapter 48

1 *ALG*, p. 260.
2 *ALG*, p, 272.
3 *ALG*, pp. 278–79, 283. Later she would say of her hope for a permanent life together with WF, "it was a foolish dream, and I didn't understand it or realize it for all those years." IMCW, p. 789.
4 Jack L. Warner with Dean Jennings, *My First Hundred Years in Hollywood* (New York, 1965), pp. 6, 185.
5 Dardis, p. 121.
6 *SLWF*, p. 162.
7 *SLWF*, p. 163.
8 Bruce F. Kawin, "Faulkner's Film Career: The Years with Hawks," in *FMF*, p. 169.
9 *ALG*, p. 284.
10 Barbara Izard and Clara Hieronymus,

Requiem for a Nun: Offstage and On (Nashville, Tenn., 1970), p. 150.
11 Shelby Foote, "Faulkner's Depiction of the Planter Aristocracy," in *SFY*, p. 56.
12 *SLWF*, p. 166.
13 Dardis, p. 125.
14 *SLWF*, p. 167.
15 *SLWF*, p. 169.
16 WF to EW, 27 April 1943. FCVA.
17 *SLWF*, p. 173.
18 *SLWF*, p. 174.
19 *Ibid.*
20 *ALG*, p. 286.
21 *SLWF*, p. 175.
22 *SLWF*, pp. 175–76.
23 *SLWF*, p. 177.
24 JFSA.
25 *ALG*, p. 301.
26 FCVA.

Chapter 49

1 *SLWF*, p. 179.
2 *SLWF*, p. 180.
3 *ALG*, p. 298.
4 Kawin, "Faulkner's Film Career," p. 180.
5 *To Have and Have Not* [screenplay], ed. Bruce F. Kawin (Madison, Wis., 1980), p. 28.
6 *SLWF*, p. 181.
7 *ALG*, p. 300.
8 Kawin, *op. cit.*, p. 53.

9 *SLWF*, p. 181.
10 *ALG*, p. 301.
11 *ALG*, p. 303.
12 *FCF*, p. 6.
13 *SLWF*, p. 182.
14 *SLWF*, p. 183.
15 Gardner, p. 23.
16 *SLWF*, p. 185.
17 *ALG*, p. 309.
18 Courtesy Warner Bros.

Chapter 50

1 *SLWF*, p. 187.
2 *SLWF*, p. 188.
3 Meriwether, "Faulkner, Lost and Found," p. 7.
4 *SLWF*, p. 188.
5 *SLWF*, p. 189.
6 *SLWF*, p. 180, but erroneously dated there as 1944 instead of 1945.
7 *SLWF*, p. 191.
8 Malcolm Cowley, "William Faulkner Revisited," *The Saturday Review of Literature*, 28 (14 April 1945), 13–16.
9 *ALG*, p. 311.
10 *SLWF*, p. 193.
11 *SLWF*, pp. 197–98.
12 *SLWF*, p. 199.
13 *NYT*, 16 Feb. 1947.
14 Stephen Longstreet, "William Faulkner in California," *Orange County Illustrated* (May 1964), p. 29.
15 *WFLP*, p. 90.
16 *FCF*, pp. 27–30.
17 *SLWF*, p. 203.
18 *ALG*, pp. 311–12.

Chapter 51

1 *SLWF*, p. 205.
2 Malcolm Cowley, ed., *The Portable Faulkner* (New York, 1946); *S&F*, p. 413.
3 *SLWF*, p. 205.
4 *SLWF*, pp. 204–05.
5 *SLWF*, p. 210.
6 *SLWF*, p. 213.
7 *BLRO*, pp. 74–75.
8 *SLWF*, p. 215.
9 *SLWF*, p. 219.
10 *SLWF*, p. 222.
11 *SLWF*, pp. 217–18.
12 Malcolm Cowley, "American Novelists in French Eyes," *The Atlantic Monthly*, 178 (Aug. 1946), 113–18.
13 *FCVA*.
14 *BLRO*, pp. 18–19.
15 Courtesy MAETV.
16 *SLWF*, p. 232.
17 *SLWF*, p. 233.
18 *SLWF*, p. 220.
19 *SLWF*, p. 228.
20 *SLWF*, pp. 229–30.
21 *SLWF*, p. 235.
22 *SLWF*, pp. 236–37.
23 *SLWF*, pp. 234–35.
24 *SLWF*, pp. 237–38.
25 *ESPL*, p. 35.
26 *SLWF*, p. 244.
27 *SLWF*, p. 245.
28 Malcolm Cowley, —*And I Worked at the Writer's Trade* (New York, 1978), p. 258.
29 *FOM*, p. 8.
30 *Robert Penn Warren Talking: Interviews 1950–1978*, eds. Floyd C. Watkins and John T. Hiers (New York, 1980), p. 132.
31 *The New Republic*, CXV (12 Aug. 1946), 176–80.
32 *SLWF*, p. 247.
33 *WFO*, pp. 128–29.

Chapter 52

1 *WFO*, pp. 137–39.
2 Courtesy MAETV.
3 *SLWF*, p. 249.
4 *SLWF*, pp. 251–52.
5 *Ernest Hemingway: Selected Letters, 1917–1961*, ed. Carlos Baker (New York, 1981), pp. 623–25.
6 *SLWF*, p. 248–49.
7 *SLWF*. p. 250.
8 *SLWF*, pp. 253–54.
9 *SLWF*, pp. 254–55.
10 *SLWF*, p. 134.
11 *SLWF*, p. 255.
12 *SLWF*, pp. 256–57.
13 *SLWF*, pp. 260–61.
14 *SLWF*, pp. 261–62.
15 *BLRO*, p. 116.
16 *SLWF*, p. 262.

Chapter 53

1 *SLWF*, p. 128.
2 *SLWF*, p. 262.
3 *SLWF*, p. 263.
4 *SLWF*, p. 264.
5 Patrick Samway, S.J., *Faulkner's "Intruder in the Dust": A Critical Study of the Typescripts* (Troy, N.Y., 1980), p. 71 and *passim*.
6 *IID*, p. 11.
7 Samway, pp. 162 and 235.
8 Dahl, p. 1029.
9 See Samway, p. 214.
10 *SLWF*, p. 266.
11 Patrick Samway, S.J., "Faulkner's Hidden Story in *Intruder in the Dust*," *Delta* (Nov. 1976), 64.
12 *SLWF*, p. 269.
13 *WFO*, pp. 68–69, 234.
14 *SLWF*, p. 270.
15 JWW to JB, 18 Sept. 1973.
16 *SLWF*, p. 276.

17 *Ibid.*
18 *The New Yorker*, XXIV (3 Oct. 1948), 106–13; *Time*, LII (4 Oct. 1948), 108.
19 *FCF*, pp. 103–04.
20 *NYT*, 7 Nov. 1938; rept. *LIG*, pp. 61–62.
21 Cowley,—*And I Worked at the Writer's Trade*, p. 258.
22 *FCF*, pp. 104–05, 107–08.
23 *SLWF*, p. 280.
24 See Albert Erskine, "A special message to the members of the First Edition Society," in *Uncollected Stories of William Faulkner*, ed. Joseph Blotner (Franklin Center, Pa., 1979).
25 *SLWF*, p. 273.
26 *SLWF*, p. 277.
27 *SLWF*, p. 277.
28 *SLWF*, p. 280.

Chapter 54

1 *SLWF*, p. 285.
2 *OXE*, 3 Feb. 1949.
3 *Ibid.*
4 *SLWF*, p. 286.
5 See Samway, *Faulkner's "Intruder,"* pp. 64–65, and Regina A. Fadiman, *Faulkner's "Intruder in the Dust": Novel Into Film* (Knoxville, Tenn., 1978), pp. 59–61.
6 For the suggestion that *Ring Dove* came from George Moore's "The Lovers of Orelay," see *HEL*, p. 54.
7 *SLWF*, p. 280.
8 *SLWF*, p. 292.
9 *OFA*, Ch. 6.
10 *OFA*, Ch. 12.
11 See *OFA*, Ch. 9, note 19.
12 Joan Williams, "Twenty Will Not Come Again," *The Atlantic*, 245 (May 1980), 60.

13 *ALG*, p. 127.
14 Williams, p. 61.
15 Walker, p. 107.
16 Williams, p. 60.
17 *MCA*, 12 Oct. 1949.
18 *ALG*, p. 317.
19 *SLWF*, p. 293.
20 *MCA*, 29 May 1949.
21 William Riggan to JB, 24 April 1981.
22 Williams, p. 63.
23 *NYT Book Review*, 6 Nov. 1949; Chicago *Tribune*, 13 Nov. 1949; *The New Yorker*, XXV (24 Dec. 1949), 58; *The Nation*, CLXIX (12 Nov. 1949), 473; *NYHT Book Review*, 6 Nov. 1949.
24 *SLWF*, p. 296.
25 Williams, pp. 61–62.
26 Courtesy MAETV.
27 *SLWF*, p. 297.

Chapter 55

1 *SLWF*, p. 304.
2 *MCA*, 19 Feb. 1950.
3 *SLWF*, p. 298.
4 *FIU*, p. 79.
5 *FIU*, p. 96.

6 *OXE*, 9 June 1949.
7 *SLWF*, p. 287.
8 *SLWF*, p. 300.
9 Williams, p. 63.
10 *ESPL*, p. 204.

11 Jackson *Daily News*, 27 March 1950.

12 *REQ*, p. 64.

13 *SLWF*, p. 302.

14 *ESPL*, p. 206.

15 Williams, p. 63.

16 *SLWF*, pp. 302–03.

17 *SLWF*, p. 305.

18 Noel Polk, *Faulkner's Requiem for a Nun: A Critical Study* (Bloomington, Ind., 1981), p. 21.

19 *NYT Book Review*, 20 Aug. 1950; *NYHT Books*, 20 Aug. 1950.

20 *ESPL*, pp. 207–08.

21 *ESPL*, pp. 209–10.

22 *The New Yorker*, XXIV (25 Nov. 1950), 29.

23 *SLWF*, p. 307; *F*, p. 1332.

24 See Dean Faulkner Wells, *The Ghost Stories of Rowan Oak* (Oxford, Miss., 1981).

25 Dr. Kjell Stromberg, "William Faulkner—1949" (Paris, Presses du Compagonage).

Chapter 56

1 Osceola (Ark.) *Times*, 22 Dec. 1966.

2 *WFO*, pp. 185–86.

3 *MCA*, 11 Nov. 1950.

4 *MBB*, p. 242.

5 *OXE*, 16 Nov. 1950; *MPS*, 11 Nov. 1950; Jackson *Daily News*, 11 Nov. 1950.

6 *MCA*, 22 Nov. 1950.

7 *OTF*, pp. 18–20; *PWWF*, pp. 132–34; *WFO*, p. 160; *MCA*, 27 Nov. 1950; *OXE*, 30 Nov. 1950.

8 *PWWF*, p. 134.

9 *MCA*, 4 and 10 Dec. 1950.

10 *PWWF*, p. 185.

11 *MCA*, 6 and 7 Dec. 1950.

12 *FCF*, p. 129.

13 Frank MacShane writes that the lighter had been given to O'Hara by the recently deceased playwright Philip Barry, and that O'Hara had meant it

to be "a symbol, a link in a chain of friendship among writers. . . ." *The Life of John O'Hara* (New York, 1980), p. 152. What WF once called his "rotten habit of inattention," especially under these circumstances, may have accounted for his mistaking the lighter's antecedents. Or it may have seemed a better story if the lighter had been O'Hara's father's.

14 *MCA*, 7 Jan. 1951.

15 *Ibid.*

16 *Les Prix Nobel en 1950* (Stockholm, 1951), p. 127.

17 *MCA*, 17 Jan. 1951.

18 Courtesy Mrs. Frederick R. Johnson.

19 *ESPL*, p. 120.

20 *MCA*, 7 Jan. 1951.

21 *WFLP*, p. 107.

22 *SLWF*, pp. 310–11.

Chapter 57

1 *SLWF*, p. 311.

2 *SLWF*, p. 312.

3 *ALG*, p. 320.

4 *SLWF*, p. 313.

5 *NYT*, 8 Feb. 1951.

6 Osceola (Ark.) *Times*, 22 Dec. 1951; *MCA*, 27 March 1951; in *ESPL*, pp. 211–12.

7 Jackson *Daily News*, 29 March 1951.

8 *SLWF*, p. 314.

9 *ESPL*, p. 123.

10 *SLWF*, p. 315.

11 *SLWF*, p. 318.

12 *SLWF*, pp. 319–20.

13 *SLWF*, p. 321.

Chapter 58

1 *NYHT*, 7 Oct. 1951; Linscott, pp. 36, 38.

2 *Time*, LVIII (24 Sept. 1951), 114; *Saturday Review*, XXXIV (29 Sept. 1951), 12. The Warren and Cowley

reviews appeared on 30 Sept. 1951 in *NYT* and *NYHT*, respectively.

3 Polk, *Faulkner's Requiem for a Nun*, pp. xii–xiii.

4 *ALG*, p. 321.

⁵ *ESPL*, p. 125.
⁶ *SLWF*, p. 323.
⁷ *SLWF*, p. 324.
⁸ *Ibid*.
⁹ *SLWF*, p. 326.

¹⁰ Polk, p. 229.
¹¹ *ALG*, p. 322.
¹² *SLWF*, p. 328.
¹³ *SLWF*, pp. 330–31.

Chapter 59

¹ *SLWF*, p. 335.
² 20 June 1942, courtesy Harvey Breit.
³ *Ernest Hemingway: Selected Letters*, pp. 768–72.
⁴ *ESPL*, p. 193.
⁵ *SLWF*, pp. 338–39.
⁶ *SLWF*, p. 338.
⁷ *SLWF*, p. 339.
⁸ *ALG*, p. 323.
⁹ *SLWF*, p. 341.

¹⁰ *Ibid*.
¹¹ *Ibid*.
¹² *FGBC*, p. 187.
¹³ *FGBC*, p. 188.
¹⁴ *PSY*, p. 70.
¹⁵ *LIG*, p. 70.
¹⁶ *SLWF*, p. 345.
¹⁷ *SLWF*, p. 344.
¹⁸ *SLWF*, p. 345; *F*, p. 1445.

Chapter 60

¹ *The New Yorker*, XXVIII (7 Feb. 1953), 21–22; Nashville *Tennessean*, 15 Feb. 1953; *NYT Book Review*, 8 Feb. 1953.
² *SLWF*, p. 347.
³ *ALG*, p. 324.
⁴ *SLWF*, p. 347.
⁵ *ESPL*, pp. 3–10.
⁶ *FGBC*, p. 203.
⁷ *Holiday*, XV (April 1954), 33–54; rept. *ESPL*, pp. 35–36.
⁸ *SLWF*, p. 347.
⁹ *SLWF*, p. 348.
¹⁰ *ESPL*, pp. 133, 140, 137–38.
¹¹ *F*, p. 1460; *SLWF*, p. 349.

¹² *SLWF*, p. 350.
¹³ Noel Polk, "The Nature of Sacrifice: *Requiem for a Nun* and *A Fable*," *Faulkner Studies* 1 (Coral Gables, Fla., 1980), 101.
¹⁴ *SLWF*, p. 352.
¹⁵ *SLWF*, p. 353.
¹⁶ *CNC*, p. 183.
¹⁷ *SLWF*, p. 354.
¹⁸ *ALG*, p. 327.
¹⁹ Samway, "Faulkner's Hidden Story," p. 64.
²⁰ *LIG*, p. 162.
²¹ *FR*, p. ix.

Chapter 61

¹ *FGBC*, p. 207.
² AP dispatch, 8 March 1954.
³ *FGBC*, p. 203.
⁴ *SLWF*, p. 362.

⁵ *FGBC*, p. 205.
⁶ *SLWF*, pp. 361–62.
⁷ *SLWF*, p. 363.
⁸ *FGBC*, p. 209.

Chapter 62

¹ *SLWF*, p. 364.
² *SLWF*, p. 365.
³ *SLWF*, p. 366.
⁴ *Ibid*.
⁵ Lewis P. Simpson, "Yoknapatawpha & Faulkner's Fable of Civilization," in *M&M*, p. 136.
⁶ Humphrey Cobb, *Paths of Glory* (New York, 1935), pp. 225, 256.

⁷ *CSWF*, p. 509.
⁸ *The Atlantic Monthly*, 194 (Sept. 1954), 79; *The New Republic*, CXXX (23 Aug. 1954), 18; *The New Yorker*, 30 (28 Aug. 1954), 78; *NYT*, 29 Aug. 1954.
⁹ Courtesy MAETV.
¹⁰ *SLWF*, p. 368.
¹¹ Courtesy MAETV.

¹² Jane Sanderson, "A Kind of Greatness," *The Delta Review*, 2 (July–Aug. 1965), 15–17.
¹³ *SLWF*, p. 371.
¹⁴ *OTF*, pp. 42–43.
¹⁵ *BW*, pp. 175–98.
¹⁶ *USWF*, p. 455.
¹⁷ *ESPL*, p. 71.
¹⁸ *SLWF*, p. 372.
¹⁹ *Ibid*.
²⁰ *ESPL*, p. 50.
²¹ *The Kenyon Review*, XVI (Autumn 1954), 661–70; *Anglia* (1955), 484–515, rept. *William Faulkner: Three Decades of Criticism*, eds. Frederick J. Hoffman and Olga W. Vickery (New York, 1963), pp. 349–81.

²² *ESPL*, p. 144.
²³ Harvey Breit, "A Walk with Faulkner," *NYT Book Review*, 30 Jan. 1955, rept. *LIG*, pp. 80–3.
²⁴ *SLWF*, p. 377.
²⁵ *SLWF*, p. 378.
²⁶ *FIU*, p. 13.
²⁷ *ESPL*, pp. 215–16.
²⁸ *MBB*, p. 268.
²⁹ *ESPL*, p. 219.
³⁰ *ESPL*, pp. 52–53, 57, 60.
³¹ Edwin Howard, *MPS*, 14 June 1955.
³² *MCA*, 14 June 1955.
³³ *SLWF*, p. 382.
³⁴ *SLWF*, p. 384.

Chapter 63

¹ *LIG*, p. 188.
² *Asahi*, 5 Aug. 1955; *Shimbun*, 5 Aug. 1955.
³ *Yomiuri*, 6 Aug. 1955.
⁴ Courtesy Dr. Leon Picon.
⁵ *LIG*, pp. 142–50.
⁶ *LIG*, p. 166.
⁷ *ESPL*, p. 78.
⁸ *ESPL*, p. 77.
⁹ *ESPL*, p. 78.
¹⁰ Courtesy Department of State.
¹¹ *Ibid*.
¹² *ESPL*, p. 84.

¹³ Prof. Walter Harding to JB, 23 Feb. 1965.
¹⁴ *ESPL*, p. 81.
¹⁵ *ESPL*, p. 223.
¹⁶ *FIU*, pp. 155, 157.
¹⁷ *SLWF*, p. 405.
¹⁸ *LIG*, p. 223.
¹⁹ Kenneth Tynan, "Papa and the Playwright," *Esquire*, 11 (May 1963), 140.
²⁰ Madeleine Chapsal, "A Lion in the Garden," *The Reporter*, 13 (3 Nov. 1955), 40, rept. *LIG*, pp. 228–31.
²¹ *SLWF*, p. 387.

Chapter 64

¹ *ESPL*, p. 149.
² *OTF*, p. 56.
³ *SLWF*, p. 388.
⁴ James W. Silver, *Mississippi: The Closed Society* (New York, 1964), p. xii.
⁵ *CNC*, pp. 195–98.
⁶ *F*, p. 1587; *SLWF*, p. 391.
⁷ *SLWF*, p. 393.
⁸ *SLWF*, pp. 392 –93.
⁹ *ESPL*, p. 87.
¹⁰ Russell Warren Howe, *The Reporter*, 14 (22 March 1956), 18–20; rept. *LIG*, p. 262.
¹¹ *ESPL*, p. 225.
¹² *SLWF*, pp. 408–09.

¹³ Linscott, pp. 38, 42.
¹⁴ *LIG*, p. 255.
¹⁵ *SLWF*, p. 396.
¹⁶ *HAM*, pp. 67–68.
¹⁷ *SLWF*, p. 399.
¹⁸ *SLWF*, pp. 399–400.
¹⁹ *ESPL*, pp. 109, 111.
²⁰ *SLWF*, p. 402.
²¹ *Ibid*.
²² *MBB*, pp. 261–62.
²³ *SLWF*, p. 404.
²⁴ *FGBC*, p. 258.
²⁵ *ESPL*, pp. 227–28.
²⁶ *FGBC*, p. 263.
²⁷ *Ibid*.

Chapter 65

1 *FIU*, pp. 12, 13–14.
2 *SLWF*, p. 409.
3 *FIU*, pp. 67, 70.
4 Athens *News*, 20 March 1957.
5 *FIU*, pp. 129–30.
6 *ESPL*, p. 152.
7 *FGBC*, p. 264.
8 Harold E. Howland, "Midnight Ride with William Faulkner," *Virginia Cardinal*, III (Nov. 1973), 12–13.
9 Unpublished portion of class conference, University of Virginia, 15 April 1957.
10 *The New Republic*, CXXXVI (27 May 1957), 20.
11 *FIU*, p. 107.
12 *SLWF*, p. 410.
13 *ESPL*, pp. 153–54.
14 *FCF*, pp. 146–47.
15 Washington *Evening Star*, 12 June 1957.
16 *FIU*, pp. 193, 195.

Chapter 66

1 *SLWF*, p. 411.
2 *ESPL*, p. 229.
3 *NYT*, 13 Oct. 1957; rept. *ESPL*, pp. 230–31.
4 *MBB*, pp. 266–67.
5 *FIU*, pp. 209–13, 216, 214.
6 *SLWF*, p. 413.
7 *SLWF*, p. 415.
8 *FIU*, pp. 241–45.
9 *FIU*, p. 268.
10 *FIU*, p. 280.
11 *FIU*, p. 282.
12 Dorothy Commins, *What Is an Editor? Saxe Commins at Work* (Chicago, 1978), p. 232.
13 *SLWF*, p. 415.
14 *SLWF*, p. 414.
15 *SLWF*, p. 416.
16 *MBB*, pp. 226–27.

Chapter 67

1 *SLWF*, p. 419.
2 *Ibid.*
3 *SLWF*, p. 421.
4 *Ibid.*
5 *PSY*, pp. 259, 353.
6 *SLWF*, p. 422.
7 *SLWF*, p. 424.
8 *SLWF*, p. 426.
9 *SLWF*, p. 422.
10 *SLWF*, p. 423.
11 *SLWF*, p. 427.
12 *MBB*, p. 258.
13 *SLWF*, pp. 429–30.
14 *SLWF*, p. 427.
15 *SLWF*, p. 431.

Chapter 68

1 Hiram Haydn, *Words & Faces* (New York, 1974), p. 88.
2 *SLWF*, p. 432.
3 *SLWF*, p. 437.
4 *FIU*, p. 61.
5 Courtesy MAETV.
6 *FIU*, p. 150.
7 *SLWF*, pp. 432–33.
8 *SLWF*, p. 434.
9 *Ibid.*
10 *SLWF*, pp. 436–37.
11 *SLWF*, p. 425.
12 *ESPL*, p. 167.
13 *SLWF*, p. 438.
14 *Saturday Review*, XLII (14 Nov. 1959), 20.
15 William Ferris and Ann J. Abadie, "The World of Yoknapatawpha: A Documentary Project," Center for the Study of Southern Culture, University of Mississippi, 1980, p. 2.
16 *NYT Book Review*, 15 Nov. 1959.
17 *SLWF*, p. 439.
18 *SLWF*, p. 440.
19 *SLWF*, pp. 440–42.
20 *ESPL*, pp. 113–14.

21 *SLWF*, p. 444.
22 Charlottesville *Daily Progress*, 26 May 1960.
23 I: Dean Faulkner Wells, 14 Dec. 1979.
24 *SLWF*, p. 448.

25 *SLWF*, p. 449.
26 *FOM*, pp. 188–89.
27 *Ibid.*
28 *SLWF*, p. 446.

Chapter 69

1 *SLWF*, p. 450.
2 John Terraine, *Haig: The Educated Soldier* (London, 1963), p. 433.
3 *SLWF*, p. 452.
4 *SLWF*, p. 453.
5 *ESPL*, p. 453.

6 Charlottesville *Daily Progress*, 27 May 1961.
7 *REV*, p. 70.
8 *SLWF*, p. 124.
9 *SLWF*, p. 455.
10 Courtesy MAETV.

Chapter 70

1 *SLWF*, p. 458.
2 *Ibid.*
3 *SLWF*, p. 459.
4 Courtesy MAETV.
5 *FWP*, p. 5.
6 *FWP*, p. 66.

7 *FWP*, pp. 75, 101–02.
8 *FWP*, p. 129.
9 *FGBC*, p. 310.
10 *FCF*, pp. 147–48.
11 *Ibid.*

Chapter 71

1 Manchester *Guardian* (28 Sept. 1962), p. 6; *The New Statesman*, LXIV (28 Sept. 1962), 405.
2 *WFO*, p. 173.
3 Williams, p. 65.
4 *SLWF*, p. 461–62.
5 *SLWF*, p. 463.
6 *WFO*, p. 194.
7 *WFO*, p. 188.
8 *MBB*, p. 3.
9 *MBB*, p. 2.

10 *MBB*, p. 6.
11 *FOM*, pp. 201–02.
12 Edwin Howard, "Foote-note on Faulkner," *The Delta Review*, 2 (20 July 1962), 37, 39.
13 William Styron, "As He Lay Dead, a Bitter Grief," *Life*, 53 (20 July 1962), 39–42.
14 *Ibid.*
15 *ESPL*, p. 206.
16 *AGB*, p. 67.

CHRONOLOGY

1897 *Sept. 25:* born, New Albany, Miss.

1898 *Dec. (or shortly thereafter):* family moves to Ripley.

1899 [*June 26:* brother Murry C. (Jack) Falkner, Jr., born.]

1901 [*Sept. 24:* brother John Wesley Thompson (Johncy) Falkner, III, born.] *Oct.:* seriously ill with scarlet fever.

1902 *Sept. 22:* family moves to Oxford.

1905 *Sept. 25:* enters first grade, Oxford Graded School.

1906 *Sept.:* skips to third grade. [*Dec. 21:* grandmother Sallie Murry Falkner dies.]

1907 [*June 1:* grandmother Lelia Dean Swift Butler dies. *Aug 15:* brother Dean Swift Falkner born.]

1909 *June:* works in father's livery stable.

1911 *Sept.:* enters eighth grade; increasing truancy.

1914 *June:* takes poetry to Phil Stone; beginning of friendship. *Sept.:* enters eleventh and final grade of Oxford High School. *Dec.:* drops out of school.

1915 *Sept.:* returns to school to play football; suffers broken nose; quits school for good sometime later that fall. *Nov.:* goes bear-hunting at "General" James Stone's camp.

1916 *Winter:* works briefly as First National Bank clerk. *Fall:* frequents U. of Miss. campus; writes verse under influence of Swinburne and Housman.

1917 *Spring:* begins supplying drawings for yearbook *Ole Miss.*

1918 *Spring:* [Estelle Oldham engaged to Cornell Franklin] tries to enlist in U.S. Army. *Early Apr.:* joins Phil Stone in New Haven, Conn. *Apr. 10:* begins work as ledger clerk, Winchester Repeating Arms Co. [*April 18:* Estelle Oldham marries Cornell Franklin.] *Mid-June:* accepted in New York by RAF as cadet, returns to New Haven, then Oxford. *July 9:* reports to Recruits' Depot, Toronto, and enters upon active service next day. *July 26:* posted to Cadet Wing, Long Branch. *Sept. 20:* posted to School of Military Aeronautics, Toronto. [*Nov. 1:* Marine Pvt. Jack Falkner wounded near Argonne Forest.] *Early Dec.:* receives discharge and returns to Oxford.

1919 *Winter:* roaming in Miss.; travels to Memphis and New Orleans. *Aug. 6:* poem "L'Apres-Midi d'un Faune" appears in *The New Republic*. *Sept.:* enters U. of Miss. as special student. *Nov.:* begins publishing poems in *The Mississippian* and Oxford *Eagle. Dec. 10:* initiated into Sigma Alpha Epsilon.

1920 *June:* wins $10 poetry prize offered by Prof. Calvin S. Brown. *Summer:* does odd jobs, helps with Boy Scout troop. *Sept.:* joins The Marionettes, university drama club. *Nov. 5:* withdraws from university. *Mid-Nov.:* commission arrives as Hon. 2nd Lt., RAF. *Late Dec.:* hand-letters six copies of *The Marionettes,* verse play.

1921 *Summer:* presents Estelle Franklin with gift volume of ts. poems, *Vision in Spring. Fall:* accepts Stark Young's invitation to visit in New York; hired as bookstore clerk by Elizabeth Prall; rents room in Greenwich Village; revisits New Haven. *Dec.:* returns home to become postmaster at university post office.

1922 [*March 13:* death of grandfather J. W. T. Falkner.] *Late summer:* replaces Rev. J. Allan Christian as scoutmaster. Poem "Portrait" published in *The Double Dealer* (New Orleans).

1924 *May:* Four Seas Co. agrees to publish for $400 *The Marble Faun,* sent in by Phil Stone. *Oct.:* compiles ts. gift booklet, *Mississippi Poems,* for Myrtle Ramey; removed as scoutmaster because of drinking. *Oct. 31:* resigns from post office after charges brought by postal inspector. *Fall:* calls on Elizabeth Prall Anderson in New Orleans and meets her husband, Sherwood Anderson. *Dec. 15:* *The Marble Faun* published.

1925 *Jan. 4:* leaves Oxford for New Orleans to sail for Europe. *Jan.:* invited by Elizabeth Anderson to stay at Andersons' apartment. *Feb. 8:* begins to contribute to New Orleans *Times-Picayune. Feb.–June:* alternates between New Orleans and Oxford; visits Pascagoula, Miss. *July 7:* sails from New Orleans with William Spratling. *Aug. 2:* debarks at Genoa; travels in Italy and Switzerland. *Aug. 13:* entrains from Geneva for Paris; takes room on Left Bank. *Oct. 6:* leaves for week in England. *Dec. 9:* boards boat train for return home.

1926 *Winter:* moves in with Spratling in New Orleans. *Jan. 27:* dates *Mayday,* hand-lettered tale composed for Helen Baird. *Feb. 25: Soldiers' Pay* published by Boni & Liveright. *Summer:* vacations at Pascagoula. *June:* dates hand-lettered gift book of poems, *Helen: A Courtship,* for Helen Baird. *Sept.:* returns to Oxford, then New Orleans. *Dec.:* collaborates with Spratling on *Sherwood Anderson & Other Famous Creoles.*

1927 *Apr. 30: Mosquitoes* published. *Summer:* returns to Pascagoula.

1928 *Sept.:* Harcourt, Brace accepts *Sartoris;* goes to New York for three months.

1929 *Jan. 31: Sartoris* published [*Apr. 29:* Estelle Franklin divorced.] *June 20:* marries Estelle in College Hill, Miss.; honeymoons at Pascagoula until late summer. *Early fall:* takes job at university power plant. *Oct. 7: The Sound and the Fury* published by Jonathan Cape and Harrison Smith.

1930 *Apr.:* begins publishing stories in national magazines; purchases house and land, naming it Rowan Oak. *June:* moves in. *Oct. 6: As I Lay Dying* published.

1931 *Jan. 11:* daughter Alabama born, lives nine days. *Feb. 9: Sanctuary* published. *Sept. 21: These 13* published. *Oct. 21:* arrives in Charlottesville for Southern Writers' Conference; goes on to New York for seven-week stay.

1932 *May 7:* arrives in Culver City, Calif., as MGM contract writer. [*Aug. 7:* father dies.] *Aug. 10:* returns home. *Oct. 3:* back to MGM for three weeks' work. *Oct. 6: Light in August* published by Harrison Smith & Robert Haas.

1933 *Feb. 2:* begins flying lessons. *Apr. 20: A Green Bough* published. *Late Apr.:* goes to New Orleans for a few weeks' scriptwriting on location. *June 24:* daughter Jill born.

1934 *Feb. 15:* flies to New Orleans for dedication of Shushan Airport. *Apr. 16: Doctor Martino and Other Stories* published. *July 1:* leaves for three-week assignment at Universal Studios.

1935 *Jan. 30:* with two others incorporates Okatoba Fishing and Hunting Club. *Mar. 25: Pylon* published. [*Nov. 10:* brother Dean killed in plane crash.] *Dec. 10:* leaves for five-week assignment at Twentieth Century-Fox; meets Meta Dougherty Carpenter, thereafter begins intimate intermittent fifteen-year relationship.

1936 *Feb. 26:* back at studio until end of May. *Late June:* returns to studio with

Estelle and Jill to resume work July 1. *Oct. 26: Absalom, Absalom!* published by Random House.

1937   [*Late May:* Estelle and Jill return to Oxford.] *Late Aug.:* returns to Oxford. *Mid-Oct.:* leaves on three-and-a-half-week trip to New York; suffers severe back burn.

1938   *Feb. 15: The Unvanquished* published; screen rights sold to MGM. *Late Feb.:* buys land and names it Greenfield Farm.

1939   *Jan.:* elected to National Institute of Arts and Letters. *Jan. 19: The Wild Palms* published.

1940   [*Jan. 27:* Mammy Caroline (Callie) Barr suffers stroke and dies four days later.] *Apr. 1: The Hamlet* published.

1941   *Late June:* organizes county aircraft warning system.

1942   *May 11: Go Down, Moses* published. *July 26:* reports for five-month segment of long-term Warner Bros. contract.

1943   *Jan. 16:* reports back for seven-month stay.

1944   *Feb. 14:* reports back again. *Late June:* Estelle and Jill join him for two months. *Dec. 12:* leaves for home.

1945   *June 7:* reports back to Warner Bros. for three and a half months' work.

1946   [*Apr. 29:* Viking Press publishes *The Portable Faulkner*, ed. by Malcolm Cowley.]

1947   *Mid-Apr.:* meets a series of six classes at U. of Miss.

1948   *July 11:* screen rights to *Intruder in the Dust* sold to MGM. *Sept. 27: Intruder in the Dust* published. *Nov. 23:* elected to American Academy of Arts and Letters.

1949   *Feb.:* helps with preparations for filming *Intruder* in Oxford. *Aug.:* meets Joan Williams. *Nov. 27: Knight's Gambit* published.

1950   *May:* receives American Academy's Howells Medal for Fiction. *Aug. 2: Collected Stories of William Faulkner* published. *Nov. 10:* notified he has won 1949 Nobel Prize for Literature. *Dec. 8:* leaves with Jill for Stockholm to receive Nobel award.

1951   *Feb. 1:* arrives in Hollywood for five weeks' scriptwriting for Howard Hawks. *Feb. 10: Notes on a Horsethief* published. *Mar.:* receives National Book Award for Fiction for *Collected Stories. Apr. 12:* leaves for three-week trip to France and England. *Early July:* leaves for one week's work in New York on stage version of *Requiem for a Nun. Sept. 12:* with Estelle, drives Jill to Wellesley, Mass., to enter Pine Manor Junior College. *Sept. 27: Requiem for a Nun* published. *Oct. 2:* leaves to spend two weeks on *Requiem* in Cambridge, Mass. *Oct. 26:* receives Legion of Honor in New Orleans. *Nov. 10:* ten days' more work in Cambridge.

1952   *May 15:* addresses Delta Council, Cleveland, Miss. *May 16:* leaves for one-month trip to France, England, and Norway. *Mid-Nov.:* leaves to work for one month on *A Fable* in Princeton and New York.

1953   *Jan. 31:* returns to New York; until Oct. alternates between there and Oxford. *Nov. 30:* leaves for Paris to begin work on *Land of the Pharaohs* for Howard Hawks, then on to Stresa and St. Moritz. *Dec. 24:* meets Jean Stein.

1954   *Jan. 1:* series of short stays in England, France, and Switzerland. *Jan. 19:* arrives in Rome. *Feb. 11:* goes to Paris for three days before joining Hawks on location near Cairo. *Mar. 29:* leaves Egypt for three weeks in France before returning to New York. *Late Apr.:* returns to Oxford. *Aug. 2: A Fable* published. *Aug. 7:* arrives in Lima for one-day stopover on way to São Paulo for six-day stay at International Writers' Conference. [*Aug. 21:* Jill marries Paul D. Summers, Jr.] *Sept.-Feb.:* alternates between Oxford and New York.

1955   *Jan. 25:* accepts National Book Award for Fiction for *A Fable. Mid-Apr.:* speaks at U. of Oregon and Montana State U. *Early May: A Fable* wins Pulitzer Prize. *July 29:* leaves for Japan on State Dept. trip. *Aug. 23:* leaves Japan for forty-eight-hour stopover in Manila on way to Italy. *Sept. 17:* leaves Italy by train for France via Munich. *Oct. 12:* arrives in Iceland for five-day stay before flying to New York. *Oct. 14: Big Woods* published. *Oct. 23:* leaves for Oxford.

1956 *Feb–Sept.:* alternates between Oxford and New York with visits to Charlottes-ville, Va. [*Apr. 15:* grandson Paul D. Summers III, born.] *Sept. 11:* to Washing-ton for four days as chairman of Writers' Group, People-to-People Program.

1957 *Early Feb.:* to New York for People-to-People Program. *Feb. 15:* to U. of Va. for second semester as writer-in-residence. *Mar. 18:* arrives in Athens on two-week mission for State Dept.; accepts Silver Medal of Greek Academy. *May 1: The Town* published.

1958 *Jan. 30:* returns to U. of Va. for another semester as writer-in-residence. *Mar. 1:* arrives in Princeton to spend two weeks at University for Council on Humanities. *Mid-Mar. onwards:* alternates between Charlottesville (later Albermarle County) and Oxford. [*Dec. 2:* grandson William Cuthbert Falkner Summers born.]

1959 *Jan. 30:* American debut of *Requiem for a Nun* on Broadway. *Mar. 14:* fractures right collarbone in fall from horse in Charlottesville. *Aug. 21:* purchases house at 917 Rugby Road, Charlottesville. *Sept. 29:* to Denver for four-day UNESCO conference. *Nov. 13: The Mansion* published.

1960 *Aug. 25:* accepts appointment to U. of Va. faculty. [*Oct. 16:* mother dies.] *Fall:* asked to wear colors of the Farmington (Va.) Hunt Club. *Dec. 28:* wills manu-scripts to the William Faulkner Foundation.

1961 *Apr. 2:* arrives in Venezuela on two-week State Dept. trip. [*May 30:* grandson A. Burks Summers born.]

1962 *Jan. 3:* injured in fall from horse in Charlottesville. *Apr. 19:* two-day visit to U.S. Military Academy at West Point. *May 24:* in New York to accept Gold Medal for Fiction of National Institute of Arts and Letters. *June 4: The Reivers* pub-lished. *June 17:* injured in fall from horse in Oxford. *July 5:* enters hospital. *July 6:* dies of heart attack at 1:30 A.M. *July 7:* buried in St. Peter's Cemetery, Oxford.

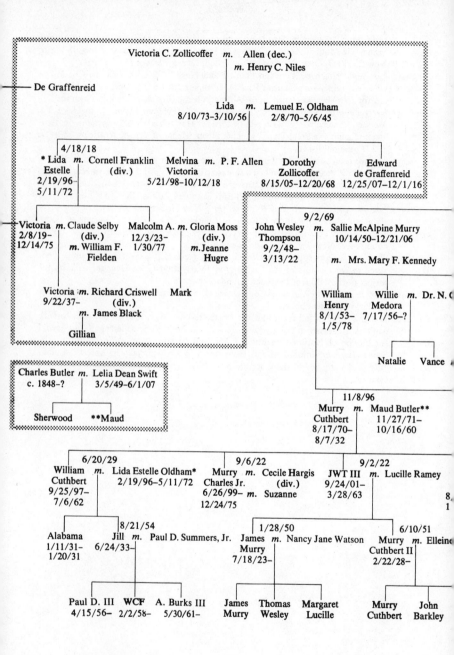

Victoria C. Zollicoffer *m.* Allen (dec.)
m. Henry C. Niles

De Graffenreid

Lida *m.* Lemuel E. Oldham
8/10/73–3/10/56   2/8/70–5/6/45

4/18/18
* Lida *m.* Cornell Franklin   Melvina *m.* P. F. Allen   Dorothy   Edward
Estelle   (div.)   Victoria   Zollicoffer   de Graffenreid
2/19/96–   5/21/98–10/12/18   8/15/05–12/20/68   12/25/07–12/1/16
5/11/72

9/2/69
Victoria *m.* Claude Selby   Malcolm A. *m.* Gloria Moss   John Wesley *m.* Sallie McAlpine Murry
2/8/19–   (div.)   12/3/23–   (div.)   Thompson   10/14/50–12/21/06
12/14/75   *m.* William F.   1/30/77   *m.* Jeanne   9/2/48–
              Fielden   Hugre   3/13/22

                                                                 m. Mrs. Mary F. Kennedy

Victoria *m.* Richard Criswell   Mark
9/22/37–   (div.)   William   Willie *m.* Dr. N. (
         m. James Black   Henry   Medora
                                                                 8/1/53–   7/17/56–?
         Gillian   1/5/78

Charles Butler *m.* Lelia Dean Swift   Natalie   Vance
c. 1848–?   3/5/49–6/1/07

Sherwood   **Maud   11/8/96
                                                                Murry *m.* Maud Butler**
                                                                Cuthbert   11/27/71–
                                                                8/17/70–   10/16/60
                                                                8/7/32

6/20/29   9/6/22   9/2/22
William *m.* Lida Estelle Oldham*   Murry *m.* Cecile Hargis   JWT III *m.* Lucille Ramey
Cuthbert   2/19/96–5/11/72   Charles Jr.   (div.)   9/24/01–
9/25/97–   6/26/99– *m.* Suzanne   3/28/63   8
7/6/62   12/24/75   1

         8/21/54   1/28/50   6/10/51
Alabama Jill *m.* Paul D. Summers, Jr.   James *m.* Nancy Jane Watson   Murry *m.* Elleine
1/11/31– 6/24/33–   Murry   Cuthbert II
1/20/31   7/18/23–   2/22/28–

Paul D. III WCF A. Burks III   James   Thomas   Margaret   Murry   John
4/15/56–   2/2/58– 5/30/61–   Murry   Wesley   Lucille   Cuthbert   Barkley

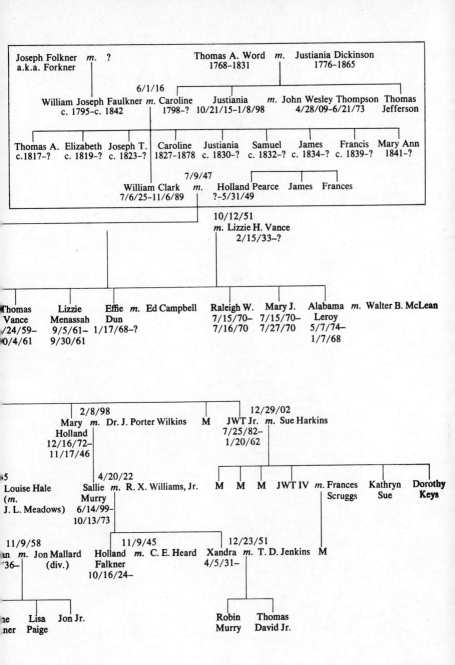

Genealogy

ACKNOWLEDGMENTS

FOR this volume, as with my earlier study, my thanks go first to Jill Faulkner Summers, William Faulkner's daughter and executrix, for her continuing help and friendship. They go also to other members of William Faulkner's family: James M. Faulkner, Murry C. Falkner II, Dean Faulkner Wells, Louise Meadow, and Mrs. Frederick R. Johnson. I should also like to thank once again all those who aided me in my work on the earlier study, laying the foundation as it did for this one.

My indebtedness to institutions and the richness of their resources has also been a personal one because of the people who did so much to help me: Dr. Ann J. Abadie of the Center for the Study of Southern Culture at the University of Mississippi; Seetha Srinivasan, Hunter Cole, and Barney McKee of the University Press of Mississippi; Joan St. C. Crane and Anne Freudenberg of the University of Virginia Library; Dr. Lola L. Szladits of the New York Public Library; Ann S. Gwyn and Wilbur E. Meneray of the Tulane University Library. I have benefited too from the resources of Louis Daniel Brodsky, private collector and scholar, and of his collaborator, Professor Robert W. Hamblin. I am privileged to thank all of them.

My sincerest gratitude goes also to the scholars who took the time to give me the benefit of their knowledge in correcting errors in the earlier study, especially: Professors Calvin S. Brown, James B. Meriwether, Tamotsu Nishiyama, Hiroshi Takahashi, and Floyd Watkins. I am particularly grateful to Professor Meriwether for taking the time to read this book in proof and for helping me to correct errors.

I have had the generous help too of scholars who shared their research with me: Professors Carlos Baker, Tom Dardis, Bruce F. Kawin, Ilse Dusoir Lind, James B. Meriwether, Franklin E. Moak, Noel Polk, Paul R. Rogers, Patrick Samway, Judith L. Sensibar, Richard J. Stonesifer, James G. Watson, and James W. Webb. I thank them for embodying the communal nature of scholarship.

Friends from other professions have also placed me in their debt for their aid and many kindnesses: William Boozer, Howard Duvall, Robert Farley, Gerald A. Gafford, Dr. M. Beckett Howorth, Jr., Lomax Lamb, Dr. Chester McLarty, Jean Stein, W. E. Stone V, Lawrence Wells, and Joan Williams.

Generous as always in friendship as well as professional skill have been Albert and Marisa Erskine and Bertha Krantz, and my special thanks go to them too.

The early portions of this book were written in surroundings so spectacular as almost to embody the beauty of the impulse that moves people to help writers do their work: the Villa Serbelloni, the Bellagio Study and Conference Center of the Rockefeller Foundation on Lake Como. Some of the last work on the book was done in Connecticut on a trip paid for by the University of Michigan Faculty Assistance Fund. Here, too, particular thanks are due.

Grateful acknowledgment is made to all the publishers cited in the notes.

Yvonne Wright Blotner worked with me to compile the index. My thanks for this long task are a mere token of all I owe her.

My last statement of indebtedness is to those who have helped me but whose names I have inadvertently omitted, with apologies but with gratitude as well.

JOSEPH BLOTNER

INDEX

All persons whose surnames are known are indexed here. In lieu of an entry for William Faulkner, a comprehensive chronology of his life has been provided, details of which can be amplified by consulting the relevant pages in the text through the dates supplied in the running heads. Selected items appearing in newspapers and periodicals are indexed where they have a particular importance, e.g., crucial acceptances or rejections of his work in magazines such as *The Saturday Evening Post*, potentially influential reviews or articles in *The New York Times* or *Time* magazine, or an article in the Oxford *Eagle* revealing changing perceptions of Faulkner. Places are also selectively indexed, e.g., important arrivals or periods of residence in New York and Paris, and passages describing the nature of Faulkner's feeling for places, such as Hollywood and Virginia. Readers seeking further detailed bibliographical and critical information are referred to John Bassett, *William Faulkner: An Annotated Checklist of Criticism*, New York, David Lewis, 1972; John Earl Bassett, *Faulkner: An Annotated Checklist of Recent Criticism*, The Kent State University Press, 1983; O. B. Emerson, *Faulkner's Early Literary Reputation in America*, Ann Arbor, Mich., UMI Research Press, 1984; Thomas L. McHaney, *William Faulkner: A Reference Guide*, Boston, G. K. Hall, 1976; James B. Meriwether, "The Short Fiction of William Faulkner: A Bibliography," *Proof: The Yearbook of American Bibliography and Textual Studies*, Vol. I (1971), 293–329; James B. Meriwether, "The Books of William Faulkner: A Revised Guide for Students and Scholars," *The Mississippi Quarterly*, XXXV (Summer 1982), 265–81; and the annual bibliographies of Faulkner studies in *American Literary Scholarship: An Annual*, Durham, N.C., Duke University Press; *MLA International Bibliography of Books and Articles on the Modern Languages and Literatures*, New York, The Modern Language Association of America; and The William Faulkner issue, *The Mississippi Quarterly*, Mississippi State, Miss.

ABOUT THE AUTHOR

JOSEPH BLOTNER grew up in Scotch Plains, New Jersey, but lived and taught in the South for fifteen years. Educated at Drew, Northwestern, and the University of Pennsylvania, he interrupted his schooling to fly with the 8th Air Force in England during World War II. He then taught at the Universities of Idaho, Virginia, and North Carolina (Chapel Hill). At Virginia he was a member, and later chairman, of the Balch Committee, under whose auspices William Faulkner became Writer-in-Residence there. His writings on Faulkner include *Faulkner in the University* (with Frederick L. Gwynn); *William Faulkner's Library: A Catalogue; Faulkner: A Biography;* and *Selected Letters of William Faulkner* as well as *Uncollected Stories of William Faulkner.* His other books are *The Political Novel, The Fiction of J. D. Salinger* (with Frederick L. Gwynn), and *The Modern American Political Novel: 1900–1960.*

Twice a Guggenheim Fellow and twice a Fulbright Lecturer in American Literature at the University of Copenhagen, Professor Blotner has lectured extensively in the United States and Europe on American literature and particularly the work of Faulkner. He and his wife, Yvonne, live in Ann Arbor, where he is Professor of English at the University of Michigan. He is currently working on a biography of Robert Penn Warren.

Grateful acknowledgment is made to the following for permission to reprint material from previously published works:

International Famous Agency: For excerpts from "Interview with William Faulkner" by Cynthia Grenier, published in *Accent*, Vol. 16, Summer 1956. Copyright © 1956 by *Accent*.

Liveright Publishing Corporation: For excerpts from *Soldier's Pay* by William Faulkner. Copyright renewed 1953 by William Faulkner. For excerpts from *Mosquitoes* by William Faulkner. Copyright 1954 by William Faulkner.

Harold Ober Associates, Inc.: For excerpts from *Letters of Sherwood Anderson*, selected and edited by Howard M. Jones. Copyright 1953 by Eleanor Anderson. Copyright renewed 1981 by Eleanor Copenhaver Anderson.

Purdue Research Foundation: For excerpts from "Conversation with William Faulkner," Vol. V, Number 4, *Modern Fiction Studies*; Winter 1959–1960. Copyright © 1960 by Purdue Research Foundation, Lafayette, Indiana.

Random House, Inc.: For selections from the copyrighted works of William Faulkner, published by Random House, Inc.

Saturday Review: For excerpts from "William Faulkner: That Writin' Man of Oxford" by Anthony Buttitta, *Saturday Review of Literature*, May 21, 1938.

Trident Press, a division of Simon and Schuster, Inc.: For excerpts from *My Brother Bill* by John Faulkner. Copyright © 1963 by Lucille Ramey Faulkner.

The Viking Press, Inc.: For excerpts from *The Faulkner-Cowley File: Letters and Memories*, 1944–1962 by Malcolm Cowley. Copyright © 1966 by Malcolm Cowley, copyright © 1966 by the Estate of William Faulkner. All rights reserved. For an excerpt from *Writers at Work: The Paris Review Interviews*, edited by Malcolm Cowley. Copyright © 1957, 1958 by The Paris Review, Inc.

Acknowledgment is also made to the following:

L. D. Brodsky: For passages from *Faulkner: A Comprehensive Guide to the Brodsky Collection*, eds. Louis Daniel Brodsky and Robert W. Hamblin.

Lee Morris: For passages from *William Faulkner: A Life on Paper*, ed. Ann Abadie.

University Press of Mississippi: For passages from *Count No 'Count: Flashbacks to William Faulkner* by Ben Wasson.

Meta D. Wilde: For passages from *A Loving Gentleman: The Story of William Faulkner and Meta Carpenter* by Meta Carpenter Wilde and Orin Borsten, New York: Simon and Schuster, 1976.